Media Law

McGRAW-HILL SERIES IN MASS COMMUNICATION

CONSULTING EDITOR
Barry L. Sherman

Media Law

FOURTH EDITION

RALPH L. HOLSINGER

Professor Emeritus, Journalism
Indiana University, Bloomington

JON PAUL DILTS

Associate Dean and Associate Professor, Journalism
Indiana University, Bloomington

THE McGRAW-HILL COMPANIES, INC.

New York   St. Louis   San Francisco   Auckland   Bogotá   Caracas
Lisbon   London   Madrid   Mexico City   Milan   Montreal   New Delhi
San Juan   Singapore   Sydney   Tokyo   Toronto

McGraw-Hill

A Division of The **McGraw·Hill** *Companies*

Media Law

Copyright © 1997, 1994, 1991, 1987 by The McGraw-Hill Companies, Inc. All rights reserved. Printed in the United States of America. Except as permitted under the United States Copyright Act of 1976, no part of this publication may be reproduced or distributed in any form or by any means, or stored in a data base or retrieval system, without the prior written permission of the publisher.

This book is printed on acid-free paper.

1 2 3 4 5 6 7 8 9 0 FGRFGR 9 0 9 8 7 6

ISBN 0-07-029710-X

This book was set in Times Roman by Graphic World, Inc.
The editors were Marjorie Byers, Fran Marino, and Larry Goldberg;
the production supervisor was Kathryn Porzio.
The cover was designed by Christopher Brady.
The photo editor was Elyse Rieder.
Quebecor Printing / Fairfield was printer and binder.

Library of Congress Cataloging-in-Publication Data

Holsinger, Ralph L.
    Media law / Ralph L. Holsinger, Jon Paul Dilts.—4th ed.
        p.   cm.—(McGraw-Hill series in mass communication)
    Includes bibliographical references and index.
    ISBN 0-07-029710-X
    1. Mass media—Law and legislation—United States.   2. Press law—
United States.   I. Dilts, Jon.   II. Title.   III. Series.
KF2750.H65   1997
343.7309' 9—dc20
[347.30399]   96-15358

ABOUT THE AUTHORS

Ralph L. Holsinger is Professor Emeritus of Journalism at Indiana University, Bloomington, where he taught for twenty-four years. He originated the School of Journalism's courses in media law and ethics. He also taught graduate-level courses on the press and the Constitution, problems in media law, and reporting the law. Professor Holsinger has conducted numerous seminars in law and editing for professional journalists and has been engaged as an expert witness in libel cases in Florida, Indiana, and Minnesota. He is a graduate of Ohio Wesleyan University with honors in economics and membership in Phi Beta Kappa. After service in North Africa and Europe in World War II, he was a reporter for newspapers in Ohio, covering three presidential campaigns and becoming a Washington correspondent before he became managing editor of the *Cincinnati Enquirer*. Professor Holsinger is a member of the Indiana Journalism Hall of Fame.

Jon Paul Dilts is Associate Dean and Associate Professor of Journalism at Indiana University, Bloomington. He is an attorney and has conducted numerous workshops on media law for lawyers, journalists, and business communicators. Professor Dilts also has been a newspaper reporter and a newspaper and magazine editor, and he is the author of a book on the history and architecture of Indiana courthouses. He has been at Indiana University for fourteen years, teaching undergraduate courses in communications law and intellectual property, as well as graduate courses on the First Amendment, international media law, and news coverage of the courts. Professor Dilts has a bachelor's degree in English from Saint Meinrad College, a master's degree in journalism from Indiana University, and a law degree from Valparaiso University. He lives in Bloomington with his wife, Anne, and their two sons, Christopher and Andrew.

CONTENTS

PREFACE

This fourth edition of *Media Law* was written amid dramatic events in the communication industry: Congress passed and President Clinton signed the Telecommunications Act of 1996, new efforts were made at libel law reform, and the Internet began to show its first true sign of maturity—litigation. Those events are reflected in this text, but reflections of a busy world are like the reflections in the windows of a glass office building. Lights, shadows, and the passing traffic shift so continuously that it is easy to be distracted from what is lasting and fundamental.

In revising *Media Law,* we have tried to be faithful to fundamentals. Free speech in cyberspace, for example, is not an issue out of context. It is an issue with a history and a tradition tied to America's deepest understandings of the First Amendment. Libel, privacy, and copyright are not concerns that Americans have only recently discovered, and there is no reason to be distracted merely because the scenery is changing. What matters is learning how to look through the reflections of passing details to the substance of what media law is about—freedom and justice in a democratic society.

In revising *Media Law,* we have tried not to lose sight of the textbook's original purpose. From the first edition to this one, *Media Law* has attempted to give students, whatever their career objectives, a solid grounding in the constitutional, statutory, administrative, and common law that applies to communication in any medium. We believe that all students benefit as citizens from an understanding of the philosophy supporting the most fundamental of their rights—liberty of speech and press—and the legal principles that both protect and limit that liberty. Thus, *Media Law* is based firmly on the cases that tell us what the law is and how it has affected real people in real time.

Some students who use *Media Law* have been kind enough to report that they like the book because of the stories it tells. We continue to tell stories because we believe that the law offers fascinating insights into the lives of people who either were caught up by the system or chose to challenge it, and who in the process put their liberty or their property at stake to make a point. Thus, *Media Law* continues to be a practical guide to coping with the legal problems likely to confront professional communicators. It also continues to offer insights into the meaning and application of the speech and press clauses of the First Amendment.

But that is not all we have tried to do with *Media Law.* The authors are committed to the belief that beyond the question, Is it legal? there is a more important question, Is it right? Thus, as with the first three editions, each chapter ends with a section, "In the Professional World," that discusses the ethical aspects of its subject matter. These sections are not intended to be exhaustive—many textbooks deal exclusively and in detail with media ethics—but they are intended to provoke thought and discussion.

Plan of the Book and New Features
of the Fourth Edition

For those of you who have used the third edition, there are some obvious changes. In response to suggestions from users of *Media Law,* we have converted the Introduction into a new chapter on the legal system, Chapter 1. We have combined the old chapters on broadcasting and cable into a new Chapter 13 and have renamed it "Electronic Media," which focuses on issues unique to broadcast, cable, and computer networks. Issues in broadcast, cable, and computer networks that are not unique to electronic media—such as libel, privacy, and copyright—are where we think they should be, in the libel, privacy, and copyright chapters. We have revised the libel chapters to approach the subject in a manner that is more linear and more in keeping with the way many say they approach it in the classroom.

To guide those teachers who will be making a transition from the third to the fourth edition, here is a chapter-by-chapter summary of some changes to watch for.

Chapter 1 is now an introduction to the book and to the law in general. It includes a new section on criminal and civil procedure and has been reorganized a bit to help students understand more clearly the various types of law. It is still relatively brief and introductory, but students will find here summaries of the various kinds of law with which the rest of the book deals; an outline of the state and federal court systems; and sections on how cases reach the Supreme Court of the United States, how it decides the cases it accepts for review, and its role in the legal system.

Chapter 2 begins with a brief survey of the history of freedom of speech and press leading to the adoption of the First Amendment and the Sedition Act of 1798. As it has in the past, this chapter introduces students to the variety of twentieth-century ideas about the First Amendment, as well as the Supreme Court's own catalogue of approaches to First Amendment decisions. The chapter, as in the third edition, includes a discussion of the Supreme Court's decisions in *Schenck* v. *United States* (the 1919 "clear and present danger" case), *Texas* v. *Johnson* (the 1989 flag-burning case), and *R.A.V.* v. *City of St. Paul* (the 1992 hate-speech case).

Chapter 3 continues the themes raised in Chapter 2 but with emphasis on political speech and on prior restraint. Changes include a somewhat stronger emphasis on *Brandenberg* v. *Ohio* (the 1969 "clear and present danger" case) and a brief discussion of the effort to stop *Business Week* from publishing a sealed court record. The chapter continues to address issues of obvious student interest: death threats, hate speech, and censorship of student publications.

We continue to devote two chapters to libel. In this edition they are Chapters 4 and 5. Users of earlier editions will notice some structural changes. Chapter 4 is concerned primarily with basic problems that do not raise First Amendment issues, such as jurisdiction and timeliness. A new section focuses on parties to libel suits and introduces *Stratton Oakmont* v. *Prodigy,* a 1995 case that raised questions about the liability of a computer network provider. Another new section discusses the settling of libel disputes by arbitration and mediation and introduces students to the Uniform Correction or Clarification Act. As in the third edition, much that is here is an attempt to explain that not all libel lawsuits, particularly those involving business communicators, raise First Amendment issues.

Consequently, the primary concern of Chapter 4 is with the common law elements and defenses in libel litigation.

Chapter 5 picks up where Chapter 4 ends—at the point where First Amendment questions insert themselves into the dispute. Chapter 5 focuses entirely on the constitutional issues in libel, beginning with *New York Times* v. *Sullivan* and extending to current concerns about protection for opinion and neutral reporting.

Chapter 6 deals with invasion of privacy and has not changed much in this edition. We have added a section that introduces students to related privacy concerns about trespass and infliction of emotional distress. But the chapter still emphasizes the four traditional torts: intrusion, private fact, false light, and appropriation.

Chapter 7, "A Fair and Public Trial," has been revised so that it launches directly into the meaning of a fair trial. Materials about criminal justice procedures, which opened the chapter in the third edition, have been moved to Chapter 1 and enlarged to include a parallel section on civil justice procedures. As might be expected, the chapter opens with a reference to the O. J. Simpson murder trial, which is now a set piece in the experience of most students who think about fair-trial issues.

Chapter 8, "The Journalist's Privilege: Confidentiality," includes new material on the use of search warrants to seize the work of electronic publishers and the role played by the Privacy Protection Act of 1980 and the Electronic Communications Privacy Act. Of interest to students may be a case from Texas, *Steve Jackson Games* v. *U.S. Secret Service,* which illustrates emerging concerns of electronic publishers.

Chapter 9, about access to government information, again opens with a discussion of the First Amendment's role in gaining access to judicial proceedings. It echoes the issues raised in Chapter 7 about public trials and in Chapter 3 about prior restraints, but the heart of the chapter is the overview of the federal Freedom of Information Act and the updated material on access to state and local government.

Chapter 10 has been renamed "Obscenity, Indecency, and Sexual Violence" and has been expanded to include material about indecency and violence on television and on the Internet. In earlier editions, issues of indecency were addressed in separate chapters on cable and broadcasting. This change, at the suggestion of students and teachers, provides a more convenient and logical opportunity to discuss issues of offensive sexual speech in the context of a discussion about obscenity.

Chapter 11, "Advertising," includes new material on advertising by professionals in light of the Supreme Court's decisions in *Ibanez* v. *Florida Department of Business and Professional Regulations* and *Florida Bar* v. *Went For It Inc.* The chapter also reflects a shift in the Court's thinking about the *Central Hudson* test and its application to the advertising of products that have not been made illegal *(Rubin* v. *Coors Brewing Co.).* On the whole, however, this chapter continues to be one written for students who are considering careers in advertising. It begins with a survey of the cases through which the Supreme Court extended First Amendment protection to commercial speech and then defined the limits of that protection. The chapter continues to deal with government regulation of false or deceptive advertising and with concerns about media rights to refuse advertising and to use advertising to promote political causes.

Chapter 12, on copyright and trademarks, includes a new section on the Internet, which is experiencing a burst of litigation as creators try to protect proprietary rights to data and software. The discussion of fair use has been expanded and includes an introduction to *American Geophysical Union* v. *Texaco,* an important Second Circuit opinion that limits the photocopying of academic journals. The section on trademarks also has been revised and updated.

Chapter 13 is a new chapter, entitled "Electronic Media." We have eliminated separate chapters on cable and broadcast and moved much of the information in those chapters to more appropriate places in the text. In this revised chapter we have focused on the issues that are truly unique to electronic media: licensing of broadcasters, emerging competition among phone companies and cable, and the impact of federal legislation, including the Telecommunications Act of 1996, on cable and the Internet.

Chapter 14, "The Media as Businesses," has changed little from the third edition, other than the usual updating. As before, the chapter focuses on four major legal concerns of media management: antitrust, distribution, taxation, and employment practices. Although we realize that the last chapter in a textbook is the first to be dropped when time gets short, we urge students not to overlook the practical issues that are raised in this chapter, such as buying manuscripts from convicted criminals, becoming too friendly with the competition, placing news racks on city streets, and getting paid for overtime.

Acknowledgments

We continue to be grateful to the late Richard G. Gray, who as chairman of Indiana University's Department of Journalism and later as dean of the School of Journalism encouraged the creation of *Media Law.* Without his support and patience, the first edition, much less the fourth, could not have happened. We are grateful, too, to Dean Gray's successor, Trevor R. Brown, who as a colleague and friend has never failed to encourage the project through what is now many years of revisions.

We are grateful, too, to all the teachers throughout the country who have used *Media Law* in their classes, some of whom we have come to know personally and some only as E-mail pen pals.

We owe thanks to everyone at Random House and McGraw-Hill who through the years has nurtured and prodded this work along, especially Hillary Jackson and Roth Wilkofsky, who edited the early editions. No one, however, has yet matched the patience of Fran Marino at McGraw-Hill, who joined us in editing the third and fourth editions. Her ability to work with us during stressful times was a lesson in forbearance and optimism. We also thank Stephanie Hiebert, whose careful copyediting caught our mistakes and compelled us to complete citations, and Larry Goldberg and Kathy Porzio, who shepherded the manuscript through the editing and production stages. Elyse Rieder and Beth Murphy faithfully found ways to make our ideas for illustrations into pertinent photos and cartoons for this edition. For this, we are grateful.

We would like to thank our colleagues at Indiana University who share our interest in media law and whose comments and suggestions, while sometimes sobering, have always been helpful: professors Linda Lawson, Paul Voakes, Charlene Brown, and Herb Terry, as well as two very fine graduate students, both lawyers, George Sullivan and John Schmitt.

Finally, we would like to thank all the professors who reviewed the third edition and offered us their suggestions for this revision. They include: Michael E. Abrams, Florida A&M University; Ed Adams, Angelo State University; John G. Cooper, Eastern Michigan University; Ronald T. Farrar, University of South Carolina; Rosalind C. Florez, University of Cincinnati; Janet McMullen, University of North Alabama; Charles J. Sennet, Northwestern University; and George Whitehouse, University of South Dakota.

Jon Dilts

Media Law

CHAPTER 1

As the title indicates, this is a textbook on media law. The term "media" was chosen deliberately to describe the broad scope of the subject matter. This text is written for all communications students, no matter what their present career goal—be it advertising, public relations, corporate communications, photography, or the gathering and dissemination of news in any medium. The "law" of the title also is used in its broadest sense. It includes constitutional law, with special emphasis on the guarantees of freedom of speech and press that are found in the First Amendment to the U.S. Constitution. The term "law" also includes statutes and administrative rules defining what communicators can and cannot do. During the twentieth century, the Supreme Court of the United States has on many occasions ruled on cases in which attempts to regulate the media have raised First Amendment questions. Under the Constitution, these decisions also are "the law of the land," and they make up a significant portion of Media Law.

This book is grounded in the belief that all communications students—not just those thinking of careers in print or electronic journalism—should understand that no society can call itself free unless it not only tolerates, but insists on, freedom of speech and press. Law and the courts not only define the limits of acceptable conduct; they

THE LEGAL SYSTEM

also protect the rights of individuals who test those limits. Thus, we start with a summary of the many meanings of the term "law" and an outline of the state and federal court systems. Students who assimilate the subject matter of this introductory chapter will find the remainder of the text easier to understand.

This chapter is a quick introduction to the nature and process of American law. It describes the sources and types of most kinds of law that affect the professional lives of writers, editors, broadcasters, advertisers, and public relations personnel. Chapter 2 outlines the development of the idea of freedom, particularly the freedom of ordinary folks to disagree with people in authority. This idea still has not been fully accepted, as is illustrated by the subject matter of Chapter 3: Our own government has, in times of stress, punished its critics, and under extreme conditions courts do sanction government censorship.

Starting with Chapter 4, the subject matter of *Media Law* may vary in its appeal, depending on career goals. However, the libel chapters are pertinent to all communications students. Although newspapers, magazines, and books have been the targets of most of the landmark libel cases, no one is exempt from being sued for defamation. One of the landmark libel cases involved a television news program, *60 Minutes*.[1] Another grew from an ill-fated credit-rating service at Dun & Bradstreet.[2] Public relations releases and advertisements have been a frequent target of libel actions. Even corporate providers of electronic bulletin boards, such as Prodigy and CompuServe, have been sued for defamation.[3] Business corporations are not always the defendants; sometimes they aggressively sue for libel individuals who circulate petitions criticizing their impact on the environment or their safety records.

Invasion of privacy, treated in Chapter 6, also is a potential source of litigation for all communicators. Once largely a problem for aggressive and nosy reporters, invasion of privacy is of increasing concern to advertisers, public relations practitioners, producers of television docudramas, and the users of computer on-line services.[4] The Supreme Court has held that persons in the pub-

---

1. Westmoreland v. CBS, 97 F.R.D. 703, 9 Med.L.Rptr. 1521 (S.D.N.Y. 1983); 596 F.Supp. 1170, 10 Med.L.Rptr. 2417 (S.D.N.Y. 1984).
2. Dun & Bradstreet v. Greenmoss Builders, 472 U.S. 479, 105 S.Ct. 2939, 86 L.Ed.2d 593, 11 Med.L.Rptr. 2417 (1985).
3. Stratton Oakmont, Inc. v. Prodigy Services Co., 23 Med.L.Rptr. 1794 (N.Y.S.Ct., Nassau County 1995). Cubby Inc. v. CompuServe, Inc., 776 F. Supp. 135, 19 Med.L.Rptr. 1525 (S.D.N.Y. 1991).
4. Howard Stern v. Delphi Internet Services Corp., 23 Med.L.Rptr. 1789 (N.Y.S.Ct., New York County 1995).

lic eye have a right of publicity that can be protected against exploitation by others.

Chapters 10 and 12, on obscenity and copyright, respectively, should be of interest to all students. In a sense, the chapter on obscenity is related to Chapter 3, on censorship, because written and pictorial materials portraying explicit sexual activity have been and continue to be the leading subjects of censorship in our society. It is unlikely that students in college and university communications courses are preparing for careers that will involve them in testing the limits of obscenity law. However, all of us need to know that well-meaning persons have used the term "obscene" loosely in seeking to ban school textbooks, to cut off public support for certain forms of art, to censor the lyrics of popular songs, or to force television, cable, and computer services to conform to community standards of decency. Thus, obscenity law should be of general interest to all who are concerned with attempts to put limits on freedom of expression.

Copyright is of general interest because all forms of expression are eligible for legal protection against unauthorized copying once they are put in tangible form. A communicator who borrows a few lines of a popular song, a photograph, a sketch, or an extended quotation from a newspaper article is a potential copyright infringer, subject to legal penalties. Chapter 12 also includes a section on trademarks, the distinctive graphics or words that become part of a business firm's identity. Such marks are protected by law.

The titles of the remaining chapters define their appeal and usefulness to the individual student. The chapters on fair trial (7), the journalist's privilege (8), and the right to know (9) are of interest mainly to reporters and editors of news, print or electronic. However, potential business communicators will find Chapter 9, on the right to know, pertinent because businesses have become major users of the Freedom of Information Act. The chapters on advertising and electronic media (11 and 13) obviously appeal to specific interests. However, all of us, as voracious users of cable and over-the-air television, and as targets of advertising, should have a general interest in the laws that regulate those media. Finally, Chapter 14, on the business aspects of the media, includes a concern about fair employment practices and the role of communications in securities fraud, making it pertinent to business communicators and public relations practitioners.

One final note: Given the rapidly changing nature of the communications media and of the business community, students who are dead set on a particular career goal probably will find themselves in an entirely different field before they retire. Those who have built the broadest base of knowledge will find a career change easier to make.

THE MEANING OF "LAW"

As used in this text, "law" has two general meanings that are quite different but nevertheless closely interrelated. The primary meaning refers to law as the legal rules by which we live. These include statutes enacted by Congress and state legislatures, ordinances adopted by local governing bodies, the rules adopted by administrative bodies at all levels; they also include the decisions of courts interpreting all of the above or applying rules based on custom, which is known as common law. In this sense, put in basic terms, laws are the words that define conduct required of us, or forbidden to us, for the common good.

In its secondary meaning, law is the system of courts, judicial processes, and legal officers through which the rules are applied. In this sense, it is a means of resolving disputes to reach an end loosely described as justice.

In the first meaning of the term, laws usually are classified by origin. The major sources of such law are described in the section that follows.

Sources of Law

Constitutional Law

Constitutional law stands at the apex of our system of laws. As the name suggests, it is derived from the constitutions, federal and state, that are the basic charters of government. From the earliest days of the Republic, supreme courts, national and state, have had the power to nullify any law that is not based on powers given the legislature by a constitution or that violates a right guaranteed by one. Thus, constitutions are not dead collections of words. They have been kept alive by courts' interpretations of what the words mean when applied to a specific set of facts in a case based on a clash of interests. These interpretations are what make up constitutional law. Because the federal Constitution is at the apex of the hierarchy of laws, constitutional questions can arise from all other kinds of law.

No one can say with certainty what any part of the U.S. Constitution means until the Supreme Court has decided what it means in a particular case. This does not mean that lower courts can't interpret the Constitution. The judge of even the lowest level of a state court has the authority—and the duty—to do so when the parties to a case raise a constitutional question. But such decisions are subject to appeal and review by courts at a higher level. The higher the court in the hierarchy, the greater is the weight carried by its decisions. The Supreme Court of the United States is the final authority on all federal constitutional questions, but even its decisions are not carved in stone. On occasion, the Court has changed its mind about the meaning or application of a constitutional principle.

The same principles govern the interpretation of the constitutions of each of the fifty-five states and territories. Here, the rule is that a state constitution means whatever that state's supreme court says it means. Such rulings are supposed to be respected by the U.S. Supreme Court, and almost always are. However, if a provision of a state constitution violates a provision of the U.S. Constitution, the Supreme Court can declare it void if it is at issue in a case accepted for review.

Common Law

Constitutional law is not involved in every legal dispute. Often the basis of a conflict is something less fundamental to human rights, such as an argument over water rights or an injury caused by carelessness. Sometimes the court is asked to settle a dispute for which there is little precedent and no guidance from the legislature. Quite often a court is asked to allow recovery for the breach of a duty that has developed not in legislative debate but from the customary practices of, say, farmers or Internet users. Examples of such duties are not to block a drainage ditch or not to allow a virus into a computer network. Courts don't ignore disputes such as these that have no clear law. They look to their own sense of justice and to their own history of decision making for guidance in resolving the dispute. Over the centuries, this process has given rise to a special kind of law—common law. Common law is created by judges and built gradually from the decisions of courts as they apply common sense and custom in reaching decisions.

Ten centuries ago, courts in medieval England began to apply commonsense principles to the resolution of disputes, often property disputes, which no statute addressed. As early as the thirteenth century, courts began to protect personal rights, such as harm to reputation, awarding compensation to victims of damaging lies. Since then, a huge body of law, based on nothing more tangible than a court's sense of what justice requires, has been established. This common law is a product of cases, decided at a particular time on a specific set of facts. However, embedded in these cases are principles that legal scholars have done their best to analyze and present in orderly form for the guidance of lawyers, judges, and students.

Because common law is a product of specific cases, it continues to grow as new kinds of unanticipated disputes arise. Its flexibility is one of its strengths. It has survived and grown because it is adaptable to changing conditions. However, most scholars hold that despite its ability to respond to new situations, common law is, at bottom, based solidly on identifiable principles and on a sound sense of what the community will or will not tolerate. Therefore, it is not unusual for a legislative body to take the principles emerging from common law and distill and codify them as statutes.

Legislation

STATUTES. Statute law is the great body of law that is a product of legislative action—by Congress at the national level, by legislatures at the state level, and by city and county councils at the local level. In theory, statutes are drafted to reflect the people's will, as perceived by elected representatives acting on their behalf. Such law provides for punishment of wrongdoing, but it also defines and makes provisions for benefits. The Social Security system, for instance, is the product of a large body of statute law. Such law is said to be prospective in that we are supposed to know what it is and guide our conduct accordingly. In reality, none of us can know, except in general terms, what is in the thousands of statutes under which we live. Federal law alone fills twenty-four volumes of the United States Code, and every session of Congress adds more.

REGULATIONS. In the past fifty years, Congress has enacted statutes stating broad objectives, leaving the details of reaching those objectives to administrative agencies. Under such statutes, Congress sets goals and creates an agency charged with seeing that they are reached. The Environmental Protection Agency, for instance, was given the duty of holding air and water pollution to specified minimums. It is up to the agency to devise specific regulations and impose them on polluters so as to meet those minimums.

When regulations are drafted and adopted in accordance with procedures prescribed by Congress and the courts, they have the effect of law. They may be enforced through the agency's own hearing system, subject to an appeal to the courts. Because of the number of agencies empowered to regulate various aspects of society, and the complexity of the problems with which they try to cope, this body of administrative agency law surpasses in volume the statutes enacted by Congress. Administrative law is of special concern to broadcasters, who are subject to rules adopted by the Federal Communications Commission, and to advertisers, who are regulated by the Federal Trade Commission and the Securities and Exchange Commission.

In the next three sections we shift our focus to systems and processes of law relevant to communicators.

Types of Law

Criminal Law

Society so abhors some conduct—such as murder, robbery, and drug abuse—that it provides for its punishment. The rules defining such infractions make up the body of

Judge Lance A. Ito questions Dennis Fung, a crime expert with the Los Angeles Police Department, during the O. J. Simpson murder trial in California in 1995. (AP/Wide World)

criminal law. With rare exceptions, criminal law is statute law. The purpose of the legislature in defining a crime and its punishment is to deter lawbreaking. All of us stand on notice that if we use illegal drugs or drive a car after having one beer too many, we risk being arrested. If the prosecutor believes the evidence against us is strong enough, we will find ourselves in court, facing a judge.

In court, our fate will be determined by application of the processes of criminal law. Our offense will be treated as an offense against society, which will be represented by the state, with the prosecutor acting as its agent. However, we will not be helpless. The Constitution requires the court to assume that we are not guilty. We have a right to be tried a jury if we so desire. If we choose not to plead guilty, the prosecutor must present enough credible evidence to prove our guilt beyond a reasonable doubt.

Criminal cases, from traffic offenses to murder, make up the bulk of the work of state trial courts. Federal trial courts try criminal cases involving violations of federal law. An earmark of criminal law is the nature of the penalty. Defendants can be deprived of property, by being required to pay a fine; of their liberty, by being sentenced to prison; or of their life, if the crime is serious enough.

Civil Law

When individuals disagree—over whether a physician's carelessness resulted in injury, whether a journalist's story defamed someone, or who was at fault in an automobile accident—they may ask a court to resolve their differences. Such disputes, and many others, become grist for the civil law system. Although the state is not an essential party to a civil proceeding, it can be involved. If the state wants part of your land for a new highway, and you don't like what it offers to pay, the state may ask a court to decide on a fair price. The state also is involved in civil actions to the extent that it provides the forum—a court—and the rules for resolving the dispute.

The purpose of a civil action is to decide whether one party or the other has been wronged, and if so, to make good the victim's loss. If a precise dollar value can be placed on the loss, the award is for actual damages. If the claimed harm can't be measured precisely because it is attributed to such intangibles as mental anguish, humiliation, pain, and suffering, the award is for compensatory damages, sometimes called general damages. If the offending party's actions are considered particularly outrageous, the court may order an award of an additional sum that is designed to punish the offender and deter other potential offenders. This type of award is for punitive damages. Some such awards can be quite large, and unlike the fines imposed in criminal cases, are paid to the victim rather than to the state.

There are important differences between civil and criminal law. Criminal law involves a legal action on behalf of the people as a whole; civil law typically involves a dispute among private parties. A defendant found guilty of violating a criminal statute may have to pay a fine that goes to government, not to the victim; a defendant found liable in a civil case may have to pay money damages to the victim, not the government. Because penalties can be so severe in criminal cases and because people should not be in doubt about what is criminal and what isn't, U.S. courts do not recognize common law crimes. All crimes are written as statutes, and they cannot be created by the courts after the fact. On the other hand, a lot of civil law is developed as common law in the courts. To find it, you may have to read court opinions rather than statutes. The Bill of Rights in the U.S. Constitution provides a special protection for defendants in criminal cases—such as the right to an attorney and the right to remain silent. These rights do not apply in civil cases. Finally, note the difference in vocabulary: Criminal defendants are found guilty or not guilty; civil defendants are found liable or not liable. Criminal defendants are prosecuted; civil defendants are sued.

Equity Law

One type of civil law, known as equity law, has assumed an identity of its own. It traces its origins to medieval England and to the belief that the king was the ultimate source of justice. When persons became embroiled in disputes that could not be resolved by reference to the common law, they looked to the king for help. Originally, the monarch himself listened to the competing claims and made a decision based on the equities—that is, on a balancing of the rights of the one against those of the other in the search for a solution that would be fair to both.

In the United States, equity cases are heard by a judge. Usually, all that the disputing parties want is an order directing one or the other to perform a duty, or to refrain from performing an act considered harmful. If the duty is one required by law, the court may resolve the matter by issuing an order called a writ of mandamus. *Mandamus* is a Latin word meaning "we command." A writ of mandamus also can be issued to prevent one of the parties from committing an act forbidden by law.

If one party to the equity action seeks a remedy not required by law, the court may resolve the dispute by issuing an injunction. A farmer who believes that a storm sewer designed to serve a proposed subdivision would pour water onto his land could ask a court to halt work on the sewer. A judge would hear arguments from both sides and might even join the discussion. The court's purpose would be to resolve the dispute with the least harm to both parties. The result could be an order to the developers of the subdivision to revise their plan for the sewer, or an injunction forbidding further work.

The Court System

The United States has fifty-six different court systems—fifty-seven if you include military courts. Each state and territory has a judicial system, which deals with law violations within its own borders and with civil lawsuits between its residents and, in some instances, between residents and nonresidents.[5] In addition, the federal government is served by a system of United States courts, which deal with violations of federal statutes and, if the amount at issue is large enough, with civil actions brought by residents of one state or territory against residents of another. U.S. courts also hear cases raising federal constitutional issues, although such cases may begin in

---

5. In addition to the 50 states, the territories include the Commonwealth of Puerto Rico, the Territory of Guam, the Virgin Islands of the United States, the Territory of American Samoa, and the Commonwealth of the Northern Mariana Islands.

state or territorial courts, too. The judicial systems are discussed in greater detail in the subsections that follow.

Courts, which apply law to real-life problems and give it meaning, are a separate and equal branch of our three-part system of government. This is true in all state, territorial, and federal jurisdictions. The legislative branch, elected by the people, enacts statutes, which presumably reflect the popular will. The executive branch, headed by governors in the states and territories and by the president in the federal system, has the duty of carrying the statutes into effect. The judicial branch, working separately and at several levels in state, territorial, and federal courts, enforces the laws and, when a question is properly raised, decides what they mean.

In keeping with their separate-but-equal status, courts generally respect the legal expertise of legislators or administrators. However, constitutional law sometimes compels the courts to assume a role that, in a sense, raises them above the other branches of government. These situations arise in legal actions when the meaning of a law is in dispute or when a litigant has alleged that a law is in violation of some provision of a state, territorial, or federal constitution. In interpreting the meaning of a law, if the language itself is not clear, courts generally try to learn the intent of the legislative body and rule accordingly. But when constitutional questions are raised, the courts, in practice, are on their own unless a majority of a higher court has ruled previously on a closely related question. If such precedents are lacking, some jurists maintain they are guided by the intent of the drafters; others, by their sense of what is just, under the circumstances. But often the intent of the drafters is difficult, if not impossible, to determine. Thus, judges have considerable latitude in writing their opinions, making it literally true that constitutions, state or federal, mean what the most recent decisions of the appropriate court of last appeal say they mean. This is an awesome power, especially when it is used to interpret fundamental individual rights guaranteed by a constitution. We will see throughout this textbook that the courts' interpretation of the guarantees of freedom of speech and press stated in the Constitution has passed through several cycles, although obviously the wording of the document has not changed. In the early twentieth century, courts construed the freedoms narrowly. Not until midcentury did the U.S. Supreme Court, under the leadership of Chief Justice Earl Warren, greatly expand the scope not only of freedom of speech and press but of other guarantees of the Bill of Rights as well. More recently, under Chief Justice William H. Rehnquist, the Court has narrowed some of the decisions of the Warren Court, including those dealing with speech and press. Such changes in direction emphasize that the courts are the ultimate guardians of our constitutional rights, however they may be interpreted.

State Courts

At the lowest judicial level, state and territorial courts dealing with minor offenses and small claims may be quite informal, not even making a record of their proceedings. Names of such courts vary from place to place. Some are called municipal courts; others, police courts, county courts, or small-claims courts.

The lowest-level trial courts of record also vary in what they are called. In most states, such courts operate at the county or parish level.[6] In some states, sparsely populated counties may be grouped together and served by one court called a district or circuit court. In a few states, lowest-level trial courts of record are called courts of common pleas. New York confuses the out-of-state beginning legal scholar by calling its basic trial courts supreme courts. Whatever the name, these courts are responsible for the great bulk of all legal work done. Here individuals are tried on murder and other criminal charges, libel actions and other suits for damages are heard, and injunctions are sought.

Each state also has one or two layers of appellate courts. The more populous states generally have an intermediate appellate court and a higher court of last resort. The intermediate courts in some states subdivide themselves into panels to hear appeals from trial courts in certain counties that make up geographical districts. In other states the panels may take turns accepting appeals, no matter where they come from. Several states have specialized appeals courts, one branch hearing criminal appeals, the other, civil.

However they are named or organized, appeals courts ordinarily do not conduct trials. Witnesses are heard and evidence is collected only in the lower trial courts. There a jury or judge decides whose version of the facts to believe. Appeals courts are concerned with questions of law, which come to them through documents supported by legal citations called briefs. Appeals courts sometimes permit lawyers representing the two sides to make limited oral arguments supporting their cases. Appeals are based on the contention that the trial judge erred in interpreting one or more points of law. Typical questions raised on appeal include, Did the judge improperly admit the defendant's confession as evidence? Were the instructions to the injury in accord with established principles of law?

Each state has a court of final appeal, which usually also oversees the functioning of the entire judicial system. The name of this court also varies. Some are called supreme courts; others, the court of appeals. Massachusetts calls its highest court the Supreme Judicial Court. Whatever its name, a state's highest court has the final word on any case that deals exclusively with interpretation of that state's constitution or statutes.

If no federal question has been raised in the courts below, a litigant who is displeased with the judgment of a state's highest court has no further recourse for appeal. However, if a federal issue, such as freedom of speech, has been raised and not resolved to the satisfaction of one of the litigants, the case may be taken to a federal court for resolution of that issue only. In no sense are state courts inferior to those in the federal system; they are coequal. According to one rule of judicial construction, in a case involving both state and federal questions, a federal court must honor a state supreme court's interpretation of the meaning of that state's constitution or statutes.

---

6. In Louisiana, a unit of government corresponding to the county is called a parish. The name harks back to the time when Louisiana was French, a heritage that explains, moreover, why Louisiana is the only state that never adopted English common law as a foundation for its legal system.

Federal Courts

Federal courts operate at three levels. At the trial level are the ninety-four U.S. district courts, which may be found in the major cities of every state. Some districts are divided into divisions, and a judge may hold court in two or more cities on a rotating basis to serve the convenience of the litigants. Districts are given straightforward geographical names. For example, the cluster of federal trial courts in New York City is identified collectively as the U.S. District Court, Southern District, New York. The Northern District is headquartered in Albany; the Eastern, in Brooklyn; and the Western, in Buffalo.

The district courts in New York, Connecticut, and Vermont make up the Second Circuit for appeal purposes. Their decisions are subject to review by the U.S. Court of Appeals, Second Circuit, which has its headquarters in New York City. There are eleven such circuits, made up of as few as three states and as many as nine. The District of Columbia has a separate U.S. circuit court, which hears many appeals from the decisions of federal administrative agencies, as well as from the U.S. District Court for the District of Columbia. A thirteenth federal circuit court, simply called the Federal Circuit, also sits in Washington, D.C. It hears appeals of cases involving government contracts and employees, patents, trademarks, and customs.

Other specialized U.S. courts include the Court of International Trade, which hears disputes over customs duties; the Claims Court, which hears disputed financial claims involving the government; a system of Bankruptcy Courts paralleling the U.S. district courts; a Court of Veterans Appeals, which hears cases involving compensation of veterans of military service, and the Court of Military Appeals, which reviews selected decisions of disciplinary tribunals in the armed services.

At the apex of the federal judicial pyramid is the Supreme Court of the United States, the only court established by the Constitution. Each of its nine justices supervises in a loose way one or more of the circuits. In practice, this responsibility means little more than that the justice has the power to hear and act on emergency appeals from his or her assigned circuit while the Court is in recess. Federal judges are appointed for life by the president, subject to approval by the Senate. Historically, federal judgeships have been used to reward faithful members of the president's political party. However, some recent presidents have made a show of consulting lawyers' organizations and others in seeking judges of merit. This approach has been especially true at the Supreme Court level, although even there presidents have sought to influence history by choosing justices who are considered likely to interpret the Constitution to their liking.

Federal district courts are trial courts. They hear cases involving violations of federal statutes. They are also the starting point for any civil suit to which the federal government is a party, as well as for many such actions that involve residents of different states. To be eligible for hearing in a federal court, the amount at issue in a diversity action must exceed $50,000, or the case must raise a question about a right guaranteed by the Constitution.

A litigant who is dissatisfied with the verdict of a district court can appeal to the appropriate circuit court of appeals for a review of disputed points of law. A circuit court's decisions are binding as precedents only within its own circuit. Thus, sometimes one circuit rules one way on a disputed point of law, and another rules just the opposite. If the matter is of any consequence, the Supreme Court usually takes one or both cases in order to resolve the difference.

Legal Procedure

Criminal Procedure

The trial of a person accused of committing a crime is a ritual, with roots embedded deep in Anglo-Saxon history. However informal the process may sometimes seem, it is surrounded by safeguards designed to prevent the defendant's being railroaded into prison on flimsy evidence or in response to public clamor.

An individual is brought into the criminal justice system in most cases by an *arrest,* which is defined as "the taking of a person into custody for the purpose of charging him with a crime."[7] At this point the nature of the crime and the identity of the suspect become known to the news media, because arrests are matters of public record. This public record is created by a process known as *booking,* the formal entry into the police records system of the date, the time, the nature of the charge, the name of the person arrested, and the name of the arresting officer.

The arrested person is now in custody, and the next step usually is *detention,* in jail or in a holding cell. If the charge is minor, the suspect may be released on posting bail, or, if he or she has strong roots in the community, on his or her own recognizance— that is, on the promise that he or she will appear for further proceedings as they are scheduled. If the crime is a serious one, the setting of bail may be the subject of a hearing conducted by a judge. If the charge is murder, a suspect may be denied bail as a matter of law.

The next step is the drafting of the *formal accusation,* or *charge.* If the suspect was arrested on a warrant, that step was taken before the arrest. The formal accusation, which takes varying forms depending on its origin, is a statement in legal language precisely defining the crime of which the suspect is accused. In federal cases involving serious crimes, the Fifth Amendment requires that the formal accusation come from a *grand jury.* A grand jury is a group of persons whose names have been chosen at random and brought together to decide whether a crime has been committed and, if so, to identify the likely suspect. At the state level, the formal accusation can come from a grand jury or from the prosecutor, acting either on his or her own or on the basis of complaints from the victim, the police, or others. A formal accusation of crime resulting from a grand jury's investigation is called a bill of *indictment,* sometimes referred to as a true bill. If the suspect is not already in custody, the indictment might be sealed until he or she can be arrested.

What happens next varies from state to state and with the manner in which the formal accusation was brought. A prompt *preliminary hearing* is generally required, although this hearing can be waived by the defendant, and it usually is if a grand jury has returned an indictment. If the hearing is not waived, the suspect is brought before a judge, and the prosecutor is required to (1) show that a crime has been committed and (2) offer sufficient evidence to convince the judge that there is a reasonable basis for connecting the accused with the crime. Such hearings are informal. The prosecution is permitted to present evidence that may not be admissible at trial. Because such information may be highly prejudicial to the defendant, the preliminary hearing has become a point of contention between the courts and the news media.

---

7. A. C. Germann, Frank D. Day, and Robert R. J. Gallati, *Introduction to Law Enforcement and Criminal Justice* (Springfield, Ill.: Thomas, 1976), p. 192.

If the preliminary hearing results in a finding of "probable cause," the next step is *arraignment*. Again the suspect is brought before a judge. The charge is read and explained, and the suspect is asked how he pleads. If the defendant pleads quilty, all that remains is sentencing. If he pleads not guilty, the next step is the trial.

Trial is the exception. In most instances, while the steps preceding trial are taking place, the prosecutor and the defense attorney are engaged in *plea bargaining*. A defendant charged with armed robbery, a serious crime, may balk at pleading guilty to that charge but may agree, through his attorney, to plead guilty to a lesser charge of simple assault. Or a defendant charged with driving under the influence, and facing a possible loss of his driver's license, may agree to plead guilty to reckless driving. Most cases are disposed of in this way because neither prosecutors' staffs nor the courts themselves could otherwise cope with the large numbers of persons charged with crime.

If the decision is made to go to trial, the defendant may choose to be tried by a judge or by a jury. If there is to be a jury, the first day or days of the trial will be concerned with the selection of its members. Prospective jurors are chosen by lot from lists of registered voters, taxpayers, or telephone customers, and are supposed to represent a cross section of the community. The judge has the duty of questioning each candidate closely to weed out those who may be prejudiced for or against the defendant. This questioning is called *voir dire*—a French phrase meaning "to say truly." During voir dire, prospective jurors are questioned closely by the judge, or sometimes by the attorneys, in the presence of the defendant and counsel for both sides. The purpose is to discover any prejudices or personal information that might unfairly influence a juror's decision.

Once the jury has been chosen, the trial itself is as rigidly structured as a Bach fugue. The following is a summary of the elements of a criminal trial:

THE OPENING STATEMENTS.   First the prosecutor and then the defense attorney tell the court their versions of the facts and the likely testimony. What is said is argument, not evidence, and the judge cautions the jury to avoid drawing conclusions from it.

THE STATE'S CASE.   The prosecutor calls witnesses whose testimony is designed to prove the defendant guilty beyond reasonable doubt.[8] Each witness is subject to cross examination by defense counsel, who will do everything possible to raise doubt about the credibility of each. If the cross-examination produces new information, the prosecutor may follow with redirect examination, which may open the witness to re-cross-examination.

This process, niggling and repetitive as it may seem, is the heart of the trial. The burden of proof is on the prosecutor, and it is a strong one. The prosecutor cannot win a guilty verdict unless the evidence convinces each member of the jury beyond a rea-

---

8.   In most civil cases, the standard of proof is "by a preponderance of the evidence," a good deal less than beyond reasonable doubt.

sonable doubt. The defense attorney's job is much simpler. All he or she must do is raise doubt in the mind of one strong-willed juror. If the defense attorney can accomplish this task, the worst he or she can expect is a hung jury—that is, a jury that cannot agree. A few states permit majority verdicts if the offense is minor, but in most cases the jury's verdict must be unanimous. If the jury cannot agree, the state must decide whether to undertake the time and expense of another trial, or dismiss the charge.

THE DEFENSE'S CASE.   If the defense attorney thinks the prosecution's case is weak, he or she will move to dismiss. If the judge agrees, the defendant is freed. If not, the defense presents its case. Its witnesses may merely attack the credibility of the state's case, or they may offer an affirmative defense, such as an alibi or a claim of self-defense. The defendant is not required to testify. Indeed, if he or she is a repeat offender, it is unlikely he or she will be called to the stand. If the defendant doesn't testify, the rules of the court forbid any mention of his or her criminal record. The court operates on the theory that a prior arrest record, or even a term in prison for a similar offense, has nothing to do with proving guilt in the current case. However, if the defendant does choose to testify, the prior record may be introduced by the prosecution to impeach his or her testimony—that is, to raise doubt in the minds of the jurors as to how far the defendant can be trusted to tell the truth.

REBUTTAL.   The prosecution may offer witnesses to respond to allegations made by the defense, or to answer questions the defense has raised. If the process discloses new evidence, the defense has an opportunity for surrebuttal.

SUMMATION OR CLOSING ARGUMENT.   After all the evidence is in, first the prosecutor and then the defense counsel offer a summary of the case. Following the defense's summation, the prosecutor has an opportunity for final rebuttal. Again, the jury is cautioned that closing statements are not evidence. Each attorney summarizes the testimony in a manner calculated to lead the jury to the desired conclusion.

INSTRUCTING THE JURY.   The judge is responsible for seeing that the trial is conducted in accord with pertinent law and constitutional safeguards. The jury's duty is to decide what the evidence means. However, that decision cannot be made without some awareness of the law. The judge may tell the jury, for instance, that it cannot find the defendant guilty if it concludes that he or she was legally insane at the moment the crime was committed. The judge probably will instruct the jury further on the legal criteria involved in determining insanity. The jury is the finder of fact. It decides which witnesses to believe, which versions of two or more conflicting stories to accept. The judge also "charges" the jury by seeking to impress it with the duty to bring in a verdict based solely on the evidence seen and heard in court.

DELIBERATIONS.   The jury retires to a jury room where it remains until it reaches a verdict. The jurors select one of their number to act as foreperson, who seeks to lead them to a verdict. If the judge's instructions on the law permit, the jury may find the defendant guilty of a lesser offense than the one charged.

MOTIONS. If the defendant is found guilty, motions are in order. Usually at this point the defense will allege that the judge erred in rulings on points of law raised during the trial. These motions provide grounds for possible appeal.

JUDGMENT. The judge issues the decision of the court. This decision may be in accordance with the jury's verdict, or it may be a judgment notwithstanding the verdict. Imposition of the penalty usually is deferred, pending an investigation designed to guide the judge to a choice of several sentences ranging from release on probation to capital punishment.

The trial process is designed to make the state prove its case by evidence that goes to the point of the offense with which the defendant is charged. Evidence that does not bear directly on the offense, or that has been obtained in violation of the defendant's rights, is not supposed to be submitted to the jury. For instance, a confession is not admissible as evidence if the defendant had not been advised beforehand of his or her Fifth Amendment right to remain silent and the right to consult a lawyer. Sometimes a hearing on the admissibility of evidence is the most important element in the criminal process. If a confession is the strongest evidence the prosecution has, a ruling excluding it from the trial may mean the defendant goes free.

Fair-trial issues are raised when the news media report the existence of evidence that cannot, under the rules, be used at the trial. Jurors are screened at the start of the trial to determine whether they have knowledge of such evidence. Once chosen, they are admonished not to read or listen to news accounts of the trial, but on occasion courts have found that news reports of inadmissible evidence were so pervasive that the jurors could not have been impartial. In such instances the defendant either must be submitted to a new trial or must be set free. Of course, mass media are not the only source of problems for a judge who is trying to ensure a fair trial. Jurors and judges are sometimes subjected to bribery, threats, courtroom disturbances, and community prejudices that are far more immediately threatening than is inappropriate publicity.

Civil Procedure

Although civil trials are similar to criminal trials, there are important differences. There are no arrests or bookings or detentions in jail, no bail or indictments, no arraignments, and no bargaining over the details of a prison sentence.

An individual is brought into the civil justice system in most cases by a *complaint* filed with the court by a plaintiff who believes the defendant has breached a duty and caused him or her harm. The duty might have been created by contract, common law, or statute. In media cases, the complaint often alleges that the defendant's conduct was tortious; that is, the defendant is accused of committing a tort, a civil wrong for which the law requires compensation. Typical torts in media law include such things as libel or invasion of privacy.

The defendant is notified of the complaint by the plaintiff and must file an *answer* to the complaint. Failing to file an answer can result in a *default judgment* against the defendant. One way to lose a libel suit quickly is to ignore a civil complaint filed with the court.

A common answer to a complaint is the simple denial that the defendant did what the plaintiff says. Sometimes the answer is accompanied by a *motion* to the court to dismiss the complaint because of lack of jurisdiction or because the complaint asserts a wrong that the law does not recognize as actionable. Frequently the answer asserts an *affirmative defense,* such as a statutory or constitutional privilege excusing the defendant from liability.

After a complaint has been filed and answered, the parties begin a process of *discovery.* This is the investigative stage of a civil suit. Both sides try to gather the evidence they need to prove or disprove the allegations in the complaint. Both sides have the right to *subpoena* any evidence relevant to the case. They may also take witnesses' *depositions* or ask them to complete questionnaires, called *interrogatories.* If there are objections to subpoenas or depositions or other investigative techniques, the court may hold a hearing to decide whether those objections are valid. For example, sometimes reporters object to a subpoena requiring them to identify confidential sources of information. Courts are willing to listen to those objections and rule on them.

The process of discovery can be time-consuming and expensive. It is not unusual for discovery in a libel suit to take several years and cost thousands of dollars in attorney fees. Often, after all the evidence in the case seems to have been gathered, one party—usually the defendant—will file a motion for *summary judgment.* The opposing party must respond or face possible sanctions. That's what psychic Uri Geller discovered when his lawyer failed to respond to a motion for summary judgment made by magician James Randi. Geller had sued Randi for libel because of comments made in the *International Herald Tribune.* When Geller didn't respond to the motion, the court entered a judgment against Geller of $149,000, representing the fees and costs incurred by the defense.[9] Generally, however, summary judgment is granted only if there is no real dispute about the events that occurred, allowing the outcome of the case to depend simply on how the judge applies the law to those events. In other words, if the parties agree about the facts, the judge can reach a judgment without a trial. The summary judgment, of course, like the judgment after a trial, can be appealed to a higher court.

If the case survives motions to dismiss or motions for summary judgment and goes to trial, the procedure is much the same as in a criminal trial. But there are important distinctions. Criminals can be convicted only by evidence that shows guilt beyond a reasonable doubt. In civil cases, defendants can be found liable even if there is some reasonable doubt. In most civil cases, the standard is *a preponderance of the evidence*—meaning simply that there is somewhat more evidence of liability than there is to the contrary. In media cases that raise First Amendment issues, such as libel, the standard can be somewhat higher, such as requiring the evidence to be *clear and convincing.* Although this standard is higher standard than a "preponderance of the

---

9.   Geller v. Randi, 23 Med.L.Rptr. 1401 (D.C. Cir. 1994).

evidence," it is still easier to meet than the criminal law's standard of proof, "beyond a reasonable doubt."

Most civil cases never go to trial. Usually they are settled by an agreement among the parties before the case gets that far. Each side assesses the likelihood of success at trial and on that basis tries to negotiate a result that will be less costly than the expense of litigation. If negotiations fail or one of the parties insists on a trial, a date is set and a jury is selected.

The trial itself is structured so that evidence can be presented and challenged in the presence of a jury whose members, as in a criminal case, are chosen at random and screened for prejudice. As in a criminal trial, opening statements are followed by the presentation of the plaintiff's case and then the defendant's case. There is an examination of witnesses, followed by cross-examinations, redirect examinations, and re-cross-examinations as necessary, all under the watchful eye of a trial judge. In civil media cases, the parties commonly call expert witnesses to testify about the standard practices of media organizations in an effort to convince the jury that the defendant did or did not engage in acceptable behavior. As in a criminal case, the trial concludes with summations and closing arguments by the attorneys.

Jury instructions in civil media cases are especially important because the law and the evidence can be highly technical. For example, in libel involving public issues and public figures, the jury can find the defendant liable only if the plaintiff's evidence clearly and convincingly indicates that the defendant acted with "actual malice." A judgment can be overturned if a judge fails to carefully instruct jurors about the difference between "actual malice" and malice demonstrated by hatred, spite, or ill will. Many jurors are surprised to learn that there is a difference.

Jurors then reach a verdict after deliberating privately. Whether the matter is civil or criminal, a judge may issue a judgment contrary to the verdict if he or she believes the jury's verdict is unreasonable. Although judges rarely overturn a verdict, their right to do so demonstrates that in the end it is the judgment, rather than the verdict, that really matters. Usually only a final judgment can be appealed to a higher court. Upon final judgment, motions to correct errors or to dismiss may be submitted to the court. Such motions are rarely granted and are intended mainly to preserve a record for appeal to a higher court on grounds that the trial was unfair.

If the judgment is in favor of the plaintiff, the judge, using the jury's verdict as his guide, will decide what kind of compensation or action is required to repair the harm done. Usually the compensation is in the form of money, but the amount is almost never as much as the plaintiff originally asked for in the complaint. If the judge thinks the defendant's actions were especially egregious, he or she may order the defendant to pay punitive damages as well. Punitive damages are intended to make an example of an especially errant defendant.

In all courts in the United States, a judgment can be appealed at least once. The power of appellate courts, however, is generally limited to reviewing the fairness of the trial and the judge's understanding of the law. Appellate courts do not retry the case, and only rarely do they challenge the facts as determined by the jury.

THE SUPREME COURT OF THE UNITED STATES

How a Case Reaches the Supreme Court

In our litigation-minded age, the Supreme Court of the United States is asked to resolve many kinds of questions. The Court is besieged with applications for review of decisions made by lower courts, which come to it in three ways:

1. By appeal

2. By application for a writ of certiorari

3. By certification

Most cases come to the Supreme Court through a petition for a writ of certiorari. The writ, if issued, is an order to the lower court to deliver its file on the case to the Supreme Court for review. If petitioners are to have any chance of success, they must assert that the lower court erred in applying a federal constitutional principle or a point of federal law to the decision of the case. Four of the nine justices must agree to take a case before a writ can be issued. In the overwhelming majority of cases, the Court refuses certiorari. Usually, no reason is given.

Until 1988, lower-court decisions holding that a state or federal law is unconstitutional could be appealed directly to the Supreme Court. The Department of Justice also could appeal adverse decisions of U.S. district courts in criminal cases. The right to appeal did not necessarily mean that the Court would hear the cases. In many instances, the Court would avoid a decision by blandly announcing that it found "no substantial federal question" at issue. Such direct appeals made up about a fifth of the five thousand cases reaching the Court each year. At the Court's request, Congress enacted a law that eliminated the right of direct appeal in all but a few instances. Under its terms, an appeal of a federal trial court decision declaring a law unconstitutional must go to the proper U.S. court of appeals. If the appellate court affirms, the losing side can file for a writ of certiorari, which the Supreme Court can grant or deny as it does with other kinds of cases. Direct appeals still can be taken in certain civil injunctive actions, which, by law, must be decided in the first instance by a three-judge district court panel. This provision applies to congressional reapportionment cases and to certain cases arising out of the Civil Rights Act of 1964, the Voting Rights Act of 1965, and the Presidential Election Campaign Fund Act of 1971. Direct appeals also are permitted in a limited number of antitrust cases if the trial judge finds that immediate equitable relief is of "general public importance in the administration of justice."

Certification seldom happens. The Court's procedures permit the circuit courts of appeal to ask it to clarify points of law essential to the decision of a pending case. The Supreme Court may choose to answer such questions, or it may ask that the case be sent up to it for decision.

By these three methods, the Court is asked to review about five thousand cases each term, which runs from the first week of October until about the end of June. Obviously such a tide of paper is more than enough to inundate the nine members of the Court, who must, by necessity, assign most of the screening to their clerks. Because there is a limit to how much work the justices can do, they have become ruthless in rejecting cases. In recent years, their formal written decisions have been limited to fewer than 140 cases a year.

How the Supreme Court Decides a Case

Cases submitted to the Supreme Court for review must be accompanied by briefs. Under the rules, these briefs must state the issues presented by the case and the questions of law that it raises. The brief must contain a summary of the action taken in the lower courts; the arguments supporting the outcome sought by the litigant; and citations to cases, statutes, or administrative rules believed to support the sought-after decision. These briefs are of the utmost importance, for they frequently shape the Court's decision.

After the justices and their clerks have studied the briefs, they decide whether to schedule oral argument. If so, the maximum time permitted each side usually does not exceed an hour. Lawyers arguing their cases to the Court can never be sure that they will get to use all of their time as they had planned. One or more of the justices may choose to question a lawyer, or even to argue a point of law.

Each Friday morning, the justices meet in private to discuss cases awaiting decision. The chief justice presides. When a given case is under discussion, he asks each justice in turn, starting with the oldest in terms of years on the Court, to present his or her views. If the case is important or deals with a topic on which the justices have strongly conflicting views, the discussion can be animated. When the time comes to vote, the oldest justice in terms of service votes first, and the balloting continues in order of seniority.

The next step, and it can be an important one, is the assignment of the case to the justice who is to write the decision of the Court. If the chief justice is a part of the majority, he makes the assignment and can give the task to himself or another justice. If the chief justice is not a part of the majority, the assignment is made by the senior justice voting with the majority. The justice charged with the writing usually circulates preliminary drafts among the justices for their comments. If the case is a close one, this step can be a crucial part of the procedure. Much depends on how the author has supported his or her conclusions on disputed points of law, or even on the author's willingness to include the views of other justices in the supporting arguments. In a few instances, an opinion that began circulation as the majority's has come out of the process as a dissent, supplanted by an argument that began as a minority view. Even though five or more justices agree on an opinion, other justices may feel moved to write concurring or dissenting opinions. In a concurring opinion, the writer agrees with the Court's decision, but does not fully agree with the legal reasoning used by the drafter of the leading opinion. When all of the opinions on a given case reach final form, the decision is announced in open court, usually on Monday of each week. Late in the term, decisions are announced more frequently.

The decisions and opinions of the Court take several forms. If the Court decides that a case does not raise new points of law but can be used as a vehicle for reiterating a point the justices thought they had decided previously, the decision may take the form of a *per curiam* opinion. (*Per curiam* is Latin meaning "for the court.") Such opinions are never signed by an individual justice, although one or more may choose to write a supplementary opinion. *Per curiam* opinions are not looked to as strong precedents, although they can help clarify a confusing point of law.

If four or more justices agree with the legal reasoning used by the justice who writes the prevailing opinion, and they sign onto it, the case reports call it "the opinion of the Court," because it reflects the reasoning of the majority and establishes precedents that all lower courts are expected to follow in deciding similar cases. It makes no difference whether such opinions are joined by only five of the justices or by all nine; a majority always speaks for the Court.

Sometimes a majority of the justices agree with the outcome of the case but disagree widely among themselves with the legal reasoning used by the author of the leading opinion. As a result, there may be no majority opinion about the rationale for the decision, although there is majority agreement with the result. Such fractured opinions are identified in the case reports as "the judgment of the Court" rather than "the opinion of the Court." Often they are referred to simply as plurality opinions. Lower courts may and do look to such judgments for guidance in deciding similar cases, but they are not required to follow them.

Sitting in front of a backdrop in the Supreme Court, the Justices pose for their annual portrait. In the front row, from the left, are Justices Antonin Scalia and John Paul Stevens, Chief Justice William H. Rehnquist, and Justices Sandra Day O'Connor and Anthony M. Kennedy. In the back row, from the left, are Justices Ruth Bader Ginsburg, David H. Souter, Clarence Thomas, and Stephen G. Breyer. (AP/Wide World)

Opinions of the justices are not always models of precision. In theory, the Court addresses only the specific questions of law raised in the proceedings of lower courts. Sometimes it accepts a case for review with the stipulation that it will address only one disputed question of law. However, sometimes the justice writing for the Court gets carried away and comments on points of law that are not at issue and may have no bearing on the outcome of the case. Such comments are known as *dicta*. In theory, dicta do not carry the force of law, but lawyers and lower-court judges may nevertheless be guided by them. Not infrequently, First Amendment discussions about the proper protection for free speech have first surfaced as dicta, later to be discarded or adopted as law in subsequent appellate opinions.

The Supreme Court and the Legal System

By now, one point should be clear. If we are to know at any particular time what the law is on any given topic, we must find out what the courts have said about it. When courts at any level make a decision interpreting the meaning of a statute, administrative rule, or constitutional principle, that decision becomes a part of the case reports that are found in law libraries and in computer data banks. Publishers of the reports hire trained lawyers as editors to analyze court decisions and distill from them legal principles, which are compiled into elaborate guides to the law. Lawyers refer to these guides in preparing their presentation of a case; judges consult them in writing decisions. Much of this textbook is based on case reports, which are used both to trace the historical origins of the more important principles of media law and to illustrate how principles are applied to new cases. Before embarking on our study, we need to know a bit more about the rules that guide judges as they decide cases.

In reaching a decision on a disputed question of law, few judges have the privilege of starting fresh. Given the volume of recorded court decisions in the more than two centuries since the United States was founded, there is no shortage of legal principles applicable to almost any case. The judge's task is to determine which ones to apply. Here, the rule of precedent comes into play. As we saw earlier, the courts are organized into a hierarchy, from the lowest-level trial courts to a court of final authority. In reaching a decision, judges of the lowest-level court in each system are supposed to follow the applicable decisions of the higher appellate courts with jurisdiction over them. Thus, an Indiana circuit court judge pondering the meaning of an Indiana statute or a clause of the state's constitution would look to the decisions of the Indiana Court of Appeals or the Indiana Supreme Court. If neither court gave clear guidance, the judge might be persuaded by a well-written brief prepared by one of the contending attorneys to apply the reasoning used by a court in another state or by a federal court. In the federal system, U.S. district court judges are bound in the first instance by applicable decisions of the U.S. Supreme Court. If there are no such decisions in point, the judge is bound by decisions of the U.S. circuit court of appeals with jurisdiction over his or her court. And if here, too, nothing applies exactly, the last resort is the decisions of other courts in the same district. If even this last resort produces no precedents directly applicable to the case in point, the judge may look to decisions of other circuits for guidance.

That is how the system is supposed to work, and usually it does. Reliance on precedent gives the legal system stability. The principle involved is called *stare decisis*—that is, a judge's taking at face value a decision on a specific point of law previously made by a higher court with jurisdiction over him or her. However, if the facts of the case at issue are not exactly like those of the ruling case, or if the question of law involved can be stated in somewhat different terms, precedent can be ignored or modified. If a lower court's decision based on what it sees as a somewhat different case is upheld on appeal, there is a new precedent. This process keeps the law flexible—too flexible, its critics say.

Thus, the meaning of the law can be stated with certainty only in terms of the latest appeals court cases. The most authoritative decisions guiding state court judges are those issued by the state's highest court; for federal courts, the decisions of the Supreme Court of the United States are the final word. And if a question is raised in any court, state or federal, about the meaning and application of a principle found in the U.S. Constitution, judges must follow precedents established by the U.S. Supreme Court. That rule was established very early in the nation's history by one of our most brillant chief justices, John Marshall, who led the Supreme Court in staking out ground it holds to this day. The origins of the rule are found in four notable decisions:

1. A federal question raised during the trial of a state case in a state court creates a right to take the case to the Supreme Court of the United States. *Cohens* v. *Virginia,* 6 Wheat. 264, 5 L.Ed. 257 (1821).

2. When the Supreme Court concludes that an act of Congress or an action of the executive violates the Constitution, the Court can declare either action null and void. *Marbury* v. *Madison,* 1 Cranch 137, 2 L.Ed. 60 (1803).

3. The Court can declare null and void a state statute, or even a section of a state constitution, that violates the federal Constitution. *McCulloch* v. *Maryland,* 4 Wheat. 316, 4 L.Ed. 579 (1819).

4. Although state courts are free to interpret and apply the federal Constitution, if the state court's decision is overruled by the Supreme Court of the United States, the latter decision prevails. *Martin* v. *Hunter's Lessee,* 1 Wheat. 304, 4 L.Ed. 97 (1816).

Through these remarkable decisions the Supreme Court gave itself the authority to determine how far the Constitution permits the federal government's power to reach. It is a power that permeates every level of our legal system.

Such authority is not used lightly. As a rule, if the Supreme Court or other courts can avoid deciding a case on constitutional grounds, they will do so. If a law or executive order does not affect fundamental rights, courts assume that it is constitutional until the weight of evidence proves otherwise. If fundamental rights, such as freedom of speech and press, are at stake, the burden of proof is turned around. The government must prove that its power to restrict these rights is found in the Constitution, and it must offer compelling reasons for doing so. In two centuries, the Supreme Court has voided fewer than 125 acts of Congress.

FOR REVIEW

1. What does it mean to say that constitutional law "stands at the apex of our system of laws"?

2. Define statute law. How does it differ from an administrative ruling? Is there any difference in their legal effect?

3. Define common law. On what is it based? Assess its strengths and weaknesses.

4. Distinguish between criminal law and civil law, giving special attention to the role of the state in each.

5. Distinguish between a fine and an award of damages in a civil action.

6. Distinguish between federal and state courts, and define their respective areas of jurisdiction.

7. Compare and contrast a criminal arraignment and a civil answer.

8. Constitutions, state and federal, establish three branches of government, which generally are described as separate but equal. List those branches and, in general, their duties. If one branch can be said to be more equal than the others, what is it, and why?

9. In your town, an individual is arrested and later found guilty in a county court for disturbing the peace. The individual was one of several who formed a human chain barring access to an abortion clinic. Could the county court's decision ultimately be reviewed by the U.S. Supreme Court? Explain.

10. Identify and list the courts functioning in your county or parish. What is the subject-matter jurisdiction of each? Where would an appeal from a decision of a trial court be taken? What is the name of the court of final appeal in your state or territory?

11. What federal district court has jurisdiction where you reside? Where does it sit? Of what circuit is that court a part? Where does the circuit sit?

12. What does it mean when the Supreme Court announces that it has granted certiorari on a case presumably decided by a lower court?

13. With respect to the U.S. Supreme Court, distinguish between a *per curiam* decision, an opinion of the Court, the judgment of the Court, a concurring opinion, and a dissenting opinion. Which offers the strongest guidance to judges of lower courts?

14. In legal terms, what is a precedent? What is its role in the legal system?

CHAPTER 2

For most of human history, when people have spoken critically of the social, religious, and political views of those in power they have done so at great personal peril. Even today, despite the advances of democratic values, which have swept away many totalitarian regimes, some national governments consider critics of official policies enemies of the state, to be tortured, imprisoned, or exiled.

FREEDOM OF SPEECH AND PRESS: HISTORY AND PHILOSOPHY

Those who believe in freedom of speech and press have long argued that only those expressive freedoms ensure the existence of a government responsive to the needs of the people. Only men and women who are free to talk about their problems can arrive at mutually acceptable solutions. Only a people tolerant enough to allow speech, even speech that offends them, can grow in wisdom. Only a government accountable to the critical oversight of its people can call itself free. Among the leading proponents of that view has been the Supreme Court of the United States, holding repeatedly that debate on public issues should be robust, uninhibited, and wide open.

Among those who would agree with the Court are those news media whose merger of journalistic idealism and economic success has broadly expanded the free-speech debate to include issues about the right of access to information, about the confidentiality of news sources, and about the separation of press and state. Yet many people believe that the Court and the news media have overstated the value of freedom in a world dominated by regional conflict and poverty, by excessive and thoughtless entertainment, and by the pervasive fear of drug-induced crime and violence. Many believe the news media should cooperate with government to help it win public approval for policies designed by officials to meet the people's needs. In this view, uninformed criticism merely creates dissatisfaction and interferes with the ability of government to perform.

The debate between those who advocate freedom of expression and those who argue for restraint continues every day, even in the United States, a nation long committed to the values of the First Amendment. Almost every American president—from Jefferson to Clinton—has complained that a negative press has made it difficult to carry out his policies. Critics of freedom of speech and press are not confined to government officials. When American Nazis wanted to march in a Jewish neighborhood, when the Ku Klux Klan wanted to erect a cross on a courthouse lawn, and when an unhappy American burned his nation's flag in protest and anger, many average Americans supported efforts to silence and punish them.

Many Americans question the value of freedom for political protests with which they disagree. Many more question the value of freedom for speech that is outside of the political process entirely. There have been popular efforts, for example, to censor or ban MTV, the lyrics of popular rock and rap songs, and movies featuring sex and violence, on the grounds that such things contribute to the decay of society. On many public college campuses, students, faculty, and administrators, offended by hateful speech, have debated whether limits should be imposed on freedoms of speech and press.

This chapter presents a brief history of the development of the idea that people ought to be free to criticize and offend. The first part highlights the forces that led to the drafting and adoption of the American Declaration of Independence and the U.S. Constitution. We will focus on the First Amendment guarantee of freedom of speech and press. The second part of the chapter examines the philosophy supporting and limiting freedoms of speech and press, along with Supreme Court decisions interpreting those freedoms.

Major Cases

- *R.A.V.* v. *City of St. Paul, Minnesota,* 112 S.Ct. 2538, 120 L.Ed.2d 305 (1992).

- *Schenck* v. *United States,* 249 U.S. 47, 39 S.Ct. 247, 63 L.Ed. 470 (1919).

- *Texas* v. *Johnson,* 491 U.S. 397, 109 S.Ct. 2533, 105 L.Ed.2d 342 (1989).

THE HISTORY OF FREEDOM OF SPEECH AND PRESS

The Idea of Freedom

The origin of the idea that people should be free to govern themselves is lost in folklore. However, we do know that the idea was brought to life for the first time in the fifth century B.C., when the city-state of Athens experimented with a form of democracy. From that experience emerged the idea that people should be free to talk about the policies of government and decide for themselves which are good and which are bad. The philosophers Socrates and Plato played active parts in Athenian democracy and reflected on their experience in writings that are studied to this day. As a soldier, Socrates fought bravely for Athens against its enemies. But he also wandered the streets questioning authority, particularly the authority based on religious belief. He acquired followers, Plato among them, and at the age of thirty-one found that even in a democracy, there are limits to freedom of speech. Tried and condemned for corrupting the morals of the young, he was sentenced to death by drinking hemlock.

Socrates was immortalized in the works of Plato, who argued that truth is best reached through a rigorous discussion from which no fact or argument is withheld. Plato believed that such discussion is essential if a government is to serve its people well. His vision of an ideal form of government survives in *Republic,* which describes a state in which the good, the beautiful, and the true prevail. However, Plato, no doubt with the fate of Socrates in mind, was realistic enough to recognize that those who achieve power in government are not always willing to submit their policies to rigorous discussion, or themselves to criticism.

The Athenian flirtation with government by the people, and with the freedom of speech that accompanied it, did not last long. But the writings of Plato gave birth to an idea that has attracted followers through the ages: Truth can best be reached through free discussion.

Ancient Rome also adopted a form of democratic, popular rule, which flourished for more than two centuries before foundering in the third century B.C. amid class conflict and civil war. Despite the ugliness that marked the last days of the Roman Republic, Roman writers and scholars left a literary legacy about the uses of freedom that is still studied by democratic theorists.

Autocracy and the Divine Right of Kings

With the deaths of Julius Caesar in 44 B.C. and Mark Antony and Cleopatra a few years later, Octavian, Caesar's grandnephew, became the undisputed ruler of the Roman Empire. In 27 B.C., assuming the title of Augustus, Octavian adopted a model for government that for the next fifteen hundred years most people in Europe and the Middle East could easily recognize: autocracy—a system in which a few persons of power impose their will on the masses.

The claim to govern with or without popular support was, by the Middle Ages, a declaration of divine right. The medieval king, so went the logic, governed the lives of his people because God made him their protector. That this was so was evidenced by his soldiers, his wealth, and his alliance with the church. Critics of a king's decisions ran the risk of losing livelihoods and property, or of being tortured or killed by the king's soldiers. And, as enemies of God, critics could be condemned to eternal damnation.

The Questioning of Autocratic Power

In fifteenth-century Europe, new technologies, religious reformation, and advances in the arts and sciences set in motion political and social forces that even the cruelest tyrants could not control.

The development of the printing press, generally attributed to a German named Johannes Gutenberg, made information accessible in ways that had never before been possible. For centuries, books had been preserved and copied laboriously by hand in monastic libraries. This service, while keeping alive the great literature of the Middle Eastern and Mediterranean civilizations, also had the effect of limiting literacy and scholarship to the literate clergy and to their allied princes.

Printing made books more readily available and created opportunities for dissent outside authorized channels. From the mid-sixteenth century on, what many of the newly literate read were controversial tracts written by religious dissenters, such as Martin Luther in Germany, Huldreich Zwingli in Switzerland, and John Calvin in Geneva. They and others argued successfully for a reformation of Christian doctrine and religious practices, and for a separation from the autocratic authority of Roman Catholicism.

Authority was being questioned in other areas, too. Throughout Europe, writers, painters, sculptors, artisans, musicians, natural scientists, and others demonstrated that one could not always look backward to ancient authority to find truth. Explorers demonstrated that Earth is not flat, despite Scripture, popular belief, and church teachings. In Italy, Galileo peered at the planets through a crude telescope and concluded that, despite many ancient writings and long-held beliefs, Earth is not the center of the universe.

The forces of inquiry, once set in motion, could not be stayed. By the seventeenth century, dissenters in England were questioning not only the authority of the Church, but that of the Crown. One king, Charles I, was beheaded in 1649, leading the English monarchy to agree to share its power with an elected parliament.

John Milton's Argument for Freedom of Speech

The transfer of power from monarchs to the people required drastic changes in political theory. When kings ruled because they were ordained by God to do so, the people were their subjects. Kings gave orders; underlings were expected to obey those orders without question. People who were rash enough to question the wisdom of a king's policies could find themselves charged with seditious libel, a crime punishable by death. But when much of a king's power was transferred to an elected parliament, the old rules came under question. Long-established lines of authority literally were turned upside down. Members of a parliament represented the people, in whom the power of the state resided. Did this not mean that the people had a right to inform themselves about government policies? And did it not mean that they could criticize those policies and the officials who enforced them without being charged with seditious libel?

One person who raised these questions was John Milton, who is remembered today mainly for such enduring classics as *Paradise Lost*. However, during the civil war that followed the beheading of Charles I, Milton served as an official of and apologist for the British parliamentary government of Oliver Cromwell. During that period, Milton came under attack from Puritan members of Parliament because he had written a tract arguing that partners in an unhappy marriage should have the right to get a divorce. Puritans, who lived strictly disciplined lives in accord with their understanding of God's will, disapproved of divorce. To compound Milton's crime, he had managed to get his tract published without first obtaining approval from a government censor. According to the law in effect at that time, nothing could be published until it had received a license from the government. The purpose was to prevent publication of books or tracts critical of government policies or officials.

As Milton's experience suggests, however, the licensing system was already breaking down in the seventeenth century as printing presses became more common. Milton responded to the attack on his works by proposing that the system of censorship be abolished. In 1644, he composed "A Speech for the Liberty Of UNLICENC'D PRINTING," which, published in essay form, bears the title *Areopagitica*. This work is a passionate yet well-reasoned argument against government censorship of written works dealing with political policy.

It is illogical to assume, Milton wrote, that any government can satisfy all its people. It is equally illogical to assume that everything a government does will be done justly. But if the people are free to talk and write about government policies, and if those who govern are willing to pay attention, the result should be an improvement in the quality of government and the well-being of the people.

However, Milton had reservations about how far freedom of expression ought to go and who could be trusted with it. Note the conflicting currents running through this passage from *Areopagitica:*

> I deny not, but that it is of greatest concernment in the Church and Commonwealth, to have a vigilant eye how Bookes demeane themselves, as well as men; and thereafter to confine, imprison, and do sharpest justice on them as malefactors; for Bookes are not absolutely dead things, but do contain a potencie of life in them to be as active as that soule was whose progeny they are; nay they do preserve as in a violl the purest efficacie and extraction of that living intellect that bred them.[1]

Milton's contribution to the advancement of freedom of expression lies in his recognition that such freedom is in the public interest. He summarized his message in a notable passage:

> And though all the windes of doctrine were let loose to play upon the earth, so Truth be in the field, we do injuriously by licencing and prohibiting to misdoubt her strength. Let her and Falshood grapple; who ever knew Truth put to the wors, in a free and open encounter.[2]

Two hundred years later, Milton's idea was put in stronger terms by another English philosopher, John Stuart Mill. In his essay "On Liberty," Mill argued that even when the power of government is backed by near-unanimous public opinion, that power should not be used to suppress dissent. He wrote:

> If all mankind minus one were of one opinion, and only one person were of the contrary opinion, mankind would be no more justified in silencing that one person, than he, if he had the power, would be justified in silencing mankind. . . . [T]he peculiar evil of silencing the expression of an opinion is, that it is robbing the human race: posterity as well as the existing generation; those who dissent from the opinion, still more than those who hold it. If the opinion is right, they are deprived of the opportunity of exchanging error for truth; if wrong, they lose, what is almost as great a benefit, the clearer perception and livelier impression of truth, produced by its collision with error.[3]

Mill recognized what Milton did not, that truth cannot always prevail, at least in the short run, against the cruel refinements of repression and propaganda used by some determined dictators. Nor could either Mill or Milton have anticipated the impasse created when both sides of a dispute take unyielding positions based on opposing principle, as in the debate over a woman's right to have an abortion. Moreover, Milton himself did not always practice what he preached. Secure in the belief that his

---

1. *Complete Poetry and Works of John Milton* (New York: Modern Library, 1950), pp. 681–682.
2. Ibid., p. 719.
3. John Stuart Mill, "On Liberty." In *J. S. Mill's* On Liberty *in Focus,* ed. John Gray and G. W. Smith (London and New York: Routledge, 1991), p. 37.

own Protestant views were correct, he had no objections to censoring the works of Catholic writers.

Milton's arguments, persuasive as they sound to modern ears, did not end political oppression in England. After 1660, when the English Parliament restored Charles II to the throne, but with less power than his father had had, English citizens continued to suffer cruel deaths for the crime of seditious libel. One of the more interesting of the many cases reported in *Howell's State Trials*[4] involved a printer, John Twyn, whose shop was raided by constables in the early hours of the morning. They found smudged page proofs of a book arguing that a king whose decrees violated the "law of God" should be called to account by the people. When Twyn refused to identify the author of the tract, he was accused of "imagining and intending the death" of the king. After a short trial, during which the judge acted both as Twyn's lawyer and his accuser, a jury found him guilty and condemned Twyn to be drawn and quartered. At the start of the procedure, the victim's "privy-members" were cut off and burned within his sight so that he would die knowing it was unlikely he could procreate in the afterlife. Twyn's head was cut off and his body hacked into four pieces. Each part was hanged above one of the several portals to the old city of London as a warning to others who might dare question such authority as the king still had.

Twyn was a victim of the Royalist backlash that accompanied the restoration of the monarch, even one who had to share power with an elected parliament. Milton, too, was a victim, but only to the extent of being driven out of public life. Not until 1695, twenty-one years after Milton's death, did Parliament take his advice and let the Printing Act expire, thus advancing the cause of free speech in England.

John Locke and the Rights of the People

There is a striking similarity between the ideas for which Twyn was executed in 1663 and those that survive in John Locke's *Two Treatises on Government,* published in 1690. Locke designed his *Treatises* to rationalize the transfer of power from a king who rules by divine right, to a parliament that represents the people. In doing so, Locke borrowed the social-compact theory of the origins of government from Thomas Hobbes, an earlier political philosopher. This theory rests on the assumption that at some time in the past people recognized that they would be better off working together than they were in a "state of nature," where every family had to provide for all its needs. In that state, the only law was the "law of the jungle," which meant, in effect, that only the strongest or the most clever survived. Hobbes theorized that at some point people had become tired of fending for themselves and had agreed to surrender some of their independence in return for security. These agreements, or compacts, marked the beginning of organized society and of rudimentary governments.

Locke expanded on Hobbes's social-compact theory and sought to formalize it. Like the unknown author of the tract for which Twyn was executed, Locke argued that those who govern should be held accountable to the people. But Locke had no illusions that the transfer of power to the people from a monarch who ruled by divine right

---

4.   15 Charles II 1663, p. 513.

would in itself end tyranny. Locke recognized that majorities also can adopt policies that oppress minorities. To counter that possibility, Locke advocated two safeguards:

1. People creating a new government should agree in advance on the powers they are willing to give it and define the limits of those powers in a written constitution.

2. The constitution should make clear that the people are not giving up all of the personal rights they enjoyed in the state of nature. Life in the political jungle may have been hard, but, Locke argued, some of its freedoms ought not be surrendered to any government.

As a further barrier against oppression by majority vote, Locke argued that the powers of government ought to be divided three ways: An elected legislature should have the power to adopt laws; an independent executive branch should have the power to carry the laws into effect; and a court system should have the power to dispense justice and determine the rights of citizens. Finally, all three branches of government should be constrained by a duty to the law of nature, which, in Locke's view, guaranteed the personal, or natural, rights retained by the people.

Under Locke's system, then, there would be a check on the will of the majority. People who believed that a law violated their natural rights could appeal to the courts for justice. If the judges decided that the law did infringe those rights, they had the duty to hold that the law was void. Further, Locke argued, the people had a right to resist officials who exceeded the powers given them by the compact.

The political wisdom of fifteen hundred years literally was turned upside down as people began to understand Locke's argument. No longer was the power to govern understood as flowing from the top down. No longer were the people expected to obey without question whatever order a monarch might give them. Authority had shifted, at least in some parts of the world, back to the people. With that authority came the right to choose rulers, and to oust them if they abused their powers. This right implied, at the least, the people's right to criticize those they had elevated to public office. In theory and increasingly in practice, the argument that kings governed by divine right was no longer reasonable. If kings governed at all, they did so legitimately by popular will, or illegitimately by brutal force of arms. Locke's views gradually prevailed in England and, later, in its American colonies.

Seditious Libel in Colonial America

When Locke wrote his *Two Treatises on Government,* the English colonies in America had been in existence for nearly a century. Already, some colonists were beginning to object to the idea of being ruled from London. Although each colony had a legislative body of some kind, the governors were appointed in London, and colonial laws were subject to veto by the British Parliament. In addition, laws enacted by Parliament were to be obeyed by the colonists just as they were in the homeland. One such law was the law of seditious libel.

John Peter Zenger defied the colonial law of seditious libel so that he might tell his *New York Weekly Journal* readers about the misdeeds of New York Governor William Cosby. Zenger's arrest in 1734 led to a jury's verdict of not guilty, striking an early blow for freedom of the press. The event is commemorated in this tapestry designed by Albert Herter. *(Bettmann)*

In 1734, that law was challenged in an action in the New York courts. John Peter Zenger, publisher of the *New York Weekly Journal,* had published articles accusing Governor William Cosby of dishonesty and oppression.[5] Cosby reacted by charging Zenger with seditious libel. Zenger spent nine months in jail awaiting trial, while his wife continued to publish the paper. When Zenger came to trial, he faced a rule of law that made it almost impossible for him to win. Under that rule, any words, whether true or false, that tended to undermine the people's faith in their government were punishable. During the trial, the judge instructed the jury that the truth of Zenger's articles was not at issue. Indeed, one of the precepts of the law of seditious libel held that the greater the truth, the greater the libel. That is, if an official was as corrupt as the offending article said he was, the report was likely to undermine his authority. In the judge's view, the only question for the jury to decide was whether the article reduced Cosby's power to govern. Under the precedents in effect at the time, there was no question that it did.

Zenger's lawyer, Andrew Hamilton, took the bold step of disregarding the judge's instructions and made Cosby's conduct the question for the jury to ponder. He told the jurors that under cases recently decided in England, they could not be punished if they ignored the judge's instructions. That was true, but Hamilton also advanced an argument that had no basis in common law, either in English or colonial courts. With great eloquence, he argued that truth ought never to be punished as libelous. The jury agreed and found Zenger not guilty.

---

5. Frederic Breakspear Farrar, "A Printer, a Lawyer, and the Free Press," *Editor & Publisher,* 3 August 1985. The article includes a facsimile of the *New York Weekly Journal* for 2 December 1734 reporting the order to burn several issues of the *Journal* because they had been declared seditious.

However, the verdict did not change the law of seditious libel. Not until after the American Revolution, half a century later, would Congress recognize truth as a defense against harmful criticism of government, and that recognition would be short-lived. However, because the Zenger decision was widely publicized and became a rallying point for foes of press censorship, the decision sent a message to British prosecutors in the American colonies. There is no record of seditious libel trials in the colonial courts after Zenger's acquittal. Thus, the case generally is regarded as the beginning of press freedom in what was to become the United States of America.

During the fifty years following the Zenger trial, the belief in freedom of speech and press was by no means universal. If the government would not act against unpopular speakers and writers, the people occasionally did. Some editors who favored English rule in the years leading up to the Revolution were victims of mob violence. However, persons who believed that the colonists were victims of oppressive laws enacted by a parliament in which they had no representation found a ready outlet for their protests in newspapers, in pamphlets, and in the pulpits of many churches. Some of those critics of English rule drew their arguments from writings used to justify England's earlier rebellion against its monarchs. Locke's works in particular were used by speakers who argued that the colonies should sever their ties to England and establish a new political order in which the rights of the people could be protected.[6]

Those arguments took tangible form in 1776 in the Declaration of Independence, which led to more than five years of war, ending with the creation of the United States of America. Both the Declaration and the Constitution, which established our present form of government in 1789, draw heavily from Locke's *Two Treatises on Government*. The first paragraph of the Declaration invokes the authority of "the Laws of Nature and of Nature's God" to justify separation from English authority. The Constitution, enacted in the name of "[w]e, the people of the United States," is a compact of the kind Locke recommended.

The Constitution and the Bill of Rights

It is impossible at this distance to imagine what it must have been like to establish a new government stretching from Maine to Georgia along the Atlantic coast two hundred years ago. Yet some things are clear. The Founders did not want a monarch, or an executive who could assume the powers of one. They believed that the people were the source of the government's power. They thought the primary responsibility for day-to-day governing should rest with the states. But they needed a central government to conduct relations with foreign countries, to protect them from foreign enemies, to create a monetary system, and to ensure the flow of commerce among the states and with other countries. However, they did not want that government to become strong enough to take away the powers of the states or certain basic liberties of the people.

---

6. Lawrence Henry Gipson, *The British Empire before the American Revolution*, vol. 13: *The Triumphant Empire* (New York: Knopf, 1967), pp. 193–194.

After the colonists had won their freedom in the Revolution, with help from the French army and navy, they tried to get along with an almost powerless central government operating under the Articles of Confederation. When it became evident that such a government was not going to work, the states elected delegates to a constitutional convention, which met in secret in Philadelphia for four months in 1787 and produced a brief document of seven articles. Including the names of its forty signers, the Constitution takes up about four pages of the *World Almanac.* Amendments added since it went into effect in 1789 take up another three and a half pages.

In simplest terms, the Constitution is a plan of government. It establishes the institutions of government: Congress, the executive branch, headed by the president, and the judiciary, headed by the Supreme Court of the United States. Numbered sections and subsections define the powers of each. Other articles define the relationship between the federal and state governments. Another prescribes the slow, deliberate procedure by which the Constitution can be amended.

As presented to the states for adoption, the Constitution said nothing about the rights of the people, including the right to speak and write freely about the actions of the central government. The drafters had acted on the theory that they were creating a central government of carefully defined, limited powers. In their view, they had given that government no authority to meddle with the rights of its citizens. The Constitution's silence on the people's rights raised suspicions in the minds of political leaders in several states. They made a point of conditioning their approval of the new union on the promise that the Constitution would be amended to protect the rights of individuals.

Within two years after the federal government began functioning in 1789, Congress proposed twelve amendments making up a bill of rights designed to prevent the new central government from trampling on the people's natural or personal rights. Interestingly, in light of the importance that the guarantee of the freedom of speech, press, and religion has assumed in our time, those freedoms were not the subject of the original First Amendment. The original First Amendment dealt with the apportionment of representatives to Congress, and the Second with their compensation. When both failed to win ratification, the original Third became the First.

In large part, the subject matter of the ten adopted amendments reflects grievances against specific injustices experienced by Americans during the latter days of British colonial rule. In some of the colonies people had been taxed to support officially approved churches; in others, believers in unapproved religious doctrines had been persecuted. Thus, the First Amendment begins by declaring that Congress is neither to tax the people to support a state church nor to interfere with the right to worship as one pleases. Next, in the same amendment, is what appears to be a flat prohibition against any attempt by Congress to limit freedom of speech or of the press. Then follows a guarantee of the right of the people to assemble peacefully and to ask government for a redress of grievances. The Third, Fourth, and Fifth amendments are designed to protect the privacy of the home and to prevent seizure of property. The Fourth through the Eighth, with some overlapping, detail the rights of persons accused of crime.

Here we focus on the First Amendment:

> Congress shall make no law respecting an establishment of religion, or prohibiting the free exercise thereof; or abridging the freedom of speech, or of the press; or the right of the people peaceably to assemble, and to petition the Government for a redress of grievances.

Strangely, there is little in the debates of the time to show what the drafters meant when they wrote and adopted that amendment. Read literally, it seems to say that Congress has no authority to limit freedom of speech or of the press. But the realities of the time suggest otherwise.

According to one view, the founders were influenced by Sir William Blackstone, whose *Commentaries on the Laws of England* was considered the definitive discussion of the meaning of the common law in the colonies as well as in England. Following Milton's lead, Blackstone condemned government censorship of the press. But he also defended the government's right to punish publishers of blasphemous, immoral, treasonable, schismatical, seditious, or scandalous libels. He wrote:

> The liberty of the press is indeed essential to the nature of a free state; but this consists in laying no previous restraints upon publications, and not in freedom from censure for criminal matter when published. Every freeman has an undoubted right to lay what sentiments he pleases before the public: to forbid this is to destroy the freedom of the press: but if he publishes what is improper, mischievous, or illegal, he must take the consequences of his own temerity.[7]

Clearly, Blackstone's view of liberty of the press was limited. By his standards, England had enjoyed liberty of the press since the Printing Act had expired in 1695, and the American colonies since 1725, when the licensing act was permitted to expire on this side of the Atlantic. But if writers knew they might suffer Twyn's fate or languish in jail like Zenger, how likely were they to share their views with the public?

Only scanty written evidence remains as to what the founders meant when they sought to protect freedom of speech and of the press. Thomas Jefferson, who wrote the Declaration of Independence, and James Madison, who wrote the First Amendment to the Constitution, seem to have rejected the English common law of seditious libel.[8] Benjamin Franklin, a member of the committee that drafted the Declaration and a delegate to the convention that drafted the Constitution, said in 1789 during a discussion of the freedom of speech clause in the Pennsylvania constitution: "[I]f by the liberty of the press were to be understood merely the liberty of discussing the propriety of public measures and political opinions, let us have as much of it as you please. On the other hand, if it means liberty to calumniate another, there ought to be some limit."[9] That he would put some limits on liberty of speech is notable in light of the

---

7. William Blackstone, *Commentaries on the Laws of England,* facsimile ed. (Chicago: University of Chicago Press, 1979), vol. 4, pp. 151–152.
8. Zechariah Chafee, Jr., *Free Speech in the United States* (Cambridge, Mass.: Harvard University Press, 1941); Leonard W. Levy, *Legacy of Suppression* (Cambridge, Mass.: Belknap Press of Harvard University Press, 1960).
9. Zechariah Chafee, Jr., *Free Speech in the United States,* Atheneum ed. (New York: Atheneum, 1969), p. 17.

fact that he was a successful printer and publisher until he became caught up in public life in 1748.

The first ten amendments to the Constitution—the Bill of Rights—took effect in 1791. At that point, the United States not only had a form of government based squarely on John Locke's *Two Treatises on Government;* it also had taken steps to guarantee the rights of the people, an idea borrowed from Thomas Hobbes. In a sense, the Bill of Rights created a law above the law to which people could appeal, through the courts, when they believed their freedom was being violated. The Supreme Court has held on numerous occasions that laws or acts of public officials that violate rights guaranteed by the first ten amendments are void.

The Sedition Act of 1798

Within a decade after the adoption of the First Amendment, the federal government's commitment to freedom of speech was put to the test, and it failed. Reacting to the possibility that inflamed passions might draw the United States into a renewed war between England and France, Congress adopted the Sedition Act of 1798, which was plainly a seditious libel law. The act made it a crime, punishable by fine and imprisonment, to engage in harmful criticism of President John Adams and his policies. However, unlike the law under which Zenger had been prosecuted fifty years earlier, persons accused under the act could use truth as a defense.

The Sedition Act had its origins in the highly charged partisan politics of the time. President Adams headed the Federalist party, which was sympathetic to England while wanting to keep the United States out of the war. The Federalists also believed in a strongly centralized government in which the president played a dominant role. In opposition were the Republicans, headed by Vice President Thomas Jefferson. Theirs was a party of small farmers and artisans who mistrusted a strong central government. Party members leaned toward the French, remembering their help in the Revolution. It soon became apparent that the Sedition Act was aimed primarily at the editors of Republican newspapers.

Viewed from the vantage point of today, the Sedition Act was obviously a serious abridgment of freedom of speech and of the press. Yet, judging from the records of the time, few people in 1798 believed that it violated the First Amendment guarantees. The debate in Congress preceding passage of the act indicates that the amendment was seen only as a protection against direct censorship. One speaker, echoing Blackstone, said that the First Amendment could not prevent punishment of an editor who published material that "offends against the law."[10] Alexander Hamilton, who had been President Washington's secretary of the treasury and remained one of the leaders of the Federalist party, defended the Sedition Act, partly because of the clause making truth a defense. In a 1799 letter, Hamilton argued that officers of government could serve effectively only if the law protected "their reputations from malicious and unfounded slanders."[11]

---

10. Robert Harper, a representative from South Carolina, 8 *Annals of Congress,* 5th Cong. 1797–1799, p. 2101.
11. *The Papers of Alexander Hamilton,* vol. 23 (New York: Columbia University Press, 1976), p. 604.

This view was shared by Justice Samuel Chase of the Supreme Court of the United States. As was the practice in those days, he also sat as a trial judge assigned to a "circuit" made up of one or more states. In his decision that found Dr. Thomas Cooper, editor of the *Sunbury and Northumberland Gazette,* guilty of sedition, Justice Chase noted that he did not know of a government that had no laws to protect itself and its officials from harmful criticism. In a passage that could have been written by some present-day politicians, he said:

> A Republican government can only be destroyed in two ways; the introduction of luxury or the licentiousness of the Press. The latter is the more slow, but more sure and certain, means of bringing about the destruction of the government. The legislature of this country, knowing this maxim, has thought proper to check the licentiousness of the press.[12]

Cooper's crime was that he wrote an editorial taking issue with President Adams's trade policies. According to Cooper, when Adams had taken office, "he was hardly in the infancy of political mistake." That statement was enough to put Cooper among the approximately twenty-five persons arrested on charges of sedition in 1798 and 1799. Fifteen were indicted, eleven tried, and ten found guilty.[13] The crime was a misdemeanor punishable by a fine or a jail term, or both. Almost all of those who were tried were editors of Republican newspapers.

The act aroused opposition. Two states, Kentucky and Virginia, passed resolutions condemning it—the former written by Thomas Jefferson, the latter by James Madison. The resolutions took the position that in passing the Sedition Act, Congress had usurped powers expressly denied it by the Constitution. The adoption of these resolutions implied that a similar act might be legal if it were drafted and adopted by the various state legislatures.

The Sedition Act expired in March 1801, at the end of Adams's term. Historians differ as to the role public resentment over its enforcement played in the election of Thomas Jefferson as president in 1800. One of the first things Jefferson did as president was to pardon all who had been convicted under the act. Because all of the victims were members of his Republican party, it is impossible to know whether he acted on a firm belief in freedom of speech or out of political motives. During his first term Jefferson took no action to prevent the trial of one of his critics, Harry Croswell, who was charged with violating New York's seditious libel law.[14]

The episode lies embedded deep within American history, but its lessons remain valid. Even in a nation with a Constitution that guarantees freedom of speech and press, the urge to suppress unpopular speakers and writers lies just beneath the surface. When foreign enemies threaten or economic hardship creates unrest, that urge may well be translated into action, official or unofficial. Experience with the Sedition Act did nothing to demonstrate how much protection the First Amendment offers to critics of government, because none of the convictions was appealed to the Supreme Court as a whole.

---

12. United States v. Cooper, 25 Fed. Cas. 631, 635 (1800).
13. Clifton O. Lawhorne, *Defamation and Public Officials: The Evolving Law of Libel* (Carbondale: Southern Illinois University Press, 1971), p. 51.
14. People v. Croswell, 3 Johns. Cas. 337 (1804).

THE PHILOSOPHY OF FREEDOM OF SPEECH AND PRESS

The belief that free discussion offers society the best hope for peaceful resolution of its differences has advanced haltingly and still is held by only a minority of the world's peoples. Such belief assumes that the participants in the debate are rational and willing to compromise on something short of each side's view of absolute truth. The alternative is suppression of one side or the other. Thus, freedom of speech is viewed as beneficial both to individuals, who otherwise might be persecuted for their beliefs, and to society, which will enjoy stability under public policies approved by a majority and acceptable to the minority.

Court decisions, even those of the Supreme Court of the United States, are reactive. They tell us what the law is at any given time. They are reached in response to real-life conflicts, in which both sides have much to gain or lose. In making decisions, judges, as we have seen, rely on legal precedents when they can. When they cannot, they must choose between legal theories offered by the parties to the action or legal philosophy, either their own or that of scholars of the law. Such scholars study the law with a view to establishing principles that will lead to just decisions and serve the public good. Thus, to the degree that it is adopted by judges, legal philosophy is prescriptive—that is, it seeks to point to where the law should be.

The speech and press clause of the First Amendment has intrigued legal scholars because its guarantees are intertwined with the larger questions of how much or how little the government should regulate the economy, business, education, natural resources, and even the personal lives of its citizens. What did the founders mean when they adopted a constitutional amendment saying, "Congress shall make no law . . . abridging the freedom of speech, or of the press"? What should those words mean as we near the end of the twentieth century? In the best of all possible worlds, if everyone were rational, reasonable, and dispassionate, the answer would be simple: There would be no need for any law limiting the freedoms of speech and press. People would solve the problems of society by talking them out and reaching a compromise acceptable to everyone. Even in our imperfect society, this is the process mandated by the Constitution, and it works most of the time.

However, as we saw in the first part of this chapter, freedom of speech and a free press create tension in the relationship between government and its citizens. In studying that relationship, First Amendment theorists have sought to demonstrate, in the tradition of John Milton, that unfettered debate, in which all are free to participate, is the best means of arriving at the truth about important public issues. However, most theorists have also recognized, as did Milton, that words can cause harm, not only to society but to individuals. Many of the differences between theorists relate to the argument over the point at which harm occurs and the degree to which even harmful speech should be protected in order to ensure that all sides are heard in the debate on public policy.

Thus, in one dimension, First Amendment theorists point to the future, telling us what ought to be. Courts work in a second dimension, the present, telling us what the law is with respect to freedom of speech and press. A third dimension, ethics, is concerned with what is right, with the moral aspects of freedom of speech and press. In some instances, theory approves and law permits speech that some believe to be harmful. For example, in theory, we need to know anything that might bear on the fitness of a candidate to hold public office. Certainly, there are no legal barriers to publishing such information. But there is a strong difference of opinion as to whether the media ought to air unproven allegations that a married candidate for president kept a mistress on his state's payroll while he was governor. Thus, there are times when media professionals must draw on their own sense of ethics in deciding what to do. In this book we discuss the ethical considerations applying to each area of media law in a section called "In the Professional World" at the end of each chapter.

First Amendment theory should not be dismissed as interesting only to lawyers and judges. In a society such as ours, each of us must decide how important it is to insist that others be permitted to speak their minds. No person's right to speak and write freely is any more secure than that of the least rational and most repulsive member of society. Once we embark on a course of silencing those whose speech we don't like, we run the risk that we may be next.

Speech as a Means of Individual Fulfillment

On the basis of their reading of Hobbes and Locke, the drafters of the Declaration of Independence found some "truths to be self-evident, that all Men are created equal, that they are endowed by their Creator with certain unalienable Rights, that among these are Life, Liberty, and the Pursuit of Happiness."[15] The idea of "unalienable rights" was carried forward and formalized in the Constitution, which, says its preamble, was adopted to "establish justice, insure domestic tranquility," and "secure the blessings of liberty to ourselves and our posterity."

Such language presumes that in establishing public policy, one person's word is as good as another's. We may not get our way, but if we have had our say, we may be more willing to accept the result. Most of us have had times when frank talk cleared the air and left us feeling better for it. Thus, freedom of speech is a means of individual fulfillment. Thomas I. Emerson, a professor at Yale who wrote one of the leading works on First Amendment theory,[16] argued that freedom of expression can be justified on that basis alone: "It derives from the widely accepted premise of Western thought that the proper end of man is the realization of his character and potentialities as a human being."[17]

In defining who can benefit from free speech, theorists and the courts have used the term "individual" broadly. It includes religious and social organizations, trade associations, political action committees, the press, and nonmedia private corporations. It also includes persons and groups who use speech to denigrate others. All have a right to participate in forging public policy.

---

15. The United States Declaration of Independence, 4 July 1776.
16. Thomas I. Emerson, *The System of Freedom of Expression* (New York: Random House, 1970).
17. Thomas I. Emerson, *Toward a General Theory of the First Amendment* (New York: Random House, 1966), pp. 4–5.

What kinds of speech should be protected? Alexander Meiklejohn, a philosophy professor who wrote widely on academic freedom before turning his attention to the First Amendment, postulated a two-tier theory of freedom of expression: at the higher level, speech devoted to public affairs; at a lower level, speech that distorts debate on public matters, speech that directly provokes illegal acts, and speech that brings harm to other individuals.[18] In his view, the people of the United States are "the electorate," the most important branch of government. Meiklejohn argued that when the electorate engages in political speech, the First Amendment means exactly what it says: "It admits of no exceptions. It tells us that Congress and, by implication, all other agencies of government are denied any authority whatever to limit the political freedom of the citizens of the United States."[19] Meiklejohn defined political speech broadly, including the discussion of economic and social issues—such as factory closings, air pollution, abortion, and racial and sexual discrimination—because all such issues involve government action at some point. As we shall see, the Supreme Court has gone a long way toward adopting Meiklejohn's position, holding on numerous occasions that the protection of political speech lies at the very core of the First Amendment.

Unquestionably, freedom of speech is an essential element of personal liberty. But if it is seen only as a means of personal fulfillment, it is on weak ground. Milton may well have believed that truth always emerges triumphant in "free and open encounter" with falsehood, but cruel experience suggests otherwise. In the nineteenth century John Stuart Mill dismissed Milton's notion as "idle sentimentality."[20] In the twentieth century, at a time when speech was being brutally suppressed in both Germany and the Soviet Union, Walter Lippmann wrote that mere tolerance is not enough to protect unpopular speakers.[21] He noted that most persons say they believe in freedom of speech, but, in his opinion, few have a strong commitment to it. Freedom of speech can survive, he concluded, only if people realize that the freedom of others is necessary to improve our own opinions. Thus, First Amendment theorists, enlarging on ideas advanced by Milton and Mill, have sought to portray freedom of speech as essential to the kind of society in which individuals can live up to their potential and engage in "the pursuit of happiness."

Freedom of Speech as a Social Value

The Search for Truth

Plato dreamed of an ideal republic in which the good, the beautiful, and the true would prevail through a process of rigorous discussion. But he also conceded that such a state might not come about "till philosophers become kings, or those now named

---

18. Alexander Meiklejohn, *Political Freedom* (New York: Harper & Row, 1960).
19. Ibid., pp. 107–108.
20. John Stuart Mill, *On Liberty* (Chicago: Gateway, 1955), p. 24.
21. Walter Lippmann, "The Indispensable Opposition," published originally in the *Atlantic Monthly* in 1939. Reprinted in Henry Steele Commager, ed., *Living Ideas in America* (New York: Harper & Row, 1951), pp. 400–403.

kings and rulers give themselves to philosophy truly and rightly."[22] Milton saw freedom of speech as a means of reaching truths that could become policies of government. Mill argued that if an opinion were so lightly regarded that it was rejected by "all mankind minus one," it should not be silenced. To do so would deprive the majority of "the opportunity of exchanging error for truth." Few present-day philosophers have been able to add much to these arguments supporting freedom of speech.

Zechariah Chafee, Jr., wrote *Free Speech in the United States,*[23] at a time when freedom was the exception, not the rule, for a majority of the world's people. He saw freedom of speech as only one of many interests that government must protect for its own good and that of society. In his view, however, freedom of speech was a most important interest, because only through the free play of ideas is truth likely to be found. If the government uses its power to suppress a point of view, "it becomes a matter of chance whether it is thrown on the false side or the true, and truth loses all the natural advantages of the contest."[24]

Emerson urged those who would forge government policy to "hear all sides of the question, especially as presented by those who feel strongly and argue militantly for a different view. He must consider all alternatives, test his judgment by exposing it to opposition, make full use of different minds to sift the true from the false."[25]

Thus, the search for truth is seen as a process of give and take, of an exchange where ideas, instead of goods, are traded. In 1919 Justice Oliver Wendell Holmes, writing to protest a decision sending several Socialists to prison, argued for a "free trade in ideas" because "the best test of truth is the power of the thought to get itself accepted in the competition of the market."[26] This statement gave rise to the expression "marketplace of ideas." However, the question of whether such a marketplace will offer takers the kind of truth that can be converted into enlightened government policy, or merely sound bites and headlines that will carry incumbents through the next election, remains open.

The Development of Government Policy

In its pure form, the search for truth is the business of philosophers, theologians, and academics. At a more practical level, theorists have argued that freedom of speech is essential to the development of government policy. No president can lead the nation very far without the support of public opinion, as Presidents Johnson and Nixon learned during the Vietnam war. Congress has divided itself into scores of committees so that it can hear from competing interests before it seeks to reconcile their views in statutes. Interest groups representing labor, business, welfare recipients, the elderly, and many others keep representatives in Washington and at state capitols for the sole purpose of using their voices, magnified by those of their employers, to influence government policy. So, it goes without question that in a free society, freedom of speech

---

22. Benjamin Jowett, trans., *Republic of Plato* (Oxford: Clarendon Press, 1908), pp. 473.
23. Chafee, *Free Speech in the United States,* Atheneum ed.
24. Ibid., pp. 31–32.
25. Emerson, *Toward a General Theory of the First Amendment,* p. 7.
26. Abrams v. United States, 250 U.S. 616, 40 S.Ct. 17, 63 L.Ed. 1173 (1919).

is vital to the forging of public policy. But does what Meiklejohn called "unregulated talkativeness" serve a valid public purpose?[27]

Chafee noted that free speech is not the only interest that government must protect. Government is also concerned with order, education, and protection against external aggression. If speech threatens to interfere with these other interests, Chafee argued, speech should weigh so heavily in the balance that it is punished only in cases when public safety is really impaired. The line between acceptable speech and unacceptable speech should be drawn, he argued, "close to the point where words will give rise to unlawful acts."[28] Thus, in Chafee's view there are times when speech can be harmful to government policy. In such instances, the courts must balance the right of the speaker against the state's interest in protecting legitimate governmental concerns. The Supreme Court has often endorsed that view, as we shall see, and has applied the balancing test in many contexts, holding sometimes the interest in free speech must give way to the protection of other interests.

In Meiklejohn's view, speech plays such an important role in the formulation of public policy that, when voiced for that purpose, it should be given absolute protection. Further, he would have government encourage debate on its policies by opening public buildings and other public places for that purpose. Such places should be as open to those who attack the government's policies as they are to those who support them.

As already noted, however, Meiklejohn relegated speech-related action and some forms of pure speech to a lower level, where they are protected not by the First Amendment but by the due process clause of the Fifth Amendment. Although he expressly rejected the application of Chafee's balancing test to speech having to do with public policy,[29] he was willing to apply it to lower-level speech. Some such speech grows out of personal relationships: One person, for instance, does not have an absolute right to defame another. Other such speech is a product of commercial relationships: Advertisers do not have a right to make false claims for their products. Meiklejohn also put on his lower level some speech directed at government. Once the debate on policy has ended and has been formalized into a statute, the people are required to obey the law until it has been changed. Speech or speech-related action in defiance of law may be punished if the punishment is carried out in accord with the due process guarantees of the Fifth Amendment.

Although Meiklejohn advocated that people with all shades of opinion should be welcomed to the debate on public policy, he also argued that some control should be imposed on the process.[30] To ensure an orderly discussion of the issues, noisy obstructionists should be removed from the forum. Nor should twenty persons be given time to say the same thing. Nor does the First Amendment mean that an individual should be permitted to use a sound truck in a residential neighborhood in the middle of the night to argue a point of view, nor demonstrators be permitted to stop traffic in rush hour to make a point. Meiklejohn argued that what was essential was not that everyone be guaranteed an opportunity to speak, but that everything worth saying

---

27.   Meiklejohn, *Political Freedom,* p. 26.
28.   Chafee, *Free Speech in the United States,* p. 35.
29.   Meiklejohn, *Political Freedom,* pp. 58–59.
30.   Ibid., p. 26.

have an opportunity to be said. In short, Meiklejohn was saying, as the Supreme Court has said consistently, that the state may regulate the *process* of debate—the time, place, and manner of speaking—but in doing so, it must be neutral as to the *content* of the speech. If it is not neutral, the governors, and not the governed, are controlling government policy.

Emerson went further, arguing that all expression, including some kinds of speech-related action, that bears on government policy should have the full protection of the First Amendment. He would protect peaceful picketing, demonstrations, the carrying of signs, and symbolic speech, such as the burning of an American flag. Emerson found no room in a system of free expression for application of the balancing test advocated by Chafee. In his view, courts considering First Amendment cases should limit themselves to defining whether the speech at issue is a form of expression on government policy. If so, it should be protected absolutely against any act of government seeking to limit it.

Emerson finished *The System of Freedom of Expression* while demonstrations against the war in Vietnam were boiling around him on the Yale campus. What he saw obviously raised questions about the viability of freedom of speech. In an epilogue, he expresses doubt that such freedom can survive if those on one side equate freedom of speech with a lack of conviction and those on the other attempt to limit speech to preserve the status quo. Another professor on another campus, Jerome Barron of the National Law Center, George Washington University, pondered the same events and came to a different conclusion. He saw the riots of that era as a symptom of a breakdown of the system used to formulate government policy. That system had turned a deaf ear to messages it did not want to hear. It excluded from the debate such groups as college students and others opposed to the war, as well as African-Americans who were chafing under the formal and informal rules of racial segregation then in force. Barron wrote a law journal article[31] and then a book[32] taking First Amendment theory to a new level.

In Barron's view, the news media are big businesses engaged in pursuit of an audience. When he was formulating his theory in the 1960s, the number of cities in which two or more newspapers were owned by publishers of differing political views was dwindling rapidly. The survivor was the one that could offer the most readers to the city's advertisers. And the survivor could not abandon the pursuit for circulation. It must compete with television stations, radio, billboards and other media, all of which also depended on advertising revenues. The constant need to placate various audiences in order to attract both subscribers and advertisers made media managers cautious. This caution was reflected in bland content that largely ignored the dispossessed members of society. Shut out of the conventional media when they sought to engage in rational debate, the dispossessed turned to violence to call attention to their grievances.

Barron argued that if the First Amendment were to have any real application to the modern world, the way we think about it needs to be turned around. At the time, the amendment played a passive role, protecting expression after it had been published or

31. Jerome Barron, "Access to the Press—A New First Amendment Right," 80 *Harv.L.Rev.* 1641 (1967).
32. Jerome Barron, *Freedom of the Press for Whom?* (Bloomington: Indiana University Press, 1973).

broadcasted. Media managers who were cautious enough not to make waves had no need for such protection. Barron advocated that the First Amendment be used as a weapon to compel the media to carry all shades of opinion. At a minimum, he said, the First Amendment should give people a right to buy advertising space to offer their views on public policy, and should give public officials and public figures a right to respond to attacks on them or their policies. At one point, he suggested that newspapers be required to publish all letters to the editor. Courts have refused to adopt Barron's theory of the First Amendment, but it has been widely discussed in university law and journalism classrooms and at meetings of editors and television news directors, and this discussion has led to voluntary decisions that have opened the media to points of view that might have been ignored thirty years ago.

The First Amendment's role in the development of public policy cannot be overstated. The Supreme Court has come very close to adopting the views of Meiklejohn and Emerson by giving almost absolute protection to political speech and by defining that term broadly.

Freedom of Speech as a Check on Government Power

Vincent Blasi, a Columbia University law professor writing at the end of the 1970s, offered a new rationale for protecting freedom of speech.[33] Noting the pervasiveness of government, and the vulnerability of officials to corruption, he argued that the First Amendment serves a valuable purpose by protecting critics from unhappy government officials. This protection is of special benefit to the news media because it encourages them to serve as a check on the power of government. Blasi's theory is based on *New York Times* v. *Sullivan*,[34] the landmark case in which the Supreme Court raised the level of proof required of government officials when they sue the media for libel. The Court held that to ensure robust debate of public policy, the First Amendment requires such plaintiffs to prove that defamatory statements aimed at them are false and that the publisher either knew they were false or acted in reckless disregard for the truth. By offering the news media such protection, Blasi wrote, the First Amendment has a "checking value" on the power of government. To further that value, Blasi said the amendment also should protect the news-gathering function of the media, particularly by giving journalists an absolute right to refuse to identify their confidential sources of information. Blasi also partially endorsed Barron's access thesis. If the news media are not doing an adequate job of exposing wrongdoing by government officials, they should be required to offer an outlet to those who do not share the biases of journalists as to what they should and should not write about.

Blasi's theory offers a rationale to support what many journalists have called a watchdog role for the press. One has only to skim through the listing of Pulitzer Prizes in journalism to learn that some news media have taken that role seriously, even without the degree of protection advocated by Blasi. However, one also must concede that at some times in some places the watchdog has been both toothless and unable or unwilling to bark.

---

33. Vincent Blasi, "The Checking Value in First Amendment Theory," *Am.B.Found.Res.J.* 521 (1977); "The Pathological Perspective and the First Amendment," 85 *Colum.L.Rev.* 449 (1985).
34. 376 U.S. 254, 84 S.Ct. 710, 11 L.Ed.2d 686 (1964).

An Application of First Amendment Theory

Suppose the Ku Klux Klan announces plans for a rally in a city park in a community where racial tensions are near the flash point. City officials are concerned because civil rights advocates have made clear their intention to disrupt the rally. How might the ideas that we have descibed in this chapter apply?

If the rally is merely a picnic—good food but no effort to express a point of view—then the gathering might be regulated or forbidden for any good reason. Those reasons might include concern about violence or something as innocuous as a concern about the weather or who will clean up afterward. But if the rally is an effort to express a point of view, even an unpopular one, then the First Amendment becomes a factor, so even questions about who will clean up become matters of importance.

Certainly, in this hypothetical situation the Klan plans by its actions and its words to make a statement that is going to offend many Americans and is going to evoke strong emotions of fear and anger on both sides. Those who show up for the rally, whether they support the Klan or are against it, are going to be willing to risk physical harm to express their points of view. Must the government stand by idly while a riot develops, just because the Klan can invoke the First Amendment?

Chafee would see the Klan's right to use the park for a rally as only one of several concerns, although an important one. Also at issue are the state's interests in maintaining order, health, and safety; keeping the park open for recreation; and preserving the park's plants and structures. Consequently, in Chafee's view, those opposed to the rally could ask the court to intervene to prevent the rally, and the court could balance the free speech rights of the Klan against the probable dangers engendered by the Klan's use of the park. If the court concluded that the possibility of violence or harm to the park outweighed any contribution to the debate on racial policy, it would have a number of options: It could issue an injunction forbidding the rally, it could order the anti-Klan forces to remain outside the park, or it could increase police protection for the Klan. In any case, the solution would involve an effort to balance the value of the Klan's speech against the value of other asserted government interests.

Meiklejohn would look at the rally in two ways. He would regard the political speech making in one way, but the surrounding elements—the robes, the hoods, the possibility of a march through the streets, the number of participants, and the likelihood of a cross being burned—in another. Whatever the speakers might have to say about race relations ought to be given the utmost protection because it would be a contribution to the debate on public policy. If police are required to protect the participants from violence, then police protection ought to be provided. But it is one thing to guarantee protection for a message and something quite different to guarantee protection for any means by which that message is expressed. If the Klan members were to wear hoods, or march through an African-American neighborhood, or burn a cross, that would be a different matter. Such actions might well be intimidating rather than communicative. They probably would provoke violence. In Meiklejohn's view, the Klan's rally could be challenged in court, and the court could well conclude that any speech-related action likely to cause violence should be forbidden.

Emerson's theory of the First Amendment would protect not only the speeches, but any peaceful action Klan members might take to draw attention to their cause. They could march, they could wear robes and hoods, and they could burn a cross if they wanted to. What they could not do is create a situation in which there is imminent danger of violence against others. But the likelihood that the speeches would spur members to action would have to be clear. By the same token, Emerson would expect the police to intervene if others should attempt violence against the Klan. In that event, police action would be directed at those who were threatening violence, not at the participants in the rally.

Barron would likely argue that there would be no need for the Klan march, or the demonstration against it, if the media had done their job by giving ample coverage to the grievances of both sides. Both sides are resorting to action because the media, and therefore the government, paid too little attention to their problems.

Blasi's gloss on the debate might be to note that the First Amendment has empowered journalists to explore questions of racial tension and government performance, to seek answers and to publish findings. And if journalists are unwilling to assume that responsibility, publishers and broadcasters should be required to open their columns and their channels to those who are. In short, vigorous and controversial media are better places for debate and expressions of outrage than are city parks and streets.

All these theories start with the assumption that members of the Klu Klux Klan are entitled to participate in the debate over public policy, as are those who hold other points of view. All the theories further assume that those who do not participate in the debate, and even the debaters themselves, will weigh the various arguments and decide for themselves what the policy ought to be. Finally, the First Amendment theorists assume that people are rational. Therefore, they believe that most people will reject extreme positions and will reach an accommodation that will be acceptable to a majority. The theories all assume that freedom of speech and press is the appropriate alternative to violence and tyranny as a means for shaping public policy.

But what about the Klan rally? In the end, as a practical matter that will be up to the court, not up to eminent scholars like Chafee, Meiklejohn, Emerson, Barron, or Blasi. In the end, it will be up to eminent jurists such as William Rehnquist, John Paul Stevens, Sandra Day O'Connor, Antonin Scalia, Anthony Kennedy, David Souter, Clarence Thomas, Steven Breyer, and Ruth Bader Ginsburg—the current members of the United States Supreme Court.

THE SUPREME COURT AND FREEDOM OF SPEECH AND PRESS

For more than a century after the Sedition Act expired in 1801, the First Amendment lay unused. Matters of freedom of speech and press were thought to be the concerns of the states, not the federal Congress. During the Civil War, in the 1860s, federal military censorship of dispatches from war zones was accepted without legal challenge. Sometimes officials prosecuted for criminal libel in state courts, but if anyone believed that military censorship or libel laws—or, for that matter, state restrictions on abolitionist and labor editors—violated the First Amendment, nothing in the case reports indicates such a view.

Not until the World War I era, early in the twentieth century, was the Supreme Court asked for the first time to interpret the amendment's guarantee of freedom of speech and press. When Congress declared war against Germany in 1917, its fear of resistance from the large number of German-Americans in this country led to quick enactment of the Espionage Act of 1917, followed by the Sedition Act of 1918. These acts made opposition to the government's war policies a crime. In 1919, in the first case of its kind, the Supreme Court upheld Congress's power to enact such laws.[35] Since then, and especially since 1945, the Supreme Court has decided scores of First Amendment speech and press cases. Its decisions have dealt not only with the right to criticize government and government officials, but with the right to picket in labor disputes, the right to demonstrate against racial and other forms of discrimination, the right to protect one's privacy, the right to protect one's reputation, the right to see sexually explicit movies, the right of political candidates to appear on radio and television, and the right of lawyers and other professionals to advertise. Many aspects of our lives have been touched by the Court's First Amendment rulings. Nevertheless, critics, including some members of the Court, have complained that the Court has not been able to settle on any consistent theory of First Amendment law. In the seventy years in which it has dealt with First Amendment cases, the Court has applied lots of theories, strategies, doctrines, and tests to guide it to a decision.

One doctrine has been clearly rejected, however: The Court has never agreed with Meiklejohn or Emerson that some kinds of speech under some circumstances should be given absolute protection. A majority has always left an exception that could be applied to limit freedom in an extreme case. Instead, the Court has developed a variety of ideas about when speech might be abridged: the bad tendency and clear and present danger tests, the theory of the balancing of interests, the preferred position theory, and a positive theory of the First Amendment, to name a few. Moreover, the Court has recognized some kinds of action as symbolic speech, protected by the First Amendment, and has expanded the concept of a public forum. It has agreed with Meiklejohn's view that government can regulate the process of speech—the time, place, and manner of the exercise of First Amendment rights—as long as the regulation is neutral as to the content of the speech and there are alternative means to get the message out. In addition, the court has developed various levels of judicial scrutiny depending on the value of the speech—strictly examining regulations that would abridge political speech while being more tolerant of regulations that would abridge commercial speech.

Bad Tendency

The theory of bad tendency comes from the kind of English common law that was used to kill poor Twyn and that justified the convictions of the Republican editors caught up in the Sedition Act of 1798. It goes like this: If words have a tendency to undermine the authority of government or to corrupt the morals of some members of society, the writer or speaker can be punished. Under this theory, there is no need to show that any harm has actually been done. The mere likelihood of harm is enough to support a conviction. This test was used, but not acknowledged, in World War I sedition cases. It is routinely applied in obscenity cases, where standards established by the Supreme Court require jurors to determine whether allegedly obscene works ap-

---

35.   Schenck v. United States, 249 U.S. 47, 39 S.Ct. 247, 63 L.Ed. 470 (1919).

peal to the prurient interest in sex, thus having a tendency to harm the morals of the recipient.

Clear and Present Danger

This test for determining the boundary between freedom and abridgment was formulated by Justice Oliver Wendell Holmes in *Schenck* v. *United States* in 1919. Charles Schenck was general secretary of the Socialist party. During World War I, he and an associate printed and distributed fifteen thousand leaflets urging resistance to the draft. The two were charged with violating the Espionage Act, found guilty, and sentenced to prison. They appealed to the Supreme Court, arguing that their right to free speech had been violated. The case was not decided until four months after the war had ended in victory for the United States and its allies. Nevertheless, the Court found, with Holmes writing a unanimous decision, that the leaflets presented a "clear and present danger" to the draft system, and thus to the nation's efforts to win the war. In time, the decision was seen as giving speech greater protection than that offered by the bad tendency test, but in its early applications, in the 1920s, the distinction was hard to see.

Schenck v. *United States,*
249 U.S. 47, 39 S.Ct. 247,
63 L.Ed. 470 (1919).

Justice Holmes said that freedom of speech depended on the circumstances. "The character of every act," he wrote, "depends upon the circumstances in which it is done. . . . [T]he question in every case is whether the words used are used in such circumstances and are of such a nature as to create a clear and present danger that they will bring about the substantive evils that Congress has a right to prevent. It is a question of proximity and degree."[36] From Holmes's point of view, Schenck's effort to obstruct the draft was such a hindrance to the war effort that it need not be endured "so long as men fight, and no Court could regard [it] as protected by any constitutional rights."[37]

Holmes illustrated his point about circumstances with a sentence that has been more frequently quoted than fully understood: "The most stringent protection of free speech would not protect a man in falsely shouting fire in a theater and causing a panic." Examined closely, the sentence is much closer to the ideas of Meiklejohn and Emerson than the affirmation of Schenck's conviction would seem to indicate. First, Holmes's example suggests that the content of the speech must be a lie. Only a deliberate misstatement of fact should be punished—not a mistaken opinion, not an illogical appeal based on emotion. Clearly, his choice of words means that there should be no punishment for the person who found a fire in a theater and whose warning saved the lives of the audience. Nor could the law punish an actor whose lines required him to shout "Fire!" The speaker must have resorted to falsehood in order to cause trouble. Second, Holmes suggests that there must be a direct connection between the false speech and a harmful act—in this instance, panic, the kind of action that leads to people getting trampled or piled up against the doors, causing injury or death.

---

36.   Ibid.
37.   Ibid.

In later cases, Holmes and Justice Louis Brandeis were to say that the meaning of the clear and present danger test was wrapped up in that one sentence about "shouting fire." Speech creates a clear and present danger only when it is obvious that it will immediately produce actions harmful to a vital interest that Congress has the authority to protect. If the test is properly applied, it puts the line between speech and action very close to action, as Chafee, Meiklejohn, and Emerson had advocated.

The Balancing of Interests

Under this theory, reminiscent of Chafee's ideas, the First Amendment interest in free discussion is seen merely as one of many interests safeguarded by the Constitution. When one interest comes into conflict with another, the courts must weigh the competing interests and decide which has the greater value to society under the circumstances. Obviously, the outcome of the contest is as subject to the personal leanings of the individual judges involved as under any other theory.

Balancing in speech cases had its formal origins in the 1950 case *American Communications Association* v. *Douds*.[38] In that case, the Court held that a labor union official's First Amendment interest in refusing to swear that he was not a member of the Communist party was not strong enough to overcome the government's interest in preventing defense-industry strikes that were politically motivated.

The balancing theory is regularly used by courts whenever competing interests come into conflict. A scales, in fact, is the symbol of justice. But when explicit constitutional rights are involved, balancing can be controversial. After all, what interests of the government could be more important than those outlined in the Bill of Rights? Justice Hugo Black wrote in the early 1960s that he could not subscribe to a legal doctrine that permitted constitutionally protected rights, such as freedom of speech, "to be 'balanced' away when a majority of the Court thinks that a State might have an interest sufficient to justify abridgment of those freedoms."[39] He and others criticized balancing as being too deferential to government and so focused on the particular facts of a particular case that it is of little use as precedent, thus earning the epithet "ad hoc balancing."

Still, a majority of the Court over the years has sided with Justice John Harlan's view that the First Amendment is not absolute, but that when "constitutional protections are asserted against the exercise of valid governmental powers a reconciliation must be effected, and that . . . requires an appropriate weighing of the respective interests involved."[40] Harlan suggested that balancing was the appropriate method to use whenever abridgment of speech was an unintended side effect of a statute that was intended to serve a nonspeech concern of government. For example, the Court in *American Communications Association* v. *Douds* evaluated a statute intended to protect a governmental interest in the production of military hardware against the right of a man not to disclose his political party affiliation if he wanted to work at the plant. And in

---

38.   339 U.S. 382, 70 S.Ct. 674, 94 L.Ed. 925 (1950).
39.   Konigsberg v. State Bar of California, 366 U.S. 36 (1961). J. Black dissenting.
40.   Konigsberg v. State Bar of California, 366 U.S. 36 (1961).

Konigsberg v. *State Bar of California*,[41] the case a decade later in which Harlan and Black squared off over the issue of balancing, a majority upheld California's denial of bar admission to an applicant who refused to answer questions about his Communist party membership.

Balancing with Strict Scrutiny

Very often, the Court has suggested that the question of whether to balance competing interests really begins with a determination about how carefully the Court should scrutinize the dispute in the first place. For example, a law that on its face explicitly abridges speech should be examined more carefully than one that on its face does not seem to abridge speech. Likewise, regulations intended to control negative effects of speech that has political value, such as a civil rights march, should be given more careful scrutiny than regulations intended to control speech of minimal political value, such as product advertising.

In other words, some speech should be subject to strict scrutiny and other speech subject to somewhat lesser scrutiny. Strict scrutiny requires the government to demonstrate that its abridgment of speech is based on a *compelling* state interest— a very difficult task, since few interests are more compelling than freedom of speech. Still, it is possible. The Court found that Tennessee had a compelling reason in 1992 when it upheld a law prohibiting political campaigning within 100 feet of polling places on election day.[42]

Four justices in *Burson* v. *Freeman* concluded that the law directly and on its face abridged political speech in a public forum, thus requiring strict scrutiny. Although campaigning for public office is speech of the most important kind, the justices concluded that the state's ban advanced a compelling interest in preventing voter intimidation and election fraud. Moreover, the ban was specific, going no farther than necessary in limiting the no-campaign zone to the immediate vicinity of polling places. Therefore, in the opinion of four members of the Court, the lower court's decision was a rare but constitutional restriction of political speech.

Four justices is not a majority, however. Only because a fifth justice agreed with the outcome, but not the reasoning, was the statute upheld. The fifth justice did not accept the view that a polling place is a public forum for political or any other kind of speech. Because the statute restricted the use of a place, not the message of a speaker, the justice believed it unnecessary to require Tennessee to show a compelling concern about political fraud. A lesser scrutiny should apply. As long as the state had reasonable grounds for limiting speech and did not discriminate on the basis of content, the statute was constitutional. It was simply a matter of balancing the state's reasonable interest in discouraging intimidation and fraud against the speaker's interest in campaigning at a specific place and time. Thus, justices can agree on the outcome of a case while understanding the extent of First Amendment protection in very different ways.

---

41.   366 U.S. 36 (1961).
42.   *Burson v. Freeman*, 112 S.Ct. 1846, 119 L.Ed.2d 5 (1992).

Balancing from a Preferred Position

Since the mid-twentieth century, members of the Court often have held that freedom of speech, guaranteed by the First and Fourteenth Amendments, and some other rights guaranteed in the Bill of Rights, occupy a "preferred position" when governments attempt to restrict them. The theory begins with the assumption, found in Hobbes and Locke, that people enjoyed certain natural rights before they entered into the compact that resulted in the Constitution.[43] Therefore, although the Constitution specifically protects natural rights, it did not create these rights. Freedom of speech is so fundamental to democracy and human dignity that it must be guarded diligently. Consequently, any encroachment by government, however well-intended, is a serious matter—so serious that the courts assume that the restriction is unconstitutional until the government proves otherwise. That this is an extraordinary protection for freedom of speech is evidenced by the fact that in other cases courts normally require the challenger—not the government—to prove that the law at issue is unconstitutional.

In speech cases, with the burden of proof on the government, the government must show (1) that the restriction on speech has been imposed to protect an interest it is entitled to protect under the Constitution, (2) that the law has been drafted in such specific terms that it will do what it is supposed to do with a minimum of harm to freedom of speech, and (3) that the government's vital interest cannot be protected without some restriction on speech. If there is more than one way to protect the government's basic interest, the government must use a method that harms the freedom of speech as little as possible.

When members of the Court approach a case in this way, they usually begin by noting that there is both a "heavy presumption" that any such restraint is unconstitutional[44] and a "heavy burden of showing justification for such restraint."[45] The emphasis is on the word "heavy." The approach generally triggers strict scrutiny by the Court, requiring the government to show that it has a compelling need to restrict the speech.

The effect of the preferred position theory has been to grant pure speech—that is, expression by words rather than by actions or by words mixed with actions—a high degree of freedom, particularly if that speech is in a political context. At times, members of the Supreme Court, in balancing the scales in favor of freedom, have come very close to the positions advocated by Meiklejohn and Emerson, especially when speech concerns the actions of government and government officials.

Symbolic Speech and Intermediate Scrutiny ─────────

Both Meiklejohn and Emerson believed that the First Amendment should protect conduct—not just words—designed to express a position on public issues. The

---

43. See the United States Declaration of Independence, 4 July 1776. For a current view, see Harry V. Jaffee, *Original Intent and the Framers of the Constitution* (Washington, D.C.: Regnery Gateway, 1994).
44. Bantam Books v. Sullivan, 372 U.S. 58, 83 S.Ct. 631, 9 L.Ed.2d 584 (1963).
45. Organization for a Better Austin v. Keefe, 402 U.S. 415, 91 S.Ct. 1575, 29 L.Ed.2d 1 (1971).

Supreme Court also has recognized that expression is not always in the form of words. For more than fifty years the Court has given almost as much protection to peaceful political action as it has to political argument. In addition, it has protected action that some people consider irritating, if not threatening.

In 1989 the Court demonstrated how far it is willing to go to protect such symbolic speech when it upheld the right to burn an American flag to make a political point. Three years later, the Court nullified a St. Paul, Minnesota, city ordinance used to prosecute a juvenile who burned a cross on the lawn of an African-American family. The Court's majority said it did not approve of cross burning, but held the ordinance void for punishing an expressive act because of its message.

The flag-burning decision was not an easy one for the Court, but it was clear that *Texas* v. *Johnson,* **491 U.S. 397, 109 S.Ct. 2533, 105 L.Ed.2d 342 (1989).** the law against desecration of the flag was not intended to prevent the dangers of open fires or to control traffic. It was intended to stop expressive conduct because government disagreed with the message. The Court split five to four. Anthony Kennedy and Antonin Scalia, both appointed by President Reagan and thought to be conservatives, joined the opinion written by William J. Brennan, Jr., appointed by President Eisenhower but generally considered to be a liberal. Justice Kennedy decided to write separately to note his "distaste for the result," but he said settled principles of First Amendment law gave the Court no right to rule otherwise, "however painful this judgment is to announce."

Justice Brennan built the majority's decision on cases dating to World War I and more specifically on precedents established in cases on symbolic speech and flag desecration that had been decided by the Court during the Vietnam war. In those cases, the Court held that the First Amendment protects the right to speak disrespectfully of the flag and urge others not to honor it,[46] to tape a peace symbol to a U.S. flag and display it in a public place,[47] or to sew a flag to the seat of one's pants.[48] The Court also held that when otherwise illegal acts are committed to express a point of view on an important public issue, they may be protected as symbolic speech. The test is whether the actor's purpose is to convey a particular message and whether his audience understands it to be a message. Further, the conduct's First Amendment value must be weighed against the state's interest in punishing it.

The symbolic speech doctrine consequently does not encompass all politically expressive action. It does not encompass, for example, kidnapping, murder, assault, or armed robbery committed with the intent to convey a political message. In those cases, the incidental burden on expression is outweighed by the interest of the government in saving lives and property. In a celebrated case during the Vietnam war era, the First Amendment, the Court decided, did not protect a man who burned his draft card to protest the war. The Court held that the government's interest in identifying men eligible for the draft overcame any First Amendment point made by the card's destruction. Under the test established in *U.S.* v. *O'Brien,*[49] the government can regulate ex-

---

46.   Street v. New York, 394 U.S. 576, 89 S.Ct. 1354, 22 L.Ed.2d 572 (1969).
47.   Spence v. Washington, 418 U.S. 405, 94 S.Ct. 2727, 41 L.Ed.2d 842 (1974).
48.   Smith v. Goguen, 415 U.S. 566, 94 S.Ct. 1242, 39 L.Ed.2d 605 (1974).
49.   391 U.S. 367, 88 S.Ct. 1673, 20 L.Ed.2d 672 (1968).

pressive conduct if the regulation is narrowly tailored to further a substantial governmental interest unrelated to expression. Further, any incidental restriction of expression must be no greater than is necessary to carry out that interest.

If you read that language carefully, you can see that the approach of the Court in symbolic speech cases, such as *O'Brien,* is a kind of intermediate scrutiny—keeping the First Amendment in a preferred position but adjusting the burden of the government to accommodate for the reality that this is not "pure speech." Rather than requiring a compelling interest to justify an incidental interference with freedom, a substantial interest might be sufficient and appropriate.

In *Johnson,* Texas authorities said the state's flag desecration law was designed to prevent breaches of the peace and to preserve the flag "as a symbol of nationhood and national unity." Brennan ruled that the state's interest was not sufficient to overcome Gregory Lee Johnson's First Amendment interest in burning a U.S. flag to protest the renomination of President Reagan. Noting that the right to express dissatisfaction with national policy is at the core of our First Amendment values, Brennan added, "If there is a bedrock principle underlying the First Amendment, it is that the government may not prohibit the expression of an idea simply because society finds the idea itself offensive or disagreeable." To forbid the use of the flag or other symbols as a means

This Seattle, Washington, resident was one of several persons who burned American flags to protest a federal anti-flag-burning law, enacted in 1989 to circumvent the Supreme Court's *Texas* v. *Johnson* decision. He was cheered by a crowd of several hundred who alternately chanted "burn baby burn" and sang the national anthem. *(AP/Wide World)*

of expression "would be to enter territory having no discernible or defensible boundaries."

Disagreeing with Brennan was Chief Justice William H. Rehnquist. Where Brennan found an expression of political ideas, Rehnquist found only "an inarticulate grunt or roar that, it seems fair to say, is most likely to be indulged in not to express any particular idea, but to antagonize others." Many in Congress share Rehnquist's view. In 1990 and again in 1995, most conservative and some liberal members of the House and Senate proposed to amend the Constitution and, by so doing, overrule the Supreme Court. The proposed constitutional amendment would have allowed states, such as Texas, to punish anyone who desecrates an American flag, even if the desecration is a form of symbolic speech. The Clinton administration opposed the constitutional amendment, which in 1995 failed in the Senate by only three votes.[50] An amendment would require ratification by at least three-quarters of the states to be added to the Constitution.

In 1992, in the cross-burning case, a unanimous Court held that an ordinance designed to punish "hate speech" violated the First Amendment. However, the justices again split, five to four.

R.A.V. v. *City of St. Paul, Minnesota,* 112 S.Ct. 2538, 120 L.Ed.2d 305 (1992).

At issue was a city ordinance that made it a crime to display a symbol, such as a swastika or a burning cross, that one knows, or has reason to know, will arouse "anger, alarm, or resentment on the basis of race, color, creed, religion or gender." The stated purpose was to protect persons "who are particularly vulnerable because of their membership in a group that historically has been discriminated against."

In the majority's view, that purpose made the ordinance a restriction of expression based on the content of the message and in clear violation of the First Amendment. The Minnesota Supreme Court had thought otherwise. It saw the ordinance as an attempt to punish the use of "fighting words," an elusive category of speech unprotected by the First Amendment and defined as insults so lacking in idea content as to be undeserving of protection. The exception for "fighting words" came from a 1942 decision of the Supreme Court, *Chaplinsky* v. *New Hampshire,* upholding New Hampshire's right to punish a criminal suspect who had cursed the police officer who arrested him.[51] However, Justice Scalia said that the Minnesota court's finding of fighting words in this instance was not enough to save St. Paul's ordinance. The law was "facially unconstitutional" because it prohibited speech on the basis of its content.

Although Scalia's opinion is not easy to read and understand, it seems to boil down to an updated version of John Milton's "let truth and falsehood grapple"; truth is more likely to be reached if proponents of conflicting doctrines are left free to use whatever rhetoric they choose, no matter how mean and nasty it may get. In Scalia's view, the St. Paul ordinance used the power of government to limit the rhetoric of those who

---

50. "Conservatives Revive Bill on Protecting Flag," *New York Times,* 22 March 1995, p. A12; "Amendment on Flag Burning Is Opposed by Administration," *New York Times,* 7 June 1995, p. A14; Katharine Q. Seelye, "House Easily Passes Amendment to Ban Desecration of Flag," *New York Times,* 29 June 1995, p. 1; Robin Toner, "Flag-Burning Amendment Fails in Senate, but Margin Narrows," *New York Times,* 13 December 1995, p. 1.

51. Chaplinsky v. New Hampshire, 315 U.S. 568, 62 S.Ct. 766, 86 L.Ed. 1031 (1942).

oppose approved positions on matters of race, color, creed, religion, or gender. That, the court said, the city could not do. It has no "authority to license one side of a debate to fight free style, while requiring the other to follow the Marquis of Queensbury Rules."[52]

Justice Byron R. White, writing for himself and three others, thought Scalia's reasoning was wrong. The four dissenting justices protested that Scalia had written the leading opinion so broadly that the majority seemed to condemn all attempts to restrict speech based on the nature of its content. They called attention to a long line of decisions, starting with Holmes's condemnation of one "who falsely shouts 'fire' in a crowded theatre," in which the Court has upheld punishment of speech because of the nature of its content. They would simply have held that the ordinance was void because it swept too broadly, reaching protected speech on such issues as race and gender, in its attempt to punish speech that inspires fear or provokes violence. Justice Harry A. Blackmun wrote separately to accuse Scalia of reaching beyond the facts of the case to write an opinion directed at "politically correct speech" and "cultural diversity."

Symbolic speech cases can draw close distinctions between speech that's protected and action that isn't. For example, the Court upheld, five to four, that a woman dancing nude in an Indiana bar could be arrested for public indecency.[53] Usually dancing would be considered a form of expression protected by the First Amendment. Public indecency usually would be considered action unprotected by the First Amendment. But what should happen when a woman dances nude in public to express an erotic message?

Chief Justice Rehnquist, writing the leading opinion for the Court and keeping the *O'Brien* case in mind, held that Indiana's public indecency statute was narrowly tailored to protect societal order and morality. The public indecency law, he said, does not ban dancing designed to convey an erotic message. It only bans public nudity. It requires only that a woman who performs such dancing in public must wear something to cover her nipples and pubic area. She can dance in as little as pasties and a G-string. That limitation, he wrote, "does not deprive the dance of whatever erotic message it conveys; it simply makes the message slightly less graphic." Thus, the law's impact on protected expression is no greater than necessary to achieve the state's purpose.

Not all of the justices were happy with that opinion, of course. Other justices would not have worried their way through such a complicated analysis. Kennedy and Scalia, who had said the Court's precedents compelled them to hold that flag burning is a protected expression of opinion, could find no precedents strong enough to compel them to uphold nude dancing. Indeed, Scalia wrote separately to say that such dancing is conduct, not speech, and therefore can be regulated as state and local authorities see fit, without regard for the First Amendment.

All of these cases illustrate the fine line that lies between protected and unprotected symbolic speech. The action must be intended to convey a message and be understood to be a message by the audience. Any restrictions placed on the expressive activity must further a substantial public interest unrelated to the content of the message, and the restriction must go no farther than is necessary to protect that interest.

---

52. The usually precise Scalia was referring to the Marquis of Queensberry, Sir John Sholto Douglas, an Englishman who supervised the writing of the rules of modern boxing in 1867.
53. Barnes v. Glen Theatre, Inc., 111 S.Ct. 2456, 115 L.Ed.2d 504 (1991).

A Positive Role for the First Amendment

Until 1980, the Court had flirted with, but generally rejected, the idea advanced by Meiklejohn and made more specific by Emerson that the First Amendment requires positive steps by government to ensure free and informed debate on its policies. More than fifty years ago, the Court noted in *Hague* v. *CIO*[54] that "time out of mind public streets and sidewalks have been used for purposes of assembly, communicating thoughts between citizens, and discussing public questions." In such places, the government's right to restrict the content of speech is very limited, the Court said. Thus, it has long been established that government has, at the least, a passive role in providing a forum for the communication of ideas.

At one time, the Supreme Court embraced Meiklejohn's belief that radio and television, as media licensed by the government, are required by the First Amendment to seek out and present both sides of public issues; for example, in 1969 the Court upheld the fairness doctrine imposed on broadcasters by the Federal Communications Commission.[55] That doctrine required broadcasters to identify controversial public issues and to offer a balanced discussion of them. However, the doctrine was abandoned by the commission in 1987 except as it applies to public referenda. An appellate court in the District of Columbia affirmed the commission's right to do so.[56] The Supreme Court has held flatly that any attempt by government to enforce "fairness" on newspapers violates the First Amendment.[57] Courts also have rejected Barron's theory that the First Amendment implies a right of access to the print media.[58] Nor has the Court found in the First Amendment any levers that can be used to pry information out of the government. It has held that the amendment protects a reporter's right to share information with the public but offers no help in getting information. Congress moved into that breach by adopting the Freedom of Information Act, establishing by law a right of access to much, but not all, of the information generated by government agencies. The Supreme Court has upheld that act in numerous decisions but has construed it rather narrowly.

In 1980 the Court handed down its First Amendment access decision in *Richmond Newspapers* v. *Virginia.*[59] The case grew out of an order by a judge who ejected journalists and other spectators from his courtroom while he conducted a murder trial. On appeal, a majority of the Court held that the First Amendment protects the right to be present in a courtroom during a trial. Chief Justice Burger reasoned that courtrooms historically have been public assemblies and therefore come within the First Amendment's guarantee of the right to assemble. That right, he said, is not absolute but can be restricted only for the most compelling reasons. Justice John Paul Stevens noted the potentially far-reaching aspects of that ruling. The Court, he said, had for the first time

---

54. 307 U.S. 496, 59 S.Ct. 954, 83 L.Ed. 1423 (1939).
55. Red Lion Broadcasting Co. v. Federal Communications Commission, 395 U.S. 367, 89 S.Ct. 1794, 23 L.Ed.2d 371 (1969).
56. Syracuse Peace Council v. Federal Communications Commission, 867 F.2d 654 (D.C.Cir. 1989).
57. Miami Herald Publishing Co. v. Tornillo, 418 U.S. 241, 94 S.Ct. 2831, 41 L.Ed.2d 730 (1974).
58. Chicago Joint Board, Amalgamated Clothing Workers of America, AFL-CIO v. Chicago Tribune Co., 307 F.Supp. 422 (N.D.Ill. 1969); affirmed, 435 F.2d 470 (7th Cir. 1970); cert. denied, 402 U.S. 973 (1971).
59. 448 U.S. 555, 100 S.Ct. 2814, 65 L.Ed.2d 973 (1980).

found in the First Amendment a right of access to news generated by organs of government. The case stands as at least a first step toward the positive role for the First Amendment postulated by Meiklejohn and Emerson. However, in the decade since, the Court has done little to expand the meaning of *Richmond Newspapers* to establish a right of access to other newsworthy government activities.

Public Forums

As noted briefly in the preceding section, the Supreme Court held more than fifty years ago that "time out of mind public streets and sidewalks have been used for purposes of assembly, communicating thoughts between citizens, and discussing public questions."[60] That holding was expanded in 1988 when the Court upheld the right of demonstrators to use streets and sidewalks in quiet residential neighborhoods.[61] In legal theory, such places are public forums, open to all for the exchange of ideas. The Court's decisions have identified and defined three kinds of forums, with different rules controlling how each may be used for political speech.

At the top of the list are traditional public forums: public streets, sidewalks, parks, and other "government property that has traditionally been available for public expression." Attempts to restrict speech in such forums are "subject to the highest scrutiny" and can "survive only if they are narrowly drawn to achieve a compelling state interest."[62] At a second level is public property that the state has opened to expressive activity by part or all of the public. These areas are called designated public forums. They include, but are not limited to, public auditoriums[63] and public schools,[64] including colleges and universities. Once a public building has been opened to the general public for the discussion of ideas, attempts to regulate such speech are subject to the same limitations as in a traditional public forum. Finally, there is public property that has not been opened for expressive activity because it is devoted primarily to a specific function of government. A post office lobby is one example. Another is the stacks of a public library. Others are offices of public officials, courtrooms, and police stations. In such places, restrictions on political expression by outsiders need only be reasonable.

Courts have found it sometimes difficult to distinguish among the three types of forums. In one instance, the Supreme Court held that a street lying within the boundaries of a military base was not a traditional public forum, even though it was freely open to motor vehicle and pedestrian traffic.[65] In another instance, *Burson* v. *Freeman,*[66] discussed earlier, the Court could not make up its mind as to whether polling places are

---

60. Hague v. CIO, 307 U.S. 496, 59 S.Ct. 954, 83 L.Ed. 1423 (1939).
61. Frisby v. Schultz, 487 U.S. 474, 108 S.Ct. 2495, 101 L.Ed.2d 420 (1988).
62. International Society for Krishna Consciousness v. Lee, 112 S.Ct. 2701, 2705, 120 L.Ed.2d 541 (1992), with reference to Perry Education Association v. Perry Local Educators' Association, 460 U.S. 37, 103 S.Ct. 948, 74 L.Ed.2d 794 (1983).
63. Southeastern Promotions v. Conrad, 420 U.S. 546, 95 S.Ct. 1239, 43 L.Ed.2d 448 (1975).
64. Tinker v. Des Moines School Dist., 393 U.S. 503, 89 S.Ct. 733, 21 L.Ed.2d 731 (1969).
65. Greer v. Spock, 424 U.S. 828, 96 S.Ct. 1211, 47 L.Ed.2d 505 (1976).
66. 112 S.Ct. 1846 (1992).

public forums. In this debate on what constitutes a public forum, courts have had perhaps the greatest difficulty in deciding on the status of airport terminals. In 1981 the Supreme Court seemed to say they are public forums.[67] Courts in the fifth, seventh, eighth, ninth, and District of Columbia circuits have so held.[68] But in 1992, a bare majority of the Supreme Court held, in *International Society for Krishna Consciousness* v. *Lee,*[69] that they are not.

At issue was a regulation adopted by the Port Authority of New York and New Jersey forbidding the solicitation of funds and distribution of leaflets in terminals at Kennedy, LaGuardia, and Newark airports. Chief Justice Rehnquist, writing for himself and four others, held that the terminals are operated as commercial facilities by an agency of government acting in a proprietary capacity. The terminals are designed to make it possible for large numbers of people to get to and from aircraft without undue inconvenience. Although terminal concourses are open to others besides air travelers, they have no history of being open for discussion of public issues. Thus, the majority concluded that they are nonpublic forums, subject to reasonable restrictions on expressive activity.

This opinion drew a strong protest from Justice Kennedy, who asserted that the Court's public forum analysis was inconsistent with the values underlying the First Amendment. He accused the majority of ignoring the realities of modern life when it based its public forum analysis on history and tradition. In a mobile society, he wrote, "an airport is one of the few government-owned spaces where many persons have extensive contact with other members of the public."

However, Kennedy went along with the majority's holding that fund-raisers would add to the congestion in the terminals and interfere with their proper use. In contrast, a majority of the Court held that the Port Authority's ban on the distribution of leaflets was unreasonable. It concluded that leafleting would have a minimal effect on the flow of passengers within the terminals, in contrast with fund-raising, which would require people to stop, listen, and decide whether to give cash or write a check to the solicitor.

Time, Place, and Manner Restrictions on Speech in a Public Forum

Governments may regulate speech in a public forum only to the extent necessary to further a compelling competing interest. Further, the regulation must be neutral with respect to the content of the speech. As the previously discussed decision in the *R.A.V.* case emphasizes, the power of government cannot be used to favor one point of view or suppress another. This is not to say that people can take over public places and use them for political purposes as they see fit. Government can control the time,

---

67. Heffron v. International Society for Krishna Consciousness, 452 U.S. 640, 101 S.Ct. 2559, 69 L.Ed.2d 298 (1981).
68. International Society for Krishna Consciousness v. Lee, 112 S.Ct. 2701, 2705, footnote 2, 120 L.Ed.2d 541 (1992).
69. International Society for Krishna Consciousness v. Lee, 112 S.Ct. 2701, 2705, 120 L.Ed.2d 541 (1992).

place, and manner of the use. Such control must be reasonable and cannot be used to prohibit speech altogether. The Court has upheld restrictions imposed to preserve order, although it has required strong evidence that a riot would be likely. The Court also has upheld restrictions designed to keep traffic moving, or to protect those outside the forum from undue disturbance, as from excessively loud amplifying systems. For instance, in 1989 the Court held that the City of New York could impose decibel limits on the sound systems used by rock bands during concerts at the band shell in Central Park.[70] Years earlier, the Court had held that cities can regulate the loudness of sound trucks used on public streets during political campaigns.[71]

But cities can't use their power to protect people from political speech they may not like, even when relations with a foreign country are involved. To prevent incidents that might invite a diplomatic protest, the city of Washington adopted an ordinance forbidding protesters of a foreign government's policies from demonstrating within five hundred feet of its embassy. In 1988, in *Boos* v. *Berry*,[72] the Supreme Court held that this ordinance violated the First Amendment. It did so because the district's attempt to regulate speech in a public forum was not content neutral, for the ordinance applied only to signs tending to bring the targeted nation into public disrepute.

On another occasion, the content-based nature of an attempt to regulate speech in a public forum was not so evident. In 1987 Forsyth County, Georgia, was the scene of a massive civil rights demonstration. The organizers chose this county because in 1912 it had forced its entire African-American population to leave the county in the wake of the raping of a white woman and the lynching of her accused assailant, who was black. Seventy-five years later, the county's population remained 99 percent white. More than twenty thousand persons, including United States senators and presidential candidates, paraded through the county seat, protesting what they saw as a policy that discouraged African-Americans from living in the county. The marchers were heckled by about a thousand counterdemonstrators, including members of the Nationalist Movement and the Ku Klux Klan. More than three thousand local and state police were used to keep the two sides apart. The cost of the protection exceeded $670,000, only a small part of which was paid by Forsyth County.

In response, the county adopted an ordinance requiring planners of parades, demonstrations, and other uses of public property to obtain a permit and pay a variable fee of not more than $1,000, based on the county administrator's estimate of the cost of maintaining public order during the event. When the Nationalist Movement sought a permit to conduct a rally protesting the observance of Martin Luther King's birthday, it was told it must pay a fee of $100. It filed a lawsuit challenging the ordinance. Ultimately, the Supreme Court held that because the size of the fee was related to the content of the message, the ordinance violated the First Amendment.[73] Justice Blackmun, writing for the five-member majority, held that the ordinance could survive only if it were narrowly drawn to further an important public purpose, in this instance, the preservation of order. Focusing on the licensing re-

---

70. Ward v. Rock Against Racism, 491 U.S. 781, 109 S.Ct. 2746, 105 L.Ed.2d 661 (1989).
71. Kovacs v. Cooper, 336 U.S. 77, 69 S.Ct. 448, 93 L.Ed. 513 (1949).
72. 485 U.S. 312, 108 S.Ct. 1157, 99 L.Ed.2d 333 (1988).
73. Forsyth County, Georgia v. Nationalist Movement, 112 S.Ct. 2395, 118 L.Ed.2d 204 (1992).

quirement, the Court found that too much was left to the sole discretion of the county administrator. The language of the ordinance required the administrator to base the fee on his estimate of the public's probable hostility to an applicant's purpose in seeking a right to use public streets. "Those wishing to express views unpopular with bottle throwers, for example, may have to pay more for their permit," the majority concluded. Thus, the ordinance was invalid both because it discriminated against speech on the basis of its content and because it gave the administrator arbitrary authority to establish the cost of a permit. That the fee could not exceed $1,000 made no difference. "A tax based on the content of speech does not become more constitutional because it is a small tax."

As these cases illustrate, when government attempts to regulate the right to use a public forum, it must do so only to protect a compelling public interest. Such regulation must be essential to the protection of that interest and must be content neutral. City officials might require demonstrators seeking a parade permit to time their use of the streets to avoid the morning and evening rush hours, but they cannot require that the parade be held at 3 A.M. or on streets in a remote industrial area. Nor can they permit a president seeking reelection to conduct a rally in the heart of the city at lunch hour and then forbid an opposing candidate to do so. Government cannot throw its power behind proponents of one point of view or use it to deny a forum to proponents of another, even when the speech in question is as repugnant as the cross burning in *R.A.V.*

In the Professional World

If history teaches any lessons, one of them surely must be that we cannot take for granted the right to say or publish what we please. Another must be that, as Milton put it, words "are not absolutely dead things, but do contain a potencie of life in them." Milton went on to compare words to the dragon's teeth of mythology, which, "being sown up and down, may chance to spring up armed men." Through history, that "potencie" has created tensions, which have fueled the urge to censor, lest unbridled speech tear apart the fabric that holds society together. The opposing view is that a society can become strong only by listening to its critics and shoring up the weaknesses they expose.

The authors of the First Amendment, guided by Milton, Locke, and others, adopted the latter view, embracing the idea that freedom of expression is one of the natural rights retained by the people when they entered the social compact. One purpose of the amendment was to place political speech beyond the reach of a majority's power to suppress ideas it does not like. That goal has been endorsed by the Supreme Court.

Halfway through World War II, when it was by no means certain that the United States and it allies would prevail over the Axis powers, the Court wrote one of its most eloquent decisions upholding the right of dissent. At issue was a law adopted by the state of West Virginia requiring all public school pupils to start the day by pledging their allegiance to the flag. The purpose was to promote loyalty to the government in a time of peril. To a handful of Jehovah's Witnesses, the flag salute was idolatry, forbidden by the tenets of their faith. When their children refused to mouth the pledge, the children were expelled from school and the parents were prosecuted for contributing to their delinquency.

The Supreme Court told the state that its law violated the freedom of speech clause of the First Amendment.[74] Justice Robert H. Jackson, writing for the Court, noted that when rulers attempt to coerce an end to dissent, they "soon find themselves exterminating dissenters." Nor is the punishment of dissenters made any more palatable when it is done by a majority for the purpose of promoting national unity. Jackson wrote:

> The very purpose of a Bill of Rights was to withdraw certain subjects from the vicissitudes of political controversy, to place them beyond the reach of majorities and officials and to establish them as legal principles to be applied by the courts. One's right to life, liberty, and property, to free speech, a free press, freedom of worship and assembly, and other fundamental rights may not be submitted to vote; they depend on the outcome of no elections.
>
> If there is any fixed star in our constitutional constellation, it is that no official, high or petty, can prescribe what shall be orthodox in politics, nationalism, religion, or other matters of opinion, or to force citizens to confess by word or act their faith therein. If there are any circumstances which permit an exception, they do not now occur to us.

Jackson's words erased a law enacted by the West Virginia legislature, but implicit in them is a recognition of the repressive force of great majorities. Whether by law or by force, many of us are moved to silence those whose views we abhor. That some such views are indeed abhorrent—racial slurs directed at African-, Asian, Hispanic, and Native Americans; sexual harassment; and callousness toward the physically handicapped are some examples—makes repression easier, even makes it seem the nobler course. Some see racial and religious slurs much as Rehnquist saw flag burning, as a "grunt or roar" designed to provoke anger rather than to express an idea. In keeping with that view, administrators at some prestigious universities either acted to punish students for discriminatory remarks or adopted rules to provide for such punishment.[75] Such actions stopped only when federal courts held that the Wisconsin and Michigan hate-speech codes violated the First Amendment guarantee of freedom of speech.[76] The Supreme Court's decision in *R.A.V.* raises doubt that any code restricting speech on the basis of its content can withstand legal challenge.

But the problem has not gone away. Student newspapers report that African-Americans, Hispanics, homosexuals, Jews, and women on college campuses are victims of both verbal and physical abuse. School administrators

---

74. West Virginia State Board of Education v. Barnette, 319 U.S. 624, 63 S.Ct. 1178, 87 L.Ed. 1628 (1943).
75. Richard Bernstein, "On Campus, How Free Should Free Speech Be?" *New York Times,* 10 September 1989.
76. Amy Dockser Marcus and Beatrice E. Garcia, "College Rules to Curb Bias Draw Challenge on Constitutional Basis," *Wall Street Journal,* 4 September 1990, and "Federal Court Rules against Ban on Hate Speech at Wisconsin U.," *New York Times,* 13 October 1991.

use both persuasion and punishment to convince students and faculty that they should serve as examples in accepting diversity and rejecting stereotypes of all kinds.

At Dartmouth, four editors of a conservative weekly newspaper, *The Dartmouth Review,* were suspended from school after President James O. Freedman accused the publication of "dangerously affecting—in fact, poisoning—the intellectual environment of our campus."[77] The *Review's* crowning offense was publication of a transcript of a rambling lecture given by a black professor of music, which was followed by a confrontation when the students sought comment from the professor.

Officially, the students were suspended not for what they wrote but for harassing a professor. However, in his speech to the faculty justifying the filing of disciplinary charges, President Freedman focused on the content of the weekly. He said, "What it has done has been irresponsible, mean-spirited, cruel and ugly." He said he felt morally obligated to respond to the publication's "bullying tactics," which, he said, "seems virtually designed to have the effect of discouraging women and members of minority groups from joining our faculty or enrolling as students." Freedman called *Review* staffers "ideological provocateurs posing as journalists." He said his own "profound commitment to protecting freedom of expression is entirely consistent with the personal and moral obligation of exercising one's own First Amendment rights in criticizing the press upon appropriate circumstances." Thus, he said, we "must not stand by silently when a newspaper recklessly sets out to create a climate of intolerance and intimidation that destroys our mutual sense of community and inhibits the reasoned examination of the widest possible range of ideas." The speech brought a standing ovation from the faculty.

Freedman was responding to a problem provoked by the *Review's* tactics. African-American students, charging that articles questioning the academic value of the music professor's classes were racially motivated, conducted rallies, forums, and marches in protest. Freedman met with students several times in an attempt to ease tensions on the campus. From his point of view, he was seeking to remove an irritant that disturbed the harmony of an integrated campus.

Although applauded on campus, Freedman's speech was deplored by critics elsewhere, including Laurence Silberman, a Dartmouth graduate and a judge of the U.S. Court of Appeals for the District of Columbia Circuit. Silberman made public the letter he wrote declining the Daniel Webster Award offered by the Dartmouth Club of Washington.[78] He said his purpose in declining the award was to indicate his "strong disapproval of the present Dartmouth atmosphere of intolerance to unfashionable opinion." Contributing to that atmosphere, he continued, is the "official position of the college that there is a morally right and wrong answer" to controversial social and political questions. "The Dartmouth Administration and many of the faculty use 'racism' and 'sexism' and other

---

77. Allan R. Gold, "Dartmouth President Faults Right-Wing Student Journal," *New York Times,* 29 March 1988.
78. Excerpts from it were published in the *Wall Street Journal,* 28 December 1988.

'isms' loosely . . . to label their critics as morally inferior." Silberman said he found that approach offensive.

There was a somewhat different result at Northwestern University when an English professor led a demonstration that prevented a Nicaraguan contra leader from speaking. She took over the stage, announced that she was a member of the International Committee Against Racism, and said she and sympathizers in the audience were not going to let the contra leader speak. They made such a clamor that the meeting was canceled. A faculty disciplinary committee concluded that the professor had "committed a grave violation of academic freedom and the right of a speaker to speak and be heard in a university." Nevertheless, the English faculty and the university's tenure committees later recommended that she be given tenure. Provost W. Raymond Mack rejected the tenure recommendation, holding that the professor had "violated widely accepted principles of academic freedom and responsibility." President Arnold W. Weber upheld Mack's decision.[79]

These instances and others raise the question asked in a *New York Times* headline: "On Campus, How Free Should Free Speech Be?" Traditionally, the core of the university has been its college of the liberal arts. That term dates to the middle of the eighteenth century, when it was translated from the Latin *artes liberales,* meaning "works befitting a free man." The word "liberal" comes from the same Latin root as "liberty": *liber,* which means "free." To be free, of course, has many meanings. In this text, "free" generally will mean the freedom to express ideas—good, bad, significant, silly, profound, trivial, and, yes, even abhorrent. But free also means the right to be free from harassment, from discrimination, from intimidation, and worse. And because words are not dead things, sometimes one person's freedom of speech becomes harassment of someone else. Philosophers seek a moral balance among these sometimes conflicting freedoms. Judges sometimes are compelled to strike a legal balance. Because ours is a society that rests ultimately on public opinion, each of us must decide which freedoms we value most.

The measure of freedom, as Justice Jackson wrote during World War II, is our willingness as individuals to permit speech that outrages us. It is easy, if one has no deep commitment to church or country, to tolerate antireligious or antigovernment diatribe. Religious and governmental authorities are remote figures, able to take care of themselves. In any event, they have been subject to criticism as far back as anyone can remember, and seem none the worse for it.

But the new kinds of criticism, especially on college campuses, attack more vulnerable targets. Equality for women, justice for minorities, and respect for homosexual preferences are values that have come to the fore relatively recently. They have not yet struck deep roots into our culture and hence seem more vulnerable to attack than the older values of church and state. When racist, sexist, and homophobic slurs appear on campus buildings overnight, are broadcast on a campus radio station, or are uttered in a classroom, real people suffer immediate real pain.

---

79. "Freedom 101 (Ltd. Enrollment)," editorial in *Wall Street Journal,* 25 February 1987.

It is understandable that people who feel vulnerable, for whatever reason, do not want to be reminded of that vulnerability. When they are, it is easy to believe that language seen as an outrageous insult will sway public opinion and sweep away such gains as have been made. But it is equally likely that such outbursts are the last shots of a dwindling rear guard reacting to what it sees as the crumbling of its values. If the new values are another step in the direction of truth, the better course would be not to suppress racist, sexist, homophobic, or anti-Semitic speech but to counter it with fact and reasoned argument. We do not need a First Amendment to protect speech that makes no one angry. Freedom is measured by how far we are willing to go to protect speech that enrages us because we consider it irresponsible and even harmful.

FOR REVIEW

1. Beginning with Plato, philosophers have recognized and sometimes been victims of tension between political authority and the right to question that authority. List and examine arguments used to justify the exercise of authority by government. Do the same for arguments supporting the right to question authority. Can the two lists be brought into harmony?

2. Milton saw words as potent forces, capable, if sown in the right soil, of "springing up armed men." If this statement is true, doesn't it support the argument that some speech is so outrageous that it ought to be suppressed? Like what? Who should have the authority to determine which speech should be suppressed? How should such authority be exercised?

3. A sometimes humorous television commentator on human foibles writes a letter in which he says he finds certain homosexual practices abhorrent. He also is alleged to have made disparaging remarks about Jews. This behavior leads to his being characterized as a bigot. Should he be removed from his program? What principles should guide your decision?

4. At this distance, what is the significance of the Zenger case? Of the Alien and Sedition acts and the enforcement of them? What factors are common to both?

5. Does the First Amendment mean what it says? Should it? Why or why not?

6. If you could be appointed to the Supreme Court, what theories would you adopt in interpreting the meaning of the speech and press clause of the First Amendment? To which of the philosophers discussed in this chapter would you look for guidance?

7. How valid is the clear and present danger test as applied to speech or writing? How precise? Was it applied in *Schenck?* What would happen if you were to use it as your guide in answering question 2 above?

8. Some Supreme Court justices, such as William O. Douglas, have believed that there is no room in First Amendment theory for a balancing test, that when the framers said "no law abridging freedom," they meant no law. Is this a realistic position? Was there a role for balancing, for instance, in the flag-burning case, or in *R.A.V.?* Was there a role for a clear and present danger test?

9. A considerable number of people in your town believe so strongly that abortion is wrong that they are determined to force the closing of the town's only abortion clinic. How far can they go under the doctrine of symbolic speech to do so?

10. Meiklejohn and, to a greater degree, Emerson believed that the First Amendment should not just protect speech but should encourage speech. Others have argued that this positive view of the amendment should go so far as to provide a right of access not only to public forums but to the media. List and examine arguments supporting a positive role for the First Amendment.

11. What is a public forum? What distinguishes a public forum from a nonpublic forum?

CHAPTER 3

A government trying to win a war, keep vital secrets, or ensure what the preamble to the Constitution calls "domestic tranquility" can take one of three courses with those whose words might cause trouble:

1. It can adopt the First Amendment theories of Emerson and Meiklejohn and take its chances that the people will reject advocates of harmful action and do what is best for the nation.

2. It can adopt laws providing for punishment of those whose words might help the enemy, or who would disclose vital secrets or try to stir up trouble.

3. It can impose censorship, thus cutting off at the source any words that might help the enemy, disclose vital secrets, or provoke harmful action. Obviously, if censorship can be made effective, it offers the most certain way of pre-

SEDITION AND CENSORSHIP

venting speech that the government considers harmful. On the other hand, it is also the most stringent possible abridgment of the freedom of speech and press guaranteed by the First Amendment.

As this book will demonstrate, the first option has been the one usually taken in the United States. On numerous occasions, the Supreme Court has held that free debate is the preferred method of resolving differences in our society.

The Court has so held even when the debaters have played fast and loose with the truth or have used language that others have found offensive. However, the Court also has upheld laws designed to punish persons whose speech is considered harmful to national security, to an orderly society, or to the rights of others. If such laws are carefully drafted to protect government interests, and if they do not restrict speech unduly, they can be enforced. People have been sent to prison for long terms because it was believed that their speech might help an enemy in time of war or might lead to an overthrow of the government in time of peace. The third course, censorship, has rarely been imposed. In modern times, the Supreme Court has held in several notable instances that censorship violates the First Amendment guarantees of freedom of speech and press, but the Court also has refused to hold that censorship can never be imposed. The Court has always left open the possibility that at some time, under certain extreme circumstances, government can use its power to suppress speech that poses a direct threat to a vital interest, such as national security.

At this point, it might be well to reflect on the difference between punishing someone for speech considered harmful and suppressing that speech altogether. People who know they might go to prison or be fined heavily if they criticize government officials too severely will think twice before they do so. But as we saw in Chapter 2, in the discussion of the Sedition Act of 1798, some people will go ahead and criticize anyway. They do so for several reasons. They know that their comments will reach the public and may even have an influence on policy in the long run. They may also reason that a possible arrest will lead more people to pay attention to their comments. And it is possible, as in Zenger's case, also described in Chapter 2, that a jury may find the critics not guilty. Thus, laws designed to punish some participants in the debate on public policy may have a deterrent effect, but they do not prevent determined speakers from being heard. That is what censorship attempts to do. Thus, the difference can be quite significant. The Supreme Court once expressed the difference in this way: Laws punishing speakers can be said to chill speech; censorship freezes it.

Direct censorship of the media has been rare in the United States. More common, starting with World War I and continuing through the Great Depression into the Cold War following World War II, has been the use of sedition law to punish those whose speech or writings were believed to pose a threat to national security.

For governments, as for individuals, the instinct for self-preservation is a powerful force. Thus, all nations have laws providing for punishment of those who would attempt to destroy them. In many nations, laws designed to prevent violent overthrow make advocating such overthrow a crime. Despite the First Amendment, the United States is no exception. Since 1940, the Smith Act[1] has made it a crime to advocate violence to effect a change in the form of government. The problem with such laws lies in drawing the line between words advocating a change in government policies or the form of government, and words designed to provoke rebellion. Advocacy of peaceful change is politics. Advocacy of violent change can be punished as sedition.

This chapter examines the use of sedition law and censorship in the United States. After the Sedition Act of 1798 was permitted to lapse in 1801, there was no federal sedition law until the United States entered World War I in 1917. During that war, nearly two thousand Socialists, pacifists, and German immigrants were punished for sedition. In the immediate aftermath of the war, in response to fears raised by the Bolshevik Revolution in Russia, sedition law was used against U.S. Communists and others who advocated an end to what they saw as capitalist oppression. Appeals from some of the convictions reached the U.S. Supreme Court, which for the first time had to decide how far the First Amendment goes in protecting unpopular speech. Some of the cases from that era remain as landmarks defining the right of individuals and groups to defy government policy or advocate changes in the form of government.

The Smith Act was adopted to counter the contending ideologies, Communist and Fascist, seeking to draw the United States into or keep it out of World War II. The act's purpose was to punish those who might be tempted to impose either form of government on the United States. The Japanese attack on Pearl Harbor in December 1941 so united the American people that few were accused of sedition during World War II, although President Roosevelt used his war powers to confine most U.S. citizens of Japanese descent to internment camps for the duration. After the war ended in 1945, prosecution of Communists was renewed during the period of mutual suspicion between the United States and the Soviet Union known as the Cold War. During the 1950s the entire leadership of the U.S. Communist party was found guilty of sedition and sent to prison. In the 1960s and 1970s, the nation's attitude toward public dissent began to shift dramatically. The Supreme Court held in 1969 that people could not be punished for advocating violent overthrow of the government unless they clearly intended to incite immediate harmful action. Since that decision, sedition law has been little used to curb political protests short of threats or terrorism.

Thus, Americans remain free to say pretty much what they please about the president, Congress, and government at all levels, as every political campaign illustrates anew. The line is drawn at death threats, particularly those directed at the president. Persons who talk openly about killing the president are likely to be arrested and, if a court concludes the talk was serious enough to present a threat, punished.

---

1.   18 U.S.C.A. § 2385.

The latter part of this chapter examines several instances in which the government sought to freeze speech by imposing a prior restraint, which is the legal term for government censorship. The first prior restraint case came to the Supreme Court in 1931, when the state of Minnesota ordered a weekly newspaper to stop publishing. In that case, and in two more recent cases, the Court erected high barriers that government must overcome before a prior restraint can be imposed. However, these barriers are not so high as to rule out prior restraint in all instances.

On one occasion, the government was able to hold up for two weeks newspaper publication of a top secret report on the Vietnam war. On another, for seven months the government prevented a magazine from publishing an article that the government believed might help other nations build a hydrogen bomb. The government has also been able to enforce contracts that prevent former CIA agents from publishing secrets learned while they were with the agency. The Supreme Court held that public school officials can censor newspapers published as part of the course work in journalism. Most recently, a federal district court judge ordered *Business Week* magazine not to publish an article based on documents that the court had sealed. Although the judge unsealed the documents three weeks later, neither the court of appeals nor the Supreme Court intervened.

Later in the book we will see that prior restraint can be imposed to protect privacy, suppress obscenity, and prevent infringement of copyright. Thus, although the Supreme Court has made censorship difficult, it has refused to hold that the First Amendment makes censorship impossible.

Major Cases

- *Abrams* v. *United States,* 250 U.S. 616, 40 S.Ct. 17, 63 L.Ed. 1173 (1919).

- *Bantam Books* v. *Sullivan,* 372 U.S. 58, 83 S.Ct. 631, 9 L.Ed.2d 584, 1 Med.L.Rptr. 1116 (1963).

- *Brandenberg* v. *Ohio,* 395 U.S. 444, 89 S.Ct. 1827, 23 L.Ed.2d 430 (1969).

- *Dennis* v. *United States,* 341 U.S. 494, 71 S.Ct. 857, 95 L.Ed. 1137 (1951).

- *Gitlow* v. *People of the State of New York,* 268 U.S. 652, 45 S.Ct. 625, 69 L.Ed. 1138 (1925).

- *Hazelwood School District* v. *Kuhlmeier,* 484 U.S. 260, 108 S.Ct. 562, 98 L.Ed.2d 592 (1988).

- *Near* v. *Minnesota,* 283 U.S. 697, 51 S.Ct. 625, 75 L.Ed. 1357, 1 Med.L.Rptr. 1001 (1931).

- *New York Times Co.* v. *United States,* 403 U.S. 713, 91 S.Ct. 2140, 29 L.Ed.2d 822, 1 Med.L.Rptr. 1031 (1971).

- *Organization for a Better Austin* v. *Keefe,* 402 U.S. 415, 91 S.Ct. 1575, 29 L.Ed.2d 1, 1 Med.L.Rptr. 1021 (1971).

- *Snepp* v. *United States,* 444 U.S. 507, 100 S.Ct. 763, 62 L.Ed.2d 704, 5 Med.L.Rptr. 2409 (1980).

- *United States* v. *Morison,* 844 F.2d 1057, 15 Med.L.Rptr. 1369 (4th Cir. 1988).

- *Yates* v. *United States,* 354 U.S. 298, 77 S.Ct. 1064, 1 L.Ed.2d 1356 (1957).

SEDITION

The Prosecution of Sedition

When Congress declared war on Germany and its allies in April 1917, many Americans doubted that it was acting wisely. To them Europe was far away, its wars no concern of ours. Consequently, some in Congress believed that the people's doubts would undermine the will to fight. Two groups were viewed with particular suspicion: the large numbers of Germans who had come to this country in the 1890s, and the Socialists, who were numerous enough to have elected mayors in several cities and who believed the war was part of an evil design to shore up declining capitalist systems.

To cope with anticipated antiwar talk from such people, Congress quickly followed up its declaration of war by adopting the Espionage Act of 1917, which made it a crime to speak or write in a way that could be seen as helping the enemy.[2] When that law turned out not to be broad enough to catch all who spoke their doubts about the war, Congress passed the much more stringent Sedition Act of 1918. That law made it a crime to talk against the draft or the sale of war bonds, or to interfere with the production of war goods, as by advocating a strike. Even to question the constitutionality of the draft or the official version of why we entered the war became a crime. Consequently, nearly two thousand espionage and sedition arrests were made in fewer than eighteen months. The attorney general reported that 877 of the arrests resulted in convictions. Other cases were dismissed after the war ended in 1918.[3] No other period in U.S. history has seen so many arrests for the crime of talking against the government.

---

2. Section 3, Title I of the 1917 Espionage Act provided: "[1] Whoever, when the United States is at war, shall willfully make or convey false reports or false statements with intent to interfere with the operation or success of the military or naval forces of the United States or to promote the success of its enemies, and [2] whoever, when the United States is at war, shall willfully cause or attempt to cause insubordination, disloyalty, mutiny, or refusal of duty, in the military or naval forces of the United States, to the injury of the service or of the United States, or [3] shall willfully obstruct the recruiting or enlistment service of the United States, to the injury of the service or of the United States, shall be punished by a fine of not more than $10,000 or imprisonment for not more than twenty years, or both." See also Zechariah Chafee, Jr., *Free Speech in the United States,* Atheneum ed. (New York: Atheneum, 1969), pp. 37–39.
3. Chafee, *Free Speech in the United States,* Atheneum ed., p. 52.

The cases were decided by applying the bad tendency theory. The decisions were based on the premise that the right of the government to preserve itself from conquest by foreign enemies and from violent overthrow by domestic enemies is foremost. Under this theory, words that have a tendency to help either kind of enemy may be punished. Convictions were based on the belief that forces that might be set in motion by seditious words must be checked at the start, before they can cause harm. In this view, liberty of speech protects reasoned discourse in which truth is used for good purposes. But when speech becomes "license" in the old sense of "licentiousness," it becomes destructive of orderly discourse and therefore punishable. Obviously, reasonable persons can disagree widely as to when liberty becomes license. Under the pressures of fear generated by the war, the field of license expanded. Judges and juries interpreted license as covering words that in ordinary times would have been dismissed as the spouting of harmless hotheads or pondered as valid debate on public policy.

A series of Supreme Court cases from the World War I era remain of interest in helping us understand the extent to which the First Amendment protects those who protest government policies. They are *Schenck* v. *United States,*[4] *Frohwerk* v. *United States,*[5] *Debs* v. *United States,*[6] and *Abrams* v. *United States.*[7] A fifth, from the mid-1920s, *Gitlow* v. *People of the State of New York,*[8] is of enduring importance because it led the Supreme Court to stretch the First Amendment, through the Fourteenth, so that it applies to state attempts to restrict freedom of speech and press.

In *Schenck,* which was summarized in Chapter 2, the Supreme Court for the first time interpreted the meaning of the First Amendment and found it to be far from an absolute guarantee of the right to speak freely, particularly in time of war. Justice Oliver Wendell Holmes, writing for the Court, took note of the bad tendency theory, saying that it permitted the government to move too easily to repress unpopular speakers. It should be replaced, he said, by a test that would permit punishment only of those speakers whose words "create a clear and present danger" of harm to an interest the government is entitled to protect. In this instance, the Court found that interest in Article I, Section 8, of the Constitution, which gives Congress the power to "raise and support armies." In the Court's view, Schenck's pamphlets urging resistance to the draft directly threatened the government's ability to do that. Had the campaign succeeded, the Court reasoned, the United States could have lost the war with Germany. Actually, there was no evidence that anyone who read Schenck's pamphlets had refused to serve. In addition, the justices knew when they decided the case, four months after the war ended, that the United States and its allies had won. These facts have led some legal scholars to conclude that despite Holmes's rhetoric, the Court really decided the case on a bad tendency theory.

In any case, Justice Holmes, a Civil War veteran who in his time had lived through four American wars, was not sympathetic to speech that could obstruct success in wartime. In *Frohwerk* v. *United States* Holmes again spoke for the

---

4. 249 U.S. 47, 39 S.Ct. 247, 63 L.Ed. 470 (1919).
5. 249 U.S. 204, 39 S.Ct. 249, 63 L.Ed. 561 (1919).
6. 249 U.S. 211, 39 S.Ct. 252, 63 L.Ed. 566 (1919).
7. 250 U.S. 616, 40 S.Ct. 17, 63 L.Ed. 1173 (1919).
8. 268 U.S. 652, 45 S.Ct. 625, 69 L.Ed. 1138 (1925).

Court in upholding the 1917 act. This case had resulted in the conviction of a newspaper editorialist for writing a series of antiwar articles published in the *Missouri Staats Zeitung.* Holmes emphasized that freedom of speech depends on the circumstances:

> [W]e think it necessary to add to what has been said in [*Schenck*] only that the First Amendment while prohibiting legislation against free speech as such cannot have been, and obviously was not, intended to give immunity for every possible use of language. [We] venture to believe that neither Hamilton nor Madison, nor any other competent person then or later, ever supposed that to make criminal the counseling of a murder within the jurisdiction of Congress would be an unconstitutional interference with free speech.

In *Debs* v. *United States,* decided on the same day, Justice Holmes wrote an opinion for the Court upholding the conviction of Eugene V. Debs, a one-time member of the Indiana Legislature who had become the leader of the Socialist party. Debs was sentenced to prison for ten years because of a speech he made at the Ohio Socialist Party Convention in June of 1918. In that speech Debs praised several persons who had been convicted of helping others avoid the draft. He said that those antidraft counselors were "paying the penalty for standing erect and for seeking to pave the way to better conditions for all mankind." Debs said he was proud of them, predicted the success of the international Socialist crusade, and told his audience, "You need to know that you are fit for something better than slavery and cannon fodder." At his trial, Debs told the jury, "I have been accused of obstructing the war. I admit it. Gentlemen, I abhor war. I would oppose the war if I stood alone."

Eugene Debs, a leader of the Socialist party, was found guilty of sedition in World War I and sentenced to prison, partly on the basis of his many speeches opposing United States participation in the war. Here, he addresses a rally in Canton, Ohio, in 1918. He received almost a million votes for president in 1920 while he was serving his sentence. (*UPI/Bettmann*)

Justice Holmes found that a jury was warranted in finding Debs's remarks to have the natural and intended effect of obstructing recruiting during wartime. "If that was intended and if, in all the circumstances, that would be its probable effect it would not be protected."[9]

The difference between "bad tendency" and "clear and present danger" seemed to mean little after the Debs case. But a few months later, in *Abrams* v. *United States,* Holmes found himself joining the Court's most liberal justice, Louis D. Brandeis, in a dissent that made clear that Holmes did have something different in mind or, at least, was developing something different from the old bad tendency approach that seemed still to satisfy the Court's majority.

Abrams v. *United States,*
250 U.S. 616, 40 S.Ct. 17,
63 L.Ed. 1173 (1919).

Holmes wrote the most eloquent of his many dissents in *Abrams,* a case involving five self-described "revolutionaries, anarchists, and socialists." Their crime had been to write and distribute pamphlets attacking President Wilson because he had sent troops to Russia to fight against the Bolsheviks during the revolution. The majority had no doubt that the five intended "to excite, at the supreme crisis of the war, disaffection, sedition, riots, and, as they hoped, revolution in this country." Nor did the majority doubt that the threat was real. The Court confirmed the twenty-year prison sentences imposed on Abrams and his associates by the trial court. Holmes, on the other hand, thought the threat was silly.

In Holmes's view the defendants' leaflets were to be given no more credence than a claim that they had found a formula to square the circle. Holmes's vehement dissent included an eloquent passage defending freedom of speech:

> But when men have realized that time has upset many fighting faiths, they may come to believe even more than they believe the very foundation of their own conduct that the ultimate good desired is better reached by free trade in ideas—that the best test of truth is the power of the thought to get itself accepted in the competition of the market; and that truth is the only ground upon which their wishes safely can be carried out. That, at any rate, is the theory of our Constitution. It is an experiment, as all life is an experiment. Every year, if not every day, we have to wager our salvation upon some prophecy based upon imperfect knowledge. While that experiment is part of our system I think that we should be eternally vigilant against attempts to check the expression of opinions that we loathe and believe to be fraught with death, unless they so imminently threaten immediate interference with the lawful and pressing purposes of the law that an immediate check is required to save the country.

That passage comes closer to defining the clear and present danger test as we have learned to understand it than does Holmes's majority opinion in *Schenck.* The passage also elaborates on the argument advanced by Milton—that the test of truth is the ability of an idea to win acceptance in free and open encounter with other ideas. But neither Holmes's eloquence nor the clear and present danger test prevented the Court from upholding the prison sentence imposed on Abrams, and Holmes did not regret

---

9. In the 1920 U.S. presidential race, Debs, while in prison, received more than 900,000 votes as the Socialist candidate. In 1921, he was released from prison by President Harding.

his decisions in *Schenck, Frohwerk,* and *Debs.* For Holmes, the clarity and presence of the danger depended on the circumstances of each case. The circumstances in *Schenck, Frohwerk,* and *Debs,* he thought, justified the result. In his dissent in *Abrams,* Holmes wrote:

> I never have seen any reason to doubt that the questions of law that alone were before this Court in the cases of [*Schenck, Frohwerk,* and *Debs*] were rightly decided. I do not doubt for a moment that by the same reasoning that would justify punishing persuasion to murder, the United States constitutionally may punish speech that produces or is intended to produce a clear and imminent danger that it will bring about forthwith certain substantive evils that the United States constitutionally may seek to prevent. The power undoubtedly is greater in time of war than in time of peace because war opens dangers that do not exist at other times. But as against dangers peculiar to war, as against others, the principle of the right to free speech is always the same. It is only the present danger of immediate evil or an intent to bring it about that warrants Congress in setting a limit to the expression of opinion where private rights are not concerned.

The circumstantial difference in *Abrams,* said Holmes, was that here nobody could seriously suppose that the "surreptitious publishing of a silly leaflet by an unknown man, without more, would present any immediate danger that its opinions would hinder the success of the government arms or have any appreciable tendency to do so."

The First Amendment and the States

In the 1920s, the fears and tensions that had led to sedition prosecutions subsided somewhat at the federal level. However, states continued prosecution of Communists; anarchists; and members of a left-wing labor union, the Industrial Workers of the World. One of these cases led to a Supreme Court decision that upset a century-old constitutional principle limiting application of the Bill of Rights to actions by the federal government. In 1833, in *Barron* v. *Baltimore,*[10] Chief Justice John Marshall had held that the Constitution had been adopted by the people of the United States "for themselves, for their own government, and not for the government of the individual states." Each state, he noted, had its own constitution when the federal Constitution was adopted. Those constitutions remained in effect, establishing the limits within which state authorities could act. Marshall went on to hold that in this instance the due process clause of the Fifth Amendment could not be invoked by a Baltimore wharf owner to collect damages against the city. From that time on, courts acted on the theory that guarantees of rights contained in other amendments, including the First, could be used to bar federal action, but not infringements by state authorities. In the latter instances, victims had to look to their individual state constitutions for help.

---

10.   7 Pet. 243, 8 L.Ed. 672 (1833).

Thus, when New York authorities prosecuted Benjamin Gitlow under a state law that made it a crime to advocate violence against the government, they did so in the belief that they need satisfy only the state constitution's free speech clause. Gitlow was a member of the left-wing section of the Socialist party. His crime was the publication of a ponderous manifesto calling for a general strike as a first step toward the toppling of the capitalist system. A New York court found him guilty of criminal anarchy and sentenced him to prison.

Gitlow v. *People of the State of New York*, 268 U.S. 652, 45 S.Ct. 625, 69 L.Ed. 1138 (1935).

The Supreme Court agreed to review the conviction and affirmed it, despite a strong protest by Justice Holmes. Remarkably, however, the Court also held that a state's attempts to restrict freedoms of speech and press are subject to review under the standards established by the First Amendment. Speaking for a majority, Justice Edward T. Sanford wrote:

> For present purposes we may and do assume that freedom of speech and of the press—which are protected by the First Amendment from abridgment by Congress—are among the fundamental personal rights and "liberties" protected by the Fourteenth Amendment from impairment by the States. We do not regard the incidental statement in *Prudential Ins. Co.* v. *Cheek,* 259 U.S. 530, 543, that the Fourteenth Amendment imposes no restrictions on the States concerning freedom of speech, as determinative of this question.

Two points in that paragraph require explanation. In deciding *Prudential* only a few years earlier, the Court had said, in language not essential to the decision, that states were not bound by the First Amendment's guarantees of freedom of speech and press. Now, in language that clearly was essential, the Court said just the opposite. Had it held otherwise, it would have had no jurisdiction over *Gitlow,* because the case dealt with a prosecution in a state court under a state law. The case could be reviewed by a federal court only if a federal question—in this instance, Gitlow's right to freedom of speech—was involved. The second point requiring explanation is Sanford's reference to the "liberties" protected by the Fourteenth Amendment. That amendment, adopted in the aftermath of the Civil War, was drafted to prevent states from adopting laws designed to deny freed slaves the rights enjoyed by white people. The language alluded to by Sanford says:

> No state shall make or enforce any law which shall abridge the privileges or immunities of citizens of the United States; nor shall any State deprive any person of life, liberty, or property without due process of law; nor deny to any person within its jurisdiction the equal protection of the laws.

With time, the *Gitlow* decision has assumed an importance far greater than it had in 1925. Then its only result was to ensure that Gitlow went to prison. But in more recent times the Supreme Court has used the rationale of *Gitlow* not only to ensure freedom of speech and press but to prevent the states from restricting most of the rights, or "liberties," guaranteed by the Bill of Rights. Sanford's seemingly casual invocation of the Fourteenth Amendment in *Gitlow* permeates much of the remainder of this book. That decision made possible the broad application of the First Amendment that protects freedom of speech and press in our time.

The Smith Act

The World War I Sedition Act was permitted to expire in the 1920s. The nation was at peace and was enjoying prosperity. By 1940, the Great Depression and the outbreak of war in Europe had brought on a new period of stress in the United States. With as many as a quarter of the nation's adults out of work, ideologues offering various economic panaceas sought changes in business and government. Communist sympathizers with Stalinist Russia and brown-shirted followers of Hitler's Nazi Germany contended for support. When the war in Europe began in 1939, strife arose between those who believed we should join forces with England and those who wanted peace at any price.

The atmosphere was made to order for those who believed that a law was needed to protect the nation from harmful talk. With little fanfare, Congress enacted the first peacetime sedition law since the Alien and Sedition Act had been permitted to expire in 1801. This law was known as the Smith Act because its language was offered as an amendment to an alien deportation bill by Howard W. Smith, a representative to Congress from Virginia. The act made it a crime to

> knowingly or willfully advocate, abet, advise, or teach the duty, necessity, desirability, or propriety of overthrowing or destroying the government of the United States, or the government of any State . . . or . . . any political subdivision therein, by force or violence, or by the assassination of any officer of any such government.

Oddly, Representative Smith's law was used little either in the short time remaining before the United States entered the war at the end of 1941 or during the four years of the war. For one thing, Japan's surprise attack on Pearl Harbor united the nation as have few events in its history. For another, Germany's invasion of the Soviet Union in 1940 made the United States an ally of the Soviet Union, thus converting U.S. Communists into ardent patriots. Remaining as potential targets of sedition law were only a few U.S. Nazis and a more numerous population of Japanese-Americans. Although history has taught that there was little to fear from the Americans of Japanese descent, the government reacted by rounding them up and putting them in detention camps until the war ended. Not until 1988 did the government partially atone for that act by agreeing to pay the surviving internees a few thousand dollars each.

The Prosecution of American Communists

With the end of World War II in 1945, America's long-standing fear of communism quickly revived. The United States and the Soviet Union had been uneasy and mistrusting allies at best. With the defeat of Germany and Japan, old suspicions were revived, creating an era of distrust that became known as the Cold War. Because at that time U.S. Communists were seen as taking orders from Moscow, they, too, became subjects of suspicion and distrust. Very quickly, covert investigations of party members by the FBI resulted in prosecutions under the Smith Act. Before the Cold War ended, nearly two hundred persons, including the entire leadership of the Communist party in the United States, had been prosecuted under federal law. Others suspected of harboring subversive ideas were targets of state sedition laws or subjects of congressional committee investigations designed to hound them out of public life.

The prosecutions of the Communists, and later of an Ohio Ku Klux Klan leader, led to three significant Supreme Court decisions that drew the line between speech that may be punished as sedition and speech that is an acceptable part of political debate: *Dennis* v. *United States,*[11] *Yates* v. *United States,*[12] and *Brandenberg* v. *Ohio.*[13]

During and after World War II, Eugene Dennis was the general secretary of the Communist party U.S.A. On the strength of reports from FBI informants who had infiltrated the party organization, Dennis and his fellow members of the Central Committee were indicted in 1948 on charges of plotting the overthrow of the government. At the time, the Communist party had a known membership of about seventy-four thousand in the United States, but such was the political climate that the party was widely believed to have hundreds of thousands of secret sympathizers.

After a trial that lasted nine months, a jury in a U.S. district court in New York City found Dennis and twelve members of the party's governing board guilty of advocating violent overthrow of the government. Prosecution witnesses testified that the leaders were preparing their followers to use force to topple the government if another depression should cause unrest. All defendants were sentenced to prison. They appealed, arguing that they were doing no more than talking about violent overthrow as one of several means of achieving power. As they saw it, such talk is protected by the First Amendment. The circuit court of appeals disagreed. The Communists took their case to the Supreme Court, which held, six to two, that the trial court jury's verdict was correct.

Four of the six justices in the majority concluded that the party represented a clear and present danger to the nation's security. They started with the premise that Congress has power under the Constitution to draft laws designed to protect the nation from armed rebellion. Theoretically, as recognized by the Declaration of Independence, there is a right to rebel against a dictatorial government. But that right has no meaning, the plurality wrote, when "the existing structure of government provides for peaceful and orderly change." This was a reminder that, in the United States, the route to power runs through the ballot box.

Dennis v. *United States,*
341 U.S. 494, 71 S.Ct. 857,
95 L.Ed. 1137 (1951).

Lawyers for Dennis argued that the language of the Smith Act swept more broadly than was needed to protect the government from those who would destroy it. They argued that if the act were strictly enforced as written, it could be used to punish classroom discussion of Communist party doctrine.

The plurality disagreed. It said the law was directed at advocacy, not discussion. Indeed, the trial judge had told the jury it could not convict the party leaders if it concluded they were engaged only in the peaceful discussion of ideas. He also had told the jury that the Smith Act did not make it a crime to study the principles of communism in colleges and universities. The plurality concluded that when Congress wrote

---

11.   341 U.S. 494, 71 S.Ct. 857, 95 L.Ed. 1137 (1951).
12.   354 U.S. 298, 77 S.Ct. 1064, 1 L.Ed.2d 1356 (1957).
13.   395 U.S. 444, 89 S.Ct. 1827, 23 L.Ed.2d 430 (1969).

the law, it was concerned with speech and writing used to plan and set in motion illegal acts against the government.

The outcome of the case hinged on the distinction between advocacy and discussion. The plurality said that speech urging illegal action against the government is advocacy of a kind not protected by the First Amendment. People are free to discuss violent overthrow as long as they don't prepare themselves to strike when the time seems ripe for successful action. But as the Court saw it, the Communist party was preparing to strike. Chief Justice Fred M. Vinson, who wrote for the plurality, used some of his strongest language in condemning the party's purpose. He said the clear and present danger test

> cannot mean that before the Government may act, it must wait until the *putsch* is about to be executed, the plans have been laid and the signal is awaited. If Government is aware that a group aiming at its overflow is attempting to indoctrinate its members and to commit them to a course whereby they will strike when the leaders feel the circumstances permit, action by the Government is required.

Justice Felix Frankfurter, usually a liberal on First Amendment rights, concurred in the Court's holding that the defendants were guilty, but not in the plurality's reasoning. He clearly was bothered by Vinson's attempt to distinguish between advocacy and discussion. The plurality said that the party leaders' crime was advocacy—in this instance, of violent overthrow of the government. Frankfurter was not willing to concede that all advocacy is illegal, nor was he certain that a clear line always can be drawn between advocacy and discussion. As he saw it, a certain degree of advocacy of change is at the heart of the political process. Therefore, courts ought to be cautious about restricting advocacy, even when its purpose is to change the form of government. However, Frankfurter concluded that Congress was within its constitutional powers in making advocacy of violent overthrow a crime. Despite his misgivings, he held that the Communist party leaders had urged such overthrow.

Justice Robert H. Jackson, the sixth member of the majority, did not share Frankfurter's doubts. Nor did he see any First Amendment issue in the case. In his view, Dennis and his associates were involved in a conspiracy to commit illegal acts against the government. Under criminal law, such conspiracies always have been punishable. He chided the other justices for making more out of the case than that.

That decision, reached at the depth of the Cold War in 1951, cleared the way for vigorous prosecution of lower-level Communist party leaders, including Oleta O'Connor Yates and other officers of the party in California. At the trial in a federal court in Los Angeles, the judge read the Supreme Court's decision in *Dennis* and told the jurors they could find the defendants guilty if they concluded that the Communists had advocated violent overthrow of the government "unrelated to [the] tendency [of their words] to produce forcible actions." The jury found the officers guilty. The judge sentenced each to five years in prison and imposed a $10,000 fine on each. When the case reached the Supreme Court in 1957, the decision was reversed. The Court said the judge had gone too far in telling the jury that the Smith Act punishes all advocacy of violent overthrow. People can talk all they want about the desirability of using vio-

Yates v. *United States,* 354 U.S. 298, 77 S.Ct. 1064, 1 L.Ed.2d 1356 (1957).

lence against government. They can even express the hope that a revolution will succeed. As Justice John Marshall Harlan put it, "The essential distinction [between legal and illegal advocacy] is that those to whom the advocacy is addressed must be urged to *do* something, now or in the future, rather than merely believe in something." The Court said there was no evidence that Yates and the other officers of the California branch of the Communist party had urged anyone to commit illegal acts.

The government made no attempt to retry the *Yates* defendants so as to offer such evidence. Indeed, with the Supreme Court's decision, Smith Act prosecutions dwindled and died. By 1961, the government's attempt to suppress its Communist critics had ended.

The decisions in *Dennis* and *Yates,* only six years apart, illustrate that even the justices of the Supreme Court, the branch of government most remote from the pressures of politics, are not altogether insulated from public opinion. In 1951, when *Dennis* was decided, Joseph Stalin was in control of the Soviet Union and the Communist party, including its branches in other countries. Investigations conducted by committees of both houses of Congress were exposing persons in labor unions, civil rights organizations, and the moving picture industry who were alleged to be either Communists or fellow travelers doing Stalin's bidding. At the time the Supreme Court was pondering its decision in *Dennis,* a court in New York City was finding Julius and Ethel Rosenberg and Morton Sobell guilty of giving the secrets of the atom bomb to the Soviet Union. The Rosenbergs were executed in 1953. In that same year, Stalin died and was succeeded as Soviet leader in 1955 by Nikita Khrushchev. In a secret speech to the Twentieth Congress of the Soviet Communist party Khrushchev denounced Stalin and announced a policy of peaceful coexistence with the West. The speech created a worldwide sensation when it was leaked to Western correspondents. By 1957, when the Court decided *Yates,* the Soviet Union and the United States were experiencing tense but improved relations. The danger of political violence by Communists that had impressed five justices of the Supreme Court as being clear and present in 1951 was not mentioned by a single justice in *Yates.* In 1959, Khrushchev became the first Soviet premier to visit the United States, where he was greeted by large and generally friendly crowds. Although the Cold War was far from over, relations between the two powers were noticeably warmer.

The Civil Rights Movement and Sedition Law

Constitutional amendments adopted during and after the Civil War abolished slavery and sought to protect the rights of freed persons,[14] but they by no means brought about equality for blacks with whites. Indeed, the Supreme Court in the 1890s had endorsed a doctrine of "separate but equal" treatment of blacks with respect to such things as railroad cars, schools, restrooms, and even drinking fountains. Under this doctrine, local governments could enforce rigid patterns of racial segregation justified

---

14.   The Thirteenth, ratified in 1865, abolished slavery. The Fourteenth, ratified in 1868, sought to prevent states from depriving blacks of rights enjoyed by other citizens. The Fifteenth, ratified in 1870, sought to protect the voting rights of blacks.

by the fiction that facilities provided for blacks were the same as those provided for whites.

In the 1950s, blacks mounted a challenge to the separate-but-equal doctrine. In 1954, in *Brown* v. *Board of Education*,[15] the Supreme Court held that public schools should be integrated. The decision proved to be only a beginning. Many whites, including governors of several southern states, resisted integration, thereby instigating boycotts, lunch counter sit-ins, demonstrations, and violence. State sedition laws were among the legal devices involved in a vain attempt to preserve segregation. In Mississippi, for instance, when William Ware tried to get blacks registered so that they could vote, he was arrested and charged with promoting anarchy. A federal trial court said the law defining anarchy as a crime was written so broadly that it could be used to punish mere advocacy or teaching of violent overthrow as an abstract theory.[16] Therefore, the Supreme Court's decision in *Yates* made the law unconstitutional.

Ironically, the arrest of a member of the Ku Klux Klan in southwestern Ohio gave the Supreme Court an opportunity to hold that all similar state laws were unconstitutional. Clarence Brandenberg, owner of a television repair shop in a Cincinnati suburb, was an officer in the Klan. In the mid-1960s, he invited a reporter from a Cincinnati television station to cover a Klan rally and cross burning. Police who saw part of Brandenberg's speech on television heard him talk about taking revenge against officials who were trying to bring about racial integration. Brandenberg was charged with violating Ohio's Criminal Syndicalism Act. A county court found him guilty. A judge sentenced him to ten years in prison and fined him $1,000. Brandenberg's appeal reached the Supreme Court, which held that the Ohio law and all others like it were unconstitutional. The Court said that the law was written so broadly that it could be used to punish people for doing no more than talk about resorting to violence, and that laws seeking to protect government against violent overthrow can survive only if they are aimed narrowly at speech directly linked to "imminent lawless action" or likely to "incite or produce such action."

Brandenberg v. *Ohio,*
395 U.S. 444, 89 S.Ct. 1829,
23 L.Ed.2d 430 (1969).

With that decision, the Court brought to an end the line of sedition cases starting with *Schenck* in 1919. In those decisions the Court has said that governments, federal and state, have a right to protect themselves against those who would resort to violence to change the system. Governments also can protect themselves against those who advocate such violence. As defined in *Dennis,* "advocacy" is broad enough to include the leaders of the Communist party whose crime was said to be creating a disciplined group primed to act when its leaders gave the signal. However, in *Yates* and *Brandenberg,* the Court said that advocacy cannot be punished unless its purpose is to incite direct and immediate violence. Any law that fails to make clear the distinction between urging people to take up arms against their government and merely talking about doing so violates the First Amendment.

15. 347 U.S. 483, 74 S.Ct. 686, 98 L.Ed. 873 (1954).
16. Ware v. Nichols, 266 F.Supp. 564 (S.D.Miss. 1967).

The Revival of Sedition Law

Although the Vietnam war in the 1960s divided the American people as have few other events since the Civil War, the Sedition Act was not invoked, even against demonstrators who tried to block access to government buildings in Washington, D.C. However, the law was revived briefly, with mixed results, during the Reagan administration. The targets included Puerto Rican nationalists, white supremacists preaching hatred of Jews and blacks, and Marxist-Leninists accused of bombing firms that do business with South Africa.

In 1985, a federal court in Chicago convicted on sedition charges four persons who the government said were members of the Armed Forces of National Liberation, a Puerto Rican group. Three members of the group had been filmed, by hidden cameras, in the act of making bombs. The group claimed responsibility for 120 bombings in New York City and elsewhere between 1974 and 1983 in which five persons were killed and about a hundred injured. According to a government attorney for the prosecution, the case did not involve a First Amendment issue. She was quoted as saying, "There is no protected right to oppose the Government by force and violence and to say so is to debase the First Amendment.[17] In 1988 and 1989, however, attempts to prosecute thirteen white supremacists in Arkansas and three avowed revolutionaries in Massachusetts failed when juries voted for acquittal.[18]

These instances serve as a reminder that the Smith Act, as interpreted by the Supreme Court in *Yates,* remains in force, and that it can be invoked when prosecutors conclude that opponents of the government are plotting action aimed at the government's overthrow. The size of the odds against success does not matter. As the Court said in *Dennis,* officials who are aware that action is being planned need not "wait until the *putsch* is about to be executed" before taking action. But, as two of the cases described here illustrate, whether a jury can be convinced that there is a real threat to the government is another matter.

OTHER RESTRICTIONS ON SPEECH ABOUT GOVERNMENT

Espionage Law and the News Media

As noted at the beginning of this chapter, when the United States entered World War I, Congress quickly enacted the Espionage Act of 1917. This law, unlike the Sedition Act of that era, was not permitted to lapse. It is still the law used to prosecute as spies people who pass military secrets to other countries. However, in 1985

---

17. Katherine Bishop, "U.S. Dusts Off an Old Law," *New York Times,* 27 March 1988.
18. "Jury Acquits 9 of Conspiracy against the U.S.," *New York Times,* 7 April 1988; "Jury Clears 3 on Sedition Charges but Is Undecided on Racketeering," *New York Times,* 28 November 1989; "Judge Declares Mistrial for 3 after Jury Deadlocks in Sedition Case," *New York Times,* 30 November 1989.

the Espionage Act was used for the first time to prosecute and convict a govern-ment employee for disclosing information to the news media rather than to agents of a foreign government.[19] Many journalists found the conviction disquieting. In the higher echelons of Washington correspondence, leaks of classified materials are al-most routine. Officials, high and low, give materials to reporters, on a selective ba-sis, to advance their own policies or disparage those of their rivals. The conviction in this case, which was upheld on appeal, can be seen as a warning to those who may be tempted to leak classified information to reporters, no matter what their mo-tives for doing so. It also raises a question as to whether reporters might be pun-ished for failure to disclose on request the identity of the source of a leak of clas-sified information.

The case began when Samuel Loring Morison, a naval intelligence analyst and a part-time correspondent for a British naval publi-cation, was looking for a way to convince the ed-itor of that publication that he should be given a full-time job. Morison worked in the Naval Intel-ligence Support Section in a room known as a "vaulted area," because all of the employees were cleared to handle "top secret" materials. One day, Morison glanced at a colleague's desk and saw photographs taken by a spy satellite of the Soviet Union's first nu-clear aircraft carrier, then under construction in a Black Sea shipyard. The borders of the photographs were stamped "Top Secret" and carried a warning that intelli-gence sources or methods could be disclosed, were the wrong persons to see them. Morison surreptitiously took the photographs, clipped off the borders, and made copies, which he sent to the editor of *Jane's Defense Weekly,* with whom he had been talking about a job. Morison also sent the editor a summary of what the U.S. Navy knew about an explosion that recently had occurred at a Soviet naval base.

United States **v.** *Morison,*
844 F.2d 1057, 15
Med.L.Rptr. 1369
(4th Cir. 1988).

When the photos were published in *Jane's* they were considered so newsworthy that other magazines and newspapers, including the *Washington Post,* republished them. When the Navy began an investigation, Morison denied ever seeing the photos and gave officers the names of two fellow employees who he said should be ques-tioned. He continued his denials even after his fingerprint was found on one of the photos. Investigators also analyzed his typewriter ribbon, finding several letters to *Jane's* and the report on the explosion. A federal district court jury found Morison guilty of espionage, and a judge sentenced him to two years in prison.

On appeal, Morison argued, with support from the *Post,* CBS, and other news or-ganizations, that he was not acting as a spy but was serving a First Amendment inter-est in providing information of public importance to the news media. His primary mo-tive, he said, was to alert the public to a significant advance in Soviet naval power, thus making people more willing to support increased expenditures for our own Navy.

19. George Garneau, "Conviction of Classified Photo Leaker Upheld," *Editor & Publisher,* 9 April 1988, p. 20+; Stuart Taylor, Jr., "Court Ruling on Leaks Could Make It a Crime to Talk to the Press," *New York Times,* 10 April 1988.

He also argued that Congress never intended that the Espionage Act be used to stifle the dissemination of legitimate news. The intent of Congress, he said, was that the law be used only against those who pass vital information to foreign powers for the purpose of harming the United States. In briefs filed with the court, the news organizations argued that upholding Morison's conviction would have a chilling effect on the First Amendment by deterring others in the government who might otherwise leak newsworthy information to the media.

The appellate court rejected all the arguments, although all three judges felt compelled to write about the First Amendment issues raised by the case. The court said the language of the Espionage Act is clear. Under its terms, it is a crime for persons with access to government secrets to disclose them to persons not entitled to receive them. Those persons need not be agents of a foreign government. Nor does the First Amendment give people a right to break the law to obtain news or disseminate it. The court's opinion said:

> . . . [I]t seems beyond controversy that a recent intelligence department employee who had abstracted from the government files secret intelligence information and had willfully transmitted or given it to one "not entitled to receive it," as did the defendant in this case, is not entitled to invoke the First Amendment as a shield to immunize his act of thievery. To permit the thief thus to misuse the Amendment would be to prostitute the salutary purposes of the First Amendment.

The court's opinion was written by Judge Donald Russell. The other members of the panel, Judges J. Harvey Wilkinson III and James Dickson Phillips, wrote separately to stress that the case raised significant First Amendment questions. Wilkinson said that "[t]he First Amendment interest in informed popular debate does not simply vanish at the invocation of the words 'national security.'" He noted that leaks sometimes serve a useful public purpose in countering the tendency "for government to withhold reports of disquieting developments and to manage news in a fashion most favorable to itself." That tendency, he said, threatens harm to the public interest because it diminishes access to "unfiltered facts." However, Morison's actions also were potentially harmful to the public interest. On his own, he gave away secrets that may have compromised "the security of sensitive government operations." Wilkinson noted that in a less than perfect world, it is essential that even democratic governments keep some things secret from their own people, lest potential enemies be given an advantage. Thus, despite misgivings, in which he was joined by Phillips, Wilkinson concluded that Morison's conviction should be affirmed.

Death Threats Directed at Public Officials

In 1994, Christopher Reincke, an eighteen-year-old college student at the University of Illinois, was arrested by federal law enforcement agents and accused of sending a message to the White House via E-mail. The message, signed "Overlord," said: "I am curious, Bill, how would you feel about being the first President to be killed on the same day as his wife?" The message said, "You will die soon." Reincke was charged with threatening the life of the president, a federal crime punishable by five years in prison and a $250,000 fine.[20]

Although the courts will tolerate speech, and even some kinds of action, aimed at demonstrating opposition to government policies, law enforcement officers and the courts have taken a serious view of threats to the lives of public officials, particularly the president. That this is so reflects a disturbing fact of political life in the latter part of the twentieth century: Some people make targets of presidents and other prominent persons. The victims of assassins include President John F. Kennedy; his brother Robert, a candidate for president; Malcolm X, a charismatic black religious leader; and the Reverend Martin Luther King, Jr., a giant among civil rights advocates. Others have survived attempts on their lives, among them former presidents Gerald Ford and Ronald Reagan; former presidential candidate and Alabama governor George Wallace, paralyzed for life from the waist down; and Vernon Jordan, another civil rights leader.

It should be no surprise, then, that courts have not been disposed to interfere with punishment of those who threaten to kill the president, if the threat has even remote credence. Presidents can be and have been portrayed in words and cartoons as inept, as liars, and as robbers of the poor—all part of the political game. But individuals have been sent to prison for threatening to kill the president, even when the person making the threat was many miles distant from his target. The statute defining the crime is 18 U.S.C. §871, adopted in 1948. Several cases illustrate the circumstances under which a threat directed at the president can result in an arrest.

To be actionable, a threat on the president's life must be made in such circumstances that it is taken seriously by those who are charged with protecting her or him from harm. When Ronald Gene Barbour, an unemployed limousine driver living in Orlando, Florida, talked about killing President Clinton, one of his neighbors believed him and called the Secret Service. Barbour later said he didn't remember making the remark, though he said he told friends he didn't like Clinton. When evidence indicated that Barbour had driven to Washington, D.C., in January 1994 and had a .45 caliber handgun in his car, he was arrested. Barbour told police he drove there by mistake after getting lost on his way to Huntington, West Virginia, where he had planned to commit suicide.[21]

In *United States* v. *Hoffman,*[22] the Seventh Circuit Court of Appeals affirmed the conviction of David L. Hoffman of Milwaukee, who sent a letter to the White House saying, "Ronnie, Listen Chump! Resign or You'll Get Your Brains Blown Out." Below those words, Hoffman had made a crude drawing of a pistol with a bullet emerging from its barrel. Despite the distance between Milwaukee and Washington, D.C., a trial court jury concluded that the threat violated the law. At the trial, Hoffman's mother testified that he was angry with the president because Reagan would not pardon Sun Myung Moon, the leader of the Unification Church, with which her son was

---

20.   Reuters, "U.S. Says Student, by E-Mail, Sent Clintons a Death Threat," *New York Times,* 26 February 1994, p. 9.
21.   Associated Press, "Man Denies Charges That He Threatened to Kill Clinton," *Herald-Times,* Bloomington, Ind., 20 February 1994, p. A7.
22.   806 F.2d 703 (7th Cir. 1986).

then affiliated. Hoffman also had been arrested for carrying a concealed weapon and had a history of psychiatric disorders. The court held that under the circumstances, reasonable people could conclude that the letter was intended as a threat and was therefore not political speech protected by the First Amendment. Quoting from *Watts* v. *United States,*[23] the court said that because the statute makes criminal a form of pure speech, it must be interpreted with the commands of the First Amendment clearly in mind. For that reason, the Supreme Court held in *Watts* that the government can obtain a conviction only if it can prove that the defendant's words were a "true threat" and not political hyperbole.

The Supreme Court concluded that there was no "true threat" in the comment made by a deputy constable in Houston, Texas, when she heard that President Reagan had survived the attempt on his life in 1981. She was working at a computer terminal in an inner room of the constable's office when she heard the news. She said to her boyfriend, who was working nearby, "If they go after him again, I hope they get him." When another deputy reported the remark to the constable, the constable fired the woman. She sued to get her job back, and the case reached the Supreme Court. In *Rankin* v. *McPherson,*[24] the Court held that under the circumstances, the comment could not be construed as a serious threat on the life of the president. The Court's majority concluded that the woman's comment, tasteless as it may have been, was an expression of political opinion protected by the First Amendment. Therefore, the constable violated the deputy's free speech rights by firing her.

These cases round out our look at the punishment of speech that threatens harm to the government or its officials. If that speech is merely critical of the government's policies, or of how officials carry out those policies, it is protected by the First Amendment. But if a speaker's words are designed to provoke harmful action, and are likely to do so, the government can punish the speaker. Such punishment is most likely when the words take the form of a death threat directed at the president under circumstances that lead authorities to take the threat seriously.

PRIOR RESTRAINT

The Supreme Court and Prior Restraint

Censorship has rarely been imposed in the United States, even in time of war. During the Civil War, the Army sometimes used its control of the telegraph system to prevent newspapers from receiving dispatches describing Union defeats.[25] However, such steps only delayed publication of the bad news. During World War I, censorship was imposed through the postal system and was directed mainly at Socialist party news-

---

23.   394 U.S. 705, 89 S.Ct. 1399, 22 L.Ed.2d 664 (1969).
24.   483 U.S. 378, 107 S.Ct. 2891, 97 L.Ed.2d 315 (1987).
25.   An interesting account of how northern newspapers covered the Civil War and bypassed army censors is found in J. Cutler Andrews, *The North Reports the Civil War* (Pittsburgh: University of Pittsburgh Press, 1955).

papers.[26] In neither world war was the Supreme Court asked to rule whether censorship violated the First Amendment guarantees of freedom of speech and press.

Not until 1931, when the nation was at peace, did the Court have its first opportunity to decide whether the First Amendment forbids censorship. When the test did come, it had nothing to do with national security. The question was, Could a newspaper be shut down because it was considered scandalous?

Authorities in Minnesota, acting under powers given them by a state law, had obtained a court order forbidding J.M. Near and Howard Guilford to publish further issues of the weekly *Saturday Press* until they promised to print only the truth, and that "with good motives and for justifiable ends." The Supreme Court ruled, five to four, that Near and Guilford could resume publication without making such a promise.[27] The decision in *Near,* written by Chief Justice Charles Evans Hughes, has become a landmark case quoted frequently by lower courts. Although the majority held that prior restraint usually violates the First Amendment guarantee of freedom of speech and press, it also suggested several specific instances in which restraint might be justified. Thus, *Near* has proved to be both a victory and a defeat for those who believe that, whatever else it does, the First Amendment ought to stand as a barrier against censorship.

Near v. *Minnesota,* 283
U.S. 697, 51 S.Ct. 625,
75 L.Ed. 1357,
1 Med.L.Rptr. 1001 (1931).

The *Saturday Press* was one of many unexpected by-products of a constitutional amendment, adopted in 1919, that prohibited the manufacture and sale of alcoholic beverages. It soon became evident that while the amendment cut off the legal sale of beer, wine, and spirits, it did not end the people's thirst for such beverages. To satisfy that thirst, an illegal newtork of distillers, brewers, distributors, and sellers came into existence. This illegal network was able to exist in part because police chose to ignore it, or because they were bribed to do so. Because laws in some states made mere possession of alcoholic beverages a crime, one of the effects of the prohibition amendment was to make lawbreakers out of everyone who wanted to drink something stronger than soda pop. Near and Guilford sought to capitalize on the situation by publishing a weekly newspaper devoted to exposing wrongdoers, of whom there obviously were many.

In one sense, the *Saturday Press* served a public purpose by pointing to public officials who were taking bribes to ignore the illegal traffic in liquor. But their critics alleged that Near and Guilford used the paper as a form of blackmail. The critics charged that some people were given a chance to keep their names out of the paper if they agreed to buy advertising or make a direct payment to the publishers. Additionally, the *Saturday Press* published derogatory comments about Jews and others. Its content and the tactics of its publishers made many people angry. As a result, Guilford was shot and wounded by unknown assailants shortly after publication began, and there were threats of further violence. After the ninth issue of the paper appeared, a

---

26. For a discussion of the actions taken by the post office to bar allegedly subversive publications from the mails, see Chafee, *Free Speech in the United States,* Atheneum ed.
27. "Scandal and Defamation! The Right of Newspapers to Defame," American Civil Liberties Union, 1931. See also Fred W. Friendly, *Minnesota Rag* (New York: Random House, 1981).

county attorney went to court and, without notice to either Near or Guilford, obtained an order shutting the paper down. In this court order, the *Saturday Press* was condemned as a nuisance devoted to fomenting violence. The publishers, with help from the *Chicago Tribune,* the American Civil Liberties Union, and the American Newspaper Publishers Association, were able to take their case to the Supreme Court of the United States.

That Court overturned the state court's order. Chief Justice Hughes, writing for the majority, saw the case as a conflict between two important interests. On one side was the First Amendment interest in freedom of speech and press, which lies at the heart of a free society. On the other side was another vitally important interest: the preservation of an orderly society. Hughes noted that states inherently have the authority to protect the health, safety, morals, and general welfare of their residents. This authority, called the "police power," is exercised in many ways. Some courts have held that this authority is of equal importance with freedom of speech and press, reasoning that if society cannot maintain itself in an orderly manner, freedom of speech and press will have little meaning. Hughes noted that the Minnesota law used to shut down the *Saturday Press* was designed to promote public safety and therefore was an exercise of the police power. Under it, a judge could suppress any publication that, in his or her opinion, might provoke violence. However, and this was critical to the judgment in *Near,* the law made no distinction between truthful and untruthful articles. Nor did it establish any clear guidelines for determining when a publication might provoke violence. In short, the law's language was so broad that the decision was entirely up to the judge's discretion. That, Hughes concluded, was "the very essence of censorship."

The chief justice then examined what Blackstone and other legal commentators had said about previous restraint. He concluded that where libel is concerned, the generally approved remedy is a suit for damages, not suppression of the libelous publication. However, Hughes continued, some commentators have argued that the First Amendment, despite its seemingly absolute terms, does not prohibit all previous restraints. He agreed that it does not.

> No one would question but that a government might prevent actual obstuction of its recruiting service or the publication of the sailing dates of transports or the number and location of troops. On similar grounds, the primary requirements of decency may be enforced against obscene publications. The security of community life may be protected against incitements to acts of violence and the overthrow of orderly government. The constitutional guaranty of free speech does not "protect a man from an injunction against uttering words that may have all the effect of force."

The majority of the Court concluded that the *Saturday Press* did not come under any of these categories and therefore had been shut down in violation of the First Amendment. The Court also held that the Minnesota law was unconstitutional because it did not define with precision when a paper might be suppressed, and because it permitted suppression of truth as well as falsehood.

We should emphasize that decisions written by five justices are as strong in establishing precedent as are decisions written by all nine. But it is also worth noting that the first time the Court was confronted by a prior restraint of a newspaper, four of the nine justices acted on the belief that abuse of First Amendment freedoms could justify prior restraint. In the opinion of the minority, Near and Guilford were engaged in the publishing business for purposes of blackmail and extortion. Such businesses, the minority reasoned, could be shut down by court order.

The decision illustrates the dilemma that lies at the heart of many First Amendment cases. Beyond question, by the standards of most publishers of the era, the *Saturday Press* was a product of bad journalism. Some of its contents were highly offensive; other parts of it were false. In short, in the eyes of many people, it was garbage, and the Minnesota court treated it as such. So did the minority in the Supreme Court, which took the position that a rag like the *Saturday Press* was not entitled to First Amendment protection. But the majority took the position that the First Amendment was designed to protect speech that some people condemn as garbage. In fact, that is the point of having constitutional protection for freedom of speech and press. No one makes an issue of speech that everyone agrees with. Nor is there likely to be a problem with publications reflecting the opinions of a majority. Only when speakers begin making someone uncomfortable do they run into problems. In *Near,* the majority held that the state could not use its power to put shabby journalists out of business, even when much of what they published was considered trash.

The *Near* decision is of continuing importance for two reasons:

1.   A majority of the Court condemned prior restraint of a newspaper on First Amendment grounds. Its reasons for doing so were not particularly strong, but the precedent was established and would be followed by other courts.

2.   A majority of the Court also suggested that under certain specified circumstances, prior restraint—censorship—might be proper. Thus, in striking down a restraint imposed to prevent libelous assertions deemed likely to provoke violence, the Court opened the way for attempts to impose censorship for other purposes. Indeed, this is what has happened, as the remainder of this chapter will illustrate. *Near,* then, must be seen in perspective as a paradox. It extended the meaning of the First Amendment in a specific case but also seemed to approve censorship under certain circumstances.

Limits to Prior Restraint

Not until 1963 did the Court pick up the issues raised in *Near* about the limits to prior restraint. Then in 1971 came a second decision, further defining procedures that must be followed if a prior restraint is to be upheld. These two cases, taken with *Near,* have erected high barriers that must be surmounted if censorship is to survive appeal to the courts.

The first of these cases, *Bantam Books* v. *Sullivan,* grew out of an attempt by the

Bantam Books **v.** *Sullivan,*
372 U.S. 58, 83 S.Ct. 631,
9 L.Ed.2d 584,
1 Med.L.Rptr. 1116 (1963).

state of Rhode Island to prevent allegedly obscene publications from reaching young people. Members of a state commission were given the authority to determine which books and magazines were suitable for children and which were not. The commission's periodical listing of works unfit for children was distributed to bookstores and other places selling books and magazines. Police officers visited the stores to check on whether the proscribed publications were being displayed where minors could get at them. To avoid being hassled, some stores stopped selling books and magazines listed by the commission, including such widely read novels as *Peyton Place* and such magazines as *Playboy*.

Bantam Books took the lead in challenging the state's action. It argued that even though the state had pursued no prosecutions, the listing system's intimidation was a form of prior restraint. Rhode Island courts disagreed, but the U.S. Supreme Court reversed. Writing for the majority, Justice William J. Brennan, Jr., drafted a standard that went beyond the Court's holding in *Near* and that since has been applied in prior restraint cases. The key passage in the Court's decision is: "Any system of prior restraints of expression comes to this Court bearing a heavy presumption against its constitutional validity. . . . We have tolerated such a system only where it has operated under judicial superintendence and assured an almost immediate judicial determination of the validity of the restraint." At a minimum, Brennan suggested, a proper system for imposing a prior restraint to prevent the distribution of materials considered harmful to minors would include notice to the subject that a restraint was contemplated. Such notice should lead quickly to an appearance before a judge who would hear both sides of the argument. At that time, the agency seeking the restraint would be required to offer a precise statement of the standard that had been applied in determining that the materials were unfit for minors. Finally, the agency would have to explain why it had found the works objectionable. A restraint could be imposed only if the judge could be convinced that it was justified. Brennan concluded that the Rhode Island law was unconstitutional because it provided none of the suggested safeguards.

Eight years later, the Supreme Court reinforced those procedures in a case involving an attempt to prevent the distribution of handbills in a Chicago suburb. *Organization for a Better Austin* v. *Keefe* originated with Jerome M. Keefe, owner of a real estate agency. The Organization for a Better Austin, a group of homeowners formed to protect the racially mixed nature of their community, accused Keefe of trying to upset that mixture by promoting "block-busting" and "panic peddling" designed to induce white owners to sell and move out. The organization prepared leaflets denouncing Keefe's sales tactics and distributed them widely in the community where Keefe lived. Contending that his privacy was being invaded, Keefe went to court and was able to get an order forbidding further distribution of the leaflets. State courts affirmed, but the Supreme Court reversed, holding that the organization was a victim of an impermissible prior restraint. The Court held that anyone seeking a prior restraint through the procedures outlined in Bantam Books "carries a heavy burden of showing justification" for its request.

Organization for a Better Austin v. *Keefe,* **402 U.S. 415, 91 S.Ct. 1575, 29 L.Ed.2d 1, 1 Med.L.Rptr. 1021 (1971).**

The key points of *Near, Bantam Books,* and *Organization for a Better Austin* may be summarized thus: Despite its seemingly absolute wording, the speech and press clause of the First Amendment does not stand as a barrier against all forms of censorship. If words have "all the effect of force," or if they obstruct the recruiting service in time of war or give away vital military secrets, if they are obscene, or incite violent overthrow of the government, they may be restrained. But such restraint cannot be casual or arbitrary. There is a "heavy presumption" that any restraint of speech or press is unconstitutional. The government can prevail only if it "carries [the] heavy burden of showing justification" for restraint. The government must show that it is trying to protect a vital interest, such as national security, that the Constitution gives it a right to protect. Or the government must show that the offending speech is of a type, such as obscenity, not protected by the First Amendment. The government must show that the restraint will accomplish its intended purpose without also restraining speech that offers no threat to a vital interest. The victim of the intended restraint must be given an opportunity to counter the government's evidence. In short, prior restraint can be imposed only after an adversary hearing before a judge and then only for compelling reasons.

The barriers erected by the Supreme Court have made judicially approved prior restraint uncommon. However, private individuals, business organizations, and government officials have persisted in trying to surmount them, as the remainder of this chapter illustrates.

The Protection of Unpopular Opinions and Hateful Speech

Starting in the 1930s, when a small religious movement, Jehovah's Witnesses, was the victim of widespread persecution in the United States,[28] the Supreme Court wrote a remarkable series of decisions banning the use of prior restraint to prevent the spread of unpopular doctrines. The precedents established by the Court have protected labor unions and civil rights advocates, along with white racists and anti-Semites.

It was not easy to be a Jehovah's Witness in the 1930s. The religious movement's literature protrayed the Roman Catholic Church as the creation of the devil, with the pope as his vicar. The salute to the flag was condemned as a form of idolatry. Further, Witnesses made themselves highly visible by going door to door or accosting people on the streets to sell or give away religious pamphlets. In reaction, city governments everywhere adopted ordinances designed to discourage the distribution of handbills or other printed matter.

An ordinance adopted in Griffin, Georgia, was typical. Under its terms, anyone who wanted to distribute pamphlets or leaflets had to get a permit from the city manager, who had the sole authority to deny, grant, or revoke a permit. Alma Lovell, a Jehovah's Witness, ignored the ordinance. When she was arrested for trying to sell tracts at two for a nickel, she was found guilty of soliciting without a license and was fined $50. The case, *Lovell* v. *Griffin*,[29] reached the Supreme Court, which held unanimously that the Griffin ordinance was an unconstitutional form of prior restraint. The Court focused on the city manager's arbitrary authority to grant or revoke a license

---

28.   For a sampling of the more than a thousand recorded instances of persecution of Jehovah's Witnesses, see Leonard A. Stevens, *Salute! The Case of the Bible vs. the Flag* (New York: Coward, 1973).
29.   303 U.S. 444, 58 S.Ct. 666, 82 L.Ed. 949 (1938).

at will. Echoing John Milton's *Areopagitica,* the Court said, "The ordinance would restore . . . licensing and censorship in its baldest form." Although on its face the ordinance did not interfere with the right of the Witnesses to publish whatever they pleased, the Court said it was a form of restraint nevertheless, because its purpose was to prevent distribution of the movement's views. The Court noted that "without circulation, the publication would be of little value."

With its decision in *Lovell* in 1938, the Court extended the protection of the First Amendment to newspaper carriers, pamphleteers, corner soapbox speakers, itinerant evangelists, and all others who seek to spread the word, on paper or orally, in public places.

Two years later, in *Thornhill* v. *Alabama,*[30] the Court extended the First Amendment's protection to peaceful picketing by labor unions. The target this time was an Alabama law that forbade loitering or picketing "without just cause or legal excuse." "Just cause" was not defined, nor was "legal excuse." Nevertheless, police concluded that several men who were picketing a wood-preserving plant had no justifiable reason for doing so, even though a strike was in progress. Police arrested the pickets and a court found them guilty. The Supreme Court reversed, holding that the law permitted the same kind of arbitrary interference with speech that the Court had condemned in *Lovell.* Under the law's terms, officials could jail pickets simply because they didn't approve of the pickets' cause.

In a real sense, the victories won by Jehovah's Witnesses in *Lovell* and by organized labor in *Thornhill* made possible the victories of the civil rights movement in the 1950s and 1960s. Courts cited those and related cases in striking down attempts to prevent or suppress the protest marches and demonstrations that brought the movement to public attention. Some of these cases reached the Supreme Court.[31] In its decisions, the Court reiterated principles in the Witnesses' and labor cases: Government cannot prevent the use of streets and other public places for the dissemination of ideas, no matter how unpopular. Government can require that demonstrations be peaceful and can limit the time, place, and manner of dissemination, but such regulation must be reasonable.

Further, the Supreme Court has held that governments cannot prevent speakers from presenting unpopular, or even repugnant, views in order to head off possible violence. A restraint to prevent bloodshed can be imposed only if the threat of violence is so imminent and so beyond the control of the authorities that no other remedy will work.

The leading case, *Carroll* v. *President and Commissioners of Princess Anne,*[32] grew out of an ugly series of events on Maryland's eastern shore when members of the National States Rights party conducted a rally in Princess Anne, a community of fewer than a thousand. The audience was subjected to a series of racist and anti-Semitic tirades. Feelings were running high, and state police were on hand to prevent a riot. There was no trouble that night, but one of the speakers promised that even stronger speeches would be made at a similar rally the next night.

---

30.   310 U.S. 88, 60 S.Ct. 736, 84 L.Ed. 1093 (1940).
31.   See, for instance, Shuttlesworth v. City of Birmingham, 394 U.S. 147, 89 S.Ct. 935, 22 L.Ed.2d 162 (1969).
32.   393 U.S. 175, 89 S.Ct. 347, 21 L.Ed.2d 325 (1968).

The second rally was not held. Early in the day, local officials went to Somerset County Circuit Court and, without notice to any members of the States Rights party or even a hearing, obtained a restraining order forbidding any further rallies in the county during the next ten days, later extended to ten months. The Supreme Court of the United States held that even a ten-day order was unconstitutional, focusing narrowly on the arbitrary nature of the proceeding in the Maryland trial court. The Court based its decision on *Bantam Books,* in which it had held that a restraint can be imposed only after an adversary hearing. It noted, quoting *Near,* that a prior restraint can be imposed to prevent an incitement to violence but concluded that there was no clear evidence of such incitement in Princess Anne.

What can a community do when advocates of highly offensive racial or religious views insist on their right to express those views under circumstances that seem designed to provoke violence? That question has no clear answer, as is illustrated by the experience of Skokie, Illinois, when self-proclaimed U.S. Nazis sought permission to conduct a rally there in the 1970s. Skokie has a predominantly Jewish population, and at the time some of its residents were survivors of Hitler's World War II death camps. Members of the Nazi group wore uniforms patterned on those worn by Hitler's infamous SS squads, who enforced his attempt to exterminate Jews. When the U.S. Nazis asked to conduct a rally on the steps of the Skokie Village Hall, residents reacted with fear and indignation. Militant Jewish groups threatened violence. Caught in the middle, the Skokie Village Council adopted three ordinances designed to make it difficult if not impossible for the meeting to be held. This action set off a series of lawsuits in both state and federal courts, resulting in decisions holding that the ordinances were unconstitutional attempts at prior re-

The U.S. Supreme Court upheld the right of a neo-Nazi organization to march in Skokie, Illinois, despite local opposition. Members of the Court were not happy with the result, as this editorial cartoon by Ben Sargent suggests, but nevertheless held that the First Amendment protects unpopular as well as popular causes. *(Ben Sargent/Universal Press Syndicate)*

straint. The Supreme Court refused to hear pleas asking that the decisions be over-turned because the rally would lead to violence.[33]

The Nazi group's right to freedom of speech and assembly was upheld. But as Justice Harry A. Blackmun noted, every court that considered the case felt a need to apologize. Blackmun argued that the Supreme Court should have taken the case, to determine how far a community must go to protect inflammatory and provocative speakers. It is interesting to compare Blackmun's view with that of Thomas I. Emerson, the First Amendment scholar whose views we summarized in Chapter 2. Emerson argued that the First Amendment imposes a duty on government to provide a forum for all shades of opinion. Blackmun, confronted with an extreme application of that argument, wrote:

> I . . . feel that the present case affords the Court an opportunity to consider whether . . . there is no limit whatsoever to the exercise of free speech. There indeed may be no such limit, but when citizens assert, not casually but with deep conviction, that the proposed demonstration is scheduled at a place and in a manner that is taunting and overwhelmingly offensive to the citizens of that place, that assertion, uncomfortable though it may be for the judges, deserves to be examined. It just might fall into the same category as one's "right" to cry "fire" in a crowded theater, for "the character of every act depends upon the circumstances in which it is done." [Quoting Holmes in *Schenck*.]

Blackmun's concern raises serious questions. How far must society go to provide a forum for those whose only purpose seems to be to stir up racial, religious, or political hatred?

For public universities, the idea of protecting hateful speech has been particularly vexing. These institutions are founded on the notion of civility and tolerance. To allow students to get away with hurling racial and sexual insults at classmates has seemed so intolerable on many campuses that rules have been written to forbid and punish such behavior. But just as on the streets of Skokie, hateful speech short of causing imminent danger of lawlessness is speech that is protected under the First Amendment. That was the lesson of *Brandenberg* v. *Ohio* in 1969 and *R.A.V.* v. *City of St. Paul* in 1992. It was also the lesson the University of Michigan learned when a federal district court judge ruled that parts of the university's policy on harassment "swept within its scope a significant amount of 'verbal conduct' or 'verbal behavior' which is unquestionably protected speech under the First Amendment."[34] The case was brought by a biopsychology graduate student who, as a teaching assistant, was afraid that under the code he could not discuss controversial theories stating that biological differences among the sexes and races made for differing personality traits and abilities. The university had adopted the code after a number of racial incidents, including the distribution of a flier declaring "open season" on African-Americans, the use of racist jokes on the campus radio station, and the display of a Ku Klux Klan uniform in a dormitory window.

---

33. Smith v. Collin, 439 U.S. 916, 99 S.Ct. 291, 58 L.Ed.2d 264, 4 Med.L.Rptr. 1590 (1978). See also 447 F.Supp. 676, 3 Med.L.Rptr. 1915 (N.D.Ill. 1978); 578 F.2d 1197, 3 Med.L.Rptr. 2490 (7th Cir. 1978); Village of Skokie v. National Socialist Party, 373 N.E.2d 21, 3 Med.L.Rptr. 1704 (Ill. 1978).
34. Jon Doe v. University of Michigan, 721 F.Supp. 852 (E.D.Mich. 1989).

In response to similar problems at the University of Wisconsin—a fraternity slave auction with pledges in blackface and the display by a fraternity of a large caricature of a black Fiji Islander at a party—the university produced a rule that would punish students for racist or discriminatory comments. A federal district court found the rule overbroad and vague. The school could ban violence and even "fighting words," but it could not ban comments short of that. "[I]n order to constitute fighting words, speech must not merely breach decorum but also must tend to bring the addressee to fisticuffs. . . . Since the elements of the UW Rule do not require that the regulated speech, by its very utterance, tends to incite violent reaction, the rule goes beyond the present scope of the fighting words doctrine.[35] The same was true at George Mason University when a fraternity staged an ugly woman contest in which fraternity members dressed up as caricatures of different types of women. When the fraternity was punished by the university for creating an environment hostile to women and African-Americans, the fraternity sued. The federal courts held that "[T]he fraternity's skit, even as low-grade entertainment, was inherently expressive and thus entitled to First Amendment protection."[36]

In light of these decisions, universities began to rethink the way tolerance and respect might be taught on campus. Six months after the University of Pennsylvania charged a student with racial harassment for calling five African-American sorority sisters "water buffalo," it decided to scrap its code barring racially demeaning speech because, in the words of the president, Claire Faigin, it is "not the best solution to the problems of racism in our community."[37]

Questions, ethical ones if not legal ones, remain. What is the best solution to the pain of hateful speech?[38] How much exposure should the media give to persons whose arguments are based on deliberate misstatement of fact or are devoid of both reason and logic? Is there an obligation to provide a forum for any kind of expression uttered in the name of any cause? These are questions that vex not only judges and university administrators, but journalists, civil rights lawyers, and anyone who cares about justice and civility.

The Protection of National Security

In two celebrated cases, the federal government has asked the courts to prevent publication of information believed harmful to national security. In the first instance the *New York Times,* the *Washington Post,* and other newspapers were prevented for about two weeks from publishing secret documents dealing with the Vietnam war. The Supreme Court ruled that the government had not met the heavy burden of proving

---

35. UWM Post v. Board of Regents of the University of Wisconsin System, 774 F.Supp. 1163 (E.D.Wis. 1991). See Chaplinsky v. New Hampshire, 315 U.S. 568, 62 S.Ct. 766, 86 L.Ed. 1031 (1942).
36. Iota Xi Chapter of Sigma Chi Fraternity v. George Mason University, 993 F.2d 386 (4th Cir. 1993).
37. "Penn Leaders Plan to Scrap Speech Code," *Herald-Times,* Bloomington, Ind., 17 November 1993.
38. One proposed alternative to speech codes suggests such alternatives as discussions, workshops, recruitment of minorities, and enforceable restrictions on conduct. Arati R. Korwar, *War of Words, Speech Codes at Public Colleges and Universities* (Nashville, Tenn.: Freedom Forum, 1994).

that the restraint was essential to the nation's security. In the second instance, a U.S. district court prevented a magazine from publishing an article purporting to describe how a hydrogen bomb is made. That episode ended indecisively when the information was disclosed in other media. At the time, both cases caused considerable controversy, but neither established enduring principles of media law.

The Pentagon Papers

The first case, known as the "Pentagon Papers" case, began in June 1971 when readers of the *New York Times* were offered the first installment of a top secret government study of how the United States became involved in the Vietnam war. The newspaper said it would publish the parts of the seven-thousand-page document that its editors believed to be of public interest. Henry Kissinger, President Nixon's national security adviser, said in his memoirs that the disclosure "came as a profound shock to the Administration."[39] That shock quickly was converted into action of an unprecedented nature. Within three days, the attorney general of the United States obtained court orders that stopped first the *New York Times* and then the *Washington Post* from publishing further installments of the documents. Only one court, the U.S. Court of Appeals for the Second Circuit, ruled that the facts justified a prior restraint. Other courts in New York City and Washington, D.C., granted government motions for temporary restraint pending the outcome of an appeal to the Supreme Court. That Court, acting with unusual speed, granted certiorari, heard arguments, and issued its decision in one week. That fact alone speaks volumes about how seriously courts view an attempt to prevent publication of government information. Normally, two to four months elapse between argument and the Court's decision, and commonly a year will pass between the Court's agreeing to take a case and its decision.

In this instance, the justices voted six to three to lift the restraint immediately. The unsigned *per curiam* decision disposed in two short paragraphs of the government's argument that the president had a right to restrain the publication of information that he believed to be harmful to national security. Quoting directly from *Near, Bantam Books,* and *Organization for a Better Austin,* the Court said it agreed with a New York federal district court and the District of Columbia Circuit Court, which had held that the government had not carried the "heavy burden" required to justify its request for a restraint. Thus, it had not overcome "the heavy presumption against" the restraint's constitutional validity. Even the three dissenters took pains to say that they opposed prior restraints in general but thought this case had moved through the courts too quickly to develop a factual basis on which to judge whether national security was indeed in

New York Times Co. v. United States, **403 U.S. 713, 91 S.Ct. 2140, 29 L.Ed.2d 822, 1 Med.L.Rptr. 1031 (1971).**

---

39. Henry Kissinger, *White House Years* (Boston: Little, Brown, 1979), p. 729. The book contains background information on the context in which the Pentagon Papers case arose. See also Floyd Abrams, "The Pentagon Papers a Decade Later," *New York Times Magazine,* 7 June 1981, p. 22, for one view of the consequences of the publication.

danger. They wanted the case returned to the lower courts for trial so that a record might be developed.

Although the decision broke no new legal ground, the case was of great importance to the news media because for the first time the Department of Justice had asked the courts to restrain the publication of government information and had succeeded temporarily in doing so. Each justice of the Supreme Court was sufficiently moved by the gravity of the action to write a separate opinion. Only two, William O. Douglas and Hugo L. Black, would have held that the press never can be prevented from publishing what it knows. Justice Brennan relied on *Near* and concluded that publication of the Pentagon Papers did not raise the same kind of danger as publication of the sailing date of transports or of troop dispositions in time of war. The three other members of the majority avoided the First Amendment issue by concluding that no law authorized the government to prevent newspapers from publishing top secret documents.

Only one of the opinions, that of Chief Justice Warren E. Burger writing in dissent, raised questions that continue to plague relations between the news media and the government. Lawyers for the *Times* had asserted in argument to the Court that the paper was serving the public's "right to know" when it began publication of the documents. Burger said he could not find that right in the First Amendment. Even if it were there, as the *Times* lawyer seemed to argue, it would not be absolute, Burger wrote, but might have to yield in some instances to other important interests. If the Court were to recognize such a right, and ground it in the Constitution, Burger asked, who would be responsible for fulfilling it? The news media? Or the government, which is the main repository of information on its own activities? Burger could not resist pointing out that the editors of the *Times* had held up publication of the papers for three months while they decided what parts of them would be published. Why, in the fulfillment of a "right to know," should the courts be required to act in a few days?

Burger's questions are good ones. They will arise in different contexts later in this book. "The right to know" is a phrase that slips easily off the tongue, especially when a journalist is denied access to information that seems important. Usually this right is asserted in a context that suggests the journalist is acting on behalf of the people, who are the ultimate possessors of a "right to know." That people who govern themselves have a right to know everything their various governments are doing is an appealing concept in a free society. If that indeed is the ultimate nature of the right, it has awesome implications, as Burger suggests. If such a right were to be found in the First Amendment, would it not compel journalists to transmit in unedited form every last word they found in public government documents and in the utterances of government officials? Would not any abridgment of that flow by an editor become a violation of the public's "right to know"? This scenario may sound far-fetched, but a constitutional right, once defined, holds a preeminent position in the legal hierarchy.

Burger also taunted the *Times* for its willingness to accept and publish documents he saw as stolen property. The *Times* editors, he wrote, should have known something was wrong when they were handed such a vast quantity of documents, clearly marked "top secret" and clearly the property of the United States government. It should have occurred to them to notify the proper government departments of their windfall and to seek declassification of the materials through proper channels. "With such an approach—one that great newspapers have in the past practiced and stated editorially to be the duty of an honorable press—the newspapers and Government might well have narrowed the area of disagreement" and settled it through litigation. Burger let fly a final arrow:

> To me it is hardly believable that a newspaper long regarded as a great institution in American life would fail to perform one of the basic and simple duties of every citizen with respect to the discovery or possession of stolen property or secret Government documents. That duty, I had thought—perhaps naively—was to report forthwith to responsible public officers. This duty rests on taxi drivers, justices and the *New York Times.*

Chief Justice Burger's belief that documents, or even copies of them, are property and therefore subject to criminal law defining theft was to surface in each succeeding session of Congress through 1977. Proposals arose to make unauthorized possession of such documents a crime. But each time, representatives of the news media and civil libertarians raised enough objections to defeat the attempt.[40] In 1987, however, in another context, the Supreme Court itself held that information is property and can be protected from theft as any other kind of property is. The Court's decision, in *Carpenter* v. *United States,*[41] upheld the conviction for securities fraud of two *Wall Street Journal* employees and a stockbroker who used information taken from the paper in advance of publication to profit from changes in securities prices. A unanimous Court held that *Journal* editors could protect information gathered by reporters for the paper's use until it is published. The decision is summarized in Chapter 12, "Copyright Law."

With the benefit of hindsight, the publication of the Pentagon Papers seems to have had little effect on the nation's security. Still, questions persist. Should information considered so vital to security that government officials stamp it "top secret" be subject to disclosure by any reporter who can lay hands on it? Or should disclosure be permitted only by "responsible" reporters, such as those employed by the *New York Times* and the *Washington Post?* If reporters may tell the world about matters the government deems secret, who else may do so?[42]

Or does the problem lie, as Justice Potter Stewart suggested, in the government's trying to keep too many secrets? When the secrecy stamp is applied, as it has been, to clippings from newspapers and magazines, doesn't this make a mockery of the classification system? And isn't the system further mocked when government officials, including presidents, selectively disclose classified information that will help them score a political point? In its brief in this case, the *New York Times* pointed to many instances of such disclosure in memoirs, in press conferences, and in "don't quote me" leaks to favored reporters.

If Congress should try to enact a law, as some members of the Court suggested, providing for punishment of the publisher of classified information, what is to be done in those instances in which a knowledgeable reporter, working with readily available information, reaches conclusions that have also been reached in a classified document?

---

40. *Congressional Quarterly Almanac* (Washington, D.C.: Congressional Quarterly), editions from 1971 through 1980.
41. 484 U.S. 19, 108 S.Ct. 316, 98 L.Ed.2d 275, 14 Med.L.Rptr. 1853 (1987).
42. See United States v. Morison, 844 F.2d 1057, 15 Med.L.Rptr. 1369 (4th Cir. 1988), discussed earlier.

"JUST REMEMBER THE RULES — NO NOISY POWER TOOLS, AND NO ABOVE-GROUND TEST SHOTS IN THE LIBRARY"

When Howard Morland wrote an article about how to build a hydrogen bomb for the *Progressive* magazine, he said that all the information came from previous material found in libraries. That became grist for Etta Hulme's cartoon in the *Ft. Worth Star-Telegram. (Etta Hulme/Ft. Worth Star-Telegram)*

Would shrewd analysis of a broad range of sensitive information thus become a crime? Despite the troubling questions raised by publication of the Pentagon Papers, the fact remains that a majority of the Supreme Court reinforced the principle that censorship is a weapon of last resort, to be used only when the danger is so serious that nothing less stringent will work.

The H-Bomb Secret

In 1979 a federal district court judge in Wisconsin thought he was confronted with a danger so serious that prior restraint was justified. Justice Department lawyers told the judge that *The Progressive* magazine was going to publish an article that would explain how to make a hydrogen bomb. In this instance the Justice Department lawyers pointed to a law that authorizes restraint to prevent disclosure of nuclear secrets.[43] The government argued that under terms of the law, all information dealing with nuclear weapons technology is "classified at birth"; that is, it must be treated as a secret as soon as it takes tangible form.

Howard Morland, the author of the article, argued that the article disclosed no secrets. He said he had obtained all of his information from published material found in

43. Atomic Energy Act, 42 U.S. Code §§ 2274, 2280.

libraries. His point, he said, was that no longer are any secrets involved in making hydrogen bombs. Because that is true, he said he and the magazine's editors hoped that publication of the article would lead to more diligent efforts to abolish nuclear weapons. Judge Robert W. Warren listened to both sides and then ruled for the government, issuing an order forbidding publication of the article. He conceded that his decision was a serious blow to First Amendment freedoms, but he said those freedoms wouldn't matter if publication of the article were to make it possible for someone to build and use a hydrogn bomb.[44]

The Progressive appealed the ruling, but the case was dropped six months later when a newspaper in Madison, Wisconsin, and several other newspapers ran a letter from a computer programmer containing essentially the same information about the working of a hydrogen bomb. The programmer had even prepared a diagram purportedly of the bomb's mechanism. Like Morland, the programmer said he had found all his information in the public domain, although he conceded that some of it had been made public by three scientists who allegedly had violated their security clearances. However, no one was punished.[45] *The Progressive* published Morland's article in the November 1979 issue under the title "The H-Bomb Secret: To Know How Is to Ask Why."

Sealed Court Documents

In a remarkable example of prior restraint, a federal district court judge in Cincinnati, Ohio, ordered *Business Week* magazine in 1995 not to publish an article about a lawsuit involving Bankers Trust Company and Procter & Gamble.[46] The article was based on court documents filed by Procter & Gamble that disclosed huge financial losses by several companies that had invested in derivatives sold by Bankers Trust. Derivatives are financial contracts whose value is linked to some underlying asset, such as stocks and bonds. Procter & Gamble claimed that it owed almost $200 million because Bankers Trust had not advised it of the risks involved in the investments. The court documents were filed under court seal as part of an agreement between Procter & Gamble and Bankers Trust, but a *Business Week* reporter, Linda Himelstein, obtained a copy from a lawyer at the firm representing Bankers Trust. Both the reporter and the lawyer said they didn't know the documents had been sealed by the court.[47]

An hour before the presses were ready to roll, Judge John Feikens issued a temporary restraining order at the request of both Procter & Gamble and Bankers Trust. Such orders are used to maintain the status quo while a court decides whether a permanent order is justified. Temporary restraining orders can last for weeks, and in this case the order effectively barred the magazine from printing the article for sev-

---

44. United States v. The Progressive, 467 F.Supp. 990, 4 Med.L.Rptr. 2377 (W.D.Wis. 1979).
45. John Consoli, "The Progressive Triumphs in H-Bomb Case," *Editor & Publisher,* 22 September 1979, pp. 9, 36.
46. Deirdre Carmody, "Magazine Pulls Article under Order," *New York Times,* 15 September 1995, p. A7.
47. "Bank Lawyer Gave Papers to Reporter," *New York Times,* 28 September 1995, p. A15.

eral weeks or risk being held in contempt of court. *Business Week*'s lawyers, who said they were unable to find Judge Feikens on the night of his order, appealed to the U.S. Court of Appeals for the Sixth Circuit. The court refused to intervene, saying that the order was only a temporary restraining order and that the appeals court had no jurisdiction, at least not yet.[48] *Business Week* then went to the U.S. Supreme Court, filing a petition with Justice John Paul Stevens. But in a sternly worded, three-page order, Stevens rebuked *Business Week*'s lawyers for failing to follow procedure by exhausting every available avenue of relief before coming to the Court. He said the magazine should have first given the judge who issued the order an opportunity to reconsider. Stevens said he thought that if the magazine "had filed a prompt motion to dissolve" Judge Feikens's order, "I assume" he "would have granted that relief."[49]

Three weeks after his restraining order, Judge Feikens, apparently looking for a way to allow publication without admitting he had been wrong, unsealed the documents but made permanent his injunction against *Business Week*'s use of the identical documents it had obtained earlier, saying the magazine had acted improperly to get them. Although *Business Week* now had, in effect, Judge Feikens's permission to publish an article using the unsealed papers, the magazine asked the appeals court to review both the permanent injunction and the finding that the magazine had obtained the papers improperly.

This time, the Court of Appeals stood with *Business Week,* saying that Judge Feikens had been wrong to issue the order barring publication or conducting a hearing into how *Business Week* got the papers.

"At no time," the court ruled, "even to the point of entering a permanent injunction after two temporary restraining orders, did the District Court appear to realize that it was engaging in a practice that, under all but the most exceptional circumstances, violates the Constitution: preventing a news organization from publishing information in its possession on a matter of public concern."[50]

Prior Restraint by Contract

The Supreme Court has held that the government can impose prior restraint to enforce a contractual relationship. It has upheld compulsory agreements between the federal government and its employees who have regular access to classified information. The Court also has held that family-planning organizations that accept federal funds can be prevented from offering abortion counseling.

As one might expect, people who go to work for the Central Intelligence Agency must agree not to disclose any information learned during their employment that would expose "intelligence sources or methods." Some of the agency's employees occupy such sensitive positions that they cannot even tell outsiders who they work

48. Deirdre Carmody, "Business Week Files Appeal to Supreme Court," *New York Times,* 20 September 1995, p. A16.

49. Patrick Reilly, "Justice Allows Restraint on Business Week," *Wall Street Journal,* 22 September 1995.

50. Iver Peterson, "Court Voids Restraint on Business Week," *New York Times,* 6 March 1996, p. C6.

for. This insistence on secrecy continues when employees leave the CIA, for whatever reason. The employment agreement has been construed to require former employees to submit to the agency for security clearance any article, book, or speech based on their previous work. The purpose is to prevent the disclosure of information learned during the course of their employment that still might be classified. The same restrictions apply to former employees of the Defense and State departments or of the White House who had regular access to classified intelligence data.

Three court decisions, one of them by the Supreme Court, have upheld the government's authority to compel such review. The leading case involved a book, *Decent Interval,*[51] written by Frank Snepp, a former CIA agent. The book described the United States's pell-mell withdrawal from Vietnam in 1975. The author did not submit the manuscript for review, although he had signed

Snepp v. United States,
444 U.S. 507, 100 S.Ct. 763,
62 L.Ed.2d 704,
5 Med.L.Rptr. 2409 (1980).

the usual employment contract when he went to work for the agency. Although the government conceded that there was no still-classified material in the book, it filed suit in a federal district court to compel Snepp to surrender his profits from the work. Lower courts disagreed as to whether he should do so, but the Supreme Court had no doubts. In a brusque *per curiam* decision, the Court held that a former agent's judgment as to what may be disclosed safely is not to be substituted for that of the CIA. The Court wrote:

> Undisputed evidence in this case shows that a CIA agent's violation of his obligation to submit writings about the agency for prepublication review impairs the CIA's ability to perform its statutory duties. Admiral Turner, director of the CIA, testified without contradiction that Snepp's book and others like it have seriously impaired the effectiveness of American intelligence operations.

As a consequence, the Court required that all Snepp's earnings from the book, estimated at $125,000 or more,[52] be placed in trust for the benefit of the government. The Court said that its order "simply requires him to disgorge the benefits of his faithlessness."

Two earlier decisions by the U.S. Court of Appeals for the Fourth Circuit[53] resulted in publication of a book containing blank spaces to reflect material deleted by the order of government censors. The book, *The CIA and the Cult of Intelligence,*[54] was written by Victor L. Marchetti, a former official of the CIA, and John Marks, a former employee of the State Department. Its purpose was to expose what the authors believed to be improper interference by the CIA in the internal affairs of other countries, most notably Chile, Cuba, and China. The book can still be found on the shelves of some libraries as an interesting example of a rare instance of court-enforced government censorship.

---

51. Frank W. Snepp, *Decent Interval* (New York: Random House, 1977).
52. "Top Court Rules CIA Has Power to Screen Writings by Past and Current Employees," *Wall Street Journal,* 20 February 1980.
53. United States v. Marchetti, 466 F.2d 1309, 1 Med.L.Rptr. 1051 (4th Cir. 1972); Alfred A. Knopf v. Colby, 509 F.2d 1362 (4th Cir. 1975).
54. Victor L. Marchetti and John Marks, *The CIA and the Cult of Intelligence* (New York: Knopf, 1974).

The Supreme Court, in *Rust* v. *Sullivan,* also held that the Department of Health and Human Services acted within its powers when it prohibited family-planning agencies that accept its Title X funds from offering abortion counseling.[55] The Court held that the prohibition does not violate the free speech rights of such agencies and their employees. Title X funds are provided by the federal government for family-planning purposes. Section 1008 of the Public Health Service Act (84 Stat. 1506, as amended) provides that none of the funds "shall be used in programs where abortion is a method of family planning." In 1989 the secretary of health and human services elaborated on that section to specify that a "Title X project may not provide counseling concerning the use of abortion as a means of family planning or provide referral for abortion as a method of family planning."[56]

Several agency recipients of Title X funding, doctors who work for them, and the state of New York asked a federal district court to nullify the restriction on First Amendment and other grounds. They argued, in effect, that Section 1008, and the secretary's elaboration of it, imposed an impermissible prior restraint on one kind of family-planning advice; that is, abortion is one alternative that might be given their clients. That court and the U.S. Court of Appeals for the Second Circuit upheld the restriction. The Supreme Court affirmed, five to four.

The challengers argued that the prohibition violated the Court's holding in a number of cases that restrictions on speech must be content neutral—that government cannot deny benefits to some people because it disagrees with their views. Chief Justice William H. Rehnquist, writing for the majority, said that reliance on such cases was misplaced: "[H]ere the government is not denying a benefit to anyone, but is instead simply insisting that public funds be spent for the purposes for which they were authorized. The Secretary's regulations do not force the Title X grantee to give up abortion-related speech; they merely require that the grantee keep such activities separate and distinct from Title X activities." In his view, when an agency asks for and receives Title X funds it enters into a contract that requires it to abide by the restrictions imposed on that funding. Thus he concluded, "The condition that federal funds will be used only to further the purposes of a grant does not violate constitutional rights."

Following the decision, President Bush modified the order to permit physicians associated with family-planning centers to offer advice on abortions. However, many of the approximately four thousand clinics offering family planning are staffed by health professionals other than physicians. Congress responded by passing a bill that would have blocked enforcement of Bush's order. The president vetoed the bill. The Senate voted to override, but a similar attempt in the House failed by ten votes.[57] During the 1992 presidential campaign, Democratic candidate Bill Clinton said he opposed the rule and would abolish it if elected. On this third day in office, President Clinton issued an executive order ending the gag rule, thus permitting health professionals employed by federally funded family-planning clinics to discuss abortion with their clients.[58] However, the principle endorsed by the Court's majority in *Rust* remains

---

55. 500 U.S. 173, 111 S.Ct. 1759, 114 L.Ed.2d 233 (1991).56.   42 CFR 59.8(a)(1).

57. Los Angeles Times News Service, "Veto Upheld; Abortion 'Gag Rule' Remains," *Indianapolis Star,* 3 October 1992.

58. Ann Devroy *(Washington Post),* "Clinton Scraps Abortion Limits," *Indianapolis Star,* 23 January 1993.

valid. The government can impose restraints on the job-related speech of employees of private agencies that accept federal funds.

Prior Restraint and Student Publications

Students who work on school publications long have been torn between two forces. One force is whatever impels them to go into journalism in the first place, ranging from a narrowly personal interest in showing off one's writing ability or in having a little fun, to an altruistic interest in helping change the world. Students who choose journalism also usually are aware that the First Amendment to the Constitution protects freedom of the press, which presumably includes school newspapers. The second force is school authorities—the publication's faculty adviser backed by the principal, the superintendent, and the board of education. At best, such authorities tolerate or may even encourage a student press that is free to explore any issue of interest to its staff. But anyone who has ever worked on a student newspaper is aware that freedom has its limits. Go too far, stir up too many people, and school authorities not only will talk about the responsibilities that go along with freedom but may enforce their view of those responsibilities on the student staff. Until 1988, despite a scattering of lower-court cases, no one involved in this tense equation could say with certainty whether the First Amendment supported the students' freedom to publish what they pleased or the school officials' right to enforce responsibility. In that year, the Supreme Court resolved those doubts. It held, five to three, that when a public school newspaper is published as part of a journalism class, school officials, not the student editors, have the ultimate authority to decide what is printed, as long as the decision is not made for political reasons. Put in its bluntest terms, the Court's decision affirmed the right of public school officials—agents of the state—to censor the work of student editors. At the time, one state, California, had a law providing for freedom of the student press. Since then, Arkansas, Colorado, Iowa, Kansas, and Massachusetts have enacted similar laws.

Under the Supreme Court ruling, student editors of many high school publications in the remaining forty-four states enjoy only as much freedom of the press as their advisers and other school officials are willing to permit. The case had its origins in May 1983, when the student editors of *Spectrum*, a newspaper serving students at Hazelwood East High School in the suburbs of St. Louis, put together the final edition for the school year. This issue included an article on teenage pregnancy, featuring interviews with several Hazelwood students who had babies. The students were not named, and the editors believed they had changed the stories enough to keep the girls from being identified. The issue also contained an article in which the writer described his reactions to being torn between divorced parents. He was particularly hard on his father. When students received their copies of *Spectrum*, neither article appeared. The two pages on which they had been dummied by the editors had been removed from the newspaper. Hazelwood East Principal Robert E. Reynolds said later, "The students and families in the articles [on pregnancy and divorce] were described in such an accurate way that readers could tell who they were. When it became clear that the articles were going to

Hazelwood School District v. Kuhlmeier, **484 U.S. 260, 108 S.Ct. 562, 98 L.Ed.2d 592, 14 Med.L.Rptr. 2081 (1988).**

tread on the right of privacy of students and their parents, I stepped in to stop the process."[59]

Reynolds stopped one process but started another. Cathy Kuhlmeier and two other *Spectrum* staffers asked a federal district court in St. Louis to override the principal. It refused to do so, but the Eighth Circuit Court of Appeals reversed the lower court. School officials then took the case to the Supreme Court, which agreed to consider it. Five justices, over vigorous protests from three others, ruled that the principal had acted reasonably, and the majority held that "no violation of First Amendment rights occurred." Justice Byron R. White, writing for the majority, said the principal was merely playing the role of a good teacher by correcting a substandard classroom exercise. That view was not shared by Justice Brennan, who wrote for the minority, and by others who commented on the decision. Brennan called the principal's action "brutal censorship." A headline in *Editor & Publisher,* the newspaper trade magazine, called the decision a "First Amendment disaster."[60]

How could there be such widely diverse views of the same action and the same decision? Within the Court, the split occurred over which of the Court's previous decisions was seen as the applicable precedent. The majority, made up of Justice White, Chief Justice Rehnquist, and Justices John Paul Stevens, Sandra Day O'Connor, and Antonin Scalia, found its guidance in *Bethel School District No. 403* v. *Fraser.*[61] In that case, the Court had approved actions by school officials who disciplined a student speaker for using vulgar language in a speech to a high school assembly, which students were required to attend. The majority said that such language was offensive to some students and inappropriate for the younger members of the student body. In the *Hazelwood* decision, White noted that in *Bethel* the Court had held that "[a] school need not tolerate student speech that is inconsistent with its 'basic educational mission,' even though the government could not censor similar speech outside the school. . . . We thus recognized that '[t]he determination of what manner of speech in the classroom or in school assembly is inappropriate properly rests with the school board' rather than with the federal courts. It is in this context that [the student editors'] First Amendment claims must be considered."

The minority, as had the lower appeals court, found its guidance in *Tinker* v. *Des Moines Independent Community School Dist.*[62] In that case the Court had told school officials they acted improperly in disciplining students for wearing black armbands to class to protest the Vietnam war. It reminded school officials, in language that has become classic, that First Amendment freedoms do not stop at the schoolhouse gate. School officials can restrict student expression only if the officials can prove that the expression seems likely to disrupt the educational process. In a considerable number of cases, as in this one, lower courts had quoted *Tinker* in upholding the right of students to publish alternative newspapers or to resist censorship of the student press.

The lower court's reliance on *Tinker* in this instance was mistaken, White said. The action approved in *Tinker*—the wearing of black armbands to protest the nation's involvement in the Vietnam war—had nothing to do with the school's educational mis-

---

59. "From Hazelwood to the High Court," *New York Times Magazine,* 13 September 1987, p. 102.
60. *Editor & Publisher,* 16 January 1988, p. 12.
61. 478 U.S. 675, 106 S.Ct. 3159, 92 L.Ed.2d 540 (1986).
62. 393 U.S. 503, 89 S.Ct. 733, 21 L.Ed.2d 731 (1969).

sion. The *Tinker* children were expressing their objections to events outside the school. Their actions were not a part of any lesson being taught in a classroom.

White noted that *Hazelwood* brought an altogether different set of facts to the Court. *Spectrum* was published as part of the work in a class for which the student reporters and editors received grades and academic credit. Whatever else the newspaper was, it was a laboratory production to which the students applied their lessons in journalism. Because *Spectrum* was intimately involved in the educational process, White and his colleagues concluded that they must look to *Bethel,* not *Tinker,* for guidance, because *Bethel,* too, had its origins in a school function—an assembly that was a part of the process of electing student body officers. As the Court saw it, the assembly was part of the educational process. Therefore, school officials could exercise control over what was said in the assembly to make certain that the speech served an educational purpose and was not inappropriate for some members of the audience. Once that line of reasoning was applied to the facts of *Hazelwood,* the next step was inevitable. *Spectrum,* too, was a part of the educational process. As such, it could be controlled by school authorities, like any other part of the educational process, without raising First Amendment questions, as long as the control served a reasonable educational purpose.

White next sought to define how far officials could go before their regulation of content might be considered unreasonable. In doing so, he expanded the scope of the decision to include not only school-sponsored publications, but also "theatrical productions, and other expressive activities that students, parents, and members of the faculty might reasonably perceive to bear the imprimatur of the school." Such activities, White said, are supervised by faculty members "and designed to impart particular knowledge or skills to student participants and audiences." At that point, in the eyes of a majority of the Court, *Spectrum* no longer was a newspaper entitled to full First Amendment protection but was a part of the school's classroom-oriented activities, over which "[e]ducators are entitled to exercise greater control." The purpose of that control, White said, is "to assure that participants learn whatever lessons the activity is designed to teach, that readers or listeners are not exposed to material that may be inappropriate for their level of maturity, and that the views of the individual speakers are not erroneously attributed to the school."

With respect to a school-sponsored newspaper, White wrote, a school may "disassociate itself," quoting from *Fraser,* "from speech that is, for example, ungrammatical, poorly written, inadequately researched, biased or prejudiced, vulgar or profane, or unsuitable for immature audiences. A school must be able to set high standards for the student speech that is disseminated under its auspices—standards that may be higher than those demanded by some newspaper publishers or theatrical producers in the 'real' world—and may refuse to disseminate student speech that does not meet those standards." Lest there be any doubt about the limits to reasonable control of course-related activities, White added, "A school must also retain the authority to refuse to sponsor student speech that might reasonably be perceived to advocate drug or alcohol use, irresponsible sex, or conduct otherwise inconsistent with 'the shared values of a civilized social order,'" again quoting from *Fraser,* "or to associate the school with any position other than neutrality on matters of political controversy."

One other question had to be answered before the Court could complete its decision. Was the newspaper a public forum? The court of appeals had said it was. If so, school officials could control the time, place, and manner of its publication, but that control would have to be content neutral. The Supreme Court had said so on many occasions. In this instance, there was no doubt that Principal Reynolds had removed the two pages because he objected to their content. He had said so. That made no difference, White wrote, because the evidence clearly proved that *Spectrum* was not a public forum. Schools are not like public streets or parks, "that 'time out of mind, have been used for purposes of assembly, communicating thoughts between citizens, and discussing public questions.'" Schools can become public forums only if officials open classrooms or auditoriums "for indiscriminate use by the general public." That had not been done with *Spectrum.* Quite to the contrary, the Hazelwood School Board had adopted a policy statement providing that "[s]chool sponsored publications are developed within the adopted curriculum and its educational implications in regular classroom activities." The policy statement paid lip service to the principle of free expression "within the rules of responsible journalism," but also stated that "school officials retained ultimate control over what constitutes 'responsible journalism.'"

The school's "Curriculum Guide" described the Journalism II course, which produced *Spectrum,* as a "laboratory situation in which the students publish the school newspaper applying skills they have learned in Journalism I." White noted further that Journalism II was taught by a faculty member "who selected the editors of *Spectrum,* scheduled publication dates, decided the number of pages for each issue, assigned story ideas to class members, advised students on the development of their stories, reviewed the use of quotations, edited stories, selected and edited the letters to the editor, and dealt with the printing company." The instructor had final authority over content but, as a matter of routine, submitted all copy to Principal Reynolds for review prior to publication.

Nevertheless, a statement of policy published at the beginning of each school year said, "*Spectrum,* as a student-press publication, accepts all rights implied by the First Amendment." Contrary to the position taken by the court of appeals, White concluded that the statement did not reflect an intent to have the newspaper serve as a public forum. All it suggested, he wrote, was "that the administration will not interefere with the students' exercise of those First Amendment rights that attend the publication of a school-sponsored newspaper." White did not attempt to define those rights except to say that because they were exercised within the framework of "a supervised learning experience for journalism students . . . school officials were entitled to regulate the contents of *Spectrum* in any reasonable manner."

The Court concluded that Principal Reynolds had acted reasonably, out of concern for privacy and for the immature students in the paper's audience, when he removed two pages from *Spectrum.* He was simply acting as a teacher to correct students who had not learned their lessons. As White put it,

> Reynolds could reasonably have concluded that the students who had written and edited these articles had not sufficiently mastered those portions of the Journalism II curriculum that pertained to the treatment of controversial issues and personal attacks, the need to protect the privacy of individuals whose most intimate concerns are to be revealed in the newspaper, and 'the legal, moral, and ethical restrictions imposed upon journalists within [a] school community' that includes adolescent subjects and readers."

By thus reducing the student newspaper to a classroom exercise, putting it on the same footing with U.S. history tests and English grammar essays, White and his colleagues were able to sum up their decision by asserting, "Accordingly, no violation of First Amendment rights occurred."

Justice Brennan wrote a strong dissent, but stopped short of endorsing absolute freedom for student editors. Standing squarely on the Court's rationale in *Tinker,* he indicated he would uphold a "narrowly tailored" right to censor student expression that "disrupts class work [or] invades the rights of others." He did not find that kind of narrow tailoring in the actions of the school principal. Brennan conceded that some kinds of speech can be "illegitimate." But when such speech is found, those who would eliminate it must use "sensitive tools" to separate it from speech protected by the First Amendment. In Brennan's view, that is not what Reynolds did. In an area where precision was called for, "the principal used a paper shredder." Brennan was joined in dissent by Justices Thurgood Marshall and Harry Blackmun. At the time of the decision, the Court had only eight members because Congress and President Reagan were deadlocked over a replacement of Justice Lewis Powell.

The dissenters did not agree that there had been "no violation of First Amendment rights." In their view, *Spectrum* was first a newspaper and only secondarily a classroom exercise. Seeing it as an outlet for student news and opinion, they would have given it First Amendment protection up to the limits established by the Court in *Tinker.* In their view, the majority's reliance on *Fraser* was nothing more than an excuse to justify "brutal censorship." To them, the principal's action "served no legitimate pedagogical purpose." If he had been trying to teach a lesson, Brennan suggested, Reynolds might have chosen "obvious alternatives, such as precise deletions or additions . . . rearranging the layout, or delaying publication. Such unthinking contempt for individual rights is intolerable from any state official. It is particularly insidious from one to whom the public entrusts the task of inculcating in its youth an appreciation for the cherished democratic liberties that our Constitution guarantees."

Despite Brennan's protests, the majority's lesson, reduced to a few words, can be summed up as follows: A public school newspaper published in connection with a class, as about half of them are,[63] is primarily an educational tool and only secondarily a limited exercise in First Amendment freedoms. Therefore, teachers and administrators can change or even delete articles that fall short of the standards of good journalism, as long as those changes or deletions serve a reasonable educational purpose. In the Court's view, student victims of administrative censorship can seek relief under the First Amendment only if they can prove that changes in their stories were made for other than educational reasons.

The decision does not affect the appreciable number of public school newspapers that are not published as part of the required work in a journalism or English course. Those papers in public schools enjoy considerable First Amendment protection. Nor does this decision have any effect on student newspapers published by private or parochial schools. Because teachers and officials of such schools are not agents of the state, and because students are under no compulsion to attend such schools, private

---

63. Mark Goodman, director of the Student Press Law Center, Washington, D.C., as quoted in Stephen Wermiel, "High Court to Review School Officials' Authority to Censor Student Newspapers," *Wall Street Journal,* 21 January 1987.

school authorities may control their student publications without raising First Amendment questions.

Since the *Hazelwood* decision, high school and college journalism instructors, with leadership from the Student Press Law Center and the Secondary Education Division of the Association for Education in Journalism and Mass Communications, have sought support in state legislatures for laws guaranteeing the freedom of the student press. They have used Section 48907 of California's State Education Code, adopted in the 1970s, as a model. The section says that school officials cannot censor a story unless it is "obscene, libelous, slanderous," or advocates "substantial disruption" of the school.[64] As noted earlier, legislatures in five other states have adopted similar codes. The Wisconsin legislature passed a student press freedom bill in 1992, but the bill was vetoed by the governor.[65] Bills have reached various stages of the legislative process but have failed to be signed into law in Arizona, Idaho, Indiana, Michigan, Minnesota, Missouri, New Jersey, Ohio, South Carolina, and Washington.

The Supreme Court's decision in *Hazelwood* stands as an important watershed in First Amendment law. Before it was handed down, it was possible to argue that a public school official's censorship of a student newspaper was in most instances an unacceptable prior restraint by an officer of the state acting in violation of the First and Fourteenth amendments. A few courts had ruled that way. No longer is it possible to take that position with respect to public school newspapers published as part of the school's course work. School officials can exercise reasonable control over the content of such newspapers to further an educational purpose. That control can take the form, as it did in *Hazelwood,* of a prior restraint.

In the Professional World

For most journalists, "sedition" and "censorship" are words found in history books or in the news from countries with governments that permit no political opposition. Few mainstream American journalists ever have had their work censored by government authorities or ever have been accused of sedition. But that fact may not be much of a test of media freedom. Most journalists in the conventional media, like most of the American people, are not at odds with the U.S. political and economic systems. They think the systems generally work well for most Americans.

However, some Americans take a different view of society. Whether they come from the left or the right of the political spectrum, they see the conventional political process as a sham. Although politicians seeking to hold or win office make a big fuss every two years, once inside the Washington, D.C., beltway they do nothing to fix the nation's ills. Instead, they talk, raise taxes, trample on civil liberties, and watch the nation accumulate debt. In the view of some

64. Allan Wolper, "California Students Protected from Censorship," *Editor & Publisher,* 6 February 1988, p. 17+.
65. Annual Report, Professional Freedom and Responsibility, David L. Adams, chairman; Secondary Education Division, Association for Education in Journalism and Mass Communications, delivered in Montreal, Quebec, August 1992.

Americans, the federal government works to shore up an economic system that makes some people rich but also oppresses the poor, pollutes the environment, rapes the country's natural resources, and keeps minority groups in poverty and bondage. In the view of some Americans, the federal government works to undermine the physical and moral health of the nation by subsidizing tobacco products, encouraging gambling and abortions, funding unjust welfare systems, and pushing Medicare and Social Security to the brink of insolvency. Some Americans believe they are witnessing the rise of a police state, intent on disarming citizens and depriving them of their property. In their view, change for the better is unlikely unless the people rise up and take control. Only then can the nation's resources be used to benefit all, rather than to enrich the few.

There are enough such opponents of the establishment to organize political parties and qualify for a place on the ballot in most states. In presidential elections in recent times, candidates have represented the Libertarian, Communist, Socialist Workers, Workers World, and Socialist parties. But unless they have the money of Texas millionaire Ross Perot or the misfortune of having spawned armed paramilitary organizations, these disaffected Americans campaign for change with little or no attention from television, wire services, newspapers, or magazines. Most people aren't even aware of the existence of minor-party candidates until they enter the voting booth and see the unfamiliar names on the ballots.

Ross Perot, a Texas entrepreneur with no previous political experience, was able to get on the presidential ballot in all fifty states in 1992 with the help of millions of dollars in television advertising paid for from his own vast fortune. He wasn't elected or appointed to anything in government, but he was able to garner almost 20 percent of the vote. Apart from his money, Perot was perceived to be talking in plain terms about what was wrong with the system and what might be done to make it work better. Not only was he able to command media attention, starting with an appearance on Larry King's nationally televised talk show on the Cable News Network, but he won the right to appear with President Bush and President-to-be Clinton in the campaign's three presidential debates. However, the other dozen or so candidates who aspired to the presidency on platforms that proposed changes in the system toiled, as usual, all but unseen and unheard. If they found a forum, it was in the publications of their small political groups, where they reached only those already converted to their causes. Was their invisibility caused by government censorship? No. They were being ignored by the mainstream media.

This example raises questions not of law, but of ethics: If the mass media lean so far on the side of safety that they give time and space only to those who work within and support the system, is there a true marketplace of ideas? Milton complained that truth and falsehood could not truly grapple if government used its power to keep some ideas out of the arena. Is the contest any less rigged when media indifference keeps them out? When Eugene McCarthy, a former U.S. senator and by no stretch of the imagination a radical opponent of the system, ran for president as an independent in 1976, he complained with elegance and wit that he was ignored by the major media. Editors responded that they were merely reflecting the perceived interests of their audience. Everyone knew McCarthy's cause was doomed from the start, so why give it any attention? The circular logic of such a position is evident.

Indifference to unpopular causes and political candidates is not the only ethical problem confronting media professionals. Polls conducted during the 1988 and 1992 campaigns and remarks by the candidates, particularly President Bush, evidenced widespread public distrust of reporters and the news media. Complaints of media bias were prevalent. Some critics even suggested that mainstream journalism was becoming subversive by paying too much attention to radical causes or disaffected Americans. Some critics complained that, in the wake of the Watergate scandal in the 1970s, journalists had adopted an adversary stance in reporting about government, and that was undermining public confidence in officials.

If it is a problem to ignore news that seems to come from the fringes of society, is it also a problem to report too much negative news that comes from the center of government? Within a week after Clinton was elected to the presidency, news stories, political columns, editorials, and television commentaries began raising questions about his ability to keep his campaign promises. If he intended to start his administration by putting people to work rebuilding highways and bridges, what would that do to his promise to reduce the deficit? When Clinton announced that members of his transition team would be forbidden to lobby government agencies after they finished their jobs, stories pointed out that the coleaders of the team not only were veteran lobbyists but were associated with organizations doing business with government. If the big stories are those that play up the failings of public officials, the flaws in policy, or the shortcomings of the government, what happens to the public trust that is essential to the working of a democratic system? The truth is, no one knows. Nor can one argue that it is not news when a president lies to the people, as Nixon did during the Watergate episode, as Johnson did about events in the Gulf of Tonkin, or as Bush may have about how much he knew about the proposed swap of arms to Iran for the release of hostages in Lebanon. Nor is there any question that policy should be debated. Few proposals for dealing with problems as persistent and complex as poverty, unemployment, racial relations, the skyrocketing cost of health care, drug abuse, and the "glass ceiling" for women are likely to offer perfect solutions. Precisely because such problems are persistent and complex, their every aspect needs to be studied critically and attacked logically. The question is, What happens to any administration's ability to deal with such problems when its proposals are overwhelmed by instant reaction? One effect may be a form of paralysis that rules out any significant change. Another effect may be a loss of faith in the ability of the system to meet the people's needs.

In the legal sense, there is nothing seditious in proclaiming that our emperors aren't wearing clothes. The First Amendment does not require that journalists be cheerleaders for government. One of the most important purposes of that amendment is to prevent government from punishing journalists and others who expose its mistakes and hoot at its follies. For more than thirty years, the courts have protected this purpose with zeal. The freedom to criticize government is near or at the absolute level advocated by Meiklejohn and Emerson.

However, should that freedom go so far, as some media lawyers argued in the *Morison* case, as to condone the publication of secret photographs stolen from the government? In that instance, a court said no. Earlier, however, the Supreme Court itself had held that the *New York Times* and other newspapers had a right to publish information taken from top secret documents obviously stolen from the U.S. government. In December 1989, as airborne troops were on their way to Panama, at least two news organizations were disseminating stories about their departure and their probable destination. Three journalists for the Cable News Network described from their hotel room the U.S. bombing of Baghdad that started the brief Gulf War of 1991. The network continued to broadcast reports from Iraq for the duration, leading some critics to charge that it had become a propaganda organ for Saddam Hussein. More recently, in 1994, all four television networks voluntarily withheld information that American planes had taken off for an invasion of Haiti until after the invasion had been called off and the Pentagon agreed that the news could be broadcast.[66]

Would it have been illegal to report that the United States had launched an invasion of Haiti? Probably not. Would it have been ethical? The question has no easy answer. At all levels of government, reporters deal with sources who offer them information "off the record" or for background. Sometimes such information is offered in the expectation that the reporter will publish it without identifying the source. But at other times, the reporter and the source agree that the information will not be disclosed to the public. On such occasions, if the information has any value to the public, hasn't the reporter self-imposed a form of prior restraint? Editors of the *New York Times* knew that President Kennedy was planning an invasion of Cuba to attempt the overthrow of Fidel Castro. At the president's request, they chose not to publish it. After the invasion had failed, both the *Times* editors and the president said they wished the newspaper had published the story. Had it done so, many lives might have been saved, and relations between the United States and Cuba might have taken a different course.

The "right to know" is a phrase that comes easily to reporters in pursuit of stories that sources are reluctant to disclose. But, as our discussion here suggests, that right is not easy to define. The questions raised by Chief Justice Burger in his dissent in the Pentagon Papers case will not go away. If there is such a right, he asked, who decides what the people have a right to know? Government officials or journalists? How much or how little of the information produced by government, or stored in its files, can be withheld without destroying our ability to govern ourselves wisely? How selectively can such information be disclosed—or reported—without skewing the outcome of debate over public policy? Does it make any difference whether information is withheld because government officials refuse to disclose it or because journalists reject it as not fitting their definition of news? In either event, the classic struggle between truth and falsehood is something less than the "free and open encounter" advocated by John Milton.

---

66. Bill Carter, "Networks Held Back News That Invasion Had Begun," *New York Times,* 20 September 1994, p. A8.

FOR REVIEW

1. What is the rationale for a sedition law in time of peace? Is the rationale valid in a democracy?

2. On its face, the First Amendment seems to stand as a barrier only against acts of Congress designed to limit freedom of speech or press. How, then, can courts use that amendment to overrule attempts by state governments to limit expression?

3. With reference to the Supreme Court's decisions in *Dennis, Yates,* and *Brandenberg,* are there circumstances in which advocacy of violent overthrow of the government might be punished? Should there be?

4. In the *Morison* case, Judge J. Harvey Wilkinson III wrote that "[t]he First Amendment interest in informed popular debate does not simply vanish at the invocation of the words 'national security.'" But he also noted that in a less than perfect world, even democratic governments must keep some things secret from their own people. How can these statements be reconciled?

5. What is the crucial fact question in determining whether someone who threatens to kill the president is likely to be prosecuted and found guilty?

6. Define a prior restraint. How can such action be justified in light of the part of the First Amendment that says, "Congress shall make no law . . . abridging the freedom of speech, or of the press"?

7. The Supreme Court's decision in *Near* v. *Minnesota* has been called both a victory and a defeat for the First Amendment. Explain.

8. What elements distinguish the Wisconsin district court's decision in the *Progressive* case from the Supreme Court's decision in the Pentagon Papers case? What questions do the cases raise?

9. Under what circumstances can information be treated as private property? Can such treatment be justified in light of the First Amendment? Why or why not?

10. Analyze the Supreme Court's decision in *Hazelwood School District* v. *Kuhlmeier* with specific reference to First Amendment values. Now, suppose that Justice Brennan's dissent had been the majority opinion of the Court. What difference might it have made in the operation of public high school student newspapers?

CHAPTER 4

THE COMMON LAW OF DEFAMATION

An Overview
Parties to a Libel Suit
The Common Law Elements of Libel

Publication/Identification/Defamation/Jurisdiction/Timeliness

THE SUPREME COURT, COMMON LAW, AND
"PUBLIC CONCERN"
COMMON LAW AND BUSINESS
ALTERNATIVES: SETTLEMENTS, ARBITRATION,
AND RETRACTIONS

For more than six centuries, courts in England and the United States have recognized the value of reputation—what others think of us. They also have recognized that reputation can be harmed by words, particularly by accusations of crime, of immorality, or of dishonesty. Therefore, as a matter of common law, courts have permitted victims of harmful words to sue their detractors and recover sums of money calculated to compensate for the loss of reputation. The great body of law that has grown out of such actions is called the law of defamation, commonly known as the law of libel and slander. In libel, the harmful words are written, printed, or otherwise put into a form that will endure and be disseminated to the public. In slander, they are spoken.

In the last half of the twentieth century, libel law has become of greater concern to journalists and other communicators than any other kind of law. During a twenty-five-year period, reaching a peak in the mid-1980s, libel actions were brought against the media in record numbers. Ironically, this surge came when the Supreme Court, in a notable series of decisions, was making libel actions more difficult for plaintiffs to win. The Court did so by removing libel involving matters of public concern from the realm of common law and making it subject to federal constitutional law. In the first and most important of its libel decisions, *New York Times* v. *Sullivan*[1] in 1964, the Court held that the First Amendment protected the *New York Times* against a libel action brought by an Alabama public official. In such instances, the Court said, public officials cannot recover damages unless they can prove that the publisher knowingly published a lie or showed reckless disregard for the truth. With that holding, the Court embarked on a

---

1. 376 U.S. 254, 84 S.Ct. 710, 11 L.Ed.2d 686, 1 Med.L.Rptr. 1527 (1964).

116

DEFAMATION: COMMON LAW FOUNDATIONS

course that revolutionized libel law. In later cases, the Court expanded the *New York Times* principle to cover public figures—people who hold no public office but have an influence on events—and, in a modified form, even private individuals.

Although most libel cases involve the news media, no one in communications is exempt from libel law. In recent years, on-line publishers, corporate communicators, advertisers, and book publishers, as well as journalists, have been targets of libel actions. A message posted on an electronic bulletin board accusing a bank of breaking the law triggered a libel suit against an on-line information company. An employer's in-plant bulletin defining sexual harassment and noting that one supervisor had been fired for that offense led to another such suit. A book based on the life of a noted Texas sheriff led to yet another lawsuit. But journalists are especially vulnerable because they are constantly involved in reporting crime and other wrongdoing. They are particularly vulnerable when they attempt to expose those in and out of government who abuse the public trust. An Indiana newspaper was sued for libel because it asked in a news item whether an automobile salvage yard should continue to hold a towing contract with the city after one of its owners was charged with receiving stolen property. The *Washington Post* spent more than five years in litigation when it looked into allegations that an oil company executive had set up his son in a tanker chartering firm that hauled the company's oil, and published its findings.

In the cases mentioned here, the defendants won, as they usually do,[2] but they spent thousands of dollars in doing so. Floyd Abrams, a New York lawyer with extensive experience in defending libel cases, has estimated that media defendants' legal costs average $150,000 in lawsuits that go to trial.[3] Some media defendants have spent as much as $600,000.[4] Professional communicators can and do buy libel insurance to guard against such costs, but the insurance, too, is expensive. Such expenses, say some reporters and lawyers, have dampened the business of investigative journalism. During a national conference of Investigative Reporters and Editors, reporters spoke of the fear their publishers have of heavy legal costs.[5]

---

2. Randall P. Bezanson, Gilbert Cranberg, and John Soloski, "Libel and the Press, Setting the Record Straight," *Iowa L.Rev.,* October 1985, pp. 215–233.
3. Floyd Abrams, "Why We Should Change Libel Law," *New York Times Magazine,* 29 September 1985, p. 34+.
4. "The Cost of Libel: Economic and Policy Implications," a report on a Cost of Libel Conference conducted by the Gannett Center for Media Studies and Columbia University's Center for Telecommunications and Information Studies in June 1986. The report was published by the Gannett Center, now The Freedom Forum Media Center, 2950 Broadway, New York, NY 10027.
5. M. L. Stein, "The Chilling Effect," *Editor & Publisher,* 4 July 1987, p. 10+.

The fact is, however, that during the past several years the number of libel actions aimed at the media has declined, in part because of Supreme Court decisions encouraging judges to grant defense motions for summary judgment.[6] In 1994, the Libel Defense Resource Center reported that the average number of libel cases tried and the number of trials lost by the media had dropped to their lowest levels since the group starting tracking them in 1980.[7] During those turbulent 1980s, the media lost about 74 percent of their cases at trial, with average jury awards climbing from $500,000 in the early 1980s to $8 million by 1991.[8] By 1993, however, media losses were down to about 54 percent of the cases tried, and average awards were down to about $1 million.[9] The Libel Resource Defense Center reported that for 1992–1993, of the eleven trials lost by media, the amount of individual awards varied from well under $1 million to as high as $7.5 million.

Media defendants lose more than half the libel cases that go to trial, but most of those losses are reversed, or the damages are reduced, on appeal. In a study of 201 appeals to the U.S. Supreme Court, the Libel Defense Resource Center found that in media cases involving libel and privacy, the Court reversed the lower-court decision almost 78 percent of the time.[10] Consequently, awards actually collected by plaintiffs, even in the 1980s, were nowhere near the multimillion-dollar figures indicated above. The amount collected averaged closer to $260,000 per lost case, or about 18 percent of the award that jurors thought they were recommending.[11]

The bottom line, nevertheless, is that defending a libel suit is costly, even if that defense is successful at trial or on appeal. Moreover, the possibility of losing a multimillion-dollar judgment has led many lawyers representing media defendants and their libel insurers to urge caution in reporting and a quick settlement of close cases rather than risk the cost of fighting them out in court.

Defamation law began to take form in the common law of England as early as the thirteenth century. That law was transported to the colonies by the English settlers and became a part of the common law of each state after the Revolution. Thus, by the middle of the twentieth century, the common law of defamation was based on nearly 700 years of court decisions and had been written into the statutes of many states. In practice, the law favored those who believed they had been defamed. When a libel suit was filed, the plaintiff needed only to establish by evidence that the defendant had published a defamatory statement of and concerning the plaintiff. In other words, the plaintiff had only to prove three elements: that there was *publication* by the defendant, that there was *identification* of the plaintiff, and that the words constituted *defamation*. Some words, in fact, were so obviously defamatory that the court required no proof beyond the words themselves. The court generally presumed that the defamatory words were false and that the plaintiff had been harmed by them. Moreover, the plain-

---

6. Mary A. Anderson, "Media Lawyers Are Sanguine about Libel Trends, Less Optimistic about Other Legal Challenges," *Presstime,* December 1988, p. 40.

7. George Garneau, "Libel Threat Dips," *Editor & Publisher,* 19 March 1994, p. 29.

8. Ibid.

9. The mean average was $1 million in 1992–1993; the median was $564,000.

10. "Few Libel Cases Were Heard by Supreme Court," *Editor & Publisher,* 8 October 1994, p. 37.

11. "Survey: Juries Hiking Libel Penalties," *Editor & Publisher,* 5 September 1992, p. 13.

tiff was not required to prove that the defendant knew the words were false or that the defendant was otherwise at fault.

The defendant could avoid paying damages only by proving with evidence in court that the offending words were true, or were a fair comment, or were otherwise privileged by law. However, even these defenses could not be relied upon with certainty. Truth couldn't protect a defendant if publication was demonstrably motivated by ill will. Opinions had to be "fair" to be defensible, and by that the courts meant they had to be based on facts, not imagination. Privilege was qualified by a requirement that the defendant prove the defamatory words were a complete and accurate report of a privileged government or judicial proceeding or that the communication was essential to a bona fide business relationship, as in the case of a defamatory letter of evaluation or a defamatory complaint to a supplier. A defendant might in the end avoid damages or reduce the size of the award by overcoming the court's presumption that real injury was done, but more frequently, a jury's only task under the common law was to determine the size of the award after the defendant failed to prove any of the defenses.

Long-established principles of law are not easily changed. But in the 1960s the Supreme Court, beginning with its decision in *New York Times* v. *Sullivan,* began to address the issue of whether traditional common law libel provided sufficient protection for those who would speak out on public issues. Should the First Amendment intervene in a libel case? When and for what reasons? In *New York Times* v. *Sullivan,* the Court held that public officials who sue for libel have to go beyond the common law requirements to win a libel suit. They have to prove with "clear and convincing" evidence that the defendant published with "actual malice," which the Court defined as publishing with knowledge of falsity or with reckless disregard for the truth. Within a decade, the Court had extended that burden to public figures. It defined public figures as people who do not hold public office but who have thrust themselves into the vortex of the discussion of a public controversy in an attempt to influence its outcome and who can reasonably be expected to do so. In later decisions, the Court held that even private individuals who are involved in matters of public concern must prove some degree of fault on the part of the defendant—usually negligence rather than actual malice. In addition, the Court dropped the presumptions of falsity and injury, requiring the plaintiff to prove those, too.

The Supreme Court's decisions during the past thirty years have literally rewritten libel law, at least in cases that raise First Amendment concerns. The Court has held that in such cases truth can never be libelous, no matter what the reason for publishing it. Further, assertions of fact are assumed to be true until the plaintiff proves their falsity. The old defense of fair comment has been pushed aside by the Court's holding that opinions—assertions not subject to being proved true or false—are protected by the First Amendment, with the caveat that any factual basis of an opinion may become the subject of litigation if it can be proven false.[12] Further, the Court has held that hyperbole—assertions that seem to be factual but are so outlandish that no reasonable

---

12. Milkovich v. Lorain Journal Co., 497 U.S. 1, 110 S.Ct. 2695, 111 L.Ed.2d 1, 17 Med.L.Rptr. 2009 (1990).

person would believe them to be such—also is protected. Common law privilege remains a defense but has been expanded to embrace the right to report and comment on almost any governmental doings.

This chapter and the next might best be treated as a unit. They summarize the court decisions that give a general structure to libel law. At one time, it seemed the Court was about to sweep away the common law of defamation, bringing all libel cases within the protection of the First Amendment. But that hasn't happened. The Court has held that states may apply most principles of common law to cases that do not involve matters of public concern. Thus, public relations practitioners, corporate communicators, advertising agencies, and under certain circumstances, news organizations run a risk of being caught in libel cases without constitutional protection. If an alleged libel arises out of internal corporate communications, or a narrowly circulated business medium, the communicators involved may find themselves carrying the burdens of proof prescribed by common law. When a communication involves a matter of public concern, however, First Amendment principles increase the plaintiff's burden and protect the defendant.

Although there are variations in details among the states, the common law and constitutional principles together are sufficiently clear to outline a fairly coherent understanding of libel law across the United States. All cases, whether they involve matters of public concern or not, require the libel plaintiff to establish jurisdiction and prove the elements of publication, identification, and defamation. If the case involves a matter of public concern, the plaintiff must further prove the elements of fault, actual injury, and falsity. The defendant can then respond by raising any technical or substantive defenses that might justify or excuse the defamatory statement. It is as simple as that.

We can begin therefore by examining the common law elements of defamation in this chapter and then move in the next chapter to an overview of the landmark First Amendment cases and the repertoire of defenses available to defendants.

Major Cases

- *Calder* v. *Jones,* 465 U.S. 783, 104 S.Ct. 1482, 79 L.Ed.2d 804, 10 Med.L.Rptr. 1401 (1984).

- *Dun & Bradstreet* v. *Greenmoss Builders,* 472 U.S. 479, 105 S.Ct. 2939, 86 L.Ed.2d 593, 11 Med.L.Rptr. 2417 (1985).

- *Garziano* v. *E. I. du Pont de Nemours & Co.,* 818 F.2d 380 (5th Cir. 1987).

- *Greenbelt Cooperative Publishing Co.* v. *Bresler,* 398 U.S. 6, 90 S.Ct. 1537, 26 L.Ed.2d 6, 1 Med.L.Rptr. 1589 (1970).

- *Hustler Magazine* v. *Falwell,* 485 U.S. 46, 108 S.Ct. 876, 99 L.Ed.2d 41, 14 Med.L.Rptr. 2281 (1988).

- *Keeton* v. *Hustler Magazine,* 465 U.S. 770, 104 S.Ct. 1473, 79 L.Ed.2d 790, 10 Med.L.Rptr. 1405 (1984).

- *Moncrief* v. *Lexington Herald-Leader,* 807 F.2d 217, 13 Med.L.Rptr. 1762 (D.C. Cir. 1986).

- *Old Dominion Branch No. 496, National Association of Letter Carriers, AFL-CIO* v. *Austin,* 418 U.S. 264, 94 S.Ct. 2770, 41 L.Ed.2d 745 (1974).

THE COMMON LAW OF DEFAMATION

An Overview

In general terms, the law of defamation is concerned with protection of reputation. *Merriam Webster's Collegiate Dictionary* defines the root word, "defame," thus: "to harm the reputation of by libel or slander." Legal reference works, reflecting decisions of the courts, attempt to be more precise. *Restatement of Torts,* which is prepared by lawyers specializing in tort law and published by the American Law Institute,[13] says: "A communication is defamatory if it tends to so harm the reputation of another as to lower him in the estimation of the community or to deter third persons from associating or dealing with him."

The problem with any definition is that it cannot anticipate the variety of ways in which allegedly defamatory words will confront the unsuspecting communicator. The *Restatement*'s definition is followed by five paragraphs of elaboration that can be boiled down to another principle: Any communicator who feels compelled to report in tangible form or in a broadcast that an identifiable person or business firm may be involved in illegal, unethical, immoral, or dishonest activity risks being sued for defamation. This does not mean that such reports should not be made. The public needs to know when individuals, particularly those in government or other influential positions, seem to be doing wrong. An employer considering an applicant for a position has a right to know if a previous employer found that candidate untrustworthy. Potential customers are entitled to know if a business firm is selling shoddy or dangerous products, or providing inferior service.

Long ago, courts recognized those needs and established defenses that could be used against defamation suits. However, when a libel suit was filed, courts assumed that the offending language was false and that if it made certain particularly serious charges, such as accusation of a crime, the victim had been harmed. Defendants carried the burden of justifying the defamation and could do so only by convincing judges or juries that one or more of three options protected them: (1) The assertions at

---

13. *Restatement of the Law, Second: Torts, 2d,* as adopted and promulgated by the American Law Institute, Washington, D.C., 19 May 1976 (St. Paul, Minn.: American Law Institute Publishers, 1977), vol. 3, § 559, p. 156.

issue were true; (2) the assertions were part of a fair and accurate account of a trial, of a legislative debate, or of some other government action or report, or in the case of a business firm, the assertions were an essential part of doing business; (3) the assertions were a fair comment on the actions of someone who had invited public attention. Comment was considered fair only if it was based on facts either stated in the article or commonly known.

Defendants who could not prove one of these defenses to a jury's satisfaction were required to pay whatever damages the judge considered appropriate, even if there was no evidence that the plaintiff had suffered loss. None of this had anything to do with the First Amendment because the common law assumed that, like obscenity, libel was outside the realm of protected speech.

Common law recognized two kinds of defamation, *libel* and *slander*. Libel is defamation stated in a tangible medium—in print, in a photograph, on a computer disk, or in some other form with a capacity to endure. Slander rises from spoken words. Because libel usually exists in a medium capable of being widely circulated, courts applying principles of common law treated it seriously. In contrast, the courts took slander much more lightly. Slanderous words usually are heard by relatively few persons, and the defamatory sting of the statement might soon be dissipated. Therefore, slander victims were required to prove they had suffered some harm before they could collect damages.

With the advent of radio in the 1920s, and its capacity to carry harmful spoken words to a large audience, the legal distinctions between libel and slander began to blur, although a few slander cases continue to arise in the business world. Today, courts treat an action in defamation directed at a radio or television station as they would a libel suit directed at a newspaper, magazine, or book publisher. Any differences concern the question of fault. A broadcaster is more likely to be found at fault for libel written into a script or found in a previously taped segment of a newscast than it is for defamatory remarks that come out of the blue from a caller to a radio talk show.

Common law divided libel into two kinds, libel per se and libel *per quod*. At one time there was a significant difference in the way courts treated them. Certain classes of words were considered harmful "on their face"—that is, per se. These included accusations of crime. To say that someone is a thief, a rapist, a drug pusher, or a murderer means that that person will be shunned by most of society. Courts in England established seven centuries ago that it is libelous on its face to accuse someone of immoral behavior. Despite the relaxation of moral standards, such accusation still is considered libelous. It also is libelous per se to label a person as mentally ill or as the victim of a loathsome disease. Although the nature of such diseases has changed with the times, there is little doubt that a person wrongfully identified as a victim of AIDS would have a cause of action.[14] Other words considered harmful on their face include assertions that a physician is a "quack," a lawyer, a "shyster," that a priest tells others secrets heard in the confessional, or that a business firm cheats its customers or can't pay its bills. There are circumstances under which all of these allegations, and others equally serious, can safely be published. Because jurors are likely to see such allega-

---

14. Sleem v. Yale University, 21 Med.L.Rptr. 1897 (M.D.N.C. 1993).

tions as particularly harmful, their appearance in copy being prepared for publication or broadcast should be treated like a flashing red light calling for the utmost caution before proceeding.

A libel *per quod* is not evident on its face. Indeed, the language may seem harmless, and to many persons it will be. But to those who know what the unstated facts are, the language is defamatory. Under the common law rules of libel *per quod,* the victim had to prove that others knew the circumstances that made the apparently harmful assertion defamatory and that he or she had suffered a loss of reputation as a consequence. West Virginia's Supreme Court found libel in headlines reporting that a candidate for governor was "enriched" by the sale of land near a new national park.[15] The candidate had done nothing wrong, and the stories made that clear, but the court said the headlines would evoke harmful comparisons with a former governor who had been found guilty of corruption because he had used his office to enrich himself. Although on its face the report that a governor had made money on a land sale appeared to be innocuous, in the context of West Virginia history it was defamatory.

Many courts still use the terms libel per se and libel *per quod* in their decisions. Judges are not likely to dismiss cases based on assertions that are libelous on their face. The distinction also may have some influence on jurors assessing damages against a losing defendant. Journalists who have no problem identifying a potential libel per se need to keep up with the news to avoid being tripped up by a libel *per quod*. A business-page story reporting a savings and loan executive's investments in race horses can take on another cast if her institution previously has appeared on a list of troubled thrifts.

Courts consider libel a *tort*—that is, a civil wrong, other than a breach of a contract, for which one may recover damages or seek an injunction. Tort law allows a party to seek compensation for harm caused by a breach of duty owed him or her by another. The duty generally arises from custom, business practice, or reasonable civility, and the usual remedy is a lawsuit for money damages. Thus, libel is usually a private matter, to be resolved by the parties involved, rather than a criminal matter involving police or prosecutors. However, legislatures can make libel a crime, and some criminal libel statutes exist.[16] Such statutes make it a crime to libel individuals, including public officials in some instances. The rationale is that the state has an interest in preventing the dissemination of false statements that may provoke violence. Such laws are rarely invoked in modern times and in some instances have been held to violate the U.S. Constitution.[17]

In the normal course of events, persons who believe they have been defamed have three options. They can do nothing, hoping that whatever damage has been done to their reputations will disappear in time. They can ask the offending medium to run a correction or let them tell their side of the story. Or they can hire a lawyer and sue. Only if they take the third option—and win in court or reach a settlement—can they be compensated financially for the harm to their reputation.

---

15.   Sprouse v. Clay Communications, 211 S.E.2d 674 (W.Va. 1975).
16.   For example, see Kans. Stat. Ann., § 21-4004 (1988).
17.   Garrison v. Louisiana, 379 U.S. 64, 85 S.Ct. 209, 3 L.Ed.2d 125, 1 Med.L.Rptr. 1548 (1964). But see Phelps v. Hamilton, 23 Med.L.Rptr. 2121 (10th Cir. 1995), construing the Kansas criminal defamation statute as constitutional.

Parties to a Libel Suit

Anyone who is alive can sue for libel. The operative word here is "alive." Although a lawsuit already in progress at the time of death may be finished by a plaintiff's estate, the dead cannot sue, and courts have held that no one can sue for them.[18] When KTAL-TV in Shreveport, Louisiana, reported that Sammie Gugliuzza had been murdered at his convenience store, it also reported that the "word on the street" was that Gugliuzza had "gambling debts and ties to organized crime." Sammie's widow and son sued, but the Louisiana Supreme Court said Gugliuzza's relatives could not protect Gugliuzza's memory. Once a person is dead, said the court, there is no longer a reputation to injure or protect.[19] That lesson was learned, too, by Mary Fitch's family in Alabama. *The Lee County Eagle* published a photograph of Mary lying on a hospital bed and described her as dying of cancer. In fact, Mary had died two years earlier. When her family sued for libel, the Alabama Supreme Court said simply that a libel claim is a personal claim, "based on a matter of and concerning the plaintiff," and therefore a claim cannot be brought after death.[20]

Although the general rule, as illustrated here, is that no one can sue on behalf of the dead, Puerto Rico, by statute, allows plaintiffs to sue on their own behalf if they can show that they were harmed by defamatory statements about the dead. Although the rule is unusual, Puerto Rico takes the position that a spouse or child who suffers social rejection because of the false and defamatory statements about a loved one should be able to seek compensation.[21]

Courts have held that formal business associations, profit and nonprofit corporations, and labor unions may sue for libel,[22] but governments may not.[23] Because libel is about damage to an individual person's reputation—whether that person is a human being or a legal entity like a corporation—only individuals who have been specifically identified have the right to sue. Large groups, consequently, cannot sue for the reputational harm to the group. For examples, racial and religious slurs do not entitle any random member of the racial group or church to file a lawsuit.

Courts have held that members of small groups, usually defined as having fewer than twenty-five members,[24] can maintain an action if the defamatory language is inclusive. One court held that nine Neiman-Marcus models had grounds for suit against the author of a book describing the models as including the best call girls in Dallas.[25] But a

---

18. McBeth v. United Press International, 505 F.2d 959 (5th Cir. 1974).
19. Gugliuzza v. KCMC Inc., 607 So.2d 790, 20 Med.L.Rptr. 1866 (La. 1992).
20. Fitch v. Voit, 624 So.2d 542, 21 Med.L.Rptr. 1863 (Ala. 1993).
21. 32 L.P.R.A. § 3142. Rodriquez v. El Vocero De Puerto Rico, Inc., 22 Med.L.Rptr. 1495, cert. denied, 114 S.Ct. 2744 (P.R. 1994).
22. *Restatement of the Law, Second: Torts 2d,* § 559 (1977).
23. City of Chicago v. Chicago Tribune, 307 Ill. 595, 139 N.E. 86 (1923); City of Albany v. Meyer, 99 Cal.App. 651, 279 P. 213 (1929).
24. O'Brien v. Williamson Daily News, 735 F. Suppl. 218 (E.D.Ky. 1990; affirmed, 931 F.2d 893 (6th Cir. 1991). But twenty-five is not a magic number; larger groups have been allowed a cause of action.
25. Neiman-Marcus v. Lait, 107 F.Supp. 96 (S.D.N.Y. 1952).

California court held that three wives of members of the Hell's Angels motorcycle gang could not maintain an action against *Playboy* for an article describing the unusual sexual activities of the gang's women, because none of the more than a hundred women was sufficiently identified.[26]

As for defendants, anyone in the chain of publication and distribution who had responsibility or the opportunity to correct or prevent the defamatory material can be named in the lawsuit, including writers, editors, managers, and the company for which they work. Even a company that provides computer access to the Internet may be included if the company claims some editorial control. Such was the case when Stratton Oakmont, Inc. sued Prodigy Services Co. for a posting on Prodigy's computer bulletin board.

A trial court in New York said that Prodigy was the publisher of the statements on its "Money Talk" bulletin board and so could be held responsible for any statements posted there, regardless of their source.[27] Among those statements was one from an unidentified bulletin board user[28] who claimed that Stratton Oakmont, a securities investment banking firm, and its president, Danial Porush, had engaged in criminal activities in connection with a stock offering. Judge Stuart L. Ain said that Prodigy could be held responsible because it had the ability to correct or prevent the defamatory material:

> First, Prodigy held itself out to the public and its members as controlling the content of its computer bulletin boards. Second, Prodigy implemented this control through its automatic software screening program, and the Guidelines which Board Leaders are required to enforce. By actively utilizing technology and manpower to delete notes from its computer bulletin boards on the basis of offensiveness and "bad taste," for example, Prodigy is clearly making decisions as to content, and such decisions constitute editorial control.

The judge contrasted this kind of control with an earlier case involving a Prodigy competitor, CompuServe. In that case,[29] CompuServe was sued for statements made in a daily electronic newspaper called *Rumorville USA*. Unlike Prodigy, however, CompuServe had no opportunity to review *Rumorville's* contents. *Rumorville* was published independently from CompuServe by Don Fitzpatrick Associates (DFA) of San Francisco, who had a management contract with Cameron Communications (CCI), which in turn had a contract with CompuServe to make *Rumorville* available to subscribers by listing it on CompuServe's "Journalism Forum." DFA would upload the electronic newspaper into CompuServe's computer, where it would be immediately available to *Rumorville* subscribers. CCI assumed responsibility for managing and controlling the contents; DFA assumed responsibility for the contents; and CompuServe blindly passed it along without editorial control.

---

26. Barger v. Playboy Enterprises, 564 F.Supp. 1151, 9 Med.L.Rptr. 1656 (N.D.Calif. 1983).
27. Stratton Oakmont Inc. v. Prodigy Services Co., 23 Med.L.Rptr. 1794 (N.Y.Sup.Ct. 1995).
28. The user was apparently a computer hacker who used the account of a Key West, Fla., man to enter the Prodigy system. "A New Twist in an On-Line Libel Case," *New York Times,* 19 December 1994, p. C10.
29. Cubby, Inc. v. CompuServe, 776 F.Supp. 135, 19 Med.L.Rptr. 1525 (S.D.N.Y. 1991).

The Common Law Elements of Libel

Persons who believe they have been wronged by the publication of a libel must assert in their petition to the court that there was (1) publication, (2) identification, and (3) defamation. These are the basic common law elements that must be proven by the plaintiff at trial. In addition, the plaintiff must be able to establish (4) that the action has been brought in a court with jurisdiction over the defendant, and (5) that the suit has been filed on time. These are fundamental requirements, and if any are unfulfilled the lawsuit will fail. There can be no successful libel suit if the libelous statements were not published, were about someone else, or were not harmful to the plaintiff's reputation.

Publication

In virtually all libel actions, publication is proved by a copy of the offending item. The item can be a printout of an E-mail message, a copy of a newspaper article or editorial, a transcript of a broadcast, a photograph, or a videotape. It is assumed from the fact of publication that someone read, heard, or saw the offending words or image. The case reports contain a few instances in which publishers have tried to argue that, owing to the paper's poor circulation, probably no one saw the story. Such arguments are rejected. In terms of the law, publication is proved if the circumstances suggest that anyone other than the author of the libel and its target saw the offending words. Cases have been based on letters typed by a secretary and seen otherwise only by the person who dictated the letter and its recipient, who was the subject of the libel. At the minimum, only three people are required as groundwork for a libel case: the libeler, the target of the libel, and a third person who read the libel or heard it broadcast. Therefore, the fact of publication is not likely to be at issue in a case involving mass media.

Identification

Occasionally, reporters have written a story in the belief that there can be no libel if no names are mentioned. And, on occasion, reporters have found out the hard way that they were wrong. A Hearst newspaper columnist lost a suit based on an item that reported gossip in Palm Beach of an affair between the wife of a wealthy pillar of society and a former FBI agent who had become a lawyer. No names were mentioned, but there was only one lawyer in Palm Beach who had been an FBI agent and who mixed with the upper levels of society. He won a judgment for $60,000.[30]

Libel cases sometimes can result from too little identification. During the Watergate burglary episode in the 1970s, several lawyers on the White House staff were found guilty of misconduct. *Time* magazine followed up by publishing an article on unprofessional conduct by lawyers in general. One lawyer whose conduct was described by

---

30. Hope v. Hearst Consolidated Publications, 294 F.2d 681 (2d Cir. 1961).

the article was Richard R. Ryder, who practiced in Virginia. He had been accused of hiding evidence for a client suspected of dealing in narcotics. Following its usual editorial style, *Time* omitted the middle initial and did not name the town in which Richard R. Ryder practiced.

Richard J. Ryder, who also practiced law in Virginia, sued *Time* for libel, asserting that he had suffered embarrassment because some persons thought he was the subject of the article. Eventually, *Time* won the case, but the magazine had to undertake the expense of defending itself in more than three years of litigation that reached the federal appeals level.[31] The action ended when a federal magistrate held that *Time* could not reasonably be expected to check the roster of lawyers in Virginia to make certain there was only one Richard Ryder.

Thus, win or lose, mistakes in identification in connection with libelous assertions can be costly. To avoid them, reporters should obtain precise identification of anyone mentioned in a story involving wrongdoing. Such identification should include exact spelling of first and last names—some Smiths spell it "Smythe"—middle initials, age, address, and occupation. This information is especially important if the last name is common in the community. The telephone directory in even a medium-sized city may show two or three Ralph Johnsons, Raymond Johnsons, or Robert Johnsons. Under such circumstances, to report simply that Ralph Johnson was arrested for assault is to invite, at the least, an outraged telephone call from the Ralph Johnsons who weren't arrested and their families.

Defamation

In many libel cases, the decisive question is whether the language at issue is defamatory; that is, whether the language is of such a natue as to lower the plaintiff in the estimation of others. At an early stage of the proceedings, a judge must look at the evidence and decide as a matter of law whether defamation is present.

Under common law, certain kinds of allegations were considered libelous per se—so damaging that they were held to be defamatory on their face. Therefore, if the item in question accused the plaintiff of committing a felony, the judge's decision was easy to make. Defamation was present, and falsity was presumed. The case could proceed, and its outcome would depend on whatever evidence of truth or privilege the defendant could muster.

The judge's decision is also easy if the item in question clearly is not defamatory. Some people can be highly insulted by accusations that strike most reasonable people as just a part of the give-and-take of life. A Minnesota newspaper ran a series of articles and editorials portraying its city's administrator as manipulating members of the city council so as to carry his policies into effect. The newspaper also conducted a study that showed that the administrator was more highly paid than persons holding similar positions in much larger and more prosperous Min-

---

31.   Ryder v. Time, Inc., 557 F.2d 824, 2 Med.L.Rptr. 1221 (4th Cir. 1976); 3 Med.L.Rptr. 1170 (1977).

nesota cities, leading the newspaper to assert in its editorials that he was overpaid. He sued for libel, alleging that he was the victim of an unfair vendetta on the part of the newspaper's publisher and editor. A district court judge granted the newspaper's motion for summary judgement, holding that the administrator was simply caught up in "vigorous public debate," adding that "not one of the challenged items libeled the plaintiff in any fashion."[32]

The judge's decision also may be easy if the defendant is notoriously evil. The U.S. Court of Appeals for the Second Circuit has held that some plaintiffs, such as criminals, have a reputation so low that they should not recover even nominal damages. Such plaintiffs are said to be "libel proof."[33] They so lack the respect of the community that nothing can lower them further in the estimation of others. Not all courts are willing to adopt such a category, however. The Third Circuit has twice rejected requests that it apply the doctrine.[34]

The problems come with statements that do not make clearly defamatory assertions but are still harmful. Suppose, for instance, that an officeholder has been accused of neglecting his duties. How is "neglect" defined? At what point does an observer's "neglect" become the officeholder's wise discretion? Do the facts point to a failure to perform duties required by law or simply to a difference of opinion as to what the officeholder should have done? In such instances, the judge may decline to rule on whether defamation is present. That question would be reserved for trial, where it would be decided by the "trier of fact," usually a jury, in the light of the evidence presented and argued by both sides. If the trial were by jury, the judge would instruct the jurors to consider the words at issue in their ordinary meanings and determine for themselves whether those words would lower the plaintiff in the esteem of the community.

Illinois[35] and Ohio[36] follow what is called the "innocent construction" rule. If a statement is capable of two meanings, one defamatory and the other not, the rule requires that the innocent meaning prevail. In making a decision, the judge must consider a statement as a whole, give the words their natural and obvious meanings, and reach a conclusion that an appellate court would find reasonable.

Twice the Supreme Court has recognized that when political speech is exaggerated to make a point it should not be taken literally. In a third instance, the Court protected the hyperbole of a crude social commentary.

In *Greenbelt Cooperative Publishing Co.* v. *Bresler,* a speaker, during a hearing on a zoning change, called a real estate developer's offer of compromise a form of blackmail. When a newspaper quoted the speaker, the developer sued for libel, arguing that he

---

32.   Dragisich v. Mesabi Daily News, County of St. Louis, Sixth Judicial District, Court file no. C3-91-102249 (1992).

33.   Guccione v. Hustler Magazine, Inc., 800 F.2d 298, 13 Med.L.Rptr. 1316 (2d Cir. 1986); cert. denied 107 S.Ct. 1303 (1987). See also Schaefer v. Wilson, 22 Med.L.Rptr. 2445 (S.D. Fla. 1994); Rogers v. Jackson Sun Newspaper, 23 Med.L.Rptr. 1670 (Tenn. Cir. 1995).

34.   Marcone v. Penthouse International Magazine for Men, 754 F.2d 1072, 11 Med.L.Rptr. 1577 (3d Cir. 1985); cert. denied, 474 U.S. 864 (1985); Schiavone Construction Co. v. Time, Inc., 847 F.2d 1069, 15 Med.L.Rptr. 1417 (3d Cir. 1988).

35.   Chapski v. Copley Press, 442 N.E.2d 195 (Ill. 1982).

36.   Yeager v. Local Union 20, 6 Ohio St.3d 369, 453 N.E.2d 666 (1983).

Greenbelt Cooperative Publishing Co. v. Bresler, **398 U.S. 6, 90 S.Ct. 1537, 26 L.Ed.2d 6, 1 Med.L.Rptr. 1589 (1970).** falsely had been accused of committing the crime of blackmail. Maryland courts agreed with him, awarding him a sizable judgment. The Supreme Court reversed, holding that the word "blackmail" could not reasonably be understood as an accusation of crime. The Court reasoned that taken in context, the word, as understood by the ordinary reader, simply summed up one opponent's strong objections to the developer's negotiating tactics. It was, in short, "rhetorical hyperbole" of a kind that could be expected of participants in a debate that could affect property values.

Old Dominion Branch No. 496, National Association of Letter Carriers, AFL-CIO v. Austin grew out of a labor dispute. When several post office employees in Richmond, Virginia, refused to join the Letter Carriers union, the union published a leaflet denouncing them as "scabs." The epithet was reinforced by a quotation attributed to author Jack London portraying scabs as traitors to their religion, their country, their families, and their class.

Old Dominion Branch No. 496, National Association of Letter Carriers, AFL-CIO v. Austin, **418 U.S. 264, 94 S.Ct. 2770, 41 L.Ed.2d 745 (1974).**

The targets of the abuse sued for libel, arguing that they had falsely been accused of treason. The Supreme Court held that the leaflet's language, strong as it was, was protected political speech. The Court said that anyone who knew anything about labor disputes would know that "traitor" was used in a "loose, figurative sense" and not as an accusation of crime. Such persons also would know that "exaggerated rhetoric was commonplace in labor disputes."

A case involving *Hustler Magazine* added another dimension to the points made in the *Bresler* and *Letter Carriers* decisions. In *Hustler Magazine v. Falwell,* the Court held that an "outrageous" insult directed at a nationally known television evangelist was protected hyperbole, even though it seemed to make an assertion of fact. At issue was a parody based on Campari liqueur's "first time" advertising campaign. In a cartoon drawn to resemble a Campari ad, *Hustler* said the Reverend Jerry Falwell's "first time" was during a drunken, incestuous rendezvous with his mother in an outhouse. The Supreme Court said the parody "suggested that [Falwell] is a hypocrite who preaches only when he is drunk." At the bottom of the page, a disclaimer in small type said, "Ad parody, not to be taken seriously."

Hustler Magazine v. Falwell, **485 U.S. 46, 108 S.Ct. 876, 99 L.Ed.2d 41, 14 Med.L.Rptr. 2281 (1988).**

Falwell did take it seriously. He sued for libel, invasion of privacy, and intentional infliction of emotional distress. The court threw out the invasion of privacy claim, but the case went to trial on the other two counts. A federal court jury in Roanoke, Virginia, where Falwell has his headquarters, found that the evangelist had not been libeled because the ad parody could not reasonably be understood as making factual assertions about him.

As for intentional infliction of emotional distress, the jury's $200,000 award for Falwell was thrown out on appeal. Chief Justice William Rehnquist, who wrote for the Supreme Court, said that the claim of intentional infliction of emotional distress was barred by the First Amendment. "Were we to hold otherwise, there can be little

Larry Flynt displays the parody advertisement in *Hustler* magazine that provoked evangelist Jerry Falwell to sue him for libel, invasion of privacy, and intentional infliction of emotional distress. A jury found for Falwell on the latter grounds, but the Supreme Court held that the advertisement expressed an opinion which, gross as it might be, was protected by the First Amendment. *(UPI/Bettmann)*

doubt that political cartoonists and satirists would be subjected to damages awards (for inflicting emotional distress) without any showing that their work falsely defamed its subject." In this case, the jury found that Falwell simply could not show he had been defamed. Defamation is not about how painful insults can be, but about whether harmful statements are statements of fact that do damage to a reputation. Hyperbole, by its very nature, is not factual material that reasonable people are expected to take literally.

Jurisdiction

In the overwhelming majority of libel actions, the lawsuit is filed in a state court having jurisdiction over the community in which the defendant is situated. But, as a result of two Supreme Court cases, publishers of magazines and national newspapers, or owners of broadcasting networks, may find themselves being sued in state or federal courts far from their headquarters. Such distance can add considerably to the cost of defending a libel action.

When the plaintiff and defendant in a libel action are domiciled in different states, the plaintiff has the option of filing suit in the state or federal court deemed to have jurisdiction over the action, if the harm done by the alleged libel is said to exceed $50,000. However, federal courts are required to apply pertinent state law to such cases, as long as the law does not conflict with constitutional principles established by the Supreme Court.

As a result of the Supreme Court's decisions, the plaintiff's lawyer also may have a choice as to the state in which to bring suit. That choice is controlled by state "long-arm" statutes and by U.S. Supreme Court decisions interpreting the due process clause of the Fourteenth Amendment. Long-arm statutes define the rules governing court jurisdiction over civil actions involving parties who live or have their headquarters in different states. In figurative terms, the statutes define how far a state court can reach out to gather in a distant defendant.

The controlling Supreme Court cases are *Calder* v. *Jones* and *Keeton* v. *Hustler Magazine*. A third case, *Moncrief* v. *Lexington Herald-Leader,* decided by the U.S. Court of Appeals for the District of Columbia Circuit, defines procedures protecting news agencies that have Washington bureaus.

In *Calder,* Shirley Jones, an actress living in southern California, was the target of

Calder v. Jones, 465 U.S. 783, 104 S.Ct. 1482, 79 L.Ed.2d 804, 10 Med.L.Rptr. 1401 (1984).

a story in the *National Enquirer.* The weekly tabloid is published from offices in Florida and has a circulation of more than four million. In 1979, when the article appeared, almost 600,000 copies were sold in California each week, more than in any other state. When Jones decided to sue the weekly for libel, her attorney filed the action in a California superior court, a trial court in the county in which she lived. The *Enquirer*'s lawyer asked that the suit be dismissed on the ground that the court had no jurisdiction over the weekly's employees, because they lived and worked in Florida. The trial court granted the motion, but the California Court of Appeal reversed. The Supreme Court accepted the case for review and affirmed the reversal, thus holding that the lawsuit could proceed in California.

The Supreme Court based its decision on two cases interpreting the Fourteenth Amendment's due process clause.[37] In those cases the Court had held that the clause "permits personal jurisdiction over a defendant in any State with which the defendant has 'certain minimum contacts . . . such that the maintenance of the suit does not offend "traditional notions of fair play and substantial justice." '"

In this instance, the Court found sufficient "contacts" in the *Enquirer*'s circulation in California and in the actions of a reporter, who had made several telephone calls to sources in California to gather and check information, and his editor, who had approved the story, knowing that it was "calculated to cause injury" in that state.

In *Keeton,* the Court stretched the idea of "minimum contacts" still further, hold-

Keeton v. Hustler Magazine, 465 U.S. 770, 104 S.Ct. 1473, 79 L.Ed.2d 790, 10 Med.L.Rptr. 1405 (1984).

ing that a libel plaintiff who lived in New York could file suit in New Hampshire against a magazine published by an Ohio corporation with its principal place of business in California. The plaintiff, Kathy Keeton, first filed suit against *Hustler* magazine and its publisher, Larry Flynt, in Ohio. The case was dismissed because that state's

---

37. Miliken v. Meyer, 311 U.S. 457, 61 S.Ct. 339, 85 L.Ed. 278 (1940); International Shoe Co. v. Washington, 326 U.S. 310; 66 S.Ct. 154, 90 L.Ed. 95 (1945).

one-year statute of limitations had expired. By the time that happened, it was too late to file in California or New York or, indeed, in any other state except New Hampshire, which then had a six-year limit for filing libel actions. (This limit has since been reduced to three years.) When Keeton filed suit in a U.S. district court in that state, the court ruled that the due process clause forbade the use of New Hampshire's long-arm statute to reach across the country and acquire personal jurisdiction over Flynt and his magazine. The judge concluded that the New Hampshire contacts of both parties were less than minimal. Keeton's only association with New Hampshire was that her name appeared as an editor on the masthead of a magazine with a limited circulation in the state. *Hustler's* contacts were limited to the circulation of 10,000 to 15,000 copies each month. The U.S. Court of Appeals for the First Circuit affirmed, holding that "the New Hampshire tail is too small to wag so large an out-of-state dog."[38]

However, a unanimous Supreme Court disagreed. The Court said New Hampshire's extra-long statute of limitations did afford Keeton an opportunity to redress whatever harm the *Hustler* story had done to her reputation in her home state of New York or anywhere else that she might be known. Further, it held that *Hustler's* sales in the state, however few, were the product of an effort on the magazine's part to reach and have an effect on New Hampshire readers. That was enough to satisfy the "minimum contacts" requirement.

In cases like those described above, courts in Florida and some other states will discourage forum shopping by applying the law of the state with the most "significant relationship" to the occurrence and the parties. Under that test, the court takes into consideration the place where the allegedly libelous article was prepared, the states in which it was circulated, the place of residence of the parties to the lawsuit, and the state in which the plaintiff was likely to have suffered the most harm to his or her reputation. An action in which Daryl Hall, an internationally famous musician and recording artist, was the defendant illustrates how the test is applied.[39] A reporter for *Music Connection,* a magazine published in California, interviewed Hall, who was in New York, by telephone. The resulting story included Hall's derogatory recollection of his association with John Madera, a songwriter, when Hall was breaking into the music business between 1969 and 1971. Madera, who lived in California when the article appeared in 1986, didn't learn about it until more than a year later. He filed a libel action in New York, where Hall lived. It was dismissed because New York's one-year statute of limitations had been exceeded. Madera also attempted to file suit in California, which also has a one-year limit. His third suit was filed in the U.S. district court in Miami, Florida, a state with a two-year statute of limitations for libel actions. Calling the filing "a clear example of forum shopping," Judge James Lawrence King granted Hall's motion to dismiss. Analyzing the basis for the lawsuit, King noted that the reporter had conducted his interview and written the offending article in California. The magazine was published in that state, and most of its subscribers live there. Only eighteen copies were mailed to Florida. King concluded that if Madera had suffered harm to his reputation, it had been in California, where he lived and worked, and not in Florida. Therefore, California, not Florida, had the "most significant relationship" to the alleged libel. Cali-

---

38.   682 F.2d 33 (1st Cir. 1982).
39.   Madera v. Hall, 717 F.Supp. 812, 17 Med.L.Rptr. 1178 (S.D.Fla. 1989).

A *Washington Times* editorial cartoon accurately reflects the attitude of the Supreme Court's majority in the *Falwell* case. Larry Flynt's portrayal of Jerry Falwell as an incestuous drunk was outrageous, Chief Justice Rehnquist wrote, so outrageous that few, if any, would believe it. It was a protected expression of opinion. *(Bill Garner/The Washington Times)*

fornia's law, then, with its one-year statute of limitations, governed the case. Because that limit had been exceeded, the action again was dismissed.

Keeton and *Calder* serve notice that magazines, national newspapers, and network broadcasters can be sued for libel in any state in which they do some part of their business or have enough of an audience to meet the "minimum contacts" requirement of the due process clause of the Fourteenth Amendment.

A significant exception applies to news organizations with Washington correspondents. The District of Columbia's long-arm statute contains language that in most instances protects correspondents and their employers from being sued for libel in D.C. courts.[40] That language was upheld by the U.S. Court of Appeals for the District of Columbia Circuit in a libel action brought in the District against the *Lexington Herald-Leader,* a Kentucky newspaper.[41] The paper's Washington correspondent had written a highly critical story about an attorney employed by the Department of Labor. When the attorney sued for libel, the *Herald-Leader* moved to dismiss, arguing that the U.S. District Court for the District of Columbia had no jurisdiction over the newspaper. The

---

40.   D.C.Code Ann. § 13-423 (1981).
41.   Moncrief v. Lexington Herald-Leader, 807 F.2d 217, 13 Med.L.Rptr. 1762 (D.C. Cir. 1986).

attorney argued that the court did have jurisdiction because the newspaper met the minimum contacts standard defined in *Keeton* and *Calder,* the newspaper had a full-time Washington correspondent and sold twenty-two mail subscriptions to D.C. residents. The district court dismissed the suit, and the appellate court affirmed, relying on the news-gathering exception in the District's long-arm statute. The appellate court noted with approval an earlier decision holding that "the mere collection of news" in Washington for publication elsewhere is not "a doing of business" in the city.[42]

Timeliness

All states have statutes of limitations, which establish periods within which tort actions must be brought. These limits are coupled in twenty-six states, the District of Columbia, and Puerto Rico[43] with what is known as "the single publication rule" to establish strict time frames within which libel actions must be brought.

The single publication rule, in effect, permits only one libel action to be based on a defamatory article or broadcast. This limitation is particularly important if the defamation occurs in a publication that circulates in two or more states or in a radio or television network program. The rule assumes that all damages, no matter where suffered, can be recovered in a single action. Further, a judgment in any one jurisdiction bars any other actions between the same plaintiff and defendant in all other jurisdictions.[44]

Under statutes of limitations, a libel action must be filed within a specified time, which varies from one to three years, depending on the state.[45] Time limits established by statute are enforced strictly. Usually, the limit is based on the date on which the matter at issue was made public, rather than when it became known to the plaintiff.[46] That distinction was decisive in *Morgan* v. *Hustler Magazine,* decided by a federal district court in Ohio.[47] In December 1975, the magazine pub-

---

42. Neely v. Philadelphia Inquirer Co., 62 F.2d 873 (D.C. Cir. 1932).
43. Compiled from *50-State Survey 1989,* Henry R. Kaufman, ed. (New York: Libel Defense Resource Center, 1989). The states are Alaska, Arizona, Arkansas, California, Connecticut, Florida, Georgia, Idaho, Illinois, Kansas, Minnesota, Mississippi, Missouri, Nebraska, New Hampshire, New Jersey, New Mexico, New York, North Dakota, Ohio, Oregon, Pennsylvania, Tennessee, Texas, Virginia, and Washington. In California, Illinois, and New York, courts have held that a paperback version of a book originally published in hardcover is a separate publication. Only Hawaii and Montana have rejected the single publication rule. In other states, neither statute nor case law has had occasion to address the question.
44. Restatement § 577A, Comment a (1971).
45. States with a one-year limit are in the majority. They are Arizona, California, Colorado, Georgia, Illinois, Kansas, Kentucky, Louisiana, Maryland, Michigan, Mississippi, Nebraska, New Jersey, New York, North Carolina, Ohio, Oklahoma, Oregon, Pennsylvania, Tennessee, Texas, Utah, Virginia, West Virginia, and Wyoming. The District of Columbia and Puerto Rico also have a one-year limit.
    A two-year limit is in effect in Alabama, Alaska, Connecticut, Delaware, Florida, Hawaii, Idaho, Indiana, Iowa, Maine, Minnesota, Missouri, Montana, Nevada, North Dakota, South Carolina, South Dakota, Washington, and Wisconsin.
    A three-year limit is in effect in Arkansas, Massachusetts, New Hampshire, New Mexico, Rhode Island, and Vermont.
46. Bradford v. American Media Operations, Inc., 23 Med.L.Rptr. 1941 (E.D.Pa. 1995). Time runs from actual date of publication rather than date on the cover.
47. 653 F.Supp. 711 (N.D.Ohio 1987).

lished photographs of Donda R. Morgan, which had been taken in 1973 when she was a fashion model. Although one of the photographs appeared on the front cover, Morgan did not learn about the publication until January 1984. She filed suit against the magazine a year later. *Hustler*'s lawyer filed a motion to dismiss, citing Ohio's one-year statute of limitations for libel actions. Morgan's lawyer argued that the limit should be tolled from the date of the discovery of the alleged libel rather than from the date of publication. He cited rulings in medical malpractice cases in which courts held that the right to file suit is measured from the patient's discovery of the alleged harm. A few states also permit the statute of limitations in libel actions to be tolled from the date of discovery. The district court held that nothing showed that Ohio courts had applied the discovery rule to libel actions. Rather, Ohio courts had adopted the single publication rule, meaning that the cause of action began with the date the magazine first reached the public. Because the magazine issue in question had been published more than nine years before Morgan filed her lawsuit, the court ruled that the statute of limitations barred her action. The court dismissed the case.

THE SUPREME COURT, COMMON LAW, AND "PUBLIC CONCERN"

Libel suits, whether they involve private disputes or matters of public concern, always fail if one of the basic, common law elements is missing. If a case is not in a timely manner, if a court lacks jurisdiction, if there is no publication, no identification, or no defamatory statement of fact, there is no case.

On the other hand, if all the fundamental elements of libel are present, the case moves forward in one of two directions: If the situation involves a private dispute among businesses or individuals, the common law shifts the burden to the defendant as soon as the plaintiff has established the basic elements. To win, the defendant must overcome the common law presumptions of falsity and injury and make whatever defense possible. If the situation involves a matter of public concern, the common law gives way to additional burdens of proof placed on the plaintiff by the First Amendment. In such a case, the plaintiff is required to prove not only publication, identification, defamation, jurisdiction, and timeliness, but also that the defendant was at fault, that the statement was false, and that there was actual injury.

Not all of this is as tidy as it sounds. It isn't always easy to know when a case involves a matter of public concern or when it is merely a private matter. Generally, cases that involve news media are not private matters, nor are cases involving public figures or public officials. These cases are likely to follow a First Amendment path, which tends to favor the defendant. On the other hand, cases that involve private figures or private businesses who are concerned about their own personal or financial affairs are likely to proceed under traditional common law rules, which tend to favor the plaintiff.

The Supreme Court gave impetus to this divergence between common and constitutional law in libel disputes when it decided a case involving the business reporting service Dun & Bradstreet. The service relies on thousands of correspondents to gather from public agencies and other sources information that has a bearing on the creditworthiness of business firms. It disseminates that information on a confidential basis to thousands of clients. With respect to those clients, Dun & Bradstreet is as much a news organization as is the Associated Press.

Dun & Bradstreet v.
Greenmoss Builders,
472 U.S. 479, 105 S.Ct.
2939, 86 L.Ed.2d 593,
11 Med.L.Rptr. 2417 (1985).

Yet when Dun & Bradstreet was sued for libel by a firm that it had erroneously reported to be bankrupt, the Supreme Court held that Vermont courts had acted properly in trying the case under the state's common law witout regard to the First Amendment. Because the Court was divided five ways, with no more than four justices signing any of the opinions, the effect of the decision was not immediately apparent.

At trial in a Vermont state court, the judge told the jury that because the credit agency's report was libelous on its face, Greenmoss did not have to prove it had been harmed, since "damage and loss [are] conclusively presumed." In doing so, the judge was applying Vermont's common law. He also told the jury it could make an award of punitive damages if it concluded that Dun & Bradstreet had acted with malice. The jury awarded the builder $50,000 in compensatory or presumed damges and $300,000 in punitive damages.

Dun & Bradstreet asked for a new trial, arguing that the judge's instruction to the jury violated the constitutional requirements imposed by the Supreme Court in First Amendment libel cases. The judge, conceding that he was in doubt as to whether the First Amendment applied to nonmedia defendants, granted the request. Greenmoss appealed to the Vermont Supreme Court, which reversed, thus reinstating the jury's verdict. The court concluded that credit-reporting firms, such as Dun & Bradstreet, are not "the type of media worthy of First Amendment protection as contemplated by [the Supreme Court's opinion in the] *New York Times.*" Therefore, the state's common law governed. This ruling permitted the trial court to assume that Greenmoss had been harmed and award punitive damages on proof of something less than actual malice. The U.S. Supreme Court agreed to review the case and upheld the judgment, five to four.

However, the Supreme Court did not adopt the Vermont court's rationale. The prevailing justices did not attempt to distinguish between media and nonmedia defendants. Nor did they say clearly that different standards apply to each in a libel case. Rather, they focused on the facts from which the case arose, reasoning that Greenmoss's credit rating was a private matter, of interest only to the contractor and the firms that did business with it. Justice Lewis Powell, writing for only two others, reasoned that because the libel arose out of a private matter, the First Amendment did not come into play. Therefore, Vermont courts had acted properly in applying the state's common law to the case.

Powell muddied the waters by suggesting that statements that are not of public concern are "not totally unprotected by the First Amendment." In context, he seemed to be referring to the doctrine of commercial speech under which a lesser degree of First

Amendment protection is afforded to purely commercial advertising than to speech dealing with public issues. In his discussion, Powell made much of the fact that Dun & Bradstreet "is solely motivated by the desire for profit" and that the speech in question was "solely in the individual interest of the speaker and its specific business audience." He saw the profit motive as an incentive to ensure the accuracy of the agency's service and a justification for penalizing its mistakes.

The four dissenting justices argued that Greenmoss's credit rating was not strictly a private matter. There was enough public interest in it, they said, to justify a holding that Greenmoss needed to prove both fault and harm. Powell accused the dissenters of trying "to constitutionalize the entire common law of libel."

A decade has elapsed since the Court's less-than-conclusive disposition of *Greenmoss*. A survey of the cases indicates that courts in nine states have held that their common law rules apply to an action brought by a private individual who is defamed in connection with a matter that is not of public interest. These states are Arizona, Florida, Idaho, Kansas, Maine, Oregon, Pennsylvania, Texas, and Wisconsin.[48]

Courts in twenty-seven states apply First Amendment principles to libel actions against private defendants growing out of the discussion of matters of public concern. In one instance, a federal court of appeals held that Du Pont was protected by a First Amendment privilege when it issued a press release announcing its decision to withdraw Teflon from the oil-additive market because it had concluded that the product was ineffective in such usage. The maker of one additive contended that it had been falsely accused of marketing a useless product, but the court held that the press release truthfully addressed a matter of public concern.[49] The record indicates that courts have opted to grant a high degree of protection to speech that addresses matters of public concern, even when private individuals are sued.

COMMON LAW AND BUSINESS

As *Greenmoss* makes clear, it would be a mistake to conclude that the common law has lost its vitality. For business communicators and for public relations practitioners, the common law of libel and slander is very much alive. An internal communication explaining why an employee was fired, an unduly harsh comment to a potential employer of a one-time employee, or a press release making harmful references to a competitor's product may lead to a lawsuit that will be decided by the application of common law. If that should happen, the court will assume that the alleged libel is false and that the plaintiff has been harmed. The defendant will be faced with the burden of proving that there was a valid justification for issuing the communication in question. If that communication involves a matter in which there is no public concern, the target of the suit can rely on only two defenses. He or she can attempt to prove that what

---

48. *50-State Survey 1990–91,* Henry R. Kaufman, ed., (New York: Libel Resource Defense Center, 1991). Ramirez v. Rogers, 540 A.2d 475 (Maine 1988).
49. Flotech v. E. I. du Pont de Nemours & Co., 627 F.Supp. 358 (D.Mass. 1985); 814 F.2d 775 (1st Cir. 1987).

was said is true, a task that can be difficult, or to prove that the communication is protected by a qualified privilege. The third common law defense, fair comment, would not apply, because by definition, such comment is protected only if it is aimed at the public actions of an individual who has sought public attention, either through a performance, a composition, or an attempt to influence public policy.

For the business communicator caught up in a libel suit involving a subject lacking a public concern, "privilege" has a narrowly defined meaning honed by court decisions in hundreds of cases. These decisions have established that business firms have a qualified privilege to share information essential to the conduct of their business. Such information includes references for employment, evaluations of job performance, credit reports, reasons for dismissals, accident investigatory reports, communications between officers of a corporation and its stockholders or its creditors, and other communications deemed essential to a bona fide business relationship.

However, if such communications are to qualify as privileged, they must be made in good faith, they must bear a reasonable relation to a proper business purpose, and they must be made without malice. In this connection, "malice" is given its common law meaning. To be protected by privilege, the communication cannot be motivated by ill will or an intent to harm the subject of a derogatory evaluation. Further, a reasonable effort must be made to limit the communication to those who have a direct interest in the derogatory information that it may contain. Some courts further restrict the scope of the privilege by holding that derogatory information about an individual cannot be volunteered but must be given only in response to an inquiry from one who needs the information for a legitimate business purpose.[50]

Many of the principles that we have discussed here are illustrated by the decision of the U.S. Court of Appeals for the Fifth Circuit in *Garziano* v. *E. I. du Pont de Nemours & Co.* applying Mississippi's common law of libel. The plaintiff, Richard Garziano, was discharged after his supervisors concluded that he had committed several acts of sexual harassment in the course of his work. When rumors about the discharge and the reasons for it circulated through the plant, the company issued a management information bulletin on sexual harassment. The bulletin referred to "the recent sexual harassment incident which resulted in an employee's termination." The remainder of the bulletin dealt with sexual harassment in general, describing the offense and prescribing procedures for reporting and investigating it. The bulletin was one of a series distributed to supervisors with instructions to share pertinent information with their subordinates. Subsequently, Garziano's termination and the reasons for it became the subject of talk not only in the plant but in the community outside.

Garziano sued Du Pont for libel. Under the state's common law, the company argued that its bulletin was protected by privilege—that is, by its right to share accurate information about company actions and policies with its employees. After a jury had awarded Garziano $93,000 in compensatory damages, Du Pont asked the trial judge to overrule. The judge refused to do so. He conceded that Du Pont did

Garziano v. *E. I. du Pont de Nemours & Co.,* 818 F.2d 380 (5th Cir. 1987).

---

50.   Courts in California and Missouri have so held. 53 *Corpus Juris Secundum,* § 77, p. 146.

have a right to inform its employees as to its policies on sexual harassment, but he said the jury apparently had concluded that the company could have done so without associating Garziano with the offense. To the extent that Du Pont did the latter, it lost the right to be protected by the privilege.

On appeal, the circuit court reversed. It did not question the application of common law to the case. It agreed with the trial judge's holding that the management bulletin was protected by privilege and held that the privilege had not been abused by distribution of the bulletin to supervisors. However, the circuit court said there was a question, unresolved at trial, as to whether the privilege was abused by dissemination of information about Garziano to persons outside the plant who had no need to know it. The court remanded the case for resolution of that point.

This case is of further interest because it illustrates an instance in which even the truth can be libelous. Under common law, truth can be the subject of a libel action if there is no reasonable justification for publishing it. Thus, the courts found that Du Pont was justified in telling its own employees why Garziano was dismissed. To that point, the company was protected by privilege—by its right to share with its employees information to which they are entitled. But as the Fourth Circuit's decision clearly suggests, Du Pont had no reason to spread that information through the community. Students should not let themselves be confused by the court's holding in this case. It is confined only to the common law as it applies to libel actions brought by private individuals over matters that do not involve a public concern. If public officials or public figures are libel plaintiffs, or if private individuals are defamed because of their involvement in public issues, all must prove falsity. For such plaintiffs, the truth can't be libelous.

Scores of cases exploring the limits of the common law qualified privilege as it applies to business communications have been decided in the last decade. In one instance, an Indiana appellate court held that a letter written by a university faculty member to a school administrator describing a student teacher as marginal and not recommended for even a part-time position was not excessively published. No copy was retained in the university's files, and only the writer, the school superintendent to whom it was addressed, and a principal had seen the letter.[51] In another instance, an Ohio appellate court held that the executive director of a child care center acted within the scope of her duties when she reported suspected child abuse by one of the center's teachers to the board of directors and to the child's mother. The court said that the report concerned not only the performance of the teacher but matters of common business interest between her and the directors.[52]

Such cases stand as reminders that libel law has not been completely brought under the realm of the First Amendment. For some professional communicators, the common law of libel, with its easy assumption of falsity and harm, is still there and can be used by private individuals whose private lives are needlessly defamed by their employers or by other nonmedia entities. Such plaintiffs need prove only identification, publication, and defamation. Harm and fault are assumed. From then on, the burden of proof is on the defendants to justify their acts, if they can.

---

51. Olsson v. Indiana University Board of Trustees, 571 N.E.2d 585 (Ind.App. 1991).
52. Lail v. Madisonville Child Care Project, Inc., 562 N.E.2d 1063, 55 Ohio App.3d 37 (Ohio App. 1989).

ALTERNATIVES: SETTLEMENTS, ARBITRATION, AND RETRACTIONS

Defending a libel suit is an event most people and most businesses would like to avoid. Libel suits are expensive, time-consuming, and sometimes very public. Consequently, during the past decade, scholars, lawyers, and insurance carriers have looked for alternatives to protracted litigation, and there have been experiments with various ways to negotiate these disputes. The most common alternative has come to be the out-of-court settlement. That is how Philip Morris ended its lawsuit with Capital Cities/ABC after ABC reported that cigarette companies lace cigarettes with extra nicotine. ABC agreed to broadcast an apology and clarification in exchange for the end of a $10 billion lawsuit.[53] A negotiated settlement is how Dr. Charles Crenshaw ended his lawsuit against the American Medical Association and the *Dallas Morning News* after complaining that he was defamed by three articles about his 1992 book, *JFK: Conspiracy of Silence.* In exchange, the *News* agreed to give Crenshaw and coauthor J. Gary Shaw space in the newspaper to rebut the book review. The AMA also settled, agreeing to publish a rebuttal to its own article and pay $200,000 to Crenshaw and Shaw.[54]

Although negotiated settlements are less expensive than are trial losses, they are not especially satisfactory for defendants who believe they are right, nor are they much less public than a trial. Another approach, familiar to the world of finance, is called alternative dispute resolution (ADR). If the angry parties can agree to be bound by private mediation, ADR is available to help resolve their disagreements early and at much less cost than that of going to trial. ADR has often worked well to settle financial disputes with a minimum of publicity, but it is less clear that it works well in disputes marked by intangible concerns about honor and pride. Gil Cranberg, a founder of the Iowa Libel Research Project, spent three years trying to find out if ADR could work as an alternative to a libel suit. With the help of the American Arbitration Association and the Washington and Lee School of Law, the Iowa project approached attorneys involved in 128 libel disputes and tried to persuade them to stay out of court. The Project offered to use its resources to determine whether assertions made in the offending article were true or false, and if the latter, to help the defendant repair the harm to the plaintiff's reputation. More than two-thirds of the attorneys contacted said they were interested in using the program, but only five ultimately participated, and only one case was resolved by arbitration. One case failed and went to court; two were settled before formal arbitration began; and one was left pending at the end of the project.[55] Cranberg concluded that arbitration can work in some cases, but it is the editor's initial reaction

---

53.   Alix M. Freedman and Elizabeth Jensen, "ABC Agrees to Run On-Air Apology to Settle Philip Morris Libel Lawsuit," *Wall Street Journal,* 23 August 1995. The *Journal* also reported that Capital Cities/ABC agreed to pay Philip Morris's attorneys' fees and litigation expenses, amounting to an estimated $15 million to $20 million.

54.   Mark Fitzgerald, "JFK Conspiracy Buff Settles Libel Suit with Dallas Morning News," *Editor & Publisher,* 4 March 1995, p. 23.

55.   Don J. DeBenedictis, "Little Interest in Libel ADR," *ABA Journal,* January 1992, p. 22.

to a complaint about a story that generally turns out to be the crucial element. A potential plaintiff's interest in an explanation and an apology, rather than money, is highest immediately after publication.[56] Later, once the anger hardens, it is difficult to move a case away from litigation or an expensive settlement. Although there has been no dash toward ADR to resolve libel disputes, the American Arbitration Association continues to offer mediation and arbitration services for those who are interested.

One libel lawyer has recommended that it is better for the media to anticipate complaints and attempt to head them off while a potentially defamatory story is being prepared. Alexander Greenfield, former counsel to the *New York Times* and *U.S. News & World Report,* wrote: "The best protection always is to get an interview or comment from a subject who is being pictured in a bad light. You may learn you have errors, learn about other sources, and deflect a lawsuit by giving the person his say and showing him a balanced picture."[57]

Floyd Abrams, a First Amendment lawyer practicing in New York City, recommends an additional step. He encourages defendants to make a prompt admission of error when it is clear that they have misstated facts. But Abrams would go further and make changes in the law that would both discourage libel suits and make it less expensive to resolve questions of truth when persons have been defamed. Abrams would start by denying plaintiffs the right to sue when the defendant makes a prompt and complete retraction. He would continue by limiting damages for emotional injury and abolishing punitive damages. This action would end the "pot of gold" potential that now encourages some lawyers to file suit hoping either to find a sympathetic jury or to force a generous settlement. To further discourage such suits, Abrams would give courts the power to require that the loser pay the winner's legal fees if the suit were brought or defended in disregard of settled principles of law. Finally, he suggests that states enact laws to permit public officials or public figures to sue for a declaratory judgment to determine the truth of what was published about them.

Those suggestions were made in 1985. They have not been put into effect. However, the National Conference of Commissioners on Uniform State Laws, a group of lawyers, legislators, and scholars who propose model statutes for adoption by the states, worked for five years to try to find a way to unify defamation laws around the nation and provide an alternative to litigation. Although most of its efforts have come to naught, there has been success in one area. In 1993, the group, with media support, proposed language for a uniform retraction law.[58] In 1995, North Dakota became the first state to enact the model Uniform Correction or Clarification Act.[59]

56. Gil Cranberg, "Don't Make Them Sue You," *ASNE Bulletin,* July/August 1992, pp. 20–21.
57. Alexander Greenfield, "Thirty Ways to Protect Yourself against Libel Lawsuits," *Editor & Publisher,* 3 June 1989, p. 56.
58. "Correction Act Adopted, Defamation Act Rejected," *Media Law Reporter News Notes,* 24 August 1993, p. 2.
59. "North Dakota Adopts Uniform Correction Act," *Media Law Reporter News Notes,* 2 May 1995, p. 2.

The Uniform Act provides, among other things, that:

— No one may maintain a libel action unless he or she has first asked for a correction or clarification.

— The request for correction or clarification must be in writing, must be specific, and must describe the circumstances that give rise to the defamatory meaning.

— If a timely and sufficient correction or clarification is made, a person may recover only provable economic loss caused by the defamatory publication, as mitigated by the correction or clarification.

— The correction or clarification must be published within forty-five days and in a place likely to reach the same audience as the original statements at issue or in some other manner if the parties agree in writing.

— Either party may ask a court to determine the sufficiency of the offered correction or clarification, and the court may determine the amount of reasonable expenses of litigation, including attorneys' fees.

Whether other states will adopt the Uniform Correction or Clarification Act or modify their existing retraction statutes[60] to conform with this law remains to be seen, but it is likely that many will. The act helps to accomplish what is often the first goal of a plaintiff—an early and clear correction. However, once a correction or clarification has been requested, the parties are still free to pursue the case to trial, to settle it, or to defer it to arbitration. In the end, the greatest advantage of the Uniform Act may be only a reduction of litigation costs, but when lawsuits have the potential of six- and seven-figure judgments, cost reduction is a significant bonus.

FOR REVIEW

1. What is the law of defamation concerned with? Distinguish between libel and slander; between libel per se and libel *per quod.*

2. Under common law, what elements had to be present to establish grounds for a lawsuit in defamation?

3. What factors control where a lawsuit in defamation may be filed? Could the jurisdiction in which a libel action is filed make a difference in its outcome? Explain.

4. You are public relations director for a department store. Employee pilferage is a problem. The store manager decides to make an example of the principal suspect and fires him. No charges are filed. The manager also wants the remaining

---

60. Retraction as a defense strategy is discussed further in the next chapter.

employees to know what happened and why, and she tells you it's your job to tell them. What do you do? Why?

5.   What are some alternatives to a libel trial? What are the advantages and disadvantages of these alternatives?

6.   Although by the time it reached the Supreme Court the central issue in *Falwell* was the intentional infliction of emotional distress, not libel, the decision nevertheless made important points with respect to libel law. What are they?

CHAPTER 5

DEFAMATION: CONSTITUTIONAL FOUNDATIONS

The constitutional ramparts erected around libel cases that involve matters of public interest make libel law one of the most complex fields of jurisprudence. As a practical matter, any plaintiff who sues an on-line publisher, broadcaster, newspaper, magazine, or book publisher can anticipate years of expensive litigation.

Yet despite the law's complexity, each libel case has a series of clearly critical points of contention. They form the basic elements of the plaintiff's case, and the failure to prove any one of them is fatal for the plaintiff. As we have seen, it is essential to establish in any libel case that the lawsuit has been filed in a timely way in a court with jurisdiction. Common law practice requires the plaintiff to assert and eventually prove that a defamatory statement of and concerning the plaintiff was published, or more succinctly, the plaintiff must prove publication, identification, and defamation. In cases that do not involve matters of public concern, the jury may assume falsehood and injury. If any element is clearly missing in the plaintiff's case, the defendant can ask that the case be dismissed for a failure to state a cause of action or for lack of jurisdiction.

In cases that do involve matters of public concern—as do most cases involving mass media—the First Amendment requires a plaintiff also to assert and eventually to prove that the defamatory statements were false and actually caused injury. Again, if any element is clearly missing in the plaintiff's case, the defendant can ask that the case be dismissed for a failure to state a cause of action. In addition, the plaintiff must establish by clear and convincing evidence that the defendant was at fault. If, even before trial, the plaintiff appears unable to do that, the judge is empowered to dismiss the case in response to a defendant's motion. Frequently, when the process of discovery is complete and the facts are not in dispute, the defendant can ask for a ruling to determine whether he or she is responsible as a matter of law for any harm done. Such a request is a motion for summary judgment and usually turns on the very technical nature of what it means to be at fault. That determination is a question of law for a judge to decide. It can be an important point of contention because public officials and public figures must prove a higher degree of fault in most states than is required of private individuals. Public officials and public figures must offer clear and convincing proof of actual malice—that the defendant knew the defamatory assertion was false or acted in reckless disregard for the truth. On the other hand, private individuals in most states must prove negligence— that the defendant acted carelessly. Consequently, much of libel law today involves close legal questions about what kind of fault the plaintiff must prove and with what kind of evidence.

Moreover, just how convincing a plaintiff's evidence is may depend on how well a defendant can offer a defense. There are a number of responses to a plaintiff, even one who has evidence of actual malice, actual injury, and falsity.

1. Although the plaintiff must establish falsity to get started, a defendant can offer his or her own evidence of the truth of the allegedly libelous assertions. Sometimes the outcome is simply a matter of whose version of the facts the jury ultimately believes.

2. The defendant also can counter by proving that the alleged defamation was drawn from privileged sources—that is, from public officials acting in an official capacity, from the proceedings of a public deliberative body, from public records, from highly placed participants in a public controversy, or from other trusted sources. Even with common law, journalists have a qualified privilege to make a fair and accurate report of an official record or proceeding, even if that public record turns out not to be true. When First Amendment concerns are involved, that privilege takes on even greater power and importance.

3. There are other important defenses as well. Some states recognize the defense of neutral reportage, a kind of privilege that allows news organizations to knowingly report the false accusations made by usually responsible but nongovernmental organizations and individuals. Moreover, almost every court recognizes that pure opinion, even if it causes harm, should be privileged, if only because opinion, by definition, cannot be proved true or false. Finally, an early and prominent retraction can go far to mitigate damages.

Overall, this chapter examines the constitutional privilege established by *New York Times* v. *Sullivan* and further defined by *Gertz* v. *Robert Welch, Inc.* and other Supreme Court decisions. So powerful is the First Amendment that it has become by far the biggest hurdle for plaintiffs, as well as the defense of choice for lawyers who represent the mass media in libel actions growing from the reporting or discussion of a public issue.

Major Cases

- *Anderson* v. *Liberty Lobby,* 477 U.S. 242, 106 S.Ct. 2505, 91 L.Ed.2d 282, 12 Med.L.Rptr. 2297 (1986).

- *Bose Corporation* v. *Consumers Union,* 466 U.S. 485, 104 S.Ct. 1949, 80 L.Ed.2d 502, 10 Med.L.Rptr. 1625 (1984).

- *Edwards* v. *National Audubon Society,* 566 F.2d 113, 2 Med.L.Rptr. 1849 (2d Cir. 1977).

■ *Gertz* v. *Robert Welch, Inc.,* 418 U.S. 323, 94 S.Ct. 2997, 41 L.Ed.2d 789, 1 Med.L.Rptr. 1633 (1974).

■ *Greenbelt Cooperative Publishing Co.* v. *Bresler,* 398 U.S. 6, 90 S.Ct. 1537, 26 L.Ed.2d 6, 1 Med.L.Rptr. 1589 (1970).

■ *Herbert* v. *Lando,* 441 U.S. 153, 99 S.Ct. 1635, 60 L.Ed.2d 115, 4 Med.L.Rptr. 2575 (1979).

■ *Hutchinson* v. *Proxmire,* 443 U.S. 111, 99 S.Ct. 2675, 61 L.Ed.2d 411, 5 Med.L.Rptr. 1279 (1979).

■ *Masson* v. *New Yorker Magazine, Inc.,* 501 U.S. 496, 111 S.Ct. 2419, 115 L.Ed.2d 447, 18 Med.L.Rptr. 2241 (1991).

■ *Milkovich* v. *Lorain Journal Co.,* 497 U.S. 1, 110 S.Ct. 2695, 111 L.Ed.2d 1, 17 Med.L.Rptr. 2009 (1990).

■ *Moldea* v. *New York Times,* 22 F.3d 310, 22 Med.L.Rptr. 1673 (D.C. Cir. 1994).

■ *New York Times* v. *Sullivan,* 376 U.S. 254, 84 S.Ct. 710, 11 L.Ed.2d 686 (1964).

■ *Old Dominion Branch No. 496, National Association of Letter Carriers, AFL-CIO* v. *Austin,* 418 U.S. 264, 94 S.Ct. 2770, 41 L.Ed.2d 745 (1974).

■ *Rosenblatt* v. *Baer,* 383 U.S. 75, 86 S.Ct. 669, 15 L.Ed.2d 597, 1 Med.L.Rptr. 1558 (1966).

■ *Rosenbloom* v. *Metromedia, Inc.,* 403 U.S. 29, 91 S.Ct. 1811, 29 L.Ed.2d 296, 1 Med.L.Rptr. 1597 (1971).

■ *St. Amant* v. *Thompson,* 390 U.S. 727, 88 S.Ct. 1323, 20 L.Ed.2d 262, 1 Med.L.Rptr. 1586 (1968).

■ *Stone* v. *Essex County Newspapers,* 367 Mass. 849, 330 N.E.2d 161 (Mass. 1975).

■ *Time, Inc.* v. *Firestone,* 424 U.S. 448, 96 S.Ct. 958, 47 L.Ed.2d 154, 1 Med.L.Rptr. 1665 (1976).

■ *Wolston* v. *Reader's Digest Association,* 443 U.S. 157, 99 S.Ct. 2701, 61 L.Ed.2d 450, 5 Med.L.Rptr. 1273 (1979).

LIBEL AND THE FIRST AMENDMENT

New York Times v. Sullivan

In 1908 Kansas was the first of several states to apply the "public principle" to libel actions.[1] Under this principle public officeholders were required to carry a heavier burden of proof than that carried by other libel plaintiffs. The public principle was grounded in the belief that persons who seek and hold public office ought to expect searching examination of their public actions. Such people enjoy advantages that private citizens do not, including access to the media, where they can respond to criticism. Courts in the public principle states reasoned, therefore, that it ought to be more difficult for public persons to win libel actions.

In 1964 the Supreme Court of the United States accepted an appeal by the *New York Times* and ruled that the First Amendment requires all state and federal courts to apply the public principle to libel suits brought by public officials. With its decision in *New York Times* v. *Sullivan,* the Court federalized important elements of libel law, moving them out of the realm of common law and state statute and into the realm of constitutional law. At the same time, the Supreme Court revolutionized libel law, shifting most of the burden of proof from the defendant onto the plaintiff in actions involving the news media and growing out of the discussion of public policy. The importance of the case cannot be overstated. An understanding of the present status of libel law must begin with an understanding of *New York Times* v. *Sullivan.*

New York Times v.
Sullivan, 376 U.S. 254,
84 S.Ct. 710,
11 L.Ed.2d 686 (1964).

The case was one of the by-products of the civil rights movement that swept the south in the late 1950s. The movement's target was a system of racial segregation, in effect since the Civil War, that forced African-Americans to live separated from other Americans. About 1955 this system came under challenge from those who sought the right to do such things as sit where they pleased in city buses or eat at lunch counters in downtown department stores. In 1960 separatists used violence against demonstrations by students at Alabama State College in Montgomery who were seeking to integrate such public facilities. In March of that year, an advertisement appeared in the *New York Times* appealing for financial support for the embattled students of Alabama State. The ad was signed by sixty-four persons, many of them prominent in public affairs, religion, trade unions, and the performing arts. Headed "Heed Their Rising Voices," the ad said in part:

> In Montgomery, Ala., after students sang "My Country, 'tis of Thee" on the State Capitol steps, their leaders were expelled from school, and truck loads of police armed with shotguns and tear gas ringed the Alabama State College campus. When the entire student body protested to state authorities by refusing to register, their dining hall was padlocked in an attempt to starve them into submission . . . .
>
> Again and again, the Southern violators have answered Dr. [Martin Luther] King's peaceful protests with intimidation and violence. They have bombed his home almost killing his wife and child. They have assaulted his person. They have arrested him seven times—

---

1. Coleman v. MacLennan, 98 P. 281 (Kans. 1908).

The man who started it all, L. B. Sullivan (center), then the police commissioner of Montgomery, Alabama, sits in court with his lawyers during his libel action against the *New York Times*. His victory there led to a reversal in the U.S. Supreme Court and a revolutionary decision immortalizing his name. *(UPI/Bettmann)*

for "speeding," "loitering," and similar "offenses." And now they have charged him with "perjury"—a *felony* under which they could imprison him for *ten years*.

Attorneys representing Police Commissioner L. B. Sullivan, one of three elected commissioners of the city of Montgomery, wrote the *Times* asserting that those two paragraphs libeled their client. In accordance with Alabama law, they asked for a retraction, a published admission from the *Times* that it had published untruths. The *Times* responded by asking the attorneys to point to specific libelous passages in the advertisement. Sullivan's response was to file a lawsuit in a Montgomery court.

At trial, Sullivan argued that the ad's general references to police pointed a finger at him because he supervised the police force. Therefore, he reasoned, the ad accused him of being responsible for padlocking the dining hall to starve the students into submission. And, since arrests ordinarily are made by police, it accused him of arresting Dr. King seven times, perhaps illegally, thus making Sullivan one of the "Southern violators." Further, he said, the ad made it look as though he had encouraged the violence directed at Dr. King and his family. Six witnesses testified that they had read the ad and concluded it was referring to Sullivan in a derogatory way.

Other witnesses testified that much of the detail in the offending paragraphs was false. The students had not sung "America"; they had sung "The Star-Spangled Banner." Only nine students were expelled, but not for leading the demonstration at the capitol. Only part of the student body had protested the expulsions, not by refusing to register, but by boycotting classes for a single day. The campus dining hall was not padlocked at any time. The only students who may have been refused service were those who did not have meal tickets, and there were few of them. Police were deployed near the campus in large numbers, but at no time did they ring the campus.

Nor were those the only errors. Dr. King had been arrested four times, not seven. Although he claimed he had been assaulted when he was arrested for loitering outside a courtroom, one of the officers involved denied at the libel trial that there had been an assault. Dr. King's house had indeed been bombed, but that had happened before Sullivan became police commissioner. No evidence ever implicated the police in the bombing. Three of Dr. King's four arrests also took place before Sullivan's election. Dr. King was indicted on two counts of perjury, for which the maximum term was five years, not ten, but he had been acquitted on both. Sullivan testified that he had nothing to do with either charge.

Clippings in the *Times*'s own files showed that some of the allegations made in the ad were false. The manager of the newspaper's advertising acceptability department testified that he had not checked the files because the ad had been prepared by a reputable agency. It had been accompanied by a letter from A. Philip Randolph, president of the Brotherhood of Sleeping Car Porters and a New York City resident, certifying that all the persons whose names appeared in the ad had given their permission. The manager said he knew and respected Randolph. He said he had approved the ad for publication because he knew nothing to cause him to believe it was false, and because it bore the endorsement of "a number of people who are well known and whose reputations [he] had no reason to question."

The jury found that Sullivan had been libeled and awarded him a judgment for $500,000. The Alabama Supreme Court affirmed. In light of the facts as presented in court, it had no other course. The decision was in accord with the common law. Sullivan and his witnesses had proved the only issue really in doubt—identification. Once identification was established, Sullivan stood accused of condoning, if not participating in, a series of felonies. Such accusations were libelous on their face. Nor did the *Times* have any defense. The proven errors undercut any attempt to establish truth. The common law's qualified privilege and fair comment were out of the question. By no stretch was the ad a fair and accurate report of facts found in official records, nor was such comment as it contained based on fact. The only question for the jury was to establish the degree of harm to Sullivan's reputation and, hence, the size of the award.

The outcome of the lawsuit in the state courts struck not only at the *Times*, but at other news media. The *Times* faced eleven other libel suits in Alabama courts in which plaintiffs were seeking more than $5 million. The Columbia Broadcasting System was defending five libel suits in southern states in which plaintiffs were asking for nearly $2 million. Most of these lawsuits were based on news coverage of the racial integration movement. Against that background the Supreme Court agreed to review the case and reversed unanimously.

Justice William J. Brennan, Jr., wrote the Court's opinion. He was joined by four others, thus giving him the majority required to establish the opinion as a precedent applicable to future cases. From the outset, he took the position that comment on the public conduct of public officials is protected by the First Amendment. His clear intent was to take the case out of the realm of Alabama's common and statute law, where the *Times* could not win, onto the higher ground of constitutional law, where, the decision would prove, it could. In the process, the Court made four fundamental changes in legal principles.

The Protection of Editorial Advertising

The first change in traditional law was made to counter Sullivan's contention that "Heed Their Rising Voices" was not protected by the First Amendment because it was a paid advertisement. In making this point, Sullivan's lawyers relied on the Supreme Court's 1942 opinion in *Valentine* v. *Chrestensen*.[2] In that case, in which the Court had held that the owner of a submarine had no right to distribute commercial advertising handbills on the streets of New York City, the majority held that advertising was not protected by the Constitution. In response to Sullivan's argument, Brennan wrote:

> The publication here . . . communicated information, expressed opinion, recited grievances, protested claimed abuses, and sought financial support on behalf of a movement whose existence and objectives are matters of the highest public concern. That the *Times* was paid for publishing the advertisement is as immaterial in this connection as the fact that newspapers and books are sold. Any other conclusion would discourage newspapers from carrying "editorial advertisements" of this type, and so might shut off an important outlet for the promulgation of information and ideas by persons who do not themselves have access to publishing facilities—who wish to exercise their freedom of speech even though they are not members of the press. The effect would be to shackle the First Amendment in its attempt to secure "the widest possible dissemination of information from diverse and antagonistic sources."[3] To avoid placing such a handicap upon the freedom of expression, we hold that if the allegedly libelous statements would otherwise be constitutionally protected from the present judgment, they do not forfeit that protection because they were published in the form of a paid advertisement.

With those words, the Court established its first new principle. Editorial advertising stands on higher constitutional ground than does ordinary commercial advertising. Editorial advertising gives people an opportunity to plead their cause in the media. It is concerned with ideas. In contrast, commercial advertising simply offers a product or a service at a price. By bringing editorial advertising under the protection of the First Amendment, the Court was raising a barrier against successful libel suits, thus encouraging publishers to accept such ads. Ten years later, the Court would extend limited First Amendment protection to commercial advertising, too.

The First Amendment and Libel Per Se

Sullivan's next argument went to the heart of the common law of libel, the concept of libel per se. Under Alabama law, a statement was libelous on its face if it imputed misconduct to a public official. If a jury found that the words at issue applied to the official, it was assumed that the words were false and that he had suffered harm to his reputation. The defendant could escape an award of damages only by proving that the allegedly defamatory allegations were harmless, were true in all respects, or were fair comment based on a solid bed of fact. If the defense tried and failed, the law further assumed that publication of a libel per se was a product of malice, in the sense of ill will. Thus, a jury could require the defendant to pay not only compensatory damages,

---

2. 316 U.S. 52, 62 S.Ct. 920, 86 L.Ed. 1262, 1 Med.L.Rptr. 1907 (1942).
3. Quoting the Court's 1945 decision in Associated Press v. United States, an antitrust case, 326 U.S. 1, 65 S.Ct. 1416, 89 L.Ed. 2013, 1 Med.L.Rptr. 2269 (1945).

a sum designed to make good the plaintiff's harm, but punitive damages, an additional sum levied as punishment.

The question thus became, Could the First Amendment be invoked to interrupt this march to a costly conclusion once a publication had been found to be libelous on its face? Sullivan's lawyers quoted from numerous decisions in which Supreme Court majorities had said that libel per se, like obscenity and other language devoid of idea content, was outside the scope of First Amendment protection. But, responded Brennan, none of those cases involved criticism of the public conduct of public officials:

> [W]e are compelled neither by precedent nor policy to give any more weight to the epithet "libel" than we have to other "mere labels" of state law. Like insurrection, contempt, advocacy of unlawful acts, breach of the peace, obscenity, solicitation of illegal business, and the other various formulae for the repression of expression that have been challenged in this court, libel can claim no talismanic immunity from constitutional limitations. It must be measured by standards that satisfy the First Amendment.
>
> The general proposition that freedom of expression upon public questions is secured by the First Amendment has long been settled by our decisions.

Brennan thus forged the second link in the progression required to reverse the Alabama courts. Even statements libelous on their face must be examined in the light of First Amendment guarantees if they arise out of the discussion of public issues. With this platform built, the Court proceeded to the heart of its decision:

> Thus we consider this case against the background of a profound national commitment to the principle that debate on public issues should be uninhibited, robust, and wide-open, and that it may well include vehement, caustic, and sometimes unpleasantly sharp attacks on government and public officials. The present advertisement, as an expression of grievance and protest on one of the major public issues of our time, would seem clearly to qualify for the constitutional protection.

The Partial Protection of False Statements

Having established that "Heed Their Rising Voices" was protected by the First Amendment, even though it had appeared as a paid advertisement and was libelous on its face, the Court had an even higher hurdle to jump. Beyond question, the ad contained false assertions of fact, and some of these were libelous. Does the First Amendment also protect falsehood?

Brennan examined the "public principle" cases and found that courts in a minority of the states had tolerated some error in the criticism of public officials. He concluded, quoting James Madison, who wrote much of the Constitution, that "some degree of abuse is inseparable from the proper use of everything; and in no instance is this more true than in that of the press." Brennan also noted that in some areas of law, the Supreme Court already had rejected the suggestion that the First Amendment protects only those statements that can be proved to be true. He added, again quoting Madison:

> [E]rroneous statement is inevitable in free debate, and . . . it must be protected if the freedoms of expression are to have the "breathing space" that they "need . . . to survive."

With those words, Brennan, writing for a majority of the Court, established a third legal principle, and a most significant one: The First Amendment excuses some falsehoods uttered in the heat of debate over the public conduct of public officials.

Brennan expanded on the reasons for the Court's new approach. The *Times* had already been ordered to pay a $500,000 judgment, which Brennan likened to a fine, and was facing other civil suits for comparable sums. Newspapers confronted with such prospects might well succumb to a "pall of fear and timidity" and mute their criticisms of public officials, Brennan said. In such an atmosphere, he noted, "First Amendment freedoms cannot survive." Nor can state libel laws be saved, Brennan added, by permitting publishers to win libel suits by proving the truth of their statements. He wrote:

> A rule compelling the critic of official conduct to guarantee the truth of all his factual assertions—and to do so on pain of libel judgments virtually unlimited in amount—leads to . . . "self-censorship." Allowance of the defense of truth, with the burden of proving it on the defendant, does not mean that only false speech will be deterred. Even courts accepting this defense as an adequate safeguard have recognized the difficulties in adducing legal proofs that the alleged libel was true in all its factual particulars . . . Under such a rule, would-be critics of official conduct may be deterred from voicing their criticism, even though it is believed to be true and even though it is in fact true, because of doubt whether it can be proved in court for fear of the expense of having to do so . . . The rule thus dampens the vigor and limits the variety of public debate. It is inconsistent with the First and Fourteenth Amendments.

The Plaintiff Must Prove Actual Malice

Brennan saved the Court's most explosive change for last:

> The constitutional guarantees require, we think, a federal rule that prohibits a public official from recovering damages for a defamatory falsehood relating to his official conduct unless he proves that the statement was made with "actual malice"—that is, with knowledge that it was false or with reckless disregard of whether it was false or not.

The term "actual malice" was not new in court decisions. But Brennan's definition of the term was new. The dictionary defines "malice" as embodying "evil intent or motive"—the desire to cause harm to another. As used in libel decisions, however, "actual malice" means precisely what the Supreme Court said it meant in *New York Times,* no more and no less. It means that the publisher of the libel acted either in the knowledge that the assertion was false or in reckless disregard of whether it was true or not.

Seldom has a single paragraph in a Supreme Court decision brought about such a revolutionary change in the law. With that paragraph, the Court shifted most of the burden of proof in libel suits brought by public officials against the news media. From this point on, public official plaintiffs in libel actions not only would have to prove publication, identification, and defamation, but they would have to prove that the publisher either knew the statements were false or had published them in reckless disregard of the truth. Further, Brennan wrote, for a majority of the Court, public official plaintiffs would have to prove actual malice with "convincing clarity." This would be a higher level of proof than the "preponderance of the evidence" test usually required in civil actions. Lawyers say the difference is between the need to prove 90 percent of the case and the need to prove only 51 percent, a wide gap indeed.

To avoid the expense of returning the case to an Alabama court for possible retrial under the new rules, the Court proceeded to hold that Sullivan could not prove that the *Times* acted with actual malice. At the most, Brennan wrote, Sullivan might be able to prove that the *Times*'s advertising department was negligent in not checking the assertions in the advertisement against clippings in the newspaper's own files. But, Brennan added, a mere failure to investigate is not reckless disregard. Such failure must be coupled with a showing that the publisher doubted the truth of the statement in question. In this instance, there was no doubt. The advertisement bore the signatures of respected persons of substance. There was no reason why anyone at the *Times* should doubt them.

The Supreme Court's decision in *New York Times* v. *Sullivan* sent lower courts everywhere a clear signal: Public officials should not be permitted to collect libel judgments from the news media except for a knowing or reckless lie. Further, the burden was on the public official plaintiff to prove knowledge of falsity or reckless disregard of truth on the part of the publisher.

It quickly became apparent that the Supreme Court's decision in *New York Times* raised significant questions:

—Sullivan was an elected public official with responsibility for overseeing a police department. The Court's decision was written with frequent reference to a "public official" and therefore seemed limited in its application. But who else on the public payroll might be classed as a public official?

—Some persons in public life have considerable influence, even though they hold no public office. Others seek influence by becoming candidates for election to public offices. Shouldn't such persons be subject to robust and uninhibited debate?

—The Court defined "actual malice" in terms that looked deceptively easy. It is the knowing lie or the assertion that is a product of a reckless disregard for the truth. But how might a public official prove either one with "convincing clarity"?

— Brennan had written that doubt on the part of the publisher is an element in reckless disregard, but how much doubt? And how can it be proved? Did the decision mean that libel plaintiffs could examine the editorial process? Could they pry into the state of mind of the reporter who had gathered the facts and written the story, and of the editors who had approved it?

There were also more subtle questions. Does the First Amendment protect discussion of persons or discussion of ideas? Could the same statement libel one person because he or she did not hold public office and not libel another because he or she did? If a public official plaintiff must prove actual malice, would he also have the burden of proving that the statement at issue was false? In view of the Court's robust commitment to freewheeling debate, even to the point of tolerating some degree of false-hood, were judges expected to dispose of more cases through summary judgment?

Cases seeking answers to some of these questions reached the Supreme Court during the decade after 1964. In its decision in three of the cases, the Court extended the scope of the *New York Times* rule, as the constitutional defense quickly came to be known. In *Rosenblatt* v. *Baer,*[4] the Court defined "public official" to include "those among the hierarchy of government employees who have, or appear to the public to have, substantial responsibility for or control over the conduct of government affairs." A public official, then, is not just anyone on a government payroll, but only those employees who make policy or who have considerable discretion as to how they carry out their duties. In *Curtis Publishing Co.* v. *Butts,*[5] the Court extended the application of the *New York Times* rule to "public figures." These it defined in part as persons who thrust themselves "into the 'vortex' of an important public controversy."

First Amendment Protection Further Defined

The *New York Times* decision was a product of a Supreme Court led by Chief Justice Earl Warren, who had been appointed by President Dwight D. Eisenhower in 1953 and presided for sixteen years during one of the most liberal eras in the history of the Supreme Court. Particularly during the 1960s, the Court greatly expanded the protections afforded by the Bill of Rights, including freedom of speech and press. The *Rosenblatt* and *Butts* decisions also were products of the Warren Court.

In 1969 Warren retired as chief justice, giving Richard M. Nixon, a Republican who had been elected president the previous year, an opportunity to make his first appointment to the Court. Nixon chose Warren E. Burger, then a judge of the United States Court of Appeals for the District of Columbia Circuit, to replace Warren. Burger was known to believe that the Warren Court had gone too far in applying federal constitutional law to cases that he thought best left to state courts for decision.[6] A year later, Burger was joined on the Court by the second Nixon appointee, Harry A. Blackmun, who had been a judge of the Court of Appeals for the Eighth Circuit in Minnesota. Blackmun replaced Abe Fortas, who had been appointed to the Court by President Lyndon B. Johnson, a Democrat. With Nixon's first two appointments, the Court began to move in a conservative direction.

During its 1970–1971 term, the Court accepted for review a libel case growing out of the arrest of a book and magazine distributor in Philadelphia on obscenity charges. In reporting the arrest, a Philadelphia radio station owned by Metromedia had referred to the distributor as a "smut peddler," even after the distributor had called the station and told its news staff that the magazines in

Rosenbloom v. *Metromedia, Inc.,* **403 U.S. 29, 91 S.Ct. 1811, 29 L.Ed.2d 296, 1 Med.L.Rptr. 1597 (1971).**

4. 383 U.S. 75, 86 S.Ct. 669, 15 L.Ed.2d 597, 1 Med.L.Rptr. 1558 (1966).
5. 388 U.S. 130, 87 S.Ct. 1975, 18 L.Ed.2d 1094, 1 Med.L.Rptr. 1568 (1967).
6. For an interesting description of the transition from the Warren to the Burger Court, see Bob Woodward and Scott Armstrong, *The Brethren, Inside the Supreme Court* (New York: Simon & Schuster, 1979).

question had been held not to be obscene by courts elsewhere. The epithet also was used to describe the distributor, Rosenbloom, after the charges against him had been dismissed. Rosenbloom sued the station for libel and won a six-figure judgment. The Supreme Court reversed, but was so badly divided that a majority could not agree on a rationale.

At issue was whether Rosenbloom should have to prove actual malice. He was not a public official, and the Court was in disagreement as to whether he was a public figure. Justice Brennan's view was decisive, although he could not get a majority of the Court to accept his position as he had in *New York Times*. Arguing that the purpose of the First Amendment is to protect the discussion of ideas and to protect the news media in the reporting of public affairs, he and three other justices concluded that Rosenbloom's status was immaterial. At the heart of the case was the bigger issue of obscenity and the attempt to control its distribution in the public interest. Rosenbloom was caught up in the attempt to resolve that issue. Therefore, he should be required to prove actual malice.

At that point, the Supreme Court had gone as far as it was going to go in extending First Amendment protection to libel defendants. Had Brennan been able to muster a majority behind his opinion, all libel plaintiffs suing the news media would have to prove actual malice. The *Rosenbloom* decision continues to be of importance because courts in a few states have adopted its rationale. Within three years, however, the Supreme Court was to accept another libel case and hold that states can permit private individuals to sue the news media for libel on a lesser showing of fault than actual malice.

In the same year that *Rosenbloom* was decided, Justices Hugo L. Black and John Marshall Harlan died. Black had taken the position that the First Amendment gives absolute protection to pure speech, including libel. Harlan, an Eisenhower appointee, was more conservative. After a long fight with the Senate, Nixon replaced them in 1972 with Lewis F. Powell, Jr., and William H. Rehnquist, both of whom at that time took the position that the Constitution should be construed in strict terms. Rehnquist, perhaps even more than Burger, has taken the position that many issues, including libel, should be resolved at the state level, without resort to federal constitutional law. Powell was to become more flexible on First Amendment issues.

Thus, there were four Nixon appointees on the Court when it decided its next significant libel case in 1974. The plaintiff was a Chicago lawyer, Elmer Gertz, who had been criticized severely by an article in *American Opinion*, the magazine of the politically conservative John Birch Society. Gertz drew the magazine's fire when he agreed to represent the parents of a youth who had been shot to death by a Chicago police officer. When police officials ruled that the shooting was unjustified, the parents sued their son's killer for damages. The magazine took the position that Gertz's role as the family's lawyer made him part of a plot to discredit the police. The writer referred to the lawyer as "Leninist Elmer Gertz" and "Communist-fronter Gertz." A photo caption referred to Gertz as a member of the "Red Guild," a reference to Gertz's earlier membership in the National Lawyers Guild. In addition to falsifying Gertz's political affiliation, the article said the police

Gertz v. *Robert Welch, Inc.,* 418 U.S. 323, 94 S.Ct. 2997, 41 L.Ed.2d 789, 1 Med.L.Rptr. 1633 (1974).

file on the lawyer was so voluminous that only "a big Irish cop" could lift it. Gertz had no police record.

When Gertz sued the magazine's publisher, Robert Welch, Inc., for libel, the district court judge who heard the case was somewhat confused as to the meaning of the *New York Times* rule. He had decided at the start of the trial that it did not apply. After the jury had returned a $50,000 judgment in Gertz's favor, he held otherwise on grounds that the article in *American Opinion* discussed an issue of public importance. The United States Court of Appeals for the Seventh Circuit affirmed the judge's ruling. Gertz, who had seen his $50,000 award wiped out, asked the Supreme Court to accept the case for review, which it did.

Justice Powell, writing for a five-member majority that included Blackmun and Rehnquist, specifically repudiated the plurality ruling in *Rosenbloom*. The Court held that the nature of the plaintiff is the crucial element in deciding whether the *New York Times* rule protects a media libel defendant. The majority's opinion in *Gertz* established precedents that both supplemented and limited *New York Times*.

LIBEL IS LIMITED TO FALSE AND DEFAMATORY ASSERTIONS OF FACT. Powell began by writing about the nature of defamation:

> We begin with the common ground. Under the First Amendment there is no such thing as a false idea. However pernicious an opinion may seem, we depend for its correction not on the conscience of judges and juries, but on the competition of other ideas. But there is no constitutional value in false statements of fact. Neither the intentional lie nor the careless error materially advances society's interest in "uninhibited, robust, and wide-open debate" on public issues. . . . They belong to that category of utterances which "are no essential part of any exposition of ideas, and are of such slight social value as a step to truth that any benefit that may be derived from them is clearly outweighed by the social interest in order and morality."[7]

In the second and third sentences of this paragraph, Powell seemed to be saying that statements of opinion are not actionable as libel. Defamatory statements, he seemed to say, are actionable only if they make a false assertion of fact. Because Gertz's lawsuit was based on demonstrably false assertions of fact, Powell's references to opinion were *dicta,* extraneous comments not essential to resolving the case. However, many lower courts subsequently looked to Powell's language for guidance, holding that the First Amendment protects the expressions of opinion, a term sometimes construed very broadly. In 1990, the Supreme Court affirmed in *Milkovich* v. *Lorain Journal Co.*[8] that statements "of opinion relating to matters of public concern," which do not contain "a provably false factual connotation, will receive full constitutional protection." However, it also said that an opinion conveying a false and defamatory assertion of fact, such as an accusation of crime, or implying such an assertion, is actionable.

STATES MAY ESTABLISH A LOWER STANDARD OF FAULT FOR PRIVATE INDIVIDUALS WHO SUE THE NEWS MEDIA FOR LIBEL. Powell next reviewed the Court's decision in *New*

---

7. Quoting Chaplinsky v. New Hampshire, 315 U.S. 568, 62 S.Ct. 766, 86 L.Ed. 1031 (1942), in which the Court held that "fighting words," in that instance insulting epithets, are devoid of idea content and hence are not protected by the First Amendment.
8. 497 U.S. 1, 110 S.Ct. 2695, 111 L.Ed.2d 1, 17 Med.L.Rptr. 2009 (1990).

York Times, focusing on the protection it gives to falsehoods uttered in the heat of debate. To retreat from that holding, he said, would run the risk of restricting debate through "intolerable self-censorship." Some error must be protected, Powell added, "to protect speech that matters."

However, Powell noted for the majority, freedom of speech and press do not stand alone. Other interests also must be protected. For instance, the justice wrote, states have a legitimate interest in providing "compensation of individuals for harm inflicted on them by defamatory falsehoods." Therefore, the Supreme Court would not foreclose the right of any state to protect an individual's reputation. Here Powell was addressing an issue raised by the case and no longer was writing dicta.

Without directly saying so, Powell was responding to critics who argued that the Supreme Court in *New York Times* had tried to bring all libel law within the scope of the First Amendment, thus overriding principles long established by state statutes and common law. Powell's words signaled the Court's intention to pull back from that extreme. At the same time, Powell emphasized that the Court did not intend to weaken the actual malice rule as it applies to public persons. "Those who, by reason of the notoriety of their achievements or the vigor and success with which they seek the public's attention, are properly classed as public figures" and government officials must offer "clear and convincing proof" of actual malice if they are to recover damages in a libel action. That requirement, the majority said, serves as "an extremely powerful antidote" for the tendency toward self-censorship induced by the common law. But, he added, the Court had concluded that states should have the right to apply a less stringent rule to private individuals who might be defamed by the media.

The majority offered a simple justification for its conclusion. Public officials and public figures are newsworthy. If they are subjected to criticism, they can fight back in print and on the air. Private individuals are less likely to reach the public with their views, even when they have been the subject of a defamatory story. Therefore, the Court concluded, they are "more vulnerable to injury, and the state interest in protecting them is correspondingly greater." On the other hand, persons who hold public office, or who try to influence public affairs, should do so in full knowledge of the likely consequences. They run "the risk of closer public scrutiny than might otherwise be the case."

PUBLIC FIGURES ARE DEFINED AND CATEGORIZED. If states were to be permitted to make it easier for some people to win libel suits, what criteria should be used to differentiate public figures from private individuals? Powell began the Court's answer to that question by dividing public figures into three categories—involuntary, all-purpose, and limited:

> Hypothetically, it may be possible for someone to become a public figure through no purposeful action of his own, but the instances of truly involuntary public figures must be exceedingly rare. For the most part those who attain this status have assumed roles of especial prominence in the affairs of society. Some occupy positions of such persuasive power and influence that they are deemed public figures for all purposes. More commonly, those classed as public figures have thrust themselves to the forefront of particular public controversies in order to influence the resolution of the issues involved. In either event, they invite attention and comment.

Even if the foregoing generalities do not obtain in every instance, the communications media are entitled to act on the assumption that public officials and public figures have voluntarily exposed themselves to increased risk of defamatory falsehoods concerning them. No such assumption is justified with respect to a private individual. He has not accepted a public office or assumed "an influential role in ordering society." He has relinquished no part of his interest in the protection of his own good name, and consequently he has a more compelling call on the courts for redress of injury inflicted by defamatory falsehood. Thus, private individuals are not only more vulnerable to injury than public officials and public figures; they are more deserving of recovery.

For these reasons we conclude that the States should retain substantial latitude in their efforts to enforce a legal remedy for defamatory falsehood injurious to the reputation of a private individual.

PRIVATE INDIVIDUALS MUST PROVE SOME DEGREE OF FAULT ON THE PART OF THE MEDIA. The phrase "substantial latitude" was used for a purpose. The Supreme Court was willing to let the states apply their own rules to libel suits directed at media by private individuals, but it was not willing to let them revert to the rules of common law in their entirety. There are limits, which Justice Powell defined:

> We hold that, so long as they do not impose liability without fault, the States may define for themselves the appropriate standard of liability for a publisher or a broadcaster of defamatory falsehood injurious to a private individual. This approach provides a more equitable boundary between the competing concerns involved here. It recognizes the strength of the legitimate state interest in compensating private individuals for wrongful injury to reputation, yet shields the press and broadcast media from the rigors of strict liability for defamation. At least this conclusion obtains where, as here, the substance of the defamatory statement "makes substantial danger to reputation apparent."

Although Powell did not define what he meant by "liability without fault," Chief Justice Burger, writing in dissent, did. Burger said that the majority had established a "new negligence standard," as indeed it had. In most states that have chosen the option offered by *Gertz,* private individuals who sue the news media for libel need show only that reporters or editors have fallen short of a recognized standard of care. State courts have varied in defining that standard. Some have applied the well-established principles of ordinary negligence, in which persons are at fault if they have failed to do what a "prudent person" would have done under the circumstances. What such a person would do is a matter for a jury to determine after listening to witnesses for both sides. Other courts have held that the performance of journalists should be measured against the standard of care that would be applied by trained reporters and editors caught up in similar circumstances. Again, the determination is one to be made by the jury after listening to witnesses deemed to have knowledge of professional practices.[9] In either event, *Gertz* has given courts the duty of doing what journalists themselves have not done in a systematic fashion: establishing professional standards for performance.

---

9. John B. McCrory, Robert C. Bernius, Robb M. Jones, and J. Gregory Bishop, "Constitutional Privilege in Libel Law." In *Communications Law 1987,* vol. 2 (New York: Practising Law Institute, 1987), pp. 787–792.

A few courts, noting Justice Powell's final line of the quotation above, "[a]t least this conclusion obtains where, as here, the substance of the defamatory statement 'makes substantial danger to reputation apparent,' " have since followed one implication of that dictum by holding that a negligence standard for private figures is allowable only when the libel is apparent on its face—that is, when the libel is libel per se. Under this approach, if a statement involving a matter of public concern is libelous *per quod,* even private plaintiffs would have to prove actual malice.[10] Whether most courts would follow this approach today is not clear. What is clear is that states have a great deal of latitude in establishing the level of fault that a private figure in a libel case must prove to win, beginning with negligence and rising to actual malice.

PRIVATE INDIVIDUALS ALSO MUST SHOW THEY HAVE BEEN HARMED UNLESS THEY CAN PROVE ACTUAL MALICE.   The Court moved next to the question of damages. If states were permitted to apply their common law standards in libel suits brought by private individuals, the sky might be the limit. At common law, courts assumed that victims of libel had been harmed. Powell noted that this assumption gave juries "largely uncontrolled discretion" to "award substantial sums as compensation for supposed damages to reputation without any proof that such harm actually occurred." If states were to revert to that standard, they would invite "juries to punish unpopular opinion rather than to compensate individuals for injury." The prospect of such awards might "inhibit the vigorous exercise of First Amendment freedoms by inviting self-censorship." To prevent this situation, Powell wrote for the Court, states could go no further in awarding damages "than compensation for actual injury. . . . [W]e hold that States may not permit recovery of presumed or punitive damages, at least when liability is not based on a showing of falsity or reckless disregard of the truth."

The Court turned next to a strong criticism of awards of punitive damages in libel suits but stopped short of outlawing them. The majority said:

> We find no justification for allowing awards of punitive damages against publishers and broadcasters held liable under state-defined standards of liability for defamation. In most jurisdictions jury discretion over the amounts awarded is limited only by the gentle rule that they not be excessive. Consequently, juries assess punitive damages in wholly unpredictable amounts bearing no necessary relation to the actual harm caused. And they remain free to use their discretion selectively to punish expressions of unpopular views. Like the doctrine of presumed damages, jury discretion to award punitive damages unnecessarily exacerbates the danger of media self-censorship, but unlike the former rule, punitive damages are wholly irrelevant to the state interest that justifies a negligence standard for private defamation actions. They are not compensation for injury. Instead, they are private fines levied by civil juries to punish reprehensible conduct and to deter future occurrence. In short, the private defamation plaintiff who establishes liability under a less demanding standard than that stated in *New York Times* may recover only such damages as are sufficient to compensate him for actual injury.

With that part of its decision, the majority seemed to be trying to bring awards of damages in libel cases under control. Recovery by private individuals would be lim-

---

10. Sobel v. Miami Daily News, 5 Med.L.Rptr. 2462 (Fla.Cir. 1980); affirmed, 395 So.2d 282 (Fla.App. 1981). Cox v. Hatch, 761 P.2d 556 (Utah 1988). Smith v. Dameron, 14 Med.L.Rptr. 1879 (Va.Cir.Ct. 1987).

ited to compensation for actual injury, unless they could prove actual malice. Public officials and public figures could recover damages only if they could prove actual malice. However, the Court could not define harm in such a way as to reduce it to a tangible measurement. Juries were left with considerable discretion. What, for instance, is the dollar value of "impairment of reputation and standing in the community"? Or of "personal humiliation, and mental anguish and suffering"? How does one prove the latter? Subsequent cases have demonstrated that some juries are willing to put six- and seven-figure values on such intangibles, despite Powell's condemnation of "private fines levied by civil juries."

The remainder of the decision was devoted to the Court's finding that Gertz was not a public figure, although he had some minimal participation in public affairs in Chicago. In essence the Court concluded that Gertz had attracted *American Opinion*'s libelous lightning not because he was trying to influence public opinion against police in general, but because he had been hired to file suit against one police officer. He was simply a lawyer doing his job. That did not make him even a limited-purpose public figure.

The case was sent back to the federal district court in Chicago. There, seven years later, the case again reached trial. In the meantime, Gertz had achieved a sort of fame as the lawyer whose lawsuit had changed the law of libel. He conceded that the case "may have made me a public figure."[11] Nevertheless, the trial was conducted on the ground that he was a private individual, as the Supreme Court had held him to be at the time the libel was published in 1969. A jury found that *American Opinion* not only had been negligent in publishing the article, but had acted with actual malice. The jurors concluded that Gertz had suffered $100,000 in actual harm. They assessed an additional $300,000 in punitive damages against Robert Welch, Inc. An appeals court affirmed the award.[12]

As a consequence of cases like *New York Times* and *Gertz,* the Court effectively expanded the elements in a plaintiff's case-in-chief beyond proving publication, identification, and defamation, to proving fault, falsity, and actual injury as well.

The Elements of Libel Enlarged

Publication and Identification

In addition to establishing jurisdiction and timeliness, a plaintiff in a libel case must assert and eventually offer evidence of publication, identification, and defamation. That requirement was true under common law and remains true in cases brought under the First Amendment. Publication usually is proved by offering a copy of the offending article or photograph, or a transcript of the broadcast. Identification is not an issue if the individual is named in the submitted material, provided that the allegedly defamatory portions are directed at the plaintiff. If the identification is not direct, there must be evidence, as in *New York Times,* that others understood the defamatory language to be directed at the plaintiff.

---

11. "Landmark Libel Case Being Quietly Retried," *Chicago Law Bulletin,* 17 April 1981.
12. Gertz v. Robert Welch, Inc., 680 F.2d 527, 8 Med.L.Rptr. 1769 (7th Cir. 1982).

Defamation

The *New York Times* rule has had little effect on proof of publication and identification, but it has made significant changes in the third essential requirement, proof of defamation. At common law, courts showed great respect for a plaintiff's assertion that he or she had been defamed by the media, or by anyone else. Courts assumed that the allegedly defamatory assertions were false and that the plaintiff had been harmed by them. The plaintiff was not required to show that the defendant was at fault in publishing the harmful facts, only that the defendant had done so. All of that changed dramatically with the Supreme Court's holding in *New York Times* and cases that followed it.

The new rule requires plaintiffs involved in libel disputes that touch on public concerns to prove that it was the defendant's fault that they were defamed by false and harmful statements. In effect, the courts expanded the common law element of defamation into three new ones: fault, falsity, and actual injury.

Fault

In *New York Times,* the Court held that comment on the public actions of public officials is protected by the First Amendment's speech and press clause, even when it is clearly defamatory. The Court ruled that such officials cannot win a libel case unless they can prove either knowledge of falsity or reckless disregard for the truth, and they must offer clear and convincing evidence of one or the other. Within a few years, the Court brought all public figures within the scope of the rule.[13] Not long after, with *Gertz,* the Court moved to require private figures to prove some kind of fault on the part of the defendant. State law could decide the level of fault, but some showing of fault—even if only negligence—had to be made. Because most states have chosen negligence as the standard of fault that private figures must prove, a major point of contention in libel cases often is the status of the plaintiff. It is to the advantage of media defendants if the court determines a plaintiff to be a public figure; it is to their disadvantage if the court determines the plaintiff to be a private figure.

Actual Injury

To be actionable the assertions at issue must be both false and actually defamatory. Justice Powell wrote in *Gertz* that the Court need not attempt to define "actual injury," but then he seemed to do just that. Such injury, he said, "is not limited to out-of-pocket loss," but includes "impairment of reputation and standing in the community, personal humiliation, and mental anguish and suffering." In assessing the value of such intangibles, "juries must be limited by appropriate instructions, and all awards must be supported by competent evidence" of injury, "although there need be no evidence which assigns an actual dollar value to the injury."

---

13.   Curtis Publishing Co. v. Butts, 388 U.S. 130, 87 S.Ct. 1975, 18 L.Ed.2d 1094, 1 Med.L.Rptr. 1568 (1967).

The court expects the plaintiff to show, at least, that there is personal humiliation and suffering caused by an actual impairment of reputation and standing in the community. Thus, there would be no grounds for action if a magazine erroneously reported that a reporter had won a Pulitzer Prize. The reporter might be embarrassed, but there is nothing defamatory about winning the most prestigious prize in journalism. There might not be grounds for action if a newspaper falsely reported that a prostitute overcharged her customers. She might be angry, but she might find it difficult to show an actual impairment of standing in the community. On the other hand, there likely would be grounds for action if a proud physician could demonstrate to a court that some of her patients thought less of her after a broadcaster falsely reported that she overcharged Medicare patients.

Falsity

After *New York Times,* lower-court judges recognized the obvious: Plaintiffs could not prove that defendants knew that statements were false without first proving falsity. The Supreme Court affirmed and extended that burden on the plaintiff to prove falsity by holding, in *Philadelphia Newspapers* v. *Hepps,*[14] that even private individuals who sue in connection with a matter of public concern must prove falsity. The majority said that to hold otherwise would have "a chilling effect . . . antithetical to the First Amendment's protection of true speech on matters of public concern."

As a consequence, anyone involved in a matter of public concern who sues the mass media for libel must now offer evidence of falsity to have a case. How much evidence? According to at least two federal appellate courts, it may be somewhat easier to prove falsity than to prove fault. Although the standard of proof for fault is that the evidence has to be clear and convincing, the U.S. Court of Appeals for the Ninth Circuit and the Court of Appeals for the Second Circuit have held that falsity need only be proved by a "preponderance of the evidence," meaning that there need be only more evidence than not that the statements were false.[15]

On the other hand, if the evidence indicates that the statements are truthful, they are not actionable, no matter how harmful they may be, nor how questionable the defendant's motives for using them. The Supreme Court held in *Garrison* v. *Louisiana,*[16] that truth "may not be the subject of either civil or criminal sanctions where the discussion of public affairs is concerned."

Thus, for a plaintiff to win a libel suit in a case that impinges on the First Amendment, the courts require proof that the allegedly libelous statements were published and the plaintiff identified and defamed, that the statements were false, that the statements actually caused injury, and that the defendant was at fault. Two of these elements, fault and actual injury, can especially determine the character and the outcome of a libel suit, so they deserve a closer look, beginning with fault.

---

14. 475 U.S. 767, 106 S.Ct. 1558, 89 L.Ed.2d 783, 12 Med.L.Rptr. 1977 (1986).
15. Rattray v. City of National City, 23 Med.L.Rptr. 1779 (9th Cir. 1995), cert. filed, City of National City v. Rattray, U.S. No. 94-2062; Goldwater v. Ginsburg, 414 F.2d 324, 1 Med.L.Rptr. 1737 (2d Cir. 1969).
16. 379 U.S. 64, 85 S.Ct. 209, 12 L.Ed.2d 1042, 1 Med.L.Rptr. 1548 (1964).

FAULT: THE STATUS OF LIBEL PLAINTIFFS ———

As already noted, it is to the media's advantage if a plaintiff is determined by the court to be a public figure. In such a case, the plaintiff has to prove by clear and convincing evidence that the defendant knew that the harmful statements were false or published them with reckless disregard for the truth. On the other hand, if the plaintiff is a private figure, in most states he or she must prove merely that the harmful statements were published negligently.[17]

Thus, in most libel suits, a judge's decision as to the status of the plaintiff can be a factor in who wins or loses. If the plaintiff is a mayor, a member of a legislative body, or a candidate for such offices, the question of status can be answered fairly easily. But if the plaintiff is a welfare department case worker, a teacher, a lawyer, or a party to a legal proceeding, status is more difficult to determine. Such status is especially difficult to define when the plaintiff also is newsworthy. The Supreme Court has offered lower courts guidance in making such determinations. The principles derived from these decisions are summarized in the sections that follow.

Public Officials ————————————————

There is no doubt that L. B. Sullivan, whose libel suit resulted in the *New York Times* rule, was a public official. He held an elective office, and as supervisor of the police department in Montgomery, Alabama, made public policy and had considerable discretion in how he carried out his duties. Therefore, what he did and how he did it had an impact on many persons and were proper subjects for public debate.

Only a minority of public officials are elected. Many are appointed to office; others are simply hired to do a job. Thus, not surprisingly, within two years after it had decided *New York Times* v. *Sullivan,* the Supreme Court sought, in *Rosenblatt* v. *Baer,* to define public officials. Baer had been manager of a county-owned ski slope in Laconia, New Hampshire. He was caught in a political dispute and had to resign. During the following ski season, Rosenblatt wrote a column for the local newspaper commenting on how much more profitable the ski slope was under the new manager. Arguing that the column implied that he had been skimming funds from the slope's till, Baer sued Rosenblatt for libel, winning a $31,500 judgment in the state courts. The Supreme Court took the case and reversed, holding that Baer was a public official who would have to prove actual malice, which he could not do. The Court's decision said:

Rosenblatt v. *Baer,* 383 U.S. 75, 86 S.Ct. 669, 15 L.Ed.2d 597, 1 Med.L.Rptr. 1558 (1966).

---

17. In a few states, notably Alaska, Colorado, Indiana, and New Jersey, courts have held that private individuals always must prove actual malice if they have been defamed during the discussion of a public issue. Gay v. Williams, 486 F.Supp. 12 (D.Alaska 1979). Diversified Management v. Denver Post, 653 P.2d 1103, 8 Med.L.Rptr. 2505 (Colo. 1982). Aafco Heating & Air Conditioning Co. v. Northwest Publications, 321 N.E.2d 580, 1 Med.L.Rptr. 1683 (Ind.App. 1974). Sisler v. Gannett Co., Inc., 104 N.J. 506, 516 A.2d 1083, 13 Med.L.Rptr. 1577 (N.J. 1986).

We remarked in *New York Times* that we had no occasion "to determine how far down into the lower ranks of government employees the 'public official' designation would extend for purposes of this rule, or otherwise specify categories of persons who would or would not be included." . . . No precise lines need to be drawn for this case. The motivating force for the decision in *New York Times* was twofold . . . There is, first, a strong interest in debate on public issues, and, second, a strong interest in debate about those persons who are in a position significantly to influence resolution of those issues. . . . It is clear, therefore, that the "public official" designation applies at the very least to those among the hierarchy of government employees who have, or appear to the public to have, substantial responsibility for or control over the conduct of government affairs.

In this instance, Baer's testimony at the trial helped the Court classify him as a public official. He said that the public had regarded him as responsible for the success or failure of the ski slope's operation. Thus, he had had both "responsibility for" and "control over" a function of government that was important in a snow state like New Hampshire.

As a consequence of the Supreme Court's decision in *Rosenblatt,* courts seek answers to two questions in deciding whether a libel plaintiff is a public official:

1. Does he or she have policy-making authority?

2. Does he or she ordinarily have access to the news media?

If the answer to both questions is yes, the person is a public official. Courts have held the following to be public officials:

—A physician who was under contract at $125,000 a year to provide medical services to prisoners in Alaska state correctional facilities.[18] The Alaska Supreme Court quoted *Rosenblatt* in holding that the public had an interest in how he performed his duties.

—The building inspector in Ocean Beach, New York.[19] Building permits were issued or denied on the basis of his recommendations.

—A territorial detective in the Virgin Islands.[20] Courts, with a few exceptions, have held that any law enforcement officer who has authority to make arrests is a public official.[21] Police officers have broad discretion in deciding whether to take persons into custody. If they decide to make an arrest, the consequences are severe, resulting in at least temporary loss of freedom for the subject of the arrest.

—The executive director of the State Human Relations Commission in Georgia.[22] Although he was appointed, not elected, he exercised broad discretion in carrying out his duties.

---

18. Green v. Northern Publishing Co., 655 P.2d 736, 8 Med.L.Rptr. 2515 (Alaska 1982).
19. Dattner v. Pokoik, 437 N.Y.S.2d 425, 7 Med.L.Rptr. 1636 (N.Y.App. 1981).
20. Zurita v. Virgin Islands Daily News, 578 F.Supp. 306 (D.V.I. 1984).
21. See Costello v. Ocean City Observer, 136 N.J. 594, 643 A.2d 1012, 22 Med.L.Rptr. 2129 (1994); Soke v. Plain Dealer, 69 Ohio St.3d 396, 632 N.E.2d 1282, 22 Med.L.Rptr. 1910 (1994).
22. Walker v. Southeastern Newspapers, 9 Med.L.Rptr. 1516 (Ga. 1982).

—The director of financial aid at Weber State College in Utah.[23] As the official responsible for administering $2 million a year in student aid, he invited public scrutiny, especially because most of the money came from public funds.

Several decisions serve as a reminder that not everyone on the public payroll qualifies as a public official for purposes of a libel suit. Courts in California and New York have held, for instance, that public school teachers do not become public officials by carrying out the duties assigned to them in the classroom.[24] The courts ruled that because teachers are expected to conform to policies set by school boards and administrators, they are employees.

The U.S. Court of Appeals for the Fourth Circuit ruled that an archaeological firm hired as a consultant to a county government was not a public official.[25] The court said that the firm was a "fact-finder . . . [with] no control over governmental affairs. It made no recommendations, participated in no policy determinations, and exercised no discretion."

The passage of time does not alter an individual's status as a public official if the alleged defamation relates to his or her activity when in office. The U.S. Court of Appeals for the Fifth Circuit said that it could see "no persuasive reason why [plaintiffs'] departure from their public positions should exempt them from meeting the *New York Times* standard when they sue for a news story on that departure."[26]

Public officials, then, may be elected or appointed, but they must be able to exercise discretion. They must be able to make public policy or make decisions that have an effect on others. They must be involved in duties in which some segment of the public has an interest and over which they have some discretionary control. Thus, persons on a public payroll who do no more than perform a job under the direction of a superior are not public officials for the purpose of a libel suit.

Public Figures

In its decision in *Gertz,* the Supreme Court recognized a class of persons known as public figures and held that they, like public officials, must prove actual malice if they sue the news media for libel. Such persons, the Court said, invite public attention and, because they are newsworthy, have ready access to the news media to respond to their critics. The Court defined three kinds of public figures:

1. All-purpose public figures. Such persons "have assumed roles of especial prominence in the affairs of society." They have "persuasive power and influence."

23.   VanDyke v. KUTV, 663 P.2d 52, 9 Med.L.Rptr. 1546 (Utah 1983).
24.   Franklin v. Lodge 1108, 97 Cal.App.3d 915, 5 Med.L.Rptr. 1977 (1979); DeLuca v. New York News, 109 Misc.2d 341, 4 Med.L.Rptr. 2313 (N.Y.Sup. 1981).
25.   Arctic Co. v. Loudoun Times Mirror Co., 624 F.2d 518 (4th Cir. 1980).
26.   Zerangue v. TSP Newspapers, 814 F.2d 1066, 13 Med.L.Rptr. 2438 (5th Cir. 1987). See also Gray v. Udevitz, 656 F.2d 588, 7 Med.L.Rptr. 1872 (10th Cir. 1981); Hart v. Playboy Enterprises, 5 Med.L.Rptr. 1811 (D.Kan. 1979); and Stripling v. Literary Guild of America, 5 Med.L.Rptr. 1958 (W.D.Tex. 1979).

2. Limited, or "vortex," public figures. These are persons who "have thrust themselves to the forefront of particular public controversies in order to influence the resolution of the issues involved."

3. Involuntary public figures. These are persons who do nothing to attract attention or influence public policy, yet find themselves in the middle of a controversy over a public issue.

The Court was trying to define more precisely a category that had emerged casually seven years earlier in its decision in *Curtis Publishing Co.* v. *Butts.*[27] In that decision, the Court had held that Edwin Walker, a retired army general who was active in trying to prevent blacks from entering southern universities, and Wally Butts, athletic director at the University of Georgia, were public figures. Therefore, they, like public officials, would have to prove actual malice if they were to prevail in a libel suit. The Court's decision offered few specific guidelines to judges seeking help in deciding whether a plaintiff was a public figure. Such guidelines are what the Court tried to provide in *Gertz.* However, several times since, the Court has seen fit to refine the guidelines further.

All-Purpose Public Figures

All-purpose public figures have continuing news value, or they exercise "persuasive power and influence" in matters of public concern. They are celebrities whose names are recognized by the general public. The public follows their ideas and actions with great interest. Because such public figures have so much influence, courts have held that the media have considerable leeway in commenting on their activities. Chief Judge Edward Allen Tamm of the U.S. Circuit Court of Appeals for the District of Columbia explained the rationale for that leeway:

The media serve as a check on the power of the famous and that check must be strongest when the subject's influence is strongest. Fame often brings power, money, respect, adulation, and self-gratification. It also may bring close scrutiny that can lead to adverse as well as favorable comment. When someone steps into the public spotlight, or when he remains there once cast into it, he must take the bad with the good.[28]

Courts have held that Johnny Carson, for many years host of the *Tonight* show on NBC television, is an all-purpose public figure.[29] So is William F. Buckley, Jr., the nationally syndicated conservative columnist and novelist.[30] Some institutions have been held to be all-purpose public figures, among them the Church of Scientology,[31] which has five million members; the Reliance Insurance Co.,[32] a billion-dollar corporation;

---

27. 388 U.S. 130, 87 S.Ct. 1975, 18 L.Ed.2d 1094, 1 Med.L.Rptr. 1568 (1967).
28. Waldbaum v. Fairchild Publications, Inc., 627 F.2d 1287, 5 Med.L.Rptr. 2629 (D.C.Cir. 1980).
29. Carson v. Allied News Co., 529 F.2d 206 (7th Cir. 1976).
30. Buckley v. Littell, 539 F.2d 882, 1 Med.L.Rptr. 1762 (2d Cir. 1976).
31. Church of Scientology v. Siegelman, 475 F.Supp. 950, 5 Med.L.Rptr. 2021 (S.D.N.Y. 1979).
32. Reliance Insurance Co. v. Barron's, 442 F.Supp. 1341, 3 Med.L.Rptr. 1033 (S.D.N.Y. 1977).

and Ithaca College,[33] a private liberal arts college that a New York court found to be pervasively involved in public affairs as an educational institution.

Several courts have held that individuals can be all-purpose public figures with respect to a limited geographic area. Kansas courts held that an attorney who had practiced in the same community for thirty-two years, during which time he had taken an active role in resolving many public issues, had become an all-purpose public figure.[34] New York courts came to the same conclusion about an individual who, for ten years, had injected himself into the attempt to resolve public controversies in his community.[35] Montana courts held that a former state chairman of the Republican party, who had written books on stocks and commodities and who had been the subject of articles in several business magazines, was an all-purpose public figure within that state.[36]

Notoriety also can define an all-purpose public figure, as a federal court demonstrated by holding that James Earl Ray, the convicted assassin of the Reverend Martin Luther King, Jr., has that status.[37]

A common theme runs through these cases. All-purpose public figures have achieved what the U.S. Circuit Court of Appeals for the District of Columbia called "celebrity in society," adding that well-known athletes and entertainers are the archetypes.[38] But that is not the end of it. To become all-purpose public figures, individuals must seek and win widespread public attention. They must achieve influence such that when they talk, people listen. They have the power to shape events. They are dominant figures, whether it be on the national stage or on the more limited platforms of their states or communities. Whatever the forum, they are quoted in the print media and appear on television. As the District of Columbia circuit court noted, not many achieve such status, but those who do must be prepared to accept criticism as well as adulation. In our society, that is the lot of those who "have knowingly relinquished their anonymity in return for fame, fortune, or influence."

Limited, or "Vortex," Public Figures

Limited public figures become so through their voluntary involvement in attempts to resolve specific public controversies. Courts, including the Supreme Court, have made the point that persons can be newsworthy without becoming public figures. Courts have said that the news media cannot create public figures simply by stirring up a controversy and drawing people into it by seeking them out and quoting them. The controversy must arise from events, and only the persons who enter a public dispute voluntarily for the purpose of resolving it to their liking are likely to be considered limited public figures if they become libel plaintiffs.

"Limited" must be understood in two ways. Usually, a limited public figure is involved only in a particular controversy. Further, media comment on the individuals

---

33. Ithaca College v. Yale Daily News Publishing Co., 105 Misc.2d 793, 6 Med.L.Rptr. 2180 (N.Y.Sup.Ct., Tompkins County, 1980).
34. Steere v. Cupp, 602 P.2d 1267, 5 Med.L.Rptr. 2046 (Kan. 1979).
35. Clements v. Gannett Co., 5 Med.L.Rptr. 1657 (N.Y.Sup.Ct., Monroe County, 1979).
36. Williams v. Pasma, 656 P.2d 212, 9 Med.L.Rptr. 1004 (Mont. 1982).
37. Ray v. Time, Inc., 452 F.Supp. 618 (W.D.Tenn. 1978).
38. Tavoulareas v. Piro, 817 F.2d 762, 13 Med.L.Rptr. 2377 (D.C.Cir. 1987).

Mobil Oil Co. President William P. Tavoulareas sued the *Washington Post* for a story that said the father had set up his son in business and then steered Mobil's tanker leases to him. The story suggested William Tavoulareas had deceived Mobil's board of directors about his ties to his son's business. A critical issue in the case was whether Tavoulareas was a public figure required to prove actual malice. *(AP/Wide World)*

involved in the controversy must be limited to the role of those individuals in that controversy if the actual malice rule is to be applied in a libel action. So, in most states, in any libel suit brought by people other than public officials or celebrities, a crucial question is, Are the plaintiffs limited public figures? In two cases out of three, the answer to that question is yes, according to one survey.[39]

In determining whether a plaintiff is a limited public figure, courts look for guidance to *Gertz* and other Supreme Court opinions. The District of Columbia circuit court's decision in *Waldbaum* v. *Fairchild Publications* also has proved to be influential.[40] There, the court found that Waldbaum, who had been discharged as president of the second largest consumer grocery cooperative in the country, was a public figure because he was deeply involved in promoting cooperatives as competitors to privately owned supermarkets and was looked to as a leader in the field.

Three principles have emerged from these cases. When there is doubt as to whether a plaintiff is a limited public figure, courts start by (1) identifying the controversy at issue. They proceed by (2) examining the plaintiff's role in the controversy. The final step is (3) determining if the alleged defamation grew out of the plaintiff's participation in the controversy.

An opinion written by Kenneth W. Starr when he was a judge on the District of Columbia circuit illustrates how those principles are applied.[41] William P. Tavoulareas, at the time president and chief operating officer of Mobil Corporation, and his son Peter, who in his twenties had become a partner in a London-based shipping firm that leased

39. Randall P. Bezanson, Gilbert Cranberg, and John Soloski, "Libel Law and the Press: Setting the Record Straight," 71 *Iowa L.Rev.* 217, October 1985. The authors analyzed 497 libel cases against media defendants.
40. Waldbaum v. Fairchild Publications, Inc., 627 F.2d 1287, 5 Med.L.Rptr. 2629 (D.C.Cir. 1980).
41. Tavoulareas v. Piro, 817 F.2d 762, 13 Med.L.Rptr. 2377 (D.C.Cir. 1987).

oil tankers to Mobil, sued the *Washington Post* and others for libel. At issue was a story in the *Post* that said the father had set up his son in business and then had steered Mobil's tanker leases to him. The story portrayed William Tavoulareas as a dominant figure who had deceived Mobil's board of directors as to his links with his son's business. Testimony offered at the trial indicated no such deceit. A jury awarded William Tavoulareas $250,000 in compensatory damages and $1.8 million in punitive damages against the *Post* and the two reporters who prepared the article.

The trial judge overturned the verdict, setting off a round of appeals that led first to an order reinstating the jury's award and ultimately to a decision by the entire circuit court panel, which ruled, with one dissent, that the *Post* and its reporters did not have to pay the defendants anything. A crucial question for the panel was whether William Tavoulareas was a public figure.

Judge Starr, writing for the court, quickly disposed of the contention that the plaintiff was an all-purpose public figure. He said that the Supreme Court had established "stringent standards applicable to this class of public figure," and the oil executive did not come within them. Tavoulareas's prominence was confined to business circles, and his celebrity in society at large did not "approach that of a well-known athlete or entertainer." The court also noted that in its *Waldbaum* decision, it had held that "[b]eing an executive within a prominent and influential company does not by itself make one a public figure."

However, Judge Starr continued, individuals may become public figures because of their involvement in "certain issues or situations." Was Tavoulareas one of them? The court said he could be, but only if he had thrust himself into the resolution of a public controversy other than that created by the *Post*'s article. Beginning its analysis of the executive's status, the court said:

> First, we isolate the controversy at issue, because the scope of the controversy in which the plaintiff involves himself defines the scope of the public personality. The controversy must be public both in the sense that "persons actually were discussing" it, and that "persons beyond the immediate participants in the dispute [are likely] to feel the impact of its resolution."

In this instance, the court said, there was a public controversy of long standing. This controversy had its origins in the oil shortages of the 1970s, when mideastern Moslem nations temporarily had cut off shipments to the United States to show their opposition to this nation's ties to Israel. As a result of those shortages, the management and structure of the oil industry came under close scrutiny. "Many reform proposals were publicly advanced and considered, including measures to break up or divest the large oil companies, increase their taxes, install government representatives on their boards of directors, and subject them to more intense public regulation." The stakes were high. The public was directly involved. At the height of the embargo, motorists waited in long lines to buy gasoline from stations able to get it. In less than a decade, the price of petroleum products more than tripled, with effects that were felt throughout the economy. The resulting controversy had not been resolved when the *Post* wrote about Tavoulareas and Mobil in 1979.

Had Tavoulareas thrust himself into that controversy? Indeed he had. Throughout much of the 1970s, Mobil had conducted an unusual advertising campaign, directed not at selling its products but at advocating its point of view. At Tavoulareas's direction, the company's public relations department prepared a series of quarter-page editorial advertisements, which were published in the nation's leading newspapers. Through them, as the court noted, "Mobil and Tavoulareas played substantial roles in spearheading a public counterattack on the movement for reform in the oil industry." As evidence of Tavoulareas's involvement in the controversy, the *Post* compiled five hundred pages of news clippings in which he was quoted. In the court's view, the collection left no doubt that "Tavoulareas was outspoken in defending the oil industry's performance, in blaming the oil crisis on government regulation and interference with the free market, and in advocating rejection of efforts to further regulate or alter the oil industry." Further, the clippings offered proof that Tavoulareas had ready access to the media, not only through Mobil's advertisements, but as a public speaker and as a witness before congressional committees.

The conclusion was inevitable. Tavoulareas had thrust himself into the vortex of the debate over public policy toward the oil industry. That made him a limited public figure. Therefore, the court said "[h]aving 'stepped into the public spotlight . . . he must take the good with the bad,' " again quoting from *Waldbaum.*

Only one question remained, but it was crucial. Was the *Post*'s article, focusing as it did on a business relationship between father and son, and between the two companies they represented, germane to the public controversy? The court backed into its answer, saying, "The alleged nepotism by Tavoulareas was not 'wholly unrelated' to a public controversy where the credibility and integrity of representatives of the oil industry had become an issue." Further, the arrangement had become so much a subject of gossip within the oil industry during the crisis years that Mobil had released its version to an oil industry trade publication before the *Post*'s article appeared. The Securities and Exchange Commission had looked into the arrangement and had asked Tavoulareas to justify it. Mobil's board of directors was so concerned with the apparent conflict of interest that it had raised questions within the company. In the end, the court found "abundant evidence of the already 'public' nature" of the subject of the *Post*'s article and its bearing on Tavoulareas's stature as an influential figure in the debate over oil policy. The upshot was that Tavoulareas could not win his lawsuit against the *Post* unless he could prove actual malice. In a decision that examined in depth the role of investigative reporting in modern journalism, the court concluded that he had not done so.

A survey of the reported cases shows many other instances in which libel plaintiffs have been held to be limited public figures. One way to achieve that status is to run for political office.[42] Another is to attempt to influence the outcome of a referendum.[43] Another is to become a controversial high school football coach.[44] Courts have ruled that newspapers,[45] their editors,[46] columnists,[47] and reporters[48] are public figures. In

---

42.   Brown v. Herald Co., 698 F.2d 949, 9 Med.L.Rptr. 1149 (8th Cir. 1983).
43.   Cloyd v. Press, 629 S.W.2d 24, 8 Med.L.Rptr. 1589 (Tenn.App. 1981).
44.   Brewer v. Rogers, 211 Ga.App. 343, 439 S.E.2d 77, 22 Med.L.Rptr. 1180 (1993).
45.   Bee Publications v. Cheektowaga Times, 107 A.D.2d 382 (N.Y.App.Div. 1985).
46.   Fried v. Daily Review, 11 Med.L.Rptr. 2145 (Calif.Ct.App. 1985).
47.   Warner v. Kansas City Star, 726 S.W.2d 384, 13 Med.L.Rptr. 1961 (Mo.Ct.App. 1987).
48.   Jensen v. Times Mirror, 634 F.Supp. 304, 12 Med.L.Rptr. 2137; on reconsideration, 647 F.Supp. 1525, 13 Med.L.Rptr. 2160 (D.Conn. 1986).

other instances, people have become limited public figures because they made a diligent effort to publicize otherwise private causes or organizations with which they were associated. Among them are the director of a drug rehabilitation center who issued statements to the press and invited a reporter to be present when a state official inspected the center's records.[49] Another was the owner of an art school who sought press coverage when his operation of the school came under fire.[50] In one unusual case, a marine biologist who trained dolphins for the Navy and the Central Intelligence Agency during the Vietnam war was held to be a public figure.[51] His work during the war was secret, but he entered the public arena later by writing articles, responding to requests for interviews, including an appearance on *60 Minutes,* and preparing brochures offering his services as a dolphin trainer.

Involuntary Public Figures

In *Gertz,* the Supreme Court used the word "hypothetically" to introduce the suggestion that some persons might become public figures "through no purposeful action" of their own. It added that "instances of truly involuntary public figures must be exceedingly rare." That prediction has proved accurate. In a half dozen or so reported cases, courts have recognized the possibility that some individuals might become public figures despite their efforts to stay out of the limelight. In only one reported instance, however, has a court ruled that a plaintiff was an involuntary public figure. The U.S. Court of Appeals for the District of Columbia Circuit held that an air traffic controller had become an "involuntary public figure for the very limited purpose" of the discussion of a crash that occurred while he was on duty.[52]

Time Lapse and Public Figure Status

The case brought by the marine biologist who trained dolphins for the CIA raised a question that has been a factor in several others. With the passage of time, can a limited public figure again become a private individual? The district court judge said that the marine biologist might indeed do so, at least with respect to some aspects of his career. However, two federal appellate courts and the Mississippi Supreme Court have held that once people become limited public figures, they remain so for purposes of comment on the controversy in which they became involved. The Sixth Circuit Court of Appeals held that a major witness in a rape trial that had led to the execution of several black youths in the 1930s remained a public figure for purposes of comment on that event more than forty years later.[53] The Fifth Circuit Court of Appeals held that an entertainer who for several years had been Elvis Presley's girlfriend still was a public figure a dozen years later with respect to her association with the

---

49. Major v. Drapeau, 507 A.2d 938, 12 Med.L.Rptr. 2032 (R.I. 1986).
50. Cooper School of Art v. Plain Dealer, 12 Med.L.Rptr. 2283 (Ohio Ct.App. 1986).
51. Fitzgerald v. Penthouse International, 525 F.Supp. 585, 7 Med.L.Rptr. 2385 (D.Md. 1981).
52. Dameron v. Washington Magazine, 779 F.2d 736, 12 Med.L.Rptr. 1508 (D.C.Cir. 1985).
53. Street v. National Broadcasting Co., 645 F.2d 1227, 7 Med.L.Rptr. 1001 (6th Cir. 1981); cert. granted, 454 U.S. 815; cert. dismissed, 454 U.S. 1095 (1981).

singer.[54] The Mississippi decision involved a man who had been a candidate for deputy sheriff in 1967 and thereafter retired from public life. The court said that for purposes of comment on that election, he remained a public figure in 1983.[55]

These examples, and the many others in the case reports, emphasize principles already presented. Individuals become limited public figures because they voluntarily involve themselves in the attempt to resolve a public controversy. Courts have said that a controversy is public when it affects people other than those directly involved in it. Further, the controversy must be of such a nature that its resolution depends to some extent on the power of public opinion. Limited public figures take their case to the media by issuing press releases and calling press conferences. They write letters to the editor. They appear on television. When they go public, they cannot expect that all that is printed or said about them will be favorable. If they are defamed by the media in connection with their advocacy, they must prove actual malice if they are to prevail.

Public Personalities

Courts in a few jurisdictions have recognized a class of persons who do not precisely fit the public figure categories described already, but who nevertheless have ready access to the media. New York courts have taken the lead in calling such persons "public personalities."[56] Courts in that state have applied the term to a belly dancer who was widely known in her community,[57] to a writer for *Sports Illustrated*,[58] and to the owner of radio stations in Buffalo.[59] Courts in a few other jurisdictions have also applied the term to sports figures.[60] In these instances, the plaintiffs were not deemed to have reached the celebrity status that would have made them all-purpose public figures. Nor had they thrust themselves into a public controversy. However, they did have access to the media and therefore could respond to their detractors. For that reason, the courts held that they would have to prove actual malice to prevail in a libel action.

Private Individuals

Libel plaintiffs who do not achieve public official or public figure status are regarded by the courts as private individuals. The distinction is important because in most states private individuals can win a libel suit by proving a degree of fault lesser than actual malice, usually negligence.

---

54. Brewer v. Memphis Publishing Co., 626 F.2d 1238, 6 Med.L.Rptr. 2025 (5th Cir. 1980); cert. denied, 452 U.S. 962 (1981).
55. Newson v. Henry, 443 So.2d 817, 10 Med.L.Rptr. 1421 (Miss. 1983).
56. James v. Gannett Co., 40 N.Y.2d 415 (1976).
57. Ibid.
58. Maule v. NYM Corp., 54 N.Y.2d 880, 7 Med.L.Rptr. 2092 (1981).
59. Howard v. Buffalo Evening News, 89 A.D.2d 793, 453 N.Y.S.2d 516, 8 Med.L.Rptr. 2592 (N.Y.App.Div. 1982).
60. Chuy v. Philadelphia Eagles Football Club, 595 F.2d 1265 (3d Cir. 1979).

Several times since 1967, when the Supreme Court first identified public figures in the *Butts* case, the Court has reviewed cases in which the status of the plaintiff was at issue. In all instances, the plaintiffs were, or had been, much in the news. In each instance, the Court held that the plaintiff nevertheless remained a private individual. The decisions are of continuing importance as reminders that newsworthiness alone does not make people public figures for libel actions.

The first of the decisions was *Gertz*. In that case, the Court held that a lawyer hired to represent a client does not, by that act alone, become a public figure. Even though the lawyer may try a case that deals directly with a public controversy, as in *Gertz*, that involvement itself does not make the lawyer a public figure. Lawyers become public figures for purposes of comment on their handling of cases only when they go beyond the normal bounds of their professional duties. Lawyers must become advocates of causes, as well as agents of their clients, if they are to become limited public figures.

Other professionals who work for fees or are hired to perform duties for or give advice to clients, including governments, also are private individuals as long as they simply do their jobs and do not enter the public forum as advocates. These professionals include engineers, accountants, physicians, consultants, marketing analysts, and the like. Although public relations practitioners might conceivably become public figures as they carry out their missions for clients, no reported cases define their status.

The second decision defining a private individual was *Time, Inc.* v. *Firestone*. The case grew out of a brief item in *Time* magazine noting that Russell A. Firestone, Jr., heir to the tire fortune, had been granted a divorce from his wife, Mary Alice, on grounds of adultery. It also noted that she had been awarded $3,000 a month in alimony. Under Florida law, a wife found to have committed adultery cannot be awarded alimony. Although the judge who had heard the divorce action said that it had "produced enough evidence of extramarital adventures on both sides to make Dr. Freud's hair curl," he had ignored most of this evidence, granting the divorce on other grounds. Mrs. Firestone sued the magazine for libel. A jury awarded her $100,000 in damages, and the Florida Supreme Court affirmed, holding that the magazine's reporter was negligent in not knowing enough law to realize that Mrs. Firestone could not have been awarded alimony if she had been found to be an adulteress. The U.S. Supreme Court took the case to review *Time's* argument that Mrs. Firestone should have been regarded as a public figure because the divorce trial had been so highly publicized that she had arranged several news conferences to answer questions from reporters.

**Time, Inc. v. Firestone,
424 U.S. 448, 96 S.Ct. 958,
47 L.Ed.2d 154,
1 Med.L.Rptr. 1665 (1976).**

The Supreme Court said that notoriety did not make her a public figure. Nor did her ready access to the media. And even though the most intimate details of her conflict with her husband were spread across the land, she was not involved in a public controversy of the kind contemplated in *New York Times* and *Gertz*. Only she, her husband, their families, and their friends had anything to gain or lose from the divorce action. The dispute was resolved by a judge, who applied the law to the evidence, not by public opinion. Moreover, Mrs. Firestone was involved in the dispute because she went to court to protect her interests, a right guaranteed by the Constitution.

From the point of view of the judicial branch, the decision made sense. Civil courts are for the use of persons who think they have been wronged. People who are thinking about filing a lawsuit, or responding to one, should not also have to think about whether those acts will open them to defamatory falsehood under a rule that makes recovery difficult. But from the point of view of the news media, the decision had an ominous note. It told journalists that they cannot be certain that highly visible news makers will be required to prove actual malice if they sue for libel. Some lawyers advise their clients in states that have adopted a negligence standard for private individuals never to assume that subjects of defamatory stories are public figures, no matter how much they have been in the news.[61]

The Supreme Court reinforced the point it made in *Firestone* when it decided two cases brought by persons who had been dragged into the news through their association with highly publicized controversies. The Court held that neither person's newsworthiness had made him either an involuntary or a limited public figure.

The first of the cases, *Hutchinson* v. *Proxmire,* was unusual in two ways. The defendant, William Proxmire, was a U.S. senator, and the suit was based on a news release from his office. Dr. Ronald Hutchinson, who relied on federal grants to finance his research in psychology, was drawn out of the obscurity of the laboratory when Senator Proxmire awarded his "Golden Fleece" to

Hutchinson v. *Proxmire,*
443 U.S. 111, 99 S.Ct. 2675,
61 L.Ed.2d 411, 5
Med.L.Rptr. 1279 (1979).

the government agencies that paid for the research. In this recognition there was no honor. The senator gave the award periodically to individuals, government agencies, and projects that he considered outrageously wasteful of public funds. In this instance, the primary targets were the Defense Department and NASA, which had given Hutchinson $500,000 to study stress. The researcher used monkeys as subjects and made thousands of feet of videotape of their facial expressions as they reacted to various kinds of stress. In Proxmire's opinion the whole project was monkey business of another kind, and he said so in a scathing press release. The story was used widely. Reporters sought out Hutchinson and published his reaction to the senator's charges.

Hutchinson sued Proxmire for libel, saying that his work had been made to appear worthless and that he had been subjected to ridicule. A judge dismissed the lawsuit, ruling that Hutchinson was a public figure and that he could not prove actual malice. An appellate court affirmed. The Supreme Court took the case and reversed.

The lower courts looked to Hutchinson's federal grants and his access to the media in deeming him a public figure. The Supreme Court looked at the nature of the controversy and how Hutchinson had become involved in it. The Court said that the key issue was not Hutchinson's research; only a few professionals in the same field knew about it. His work was not controversial until Proxmire made it so. The real public controversy was over the spending of public funds. Hutchinson did not enter that debate until Proxmire made an issue of his grants. Thus, the scientist was an unwilling player in Proxmire's game. He remained a private individual and thus needed prove only negligence to prevail. Proxmire eventually settled with Hutchinson for $10,000.

---

61. Alexander Greenfield, "Thirty Ways to Protect Yourself against Libel Lawsuits," *Editor & Publisher,* 3 June 1989, p. 56.

In the second case, *Wolston* v. *Reader's Digest Association,* the Supreme Court said that involvement in criminal conduct, without more, does not make one a public figure. Wolston had a brief brush with the law during the McCarthy era after World War II, when he failed to appear before a federal grand jury and was held in criminal contempt.

Wolston v. *Reader's Digest Association,* 443 U.S. 157, 99 S.Ct. 2701, 61 L.Ed.2d 450, 5 Med.L.Rptr. 1273 (1979).

Like many others who lived through those times, Wolston was more a victim of circumstances than a shaper of events. He was born in Russia, came to the United States after the Russian Revolution, became a citizen, served in the U.S. Army during World War II, and remained in government service afterward. He was the nephew of a couple who pleaded guilty to espionage for the Soviet Union in 1958. For that reason he was called by the grand jury. No charges were filed against him. However, years later a book published by *Reader's Digest* listed him, his aunt, and his uncle among those who had been identified as Soviet spies or who had been found guilty of perjury or contempt in connection with charges of spying during and after World War II. Wolston sued the book's publisher for libel. A federal district court judge dismissed the case, ruling that Wolston was a public figure and could not prove actual malice. The judge said that Wolston had become a public figure when he pleaded guilty to criminal contempt and became the subject of news stories in Washington, D.C., and New York City.

The Supreme Court said that he did not. The Court said that Wolston had done nothing on his own to thrust himself into the post-World War II controversy over Soviet spying. He had been brought into the controversy by the FBI and the grand jury. His failure to appear was not an act of defiance designed to call attention to a cause. The reason he hadn't appeared was that he was ill. When he appeared in court of his own volition the following day, Wolston offered to testify, but the judge reacted by finding him in contempt. None of that made him a public figure. Nor did the news stories, which merely reported an event in which Wolston was an unwilling participant. To emphasize the point, Justice Rehnquist wrote for the Court's majority: "[W]e reject the further contention of respondents that any person who engages in criminal conduct automatically becomes a public figure for purposes of comment on a limited range of issues related to his conviction. . . . To hold otherwise would create an 'open season' for all who sought to defame persons convicted of crime."

In each of these cases, the Court said that libel plaintiffs who are not otherwise famous do not become public figures merely because they do something—or something is done to them—that makes them newsworthy. Likewise, courts have held that people who are engaged in private business, or who are employed by business firms, are private individuals unless they enjoy unusual prominence or, like Tavoulareas, seek to influence the outcome of a public controversy. The following have been held to be private individuals: a broker who sought investors in a proposed tax-exempt mutual fund;[62] a businessman who was "in the public eye in regard to certain of his business ventures," but who was accused of wrongdoing apart from those ventures;[63] a corpo-

---

62.   Jadwin v. Minneapolis Star, 367 N.W.2d 476, 11 Med.L.Rptr. 1905 (Minn. 1985).
63.   Mead Corporation v. Hicks, 448 So.2d 308, 10 Med.L.Rptr. 1030 (Ala. 1983).

ration's general counsel, who was involved in a stockholder's dispute that was held to be a private controversy;[64] a seller of Olympic souvenirs;[65] and a milk producers association that did not initiate news coverage of a controversy over a request for a federal loan guarantee.[66]

It is also worth noting that courts have found the following to be private individuals: a former Miss Wyoming, who participated in the Miss America contest and who alleged that she was identified as the subject of a short story attributing amazing sexual powers to a "Miss Wyoming";[67] the author of novels on human sexuality, when her name was used in connection with the nude photo of another person;[68] and a woman who was photographed on the street during filming of a televised documentary on prostitution.[69]

This sampling of the reported decisions, and the four landmark Supreme Court cases that we have discussed, tell us that people do not become public figures for purposes of a libel suit simply because they are in the news. These cases serve as a reminder that the news media may be able to create all-purpose public figures or public personalities but are not likely to create limited public figures by dragging ordinary people into the news. All-purpose public figures are celebrities; in the language of one decision, their names are "household words." Such figures can be created by constant exposure on television screens, in newspapers, or in magazines. They are recognized wherever they go, and people talk about them. If that talk is sometimes harshly critical, such is the price of fame.

Limited public figures are linked to events. They are people who take up causes and by doing so seek to change the course of human affairs. By their efforts, they may force the closing of a landfill, limit the flight patterns at an airport, win approval of zoning for satellite television dishes, urge a boycott of an abortion clinic, or force other changes that have an effect on their neighbors or on society at large. Because they have an effect on others, they must expect criticism in connection with their attempts to change the course of events.

FAULT: DEFINING THE STANDARDS

Let's assume that from the point of view of a communications medium, the worst has happened. The matter at issue has been found to contain a false and defamatory assertion of fact. Thus, the judge has rejected a motion to dismiss. The judge also has ruled on the status of the plaintiff: public official, public figure, or private individual. That ruling will have a major influence on the next point of contention: To what degree was the communications medium at fault? In all states, if the judge has ruled that

---

64. Denny v. Mertz, 106 Wis.2d 636, 318 N.W.2d 141, 8 Med.L.Rptr. 1369; cert. denied, 459 U.S. 883 (1982).
65. Zates v. Richman, 86 A.D.2d 746 (N.Y.App.Div. 1982).
66. Eastern Milk Producers Cooperative v. Milkweed, 8 Med.L.Rptr. 2100 (N.D.N.Y. 1982).
67. Pring v. Penthouse International, 695 F.2d 438, 8 Med.L.Rptr. 2409 (10th Cir. 1982).
68. Lerman v. Chuckleberry Publishing, 521 F.Supp. 228, 7 Med.L.Rptr. 2282 (S.D.N.Y. 1981).
69. Clark v. ABC, 684 F.2d 1208, 8 Med.L.Rptr. 2049 (6th Cir. 1982).

the plaintiff is a public official or public figure, the plaintiff must offer clear and convincing evidence of actual malice on the part of the defendant. In four states, private individuals also must offer evidence of actual malice if the alleged libel grew out of a matter of public interest. And in a few states, private individuals may have to prove actual malice if there is a combination of libel *per quod* and a matter of public concern. In most states, however, private individuals can win the lawsuit by proving a lesser degree of fault, usually negligence, defined either as a failure to use ordinary care or to follow professional standards for reporting and editing. Such fault is much easier to prove than is actual malice. If such plaintiffs can prove actual malice, they also may claim punitive damages.

We will look first at the standard of fault that the various states require private individuals to prove and then examine the leading decisions defining actual malice and negligence.

State Standards and the *Gertz* Option

Courts in thirty states, the District of Columbia, Guam, Puerto Rico, and the Virgin Islands have accepted the option offered by the Supreme Court in *Gertz* and permit private individual plaintiffs to prevail by proving negligence.[70]

Four states require private individuals to prove actual malice if the defamation grows out of the reporting of or comment on a public issue. In 1979 a federal district court in Alaska held actual malice to be the standard in that state.[71] In 1987, however, another district court, noting some uncertainty reflected in an Alaska Supreme Court decision,[72] suggested that the actual-malice standard could change if the right case came before the supreme court.[73] The Colorado Supreme Court[74] and the Indiana appellate courts[75] have adopted actual malice, taking the position that the First Amendment and the freedom of speech clause of their state constitutions protect the discussion of public issues, no matter the status of the individuals involved. New Jersey adopted actual malice, basing its position on that state's common law.[76]

New York requires private individuals to prove by the preponderance of the evidence that the publication was made "in a grossly irresponsible manner" without re-

---

70. *Communications Law 1994,* vol. 1 (New York: Practising Law Institute, 1994), pp. 365–377. The states include Alabama, Arizona, Arkansas, California, Delaware, Florida, Georgia, Hawaii, Illinois, Iowa, Kansas, Kentucky, Maryland, Massachusetts, Michigan, Minnesota, Mississippi, New Mexico, North Carolina, Ohio, Oklahoma, Oregon, Pennsylvania, Tennessee, Texas, Utah, Vermont, Virginia, Washington, and Wisconsin.
71. Gay v. Williams, 486 F.Supp. 12 (D.Alaska 1979).
72. Schneider v. Pay 'n Save Corp., 723 P.2d 619 (Alaska 1986).
73. Sisemore v. U.S. News & World Report, 662 F.Supp. 1529 (D.Alaska 1987).
74. Walker v. Colorado Springs Sun, 188 Colo. 86, 538 P.2d 450 (Colo. 1975); cert. denied, 423 U.S. 1025 (1975); Diversified Management v. Denver Post, 653 P.2d 1103, 8 Med.L.Rptr. 2505 (Colo. 1982).
75. Bandido's Inc. v. Journal Gazette, 575 N.E.2d 324, 19 Med.L.Rptr. 1178 (Ind.App. 1991); Cochran v. Indianapolis Newspapers, 372 N.E.2d 1211 (Ind.App. 1978); Aafco Heating & Air Conditioning Co. v. Northwest Publications, 321 N.E.2d 580, 1 Med.L.Rptr. 1683 (Ind.App. 1974).
76. Sisler v. Gannett Co., Inc., 104 N.J. 506, 516 A.2d 1083, 13 Med.L.Rptr. 1577 (N.J. 1986).

gard for the standards ordinarily followed by responsible journalists.[77] This standard is something more than carelessness but does not require proof that the publisher had serious doubt. New York's court of claims, in a dictum, volunteered some guidance as to the meaning of the term. The court said that editors of the student newspaper at a state university were grossly negligent in running a letter to the editor without checking to make certain it was written by the students whose names were signed to it.[78] The letter, which identified the signers as members of the gay community who were coming out of the closet, bore the names of two students who had not written it. When the two named students sued for libel, the claims court said that the failure of the newspaper's editors to verify the identity of the writers, coupled with the lack of consistent procedures for verifying letters to the editor, was "grossly irresponsible."

Although in an early decision the Illinois Supreme Court seemed to have adopted an actual-malice standard for private individuals caught up in matters of "vital public concern,"[79] the court now has adopted the negligence option offered by *Gertz*. In a decision that was left undisturbed by the supreme court, an appellate court held that private plaintiffs need not always prove actual malice, even when the defamatory statement concerns a matter of public interest.[80]

Virginia and Florida courts also are ambivalent on the standard of fault required of private individuals. The Virginia Supreme Court said that if the language at issue "makes substantial danger to reputation apparent," presumably a reference to libel per se, the plaintiff need prove only negligence. But if substantial danger is not apparent, which is a determination to be made by the trial court, the plaintiff must offer clear and convincing evidence of actual malice. And in a departure from the usual common law position, the Virginia court held that the standards should apply regardless of whether the publication in question relates to a matter of public concern.[81] Likewise, Florida courts have taken the position that in actions involving libel *per quod,* a private plaintiff can be required to prove actual malice, presumably because in such situations the media cannot be presumed to have foreseen that the statements were damaging.[82]

In a case that did not require the court to resolve the issue, the Idaho Supreme Court said that a private plaintiff need not prove actual malice to recover for "actual injury" to reputation, thus indicating that it might adopt a negligence standard.[83] Also in dicta, the supreme courts of Maine and Rhode Island said that neg-

---

77. Chapadeau v. Utica Observer-Dispatch, 38 N.Y.2d 196, 379 N.Y.S.2d 61, 341 N.E.2d 569, 1 Med.L.Rptr. 1693 (1975). See also Gaeta v. New York News, Inc., 62 N.Y.2d 340 (1984); Weiner v. Doubleday & Co., 74 N.Y.2d 586 (1989), cert denied, 495 U.S. 930, 110 S.Ct.2168 (1990); Greenberg v. CBS, 69 A.D.2d 693 (N.Y. 2d Dept. 1979).
78. Mazart v. State, 441 N.Y.S.2d 600 (1981).
79. Farnsworth v. Tribune Co., 43 Ill.2d 286, 253 N.E.2d 408 (Ill. 1969).
80. Davis v. Keystone Printing Service, 155 Ill.App.3d 309, 507 N.E.2d 1358, 14 Med.L.Rptr. 1225 (Ill.App. 1987). See also Troman v. Wood, 62 Ill.2d 184, 340 N.E.2d 292 (1975).
81. The Gazette v. Harris, 229 Va. 1, 325 S.E.2d 713, 11 Med.L.Rptr. 1985 (Va. 1985). See also Smith v. Dameron, 14 Med.L.Rptr. 1879 (Va.Cir.Ct. 1987); Fleming v. Moore, 221 Va. 1, 325 S.E.2d 713, 7 Med.L.Rptr. 1313 (Va. 1981). In the latter case, the court applied actual malice as a requirement for punitive damages in a nonmedia case.
82. Sobel v. Miami Daily News, 5 Med.L.Rptr. 2462; affirmed, 395 So.2d 282 (Fla.Ct.App. 1981).
83. Wiemer v. Rankin, 117 Idaho 566, 790 P.2d 347, 17 Med.L.Rptr. 1753 (Idaho 1990).

ligence was the standard of fault required of private individuals who sue the media for libel.[84] Missouri courts require private individuals to show that the media were at fault, but the cases do not define what that means.[85] The Connecticut Supreme Court has declined to define the fault standard for private figures until the issue is squarely presented.[86]

Actual Malice

In *New York Times,* the Supreme Court defined actual malice as publishing with knowledge of falsity or with reckless disregard for the truth. Knowledge of falsity is clear-cut and results in deliberate publishing of a lie. In a few instances plaintiffs have been able to prove such publication.[87]

Much more common have been cases in which plaintiffs have proved reckless disregard. In *New York Times,* the Supreme Court made only a general attempt to define the term. The Court noted that the advertisement was signed by persons who were distinguished in various fields. The advertising staff of the *Times* would have no reason to doubt their version of the facts. It was true, the Court noted, that clippings in the *Times*'s own library contradicted statements in the ad, but in the absence of a "serious doubt," the advertising director's failure to check the files was not reckless disregard. At worst, the Court held, it was no more than negligence.

The key words in the preceding paragraph are "serious doubt." Subsequent decisions defining reckless disregard have focused on these words. The critical questions in establishing reckless disregard are, Did the defendant seriously doubt the truth of the libelous allegation? Were the sources or the nature of the evidence such that the defendant should have had serious doubt about the allegations? Thus, reckless disregard has its roots in the defendant's state of mind. Because one's state of mind is difficult to ascertain under the best of circumstances, the finding of reckless disregard is a subjective process. It is based on such evidence as the plaintiff can muster pointing to what the defendant knew or did not know when the libelous material was being prepared and when the decision was reached to publish it.

Four years after its decision in *New York Times,* the Supreme Court felt compelled to define further what it meant by "actual malice," and particularly by "reckless disregard." It accepted for review a Louisiana case, *St. Amant* v. *Thompson,*[88] and made it the definitive guide to the meaning of the term. Four subsequent decisions have offered additional guidance. They are *Herbert* v. *Lando,*[89] *Bose Corp.* v. *Consumers*

---

84. Hudson v. Guy Gannett Broadcasting Company, 521 A.2d 714, 13 Med.L.Rptr. 2189 (Me. 1987); and DeCarvalho v. Outlet Co., 579 A.2d 469 (R.I. 1990).
85. McQuoid v. Springfield Newspapers, 502 F.Supp. 1050 (W.D.Mo. 1980); Joseph v. Elam, 709 S.W.2d 517 (Mo.Ct.App. 1986); Williams v. Pulitzer Publishing Co., 706 S.W.2d 508 (Mo.Ct.App. 1986).
86. Goodrich v. Waterbury Republican, 188 Conn. 107, 448 A.2d 1317 (1982).
87. Most notably, Goldwater v. Ginzburg, 414 F.2d 324, 1 Med.L.Rptr. 1737 (2d Cir. 1969). The successful plaintiff, for many years a U.S. senator from Arizona, was the Republican candidate for president in 1964.
88. 390 U.S. 727, 88 S.Ct. 1323, 20 L.Ed.2d 262, 1 Med.L.Rptr. 1586 (1968).
89. 441 U.S. 153, 99 S.Ct. 1635, 60 L.Ed.2d 115, 4 Med.L.Rptr. 2575 (1979).

Union,[90] *Anderson* v. *Liberty Lobby,*[91] and *Masson* v. *New Yorker Magazine, Inc.*[92] In these decisions, the Court made the following points:

—"Actual malice" means what the Supreme Court said it means. It is knowledge of falsity or reckless disregard of the truth. It does not embody the traditional meaning of "malice" as ill will or intent to harm.

—Public officials or public figures cannot prevail in a libel suit unless they prove actual malice with clear and convincing evidence. No plaintiff, public or private, can be awarded punitive damages in the absence of proof of actual malice.

—Actual malice is a subjective standard. This is particularly true of reckless disregard. Therefore, the Court held in *Herbert* that libel plaintiffs must be permitted to inquire into the state of mind of defendants, even if they are journalists. In practical terms, then, journalists can be required to justify the editorial decisions that went into preparation of allegedly libelous material.

—Key elements in reckless disregard are "serious doubts" about the truth of the publication or "a high degree of awareness of their probable falsity."[93] The existence of such doubt or awareness need not be proved directly. It may be inferred from the circumstances, such as the nature of the defendant's sources, ready access to information contradicting the libelous assertion, and deadline pressures.

—The determination of actual malice is a mixed question of law and fact. If a plaintiff can offer no factual evidence pointing to knowledge of falsity or reckless disregard, the court may grant a defendant's motion for summary judgment. If the facts are in doubt, the question is submitted to a jury. However, in a remarkable decision, *Bose Corp.* v. *Consumers Union,* the Supreme Court held that a jury's factual findings of actual malice can be reviewed by an appellate court, which is free to come to its own conclusions as to the meaning of the evidence.

—The Court took this rationale a step further in *Liberty Lobby.* It encouraged judges to grant motions for summary dismissal if they conclude that the plaintiffs are unable to offer clear and convincing evidence of actual malice. Since then, one court has said that the effect of the decision was to extend to all jurisdictions the Second Circuit's liberal policy toward summary dismissal of public official–public figure libel suits.[94]

—In *Masson,* the Court held that the deliberate alteration of direct quotations so as to reflect unfavorably on the source to whom the quotations are attributed can be used as evidence of actual malice.

90. 466 U.S. 485, 104 S.Ct. 1949, 80 L.Ed.2d 502, 10 Med.L.Rptr. 1625 (1984).
91. 477 U.S. 242, 106 S.Ct. 2505, 91 L.Ed.2d 202, 12 Med.L.Rptr. 2297 (1986).
92. 501 U.S. 496, 111 S.Ct. 2419, 115 L.Ed.2d 447, 18 Med.L.Rptr. 2241 (1991).
93. Garrison v. Louisiana, 379 U.S. 64, 85 S. Ct. 209, 13 L.Ed.2d 125, 1 Med.L.Rptr. 1548 (1964).
94. Contemporary Mission v. New York Times Co., 665 F.Supp. 248, 14 Med.L.Rptr. 1921 (S.D.N.Y. 1987).

The *St. Amant* case had its origins in the broadcast of a political appeal over a Baton Rouge television station. Phil St. Amant, a candidate for public office, accused his opponent of accepting bribes. In doing so, he read a sworn statement from a Teamsters Union member that portrayed Herman Thompson, a deputy sheriff, as an intermediary in the bribery. Thompson sued St. Amant for libel and won a $5,000 judgment before Louisiana courts became hopelessly bogged down in trying to define actual malice. The Supreme Court agreed to take the case, holding that Thompson was not entitled to damages, because there was no reckless disregard on St. Amant's part. Justice Byron R. White wrote the decision, in which he was joined by seven others.

St. Amant v. Thompson, 390 U.S. 727, 88 S.Ct. 1323, 20 L.Ed.2d 262, 1 Med.L.Rptr. 1586 (1968).

White started by emphasizing that reckless disregard is a product of the factual situation of each case, but it begins with evidence of doubt:

> There must be sufficient evidence to permit the conclusion that the defendant in fact entertained serious doubts as to the truth of his publication. Publishing with such doubts shows reckless disregard for truth or falsity and demonstrates actual malice.
>
> It may be said that such a test puts a premium on ignorance, encourages the irresponsible publisher not to enquire, and permits the issue to be determined by the defendant's testimony that he published the statement in good faith and unaware of its probable falsity. . . .
>
> The defendant in a defamation action brought by a public official cannot, however, automatically insure a favorable verdict by testifying that he published with a belief that the statements were true. The finder of fact must determine whether the publication was indeed made in good faith. Professions of good faith will be unlikely to prove persuasive, for example, where a story is fabricated by the defendant, is the product of his imagination, or is based wholly on an unverified anonymous telephone call. Nor will they be likely to prevail when the publisher's allegations are so inherently improbable that only a reckless man would put them in circulation. Likewise, recklessness may be found where there are reasons to doubt the veracity of the informant or the accuracy of his reports. . . . Failure to investigate does not in itself establish bad faith.

With its decision in *St. Amant,* the Court did what it could to tell lower courts how to know actual malice when they see it. The standard does not require reporters and editors to check every conceivable loose end as a story is being developed, especially if it is "hot news" where time is of the essence.[95] Mere failure to check will not, of itself, prove reckless disregard. But if such failure is coupled with the publisher's doubt, or with evidence suggesting that he or she should have had doubts, then there can be reckless disregard. At that point, courts look at the events leading to publication. Who were the sources of information? What was known of their reputation for honesty? How many sources were there? Why did the publisher accept information from one source and reject contradictory information from another? Were the published allegations "so inherently improbable that only a reckless man would put them in circulation"?

The answers to some of these questions lie in the editorial process—in the decisions that reporters and editors make in gathering and presenting news and comment. That

---

95. Curtis Publishing Co. v. Butts, 388 U.S. 130, 87 S.Ct. 1975, 18 L.Ed.2d 1094, 1 Med.L.Rptr. 1568 (1967).

process requires judgment, which is a factor of the state of mind of the participants. Obviously, individuals can and do disagree over news values and over the truth or falsehood of allegedly defamatory statements. What seems obviously true to a person with one point of view may seem like an improbable falsehood to a person with another point of view.

Herbert v. *Lando* grew out of a libel plaintiff's efforts to obtain the answers to state-of-mind questions. Anthony Herbert, a retired army officer who had served in Vietnam, was the subject of a segment of *60 Minutes* produced by Barry Lando of CBS News and narrated by Mike Wallace. Herbert said that the segment, which dealt with atrocities allegedly committed by American troops, made him appear to be a liar. He sued for libel and, because he conceded that he was a public figure, sought to prove actual malice.

Herbert v. *Lando,*
441 U.S. 153, 99 S.Ct. 1635,
60 L.Ed.2d 115,
4 Med.L.Rptr. 2575 (1979).

During the process of discovery, Herbert's lawyer questioned Lando at length about the news judgments that had shaped the telecast. (Discovery is a pretrial process that involves the questioning of potential witnesses under oath to narrow the issues that need to be resolved at trial.) Lando was asked why he had believed some sources but not others, and why he had used some information harmful to Herbert while rejecting information favorable to the officer. The lawyer also asked for details of the discussions between Lando and Wallace, and with others, that went into the shaping of the telecast. Lando refused to answer such questions, arguing that freedom of the press would be restricted if reporters and editors could be compelled to answer questions about their state of mind during the editorial process. A district court judge ordered Lando to answer the questions, but a federal appeals court reversed, holding that the First Amendment stood as a barrier against such questions. The Supreme Court agreed to review the decision. It held that the appeals court was wrong; Lando had to answer the questions.

Justice White, joined by six others, said that *New York Times* had erected a strong safeguard for the media by requiring public official–public figure plaintiffs to prove actual malice. To do so, they must show that the defendant acted either with knowledge that the alleged libel was false, or with serious doubts about its truth. Both knowledge and doubt are states of mind. White concluded that if the Court were to shut off all inquiry into the editorial decision-making process, including the state of mind of defendants, proving actual malice would become virtually impossible. Despite the Supreme Court's decision in his favor, on remand Herbert was unable to prove actual malice.[96]

The *Herbert* decision has been a factor contributing to the expense of taking a libel suit to trial. Journalists who become involved in libel actions can anticipate hours of questioning by plaintiffs' lawyers seeking reasons for every decision made by reporters and editors in developing the offending material.[97] Plaintiffs now commonly

---

96. *Herbert* v. *Lando*, 781 F.2d 298, 12 Med.L.Rptr. 1593 (2d Cir. 1986).
97. For examples of the detailed "state-of-mind" questions asked in a typical case, see Gilbert Cranberg, "Malice in Wonderland" (Iowa City, Iowa: Iowa Center for Communication Study, 1992).

ask during discovery for the names of all persons who played any role in preparing allegedly defamatory material. These persons can be asked about what they said to each other, with focus on whether they raised doubts about any element of the story. Further, reporters can be asked to identify their sources of information and even to produce transcripts of their notes or copies of any audiotapes of interviews. If the offending story was based on an investigation of any consequence, discovery can result in the preparation of thousands of pages of depositions, which is quite expensive. Questions are likely to focus on such matters as why reporters believed some sources but not others, why they followed up some leads but ignored others, what state of mind with respect to the plaintiff shaped the story, and what the intent was in deciding to publish at all. Courts have the duty of assessing the facts produced by such questioning and deciding whether they point to the presence or absence of a serious doubt.

The *Bose* decision also dealt with the process involved in proving actual malice. In this case, the issue was how far appeals courts can go in reviewing the facts that have led a trial court to conclude that a media defendant acted in actual malice.

Bose Corporation v. Consumers Union, 466 U.S. 485, 104 S.Ct. 1949, 80 L.Ed.2d 502, 10 Med.L.Rptr. 1625 (1984).

The case had its origins in a *Consumer Reports* magazine article evaluating the quality of stereo speakers. Included was the Bose 901 speaker, which had only recently come into production. The magazine's engineers found that this speaker had some virtues but that it was incapable of allowing the listener to pinpoint the location of individual instruments in an orchestra because the speakers made some of them seem "to wander about the room."

Bose sued Consumers Union, the magazine's publisher, for libel, alleging that the statement about the instruments' tending "to wander about the room" was false and defamatory. During discovery, the engineer who had written the review testified that in reality, the sound of a solo instrument seemed to move back and forth along the wall between the two speakers of his stereo system. The judge examined excerpts from other articles written by the engineer and concluded that he was expert enough in the English language to know that his use of "about" would convey a different impression. The judge further concluded that the engineer had used that word deliberately and thus had knowingly falsified his report. A jury awarded Bose $115,296 in damages.

On appeal, a circuit court agreed that the article was both false and defamatory. It conceded that the engineer's language may have been imprecise, but it could find no evidence proving knowledge of falsity or reckless disregard for the truth and thus reversed the lower court's decision. Bose took his case to the Supreme Court, arguing that the circuit court had violated the Federal Rules of Civil Procedure by overturning the trial court's findings of fact with respect to actual malice. At issue was Rule 52(a), which provides: "Findings of fact shall not be set aside [by an appeals court] unless clearly erroneous, and due regard shall be given to the opportunity of the trial court to judge the credibility of the witnesses."

The Supreme Court affirmed the circuit court's decision, holding that in media libel cases the First Amendment requires appellate courts to "make an independent examination of the whole record." If the appellate court is not satisfied that the plaintiff offered clear and convincing proof of actual malice, the court has the power to reverse a contrary conclusion by the trier of fact, whether it be a judge or a jury.

Not all courts agreed on the thrust of this decision. Some read it as encouraging greater use of summary judgment to dispose of libel actions short of trial, unless the plaintiff could offer clear and convincing proof of actual malice. Others continued to permit cases to go to trial if there was even minimal proof of the defendant's fault. Two years later, in *Anderson* v. *Liberty Lobby,* the Supreme Court signaled that the former reading is correct.

The question at issue in *Liberty Lobby* was whether that organization, a self-described "citizens' lobby," had presented clear and convincing evidence of actual malice during the preliminary stages of its libel suit against columnist Jack Anderson. A magazine published by Anderson had carried three articles portraying Liberty Lobby and Willis Carto, its founder and treasurer, as neo-Nazi, anti-Semitic, racist, and Fascist. One of the articles called the author of a book published by Liberty Lobby "an American Hitler."

Anderson v. *Liberty Lobby,* 477 U.S. 242, 106 S.Ct. 2505, 91 L.Ed.2d 282, 12 Med.L.Rptr. 2297 (1986).

After discovery, Anderson asked the U.S. District Court for the District of Columbia for summary judgment under Rule 56 of the Federal Rules of Civil Procedure. Under that rule, judges are to grant motions for summary judgment if the pleadings present no genuine disagreement over the meaning of material facts and the law supports the position taken by the moving party. In this instance, that Liberty Lobby and Carto were public figures was accepted as fact. Thus, they would have to prove actual malice. Liberty Lobby argued that some of the sources quoted in the articles were unreliable and that the author had not verified their information before publishing it. Liberty Lobby also offered evidence that the magazine's editor had said the articles were "terrible" and "ridiculous." Anderson's lawyers gave the court depositions that detailed the research that had gone into preparation of the articles and the author's belief that the facts in the articles were truthful and accurate. An appendix listed the sources for each of the statements alleged to be libelous. The district court judge held that the author's thorough investigation and his reliance on numerous sources precluded a jury's finding of clear and convincing evidence of actual malice. Therefore, he dismissed the lawsuit.

On appeal, the circuit court held that the judge had acted properly with respect to most of the disputed passages. However, it said that with respect to nine of them, "a jury could reasonably conclude that the . . . allegations were defamatory, false, and made with actual malice." Further, it held that to defeat a motion for summary judgment, the plaintiffs did not have to show that a jury could find actual malice with "convincing clarity." All that is required is enough evidence to support a reasonable likelihood that a jury might do so.

The Supreme Court disagreed and reversed. Justice White, writing for six justices, held that in *Liberty Lobby,* the District of Columbia Circuit Court had taken too narrow a view of the proof required to support dismissal of the libel suit. Rule 56, he said, requires judges ruling on a motion for summary judgment to apply the same standard of proof that would be required at trial. Thus, in this instance, unless Liberty Lobby could show clear and convincing evidence of actual malice, the lawsuit should be dismissed. The Court thus supported the view that judges considering libel cases brought by public officials or public figures should hold them to a high level of proof of fault if they are to avoid having their cases dismissed.

Because the majority also said that it did not intend to "denigrate the role of the jury," "authoriz[e] trial on affidavits," or "suggest that trial courts should act other than with caution in granting summary judgment," the effect of the decision was not immediately apparent. Brennan, who usually was the Court's most liberal justice on libel questions, said he was unable to discern how the majority's standard was to be applied by trial judges. The two most conservative members, Rehnquist and Burger, said the same.

Whatever the shortcomings of the Court's decision in *Liberty Lobby,* judges in the U.S. Second and Third circuits seem not to have any trouble with it. Judge Vincent L. Broderick of the U.S. district court in New York City granted summary judgment to the *New York Times* in a libel suit brought by a religious group, Contemporary Mission. Citing *Liberty Lobby,* Judge Broderick said that in the absence of clear and convincing evidence of actual malice, he was required by that decision to dismiss the case. He noted, "The Second Circuit has construed *Liberty Lobby* to be a demonstration of the Supreme Court's 'willingness to dispose of libel claims brought by public figure plaintiffs on summary judgment.' "[98] So, too, has the Third Circuit.[99]

In 1991, however, the Supreme Court held that the Ninth Circuit Court of Appeals erred when it upheld a district court's grant of summary judgment for *New Yorker* magazine in a libel action brought by a psychoanalyst who was the subject of one of its profiles. Jeffrey M. Masson, the analyst, complained that the profile's author, Janet Malcolm, had falsely attributed to him direct quotations that made him appear to be a mean-spirited egotist, self-serving, arrogant, and self-destructive. During discovery, Malcolm conceded that, although she had taped more than forty hours of interviews with Masson, she had in some instances altered grammar and syntax to make the quotations more readable and that, in other instances, she had reconstructed from notes conversations that had not been recorded. She insisted that even though the quotations attributed to Masson may not have reflected precisely what he said, they accurately conveyed his meaning. *New Yorker* published the profile as a two-part series in December 1983, and a year later Alfred A. Knopf published it as a book, *In the Freud Archives.*

Masson sued Malcolm, the magazine, and the book publisher for libel. He claimed that six direct quotations attributed to him were invented by Malcolm and were defamatory. A U.S. district court judge in San Francisco, citing *Bose* and *Liberty Lobby,* granted summary judgment to the defendants,[100] and the U.S. Court of Appeals for the Ninth Circuit affirmed.[101] The courts were not concerned that Malcolm had altered or invented quotations. Misquoting someone is not in itself proof of actual malice or even proof that the substance of the quote is false or defamatory. Even if Masson could show that the quotes had been invented or altered, both courts concluded that he could

98. Contemporary Mission v. New York Times Co., 665 F.Supp. 248, 258 n. 1, (S.D.N.Y. 1987). The quotation is from Guccione v. Hustler Magazine, 800 F.2d 298, 13 Med.L.Rptr. 1316 (2d Cir. 1986); cert. denied, 479 U.S. 1092, 107 S.Ct. 1303, 94 L.Ed.2d 158 (1987).
99. Jenkins v. KYW, 829 F.2d 403, 14 Med.L.Rptr. 1718 (3d Cir. 1987); Dunn v. Gannett New York Newspapers, Inc., 833 F.2d 446, 14 Med.L.Rptr. 1871 (3d Cir. 1987).
100. 686 F.Supp. 1396 (N.D.Calif. 1987).
101. 895 F.2d 1535 (9th Cir. 1989).

A wind-swept Jeffrey Masson stands in front of the Supreme Court building. The psychiatrist sued *New Yorker* magazine and writer Janet Malcolm for libel in a celebrated case that caused the Supreme Court to discuss the role of quotation marks in a story. In the end, a jury found Masson had not been able to prove actual malice, even if the quotes were doctored. *(Tracy Woodward/Washington Times Photo Agency)*

not show by clear and convincing evidence that Malcolm knew she was saying something untrue about Masson's character or personality when she misquoted him.

However, the Supreme Court wasn't so sure that the facts were as clear as the lower courts seemed to think. The Court held that some of the quotes raised questions about whether they were or were not defamatory or whether Malcolm knew her portrayal of Masson was inaccurate. But the Supreme Court, too, didn't think that misquoting was in itself clear and convincing evidence of actual malice by Malcolm. In writing the Court's opinion, Justice Anthony M. Kennedy took the opportunity to comment on the use of direct quotations by journalists. He started with a premise that is endorsed by most editors: Quotation marks "indicate to the reader that the passage reproduces the speaker's words verbatim." Such passages lend both authority and credibility to the article in which they appear.

Masson v. *New Yorker Magazine, Inc.,* **501 U.S. 496, 111 S.Ct. 2419, 115 L.Ed.2d 447, 18 Med.L.Rptr. 2241 (1991).**

Writers who put quotation marks around words that were not uttered by the attributed source risk libel from two directions, Kennedy wrote. A source can be libeled if the quotation attributes a false factual assertion to the speaker. Or a doctored quotation can harm the source by indicating "a negative trait or attitude the speaker does not hold." Either way, the victim of the falsely attributed quotation may be subject to ridicule or loss of esteem. But that doesn't mean that doctoring quotations is actual malice or even that the doctored quotation asserts something false or defamatory.

Kennedy recognized that even when writers have the best of intentions, the use of quotation marks is no guarantee that the speaker's exact words are used. A slip in grammar or word usage may have been corrected. Redundancies may have been eliminated. Wordiness may have been reduced. Such "minor changes," Kennedy wrote, "do not amount to falsity for purposes of proving actual malice." Nor do even significant changes prove actual malice if those changes do not so alter the speaker's words as to make them both false and defamatory.

In this instance, however, the Court said, the record contained "substantial" evidence that would support a jury's finding that Malcolm altered the quotations to portray Masson in a negative way that she knew not to be accurate. Many of the disputed passages resembled remarks appearing on tapes of the interviews with Masson but contained significant additions or deletions. Malcolm had had ample time to compare her version of what Masson said with the taped version of his statements. Malcolm had told the editor of the *New Yorker* that "all of the quotations were from the tape recordings." When this proved not to be the case, her explanations of the time and place of the conversations that she had not recorded, but that supposedly supported the alterations, were inconsistent. Also inconsistent were her explanations of changes made during the progression from typewritten notes, to manuscript, to galley proofs, to the completed article. All these discrepancies, the Court concluded, raised questions of fact for a jury to resolve. Because the Supreme Court thought that under these circumstances there was a factual dispute about the nature of the quotes, the case went back to the district court in San Francisco for trial.[102]

Knopf was released from the suit because it had relied, the Court said, on the magazine's "sterling reputation for accuracy and its fact-checking procedure." The court's decision with respect to Knopf was in line with other decisions, which have held that there can be no actual malice in relying on the accuracy of news provided by a highly respected journalist.[103] Nor is there actual malice in relying on a wire service, especially against a deadline,[104] or on articles previously published without question as to their accuracy.[105] There is no actual malice when reporters unknowingly obtain false information from police reports, from reports of other government agencies, or in interviews with public officials if the resulting article accurately reflects the source material.[106] Careful research, coupled with reliance on recognized authorities, resulted in a finding that there was no actual malice.[107]

Time magazine won a celebrated case when Ariel Sharon, then the Israeli defense minister, was unable to prove actual malice, even though he was able to prove that the

---

102. At trial the jurors aborted the case when they deadlocked on the issue of damages after finding Masson was the victim of libel by Malcolm but not by the *New Yorker.* The court ordered a second trial and dismissed the *New Yorker* from the case, leaving only Malcolm. At the second trial the jurors found no evidence of actual malice by Malcolm. David Margolick, "Psychoanalyst Loses Libel Suit against a New Yorker Reporter," *New York Times,* 3 November 1994, p. A1.
103. Loeb v. Globe Newspaper Co., 489 F.Supp. 481, 6 Med.L.Rptr. 1235 (D.Mass. 1980).
104. Curtis Publishing Co. v. Butts, 388 U.S. 130, 87 S.Ct. 1975, 18 L.Ed.2d 1094, 1 Med.L.Rptr. 1568 (1967). In Nelson v. Associated Press, 667 F.Supp. 1468, 14 Med.L.Rptr. 1577 (S.D.Fla. 1987), this is called "the wire service defense."
105. Dupler v. Mansfield Journal Co., 64 Ohio St.2d 116, 413 N.E.2d 1187, 6 Med.L.Rptr. 2362 (Ohio 1980).
106. Catalano v. Pechous, 83 Ill.2d 146, 419 N.E.2d 350, 6 Med.L.Rptr. 2511 (Ill. 1980).
107. Yiamouyannis v. Consumers Union, 619 F.2d 932, 6 Med.L.Rptr. 1065 (2d Cir. 1980).

magazine falsely accused him of condoning the massacre of hundreds of civilians by Christian Phalangist militia during the Israeli occupation of Lebanon in 1982. The reporter involved had spent many years in Israel and got his information from a trusted source who had always been reliable. Sharon's reputation was such that many in his own country believed him capable of doing what *Time*'s story said he had done.[108]

Journalists who have placed greater reliance on the word of criminals than on more reputable sources, including a former mayor of San Francisco, have been found guilty of actual malice.[109] Reliance on gossip, rumor, and eavesdropping also can get journalists in trouble. Oklahoma courts found actual malice in an incredibly botched story written by a young photographer who had spent the night in a sheriff's office waiting to go along on a drug raid.[110] The photographer overheard parts of telephone conversations and police radio chatter that led him to believe that a police officer had kidnapped a teenager at gunpoint. Without asking questions of anyone, the photographer wrote a story that, even more incredibly, was accepted by an editor who doubted its truth but published it anyway. A jury concluded that the chain of error amounted to reckless disregard for the truth.

The Supreme Court upheld a libel judgment against a Hamilton, Ohio, newspaper that had been ordered to pay a former candidate for municipal judge $5,000 in compensatory damages and $195,000 in punitive damages.[111] Shortly before the election, the newspaper reported that the candidate had used "dirty tricks" to cause an investigation of bribery allegations involving employees of one of his opponents. When the candidate sued for libel, he was able to prove that he had done nothing of the kind. In preparing the story, the newspaper had relied heavily on an interview with a woman who also had given her story to another newspaper. That newspaper found the story so lacking in credibility that it refused to publish it. Evidence showed that the Hamilton newspaper's reporter had not interviewed a key participant in the alleged bribery and had not listened to a tape recording of a meeting at which the episode had been discussed. On appeal, the Supreme Court reaffirmed the definition of actual malice found in its earlier decisions and held unanimously that in this instance the lower courts had applied those standards properly.

For centuries, "malice" in connection with libel meant ill will, spite, or an intent to cause harm. That history has been hard to overcome. Despite the Supreme Court's insistence that actual malice has nothing to do with how the writer feels about his or her subject, courts in two states, Indiana[112] and Texas,[113] have held that evidence of ill will can be introduced as part of the proof of actual malice. Courts in those states have adopted the theory that a reporter who has shown a dislike for persons involved in an unfavorable story is likely to have "a state of mind highly conducive to reckless disregard of falsity."

108. For an extended analysis of the Sharon case and that brought by General William Westmoreland against CBS and *60 Minutes,* see Renata Adler, "Annals of Law: Two Trials," *New Yorker,* 16 June 1986, p. 42+, and 23 June 1986, p. 34+.
109. Alioto v. Cowles Communications, 430 F.Supp. 1363, 2 Med.L.Rptr. 1801 (N.D.Calif. 1977).
110. Akins v. Altus Newspapers, 609 P.2d 1263, 3 Med.L.Rptr. 1449 (1977).
111. Harte-Hanks Communications v. Connaughton, 491 U.S. 657, 109 S.Ct. 2678, 105 L.Ed.2d 562, 16 Med.L.Rptr. 1881 (1989).
112. Cochran v. Indianapolis Newspapers, 372 N.E.2d 1211, 3 Med.L.Rptr. 2131 (Ind.App. 1978).
113. Frank B. Hall & Co. v. Buck, 678 S.W.2d 612 (Tex.Ct.App. 1984); cert. denied, 472 U.S. 1009 (1985).

Negligence

In response to the Supreme Court's decision in *Gertz,* at least thirty states,[114] the District of Columbia, and the territory of Puerto Rico permit private individuals to prevail in libel suits if they can prove negligence on the part of the media. Convincing evidence that the persons responsible for the defamatory matter failed to exercise reasonable care in doing their jobs is proof of negligence. Proof of doubt, serious or otherwise, is not required. Although the state of mind of the defendants is subject to examination, it is not decisive. The focus in determining whether reporters or editors are negligent is on their conduct.

Restatement of Torts 2d, which reflects the conclusions of lawyers who practice torts law, offers the following definition of negligence:

> Negligence is conduct that creates an unreasonable risk of harm. The standard of conduct is that of a reasonable person under like circumstances. . . .
>
> The defendant, if a professional distributor of news, such as a newspaper, a magazine, or a broadcasting station, or an employee, such as a reporter, is held to the skill and experience normally possessed by members of that profession. Customs and practices within the profession are relevant in applying the negligence standard, which is, to a substantial degree, set by the profession itself, though a custom is not controlling.[115]

Restatement enlarges on these generalities by noting three factors that must be taken into consideration in determining whether a reporter or editor was negligent:

1. *Was time of the essence?* "Was the communication a matter of topical news requiring prompt publication to be useful, or was it one in which time and opportunity were freely available to investigate? In the latter situation, due care may require a more thorough investigation." This statement is a recognition of the "hot news" principle.

2. *What interest was being promoted by the publication?* Was the subject essential to an understanding of a public issue? Would it help people make up their minds about a candidate for public office? Or was it merely gossip? The latter has little public purpose, but great capacity for harm. Therefore, the publisher ought to go to great pains to ensure its accuracy. A lesser standard of care might prevail in the first two instances.

3. *How extensively would the private individual's reputation be damaged if the defamatory statement proved to be false?* This question could involve considerations of whether the plaintiff had any reputation to lose, how widely the alleged libel was circulated, and its nature.

Like actual malice, negligence must be determined in the light of the facts of each case. Courts trying libel cases brought by private individuals have shown willingness to seek guidance from expert witnesses, including reporters and editors, journalism

---

114.　For a list of those states, see page 178.
115.　*Restatement of the Law, Second: Torts 2d* (St. Paul, Minn.: American Law Institute Publishers, 1977), vol. 3, § 580B(g), pp. 227, 228.

professors, consultants, and others who can demonstrate sufficient knowledge of reporting and editing practices to withstand challenge by counsel. Reflecting the lack of agreement on the standard of care expected by journalists, each side can usually produce experts who support its position. In the end, then, the decision is one for the trier of fact—that is, a jury or a judge. Thus, the *Gertz* decision has put nonjournalists in the position of deciding the standard of care expected of reporters and editors.

Courts in Florida and Kansas expect reporters and editors to know enough law to cover legal proceedings accurately. In Florida, the supreme court said that a *Time* magazine reporter was negligent in reporting the Firestone divorce, referred to earlier. The reporter should have known, the court said, that Mrs. Firestone could not have been awarded alimony if she had been found guilty of adultery.[116] In Kansas, the supreme court held that a reporter and her editor were negligent in preparing a story on a farmer accused of starving his hogs.[117] The story said that the farmer had pleaded guilty to the charge, when, in fact, the charge had only been filed. Both the Florida and Kansas courts used strong language in condemning the reporters' ignorance of the law. Noting the great harm to reputation that can come from mistakenly reporting that a person is guilty of a crime, the Kansas court said the least a journalist can do is "use due care in gathering and reporting court proceedings."

The highest court of Massachusetts also found negligence in a cub reporter's coverage of a court proceeding. The case is of special interest because it illustrates the distinction between negligence and actual malice, both of which, in this instance, were found in the same case. The reporter's problem came not from a lack of knowledge of the law but from timidity. Not knowing that a table was reserved for reporters at the front of the courtroom, the reporter sat at the back of the spectators' section during a narcotics trial. From there, he had difficulty hearing the witnesses. One of the defendants was the twenty-year-old son of the operator of the public school lunchrooms. When the prosecutor asked the town marshal who possessed the drugs in question, the reporter thought he heard the marshal respond, "Mr. Stone." The reporter assumed that the reference was to the father—the only Mr. Stone he knew. Without checking further with the marshal or the prosecutor, the reporter used the father's first name in his story.

Stone v. *Essex County Newspapers, Inc.,* **367 Mass. 849, 330 N.E.2d 161 (1975).**

When the reporter submitted the story to his editor, the latter expressed surprise. He had known the elder Stone for twenty years and had never known him to do wrong. He asked the reporter if he was sure. The reporter said the marshal had said on the witness stand that Mr. Stone possessed the drugs. The editor had also known the marshal for a long time and knew he could be trusted. With a deadline approaching, the editor cleared the story for publication.

Stone sued for libel. The Massachusetts Supreme Judicial Court ruled that if Stone were held to be a public figure, there could be no recovery from the reporter. The reporter's failure to sit where he could hear clearly, coupled with his failure to ask someone for Stone's first name, was "gross carelessness," but it did not rise to the

---

116. Firestone v. Time, Inc., 405 So.2d 172 (Fla. 1974).
117. Gobin v. Globe Publishing Co., 531 P.2d 76 (Kans. 1975).

level of reckless disregard. He was new to the town and to his job. He did not know many people and had no reason to doubt that the Stone mentioned in court was the only Stone he knew. But the editor's reaction to the reporter's story was enough in itself to prove actual malice. He did have doubts, and they could have been removed by a telephone call. His failure to react to his doubts was enough to establish reckless disregard.

An Illinois appeals court held that a reporter was negligent in placing too much reliance on a complaint filed in connection with a civil suit.[118] The reporter compounded his problem by omitting some of the detail in the complaint in order to make a better story. The resulting article was headlined: "SAVED PARROT, LET WOMAN DIE, SUIT SAYS." The defendant in the suit had indeed saved his parrot when he awakened to find his house on fire, but he had been unable to reach a woman who was asleep in an upstairs room, and he had tried in vain to awaken her. These facts were stated more clearly in the petition to the court than they were in the news story. When the man who had rescued the parrot filed a libel suit, the appeals court ruled that the discrepancy between the story and the facts in the petition, which was the reporter's sole source, permitted "an inference of negligent reporting." The court said that the facts chosen for the story portrayed such callous conduct that the reporter should have made "a reasonable investigation" to make sure they were true.

The decision serves as a reminder that pleadings filed in connection with civil suits should be handled with care. Allegations made in pleadings present only one side of the case, and that usually in absolute terms. One purpose of a civil suit is to let a jury or judge determine where, between the extremes, the truth lies.

An Arizona court found a reporter negligent in relying on a disgruntled employee for information harmful to her boss.[119] The reporter had checked the information with other sources but had stopped short of confirming the employee's assertion that the Better Business Bureau had received more complaints about her boss's firm than about anyone else. In the end, the finding of negligence made no difference. At trial, a jury found that the story was substantially true.[120] Courts have found that reporters are not negligent if they rely on the word of a police officer[121] or an officer of the immigration service,[122] even if the information proves to be incorrect.

State courts vary in the standard of proof required to show negligence. However, a survey of the cases indicates that the majority are holding that negligence need be shown only by the preponderance of the evidence. At law, this burden is less than the "clear and convincing evidence" required of public officials and public figures. Thus, in most of the states that have adopted a negligence standard, private plaintiffs not only may win libel suits against the media on a lesser showing of fault, but the rules of evidence make it easier for private plaintiffs to prove negligence.

Obviously, people can and do differ over what is "reasonable care." However, reporters who have been trained well, or who have worked for careful editors, are not likely to be found negligent. Nor are public relations practitioners and advertising

---

118.   Newell v. Field Enterprises, 415 N.E.2d 434, 6 Med.L.Rptr. 2450 (Ill.App. 1980).
119.   Peagler v. Phoenix Newspapers, Inc., 560 P.2d 1216, 2 Med.L.Rptr. 1687 (Ariz. 1977).
120.   Peagler v. Phoenix Newspapers, Inc., 640 P.2d 1110, 8 Med.L.Rptr. 1209 (Ariz. 1982).
121.   Wilson v. Capital City Press, 315 So.2d 393 (La.App. 1975).
122.   Karp v. Miami Herald Publishing Co. 359 So.2d 580, 3 Med.L.Rptr. 2581 (Fla.App. 1978).

copywriters who adhere to the standards of their professions. Prudent professional communicators rely on documentary evidence where it is available. They know that even the best of memories can falter and that participants in a dispute usually make their side look good when they talk to outsiders. Thus, potentially defamatory assertions should be checked against other sources before they are passed along to the public. Courts have held on numerous occasions that negligence begins with a failure to check facts, especially the "little" facts, such as the correct spelling of names, street addresses, and the precise wording of court records.

ACTUAL INJURY

Proving Harm

In *Gertz,* the Supreme Court held that if states elect to permit private individuals to win libel actions by proving something less than actual malice, they also must require such plaintiffs to prove that they have been harmed. This point of contention is perhaps the easiest for a plaintiff to prove. With proof of harm, private plaintiffs are entitled to recover such monetary damages as may be required to make good their loss. The terms used to describe such awards vary from state to state, but they are commonly referred to as *actual damages* or *compensatory damages.*

As Powell noted in *Gertz,* plaintiffs can demonstrate injury by showing that they have lost a job or income as a consequence of the publication of defamatory assertions about them. In such instances, plaintiffs' lawyers may call accountants and actuaries as witnesses to calculate the loss. The jury is then asked to require defendants to make the loss good. Plaintiffs who can prove that they were humiliated to a point that made them ill are permitted to seek recovery of out-of-pocket expenses for medical care, including psychiatric counseling. Jury awards to cover such calculable losses are called *special damages.*

However, Powell also wrote that "actual injury is not limited to out-of-pocket loss." It includes "impairment of reputation and standing in the community, personal humiliation, and mental anguish." These are intangibles that can be proved only through testimony from the victim or from sympathetic witnesses. Few, if any, standards help a jury place a precise value on these elements. This lack gives plaintiffs' lawyers an opening to play on the sympathies of jurors who may have their own reasons for feeling antagonistic toward media defendants. As noted earlier in this chapter, more than half the libel suits that go to a jury result in verdicts for the plaintiff, and some of these have run into millions of dollars.

A survey of the cases shows that only a few such awards have survived modification if they are appealed. Appellate judges, who do not hear the rhetoric a plaintiff's lawyer used to sway the jury, insist on convincing proof of loss of reputation to support an award of damages. The Arkansas Supreme Court summed up the legal principle involved in its decision in *Little Rock Newspapers* v. *Dodrill:*[123] "It is settled law

---

123.   281 Ark. 25, 660 S.W.2d 933, 10 Med.L.Rptr. 1063 (Ark. 1983).

that damage to reputation is the *essence of libel* and protection of reputation is the fundamental concept of the law of defamation. . . . Such injury to the reputation is a *prerequisite* to making out a case of defamation."

Further, appellate courts have been reluctant to accept a plaintiff's unsupported testimony of loss of standing in the community. In rejecting a claim for damages against the Macmillan Publishing Co., a New York appellate court said that the plaintiff had been "unable to come forth with any proof of loss of reputation because he knows of no one who believes he was a child molester or thinks less of him due to the publication."[124] A U.S. district court in Texas rejected a claim for compensatory damages after the plaintiff's friends and acquaintances had testified to his good character and excellent reputation and offered no evidence that anyone thought less of him after reading the allegedly defamatory article. The court said that a "mere tendency to injure without proof of injury cannot support a finding of defamation."[125]

Courts are divided on the proof that must be offered to support a claim for damages for mental anguish, humiliation, or sorrow. In the cases cited in the preceding paragraph, the courts held that without proof of loss of reputation, there could be no recovery for mental anguish. However, in at least three states, Louisiana, Maryland, and Florida, courts have held that mental distress alone is compensable if convincing proof is offered.[126]

The Vexing Question of Punitive Damages

In addition to special damages and actual or compensatory damages, courts may impose exemplary, or punitive, damages, which are designed to punish the defendant for its callousness and to serve as a deterrent to others who might be tempted to be reckless with the truth. In *Gertz*, the Supreme Court had harsh words for punitive damages awards, calling them "private fines levied by civil juries to punish reprehensible conduct and to deter future occurrence." The Court said that if states permitted private libel plaintiffs to win suits against the media by showing some degree of fault short of actual malice, they could not also permit juries to award punitive damages on the same basis. Private plaintiffs can recover punitive damages, the Court said, only if they can prove actual malice. This is the rule in those states that have adopted the option offered in *Gertz*, particularly if a news medium is the defendant or if the libel occurs as part of the discussion of a public issue.

From the defendant's point of view, a major problem with punitive damages is that there are no clear guidelines for juries to follow in awarding them. Powell noted in *Gertz* that in some instances jurors probably impose damages "to punish expressions of unpopular views." Studies conducted by the Libel Defense Resource Center lend credence to Powell's observation. One study showed that the average damage award by juries in libel cases jumped from $431,000 in 1987–1988 to $4.5 million in

---

124. Salamone v. Macmillan Publishing Co., 77 A.D.2d 501 (N.Y.App.Div. 1980).
125. Reveley v. Berg Publications, Inc., 601 F.Supp. 44 (W.D.Tex. 1984).
126. Freeman v. Cooper, 390 So.2d 1355 (La.App. 1980); affirmed, 414 So.2d 355 (La. 1982); Hearst Corp. v. Hughes, 297 Md. 112, 466 A.2d 486, 9 Med.L.Rptr. 2504 (Md. 1983); and Miami Herald v. Ane, 458 So.2d 239, 10 Med.L.Rptr. 2382 (Fla. 1984).

1989–1990.[127] The study included a then record libel judgment of $34 million, including $31.5 million in punitive damages, against the *Philadelphia Inquirer* in a libel case that ran from 1973 to 1990. Although the court initially sustained the damage award,[128] it changed its mind in 1995, saying that it wanted to reconsider the award in what was by then a twenty-two-year-old case with origins going back to a 1963 homicide investigation.[129]

The average damage award doubled, to $9 million, in 1990–1991, owing in part to a $58 million judgment against Belo Broadcasting and its Dallas television station, WFAA-TV.[130] The broadcaster and its libel insurer elected to settle rather than fight further. The plaintiff was a former district attorney who sued over a newscast criticizing his dismissals of drunken driving charges. Robert W. Decherd, Belo's chairman, said that the "sheer size" of the judgment, coupled with the interest that would have had to be paid on it if the appeal failed, forced the decision. At about the same time, Harte-Hanks Communications, Inc., of San Antonio also elected to settle rather than appeal a $29-million judgment.[131]

Such awards are subject to review by appellate courts and in about three cases out of four are modified or reversed, according to the Libel Defense Resource Center studies. But even at the appellate level, there are no firm rules for determining when an award is excessive. For instance, the *Pittsburgh Post-Gazette* was rebuffed at every level when it sought review of an award of $2 million in punitive damages. Neither the Pennsylvania nor the U.S. Supreme Court would consider the appeal.[132] The sum was ten times the jury's award of $200,000 in actual damages to a former commonwealth court judge. Further, Pennsylvania law, like statutes in some other states, forbids the newspaper's libel insurer to pay any part of punitive damages. By the time the case ended in 1989, interest and fees had raised the award to $2.7 million.

Several times the Supreme Court has agreed to consider cases in which the size of a punitive damages award was at issue. In *Browning-Ferris Industries* v. *Kelco Disposal*[133] a Vermont jury found that a waste disposal firm used unfair methods to drive a competitor out of business. The jury awarded the failed firm $51,146 in compensatory damages and $6 million in punitive damages, and the award was upheld on appeal in the Vermont state courts. In going to the Supreme Court, the loser of the lawsuit argued that the award of punitive damages was an "excessive fine" of the kind prohibited by the Eighth Amendment.[134] The Supreme Court ruled, seven to two, that the amendment was intended to limit fines imposed by government to punish individ-

127. Alex S. Jones, "Libel Study Finds Juries Penalizing News Media," *New York Times,* 26 September 1991.
128. "$34 Million Libel Award against Philadelphia Inquirer Is Upheld," *Wall Street Journal,* 11 September 1992.
129. "Inquirer Gets Second Chance in Sprague Libel Case," *Editor & Publisher,* 11 February 1995, p. 19.
130. "Survey: Juries Hiking Libel Penalties," *Editor & Publisher*, 5 September 1992, p. 13.
131. Jones, "Libel Study," n. 127.
132. Peter Pae, "Pittsburgh Paper Sues to Get Insurer to Cover Damages," *Wall Street Journal,* 13 July 1989.
133. 492 U.S. 257, 109 S.Ct. 2909, 106 L.Ed.2d 219 (1989).
134. The amendment says, "Excessive bail shall not be required, nor excessive fines imposed, nor cruel and unusual punishments inflicted."

uals for criminal acts and therefore does not apply to jury awards in civil actions. The Court left open the question as to whether excessive awards of punitive damages might violate the due process clause of the Fourteenth Amendment. Five justices have at one time or another raised questions as to whether awards of punitive damages that are far out of proportion to the actual damage that led to the lawsuit violate that clause.[135]

However, when the Court accepted a case based squarely on the due process clause, it declined the invitation to put a limit on punitive damages or even to offer lower courts "bright-line" criteria for determining when such awards may be excessive.[136] Instead, the Court backed into its decision by saying that rules of common law that are evolved by state courts for evaluating and limiting awards of damages are not unconstitutional on their face. However, Justice Blackmun, writing for a majority, said, "General concerns of reasonableness and adequate guidance from the court when the case is tried to a jury properly enter into the constitutional calculus," thus indicating that at some point there is a due process limit on punitive damages. In that case, growing out of an agent's pocketing of premiums intended to buy health insurance, a jury's award of $840,000 in punitive damages—about three and a half times the award of compensatory damages—was upheld.

In 1994 the Court again expressed its concern about punitive damages, holding that states must make some form of judicial review available.[137] Writing for the majority, Justice John Paul Stevens said that because "punitive damages pose an acute danger of arbitrary deprivation of property," some judicial review for excessiveness is required as a matter of due process. But the Court did not define the required standard of review any more specifically than it currently is: So long as the lower courts provide some meaningful constraints on jury discretion and so long as awards are not grossly out of proportion to the severity of the offense, lower courts are free to fashion damages sufficiently high to dissuade others from committing similar acts.[138]

Five states prohibit awards of punitive damages in libel cases. They are Massachusetts,[139] Michigan,[140] New Hampshire,[141] Oregon,[142] and Washington.[143] In Oregon and Washington, the ban is found in the state constitution. In New Hampshire, recovery is prohibited by statute. In the other states, the prohibition is grounded in common law.

---

135. Stephen Wermiel, "Punitive Damage Amounts in Civil Lawsuits Aren't Restricted, Justices Rule," *Wall Street Journal,* 27 June 1989.
136. Pacific Mutual Life Insurance Company v. Haslip, 499 U.S. 1, 111 S.Ct. 1032, 113 L.Ed.2d 1, 18 Med.L.Rptr. 1753 (1991).
137. Honda v. Oberg, 114 S.Ct. 2331, 129 L.Ed.2d 336 (1994). Linda Greenhouse, "Punitive Damage Awards by Juries Must Be Subject to Judicial Review, Justices Rule," *New York Times,* 25 June 1994, p. 9.
138. Pacific Mutual Life Insurance Co. v. Haslip, 111 S.Ct. 1032 (1991). See also Sprouse v. Clay Communications, 211 S.E.2d 674 (W.Va. 1975); cert denied, 423 U.S. 882 (1975).
139. Stone v. Essex County Newspapers, 367 Mass. 849, 330 N.E.2d 161 (Mass. 1975).
140. Peisner v. Detroit Free Press, 364 N.E.2d 600, 11 Med.L.Rptr. 1553 (Mich. 1985).
141. RSA 508:16 (Supp. 1986).
142. Wheeler v. Green, 286 Ore. 99, 593 P.2d 777, 5 Med.L.Rptr. 1132 (Ore. 1979).
143. Taskett v. KING Broadcasting, 86 Wash.2d 439, 546 P.2d 81, 1 Med.L.Rptr. 1716 (1976); Farrar v. Tribune Publishing Co., 57 Wash.2d 549, 358 P.2d 792 (1961).

DEFENSES ⎯⎯⎯⎯⎯⎯⎯⎯⎯⎯⎯⎯⎯⎯⎯⎯⎯⎯

At common law, the principle defenses to a libel suit were three: truth, fair comment, and qualified privilege. Those defenses are still available in cases that raise First Amendment concerns, but the First Amendment also has had the effect of transforming those defenses into something more powerful than they were at common law.

Opinion ⎯⎯⎯⎯⎯⎯⎯⎯⎯⎯⎯⎯⎯⎯⎯⎯⎯⎯

The constitutional protection of opinion in libel cases is based on an almost offhand observation by Justice Lewis F. Powell, Jr., in *Gertz*. Writing for a majority of the Supreme Court, he said that "there is no such thing as a false idea." Opinion, he added, no matter how "pernicious" or mistaken it may seem, should be countered by debate, not by a judge or jury deciding a libel suit. At the time, most courts and legal scholars considered the passage a dictum because it was not essential to the Court's decision. Thus, the passage did not establish a precedent that lower courts were required to apply. However, within a few years some judges were citing Powell's language to support decisions dismissing libel cases based on editorials, commentary, and other assertions of opinion. By 1984 the trend had assumed such force that the U.S. Court of Appeals for the Ninth Circuit asserted flatly that defamation actions cannot be based on statements of opinion.[144] In that same year, the U.S. Court of Appeals for the District of Columbia Circuit, sitting *en banc* (the entire panel of judges participated), went a step further and held that the distinction between fact and opinion is a question of law to be decided by a judge.[145] In the past decade, panels in all twelve federal circuits have held that opinion is not actionable as a matter of law.[146] In many instances, the decisions applied pertinent state law, reflecting the fact that state courts, too, were holding that either the First Amendment or the free speech clauses of their own state constitutions protected expressions of opinion.

The Supreme Court did not directly address the constitutional status of opinion until it decided the *Falwell* case discussed in Chapter 4. Indeed, both Rehnquist and former Chief Justice Warren E. Burger had written in one instance that *Gertz* had not es-

---

144. Church of Scientology of California v. Flynn, 744 F.2d 694 (9th Cir. 1984).

145. Ollman v. Evans, 750 F.2d 970, 11 Med.L.Rptr. 1433 (D.C.Cir. 1984); cert. denied, 471 U.S. 1127, 11 Med.L.Rptr. 2015 (1985).

146. Fudge v. Penthouse International, Ltd. 840 F.2d 1012, 14 Med.L.Rptr. 2353 (1st Cir. 1988); cert. denied, 109 S.Ct. 65 (1988). Mr. Chow of New York v. Ste. Jour Azur, 759 F.2d 219, 11 Med.L.Rptr. 1713 (2d Cir. 1985). Jenkins v. KYW, 829 F.2d 403, 14 Med.L.Rptr. 1718 (3d Cir. 1987). Potomac Valve & Fitting, Inc. v. Crawford Fitting Co., 829 F.2d 1280 (4th Cir. 1987). Mitchell v. Random House, Inc., 865 F.2d 664 (5th Cir. 1989). Street v. National Broadcasting Co., 645 F.2d 1227, 7 Med.L.Rptr. 1001 (6th Cir. 1981). Woods v. Evansville Press Co., Inc., 791 F.2d 480, 12 Med.L.Rptr. 2174 (7th Cir. 1986). Janklow v. Newsweek, Inc., 788 F.2d 1300, 12 Med.L.Rptr. 1961 (8th Cir. *en banc* 1986); reversing 759 F.2d 644, 11 Med.L.Rptr. 1995 (1984); cert. denied, 479 U.S. 883 (1986). Church of Scientology of California v. Flynn, 744 F.2d 694 (9th Cir. 1984). Rinsley v. Brandt, 700 F.2d 1304, 9 Med.L.Rptr. 1225 (10th Cir. 1983). Keller v. Miami Herald, 778 F.2d 711, 12 Med.L.Rptr. 1561 (11th Cir. 1985). Ollman v. Evans, 750 F.2d 870, 11 Med.L.Rptr. 1433 (D.C.Cir. 1984); cert. denied, 471 U.S. 1127, 11 Med.L.Rptr. 2015 (1985).

tablished a federal rule with respect to opinion.[147] However, in *Falwell,* Rehnquist wrote, echoing Powell in *Gertz,* "The First Amendment recognizes no such thing as a 'false' idea." Expanding on that theme, Rehnquist analyzed several of the Supreme Court's libel decisions, concluding that even when critics of a public person are moved by "motives that are less than admirable," their opinions are protected by the Constitution. That also is true, Rehnquist added, when the unfavorable opinion is inspired by hatred or ill will. Because he was writing for a unanimous court, and because the *Hustler* cartoon did express an opinion of sorts, Rehnquist thus seemed to put the full weight of the Supreme Court behind the principle that the First Amendment gives absolute protection to expressions of opinion.

That principle still holds true, but with a caveat. If the opinion is based on, or even implies, a false and defamatory assertion of fact, it can be actionable. Chief Justice Rehnquist, who had so strongly defended opinion, no matter how shabby, in *Falwell,* suggested in *Milkovich* v. *Lorain Journal Co.* that opinion was not to be understood as a court-created separate defense to libel, but rather as the simple absence of what defamation is: false facts that harm reputations. Statements that are not explicitly or implicitly factual or statements that cannot be proven to be false, are not actionable, whether they be called opinion or anything else.

Milkovich v. *Lorain Journal Co.,* **497 U.S. 1,
110 S.Ct. 2695,
111 L.Ed.2d 1,
17 Med.L.Rptr. 2009 (1990).**

In Milkovich, the Court rejected the Ohio courts' conclusion, based on a line of cases inspired by *Gertz,* that the First Amendment simply exempted opinion from the application of defamation laws. Rehnquist said that Powell's dictum in *Gertz* "was merely a reiteration of Justice Holmes' classic 'marketplace of ideas' concept" and was not "intended to create a wholesale defamation exemption for anything that might be labeled 'opinion.'" In sending the case back to the Ohio courts, the Court said that *New York Times,* as interpreted by the *Greenbelt–Old Dominion–Falwell* line of cases, had given opinion all the First Amendment protection it needs.

Milkovich had been in the Ohio courts since 1974 and had reached the U.S. Supreme Court twice previously.[148] The dispute began when a sports columnist disagreed with a court decision upholding a high school wrestling team's right to compete in a state tournament. The Ohio High School Athletic Association had declared the team ineligible after finding that its coach had provoked an altercation at a wrestling match. The coach and his school asked a court to overturn the order, which it did. J. Theodore Diadiun, who wrote a column, "TD Says," for the *Lake County News Herald,* published by the *Lorain Journal,* had been at the wrestling match, but did not attend the hearing in court. Relying on what he was told by the association's director, he wrote, "Anyone who attended the meet . . . knows in his heart that Milkovich and Scott lied at the hearing after each having given his solemn oath to tell the truth." Their actions, he wrote, taught students a lesson: "If you get in a jam, lie

---

147. Miskovsky v. Oklahoma Publishing Co., 459 U.S. 923, 103 S.Ct. 235, 74 L.Ed.2d 186, 8 Med.L.Rptr. 2302 (1982).

148. Certiorari was denied on both occasions: 449 U.S. 966, 101 S.Ct. 380, 66 L.Ed.2d 232 (1980); and 474 U.S. 953, 106 S.Ct. 322, 88 L.Ed.2d 305 (1985).

your way out of it." Michael Milkovich was the wrestling coach at Maple Heights High School and H. Donald Scott was superintendent of the school. Both sued for libel. Scott gave up his quest for damages in 1986 when the Ohio Supreme Court, ruling that the column was constitutionally protected opinion, sustained the *News-Herald*'s motion for summary judgment.[149] Alone, the caption "TD Says," the court stated, "would indicate to even the most gullible reader that the article was, in fact, opinion" and therefore not actionable. Milkovich persisted in his suit, arguing that the column falsely accused him of the crime of perjury—that is, of lying to a court under oath. When an Ohio appellate court felt itself bound by the state supreme court's decision in *Scott* and dismissed the suit, Milkovich appealed to the U.S. Supreme Court, which reversed.

The Court said that Milkovich had a point. The case should be permitted to go to trial because "a reasonable fact finder could conclude that...the column" implied that Milkovich had perjured himself. The writer did not use the kind of loose, figurative, or hyperbolic language that the Court had found acceptable in *Bresler, Letter Carriers,* and *Falwell.* Nor did the column as a whole negate the impression that Diadiun was accusing Milkovich of lying. Rehnquist expanded on that point:

> If a speaker says, "In my opinion John Jones is a liar," he implies a knowledge of facts which lead to the conclusion that Jones told an untruth. Even if the speaker states the facts upon which he bases his opinion, if those facts are either incorrect or incomplete, or if his assessment of them is erroneous, the statement may still imply a false assertion of fact. Simply couching such statements in terms of opinion does not dispel these implications; and the statement, "In my opinion Jones is a liar," can cause as much damage to reputation as the statement, "Jones is a liar."

In 1991, nine months after the Supreme Court had acted, attorneys for Milkovich and the *News-Herald* announced that the newspaper had agreed to pay Milkovich $116,000 to settle the dispute.[150] The newspaper's publisher said it had spent $500,000 defending the lawsuit and estimated that it would have cost more than twice the amount of the settlement to continue the litigation.

Since *Milkovich,* courts have moved in two directions. Some are more cautious, seeing the decision as a mandate to scrutinize carefully libel cases based on statements of opinion. Others continue to give broad protection to statements of opinion, relying on the principle that courts may not narrow the limits of freedom established by the Supreme Court, but they may expand them.[151] Courts in several states, including Ohio, have indicated that *Milkovich* did not significantly change anything.[152]

In practice, courts continue to decide cases after *Milkovich* in much the way they would have decided them before.[153] In *Morningstar Inc.* v. *Los Angeles Superior Court,* the California court of appeals said that before "*Milkovich,* the California

---

149. Scott v. News-Herald, 25 Ohio St.3d 243, 496 N.E.2d 699, 13 Med.L.Rptr. 1241 (1986).
150. "N-H Settles Milkovich Suit," *Lake County News Herald,* 2 April 1991.
151. Immuno AG. v. J. Moor-Jankowski, 567 N.E.2d 1270; cert. denied, 111 S.Ct. 2261 (1991).
152. Vail v. The Plain Dealer Publishing Co., 72 Ohio St.3d 279, 23 Med.L.Rptr. 1881 (Ohio 1995); Snider v. National Audubon Society, Inc., 20 Med.L.Rptr. 1218 (E.D.Cal. 1992); Shearson Lehman Hutton, Inc. v. Tucker, 806 S.W.2d 914 (Tex.App. 1991); Don King Productions, Inc. v. Douglas, 742 F.Supp. 778 (S.D.N.Y. 1990).
153. *Communications Law 1994,* vol. 1, p. 29.

courts had employed a 'totality of the circumstances' test to differentiate between fact and opinion. . . . *Milkovich* did not substantially change [this] principle; it underscored that in cases such as this, raising First Amendment issues, a reviewing court must make an independent examination of the whole record in order to ensure that there is no infringement of free expression."[154]

In the influential District of Columbia Circuit Court of Appeals, too, the court has held that circumstances matter. That court has interpreted *Milkovich* to mean that claims of "opinion" should be approached with caution lest they be camouflage for false facts stated indirectly, but that honest opinion itself is safeguarded by the First Amendment. In *Moldea* v. *New York Times,* the court held that context is critical in determining whether opinion is protected.

Moldea v. New York Times, **22 F.3d 310, 22 Med.L.Rptr. 1673 (D.C. Cir. 1994).**

The case arose when an article in the *New York Times Book Review,* a supplement to the Sunday edition, criticized a book by Dan E. Moldea titled *Interference: How Organized Crime Influences Professional Football.* The *Times* reviewer, Gerald Eskenazi, said, among other things, that the book contained "too much sloppy journalism to trust" most of it. Moldea viewed the assertion as an attack on his reputation and sued. The federal district court granted summary judgment in favor of the *Times.*[155] Moldea appealed, and the court of appeals at first overruled the district court in *Moldea (I),*[156] and then, in a remarkable move, changed its mind in *Moldea (II).* Judge Edwards wrote in the opening paragraph of his opinion for the court in *Moldea (II):*

> I often have been struck by Justice Stewart's concurring statement in *Boys Markets, Inc. . . .,*[157] a case in which the Court reconsidered and overruled an earlier decision. Justice Stewart remarked that, "[i]n these circumstances the temptation is strong to embark on a lengthy personal *apologia.*" This remark has special poignancy for me now, because it underscores the distress felt by a judge who, in grappling with a very difficult legal issue, concludes that he has made a mistake of judgment.[158]

The court's mistake, said Judge Edwards, was not paying attention to the context in which the critical remarks were made.

> A writer may not commit libel at will merely by labeling his work a "review." *Moldea* (I) is short-sighted, however, in failing to take account of the fact that the challenged statements were evaluations of a literary work which appeared in a forum in which readers expect to find such evaluations. As the Supreme Court has recognized, writers must be given some leeway to offer "rational interpretation" of ambiguous sources. See *Masson* v. *New Yorker Magazine, Inc.,* 111 S.Ct. 2419, 2434 [18 Med.L.Rptr. 2241] (1991). Thus, when a reviewer offers commentary that is tied to the work being reviewed, and that is a supportable interpretation of the author's work, that interpretation does not present a verifiable issue of fact that can be actionable in defamation.

---

154. Morningstar Inc. v. Los Angeles Superior Court, 23 Cal.App. 676, 29 Cal.Rptr.2d 547, 22 Med.L.Rptr. 1521 (1994).
155. Moldea v. New York Times, 19 Med.L.Rptr. 1931 (1992).
156. Moldea v. New York Times, 15 F.3d 1137, 22 Med.L.Rptr. 1321 (1994).
157. 398 U.S. 235, 255 (1970).
158. Moldea v. New York Times, 22 F.3d 310, 22 Med.L.Rptr. 1673 (D.C. Cir. 1994).

The *Times* review was protected opinion, said the court, because it *was* a book review. It *was* a critic's interpretation and was rationally supportable (even if wrong) by reference to the text he was evaluating. By contrast, if the review stated "that *Interference* was a terrible book because it asserted that African-Americans make poor football coaches," when in fact the book never expressed such a notion, "the usual inquiries as to libel would apply: a jury could determine that the review falsely characterized *Interference,* thereby libeling its author by portraying him as a racist (assuming the other elements of the case could be proved)."[159]

Despite misgivings among the courts about whether opinion is a true defense or merely a reflection of the requirement that a plaintiff prove falsity, the First Amendment's protection for opinion has become a strong and frequently used response to a libel complaint. It is the defense of choice in cases involving comment on matters of public interest, supplanting the old common law defense of fair comment. The only caveat is that if an opinion does assert or imply any false and defamatory facts directed at an identifiable individual, then labeling it "opinion" won't be enough to save it from judicial scrutiny.

Retraction

As of this writing, only Utah has adopted the Uniform Correction or Clarification Act discussed in Chapter 4, but in a majority of states, a news medium's honest retraction of a defamatory error usually lowers an award of damages, even if it doesn't necessarily ward off a libel suit once the plaintiff is determined to go forward. In ten states, the District of Columbia, and Puerto Rico, courts have held as a matter of common law that a full and prompt retraction, given prominent display in the offending medium, can be introduced at trial and considered by the jury in fixing the award of damages.[160] In at least three states, the prompt publication of a retraction has led to a finding that the material had not been published with actual malice.[161] Additionally, West Virginia has said that punitive damages would be inappropriate in cases where there has been a "prompt, prominent and abject apology."[162] In thirty-one states,[163] legislatures have enacted statutes defining the nature and effect of a retraction. Tennessee appears on both lists because its courts have recognized a common law right to introduce a retraction in mitigation of damages, and it has a statute that prohibits an award of punitive damages if a proper retraction is made.

---

159. Ibid at 22 Med.L.Rptr. 1677.
160. The states are Arkansas, Colorado, Kansas, Louisiana, Maryland, New York, Pennsylvania, South Carolina, Tennessee, and Washington.
161. Powell v. Toledo Blade, 19 Med.L.Rptr. 1727 (Ohio Ct. Common Pleas 1991); Cape Publications v. Teri's Health Studio, 385 So.2d 188 (Fla.Ct.App. 1980); Kerwick v. Orange County Publications, 53 N.Y.2d 625 (1981).
162. Hinerman v. Daily Gazette Co., 188 W.Va. 157, 423 S.E.2d 560, 20 Med.L.Rptr. 2169 (1992); cert. denied, 113 S.Ct. 1384 (1993).
163. Alabama, Arizona, California, Connecticut, Florida, Georgia, Idaho, Indiana, Iowa, Kentucky, Maine, Massachusetts, Michigan, Minnesota, Mississippi, Montana, Nebraska, Nevada, New Jersey, North Carolina, North Dakota, Ohio, Oklahoma, Oregon, South Dakota, Tennessee, Texas, Utah, Virginia, West Virginia, and Wisconsin.

Courts in Arizona[164] and Ohio[165] have held that laws requiring retractions are unconstitutional. The Arizona court acted on state constitutional grounds. The Ohio court cited the U.S. Supreme Court decision in *Miami Herald* v. *Tornillo.*[166] In that case, the Court had held that compelling a newspaper to publish material its editors would choose not to publish is a form of prior restraint.

Retraction statutes vary. At one end of the scale they provide only, as in common law, that a proper retraction can be used in an attempt to lower the award of damages. At the other end of the scale, Indiana, Mississippi, North Carolina, North Dakota, South Dakota, Utah, and Wisconsin require plaintiffs to seek a retraction before filing a libel suit. Commonly, the statutes limit plaintiffs to recovery of actual or general damages if a timely and complete retraction is made. Actual damages are defined in some statutes as provable financial loss. General damages include compensation for such intangibles as humiliation and embarrassment, or being shunned in the community.

Editors, producers, insurance carriers, and the lawyers who advise them, sometimes differ about the wisdom of publishing retractions. If the alleged libel involves a simple mistake in fact resulting from a misunderstanding, or reliance on an uninformed or malicious source, most would agree that a retraction should be made, especially if that would settle the issue. However, stories that often lead to libel suits are the result of complex investigations into the conduct of public officials or public figures. Or they grow out of the coverage of highly charged disagreements over public policy. In such instances, a retraction may only make things worse. It would not be in the defendant's interest to say that the sources used by the reporter did not say what they were quoted as saying. Nor would it be in the defendant's interest to say that the sources were quoted accurately but the reporter knew they were lying. In such instances, lawyers usually advise against a retraction that would amount to an admission of actual malice.

Neutral Reportage

Since 1977, courts in a few jurisdictions have recognized a First Amendment privilege for news media that are confronted with highly charged and newsworthy public controversies. In these jurisdictions, courts have held that when accusations are being flung back and forth, it is unreasonable to expect the media to investigate all of them and make reasonably certain that they are true. Therefore, as long as the media offer a neutral report of the accusations and the reactions of the participants in the controversy, the media are protected. The protection will prevail even when reporters and editors may have had serious doubts about the truth of the accusations, meaning, of course, that the defense could even overcome a showing of actual malice. Such protection, called the privilege of neutral reportage, has not won general approval. Courts in a few jurisdictions have rejected it. The Supreme Court has been silent on the issue.[167]

---

164. Boswell v. Phoenix Newspapers, Inc., 152 Ariz. 9, 730 P.2d 186, 13 Med.L.Rptr. 1785 (1986).
165. Beacon Journal Publishing Co. v. Lansdowne, 11 Med.L.Rptr. 1094 (C.P. 1984).
166. 418 U.S. 241, 94 S.Ct. 2831, 41 L.Ed.2d 730, 1 Med.L.Rptr. 1898 (1974).
167. However, in a brief concurring opinion in *Harte-Hankes,* Justice Blackmun suggested that the newspaper's lawyer was "unwise" in not relying on the privilege of neutral reporting as a defense. Blackmun said the facts of the case "arguably might fit within it."

The privilege was recognized first in 1977 by the U.S. Court of Appeals, Second Circuit, in *Edwards* v. *National Audubon Society*. The case began when a reporter for the *New York Times* read an editorial in a publication of the Audubon Society. The editorial said that some scientists who were defending the continued use of DDT as an insecticide were "paid liars." The reporter considered

Edwards v. *National Audubon Society,* 566 F.2d 113, 2 Med.L.Rptr. 1849 (2d Cir. 1977).

the allegation newsworthy, but so broad that it could hit a lot of innocent targets. He asked the society to be more specific. A vice president of the society gave him five names but insisted, as did the editor of the publication, that he did not know that the named scientists were in fact "paid liars." What he did know was that the five continued to cite the society's annual bird count as proof of their assertion that DDT was not harmful to bird life. In the society's view, the count was increasing year by year not because there were more birds, but because more watchers were participating in the count. The vice president said that the five scientists he had named had ignored the society's efforts to impress them with this point. This list included three professors at highly regarded state universities, a Nobel Prize winner who had developed high-yield varieties of food grains, and a lecturer for the National Agricultural Chemical Association. The *Times* reporter sought comment from the five and obtained it from three of them. The resulting news story used the expression "paid to lie," attributed to an Audubon Society spokesperson, and gave the reaction of the scientists. The three university professors sued the society and the *Times* for libel. A jury awarded two of them $20,000 each and the third $21,000.

On appeal, the circuit court reversed, holding that the *Times* was protected by an absolute constitutional privilege based on a right of neutral reportage. It defined that right:

> At stake in this case is a fundamental principle. Succinctly stated, when a responsible, prominent organization like the National Audubon Society makes serious charges against a public figure, the First Amendment protects the accurate and disinterested reporting of those charges, regardless of the reporter's private views regarding their validity. . . . What is newsworthy about such accusations is that they were made. We do not believe that the press may be required under the First Amendment to suppress newsworthy statements merely because it has serious doubts regarding their truth. Nor must the press take up cudgels against dubious charges in order to publish them without fear of liability for defamation. . . . The public interest in being fully informed about controversies that often rage around sensitive issues demands that the press be afforded the freedom to report such charges without assuming responsibility for them.

Edwards and subsequent decisions of other courts yield four elements that are essential to establish the privilege of neutral reportage:

1. A public controversy must exist, or it must be created by serious and newsworthy charges.

2. The allegations at issue must be made by a responsible person or organization, probably rising to the level of a public official or public figure.

3. The assertion at issue must be directed at a public official or a public figure.

4. The assertion must be reported accurately and neutrally.

Courts adopting the *Edwards* precedent have emphasized the first two points: The controversy must exist independently of the news media, and the assertions at issue must be initiated by someone of stature who is seen by the media as both responsible and newsworthy. The media's role must be confined to that of a disinterested observer resisting the temptation to take sides or to add fuel to the controversy.

In *McManus* v. *Doubleday & Co.,*[168] a federal district court in New York City held that neutral reportage did not apply to charges resulting from investigative reporting. The court held that the charges were solicited by the reporter and that "no controversy raged around the libelous statement before the reporter entered the scene." The court emphasized that "journalist-induced charges" do not come under the protection of the Edwards privilege. Nor does a news story "particularly lacking in balanced reporting."[169]

The privilege of neutral reportage has been recognized in Arizona,[170] California,[171] Florida,[172] Georgia,[173] Indiana,[174] New Jersey,[175] Ohio,[176] Texas,[177] Vermont,[178] and Washington.[179] The federal district court with jurisdiction over Wyoming has recognized the privilege, and state courts have twice referred favorably to it in dicta.[180] Alabama courts also have recognized the privilege in dicta.[181]

Illinois appellate courts have both accepted and rejected the neutral reportage privilege. A down-state court was one of the early endorsers of *Edwards,*[182] but Chicago-area courts have twice rejected it in dicta.[183]

State Courts in Kentucky,[184] Michigan,[185] New York,[186] Pennsylvania,[187] and South Dakota[188] have rejected the doctrine of neutral reportage. In their view, the privilege

---

168. 513 F.Supp. 1383, 7 Med.L.Rptr. 1475 (S.D.N.Y. 1981).
169. Cianci v. New Times Publishing Co. 639 F.2d 54, 6 Med.L.Rptr. 1625 (2d Cir. 1980).
170. Godbehere v. Phoenix Newspapers, Inc., 15 Med.L.Rptr. 2052 (Ariz.Super.Ct., Maricopa County, 1988).
171. Barry v. Time, 584 F.Supp. 1110, 10 Med.L.Rptr. 1809 (N.D.Cal. 1984).
172. Brake & Alignment Supply v. Post-Newsweek, 472 So.2d 517, 11 Med.L.Rptr. 2183 (Fla.Dist.Ct.App. 1985).
173. Minton v. Thomson Newspapers, 175 Ga.App. 525, 33 S.E.2d 913, 12 Med.L.Rptr. 1301 (1985).
174. Woods v. Evansville Press Co., 11 Med.L.Rptr. 2201 (S.D.Ind. 1985); affirmed on other grounds, 791 F.2d 480 (7th Cir. 1986).
175. Lavin v. New York News, 757 F.2d 1416, 11 Med.L.Rptr. 1873 (3d Cir. 1985).
176. Horvath v. The Telegraph, 8 Med.L.Rptr. 1657 (Ohio App. 1982).
177. Brady v. Cox Enterprises, Inc., 782 S.W.2d 272, 17 Med.L.Rptr. 1273 (Tex.Ct.App. 1990).
178. Burns v. Times-Argus Association, 139 Vt. 381, 430 A.2d 773, 7 Med.L.Rptr. 1212 (Vt. 1981).
179. Senear v. Daily Journal American, 8 Med.L.Rptr. 2489 (Wash.Sup.Ct., King County, 1982).
180. Whitaker v. Denver Post, 4 Med.L.Rptr. 1351 (D.Wyo. 1978); McMurray v. Howard Publications, 612 P.2d 14, 6 Med.L.Rptr. 1814 (Wyo. 1980); and MacGuire v. Harriscope Broadcasting Corp., 612 P.2d 830, 6 Med.L.Rptr. 1257 (Wyo. 1980).
181. Wilson v. Birmingham Post, 482 So.2d 1209, 12 Med.L.Rptr. 1668 (Ala. 1986).
182. Krauss v. Champaign News Gazette, 59 Ill.App.3d 745, 375 N.E.2d 1362, 3 Med.L.Rptr. 2507 (Ill. 1978).
183. Newell v. Field Enterprises, 91 Ill.App.3d 735, 415 N.E.2d 434 (Ill.App. 1980); and Tunney v. American Broadcasting Co., 109 Ill.App.3d 769, 441 N.E.2d 86 (Ill.App. 1982).
184. McCall v. Courier-Journal and Louisville Times, 623 S.W.2d 882, 7 Med.L.Rptr. 2118 (Ky. 1981).
185. Postill v. Booth Newspapers, 118 Mich.App. 608, 325 N.W.2d 511, 8 Med.L.Rptr. 2222 (Mich.App. 1982).
186. Hogan v. Herald Co., 84 A.D.2d 470, 446 N.Y.S.2d 836, 8 Med.L.Rptr. 1137 (N.Y.App.Div. 1982; affirmed, 58 N.Y.2d 630. 458 N.Y.S.2d 556, 444 N.E.2d 1002, 8 Med.L.Rptr. 2567 (1982).
187. Braig v. Field Communications, 456 A.2d 1366, 9 Med.L.Rptr. 1057 (Pa.Super.Ct., Philadelphia, 1983).
188. Janklow v. Viking Press, 378 N.W.2d 875, 12 Med.L.Rptr. 1539 (S.Dak. 1985).

gives the media an opening to publish dubious false and defamatory accusations simply because someone made them. To embrace that doctrine, these courts have said, they would have to ignore all that the U.S. Supreme Court has said about actual malice. In their view, the news media have no right to circulate defamatory allegations they know to be false, or about which they have serious doubt, no matter who makes them.

It is worthy of note that although *Edwards* was decided by the U.S. Court of Appeals for the Second Circuit, which sits in New York City, New York's state courts have refused to be bound by that decision. And one U.S. district court judge within the circuit ruled that *Edwards* should be given a narrow interpretation.[189] He said that any claim for protection under the neutral reportage privilege should be given careful scrutiny to make certain that all four factors on which that decision was based are present. At a minimum, then, the squabble must have begun without instigation from a news medium, it must be over an issue of genuine public importance, the defamatory accusations must have been made by public officials or public figures and directed at others of the same stature, and the news media must have played the story straight down the middle. Anything short of that is not neutral reportage.

The Fair-Report Privilege

Although the constitutional privilege created by *New York Times* v. *Sullivan* is the defense of choice for lawyers defending communications media against libel suits, the common law defense of qualified privilege is still useful. The purpose of the privilege is to protect the news media when they act as the eyes and ears of the general public in covering the actions of government agencies and the statements of government officials. Under common law, such reports had to be fair and accurate or the privilege was lost. With the added protection afforded by the actual malice holding in *New York Times,* and the negligence option offered by *Gertz,* the qualified privilege defense has become much stronger. However, courts in several states have upheld libel verdicts arising from the erroneous reporting of judicial proceedings.[190] In effect, the courts have told reporters that if they cover the courts, they better know enough law to make sure their stories are accurate. However, if reporters use care in reporting official proceedings and in taking information from public records, they can rely on the defense of qualified privilege to protect them in libel actions. Courts sometimes refer to this as the fair-report privilege.

In general, the privilege covers accurate reports of statements made at public meetings;[191] of official proceedings of public agencies, even when they are not open to the public;[192] of court proceedings, including statements made to a grand jury;[193] and of

189. Lasky v. ABC, 631 F.Supp. 962, 13 Med.L.Rptr. 1379 (S.D.N.Y. 1986).
190. See Firestone v. Time, Inc., 405 So.2d 172 (Fla. 1974) and Gobin v. Globe Publishing Co., 531 P.2d 76 (Kans. 1975).
191. Kilgore v. Younger, 102 Cal.App.3d 744, 162 Cal.Rptr. 469 (1980); affirmed, 30 Cal.3d 770, 640 P.2d 793, 180 Cal.Rptr. 657 (1982).
192. White v. Fraternal Order of Police, 909 F.2d 512 (D.C.Cir. 1990).
193. Reeves v. American Broadcasting Cos., 719 F.2d 602 (2d Cir. 1983).

proceedings in a family court not open to the public.[194] A federal district court in Colorado, interpreting that state's law, held that letters written to a state agency, to various county officials, and even to a newspaper in connection with a rezoning proceeding carried absolute protection. Since they had been written in response to a zoning board's request for facts on which to base its decision, they became a function of government and were thus privileged.[195]

Statements made by public officials, including law enforcement officers, are protected by absolute privilege when the officials are acting in an official capacity. But some courts have held that police incident reports are not protected by privilege,[196] nor are private statements about suspects made to reporters by police officers.[197] A federal district court in Pennsylvania held in *Williams* v. *WCAU-TV* that the station was protected by privilege when it televised the arrest of a suspected bank robber, even though the suspect later was released after police concluded that he had no connection with the robbery. The court held that the arrest was an official action protected by the state's law defining privilege.[198]

Courts also operate under absolute privilege. Absolute privilege protects witnesses, lawyers, and judges in their testimony or comment during any legal proceedings. A federal court in Illinois held that a letter written to a judge by a psychologist in connection with a child custody proceeding was absolutely privileged because it was relevant to the proceeding.[199] In California, depositions taken in advance of a trial are protected by an absolute privilege. A state appellate court reasoned, in a libel case brought against the *Fresno Bee,* that depositions are as much a part of a trial as is testimony given in open court.[200] Therefore, the court held, the *Bee* was protected by a qualified privilege when it published a fair and accurate account of a deposition made by one of its own reporters. In the taking of a deposition, lawyers for one side in a legal action question under oath prospective witnesses for the other side in an attempt to narrow the issues at trial.

The defense of qualified privilege can be lost. Both a U.S. district court and the Third Circuit Court of Appeals held that a *Time* magazine reporter forfeited the privilege when he omitted part of a leaked confidential FBI report from an article. The article, paraphrasing the report, said that the name of the principal owner of a construction company had "appeared several times in the bureau's reports on the 1975 disappearance of Teamster Boss Jimmy Hoffa." The FBI report also said that none of the references to the owner "suggested any criminality or organized crime associations." The reporter testified that he had omitted the disclaimer because he didn't believe it, although three of his sources within the agency told him they had gone through the files and found nothing to connect the owner with Hoffa's disappearance. In holding that the "omission presents a clear example of an unfair report that does not deserve

194. Dorsey v. National Enquirer, 952 F.2d 250 (9th Cir. 1992).
195. Walters v. Linhof, 559 F.Supp. 1231, 9 Med.L.Rptr. 1477 (D.Colo. 1983).
196. Rouch v. Enquirer & News, 137 Mich.App. 39, 357 N.W.2d 794 (1984); Stone v. Banner Publishing Co., 677 F.Supp. 242 (D.Vt. 1988); Wilson v. Birmingham Post Co., 482 So.2d 1209 (Ala. 1986).
197. Weimer v. Rankin, 117 Idaho 566, 790 P.2d 347 (1990).
198. 555 F.Supp. 198, 9 Med.L.Rptr. 1073 (E.D.Pa. 1983).
199. Bond v. Pecaut, 561 F.Supp. 1037 (D.Ill. 1983).
200. McClatchy Newspapers, Inc. v. Superior Court, 189 Cal.App.3d 961, 234 Cal.Rptr. 702, 13 Med.L.Rptr. 2281 (Calif. 1987).

the qualified privilege to reproduce a libel," the circuit court said it would let a jury decide whether the omission was actual malice.[201]

When people file lawsuits, they generally accuse a defendant of terrible things and ask for huge sums of money in compensation. While it is unethical for a lawyer to file a frivolous lawsuit, that doesn't mean that everything alleged in the petition will turn out to be true in the end. Does privilege protect the reporting of false information found in a complaint initiating a lawsuit? In the majority of the states that have ruled on the question, courts have held that such petitions are not protected by privilege until a court has taken some legal notice of them. A decision made on a motion, either by the defense or the plaintiff, constitutes such legal notice. In these states, reporters who act too soon in basing a story on defamatory material taken from a petition filed in court may not be able to rely on qualified privilege as a defense.

Courts in a few states have held that pleadings in a lawsuit are privileged when they are filed with the clerk.[202] An Illinois appeals court listed four reasons for reaching this decision:

1. The public has an interest in knowing what goes on in court, especially since many of society's problems are being addressed through litigation. Courts have been asked, for instance, to resolve issues affecting minority job rights, university admissions policies, wages paid to women, water and air pollution, and the safety of automobiles.

2. The majority of states have taken the position that by deferring privilege until some judicial action has been taken, they will discourage the filing of suits for the sole purpose of putting defamatory accusations in circulation.

3. Starting in 1927,[203] courts have recognized a growing public awareness of the reality of what happens in court. Most persons know that those who file suit base that filing on a one-sided version of the facts. Thus, most readers will apply more than a few grains of salt to allegations contained in a story of a suit's being filed.

4. In all states, the filing of most suits produces a public record. Petitions are filed in the office of the clerk of courts, where they are open to inspection by anyone. Thus, all publication does is extend the range of knowledge of the filing. In some states, records of paternity proceedings, of charges of incest, and, in a few states, of some kinds of divorce proceedings are sealed by law; therefore, they are not public records. Most juvenile courts also operate under a cloak of secrecy that can be breached only by order of the court.

201. Schiavone Construction Co. v. Time, Inc., 569 F.Supp. 614, 9 Med.L.Rptr. 2095 (D.N.J. 1983); reversed and remanded, 735 F.2d 94, 10 Med.L.Rptr. 1831 (3d Cir. 1984); 12 Med.L.Rptr. 1153 (D.N.J. 1985), denying Time's motion for summary judgment; 13 Med.L.Rptr. 1664 (D.N.J. 1986), granting Time's motion for summary judgment; affirmed in part, reversed in part, and remanded 848 F.2d 43, 15 Med.L.Rptr. 1417 (3d Cir. 1988). See also Bufalino v. Associated Press, 692 F.2d 266, 8 Med.L.Rptr. 2384 (2d Cir. 1982).
202. For a discussion of this topic, see Newell v. Field Enterprises, 415 N.E.2d 434, 6 Med.L.Rptr. 2450 (Ill. 1980).
203. Campbell v. New York Evening Post, 157 N.E. 153 (N.Y. 1927).

At least one state court has held that court documents obtained from one of the party's lawyers, rather than directly from the court, are not privileged, in *Shahvar* v. *Superior Court.*[204] Elias Shahvar's attorney faxed to the *San Francisco Examiner* on a Friday a copy of a complaint he planned to file on the following Monday with the court. On Sunday, the newspaper published a story about Shahvar's lawsuit against Ellen and Gerald Sigal. The Sigals responded by suing Shahvar for libel, and when Shahvar tried to assert the privilege generally accorded a court document, the appellate court ruled that the libel action was not based on the document filed with the court but on the document faxed to the *Examiner.* The former was privileged; the latter was not. "Shahvar's communications of his allegations to a third party, the *Examiner,* was unrelated to this litigation and therefore not covered by the litigation privilege."[205]

In general, however, professional communicators who are covering the actions of government and the activities of public officials enjoy double protection against libel suits. A story that accurately reflects a statement or action cloaked by absolute privilege is protected by qualified privilege. If the situation turns out not to have been privileged, or if some detail proves not to be accurate, the *New York Times* rule comes into play. At that point, the reporter's performance comes under examination. A plaintiff who is a public official or public figure must offer clear and convincing evidence of actual malice. Private individuals in the states that have adopted the option offered by *Gertz* must prove negligence. In a few federal circuits, and in some states, reporters of public controversies enjoy the additional privilege of neutral reportage.

In the Professional World

New York Times v. *Sullivan* has accomplished one of the purposes of the justices who wrote the decision. By the mid-1990s, it had effected a noticeable decrease in the number of libel suits brought against the news media. But critics in and out of the media were asking if that decrease had been bought at too high a price. *New York Times, Gertz,* and their many progeny have converted libel actions into elaborate and expensive rituals that only wealthy litigants can afford. Further, such is the public mood in the final years of the twentieth century that taking a libel suit to trial is likely to result in a sizable judgment that can be reduced or eliminated only by a costly and time-consuming appeal. This situation has led some publishers, prodded by their libel insurer, to settle close lawsuits to avoid such travail. Some news organizations have chosen to play it safe by discouraging investigative reporting, lest it lead to expensive legal action.

On the other hand, the decisions have raised the plaintiff's costs, too, and have increased the likelihood that a judge will grant a motion to dismiss, thus preventing the case from reaching a jury. Consequently, some victims of false and defamatory falsehoods hesitate to start a process that may or may not result, many months or even years later, in clearing their names. That reluctance is

---

204.   25 Cal.App. 653, 30 Cal. Rptr. 2d 597, 22 Med.L.Rptr. 1893 (1994).
205.   Ibid at 22 Med.L.Rptr. 1894. For a contrary view, see Field v. Kirton, 856 F.Supp. 88 (D.Conn. 1994), protecting a press release based on court pleadings.

based on a fact that troubles many, including some journalists: The law permits the news media to defame public officials, public figures, and even private individuals, and get away with it. Proving fault is difficult at best. The Supreme Court has made proving actual malice even more difficult by requiring appellate courts to review conclusions of fact reached by the trial jury. It is not surprising, then, that lawyers, academics, and others are advancing proposals designed to cut short or bypass the legal process required to establish the truth or falsehood of an alleged defamation.

No quantitative evidence supports the belief that the current state of libel law has dampened the media's willingness to air controversial public issues. Nevertheless, there is anecdotal evidence that, when lesser figures are involved, some publishers are pulling in their horns. One session of a meeting of Investigative Reporters and Editors was devoted to a discussion of the chilling effect of libel actions. Sam Klein, a lawyer whose main client is the *Philadelphia Inquirer,* was quoted as saying there is a chill "in the sense that people have to take second, third and fourth looks at stories." He also said he knew of newspapers that no longer do any investigative reporting, out of fear of being sued for libel. Bill Marimow, who has won two Pulitzer prizes as a reporter for the *Inquirer,* said he has changed his interviewing methods to avoid libel cases. He said he has become more open with sources he is investigating and as a result may not always get as much of the story as he might have previously.

Floyd Abrams, a specialist in First Amendment law who has represented the *New York Times* and other major media clients, also said that fear of the costs of libel actions has deterred investigative reporting. He wrote that an article reporting "serious misconduct in the scientific community," including the publication of false and misleading statements by distinguished scientists, was withheld because it might have led to a lawsuit.[206] He cited other instances in which articles and books by reputable journalists either had to be toned down before publication or were not published at all because of legal concerns.

Others have argued that the real problem is not the stifling of hard-hitting, investigative journalism, but that *New York Times* v. *Sullivan* has encouraged poorly prepared reporters to practice in a shoddy way. The late Clark R. Mollenhoff was one who so argued. For many years an investigative reporter for the *Des Moines Register,* Mollenhoff won three Sigma Delta Chi Distinguished Service awards and a Pulitzer Prize before he became a journalism professor at Washington and Lee University. On the twenty-fifth anniversary of *New York Times* he wrote an article asserting that the decision has done more harm than good.[207] He said he had cheered the Court's holding when it was made in 1964 but had since come to the conclusion that the actual malice rule has encouraged sloppy journalism. In his view, the rule permits editors to justify their failure to fully corroborate damaging charges against public officials and public figures by saying that their lack of doubt gave them no reason for digging deeper. With the

---

206. Floyd Abrams, "Why We Should Change the Libel Law," *New York Times Magazine,* 29 September 1985, p. 34+.
207. Clark R. Mollenhoff, "25 Years of *Times v. Sullivan,*" *Quill,* March 1989, p. 27+.

bluntness for which he was known as a reporter, Mollenhoff wrote: "It has been said that patriotism is the last refuge of scoundrels. *New York Times* v. *Sullivan* similarly has provided a significant refuge for a few willful falsifying scoundrels, for larger numbers of scoop-minded incompetents, and for many reporters and editors who are just plain lazy." That commentary may be too extreme, but Mollenhoff's reservations about the effect of *New York Times* are shared by Justice White, who helped write the decision. Concurring in the Court's judgment in *Greenmoss,* White wrote: "I have become convinced that the Court struck an improvident balance in the *New York Times* case between the public's interest in being fully informed about public officials and public affairs and the competing interest of those who have been defamed in vindicating their reputation."

In White's view, as in Mollenhoff's, the culprit is the actual-malice rule. It gives First Amendment protection "to false statements of fact about public officials." In White's view, such statements frustrate the core value of the amendment, which is protection of "that flow of intelligence" essential to our ability to govern ourselves through our elected representatives. That value, White wrote, is "even more disserved when the statements falsely impugn the honesty of those men and women and hence lessen the confidence in government." And yet officials who are the victims of false charges can't even get into court unless they can make out "a jury case of a knowing or reckless falsehood." That means, White concluded, that "[t]he lie will stand, and the public continue to be misinformed about public matters." The justice placed little stock in the remedy that is at the heart of *New York Times* and *Gertz:* the Supreme Court majority's assumption that public officials and public figures are powerful enough to reach the public in a convincing fashion with their version of the truth. Quoting from Brennan's opinion in *Rosenbloom,* White wrote, "It is a rare case where the denial overtakes the original charge. Denials, retractions, and corrections are not 'hot' news, and rarely receive the prominence of the original story."[208]

Has *New York Times* outlived its usefulness? There are those who think so and who are making suggestions for other means of counteracting defamatory falsehoods. One set of suggestions grew out of a study of media credibility commissioned by the Associated Press Managing Editors Association and a similar study conducted for the *Los Angeles Times* by its media reporter, David Shaw. Both studies recommended that reporters and editors set higher standards of professional performance, insist that these standards be met, and tell their readers what they do and why.[209] Noting that the news media are perceived as powerful institutions, Shaw argued that they should perform with the same degree of openness that they demand from the institutions they cover. In his view, journalists ought to tell their audience how they developed controversial stories and why those stories took the form they did. This disclosure is precisely what

---

208. Dun & Bradstreet, Inc. v. Greenmoss Builders, Inc., 472 U.S. 479, 105 S.Ct. 2939, 86 L.Ed.2d 593, 11 Med.L.Rptr. 2417 (1985).
209. "APME Credibility Research: What the Research Means," presentation by panel made up of Roberto Goizueta, chairman of the board, Coca-Cola Co.; Norman Isaacs, former chairman, National News Council; and David Shaw, media reporter, *Los Angeles Times,* at the APME annual meeting in San Francisco, 29 October 1985.

plaintiff's lawyers ask for when they pursue a libel action against a media defendant.

A study by three University of Iowa professors of libel plaintiffs and all libel and privacy cases decided between 1974 and 1984 suggested that such openness might help if it is coupled with a greater willingness to admit the occasional serious mistake.[210] The study showed that most libel plaintiffs said they went to court only after they had sought a correction and had been rebuffed, sometimes rudely. In a summary of their findings, the authors said, "In a significant proportion of the cases, the *way* people were treated when they contacted the media seems to account for, or be a factor in, their anger and decision to sue."

David Lawrence, Jr., then the publisher of the *Detroit Free Press* and later with the *Miami Herald,* responded to that finding in a talk to an Inland Daily Press Association meeting in Chicago.[211] He said "Journalists are people with great power that can be used for good and bad and, in many cases, the public resents that power. We're often seen as arrogant people who own the printing press and always have the last word." That arrogance often shows up, Lawrence said, when someone calls to complain about being mistreated or misrepresented in a story. At such times, he said, "It is arrogant for a newspaper to be anything but courteous. Journalists tend to think they are right most of the time, but it is important to acknowledge errors of fact, tone or context." He recommended that reporters and editors make themselves accessible to critics of their stories and that they treat them with compassion.

Meanwhile, *New York Times,* supplemented by *Gertz,* stands as a precedent that has brought under the protective shield of the First Amendment media coverage of public officials, public figures, and private individuals caught up in matters of public importance. Behind that shield, the media can report on or participate in the debate on public policy. For media professionals willing to take care to ensure that their accounts are both accurate and fair, that shield offers nearly absolute protection from libel judgments, but not from expensive libel suits. For the "willful falsifying scoundrels," "scoop-minded incompetents," and the "plain lazy," it offers lesser protection, depending on the ability of their victims to prove actual malice or negligence. At bottom then, libel becomes a question of ethics. The law permits the media to defame individuals and institutions and get away with it. Until the Supreme Court says otherwise, that is the reality faced by all who are caught in the media's spotlight. The critical question is, Should any professional communicator take comfort in avoiding liability only because the subject of a defamatory report could not prove fault?

FOR REVIEW

1. Define defamation. Who carries the burden of proving defamation? Assuming that defamation can be proved, what remains to be proved by libel plaintiffs if they are to win their lawsuits?

---

210. Bezanson, Cranberg, and Soloski, "Libel Law and the Press," p. 215+.
211. Debra Gersh, "Arrogance in Journalism," *Editor & Publisher,* 13 December 1986, p. 24+.

2. Is an accusation of crime always grounds for a libel action? Explain.

3. What criteria are used to distinguish between an assertion of opinion and a statement of fact? What did the Supreme Court's decision in *Milkovich* contribute to that determination?

4. Define a public official for purposes of a libel action. Illustrate.

5. Distinguish between an all-purpose and a limited public figure. Discuss the role of the news media in creating public figures. What criteria do courts use in determining whether a libel plaintiff is a limited public figure?

6. What standard of proof does your state require of private individuals who sue the news media for libel?

7. What is actual malice? How is it proved? What element is virtually essential to its proof? Illustrate by reference to a case in which actual malice was or was not proved.

8. A public official–public figure libel plaintiff offers proof that a publication's reporters and editors were out to get him or her, that their position was that of an adversary, not neutral fact finders. The plaintiff also offers proof of some errors in the stories. Does this evidence prove actual malice? Should it? Why or why not?

9. Distinguish between negligence, as it is defined in libel cases, and actual malice. Illustrate by reference to a case in which negligence was proved.

10. What is meant by the term "neutral reportage"? Is the concept compatible with the Supreme Court's definition of actual malice? Why or why not?

11. With respect to the news media, what is a qualified fair-report privilege? What is its value? Does the term have the same meaning for nonmedia libel defendants? Explain.

12. The news media and other professional communicators have had more than thirty years of experience with *New York Times* and its progeny. On the whole, have the rules flowing from that decision strengthened or weakened the First Amendment's guarantee of freedom of the press? Have they served the public well or badly? If you could sit on the Supreme Court, would you change any element of libel law? If so, what? Why?

CHAPTER 6

When television cameras zoom in on people who have just learned that their relatives were victims of an airplane crash, or when newspapers report, without apparent reason, that the man who deflected a shot aimed at the president is a homosexual, many people ask why. Are not such examples of journalistic enterprise an invasion of privacy?

It is not easy to answer the question when it is raised by critics of media performance. Twentieth-century law recognizes that people have a right to be left alone. Persons who suffer humiliation or embarrassment because of the acts of others have a legal right of redress in most states. Problems arise, however, because the law varies widely from state to state and because the law recognizes that at some point an individual's right to privacy limits the media's First Amendment right to inform the pub-

INVASION OF PRIVACY

lic. The problem is further compounded by a wide difference between the perception of the general public and that of media and legal professionals as to what is an invasion of privacy. Polls show, for instance, that a majority of the public mistakenly thinks that it is an invasion of privacy to publish photographs of accident victims, to report that a person committed suicide, or to give the addresses of burglary victims.[1] Other studies link the media's poor credibility with a widespread public perception that journalists wantonly invade privacy.[2]

This public perception produces a steady business in privacy lawsuits directed at media organizations, although the suits are by no means as frequent as libel actions, nor do plaintiffs have the same degree of success. Judgments, moreover, against media professionals are rare. Still, the number of actions, and the cost of defending them, make privacy law a major concern not only for newspapers and television, but also for photographers, advertisers, and public relations professionals.

Unlike the law of defamation, which has roots at least seven hundred years old, the law of privacy is of fairly recent origin. It was not recognized as a branch of tort law until early in the twentieth century[3] and still has not been recognized as an actionable tort in all states. It is a product of both common law and state statutes. The law of privacy, to a much greater extent than the law of defamation, varies from state to state. However, there is enough consistency among the court decisions to allow for some reasonably clear principles and working guidelines.

The law of privacy is concerned primarily with actions that intrude into personal space. In the broad sense, privacy law includes such things as trespass, harassment, eavesdropping, wiretapping, telling secrets, and exploiting reputations. Not surprisingly, the most frequent defendants are reporters, advertisers, employers, bill collectors, private detectives, and public relations practitioners.

Much of what media professionals understand about privacy law they owe to the late Professor William L. Prosser. He taught generations of media lawyers to think of privacy law as a complex of four torts: appropriation, intrusion, public disclosure of

---

1. Sam Cremin, "Public Tells When News Media Invade Privacy," *Editor & Publisher,* 19 May 1979, p. 13.
2. *Journalists and Readers: Bridging the Credibility Gap,* survey commissioned by the Associated Press Managing Editors Association and conducted by MORI Research, Inc., Minneapolis, October 1985.
3. The first states to recognize invasion of privacy were New York by statute in 1903 and Georgia by court opinion in 1905. Of historical interest are Roberson v. Rochester Folding Box Company, 171 N.Y. 538, 64 N.E. 442 (N.Y. 1902) and Pavesich v. New England Life Insurance Co., 122 Ga. 190, 50 S.E. 68 (Ga. 1905).

private facts, and false light in the public eye.[4] Prosser noted that these four torts have little in common except a name and their ability to interfere with the right of a person to be left alone. Because the invasion is understood to be personal, the plaintiffs are always real, living individuals, never corporations, churches, associations, or the deceased.

In the late 1990s, one might suspect that the Prosser list is too short. Rather than four, there might be six or eight distinct torts, including such wrongs as infliction of emotional distress and the invasion of publicity rights. Regardless, it is clear that poking deeply into private lives can trigger litigation that redresses a variety of privacy-related interests. In gathering information, it is entirely possible to trespass onto other people's property, intrude into their private lives, deceive them, embarrass them, and misappropriate their image for commercial advantage. One lawsuit might allege all of those wrongs, and each accusation would have to be defended.

Government, too, has become involved in protecting privacy. Both the federal and state governments have statutes intended to protect the privacy of information held by their agents, such as tax returns and welfare reports. Moreover, many states have enacted statutes permitting reformed criminals to expunge or seal records dealing with their offenses. Such laws have made it difficult in some instances for journalists to investigate allegations of wrongdoing, or the performance of police, prosecutors, and judges. In addition, juvenile law routinely provides that the crimes of children are to be treated as private matters, to be settled in closed courts without public records.

This chapter will present a number of significant cases, each of which illustrates one or more of the general principles that guide media professionals.

Major Cases

- *Bahr* v. *Statesman Journal Co.,* 51 Or.App. 177, 624 P.2d 664, 7 Med.L.Rptr. 1099 (Or.App. 1981).

- *Cantrell* v. *Forest City Publishing Co.,* 419 U.S. 245, 95 S.Ct. 465, 42 L.Ed.2d 419, 1 Med.L.Rptr. 1815 (1974).

- *Carson* v. *Here's Johnny Portable Toilets,* 698 F.2d 831, 9 Med.L.Rptr. 1153 (6th Cir. 1983).

- *Cher* v. *Forum International, Ltd.,* 692 F.2d 634, 8 Med.L.Rptr. 2484 (9th Cir. 1982).

- *Cox Broadcasting Co.* v. *Cohn,* 420 U.S. 469, 95 S.Ct. 1029, 43 L.Ed.2d 328, 1 Med.L.Rptr. 1819 (1975).

---

4. William L. Prosser, *Law of Torts,* 4th ed. (St. Paul, Minn.: West Publishing Co., 1971), pp. 802–818.

■ *Diaz* v. *Oakland Tribune, Inc.,* 139 Cal.App.3d 118, 188 Cal.Rptr. 762, 9 Med.L.Rptr. 1121 (Cal.Ct.App. 1983).

■ *Dietemann* v. *Time, Inc.,* 284 F.Supp. 425 (C.D.Cal. 1968); 449 F.2d 245, 1 Med.L.Rptr. 2417 (9th Cir. 1971).

■ *The Florida Star* v. *B.J.F.,* 491 U.S. 524, 109 S.Ct. 2603, 105 L.Ed.2d 443, 16 Med.L.Rptr. 1801 (1989).

■ *Jenkins* v. *Dell Publishing Co.,* 251 F.2d 447 (3d Cir. 1958).

■ *Kimbrough* v. *Coca-Cola/USA,* 521 S.W.2d 719 (Tex. 1975).

■ *Matter of Application to Adjudge Providence Journal Co. and Its Executive Editor, Charles M. Hauser, in Criminal Contempt,* 820 F.2d 1342 (1st Cir. 1986).

■ *Miller* v. *National Broadcasting Co.,* 187 Cal.App.3d 1463, 232 Cal.Rptr. 668 (Cal.App. 1986).

■ *New Bedford Standard-Times Publishing Co.* v. *Clerk of Third Dist. Court,* 377 Mass. 404, 387 N.E.2d 110, 4 Med.L.Rptr. 2393 (Mass. 1979).

■ *Newspapers, Inc.* v. *Brier,* 89 Wis.2d 417, 279 N.W.2d 179, 5 Med.L.Rptr. 1524 (Wis. 1979).

■ *Oklahoma Publishing Co.* v. *District Court in and for Oklahoma County,* 430 U.S. 308, 97 S.Ct. 1045, 51 L.Ed.2d 355, 2 Med.L.Rptr. 1456 (1977).

■ *Shields* v. *Gross,* 7 Med.L.Rptr. 2349 (N.Y.Sup.Ct. 1981); modified, 451 N.Y.S.2d 419, 88 A.D.2d, 846, 7 Med.L.Rptr. 2349 (App.Div. 1982); affirmed as modified, 58 N.Y.2d 338, 461 N.Y.S.2d 254, 448 N.E.2d 108, 9 Med.L.Rptr. 1466 (Ct.App. 1983); 563 F.Supp. 1253, 9 Med.L.Rptr. 1879 (S.D.N.Y. 1983).

■ *Sidis* v. *F-R Publishing Corp.,* 113 F.2d 806, 1 Med.L.Rptr. 1775 (2d Cir. 1940).

■ *Time, Inc.* v. *Hill,* 385 U.S. 374, 87 S.Ct. 534, 17 L.Ed.2d 456, 1 Med.L.Rptr. 1791 (1967).

■ *Virgil* v. *Time, Inc.,* 527 F.2d 1122, 1 Med.L.Rptr. 1835 (9th Cir. 1975).

■ *Zacchini* v. *Scripps-Howard Broadcasting,* 433 U.S. 562, 97 S.Ct. 2849, 53 L.Ed.2d 965, 2 Med.L.Rptr. 2089 (1977).

THE COMMON LAW OF PRIVACY

Unlike libel law, which traces its lineage through at least six centuries of common law, the law of privacy is one of the few fields of law that can date its birth to a law journal article. The courts have drawn many of its principles from an article written by two Boston lawyers, Samuel D. Warren and Louis D. Brandeis, published in the *Harvard Law Review* in 1890.[5] Twenty-six years later, Brandeis was appointed to the Supreme Court of the United States, where his concern with privacy was reflected in some of his opinions.

When the article was written, Warren and Brandeis were young lawyers with entree to Boston's top social circles. In their opinion, journalists were devoting too much attention to what happened in those circles. They wrote in protest:

> Instantaneous photographs and newspaper enterprise have invaded the sacred precincts of private and domestic life; and numerous mechanical devices threaten to make good the prediction that "what is whispered in the closet shall be proclaimed from the housetops." . . .
>
> Of the desirability—indeed the necessity—of some . . . protection there can be, it is believed, no doubt. The press is overstepping in every direction the obvious bounds of propriety and decency. Gossip is no longer the resource of the idle and vicious, but has become a trade, which is pursued with industry as well as effrontery. To satisfy a prurient taste the details of sexual relations are spread broadcast in the columns of the daily papers. To occupy the indolent, column upon column is filled with idle gossip, which can only be procured by intrusion upon the domestic circle.

The article suggested that the same principles that give property owners the right to protect their houses and lands from trespassers should give all persons the right to protect themselves from intrusion into their private affairs. The authors argued for a right to be left alone, for a right to control the extent to which others can pry into an individual's private life.

Within a decade, courts began to recognize such a right. Some of the early cases were decided on the theory of trespass, as the authors had suggested. Others were decided on the theory that an individual's identity is a form of property that an individual can control.

Some courts rejected the Warren and Brandeis reasoning, most notably the New York Court of Appeals in *Roberson* v. *Rochester Folding Box Co.*[6] The action had been brought by a young woman whose portrait was used without her permission to advertise flour. She won an order from a trial court preventing further use of her likeness, but the appeals court reversed, holding that it could find no precedents to support a right of privacy. The legislature reacted in 1903 by enacting a law designed to prevent such exploitation.[7]

Today, all but two states protect a right of privacy, either as defined by statute, as in New York, or by the state's common law, or by a combination of the two. However, courts in Minnesota continue to refuse to recognize a legal remedy for an

---

5. Samuel D. Warren and Louis D. Brandeis, "The Right to Privacy," 4 *Harv.L.Rev.* 193, 15 December 1890.
6. 64 N.E. 442 (N.Y. 1903).
7. New York Civil Rights Law §§ 50–51.

invasion of privacy and those in North Dakota have had no occasion to do so. Some states, although they have had no media-related privacy cases, have recognized the tort in cases involving the duty of business firms to treat customers or employees with respect.

THE FOUR TORTS OF INVASION OF PRIVACY

The phrase "invasion of privacy" seems simple, but under legal analysis in the courts the concept has proved to be highly complex—so much so that Professor Prosser, who for more than two decades was a leading authority on torts law, finally concluded that invasion of privacy is not one tort but four. His conclusions are embodied in the *Restatement of Torts*.[8] The four kinds of invasion of privacy include:

1. Intrusion upon the plaintiff's physical and mental solitude or seclusion

2. Public disclosure of private facts

3. Publicity that places the plaintiff in a false light in the public eye

4. Appropriation, for the defendant's benefit or advantage, of the plaintiff's name or likeness

Although the four torts share a common name, they are clearly distinct and can be briefly summarized.

Intrusion into Mental or Physical Solitude

Intrusion into a person's mental or physical solitude is closely related to trespass. The difference is that trespass violates a person's property, whereas intrusion violates the person. Intrusion involves entry without permission into another's personal space and in a manner that is highly offensive. Journalists who use subterfuge to gain entrance to a private home are especially vulnerable to suit as intruders. A photographer who harasses a newsworthy subject also may be an intruder. So may an eavesdropper or wiretapper.

Significantly, publication is not required before a plaintiff can bring an action for intrusion. Courts have held that the harm lies in the act of intrusion itself. Moreover, most courts reject an argument that the First Amendment can justify an intrusion, though some have held that First Amendment interests at least must be balanced against the victim's right to privacy.

---

8. *Restatement of the Law, Second: Torts 2d* (St. Paul, Minn.: American Law Institute Publishers, 1977), § 652A.

Forty-six states, the District of Columbia, and Puerto Rico recognize intrusion, at least by implication if not explicitly, as a cause of an action for invasion of privacy.[9] Other states either don't recognize the tort or have not yet addressed the issue.

Disclosure of Private Fact

A disclosure of private fact occurs when a medium, without consent, disseminates personal information that a reasonable person would find to be highly offensive and not of legitimate public concern. California courts held, for example, that a newspaper column commenting on a college student body leader's sex change operation was a disclosure of embarrassing private fact.[10] Unlike libel law, where provable truth is an absolute defense, truth is no defense at all for disclosure. Even if true, the information may be much too private to be reported. However, newsworthiness is a defense. The fact that the information was taken from the public record of a governmental agency is also a defense. The principal problem with this tort lies in defining what is newsworthy. Some courts leave this determination to a jury, but generally courts have taken a broad view of newsworthiness. For example, following journalistic conventions, a photo of a nude woman taking a bath is probably not newsworthy,[11] a photo of a topless Duchess of York cavorting near St. Tropez might be, and a photo of a nearly nude woman fleeing to waiting police after being held hostage almost certainly would be.[12]

Forty-one states, the District of Columbia, and the Virgin Islands have recognized disclosure of private fact as an actionable tort.[13] However, in all but a few of the reported cases involving media defendants, courts held that publication was justified, either because the facts in question were not sufficiently outrageous, were newsworthy, or had been found in public records.

False Light

By definition, a person can be put in a false light only through publicity. He or she must be the subject of a publication, tape, film, or broadcast that distorts his or her per-

---

9. The states are Alabama, Alaska, Arizona, Arkansas, California, Colorado, Connecticut, Delaware, Florida, Georgia, Idaho, Illinois, Indiana, Iowa, Kansas, Kentucky, Louisiana, Maine, Maryland, Massachusetts, Michigan, Mississippi, Missouri, Montana, Nebraska, Nevada, New Hampshire, New Jersey, New Mexico, New York, North Carolina, Ohio, Oklahoma, Oregon, Pennsylvania, Rhode Island, South Carolina, South Dakota, Tennessee, Texas, Utah, Vermont, Virginia, Washington, West Virginia, and Wisconsin. This list and those in the following sections were compiled from Victor A. Kovner, Harriette K. Dorsen, and Suzanne L. Telsey, "Recent Developments in Intrusion, Private Facts, False Light, and Commercialization Claims," In *Communications Law 1993* (New York: Practising Law Institute, 1993), pp. 883–939.
10. Diaz v. Oakland Tribune, 139 Cal.App.3d 118, 188 Cal.Rptr. 762 (Ct.App. 1st Dist. Div. 3 1983).
11. McCabe v. Village Voice, 550 F.Supp. 525 (E.D.Pa. 1982).
12. Cape Publications v. Bridges, 431 So.2d 988, 8 Med.L.Rptr. 2535 (Fla.Ct.App. 1982), cert. denied, 464 U.S. 893 (1983).
13. The states are Alabama, Arizona, Arkansas, California, Colorado, Connecticut, Delaware, Florida, Georgia, Hawaii, Idaho, Indiana, Iowa, Kansas, Kentucky, Louisiana, Maine, Maryland, Massachusetts, Michigan, Mississippi, Missouri, Nevada, New Hampshire, New Jersey, New Mexico, North Carolina, Ohio, Oklahoma, Oregon, Pennsylvania, Rhode Island, South Carolina, Tennessee, Texas, Vermont, Virginia, Washington, West Virginia, Wisconsin, and Wyoming.

sonality. Thus, this branch of the tort is related to defamation and at some point merges into it. But unlike defamation, a false-light action can be based on neutral or even flattering statements. A baseball pitcher, a member of that sport's hall of fame, was able to stop publication of a book that falsely portrayed him as a war hero.[14] The essential element of false light is that individuals must be portrayed as something other than they are to the point of embarrassment. To portray a Unitarian as a fundamentalist member of the Moral Majority, or vice versa, would defame neither, but probably would embarrass both. Such portrayal, then, could result in an action for false-light invasion of privacy.

In two cases brought by private individuals, the Supreme Court held that false-light plaintiffs must prove actual malice—knowledge of falsity or reckless disregard for the truth—if they were to prevail. Both of these cases preceded the famous libel case, *Gertz* v. *Robert Welch,* and the Supreme Court has had no occasion since to rule on whether private individuals may prevail on a lesser showing of fault. In recent cases, however, courts in some states have held that private false-light plaintiffs need prove only negligence. The point is that courts treat false-light actions much like actions in libel, which means that the First Amendment stands as a strong barrier against a successful suit.

Thirty-five states and the District of Columbia have recognized, at least by implication, false-light invasion of privacy as an actionable tort.[15] Texas rejected false light in 1994.[16] A decade earlier, North Carolina had rejected false light, its state supreme court holding that a plaintiff should not be compensated for mere embarrassment.[17] The Sixth Circuit Court of Appeals has more than once held that Ohio does not recognize false-light invasion of privacy as an actionable tort.[18] When the Wisconsin legislature enacted a privacy statute in 1977, it removed by amendment a section that would have permitted recovery for false light.[19]

Appropriation and the Right of Publicity

Appropriation involves the unauthorized use of one person's name or likeness to benefit another. Commonly appropriation occurs in an advertisement or in other promotional material designed to help the user make a profit. Thus, it is of particular importance to advertising and public relations professionals. Courts act on the theory that a person whose identity has been used without consent to sell a product is entitled to a share of the user's profit. Advertisers can avoid a lawsuit for appropriation by getting written consent from any person whose name or likeness will appear in an adver-

---

14. Spahn v. Julius Messner, 18 N.Y.2d 324 (N.Y. 1966); 21 N.Y.2d 124 (N.Y. 1967).
15. The states are Alabama, Arizona, Arkansas, California, Colorado, Connecticut, Florida, Georgia, Idaho, Illinois, Iowa, Kansas, Kentucky, Louisiana, Maine, Maryland, Michigan, Montana, Nebraska, Nevada, New Hampshire, New Jersey, New Mexico, New York, Oklahoma, Oregon, Pennsylvania, Rhode Island, South Carolina, South Dakota, Tennessee, Vermont, Virginia, Washington, and West Virginia.
16. Cain v. Hearst Corp., 22 Med.L.Rptr. 2161 (Texas S.Ct. 1994).
17. Renwick v. News and Observer, 310 N.C. 312, 312 S.E.2d 405 (N.C. 1984).
18. Suarez Corp. v. CBS, Inc., 23 F.3d 408, 22 Med.L.Rptr. 1711 (6th Cir. 1994); Angelotta v. American Broadcasting Corp., 820 F.2d 806 (6th Cir. 1987).
19. Wis.Stat. § 895.50.

tisement or other promotional material. Such consent is a contract, which can be drawn broadly to cover any use, or narrowly to cover a specific use. Usually, the contract includes the amount of a fee or other consideration to be paid to the person whose name or likeness is used.

Forty-one states and the District of Columbia recognize, at least by implication, the right to protect one's name or likeness against appropriation by others.[20] In recent years courts have broadened the scope of appropriation to create what is now called the right of publicity. Unlike traditional appropriation, which provides a remedy against exploitation of personal identity, the right of publicity protects a property interest in the value of a famous name or likeness. Because publicity rights protect property rather than persons, and because property can generally be sold, inherited, or given away, publicity rights cases are often brought by companies or individuals who own rights to a name or image, rather than by the actual person whose name or image has been misused. In fact, the person exploited may well be dead, with no right of privacy and no ability to sue, as would be the case with Elvis Presley or Marilyn Monroe, or the "person" may not be a person at all, but a famous dog or a horse, for example.

Courts simply have recognized that entertainers, athletes, actors, and others whose names become household words acquire an identity of commercial value that appropriation is inadequate to protect. In fact, for many celebrities, privacy may be what they least want. The public exposure of their image, not their ability to be invisible to the commercial world, is what provides their livelihood. Moreover, image is understood in an expansive sense; it can include any combination of words or actions; for example, it could be a circus act or the peculiar way a singer uses her or his voice.

The right to publicity might be understood better as a relative of copyright and trademark, except that its origin is in appropriation, and the two continue to overlap significantly. Appropriation and the right to publicity diverge only at the point when a personal image becomes a commercially valuable public image and achieves a kind of existence all its own. Courts do not always make it clear, moreover, whether it is privacy or publicity that is at stake in a decision. Consequently, even noncommercial uses of a commercially valuable image might result in liability for damages. News media, for example, under some circumstances may need permission to reproduce a commercially valuable image, such as a carnival act or a football game, in a news program. Although such use raises First Amendment questions, these questions generally are about how much, rather than what, can be used for news purposes.

Defenses

PUBLICATION.   Invasions of privacy occur in four quite different ways, but only intrusion does not require publication to be involved. Accordingly, the fact that in-

---

20. The states are Alabama, Alaska, Arizona, Arkansas, California, Connecticut, Florida, Georgia, Hawaii, Illinois, Indiana, Iowa, Kansas, Kentucky, Louisiana, Maine, Maryland, Massachusetts, Michigan, Mississippi, Missouri, Montana, Nebraska, Nevada, New Jersey, New Mexico, New York, North Carolina, Ohio, Oklahoma, Oregon, Pennsylvania, Rhode Island, South Dakota, Tennessee, Texas, Utah, Vermont, Virginia, West Virginia, and Wisconsin.

formation obtained in an intrusive manner was not published is no defense. On the other hand, there can be no action for disclosure of private fact, false light, or appropriation unless some information has been shared with the public.

CONSENT.   Where there is consent, there is no invasion. Consent can be explicit, as with a model release, or it can be implicit, as in an interview. Consent can be limited or withdrawn. As a defense, it is worthwhile only if given willingly and competently. One should always be wary of consent from minors or mental patients, or from those who would give permission for others, such as for spouses, tenants, or clients.

TRUTH.   The four torts differ in the role truth plays as a defense. Truth is irrelevant in an intrusion case; the focus is on the alleged intruder's methods. Truth works against defendants in disclosure cases. The plaintiff has no cause of action unless the information at issue is true. Obviously, then, truth alone is not a defense. The defendant can prevail only if the facts were taken from a public record or are held to be newsworthy. However, truth is an absolute defense in a false-light action. Just as persons cannot be libeled by publication of the truth about them, neither can they be put in a false light by the truth. With appropriation, or violation of the right of publicity, as with intrusion, truth is not a factor.

IDENTITY.   Invasion of privacy is a personal tort—a right that belongs to the person wronged and to no one else. False-light cases especially can turn on a question of whether the report was of and concerning the plaintiff. In appropriation cases, there is sometimes a question as to whether a collateral item, such as a race car or a basketball jersey, is sufficiently identified with the plaintiff to substitute for his or her name or image.

PUBLIC RECORDS.   If something has been made public by government, a plaintiff's argument generally should be with the government, not with the media. In false-light cases, even untruthful information found in the public record may be defensible, as it would be in libel. The gravamen of the defense is that what is already public cannot be private.

NEWSWORTHINESS.   Newsworthiness is the most notable defense in a private-fact case. It is a justification for the invasion based on the public's interest in the issues or in a free press generally. It is a common law surrogate for the First Amendment and speaks to the same concern—the public's need for information about the people and issues of the time. The first caveat is that although a jury might place great value on the expert news judgment of professionals, the jurors' sense of what is newsworthy is what often prevails. The second caveat is that a story's value as news rarely matters in cases of intrusion or false light, although it might have some value in publicity cases.

INTRUSION ══════════════════════════════

From the earliest recorded days of Anglo-Saxon jurisprudence, courts have shown great respect for private property. This respect is recognized in two places in the Bill of Rights. The Third Amendment forbids the quartering of troops in private homes. The Fourth protects individuals and their property "against unreasonable searches and seizures." Moreover, the sanctity of property has long been recognized in the common law of trespass. Property owners can take action against those who enter their premises without consent. Intrusion, as grounds for a civil action in invasion of privacy, is an extension of the law of trespass and closely related to other wrongs, such as conversion and theft.

Professional communicators who keep in mind the origins of this branch of privacy law use caution whenever it seems necessary to enter private property to obtain information or to make a photograph. In most instances, there are no problems. Most people are willing to consider a request for an interview, whether for print or for broadcast. If the request is granted, it is usually accompanied by an invitation to enter the source's home, office, or place of business. The vast majority of requests for information raise no privacy questions. But when the possessor of vital information, or a person suspected of violating the law, is unwilling to be interviewed or photographed, there can be problems.

Intrusion by Deception

The classic intrusion case, *Dietemann* v. *Time, Inc.,* involved a most reluctant source, a plumber who was believed to be practicing medicine without a license. He worked in his home and was careful to admit only persons he knew or who were referred to him by someone he knew. When an editor in the Los Angeles bureau of *Life* magazine heard about the plumber, he assigned a female reporter and a male photographer to pose as husband and wife seeking treatment from him. The couple consulted the district attorney, who decided to use them to get information that could be used in a criminal prosecution. The reporter and photographer agreed to cooperate.

Dietemann v. Time, Inc., **284 F. Supp. 425 (C.D.Cal. 1968); 449 F.2d 245, 1 Med.L.Rptr. 2417 (9th Cir. 1971).**

The reporter packed a radio transmitter in her handbag and the man wore a tie-clip camera. They gained admission to the plumber's home by posing as friends of previous patients. After an examination, the plumber told the reporter she had cancer as a result of eating rancid butter eleven years, nine months, and seven days earlier. He prescribed a cure of minerals, herbs, and other harmless substances. Every word was transmitted to a tape recorder in a police car parked nearby, while the photographer was getting pictures of the diagnostic process. The plumber was arrested and charged with practicing medicine without a license. He pleaded no contest.

Life's article appeared after the arrest but before the plea. The plumber sued for invasion of privacy, and a federal district court in Los Angeles awarded him $1,000 in damages. On appeal, the Ninth Circuit Court of Appeals affirmed. Both courts recognized there was a public interest in stopping Dietemann's crude practice of medicine, but they held that that fact did not justify the intrusion. The court of appeals condemned the *Life* team's reporting methods in strong terms:

Although the issue has not been squarely decided in California, we have little difficulty in concluding that clandestine photography of the plaintiff in his den and the recordation and transmission of his conversation without his consent resulting in his emotional distress warrants recovery for invasion of privacy. . . .

Plaintiff's den was a sphere from which he could reasonably expect to exclude eavesdropping newsmen. He invited two of defendant's employees to the den. One who invites another to his home or office takes a risk that the visitor may repeat all he hears and observes when he leaves. But he does not and should not be required to take the risk that what is heard and seen will be transmitted by photograph or recording, or in our modern world, in full living color and hi-fi to the public at large or to any segment of it that the visitor may select.

Life's lawyers argued that the First Amendment protected the gathering of news as well as its dissemination. They argued that cameras and recording devices have become indispensable tools in investigative reporting. The court swept this argument aside:

> The First Amendment has never been construed to accord newsmen immunity from torts or crimes committed during the course of newsgathering. The First Amendment is not a license to trespass, to steal, or to intrude by electronic means into the precincts of another's home or office. It does not become such a license simply because the person subjected to the intrusion is reasonably suspected of committing a crime.

The court thus condemned several methods that might be used by reporters who believe that anything goes in pursuit of a good story. Foremost was the use of deception to gain entrance to Dietemann's house. There, if anywhere, Dietemann had the greatest expectation of privacy. Although he also used his house as an office, he normally accepted patients only if he knew them or knew someone who would vouch for them. Two other tools of the investigative reporter—the hidden microphone, connected by radio to a tape recorder, and the hidden camera—also were condemned by the court. We will see that there are times when reporters legally may use both, but in this instance they were faulted because they were used in conjunction with a deceptive entry into private property.

The Camera and Intrusion

Photographers safely may use a camera to record anything they see from a public place, provided they do not make nuisances of themselves. If people willingly take off their clothes or make fools of themselves in other ways, in places that can be seen from a public street or other public property, they are fair game. But when photographers go onto or fly over private property to take photographs or harass their subjects, they may be open to an action in intrusion.

The rule of thumb is that when private property can be seen from public property, or a place normally open to the public, the camera may safely record what happens there. The Louisiana Supreme Court held that the *Crowley Post-Signal* did not intrude when it published a photograph of one of the city's older homes along with a caption referring to it as "a bit weather worn and unkempt."[21] The photo had been taken from the street. The Washington Supreme Court came to a similar conclusion in a privacy action against KING Broadcasting.[22] The action was brought by a pharmacist who was

---

21. *Jaubert v. Crowley Post-Signal*, 375 So.2d 1386 (La. 1979).
22. *Mark v. KING Broadcasting*, 635 P.2d 1081 (Wash. 1981).

charged with fraud. When the pharmacist refused to be interviewed, a KING-TV camera operator stood in an alley alongside the store and photographed him through a window. Because the alley was open to the public, the court held that there was no intrusion; the pharmacist could have been seen by anyone passing by.

As for private property, a Florida court has held that there are times when photographers may safely enter, depending on who is in control of the property at the time. The case, *Florida Publishing Co.* v. *Fletcher,*[23] involved a newspaper photographer who had gone with firefighters into a house where a young girl had died from smoke inhalation. A fire marshal asked the photographer to record the scene for the department's investigatory file. One of the photos was published in the photographer's paper, the *Florida Times-Union.* The girl's mother, who was not home at the time of the fire, sued the newspaper for intrusion. In deciding that she had no cause of action, the state supreme court noted that photographers and reporters in Florida customarily accompany police and firefighters to newsworthy events. The court said that this custom implied consent by authorities for news media to enter private property controlled by police or firefighters. The fire marshal, not the dead girl's mother, was in control of the house during the fire.

However, there could be a different result in places where "sidekick journalism" is not customary or in instances when officials are arguably not in control of the premises. For example, a California appellate court held in *Miller* v. *National Broadcasting Co.* that there was an intrusion when an NBC camera crew followed paramedics into a home and recorded their futile attempt to save the life of a heart attack victim. An NBC producer had obtained permission from the Los Angeles Fire Department to accompany paramedics to obtain material for a documentary on their work. On ten to fifteen occasions the filming took the crew into private homes. In only a few instances did anyone question the crew's right to be there.

Miller v. *National Broadcasting Co.,* **187 Cal.App.3d 1463, 232 Cal.Rptr. 668 (Cal.App. 1986).**

No questions were asked either when the crew followed paramedics into the home of Dave and Brownie Miller, although the camera crew passed Mrs. Miller in the hall outside the couple's bedroom, where Dave Miller had suffered a heart attack. Weeks later, as Mrs. Miller tried to tune in a soap opera on television, she was startled by a promotional spot for a documentary. It briefly showed paramedics trying to revive her late husband. She called the station to protest, then filed suit for trespass and intrusion.

A trial court dismissed the case, but the appellate court reversed. Noting that Miller was not a public person, the court wrote: "In our view, reasonable people could regard the NBC camera crew's intrusion into Dave Miller's bedroom at a time of vulnerability and confusion . . . as 'highly offensive' conduct." The court said that to require NBC to ask permission from residents before following paramedics into private homes ought not have "a chilling effect on the exercise of First Amendment rights. To hold otherwise might have extraordinarily chilling implications for all of us."[24]

---

23. 340 So.2d 914 (Fla. 1976).
24. See also *Ayeni* v. *CBS, Inc.,* 848 F. Supp. 362, 22 Med.L.Rptr. 1466 (E.D.N.Y. 1994). The CBS crew was not protected by a search warrant when accompanying federal agents. *Ayeni* v. *Mottola,* 22 Med.L.Rptr. 2225 (2d Cir. 1994). The federal agent who permitted the CBS crew to videotape on private property may be held personally liable.

Jacqueline Onassis walks down Madison Avenue in New York City with photographer Ron Galella pursuing her. Mrs. Onassis, the widow of President John F. Kennedy, finally asked a court to keep Galella away from her and her children. The court didn't stop Galella from making photographs but ordered him to keep at least 25 feet away. *(Ron Galella Ltd., photo by Joy Smith)*

As a general rule of trespass law, anyone is free to go onto those parts of another's property where consent is implied by the surrounding circumstances. The implication can arise from sidewalks approaching front doors, welcome mats, or the general friendliness of the neighborhood. But if what journalists do on private property—even with the implied or explicit consent of those in control of the property—is later found to be highly offensive to persons of ordinary sensibilities, they still might find themselves on the losing end of an intrusion action.

How photographers behave is important because intrusion is a tort that, like trespass, is not often justified by the mere fact that the photo turns out to be newsworthy. In one case, a photographer's method of operation, even when photographing a celebrity from a public street, was found to be an intrusive nuisance justifying control over his actions.

For more than a decade, freelance photographer Ron Galella followed Jacqueline Onassis and her children whenever they ventured into public. He would bump into them on the streets and then record their reactions. He used telephoto lenses and ingenious vantage points to photograph their activities on private property. He would appear in the middle of the night to photograph Onassis emerging from friends' apartments or to catch her with male friends. Eventually, she became fed up with Galella's antics and asked a court to stop them. The court did not go that far, but it did impose limits on how close the photographer could get to his subject. When Galella continued to harass Onassis, the court gave him a choice: He could keep his distance or go to jail.[25] He chose the former, promising not to take another picture of Onassis "as long as I live."[26]

---

25. *Galella v. Onassis,* 353 F.Supp. 196 (S.D.N.Y. 1972), 487 F.2d 986 (2d Cir. 1973, 8 Med. L. Rptr. 1321 (S.D.N.Y. 1982).
26. *Facts on File,* 18 June 1982, p. 447.

Tape Recording and Wiretapping

As the Ninth Circuit Court said in *Dietemann,* modern technology has made it possible for reporters and others to record and photograph interviews without the subject's knowledge. And as we saw in *Dietemann,* surreptitious recording is a factor that, combined with other deceptive practices, can support a finding of intrusion.

Federal law generally permits a journalist, or anyone else, to record conversations surreptitiously if there is no intent to commit a criminal or tortious act. The reason for this privilege is that the Federal Wiretap Statute[27] requires that the permission to intercept an oral or wire communication come from one, but not necessarily all, of the participants. Consequently, journalists conducting interviews can give themselves permission to record their phone conversations.

Usually, however, it isn't federal law that a reporter needs to be concerned about when recording telephone interviews without permission. It is state law. Ten states now prohibit the secret recording of telephone conversations by any participant: California, Florida, Illinois, Maryland, Massachusetts, Montana, New Hampshire, Oregon, Pennsylvania, and Washington.[28] Nor does it make a difference if the call was placed from a state that doesn't prohibit secret recording.[29] New York law forbids the interception of conversations on cordless phones,[30] but that restriction isn't true everywhere. In the Eighth Circuit, the court has found that no one using a cordless phone has the right to expect much privacy.[31]

It should go without saying that listening in on telephone conversations to which a journalist is not a party is a serious violation of both law and ethics. Under those circumstances, the Federal Wiretap Statute imposes a maximum fine of $10,000 and up to five years in prison. The publishing of information obtained in violation of the statute also is a crime.

But does that mean that wiretap information can never be published, even if it is newsworthy? The U.S. Court of Appeals for the First Circuit has held that if a newspaper obtains wiretap information legally, the paper may publish it without violating the law. Under extreme circumstances, the paper may even do so in defiance of a court order prohibiting publication.

The *Providence Journal* used the Freedom of Information Act to obtain transcripts made in the 1960s of telephone conversations by the late Raymond L. S. Patriarca and his son, Raymond J., both reputedly involved in criminal activity. The FBI had used illegal wiretaps to monitor their telephone calls. An attorney for Raymond J. Patriarca, arguing that publication of the transcripts would violate the privacy rights of his client and of others, obtained an order from a U.S. district court in Providence forbidding the *Journal* to use information from them. After consulting the newspaper's lawyer, *Journal* Executive

Matter of Application to Adjudge Providence Journal Co. and Its Executive Editor, Charles M. Hauser, in Criminal Contempt, 820 F.2d 1342 (1st Cir. 1986).

---

27. 18 U.S.C. §§ 2510–2520.
28. Kovner, Dorsen, and Telsey, "Recent Developments," p. 25.
29. See Brown v. News Group Publications, 563 F. Supp. 86, 9 Med.L.Rptr. 1851 (M.D.Pa. 1983).
30. People v. Fata, 559 N.Y.S.2d 348 (1990); N.Y. Penal Law § 250.
31. Tyler v. Berodt, 877 F.2d 705 (8th Cir. 1989); cert. denied, 110 S.Ct. 723 (1990).

Editor Charles M. Hauser concluded that the order was unconstitutional and approved publication of a story based on the transcripts.

A week later, the district court judge came to the same conclusion and lifted the order. Nevertheless, at the instigation of Patriarca's attorney, the judge found the *Journal* and Hauser in contempt for disobeying his order. He fined the paper $100,000 and sentenced the editor to eighteen months in prison (suspended) and to two hundred hours of public service.

A three-judge panel of the U.S. Court of Appeals for the First Circuit reversed, holding that a "party subject to an order that constitutes a transparently invalid prior restraint on pure speech may challenge the order by violating it."[32] The court said that the only conceivable danger was to Patriarca's privacy and the remedy for that was an action for damages after publication, not a restraint.

On rehearing *en banc,* the full court adopted the panel's opinion but suggested that in the future a publisher confronted with such an order ought to make a good-faith effort to seek emergency relief from an appellate court. "If timely access to the appellate court is not available or if timely decision is not forthcoming, the publisher may then proceed to publish and challenge the constitutionality of the order in contempt proceedings."[33] The U.S. Supreme Court agreed to review the decision but took no action after deciding that the special prosecutor representing the government lacked legal authority to make an appeal.[34]

The *Providence Journal* took a bold position and prevailed, but remember that the newspaper had obtained the copies of illegal FBI wiretaps from government sources by using the Freedom of Information Act. The *Oswegonian,* a student newspaper at State University of New York, Oswego, also took a bold position when it published a transcript of an illegal recording of a phone conversation between a police chief and a local businessman. However, unlike in the case of the *Providence Journal,* this recording was leaked to the newspaper by a political candidate for political purposes. When the local businessman sued the student newspaper for damages under the Federal Wiretap Statute, the court refused to dismiss the claim.

This case was different, said the judge, because neither public records nor rights of access to government information were involved, the editors knew they were dealing with conversations between unconsenting parties, and the conversations were not matters of public significance or import. The Federal Wiretap Statute "clearly prohibits knowing disclosure by third parties without regard for participation in the illegal interception, and no exception is made for media," said the court.[35] In a curious twist of fate, however, the court did find an exception for a rival newspaper, the *Palladium Times,* which published the same information the day after the *Oswegonian* had published its article. The lawsuit against the *Palladium Times* was dismissed because the material by then had entered the public domain, as a result of its publication in the *Oswegonian.* The lesson is this: Be especially careful when someone gratuitously

---

32. Matter of Application to Adjudge Providence Journal Co. and Its Executive Editor, Charles M. Hauser, in Criminal Contempt, 820 F.2d 1342 (1st Cir. 1986).
33. Ibid. at 1354.
34. United States v. Providence Journal Company, 485 U.S. 693, 108 S.Ct. 1502, 99 L.Ed. 785 (1988).
35. Natoli v. Sullivan, 159 Misc.2d 681, 606 N.Y.S.2d 504, 21 Med.L.Rptr. 2097, at 2101 (N.Y.Sup. 1993).

gives you an illegally recorded, private telephone conversation. It may come with a hidden price that you might not want to pay.

Copied or Stolen Documents

Letters, reports, memoranda, and other written materials prepared by an individual are that person's private property. Using them without consent can give rise to lawsuits ranging from copyright infringement to theft. Looked at from the journalist's point of view, however, the information contained in copied or stolen documents may be something other than purely private property; it may be news. Can a journalist report such news without incurring liability? The answer depends on what the reporter did to get the information. Two cases involving the legendary investigative reporter and Washington columnist Drew Pearson make the point.

The first case, *Liberty Lobby* v. *Pearson,*[36] decided by the U.S. Court of Appeals for the District of Columbia Circuit in 1968, involved information contained in documents stolen from a private lobbying organization and given to Jack Anderson, then Pearson's assistant. When the organization asked a federal court to prevent further publication of information from its files, the court refused to do so. On appeal, the circuit court held that Liberty Lobby was not entitled to relief unless it could prove that it owned the documents in Pearson's possession and could also show that either Pearson or Anderson had taken them from the files. The court also held that there was a public interest in publication that, in a close case, would require a ruling in Pearson's favor.

The second case, *Pearson* v. *Dodd,*[37] involved information taken from the files of a U.S. senator. Thomas Dodd of Connecticut was suspected of dipping into campaign funds to pay for his living expenses. Disgruntled members of his office staff copied documents supporting these suspicions and gave them to Pearson and Anderson, who published information taken from them. Dodd sued the columnists for intrusion and for conversion, a tort closely related to theft. A federal district court held that there had been a conversion, but an appeals court reversed, dismissing both counts of the lawsuit. It wrote:

> If we were to hold Pearson and Anderson liable for invasion of privacy on these facts, we would establish the proposition that one who received information from an intruder, knowing it has been obtained by improper intrusion, is guilty of a tort. In an untried and developing area of tort law, we are not prepared to go so far. A person approached by an eavesdropper would perhaps play the nobler part should he spurn the offer and shut his ears. However, it seems to us that at this point it would place too great a strain on human weakness to hold one liable in damages who merely succumbs to temptation and listens.

There was no conversion, the court held, because the documents themselves had never left Dodd's office. Thus, there had been no taking of property. The senator had not been deprived of the use of the documents, even though he had been embarrassed when the information they contained left his office through the magic of a handy copying machine.

---

36. 390 F.2d 489 (D.C. Cir. 1968).
37. 410 F.2d 701 (D.C. Cir. 1969); cert. denied, 395 U.S. 947 (1969).

Generally, if reporters accept leaked information and publish or broadcast it, they have done nothing illegal, even if others have. But if they steal documents or arrange a theft, they may be guilty of a crime, regardless of the newsworthiness of the information. Likewise, if they deprive others of their property or intrude into their private space to copy the information, they are liable for the damages that the deprivation or intrusion causes. Moreover, if a reporter possesses the only copies of the documents, and thus the rightful owner cannot use them, the reporter is liable for whatever damages their continued possession causes the lawful owner. For example, when in 1988, ABC News broadcast a report on the U.S. Army's Bradley Fighting Vehicle and displayed documents taken from the FMC Corporation, the Seventh Circuit Court of Appeals held that retention of the originals or the only known copies could give rise to an action for conversion by FMC, but retention of mere copies could not, citing *Pearson* v. *Dodd*.[38] And, as we have already seen, the publishing of information from an illegal wiretap may run afoul of the Federal Wiretap Statute.

DISCLOSURE OF EMBARRASSING PRIVATE FACT

Courts have held that news media can be required to pay damages to persons humiliated by the publication of private facts. If such publication would outrage the community's notions of decency, as measured by a jury, the publication can be an invasion of privacy. But courts also have held that the media cannot be found liable if the allegedly private facts, no matter how outrageous, are newsworthy or are taken from a public record. For journalists, the problem lies in the further holding by some courts that juries should decide when allegedly private facts become newsworthy. Thus, this branch of the tort is marked by considerable uncertainty. However, the news media have won more private-fact cases than they have lost. In the process, some guideposts have emerged to help journalists assess the hazards.

Constitutional Limits

On two occasions the Supreme Court has upheld the right of the media to publish the names of rape victims, despite state laws forbidding such publication. On a third, the Court upheld the right of West Virginia newspapers to publish the name of a juvenile offender, despite a law making such publication a crime. In each instance, however, the Court also said it was not upholding the media's right to publish all facts, whatever their source or however outrageous they might be, about individuals. Thus, the Court has kept open the right to sue for disclosure of embarrassing private fact, but the Court has imposed First Amendment limits on that right.

---

38.   FMC Corp. v. Capital/ABC Inc., 915 F.2d 300, 18 Med. L. Rptr. 1195 (9th Cir. 1990).

The landmark decision is *Cox Broadcasting Co.* v. *Cohn*. The case grew out of the rape and murder of a seventeen-year-old girl in At-

Cox Broadcasting Co. v.
Cohn, 420 U.S. 469, 95
S.Ct. 1029, 43 L.Ed.2d 328,
1 Med.L.Rptr. 1819 (1975).

lanta. In compliance with a state law making it a crime to publish or broadcast the name of a rape victim, the news media did not identify her. Eight months later, the six men accused of the crime appeared in court. As part of a plea bargain, five of them pleaded guilty to attempted rape. The sixth pleaded not guilty. A reporter for WSB-TV, the Cox station in Atlanta, was present. He asked the court clerk to show him the indictments so that he could get the names and the details of the charge correctly. Each indictment carried the victim's name, which the reporter also copied into his notes. On the news that evening, WSB-TV disclosed her name to the public for the first time.

Normally, an action for disclosure of private fact can be brought only by the victim. But a provision in the Georgia statute forbidding publication of the name of a rape victim makes it possible for close relatives to start a civil action in a deceased victim's behalf. In this case, the victim's father sued Cox Broadcasting for invasion of privacy, alleging disclosure of private fact. A trial court brushed aside First Amendment arguments and awarded summary judgment to the plaintiff, Cohn. The only question for the jury, the court ruled, was the amount of the judgment. Cox appealed, and the state supreme court upheld the verdict, ruling that the statute declares as state policy that a rape victim's name is not a matter of public concern. The statute, the state supreme court said, places a limited, but legitimate, limitation on freedom of the press. Cox Broadcasting appealed to the U.S. Supreme Court, which took the case.

Justice Byron R. White, writing for himself and five other justices, focused the Court's decision on the question raised by the facts of the case: Could the news media be held liable for publishing facts found in the public records of a court? The majority held that a state neither can prevent such publication nor can it define such publication as an invasion of privacy. The Court gave two reasons for its holding:

1. The news media perform a valuable public service by covering news of government, including the courts. Obtaining such information is something few people have the time or the inclination to do for themselves. Therefore, the media, as surrogates for the general public, should not have needless limits placed on their coverage. In this instance, news of the crime of rape was of legitimate concern to the public.

2. Of particular importance is the right of the news media to report matters on the public record. Courts have recognized a press privilege to report the events of judicial proceedings. The majority concluded that there can be no liability for the accurate reporting of matters taken from public records, especially those of the courts.

Repeatedly, the Court emphasized that its holding was a narrow one, limited solely to the facts of the case. The Court held that the young woman's name was both on the public record and an element of a legitimate news event—a particularly brutal gang rape. Further, the majority made a point of noting that in no way was the authority of states to seal court records containing embarrassing facts being limited. The majority also noted that records of juvenile courts generally are considered private, subject to release only by a judge's order.

Only four years later, however, in *Smith* v. *Daily Mail Publishing Co.,*[39] the Supreme Court struck down a West Virginia law making it a crime for newspapers to publish the names of juvenile offenders. In that instance, the name of a junior high school student who had shot another student to death in a school parking lot was obtained not from a public record but from police, a prosecutor, and other students at the scene. The Court noted that the name had been obtained lawfully and that the juvenile was involved in a matter of public significance. The Court held that the state's interest in seeking rehabilitation of juvenile offenders by shielding them from public knowledge was not sufficient to override the First Amendment interest in publication of offenders' names.

More recently, the Supreme Court struck down a Florida law making it a misdemeanor to publish the names of rape victims. At the same time, it reversed a judgment awarding the victim $100,000 for invasion of privacy. The Court took this action even though another Florida statute was designed expressly to keep the names of rape victims off the public record, as the Court had suggested in *Cox.*

The case had its origins in a series of mistakes. A reporter-trainee employed by the

The Florida Star v. B.J.F., 491 U.S. 524, 109 S.Ct. 2603, 105 L.Ed.2d 443, 16 Med.L.Rptr. 1801 (1989).

Florida Star, a weekly serving Jacksonville's black community, was sent to the sheriff's office to gather material for the newspaper's "Police Reports." Among the items made available to her and other reporters was a complaint by a woman who had been raped and robbed in a city park on her way to a bus stop. Under Florida law, the victim's name should not have been in the report, but it was. In any event, signs in the press room reminded reporters that the names of the victims of sex crimes are not matters of public record, and the *Florida Star*'s policy was not to use names of such victims. Nevertheless, the newspaper's one-paragraph item on the rape included the victim's name.

When the victim, identified only as B.J.F., sued for damages, the sheriff's department settled with her for $2,500. The newspaper elected to go to trial. B.J.F. testified that she had suffered emotional distress from seeing the assault described in print. The news item said that the assailant had undressed her and had had sexual intercourse with her before he fled. She also testified that a man had called her home and told her mother he would rape her again. As a result, B.J.F. said that she had had to change her telephone number and her residence, seek police protection, and obtain mental health counseling. At the end of this testimony, the trial judge ruled that the newspaper's conduct was negligent on its face, leaving the jury to decide only the amount of the damages. The jury awarded B.J.F. $75,000 in compensatory damages and $25,000 in punitive damages. The newspaper appealed, arguing that it ought not be held liable for publishing truthful information freely made available to it by police. The Florida

---

39.   443 U.S. 97, 99 S.Ct. 2667, 61 L.Ed.2d 399 (1979).

Supreme Court summarily affirmed the jury's award. The U.S. Supreme Court took the case on appeal and reversed, six to three.

As it had in *Cox,* the Court rejected the argument that the news media should never be held liable for publishing truthful information. It also rejected the suggestion that the rationale used in *Cox* should be applied to this case. Justice Thurgood Marshall, writing for the majority, noted that in *Cox* the rapists had been arrested and were involved in court proceedings, which usually are open to the public. In this instance, there had been no arrest. Further, by law the name of the victim was not part of the public record.

In Marshall's view, what the *Florida Star* did when it published B.J.F.'s name was on the same legal footing as the *Daily Mail*'s publication of the name of the juvenile offender in *Smith.* The paper had published truthful information that it had obtained lawfully, even if it was obtained by mistake. Under such circumstances, the state can punish the media only to protect a narrowly tailored state interest of the highest order. Marshall said that such an interest might be found in the need to protect a rape victim from retaliation or some other harm. The majority did not find that kind of interest in B.J.F.'s case.

Justice White, who had written the *Cox* decision, led the dissent in *B.J.F.,* flatly rejecting the majority's reasoning. He said he found no support for it in *Cox, Smith,* or anywhere else. Nor could he find any public interest in publishing the names, addresses, and phone numbers of crime victims or in holding newspapers free from blame when a state's efforts to protect a victim's privacy have failed.

The *Florida Star* ruling makes it difficult for a crime victim to expect to be able to keep his or her name off the air or out of the paper. When Nancy Tatum shot and killed Shedrick Hill, Jr., after he broke into her home, she relied on a Georgia statute making it unlawful for any news medium to print or broadcast the identity of a woman who may have been raped or may have been assaulted with intent to rape.[40] After the *Macon Telegraph* published her name, despite the statute, she sued for invasion of privacy, and a jury awarded her $100,000 in damages. Although the Georgia Court of Appeals affirmed the jury verdict,[41] the Georgia Supreme Court, citing *Florida Star,* found the Georgia statute unconstitutional. Under these circumstances, it said, Tatum could expect little privacy.

The circumstances of the crime were this: At about 4 A.M. on a Saturday morning, Tatum woke to find Hill in her bedroom, a knife in his hand, his trousers unzipped, and his penis exposed. Tatum shot Hill with a shotgun. The police investigation concluded that Tatum acted in self-defense, and although the investigating officers gave Tatum's name to the *Macon Telegraph* reporters, they admonished them not to publish it. The paper did anyway, under a headline that read: "Macon Woman Kills Attacker in Bedroom." The Georgia Supreme Court ruled that under these facts—a dramatic homicide by a woman with a shotgun, and her identity lawfully obtained by the press—Tatum "lost her right to keep her name private. When she shot Hill, Tatum be-

---

40.   OCGA 16-6-23.
41.   Macon Telegraph Publishing Co. v. Tatum, 208 Ga.App 111, 430 S.E.2d 18, 21 Med.L.Rptr. 1116 (1993).

came the object of a legitimate public interest and the newspaper had the right under the Federal and State Constitutions to accurately report the facts regarding the incident, including her name."[42]

These decisions leave the media free to use the names of victims of sex crimes if they choose to do so. Most editors do not,[43] with notable exceptions. For example, the issue of naming rape victims arose in two trials of national interest in 1991. The trials involved boxer Mike Tyson in Indianapolis and William Kennedy Smith in West Palm Beach. Tyson was convicted of raping a beauty pageant contestant in his Indianapolis hotel room; Smith, the nephew of Massachusetts Senator Edward M. Kennedy, was acquitted of raping a Florida woman whom he had taken to the Kennedy family estate in Palm Beach.

Most media, including the Associated Press, did not identify the victims. Television networks used electronic masking to cover the victims' faces. In the Smith case, however, the *Globe,* a supermarket tabloid based in Boca Raton, Florida, printed the victim's name and picture before Smith was charged with a crime. NBC, the *New York Times,* and others quickly followed the *Globe*'s lead. At the time, Palm Beach County State Attorney David Bludworth accused the *Globe* of violating a 1911 Florida law forbidding the printing of the identities of sex-crime victims. A local judge dismissed the case, and the appellate court affirmed the dismissal, ruling the state statute unconstitutional, a ruling consistent with *Cox Broadcasting* v. *Cohn* and *Florida Star* v. *B.J.F.*[44] In the Tyson case, the *Louisville Courier-Journal* identified the victim, as it also had in the Smith case. The policy of the paper was not to identify a rape victim except "in the most extraordinary circumstances."[45] The paper's editorial leadership believed these were extraordinary circumstances.

Even when using very old public records, media run little risk of losing privacy actions, except in California. Courts in Kansas and Iowa, among other states, have held that the lapse of time does not take away the right to publish embarrassing facts found in such records. The Kansas case involved a "Looking Backward" column's use of items reporting the discharge of a police officer ten years earlier.[46] The Iowa case grew out of a report that a young woman had been forced to undergo sterilization while she was a ward of a county home.[47] However, California courts still cite two early cases holding that the state's interest in rehabilitation of wrongdoers is sufficient to justify privacy actions against media that recall a subject's criminal past. The first, *Melvin* v. *Reid,*[48] was against the producer of a movie based on a crime committed by a prosti-

---

42. Macon Telegraph Publishing Co. v. Tatum, 22 Med.L.Rptr. 1126, 1127 (Ga. 1993).
43. A 1987 survey indicated that fewer than 3 percent of newspaper editors identify victims of sexual assaults, "Survey Finds Trend Away from Detailed Identification," *ASNE Bulletin,* July/August 1987, p. 5. In another survey in 1990, 92 percent of journalists questioned said they would never identify the victims of sexual assault, but 45 percent would consider a policy of asking rape victims whether they wanted their names included as part of a rape story. "SPJ Survey Finds Editors Worried," *Quill,* November/December 1990, p. 7.
44. Florida v. Globe Communications Corp., 622 So.2d 1066, 21 Med.L.Rptr. 2129 (Fla.App.Ct. 1993).
45. *News Policies, The Louisville Courier-Journal and The Louisville Times* (Louisville, Ky.: Gannett Newspapers, 1986), p. 44.
46. Rawlins v. Hutchinson Publishing Co., 543 P.2d 988 (Kans. 1975).
47. Howard v. Des Moines Register & Tribune, 283 N.W.2d 289 (Iowa 1979).
48. 112 Cal.App. 285 (1931).

tute many years earlier. The second involved a story in *Reader's Digest* about a truck driver named Briscoe who, eleven years earlier, had been arrested for hijacking.[49]

The Measure of an Embarrassing Private Fact

Cox and the related Supreme Court cases deal with two dimensions of the tort of disclosure of embarrassing private fact. In *Cox,* the Court said that matters found in official public records, particularly those of the courts, can't be used as grounds for a disclosure action. Simply put, the decision says that public facts aren't private. *Smith* and *B.J.F.* carry the principle further. In those cases, the Court said that the state can't punish the media for disclosing some embarrassing facts not on the public record if those facts were obtained legally and if the state can't demonstrate some strong reason for restricting their use. What, then, is an embarrassing private fact that will support a privacy suit if it is made public?

The Iowa Supreme Court said, in *Howard* v. *Des Moines Register & Tribune,* that a publication is actionable if (1) it concerns "the private, as distinguished from the public, life of the individual" and (2) it "is not of legitimate concern to the public."[50] The second element was quoted from *Restatement of Torts,*[51] which also says that the facts in question must "be highly offensive to a reasonable person." What would offend a reasonable person usually is for a jury to decide.

Once they have determined that private fact is at issue, courts often look to *Sidis* v. *F-R Publishing Corp.* for guidance as to whether it is actionable. At issue was a profile in the *New Yorker* magazine of William James Sidis, whose mathematical genius was such that he had attracted widespread attention as a child. He was graduated from Harvard at sixteen. He soon tired of life in the spotlight, however, and retreated from the academic world, became a recluse, and earned a bare existence as a clerk. More than twenty years later, a *New Yorker* writer caught up with Sidis. The resulting article was sympathetic in tone but ruthless in detailing Sidis's rise and fall. He found it deeply offensive and sued the magazine for invasion of privacy. The courts were sympathetic, too, but not enough so to find in Sidis's favor. The appeals court noted that Sidis was not an ordinary person, but a genius who, at one time, had attracted widespread public attention. That exposure had made him a public figure. As such, he had lost most of his claim to a right of privacy. True, he had retreated into obscurity, but that, too, the court said, was a matter of public concern. The article in the *New Yorker* sketched the life of an unusual person, and it had considerable popular interest. The court added:

Sidis **v. *F-R Publishing Corp.,* 113 F.2d 806, 1 Med.L.Rptr. 1775 (2d Cir. 1940).**

> We express no comment on whether or not the newsworthiness of the matter printed will always constitute a complete defense. Revelations may be so intimate and so unwarranted in the view of the victim's position as to outrage the community's notion of decency. But

---

49.   Briscoe v. Reader's Digest Association, 483 P.2d 34 (1971).
50.   Howard v. Des Moines Register & Tribune, 283 N.W.2d 289 (Iowa 1979).
51.   § 652D.

when focused upon public characters, truthful comments upon dress, speech, habits, and the ordinary aspects of personality will usually not transgress this line. Regrettably or not, the misfortunes and frailties of neighbors and "public figures" are subjects of considerable interest and discussion to the rest of the population. And when such are the mores of the community, it would be unwise for a court to bar their expression in the newspapers, books and magazines of the day.

The publication of private facts is actionable, then, only if the disclosure would outrage the community's notion of decency. The measure is not what would offend a sensitive person, like Sidis, but that composite known as the community, or the average person. A California jury found such outrage in a column that appeared in the *Oakland Tribune.* Columnist Sidney Jones thought there was news in his discovery that the female student body president of the College of Alameda had had a sex change operation. He wrote that the students would be surprised to learn that the president, Toni Ann Diaz, "is no lady, but in fact is a man whose real name is Antonio." The item added that students enrolled in a physical education class with her "may wish to make other showering arrangements." Diaz sued the newspaper and the columnist for invasion of privacy, alleging that the item disclosed private fact and was highly offensive. An Alameda County jury agreed, awarding her a $750,000 judgment against the *Tribune* and $5,000 against the columnist.

Diaz v. *Oakland Tribune, Inc.,* 139 Cal.App.3d 118, 188 Cal.Rptr. 762, 9 Med.L.Rptr. 1121 (Cal.Ct.App. 1983).

A California appeals court reversed, not because it disagreed with the result, but because it concluded that the judge had not properly instructed the jury on the burden of proof. The court noted that the gist of the column was true. Toni had been Antonio until undergoing surgery. Then she had gone to great lengths to change all the usual forms of identification to show her as a woman. Only her closest relatives knew what had happened. The columnist had acted on a tip from confidential sources. The information was confirmed by Oakland police, who had arrested Antonio Diaz some years before. The columnist did not talk to Toni Diaz.

The *Tribune,* seeking support from *Cox Broadcasting,* argued that because the arrest of Antonio Diaz had led to a trial at which he was acquitted, its item was based at least in part on the public record of a court. The sex change was confirmed not only by police, but by later records in the name of Toni Diaz. The California court held that all such records were beside the point. The fact at issue was the sex change operation, and that was not on the public record of a court.

The court also held that the publication of a private fact is an invasion of privacy if the fact in question would be offensive and objectionable to a reasonable person and if it were not of legitimate public concern. The latter was the court's way of saying that even an offensive fact would be protected if it were newsworthy. The trial judge had told the jury that the newspaper had the burden of proving that Diaz's sex change was newsworthy. That, the appeals court ruled, was error. The judge should have required Diaz to prove that her operation was not newsworthy. The court said that that burden was mandated by the same First Amendment interest found in the *New York Times* libel rule. Those who would restrict the flow of news must carry the burden of proving a need to do so.

In sending the case back for retrial, the court said that the jury, given proper instructions as to the burden of proof, would have to balance the competing interests and decide whether the item was newsworthy. That decision, the court said, "depends upon contemporary community mores and standards of decency," which is the kind of factual judgment best left to a jury. However, the appeals court volunteered the opinion that the item was not newsworthy and said that the jury was correct in its finding that the columnist had acted with malice when he added the sentence about showering arrangements. He knew, or should have known, that Diaz was not enrolled in a physical education class. The sentence could have had no other purpose than to make fun of her. That, the court said, was enough to support the jury's award of punitive damages.

The record does not show what happened on remand. Nor do the case records show many instances in which plaintiffs have been able to bring successful disclosure actions against news media. In the few instances resulting in awards for damages, disclosure was coupled with other factors, such as intrusion.

For example, the Alabama Supreme Court upheld a $4,166 judgment against the *Cullman Daily Times Democrat* based on a photograph taken at a county fair. The photo showed Mrs. Flora Bell Graham as she emerged from the fun house with her two young sons. An air jet had blown her skirt to her shoulders, and she was frantically trying to hold it down. The newspaper's editors thought the photo caught the spirit of the fair and used it on page 1. Mrs. Graham said she was mortified and sued the newspaper for disclosure of private fact. The newspaper argued that the photo had been taken in a public place and was newsworthy. The supreme court held in *Daily Times Democrat* v. *Graham*[52] that it could find nothing newsworthy in a photo of Mrs. Graham's underpants. Further, it noted that they were exposed against her will. The court concluded that the jury properly concluded that such exposure outraged the public's sense of decency.

A New Mexico court awarded a prison guard $200,000 for a story that appeared in the *Dallas Times Herald* describing his experiences as a hostage during a riot.[53] Prisoners had beaten, stabbed, and sexually assaulted him. The reporter had obtained much of the information by entering the guard's hospital room and eavesdropping on his conversation with a friend. The guard said he was very upset by publication of details of the assault and by a part of the story saying that he and his wife were living in near poverty. In this instance, the disclosure of embarrassing private fact was coupled with an intrusion.

The cases discussed thus far tell us that an individual has no cause of action for disclosure if the facts in question were taken from a public record, particularly the public record of a court. If a plaintiff's case is to survive, the embarrassing facts must have come from nonpublic sources, and they must be of such a nature as to outrage the community's sense of decency. But as the courts noted in *Sidis* and *Diaz,* even outrageous facts are protected if they possess considerable popular news interest, if they are of legitimate public concern, or if the subject of the article is a public figure. The

---

52.   276 Ala. 380, 162 So.2d 474 (Ala. 1964).
53.   "Dallas Times Herald Loses $200,000 Suit." *Editor & Publisher,* 16 October 1982, p. 57; Schmitt v. Dallas Times Herald, No. 5781-582 (N.M.Dist.Ct., Santa Fe County).

record offers abundant proof that these elements offer the media powerful defenses against disclosure actions.

Newsworthiness and the Public Interest

From the beginning, courts have recognized a conflict between an individual's interest in privacy and the public's interest in being informed. When the Georgia Supreme Court recognized a common law right of privacy more than ninety years ago, it grappled with that conflict. The court said, in *Pavesich* v. *New England Life Insurance Co.,*[54] that it believed the right of privacy to be a natural right. But it also said that one of the stumbling blocks to its enforcement is that "it would inevitably tend to curtail the liberty of speech and of the press," which also is a natural right. The court added, "It will therefore be seen that the right of privacy must in some particulars yield to the right of speech and of the press." This has proved to be the case. In federal and state courts, newsworthiness of information deemed to serve a public interest has become the strongest defense against an action for disclosure of embarrassing private fact.

Courts have tended to define newsworthiness broadly. In a decision that is still cited as a precedent, the U.S. Court of Appeals for the Third Circuit offered one of the broadest definitions of newsworthiness in *Jenkins* v. *Dell Publishing Co.* The plaintiff was a widow who was noteworthy only because her husband had been beaten to death on the street by a pack of young hoodlums, leaving her with six young children. Immediately after the incident, Mrs. Jenkins agreed to pose with her children for a Pittsburgh newspaper photographer. The picture appeared the next day along with a story about the murder of her husband. Three months later, the widow was shocked to find the same photograph in *Front Page Detective* magazine, along with a brief, factual account of the murder. She sued the publisher for invasion of privacy, alleging, among other things, that the facts of her tragic loss were offered as entertainment for the magazine's readers, causing her embarrassment. A federal district court dismissed the action, and the appeals court affirmed, holding that "information and entertainment are not mutually exclusive categories." The court then sought to define news:

Jenkins v. *Dell Publishing Co.*, 251 F.2d 447 (3d Cir. 1958).

> A large part of the matter that appears in newspapers and news magazines today is not published or read for the value or importance of the information it conveys. Some readers are attracted by shocking news. Others are titillated by sex in the news. Still others are entertained by news which has an incongruous or ironic aspect. Most news is in various ways amusing, and for that reason of special interest to many people. Few newspapers or news magazines would long survive if they did not publish a substantial amount of news on the basis of entertainment value of one kind or another. This may be a disturbing commentary upon our civilization, but it is nonetheless a realistic picture of society which courts shaping new juristic concepts should take into account.

---

54. 50 S.E. 68 (Ga. 1905).

The U.S. Court of Appeals for the Ninth Circuit also has dealt with the line between news and entertainment. In a case brought by a noted body surfer, *Virgil* v. *Time Inc.,* that court was less generous with the news media than the *Jenkins* court, but its decision, too, has become a frequently cited precedent.

Virgil v. Time Inc., 527 F.2d 1122, 1 Med.L.Rptr. 1835 (9th Cir. 1975).

Mike Virgil was said to be the most reckless member of a group who surfed at the Wedge, reputed to be the world's most dangerous spot for body surfing. *Sports Illustrated* assigned a writer to do a story on the spot, with Virgil as its focus. Virgil, his wife, and others spoke freely with the writer. The completed article was rich in unusual facts about an unusual character. The article left no doubt that Virgil was as reckless on land as he was in the water. It said he had dived down a flight of stairs at a ski resort to "impress these chicks all around." He burned the back of his hand to win a bet that, with a cigarette, he could burn a hole in a dollar bill resting on his hand. He ate spiders and insects. He injured himself deliberately on construction jobs so that he could draw workers' compensation while he continued surfing.

When one of the magazine's researchers telephoned Virgil to check on such details, he had second thoughts and asked that they not be published. Reasoning that whatever an adult says to a reporter is fair game, *Sports Illustrated* published the story. Virgil sued for invasion of privacy. A federal district court dismissed, but the appeals court reversed and remanded, holding that it thought a jury should decide whether details of Virgil's life out of the water were newsworthy. The court also held that one who speaks freely with a reporter does not necessarily consent to publication. If the subject of a story is given a chance to review it, as in this instance, and changes his or her mind about some of the revelations, the court said, "[T]he consequent publicity is without consent." Nevertheless, the court said that Virgil could not recover damages if a jury decided that the public had a legitimate interest in the facts, that the facts had previously become public knowledge, or that they would not be offensive to a reasonable person of ordinary sensibilities.

Despite the circuit court's decision, Virgil never got a chance to present his case to a jury. On remand, the U.S. District Court for the Southern District of California granted summary judgment to *Sports Illustrated.*[55] Applying the circuit court's prescribed test of newsworthiness, the district judge concluded that no reasonable juror could find the story highly offensive. He conceded that the facts would embarrass Virgil, but he said they were neither morbid nor sensational. Nor were they published without reason. The writer had a purpose, which was to give his readers an insight into Virgil's daring style of body surfing. Thus the story fulfilled a legitimate public interest.

The *Diaz* court also had offered jurors guidelines for determining when private facts become newsworthy, borrowing from the earlier decision in *Briscoe.*[56] It said that the jury should "consider (1) the social value of the facts published, (2) the depth of the article's intrusion into ostensibly private affairs, and (3) the extent to which the party voluntarily acceded to a position of public notoriety."

55.   Virgil v. Sports Illustrated and Time Inc., 424 F.Supp. 1286 (S.D. Calif. 1976).
56.   Briscoe v. Reader's Digest Association, 483 P.2d 34, at 43 (Calif. 1971).

Strict application of such guidelines has made it difficult for plaintiffs to win suits for disclosure of embarrassing private fact. Even when they have been able to convince a jury that the disclosure was not newsworthy, appeals courts have shown a disposition to hold otherwise. One case, *Cape Publications, Inc.* v. *Bridges,*[57] illustrates the point. A woman was held hostage by her estranged husband. She escaped and ran into the street clutching a hand towel that just managed to conceal the fact that she was nude. A photographer for *Cocoa Today* took her picture as she fled, and the newspaper used it. She convinced a jury that the photo was not newsworthy and that the newspaper exceeded the limits of decency in causing her extreme embarrassment. The jury awarded her $10,000. The appellate court reversed, holding:

> Just because the story and photograph may be embarrassing or distressful to the plaintiff does not mean the newspaper cannot publish what is otherwise newsworthy. At some point, the public interest in obtaining information becomes dominant over the individual's right of privacy.

This examination of newsworthiness and the public interest ends where it began: When an individual's asserted right of privacy collides with the public's right to be informed about matters of public interest, the latter almost always prevails. Courts have recognized that the public has a legitimate interest not only in the fate of nations but in human frailties, foibles, and misfortunes.

Defenses against a disclosure action are not absolute, but they are nearly so. Successful plaintiffs must prove that the facts in question were not found in the public record, that they themselves did not make these facts public, that they would outrage the community's sense of decency, and that their revelation serves no legitimate public interest. These are formidable barriers, but they reserve for the media what is perhaps the most important question of all: How far should the media go in publishing private facts that would embarrass any self-respecting person? In a free society, such questions can be answered only by those who are in the business of public communication. The ethical dimension of these questions are discussed at the end of this chapter.

FALSE LIGHT

False light is a problem for any communicator who blends fact and fiction. The harm comes in portraying individuals as better or worse than they really are to a point that would be offensive to a person of ordinary sensibilities. The point to remember is that such portrayal need not be defamatory. If it is, courts have held that it should be the subject of a libel action, not a lawsuit for invasion of privacy.

Many of the legal principles that apply to libel actions also apply to false-light litigation. A person cannot be put in a false light by the truth, so an action for false-light invasion of privacy, like an action for libel, must be grounded in a false assertion of fact. In libel actions, the false assertion of fact must be defamatory. In a false-light

---

57. 423 So.2d 426 (Fla.App.Ct. 5th Dist. 1982).

action, however, there is no defamation. There is nothing defamatory about being poor or soured on life, but to portray a person as one or both could result in a lawsuit for false-light invasion of privacy. The Supreme Court has held in two cases that plaintiffs in false-light actions must prove actual malice on the part of media defendants. Because the first of the decisions preceded the landmark *Gertz* case, and the second clearly involved actual malice, the Court left open the degree of fault that must be proved by a private individual. Lower courts, in some instances, have required all false-light plaintiffs, public or private, to prove actual malice. In the most recent cases, however, courts in some jurisdictions have been distinguishing between public official–public figure plaintiffs and private individuals. The latter have been permitted to prevail on some lesser showing of fault, usually negligence.

Distortion of an individual's personality lies at the heart of a false-light action. A professional communicator who is careful with facts and slow to jump to broad characterizations has little to fear from this branch of the tort. Communicators run a risk only if they are the kind of writers who purport to portray thought processes and who recreate conversations that may not have occurred. This is the stuff of television docudramas and historical fiction. To pass muster, such writing must be the product of sufficient research to ensure that fictionalized passages are true to the character of the persons portrayed, and readers must be told that portions of the work have been fictionalized.

The first false-light case to reach the Supreme Court, *Time Inc.* v. *Hill,* grew out of a drama review in the old weekly version of *Life* magazine. The play *The Desperate Hours* portrayed the experiences of a couple and their two children. The four were held hostage in their home by several escaped convicts. The play was based on a book by Joseph Hayes, who said he had taken his inspiration from several such real-life incidents. One of these incidents involved Mr. and Mrs. James Hill and their five children, who had been held hostage in their home in suburban Philadelphia. The three escaped convicts who invaded their home treated the family courteously during a nineteen-hour standoff with the police. When the convicts left the house, two of them were shot and killed by police. The Hills were so shocked that they moved to Connecticut and resisted all efforts to publicize the experience.

Time Inc. v. *Hill,* 385 U.S. 374, 87 S.Ct. 534, 17 L.Ed.2d 456, 1 Med.L.Rptr. 1791 (1967).

When *The Desperate Hours* was playing in Philadelphia on its way to Broadway, an editor for *Life* had what seemed like a bright idea. Why not take the actors to what had been the Hill home and photograph them enacting several of the more dramatic scenes from the play? This exercise would show the magazine's readers that the play was not altogether fiction. The play's producer and the new owner of the house were willing. Three of the resulting photographs accompanied a review of the play in an issue of *Life*. One showed a son being beaten by one of the convicts. Another showed the daughter biting a convict's hand to make him drop a gun. A third showed the father throwing the gun through a door. None of these things had happened to the Hills, and the copy written by the reviewer did not say that they had. But the editor who prepared the copy for publication changed both the review and the photo captions to make a direct association with the Hill family. He did so, he testified later, to jazz up the material. The changes gave readers the impression that the photographs portrayed the Hill family's experiences with the hostages. Hill sued for false-light invasion of privacy, setting in motion a legal yo-yo that remained in motion during more than a decade of litigation.

In the first round of the legal action, the Hills won a $75,000 judgment. An appellate court held that that amount was excessive. They then won a judgment for $30,000, which the appellate court affirmed. Time Inc. asked the Supreme Court to consider the case, arguing that its First Amendment rights were involved. The Supreme Court agreed that they were. Holding that the New York courts had not shown a proper regard for freedom of the press, the Court sent the case back for retrial.[58] It said that the Hills could win only if they could prove actual malice. At that point, they gave up.

At the time, the effect of the *Hill* decision was open to question. The Court, in deciding that *Life* should prevail over the Hill family, was divided six to three over the reason why. Only three members of the majority endorsed the actual-malice requirement. One member of the majority preferred a negligence standard. Two others would have held that the First Amendment ruled out all false-light claims.

Seven years after *Hill,* the Supreme Court reviewed a second false-light case, *Cantrell* v. *Forest City Publishing Co.* Mrs. Melvin Aaron Cantrell had been left a widow ten days before Christmas in 1967 when her husband was one of the forty-four victims of the collapse of Silver Bridge, crossing the Ohio River at Point Pleasant, West Virginia. Several months later, a reporter for the *Cleveland Plain Dealer* decided to write a follow-up story on some of the survivors. He included Cantrell because she had been the focus of one of the prize-winning stories he had written at the time of the disaster. She was not at home, but the reporter did interview several of her minor children. The resulting story, portraying the mother as embittered by broken promises and living in abject poverty, was written as though the reporter had talked with Cantrell. One passage described her as wearing "the same mask of nonexpression she wore at the funeral." *Plain Dealer* editors featured the story in the newspaper's Sunday magazine.

> *Cantrell* v. *Forest City Publishing Co.,* 419 U.S. 245, 95 S.Ct. 465, 42 L.Ed.2d 419, 1 Med.L.Rptr. 1815 (1974).

Cantrell sued for invasion of privacy, alleging that she had been placed in a false light. A federal district court jury awarded her a $60,000 judgment. The circuit court of appeals reversed, but the U.S. Supreme Court restored the original verdict. Eight justices held that a properly instructed jury had come to the correct conclusion in finding actual malice. There was enough evidence within the story to prove that the reporter's word portrait of Cantrell was false. The story indicated that he had seen her and perhaps had talked with her, but he had done neither.

Cantrell was decided about six months after the libel case of *Gertz* v. *Robert Welch.*[59] The majority took note of *Gertz* but saw no need to decide whether the reasoning in *Gertz* with respect to private individuals should be applied to Cantrell. Clearly, she was a private individual, but it was also clear that the *Plain Dealer*'s re-

---

58. For an interesting narrative about the role Richard Nixon played as an attorney in the appellate portion of the Hill case, see "Annals of Law: The Hill Case," *New Yorker,* 17 April 1989, pp. 90–110.

59. 418 U.S. 323, 94 S.Ct. 2997, 41 L.Ed.2d 789, 1 Med.L.Rptr. 1633 (1974).

porter had been caught in an intentional falsehood. Initially, lower courts confronted with false-light cases adopted the *Hill* rationale and required all plaintiffs to prove actual malice. Courts have so held in Arkansas,[60] California,[61] Colorado,[62] Connecticut,[63] Kentucky,[64] Maine,[65] New Jersey,[66] Oklahoma,[67] and Oregon.[68]

Courts in other jurisdictions have looked to *Gertz* for guidance and have held that only public official or public figure plaintiffs need prove actual malice: the U.S. Court of Appeals for the Fifth Circuit, applying Texas law,[69] and for the Sixth Circuit, applying Michigan law[70]; the U.S. district courts in the District of Columbia,[71] Illinois,[72] Kansas,[73] and Maryland;[74] the supreme courts in West Virginia[75] and Iowa[76]; the court of appeals in Michigan;[77] and an intermediate appellate court in New York.[78]

Besides the courts that have chosen sides on the question of whether *Gertz* or *Hill* should control in a false-light case, others have simply not recognized false light as a tort. The supreme court of North Carolina held that the First Amendment bars false-light actions.[79] Indiana,[80] Missouri,[81] Minnesota,[82] Ohio,[83] and Texas[84] have so far not recognized the tort. Some other states have not had the opportunity to decide the issue or have avoided it because there were other grounds for decisions.

---

60. Dodrill v. Arkansas Democrat, 590 S.W.2d 840, 5 Med.L.Rptr. 1385 (Ark. 1979), cert. denied, 444 U.S. 1076 (1980).
61. Fellows v. National Enquirer, 165 Cal.App.3d 512, 211 Cal.Rptr. 809 (2d Dist. 1985), review granted, 215 Cal.Rptr. 853, 701 P.2d 1171 (Calif. 1985), superseded by 42 Cal.3d 234, 228 Cal.Rptr. 215, 721 P.2d 97 (Calif. 1987).
62. McCammon and Associates v. McGraw-Hill, 716 P.2d 490, 12 Med.L.Rptr. 1847 (Colo.App. 1986).
63. Goodrich v. Waterbury Republican-American, 188 Conn. 107, 8 Med.L.Rptr. 2329 (1982).
64. McCall v. Courier-Journal, 623 S.W.2d 882, 7 Med.L.Rptr. 2118 (Ky. 1981), cert. denied, 456 U.S. 975 (1982).
65. Dempsey v. National Enquirer, 687 F.Supp. 692 (D.Me. 1988).
66. Machleder v. Diaz, 618 F.Supp. 1367, 12 Med.L.Rptr. 1193 (S.D.N.Y. 1985), reversed on other grounds, 801 F.2d 46, 13 Med.L.Rptr. 1369 (2d Cir. 1986), cert. denied 107 S.Ct. 1294 (1987).
67. Colbert v. World Publishing, 747 P.2d 286, 14 Med.L.Rptr. 2188 (Okla. 1987).
68. Dean v. Guard Publishing Co., 73 Ore.App.656, 699 P.2d 1158 (Ore.App. 1985), 14 Med.L.Rptr. 2100 (1987).
69. Wood v. Hustler Magazine, 736 F.2d 1084, 10 Med.L.Rptr. 1497 (5th Cir. 1984), cert. denied, 105 S.Ct.783 (1985).
70. Bichler v. Union Bank, 715 F.2d 1059, 9 Med.L.Rptr.2033, vacated, 718 F.2d 802, affirmed, 745 F.2d 1006 (6th Cir. 1984).
71. Dresbach v. Doubleday, 518 F.Supp. 1285, 7 Med.L.Rptr. 2165 (D.D.C. 1981).
72. Cantrell v. ABC, 529 F.Supp. 764 (N.D.Ill. 1981).
73. Rinsley v. Brandt, 446 F.Supp. 850 (D.Kans. 1977).
74. Fitzgerald v. Penthouse International, 525 F.Supp. 585, 7 Med.L.Rptr. 2385 (D.Md. 1981).
75. Crump v. Beckley Newspapers, 320 S.E.2d 70, 10 Med.L.Rptr. 2225 (W. Va. 1983).
76. Jones v. Palmer Communications, 440 N.W.2d 884, 16 Med.L.Rptr. 2137 (Iowa 1989).
77. Dietz v. Wometco West Michigan TV, 160 Mich.App. 367, 407 N.W.2d 649, 14 Med.L.Rptr. 1629 (1987).
78. Fils-Aime v. Enlightenment Press, 133 Misc.2d 559, 507 N.Y.S.2d 947, 13 Med.L.Rptr. 1971 (N.Y.App.Term 1986).
79. Renwick v. News and Observer, 312 S.E.2d 405, 10 Med.L.Rptr. 405 (N.C. 1984).
80. Perry v. Columbia Broadcasting Co., 499 F.2d 797 (7th Cir.), cert. denied, 419 U.S. 883 (1974).
81. Dupree v. Iliff, 860 F.2d 300, 15 Med.L.Rptr. 2225 (8th Cir. 1988); Renner v. Donsbach, 18 Med.L.Rptr. 1930 (W.D.Mo. 1990).
82. Price v. Viking Press, 12 Med.L.Rptr. 1689 (D.Minn. 1985).
83. Angelotta v. ABC, 820 F.2d 806, 14 Med.L.Rptr. 1185 (6th Cir. 1987). But see Morgan v. Hustler Magazine, 653 F.Supp. 711, 13 Med.L.Rptr. 2226 (N.D.Ohio 1987) (decided a few months before Angelotta).
84. Cain v. Hearst Corp., 22 Med.L.Rptr. 2161 (Tex.S.Ct. 1994).

Most reported false-light actions fall into one of three categories:

1. False material is added to an otherwise accurate story, resulting in a distorted portrayal of the subject.

2. A photograph or videotape is used to create a highly offensive portrayal of the subject.

3. Living people, either as themselves or thinly disguised, are portrayed in fictional works.

The classic case illustrating the first of these categories is *Spahn* v. *Julian Messner,*[85] which was decided by New York's highest court. Warren Spahn was one of the best baseball pitchers of the late 1950s. A winner of baseball's top pitching award, he has long since entered baseball's hall of fame. At the height of his career, Spahn became the subject of a biography to be published by Messner. The writer was not content to describe Spahn's career as it was, but said that Spahn was a World War II hero, which he wasn't, and generally made him out to be larger than life. The pitcher brought suit for false-light invasion of privacy and eventually was able to win an injunction preventing distribution of the book.

The use of a photograph in a context that would make it highly offensive is illustrated by *Wood* v. *Hustler Magazine, Inc.,*[86] decided by the U.S. Court of Appeals for the Fifth Circuit. Lajuan Wood and her husband Billy took nude photographs of each other during an outing in a remote section of a Texas state park. They kept the prints in a dresser drawer in their bedroom. A neighbor thought it would be a great joke to send a photo of Lajuan to *Hustler* magazine for its "Beaver Hunt" section. He stole the print long enough to make a copy. The neighbor's wife, pretending to be Lajuan, sent the copy to *Hustler,* along with a letter saying that her secret fantasy was "to be screwed by two bikers." The editors of *Hustler* have a policy of calling persons who submit photos to it to verify that senders are who they claim to be and do indeed want the photos published. In this instance, the policy was not followed strictly. The call to the neighbor's wife, pretending to be Lajuan, was perfunctory.

The Woods learned what had happened when friends began to tease them. Both sued *Hustler* for invasion of privacy. Lajuan said she was so mortified by the experience that she had to have six weeks of psychological counseling. A jury awarded her $150,000 in damages and her husband $25,000. The court of appeals threw out the award to the husband, holding that he could not collect damages for an invasion of his wife's privacy. But the court said there was no doubt that Lajuan had been put in a false light. It held further that as a private individual, she had only to prove that the editors of *Hustler* were negligent in checking the identity of the person who had submitted the photograph. Such negligence was evident, the court said, from the fact that they had not followed their own procedures.

---

85. 221 N.E.2d 543 (N.Y. 1966).
86. 736 F.2d 1084 (5th Cir. 1984).

Fictionalization has been a problem largely for television docudramas, which are mixtures of fact and fiction; for cinema; and for novels. The cases indicate that if the subject is a public figure and the work deals with matters of public concern, courts will protect all but the grossest distortions. Because truth is elusive and varies with the beholder, the First Amendment gives strong protection to works dealing with public figures and historical events.

Problems have arisen with the portrayal of peripheral figures, persons who surround public figures and play the supporting roles. For instance, an attorney who had represented a prominent figure in organized crime was found to have a false-light claim against the publisher of a novel in which his name was used.[87]

Taken as a whole, the reported cases convey a straightforward message. Professional communicators who use words or pictures to portray individuals, and who take care to make certain that their work shows the individuals as they are, have little to fear. If the subject of the work is a public figure or an event of public importance, the law will tolerate a good deal of material distortion before it will uphold a false-light privacy claim. That latitude provides some breathing space for public comment on public issues but should provide little comfort to a communicator who deliberately falsifies the life and personality of an individual.

APPROPRIATION AND THE RIGHT OF PUBLICITY

Appropriation, which for years was confined to providing a remedy for the commercial misuse of a person's name or likeness, has more recently branched to include not only this right of personal privacy but also the right to control publicity. This means that individuals, particularly celebrities, have the right to control how others use the value of their notoriety. The courts have come to recognize that a widely known name or likeness is a form of property, not just personality, and has a value that the possessor alone should be permitted to exploit.

The principal and strongest defense against an action for appropriation or violation of the right of publicity is consent, preferably in writing. From the user's point of view, the best consent is written broadly enough to cover any conceivable use of a subject's identity in perpetuity. Short of broad consent, any use of identity for commercial gain should be accompanied by the subject's specific consent. Consent can be implied in some instances, but usually only in connection with a news event or interview, or only if commercial gain is incidental to the use.

Because this branch of invasion of privacy almost always hinges on the user's commercial gain, it is of concern mainly to advertisers, public relations practitioners, and photographers. In only a few instances has news or feature content been at issue in an appropriation or right-of-publicity action.

---

87.   Polakoff v. Harcourt Brace, 413 N.Y.S.2d 537 (1st Dept. 1979).

Appropriation

In its usual form appropriation is fairly simple. An unsuspecting person who finds his or her name or photograph in a commercial advertisement has a cause of action for damages. Courts usually fix the award by determining what a model would receive for the same usage. In some instances, an attempt is made to calculate the commercial value of the subject's endorsement. On occasion, appropriation becomes intertwined with false light, as when a young woman who posed for an advertisement for sheets found that the photograph had been altered in another usage to make it look as though she were in bed reading a pornographic novel. In such instances, the award for damages might be higher than if appropriation alone were involved.

The experience of John Kimbrough, a former football player at Texas A & M University, illustrates the typical appropriation case. In it, a Texas appellate court held that a jury should decide whether Kimbrough's consent had been exceeded and, if so, how much he should receive in damages. The circumstances of the case were as follows: Kimbrough was notified that he had been selected as his school's best former football player. As a result, *Texas Football* magazine and Coca-Cola had commissioned an artist to paint his portrait. He would get the original. One print would go to Texas A & M for permanent display; another would be placed in the Texas Football Hall of Fame. The letter also said in part:

Kimbrough v. *Coca-Cola/USA,* 521 S.W.2d 719 (Tex. 1975).

> There is also contemplated use of these paintings [athletes from other Southwest Conference schools also were being honored] in a series of institutional advertisements in behalf of college football in Dave Campbell's *Texas Football* magazine.
>
> While no endorsement of any product is implied in the institutional nature of the proposed usage, we would not, of course, approach a project of this type without your complete approval.

Kimbrough replied that he was honored at being chosen and would sit for his portrait. Sometime later his daughter called to tell him that she had found a reproduction of his portrait in the program for the Southern Methodist–Wake Forest football game as part of an advertisement for Coca-Cola. Kimbrough reacted by suing everyone connected with the promotion for invasion of privacy. A state district court in Dallas dismissed the action, but an appeals court reversed.

Coca-Cola based its case on two grounds: (1) As a public figure, Kimbrough had lost any claim to a right of privacy and (2) in any event, he had given his consent. The court said that although public figures do surrender much of their privacy, they still are entitled to protection against appropriation for commercial purposes. The court also concluded that the ambiguous wording of the original letter raised a jury question as to whether Kimbrough's consent had been exceeded. Here there was a real possibility that his consent had been for noncommercial uses only.

Consent Agreements

Professional advertisers, photographers, and public relations practitioners usually know enough about their business to obtain consent from their subjects. For that reason most appropriation actions are based on attempts to revoke or limit consent or on allegations that the consent was exceeded. Some plaintiffs have learned that consent given too readily and too broadly not only can embarrass them but can deny them legal relief, as the following episode illustrates.

When Brooke Shields, the actress and model, was ten years old, she posed for a series of nude photographs taken by Gary Gross for Playboy Press. She was portrayed in and out of a bathtub for a book, *Sugar and Spice,* designed "to depict the woman in the little girl to highlight the sensuality of prepubescent youth." Brooke was photographed with the cooperation of her mother, Teri Shields, who signed a standard model release and in return received $450. Neither the photos of Brooke nor the book in which they appeared was in any way pornographic. Larger-than-life reproductions of two of the bathtub photos were displayed for weeks in the windows of a Fifth Avenue store in New York City.

Shields v. Gross,
**7 Med.L.Rptr. 2349
(N.Y.Sup.Ct. 1981).**

Five years later, after Brooke had begun to appear in movies in which she played sensual roles, the nude photos resurfaced. Some appeared in a magazine published in France. Others were used in various American magazines. When "publications of dubious respectability" began proclaiming that they offered photographs of "Brooke Shields naked," Mrs. Shields tried to buy the negatives from Gross. When that failed, she went to court, asking that the photographer be prevented from selling or using the nude photographs of her daughter. The court granted her a temporary injunction, heard her lawyer's arguments, then turned her down flat, except to put into legal form Gross's agreement not to sell the photos to pornographic magazines or those designed to appeal predominantly to a prurient interest.

Judge Edward J. Greenfield of the New York Supreme Court—a trial court—told Mrs. Shields in blunt language that she could not have it both ways. She could not exploit her daughter's "extraordinary genes," her "exceptional beauty and engaging personality," and then complain when others sought to cash in on the same qualities. He reminded Mrs. Shields that the release she had signed so eagerly, without even reading it, had given Gross an absolute right to use and publish the products of the photo session in any way he liked. She also had waived her right "to inspect or approve" the finished photographs and had agreed to give up any right to recover damages for their use, even if that use "should subject me to ridicule, scandal, reproach, scorn or indignity." In short, she would have to be satisfied with the $450, while Gross was free to sell the photos for whatever the market would offer.

Mrs. Shields proved to be a persistent adversary. She appealed first to the supreme court's appellate division, which found in her favor and gave her part of what she sought, and then to the state's highest court, which rebuffed her by restoring the trial court's order.[88] This litigation took two years to move through the courts, during which time a series of temporary injunctions prevented Gross from further sales of the photographs. When Mrs. Shields lost her last round in the

---

88.   Shields v. Gross, 451 N.Y.S.2d 419, 88 A.D.2d 846, 7 Med.L.Rptr. 2349 (N.Y.App. 1982); affirmed as modified, 58 N.Y.2d 338, 461 N.Y.S. 254, 448 N.E.2d 108, 9 Med.L.Rptr. 1466 (N.Y. 1983).

state courts, she went immediately to the U.S. district court in New York City. The judge dismissed her suit summarily, accusing her lawyer of abusing the legal system to deny Gross profits that were rightfully his under terms of the consent.[89]

The conflict between photographers and subjects is clear. On the one hand, it is in the best financial interests of photographers and advertisers who use live models to ask for the broadest possible terms of consent. On the other hand, it is in the best interests of persons asked to sell their names and likenesses to others to limit the terms of the consent to a specific use. It is a general rule of law, as the New York Court of Appeals reminded Mrs. Shields, that "a defendant's immunity from a claim for invasion of privacy is no broader than the consent executed to him." In short, for purposes of advertising or trade, people have full control over how much of their privacy they are willing to surrender and on what terms.

The Right of Publicity and the Press

In the early 1950s appropriation began to divide itself into two torts: one protecting privacy and one protecting publicity.[90] The essential difference is that appropriation is about people and right of publicity is about property. That differentiation raises interesting questions about the use of this property. As a form of property, a publicity right is generally analogous to other kinds of property. One might therefore reasonably expect to be able to prevent others from using it, or to license it, or to transfer it to others. Moreover, property owners can generally prevent not only commercial exploitation of their property, but any use of their property without consent. To what extent, then, has the right of publicity so mutated from appropriation that even noncommercial uses can cause liability for damages?

Until 1977, courts generally held that there could be no liability if a person's name or photograph was used primarily for news purposes. Although editors choose news, feature, photo, and other content with the expectation that it will help the publication prosper, the courts maintained that it does not follow that persons who are featured have been victims of appropriation. Courts were even willing to tolerate some use of a newsworthy person's identity to promote sales of a newspaper or magazine. Courts took the view that such use was merely incidental to the real purpose of the publication—to disseminate information. For instance, a New York court held that Joe Namath, then a highly successful football quarterback, could not recover from *Sports Illustrated* when his photo was used to promote the magazine.[91] The photo had originally appeared on the cover of one issue of the magazine. That cover was one of several included in the promotional brochure. The court held that Namath's likeness was being used only to show prospective readers the kind of editorial content they could expect to enjoy if they became subscribers.

---

89. Shields v. Gross, 503 F.Supp. 533 (S.D.N.Y. 1983).
90. Haelan Laboratories, Inc. v. Topps Chewing Gum, Inc., 202 F.2d 866 (2d Cir. 1953).
91. Namath v. Sports Illustrated, 48 A.D.2d 487, 1 Med.L.Rptr. 1843 (N.Y. 1st Dept. 1975); affirmed, 352 N.E.2d 584 (1976).

In 1977, however, the U.S. Supreme Court ruled that a news program that had broadcast an entire carnival act without consent was liable for damages to the owner of the act. The plaintiff, Hugo Zacchini, made his living by being shot out of a huge cannon into a net three hundred yards away. When he appeared at the Geauga County Fair in Chardon, Ohio, a crew from WEWS-TV in Cleveland recorded his dramatic, fifteen-second flight. Zacchini asked that the act not be recorded and protested that the station was stealing his act, but that night it was broadcast as part of the news from the fair. Zacchini sued, asking for $35,000 as the value of the performance. Three Ohio courts came to as many different conclusions as to the merits of his suit, with the state supreme court holding that because the act had news value, the station had a right to show it. Zacchini took his case to the U.S. Supreme Court, which reversed, holding that the station had appropriated the act, violating the performer's "right of exclusive control over the publicity given to his performance."

Zacchini v. *Scripps-Howard Broadcasting,* 433 U.S. 562, 97 S.Ct. 2849, 53 L.Ed.2d 965, 1 Med.L.Rptr. 2089 (1977).

The Court conceded that the station's newscast was protected in its entirety by the First Amendment. It conceded also that there was news value in the fact that Zacchini had performed at the fair. However, Justice White, writing for six members of the Court, held that the First Amendment could not be stretched to justify appropriation of the entire act. He compared the newscast with the usual form of appropriation:

> [T]he broadcast of petitioner's entire performance, unlike the unauthorized use of another's name for purposes of trade or the incidental use of a name or picture by the press, goes to the heart of petitioner's ability to earn a living as an entertainer. Thus in this case, Ohio has recognized what may be the strongest case for a "right of publicity"—involving not the appropriation of an entertainer's reputation to enhance the attractiveness of a commercial product, but the appropriation of the very activity by which the entertainer acquired the reputation in the first place.

The Court's minority argued in vain that the small segment of the newscast devoted to the Human Cannonball's flight contributed little, if anything, to the station's revenue and should be treated as an incidental use.

In another case involving what was technically a noncommercial use of a celebrity interview, the Ninth Circuit Court of Appeals held in *Cher* v. *Forum International, Ltd.,* that *Forum* magazine could be held liable for the unauthorized use of a taped interview bought from a freelance writer.

Cher v. *Forum International, Ltd.,* 692 F.2d 634, 8 Med.L.Rptr. 2484 (9th Cir. 1982).

The writer originally had been hired by *Us* magazine to interview Cher for a cover story. Cher had consented, but had retained the right to approve any other uses of the material. The interview did not go as Cher expected, and she asked *Us* not to base an article on it. Subsequently, the writer sold copies of the tape to *Forum* and to the *Star,* a tabloid sold at supermarket checkout counters. Both magazines prepared articles and promoted them heavily. *Forum* used Cher's photo on the cover, along with promotional copy that said, "There are certain things that Cher won't tell *People* and would never tell *Us*." The magazine invited readers to "join Cher and *Forum*'s hundreds of thousands of other adventurous readers today." The *Star*'s cover promotional copy was more direct. It simply said, seeming to quote Cher, "My Life, My Husbands, and My Many, Many Men."

Cher reacted by suing both magazines for violating her right of publicity. A trial court held in her favor and awarded her $600,000. The appellate court cleared the *Star*, but upheld a judgment against *Forum* for $269,117. Although both articles were written in the first person, as though by Cher herself, the court said that the *Star*'s deceit was not great enough to overcome the news value of the story. However, the court said that *Forum* had not only misrepresented the exclusive nature of the interview—Cher had intended it originally for *Us*—but indicated in its promotional material that Cher had endorsed the magazine. This, the court held, amounted to exploitative appropriation of the publicity value of Cher's identity.

Identity

Courts dealing with right-of-publicity cases have shown some doubt as to the definition of the identity a celebrity may protect. This confusion is illustrated by a disagreement within a three-judge panel of the U.S. Court of Appeals for the Sixth Circuit. The suit was brought by John W. Carson, introduced for thirty-five years with a drawn out "Here's Johnny!" to viewers of NBC's *Tonight* show. The owner of a Michigan firm that manufactured and distributed portable toilets admitted that he had had that introduction in mind when he named his company Here's Johnny Portable Toilets. Lest there be any doubt, he added to his advertising the phrase, "The World's Foremost Commodian," considering it "a good play on a phrase."

Carson alleged that the firm's name infringed the "Here's Johnny" trademark identifying a line of clothing made by a firm in which he held a minority interest. He also said that he was embarrassed because he found it odious to be associated with the manufacturer's product. The court rejected both grounds as a basis for suit but held that the firm clearly was exploiting Carson's identity to its advantage, thus violating his right of publicity. He alone had the right to exploit his name for commercial advantage.

Carson v. *Here's Johnny Portable Toilets*, 698 F.2d 831, 9 Med.L.Rptr. 1153 (6th Cir. 1983).

The firm had argued that it was not using Carson's name. It noted that toilets have been known as johns for many years. "Here's Johnny," it asserted, is a phrase commonly used and therefore not subject to protection. The court conceded that the phrase was not strongly enough identified with Carson's line of clothing to become protected as a trademark. But it said that each of his appearances since 1957 had been preceded by a distinctive "Here's Johnny," thus indelibly making those words a symbol of his identity. Therefore, the firm's use of "Here's Johnny" in its name violated Carson's right of publicity, and he was entitled to prevent such use or get paid for it.

Judge Cornelia G. Kennedy argued in dissent that the majority went much too far in defining the identity Carson is entitled to protect. She argued that the sentence in question is a part of the public domain and thus can be used by anyone.

She warned that the court's decision could open the way for an almost limitless expansion of a celebrity's identity, leading to many more claims under a right of publicity.

Her warning may have been prophetic. For example, citing the Carson case, the Ninth Circuit Court of Appeals held in *White* v. *Samsung Electronics America, Inc.*[92] that a female-shaped robot wearing a long gown, blonde wig, and large jewelry while standing in front of a game board turning letters appropriated the identity of Wheel of Fortune's Vanna White. Samsung used the robot in an advertisement without White's permission. "It is not important *how* the defendant has appropriated the plaintiff's identity," said the court, "but *whether* the defendant has done so."

Even the sound of a voice can be so sufficiently linked with a singer's identity that to use it would be to appropriate unjustly the value of the singer's identity. Bette Midler argued that idea successfully when she sued Ford Motor Company for a commercial in which Ula Hedwig imitated the Midler sound style.[93] Neither Midler's name nor picture was used, only the imitation of the way she sang "Do You Wanna Dance." In reversing the trial court's summary judgment for Ford Motor Company, the U.S. Court of Appeals for the Ninth Circuit held that "when a distinctive voice of a professional singer is widely known and is deliberately imitated in order to sell a product, the sellers have appropriated what is not theirs." Judge Noonon wrote:

> A voice is as distinctive and personal as a face. The human voice is one of the most palpable ways identity is manifested. We are all aware that a friend is at once known by a few words on the phone. At a philosophical level it has been observed that with the sound of a voice, "the other stands before me."

Survivability

Publicity rights can be at least as valuable to a celebrity's heirs as they were to the celebrity while alive. In some cases, the right to exploit the name of the deceased may be the most valuable asset in the estate. To protect that intangible property interest, some states, such as California, Florida, Georgia, Nebraska, Oklahoma, Tennessee, Utah, and Virginia, have statutes providing that publicity rights survive the death of the celebrity. California law is the most generous, permitting the heirs of a celebrity to protect and profit from his or her right of publicity for fifty years after the celebrity's death.

Courts are divided over whether the right of publicity survives death in the absence of a statute. Illustrative of those holding that it does is a decision of the U.S. Court of Appeals for the Eleventh Circuit. This court held, in *Martin Luther King, Jr., Center for Social Change, Inc.* v. *American Heritage Products, Inc.*,[94] that the right of publicity in the identity of the civil rights leader survived his assassination and, like any other form of property, could be protected by his heirs.

---

92.   971 F.2d 1395, 20 Med.L.Rptr. 1457 (9th Cir. 1992); rehearing denied, 989 F.2d 1512, 21 Med.L.Rptr. 1330 (9th Cir. 1993); cert. denied, 113 S.Ct.2443, 124 L.Ed.2d 660 (1993).
93.   Midler v. Ford Motor Co., 849 F.2d 460, 15 Med.L.Rptr. 1620 (9th Cir. 1988); Midler v. Young & Rubicam, 19 Med.L.Rptr. 2190 (9th Cir. 1991 unpublished).
94.   694 F.2d 674 (11th Cir. 1983).

How far the courts will go in expanding publicity rights is anyone's guess. What is clear is that the media are on notice that the taking of intellectual property, whether protected by copyright, trademark, or publicity rights, has limits, even for news purposes. Advertisers, even those who promote not-for-profit causes, may take nothing without consent; news media may take only what is fair and necessary to inform and explain. The principle is clear even if the details are still developing: Those who are able to exploit the value of their fame control the right to profit from it.

PRIVACY: BEYOND THE FOUR TORTS

It is tidy but a bit too simple to say that all of privacy law is captured in the four torts described by Professor Prosser. Reporters and photographers should also be alert to privacy problems that arise in the forms of trespass and the infliction of emotional distress.

Trespass

As already noted, the difference between intrusion and trespass is that intrusion violates a person, whereas trespass violates a person's property. Another important difference is that trespass, in addition to being a tort, is a crime. For example, UPI stringer Craig Santy was arrested and jailed briefly on trespassing charges after walking unhindered onto Michael Jackson's ranch in Santa Ynez, California, where he mingled among members of a television crew and read Jackson's planned speech on a TelePrompTer. It made no difference that Santy was working on a news story, that Jackson was in the process of setting up for a live television broadcast to respond to allegations that he had molested a fourteen-year-old boy, or that Santy was praised by his editor for his resourcefulness in getting a scoop on the Jackson speech. Santy was charged with the crime of being on private property where he had no permission to be. He later agreed to plead no contest to a reduced charge and was fined $200.[95]

Under common law rules, any unauthorized entry onto another's private land is a trespass. It doesn't matter if a news event is occurring on that land; the property remains private. In some cases, when police or firefighters have seized control of a property, they can give permission for reporters to enter,[96] and often when there are no indications that visitors are unwelcome, a reporter may reasonably assume that visitors are welcome. When faced with a direct command by a property owner or lessee to leave, however, reporters have little choice but to comply. Moreover, courts have long held that it can be a trespass to enter the airspace above a person's land,[97] or to tunnel below it if that would cause damage to or interference with the use of the surface.[98]

---

95. George Garneau, "He Got the Story—Then Was Arrested," *Editor & Publisher,* 5 February 1994, p. 16.
96. Fletcher v. Florida Publishing Co., 319 So.2d 100 (Fla.App. 1975); 340 So.2d 914, 2 Med.L.Rptr. 1088 (Fla. 1977); cert. denied, 97 S.Ct. 2634 (1977).
97. Smith v. New England Aircraft Co., 270 Mass. 511, 170 N.E. 385 (1930).
98. Boehringer v. Montalto, 142 Misc. 560, 254 N.Y.S. 376 (1931).

Infliction of Emotional Distress

Courts rarely sustain efforts to recover damages for emotional distress caused by media. Still, the infliction of emotional distress can be a troubling concern and can arise in a number of ways.

Sacramento station KOVR-TV and reporter Mark Saxenmeyer ended up in court after telling neighborhood children about the death of their playmates. Saxenmeyer and a camera crew knocked on the door of a house next to one where a mother had just murdered her two children before committing suicide. Three children, ages five, seven, and eleven, answered the door. There were no adults at home. According to the complaint, Saxenmeyer told the children about the murders and attempted to interview them on camera. A three-judge appeals panel described the incident as an "intrusive, uninvited encounter by adult strangers with children of tender years not in a public place." The court called it a "shameless exploitation of defenseless children."[99]

Certainly newspeople need to be alert to the impact of their actions. But anyone in communications, even in public relations, can be caught off guard by a complaint that his or her actions have caused emotional harm. Yale University's alumni office was forced to defend itself against a claim of negligent infliction of emotional distress for publishing in an alumni directory that an alumnus of the class of 1975 had come to terms with his homosexuality.

At the request of the Class of 1975, Yale mailed questionnaires to members of the class asking for information that could be used in connection with a planned class reunion. As the questionnaires came in, they were processed and published in a class directory entitled *Yale 1975—Fifteen Years Out.* The books were then mailed to members of the class. One of the questionnaire responses that was published in the book included the following statement: "I have come to terms with my homosexuality and the reality of AIDS in my life. I am at peace." It bore the name of alumnus Dimitri K. Sleem. But it had not come from Sleem; it had come from somebody with a bad idea for a practical joke.

The editors made no attempt to verify the response from "Sleem." Sleem thought that it was negligent not to check and sued for libel and for emotional distress. The federal district court denied Yale's motion for summary judgment.[100] The court then described what Sleem would need to do if the case were to go to trial. He would have to prove the following:

1. That the editors were negligent—that is, that they had not behaved in a manner one would expect a reasonably prudent person to behave.

2. That it was reasonably foreseeable that such negligence would cause severe emotional distress.

3. That the negligence did cause severe emotional distress.

99. "TV Newsman Can Be Sued for Telling Youngsters about a Murder," *Editor & Publisher,* 25 March 1995, p. 34–35.

100. *Sleem v. Yale University,* 843 F.Supp. 57; 21 Med.L.Rptr. 1897 (M.D.N.C. 1993).

Although no date for trial was set, the court apparently thought it was at least possible to prove to a jury that a defendant could be responsible for the emotional harm caused by a lack of care.

Most courts, however, don't look favorably on claims that writers and editors negligently inflicted emotional distress. Cases are often dismissed because the result was unforeseeable or not severe enough to justify a lawsuit. When the allegation is that the emotional distress was intentional, rather than merely negligent, courts tend to evaluate whether the behavior of the media was truly outrageous or whether there was actual malice.[101] Some states, such as Alabama[102] and Texas,[103] simply refuse to recognize the tort of negligent infliction of emotional distress.

PRIVACY AND GOVERNMENT RECORDS ———

At one level, the Supreme Court's 1975 decision in *Cox,* followed by *Smith* and *Globe Newspapers,* expanded the media's right to use names and facts. Anything found in the public record can be used without invading someone's right of privacy. At another level, however, the decisions may have restricted information in the public domain. The Court suggested in *Cox* that Georgia might have prevented publication of the name of the rape victim by sealing the records in which it was found. Indeed, at the time that decision was written, federal and state legislative bodies were enacting statutes designed to restrict access to government files containing certain personal information. These statutes took two forms.

One form, exemplified by the federal Privacy Act of 1974, is designed to prevent disclosure by government agencies of personal data about employees and others on whom files are kept. Because such laws restrict media access to information, their effect will be examined in Chapter 9, which deals with that topic.

The second form of statutory protection deals with the kinds of information that journalists have always considered public: police and court records of adult offenders. In most states, statutes provide that under certain circumstances public records of arrests, and even of convictions, can be either sealed or expunged. These laws vary in their scope but generally cover arrests that do not result in convictions or guilty pleas, long-past convictions of persons who have reformed, and records of juvenile offenses. The purposes of these laws, which have been adopted by forty-eight states, the District of Columbia, and Puerto Rico, are to encourage rehabilitation of wrongdoers and to protect the privacy of persons who have been arrested but never convicted. In a sense, these laws are a legislative adoption of the reasoning used by the California courts in *Melvin* and *Briscoe,* which were mentioned earlier in this chapter. At some point, a person caught in a law violation, but who reformed thereafter, should no longer have to fear having that infraction called to public attention.

---

101. Hustler Magazine v. Falwell, 485 U.S. 46, 108 S.Ct. 876, 99 L.Ed.2d 41, 14 Med.L.Rptr. 2281 (1988).
102. Fitch v. Voit, 21 Med.L.Rptr. 1045 (Ala.Cir.Ct. 1993); affirmed, 21 Med.L.Rptr. 1863 (Ala. 1993).
103. Tackett v. KRIV-TV, 22 Med.L.Rptr. 2093 (S.D.Tex. 1994).

Journalists see such laws as restrictions on freedom of the press. Persons have been known to revert to crime after many years of normal life. Should journalists be denied the opportunity to inform the public that one of the candidates for director of a day care center was once arrested on suspicion of child molesting? Or that a candidate for county auditor was once convicted of embezzlement? Journalists argue that they cannot properly assess the performance of police, prosecutors, and judges unless they can have access to all arrest and disposition records. For instance, it would be difficult to check reports that a prosecutor took it easy on men accused of beating their wives or girlfriends if the records of arrests not resulting in prosecution were sealed.

Expunging or Sealing of Criminal Records

The Illinois statute represents one of the common forms an expungement law takes.[104] The pertinent part states:

> All photographs, fingerprints, or other records of identification so taken shall, upon the acquittal of a person charged with the crime, or, upon his being released without being convicted, be returned to him. Whenever a person, not having previously been convicted of any criminal offense or municipal ordinance violation, charged with a violation of a municipal ordinance or a felony misdemeanor, is acquitted or released without being convicted, the Chief Judge of the circuit wherein the charge was brought, or any judge of that circuit designated by the Chief Judge, may upon verified petition of the defendant order the record of arrest expunged from the official records of the arresting authority.

A Massachusetts law went further, establishing elaborate safeguards designed to keep anyone but police and courts from having access to criminal dossiers on individuals. Under the law, there is public access only to the day-to-day records of arrests and of public judicial proceedings. Any compilation of records in alphabetical order or any alphabetized index to police or court files is available only to law enforcement officers.

The *New Bedford Standard-Times* saw the Massachusetts law as an obstacle when

New Bedford Standard-Times Publishing Co. v. Clerk of Third Dist. Court, 377 Mass. 404, 387 N.E.2d 110, 4 Med.L.Rptr. 2393 (Mass. 1979).

it undertook an investigation of individuals believed to be in violation of building, sanitary, or housing regulations. Its reporters were unable to check the records readily to see whether any given individual had been arrested or even convicted in the past. To do so, reporters would have had to go through docket books day by day, looking for individual names. The newspapers asked, therefore, to look at an alphabetical case file compiled by the clerk of the Third District Court of Bristol County to make the court's work easier. Cards in that file contained a reasonably complete arrest and disposition record for each offender. When the clerk refused the request, the *Standard-Times* filed suit, arguing that the section of the law barring public inspection of alphabetical files was unconstitutional. The newspaper was rebuffed both by a district court and by the Massachusetts Supreme Judicial Court.

---

104.   Ill.Rev.Stat. 1975, ch. 38, par. 206-5.

The court viewed the dispute narrowly. The only question, it said, was how far the state should go in making it easy for the newspaper to obtain information from public records. The court conceded that the newspaper had difficulty in assembling arrest records, particularly of offenses that had occurred in the distant past. This was as it should be, the court concluded, for there is less news value in long-past convictions. In any event, the legislature had decided that the public interest in rehabilitation of offenders requires protection of their privacy. The court held that the right of privacy "weighs more heavily" than the purpose of the newspaper's investigation.

But judicial attitudes can vary. The Supreme Court of Wisconsin, in *Newspapers, Inc.* v. *Breier,* held that the privacy interest of criminal suspects was limited. It ruled that the Milwaukee police chief could not deny reporters access to his department's daily arrest log, or "blotter."

Newspapers, Inc. v. *Breier,* 89 Wis.2d 417, 279 N.W.2d 179, 5 Med.L.Rptr. 1524 (Wis. 1979).

Chief Harold A. Breier took the position that an arrest does not mean that the suspect is guilty. The prosecutor may decide that there is not enough evidence to take the suspect to court, or, even if there is enough evidence, a court may acquit. Therefore, publication of the details of an arrest, including the name of the suspect, may only result in needless embarrassment of an innocent person. Therefore, the chief adopted a policy of releasing the names of arrested persons only on demand; but even then, police would not release the nature of the charge.

Joseph W. Shoquist, managing editor of the *Milwaukee Journal,* took the chief to court, arguing that arrest records are public records. The trial court would have permitted a forty-eight-hour delay in the release of arrest records, but the state's highest court said that even that delay was too much. The power to arrest, it said, "is an awesome weapon for the protection of the people, but it also is a power that may be abused." One way of preventing abuse is to make the people aware of it when it happens. Under the chief's policy, even as modified by the trial court, this could not be done. The Wisconsin Supreme Court said that it would be "a travesty of our judicial and law enforcement system" to report that persons had been arrested, but fail to give the reasons for it.

But what happens if an arrest record is expunged or withheld lawfully and the media, learning of it from others, reports it anyway? Is that an invasion of privacy? It is unlikely that most courts would find it to be so as long as the reported information was newsworthy. Expungement orders in themselves do not require secrecy. They make arrest information more difficult to obtain, but they do not protect defendants from the truthful revelation of their pasts.

Les Bahr, a candidate for county commissioner in Oregon, once sued the *Statesman Journal* for reporting that he had been convicted of a crime. He had been, but the record had been expunged. Moreover, the Oregon expungement law specified that a person whose record had been removed from the public files could say, if asked, "I have no criminal record." Bahr used that response when a reporter asked him if he had been convicted of embezzlement several years previously. In fact, Bahr had been convicted and had served four

Bahr v. *Statesman Journal Co.,* 51 Or.App. 177, 624 P.2d 644, 7 Med.L.Rptr. 1099 (Ore.App. 1981).

months in jail. When he had gone three years without committing another offense, his record was expunged.

When the reporter, relying on the newspaper's files, reported Bahr's conviction for embezzlement, the candidate sued for libel. The trial court granted the newspaper's request for dismissal, and the appellate court affirmed. Would it have made a difference if Bahr had sued for invasion of privacy rather than libel? Probably not. A part of Judge Betty Robert's decision for the defendant offers an interesting commentary on Oregon's expungement law:

> The statute does not . . . impose any duty on members of the public who are aware of the conviction to pretend that it does not exist. In other words, the statute authorizes certain persons to misrepresent their own past. It does not make that misrepresentation true.

Nor, the media might argue, does it make a conviction for embezzlement by a candidate for public office valueless as news.

Juvenile Offenders

All states have laws restricting the release of information that would identify juvenile offenders.[105] In their usual form, the statutes forbid the release of such information by the juvenile system unless it is authorized by a judge. The rationale is that young offenders should be given every opportunity to be rehabilitated and should not be haunted for the rest of their lives by the mistakes of their youth. In a few states, courts and legislatures have attempted to protect juveniles further by imposing penalties on the news media for disclosing their names. In two decisions, the U.S. Supreme Court has held that such attempts impose an impermissible prior restraint if the juvenile was identified in open court or if the state's only interest is rehabilitation of the offender.

One of the cases, *Smith* v. *Daily Mail Publishing Co.,* was discussed earlier in the chapter. In it, the Supreme Court struck down a West Virginia law making it a crime for newspapers to disclose the names of juvenile offenders. The asserted state interest was in rehabilitation. The decision in the second case, *Oklahoma Publishing Co.* v. *District Court in and for Oklahoma County,* struck down a judge's order forbidding publication of the name and photograph of an eleven-year-old boy who was accused of murder. When the boy was taken into custody, the judge permitted reporters to attend the hearing, at which the offender's name was used. When the boy was taken out of the courthouse, newspaper and television photographers recorded the scene. News reports of the arrest in all media identified the suspect.

Oklahoma Publishing Co. v. District Court in and for Oklahoma County, 430 U.S. 308, 97 S.Ct. 1045, 51 L.Ed.2d 355, 2 Med.L.Rptr. 1456 (1977).

When the boy was arraigned at a closed hearing four days later, the judge issued an order forbidding the news media to use the name or photograph of any minor child

---

105. For a summary of state statutes, see Reporters Committee for Freedom of the Press, "Access to Juvenile Courts: A Reporter's Guide to Proceedings and Documents," published as an insert in *The News Media & the Law,* Fall 1991, 12 pages.

involved in a pending proceeding. The news media appealed the judge's edict, arguing that the boy's identity already was common knowledge, owing largely to the court's own actions. Pointing to *Cox* v. *Cohn,* they argued that a name made public during the official proceedings of a court could not later be made private. The Oklahoma Supreme Court rejected that argument, but on further appeal, the U.S. Supreme Court reversed, issuing only a brief *per curiam* decision. The Court noted that the news media had obtained their information legally, with the state's implicit approval. Therefore, the judge's subsequent order was a clear violation of the First Amendment's guarantee of freedom of the press.

The Supreme Court's decision in *Cox,* discussed earlier, clearly immunizes the media from successful actions for disclosure of facts found in the public records of courts or disclosed in open court. Subsequent decisions have extended the *Cox* rationale to protect media reliance on contacts found in other kinds of public records, if they are obtained legitimately. But *Cox* also stands for the proposition that courts and legislatures may protect the privacy of rape victims and others by sealing records or closing proceedings if these measures can be taken effectively and with judicial concern for First Amendment interests.

The real issue today may be not so much whether a court can seal its records but whether it also can restrain the reporting of information—such as juvenile names—obtained by the media from other sources.

In the Professional World

When professional journalists get together, few topics arouse more discussion than invasion of privacy. These discussions usually are inconclusive because opinions and practices with respect to the line between private fact and news vary widely. A stakeout employed by one newspaper to find out with whom a presidential candidate spent the night was seen as "sneaky snooping" by a former editor of the *New York Times.*[106] An elaborate subterfuge used by another newspaper to catch city employees in the act of taking bribes was condemned as unethical by editors of other newspapers.[107] Sometimes the conflict between good journalism and unacceptable ethics occurs in the same individual. One editor said that he would nominate for a Pulitzer Prize a photograph he considered a grossly insensitive intrusion into a family's grief.[108]

Codes of ethics adopted by organizations of journalists contain sections on privacy. The code embraced by the Society of Professional Journalists says, "The news media must guard against invading a person's right to privacy." That statement is followed by a less strongly worded sentence that says, "The media should not pander to morbid curiosity about details of vice and crime." The Associated Press Managing Editors Association code also advises respect for the

---

106. A. M. Rosenthal, "Attack on the Herald," *Louisville Courier-Journal,* 8 May 1987.
107. H. Eugene Goodwin, *Groping for Ethics in Journalism* (Ames: Iowa State University Press, 1983), pp. 135–136, 138–140.
108. Bob Greene, "News Business and Right of Privacy Can Be at Odds." In *1985–86 Journalism Ethics Report* (Chicago: National Ethics Committee, Society of Professional Journalists, 1986), p. 15.

individual's right of privacy. The code of the Radio-Television News Directors Association is somewhat broader. It says that "broadcast journalists shall at all times display humane respect for the dignity, privacy and the well-being of persons with whom the news deals." Such language obviously leaves the individual professional wide latitude in dealing with questions of privacy.

As we have seen, the law of privacy also gives journalists a wide field in which to work. Courts have shown little sympathy for reporters who trespass or break the law to get a story. In *Dietemann,* two federal courts condemned a reporter's and a photographer's use of deception. However, the decision is clouded by the fact that the deception was used to gain entry to the private sanctuary offered by Dietemann's home. Courts have not condemned other kinds of deception used to obtain news stories. Journalists who are usually quick to condemn the deception of others have on occasion used subterfuge themselves.

In one instance, editors of the *Chicago Sun-Times* asked two reporters to buy and operate a tavern, The Mirage, to investigate tips that city building inspectors were shaking down owners of small businesses. The "barkeepers" soon learned that the tips were true. They could not stay open without paying off electrical and plumbing inspectors. Hidden microphones and cameras recorded the transactions. The operation produced stories that ran for weeks.

Were these stories the fruits of unusual enterprise? Or were the unwary officials led into a trap and baited into making demands they might not otherwise have made? If dishonesty was indeed rampant in city officialdom, could it have been exposed only by tactics that were not quite on the level themselves? Those questions were raised by David Halvorsen, then managing editor of the *San Francisco Examiner,* who asked two editors of stature to respond.[109] Clayton Kirkpatrick, whose *Chicago Tribune* was scooped by the series, defended his competitor's methods. He said he was convinced that there was no entrapment. There are times, he said, when direct, convincing evidence of wrongdoing can be obtained only through the reporter's involvement. He saw the Mirage operation as different only in degree from instances in which reporters posing as ordinary consumers obtain evidence on dishonest television and automobile repair services.

Eugene Patterson of the *St. Petersburg Times* disagreed. Like Kirkpatrick, he recognized that on some occasions reporters need not proclaim who they are. A newspaper's restaurant critic can best serve by seeming to be an ordinary diner. Applying what he called "a scale of distinctions," Patterson said that his newspaper would not ask reporters to go undercover to investigate conditions in nursing homes. He said he believed that with hard work, open reporting methods could get the same information. He said, "We've inflicted pretty high ethical standards on public and private institutions with our editorials in recent years, and I worry a lot about our hypocrisy quotient if we demand government in the sunshine and practice journalism unnecessarily in the shade." However, Patter-

---

109. *Bulletin of the American Society of Newspaper Editors,* September 1979, p. 12.

Former U.S. Senator Gary Hart's political career ended after the news media began to draw attention to his personal life, particularly his relationship with Donna Rice, an actress and model who was not his wife. At the time Hart was the leading Democratic party candidate for President. Today, he lives in Colorado, works as an international trade lawyer, and has a weekly radio talk show called *Heartland.* Rice, now married to a business executive in northern Virginia, leads a grassroots political organization, Enough is Enough, that crusades against pornography in cyberspace. *(Brian Brainerd/NYT Pictures)*

son reserved the right to use deception if that proved to be the only way to obtain a story of "vital public interest."

Where the dissemination of private facts is at issue, journalists differ widely. The *Diaz* case represents one extreme. Some editors take the position that people who seek the public's approval, either by entering politics or by becoming celebrities, have little or no right of privacy. Others still act on the belief that even persons of prominence are entitled to raise a family, drink, or philander in private as long as what they do does not affect their duty to the public. In this area, journalistic ethics have changed markedly in the past generation. When John F. Kennedy was president, every Washington correspondent who was halfway alert heard stories of Kennedy's womanizing, but no one reported it. Nor was there anything in the media about Lyndon B. Johnson's "drinking a quart a day."[110] The White House correspondents of the time focused their reporting on what both men did as presidents. What they did in private was treated as gossip that the correspondents shared with one another and used to regale their editors on their occasional trips to Washington.

Contrast the easygoing tolerance of that period with what happened to Gary Hart in 1987. On May 1 of that year, Hart was, according to all the polls, the leading contender for the Democratic nomination for president of the United

---

110. Patrick J. Buchanan, *Right from the Beginning* (Boston: Little, Brown, 1988), p. 275.

States. That same day, editors of the *Miami Herald,* acting on a tip telephoned from an anonymous source, put a reporter on a flight to Washington, D.C., with instructions to look for an attractive, young aspiring actress who supposedly was on her way to spend a weekend with the candidate. That night and the next day, *Herald* reporters kept Hart's Georgetown townhouse under surveillance. They did not try to hide what they were doing. One of them even attempted to interview Hart.

In its editions of Sunday, May 3, the *Herald* proclaimed in a page-1 story that, with his wife in Colorado, Hart had spent "Friday night and most of Saturday" at home with a young woman from Miami. On that same Sunday, the *New York Times Magazine*'s lead story was a profile of Hart. It portrayed him favorably as a candidate with original ideas for coping with some of the nation's more serious problems. Hart's stature is further attested to by the fact that he was to speak to the American Society of Newspaper Editors on May 5. He kept that date. But by then the editors were far more interested in what he had to say about how he had spent the previous weekend than they were in his ideas for the presidency. Hart denied that he had done anything wrong. He said that the reporters' incomplete surveillance had failed to detect the woman's departure through a back door. Nevertheless, before the week was out, Hart had abandoned his campaign for the presidential nomination and returned to Colorado with his wife.

In retrospect, it is too simplistic to contrast the media's treatment of John Kennedy with that of Gary Hart and conclude that the latter was the victim of sneaky, gossip-mongering reporters. In advance of that fateful weekend, Ellen Goodman, a syndicated columnist for the *Boston Globe,* had written about Hart and "the sex issue."[111] She argued that a candidate's sexual affairs are pertinent to an assessment of character. Noting "the old-boy tolerance of dalliance" that led reporters to ignore JFK's affairs, she said that times have changed. Women have been admitted into the system, bringing with them an awareness that "you do learn something important about the character of a man from revelations of his sexual behavior." Such behavior, she wrote, is "part of a whole portrait of a man," particularly one who is seeking the nation's highest office. The president is "not just a chief executive, but a chief figurehead, chief role model, chief moral leader—in short, chief American. We ask a great deal. Anyone who runs for the office today has to know that there is no room in the job description for chief womanizer."

Goodman was one of those who wrote after the event to defend the surveillance conducted by the *Herald*'s reporters and the newspaper's use of their story. A *New York Times* editorial refused to condone the reporters' methods but said that the story served the public interest. The editorial said that Hart had made himself a special case because of his emphasis on character at a time when members of his own staff were talking about his vulnerability on the womanizing issue.[112] David Broder of the *Washington Post,* whose political columns almost invariably take the high road, also found the methods flawed but justified in this

---

111. Ellen Goodman, "Sex and Politics," *Louisville Courier-Journal,* 21 April 1987.
112. "More than Scandal," *New York Times,* 6 May 1987.

instance. The findings answered important public questions about "Hart's truthfulness, his self-discipline, his sense of responsibility to other people—indeed, his willingness to face hard choices and realities."[113]

Others of equal stature strongly condemned the *Herald*'s methods and their deeper implications. Among them were three *New York Times* columnists: Tom Wicker, William Safire, and A. M. Rosenthal, former executive editor of the newspaper. Wicker and Safire argued that even candidates for high office are entitled to some degree of privacy. Wicker argued that candidates should be judged by their positions on important issues, not on who they may or may not have slept with.[114]

Rosenthal wrote that during his twenty years as a reporter, he would have refused an assignment to hide outside a politician's house to find out whether he was in bed with somebody. As an editor for twenty-three more years, he would not have made such an assignment or allowed one of his subordinates to do so. In his opinion, the *Herald*'s editors were mistaken when they ordered the stakeout of Gary Hart's home. Calling for journalists to be as open in gathering news as they expect others to be in carrying out their duties, he concluded:

> In part this is simply a matter of taste. It is not to my taste to hang outside somebody's house in the middle of the night to see who goes in and out. It shows a lack of self-respect, a commodity a journalist does not give up when he gets a press card. It is also a matter of protection of journalism and the First Amendment, both of which have plenty of enemies as it is. If reputable papers such as the *Miami Herald* indulge in sneaky snooping that its editors would never tolerate around their own home, that is bad. But if the rest of the newspaper business justifies it, that's worse. We are begging the nation to treat us as unworthy of respect. In time, without any question, we will lose the support of the American public in the constant struggles against those who would erode the First Amendment. We cannot claim it was designed for voyeurs.[115]

Many editors, not all of them producing supermarket checkout tabloids, disagree. Stakeouts of the homes of newsworthy people are common in television journalism. Usually such surveillance produces no real news. But in Gary Hart's case, the stakeout did produce news and that news brought down a leading candidate for one party's presidential nomination. Whether, as Ellen Goodman suggests, he would eventually have fallen victim to his character flaws cannot be known. Nor is any connection established between a political leader's sexuality and his or her ability to govern. As Anthony Lewis, also a columnist for the *New York Times,* observed, eminent statesmen in both Britain and the United States, including Franklin D. Roosevelt, Dwight Eisenhower, and Winston Churchill, have not been saintly Puritans in their private lives.[116]

---

113.   David Broder, "Too Often, the Media Don't Go Far Enough," *Herald-Telephone,* Bloomington, Ind., 13 May 1987.
114.   Tom Wicker, *Louisville Courier-Journal,* 7 May 1987, and William Safire, "Keyhole Journalism," *Louisville Courier-Journal,* 12 May 1987.
115.   A. M. Rosenthal, "Attack on the Herald," *New York Times,* 8 May 1987.
116.   *Louisville Courier-Journal,* 6 May 1987.

When private individuals are drawn into the news, the definition of a right of privacy becomes even more difficult. This situation is illustrated by the experience of John Harte, a photographer for the *Bakersfield Californian,* and his managing editor, Bob Bentley. Harte was present when the body of a five-year-old drowning victim was dragged from a lake. He photographed the victim's father, mother, and older brother at the moment the body bag was opened to reveal the boy's face. In the photograph, the father is crouched over the body, his fists pressed tightly against his eyes. The older brother stands screaming in his mother's arms. Her face is distorted by a sob. The *Californian* published the photograph. In the next two days, the newspaper received more than five hundred telephone calls from people protesting what they saw as an invasion of the family's privacy. A bomb threat forced evacuation of the newspaper building. Bentley wrote a column, apologizing to the paper's readers. If he had it to do over, he said, he would not have run the photograph. He told Bob Greene, columnist for the *Chicago Tribune:*

> To me, this case is the strongest validation I've ever seen that newspapers are out of touch with their readers. We did something we thought was right, and the overwhelming majority of our readers thought it was wrong. They told us that by printing the picture, we had violated that child's memory. . . . By running that picture we alienated the hell out of our readers, and if we don't respond to that, we're stupid.

Photographer Harte disagreed. "I'm proud of the shot," he said, adding that it stood as a powerful reminder to others to be careful in the water. Bentley did not fault the photographer for taking the picture or for being proud of it. He agreed that it was a powerful and dramatic shot, so good that he told Greene he intended to nominate it for a Pulitzer Prize. As for Harte, as late as 1994 he was still photographing the dangers of water. That year, a sheriff's deputy arrested him for disobeying orders to remain behind a chain-link fence while rescue workers retrieved the body of a drowned eight-year-old boy from a canal. Judge Charles Pfister dismissed the charges against Harte, saying that he had a right to "be present and to view and photographically record the recovery of the body."[117]

The dilemmas represented by the clash of legal rights, aesthetic perceptions, and personal privacy are all too common in the professional world. Questions of privacy present more hard decisions than any others. Policies can be adopted and guidelines drafted, but they cannot cover all eventualities.

Any generalizations about journalism professionals and their attitudes toward privacy are likely to be fallacious. Yet, one observation may be more valid than not. In recent years, journalists have been talking more about ethical considerations than once was the case. The Associated Press Managing Editors Association and the Society of Professional Journalists issue annual reports surveying what they see as ethical lapses of the media. Each issue of *Quill,* the Society's magazine, has a section on ethics. *Editor & Publisher* (the newspaper trade magazine) and *Broadcasting* magazine have occasional articles on the subject. The list of

---

117. "Photographer Crosses Police Barrier; Faces Year in Jail," *Editor & Publisher,* 5 November 1994, p. 21; "Judge Dismisses Charges against Photographer," *Editor & Publisher,* 24 December 1994, p. 3.

textbooks designed for college courses on journalism ethics has grown impressively in the past decade. Seminars on journalism ethics are popular with journalists and the general public. All this activity suggests that many journalists are becoming less concerned about how much the law will let them get away with and more concerned with what a sense of compassion tells them they should do.

FOR REVIEW

1. What is meant by the right of privacy? Why is the concept of particular interest to journalists?

2. List and define the four branches of invasion of privacy identified by William L. Prosser. Distinguish each from the others in terms of the elements of the offense.

3. How far can a reporter go in gathering news that takes place on private property? In obtaining information from reluctant news sources?

4. Define the limits of a photographer's right to take and use pictures for news purposes. Would the limits be any different if the photographs were to be used for feature purposes?

5. How have the courts defined an "embarrassing private fact"? How far can the news media go in reporting intimate details of a news subject's life?

6. What meaning does *Cox* v. *Cohn* have for journalists? To what extent, if any, was this meaning modified by the Supreme Court's decision in *Florida Star?* Had you been on the Court, how would you have voted in these cases? On what rationale would your vote have been based?

7. Does the term "public figure" have the same meaning in connection with invasion of privacy as it has in connection with libel?

8. Distinguish between false light and libel. What is the meaning of the *Hill* and *Cantrell* decisions?

9. List and justify a set of rules for use by an advertising agency planning to use identifiable persons in an advertising campaign.

10. What meaning does the right of publicity have in law? What hazards does this right raise for television news directors? For writers of magazine articles?

11. Expand on the meaning of newsworthiness, illustrating with examples from cases.

12. Expand on the meaning of consent, illustrating with examples from cases.

13. What is an expungement law? A sealed record? How do they relate to the work of the journalist?

14. In all states, records of juvenile offenders are kept secret unless released by a judge. Does this mean that the news media can be kept from disseminating names of juveniles who have committed crimes? Why or why not?

CHAPTER 7

THREATS TO A FAIR TRIAL

Defining an Impartial Jury
Causes of an Unfair Trial

ENSURING A FAIR TRIAL

The Supreme Court Prescribes Remedies
Voir Dire
Restraining Participants in a Trial
Restraining the News Media
Access to Court Proceedings

Trials of Criminal Cases/Jury Selection and Pretrial Hearings

Protecting Jurors

CONDUCTING A FAIR TRIAL IN PUBLIC

Nonprejudicial Publicity
The Photographer and the Courtroom

It's nearly impossible to talk about trial publicity without beginning with the O. J. Simpson case. No trial in the history of the country has generated so much sustained and dramatic publicity. The arrest, trial, and acquittal of a celebrity after an especially horrible double murder was a matter of enormous public interest, and the media accommodated that interest with live cable and broadcast coverage, with daily newspaper articles and magazine features, and with books and Internet services devoted to the trial. The case created its own world of stars, consultants, and late-night comedy. But was all that publicity fair to Simpson? Was it fair to the American public? Was it fair to the legal system?

Spectacular coverage of sensational crime has a long history in American journalism. The Simpson case is the latest and the biggest, but even as long ago as the 1920s and 1930s sensational crime was a reporter's weapon of choice for capturing reader interest. In those days, prohibition, which spanned the twenties, and the depression, which ended them, spawned gangland wars and such figures as Al Capone, John Dillinger, Pretty Boy Floyd, and Bonnie and Clyde. Their crimes were the subjects of breathlessly written stories bannered under screaming page-1 headlines. When suspects were arrested, particularly on murder charges, reporters outdid each other in try-

A FAIR AND PUBLIC TRIAL

O.J. Simpson's murder trial has reopened the journalistic debate about news media coverage of sensational trials. Simpson was acquitted by a jury, but some critics charge that lawyers and witnesses used the trial for its publicity value and often played to the television audience. Here, a *Chicago Tribune* editorial cartoon suggests that the "real jury" may not have been in the courtroom at all. *(MacNelly/Tribune Media Services)*

ing to scoop the competition, gather evidence, and prove the guilt of any likely suspect. These trials by newspaper captured public interest and helped reporters make names for themselves and for the prosecutors and police officers who helped them. Defense attorneys, in response, built backfires by feeding reporters any shred of evidence they thought could prove their clients' innocence. Most judges simply looked the other way. Only an occasional libertarian argued that the publicity was so prejudicial that it violated a suspect's constitutional right to a fair trial in a courtroom.

From that perspective, the Simpson case was remarkably controlled. Television was continuous and live, but it was limited to a single camera and jurors were never shown. In fact, the identities of the jurors remained confidential as long as they served. Judge Lance Ito set the rules and even excluded reporters who failed to follow them. He fined attorneys for misconduct. Meanwhile the media incessantly debated its role in the case and reported its own excesses.[1] That there were excesses was obvious to anyone who lived through those months of the Simpson trial, but problems with the inaccurate reporting of leaked evidence, the tainting of witnesses with premature publication of their books, and the nightly media second-guessing about defense and prosecution strategy all operated on a level of consciousness and earnestness far different from the mongering of the 1930s.

During that earlier time, reporters were far less circumspect about their coverage of sensational crimes. Today, even the hungriest crime reporter knows that little is to be gained in glorifying or demonizing defendants. Audiences are better educated and sophisticated than were their grandparents. They may be curious about sensational crimes, but they are more likely to want to link them to larger social issues—police brutality, racism, the death penalty, and societal violence. If they were really interested in enjoying the drama of crime, they could find plenty of that in prime-time television fiction—and it is generally a lot more exciting than the real thing.

A more important factor in the decline of overt and intentional trial by media was the Warren Court. The term is a tribute to Earl Warren, who was appointed Chief Justice of the United States by President Eisenhower in 1953 and who served until 1969. Under his leadership, the Supreme Court did more to enlarge and protect the rights of criminal suspects than in any other time in its history. Two of its decisions, *Irvin* v. *Dowd*[2] in 1961 and *Sheppard* v. *Maxwell*[3] in 1966, served notice on judges everywhere that they should not permit prejudicial publicity in the news media to interfere with a suspect's right to a fair trial. The Court found that mandate in the Sixth Amendment:

> In all criminal prosecutions, the accused shall enjoy the right to a speedy and public trial, by an impartial jury of the State and district wherein the crime shall have been committed, which district shall have been previously ascertained by law, and to be informed of the nature and cause of the accusation; to be confronted with the witnesses against him, to have compulsory process for obtaining witnesses in his favor, and to have the assistance of counsel for his defense.

In this chapter, we will focus on just four words of this amendment: "impartial jury" and "public trial." We will see that, starting with *Irvin,* the Court sought to define what trial by an impartial jury means. In the process, it established criteria for determining whether a trial has been fair. With the *Sheppard* decision five years later, attention shifted to the measures judges should take to ensure that a defendant gets a fair trial. In response to media coverage of the Sheppard trial, some judges experimented with restraints, sometimes called gag orders, designed to stop prejudicial information at the source. These restrictions had two targets: the participants in the

---

1. See, for example, Jacqueline Sharkey, "Judgment Calls, The Media's O. J. Obsession," *American Journalism Review,* September 1994, pp. 18–27.
2. 366 U.S. 717, 81 S.Ct. 1639, 6 L.Ed.2d 751, 1 Med.L.Rptr. 1178 (1961).
3. 384 U.S. 333, 86 S.Ct. 1507, 16 L.Ed.2d 600, 1 Med.L.Rptr. 1220 (1966).

trial—attorneys for both sides, witnesses, and court employees—and the reporters covering court proceedings.

Appellate courts have since upheld restraint of participants, but only when the threat to a fair trial is clear. The Supreme Court, on the other hand, has held that journalists can be subjected to restraint only under the most unusual circumstances. But the Court also has suggested that judges might solve their publicity problem by closing some proceedings, in an effort to keep highly prejudicial information from the public. That suggestion immediately raised questions about the meaning of the Sixth Amendment's guarantee of a public trial and the First Amendment rights of the public to attend court proceedings. In resolving the issues, the Supreme Court held that the Sixth Amendment does not require an open proceeding if the defendant does not want one, but that the First Amendment does imply a right of access to court proceedings by journalists and the public. Consequently, that First Amendment right can be overcome only by evidence that the defendant cannot get a fair trial without closure or that the court is faced with a compelling privacy interest of a juror or witness.

Reduced to this brief outline, the Court's struggle to ensure that trials are both fair and open to the public is stripped of the strong feelings that it aroused at the time and continues to arouse. Lawyers and judges stand behind the Sixth Amendment, arguing that circulation-hungry newspapers and ratings-hungry broadcasters trample on the rights of criminal suspects. Opposing them, reporters and editors stand behind the First Amendment, arguing that courts and the bar trample on the people's right to be informed. Relations between the two sides were so strained at one point in the 1960s that it was news when a press-bar committee was formed in the state of Washington to attempt to reach a middle ground.[4] Skirmishes still are heatedly fought, but there has developed over the past thirty years a better understanding about what needs to be done if defendants are to be assured a fair and public trial and the people are to be informed fully of the activities of the justice system. This chapter, therefore, is a study of what happens when two rights, each directly guaranteed by the Bill of Rights, come into conflict.

Major Cases

- *Chandler* v. *Florida,* 449 U.S. 560, 101 S.Ct. 802, 66 L.Ed.2d 740, 7 Med.L.Rptr. 1041 (1981).

- *Gannett* v. *DePasquale,* 443 U.S. 368, 99 S.Ct. 2898, 61 L.Ed.2d 608, 5 Med.L.Rptr. 1337 (1979).

- *Gentile* v. *State Bar of Nevada,* 501 U.S. 1030, 111 S.Ct. 2720, 115 L.Ed.2d 888 (1991).

---

4. Fair-trial–free-press guidelines were first proposed to the press by the American Bar Association in the late 1960s. The proposal was initially greeted with hostility by the national press. Nevertheless, publishers and broadcasters in about thirty states eventually joined local fair-trial–free-press conferences organized by bar associations to develop voluntary guidelines.

■ *Globe Newspaper Co.* v. *Superior Court, County of Norfolk,* 457 U.S. 596, 102 S.Ct. 2613, 73 L.Ed.2d 248, 8 Med.L.Rptr. 1689 (1982).

■ *Irvin* v. *Dowd,* 366 U.S. 717, 81 S.Ct. 1639, 6 L.Ed.2d 751, 1 Med.L.Rptr. 1178 (1961).

■ *Mu'Min* v. *Virginia,* 500 U.S. 415, 111 S.Ct. 1899, 114 L.Ed.2d 493 (1991).

■ *Murphy* v. *Florida,* 421 U.S. 794, 95 S.Ct. 2031, 44 L.Ed.2d 589, 1 Med.L.Rptr. 1232 (1975).

■ *Nebraska Press Association* v. *Stuart,* 427 U.S. 539, 96 S.Ct. 2791, 49 L.Ed.2d 683, 1 Med.L.Rptr. 1064 (1976).

■ *New Mexico Press Association* v. *Kaufman,* 98 N.M. 261, 648 P.2d 300, 8 Med.L.Rptr. 1713 (N.Mex. 1982).

■ *Patton* v. *Yount,* 467 U.S. 1025, 104 S.Ct. 2885, 81 L.Ed.2d 847 (1984).

■ *Press-Enterprise Co.* v. *Superior Court of California, Riverside County,* 464 U.S. 501, 104 S.Ct. 819, 78 L.Ed.2d 629, 10 Med.L.Rptr. 1161 (1984).

■ *Press-Enterprise Co.* v. *Superior Court of California, Riverside County,* 478 U.S. 1, 106 S.Ct. 2735, 92 L.Ed.2d 1, 11 Med.L.Rptr. 1297 (1986).

■ *Richmond Newspapers* v. *Virginia,* 448 U.S. 555, 100 S.Ct. 2814, 65 L.Ed.2d 1973, 6 Med.L.Rptr. 1833 (1980).

■ *Sheppard* v. *Maxwell,* 384 U.S. 333, 86 S.Ct. 1507, 16 L.Ed.2d 600, 1 Med.L.Rptr. 1220 (1966).

■ *United States* v. *Dickinson,* 465 F.2d 496, 1 Med.L.Rptr. 1338 (5th Cir. 1972).

■ *Waller* v. *Georgia,* 467 U.S. 39, 104 S.Ct. 2210, 81 L.Ed.2d 31, 10 Med.L.Rptr. 1714 (1984).

THREATS TO A FAIR TRIAL

Defining an Impartial Jury

The concern with prejudicial publicity and its presumed effect on the right to a fair trial is not new. Aaron Burr, a former vice president of the United States, raised the question in 1807 when he was tried for treason because of his alleged part in a conspiracy to set up an independent nation somewhere between the Ohio and Mississippi rivers. He asked that the indictment be dismissed, arguing that inflammatory articles in the *Alexandria* (Va.) *Expositor* and other newspapers had turned the minds of potential jurors against him. Chief Justice John Marshall, sitting as a trial judge, rebuffed that argument, setting standards used to this day in selecting juries. He wrote in *United States* v. *Burr:*[5]

> The great value of trial by jury certainly consists in its fairness and impartiality. Those who most prize the institution prize it because it furnishes a tribunal which may be expected to be uninfluenced by an undue bias of the mind. I have always conceived [that] . . . an impartial jury . . . must be composed of men who will fairly hear the testimony which may be offered to them, bring in their verdict according to that testimony, and according to the laws arising on it.

Marshall noted the obvious: Persons who have made up their minds in advance about the defendant's guilt or innocence cannot be impartial. This does not mean, he added, that potential jurors must be completely ignorant of the defendant or of the crime. Even in the society of 1807, that would be too much to expect. Therefore, jurors can be considered impartial if they hold "light impressions [as to guilt or innocence] which may fairly be supposed to yield to the testimony which may leave the mind open to a fair consideration of that testimony." An impartial juror, then, is one whose mind is not made up in advance, but who is willing to listen to the evidence and evaluate it fairly. In Burr's case, jurors chosen by Marshall's criteria listened to the evidence for six months and found the defendant not guilty.

The passage of nearly two centuries has not materially changed Chief Justice Marshall's definition of an impartial jury. It is made up of men and women whose minds are open to the testimony offered in court and who will base their decision solely on that evidence. In the America of the early 1800s, sources of information that might prejudice members of a jury were confined largely to the weekly newspapers and to word of mouth. Today, we are surrounded by communications media that use graphic devices, market research, and the latest discoveries of the communications theorists in an attempt to get us to pay attention to them. Not surprisingly, these changes have raised new questions about the influences that can prevent people from being impartial jurors.

Some of these questions have focused on what makes a potential juror biased. In a University of Chicago study, judges noted that suspects were denied a fair trial because jurors had read or heard about confessions that were made in violation of constitutional safeguards. Other jurors were prejudiced by reading or hearing about the results of lie detector tests, which are not admissible as evidence; about the defendant's prior criminal record; or about evidence seized in violation of the suspect's right of privacy.[6] By an overwhelming majority, these judges said they believed it "inappropriate" for the news media to publish such information in advance of a trial. However, they also said, as Marshall had many years earlier, that they did not believe that jurors need to be altogether ignorant of the facts of a case to be impartial.

Studies of jury performance are inconclusive. Some people believe that publicity has little real impact on jurors. One researcher concluded that "the jury is a pretty stub-

---

5. 25 Fed.Cas. 49 (No.14,692g)(1807).
6. Fred S. Siebert, "Trial Judges' Opinions of Prejudicial Publicity." In Chilton R. Bush, ed., *Free Press and Fair Trial* (Athens: University of Georgia Press, 1970), pp. 2–19. The poll was conducted by the National Opinion Research Center at the University of Chicago.

born, healthy institution not likely to be overwhelmed either by a remark of counsel or a remark of the press."[7] A federal appeals court judge in Chicago once told an audience of newspaper editors that he had learned during his days as a trial judge that most potential jurors didn't pay much attention to stories of crime. He said that very few made up their minds as to guilt or innocence because of what they read.[8] A probability study in the late 1980s found that the conditions necessary for media coverage to prejudice jurors to the extent that they would be unable to decide a case based on the evidence are likely to occur in only one of every ten thousand cases.[9]

However, in a significant number of court opinions since 1960, federal and state courts have found that pervasive media publicity given to inadmissible evidence and prior criminal records has caused jurors to come to the trial with their minds closed and their opinions as to guilt or innocence already formed. Thus, they have not been impartial jurors, as required by the Sixth Amendment. As a result, some criminal defendants have been set free, and others have had to go through new trials.

Causes of an Unfair Trial

A little-noted decision of the Warren Court in 1959 marked the beginning of a new attitude toward trial by mass media. In *Marshall* v. *United States,*[10] the Supreme Court reversed a federal conviction of a drug dealer. The Court held that the jurors had been improperly influenced by reading in their newspaper that Marshall had been convicted twice previously. The decision had limited impact because it involved only the federal court system, which, compared with state courts, was not heavily involved in criminal cases.

Two years later, however, the Court won a great deal of attention with its reversal of a murder conviction that came to it from the state courts in Indiana. With its decision in *Irvin* v. *Dowd*, the Court established a principle of constitutional law applicable to all courts, state or federal. The Court held that verdicts reached by jurors who have been influenced by prejudicial publicity violate the Sixth Amendment guarantee of trial by an impartial jury. The *Irvin* decision led to three others in the next five years, making clear the Court's insistence that criminal suspects be tried in the courts rather than in the news media. Each case dealt with a different aspect of media interference with a fair trial. Each case also reversed a con-

Irvin **v.** *Dowd,* **366 U.S. 717, 81 S.Ct. 1639, 6 L.Ed.2d 751, 1 Med.L.Rptr. 1178 (1961).**

---

7. Walter Wilcox, "The Press, the Jury and the Behavioral Sciences." In Chilton R. Bush, ed., *Free Press and Fair Trial* (Athens: University of Georgia Press, 1970), pp. 67–102, quoting Harry K. Kalven, Jr., coauthor with Hans Zeisel of *The American Jury* (Boston: Little, Brown, 1966).
8. "Notable and Quotable," *Wall Street Journal,* 5 May 1976, quoting Judge William J. Bauer of the U.S. Court of Appeals, Seventh Circuit, in a speech to the American Society of Newspaper Editors. See also Newton N. Minow and Fred H. Cate, "Who Is an Impartial Juror in an Age of Mass Media?" 40 *Am.Univ.L.Rev. 2, Winter 1991, p. 658:* "The recent inability of the jury to reach a verdict on twelve counts in the cocaine and perjury trial of District of Columbia Mayor Marion Barry should give pause to those who believe that a jury is easily swayed by the press."
9. Ralph Frasca, "Estimating the Occurrence of Trials Prejudiced by Press Coverage," *Judicature,* October–November 1988.
10. 360 U.S. 310, 79 S.Ct. 1171, 3 L.Ed.2d 1250 (1959).

viction, leading some editors to accuse the Supreme Court of placing a higher value on the rights of criminals than on a free press.

In *Irvin* the defendant, Leslie Irvin, was accused of killing six persons in and near Evansville, Indiana. He showed so little remorse for what he had done that one newspaper story compared his actions to those of a mad dog. Copyeditors picked up the phrase, producing headlines about "Mad Dog Irvin." By the time the case came to trial, surveys showed that practically everyone within reach of the Evansville newspapers and broadcasting stations had heard about Irvin and believed him guilty. In an attempt to escape the effects of the publicity, the trial was moved from Evansville to nearby Gibson County. But there, too, questioning revealed that most prospective jurors knew about the murders. A jury quickly found the defendant guilty and sentenced him to death.

When the Supreme Court agreed to review the verdict, Irvin's attorney offered evidence showing that nine of the twelve jurors had made up their minds as to the defendant's guilt before they had heard any of the testimony. The Court held that in the face of such overwhelming evidence of media-created prejudice, a fair trial was impossible. Irvin was retried in central Indiana, many miles from Evansville and again was found guilty. He was sentenced to a life term in prison.

The next two fair-trial decisions of the Supreme Court involved television coverage—in one instance, of a confession made in a jail cell; in the other, of the trial itself. In the first case, *Rideau* v. *Louisiana,*[11] the Court held that the inclusion of the confession on three newscasts in two days created an "atmosphere of prejudice" that made selecting an impartial jury impossible. In the second, *Estes* v. *Texas,*[12] the Court speculated that the mere presence of television cameras in the courtroom had influenced the participants in such a way as to make a fair trial impossible. In neither case did the Court require evidence, as it had in *Irvin,* that jurors actually were prejudiced against the defendants.

In neither case was there much doubt as to the defendant's guilt, and both were convicted when they were tried again. Wilbert Rideau had robbed a bank in Lake Charles, Louisiana. He took three of the bank's employees as hostages on his getaway and killed one of them before he was captured. The morning after his arrest, Rideau was visited in his jail cell by the sheriff, who was followed by a television camera crew. With the sheriff asking the questions, Rideau talked about the robbery, freely admitting that he had killed one of the hostages. When the Supreme Court reviewed his conviction, Justice Potter Stewart wrote that for the tens of thousands of people who had seen the telecasts, Rideau's trial had taken place in his jail cell, and his own words had proved his guilt. The Court held that where there is pervasive exposure to such prejudicial publicity, a trial cannot be fair.

Billie Sol Estes was one of the most prominent young businessmen in Texas when he was charged with swindling hundreds of farmers out of millions of dollars. He had made *Time* magazine's man-of-the-year list and was a friend of two presidents of the United States. Under rules of court then in effect only in Texas and Colorado, television and still photographers were permitted in the courtroom during Estes's prelimi-

---

11.   373 U.S. 723, 83 S.Ct. 1417, 9 L.Ed.2d 229, 1 Med.L.Rptr. 1183 (1963).
12.   381 U.S. 532, 85 S.Ct. 1628, 14 L.Ed.2d 543 (1965).

nary hearing and again during his trial. Although at the trial the photographers operated from behind a wall, out of sight of most participants and spectators, five members of the Supreme Court concluded that the jurors may have been distracted by the cameras and their "telltale red lights." Justice Tom C. Clark, who wrote the Court's opinion, cited no evidence to support the majority's belief that the presence of the cameras converted Estes's trial into a theatrical event. However, Clark concluded: "A defendant on trial for his life is entitled to his day in court, not in a stadium, or a city or a nationwide arena. The heightened public clamor resulting from radio or television coverage will inevitably result in prejudice. Trial by television is, therefore, foreign to our system."

The day was saved for photojournalism by Justice John Marshall Harlan, the fifth member of the majority. He agreed that the presence of cameras had kept Estes from getting a fair trial in this instance. But he was unwilling to conclude, as the other four had, that courtroom cameras would in all circumstances prevent a fair trial.

The Supreme Court's fourth fair-trial case in the 1960s was to become its most celebrated decision in this area of law. In *Sheppard* v. *Maxwell*, the Court not only reversed the murder conviction of a socially prominent surgeon but told the judges what they must do to prevent prejudicial publicity from interfering with the right to a fair trial. Dr. Sam Sheppard had been found guilty in 1954 of murdering his wife and had served ten years in the Ohio State Penitentiary before the Supreme Court accepted his case for review. From the beginning, the doctor had asserted his innocence. He said that his wife had been beaten to death by a bushy-haired stranger whom he had surprised in the act and who had fled from the house onto a beach along nearby Lake Erie. Because no one else had seen such a stranger, and because it was known that Sheppard and his wife were having marital problems, he quickly became the center of suspicion. When police did not act on that suspicion, Cleveland's three newspapers demanded they do so. One headline proclaimed, "Somebody Is Getting Away with Murder." Another demanded, "Why Isn't Sam Sheppard in Jail?" His arrest followed within hours.

During the weeks leading up to Sheppard's trial, Cleveland's newspapers and radio and television stations laid down a barrage of stories designed to prove his guilt. It was alleged that he had had extramarital affairs and that his wife had lived in fear of him but had refused to give him a divorce. One story reported as fact that Sheppard had delayed reporting his wife's murder while he washed away a trail of blood leading from the bedroom and disposed of the murder weapon. When jurors were chosen for the trial, the newspapers published their names and addresses. All of the jurors said they received letters and telephone calls from persons trying to influence them. So many reporters wanted to cover the trial that the judge, Herbert Blythin, ordered an extra press table set up inside the bar of the court. The press table was so close to the defense table that Sheppard had to confer with his lawyers in a whisper to avoid being overheard. Newspaper and radio reporters took over adjacent courthouse offices. Television cameras kept a vigil on the sidewalk outside the courthouse, where interviews were conducted with witnesses. The judge would not permit cameras in the courtroom while court was in session, but he made an arrangement with photogra-

Sheppard v. *Maxwell,* 384 U.S. 333, 86 S.Ct. 1507, 16 L.Ed.2d 600, 1 Med.L.Rptr. 1220 (1966).

phers that made the ban a mockery. At each recess, they would burst through the doors, cameras ready, and take their pictures before the witness could leave his chair.

Through more than six weeks of trial, the jurors were permitted to go home each evening. Judge Blythin told them not to read, view, or listen to any reports about the case but made only the most perfunctory attempts to find out whether his order was being obeyed. If the jurors did disobey him, they read and heard about an altogether different trial from the one conducted in the courtroom. News media, local and national, consistently reported "evidence" from "witnesses" who were not called to testify. Newscasters of prominence argued on radio that the evidence proved Sheppard guilty long before the trial had ended.

Shortly before Christmas, 1954, the jury found Sam Sheppard guilty of the murder of his wife. He was sentenced to life in the penitentiary. He appealed to both the Ohio and U.S. Supreme Courts, arguing that prejudicial publicity had prevented his getting a fair trial. With the *Irvin* decision still seven years in the future, both courts rejected his plea. But in 1964, with the groundwork laid by the *Irvin* and *Rideau* decisions, Sheppard's family hired a prominent defense attorney, F. Lee Bailey, who was able to persuade a newly appointed U.S. district court judge in Dayton, Ohio, to order Sheppard's release on the ground that his conviction was the product of a media carnival that not only had polluted the atmosphere with inadmissible evidence but had violated the serenity of the courtroom. An appeals court disagreed, but the Supreme Court reversed, upholding the district judge's order that Sheppard be given a new trial or set free. In holding that Sheppard had been the victim of a biased jury, the Court reiterated a basic principle of jurisprudence: A judge's first duty is to make certain that a trial is conducted fairly, solely on the basis of admissible evidence.

Justice Clark, writing for seven members of the Court, started with praise for "a responsible press." Over the years, he said, the media have guarded "against the miscarriage of justice by subjecting police, prosecutors, and judicial process to extensive scrutiny and criticism." Clark endorsed that coverage, noting that the press had been "the handmaiden of effective judicial administration."

He turned next to Judge Blythin's conduct of the trial. Here he was more critical, holding that the judge had not done as much as he should have to protect the jurors from media influences. Indeed, the judge had permitted the media to turn the jurors into celebrities of a sort by publicizing their names, addresses, and photographs. As a result, the jurors had been exposed "to expressions of opinion from both cranks and friends." Additionally, by giving reporters and photographers almost free rein in and around the courtroom, the judge had deprived Sheppard of the "judicial serenity and calm to which [he] was entitled." Clark wrote:

> The fact is that bedlam reigned at the courthouse during the trial and newsmen took over practically the entire courtroom, hounding most of the participants in the trial, especially Sheppard. [T]he judge lost his ability to supervise the environment. The movement of the reporters in and out of the courtroom caused frequent confusion and disruption of the trial.

Thus, the Court, which had found television cameras a distracting influence in *Estes,* found reporters and photographers, whatever their medium, to be a problem when they were permitted to take over the courtroom and its environs. Because reporters entered and left the courtroom as they pleased, because photographers congregated in the corridors, ready to pounce when the courtroom doors were opened, because witnesses and other participants were fair game for on-the-spot interviews, the "judicial serenity" that should have surrounded the trial was lost. Further, by giving publicity to members of the jury, the media had ensured that they would be subjected to pressure from anyone who felt moved to pick up a telephone and call them. All this was in addition to a massive barrage of prejudicial tips, rumors, and speculation pointing to Sheppard's guilt. The Court concluded that a trial conducted under such circumstances could not possibly have been fair. Sam Sheppard's life sentence was set aside. He was entitled to a new trial.

Sam Sheppard was freed from prison and retried late in 1966. Witnesses had died. Memories had faded. A jury acquitted him. Sheppard tried to resume his practice of osteopathy but was the subject of several malpractice suits. He quit his practice and turned to other things. Immediately after his release from prison, he married a German immigrant with whom he had corresponded. That union ended in divorce. Not long before he died of liver disease in 1970, Sheppard had become a professional wrestler in the stable of a promoter working out of Columbus, Ohio. He had married the promoter's nineteen-year-old daughter, who became his widow. A book and a television movie later portrayed him as the innocent victim of a vendetta inspired by the *Cleveland Press*.[13] Others remained convinced that the first jury was right.

The problem of prejudicial publicity seemed so serious that the Court moved in five years from a holding that convictions should be set aside only if the defendant could show that the publicity actually had prejudiced a jury, to a holding that allowed reversal if the defendant could show that prejudicial publicity had permeated the area. Trial judges now seemed to understand that an appellate court would decide on a case-by-case basis whether publicity before and during a trial, coupled with distracting conduct on the part of the media, raised a presumption that jurors were prejudiced. If so, based on that presumption, there would be a new trial or the suspect would be freed. All four decisions, and the earlier *Marshall* decision as well, accepted as a fact that publicity given to such things as prior criminal records—Irvin had a long one, for example—and inadmissible evidence has an unacceptable influence on jurors. At the time, judges reading the Supreme Court's decisions began to act on the assumption that juror exposure to news stories of any kind dealing with the case at hand made a fair trial unlikely.

Given the pervasive penetration of the media in modern society, questions have arisen about the trial system itself. Could not a clever criminal inevitably escape punishment by committing a crime on television, as when Jack Ruby shot Lee Harvey Oswald on national television in 1963? Indeed, by the mid-1990s, Americans would see some remarkable television involving remarkable defendants, including Mayor Marion Barry of Washington, D.C.; automaker John Z. DeLorean; Panamanian strongman Manuel Noriega; a group of Los Angeles police officers accused of beating Rodney King; and, of course, O. J. Simpson. What could judges do to ensure that defendants in highly publicized cases were tried in the courtroom rather than in the media?

---

13.   Jack H. Pollack, *Dr. Sam: An American Tragedy* (Chicago: H. Regnery Co., 1972). The television movie *Guilty or Innocent: The Sam Sheppard Murder Case* was presented by NBC on 17 November 1975.

ENSURING A FAIR TRIAL

The Supreme Court's decision in *Sheppard* went beyond its previous fair-trial decisions in that the Court prescribed steps that trial judges might take to counteract prejudicial media publicity. In doing so, the Court recognized that reversal, and a new trial years after the crime had been committed, did not always lead to justice.

The prescriptions in *Sheppard* began with such basic remedies as a more vigorous voir dire, which always had been part of the jury selection procedure, and change of venue, the moving of the trial to another locality not reached by news stories about the crime and the defendant. These remedies have aroused little controversy, but some of the others have. For instance, some judges reading *Sheppard* have imposed so-called gag orders—court orders directing witnesses, lawyers, defendants, and others involved in a trial not to talk to outsiders about the case. Such orders, which are classic prior restraints, have also been imposed on journalists who have become aware of prejudicial information through court proceedings. Judges have sought, too, to cut off prejudicial publicity by closing legal proceedings at which prejudicial information might be discussed. The latter measures have led to serious conflicts between the legal establishment, as it has sought to protect the Sixth Amendment rights of defendants, and journalists, as they have sought to protect First Amendment freedoms. At least half a dozen times in the thirty years after *Sheppard,* the Supreme Court has felt compelled to try to resolve various aspects of that conflict.

The Supreme Court Prescribes Remedies

In the *Sheppard* decision, the Supreme Court concluded that Judge Blythin had lost control of the proceedings. Because he had given reporters and photographers free rein in and out of the courtroom, he had sacrificed the "judicial serenity and calm" that are essential to a fair trial. Thus, Sam Sheppard was entitled to a new trial at which his right to trial by an impartial jury must be protected.

At that point in the decision, Justice Clark turned to a discussion of remedies that Judge Blythin could have used to ensure a fair trial. Clark wrote that the judge had compounded the problems arising from the conduct of reporters and photographers by making no effort to cut off prejudicial news stories at their source. At the start of the trial, Blythin had announced "that neither he nor anyone else could restrict prejudicial news accounts." He repeated the view many times thereafter. But, said Clark, Blythin looked at the wrong target when he saw the news media as the sources of that problem. What he should, and could, have done, was to take steps to prevent prejudicial information from reaching the news media. Clark made some specific suggestions:

> The carnival atmosphere at trial could easily have been avoided since the courtroom and courthouse premises are subject to the control of the court. . . . Bearing in mind the massive pretrial publicity, the judge should have adopted stricter rules governing the use of the courtroom by newsmen, as Sheppard's counsel requested. The number of reporters in the courtroom itself could have been limited at the first sign that their presence

would disrupt the trial. They certainly should not have been placed inside the bar. Furthermore, the judge should have more closely regulated the conduct of newsmen in the courtroom. . . .

Secondly, the court should have insulated the witnesses. All of the newspapers and radio stations apparently interviewed prospective witnesses at will, and in many instances disclosed their testimony. . . .

Thirdly, the court should have made some effort to control the release of leads, information, and gossip to the press by police officers, witnesses, and the counsel for both sides. Much of the information thus disclosed was inaccurate, leading to groundless rumors and confusion. . . .

Defense counsel immediately brought to the court's attention the tremendous amount of publicity in the Cleveland press that "misrepresented entirely the testimony" in the case. Under such circumstances, the judge should have at least warned the newspapers to check the accuracy of their accounts. . . . The prosecution repeatedly made evidence available to the news media which was never offered in trial. Much of the "evidence" disseminated in this fashion was clearly inadmissible. The exclusion of such evidence in court is rendered meaningless when the news media make it available to the public. . . .

More specifically, the trial court might well have proscribed extra judicial statements by any lawyer, party, witness, or court official which divulged prejudicial matters, such as the refusal of Sheppard to submit to interrogation or take any lie detector tests; any statement made by Sheppard to officials; the identity of prospective witnesses or their probable testimony; any belief in guilt or innocence; or like statements concerning the merits of the case. . . . [T]he court could also have requested the appropriate city and county officials to promulgate a regulation with respect to dissemination of information about the case by their employees. In addition, reporters who wrote or broadcast prejudicial stories could have been warned as to the impropriety of publishing material not introduced in the proceedings. . . . In this manner, Sheppard's right to a trial free from outside interference would have been given added protection without corresponding curtailment of the news media. Had the judge, the other officers of the court, and the police placed the interest of justice first, the news media would have soon learned to be content with the task of reporting the case as it unfolded in the courtroom—not pieced together from extrajudicial statements.

. . . Given the pervasiveness of modern communications and the difficulty of effacing prejudicial publicity from the minds of jurors, the trial courts must take strong measures to ensure the balance is never weighed against the accused. And appellate courts have the duty to make an independent evaluation of the circumstances. Of course, there is nothing that proscribes the press from reporting events that transpire in the courtroom.

Clark ended by mentioning other steps that judges might take in cases like this one, "where there is a reasonable likelihood that prejudicial news prior to trial will prevent a fair trial." The start of the trial can be postponed until the publicity dies down, or the judge can order a change of venue—that is, transfer of the trial to a court not reached by the publicity. If prejudicial publicity continues during the trial, the judge can sequester the jury or declare a mistrial and start over. But Clark emphasized that the cure lies with trial judges, who must "protect their processes from prejudicial outside interferences."

Courts have found ten remedies implicit or explicit in Justice Clark's decision. Six of these either were noncontroversial because they had always been part of the trial process, or have been upheld so firmly by appellate courts that they have become taken for granted. The other four remain controversial. Here is a summary of the ten remedies:

1. Continuance to allow the effect of an initial burst of publicity to subside. However, the Supreme Court has ruled that undue delay violates the speedy trial clause of the Sixth Amendment.[14] Rules of court now require dismissal of cases that do not reach trial within a specified time after arraignment, unless the delay is attributable to the defense. Six months is a common limit.

2. Change of venue, now quite common.

3. Rigorous use of voir dire to screen prospective jurors who have made up their minds as a result of pretrial publicity.

4. Restrictions on the number of reporters who are permitted to cover trials that attract massive attention in the media, and on the comings and goings of reporters in the courtroom while court is in session.

5. Banishment of photographers from the courtroom and its environs. However, there have been significant changes in attitude on the part of judges in more than half the states, and of the Supreme Court itself, with respect to the photographing of trial proceedings.

6. Sequestration of the jury. Most judges consider this a tool of last resort. Jurors resent being kept virtual prisoners for the duration of a trial, especially if it is a long one.

The remedies that have generated the most controversy are:

7. Gag orders directed at participants in the trial, including attorneys. Appellate courts have upheld the right of trial judges to order participants in the proceedings to refrain from talking to reporters and others, provided a sufficient need is demonstrated.

   Additionally, attorneys who talk to reporters and disclose prejudicial information are subject to discipline by the courts. The code of ethics of the American Bar Association defines the kinds of information likely to be prejudicial and establishes guidelines for the release of information by lawyers involved in criminal cases.[15] The Supreme Court has held that carefully crafted restrictions on an attorney's comments do not violate the First Amendment.[16]

---

14. Barker v. Wingo, 407 U.S. 514, 92 S.Ct. 2182, 33 L.Ed.2d 101 (1972).
15. American Bar Association Legal Advisory Committee on Fair Trial and Free Press, *The Rights of Fair Trial and Free Press* (1969). Lawyers should confine their public disclosures to factual information of the kind likely to be admitted as evidence at trial. Lawyers are not supposed to talk about things such as confessions, tests, the possibility of a guilty plea, and witnesses and their likely testimony, because these are matters to be resolved during the trial process.
16. Gentile v. State Bar of Nevada, 111 S.Ct. 2720, 115 L.Ed.2d 888 (1991).

8. Gag orders directed at reporters. The suggestion of this restriction led to a decision of the Supreme Court that makes it difficult, if not impossible, for judges to justify such orders.

9. Closing to the press and public of certain parts of the trial process—preliminary hearings, bail hearings, and hearings on the admissibility of evidence. After four Supreme Court decisions in this area, the controversy continues, but the decisions make clear that court proceedings presumptively are open. They are to be closed only as a last resort to ensure a fair trial.

10. Refusing to release the names and addresses of jurors to the news media.

By applying these remedies conscientiously, trial court judges have reduced considerably the number of reversals based on prejudicial publicity.

Voir Dire

In its *Sheppard* decision, the Supreme Court urged trial judges to conduct a rigorous examination of potential jurors to screen out those who have already made up their minds as to a defendant's guilt or innocence. The process, called voir dire, is the courts' first line of defense against trial by the media. Appellate courts have given judges considerable leeway in how they conduct voir dire and in dismissing potential jurors who they believe may not be able to reach a verdict based solely on the evidence heard in court.

In 1991 the Supreme Court endorsed that position, noting that its cases "have

Mu'Min v. Virginia, **500 U.S. 415, 111 S.Ct. 1899, 114 L.Ed.2d 493 (1991).**

stressed the wide discretion granted to the trial court in conducting voir dire in the area of pretrial publicity and in other areas of inquiry that might tend to show juror bias." At issue was a trial judge's refusal to ask prospective jurors about the specific content of news stories naming a murder defendant, Dawud Majid Mu'Min. In 1988, while he was serving a forty-eight-year sentence for first-degree murder, Mu'Min walked away from a highway work detail long enough to rob and murder the owner of a store in Prince William County, Virginia. He was again charged with first-degree murder, and a trial date was set.

As that date approached, Mu'Min's lawyer asked for a change of venue, submitting as grounds for his request forty-seven newspaper stories relating to the murder that had been published in the previous four months. When his motion failed, the lawyer submitted sixty-four proposed voir dire questions to the judge along with a request that the judge examine each proposed juror separately. The proposed questions asked about specific content of the newspaper stories. The judge rejected the request. Instead, he began his voir dire by asking the original panel of twenty-six prospective jurors whether they had read or seen any news stories about the offense or the defendant. Sixteen said they had. The judge then asked whether what they had read or seen would influence their impartiality. Only one said that it would and was dismissed for cause. The judge then divided the panel into groups of four for further questioning. Any prospect who had read or heard about the case or who had discussed it with anyone was questioned further about his or her attitude toward the defendant, toward the Islamic faith, and toward the death sentence. This line of questioning led to the dismissal of several others.

Of the twelve jurors ultimately seated, eight said that they had read or heard something about the case but insisted that they had not formed an opinion as to Mu'Min's guilt or innocence. The jury found Mu'Min guilty of murder and recommended that he be sentenced to death. The Virginia Supreme Court upheld the verdict and the sentence. Mu'Min's lawyer appealed to the U.S. Supreme Court, arguing that some of the Court's fair-trial decisions had established a defendant's constitutional right to insist that certain types of specific questions be asked during voir dire.

Chief Justice Rehnquist, writing for three others, noted that in at least two instances the Court had held that the Sixth Amendment required specific questions to be asked when there is a possibility that potential jurors may be influenced by racial prejudice. But the chief justice said that the Court had not made a similar ruling in any of its cases dealing with prejudicial publicity. Nor would it do so in this instance. The Court's cases, Rehnquist said, "have stressed the wide discretion granted to the trial court in conducting voir dire. . . . Particularly with respect to pretrial publicity, we think this primary reliance on the judgment of the trial court makes good sense. The judge of the court sits in the locale where the publicity is said to have had its effect, and brings to his evaluation of any such claim his own perception of the depth and extent of news stories that might influence a juror." The Court concluded in this instance that the trial judge had made a rigorous effort to find out whether prospective jurors had made up their minds. The plurality held that the Sixth Amendment does not compel a judge to ask specific questions prepared by the defense to determine whether exposure to publicity has prejudiced potential jurors. Justice O'Connor wrote separately to endorse that conclusion, thus making it the majority holding.

Restraining Participants in a Trial

In *Sheppard,* Justice Clark suggested that Judge Blythin should have tried to cut off some of the flood of prejudicial publicity at its source by "proscribing extrajudicial statements by any lawyer, party, witness or court official." Clark's theory was that the media don't create news; they only report what sources are willing to disclose. If there are no prejudicial disclosures, there will be no prejudicial stories.

Limiting prejudicial publicity at its source sometimes is easier said than done. A judge can enforce a gag order against persons within the jurisdiction of the court, including employees of the court, witnesses,[17] parties to the action,[18] and the attorneys representing them. However, the judge must make a finding, based on evidence, that there is "a clear and present danger, or a reasonable likelihood, of a serious and imminent danger to the administration of justice."[19] Such findings must be made on a

---

17. *In re Russell*, 726 F.2d 1007 (4th Cir. 1984).
18. *United States v. Tijerina*, 412 F.2d 661 (10th Cir. 1969).
19. 16 *Corpus Juris Secundum,* 1981 Supp., p. 264.

case-by-case basis. For instance, the U.S. Court of Appeals, Seventh Circuit, rejected an attempt by a lower court to impose a general gag order for all trials by issuing a "standing order" of the court.[20]

What a lawyer can say to the media may be restricted by the rules that govern his or her membership to the bar. The Supreme Court, in striking down a Nevada rule limiting attorney comments, noted that such rules do not violate the First Amendment rights of attorneys if they are precisely drawn.

The Court held that lawyers may be disciplined if they know, or should know, that their comments will have a "substantial likelihood" of prejudicing a criminal proceeding to which they are a party. The effect of the decision is to give more weight to a suspect's Sixth Amendment right to trial by an impartial jury than to his or her lawyer's First Amendment right of free speech.

Gentile v. *State Bar of Nevada,* **501 U.S. 1030, 111 S.Ct. 2720, 115 L.Ed.2d 888 (1991).**

Thus, the decision is likely to reduce the burden of proof required to persuade a court to issue gag orders directed at counsel in criminal cases. Chief Justice Rehnquist, writing for himself and four others, said that *In re Sawyer,*[21] and *Sheppard* v. *Maxwell* "plainly indicate that the speech of lawyers representing clients in pending cases may be regulated under a less demanding standard than that established for regulation of the press in *Nebraska Press Association v. Stuart.*"

The case began when Dominic P. Gentile, a Nevada lawyer, called a press conference to discuss the indictment in Las Vegas of one of his clients on drug-related charges. He intimated that his client was being blamed for a crime that had been committed by police officers. At trial six months later, the client was found not guilty. Afterward, the State Bar of Nevada filed a complaint alleging that Gentile had violated Nevada Supreme Court Rule 177 regulating pretrial publicity. The rule, identical to the American Bar Association's Model Rule of Professional Conduct 3.6, prohibits a lawyer from making "an extrajudicial statement that a reasonable person would expect to be disseminated by means of public communication if the lawyer knows or reasonably should know that it will have a substantial likelihood of materially prejudicing an adjudicative proceeding." The rule then lists examples of the kinds of statements likely to be prejudicial. A subsection lists a number of statements that attorneys safely may make to the press because they are not considered prejudicial. The state bar's disciplinary board held that Gentile had violated the rule and recommended that he be privately reprimanded. The state supreme court affirmed.

The U.S. Supreme Court reversed on narrow grounds. It held that the rule, as interpreted by the Nevada Supreme Court, was void for vagueness. Specifically, the U.S. Supreme Court focused on the "safe harbor" subsection, which Gentile had interpreted as giving him the right to explain the "general" nature of his defense as long as he offered no "elaboration." The Court said that the words in quotation marks "are both classical terms of degree," lacking a settled meaning. Therefore, the words laid a trap for the unwary, as in this instance.

---

20.   In re Oliver, 452 F.2d 111 (7th Cir. 1971).
21.   360 U.S. 622, 79 S.Ct. 1376, 3 L.Ed.2d 1473 (1959).

However, a majority of the Court also held that aside from the "safe harbor" subsection, the main body of Rule 177, and the ABA Model Rule from which it was copied, do not violate the First Amendment's guarantee of freedom of speech. The Court thus indicated its approval of rules in effect in all but a few states. The Court noted that thirty-two states have rules either identical to the Model Rule or nearly so.[22]

Eleven states have adopted a rule that applies a more stringent "reasonable likelihood of prejudice" standard to lawyer speech on pending cases.[23] Only Virginia requires a showing that a lawyer's comments are a clear and present danger to a defendant's right to a fair trial. Illinois, Maine, North Dakota, Oregon, and the District of Columbia have adopted standards that the Court said "arguably approximate 'clear and present danger.'"

Restraining the News Media

Some trial judges who read *Sheppard* and tried to follow the Supreme Court's mandates concluded that the Supreme Court might condone prior restraint of the media if that were necessary to ensure a fair trial. Two decisions from the 1970s remain worthy of note. One prescribes the proper course of action for journalists confronted with an order not to publish prejudicial information. The other makes such a court order highly unlikely, although not impossible.

In the first case, *United States* v. *Dickinson,* a federal district court judge in Baton Rouge, Louisiana, was confronted with a highly charged situation. A young man active in the civil rights movement during the early 1970s was accused of conspiring to kill the mayor of the city. The judge had to conduct a preliminary hearing to determine if there was enough evidence to hold the suspect for trial. He knew that police would offer evidence at that hearing that might not be admissible at the trial but would point strongly at the man's guilt. He also knew that reporters would be present, ready to spread that evidence through the city. Thinking ahead to the problem of selecting an impartial jury if the man were tried, the judge concluded that his only recourse was to cut off harmful publicity at its source. He ordered the reporters present not to publish anything about the hearing except his decision, which was to hold the man for trial.

United States v. *Dickinson,* 465 F.2d 496, 1 Med.L.Rptr. 1338 (5th Cir. 1972).

Reporters for the two Baton Rouge newspapers consulted their editors, who told them to write stories covering the hearing in full. The editors reasoned that the public was more likely to be inflamed by a lack of facts than by a straightforward account of the evidence presented at the hearing. Without the facts, rumor would take over. When the stories were published, the judge held the reporters in contempt for violating his

---

22. Those states are Arizona, Arkansas, Connecticut, Delaware, Florida, Idaho, Indiana, Kansas, Kentucky, Louisiana, Maryland, Michigan, Minnesota, Mississippi, Missouri, Montana, Nevada, New Hampshire, New Jersey, New Mexico, New York, Oklahoma, Pennsylvania, Rhode Island, South Carolina, South Dakota, Texas, Utah, Washington, West Virginia, Wisconsin, and Wyoming.

23. Those states are Alaska, Colorado, Georgia, Hawaii, Iowa, Massachusetts, Nebraska, North Carolina, Ohio, Tennessee, and Vermont.

order and fined each $300. They appealed to the U.S. Court of Appeals for the Fifth Circuit.

Chief Judge John R. Brown held that "even the merest breeze blowing across the First Amendment" was enough to lead to the conclusion that the gag order was improper. It was a prior restraint, based not on a heavy showing of necessity, but on a series of improbable assumptions that the suspect would go to trial, that the prejudicial publicity, if any, would be pervasive, and that voir dire would not work. Further, the court held, the public had a right to know as much as the media could learn about a situation as highly charged as that which had prevailed in Baton Rouge.

With that said, the court also held that journalists, like everyone else, must obey a judge's order or appeal to a higher court for relief. The First Amendment gives them no special right to disobey a judge, even when they are convinced he or she is wrong.

On remand, the trial judge stuck to his guns, reimposing the $300 fines. He conceded that his order may have been improper but reiterated that he would not tolerate defiance. On further appeal, the appellate court upheld the fines. The Supreme Court refused to review.[24]

Despite the part of the *Dickinson* decision that condemned prior restraint, trial judges persisted in trying to tell reporters what to *Nebraska Press* omit from their stories. The most notable of these *Association* v. *Stuart,* attempts took place in a small county seat in west- **437 U.S. 539, 96 S.Ct. 2791,** ern Nebraska in 1975. Erwin Charles Simants had **49 L.Ed.2d 683, 1** killed six members of the Henry Kellie family and **Med.L.Rptr. 1064 (1976).** then had confessed to anyone who would listen. One of the victims was a ten-year-old girl, who also had been raped. These events took place in Sutherland, a town with a population of 840 in Lincoln County, which has a population of 36,000, of whom 24,000 live in North Platte, the county seat. The crime was highly publicized by the media in the county and elsewhere.

When Simants was scheduled to appear in court in North Platte for a preliminary hearing, his attorney and the county attorney joined in asking district court Judge Hugh Stuart to issue an order restricting what could be reported about the case. They said that details highly prejudicial to Simants would be presented at the hearing. They considered these details so inflammatory that it probably would be impossible to select an impartial jury when Simants came to trial. The judge agreed and issued a restrictive order.

The news media, represented by the Nebraska State Press Association, appealed to a higher court in Lincoln, the state capital, for relief. The court noted that the press association and most of the state's media had adopted a set of voluntary guidelines, patterned on the *Sheppard* decision and the American Bar Association guidelines, for the coverage of news of crime and the courts. Media subscribing to these guidelines promised not to publish information that might prejudice a defendant's right to a fair trial. The appellate court said that it would make the guidelines mandatory by adopting them as rules of the court. Finding clear and present danger to Simants's right to

---

24.   476 F.2d 373 (5th Cir. 1973), cert. denied, 414 U.S. 979 (1973).

a fair trial, the court issued an order, to be in effect until a jury was chosen, prohibiting media within the trial court's jurisdiction from mentioning the defendant's several confessions. The order also forbade publication of medical information indicating that some of the victims had been sexually assaulted. Finally, the appellate court also ordered the media not to report that they were operating under a gag order.

Appeals were filed in all directions, with the U.S. Supreme Court eventually agreeing to consider the case. Its decision in *Nebraska Press Association* v. *Stuart* erected three high hurdles between courts and a prior restraint of the news media in the interest of ensuring a fair trial.

Chief Justice Warren E. Burger wrote for a Court that was unanimous in condemning Judge Stuart's order but was divided as to whether all such orders violate the First Amendment. The chief justice began by noting that the drafters of the Bill of Rights had guaranteed both freedom of the press and the right to trial by an impartial jury. When the two rights conflict, how can each be preserved without harming the other? Burger suggested that voluntary press-bar guidelines like those in effect in Nebraska and several other states offered one answer. However, such guidelines may fail when the need for them is greatest. The chief justice noted that "even the most ideal guidelines are subjected to powerful strains when a case such as Simants' arises." Some editors will observe them. Others will not.

Confronted with that fact, Judge Stuart sought to protect Simants's Sixth Amendment right to a fair trial by restraining the media's First Amendment rights. The Court held that Stuart had gone too far. At the same time, Chief Justice Burger rebuffed those who would resolve the fair-trial issue by holding that First Amendment rights should never be restricted. He wrote:

> The authors of the Bill of Rights did not undertake to assign priorities as between First Amendment and Sixth Amendment rights, ranking one as superior to the other. . . . [I]f the authors of these guarantees . . . were unwilling or unable to resolve the issue by assigning to one priority over the other, it is not for us to rewrite the Constitution by undertaking what they declined. It is unnecessary, after nearly two centuries, to establish a priority applicable to all circumstances.

The Court proceeded to hold that gag orders could be imposed on the media only as a last resort to ensure a fair trial. Such orders can be imposed, a majority of the Court held, only if three conditions are met. A judge proposing a restraint on the media must offer convincing evidence of these three criteria:

1. There is, or is likely to be, widespread prejudicial publicity.

2. None of the usual methods of ensuring a fair trial—voir dire, change of venue, continuance, and the like—will work.

3. The prior restraint will stop the flow of prejudicial publicity.

The chief justice said that Judge Stuart had satisfied only the first of these criteria. There was ample evidence of widespread prejudicial publicity and the promise of more. But Judge Stuart could only speculate on the effect of that publicity. There was no evidence to prove that rigorous voir dire or a change of venue could not result in selection of an impartial jury. Nor was there any evidence that a gag order imposed on the media would cut off news of the confessions or of the sordid nature of the crime. Word of mouth, Burger noted, would spread such information quickly through a town of only 840 persons. The news also had been poured into the county by outside broadcasting stations and newspapers. Therefore, Judge Stuart's order was an improper restraint, violating the First Amendment.

Meanwhile, Simants had been tried before a jury in North Platte, with Judge Stuart presiding, and had been found guilty of murder. The Nebraska Supreme Court reversed, finding that the Lincoln County sheriff not only had lobbied the jury for a conviction but had played cards with the jurors during the trial. On retrial in Lincoln, with Judge Stuart again presiding, Simants was found not guilty by reason of insanity.

In 1983, a U.S. district court judge in California attempted to comply with the *Nebraska Press Association* guidelines in imposing a gag order on CBS News. John DeLorean, a former General Motors executive who had organized a British company to build a sports car carrying his name, was about to go on trial for conspiracy to sell cocaine. Federal agents had videotaped him apparently in the act of making the deal. Government prosecutors alleged that he had resorted to the cocaine deal to raise money to save his failing automobile business.

A few days before the trial was to begin, KNXT, the CBS affiliate in Los Angeles, broadcast excerpts from the government's videotape. One segment showed DeLorean examining a shipment of cocaine in a hotel room. Another showed FBI agents arresting him. The station said that it would show other segments later. Judge Robert M. Takasugi postponed the start of the trial and issued an order forbidding CBS News from broadcasting any part of the tape. He said he feared that the portion already shown would make it difficult for him to find an impartial jury.

CBS complied with the court order and immediately appealed. On appeal, the U.S. Court of Appeals, Ninth Circuit, overruled Judge Takasugi. It held that his gag order was an unconstitutional prior restraint. The court said that the judge had failed to prove that further publicity would so distort the views of potential jurors that an impartial panel could not be seated.[25] In fact, later the judge was able to pick an impartial jury, and after many weeks of trial the jury found DeLorean not guilty. The jury concluded that federal agents, not DeLorean, had initiated the cocaine transaction.[26]

The CBS case illustrates the difficulty any court is likely to have in fulfilling the criteria established in *Nebraska Press Association.* The likelihood of prejudicial publicity is easy to illustrate. But how does a judge prove in advance that such ordinary measures as change of venue and voir dire will not result in finding a dozen persons who can decide the case on its merits? And with satellites, cable, computers, and even the mails bringing in news reports and commentary prepared by individuals who need not come within hundreds of miles of the judge who issues a gag order against the media, how can prejudicial information be cut off by court order? A judge cannot reach beyond the limits of the court's jurisdiction and punish those who disseminate information that he or she has proscribed. For these

---

25. Columbia Broadcasting Systems, Inc. v. U.S. District Court, Central District of California, 729 F.2d 1174 (9th Cir. 1984).
26. "DeLorean: Not Guilty," *Newsweek,* 27 August 1984, pp. 22–23.

reasons, any order restricting the media's right to report what is known about a pending criminal case is unlikely to survive an appeal to the next higher court. Yet, to publish in defiance of a court order before an appeal is made or while one is pending can be disastrous.

In 1990, federal district Judge William Hoeveler ordered CNN not to broadcast a recording of telephone calls made from jail by General Manuel Antonio Noriega, a former Panamanian leader who had been arrested by American armed forces after the U.S. invasion of Panama. Noriega had been brought to the United States to stand trial in Miami on international drug trafficking charges. Judge Hoeveler ordered CNN to turn the tapes over to him to determine whether they might jeopardize the Noriega trial.[27]

Believing Judge Hoeveler's gag order to be an unconstitutional prior restraint, and acting on the advice of its lawyers, CNN broadcast some of the conversations in a story intended to raise questions about the actions of the federal officers who had recorded the conversations. Judge Hoeveler, believing that his order had been intentionally defied, charged CNN with criminal contempt of court and ordered the network to stand trial.[28]

CNN then sought help from the 11th Circuit Court of Appeals, asking for a writ of mandamus against Judge Hoeveler. The appellate court, troubled by CNN's refusal to obey Judge Hoeveler's order to give him the tapes, denied CNN's request. The court said that Judge Hoeveler had a delicate, difficult, and important task requiring him to balance the rights of a free press and a fair trial. "However, CNN has shackled the district court by refusing that court's reasonable request to review the audio tapes it has in its possession and which CNN desires to broadcast." "No litigant," said the court, "can continue to violate a district court's order and attempt to have that district court's order reviewed at the same time."[29]

CNN appealed to the U.S. Supreme Court, which denied certiorari, although Justices Marshall and O'Connor dissented.[30] They argued that any prior restraint—however short—came with a heavy presumption of its unconstitutionality. In this case, they would have first required Judge Hoeveler to show that the gag order was necessary to protect Noriega's right to a fair trial. Without such a showing, the order should have been deemed a violation of the First Amendment.

Judge Hoeveler's position, of course, was that he couldn't do any of that unless CNN first gave him the tapes to review and the time to review them. He believed that CNN should not decide on its own whether its broadcast was protected by the

---

27. There were two written orders. The first ordered CNN not to broadcast the tapes until the court had a chance to review them and reach a decision about their impact on the fairness of the trial. The second clarified the first order and specified that the restraint would last ten days or until such lesser time as was needed to review the tapes. The orders further directed CNN to deliver the recordings to Judge Hoeveler. See In re Cable News Network, Inc., 917 F.2d 1543, 18 Med.L.Rptr. 1352 (11th Cir. 1990); cert. denied, Cable News Network, Inc. v. Noriega, 111 S.Ct. 451, 18 Med.L.Rptr. 1358 (1990).
28. "CNN's President Says Defiance Was Not Intent in Noriega Case," *New York Times,* 16 September 1994, p. A11.
29. In re Cable News Network, Inc., 917 F.2d 1543, 18 Med.L.Rptr. 1352, 1358 (11th Cir. 1990); cert. denied, Cable News Network, Inc. v. Noriega, 111 S.Ct. 451, 18 Med.L.Rptr. 1358 (1990).
30. Cable News Network, Inc. v. Noriega, 111 S.Ct. 451, 18 Med.L.Rptr. 1358 (1990).

Constitution, and that if CNN defied a court order to produce the tapes, it could be found guilty of contempt, even if he later determined that his caution was unfounded.

In driving that lesson home, Judge Hoeveler pursued the contempt citation against CNN, and after a four-day trial, he found the news network guilty, ordering it to pay a hefty fine or publicly apologize and be fined far less.[31] CNN apologized:

> On further consideration, CNN realizes that it was in error in defying the order of the court and publishing the Noriega tape while appealing the court's order. We do now and always have recognized that our justice system cannot long survive if litigants take it upon themselves to determine which judgments or orders of court they will or will not follow. Ours is a nation of laws under which the very freedoms we espouse can be preserved only if those laws are observed. In the event unfavorable judgments are rendered, the right of appeal is provided. This is the course on which we should have relied. We regret that we did not.[32]

Access to Court Proceedings

Precisely because of the unlikelihood of prior restraint of the media, condemned in *Nebraska Press Association,* some courts began using a new technique: the closing of court proceedings at which prejudicial information was likely to be disclosed. Historically, trials have been open to the public. Moreover, the Sixth Amendment guarantees defendants the right not only to trial by an impartial jury but "to a speedy and public trial." In *Sheppard,* Justice Clark had noted, almost as an aside, "Of course, there is nothing that proscribes the press from reporting events that transpire in the courtroom." Nor was there any reason in 1966 to doubt that court proceedings would be conducted in public in all but the most unusual circumstances, usually involving divorce and custody cases or embarrassing testimony in sex-crime trials.

By 1976, when *Nebraska Press Association* was decided, some judges, in their attempt to ensure a fair trial, had begun to experiment with closing pretrial proceedings. The most common closures were of preliminary, sometimes called probable cause, hearings, where police and prosecutors can offer evidence that would not be admissible at a formal trial. The gag order in *Nebraska Press Association* was issued at such a hearing. In his decision in that case, Chief Justice Burger took note of the experiments with closing in a way that seemed to approve them. He wrote:

> The county court could not know that closure of the preliminary hearing was an alternative open to it until the Nebraska Supreme Court so construed state law, but once a public hearing had been held, what transpired there could not be subject to prior restraint.

Burger was referring to a decision of the Nebraska court holding that the judge who had conducted the preliminary hearing, and who had imposed the original gag order, might have solved his problem by conducting the hearing in private. Some

---

31. "CNN Found in Contempt for Tapes Broadcast," *New York Times,* 2 November 1994, p. A8.
32. "CNN Is Sentenced for Tapes and Makes Public Apology," *New York Times,* 20 December 1994, p. A8. General Noriega, meanwhile, was convicted of drug trafficking and other charges and sentenced to forty years in prison.

judges read the first part of the sentence quoted above and found in it the Supreme Court's endorsement of such closings. One such judge was Daniel DePasquale, of the Seneca County Supreme Court, a trial court in upstate New York. DePasquale was confronted with the duty of conducting a highly unusual murder case—one without a corpse. The case began when Wayne Clapp, a former police officer, disappeared from his home near Rochester. He had gone fishing on Lake Seneca, forty miles away, with two male companions. When Clapp failed to return, police began a search. His boat, riddled with bullets, was found on Lake Seneca, and his pickup truck was found outside a motel in Jackson, Michigan. Officers arrested Kyle Greathouse and his wife, both sixteen, and David Ray Jones, twenty-one, who were in the motel. The suspects surrendered Clapp's credit cards and a .357 Magnum revolver. They also made statements to police describing how and why they had killed Clapp. Police returned the trio to Seneca County, New York, where the two men were charged with murder.

As the trial date approached, the defendants' attorneys filed two motions with the county court. One asked that the statements be suppressed on the ground that they had not been given voluntarily. The other asked for suppression of the credit cards and the revolver. When these motions came up for a hearing, the attorneys made a third motion. Pointing to seven news stories that had appeared in the two Rochester newspapers, they argued that "the unabated buildup of adverse publicity has jeopardized the ability of the defendants to receive a fair trial." They asked that spectators, including reporters, be excluded from the suppression hearing. The district attorney made no objection, and Judge DePasquale granted the request. Only one reporter, Carol Ritter, a correspondent for the Rochester newspapers owned by the Gannett Company, was present. She left the courtroom at the judge's request, and the hearing proceeded behind closed doors. Judge DePasquale ruled that the credit cards, the Magnum, and the confessions had been obtained in violation of the defendants' rights and therefore could not be used as evidence. The prosecutor concluded that without such evidence and without the body of the victim, he could not persuade a jury to convict the suspects of murder. This situation led to an agreement under which Greathouse and Jones pleaded guilty to lesser offenses and served short terms in prison.[33]

Meanwhile, Gannett's attorney had filed a motion with Judge DePasquale asserting Ritter's right to cover the suppression hearing, even though it had been completed, and asking for a transcript of the proceeding. At the hearing on the motion, DePasquale said that he, too, believed the press had a constitutional right of access to court proceedings. He said it was unfortunate that Ritter had not objected at the time the closure motion was made. However, he said her right under the First Amendment was not absolute and would have to be balanced against the right of the defendants to a fair trial. In this instance, he said he would hold that the right to a fair trial outweighed the reporter's right to cover the suppression hearing. He also refused to release the transcript, on the ground that it contained information that would make it difficult if not impossible for Greathouse and Jones to get a

---

33. Gannett v. DePasquale, 43 N.Y.2d 373 (N.Y. 1977).

IRAN   AFGHANISTAN   AMERICAN

News media reaction to the decision in *Gannett* v. *DePasquale* was almost entirely negative, as this editorial cartoon by Don Wright illustrates. Editors and producers were afraid of widespread attempts to close criminal proceedings, and, in fact, nearly a hundred criminal proceedings were successfully closed to the public during the first year after the *Gannett* decision. *(Don Wright/Tribune Media Services)*

fair trial. At the time, the prosecutor had not yet agreed to the plea agreement noted above.

Gannett's unsuccessful appeals to New York's higher courts led eventually to the Supreme Court, resulting in a sweeping decision that divided the justices as have few others and that created a furor in the media and the legal profession. The Court held, five to four, in *Gannett* v. *DePasquale,* that the judge had acted properly.

**Gannett v. DePasquale,
443 U.S. 368, 99 S.Ct. 2898,
61 L.Ed.2d 608, 5
Med.L.Rptr. 1337 (1979).**

Gannett based its appeal on the Sixth Amendment's guarantee of "the right to a speedy and public trial," which proved to be a poor choice. Justice Potter Stewart noted that the right to a public trial, like the right to trial by jury, was designed to protect defendants. Defendants who choose to waive a jury trial, or to be tried in private, may do so if the trial judge approves. If such requests are made, Justice Stewart wrote, the Sixth Amendment gives the media and the public no right to object. They may or may not have such a right under the First Amendment. If so, the right is not absolute, and Judge DePasquale fulfilled any duty he may have had under it by listening to Gannett's request for a transcript of the testimony.

Thus, within a few paragraphs a dispute over the right to attend a hearing had been converted into a devastating blow aimed at those who believe that justice is more likely to be done in the open than behind closed doors. In the year after *Gannett* was decided, defendants in forty-nine cases asked to have all or parts of their trial closed, and about half the requests were granted.[34]

Justice Harry A. Blackmun, who wrote for the four dissenters in *Gannett,* called the decision "an unfortunate one." Even some of the justices who supported Stewart's conclusion wrote to express their doubts about his reasoning. Some argued that the decision should have been grounded in the First Amendment. Within a year, the Supreme Court seized the opportunity to clarify the *Gannett* decision.

Trials of Criminal Cases

Since early 1976, a troublesome murder case had been bouncing through the Virginia courts. It began with the stabbing death of a motel manager in Hanover, a hamlet twenty miles north of Richmond. A Hanover County grand jury indicted John Paul Stevenson on a charge of murder, on the basis of the principal piece of evidence connecting Stevenson with the crime, a bloodstained shirt. Although the shirt belonged to Stevenson, he contended that police had seized it in violation of his rights. The shirt was introduced as evidence at the trial, and a jury found Stevenson guilty of second-degree murder. On appeal, the Virginia Supreme Court ruled that the shirt should not have been used as evidence and ordered a new trial. Two subsequent trials resulted in mistrials. When Stevenson's fourth trial began, his lawyer asked that it be closed to the public. He argued that a member of the victim's family seemed to be coaching the witnesses. The prosecutor made no objections to the closing. The judge noted that the courtroom was not well designed. The jurors could see the spectators and, the judge reasoned, might be influenced by them. When he ordered the courtroom cleared, two reporters for the Richmond newspapers were among those evicted.

At the time, the *Gannett* case had not been decided by the Supreme Court. The Virginia judge acted on his reading of a state law authorizing judges in criminal trials to "exclude from the trial any persons whose presence would impair the conduct of a fair trial, provided that the right of the accused to a public trial shall not be violated."[35]

There is nothing unusual in the statute. As the Supreme Court reminded judges in *Sheppard,* courts have always had a duty to keep prejudicial influences out of the courtroom. However, even a cursory survey of the cases in this area leads to the conclusion that the right to exclude individuals from the courtroom has been used infrequently and limited narrowly. Attempts by judges to stretch the rule into a blanket exclusion order usually were rebuffed.[36]

In the Virginia case, counsel for the Richmond newspapers asked the trial judge later that day for a hearing on the closure order. He agreed to hear the lawyer's argument, listened to him in private, and ruled that the trial would proceed behind closed doors. The trial ended the next day when the judge granted a defense motion to strike

---

34. *News Media and the Law,* August/September, November/December 1979, pp. 7–9, 10–23.
35. Va.Code § 19.2–266.
36   E. W. Scripps Co. v. Fulton, 125 N.E.2d 896 (Ohio 1955), and Oliver v. Postel, 282 N.E.2d 306 (N.Y.App. 1972).

the prosecution's case from the record. The judge then found Stevenson not guilty. His written order gave no reason for his decision.

When the state supreme court rejected an appeal of the closure order, the Richmond newspapers took their case to the U.S. Supreme Court. The petition reached the Court within weeks after *Gannett* had been decided. The Court seized the opportunity to limit that decision and held, with only one dissent, that the Virginia judge had acted improperly. Justice Powell, who had practiced law in Richmond, took no part in the case.

Richmond Newspapers v. Virginia, **448 U.S. 555, 100 S.Ct. 2814, 65 L.Ed.2d 1973, 6 Med.L.Rptr. 1833 (1980).**

The Court's seven-to-one decision in *Richmond Newspapers* v. *Virginia* was not nearly as unanimous as the vote suggests. Although the majority found common ground in holding that the closure was unwarranted, the justices wrote six different opinions to explain why they did so. Some clearly would have preferred to ground the decision in the Sixth Amendment guarantee of a public trial. But the leading opinion, written by Chief Justice Burger and signed by Justices Stevens and White, was grounded in the First Amendment. The justices reasoned that because of the historical origins of trials and a long tradition of openness, trials have become public assemblies where the business of government is conducted. Therefore, the freedom of assembly clause of the First Amendment gives journalists and the public a right to attend trials. Although not absolute, this freedom does give people a right to argue against a motion to close a trial or any part of it, with the presumption in favor of openness.

This decision represented an important advance in First Amendment theory. Previously, as Justice Rehnquist had pointed out in *Gannett,* the Court had steadfastly rejected the argument that the right to disseminate news implies a right to gather it. In a few of its previous decisions the Court had spoken in general terms about First Amendment protection for news gatherers, but it had not upheld any specific right.

But in *Richmond Newspapers,* Chief Justice Burger, noting that a "core purpose" of the First and Fourteenth amendments is to assure "freedom of communication on matters relating to the functioning of government," moved to a position he had not previously taken. He concluded that this freedom must imply a right to gather news on the functioning of government. Specifically, he said that because trials are a function of government and because they have traditionally been open, they are public assemblies that the public has a right to attend. It is not an absolute right, and the chief justice described it as follows:

> What this means in the context of trials is that the First Amendment guarantees of speech and press, standing alone, prohibit government from summarily closing courtroom doors which had long been open to the public at the time that amendment was adopted. . . .
> It is not crucial whether we describe this right to attend criminal trials to hear, see, and communicate observations concerning them as a "right of access," or a "right to gather information," for we have recognized that "without some protection for seeking out news, freedom of the press could be eviscerated." . . . The explicit, guaranteed rights to speak and to publish concerning what takes place at a trial would lose much meaning if access to observe the trial could, as it was here, be foreclosed arbitrarily.
> Subject to the traditional time, place, and manner restrictions, . . . streets, sidewalks, and parks are places traditionally open, where First Amendment rights may be exercised . . .; a

trial courtroom also is a public place where the people generally—and representatives of the media—have a right to be present, and where their presence historically has been thought to enhance the integrity and quality of what takes place. . . .

We hold that the right to attend criminal trials is implicit in the guarantees of the First Amendment; without the freedom to attend such trials, which people have exercised for centuries, important aspects of freedom of speech and "of the press could be eviscerated."

Burger concluded by holding that the Virginia judge had not given enough attention to the remedies recommended in *Sheppard* before he decided to close the courtroom in an effort to ensure a fair trial. He added:

Absent an overriding interest articulated in findings, the trial of a criminal case must be open to the public. Accordingly, the judgment under review is reversed.

Although Justice White signed Burger's opinion, he could not resist chiding the chief justice for voting with the majority in *Gannett*. If Burger had endorsed the minority view in that case, the Court would have construed the Sixth Amendment "to forbid excluding the public from criminal proceedings except in narrowly defined circumstances." Thus it could have avoided the First Amendment issue.

Justice Stevens, who also put his name on Burger's opinion, wrote separately to expand on White's reservations about the creation of a new First Amendment right of access. Noting that the Court previously had rejected suggestions that the amendment implies such a right, he added:

Today, . . . for the first time, the Court unequivocally holds that an arbitrary interference with access to important information is an abridgment of the freedoms of speech and of the press protected by the First Amendment.

Justice Stewart, who was seeing much of his year-old opinion in *Gannett* reduced to dicta, concurred in the Court's judgment. He said that his earlier decision had left open the question as to whether other parts of the Constitution might guarantee a right of access. That right had now been found in the First Amendment, and he was willing to go along with that.

Justice Blackmun, who had led the dissenters in *Gannett,* made no effort to hide his exasperation with both Stewart and the chief justice. With his position—that the Sixth Amendment gives the public some right of access to court proceedings—rejected, he concurred in the Court's finding. He wrote that he was happy to see the Court paying some attention to legal history, and added:

It is gratifying . . . to see the Court wash away at least some of the graffiti that marred the prevailing opinion in *[Gannett.]* No less than twelve times in the primary opinion in that case, the Court (albeit in what seems now to have become clear dicta) observed that the Sixth Amendment closure ruling applies to the *trial* itself. The author of the first concurring opinion [Burger] was fully aware of this and would have restricted the Court's observations and rulings to the suppression hearing. Nonetheless, he *joined* the Court's opinion with its multiple references to the trial itself; the opinion was not a mere concurrence in the Court's judgment. And Mr. Justice Rehnquist, in his separate concurring opinion, quite understandably observed, as a consequence, that the Court was holding "without qualification," that "members of the public have no constitutional right under the Sixth and Fourteenth Amendments to attend criminal trials." The resulting confusion among commentators and journalists was not surprising.

Justice Rehnquist alone remained unconvinced. He believed that his colleagues were mistaken, and he said so bluntly:

> In the Gilbert and Sullivan operetta Iolanthe, the Lord Chancellor recites:
> "The law is the true embodiment of everything that's excellent.
> It has no kind of fault or flaw, And I, my lords, embody the law."
> It is difficult not to derive more than a little of this flavor from the various opinions supporting the judgment in this case. . . .
> . . . I do not believe that either the First or Sixth Amendments, as made applicable to the States by the Fourteenth, require that a State's reasons for denying public access to a trial, where both the prosecuting attorney and the defendant have consented to an order of closure approved by the judge, are subject to any additional constitutional review at our hands.

However, Rehnquist stood alone. As Stevens emphasized in his concurring opinion, the Court, for the first time, had found in the First Amendment a right of the press and public to attend trials. It is not an absolute right, but the various opinions make clear that it is a right that can be abridged only by a strong showing of evidence that the defendant's right to a fair trial can be protected only by closing the courtroom. Further, representatives of the public and the news media have a right to argue against closing.

The issues of access presented in *Gannett* and *Richmond Newspapers* split the Court as have only two other First Amendment questions: the definition of obscenity, and the prior restraint imposed in the Pentagon Papers case. The justices wrote twelve different opinions in the two access cases. Through all the disagreements and reservations expressed in those opinions, however, one point comes clear: Eight of the nine justices concluded in varying degree that some right of access to news sources is implicit in the First Amendment and can be applied to the states through the due process clause of the Fourteenth. Rehnquist was the only holdout.

Jury Selection and Pretrial Hearings

Reacting to the confusion created in the minds of judges by its decisions in *Gannett* and *Richmond Newspapers,* the Supreme Court has on four occasions since felt compelled to take cases involving access to criminal justice proceedings. In each instance, the Court has expanded the scope of its holding in *Richmond Newspapers* and greatly restricted the reach of *Gannett.*

In the first of the cases, *Globe Newspaper Co.* v. *Superior Court, County of Norfolk,*[37] decided in 1982, the Court held that a Massachusetts law closing courtrooms during the testimony of certain sex-crime victims violated the First Amendment.

In the second, *Press-Enterprise Co.* v. *Superior Court of California, Riverside County [Press-Enterprise (I)],*[38] decided in 1984, the Court held that because the voir dire traditionally is part of the trial, it too must be conducted in the open unless convincing evidence shows that it must be closed to ensure a fair trial.

---

37.   457 U.S. 596, 102 S.Ct. 2613, 73 L.Ed.2d 248, 8 Med.L.Rptr. 1689 (1982).
38.   464 U.S. 501, 104 S.Ct. 819, 78 L.Ed.2d 629, 10 Med.L.Rptr. 1161 (1984).

In the third, *Waller* v. *Georgia,*[39] also decided in 1984, the Court held that a pretrial suppression hearing can be closed over the defendant's objections only if there are compelling reasons to do so. More important, the Court held that the people's First Amendment right of access to such proceedings rests on the same factors as the defendant's Sixth Amendment right to a public trial.

In the fourth, *Press-Enterprise Co.* v. *Superior Court of California, Riverside County [Press-Enterprise (II)],*[40] the Court held that the qualified First Amendment right of access to criminal proceedings extends to preliminary hearings as conducted in California. In that state, such hearings can involve the taking of considerable testimony, becoming, in effect, a preview of the trial.

The effect of these decisions has been to reinforce the conclusion that all court proceedings are presumed to be open; that closing, even of nontrial hearings, is the exception; and that each closing must be justified by evidence showing that a fair trial is unlikely unless the proceeding is closed.

At issue in *Globe Newspaper* was a Massachusetts law that required judges presiding at the trials of certain sex crimes to exclude the public and the media during the testimony of victims under the age of eighteen. The Court held six to three that any such arbitrary closing of a courtroom during a trial violates the First Amendment right of access defined in *Richmond Newspapers.*

Globe Newspaper Co.
v. Superior Court, County
of Norfolk G, **457 U.S.**
596, 102 S.Ct. 2613,
73 L.Ed.2d 248,
8 Med.L.Rptr. 1689 (1982).

The law had been invoked during the trial of a man accused of raping three girls, all of whom were under eighteen. When it came time for the victims to testify, the judge closed the courtroom, despite objections by a reporter for the *Boston Globe.* In response to that challenge, the state sought to justify the law on two grounds: It protected "minor victims of sex crimes from further trauma and embarrassment," and it encouraged those victims "to come forward and testify in a truthful and credible manner."

The Supreme Court's majority conceded that both interests were important but held that they can be served by measures less restrictive than a mandatory statute. The Court said that although the right of access to criminal trials is not absolute,

> the circumstances under which the press and public can be barred from a criminal trial are limited; the State's justification in denying access must be a weighty one. Where, as in the present case, the State attempts to deny the right of access in order to inhibit the disclosure of sensitive information, it must be shown that the denial is necessitated by a compelling governmental interest, and is narrowly tailored to serve that interest.

In this instance, the law swept too broadly. The Court said that Massachusetts could protect minors as witnesses through judicial action on a case-by-case basis. In that way, the judge could weigh the interests in privacy and a fair trial against the public's interest in the testimony and reach a suitable decision. Thus, the Court did not rule out the possibility that the courtroom could be closed during the testimony of the young

---

39.   467 U.S. 39, 104 S.Ct. 2210, 81 L.Ed.2d 31, 10 Med.L.Rptr. 1714 (1984).
40.   478 U.S. 1, 106 S.Ct. 2735, 92 L.Ed.2d 1, 11 Med.L.Rptr. 1297 (1986).

victims, but said that such action could be taken only after a hearing at which the media could plead their case. Then the judge would have to conclude, on the basis of clear evidence, that the victims would not testify fully unless reporters and the public were barred.

Press-Enterprise (I) had its origins in the selection of a jury for the trial of a suspect accused of rape and murder. The crime was the

Press-Enterprise Co. v. Superior Court of California, Riverside County, 464 U.S. 501, 104 S.Ct. 819, 78 L.Ed.2d 629, 10 Med.L.Rptr. 1161 (1984). subject of intense media coverage, and the judge took special pains to make certain that the voir dire was as searching as possible. The first three days were conducted in open court. Then the prosecutor asked that the process be closed, arguing that otherwise the prospective jurors might not respond to questions with sufficient candor to disclose their biases. The judge agreed, and the questioning continued in private for six weeks before a jury was seated.

When the *Press-Enterprise* sought a copy of the transcript of the voir dire, the defendant's attorney objected, arguing that some of the transcript would violate the jurors' right of privacy. The prosecutor joined in the objection, arguing that prospective jurors had answered questions under an "implied promise of confidentiality." The judge upheld the objections, noting that much of the transcript was dull and boring and that a few persons had disclosed matters that might prove embarrassing if made public. The *Press-Enterprise* appealed, but was rebuffed by two state appellate courts.

The Supreme Court overruled the California courts, with Chief Justice Burger writing for the majority. Reviewing much of the same historical ground he had covered in *Richmond Newspapers,* Burger concluded that jury selection, like the trial itself, traditionally has been conducted in public. In his view, open proceedings are more likely to ensure fairness than they are to promote prejudice. The chief justice wrote:

> No right ranks higher than the right of the accused to a fair trial. But the primacy of the accused's right is difficult to separate from the right of everyone in the community to attend the *voir dire* which promotes fairness.

However, the Court stopped short of holding that jury selection never should be conducted in private. It established the following guidelines:

> Closed proceedings, although not absolutely precluded, must be rare and only for cause shown that outweighs the value of openness. . . . The presumption of openness may be overcome only by an overriding interest based on findings that closure is essential to preserve higher values and is narrowly tailored to serve that interest. The interest is to be articulated along with findings specific enough that a reviewing court can determine whether the closure order was properly entered.

This passage has been cited frequently by lower courts seeking guidance in access cases.[41]

---

41.   For example, see Cable News Network v. United States, 824 F.2d 1046 (D.C. Cir. 1987).

The Supreme Court itself reiterated the *Press-Enterprise (I)* test in its decision in *Waller* v. *Georgia* and went further by holding that the Sixth Amendment, too, gives the press and public a right to argue against closing judicial proceedings. Guy Waller was one of thirty-six persons charged with illegal gambling after police had used court-approved wiretaps to listen to their telephone conversations. In advance of the trial, Waller and several other defendants asked that the wiretap evidence be suppressed. The prosecutor moved that the hearing be closed because it might reveal information that would violate the privacy of persons who had not been charged with gambling. He also said that some of the disclosures might violate the right of other defendants to a fair trial. Over objections from defense attorneys, the judge granted the motion.

Waller v. Georgia, 467 U.S. 39, 104 S.Ct. 2210, 81 L.Ed.2d 31, 10 Med.L.Rptr. 1714 (1984).

The hearing lasted seven days. Only two and a half hours were devoted to playing tapes of the wiretaps. Only one person who had not been indicted was named in court. The judge ruled that about half the evidence seized in response to what police heard on the wiretaps was inadmissible. A jury subsequently found the defendants guilty of gambling. They appealed, arguing that their Sixth Amendment right to a public trial had been violated by the closing of the suppression hearing. The Georgia Supreme Court denied their appeal, holding that the trial judge had acted properly.

The U.S. Supreme Court disagreed. Looking to *Globe, Richmond, Press-Enterprise,* and even to some of the opinions in *Gannett* for guidance, the Court concluded that although the three most recent decisions rested primarily on First Amendment grounds, the Sixth Amendment also implies the right of the press and public to attend not only a trial but suppression hearings as well. Indeed, the Court said that the "need for an open proceeding may be particularly strong with respect to suppression hearings." It noted that a "challenge to the seizure of evidence frequently attacks the conduct of police and prosecutor." Because the public has a strong interest in the exposure of police misconduct, suppression hearings generally should be open to public scrutiny, the Court said.

The effect of the decision has been to give the media and the public a right to intervene when a motion is made to close a suppression hearing, even when the motion is based on the defendant's Sixth Amendment right to a fair trial.

With its decision in *Press-Enterprise (II)* in 1986, the Supreme Court completed the undoing of the mischief caused by Stewart's opinion in *Gannett*. In this instance, a trial judge had closed the preliminary hearing of a nurse accused of administering massive and fatal doses of a heart stimulant to twelve persons. The hearing, to determine whether there was enough evidence to bring the nurse to trial, lasted forty-one days. Journalists

Press-Enterprise Co. v. Superior Court, 478 U.S. 1, 106 S.Ct. 2735, 92 L.Ed.2d 1, 13 Med.L.Rptr. 1001 (1986).

were denied not only access to the hearing but also access to a transcript after the hearing had been completed. California appellate courts upheld the decision of the trial judge, but on further appeal the U.S. Supreme Court reversed, seven to two.

Writing for the majority, Chief Justice Burger noted that more than nine in ten criminal cases are resolved without going to trial. In the usual procedure, the defendant agrees to plead guilty to a lesser charge, as in *Gannett*. As a consequence, Burger wrote, "the preliminary hearing is often the final and most important step in the criminal proceeding, . . . [and] in many cases provides the sole public observation of the criminal justice system."

The majority held that in this instance the judge's closing of the hearing violated a long tradition "of access to preliminary hearings of the type conducted in California." Burger concluded, as he had in *Richmond Newspapers* with respect to trials, that such hearings can be closed only if the defendant can prove a compelling reason for doing so. Such proof must demonstrate "a substantial probability that the defendant's right to a fair trial will be prejudiced by publicity that closure would prevent, and [that] reasonable alternatives to closure cannot adequately protect the defendant's fair trial rights." Burger suggested that careful voir dire usually can weed out potential jurors who might have been prejudiced by exposure to pretrial publicity. In any event, he concluded, closure of an entire forty-one-day hearing "would rarely be warranted."

At the time, some observers raised questions about the scope of the decision because Burger repeatedly used the clause "as conducted in California" to describe the kind of preliminary hearing at issue. Those doubts have been dispelled by subsequent lower-court decisions. For instance, the U.S. Court of Appeals for the Second Circuit relied on *Press-Enterprise (II)* and *Waller* in holding that journalists have a right of access not only to pretrial proceedings but to papers filed in conjunction with them.[42]

The court made this decision in a case involving Mario Biaggi, a member of Congress, and Meade Esposito, former chair of the executive committee of the Kings County Democratic Committee in Brooklyn. Both were accused of accepting bribes. They sought to suppress introduction of evidence obtained by electronic surveillance. The judge ruled that assertions made in written motions submitted to him proved that the surveillance had been properly authorized. However, he also ordered the papers sealed to protect the defendants' right to a fair trial and the privacy of persons who had not been indicted. Under challenge from the *New York Times,* the *New York Daily News,* and the Associated Press, the judge refused to grant a hearing on his order. The appellate court said that he should have done so. It also held that the public's and the media's qualified First Amendment right to attend a trial had been extended to nontrial hearings by the Supreme Court's decision in *Press-Enterprise (II).* That right also applies to the inspection of written motions, the court said. Release of some parts of the papers might unduly violate the privacy of others. If so, the judge could not so decide without granting the media appellants a hearing, and he would have to justify any decision to keep documents under seal.

Closure of suppression hearings, and even of some part or all of a trial, to ensure a defendant's right to a fair trial remains an option open to judges in highly publicized cases. However, the Supreme Court has repeatedly made it clear that closure is exceptional. In 1993 the Supreme Court held that even a criminal court rule providing a defendant with an optional private hearing to determine probable cause is unconstitutional. The Court, in a *per curiam* opinion, said that such a rule in Puerto Rican courts is irreconcilable with the principles of *Press-Enterprise (II).*[43] The Court also has left no doubt that journalists and the public have a right to object to closure. If an objec-

---

42.   New York Times Co. v. Biaggi, 828 F.2d 110 (2d Cir. 1987).
43.   El Vocero de Puerto Rico v. Puerto Rico, 113 S.Ct. 2004, 21 Med.L.Rptr. 1440 (1993).

tion is offered as a motion to the court, judges are required to stay the proceeding until a formal hearing can be conducted. Closure then can be ordered only if there is convincing evidence that a fair trial cannot be had otherwise.[44]

Protecting Jurors

In its *Sheppard* decision, the Supreme Court said that Judge Blythin had not protected the jurors from the media. The Court said that the judge had permitted the media to turn the jurors into celebrities by publicizing their names, addresses, and photographs. Consequently, the jurors were subjected to pressure from persons who sought to influence the jury's verdict. As a result of the Court's criticism, trial judges have tried various measures, including prior restraint, to protect jurors from the media. Some courts have sought to prevent disclosure of the names and addresses of jurors, and others have forbidden the sketching or photographing of them. Judges also have tried to prevent journalists and lawyers from interviewing jurors after they have reached their verdict.

Orders seeking to ensure the anonymity of jurors are justified on the ground that they will protect the panel from coercion. The few decisions in this area indicate that such orders will be upheld if the probability of coercion is high, if the restraint will indeed protect the identity of the jurors, and if there is convincing evidence that other less restrictive measures will not ensure a fair trial. These tests are derived from the Supreme Court's decision in *Nebraska Press Association*.

In a leading case, the New Mexico Supreme Court held that a trial judge acted improperly when, without notice and without a hearing, he ordered the media not to publish the names and addresses of jurors in the trial of one of several prisoners accused of leading a riot at the state penitentiary. The judge acted at the request of the defendant, who said he was afraid people might try to influence the jury against him. The prosecutor agreed with the request, saying that he too was afraid of jury tampering, because it had happened in the trial of another of the defendants.

State, ex rel. New Mexico Press Association v. Kaufman, 98 N.M. 261, 648 P.2d 300, 8 Med.L.Rptr. 1713 (N.Mex. 1982).

Associations representing the state's newspapers and broadcasters appealed. A unanimous supreme court said that "mere speculation that publishing the names of jurors might expose them to intimidation" was not enough. Citing *Richmond Newspapers,* the court held that the trial judge had erred at the start by not giving the media notice of the defendant's request and an opportunity to contest it. Indeed, it said, "[a]nyone present should be given an opportunity to object."

---

44. The fact that convincing evidence of the likelihood of unfairness is possible has been repeatedly demonstrated. See Sacramento Bee v. United States District Court, 565 F.2d 477, 7 Med.L.Rptr. 1929, rehearing denied, 7 Med.L.Rptr. 2376 (9th Cir. 1981); Federated Publications v. Swedberg, 633 P.2d 74, 7 Med.L.Rptr. 1865 (Wash. 1981); In re South Carolina Press Association, 946 F.2d 1037, 219 Med.L.Rptr. 1432 (4th Cir. 1991).

The court then turned to the standards to be applied in deciding whether jurors' names can be kept out of the media. Citing *Nebraska Press Association,* the court said that the judge should begin by examining "the nature and extent of the evil" that would come from publication. Then the judge should ask if effective alternatives to a gag order are available. The final question is whether the order will work. In this instance, the court said that although a great deal of publicity did surround the trial, no firm evidence indicated that anyone would try to intimidate the jury. The judge himself had recognized that an effective alternative was available when he had considered and rejected a motion to sequester the jury. Finally, no evidence indicated that his order would prevent people from identifying the jurors. Their names had been read in open court. The jury list, including addresses and telephone numbers, was on file in the office of the clerk of courts. Under New Mexico law, the list was a public record.

However, the court stopped short of saying that trial judges could never restrain publication of jurors' names. The court held "that a prior restraint on publication . . . must be based upon imperative circumstances supported by a record that clearly demonstrates that a defendant's right to a fair trial will be jeopardized and that there are no reasonable alternatives to protect that right."

In some instances, that standard of proof has been met. A federal district court in Nevada held that a judge acted properly in prohibiting the publication of the names of jurors who were called to impose a sentence on a man whom another jury had convicted of murder.[45] But the court emphasized that the case was an exceptional one. The conviction was controversial and had generated much public criticism and discussion. The likelihood that jurors would be subjected to pressure was high. Since the judge's order expired with the jury's decision on sentencing, the district court concluded that no public purpose would be served by publication of the names on the first day of the trial rather than the last. This was particularly true, the court said, because the only use the public might make of the names was an improper one—jury tampering.

A Delaware judge went so far as to identify prospective jurors only by number to protect them from publicity. He acted after the *Wilmington News-Journal* had published profiles of jurors in another sensational murder case. In that instance, the judge sealed the jury list after the first ten members of the panel said they did not think they could render a fair verdict if they became subject to media attention. After the jury was seated, the judge released the names, but he also lectured the newspapers on what he saw as the hazards of publishing jury profiles.[46] Jury service, he said, is "the heart of American justice," adding: "With all its strengths, it (the jury), like any other human component, is not immune to injury by vivisection. The media's ability to cut often exceeds its ability to repair the damage it may inflict."

A California judge in Los Angeles, facing what has since been called the trial of the century, permitted reporters covering the O. J. Simpson case to publish jury profiles of prospective jurors.[47] However, jurors could be identified only by badge number, and to assure continued protection of jury anonymity, Judge Lance Ito ordered reporters

---

45. Schuster v. Bowen, 347 F.Supp. 319 (D.Nev. 1972).
46. Bruce W. Sanford, "Jurors in the Spotlight," *Quill,* November 1989, pp. 12–13.
47. David Margolick, "Simpson Jury Pool Offers a Self-Portrait," *New York Times,* 14 October 1994, p. A10.

not to identify any potential juror, even by badge number, while being questioned during voir dire,[48] nor to photograph or televise the faces of jurors during the trial.

With respect to an order forbidding the televising or sketching of jurors, the Arizona Supreme Court applied the *Nebraska Press Association* test and concluded that such an order could not be justified under the circumstances of a case there.[49] The court found that the danger posed by televising the sketches—that the jurors would base their verdict on fear—was not grave. The court said that an alternative to the restraint was available: Potential jurors who conceded they might be influenced by fear could be excused. Finally, the order was ineffective because it did not apply to publication of sketches by newspapers. However, in another instance, the Fourth Circuit let stand an order forbidding the sketching of prospective jurors in the courthouse.[50]

Appellate courts generally have not looked with favor on attempts by trial judges to prevent reporters and others from talking to jurors about the verdict. In a notable exception, the Fifth Circuit Court of Appeals upheld an order prohibiting reporters from asking jurors how other members of the jury had voted and from making repeated requests for interviews with jurors who had refused to talk.[51] The court said that the trial court had not abused its discretion in forbidding the badgering of jurors. Further, the court said that the vote of a juror who refused to be interviewed is information "not available to the public at large." Therefore, there is no violation of First Amendment rights in forbidding reporters to seek such information.[52]

Federal circuit courts, including the Fifth, have held that orders forbidding reporters and others to talk to jurors must be narrowly tailored to serve an important interest if they are to pass First Amendment analysis. The Fifth Circuit ruled that an order forbidding any person to interview jurors without the trial judge's permission swept too broadly.[53] The trial court's order said that permission to interview would be granted only on a showing of good cause. The appellate court said that "the First Amendment right to gather news" was reason enough to overrule such a vaguely phrased order. The Third Circuit struck down an order forbidding reporters from attempting to persuade jurors to be interviewed. The court said that such a restriction cannot stand in the absence of any finding by the trial court that the attempts were harassing or intrusive. However, the court noted that jurors are not required to give interviews and may be forbidden from divulging how other jurors voted.[54] The Tenth Circuit struck down a double-barreled edict forbidding jurors from discussing a highly publicized armed robbery case and ordering everyone, including reporters, to "stay away from the jurors."[55] The court said that the judge had failed to meet the heavy burden of proving that the restraint was necessary.

---

48. Kenneth B. Noble, "Simpson Judge Reverses Ruling and Reopens Trial to the Media," *New York Times,* 22 October 1994, p. A1.
49. KPNX Broadcasting Co. v. Maricopa County Superior Court, 139 Ariz. 246, 678 P.2d 431 (Ariz. 1984).
50. Society of Professional Journalists v. Martin, 556 F.2d 706 (4th Cir. 1977), cert. denied, 434 U.S. 1022 (1978).
51. United States v. Harrelson, 713 F.2d 1114 (5th Cir. 1983), cert.denied, 465 U.S. 1041 (1984).
52. See also United States v. Giraldi, 858 F.Supp. 85 (1994).
53. In re Express-News Corp., 695 F.2d 807 (5th Cir. 1982).
54. U.S. v. Antar, 38 F.3d 1348, 22 Med.L.Rptr. 2417 (5th Cir. 1994).
55. United States v. Sherman, 581 F.2d 1358 (9th Cir. 1978).

Like the Supreme Court's decision in *Nebraska Press,* these cases leave open the possibility that a judge can issue orders designed to protect jurors from the media. But if the orders are to survive First Amendment scrutiny, they must be narrowly drawn and clear evidence must show that the orders will protect the defendant's right to a fair trial that otherwise would be in jeopardy. It is equally clear that if orders protecting the anonymity of jurors are to work, courts also must seal jury lists and conduct the voir dire in such a way as to avoid naming the jurors.

CONDUCTING A FAIR TRIAL IN PUBLIC

The previous sections of this chapter tell the story of conflict and accommodation between the public's right of access to criminal proceedings and the defendant's right to a fair trial. Throughout the conflict, journalists have portrayed themselves as defenders of the First Amendment and the people's right to know. Criminal defense lawyers have portrayed themselves as the protectors of misfits who wrongly would be deprived of their liberty or their lives if the Sixth Amendment did not shield them from publicity.

Nevertheless, the story of accommodation is one about how the courts have managed to reconcile these conflicting constitutional positions. Judges, literally caught in the middle, have fashioned legal principles that seem to work reasonably well, for when the media, print and electronic, give saturation coverage to major crime stories, it is evident that defendants can, even in the most highly publicized cases, get a fair trial. A fair and public trial is possible in part because the courts recognize that not all publicity is prejudicial, that proceedings conducted in public view are inherently less likely to be subject to abuse, and that judges do have the authority to control their courtrooms in the interest of fairness and justice.

Nonprejudicial Publicity

Need jurors be completely uninformed about the case they are asked to decide? That question has confronted judges since Chief Justice Marshall dealt with it in the *Burr* case. In that instance, Marshall said the jurors need not be completely uninformed, but they do need to have their minds open to the testimony they will hear in the courtroom. He recognized that some defendants, like former Vice President Burr, might be so widely known that only the least intelligent or least involved members of society would have no knowledge of them. Could such persons be entrusted with resolving difficult cases? Would they be likely to understand the issues and give them serious attention?

The Supreme Court has answered those questions in the context of at least two cases in which defendants had been found guilty of highly publicized crimes. In each instance, the Court sustained the convictions, holding that factual information about suspects and the crimes for which they were being tried was not in itself prejudicial. The decisions reinforced the position taken by many judges that impartial jurors need not be uninformed and that rigorous voir dire will eliminate those who have fixed opinions as to guilt or innocence.

The first case involved Jack Murphy, one of the most flamboyant criminals of the mid-twentieth century. Murphy first gained media attention in 1964 for his role in stealing the Star of India sapphire from an elaborately protected case in a New York City museum. That episode became the subject of a movie. Later, Murphy went to Miami Beach, where he became known as Murph the Surf.

Murphy v. *Florida,* **421 U.S. 794, 95 S.Ct. 2031, 44 L.Ed.2d 589, 1 Med.L.Rptr. 1232 (1975).**

He was handsome and handy with women. He used those attributes to gain entry to the homes of the wealthy, from which he took jewels and cash. One such episode resulted in murder, for which Murphy was convicted. All these escapades were given heavy news coverage. When Murphy resumed his criminal career after a prison term, police captured him and three accomplices as they fled from a robbery in a Miami Beach home.

At the trial, Murphy's lawyer argued that news coverage of his client's activities made a fair trial impossible. He supported that position by offering the court a voluminous file of newspaper clippings and transcripts of news broadcasts. The judge conducted a careful voir dire and seated a jury that he believed to be impartial. Murphy's lawyer took little part in the trial, resting his case on the belief that any conviction would be reversed on appeal because of publicity given to his client. The jury convicted Murphy. A state appellate court confirmed. Murphy's lawyer turned to the federal courts for relief, arguing that his client was a victim of the news media. When he was rebuffed there, he went to the U.S. Supreme Court, which, in *Murphy* v., *Florida,* affirmed the conviction with only one dissent.

Justice Thurgood Marshall wrote for the Court. He said that the earlier decisions in *Irvin, Rideau, Estes,* and *Sheppard* do not stand for the proposition that juror exposure to factual information about a defendant and his or her crime is prejudicial on its face. Reasoning as Chief Justice John Marshall had in *Burr,* he wrote that jurors need not come into the courtroom "wholly ignorant of the facts, for this would establish an impossible standard." Thurgood Marshall added that voir dire must be used diligently to find whether exposure to factual information has led a potential juror to a fixed conclusion about the defendant's guilt or innocence. Further, the judge selecting the jury must look beyond the courtroom into the community. Only if the "general atmosphere . . . is sufficiently inflammatory" should the judge disregard a prospective juror's assertions of impartiality.

The Court found no evidence of such an atmosphere in Miami. Nor could it find anything in the clippings submitted by Murphy's lawyer likely to arouse strong emotions against his client. The news clippings merely recited the facts of a criminal career. This decision sent a clear message to trial and appeals courts. A mere showing of factual news stories will not alone support the conclusion that an impartial jury cannot be had. Reinforcing a point made by Justice Clark in *Irvin,* the Court emphasized that jurors need not be completely ignorant of a case to be fair. Beyond that, the Court was reiterating its faith in the ability of careful, conscientious judges to use voir dire to screen out potential jurors who would resist the impressions conveyed by the evidence.

Murphy remained in prison until 1986, when he was paroled at the age of forty-eight on the condition that he remain on probation for the rest of his life. He said he had undergone a religious conversion and would "make his peace preaching" and his living by lecturing and selling surfing paintings.[56]

Nearly a decade later, the Court reinforced its decision in *Murphy,* upholding the conviction of a high school teacher, Jon E. Yount, who had twice been found guilty of the stabbing death of a female student. Upon his arrest, the teacher confessed. At trial, he pleaded temporary insanity, but a jury found him guilty and the judge sentenced him to life in prison. On appeal, the Pennsylvania Supreme Court held that Yount had not been adequately represented by counsel when he made his confession. The court ordered a new trial. All these events were widely publicized.

Patton v. *Yount,* 467 U.S. 1025, 104 S.Ct. 2885, 81 L.Ed.2d 847 (1984).

Because of the publicity, the nature of the crime—the victim had been left in the woods to die—and the small size of the community in which the crime occurred, virtually everyone called for jury duty in the second trial was familiar with the facts. Nevertheless, the trial judge refused repeated motions for a change of venue. He conducted a thorough voir dire, questioning 163 prospective jurors before settling on a panel that he believed to be free of fixed opinions. That jury, too, found the defendant guilty, and Yount again was sentenced to life in prison.

Like Sam Sheppard, Yount served ten years of his sentence before he was able to convince a court that publicity had kept him from getting a fair trial. The U.S. Court of Appeals for the Third Circuit noted that the voir dire had disclosed that all but two of the 163 persons questioned had heard of the case and more than three-fourths of them had had some opinion as to Yount's guilt. These were higher proportions than those that had led the Supreme Court to reverse the conviction in *Irvin.* The court ordered a new trial.

The Supreme Court agreed to review the decision and reversed, six to two. The Court took the case, it said, "to consider the problem of pervasive media publicity that now arises so frequently in the trial of sensational criminal cases." The majority noted that four years had elapsed between the two trials. Jury selection for the second trial had occurred "at a time when prejudicial publicity was greatly diminished and community sentiment had softened." The two newspapers published in the county in which the trial was held had published only a few articles about it, and "many of these were extremely brief announcements." During the voir dire, papers had printed daily articles, "but these too were purely factual, generally discussing not the crime or prior prosecutions, but the prolonged process of jury selection."

The majority concluded that there was neither "the barrage of inflammatory publicity" condemned in *Sheppard* and *Murphy* nor the "huge . . . wave of passion" that led to the reversal in *Irvin.* The majority made much of the passage of time as an antidote for prejudicial publicity, stating that the voir dire had indeed revealed that many of the jurors had held opinions about Yount's guilt, but "time had weakened or eliminated any conviction they had had." Nor had old passions been revived by the kind of

---

56.   Associated Press, "'Murph the Surf' Is Now Back on Free Turf," *Louisville Courier-Journal,* 11 November 1986.

publicity that preceded the second trial. The Court concluded that the judge had used the voir dire reasonably to select those "who had forgotten or would need to be persuaded again."

Thus, in *Patton* as in *Murphy,* the Court said that it is not the amount of publicity about a crime, but the nature of that publicity, that determines whether the atmosphere has been so infected with prejudice as to make a fair trial impossible. If the news stories are factual in nature, and if there is no attempt on the part of the news media to convict the defendant before trial, a fair trial in the courtroom is possible, even though prospective jurors have read or heard the stories. The law does not expect jurors to be ignorant of the facts. It does require that their minds be open to the evidence and that they base their decision on it. Any less realistic standard would make it virtually impossible for defendants in highly publicized criminal cases to be tried at all.

The Photographer and the Courtroom

The Supreme Court's decision in *Estes* condemned still and television photographers as contributors to an atmosphere of prejudice in the courtroom. The Court came within one vote of holding that the presence of photographers would always make a fair trial impossible by denying the defendant the due process guaranteed by the Fifth and Fourteenth Amendments. At that point, in 1965, the future of courtroom photography appeared bleak.

The *Estes* case occurred because at the time Texas, with Colorado, was one of two states that permitted photographers to use their cameras in courtrooms. The decision was, in part, a reaction to the obtrusive nature of the still and television cameras then in use. Photographic equipment was bulky, sometimes noisy, and required special lighting. However, technical advances even then were leading to smaller cameras and to film and videotape that could be used in available light. Justice John Marshall Harlan took note of these advances in writing his concurring opinion in *Estes.* Although he agreed with four other justices in holding that the use of cameras in the courtroom had kept Estes from getting a fair trial, he was not willing to join them in holding that that would always be the case. Harlan argued that further advances in technology might permit unobtrusive photography in the courtroom. Therefore, he wrote, he was unwilling to close the door on future experimentation with courtroom photography.

In time, Florida was one of several states that took up Harlan's invitation to experiment further with photojournalism in courtrooms. The Florida Supreme Court decided, in response to a request from the Post-Newsweek television stations in Jacksonville and Miami, to permit televising of court proceedings on an experimental basis.[57] Reaction was favorable, and the rule was made permanent.[58]

The guidelines regulating photography in Florida are quite strict.[59] Only one camera and one operator are permitted inside the courtroom. Once placed, the camera can-

---

57. Petition of the Post-Newsweek Stations, Florida, Inc., 327 So.2d 1 (Fla.App. 1976), 347 So.2d 402 (Fla. 1976).
58. 370 So.2d 764 (Fla. 1979).
59. Post-Newsweek Stations, 370 So.2d 764, at 778–779, 783–784 (Fla. 1979).

A television camera focuses on a panel of judges for the Courtroom Television Network. Forty-seven states and some federal courts now allow the use of cameras in the courtroom, but much of that coverage is limited to appellate courts, which ordinarily do not hear witnesses or take testimony. *(Courtesy Courtroom Television Network)*

not be moved during the trial. Nor can the operator change lenses, film, or videotape while court is in session. Sound may be recorded only through the court's own audio pickup system. Operators are forbidden to record conferences between the lawyers, between parties and counsel, and with the judge. The judge can, without being subject to appeal, forbid televising or recording of the testimony of certain witnesses. The jury cannot be filmed under any circumstances. In short, television is limited to covering only what members of the jury can see and hear, and sometimes not all of that. Judges are admonished that their first obligation is to ensure the defendant a fair trial. Judges who conclude that television would prevent a fair trial can keep cameras out of the courtroom.

During the experimental period a judge of a Dade County court permitted limited televising of a trial that had attracted a great deal of attention. Two Miami Beach police officers were charged with burglary after an amateur radio operator had heard them talking over their portable radios while they committed the crime. When they were brought to trial, a television camera recorded part of the testimony of the radio operator. It also recorded the closing arguments of counsel for both sides. Only two minutes and fifty-five seconds of videotape were used on the air, and the editor selected only those parts depicting the prosecution's side. When the police officers, Noel Chandler and Robert Granger, were found guilty, they used the presence of the television camera as the basis for an appeal. They got nowhere in the Florida courts, but on further appeal the Supreme Court took their case. In *Chandler* v. *Florida,* the Court affirmed the convictions.

Chandler v. *Florida,*
449 U.S. 560, 101 S.Ct. 802,
66 L.Ed.2d 740,
7 Med.L.Rptr. 1041 (1981).

The attorney for Chandler and Granger argued that the Supreme Court had held in *Estes* that no televised trial could be fair. Chief Justice Warren Burger, writing for a majority of the Court, rejected that argument. He noted that only four justices had taken that position. The fifth member of the majority in *Estes,* Justice Harlan, had confined his reasoning to the facts of that case. Although Harlan agreed that the presence of cameras had kept Estes from getting a fair trial, he had made a point of noting that smaller, less obtrusive cameras might not interfere with a fair trial in the future. Focusing on Harlan's concurring opinion in *Estes,* Chief Justice Burger said that the burden was on Chandler's and Granger's attorney to prove that their trial had not been fair.

The chief justice's conclusions in *Chandler* can be summarized as follows: The Supreme Court has no supervisory authority over state courts. Therefore, they are free to permit photography in the courtroom if they wish. The only limiting provisions at the federal level are the clause in the Sixth Amendment to the Constitution guaranteeing trial by an impartial jury and the clause in the Fourteenth Amendment forbidding deprivation of life, liberty, or property without due process of law. As long as the presence of cameras cannot be shown to violate either of those provisions, federal courts have no basis for interfering.

There is no firm evidence, Burger continued, to prove that the mere presence of cameras in the courtroom has an effect on the participants. It follows that federal courts cannot ban state experiments with photographic coverage of trials on the mere suspicion that prejudice will somehow occur. Therefore, the Supreme Court had no basis for concluding that the trial of Chandler and Granger had been inherently unfair.

Nor, the Supreme Court concluded, could the defendants offer facts to prove that they had been the victims of a prejudiced jury. Jurors were asked during voir dire whether the presence of cameras would keep them from deciding the case solely on the basis of the evidence. The fact that a jury was seated demonstrated that the judge and lawyers for both sides believed the jurors could do so.

The Supreme Court's decision in *Chandler* clearly rejected the many assumptions about the effects of television that are found in the leading opinion in *Estes*. The effect of *Chandler* has been to encourage state courts to adopt rules permitting still photographers and television crews to cover their proceedings, and by 1995, courts in forty-seven states had done so.[60] Some have limited photo coverage to appellate courts, which ordinarily do not hear witnesses and take testimony. In all instances, rules of court give the judge broad authority to regulate the use of cameras to avoid a disturbance or other interference with the fairness of the proceeding.

The Federal Rules of Criminal Procedure continue to forbid photography in federal courts, although some federal courts have experimented with cameras in civil cases.[61] Alcee Hastings, a federal district court judge in Miami who was accused of accepting bribes, challenged the criminal rules by asking that his trial be covered by television.

---

60. Only Indiana, Mississippi, and South Dakota still bar cameras from state courts. *News Notes, Media Law Reporter,* June 6, 1995, p. 2.

61. In re Judicial Conference Guidelines, 18 Med.L.Rptr. 1270 (U.S. Judicial Conference 1990). This authorization for a pilot program in civil cases expired in June 1994. In September the Federal Judicial Conference of the United States voted against allowing cameras in federal courts. In March 1995 the conference softened its rejection by expressing a willingness to consider new proposals for pilot programs and studies. *News Notes, Media Law Reporter,* June 6, 1995, p. 2 (Washington, D.C.: Bureau of National Affairs).

The Eleventh Circuit Court of Appeals held that only a minimal First Amendment interest would be served by such coverage and rejected his request.[62] Hastings was tried without the presence of cameras and was acquitted. On another occasion, the Supreme Court refused to review a decision of the U.S. Court of Appeals for the Sixth Circuit upholding a district judge's refusal to permit photographic coverage of the trial of Teamsters Union officials on embezzlement charges.[63] Television and radio stations and still photographers had argued that photo and audio coverage of the trial would serve an important First Amendment interest. The trial court judge said that the ban on such coverage served "the significant government interest of promoting fair and accurate fact-finding by assuring that litigants and witnesses are not distracted by media shyness or showboating."

Thus, although the First Amendment ensures that the public and reporters have a right of access to courtrooms and news of the courts, the Amendment does not go so far as to mandate a right to photograph court proceedings. However, neither the fair-trial clause of the Sixth Amendment nor the due process clauses of the Fifth and Fourteenth stand as barriers against photographs. The Constitution is neutral toward photography in the courtroom as long as the judge takes proper steps to ensure a fair trial. Judges remain divided as to whether the presence of cameras, particularly television cameras, distorts the conduct of the trial, although by now most seem willing to accept them.

In the Professional World

A criminal trial is not a sporting event, nor is it a television drama. In fact, most trials tend to be more boring than dramatic. They drone to a conclusion, unattended by anyone except a few friends and relatives of the defendant and the victim, and courthouse hangers-on. Only the celebrated case, involving a prominent defendant or victim, or a particularly monstrous crime, attracts full-time attention from the news media. Most of us can easily list the defendants in the big cases: O.J. Simpson, acquitted of murdering his wife and her friend in Los Angeles; Susan Smith, convicted of drowning her children in Union, South Carolina; Timothy McVeigh, accused of bombing a federal building in Oklahoma City; Michael Jackson, accused of molesting young boys. Few of us can remember the names of the hundreds of burglars, molesters, embezzlers, robbers, rapists, and thieves mentioned briefly on the news as they made their way routinely through the criminal justice system. Yet, whether the case is boring or celebrated, it harbors this important reality: The defendant is gambling his or her freedom, and perhaps even his or her life, on the outcome. Criminal trials are serious business.

With most news media, truly sensational coverage of the police beat and the courts can be found only in the supermarket and television tabloids or the mi-

---

62.   United States v. Hastings, 695 F.2d 1278 (11th Cir. 1983).
63.   "Supreme Court Rejects Appeal in Courtroom Camera Case," *Editor & Publisher,* 10 December 1988, p. 25.

crofilmed copies of front pages from another era. Police and court beats are more often covered with an eye for stories that illustrate trends, that will alert the public to problems with a particular kind of crime, or that will serve as a check on the performance of police, prosecutors, and judges. Much crime information is reduced to a listing for the record of offenses reported, of arrests made, and of court actions taken.

The occasional, celebrated case is what raises tensions between the legal system and the media. Judges who must try such cases are very much aware of the duty imposed by *Sheppard*.[64] Judges must do all they can to protect the defendant's rights or risk having the verdict overturned on appeal. No judge likes being overruled by a higher court. And prosecutors must be cautious in talking with reporters, lest they disclose information that might be seen later as grounds for reversal. If there has been any publicity at all, defense attorneys are under an obligation at the start to seek a change of venue. If that fails, they are likely to appeal a conviction on grounds that the publicity prevented the defendant from getting a fair trial. A defense lawyer who does not raise such questions runs the risk of being accused of offering inadequate counsel. These pressures on the lawyers and the judge may well result in pressures on the news media also, as the cases in this chapter illustrate.

These cases also illustrate that the media are free to publish or broadcast any scrap of information they can learn about the crime, the suspect, the victim, and the possible witnesses. A judge seeking to order the media not to use information in their possession is unlikely to meet the test prescribed in *Nebraska Press Association*. Editors who supervise coverage of a celebrated case act in the knowledge that the only restraints are those they impose on themselves.

All of the major professional organizations representing journalists, print or electronic, have adopted codes of ethics. All recognize that prejudicial publicity can interfere with the right to a fair trial and suggest that it be minimized. However, all of these codes are written in general terms, and journalists have resisted attempts to enforce them.

As cases like *Murphy* and *Patton* suggest, much crime and court coverage is not sensational and prejudicial. It is not unusual for the media to withhold such information as a defendant's prior criminal record, either until the trial ends or the record has been introduced in court. Many editors understand that coverage that results in a change of venue or a reversal of a conviction only adds to the costs of supporting the courts, costs the taxpayers must bear.

Yet there are limits to the self-restraint of even the most conscientious editors. In a competitive market, if one outlet uses leaked information, no matter how prejudicial, others will scramble to get it, too. KNXT's use in Los Angeles of a videotape supposedly showing John DeLorean caught up in a cocaine deal was followed by news stories describing the taped scene in detail. Even the supermarket tabloids can have an impact on what gets coverage. Mainstream reporters

---

64. Judge Lance Ito in the Simpson murder case may have had a special reason to be aware of the *Sheppard* decision. Sam Sheppard's lawyer, F. Lee Bailey, was a member of the Simpson defense team.

might complain about the *National Enquirer,* but they apparently kept an eye on the publication during the Simpson trial. It was from the *National Enquirer* that they learned and then reported that O.J. Simpson had purchased a fifteen-inch stiletto, and that for a television program called *Frogmen* he had been trained in techniques for muffling screams while slitting a throat.[65] Regardless of how it gets there, once information finds its way into the stream of public discussion, it is apparently fair game.

Nor is competition the only factor that may lead editors and producers to ignore a code of ethics. When someone runs amok, kills several persons, and then talks about it, as in *Nebraska Press Association,* it is illogical to believe that no one will publish or broadcast those facts. As the Supreme Court said, if the facts aren't used by the media, word of mouth not only will circulate them, but enlarge on them. The potential for harmful rumor was a factor in the editor's decision to publish in *Dickinson.* If the police think seriously enough that someone is plotting to kill the mayor that they make an arrest to prevent it, the public ought to know. In that instance, the editors thought the facts might defuse racial tensions that already were running high. Clearly, there are times when the news media should make every effort to get the facts of a crime and share them with the public, with as much detail and video as is available.

But can there be too much detail and too much video? Do televised trials, for example, really serve the public interest—especially trials that continue for months? Millions of Americans watched the Simpson trial day after day. Did that gavel-to-gavel coverage serve the public interest in fairness, justice, and judicial accountability?

Fred Graham thinks so. Graham, a lawyer, is the chief anchor for Court TV and a former Supreme Court reporter for the *New York Times* and correspondent for CBS News. Graham thinks that cameras in the courtroom saved the Simpson trial from disaster. "The Simpson case . . . settled down because viewers complained about the mess they were watching, prompting Judge Ito to take necessary steps. Blaming the televised coverage for the trial's early chaos and then calling for a ban on cameras in all courtrooms is a classic case of blaming the messenger," wrote Graham in an Op-Ed piece in the *New York Times* published near the end of the trial.[66]

Moreover, Graham thinks the coverage led to public debate about important issues that had received little public attention previously: "Does money count too much in a defense? Are lawyers given too much leeway to try to confuse the issues and obscure the truth? Should juries be picked by lot rather than by the lawyers? Should the unanimous jury be replaced by, say, a 10 to 2 vote?[67] In short, Graham thinks that the kind of live, continuous coverage the nation experienced in the O.J. Simpson case is, in the end, good for a democratic society.

---

65. David Margolick, "The Enquirer: Required Reading in Simpson Case," *New York Times,* 24 October 1994, p. A6.
66. Fred Graham, "The Ground Glass of Reality," *New York Times,* 5 July 1995.
67. Ibid.

Jane Kirtley thinks so, too. Kirtley, a lawyer and executive director of the Reporters Committee for Freedom of the Press, wrote in *USA Today:* "The bottom line is that cameras in the courts are good news for our democracy. They strengthen public understanding and public confidence in the judicial system."

If you doubt that, think about the impact of camera coverage on the public reaction to the acquittal of William Kennedy Smith. Because cameras were allowed in the trial, members of the public could see how the prosecution and the defense presented their cases. They could assess the credibility of the witnesses. And they could judge for themselves whether justice was done.[68]

But not everyone is convinced. Kathryn Ross, a criminal defense attorney in Lynnwood, Washington, responded to Kirtley this way:

In most cases, cameras should not be in courtrooms. Here's why:

- The broadcasting of pretrial hearings involving the admissibility of evidence can prejudice potential jurors by exposing them to evidence that may not be allowed at the trial.
- Witnesses who hold information favorable to the defendant may be fearful of being identified with a person accused of a heinous crime. Being photographed could endanger a witness and even cause the witness to alter testimony.
- . . . [Most defendants] do not have experience presenting themselves in public situations. Regardless of how truthful they may be, being photographed can increase defendants' nervousness and create an appearance of deception.
- Cameras during the trial can make jurors justifiably afraid that they will be identified and harassed if they return an unpopular verdict.
- Cameras may (adversely) affect the performance of lawyers . . . and it would then deprive the defendant of effective counsel and a fair trial.[69]

The debate about the proper coverage of police and courts will continue, but one thing is clear: The media are the means by which most people learn to understand how justice works or doesn't work in the United States. If the system seems to be working, there is little more the media need do than make the system visible and understandable. But if the system is not working properly, different considerations come into play. If the police are corrupt, the prosecutors lazy, and judges incompetent, then the public needs to know. One way to expose such problems is for the news media to dig out the facts pointing to the guilt of suspects who go free or to the innocence of a suspect who is wrongfully convicted. In such situations, editors can hope that, given the facts, the voters will set things right at the next election.

---

68. Jane Kirtley, "Do TV Cameras Belong in the Courtroom? Yes," *USA Today,* 10 August 1994, p. A9.
69. Kathryn Ross, "Do TV Cameras Belong in the Courtroom? No," *USA Today,* 10 August 1994, p. A9.

In any event, as the cases in this chapter suggest, whether they are covering the occasional highly newsworthy crime or the routine, competent journalists are aware that someone, at some point, may try to hide things from them. When that happens, reporters usually are quick to assert a right of access, even though they may decide not to use the information they obtain. As the earlier cases in this textbook tell us, the First Amendment long has meant that each of us, journalist or not, has a right to decide what information we will share with others. The cases in this chapter also tell us that the First Amendment gives us the right to insist on reasonable access to news of the courts.

FOR REVIEW

1. Distinguish between a hearing and a trial. As far as a right of access is concerned, is that difference significant?

2. Plea bargaining sometimes becomes an issue in states where judges and prosecutors are elected. Why might that be?

3. Define "voir dire." What is its purpose?

4. Define "impartial juror." Why is the term important?

5. What kinds of information are considered likely to induce prejudice in jurors?

6. Outline and define the procedures that a judge is expected to take to ensure a defendant's right to a fair trial (*Sheppard* v. *Maxwell*).

7. What did the Supreme Court's decision in *Murphy* v. *Florida* contribute to the definition of a fair trial?

8. What is meant by the term "gag order"? Is such an order ever proper?

9. Assess the likelihood that a gag order might be imposed on journalists covering a trial. What should be done if such an order is issued? Why?

10. What is meant by a First Amendment right of access to the courts? How did the Supreme Court rationalize such a right? Why did some justices have reservations about it?

11. You are a photographer confronting a judge who does not permit photography in her courtroom. What arguments would you use in an attempt to persuade her to change her mind? Now you are the judge. Given that you have a principled belief that cameras do not belong in the courtroom, how would you respond to the arguments you have advanced as a photographer? If you were the defendant in a highly publicized criminal trial, what position would you urge your lawyer to take with respect to cameras in the courtroom? Why?

12. You have received a summons to jury duty in the trial of a highly placed cocaine distributor. What position would you take with respect to an open voir dire and release of your name and address to the news media? If you were a reporter covering that trial, what is the likelihood that you could insist and obtain an open voir dire and access to the names and addresses of the jurors? In each of your roles, refer to appropriate legal precedents.

CHAPTER 8

It is a legal principle of long standing that justice demands the right to each person's evidence and consequently that the courts have authority, grounded in the Constitution, to summon as witnesses anyone who may have direct knowledge of a crime or the subject matter of a civil action. The Sixth Amendment, which gives suspects a right to a public trial by an impartial jury, also gives them the right "to have compulsory process for obtaining witnesses" in their behalf. This is a reference to the subpoena power—the power of a court to issue an official order summoning witnesses to appear and testify. This power is available to all who are directly involved in a legal proceeding, civil or criminal, including plaintiffs, defendants, prosecutors, grand juries, and judges. Anyone who refuses to obey an order to appear is in contempt and may be punished by the judge. The subpoena power is based on the theory that a court is more likely to reach a proper verdict if it hears evidence from all who have knowledge of the facts of the case than it is if some are excused.

THE JOURNALIST'S PRIVILEGE: CONFIDENTIALITY

Therefore, the courts have been reluctant to grant exceptions to the principle that all should testify. Certain exceptions, called "privileges," have been granted in recognition of special circumstances. The strongest of these is found in the Fifth Amendment, which says, in part: "No person . . . shall be compelled in any criminal case to be a witness against himself." This exception was put into the Constitution as a guard against the use of torture to force confessions, and it means what it says: No matter how guilty a suspect may be, any confession must be completely voluntary and made in full knowledge of the consequences. If suspects do not want to plead guilty, they have the right to remain silent and make the prosecutor prove the charges against them.

Courts have recognized other privileges to respect confidential relationships. Some states have written these privileges into rules of court or into statutes. The most common is the husband-wife privilege. Few courts require one spouse to testify against the other. Other common law privileges protect lawyer-client, physician-patient, and cleric-penitent relationships. The courts recognize that lawyers cannot adequately protect clients who tell them less than the truth. Physicians may make wrong diagnoses if patients withhold information. Priests cannot grant full absolution to penitents who do not confess fully. In all instances, the receivers of the information are bound by codes of ethics not to disclose it to others without the permission of the giver. Generally, courts have converted these codes into privileges, but they are not absolute. Physicians, for instance, are required to report suspicious wounds and suspected child abuse to authorities, and certain contagious diseases to the board of health.

For years, journalists sought, with little success, to have courts recognize their confidential relationship with some of their news sources and protect it as privileged. They argued that they serve a public purpose when they investigate wrongdoing, particularly on the part of public officials, and call public attention to it. They argued further that some of their information comes from sources who would disclose it only on the condition that the reporter not identify them. Such sources feared they might lose their jobs or suffer physical harm if their identity became known to anyone other than the reporter. Through the years, the promise to protect a source has become part of the journalistic code. Journalists who were asked to identify confidential sources argued that were they to do so, few sources would trust them again, and their effectiveness would be ended. Until recent times, few courts recognized a privilege for journalists. As a consequence, a number of reporters and editors have gone to jail or paid fines rather than break their word to a source.

As far back as 1896, the Maryland legislature gave enough credence to the journalists' arguments to enact a law defining reporters and giving them a right in some in-

A fire bomb is thrown at a passing motorist during a riot in Los Angeles after a jury's acquittal in 1992 of four police officers charged with the beating of an African-American suspect named Rodney King. This was one of the photographs subpoenaed by police seeking to identify rioters. *(Bob Tur and Robert Clark, © 1992 Los Angeles News Service)*

stances to protect their sources. Such statutes are called shield laws. More than half the states now have such laws. They range from near absolute to limited in their protection.

Journalists who were served with subpoenas to appear as witnesses also argued for recognition of either a common law privilege or one grounded in the First Amendment. Until 1972, they did so with little success. In that year, in *Branzburg* v. *Hayes*,[1] the Supreme Court told three reporters that they were like everyone else and would have to honor subpoenas ordering them to appear before grand juries seeking information about possible crime. In doing so, the Court appeared to reject the reporters' argument that the First Amendment should give some protection to their promises to confidential sources. However, the justices were so divided in their reasoning that many courts now read the decision as creating a limited First Amendment privilege for journalists. Some state courts, reluctant to invoke the First Amendment, have held that journalists have a common law right to protect confidential sources.[2]

Statutory and court-granted privileges raise four questions:

1. Who is entitled to invoke the privilege? This question requires the definition of a reporter and raises questions as to who is entitled to be considered as one.

---

1.   408 U.S. 665, 92 S.Ct. 2646, 33 L.Ed.2d 626, 1 Med.L.Rptr. 2617 (1972).
2.   For example, Senear v. The Daily Journal American, 97 Wash.2d 148, 641 P.2d 1180 (1982).

2.   What is protected? The privilege commonly enables journalists to refuse to identify confidential sources. It may also permit them to protect confidential information.

3.   How far does the privilege extend? In the usual context, it can be used to challenge a subpoena, whether to appear before a grand jury or as a witness in a trial, or to produce documents or photographs. However, courts also have authorized search warrants permitting police to search newsrooms and have directed subpoenas at third parties to get information about journalists.

4.   To what kinds of situations can the privilege be applied? Most commonly, journalists are asked to testify because they have reported information indicating that they have direct knowledge of a crime or the subject matter of a civil action. But in some instances, as in libel cases, the journalist may be a party to the action.

A study conducted over five years by the Reporters Committee for Freedom of the Press indicates that the number of subpoenas being issued to news media is apparently on the increase.[3] Of 900 television stations and newspapers responding to its survey, 469, or slightly more than 52 percent of the news organizations, said that they had been subpoenaed in 1993. That figure was up from about 47 percent in 1989 and was well above the low of 44 percent in 1991. The companies reported that during 1993, they had received 3519 subpoenas, with television getting about 70 percent of them. Of the subpoenas served, about 25 percent were for copies of material that had been shown on the air. Outtakes and raw footage accounted for another 25 percent. About 13 percent of the subpoenas sought news stories that had been published, and about 11 percent asked for reporters' notes. Seven percent demanded live testimony from reporters, and the remainder asked for drafts of stories, photographs, negatives, and internal memos.

Managers at two television stations and one newspaper office said that their newsrooms had been searched by police during 1993. Newspapers in Arizona and California reported that they had been fined for refusing to comply with subpoenas. Other respondents reported that four reporters had been jailed for resisting subpoenas, three in South Carolina in 1991 and one in Ohio in 1993. The reporter in Ohio, Lisa Abraham, had served twenty-two days in jail after refusing to testify before a grand jury about an interview she had had with a county engineer. The engineer was accused of circumventing bidding procedures and other violations.

The jailing of reporters is rare, but it continues to occur. As late as 1995, a judge in Columbia, South Carolina, ordered Twila Decker, a reporter for *The State,* jailed for refusing to disclose the source of a leaked psychiatric report concerning Susan Smith, a woman convicted of drowning her two sons by rolling her car into a lake with the boys strapped inside. The murder investigation and subsequent trial received national media attention.

---

3.   Debra Gersh Hernandez, "An Epidemic Called Subpoena," *Editor & Publisher,* 25 March 1995, p. 13.

Respondents to the Reporters Committee study said that they had complied with about half the subpoenas and had successfully evaded or negotiated the rest. Only one subpoena in ten was challenged with a motion to quash, but those challenges, based either on a shield law, common law, or a First Amendment privilege, succeeded in four cases out of five. In almost all those cases, courts sought answers to three questions when deciding whether to quash the subpoenas:

1. Does the journalist have information bearing directly on the case?

2. Can the information be obtained from other sources?

3. Is the information crucial to the determination of the case?

In some jurisdictions, courts impose a fourth condition: They require the party seeking disclosure to prove that its action is not frivolous. Often courts are simply not inclined to enforce a subpoena against a news organization when the information is readily available elsewhere, is redundant to information already obtained, or does not seem to be particularly relevant to the case at hand.

Major Cases

- *Branzburg* v. *Hayes,* 408 U.S. 665, 92 S.Ct. 2646, 33 L.Ed.2d 626, 1 Med.L.Rptr. 2617 (1972).

- *Bruno & Stillman* v. *Globe Newspaper Co.,* 633 F.2d 583, 6 Med.L.Rptr. 2057 (1st Cir. 1980).

- *Cohen* v. *Cowles Media Company,* 501 U.S. 663, 111 S.Ct. 2513, 115 L.Ed.2d 586, 18 Med.L.Rptr. 2273 (1991).

- *Commonwealth* v. *Corsetti,* 387 Mass. 1, 8 Med.L.Rptr. 2113 (Mass. 1982).

- *Grand Forks Herald* v. *District Court,* 322 N.W.2d 850, 8 Med.L.Rptr. 2269 (N.D. 1982).

- *In re Vrazo,* 423 A.2d 695, 176 N.J.Super.Ct. 455, 6 Med.L.Rptr. 2410 (1980).

- *Miller* v. *Transamerican Press, Inc.,* 621 F.2d 721, 6 Med.L.Rptr. 1598 (5th Cir. 1980).

- *Reporters Committee for Freedom of the Press* v. *American Telephone & Telephone Co.,* 593 F.2d 1030, 4 Med.L.Rptr. 1177 (D.C. Cir. 1979), cert. denied, 440 U.S. 949 (1979).

■ *United States* v. *Cuthbertson,* 630 F.2d 139, 6 Med.L.Rptr. 1545 (3d Cir. 1980); 651 F.2d 189, 7 Med.L.Rptr. 1377 (3d Cir. 1981).

■ *Zurcher* v. *Stanford Daily,* 436 U.S. 547, 98 S.Ct. 1970, 56 L.Ed.2d 525, 3 Med.L.Rptr. 2377 (1978).

THE ORIGINS OF THE PRIVILEGE

Reporters and Grand Juries

The Supreme Court's decision in *Branzburg* v. *Hayes* was widely viewed by journalists as a slap in the face. Three reporters had asked the Court to give them a qualified First Amendment privilege to protect them from grand jury subpoenas, and the Court had turned them down. The leading opinion told them that, like any other persons who were properly summoned, they would have to appear and testify. However, that leading opinion was signed by only four justices. The fifth member of the majority in the five-to-four decision invited journalists who felt harassed by the legal process to challenge subpoenas by filing a motion to quash—that is, to request a hearing on the propriety of the subpoena. Three of the four justices in the minority would have granted the reporters a qualified privilege, while the fourth would have made the privilege absolute.

Branzburg v. Hayes, 408 U.S. 665, 92 S.Ct. 2646, 33 L.Ed.2d 626, 1 Med.L.Rptr. 2617 (1972).

Very quickly, as journalists acted on the invitation to challenge subpoenas, lower courts began reading *Branzburg* as establishing a qualified First Amendment privilege very much like the one the Court had told the three reporters they could not have. Thus, in an ironic way, *Branzburg* v. *Hayes* has become one of the more important decisions expanding the rights of journalists. Although journalists can't count on it in every instance, this decision has given them additional credibility when they promise sources that their names will not be revealed to authorities.

The three reporters who were brought together in *Branzburg* came from widely separated parts of the country and had only a few things in common: They were investigative reporters, they were interested in people who lived at the fringes of society, and they had won the trust of their sources. As a result, they were able to produce stories offering insights into lifestyles that were viewed with distrust by much of the public.

Paul Branzburg was a reporter for the *Louisville Courier-Journal.* He won entry to the subculture of drug abusers in Louisville and Frankfort, the Kentucky capital, and wrote a series of revealing stories for his newspapers, in which he sought to describe why the children of middle-class Kentuckians were using narcotics. Earl Caldwell was one of the first black reporters employed by the *New York Times.* Assigned to the newspaper's west coast bureau, he won the confidence of Black Panthers in the San Francisco area. At a time when that organization was widely believed to be plotting guerrilla warfare, Caldwell was able to explore the forces that moved some African-Americans to take up arms. He found that the Panthers had some real grievances and sought some positive goals. Paul Pappas was a reporter-photographer for a television station in New Bedford, Massachusetts. In a city torn by racial strife, he, too, won the confidence of a Black Panther group. Members, fearing that police would attack their headquarters and kill them, let Pappas spend a night with them on the condition that he would report nothing unless the attack took place. When it didn't, he kept his word.

All three reporters were served with subpoenas by grand juries investigating criminal activity. Branzburg was asked to tell county grand juries in Louisville and Frankfort what he knew about the traffic in illegal drugs. Kentucky had a shield law[4] that protected reporters who refused to identify confidential sources of information. When Branzburg tried to use it, two separate state courts held that he could not. His stories, and the photographs illustrating them, made clear that Branzburg had been present when drug laws were violated. That made him an eyewitness to crime. He was the source of much of the information in his stories, and there was nothing confidential about his identity. Therefore, the courts ruled that he would have to appear before the grand juries and name the persons who had committed crimes in his presence.

Caldwell was subpoenaed to appear before a federal grand jury in San Francisco looking into charges that the Black Panthers were plotting to kill President Nixon. He argued that if he were to appear before the jury, he would forever lose the trust of his sources, even though he said nothing. That would cut off important information about the African-American community, having a "chilling effect" on First Amendment freedoms. Both a federal district court and the Ninth Circuit Court of Appeals were willing to permit Caldwell to refuse to identify his sources, but they were not willing to grant him an absolute right to refuse to meet with the grand jury.

Pappas worked in a state that had no shield law. When he was asked to appear before a county grand jury and tell about his night in the Panther headquarters, he asked the courts to excuse him. Massachusetts' highest court held that he would have to honor the summons or be held in contempt.

The Supreme Court took all three cases and treated them as one. It held that the reporters must honor the summonses and tell the grand juries what they knew. Aside from that conclusion, however, the Court's message was not at all clear. The justices wrote four opinions in which they differed sharply over how far the First Amendment should go in protecting news gathering. Because the justices were split so many ways, and so evenly, in their reasoning, lower courts have been able to read *Branzburg* as both rejecting and supporting the journalist's privilege, with most courts adopting the latter view.

To understand how this single decision can result in opposite interpretations, we need to study the opinions of the justices. Justice Byron R. White wrote the opinion of the Court, in which he was joined by three others. He began by making an important concession, one that has been quoted frequently in court decisions, most notably in *Richmond Newspapers* v. *Virginia,* which we discussed in Chapter 7. Noting that the reporters had argued that the First Amendment ought to protect them in gathering

---

4.   Ky.Rev.Stat. 421.100.

the news as well as in disseminating it, White wrote that he did not question the amendment's value to society. He added:

> Nor is it suggested that news gathering does not qualify for First Amendment protection; without some protection for seeking out the news, freedom of the press could be eviscerated.

White followed that concession by defining the issue in this case in narrow terms and by holding that no important First Amendment interests were at stake. He wrote:

> The sole issue before us is the obligation of reporters to respond to grand jury subpoenas as other citizens do and to answer questions relevant to an investigation into the commission of a crime. Citizens generally are not constitutionally immune from grand jury subpoenas; and neither the First Amendment nor any other constitutional provision protects the average citizen from disclosing to a grand jury information that he has received in confidence.

Nor, White said, should journalists enjoy such a constitutional immunity, despite their claims that their ability to gather news might suffer if reporters could not guarantee protection to their confidential sources. He added, "It is clear that the First Amendment does not invalidate every incidental burdening of the press that may result from the enforcement of civil or criminal statutes of general applicability."

White then turned to an examination of the role that grand juries play in the criminal justice system. Grand jurors sift allegations from many sources and then decide whether individuals should be charged with a crime. To aid them in reaching their decision, jurors have broad power to subpoena witnesses. Such power is granted, White said, to further the "longstanding principle that 'the public . . . has a right to every man's evidence.'"

At this point, White turned to the testimonial privileges noted at the start of this chapter: the Fifth Amendment privilege against self-incrimination; and the common law privileges cloaking marital, physician-patient, lawyer-client, and cleric-penitent relationships. Such testimonial privileges are so deeply rooted, he said, as to be almost beyond challenge. Then he wrote:

> We are asked to create another [privilege] by interpreting the First Amendment to grant newsmen a testimonial privilege that other citizens do not enjoy. This we decline to do.

In rejecting the reporters' argument, White and the three justices who joined him balanced the public's interest in law enforcement against the journalists' interest in access to sources of news. Because they were not convinced that confidential sources play an important role in news gathering, the justices came down on the side of law enforcement. They took the position that it is better to do something about crime than to write about it. In their view, anyone, including reporters, with direct knowledge of a crime has a duty to share that knowledge with law enforcement officers.

White further justified the plurality's position by arguing that a testimonial privilege grounded in the First Amendment could be abused by journalists who might use "a private system of informers" to threaten "the citizen's justifiable expectations of privacy." Further, such a privilege would give media informants a degree of protection higher than that of police informants. The latter have no constitutional protection,

White noted. If a police informant's testimony is sought by a grand jury or is needed in court, police either must identify the informant or drop the prosecution.

Nor were White and his colleagues willing to grant journalists a qualified privilege based on common law rather than on the First Amendment. To do that, they said, would "embark the judiciary on a long and difficult journey to . . . an uncertain destination." Courts would have to determine who would be entitled to claim the privilege. That would put the courts in the position of deciding who is a bona fide journalist. Such decisions would be made difficult by the fact that the Supreme Court has held that freedom of the press is a "fundamental personal right not confined to newspapers and periodicals." Lecturers, political pollsters, novelists, academic researchers, and dramatists also gather information and offer it to the public.

However, the plurality said it had no objection to legislators attempting to define journalists and to grant them a testimonial privilege by statute. Thus, the four justices gave their approval to the shield laws then in effect in seventeen states.

Only at the end did White and his associates temper their strong rejection of a journalist's privilege. They wrote:

> Finally, as we have earlier indicated, news gathering is not without its First Amendment protection, and grand jury investigations, if instituted or conducted other than in good faith, would pose wholly different issues for resolution under the First Amendment. Official harassment of the press undertaken not for purposes of law enforcement but to disrupt a reporter's relationship with his news sources would have no justification. Grand juries are subject to judicial control and subpoenas to motions to quash. We do not expect courts will forget that grand juries must operate within the limits of the First Amendment as well as the Fifth.

Justice Lewis F. Powell, Jr., voted with White and his colleagues to hold that the three journalists had no right to refuse to answer a grand jury's questions. But he wrote separately to enlarge on the point made in the preceding paragraph. That he did so has proved to be of utmost importance to journalists who receive subpoenas, not only to testify before grand juries, but in other legal proceedings, both criminal and civil. The majority of the courts considering challenges to such subpoenas have found in Powell's concurrence support for a qualified journalist's privilege. Therefore, Powell's reasoning merits careful attention.

The justice noted that a majority of the Court had declined to give journalists an absolute privilege that would protect their refusal to testify in any legal proceeding. However, not even the plurality had said that journalists must testify under all circumstances. It had conceded that the right to gather news has some degree of First Amendment protection. Public officials and courts must respect that right, Powell wrote. If they should not, the justice invited journalists to seek redress in court:

> If a newsman believes that the grand jury investigation is not being conducted in good faith he is not without remedy. Indeed, if the newsman is called upon to give information bearing only a remote and tenuous relationship to the subject of the investigation, or if he has some other reason to believe that his testimony implicates confidential source relationships without a legitimate need of law enforcement, he will have access to the court on a motion to quash and an appropriate protective order may be entered. The asserted claim to privilege should be judged on its facts by the striking of a proper balance be-

tween freedom of the press and the obligation of all citizens to give relevant testimony with respect to criminal conduct. The balance of these vital constitutional and societal interests on a case-by-case basis accords with the tried and traditional way of adjudicating such questions.

In short, the courts will be available to newsmen under circumstances where legitimate First Amendment interests require protection.

Powell thus sought to define how far the First Amendment might go in protecting the right to gather news. He suggested that grand juries ought not subpoena journalists unless there is reason to believe that the latter have some substantial knowledge of the subject of the investigation. Further, Powell suggested that grand juries should respect the confidentiality of reporters' sources unless "a legitimate need of law enforcement" requires disclosure. These suggestions were stated with more precision by Justice Potter Stewart, in dissent with two others. The language was blunt:

> The Court's crabbed view of the First Amendment reflects a disturbing insensitivity to the critical role of an independent press in our society. . . . While Mr. Justice Powell's enigmatic concurring opinion gives some hope of a more flexible view in the future, the Court in these cases holds that a newsman has no First Amendment right to protect his sources when called before a grand jury. The Court thus invites state and federal authorities to undermine the historic independence of the press by attempting to annex the journalistic profession as an investigative arm of government. Not only will this decision impair performance of the press' constitutionally protected functions, but it will, I am convinced, in the long run, harm rather than help the administration of justice.

White, writing for the plurality, had responded to the arguments advanced by Branzburg, Caldwell, and Pappas by focusing on the role of the grand jury. Stewart and his colleagues focused on the role of the news media. They seized on the majority's recognition that news gathering has some First Amendment protection and enlarged on that theme:

> A corollary of the right to publish must be the right to gather news. . . .
>
> . . . News must not be unnecessarily cut off at its source, for without freedom to acquire information the right to publish would be impermissibly compromised. Accordingly, a right to gather news, of some dimensions, must exist. . . .
>
> The right to gather news implies, in turn, a right to a confidential relationship between a reporter and his source. This proposition follows as a matter of simple logic once three factual predicates are recognized: (1) newsmen require informants to gather news; (2) confidentiality—the promise or understanding that names or certain aspects of communications will be kept off the record—is essential to the creation and maintenance of a newsgathering relationship with informants; and (3) an unbridled subpoena power—the absence of a constitutional right protecting, in any way, a confidential relationship from compulsory process—will either deter sources from divulging information or deter reporters from gathering and publishing information.
>
> It is obvious that informants are necessary to the newsgathering process as we know it today. If it is to perform its constitutional mission, the press must do far more than merely print public statements or prepared handouts. Familiarity with the people and circumstances involved in the myriad background activities that result in the final product called "news" is vital to complete and responsible journalism, unless the press is to be a captive mouthpiece of "newsmakers."

It is equally obvious that the promise of confidentiality may be a necessary pre-requisite to a productive relationship between a newsman and his informants. An office-holder may fear his superior; a member of the bureaucracy, his associates; a dissident, the scorn of majority opinion. All may have information valuable to the public discourse, yet each may be willing to relate that information only in confidence to a reporter whom he trusts, either because of excessive caution or because of a reasonable fear of reprisals or censure for unorthodox views. The First Amendment concern must not be with the motives of any particular news source, but rather with the conditions in which informants of all shades of the spectrum may make information available through the press to the public. . . .

. . . Commentators and individual reporters have repeatedly noted the importance of con-fidentiality. And surveys among reporters and editors indicate that the promise of nondis-closure is necessary for many types of news gathering.

Finally, and most important, when governmental officials possess an unchecked power to compel newsmen to disclose information received in confidence, sources will clearly be deterred from publishing it, because uncertainty about exercise of the power will lead to "self-censorship." . . . The uncertainty arises, of course, because the judiciary has tradition-ally imposed virtually no limitations on the grand jury's broad investigatory powers.

Stewart sought to avoid the uncertainty and the resulting self-censorship by propos-ing a three-point test that must be met before a journalist could be required to testify. He wrote:

Accordingly, when a reporter is asked to appear before a grand jury and reveal confi-dences, I would hold that the government must (1) show that there is probable cause to be-lieve that the newsman has information that is clearly relevant to a specific probable viola-tion of law; (2) demonstrate that the information sought cannot be obtained by alternative means less destructive of First Amendment rights; and (3) demonstrate a compelling and overriding interest in the information.

This is not to say that a grand jury could not issue a subpoena until such a showing is made, and it is not to say that a newsman would be in any way privileged to ignore any sub-poena that was issued. Obviously, before the government's burden to make such a showing were triggered, the reporter would have to move to quash the subpoena, asserting the basis on which he considered the particular relationship a confidential one.

No doubt the courts would be required to make some delicate judgments in working out this accommodation. But that, after all, is the function of courts of law. Better such judg-ments, however difficult, than the simplistic and stultifying absolutism adopted by the Court in denying any force to the First Amendment in these cases.

Justice William O. Douglas wrote separately in dissent to advance an absolute view of the First Amendment. He would have held that journalists have a constitutional right to refuse to take part in any legal proceeding. If they chose to testify, they could do so on their own terms.

Judges applying *Branzburg* have found the elements of a First Amendment jour-nalist's privilege in three places:

1. White and the three justices who voted with him recognized that news gath-ering has some First Amendment protection. Although unwilling to convert that protection into a privilege in this case, he warned that "[o]fficial harass-ment of the press . . . would have no justification." Where a legitimate inter-

est in coping with crime ends and harassment begins is, of course, a matter of judgment.

2. Powell, whose vote made the decision possible, emphasized White's warning against harassment. He made the further points that journalists ought not be asked for "information bearing only a remote and tenuous relationship to the investigation," and ought not be asked to identify confidential sources without good reason.

3. Where White and Powell were vague, Stewart was specific. The former can be read as recognizing that a privilege exists. Stewart had no doubts. The three-point test he suggested for determining when the privilege can be invoked has been adopted almost verbatim by many courts. In most jurisdictions, persons seeking a journalist's testimony must prove that the journalist has firsthand information about the matter at issue, that the information can't be obtained from other sources, and that it is essential to a proper resolution of the case.

The Privilege in the Federal Courts

In reaction to the Supreme Court's decision in *Branzburg,* Congress considered adoption of a federal shield law. But when journalists themselves were unable to agree on how far such a law should go, or even on the need for any such law, the proposal was dropped.[5] At about the same time, the U.S. Department of Justice adopted guidelines designed to limit the use of journalists as witnesses before federal grand juries and in trials in federal courts.[6]

The guidelines start with the premise that federal law enforcement officers will make no attempt to subpoena journalists until they have made "all reasonable attempts . . . to obtain information from nonmedia sources." If such attempts fail, the next step is negotiation with the media. If that fails, a subpoena cannot be issued without "the express authorization of the Attorney General."

That authorization is not to be given in criminal cases unless information from nonmedia sources indicates that a crime has been committed and that a reporter has information directly bearing on a suspect's guilt or innocence. Even then, the government is not supposed to issue a subpoena to the reporter unless it has been unable to get that information from nonmedia sources. Questioning of reporters who are subpoenaed is to be limited to verification of published information and to establishing its accuracy. The directive advises government attorneys to avoid the appearance of harassing journalists and to limit their requests to specific kinds of information. The same restrictions apply to civil cases, with the added provision that journalists are not to be drawn into such lawsuits unless the issue is "of substantial proportions."

Clearly, the attorney general's guidelines are based on the Stewart-Powell opinions in *Branzburg.* How diligent Justice Department attorneys have been in observing the

---

5. Martin Arnold, "Watergate Stalls Press Shield Law Effort," *Louisville Courier-Journal,* 4 July 1973.
6. 28 C.F.R. pt. 50.

guidelines has been the subject of debate in a committee of Congress[7] and of a few court cases. In 1992 a federal prosecutor made no effort to follow the guidelines when he sought confidential FBI documents from three reporters. The prosecutor said he wanted to test the documents for fingerprints in an attempt to determine who had sent the documents to the reporters through the mail. He said that if he were to follow the guidelines, the procedure could jeopardize the secrecy of grand jury proceedings.[8] A federal district court judge in Pittsburgh quashed the subpoenas, holding that the prosecutor had made no effort to trace the leak through other sources. That decision was upheld by the narrowest of margins when the full panel of the U.S. Third Circuit Court of Appeals in Philadelphia split six to six on the prosecutor's appeal.[9]

Whatever their effect, the guidelines have been overshadowed by court decisions interpreting *Branzburg.* At least ten federal circuit courts have read the decision as giving journalists some First Amendment protection against being subpoenaed as witnesses. Only the Sixth Circuit has held that *Branzburg* created no First Amendment privilege for journalists.[10] However, the court tempered its holding by noting that under some circumstances journalists may have a common law right to ask that their testimony be excluded, using a balancing of interests test. The test would balance journalists' interest in freedom of the press against the courts' interest in seeing that justice is done.

The Second Circuit, composed of Connecticut, Vermont, and New York, was one of the first to find a First Amendment privilege in *Branzburg.* In subsequent decisions it has forged strong protection for journalists subpoenaed as witnesses in both civil and criminal cases. The court's first decision, *Baker* v. *F & F Investment,*[11] tested a magazine reporter's right to protect his confidential sources of information. The reporter, Alfred Balk, had written an article on racial blockbusting for the *Saturday Evening Post.* Relying, in part, on information obtained from sources who asked not to be identified, Balk described tactics used by some real estate firms to provoke panic selling of homes whenever an African-American family moved into the neighborhood. The real estate firms involved would buy from the white owners at low prices and sell to black families at much higher prices.

Baker, representing himself and other African-American buyers, sued F & F, seeking damages as alleged victims of racial discrimination. Seeking support for his case, Baker asked a federal district court in New York City to compel Balk to identify the sources interviewed for his article. The court refused to do so. Relying on the three-point test advanced by Stewart in *Branzburg,* the court held that Baker had not shown that he could not obtain the information from other sources. That reliance was affirmed on appeal. The court held that in a civil action, which *Baker* was, a journalist's First Amendment interest in freedom of the press carries more weight than in a grand jury proceeding, which was at issue in *Branzburg.*

7. *Newsmen's Privilege:* Hearings, Subcommittee on Courts, Civil Liberties, and the Administration of Justice, Committee on the Judiciary, House of Representatives, 94th Cong., 1st sess., on H.R. 215, 23 and 24 April 1975, pp. 6–36, 94–102.
8. Milo Geyelin and Arthur S. Hayes, "News Sources' Confidentiality Challenged," *Wall Street Journal,* 15 May 1992.
9. In re Grand Jury Subpoena of Williams, 963 F.2d 567, 20 Med.L.Rptr. 1232 (3d Cir. 1992).
10. Storer Communications v. Giovan, 810 F.2d 580, 13 Med.L.Rptr. 2049 (6th Cir. 1987).
11. 470 F.2d 778, 1 Med.L.Rptr. 2551 (2d Cir. 1972); cert.denied, 411 U.S. 966 (1973).

The Second Circuit later endorsed the application of the Stewart test to a criminal case. In *United States* v. *Burke,*[12] the defendants issued a subpoena for notes, tapes, and other materials in the possession of a reporter who had written a story based on an interview with a key prosecution witness.

The trial judge rejected the request, holding that reporters have a qualified First Amendment privilege to protect the methods they use to gather news. Referring to Stewart's dissent in *Branzburg,* the judge said that the defendants could defeat that privilege only by making a strong showing of a compelling need for the reporter's notes, which they could not do. On appeal, the Second Circuit affirmed, holding that the standard of review it had established in *Baker* for civil cases applies to criminal cases as well.

More recently, the Second Circuit reminded the news media that, even when a testimonial privilege is given a strong First Amendment endorsement, journalists may be required to testify. In 1993, in a case similar to *Branzburg,* the court required reporters who were eyewitnesses and had clearly relevant information to testify. In the case, *United States* v. *Cutler,*[13] a prosecutor served subpoenas on journalists who had contact with Bruce Cutler, a defense lawyer under court order not to talk to the press about his client John Gotti. Authorities had reason to suspect that Cutler had defied the order, so the prosecutor subpoenaed notes, outtakes, and testimony from reporters about their contacts with Cutler. Because the reporters witnessed Cutler's alleged offense, the court refused to quash the subpoenas. The result has caused concern among some media lawyers that the Second Circuit's long-standing support for a strong First Amendment privilege may be eroding.[14]

Other federal circuit courts have recognized a qualified First Amendment privilege as follows:

— The District of Columbia Circuit. In an early libel case, the court recognized the existence of the privilege but upheld a district court's finding that it must yield to a libel plaintiff's need to identify a reporter's confidential sources.[15] The court said that the identity of the sources went to the heart of the plaintiff's ability to prove actual malice. In a privacy case, the court held that the plaintiff would have to exhaust all available alternative sources before he or she could question a reporter about who leaked information found in confidential government records.[16]

— The First Circuit. In a libel case, the court vacated a district court's order compelling a reporter for the *Boston Globe* to identify his confidential sources of derogatory information about a shipbuilding firm.[17] The court remanded with

12. 7 Med.L.Rptr. 2019 (E.D.N.Y. 1981); affirmed, 700 F.2d 70 (2d Cir. 1982); cert. denied, 464 U.S. 816, 104 S.Ct. 72 (1983).
13. 6 F.3d 67, 21 Med.L.Rptr. 2075 (2d Cir. 1993).
14. George Freeman, "Reporter's Privilege, Recent Developments." In *Communications Law 1994,* vol. 3 (New York: Practising Law Institute, 1994), p. 433.
15. Carey v. Hume, 492 F.2d 631 (D.C. Cir. 1974); cert. dismissed, 417 U.S. 938 (1974). See also Clyburn v. News World Communications, Inc., 903 F.2d 29 (D.C. Cir. 1990).
16. Zerilli v. Smith, 656 F.2d 705, 7 Med.L.Rptr. 1121 (D.C. Cir. 1981).
17. Bruno & Stillman v. Globe Newspaper Co., 633 F.2d 583, 6 Med.L.Rptr. 2057 (1st Cir. 1980).

instructions that, in effect, asked the trial judge to determine whether the reporter's information was essential to resolution of the dispute and had indeed been obtained in confidence. In a subsequent case, the court indicated that First Amendment concerns are less important in cases involving nonconfidential sources.[18] The court also has applied the privilege to a criminal case, quashing without a written decision a subpoena issued to a *New York Times* reporter.[19]

— The Third Circuit. The court recognized a qualified First Amendment privilege in both civil and criminal actions. In setting the precedent, the court reversed a district judge's finding that a reporter for the *Delaware County Daily Times* was in contempt because she had refused to disclose her sources. She had written that a police officer, who was a candidate for mayor of Chester, Pennsylvania, had been suspended and reprimanded on several occasions, although there had been no public announcement of the offenses. The court said that the officer would have to show that the identity of the reporter's sources was essential to carrying through his suit against the mayor and others for violating his civil rights.[20] Twice in a criminal case, the court held that CBS News had a right to withhold outtakes—unused sections of videotaped interviews—sought by the defendant in a fraud case. The court said it had not been shown that the same evidence could not be obtained from other sources.[21] The decisions are of particular interest to photographers and television journalists because in the first of the decisions the court held that the privilege protects unpublished photographs as well as the identity of confidential sources.

— The Fourth Circuit. Whatever First Amendment protection there is in the Fourth Circuit seems to be based almost entirely on Justice Powell's concurrence in *Branzburg*. As such, a journalist would be required to show evidence of government harassment or bad faith. In one case, the court upheld a contempt order for four reporters who had refused to testify for the prosecution in a bribery case against a South Carolina state senator.[22] The reporters had written a story about the senator's denial that he had accepted a $2,800 bribe from a lobbyist for parimutuel betting. The majority opinion held: "[A]bsent evidence of governmental harassment or bad faith, the reporters have no privilege different from that of any other citizen not to testify about knowledge relevant to a criminal prosecution."

— The Fifth Circuit. The court recognized a qualified First Amendment privilege, but in applying the three-point test it has held that the privilege must yield

---

18. United States v. LaRouche, 841 F.2d 1176 (1st Cir. 1988).
19. United States v. Collatos, Crim. No. 82-264-G (D.Mass. 1982).
20. Riley v. City of Chester, 612 F.2d 708, 5 Med.L.Rptr. 2161 (3d Cir. 1979).
21. United States v. Cuthbertson, 630 F.2d 139, 6 Med.L.Rptr. 1545 (3d Cir. 1980), cert. denied, 449 U.S. 1126 (1981); 651 F.2d 189, 7 Med.L.Rptr. 1377 (3d Cir. 1981), cert. denied, 454 U.S. 1056 (1981). See also In re Grand Jury Subpoena of Williams, 963 F.2d 567, 20 Med.L.Rptr. 1232 (3d Cir. 1992).
22. In re Shain (U.S. v. Long), 978 F.2d 850 (4th Cir. 1992).

when the identity of the reporter's sources is essential to proof of actual malice in a libel case.[23]

— The Tenth Circuit. The case was a civil rights action brought by the family of a young woman who said that she had become contaminated by plutonium radiation while working at a plant processing the material. After her death in an automobile accident, a television producer made her the subject of a documentary. The company she had worked for, the defendant in the lawsuit, asked the producer to identify his confidential sources and to disclose any information that had not been telecast. When the producer moved to quash the subpoena, a district court ruled that he was not a journalist and would have to respond to the company's questions. The Tenth Circuit reversed, holding that television producers are journalists and that the company could get the information only if it met a test similar to Justice Stewart's in *Branzburg*.[24]

The Seventh, Eighth, and Ninth Circuits have had no occasion to rule on requests for a journalist's privilege, nor has the Eleventh, which was carved out of the Fifth Circuit in 1981. However, district courts in each of these circuits have recognized and applied the privilege.

In their decisions, circuit court judges have focused on Powell's concurring opinion in *Branzburg,* reading it and the arguments advanced by the four dissenters as requiring First Amendment scrutiny of subpoenas issued to journalists. This focus has resulted in the application of a balancing test, on a case-by-case basis, to motions to quash. The essential queries in each instance are, Can the party seeking the journalist's testimony effectively present his or her case without it? and Can other sources of the same information be found?

The U.S. Court of Appeals for the Sixth Circuit, in a decision that so far stands alone, flatly rejected the reasoning outlined above. Upholding a contempt citation that kept a television reporter in jail for twenty-four hours, the court declared flatly that the majority in *Branzburg* "rejected the existence of . . . a first amendment testimonial privilege." Judge Alan E. Norris, writing for a three-member panel, said that he found nothing in Powell's concurring opinion that either limited or expanded the plurality opinion written by Justice White.[25] In his view, " Justice Powell's opinion certainly does not warrant the rewriting of the majority opinion to grant a first amendment testimonial privilege to news reporters."

The reporter in this case was Brad Stone, who worked for a television station in Detroit. He was assigned a story on youth gangs and interviewed several members on camera before he concluded that he was learning nothing that was of any use. Subjects told him they would talk candidly only if he promised that they could remain anonymous on the air. Stone's five-part report was edited so as to hide the identity of the youths he had interviewed.

---

23. Miller v. Transamerican Press, 621 F.2d 721, 6 Med.L.Rptr. 1598 (5th Cir. 1980); cert. denied, 450 U.S. 1041, 101 S.Ct. 1759, 68 L.Ed.2d 238 (1981).
24. Silkwood v. Kerr-McGee Corp., 563 F.2d 433, 3 Med.L.Rptr. 1087 (10th Cir. 1977).
25. Storer Communications v. Giovan, 810 F.2d 580, 13 Med.L.Rptr. 2049 (6th Cir. 1987).

The reporter's problems began when a grand jury investigated the murder of a police officer. Several informants told a detective that the assailants were youth gang members who had been videotaped when Stone made his first interviews. The informants said that they could identify the suspects, but they also said that they would not testify. Eyewitnesses to the killing said that they could identify the assailants if they were shown photographs of them. The prosecutor issued a subpoena for Stone's outtakes in the belief that they were the key to identifying the officer's killers. The television station filed a motion to quash. The trial judge held that Stone was not protected by Michigan's shield law, which at that time was written so as to protect only reporters for the print media. (The law has since been amended to cover all news gatherers.)[26] Nor, the judge said, was Stone protected by a constitutional privilege. When Stone refused to appear before the grand jury with his outtakes, he was found in contempt and was ordered to be jailed either until he did agree to appear or until the grand jury's term expired nearly a year later.[27] Stone was released the next day after he appealed to the federal courts for help.

Stone's lawyers based their appeal on two grounds. They argued that he was protected by a First Amendment privilege created by the Supreme Court in *Branzburg*. They also argued that the Michigan shield law violated the equal protection clause of the Fourteenth Amendment, because it was written to apply only to print journalists. Judge Norris, of the Sixth Circuit, rejected both arguments. In disposing of the first, he quoted from White's opinion in *Branzburg:* "[T]he Constitution does not, as it never has, exempt the newsman from performing the citizen's normal duty of appearing and furnishing information relevant to the grand jury's task." In Norris's view, Powell's pivotal concurrence did not question or modify that premise, although Norris recognized that other judges believe that it did. The judge wrote, "[W]e decline to join some other circuit courts, to the extent that they . . . have . . . adopted the qualified privilege balancing process urged by the three *Branzburg* dissenters and rejected by the majority."

Instead the court relied on a treatise on evidence written by John Henry Wigmore, one of the recognized authorities on the topic.[28] Wigmore's general thesis is that justice is most likely to be done if juries are able to consider all available facts bearing on a case. Thus, privileges excusing those who can provide such facts should be kept to a minimum. In accord with that view, the Sixth Circuit ruled, as had White, that society has little to gain from protecting a confidential relationship between journalists and their sources. In this instance, the court concluded, any interest that Stone might have in protecting his sources and their information was far outweighed by society's interest in identifying a police officer's killer.

Nor did the court find any support for the argument that the equal protection clause requires courts to give television journalists the same privilege that the legislature gave print journalists when it drafted the shield law. The court said that the equal protection of laws guaranteed by the Fourteenth Amendment applies only to "basic, fun-

---

26. Mich.Comp.Laws Ann. § 767.5a.
27. Storer Communications v. Giovan, 13 Med.L.Rptr. 1901 (Mich.Ct.App. 1986).
28. John Henry Wigmore, *Evidence in Trials at Common Law* (Boston: Little, Brown and Company, 1961), vol. 8, § 2286.

damental rights." Because journalists have no constitutional right to refuse to testify when summoned by a grand jury, the equal protection clause simply did not apply to Stone's situation.

The Sixth Circuit's decision in this case, titled *In re Grand Jury,* stands as the precedent for federal courts in Kentucky, Michigan, Ohio, and Tennessee. Prior to that decision, a U.S. district court in Detroit had recognized the privilege in a case involving a reporter,[29] but had held that the privilege did not protect an academic researcher.[30]

The circuit court decisions, taken as a whole, tell us that in the federal court system, journalists who argue that a First Amendment privilege protects their right to gather news are more likely than not to be told that it does. However, this protection does not guarantee that they will be excused from testifying before grand juries, or in civil or criminal proceedings. It does mean that those who seek their testimony must prove that the reporters have information that will help them, that such information is essential to the resolution of the case, and that it is not readily available from other sources.

State Shield Laws

At the time of the *Branzburg* decision in 1972, seventeen states had shield laws granting a testimonial privilege to journalists. Since then, twelve other states and the District of Columbia have enacted such laws. State courts declared the California and New Mexico laws unconstitutional, but California voters rewrote a shield law into their constitution, and the New Mexico Supreme Court adopted a shield law as a rule of court. New Mexico's legislature also reenacted the law to apply to nonjudicial proceedings. Therefore, as of this writing, twenty-nine states and the District of Columbia have constitutional provisions, statutes, or rules of court defining a testimonial privilege for journalists. They are Alabama,[31] Alaska,[32] Arizona,[33] Arkansas,[34] California,[35] Colorado,[36] Delaware,[37] District of Columbia,[38] Georgia,[39] Illinois,[40] Indiana,[41] Kentucky,[42] Louisisana,[43] Maryland,[44] Michigan,[45] Minnesota,[46] Montana,[47]

---

29. McArdle v. Hunter, 7 Med.L.Rptr. 2294 (E.D.Mich. 1981).
30. Wright v. Jeep Corp., 547 F.Supp. 871, 9 Med.L.Rptr. 1020 (E.D.Mich. 1982).
31. Ala.Code § 12-21-142 (1986).
32. Alaska Stat. §§ 09.25.150–.220 (1983 and Supp. 1990).
33. Ariz.Rev.Stat.Ann. § 12-2237 (1982); Ariz.Rev.Stat.Ann. § 12-2214 (1982 and Supp.).
34. Ark.Code Ann. § 16-85-510 (1987).
35. Calif.Evid.Code § 1070 (Supp. 1991); Calif. Const. Art. 1, § 2 (1983).
36. Colo.Rev.Stat. §§ 13-90-119 and 24-72.5-101 to 106 (Supp. 1990).
37. Del.Code Title 10, §§ 4320–4326 (1974).
38. D.C.Code Ann. § 16-4701 to 16-4704.
39. Ga.Code Ann. § 24-9-30 (1991 Supp.).
40. Ill.Ann.Stat. ch. 110, par. 8-901 to 8-909 (1984 and 1991 Supp.).
41. Ind.Code § 34-3-5-1 (1986).
42. Ky.Rev.Stat. 421.100 (1990).
43. La.Rev.Stat.Ann. §§ 45:1451-1454, 45:1459 (1982 and 1991 Supp.).
44. Md.Cts. and Jud.Proc.Code Ann. § 9-112 (1989).
45. Mich.Comp.Laws § 767.5a (1982 and 1991 Supp.).
46. Minn.Stat.Ann. §§ 595.021–.025 (1988).
47. Mont.Code Ann. §§ 26-1-901 to 903 (1989).

Nebraska,[48] Nevada,[49] New Jersey,[50] New Mexico,[51] New York,[52] North Dakota,[53] Ohio,[54] Oklahoma,[55] Oregon,[56] Pennsylvania,[57] Rhode Island,[58] South Carolina,[59] and Tennessee.[60]

The statutes vary widely. Each of them defines the kinds of journalists who are eligible for the privilege. The broadest definitions include anyone who gathers information for dissemination to the public through a medium of communication. California's law has been interpreted as not protecting freelance writers.[61] Some laws permit journalists to protect only confidential sources of information. In some such instances, the shield becomes operative only if the information obtained from such sources is published or broadcast. Other statutes protect not only sources, but information, whether or not it is published or broadcast. After the New York Court of Appeals ruled that the state's shield law protected only the identity of confidential sources or information provided by such sources,[62] the legislature amended the law to grant a qualified privilege to reporters' notes, audio or video outtakes, and newsroom files.[63]

A few shield laws are inoperative if the journalist is the target of a libel suit. Other laws require disclosure of information if a judge concludes that a fair trial is impossible without it. New Jersey's law, as interpreted by the state's supreme court, may be the strongest. The court held in one instance that the law protected a journalist who had witnessed the commission of a nonviolent crime.[64] Pennsylvania's supreme court has observed that state's shield law is "well nigh absolute."[65] Indiana's law, which is limited to protecting the identity of confidential sources, has been held to be absolute, even when the journalist is a defendant in a libel action.[66] Nevada's law also has been construed as absolute in its protection of confidential sources of libelous information.[67] However, the majority of the state shield laws grant qualified privileges that require courts to balance the court's need for a journalist's evidence against the journalist's interest in gathering news. The applicability of the journalist's privilege in libel cases will be discussed more fully later in this chapter.

As of this writing, courts in twenty-five states and the District of Columbia have looked to *Branzburg,* to their own state constitutions, or to common law to find a qual-

---

48. Neb.Rev.Stat. §§ 20-144 to 147 (1987).
49. Nev.Rev.Stat. § 49.275 (1986).
50. N.J.Stat.Ann. §§ 2A:84A-21, 21.1 to 21.8, 21a, 29 (1976, 1991 Cumm.Supp.).
51. N.M.Stat.Ann. § 38-6-7 (1978 and Supp. 1987), applying to nonjudicial proceedings. In judicial proceedings, a journalist's privilege is defined by Supreme Court Rule of Evidence 11-514 (1982).
52. N.Y. Civil Rights Law § 79-h (McKinney 1981, 1991 Supp.).
53. N.D.Cent.Code § 31-01-06.2 (1978 and 1991 Supp.).
54. Ohio Rev.Code Ann. §§ 2739.04, 2739.12 (1981 and 1990 Supp.).
55. Okla.Stat.Ann. Title 12, § 2506 (1980 and 1991 Supp.).
56. Ore.Rev.Stat. §§ 44.510–.540 (1989).
57. Pa.C.S.A. §5942 (1982 and 1991 Supp.).
58. R.I.Gen.Laws §§ 9-19.1-1 to 1-3 (1985).
59. S.C.Code Ann. § 19-11-100 (Law.Co-op.Supp. 1992).
60. Tenn.Code Ann. § 24-1-208 (1980 and 1990 Supp.).
61. In re Van Ness, 8 Med.L.Rptr. 2563 (Calif.Super.Ct. 1982).
62. Knight-Ridder Broadcasting v. Greenberg, 70 N.Y.2d 151 (1987).
63. N.Y. Civil Rights Law § 79-h (1993).
64. In re Vrazo, 176 N.J.Super.Ct. 455, 423 A.2d 695, 6 Med.L.Rptr. 2410 (1980).
65. In re Taylor, 412 Pa. 32, 193 A.2d 181, 1 Med.L.Rptr. 2675 (1963).
66. Jamerson v. American Newspapers, 469 N.E.2d 1243 (Ind.Ct.App. 1984).
67. Laxalt v. McClatchy, 116 F.R.D. 438, 14 Med.L.Rptr. 1199 (D.Nev. 1987).

ified testimonial privilege for journalists. They are Alabama,[68] Alaska,[69] California,[70] Connecticut,[71] Delaware,[72] District of Columbia,[73] Florida,[74] Idaho,[75] Illinois,[76] Indiana,[77] Iowa,[78] Kansas,[79] Louisiana,[80] Maine,[81] Massachusetts,[82] Michigan,[83] New Hampshire,[84] New York,[85] North Carolina,[86] Oklahoma,[87] Texas,[88] Vermont,[89] Virginia,[90] Washington,[91] West Virginia,[92] and Wisconsin.[93] The New Jersey Supreme Court also has recognized a qualified privilege, but only in dicta.[94] A comparison of this list with the one above shows that in ten states and the District of Columbia journalists who receive an unwanted subpoena can base a motion to quash on both a shield law and a court-created privilege. One way or another, forty-four states and the District of Columbia have recognized a journalist's privilege of some degree.

Like shield-law protection, court-granted privileges vary widely in their application. Most are based on a test similar to that proposed by Stewart in *Branzburg*. Florida courts have been among the most active in considering and granting journalists' requests to protect both their sources and their confidential information. Relying on that state's constitution and common law and on the First Amendment, Florida courts have created an absolute journalist's privilege in civil cases[95] and have consis-

---

68. Norandal USA v. Local Union Co. 7468, 13 Med.L.Rptr. 2167 (Ala.Cir.Ct. 1986).
69. Nebel v. Mapco Petroleum, 10 Med.L.Rptr. 1871 (Alaska 1984).
70. Mitchell v. Marin County Superior Court, 37 Cal.3d 268, 690 P.2d 625, 208 Cal.Rptr. 152, 11 Med.L.Rptr. 1076 (1984).
71. Conn. Labor Relations Board v. Fagin, 370 A.2d 1095, 2 Med.L.Rptr. 1765 (Conn.Super.Ct. 1976); Goldfeld v. Post Publishing Co., 4 Med.L.Rptr. 1167 (Conn.Super.Ct. 1978).
72. Delaware v. McBride, 7 Med.L.Rptr. 1371 (Del.Super.Ct. 1981).
73. Braden v. News World Communications, 18 Med.L.Rptr. 2040 (D.C.Super.Ct. 1991).
74. Morgan v. State, 337 So.2d 951, 1 Med.L.Rptr. 2589 (Fla. 1976).
75. In re Wright, 700 P.2d 40 (1985).
76. Illinois v. Palacio, 607 N.E.2d 1375 (Ill.App. 1993); appeal denied, 151 Ill.2d 573, 616 N.E.2d 344 (1993).
77. In re Stearns, 489 N.E.2d 146, 12 Med.L.Rptr. 1837 (Ind.Ct.App. 1986).
78. Winegard v. Oxberger, 258 N.W.2d 847, 3 Med.L.Rptr. 1326 (Iowa 1977); cert. denied, 436 U.S. 905 (1978).
79. State v. Sandstrom, 224 Kans. 573, 581 P.2d 812, 4 Med.L.Rptr. 1333 (1978); cert. denied, 440 U.S. 929 (1979).
80. In re Ridenhour, 520 So.2d 372, 15 Med.L.Rptr. 1022 (La. 1988); Louisiana v. Fontanille, 1994 La.App.Lexis 191 (La.App. 1994).
81. In re Letellier, 578 A.2d 722 (Me. 1990).
82. In the Matter of a John Doe Grand Jury Investigation, 410 Mass. 596, 19 Med.L.Rptr. 1091 (1991).
83. Schultz v. Reader's Digest Association, 468 F.Supp. 551, 4 Med.L.Rptr. 2356 (E.D.Mich. 1979).
84. Opinion of the Justices, 117 N.H. 386, 373 A.2d 644, 2 Med.L.Rptr. 2083 (1977).
85. O'Neill v. Oakgrove Construction, Inc., 71 N.Y.2d 521, 523 N.E.2d 277, 528 N.Y.S.2d 1, 15 Med.L.Rptr. 1219 (N.Y. 1988).
86. North Carolina v. Smith, 13 Med.L.Rptr. 1940 (N.C. 1987).
87. Taylor v. Miskorsky, 640 P.2d 959, 7 Med.L.Rptr. 2408 (Okla. 1981).
88. Dallas Oil and Gas v. Mouer, 533 S.W.2d 70 (Ct.Civ.App. 1976). But see Texas ex rel. Healey v. McMeans, 22 Med.L.Rptr. 1705 (Tex.Crim.App. 1994).
89. State v. St. Peter, 132 Vt. 226, 315 A.2d 254, 1 Med.L.Rptr. 2671 (1974).
90. Brown v. Commonwealth, 214 Va. 755, 204 S.E.2d 429 (Va.1974); cert. denied, 419 U.S. 966 (1974).
91. Washington v. Rinaldo, 102 Wash.2d 749, 689 P.2d 392, 10 Med.L.Rptr. 2448 (1984).
92. State, ex rel. Hudok v. Henry, 389 S.E.2d 188 (W.Va. 1990).
93. Zelenka v. State, 83 Wis.2d 601, 266 N.W.2d 279, 4 Med.L.Rptr. 1055 (Wis. 1978); overruled, 103 Wis.2d 228, 307 N.W.2d 628 (1981).
94. State v. Boiardo, 82 N.J. 446, 414 A.2d 14 (1980); 83 N.J. 350, 416 A.2d 793 (1980). Resorts International, Inc. v. New Jersey Monthly, 89 N.J. 212, 445 A.2d 395, cert. denied, 459 U.S. 907 (1982).
95. Coira v. Depoo Hospital, 48 Fla.Supp. 105, 4 Med.L.Rptr. 1692 (Fla.Cir.Ct. 1978).

tently applied the three-point Stewart test in criminal cases.[96] As of 1994, Florida courts had decided seventy-nine journalist's privilege cases, more than in any other state.[97]

Hawaii is the only state that has no shield law and has refused to recognize a journalist's privilege.[98] In only five states—Mississippi, Missouri, South Dakota, Utah, and Wyoming—are there neither shield laws nor cases of record clearly defining or rejecting a journalist's privilege. Two Mississippi trial courts recognized a privilege in unreported cases,[99] and a Missouri court gave implied recognition to a qualified privilege but found it inapplicable.[100]

The dimensions of the protection granted by state shield laws and by the decisions of state courts will be examined in subsequent sections of this chapter. However, journalists are advised to acquaint themselves with decisions of the courts in the states where they are employed.

QUALIFYING FOR THE PRIVILEGE

The Definition of a Journalist

Shield laws generally define journalists in broad terms, including anyone who is able to get news or comment in print with a recognized publisher, on the air over a radio or television station, or even on the Internet. In the past, a few of the laws have extended protection only to persons who are employed by a publisher or broadcaster or who are paid on a freelance basis. Such laws raise questions as to whether they cover student newspapers, publications produced by community organizations, and other media with nonpaid staffs. The modern tendency is to broaden the laws to cover anyone whose primary purpose is to gather information for dissemination to the public. For instance, the New York law was amended to include freelancers, still and movie photographers, authors of books, employers of journalists, and persons connected with noncommercial media.[101]

Where the law leaves doubt as to whether the person who receives a subpoena qualifies as a journalist, courts look at the circumstances. If such persons are acting as journalists and are seeking information for dissemination to the public, courts have tended to hold that they can invoke the privilege. If not, they may not be protected, as the following three cases illustrate.

---

96. Florida v. Peterson, 7 Med.L.Rptr. 1090 (Fla.Cir.Ct. 1981).
97. James C. Goodale, Joseph P. Moodhe, Lisa G. Markoff, and Rodney W. Ott, "Reporter's Privilege Cases." In *Communications Law 1994,* vol. 2 (New York: Practising Law Institute, 1994), pp. 937–1008.
98. In re Goodfader's Appeal, 45 Haw. 317, 367 P.2d 472, 1 Med.L.Rptr. 2597 (1961); DeRoburt v. Gannett Co., 507 F.Supp. 880 (D.Haw. 1981).
99. Hawkins v. Williams, a civil case in Hinds County (1983); and Mississippi v. Harden, a criminal case in Yalobusha County (1983).
100. CBS, Inc. v. Campbell, 645 S.W.2d 30, 8 Med.L.Rptr. 2529 (Mo.Ct.App. 1982).
101. N.Y. Civil Rights Law § 79-h (McKinney 1981).

The definition of a journalist became an issue during the discovery process that preceded the trial of General William Westmoreland's libel action against CBS News.[102] The general contended that he had been defamed by a segment of *60 Minutes,* which portrayed him as part of a conspiracy to understate enemy troop strength in Vietnam. When complaints were made about the segment, CBS conducted an internal study, which concluded that some of its news policies had been violated in preparing the report. During pretrial discovery, Westmoreland's lawyers asked for a copy of the study, along with notes and materials used in preparing it. When CBS resisted, the district court ordered the information released, holding that the writer of the study was not engaged in news gathering. Later, the order was modified to exempt sources who had spoken to the writer under promises of confidentiality.

An Indiana appellate court denied a claim of privilege under that state's shield law to a part-time reporter. The court held that the reporter was performing as an activist, not a journalist, when she obtained a copy of a confidential Environmental Protection Agency report. As further evidence of her nonjournalistic role, the court noted that she had not used the report in the newspaper to which she contributed articles but had given it to a television reporter. The television station's use of the report led to a libel suit. The court said that the woman would have to answer the plaintiff's questions about who had given her the EPA document.[103]

The Second Circuit held in a case called *von Bulow* v. *von Bulow* that the privilege can be invoked only by journalists who begin their news gathering with a demonstrable intent to publish their work. In this instance, the court refused to protect a manuscript produced by a freelance writer who had no record of previous publication, even though the writer had obtained a contract from a publisher after the project began.[104]

However, a federal district court judge in Philadelphia held that Standard & Poor's, a firm that publishes newsletters rating the creditworthiness of public companies and their securities, qualified for a journalist's privilege under the First Amendment.[105] Thus, the company was permitted to assert a qualified privilege during discovery in a lawsuit to which it was not a party.

In shield-law states, the definition of a journalist entitled to invoke the privilege is a matter of interpretation of the statutory language. If the statute is written broadly to cover all who gather information for dissemination to the public, it will protect student journalists and, presumably, communicators who prepare news releases for corporate employers. Such laws also may protect academic researchers. If the statute is written in terms that protect contributors to "bona fide news organizations," student journalists may be protected only if they have an affiliation with a regularly published student newspaper. As the *von Bulow* case indicates, persons who gather information on their own in the hope that they might find a publisher may not be protected. Where the shield is a product of common law or the First Amendment, who is covered is determined by how the judge or judges involved define a journalist.

---

102. Westmoreland v. CBS, 97 F.R.D. 703, 9 Med.L.Rptr. 1521 (S.D.N.Y. 1983); 596 F.Supp. 1170, 10 Med.L.Rptr. 2417 (S.D.N.Y. 1984).
103. Northside Sanitary Landfill v. Bradley, 462 N.E.2d 1321 (Ind.App. 1984).
104. Von Bulow v. von Bulow, 811 F.2d 136, 13 Med.L.Rptr. 2041 (2d Cir. 1987); cert. denied, 481 U.S. 1015 (1987).
105. In re Scott Paper Co. Securities Litigation, 145 F.R.D. 366, 20 Med.L.Rptr. 2164 (E.D.Pa. 1992).

The Definition of a Confidential Source

Codes of ethics of all major news organizations caution against the use of anonymous sources. But they also recognize that, at times, promises of confidentiality must be made—and kept—to obtain news of public importance. The "Statement of Principles" of the American Society of Newspaper Editors (ASNE) puts it this way: "Pledges of confidentiality to news sources must be honored at all costs, and therefore should not be given lightly. Unless there is clear and pressing need to maintain confidences, sources of information should be identified."

In the day-to-day give and take between reporters and their sources, it is not always clear when information is offered in confidence or when a source couples an offer of newsworthy information with a request not to be identified. "Don't quote me" slips so easily off the tongue of so many sources that reporters may not even acknowledge it. However, courts interpreting shield laws and applying common law or First Amendment privileges are insisting that journalists offer evidence that their relationship with their sources was indeed confidential. More and more courts are treating an agreement on confidentiality as a contract. Therefore, a key question when journalists seek to quash a subpoena asking for the identity of a confidential source or for unpublished information is, Did the journalist and the source reach an agreement on confidentiality before the information was disclosed?

That question was crucial to the First Circuit's decision in *Bruno & Stillman* v. *Globe Newspaper Co.,* referred to earlier. When the

Bruno & Stillman v. Globe Newspaper Co., 633 F.2d 583, 6 Med.L.Rptr. 2057 (1st Cir. 1980).

Boston Globe ran a series of articles commenting unfavorably on fishing vessels made by the company, Bruno & Stillman sued for libel. During discovery, the company asked the reporter to give it the notes and materials he had used in preparing his stories. (Discovery is a pretrial process in which lawyers obtain information from participants and potential witnesses in an effort to gather evidence and narrow the issues to be resolved at trial.) The newspaper surrendered about fifteen hundred pages of the reporter's handwritten notes, but it refused to disclose the identity of three confidential sources and the unpublished information they had given the paper. A federal district court ordered disclosure of the withheld information.

On appeal, the circuit court remanded with instructions that the district court apply a balancing test before deciding whether to repeat the disclosure order. If it should again decide that the reporter's information was needed, it should proceed to an examination of the circumstances under which he had obtained it. If the reporter could prove that the information had been obtained under a promise of confidentiality, that promise would be given consideration. If there was doubt as to whether confidentiality had been promised in advance of disclosure, the appellate court suggested that the trial judge examine the notes in the privacy of his chambers to determine whether they were relevant. The court also suggested other options, including full development of information from nonconfidential sources, that could lead to resolution of the case by summary judgment without violating the confidentiality of the reporter's sources. Only as a last resort, the appellate court suggested, should disclosure be ordered.

Nevertheless, the court clearly was troubled by the nature of the relationship between the *Globe*'s reporter and his sources. At what point, and on whose initiative, had that relationship become confidential? The court observed:

> Not all information as to sources is equally deserving of confidentiality. An unsolicited letter may be received with no mention of an interest in anonymity; such a letter may casually mention the wish for confidential treatment; it may specifically condition use on the according of such treatment; or it may defer communication of any substance until a commitment to confidentiality is received. Oral communications could also range from the cavalierly volunteered to the carefully bargained-for undertaking. . . . In the present case a number of facts need to be sorted out and others need to be developed. For example, although one source sent an unsolicited letter, there was a subsequent promise to protect not only all notes of conversation with the source but the initial letter. Whether and to what extent such a *nunc pro tunc* undertaking merits protection by the court is a matter for its discriminating judgment. The existing record is silent as to the reasonable expectation of confidentiality on the part of the other two sources.

The term *"nunc pro tunc"* refers to an attempt to modify an existing arrangement, and then to proceed on the assumption that the modifications had been in effect from the beginning. In this instance, information about Bruno & Stillman had been offered to the reporter without any request for confidentiality. At a later date, the source and the reporter did enter into a confidential relationship. The question the court raised was whether that relationship could be made retroactive to include the material offered originally. In this instance, the court chose not to push that question too hard, opting instead for a course on remand that gave the district court leeway to avoid violating the reporter's claim to privilege.

A reporter's promise of confidentiality in exchange for a source's information can sound a lot like two people making a contract. If a court interprets the agreement that way, it may well become as binding as any other formal contract. The U.S. Supreme Court upheld a Minnesota court's ruling that treated the disclosure of a confidential source as similar to a breach of contract. That decision allowed the source to sue for damages.

The case began when Dan Cohen, working as a public relations consultant to a candidate for governor, made a deal with reporters for the *St. Paul Pioneer Press Dispatch,* the Minneapolis *Star Tribune,* and two other news organizations: If the reporters would promise not to identify him as their source, he would give them copies of documents showing that the opponent's running mate had admitted shoplifting $6 worth of merchandise twelve years earlier. The reporters agreed. However, the editors of the Minneapolis and St. Paul newspapers overruled the reporters and identified Cohen. The *Star Tribune* also denounced him in an editorial.[106] Cohen was fired by the advertising agency for which he worked, and the candidate he represented lost by a large margin. Cohen sued the newspapers, arguing that they had violated an oral contract. A jury in Hennepin County court agreed, awarding him $200,000 in actual damages and $250,000 from each newspaper in punitive damages.

On appeal, the Minnesota Court of Appeals voted two to one to uphold the award of the actual damages but overturned the award of punitive damages.[107] The majority

---

106. Albert Scardino, "When the Press Breaks a Promise," *New York Times,* 31 July 1988.
107. Mark Fitzgerald, "Confidentiality Is a Contract," *Editor & Publisher,* 9 September 1989, p. 11.

held that the reporters' promise of confidentiality was like a contract and could be enforced without violating the newspapers' First Amendment rights. Judge Marianne Short wrote: "Were we not to enforce the newspapers' promises of confidentiality, confidential sources would have no legal recourse against unscrupulous reporters or editors. Ultimately, news sources could dry up, resulting in less newsworthy information to publish."

The Minnesota Supreme Court reversed but was reversed in turn by the U.S. Supreme Court, five to four. Justice White, writing for the majority, held that Minnesota's promissory estoppel law permits suits for damages against news media who break promises to confidential sources. In the absence of a written contract, the promissory estoppel doctrine "creates obligations never explicitly assumed by the parties." Or, as Justice White wrote, "Minnesota law simply requires those making promises to keep them."

Cohen v. *Cowles Media Company,* **501 U.S. 663, 111 S.Ct. 2513, 115 L.Ed.2d 586, 18 Med.L.Rptr. 2273 (1991).**

The Court held that the First Amendment does not shield the news media from lawsuits based on laws of general applicability, in this instance the common law of promissory estoppel. Pointing to a number of cases in which the Court has held that the media are subject to antitrust, labor, wages and hours, and tax laws, White concluded, "It is therefore beyond dispute that '[t]he publisher of a newspaper has no special immunity from the application of general laws. He has no special privilege to invade the rights and liberties of others.'"[108] White also rejected the argument that in publishing Cohen's name, the newspapers were publishing information they had obtained legally. White said that the newspapers had obtained Cohen's name "only by making a promise which they did not honor."

On remand, the Minnesota Supreme Court reinstated the trial court's award of $200,000 to Cohen.[109] Since 1991, at least six similar cases have been brought by news sources seeking damages on grounds that a promise of confidentiality was violated by the media.[110] The Supreme Court's decision in *Cohen* lends emphasis to the quotation from ASNE's "Statement of Principles" at the start of this section: "Pledges of confidentiality to news sources must be honored at all costs, and therefore should not be given lightly." Such pledges also should be given sparingly, and with a clear understanding by all parties as to the terms and limits of the pledge.

---

108. Quoting Associated Press v. NLRB, 301 U.S. 103, 57 S.Ct. 650, 81 L.Ed. 953, 1 Med.L.Rptr. 2689 (1937).
109. Jacob M. Schlesinger and William M. Bulkeley, "Award to Newspaper Source Is Upheld," *Wall Street Journal,* 7 February 1992.
110. Ruzicka v. Conde Nast Publications, 939 F.2d 578, 19 Med.L.Rptr. 1048 (8th Cir. 1991); Ruzicka v. Conde Nast Publications, 999 F.2d 1319, 21 Med.L.Rptr. 1821; (8th Cir. 1993); Morgan v. Celender, 780 F.Supp 307, 19 Med.L.Rptr. 1862 (W.D.Pa. 1992); Anderson v. Strong Memorial Hospital, 573 N.Y.S.2d 828 (Sup.Ct. 1991); Widmon v. Berwick Universal Pictures, 803 F.Supp. 1167, 20 Med.L.Rptr. 1851 (N.D.Miss. 1992); Multimedia WMAZ, Inc. v. Kubach, 443 S.E.2d 491 (Ga.App. 1994).

Who Controls the Privilege?

The journalist's privilege, like all privileges granted by statute or by a court, can be waived. The waiver can be intentional, if the journalist agrees to testify in a legal proceeding, or it can be inadvertent. If there is disagreement over an intentional waiver, most courts have held that the privilege is personal to the journalist or news organization protected by it and can be waived only by the holder. Two decisions, one by the U.S. Third Circuit and the other by the New Jersey Supreme Court, illustrate the majority position with respect to control over the right to waive the privilege.

In *United States* v. *Cuthbertson,* the Third Circuit held that CBS retained control over its outtakes even though the government had obtained waivers from witnesses who appeared in some of them. The outtakes were videotapes of interviews, not used in a *60 Minutes* episode, that examined complaints about Cuthbertson's franchising of Wild Bill's Family Restaurants. When a federal grand jury indicted Cuthbertson on charges of conspiracy and fraud, his lawyers issued a subpoena to CBS News asking for all outtakes rejected in preparing the program. The lawyers did so in the belief that the unused tape included interviews with persons who might appear as witnesses for the government and that the tape might be helpful in impeaching their testimony. At the same time, the government obtained from all of its witnesses waivers agreeing to release of the outtakes.

United States v. *Cuthbertson,* 630 F.2d 139, 6 Med.L.Rptr. 1545 (3d Cir. 1980); 651 F.2d 189, 7 Med.L.Rptr. 1377 (3d Cir. 1981).

When CBS moved to quash the subpoena, the trial judge ruled that the news organization would have to let him review any outtakes in which the government's witnesses appeared. If he concluded that any of the footage might be helpful to the defense, he would turn those parts of the outtakes over to Cuthbertson's lawyers. CBS rejected the request. The judge found the network in contempt and ordered it to pay a fine of a dollar a day until it complied with his order.

On appeal, the Third Circuit reversed. It held that, despite the waivers from many of the persons appearing in the outtakes, CBS retained control over the tape. The outtakes were subject to subpoena, but need be made available only if Cuthbertson's lawyers proved that they could not otherwise get the information that the outtakes contained. The decision's importance lies in the protection that the court gave the newsgathering process. It said:

> The compelled production of a reporter's resource materials can constitute a significant intrusion into the news gathering and editorial processes. . . . Like the compelled disclosure of confidential sources, it may substantially undercut the public policy favoring the free flow of information to the public that is the foundation of the privilege. . . . Therefore, we hold that the privilege extends to unpublished materials in the possession of CBS.

In *New Jersey* v. *Boiardo,*[111] that state's supreme court came to a similar conclusion. In this instance, a key government witness in a criminal case had written a

---

111. 83 N.J. 350, 416 A.2d 793, 6 Med.L.Rptr. 1337 (N.J. 1980).

letter to a reporter, apparently complaining that the prosecutor had reneged on a promise of leniency offered in return for the witness's cooperation. During the trial, the witness testified as to the contents of the letter. However, when the defendant's attorney sought to subpoena the letter in the belief that it might help him raise questions about the witness's truthfulness, the reporter moved to quash. The defendant's lawyer argued that the witness had waived any privilege that might have protected the letter, including the reporter's, when he testified as to its contents. The supreme court said that the witness's willingness to testify had no effect because the state's shield law grants a testimonial privilege only to journalists. For that reason, the court held that the privilege cannot be waived by anyone else, including the person who provided the privileged information. Therefore, the reporter did not have to surrender the letter.

Courts have held that journalists can waive their privilege involuntarily by agreeing to testify as to some aspect of the protected information. In a few instances, judges have held that reporters waived the privilege simply by testifying that they wrote the story in question and believed it to be accurate.[112] Journalists who choose, for whatever reason, to respond to a subpoena and testify about some aspects of a story based on confidential information or derived in part from confidential sources are advised to seek a stipulation as to what they can say without being held to have forfeited their privilege.

Some shield laws are written in terms that grant a privilege both to journalists and to news organizations, which can lead to conflicting views as to who has the right to waive the privilege. In one instance, a California court held that *National Enquirer* waived, in part, a privilege claimed by two of its reporters when they were subpoenaed by a grand jury.[113] The tabloid did so by giving to the grand jury copies of tape recordings made by the reporters and a transcript of an interview with the woman who was with John Belushi, a comedian and actor, when he died of a drug overdose. The court held that by surrendering the materials, the editors had waived the reporters' privilege with respect to all information in the tapes and transcript. A second California court ruled in another case that the relationship between the publisher of *Penthouse* magazine and two of its reporters was so close that they were "a single entity" for purposes of waiving a privilege.[114] However, a federal district court in Virginia questioned a publisher's right to overrule a reporter's willingness to waive privilege.[115]

Ideally, the question as to whether journalists should waive any claim to privilege should be resolved by consultation among the journalist whose testimony is sought, his or her superiors, and their legal counsel. If the reporter has promised not to identify a source, the source also should be involved in the discussion. In several instances,

---

112.   Commonwealth v. Corsetti, 387 Mass. 1, 8 Med.L.Rptr. 2113 (Mass. 1982); and Bunting v. Municipal Court, unpublished (Calif.Super.Ct. 1982).
113.   In re Brenna, 8 Med.L.Rptr. 2561 (Calif.Super.Ct. 1982).
114.   Dalitz v. Penthouse, 168 Cal.App.3d 468, 214 Cal.Rptr. 254, 11 Med.L.Rptr. 2153 (Calif.Ct.App. 1985).
115.   Bauer v. Brown, 11 Med.L.Rptr. 2168 (W.D.Va. 1985).

reporters have averted being jailed[116] or have been released from jail because their sources agreed to be identified.[117]

THE SCOPE OF THE PRIVILEGE

Journalists in Criminal Proceedings

Journalists who break the law are treated like any other violators: They are subject to arrest, and if arrested, they have no more and no less protection than anyone else. The only privilege available to a journalist who is accused of committing a crime is that offered by the Fifth Amendment's right to remain silent.

Journalists whose stories disclose a direct knowledge of a crime or the suspect open themselves to being summoned as witnesses, either before a grand jury or at trial. If that should happen, in most jurisdictions journalists have three options: They can agree to testify without qualification, or they can hire a lawyer who may advise either the filing of a motion to quash or an attempt to reach an agreement as to the limits of the reporter's testimony. The latter might include an offer to let the judge look at the contested materials in the privacy of his or her office and reach a conclusion as to whether disclosure is justified. The purpose of a motion to quash is to obtain an order excusing the reporter from testifying. However, if the accuracy of the reporter's story is at issue, a motion to quash may leave the court with the impression that the reporter is unwilling to defend the story. In such instances, the best course may be an attempt to limit the reporter's testimony and to rule out questions about confidential sources or information.

Denial of a motion to quash can be appealed. If such appeal or an attempt to limit the testimony fails, reporters are confronted with a difficult choice of options. One is to seek permission to identify their confidential sources or to testify as to information imparted in confidence. The other is to defy the court and be held in contempt, a holding that is also subject to appeal. At that stage, the cases show that some reporters have escaped punishment because the grand jury's investigation was dropped or completed, or because the grand jury had obtained enough information from other sources to support an indictment. Because the basis for the privilege varies, and because the privilege is granted or denied on a case-by-case basis, the cases chosen for treatment in this section should be considered only illustrative.

Grand Jury Subpoenas

A review of the cases shows that journalists are least likely to be able to avoid testifying if they have witnessed a crime. However, journalists have prevailed in a few

---

116. Caldero v. Tribune Publishing Co., 98 Idaho 288, 562 P.2d 791, 2 Med.L.Rptr. 1490; cert. denied, 434 U.S. 930 (1977).
117. "Reporter Freed, Promise Kept," *USA Today,* 11 July 1990.

instances by arguing that the grand jury must prove that there is an overriding need for their testimony or that they are exempted by the language of a state shield law, as in the following case.

Fawn Vrazo, a reporter for the *Philadelphia Bulletin,* wrote a series of stories on corruption in government in southern New Jersey.

In re Vrazo, **423 A.2d 695, 176 N.J.Super.Ct. 455, 6 Med.L.Rptr. 2410 (1980).** It appeared from her stories that she had talked with "ghost" employees—people who were on the state payroll but who were not doing any work. Vrazo's stories did not identify such individuals. A grand jury looked into the allegations and summoned Vrazo to testify. Her stories relied heavily on confidential sources, but they also indicated that the reporter had interviewed several persons in their homes at times when they were being paid for work they obviously were not performing. If these interviews had taken place, Vrazo was an eyewitness to crime.

Vrazo moved to quash the summons, citing New Jersey's strong shield law. The prosecutor argued that the law did not protect reporters who were eyewitnesses to a crime. He argued further that Vrazo had waived any claim to privilege with respect to information by publishing some of it. The state's superior court rejected both arguments. It held that the eyewitness exception applied only to crimes involving physical violence or property damage. Further, the law defines a journalist's privilege as protecting both sources and information. The court held that the privilege could not be waived as far as the grand jury was concerned by the disclosure of privileged information in the newspaper. Vrazo was not required to testify.

In Florida, which has no shield law, the state supreme court reversed a lower court's finding that a reporter was in contempt for refusing to identify a confidential source to a grand jury. The source had told the reporter that a third person had filed a complaint with the state ethics commission naming several public officials. Revealing that information put the source in violation of a state law that made disclosure of such complaints a crime. However, the supreme court concluded that the First Amendment interest in disclosing the complaint was strong enough to override the state's interest in protecting the reputations of the officials.[118] Therefore, the reporter could protect his source.

Florida courts came to the opposite conclusion in another case. Tim Roche, a reporter for the *Stuart News,* refused to identify a source who had given him a copy of a confidential court order terminating a mother's custody of her child. The mother had been found guilty of child abuse. A state law makes it a crime to disclose such orders or to publish their contents. State prosecutors subpoenaed Roche, took him to court, and asked him to identify his source. When he refused to do so, the judge found Roche in contempt and sentenced him to thirty days in jail. On appeal, Roche contended that both the child's mother and its foster parents had been widely interviewed, and that prosecutors had made no attempt to identify the source by other means. The Florida Court of Appeals affirmed the sentence, holding that the interests served by conducting custody proceedings in private had been violated by Roche's articles, thus voiding

---

118.   Tribune Co. v. Huffstettler, 12 Med.L.Rptr. 2288 (Fla. 1986).

his privilege. The Florida Supreme Court refused to review the decision, and the U.S. Supreme Court denied certiorari.[119]

Reporters who have not seen a crime committed, but who have talked to those who have, may have to testify if they are summoned by a grand jury. The experience of Paul Corsetti, a reporter for the *Boston Herald,* illustrates what can happen when a journalist bases a story on a conversation with a criminal. Corsetti talked by telephone with a man suspected of murder. He wrote that the man had confessed to the crime. A grand jury summoned Corsetti to testify about the interview. Corsetti filed a motion to quash, arguing that the grand jury could get the same information from a police officer. A judge concluded that Corsetti's testimony would indeed duplicate the officer's, but ordered the reporter to testify anyway. Massachusetts has no shield law, and at the time, its courts had not recognized a journalist's privilege. On appeal, the state's highest court ruled that because the grand jury had completed its work, there was no reason to decide the case.[120] However, that ruling did not end Corsetti's problems.

Reporters whose stories disclose knowledge of a crime run a risk not only of being summoned by a grand jury, but of being called as witnesses by the prosecution. Again, journalists who wish to be excused must seek relief through either a state shield law or the court's willingness to recognize a common law or constitutional privilege. Paul Corsetti's experience, which began with a summons to testify before a grand jury, illustrates the worst that can happen, as the next section describes.

Journalists as Prosecution Witnesses

When the murder suspect with whom Corsetti had talked was brought to trial, the prosecutor summoned the reporter as a witness. Corsetti appeared in court as ordered but testified only that he had written the story that appeared in the *Boston Herald.* When he was pressed for details of his interview with the suspect, Corsetti said that he had promised he would not testify in court as to the substance of the conversation. The judge found Corsetti in contempt and sentenced him to ninety days in jail, the maximum permitted by law. On appeal, the Massachusetts Supreme Judicial Court indicated that it might be willing to recognize a journalist's common law privilege but had no need to do so in this instance. Corsetti had identified his source and had disclosed much if not all of the information when he wrote the article. Therefore, he had waived any claim to a privilege. Corsetti spent about a week in jail before the governor commuted his sentence to time served and ordered his release.

Commonwealth v. *Corsetti*, 387 Mass. 1, 8 Med.L.Rptr. 2113 (Mass. 1982).

In a Pennsylvania case, neither the state's shield law nor the court's recognition of a qualified privilege protected a reporter who had interviewed a man suspected of

---

119.   In re Investigation: Florida Statute 27.04 (Roche v. State), 589 So.2d 978, 19 Med.L.Rptr. 1632 (Fla.App. 1991); review denied, 599 So.2d 1279 (Fla. 1992); cert. denied, 113 S.Ct. 1027 (1992).
120.   Corsetti v. Commonwealth, 411 N.E.2d 466 (Mass. 1980).

murdering his estranged wife. The reporter discussed her interview with police officers and gave them information that she had not included in her story for the Allentown *Morning Call.* The story was of interest to the prosecutor because it exposed inconsistencies in the suspect's alibi and revealed possible motives for the murder. When the prosecutor summoned the reporter as a witness, she filed a motion to quash. The trial court judge ruled that she had waived the privilege granted by the state's shield law when she identified her source in her story and discussed her information with police officers.[121]

Reporters involved in two cases in Florida were able to avoid testifying by invoking that state's common law privilege. In *Florida* v. *Taylor,*[122] the reporter had talked to a suspect at the scene of the crime. When the prosecutor summoned the reporter as a witness, the reporter filed a motion to quash, which was upheld by a state circuit court. The court held that the prosecutor had failed to show that the reporter's evidence was relevant and that it could not be obtained from other sources. In the second case, *Tribune Co.* v. *Green,*[123] a state appellate court applied the same test and held that the reporter, who also had interviewed a suspected criminal, should not be required to testify.

The California Supreme Court held that the state's shield law, which is a part of the state constitution, does not offer absolute protection to journalists who have witnessed a crime.[124] If what they saw or heard is essential to a defendant's case, they must testify or be in contempt. A reporter and a photographer for the *Los Angeles Times* were present during a drug and theft investigation when police made an arrest in a shopping mall. An officer searched the suspect, found a set of brass knuckles, and charged the suspect with carrying a concealed weapon. At trial, the public defender argued that the charge should be dismissed because the search had been made without the suspect's consent. Police said that consent had been given.

When both the prosecutor and the defense attorney summoned the reporter to resolve the dispute, she refused to testify, even though no promise of confidentiality had been made. The judge ordered her jailed. She spent six hours in a cell before she was released on $1,000 bond. An appellate court upheld the judge's order. In a separate proceeding, the photographer also was found in contempt.

The supreme court affirmed the appellate court's decision, noting that the suspect's defense "will rise or fall" on whether he consented to the search. The court held that what the journalists saw and heard was neither confidential nor sensitive. Nor would their testimony "even remotely" hinder their ability to gather information in other instances. "All that is being required of them is to accept the civil responsibility imposed on all persons who witness alleged criminal conduct."

---

121. Pennsylvania v. Banner, 17 Med.L.Rptr. 1434 (Ct.Comm.Pleas 1989).
122. 9 Med.L.Rptr. 1551 (Fla.Cir.Ct.1982).
123. 440 So.2d 484, 10 Med.L.Rptr. 1034 (Fla.Dist.Ct.App. 1983).
124. Delaney v. Superior Court, 202 Cal.App.3d 1019, 249 Cal.Rptr. 60, 15 Med.L.Rptr. 1815 (Calif.Ct.App. 1988); affirmed on other grounds, 50 Cal.3d 785, 789 P.2d 934, 17 Med.L.Rptr. 1817 (1990).

Journalists as Defense Witnesses

When a reporter is believed to have evidence that will help prove a criminal defendant not guilty, two constitutional rights may come into conflict. A clause in the Sixth Amendment gives a criminal defendant the right "to have compulsory process for obtaining witnesses in his favor." That process is exercised through the subpoena power. Its purpose is to ensure a fair trial by giving the court access to any testimony bearing on the defendant's guilt or innocence. Nevertheless, courts in many jurisdictions consider requests for a privilege when defendants seek testimony from journalists.

An early decision of an Ohio appeals court in *In re McAuley*[125] illustrates. A reporter for the *Cleveland Plain Dealer* had written that a murder was arranged by Mafia chieftains. When a suspect in the murder was brought to trial in California, he sought a subpoena to compel identification of the reporter's confidential sources and information. He argued that the information would show that he was not the Mafia figure who had arranged for the murder. An Ohio trial court judge refused to issue the subpoena, and the appeals court affirmed, holding that the defendant had failed to prove that the reporter was a necessary and material witness. The court said that the reporter's First Amendment privilege could be overcome only if the defendant were able to show that (1) the material sought from the reporter would help establish guilt or innocence, (2) alternative sources of helpful information had been exhausted, (3) an effort had been made to obtain the reporter's testimony as to nonconfidential information, and (4) a judge had been asked to examine confidential information in private to determine if it was relevant.

The Oregon Court of Appeals held that the *Portland Oregonian* did not have to release seventy unpublished photographs sought by lawyers defending three women who had been arrested during an antinuclear demonstration.[126] The court reversed a contempt order issued when a county district judge fined the paper $300 and ordered its editor jailed for refusing to surrender photographs taken during a demonstration in Portland's Pioneer Square. The appeals court noted that the women had made no attempt to explain how the photos might work in their favor. Therefore, they had not complied with the terms of Oregon's shield law, which protects unpublished information unless it is needed by the defendant to ensure a fair trial.

In a California case, the Court of Appeals overturned a superior court's contempt order that could have sent Erin Hallissy of the *Contra Costa Times* to jail. Hallissy had interviewed a suspected murderer, and she reported that he told her he had killed other persons than those named in the charges against him.[127] The suspect's attorney issued a subpoena for Hallissy's notes, saying that he needed them to show contradictions and inconsistencies in his client's statements, which were the principal evidence against the suspect. When Hallissy refused to surrender her notes, a judge found her in contempt. The appellate court held that the attorney had not proved that Hallissy's notes contained evidence necessary to his case. The court's decision also

125.   630 Ohio App. 5, 408 N.E.2d 697 (1979).
126.   Oregon, ex rel. Meyer v. Howell, 86 Ore.App. 570, 740 P.2d 792 (1987).
127.   Hallissy v. Superior Court, 200 Cal.App.3d 1038, 15 Med.L.Rptr. 1325 (Calif.Ct.App. 1988).

noted that the suspect had made similar admissions to other persons who could be called as witnesses.

The balancing test can go against journalists. The U.S. Court of Appeals, First Circuit, ruled that a trial judge acted properly when he ordered NBC News to let him examine outtakes of an interview with a prospective key witness in the trial of Lyndon LaRouche, a right-wing activist accused of political campaign irregularities. LaRouche's attorney had argued that some of the material in the outtakes might help him in cross-examination of the witness. The judge asked to look at the materials to see if that was the case. NBC appealed the order, which was upheld. The appellate court recognized that "there is a lurking and subtle threat to journalists and their employers if disclosure of outtakes, notes, and other unused information becomes routine and casually compelled," but the court held that, in asking to review the materials himself rather than ordering them handed over in their entirety to LaRouche's attorney, the district court judge had shown "proper sensitivity" to the competing constitutional interests.[128]

The most celebrated loser in a contest with defense attorneys was Myron Farber, a reporter for the *New York Times.* He spent forty days in jail in 1978 rather than let a New Jersey state court judge examine his notes on a murder investigation.

Farber had written a series of stories about the deaths of several patients in a New Jersey hospital. As a result, a grand jury indicted a former physician at the hospital on a charge of murder. The physician's lawyer subpoenaed Farber as a witness, alleging that he had information that would help the defendant's case. Subpoenas also were issued for Farber's notes and for any memoranda in the newspaper's files bearing on the investigation. The judge was willing to examine the materials in private to see whether any of them would help the physician. When Farber and the *Times* refused his offer, the judge found both in contempt, sending the reporter to jail and fining the newspaper $5,000 a day until each complied with his order.[129] Farber's jail term and the *Times*'s fine ended when a jury found the physician not guilty. Governor Brendan Byrne pardoned Farber and the newspaper. He also returned $101,000 of the fine. Subsequently, the legislature strengthened the state's shield law so as to give a near-absolute privilege to journalists.

The cases in the preceding sections make several points for journalists who cover the crime beat: If a reporter's investigations point to a crime for which no arrests have been made, the reporter faces the possibility of being summoned by the prosecutor or a grand jury to tell what he or she knows. If police have made an arrest and a reporter's stories contain information the police do not have or raise doubts about a defendant's guilt, the reporter faces the possibility of being summoned as a witness by one or both sides if the case goes to trial. Reporters who witness a crime or who are present when police make an arrest are particularly vulnerable to a summons. Reporters whose crime stories are based on information from confidential sources may be asked to identify those sources.

Although the reported cases indicate that reporters who contest subpoenas prevail in most instances, there is no certainty that they will do so. Reporters have

---

128.   U.S. v. LaRouche Campaign, 841 F.2d 1176 (1st Cir. 1988).
129.   In re Farber, 394 A.2d 330, 4 Med.L.Rptr. 1360 (N.J. 1978).

gone to jail or been fined for refusing to disclose information sought by the criminal justice system. Each case, even in strong shield-law states like California and New Jersey, is decided on its own facts, and the outcome cannot be predicted with certainty. A journalist's worst course is to ignore a subpoena. That will lead inevitably to a contempt citation. Where a proper challenge is mounted, however, courts will balance the reporter's First Amendment, common law, or shield-law claim of privilege against the public's interest in justice. Key questions in striking the balance are:

— Does the reporter have evidence bearing on the case?

— Can similar evidence be obtained from other sources?

— If the evidence cannot be obtained from other sources, is the reporter's evidence crucial to proper resolution of the case?

Journalists in Civil Actions

Journalists who are summoned in connection with a civil action, other than a libel suit in which the journalist is a defendant, will find courts likely to honor the journalist's privilege. In most instances, courts urge the parties to seek information from other sources, and some courts have been quite strict in holding that the search for such sources must be exhaustive. Such has been the case even when the government is one of the parties to the civil action. The following cases exemplify the majority holdings.

When five states brought a civil antitrust action against seventeen oil companies, they acted on the theory that price movements were coordinated through a trade publication, *Platt's Oilgram Price Report.* Consequently, the states obtained a subpoena directing the newsletter and two of its reporters to provide the names of their confidential sources of price information. In response to a motion to quash, a U.S. district court judge in New York ordered disclosure. One reporter gave the court four names. The other refused. The court held the newsletter's publisher, McGraw-Hill, in contempt and imposed a fine of $100 a day until McGraw-Hill complied with its order.

On appeal, the U.S. Court of Appeals, Second Circuit, reversed. Its decision was emphatic.[130] The court said that journalists could not be forced to identify confidential sources unless there was "a clear and specific showing that the information is highly material and relevant, necessary or critical to the maintenance of the claim, and not obtainable from other available sources." In this instance, the court said that the states had offered no evidence that the newsletter was involved in any price-fixing scheme. It was not enough to suggest that the reporters may have been unknowing conduits for information through which the oil companies fixed prices.

Playboy magazine was able to invoke California's shield law when it was caught in the middle of a dispute between the comedy team of Cheech and Chong and their former accountants. The comedians sued the accounting firm for damages, charging it

---

130.   In re Petroleum Products Antitrust Litigation, 680 F.2d 5 (2d Cir. 1982).

with fraud. While the case was pending, a *Playboy* writer interviewed the comedians. During the interview, Richard (Cheech) Marin allegedly made statements about the accountants. When the interview was published, two things happened. First, the accountants subpoenaed *Playboy,* asking for all notes and tape recordings taken in connection with the interview. They were seeking information that could be used to cast doubt on Marin's testimony at trial and to support their side of the case. Second, in response to publication of the article, Marin said that he had not made some of the statements attributed to him. *Playboy* moved to quash the subpoena. A state appeals court ordered the subpoena dismissed. The court said that California's shield law protected any unpublished information known to the interviewer or any unpublished information in documentary form.[131] However, it also ordered the magazine to give the accountants the address and telephone number of the writer.

A few courts have balked at excusing journalists who are asked to testify in civil actions but have held that they could assert a privilege on a question-by-question basis. This ruling is illustrated by a federal district court's decision in *Continental Cablevision, Inc.* v. *Storer Broadcasting Corp.*[132] The two firms were competitors for a cable television franchise in Florissant, Missouri, a suburb of St. Louis. When Continental's bid was rejected by the city council, the firm sued Storer for libel, based on a written statement given to members of the council. As part of its pretrial discovery, Continental issued a subpoena to a *St. Louis Globe-Democrat* reporter who had written a story about Storer's statement. She moved to quash. Referring to *Branzburg,* the court recognized a First Amendment privilege but held that the reporter would have to respond to the subpoena and submit to questioning by Continental's lawyer. At that point, the balancing test proposed by Stewart would come into play. With help from her lawyer, the reporter would decide which questions she would answer and which she would not, following detailed guidelines set by the court.

Although courts have shown a willingness to excuse reporters who seek to avoid testifying in civil cases, they have not shown a similar regard for photographers who seek to prevent litigants from subpoenaing their unpublished photographs. A decision of the North Dakota Supreme Court in a case brought by the *Grand Forks Herald* illustrates.

Grand Forks Herald v. *District Court,*
322 N.W.2d 850,
8 Med.L.Rptr. 2269
(N.D. 1982).

One of the newspaper's photographers had taken several pictures of an accident, which became the subject of an action for damages. Only one of the photos was published. One of the parties to the damage suit sought the others, thinking that they might help his case. When the newspaper resisted, the supreme court ruled against it, noting that the litigant had tried without success to find other photographs of the accident. Further, the court held that there was nothing confidential involved. The photographer had taken the pictures in a public place. His editors might have selected any one, or all of them, for publication. Further, the photos

---

131.   Playboy Enterprises, Inc. v. Superior Court, 201 Cal.Rptr. 207, 10 Med.L.Rptr. 1569 (Calif.App. 1984).
132.   583 F.Supp. 427, 10 Med.L.Rptr. 1641 (E.D.Mo. 1984).

offered evidence that would not be presented in any other way. Finally, requiring surrender of the photos would be less intrusive into First Amendment rights than requiring the photographer to testify as to what he had seen at the site of the accident.

In at least ten other reported cases, courts have required news organizations to surrender unpublished photographs, either still or video, for use in legal proceedings. In some instances, usage has been limited to attorneys in preparing their cases.[133] Other courts have followed reasoning similar to that above, holding that the taking of photographs in a public place does not imply a promise of confidentiality.[134] However, some courts have reasoned that the taking of photographs is a part of the news-gathering process and may be protected by privilege.[135]

Libel and Confidential Sources

When journalists' reliance on confidential sources subjects them to a libel suit, courts vary widely in their response to plaintiffs' attempts to compel identification of the sources. Some courts will not permit defendants to use information from such sources as part of their defense. A few have instructed juries to decide cases on the assumption that the source did not exist. The current tendency is for courts to apply variations of Justice Stewart's three-point balancing test from *Branzburg.*

The first two of these three approaches can be traced to the Supreme Court's 1979 decision in *Herbert* v. *Lando,*[136] which is summarized in Chapter 5. In that case, the Court held that journalists who are sued for libel do not have a privilege to protect their editorial processes. These are the decisions that go into the shaping of a story—to include some facts while omitting others, and to believe some sources more than others. In *Herbert,* the court held that libel plaintiffs can ask detailed questions about such decisions during discovery leading up to trial and during the trial itself. The court said that it made the ruling in order to avoid making it impossible, or nearly so, for plaintiffs to prove the requisite degree of fault.

Some courts have interpreted that decision as applying not only to the editorial process, but to the identity of confidential sources. This reading has led these courts to impose harsh restrictions on media defendants in libel actions growing from stories in which confidential sources were used. One of these approaches, to deny the defendant the use of any information obtained from such sources, has been applied in shield-law states.

In New York, for instance, a court of appeals ruled that CBS could not be compelled to identify any of the confidential sources it had used in preparing a segment of *60 Minutes* entitled "Over the Speed Limit."[137] The segment included an interview with an unidentified woman who said that a physician whom she identified

---

133. Galloway v. CBS, a California libel case summarized in *News Media & The Law,* September–October 1983, pp. 47–48.
134. Outlet Communications, Inc. v. State, 588 A.2d 1050, 18 Med.L.Rptr. 1983 (R.I. 1991); CBS, Inc. v. Jackson, 578 So.2d 698, 18 Med.L.Rptr. 2110 (Fla. 1991).
135. As in Cuthbertson, discussed earlier in this chapter.
136. 441 U.S. 153, 99 S.Ct. 1635, 60 L.Ed.2d 115, 4 Med.L.Rptr. 2575 (1979).
137. Greenberg v. CBS Inc., 69 A.D. 693, 419 N.Y.S.2d 988, 5 Med.L.Rptr. 1470 (N.Y.App. 1979).

had prescribed more than eighty diet pills a day to help her lose weight. When the physician sued for libel, CBS tried to support the patient's allegation by offering affidavits from other confidential sources. CBS acted in the belief that New York's shield law gave it absolute protection against being required to identify its sources. The appeals court conceded that because of the shield law, the trial court could not make CBS identify any of the sources. However, the appeals court held that when the case went to trial, CBS would have two options: It could continue to stand behind the shield law, in which instance it could not defend itself by offering evidence that it had obtained from confidential sources. Or it could waive the shield law, identify its sources, and use the evidence from these sources to refute the physician's assertion that CBS had been grossly negligent in preparing the segment.

More than a decade ago, state courts in California and New Hampshire and a federal district court in Hawaii imposed even more severe restrictions on libel defendants who sought to protect confidential sources of defamatory information. In each instance, the trial judge instructed the jury to assume that no source existed. This was tantamount to a finding that the defendant had made up the story, thus acting with actual malice.

The California case[138] was based on a story in *Penthouse* alleging that the owners of a luxury golfing resort had ties to organized crime. The New Hampshire case was brought by a police chief who was the subject of a newspaper article in which an unidentified source said that he had failed a lie detector test. When the chief sued for libel, he said he could not prove actual malice unless he knew who the source was. The newspaper insisted on keeping its source confidential. Although the state had no shield law, the New Hampshire Supreme Court said that it would not compel disclosure unless the chief could offer proof that the story was false. Then, holding that the chief had offered such proof, the court said that if the reporter chose to go to jail rather than identify the source, the trial judge should proceed on the assumption that no source existed.[139] The case brought to the federal district court in Hawaii grew out of articles in the *Pacific Daily News,* published in Guam, criticizing the president of the island of Nauru. When the president sued for libel and asked the newspaper to identify its confidential sources, the district judge gave the newspaper sixty days to comply or face the prospect of going to trial under instructions to the jury that the sources did not exist.[140] Two years later the case was dismissed.

More commonly, courts have shown a willingness to look past *Herbert,* if the key issue is identity of a source, and apply a balancing test. The first step in the test requires plaintiffs to prove that they were victims of a defamatory falsehood. Some courts have required plaintiffs to prove that their suits are not frivolous or brought for purposes of harassment. Only after the issue has been joined have courts moved to the question of whether the identity of confidential sources is essential to the plaintiff's

138.   Rancho La Costa, Inc. v. Penthouse, 165 Cal.Rptr. 347, 6 Med.L.Rptr. 1540 (Calif.Super.Ct. 1980).

139.   Downing v. Monitor Publishing Co., 415 A.2d 683, 6 Med.L.Rptr. 1193 (N.H. 1980).

140.   DeRoburt v. Gannett Co., 507 F.Supp. 880, 6 Med.L.Rptr. 2473 (D.Hawaii 1981).

effort to prove negligence or actual malice. Even then, some courts have required plaintiffs to prove that they have exhausted alternative methods of identifying the source of the defamatory falsehood.

A case frequently cited as a precedent grew out of an article in a trade publication re-

Miller v. *Transamerican Press, Inc.,* 621 F.2d 721, 6 Med.L.Rptr. 1598 (5th Cir. 1980).

porting that a trustee of the Teamsters' pension fund had mishandled the fund's assets. The article was based on information from a confidential source. The trustee sued the magazine for libel and sought, during discovery, to learn the identity of the source. On three occasions, a federal district court ruled that

the trustee could not compel discovery from the writer or the magazine's editor until he could prove that the information was not available from other sources. A fellow trustee gave the plaintiff a sworn statement saying he knew nothing to indicate that the fund's assets had been mishandled. This statement, together with a sworn statement from the plaintiff asserting that the article was false, was accepted by the court as proof of falsity. The trial judge then ruled that the trustee could not prove actual malice unless he knew who the source was. Because the identity of the source went to the heart of the trustee's case, the judge ordered Transamerican to name its source. On appeal, the Fifth Circuit Court modified the order, limiting disclosure to the trustee's lawyer. On rehearing, the circuit court said that its order would not go into effect until the plaintiff had made reasonable, but unsuccessful, efforts to identify the source on his own and had established that his case could not proceed unless the source was identified.

In several more recent cases, however, judges have held that shield laws give journalists an absolute right to protect their sources and that their doing so should not be held against them. An Indiana appeals court did so in a libel action brought by a former police chief. When the reporter refused to identify the source of comments disparaging the chief's leadership, the chief argued that the refusal impaired his right to protect his reputation. He also asked the court to rule that the jury should be instructed that the reporter had no source. The court of appeals ruled against the chief on both counts. The newspaper won the lawsuit.[141]

A New Jersey court held that that state's shield law protected the identity of the writer of a letter to the editor that was published without a signature.[142] The newspaper had a policy of publishing letters without a signature as long as the writer's name was on file. When one such letter became the subject of a libel suit, the trial judge ruled that the shield law protected only sources sought out by journalists, not those who voluntarily offered information, as in letters to the editor. He also ruled that the law did not cover editors or the newspaper itself. The appellate court overruled the judge on both counts.

A federal court interpreting Nevada's shield law held it to be the strongest in the country.[143] In a case brought against the McClatchy newspapers of California by a former U.S. senator from Nevada, Paul Laxalt, the court said that the plaintiff could not

---

141. Jamerson v. Anderson Newspapers, 169 N.E.2d 1243 (Ind.Ct.App. 1984).
142. Gastman v. North Jersey Newspapers Co., 254 N.J.Super.Ct. 140, 603 A.2d 111, 19 Med.L.Rptr. 2187 (App.Div. 1992).
143. Laxalt v. McClatchy, 116 F.R.D. 438, 14 Med.L.Rptr. 1149 (D.Nev. 1987).

require the newspapers' reporters to disclose their sources of derogatory information about him.

Thus, even in libel actions based on allegations made to journalists by confidential sources, some courts recognize the existence of a journalist's privilege and in many instances are honoring it.

SEARCH WARRANTS AND THIRD-PARTY SUBPOENAS

Subpoenas directed at journalists and publishers are not the only legal instruments used by prosecutors, judges, and attorneys in their attempts to get confidential information. Search warrants also have been used, as have subpoenas directed at third parties who have information that might identify a journalist's sources. Search warrants are authorized by the Fourth Amendment, which was drafted to protect people's property and possessions from arbitrary seizure by police. The amendment says that searches of private property can be made only if authorized for good cause by a magistrate. Usually, warrants are issued only to seize evidence of a crime—such things as a stash of drugs, stolen property, or weapons believed to have been used in committing a crime. Third-party subpoenas sometimes are served on banks to obtain financial information about a suspected criminal, or on the telephone company to obtain records of a user's long-distance calls.

The Privacy Protection Act of 1980

Search warrants seldom are a problem for the news media. Few publishers are involved in crime, and newsrooms are unlikely hiding places for criminal contraband. However, the era of political activism of the 1960s and 1970s, which reached a climax during the latter years of the Vietnam war, brought police search teams into newsrooms in disturbing numbers. And in the 1990s, the growth of on-line publishing has produced a number of highly publicized police searches of computer systems. Usually, the police have been seeking evidence of copyright violations, pirated software, pornography, information about confidential sources, or photographs that would help identify persons who caused personal injury or property damage during riots. In the most notable of these searches, police rummaged through desk drawers and wastebaskets in the office of the *Stanford Daily,* a college newspaper in California. Police were seeking photographs that would help them identify students and others who had occupied the Stanford University Hospital and who had severely beaten several police officers. The searchers found nothing that would help, but their actions led first to a significant Supreme Court decision and then to congressional enactment of the Privacy Protection Act of 1980.

"DO WE YELL 'DON'T MOVE,' 'THIS IS A RAID,' OR 'STOP THE PRESSES'?"

The decision in *Zurcher* v. *Stanford Daily* alarmed the news media, which roundly criticized the Court's opinion. Congress responded with legislation to provide more protection for news media than they could now expect from either the First or Fourth Amendment. Although news organizations today are often subpoenaed to produce evidence, search warrants are rare and in most cases illegal. (*Wayne Stayskal/Tribune Media Services*)

The Supreme Court decision, in *Zurcher* v. *Stanford Daily,* was seen at the time as a serious blow to First Amendment freedoms. The editors of the newspaper had reacted to the search by filing suit against those responsible, alleging violation of freedom of the press and abuse of the search warrant provision of the Fourth Amendment. They argued that because there was no evidence that anyone on the *Daily* had been involved in a crime, the police should have used a subpoena, not a search warrant, to obtain the unused photographs. Lower federal courts found in the students' favor, but the Supreme Court reversed.

Zurcher v. *Stanford Daily,*
436 U.S. 547, 98 S.Ct. 1970,
56 L.Ed.2d 525, 3
Med.L.Rptr. 2377 (1978).

Justice White, writing for a majority of the Court, noted that search warrants had been used on other occasions to seize printed materials. His reference was to instances, mainly during the Cold War era after World War II, when police had seized books and pamphlets alleged to be subversive. The court held that any First Amendment interest in protecting the newsroom from police intrusion had been taken into account by the magistrate who had issued the search warrant.

White noted further that the Fourth Amendment requires only that the warrant describe specifically the place to be searched. He found nothing in that language exempting newsrooms. If police believe that helpful evidence can be found in a particular place, and if they further believe that a subpoena would result in destruction of that evidence, issuance of a search warrant is justified. The First Amendment, in the Court's view, cannot create sanctuaries beyond the reach of the police.

The decision encouraged police and prosecutors to conduct twenty-three other newsroom searches in ten states within the year after it was handed down.[144] It also helped persuade Congress to enact the Privacy Protection Act of 1980.[145] The law, which applies to federal, state, and local law enforcement agencies, strictly limits the circumstances under which a warrant can be issued to search for the "work products" and "documentary materials" of persons "engaged in First Amendment Activities." Translated from legal jargon, the act protects photographs, audiotapes and videotapes, notes on interviews, drafts of articles, and notes used in preparation of articles.

The law does not raise absolute barriers against searches, however. A warrant can be issued to seize any materials if there is probable cause to believe a publisher is using them to commit a crime or if seizure is necessary to prevent death or serious injury.

Further, "documentary materials"—such things as photos and recordings that do not involve the mental impressions, conclusions, opinions, or theories of the person who created the material—can be seized if there is reason to believe they would be destroyed in response to a subpoena or if they have not been handed over in response to a court order and further delay would stand in the way of justice. In addition to the federal search protection statute, nine states have enacted similar legislation: California, Connecticut, Illinois, Nebraska, New Jersey, Oregon, Texas, Washington, and Wisconsin.

A case in Missouri in 1994 illustrates that the federal statute does have clout, though it may not always prevent a search.[146] During the 10 P.M. newscast at WDAF-TV in Kansas City, Missouri, a prosecuting attorney and a police officer seized a fourteen-minute videotape. They arrived with a search warrant rather than a subpoena because, the prosecutor explained later, Missouri law did not permit her to get a subpoena unless there was a "pending case." Since the tape did not yet involve a "pending case" and the station had refused to turn over the tape without a subpoena, she followed what she thought was the most expedient means to get the tape. In the presence of an armed police officer, the station gave up the tape; later the station sued, claiming violation of the Privacy Protection Act of 1980.

The tape had been purchased by the station from a tourist for $150. It showed a man dragging a woman into an apartment building and emerging alone without her. The woman was later found shot to death in the building's lobby. Because police had used a search warrant rather than a subpoena, the federal district court awarded the station $1,000 in damages and ordered the return of the tape. The judge enforced the penalty even though there was no evidence of any real damage to the station's ability to gather and disseminate news, and even though Missouri law didn't permit a subpoena. Judge Fernando Gaitan, Jr., told prosecutor Claire McCaskill that Missouri had had plenty of time—since 1980—to provide any necessary legal machinery for the issuance of subpoenas, and that if she knew of an exception that would permit a

---

144. *News Media Update,* 19 October 1981.
145. 42 U.S.C. §§ 2000aa–2000aa-12 (1976 and Supp.IV 1980).
146. Sandra Davidson Scott, "Storming a Newsroom with a Search Warrant," *Editor & Publisher,* 18 March 1995, p. 18.

search in this case, she should have made that clear to a magistrate before, not after, a search was conducted.

The leading case involving an on-line publisher[147] occurred when federal agents raided Steve Jackson Games, a company that designed and published role-playing games and operated a computer bulletin board. Police suspected that an employee of the company was a member of an illegal hacker group called Legion of Doom. Armed with what appeared to be a warrant, the agents searched the offices and seized the on-line computer system, spare parts, and a laser printer, among other things. They also confiscated the printed copies of a game manual then under development, *GURPS Cyberpunk,* which police thought was a manual for illegal hackers.

The company sued the government under the Privacy Protection Act because the search affected materials being prepared for publication; the company also sought protection under the federal Electronic Communications Privacy Act because it operated as an electronic publisher.[148] The trial court awarded Steve Jackson Games $51,000 in damages; it also awarded $1,000 each to several persons who had been using the system at the time of the seizure. The Court of Appeals for the Fifth Circuit affirmed.

The Electronic Communications Privacy Act

In *Steve Jackson Games* the court applied not only the Privacy Protection Act but also a federal statute written in the 1980s specifically to protect the privacy of computer-based communications, such as E-mail and stored messages. The Electronic Communications Privacy Act treats government interceptions of private electronic communications as a "search" in the Fourth Amendment sense. Accordingly a search warrant is required before police can examine on-line or stored messages that were intended to be private. To intercept on-line, real-time transmissions over the Internet, for example, government agents must have a search warrant that specifies, among other things, exactly what the criminal activities are suspected to be, exactly which system they want to intercept, how long the interception will last, and why other means of obtaining the information would be unlikely to succeed or would be too dangerous.[149]

To require disclosure of stored messages less than 180 days old—the situation for most E-mail—the requirements for a warrant are only a bit less vigorous. If E-mail or other stored messages are more than 180 days old, the act allows the government the option of obtaining a search warrant if it can meet the high standards of specificity, or if it can't, of using a subpoena.[150] The subpoena is easier for law enforcement agents to obtain, but it also gives the person being subpoenaed an opportunity to object. Finally, the act limits the ability of government to obtain information from system operators about the activities of on-line users unless the agents can meet the requirements for a search warrant.[151]

---

147.   Steve Jackson Games, Inc. v. U.S. Secret Service, 816 F.Supp. 432 (W.D.Tex. 1993), affirmed, 36 F.3d 457 (5th Cir. 1994).
148.   18 U.S.C. 2510 (1988).
149.   18 U.S.C. 2518 (1988).
150.   18 U.S.C. 2703 (1988).
151.   18 U.S.C. 2703 (1988).

When the Electronic Communications Privacy Act and the Privacy Protection Act are combined—as they are when electronic communications are used for First Amendment purposes—they can provide a powerful deterrent to unlawful searches of electronic newsrooms. In most instances the Privacy Protection Act forbids search warrants, but even when they are permitted, the Electronic Communications Privacy Act sets high standards for obtaining a warrant. In addition, although the Privacy Protection Act allows material taken unlawfully to be used as evidence in court, when the Electronic Communications Act also applies, the evidence is excluded. Both acts allow injured parties to sue the government, and the Privacy Protection Act allows injured parties to sue the individual agents or police officers executing the unlawful search.

Any problems with these statutes generally stem from ignorance by police of their existence. Lance Rose, an attorney who has been practicing on-line law for more than a decade, says that most police agencies would follow the rules if they understood them, but "many law enforcement agents are not familiar with either online culture or the laws that apply to networks and online systems. When a government agent tosses a seized online system computer in the back seat of his car, he or she may not realize it contains private messages. . . . To date, most agents and police officers have not been taught that properly executing a search warrant for online system files means interfering as little as possible with the daily operations of the online system."[152] Sympathetic judges, sometimes equally befuddled by new technology, often have been willing to give police the benefit of the doubt when they believe that police acted in good faith and ignorance.[153]

Limitation on Privacy of Phone Records

More than a decade ago several journalists learned that Justice Department attorneys had been studying a listing of their long-distance calls. The listings, showing the telephone numbers of persons called by the journalists, had been obtained under subpoena to the telephone companies serving the reporters' homes and offices. The attorneys sought the records in an attempt to find out who had given the Pentagon Papers to the *New York Times;* how Jack Anderson had obtained copies of a classified report on relations among the United States, India, and Pakistan; and how the *Times* had obtained an income tax audit and access to secret grand jury proceedings.

Believing that such subpoenas were both an invasion of privacy and a violation of First Amendment freedoms, a group of journalists challenged the practice in court. However, the U.S. Court of Appeals for the District of Columbia Circuit upheld the Justice Department's position. Its decision rejected both grounds for the lawsuit. The court said that the search warrant provision of the Fourth Amendment implies a right of privacy that will be protected as long as people stay on their own property. But when people venture off their

Reporters Committee for Freedom of the Press v. *American Telephone & Telegraph Co.,* **593 F.2d 1030, 4 Med.L.Rptr. 1177 (D.C. Cir. 1979); cert. denied, 440 U.S. 949 (1979).**

---

152. Lance Rose, *Netlaw* (New York: Osborne McGraw-Hill, 1995), pp. 231–232.
153. Steve Jackson Games, Inc. v. U.S. Secret Service, 816 F.Supp. 432 (W.D.Tex. 1993), affirmed, 36 F.3d 457 (5th Cir. 1994).

property, or even use the telephone to call others, they give up some of their privacy. In this instance, the telephone company had made records of long-distance calls for billing purposes. Those records belonged to the company, not to the callers. Because the callers gave up their expectations of privacy when they placed the calls, they could not prevent the phone company from surrendering its records to the government under subpoena.

The circuit court referred to White's opinion in *Branzburg* in rejecting the reporters' First Amendment argument. The government's purpose in seeking the long-distance billing records was to investigate a crime. In this instance, it seemed likely from the stories they had written that these journalists had sought information from persons who had committed crimes. As long as the investigation had been conducted in good faith, the subpoena for the long-distance records did not violate the journalists' First Amendment interests.[154]

The following year, the *New York Times* learned that the Justice Department was investigating a department employee suspected of leaking grand jury information to the media. The *Times* also learned that the Justice Department had subpoenaed Southern Bell's records of phone calls from the newspaper's Atlanta bureau and from the home of its bureau chief. More disturbingly, the *Times* learned that the Justice Department had asked Southern Bell to wait ninety days before informing the *Times*. The net result was that the Justice Department had been able to legally subpoena *Times* phone records without notice or an opportunity to object.

After protests by the *Times* and other media, the Justice Department agreed to adopt guidelines that would reduce the likelihood of clandestine subpoenas for records of journalists' long-distance calls.[155] Except in unusual circumstances, department attorneys are supposed to seek a journalist's consent to obtain records. If that fails, a subpoena can be issued only with the attorney general's approval. The department can proceed in criminal cases if it has "reasonable grounds to believe, based on information obtained from nonmedia sources, that a crime has occurred, and that the information sought is essential to a successful investigation." Subpoenas also may be issued in a civil action if the case is of "substantial proportions" and there is reason to believe that the information is "essential to [its] successful completion."

Justice Department guidelines are helpful, but they do not bind other law enforcement agencies or private parties seeking evidence. For example, Procter & Gamble Co., the Cincinnati-based producer of a wide range of consumer products, subpoenaed long-distance records in a futile attempt to find out who in its employ had leaked information to a *Wall Street Journal* reporter.[156] The company contended that articles reporting that the head of its food and beverage division had resigned under pressure and that the company was considering sale of the division disclosed business and trade se-

---

154. The New Jersey Supreme Court, critical of the *Reporter's Committee* decision, has held that the state constitution protects an individual's privacy interest in telephone toll records, even if the First Amendment does not. State v. Hunt, 91 N.J. 338, 450 A.2d 952 (1982).
155. 28 C.F.R. § 50.10.
156. James S. Hirsch, "P&G Says Inquiry on Who Leaked News Was Proper," *Wall Street Journal,* 13 August 1991; James S. Hirsch, "P&G Search for News Leak Led to Sweep of Phone System Wider Than Thought," *Wall Street Journal,* 15 August 1991; Gabriella Stern, "Procter & Gamble Says Its Investigation of News Leak Won't Lead to Prosecution," *Wall Street Journal,* 19 August 1991.

crets. An Ohio law adopted in 1967 makes it a crime to disclose such secrets. Acting through a Cincinnati police officer who was moonlighting as a Procter & Gamble security officer, the company persuaded Cincinnati police to issue a subpoena asking for "all 513 area-code numbers" of telephones whose users had dialed the office or home telephone of the *Journal* reporter. A second subpoena asked for 606 area-code numbers. These area codes are assigned to the Cincinnati metropolitan area, including northern Kentucky. Disclosure of the request created a furor in media circles that subsided only after the company announced in a letter to a *Journal* lawyer that the search had failed to "turn up sufficient information to prosecute."[157]

In the Professional World

Journalists who investigate wrongdoing enter a legal and ethical minefield. If they do their work well, they may win a Pulitzer Prize for meritorious public service. That's what the *Washington Post* did for showing that a burglary at Democratic headquarters was linked to President Nixon's personal staff. Without the help of a still-unidentified source known as Deep Throat, that connection might not have been traced. That same newspaper had to return a Pulitzer Prize when its editors discovered that one of its reporters had made up a touching story about a young boy who was being injected with heroin by his mother and her boyfriend. That story, too, was based on reports from anonymous sources. When Washington police began looking for the boy to save him from almost certain death, the reporter still refused to identify him and her editors backed her up. Only when the story won the prize was the deception discovered.

The *Washington Post* editors were not the first, nor the last, editors to be duped. Editors at the *New York Times,* the *New York Daily News,* and *New Yorker* magazine have run, as fact, stories later discovered to be part fiction because quoted sources did not exist. No doubt other editors have been taken in, too. The temptation to make a good story better, to achieve superficial balance, or to cover for a missing fact is more than some writers can resist. Unfortunately, there is more than a little truth in the cynical newsroom advice, "Never let the facts stand in the way of a good story."

Because of such temptations, both professional editors and the courts have looked askance at stories based on anonymous sources. When Carl Bernstein and Bob Woodward were developing their prize-winning Watergate stories for the *Washington Post,* editors of the newspaper said that no fact obtained from a confidential source was published unless it was corroborated by at least two other sources. The Associated Press stylebook cautions against using material from sources who do not wish to be identified. Many newspaper editors permit the use of anonymous sources only if their information serves an important public purpose and cannot be obtained on the record. Professionals are aware that

---

157. Mark Fitzgerald, "No Soap," *Editor & Publisher,* 24 August 1991, p. 13.

not all sources who insist on anonymity are motivated by the highest principles of public service. Many are self-serving and are engaged in nothing more noble than an attempt to use the news media to get even for a real or imagined wrong.

The threshold question, then, for journalists is whether and to what extent they will rely on confidential sources. Some news organizations advise reporters to promise confidentiality only with an editor's approval. This approval is usually based on evidence that the story can't be obtained otherwise. Even then, information obtained from confidential sources is treated with care and may not be used unless it can be confirmed by on-the-record sources. As the cases discussed in this chapter indicate, courts are more likely to grant the journalist's privilege when they are convinced that the source and the reporter reached a clear agreement on confidentiality. However, lawyers advise reporters to leave room for reconsideration if the reporter is cited for contempt. It is one thing to break a good story. It is another to become a martyr for it.

If a journalist's investigation, with or without the help of confidential sources, does uncover evidence of wrongdoing, new ethical and legal problems arise. Once the story or stories have been published, is the journalist's responsibility to society ended? As this chapter makes clear, courts in most states, in most instances, answer that question with a qualified yes. They do so in recognition of the fact that if a reporter, working without the subpoena power, can uncover wrongdoing, then police, prosecutors, and grand juries, with all the resources at their command, ought to be able to do so, too. This is especially true if the journalist has done a thorough reporting job.

Since the purpose of journalism is public exposure, all the facts that police need to investigate a case ought to be in the newspaper or magazine, or in the televised newscast. However, as the cases in this chapter again suggest, that is not always the situation. Drug pushers made sales and converted marijuana into hashish in Paul Branzburg's presence. They would not knowingly do so in a police officer's presence. When the reporter may be the only witness to a crime, does his or her duty to society end with the production of a no-names story? That question clearly troubled Justice White when he wrote his opinion in *Branzburg*. In his view, "The crimes of news sources are no less reprehensible and threatening to the public interest when witnessed by a reporter than when they are not." In fashioning testimonial privileges, courts think of the worst possible "what ifs": What if a reporter was the only person who knew who shot the governor—and for whatever reason chose not to testify?

The other side of the coin is illustrated by the *Farber* case. There, Myron Farber's stories for the *New York Times* resulted in revival of a long-dormant murder investigation and the arrest of Dr. Mario E. Jascalevich. The stories relied heavily on unidentified sources and may or may not have revealed all that the reporter knew about the case. Acting on the theory that the identity of some of the sources and unpublished information might help his client, Dr. Jascalevich's lawyer issued a subpoena for Farber, his notes, and such notes as the *Times* itself might have. Standing on First Amendment principle, Farber and the *Times* resisted to the point of being held in contempt. Farber spent forty days in jail, and the *Times* was fined heavily to defend a principle. In the end, the jury found the doctor not guilty. But what if Farber had been hiding the only evidence that would have proved his innocence?

As this brief look at the ethical dilemmas suggests, professional journalists tend not to nod politely when a potential news source says, "Don't quote me, but . . ." or "This is off the record." Journalists react by trying to find out why such a request is made and to get some idea of the subject matter that prompts it. Skilled reporters do not readily make promises of confidentiality.

Sophisticated news sources and reporters have developed commonly understood terms that convey degrees of meaning with respect to confidentiality. "Off the record" means that the source does not want to see the information in print or hear it on the air. The reporter is expected to use it only for guidance to avoid misstating the thrust of the news. Information offered "for background only" is designed to help the reporter understand a complex situation and may be reflected, but not directly included, in the story. If the source offers information "not for attribution," he or she wants to see it in print or hear it on the air but does not want to be connected with it. Public officials sometimes use this means to "float a trial balloon"—that is, to disclose a policy option and see how the public reacts to it before making it official. If the policy is shot down, the reporter, not the official, takes the flak.

Journalists are of two minds about confidential sources and information. Scoop-minded columnists and producers of "insider" magazine shows for television could not survive without them. Nor could investigative reporters for any medium. Indeed, we would not know as much as we do about the inside doings of government at any level if it were not for good reporters' "informed sources." Part of the art of reporting is knowing who to go to for the straight story when the official, on-the-record version is laced with double-talk.

At the other extreme are the reporters who receive all off-the-record requests with skepticism or even distrust. They are afraid of being used, and they don't want to have their hands tied if they can get the same information on the record. This difference of opinion among journalists is part of the reason there is no federal shield law. Reporters and editors who have testified before committees of Congress could not agree not only on how far the law should go, but on whether there should be one at all.

The opinions written by Justices White and Stewart in *Branzburg* reflect the differences among journalists. In White's view, confidential sources play a minor role in journalism. To him, it was incredible that a press that had flourished for more than 150 years without the ability to protect its sources suddenly had need for a First Amendment privilege. To Stewart, White's view was a "crabbed view" that might reduce the news media to serving as a transmission belt for the official views of official sources. In Stewart's view, confidential sources are important because now and then one of them helps the news media expose incompetence, mistaken policies, or outright wrongdoing on the part of public officials. In Stewart's eyes, the possibility for abuse is a small price to pay for the public benefit that flows from the use of even a limited journalist's privilege.

FOR REVIEW ▬▬▬▬▬▬▬▬▬▬▬▬▬▬▬▬▬▬▬▬▬▬▬▬▬▬▬▬

1. What is the journalist's privilege? Describe and justify other testimonial privileges recognized by the courts. Analyze the differences and similarities between the journalist's privilege and the other testimonial privileges.

2. What did the Supreme Court decide with respect to the three journalists who were involved in *Branzburg* v. *Hayes?* Identify the elements in that case that can be construed as creating a journalist's privilege.

3. List and discuss arguments for and against the journalist's privilege. What is your opinion? Justify it.

4. What is a shield law? If your state has one, what are its terms?

5. Has your state recognized a privilege for journalists other than that established by a shield law? If so, what are its terms?

6. You and your roommate stop in a convenience store to pick up a case of soda and some chips. While your roommate is scanning the magazine rack, you see a man approach the cashier, raise a revolver, point it at her, and force her to empty the cash drawer into a paper sack. Before you can say anything, he is gone. You are a reporter for the student newspaper. Your roommate is not. Undoubtedly, you have a story. What would you do if the police or the prosecutor were to ask you to help them identify a suspect? Why? Would your answer be any different if your roommate also had seen the robbery? Or if the robber had shot the cashier?

7. You are doing a story on campus racism for your student newspaper. You manage to gain the confidence of a group that satirizes "political correctness" by staging incidents directed at professors and student leaders who are known for their ardent championing of the rights of women and minorities. You do so by promising that your stories will fairly reflect their views without identifying any individual without his or her permission. One evening, after a few beers, several members of the group suggest "a little fun" by painting "KKK" and racial epithets on the outside walls of a house occupied by a predominantly black fraternity. Members of the fraternity have been on guard against such an occurrence and jump your group. There is a fight, and one of the African-American students suffers a serious injury when he is struck by one of your group and falls, hitting his head on the corner of a concrete porch step. You see it happen and know who struck the blow. You get away undetected, but some of the others are caught and arrested. Do you write a story describing what happened? What should you do? Suppose that you write a story and police decide to press charges against whoever struck the injured man. What do you do if an officer questions you? If you are summoned to testify before a grand jury? Or in a civil suit brought by the victim against his attacker? If you choose to exercise a journalist's privilege in any of the above eventualities, what factors would determine whether the privilege is upheld in court?

CHAPTER 9

As its Preamble declares, the Constitution established a government of the people. It is easy to postulate, then, that the authors must have intended, in part, to provide for access to information about government. After all, if the people are to make wise decisions about how they are to be governed, they must have access to information about the performance of government and government officials. This idea is embodied today in the phrase "the right to know."

However, if the founders intended that there be public access to government information, they did not write that intention into the Constitution. Nor did they act as if they believed that government should be conducted in the open. The Constitutional Convention itself was conducted in secrecy. Once the finished product had been announced to the public and the new government established, the Senate met behind closed doors for the first five years of its existence.[1] Only two paragraphs in the Constitution mandate any degree of openness on the part of the federal government. Both are found in Article I, which established the Congress and defined its powers:

---

1. Robert A. Diamond, ed., *Origins and Development of Congress* (Washington, D.C.: Congressional Quarterly, 1976), pp. 178–180.

THE RIGHT TO KNOW

Each House shall keep a journal of its proceedings, and from time to time publish the same, excepting such parts as may in their judgment require secrecy; and the yeas and nays of the members of either House on any question shall, at the desire of one-fifth of those present, be entered on the journal. [Section 5, paragraph 3]

No money shall be drawn from the Treasury, but in consequence of appropriations made by law; and a regular statement and account of the receipts and expenditures of all public money shall be published from time to time. [Section 9, paragraph 7]

The first requirement is met by publication of the *Journal,* a summary listing of actions taken by both houses of Congress, and, in an expanded form, by the *Congressional Record.* The second requirement is met by publication of the annual budget, which includes actual receipts and expenditures by categories in the previous fiscal year, an estimate for the current year, and planned spending for the next year. That is all the information the Constitution requires the government to give its people.

Until 1966, citizens who approached government officials in quest of information had to be content with what they got. Vance Trimble, a reporter for the Scripps-Howard News Service, learned that even the First Amendment was no help to him when he tried to find out whether members of the Senate were violating the law by putting relatives on their office payrolls.[2] He had won a prize for distinguished reporting with a series of articles naming House members who illegally funneled tax money to their relatives. But when he sought the same information from the clerk of the Senate, Felton Johnston, he was turned down flat. When Trimble went to the U.S. District Court for the District of Columbia for an order directing Johnston to let him examine the Senate payroll, Judge Alexander Holtzoff told him the court could not create a duty where neither the Constitution nor Congress had established one. The First Amendment, he said, would protect Trimble in publishing any news he might find, but it could not be used to pry news from reluctant officials. Nor would Article I, section 9, paragraph 7 help him. The Senate payroll, in total amount—without names—was in the budget, as that paragraph required.

A present-day Vance Trimble still would find himself unable to use the First Amendment to compel a congressional employee to let him look at the Senate payroll. But there are a couple of tools he might use today to obtain information from government that were not available in 1959. If the information sought is held by the judiciary, for example, he might cite the Supreme Court's 1980 holding in *Richmond Newspa-*

---

2. *Trimble v. Johnston,* 173 F.Supp. 651, 1 Med.L.Rptr. 2329 (D.D.C. 1959).

pers v. *Virginia.*[3] That opinion recognized a First Amendment right to attend trials. Since then, courts have interpreted the First Amendment as requiring access to most judicial proceedings and even to some court records. Unfortunately for present-day Trimbles, the courts, reluctant to tread too daringly onto the turf of the other two branches of government, have not stretched the First Amendment into a general right of access. Congress, on the other hand, has opened many of the records and most of the meetings of federal administrative agencies.

Congress passed the Freedom of Information Act in 1965 and has amended it several times since. The act established that records of federal agencies are available to the public on demand unless they fall within one of nine exemptions. The act does not reach records of the Office of the President,[4] of the courts, or of the Congress itself, but it reaches a lot of government information held by such bodies as the Federal Bureau of Investigation, the Food and Drug Administration, and the Federal Trade Commission. Today, journalists, scholars, business firms, and the general public use the act routinely to obtain records that once might have been withheld at a government worker's whim.

This chapter begins with a survey of the decisions in which the courts have ruled on a claimed First Amendment right of access to government information. The major part of the chapter examines the court decisions defining the limits of the Freedom of Information Act, with particular attention to the nine exemptions. The exemptions give agencies rather wide discretion to withhold information sought by journalists and others, and the courts have supported them more often than not. Congress also has adopted a "Government in the Sunshine" Act, which requires that federal administrative decision-making bodies meet and act in public.

The latter part of the chapter deals in a general way with the open-records and open-meetings laws in effect in all fifty states. Although these laws vary in detail, all are based on the same principle as the federal law—that government be conducted in the open so that the people can check the performance of those who hold public office.

Major Cases

■ *Butterworth* v. *Smith,* 494 U.S. 624, 110 S.Ct. 1376, 108 L.Ed.2d 572, 17 Med.L.Rptr. 1569 (1990).

■ *Chrysler Corp.* v. *Brown,* 441 U.S. 281, 99 S.Ct. 1705, 60 L.Ed.2d 208, 4 Med.L.Rptr. 2441 (1979).

■ *Consumer Product Safety Commission* v. *GTE Sylvania, Inc.,* 447 U.S. 102, 100 S.Ct. 2051, 64 L.Ed.2d 766, 6 Med.L.Rptr. 1301 (1980).

---

3. 448 U.S. 555, 100 S.Ct. 2814, 65 L.Ed.2d 973, 6 Med.L.Rptr. 1833 (1980).
4. National Security Archive v. U.S. Archivist, 909 F.2d 541, 17 Med.L. Rptr. 2265 (D.C. Cir. 1990).

- *Department of Justice* v. *Reporters Committee for Freedom of the Press,* 489 U.S. 749, 109 S.Ct. 1468, 103 L.Ed.2d 774, 16 Med.L.Rptr. 1545 (1989).

- *Department of the Air Force* v. *Rose,* 425 U.S. 352, 96 S.Ct. 1592, 48 L.Ed.2d 11 (1976).

- *Federal Bureau of Investigation* v. *Abramson,* 456 U.S. 615, 102 S.Ct. 2054, 72 L.Ed.2d 376, 8 Med.L.Rptr. 1561 (1982).

- *Forsham* v. *Harris,* 445 U.S. 169, 100 S.Ct. 978, 63 L.Ed.2d 293, 5 Med.L.Rptr. 2473 (1980).

- *Kissinger* v. *Reporters Committee for Freedom of the Press,* 445 U.S. 136, 100 S.Ct. 960, 63 L.Ed.2d 267, 6 Med.L.Rptr. 1001 (1980).

- *Public Citizen* v. *U.S. Department of Justice,* 491 U.S. 440, 109 S.Ct. 2558, 105 L.Ed.2d 377 (1989).

- *Seattle Times Company* v. *Rinehart,* 467 U.S. 20, 104 S.Ct. 2199, 81 L.Ed.2d 17, 10 Med.L.Rptr. 1705 (1984).

- *U.S. Department of Justice* v. *Tax Analysts,* 492 U.S. 136, 109 S.Ct. 2841, 106 L.Ed.2d 112, 16 Med.L.Rptr. 1849 (1989).

- *U.S. Department of State* v. *Washington Post Co.,* 456 U.S. 595, 102 S.Ct. 1957, 72 L.Ed.2d 358, 8 Med.L.Rptr. 1521 (1982).

THE RIGHT OF ACCESS TO GOVERNMENT INFORMATION

The First Amendment and the Right of Access

In 1959 a federal judge surveyed the Supreme Court's First Amendment decisions and told Vance Trimble he could find nothing in them to require government officials to divulge any information they wished to withhold. Twenty-one years later, Chief Justice Warren Burger, writing for the Court in *Richmond Newspapers* v. *Virginia,*[5] said, for the first time, that the First Amendment gives the public a right to attend and report on at least one important governmental function—the trial of a criminal defendant. Justice John Paul Stevens hailed the decision as "a watershed case." He saw it as opening the door to a recognition that the First Amendment provided a right to

---

5. 448 U.S. 555, 100 S.Ct. 2814, 65 L.Ed.2d 1973, 6 Med.L.Rptr. 1833 (1980).

gather news. He said, "[T]he Court unequivocally holds that an arbitrary interference with access to important information is an abridgment of the freedoms of speech and of the press protected by the First Amendment."

Although the scope of a constitutional right of access to information remains to be fully defined, it has not been carried as far as Justice Stevens suggested it might be. Neither, however, is it entirely limited to the observing of criminal trials. In *United States* v. *Carpentier,*[6] for example, a federal district court in New York held that the First Amendment provided a right of access to evidence admitted at trial, in this case an audiotape made by undercover FBI agents. The tapes indicated that seven members of the House of Representatives, a senator, and several local government officials were willing to take bribes to do favors for foreign nationals. Voice recordings of one transaction were admitted in evidence during the trial, but they were not played in court. At the end of the trial, the defendants' attorney moved to seal the tape for sixty days. The *New York Times* and the *New York Daily News* objected. The court, reviewing a line of Supreme Court cases ending with *Richmond Newspapers,* found "an emerging right of the public to know what happens in court." It ordered the tapes released.

Five years later, a panel of the U.S. appeals court in Boston surveyed *Richmond*'s progeny,[7] and found that the "emerging right" seen by the New York district court had moved in two directions. In one direction, courts had found a strong right in the First Amendment for the news media and the public to insist that judicial proceedings be conducted in public. These included jury selection, preliminary hearings, hearings on the admissibility of evidence, and hearings on the setting of bail.

But the appellate court panel found that the Supreme Court's decision in *Richmond* and its progeny had added very little to the long-standing common law right of access to records generated by court proceedings. Under common law, decisions of judges, transcripts of testimony given in open court, and any exhibits admitted as evidence at trial are records open to inspection by anyone, with some important exceptions. Information gathered to guide judges in sentencing convicted criminals is typically confidential, often under a state statute. Reports on the conduct of criminals released on probation are also confidential. Moreover, the common law provides no help for reporters seeking documents related to court proceedings but not yet part of the court record, such as discovery materials collected by lawyers preparing a case.[8] Most important, the common law permits sensitive court records to be sealed "for good cause shown" at the request of either party with the approval of the judge. Typically a "good cause" could be to protect national security, privacy, or trade secrets; to safeguard an ongoing criminal investigation; or to facilitate settlement of a troublesome lawsuit.

The news media have had mixed results in arguing that the First Amendment implies a right of access to records of the kinds listed above. In criminal cases, where there is a clear public interest in law enforcement, the common law's "good cause

---

6.   526 F.Supp. 292, 7 Med.L.Rptr. 2332 (E.D.N.Y. 1981); affirmed, 689 F.2d 21 (2d Cir. 1982); cert. denied, 459 U.S. 1108 (1983).
7.   Anderson v. Cryovac, Inc., 805 F.2d 1, 13 Med.L.Rptr. 1721 (1st Cir. 1986).
8.   McCarthy v. Barnett Bank, 876 F.2d 89, 16 Med.L.Rptr. 2016 (11th Cir. 1989); Tavoulareas v. Washington Post, 724 F.2d 1010, 10 Med.L.Rptr. 1129 (D.C. Cir. 1984); Tavoulareas v. Piro, 759 F.2d 90 (D.C. Cir. 1985); Tavoulareas v. Piro, 763 F.2d 1472 (D.C. Cir. 1985).

shown" often comes close to a First Amendment standard.[9] In civil cases, however, news media have had much less success in expanding access rights beyond the common law's deference to a judge's reasonable discretion.[10]

Several courts have held that there is little, if any, First Amendment right to challenge orders sealing discovery documents.[11] The U.S. Court of Appeals for the Sixth Circuit, for example, upheld a district judge's decision not only to seal the records of a fourteen-day "trial" but also to impose a gag order on the six "jurors" who decided it. The Supreme Court declined to review the circuit court's ruling.[12] The "trial" was conducted as part of a fact-finding process intended to encourage a settlement among three Ohio electric power companies and General Electric about liability for the safety of parts provided for an abandoned nuclear generating plant. To resolve the questions at issue, the parties agreed to submit them to a U.S. district court jury in Cincinnati for optionally binding decisions. Two months after the hearing, the parties announced that they had reached agreement on a settlement. General Electric issued a press release saying that the jury had not found it liable on any of the claims made against it.

Newspapers in Cincinnati, Dayton, and Columbus sued to obtain access to the records. The district court judge dismissed the action. He conceded that the proceeding had seemed to be a trial, but in reality it was only part of a pretrial procedure leading to a settlement. Such procedures, he said, are not open to the public but are private actions among the parties. The court of appeals agreed, holding that the First Amendment "does not attach to summary trial proceedings."

Courts, as one might expect, routinely encourage parties to settle their civil disputes without a trial. But whether it is appropriate for a court to agree to seal records in order to encourage settlement is a matter of considerable disagreement among judges and reporters. What gives hope to First Amendment advocates is that in deciding whether the possibility of a quick settlement is a sufficiently "good cause" to justify sealing records, courts are likely to consider whether the dispute is a mostly private

---

9. Minnesota v. Swart, Med.L.Rptr. 1703 (Minn.App. 1992) finding that access "to records revealing the identities of jurors may be denied only in the 'interest of justice,' upon showing of 'exceptional circumstances peculiar to the case'"; In re State-Record Co., 917 F.2d 124, 18 Med.L.Rptr. 1286 (4th Cir. 1990) holding that sealing of case records was in error because the trial court applied a "reasonable likelihood" test rather than "substantial probability" of prejudice; United States v. Smith, 776 F.2d 1104, 12 Med.L.Rptr. 1345 (3d Cir. 1985) holding that access is protected by the First Amendment and the common law; Tribune Co. v. United States, 480 U.S. 931 (1987) holding that the standard for sealing is a "compelling governmental interest" and that the order must be narrowly tailored to serve that compelling interest.

10. For example, see Cipollone v. Liggett Group Inc., 785 F.2d 1108 (3d Cir. 1986); In re Reporters Committee for Freedom of the Press, 773 F.2d 1325, 12 Med.L.Rptr. 1073 (D.C. Cir. 1985); Webster Groves School District v. Pulitzer Publishing Co., 898 F.2d 1371, 17 Med.L.Rptr. 1633 (1990). "The Supreme Court never has found a First Amendment right of access to. . . . the court file in a civil proceeding."

11. Anderson v. Cryovac, Inc., 805 F.2d 1, 13 Med.L.Rptr. 1721 (1st Cir. 1986); Tavoulareas v. Washington Post Co., 737 F.2d 1170, 10 Med.L.Rptr. 2360 (D.C. Cir. 1984); and Courier-Journal and Louisville Times Co. v. Marshall, 828 F.2d 361, 14 Med.L.Rptr. 1561 (6th Cir. 1987). All deal with discovery in civil actions. A Florida appellate court cited Seattle Times Co. v. Rhinehart, 467 U.S. 20, 104 S.Ct. 2199, 81 L.Ed.2d 17, 10 Med.L.Rptr. 1705 (1984), in upholding a denial of access to discovery in a criminal case, and Palm Beach Newspapers, Inc. v. Burk, 504 So.2d 378; rev. denied, 506 So.2d 1037, 13 Med.L.Rptr. 2087 (Fla. 1987); cert. denied, 484 U.S. 954 (1987).

12. George Garneau, "Supreme Court Upholds Sweeping Secrecy," *Editor & Publisher,* 4 March 1989, p. 22.

action—as it did in the General Electric case—or whether there is a countervailing public concern. In the latter case, courts are frequently reluctant to seal records, even when doing so would produce a settlement.

The Iowa Supreme Court shed light on this issue when, without ever mentioning the First Amendment, it ruled on public policy grounds that a written settlement agreement between a school district and a school principal could *not* be sealed.[13] The dispute arose when Dr. Bobbretta Williams was assigned to be principal of an elementary school in Des Moines. Shortly thereafter, about seventy parents and teachers complained about her performance to the director of elementary education. At a public meeting, Williams challenged the complaints, saying that she was the victim of racist and sexist slurs and that most of the parent and teacher unhappiness related to needed changes she had made in the school. Parents and some teachers then formed a group to try to resolve dissension, the superintendent appointed two investigatory committees, and Williams filed a series of civil rights complaints with the school district and with the Iowa Civil Rights Commission.

At the end of the school year, Williams and the school district announced that they had reached a settlement in which Williams agreed to dismiss her discrimination complaints against the school and agreed to resign in exchange for $49,500. The settlement was announced in a press release, but the settlement and the supporting documents were not made available to the media. The *Des Moines Register* sued for access, and in response, the state supreme court ordered the trial court to disclose the settlement agreement and any supporting documents not otherwise protected under Iowa law. "The written settlement agreement," the court said, "like most items in dispute, possesses some ingredients of both a purely public nature and also of a personal matter the legislature has designated as confidential. But the outstanding characteristic of the settlement agreement was that public funds were being paid to settle a private dispute."

The Iowa court's opinion suggests that courts, even under the common law, are likely to refuse a request to seal records when there is a clear public interest involved—as there would be in cases involving the use of public funds, oversight of government, or criminal activity. On the other hand, courts are likely to presume openness but be less scrupulous when the interests are largely thought to be non-public—as might be the case in civil disputes about contracts, tort liability, or divorce.[14]

These tendencies of the courts are further suggested by two appellate opinions in criminal cases—one federal and one state—involving probation and presentencing reports, documents one might think likely to be sealed for the "good cause" of privacy and judicial efficiency. However, both courts found that the public's interest in crimi-

---

13. Des Moines School District v. Des Moines Register & Tribune Co., 20 Med.L.Rptr. 1355 (Iowa 1992).

14. In re Keene Sentinel, 612 A.2d 911, 20 Med.L.Rptr. 1770 (N.H. 1992) finding divorce records presumptively open under the New Hampshire constitution. Lund v. Lund, 20 Med.L.Rptr. 1775 (Minn.App. 1992) finding divorce records presumptively open under Minnesota common law. Holland v. Eads, 20 Med.L.Rptr. 1839 (Ala. 1992) finding that a trial judge had not abused his discretion in agreeing to seal the records of a settlement between an individual and a car dealership in the interest of ending protracted and expensive litigation involving trade secrets.

nal justice was a clear and countervailing factor—so clear and countervailing that each court invoked not just common law, but the First Amendment.

The Ninth Circuit held in *United States* v. *Schlette*[15] that journalists have a First Amendment interest in examining documents prepared to guide a judge in sentencing a convicted criminal and in probation reports prepared when a convict is released before the end of his or her sentence. Such records are generally considered confidential, but in this instance Roland Schlette had threatened to kill the prosecutor who was responsible for sending him to prison for twenty years for arson. Years later, when Schlette was released on probation, he carried out the threat, then took his own life. The *Marin* (Calif.) *Independent Journal* and the victim's family asked to examine court and probation records on Schlette to see if anything in them should have led officials either to keep him in prison or warn the prosecutor. The request was refused. An appeal was taken to a federal judge, who happened to be the same one who had approved Schlette's release. She denied the request, ruling that such records are prepared only for the judge's guidance. On further appeal, the Ninth Circuit panel reversed, holding, "The newspaper has a legitimate interest in explaining to a concerned public the means by which sentencing decisions are made."

In the second instance, the Maryland Court of Special Appeals held that a trial judge had to consider the First Amendment access rights of the public and the media before he or she could seal a presentence investigation report admitted as evidence during the penalty phase of a murder trial.[16] The court made this ruling even though the report was confidential by state statute. The court said that to justify a court-ordered seal, the trial judge had to notify the public of the request to seal the record and had to provide an opportunity for citizens, including the media, to object. "Those objecting to the disclosure of the report have the burden of persuading the court that 'the interest sought to be protected' requires that the report or portions of it, although in evidence, should be sealed."

Nevertheless, the U.S. Supreme Court has held in five opinions that the First Amendment adds nothing to the common law rights of presumed access to judicial records nor creates any general First Amendment right of access outside the judicial system.

The most dramatic defeat for the news media was the Supreme Court's holding in *Seattle Times* v. *Rhinehart,* that protective orders were proper to prevent a newspaper from publishing information its lawyers had collected while attempting to defend against a libel suit. The decision is noteworthy both because it justified a prior restraint and, more important here, because it was consistent with earlier decisions in which the Supreme Court had found no First Amendment right of access to government information.

Seattle Times Company v. Rhinehart, 467 U.S. 20, 104 S.Ct. 2199, 81 L.Ed.2d 17, 10 Med.L.Rptr. 1705 (1984).

In *Seattle Times,* the Court was confronted with the question of access to records produced during discovery. Complicated cases, as are most libel suits, can produce

---

15. 842 F.2d 1574, 15 Med.L.Rptr. 1305 (9th Cir. 1988).
16. Baltimore Sun v. Thanos, A.2d 565, 20 Med.L.Rptr. 1317 (Md.Ct.Spec.App. 1992).

thousands of pages of information, much of which may never be submitted to a court. Some of this information might be newsworthy—if the media can gain access to it. In this instance, a judge in Washington state had ruled that the newspaper could not use discovery documents as a source of news. Those documents were compiled by the *Times*'s lawyers defending the paper against a libel suit brought by Keith Rhinehart, the leader of a small religious group, the Aquarian Foundation. Rhinehart contended that articles in the *Times* describing the group's activities had subjected him and his followers to ridicule and scorn. Rhinehart asked for $14.1 million in damages. Part of that sum was based on the claim that donations to the Aquarians had declined sharply after the newspaper articles appeared.

The claim about declining gifts gave the newspaper's lawyers an opening they sought to exploit. As a part of the pretrial process of discovery, they asked Rhinehart to give them the names and addresses of the group's members and of any other persons who had given money to him or the Aquarians. The lawyers took the position that such data would prove or disprove the Aquarians' alleged losses. The process also would give the lawyers the names of people who could be questioned to find out whether they had left the church because of what they had read in the *Times*. Rhinehart's lawyer resisted the newspaper's request.

The judge supervising the discovery process concluded that the newspaper's lawyers needed access to the membership and contribution lists if they were to prepare their defense properly. But he said that such information was to be used only by them and was not to be given to their client for publication, although the newspaper was free to publish the names of members or contributors if it could get them from sources other than the discovery documents. Neither party to the libel action was pleased with the order. Both sides appealed to the Washington Supreme Court, which affirmed the judge's order.[17] The *Times* took its case to the U.S. Supreme Court, which ruled against it unanimously.

Lawyers for the *Times* argued that information gathered through the civil discovery process is like any other information and therefore is "protected speech" for First Amendment purposes. In their view, the newspaper could be restrained only if the judge could prove convincingly that his order served an overriding public interest. In this case, the lawyers argued, the public interest favored the newspaper because the people had a right to know how the religious group functioned.

Justice Lewis F. Powell, Jr., writing for the Court, did not agree. He focused the Court's decision narrowly on the nature of discovery and its purpose. Through discovery, lawyers gather information that will help them prepare for trial or reach a settlement. Discovery is conducted under court-enforced rules to expedite the judicial process. "Pretrial depositions and interrogatories [components of the discovery process] are not public components of a civil trial," he wrote. "Discovery rarely takes place in public." Pretrial questioning is arranged to suit the convenience of the witnesses and the lawyers for both sides; questioning often takes place in a law firm's conference room with a legal stenographer as the only outsider present. Because the process is informal and investigative, it is likely to produce some information with

---

17.   Rhinehart v. Seattle Times, 98 Wash.2d 226, 654 P.2d 673, 8 Med.L.Rptr. 2537 (Wash. 1982).

only a remote bearing on the issues being readied for trial and other information with the propensity to intrude on privacy and candor.

The Court noted that court rules in the federal system and in some states require that discovery documents be filed with the clerk of the court. But even in those jurisdictions, the Court said, the rules also give trial courts authority to order that certain records not be filed or to seal those that are. Such orders, the Court added, "are not a restriction on a traditionally public source of information."

In the end, the Supreme Court gave no comfort whatsoever to those who believe that the sealing of pretrial documents is a prior restraint to be imposed only after strict analysis of the public's First Amendment interests. Powell said that a Washington rule of court that gives judges authority to issue protective orders only for good cause "requires, in itself, no heightened First Amendment scrutiny." Powell wrote: "The trial court is in the best position to weigh fairly the competing needs and interests of parties affected by discovery. The unique character of the discovery process requires that the trial court have substantial latitude to fashion protective orders." In any event, Powell concluded, the judge had not tried to extend his order to prevent the *Times* from publishing information it was able to gather on its own. Therefore, "it does not offend the First Amendment."

Rhinehart is consistent with four other Supreme Court opinions that have failed to find any general First Amendment right of access to records or nonjudicial proceedings. The Court held in *Nixon v. Warner Communications, Inc.*[18] that several news and entertainment organizations could not copy the famous Nixon Watergate audiotapes, even though they had been admitted as evidence in the trial of several of the president's top aides. The Court concluded that Nixon was justified in his fear that the tapes, secretly made recordings of conversations in his Oval Office, might be exploited for commercial purposes. The Court said that the trial judge's orders sealing the tapes did not restrict the public's right to know, because transcripts of the tapes had been widely distributed. Actually, prior to 1996, only 63 of 3700 hours of recordings were ever made public.[19]

The other Supreme Court decisions on the First Amendment and a right of access dealt with requests by journalists to visit prisons and interview prisoners. In *Pell* v. *Procunier*[20] and *Houchins* v. *KQED*,[21] the Court held that journalists have no more right to visit jails or prisons than does anyone else. The Court said that there is no First Amendment right of entry to places where prisoners are kept. In *Saxbe* v. *Washington Post Co.*,[22] the Court held that there is no right to interview prisoners, even when they are willing to be interviewed. The Court said that the principal duties of prison officials are to maintain order and encourage rehabilitation. Therefore, if prison officials conclude that an interview would detract from these duties, the officials can forbid it.

---

18.   435 U.S. 589, 98 S.Ct. 1306, 55 L.Ed.2d 570, 3 Med.L.Rptr. 2074 (1978).
19.   In April, 1996, the Nixon estate agreed to a phased release of virtually all the tapes, which have been stored at the National Archives. Robert L. Jackson, "Rest of Nixon White House Tapes to be Made Public," *Los Angeles Times,* 13 April 1996, p. A1.
20.   417 U.S. 817, 94 S.Ct. 2800, 41 L.Ed.2d 495, 1 Med.L.Rptr. 2379 (1974).
21.   438 U.S. 1, 98 S.Ct. 2588, 57 L.Ed.2d 553, 3 Med.L.Rptr. 2521 (1978).
22.   417 U.S. 843, 94 S.Ct. 2811, 41 L.Ed.2d 514, 1 Med.L.Rptr. 2314 (1974).

The sense of the case law is that whatever right of access to government information may be implicit in the First Amendment is limited primarily to the right to attend trials and other associated court proceedings. Sometimes courts have upheld a constitutional, common law, or public policy right of access to court documents, particularly documents admitted as evidence or made a part of the court's record. Outside the courts, however, there is little evidence that the First Amendment, by itself, is able to do much to open the process of government to public view.

THE FREEDOM OF INFORMATION ACT

Governments at all levels both acquire and create vast amounts of information. Much of it is routine and of little interest. Few people care, for instance, who has been issued which license plate number. Some information is highly personal. The Internal Revenue Service has tax files showing the reported income of everyone who has ever filed a return. Many business firms and journalists might find such information interesting, and even helpful, but the IRS is forbidden by statute from sharing it with the public. Other information is classified as secret by executive order because disclosure might harm national security. The Defense Department has contingency plans for troop deployment in case of another war. It might be enlightening for citizens to know what these plans are, but exposure would ensure defeat if such plans had to be used in real combat.

However, not all information in government files is boring or private or dangerous. Governments hold vast amounts of information that can best serve a public interest if it is released. Government agencies collect information on the safety of products ranging from face creams to prescription drugs to automobiles. The Department of Agriculture assesses periodically the expected annual production of farm crops and the number of animals being readied for market. Other agencies collect voluminous data measuring every aspect of the economy. These kinds of information are released routinely. As any Washington correspondent will attest, federal agencies release a torrent of information every day, far more than any one news medium can keep up with.

Without question, the government of the United States is one of the most open in the world. Yet, aside from the kinds of information for which the need for secrecy is apparent, there have been times when the public has been denied access to data in which it has had a legitimate interest. Usually such information is withheld because it would point to inefficiency, stupidity, or outright wrongdoing on the part of government officials. Until 1966, reporters seeking such information had no legal means of getting access to it. Their alternative was to cultivate sources in Congress or in the agencies who might be willing to "leak" the desired data. Then Congress passed the Freedom of Information Act (FOIA),[23] which declared as a policy of government that the public should have access to information in the files of federal government agencies.

---

23. 5 U.S.C. §552.

The act requires that federal agencies make available for inspection and copying all of their records, including the decisions of administrative tribunals, policy statements, and staff manuals of instructions affecting the public. To make the search for information easier, each agency is supposed to publish an index to its files and update it every three months. In response to FOIA requests, agencies may delete information that clearly would invade an individual's privacy but must explain such deletions in writing. The agency also may refuse to release information that it believes is covered by one of the nine exemptions. However, even when documents are withheld, the agency is required to describe them in a general way and give its reasons for denying access to them. This requirement was mandated by the U.S. Court of Appeals for the District of Columbia Circuit in *Vaughn* v. *Rosen*.[24] Appropriately, such a report is called a *Vaughn* index.[25]

Requests for information do not have to be justified and must be disposed of within ten working days. If the agency decides not to release information, the seeker is entitled to appeal to an agency review officer, and the appeal must be granted or denied within twenty working days. Thus, the maximum delay, if the law is observed, is limited to thirty working days, or six full weeks. However, because some agencies have been swamped with large numbers of requests, or with requests for huge volumes of documents, the law permits a ten-day extension. The seeker must be notified of the delay in writing and must be given a reason.

If the time limits are not met, or if the seeker meets a final refusal, the next step is to appeal to a federal district court. Such appeals must be given expedited treatment. If the plaintiff wins, the government must pay all costs, including attorneys' fees. However, in some cases, judges have refused to award legal fees to plaintiffs who have obtained information that will aid them in their businesses. Business firms have become major users of the Freedom of Information Act.

Agencies are permitted to charge fees for providing copies of records, but the law says that these fees must be reasonable and limited to recovery of direct costs. If a request is deemed to be in the public interest, the agency can reduce its fees or even waive them altogether.

The act defines the covered agencies as follows:

> [T]he term "agency" . . . includes any executive department, military department, Government controlled corporation, or other establishment in the executive branch of the Government (including the Executive Office of the President), or any independent agency.

The Freedom of Information Act cannot be used to obtain documentary information in the possession of the following:

— The president and his immediate advisers[26]

---

24.   484 F.2d 820 (D.C. Cir. 1973); cert. denied, 415 U.S. 977, 94 S.Ct. 1564, 39 L.Ed.2d 873 (1974).
25.   See Oakland Tribune, Inc. v. U.S. Small Business Administration, 17 Med.L.Rptr. 1315 (N.D. Cal. 1989).
26.   Rushforth v. Council of Economic Advisers, 762 F.2d 1038, 11 Med.L.Rptr. 2075 (D.C. Cir. 1985); National Security Archive v. U.S. Archivist, 17 Med.L.Rptr. 2265 (D.C. Cir. 1990).

— Congress, its committees, and the few agencies under its direct control, principally the Library of Congress, the Copyright Office, and the General Accounting Office

— The federal judicial system

The nine exemptions are as follows:

1. Materials properly classified under executive order "to be kept secret in the interests of national defense or foreign policy."

2. "Internal personnel rules and practices of an agency."

3. Materials exempted from disclosure by a specific statute worded in such a way as to leave no doubt of the intent of Congress.

4. "Trade secrets and commercial or financial information obtained" with the assurance that it will be kept confidential.

5. "Inter-agency or intra-agency memorandums or letters" that would not ordinarily be available to outsiders except in connection with a lawsuit.

6. "Personnel and medical files and similar files the disclosure of which would constitute a clearly unwarranted invasion of privacy."

7. "Investigatory records compiled for law enforcement purposes." However, the law requires disclosure of records that will not interfere with an ongoing investigation, identify confidential sources or methods of gathering information, invade privacy, interfere with a fair trial, or endanger lives.

8. Materials bearing on the operating conditions, regulation, or supervision of financial institutions.

9. "Geological and geophysical information and data, including maps, concerning wells."

We must emphasize that the Freedom of Information Act does *not* apply to state and local government. These institutions are covered by their own laws, which vary from state to state. However, the federal law does cover local branches of federal agencies, several of which are to be found in most cities.

One other limit on access to information at the federal level needs to be noted. The Privacy Act of 1974[27] applies directly to the Freedom of Information Act. The Privacy Act limits access to personal files collected by government. Such files are defined as those that link an individual's name with "his education, financial transactions, medical history, and criminal or employment history." You might think of it as the tenth exemption.

---

27.   5 U.S.C. § 552a.

The Privacy Act was a product of the concern about abuse of computerized record-keeping systems. The act establishes procedures under which each of us can examine any files kept on us by the federal government and correct errors found there. It also establishes civil and criminal procedures that can be used to prevent or punish invasion of privacy resulting from misuse of personal records kept by the government. The law forbids agencies of government to keep records bearing on how an individual uses First Amendment rights, unless such information is pertinent to a bona fide law enforcement activity. It also forbids the sale of names and addresses to compilers of mailing lists.

Differences of opinion about the exemptions to the FOIA have led to hundreds of lawsuits, more than twenty of which have reached the Supreme Court. The Court has held that the exemptions should be construed as written, in line with traditional rules of statutory interpretation. As a consequence, a majority of the lower-court decisions during the decade after the act was revised ran against the seekers of access to information. However, the large volume of court decisions has helped define the exemptions with such precision that the number of appeals has declined significantly. Time also has brought about changes in users of the FOIA.

The act originally was championed by journalists. It has allowed the news media to expose shortcomings of government that once might have remained hidden. In subsequent years, however, business firms seeking information about government purchases and about competitors have become major users of the act. So, too, have law violators who have used the act in an attempt to find out how much the FBI and the Drug Enforcement Administration know about their activities.[28]

INTERPRETING THE FREEDOM OF INFORMATION ACT

Court decisions interpreting the FOIA fall into three categories:

1. Those that define an "agency record." The first hurdle facing a seeker of information from the government is to know what records an agency has. The requested information must be contained in an identifiable record legally in the agency's possession. Otherwise, it cannot be obtained.

2. Those that define the ability of third parties, usually business firms that have supplied information to the government, to prevent disclosure of an agency record.

3. Those that define the nine exemptions. By far the largest number of cases are in this category. In line with the judicial rules of statutory interpretation,

---

28. U.S. Congress, House Subcommittee on Government Operations, *Freedom of Information Act Oversight,* 97th Cong., 1st sess., 15 July 1981, p. 165. Assistant Attorney General Jonathan C. Rose testified that 40 percent of the requests received by the Drug Enforcement Administration were believed to come from prisoners and another 20 percent from law violators not in custody.

the Supreme Court has insisted that the language of the exceptions must he interpreted literally and in accord with the intent of Congress.

Defining an Agency Record

The Supreme Court held in two instances that the Freedom of Information Act can be used only to obtain records in the physical possession of an agency. In a third instance, the Court held that an agency must hand over documents obtained from other agencies, even though the person making the request also might have obtained them from the originating agencies. As a result of these decisions, the threshold question in any attempt to use the FOIA is, Does the document being sought meet the criteria defining an agency record? To meet the criteria, the document must legally be in the agency's physical possession, and its subject matter must be pertinent to the agency's mission.

In the first of three Supreme Court cases, journalists sought access to notes of telephone conversations made while Henry Kissinger was serving, first, as foreign policy adviser to President Nixon, and later as secretary of state. The Supreme Court held that neither set of notes need be released. The Court ruled that the notes made while Kissinger was an adviser to the president were not subject to the FOIA, because the president and his immediate advisers were exempt from its

Kissinger v. *Reporters Committee for Freedom of the Press*, **445 U.S. 136, 100 S.Ct. 960, 63 L.Ed.2d 267, 6 Med.L.Rptr. 1001 (1980).**

terms. Ordinarily, notes made of the secretary of state's conversations would be subject to disclosure because the Department of State is an "agency" within the scope of the act. In this instance, however, the notes had been transferred to the Library of Congress under terms that gave Kissinger strict control over their release. Kissinger, who left office before the legal action began, had acted in good faith in consigning his official papers to the Library, but subsequently enacted law had made such transfers illegal. The Reporters Committee for Freedom of the Press pointed to this fact in asking a federal district court to compel the State Department to regain custody over the former secretary's papers. The district court issued such an order, and the order was upheld by a circuit court of appeals.

The Supreme Court held that both courts were wrong. Nothing in the Freedom of Information Act, the Supreme Court ruled, requires an agency to sue a third party to recover records no longer in its possession, even though the transfer to that third party may have been illegal. The act, the Court held, applies only to records in the physical possession of an agency. The act's terms cannot be used to compel an agency to release records that it does not have. Nor, the Court held, does the law give persons outside of government the right to sue to compel an agency to return documents it might be holding illegally. Only the attorney general can initiate such action. In this instance, he did not choose to do so. Nor could the reporter obtain Kissinger's notes from the Library of Congress without Kissinger's permission, because as an agency of Congress, the Library is not covered by the FOIA. One effect of the decision was to prevent other authors from using information that Kissinger chose to disclose in his memoirs, the first volume of which was published while this case was making its way through the courts.[29]

The second case, *Forsham* v. *Harris,* involved an attempt to gain access to raw data collected by a private organization hired by the government to study thousands of diabetes patients. The focus of the study was on the side effects of drugs used to control the disease. Under its contract, the research organization was required to summarize its findings and report periodically to the Department of Health, Education, and Welfare (HEW). Although the department had the right to obtain the raw data gathered during the study, it did not do so.

Forsham v. Harris, 445 U.S. 169, 100 S.Ct. 978, 63 L.Ed.2d 293, 5 Med.L.Rptr. 2473 (1980).

When the summaries indicated that the oral medicines commonly used as an alternative to injected insulin might cause heart disease, the study became a subject of controversy. The committee on the Care of the Diabetic and other groups resorted to the FOIA to compel HEW to obtain and release the raw data so that other researchers could analyze it and come to their own conclusions. When HEW refused to do so, the groups went to court. HEW's decision was upheld.

The Supreme Court ruled that a private organization, even one working under a $15-million contract with the government, is not an "agency" as defined by the FOIA. Nor can that act be used to compel a federal agency to obtain data from a private contractor if it does not choose to do so.

Finally, in another case, the Supreme Court held that U.S. district court opinions and orders received by the Department of Justice in litigating tax cases become agency records. Therefore, they must be made available for copying on request by individuals or business firms, even though the documents also can be obtained directly from the clerks of the district courts. This ruling, in *U.S. Department of Justice* v. *Tax Analysts,* was of direct benefit to the publisher of a weekly magazine, *Tax Notes,* sold to tax attorneys, accountants, and economists. The publisher also provided full text of the decisions in microfiche and published a daily electronic database, including summaries and full texts of federal court tax decisions.

U.S. Department of Justice v. Tax Analysts, 492 U.S. 136, 109 S.Ct. 2841, 106 L.Ed.2d, 112, 16 Med.L.Rptr. 1849 (1989).

The publisher sought the decisions from the Justice Department because it did not always receive prompt service from the clerk of the federal courts and from lawyers involved in tax cases. The department rejected the request, arguing that the decisions were not agency records because they were not prepared by it but were obtained from the courts, which are not covered by the Freedom of Information Act. Justice Thurgood Marshall, joined by seven others, said that the Supreme Court decisions have established that an "agency record" is one either created or obtained by an agency subject to the FOIA. Once a document becomes an agency record, it cannot be withheld unless it is subject to one of the nine exemptions. The fact that Tax Analysts could have obtained the decision directly from the court was not relevant. Marshall said that an

---

29. Henry Kissinger, *White House Years* (Boston: Little, Brown, 1979). The second volume, *Years of Upheaval,* was published in 1982.

agency cannot meet its obligations under FOIA "simply by handing requesters a road map and sending them on scavenger expeditions throughout the nation."

Defining the Ability of Third Parties to Prevent Release of Information

In an action brought by Chrysler Corporation, the Supreme Court held that the nine exemptions contained in the Freedom of Information Act can be enforced only by the government. In order to obtain a weapons contract, Chrysler had to file data with the Defense Department showing that it did not discriminate against women and minorities. When a labor union sought release of the data under the FOIA, Chrysler filed suit, arguing that disclosure was forbidden by Exemption 4, which protects trade secrets and commercial and financial information. It said that the employment figures could be used unfairly by the unions representing its employees or by its competitors.

Chrysler Corp. v. *Brown,* 441 U.S. 281, 99 S.Ct. 1705, 60 L.Ed.2d 208, 4 Med.L.Rptr. 2441 (1979).

Chrysler won a partial victory in the lower courts, but the Supreme Court reversed, holding that the company was seeking a remedy in the wrong forum and with the wrong means. The purpose of the FOIA, the Court said, is to encourage release of information. And although the act does exempt certain kinds of information from disclosure, language in the act is permissive, not mandatory. Thus, if an agency in its discretion decides to release information arguably subject to one of the exemptions, it can do so. If, as in this instance, a corporation or an individual believes that it would be harmed by such release, it should first seek relief through the agency's administrative procedures. Only if such an attempt fails can the victim resort to the courts. However, the Supreme Court said that such action would have to be based on some law other than the FOIA.

The decision conveyed two messages to government officials and to users of the FOIA. In the narrower sense, the decision said that third parties cannot invoke the act to prevent release of information they have given to a covered government agency. In a broader sense, the Court also told government officials that the exemptions are not mandatory. If officials decide to release information within the scope of one of the exemptions, they can do so, provided that some other restrictive law does not apply.

Defining the Nine Exemptions

The nine exemptions were crafted with two objectives: (1) to permit the government to protect secrets it must keep if it is to carry out its functions; (2) to protect the privacy of government employees and of persons or business firms who provide information to the government. The first objective covers such things as secrets bearing on national security, current investigations by law enforcement officers, the working papers of government lawyers, and memoranda proposing government policies. The second objective covers such things as personnel records, medical records, trade secrets, financial data used in compiling economic statistics, tax returns, and other kinds of information obtained in confidence. What follows is a sampling of the decisions interpreting seven of the nine exemptions. There are no media-related cases involving the last two, which pertain to the regulation of financial institutions and to geological data concerning wells.

CLASSIFIED INFORMATION.   In a world bristling with political, economic, and religious animosities, government must try to keep some secrets. The Defense and State departments particularly generate information every day that other governments would dearly love to have. The ultimate responsibility for keeping such information limited to those who must have it rests with the president. By executive order, each president in modern times has established guidelines to be followed in deciding what kinds of information need to be safeguarded by being classified as "Confidential," "Secret," or "Top Secret." In general, access to such information is limited to those who must have it so that they can carry out their duties. It is a crime for a person authorized to have access to restricted materials to disclose them to an unauthorized person.

The most recent executive order provides for automatic declassification of many documents more than twenty-five years old. Documents not automatically declassified after twenty-five years include those revealing confidential sources, cryptologic or weapons systems, war plans still in effect, and those involving foreign governments, such as diplomatic relations or international treaties. Also exempt from automatic declassification are documents that might assist the development and use of weapons of mass destruction, impair the ability to protect the president and other officials, or compromise national security and emergency preparedness.[30]

The FOIA permits courts to examine classified documents to determine whether they were classified properly. However, such a judicial inspection has not resulted in any widespread release of information dealing with foreign policy and defense. In determining whether documents have been classified properly, courts give great weight to affidavits from government officials asserting a need for secrecy. Although judges can, and have, examined documents in the privacy of their chambers to resolve doubts, the message implicit in the decisions is that most judges believe that the declassification of secret documents is a job for experts, not for judges, who may be uninformed about foreign policy or the intricacies of national defense.

The Supreme Court has upheld the view that great weight must be given to the claims of officials who assert a need for secrecy. In *Weinberger* v. *Catholic Action of Hawaii/Peace Education Project,*[31] the Court upheld the Navy's refusal to prepare an environmental impact statement for a weapons storage area in Hawaii. The only claimed environmental impact was that which would come from an accidental detonation if the Navy decided to store nuclear weapons in the facility. By law, the location of nuclear weapons storage depots was classified. The mere filing

---

30. Debra Gersh Hernandez, "Declassifying Government Information," *Editor & Publisher,* 22 April 1995, p. 89. Tim Weiner, "U.S. Plans Overhaul to Open Millions of Records," *New York Times,* 18 March 1995, p. 1.
31. 454 U.S. 139, 102 S.Ct. 197, 70 L.Ed.2d 298 (1981).

of an impact statement, which would be open to inspection under the Freedom of Information Act, would have confirmed supposition about the depot's purpose. Thus, Justice Rehnquist wrote, the Court would have to take the Navy's word for its claim that it had complied with environmental protection law "to the fullest extent possible." Any more than that was "beyond judicial scrutiny" for security reasons.

Certainly, reporters and others seeking to force access to classified documents under the FOIA do not face an impossible task, but most of the assumptions work against them if there is government opposition.

INTERNAL PERSONNEL INFORMATION.   Every agency of government has a body of rules to guide its employees as they carry out their duties. Some rules may be so picayune as to limit what may be stacked on desks. Others may detail procedures to be followed in auditing income tax returns. Each agency also maintains files on its employees, which include such things as educational background, work history, and pertinent medical data. The question is, How far does Exemption 2 go in shielding the internal operations of an agency from public view?

The Supreme Court dealt with that question when it decided *Department of the Air Force* v. *Rose,* an access suit brought by the student editors of the *New York University Law Review.* In preparing an article about disciplinary procedures at the service academies, the editors asked for summaries of honor and ethics hearings. These informal proceedings had been conducted by the academy students themselves to look into allegations that cadets had lied, cheated, or otherwise broken the strict code of conduct governing them. The Air Force refused to hand over summary reports of these proceedings at the Air Force Academy, even with the names of the offending cadets deleted. It argued that the offenders still might be identifiable, with consequences that would haunt them the rest of their lives. Disclosure, the Air Force contended, would violate Exemptions 2 and 6. The latter permits agencies to withhold records that would pose "a clearly unwarranted invasion of personal privacy."

Department of the Air Force v. *Rose,* 425 U.S. 352, 96 S.Ct. 1592, 48 L.Ed.2d 11 (1976).

Lower courts disagreed on withholding, but the Supreme Court ruled that the summaries should be released without the names. Justice William J. Brennan, Jr., wrote that neither exemption should be read as an absolute barrier against disclosure. Each requires a balancing of the public's interest in the requested information against the agency's or the individual's interest in withholding it.

In this case, the Court held, the public had an interest in cheating and dishonesty in the service academies. Some cadets had been discharged. Others were being disciplined. The summaries in question were posted routinely on bulletin boards within the living areas of all three service academies. Clearly, rumor abounded. Therefore, release of the facts, carefully edited to protect individual cadets, was in the public interest.

With this decision as their guide, lower courts have ordered the release of such things as manuals used to guide Internal Revenue Service agents in approving or disallowing certain deductions. However, courts have also required those seeking access to agency rules to prove that an important public interest will be served by disclosure.[32]

Information exempted by law.   In about a hundred instances, Congress has written provisions into federal law prohibiting disclosure of certain kinds of information. In many such instances, the intent is to protect an individual's privacy. Thus, there is considerable overlap between Exemptions 3 and 6, which permits agencies to withhold information to protect privacy. Court decisions interpreting both exemptions show a reluctance by both federal agencies and the courts to release data that would permit others to intrude into an individual's private life.

One Exemption 3 case that reached the Supreme Court did not involve privacy.

Consumer Product Safety Commission v. GTE Sylvania, Inc., **447 U.S. 102, 100 S.Ct. 2051, 64 L.Ed.2d 766, 6 Med.L.Rptr. 1301 (1980).**

At issue was an attempt by Consumers Union, publisher of *Consumer Reports* magazine, to obtain government data on possibly dangerous television sets. The magazine's editors learned that the Consumer Product Safety Commission was investigating reports that some people had been injured when the picture tube of their television set had exploded. When *Consumer Reports* asked the agency for its data, the commission was willing to release it, but some television manufacturers objected. Led by GTE Sylvania, Inc., they went to court arguing that the law under which the Consumer Product Safety Commission operated forbade disclosure. The U.S. District Court in Delaware agreed and issued an order forbidding the commission from releasing the data sought by *Consumer Reports.* The magazine countered by filing suit to compel release of the data in compliance with the Freedom of Information Act. Both actions reached the Supreme Court.

In *Consumer Product Safety Commission v. GTE Sylvania, Inc.,* the Court upheld the Delaware court's order forbidding release of the information. It noted that the law establishing the commission had put restrictions on the release of information reflecting unfavorably on a product. Under the law, such information cannot be released until the manufacturer has been notified and given an opportunity to defend its product. The commission's news release describing the problem is required to include the manufacturer's response. Nor can the commission issue any release until it is satisfied that its report is accurate and that disclosure is "fair in the circumstances and reasonably related" to the purpose of the law, which is to protect consumers from hazards. The Supreme Court held that the commission had not complied with the law when it had expressed its willingness to give *Consumer Reports* unfavorable information about television sets.

The commission reminded the Court that it had held in the *Chrysler* case that agencies of government are permitted to release information covered by the exemptions if they choose to do so. In some instances, that could be done, Justice Rehnquist replied, but not here. The law establishing the commission specifically limited the circum-

---

32.   Buffalo Evening News v. U.S. Border Patrol, 791 F.Supp. 386, 20 Med.L.Rptr. 1553 (W.D.N.Y. 1992).

stances under which it could release information. That law must be obeyed. Therefore, the injunction issued by the district court was proper.

Most Exemption 3 cases decided by the courts have involved section 6102 of the Internal Revenue Code, which forbids release of tax return information to a third party. Courts will permit release of such information only if the data are presented in a way that will not identify individual taxpayers.

TRADE SECRETS AND OTHER CONFIDENTIAL DATA.   The Supreme Court has not ruled directly on this exemption, but the Circuit Court of Appeals for the District of Columbia held that a consumer advocacy group was not entitled to Food and Drug Administration records on intraocular lenses, because the records contain trade secrets.[33] The lenses are implanted in a patient's eye to correct vision after cataract operations. A federal district court upheld the refusal of the Federal Aviation Administration to give aircraft certification records to the Air Line Pilots Association.[34] The court held that disclosure would result in considerable competitive harm to the McDonnell-Douglas Corporation.

MEMORANDA.   Stripped of its legal terminology, Exemption 5 applies primarily to working papers in the preparation of a legal case or to memoranda exchanged by government officials in laying the groundwork for decisions on policy. If release of such information would give persons in litigation with the government, or persons subject to proposed governmental policy, an unfair advantage, withholding is justified. Exemption 5 has been the subject of more than two dozen federal court decisions, almost all of which have upheld an agency's refusal to release memoranda.[35] Several of these cases have reached the Supreme Court, and the Court has supported an agency's refusal to release information.

The first of these decisions, *Federal Open Market Committee* v. *Merrill,*[36] permitted the Federal Reserve Board to delay for one month the public disclosure of its decisions on buying or selling government securities. Such decisions, made monthly, have an effect on interest rates, the availability of credit, and the value of the dollar in foreign exchange. The Supreme Court agreed with the Federal Reserve Board's contention that prompt release of its buying and selling plans would thwart its purpose, which is to keep the economy on an even keel.

The second Supreme Court decision, in *Federal Trade Commission* v. *Grolier, Inc.,*[37] protected the working papers of government lawyers. The commission had sued Grolier, alleging that its sales representatives were using deceptive methods to sell encyclopedias. The lawsuit was dismissed before it reached trial. Grolier then filed a request under the Freedom of Information Act for memoranda prepared by FTC lawyers in preparation for trial. The firm's admitted purpose was to find out how much the

---

33. Public Citizen Health Research Group v. Food and Drug Administration, 704 F.2d 1280 (D.C. Cir. 1983).
34. Air Line Pilots Association v. Federal Aviation Administration, 552 F.Supp. 811 (D.D.C. 1982).
35. For example, see Access Reports v. Justice Department, 926 F.2d 1192, 18 Med.L.Rptr. 1840 (D.C. Cir. 1991).
36. 443 U.S. 340, 99 S.Ct. 2800, 61 L.Ed.2d 587, 5 Med.L.Rptr. 1221 (1979).
37. 462 U.S. 19, 103 S.Ct. 2209, 76 L.Ed.2d 387, 9 Med.L.Rptr. 1737 (1983).

agency had learned about sales methods through its surveillance of Grolier's sales representatives. Two lower courts ordered disclosure of the data on grounds that the litigation had ended, thus ending any need to protect strategy planned for the trial. The Supreme Court overruled the lower courts, holding that the wording of Exemption 5 says nothing about the status of litigation; it protects the working papers of government lawyers at all times.

The third decision, *United States* v. *Weber Aircraft Corp.,*[38] upheld the Air Force's refusal to disclose statements obtained during investigation of an aircraft accident. The pilot, who had suffered serious injuries, sued Weber, manufacturer of the plane's ejection seat, for damages. To support his case, he sought access to the data collected by Air Force investigators. The Air Force readily released factual information gathered under oath during its attempt to find the cause of the crash, but it refused to surrender supplementary data gathered in an attempt to prevent similar accidents in the future. Much of that data was gathered under assurances that the identity of the sources would not be made public. The Supreme Court held that confidential statements gathered in an attempt to formulate safety regulations clearly are intra-agency memoranda of the kind Congress sought to protect when it approved Exemption 5 and therefore do not have to be released.

Sometimes the working papers or memoranda held by an agency are generated from the Office of the President. Since George Washington, presidents have asserted an executive privilege to protect communications with advisers. The privilege is based on the assumption that the president and his advisers might not be completely candid if they thought their communications would be made public. On numerous occasions, presidents have invoked the privilege to justify a refusal to release information sought by Congress. Courts generally have respected that privilege but also have reserved the right to decide when the privilege has been invoked properly. The U.S. Court of Appeals for the District of Columbia Circuit, in *Public Citizen* v. *Burke,*[39] for example, held that Attorney General Edwin Meese III was mistaken when he told the General Services Administration (GSA) to honor all claims of executive privilege made by former presidents whose records were under the agency's control. The principal beneficiary of the order was Richard Nixon, who had been attempting to prevent release of some of the many records accumulated during his presidency. The court said that claims to executive privilege must be asserted and decided on a case-by-case basis. The court also told the GSA that, as archivist for the government, it had a duty to disclose information. Executive privilege by itself does not override an agency's discretion, created by Exemption 5, to release or withhold information.

DISCLOSURES THAT INVADE PERSONAL PRIVACY.   The concern for individual privacy written into Exemption 6 is not absolute. It erects a barrier only against a clearly unwarranted invasion of personal privacy, thus requiring agencies and the courts to balance an individual's interest in privacy against the public interest served by release of data.[40]

---

38.   465 U.S. 792, 104 S.Ct. 1488, 79 L.Ed.2d 814, 10 Med.L.Rptr. 1477 (1984).
39.   843 F.2d 1473 (D.C. Cir. 1988).
40.   Department of the Air Force v. Rose, 425 U.S. 352, 96 S.Ct. 1592, 1 Med.L.Rptr. 2509 (1976).

A leading case interpreting Exemption 6 is *U.S. Department of State* v. *Washington Post Co.* It began when a reporter for the *Post* received a tip that two officials prominent in Iran's revolutionary government held valid United States passports. The *Post* asked the State Department for information in its files that would prove or disprove the tip. The department refused, citing Exemption 6. Although passport data does not qualify as "personnel or medical files," the department's lawyers argued that it qualifies as "similar files the disclosure of which would constitute a clearly unwarranted invasion of personal privacy." When lower federal courts rejected that argument, the State Department took its case to the Supreme Court.

U.S. Department of State v. Washington Post Co., 456 U.S. 595, 102 S.Ct. 1957, 72 L.Ed.2d 358, 8 Med.L.Rptr. 1521 (1982).

Writing for the Court, Justice Rehnquist noted that Exemption 6, unlike the other eight, is written in general rather than specific terms. This means, he reasoned, that Congress intended that agencies and courts give special consideration to protecting data bearing on personal privacy. Quoting from a congressional report, he wrote that "the exception [was] intended to cover detailed Government records on an individual which can be identified as applying to that individual." Since passport files provide information about individuals, they are among those "similar files" that Congress intended to cover. The only question remaining was whether releasing the information would be an unwarranted invasion of privacy.

In this instance, the Court gave great weight to the State Department's claim that disclosure of any information about the two Iranians might very well sign their death warrants. Not long after the *Post* made its original request, the Iranian government's rabid anti-Americanism led to the seizure of the United States Embassy in Teheran and the taking of its employees as hostages. The Supreme Court directed the district court to conduct another hearing on the *Post's* request, at which it should consider the danger to the Iranians' lives. Such danger, the Court said, was an important element in determining whether these "similar files" contained private information that ought to be withheld from the public.

Danger was also a factor in the Supreme Court's decision in *State Department* v. *Ray*.[41] In that case, an immigration lawyer filed an FOIA request to get documents concerning Haitians who had been interviewed by the U.S. State Department after being involuntarily returned to Haiti. The Haitians had attempted to enter the United States illegally but had been intercepted by the Coast Guard. The State Department conducted the interviews to determine whether the Haitian government was complying with an agreement not to prosecute the returnees.

The State Department provided ninety-six pages of material, but individual names and other identifying information had been removed on the grounds of Exemption 6. The Eleventh Circuit Court of Appeals affirmed a court order requiring the State Department to provide the information. The Supreme Court reversed.

Six of the justices said that the "privacy interest in protecting these individuals from any retaliatory action that might result from a renewed interest in their aborted attempt to emigrate must be given great weight. Indeed, the very purpose of respondents'

---

41.   502 U.S. 164, 112 S.Ct. 541, 116 L.Ed.2d 526, 19 Med.L.Rptr. 1641 (1991).

FOIA request is to attempt to prove that such a danger is present today." However, Justices Scalia and Kennedy would have been happier had the Court limited its discussion to present dangers rather than the danger that "might result from a renewed interest." The two justices, in their concurring opinion, expressed concern that the Court was becoming unnecessarily speculative about what dangers people might face if there were some derivative use of personal information.

Lower courts have relied on Supreme Court precedent in expanding the scope of the kinds of "similar files" entitled to privacy. Accordingly, federal appellate courts have held that a voice recording of the Challenger astronauts as they were dying is a "similar file,"[42] and that details of VA-guaranteed loans on homes,[43] the mailing addresses of Social Security employees,[44] and the names and addresses of persons with government permits to boat on a scenic river[45] are all similar files.

Once it is clear that Exemption 6 files or similar files are involved, the question is how to properly balance the public's interest and the privacy claims. In doing that, the Supreme Court has offered a standard that

> focuses on the citizens' right to be informed about "what their government is up to." Official information that sheds light on an agency's performance of its statutory duties falls squarely within that statutory purpose. That purpose, however, is not fostered by disclosure of information about private citizens that is accumulated in various governmental files but that reveals little or nothing about an agency's own conduct.[46]

It is when the public's interest in the functioning of government weighs heavily in the balance that an invasion of personal privacy is likely to be justified. In that spirit the U.S. Court of Appeals for the District of Columbia ordered released to a reporter the names and amounts of prescription drugs supplied to the Office of the Attending Physician of the Congress.[47] The reporter was investigating allegations that members of Congress were obtaining undue amounts of prescription medicine commonly used by drug abusers. Because the Office of the Attending Physician obtained its supply from the National Naval Medical Center, records of the center were subject to the FOIA. The center refused the reporter's request, arguing that specific drug orders might be traceable to individual members of Congress. The appellate court ruled that that possibility was too remote to overcome the public's interest in knowing what quantities of various medicines were being dispensed to members of Congress.[48]

---

42. New York Times Co. v. NASA, 920 F.2d 1002, 18 Med.L.Rptr. 1465 (D.C. Cir. 1990). A federal district court subsequently found release of the Challenger recording to constitute a clearly unwarranted invasion of privacy when privacy interests of the surviving families were balanced against the public's interest in understanding the activities of government, New York Times Co. v. NASA, 782 F.Supp. 628, 19 Med.L.Rptr. 1688 (D.D.C. 1991).
43. Heights Community Congress v. Veterans Administration, 732 F.2d 526 (6th Cir. 1984).
44. American Federation of Government Employees, AFL-CIO, Local 1923 v. U.S. Department of Health and Human Services, 712 F.2d 931 (4th Cir. 1983).
45. Minnis v. U.S. Department of Agriculture, 737 F.2d 784 (9th Cir. 1984).
46. Department of Justice v. Reporters Committee for Freedom of the Press, 489 U.S. 749, 109 S.Ct. 1468, 103 L.Ed.2d 774, 16 Med.L.Rptr. 1545 (1989).
47. Arieff v. U.S. Department of the Navy, 712 F.2d 1462, 9 Med.L.Rptr. 2302 (D.C. Cir. 1983).
48. See also Gannett River States Publishing Corp. v. National Guard, 20 Med.L.Rptr. 1183 (S.D.Miss. 1992). Release of National Guard records about disciplinary action taken against soldiers following a training accident is not an unwarranted invasion of privacy.

INVESTIGATORY RECORDS. Because the battleground over the meaning of Exemption 7 lies in the terms under which disclosure can be denied, a reading of its full text, 5 U.S.C. § 552(b)(7), is useful. The exemption permits withholding of

> records or information compiled for law enforcement purposes, but only to the extent that the production of such law enforcement records or information
>
> (A) could reasonably be expected to interfere with enforcement proceedings,
>
> (B) would deprive a person of a right to a fair trial or an impartial adjudication,
>
> (C) could reasonably be expected to constitute an unwarranted invasion of personal privacy,
>
> (D) could reasonably be expected to disclose the identity of a confidential source, including a state, local, or foreign agency or authority or any private institution which furnished information on a confidential basis, and, in the case of a record or information compiled by criminal law enforcement authority in the course of a criminal investigation or by an agency conducting a lawful national security intelligence investigation, information furnished by a confidential source,
>
> (E) would disclose techniques and procedures for law enforcement investigations or prosecutions, or would disclose guidelines for law enforcement investigations or prosecutions if such disclosure could reasonably be expected to risk circumvention of the law, or
>
> (F) could reasonably be expected to endanger the life or physical safety of any individual. . . .

What all this boils down to is this: Investigatory agencies, foremost among them the FBI, have been given many reasons to withhold information from the public. They can do so to protect confidential sources, to protect the right of suspects to a fair trial, to prevent disclosure of techniques that might help persons evade arrest, to protect the privacy of persons named in records, and to protect the lives of law enforcement officers or informants.

The language of the exemption has led to more than six Supreme Court opinions. In at least two of those, the Court has held that the protection of privacy found in Exemption 7 is stronger than that found in Exemption 6.[49] The latter provides for release of records unless such release would "constitute a clearly unwarranted invasion of personal privacy," but Exemption 7 gives investigatory agencies authority to refuse release of any record that "could reasonably be expected to constitute an unwarranted invasion of personal privacy." Although it may sound like a quibble over words, Justice Scalia explained that the difference is that an Exemption 6 case must focus "solely upon what the requested information *reveals,* not upon what it might lead to."[50] On the other hand, an Exemption 7 case may be far more speculative about what harm might develop from disclosure of private information.

The first of the Supreme Court's Exemption 7 cases, *National Labor Relations Board* v. *Robbins Tire and Rubber Co.,*[51] grew out of a labor dispute, making it clear that police agencies were not the only ones entitled to the exemption. Robbins Tire was defending itself in an NLRB hearing against charges that it treated its workers un-

---

49. State Department v. Ray, 502 U.S. 164, 112 S.Ct. 541, 116 L.Ed.2d 526, 19 Med.L.Rptr. 1641 (1991); Department of Justice v. Reporters Committee for Freedom of the Press, 489 U.S. 749, 109 S.Ct. 1468, 103 L.Ed.2d 774, 16 Med.L.Rptr. 1545 (1989).
50. State Department v. Ray, 19 Med.L.Rptr. 1641, 1649 (1991). Emphasis is Justice Scalia's.
51. 437 U.S. 214, 98 S.Ct. 2311, 57 L.Ed.2d 159, 3 Med.L.Rptr. 2473 (1978).

fairly. In preparing its case, Robbins Tire asked the agency for transcripts of NLRB interviews with employees who were to testify at the hearing. The board refused the request. The Supreme Court upheld the refusal, citing subsections (A) and (B) of the exemption. The Court said that disclosure might lead to coercion of the witnesses, thus interfering with the proper resolution of the dispute.

In another opinion, *John Doe Agency* v. *John Doe Corp.,*[52] the Court clarified the meaning of "records compiled" for law enforcement purposes. In that case, the Court held that records become subject to the limitations of Exemption 7 once they have been acquired by an investigatory agency. At issue was an attempt by a defense contractor to obtain records of an audit conducted by the Defense Contract Auditing Agency some years previously. At the time, the audit was routine. But when the contractor became suspected of fraud, the records were transferred to the FBI. The contractor asked for copies to use in its defense, arguing that the records were subject to release under the FOIA because they had not originally been made for law enforcement purposes. A U.S. circuit court agreed. The Supreme Court reversed, saying that the language of the act speaks only of records "compiled for law enforcement purposes." A compilation "is something composed of materials collected or assembled from various sources or other documents." The law says nothing about a record's original purpose. Once information becomes part of a file assembled as part of an investigation, that information is subject to Exemption 7. In this instance, the Court said that release might interfere with enforcement proceedings and told the company it would have to rely on the discovery process to obtain information it needed to prepare its defense.

Two other Exemption 7 cases have directly affected the ability of journalists to gather news. The first, *Federal Bureau of Investigation* v. *Abramson,* was brought by a journalist who was investigating allegations that President Nixon had used federal agencies for political purposes. Specifically, the reporter, Howard Abramson, had been told that Nixon had asked the FBI to collect information on people whom he considered to be his political enemies. Abramson asked the FBI to give him all documents in its files that pertained to such individuals. The FBI rejected the request, stating that release of such data would be an unwarranted invasion of privacy and thus could be withheld under both Exemption 6 and Exemption 7(C). When Abramson appealed to a U.S. district court for help, the FBI gave him eighty-four pages of information, from which some names and facts had been deleted.

Federal Bureau of Investigation v. *Abramson,* **456 U.S. 615, 102 S.Ct. 2054, 72 L.Ed.2d 376, 8 Med.L.Rptr. 1561 (1982).**

Abramson did not get what he wanted most—sixty-three pages of information about eleven political figures, all contained in a memorandum sent personally by J. Edgar Hoover, who for almost half a century had been chief of the FBI, to John D. Ehrlichman, one of the president's closest aides. When Abramson again went to court, he was rebuffed, but the court of appeals reversed, holding that, because the White House was not involved in law enforcement, the Hoover memorandum could not have been compiled for law enforcement purposes. Therefore, the FBI had no justification for withholding it.

---

52.   493 U.S. 146, 110 S.Ct. 471, 107 L.Ed.2d 462, 17 Med.L.Rptr. 1225 (1989).

FEDERAL BUREAU OF INVESTIGATION

Form No. 1
THIS CASE ORIGINATED AT PITTSBURGH, PA.   NY FILE NO. 100-35770 MC

REPORT MADE AT	DATE WHEN MADE	PERIOD FOR WHICH MADE	REPORT MADE BY
NEW YORK, N.Y.	2/22/43	10/15/42; 1/8, 25,27/43	▮▮▮▮ b7C

TITLE	CHARACTER OF CASE
PITTSBURGH COURIER; DISSEMINATION OF JAPANESE PROPAGANDA AMONG THE NEGROES.	INTERNAL SECURITY — J SEDITION

SYNOPSIS OF FACTS:

ROGERS and SCHUYLER, prominent negro journalists, presently writing for the PITTSBURGH COURIER, are respected by the people of HARLEM for their ability as writers in support of the colored race. Both are strong in their racial views. However, there is no indication that they are disloyal to the US, with the exception that SCHUYLER has written pro-Japanese articles and has not been known to have written any anti-Japanese material. ROGERS, on the other hand, has written anti-Japanese articles before and since the declaration of war against Japan. ▮▮▮▮▮▮▮▮▮▮▮ b7C
▮▮▮▮ interviewed and has no knowledge of pro-Japanese writers among the negroes, but does know of pro-Japanese sentiment. ▮▮▮ b7D

—REC— b7C

REFERENCE   Reports of Special Agent ▮▮▮▮▮ dated at Pittsburgh, Pennsylvania, August 2?, 1942 and November 20, 1942.

DETAILS   NEW YORK, N.Y.

A review of the files of the New York Office in the above captioned matter sets forth the following information as taken from New York File 100-24049, entitled ▮▮▮▮▮▮▮

COPIES DESTROYED ▮▮▮▮▮▮   b7C

APPROVED AND FORWARDED E. E. ▮▮▮▮   SPECIAL AGENT IN CHARGE   FILE   DO NOT WRITE IN THESE SPACES   DEPT. OF JUSTICE

FILE 100-31159- ▮▮

COPIES OF THIS REPORT
5— ▮▮▮ 43
5 — Bureau
5 — Pittsburgh
3 — New York

APPROPRIATE AGENCIES
AND FIELD OFFICES
ADVISED

This is the first page of an FBI investigation report obtained through the Freedom of Information Act by Patrick S. Washburn for his book, *A Question of Sedition: The Federal Government's Investigation of the Black Press During World War II.* Washburn, now a professor at Ohio University, obtained this and many other documents while a student studying government attitudes toward the African-American press. *(FBI)*

On further appeal, five justices of the Supreme Court disagreed with the circuit court's reasoning. They held that the court had lost sight of the origins of the data in the memorandum and thus had been led into error. It was true, the five conceded, that the *document* sent to the White House was not an investigatory record, nor had it been compiled for law enforcement purposes. But the *information* it contained had been collected by the FBI, a law enforcement agency, presumably for investigatory purposes. Congress had written the exemption to protect information, not only records conveying information. Because all the information on the pieces of paper sent to Ehrlichman had been compiled for law enforcement purposes, it was protected by Exemption 7. Further, no one had argued in court that the data would not invade privacy. Therefore, the FBI was correct in concluding that its release might reasonably lead to an unwarranted invasion of privacy.

In *Abramson,* it was clear that few, if any, of the people on Nixon's enemies list were criminals. They were private citizens whose problem was that the president didn't like them and was looking for information that could be used to embarrass them. But what if the investigation had actually involved known criminals? The Supreme Court, six years after *Abramson,* said it made no difference. The Court held that Exemption 7(C) would also justify an FBI refusal to release compilations of arrests and convictions of criminals. These records were known to law enforcement officers and journalists as "rap sheets," and for years the Justice Department had shared them regularly with police agencies and courts. On occasion, it had also released them to the news media, to employers, and to the public.

The Supreme Court held unanimously in *Department of Justice* v. *Reporters Committee for Freedom of the Press* that reporters have

Department of Justice v. Reporters Committee for Freedom of the Press, 489 U.S. 749, 109 S.Ct. 1468, 103 L.Ed.2d 774, 16 Med.L.Rptr. 1545 (1989).

no right under the FOIA to obtain rap sheets from the Justice Department if it decides to withhold them. Justice John Paul Stevens, writing for the Court, said that Justice Department officials were correct in concluding that disclosure "could reasonably be expected to constitute an unwarranted invasion of personal privacy."

The decision ended an eleven-year effort on the part of the Reporters Committee and CBS correspondent Robert Schakne to obtain the rap sheet on Charles Medico, whose Medico Industries allegedly had obtained defense contracts in exchange for contributions to the late Daniel J. Flood, a member of the House of Representatives from Pennsylvania. The FBI released rap sheets on Medico's three brothers after they died but withheld its compilation on Charles, prompting Schakne's lawsuit.

In upholding the Justice Department's decision, Stevens focused on what he saw as the purpose of the FOIA. He wrote that its "central purpose is to ensure that the *government's* activities be opened to the sharp eye of public scrutiny, not that information about *private citizens* that happens to be in the warehouse of the government be so disclosed." He noted that the FBI has rap sheets on twenty-four million persons and that they are kept up to date and on file until the subject dies or reaches the age of eighty. Conceding that much of the information could be found elsewhere, Stevens said that the federal government's computerized record system has created "a vast difference" between its files and the public records of county courts and police stations. At the heart of that difference is the federal government's ability to collect and bring together vast amounts of information on any one individual. As the Court saw it, that ability has a potential for abuse that could be invasive of privacy rights. Thus, Stevens concluded, the decision to withhold Medico's rap sheet was supported by Exemption 7(C). All that was required was a reasonable expectation that disclosure might constitute an unwarranted invasion of privacy. Had the Justice Department chosen to rely on Exemption 6, it would have had to find that disclosure "would constitute" a clearly unwarranted invasion of privacy.

Stevens also noted that the Privacy Act forbids disclosure by government of personal records without the consent of the individual involved. He saw this limitation as further evidence that individuals have a significant privacy interest even in their criminal histories. The Court concluded: "The privacy interest in a rap sheet is substantial. The substantial character of that interest is affected by the fact that in today's society the computer can accumulate and store information that would otherwise have surely been forgotten long before a person attains the age of eighty."

Jane Kirtley, executive director of the Reporters Committee for Freedom of the Press, said that she saw two very troubling results flowing from the decision.[53] In her view, the Court was saying that when information taken from readily available paper records is compiled in a computer, it is altered in nature and becomes private. She said, "If they can find this transformation happens to something that is so obviously of public interest—like a conviction—I don't think there is any limit on where they will find a privacy interest of an individual." Her second concern was with the purpose Stevens ascribed to the FOIA. She said that if his view is accepted, it could cut off access to great bodies of data gathered by government but not directly concerned with its operation.

Kirtley is correct in her conclusion that if "public interest" in FOIA cases means only the interest in the functioning of a specific government agency, the scope of available information would be substantially narrowed. That was made clear by the Third Circuit Court of Appeals when it held that the FBI properly had refused to give documents to Vincent Landano because there was no federal "FOIA-related public interest in discovering wrongdoing by a *state* agency."[54]

Landano had been convicted in a New Jersey court of the murder of a police officer during a robbery of a check-cashing center. Landano, who maintained his innocence, believed that state prosecutors had violated his rights by hiding evidence that would have cleared him. He believed that the FBI had information that would help, and he asked for FBI files relating to his case, citing the FOIA. The FBI had investigated the murder and had a 726-page file. The agency gave Landano 324 pages, some of which were redacted, and withheld the rest, citing Exemption 7(C) to protect personal privacy and Exemption 7(D) to protect confidential sources.

A federal district court rejected the FBI's 7(C) and 7(D) claims and ordered release of the information. However, on appeal, the Third Circuit Court of Appeals reversed the district court on the 7(C) claim, upholding the FBI and citing *U.S. Department of Justice* v. *Reporters Committee for Freedom of the Press* and *U.S. Department of State* v. *Ray.* The question of public interest, the appellate court said, turns on the requested document's relationship to the purpose of the Freedom of Information Act, which is to open a federal agency to the light of public scrutiny. Since Landano's complaint was with the operations of state prosecutors, not with the federal agency, there could be no FOIA-related public interest that outweighed the privacy interests of individuals named in the FBI file. Accordingly, the FBI could refuse access.

---

53. George Garneau, "Locked Away from Public View," *Editor & Publisher,* 1 April 1989, p. 9.
54. Landano v. Justice Department, 956 F.2d 422, 19 Med.L.Rptr. 2129 (3d Cir. 1992); vacated and remanded, 113 S.Ct. 2014, 21 Med.L.Rptr. 1513 (1993).

As for the FBI's 7(D) claim of protection for confidential sources. The U.S. Supreme Court, which next picked up the case, held that although there could be no blanket presumption that all FBI informants were confidential sources, confidentiality could be inferred from circumstances, and if the circumstances warranted, 7(D) also could justify the FBI's refusal to provide information.

Landano's was the case of a criminal convict who hoped to get out of prison by finding evidence in federal files that would incriminate New Jersey prosecutors. Would it have made any difference if he had been a reporter fishing for files on federal wrongdoing? Within sixty days after the circuit court published the *Landano* opinion, a federal district court in New York cited *Landano* to explain why a Buffalo newspaper reporter could not have the names and addresses of aliens apprehended by the U.S. Border Patrol.[55] Although the newspaper argued that its interest was with the operations of a federal agency, the court decided that the public interest in agency operations did not outweigh the privacy interests of individuals who were not part of the agency but who were nevertheless named in its files. The newspaper's mere *suspicions* of border patrol misconduct, said the court, were not enough to justify the release of names of apprehended aliens who might be stigmatized by being associated with a criminal investigation.[56]

"GOVERNMENT IN THE SUNSHINE"

In 1976 Congress enacted the "Government in the Sunshine" Act.[57] It was a straightforward attempt to open most of the decision making of federal administrative agencies to the public. Generally, the act has served that purpose, and courts have had to deal with few cases alleging that its terms have not been met. The law applies to

> any agency . . . headed by a collegial body composed of two or more individual members, a majority of whom are appointed to such position by the President with the advice and consent of the Senate, and any subdivision thereof authorized to act on behalf of the agency.

The list of such agencies is long. It includes some obvious ones, like the Federal Communications Commission and the Federal Trade Commission, along with some obscure ones, like the Harry S. Truman Scholarship Foundation and the Overseas Private Investment Corporation.[58] In effect, a meeting takes place any time a quorum gets together to discuss or act on any item that is properly the business of the agency. No such meetings are to be held without prior notice to the public.

There are exceptions, of course. These roughly parallel the exemptions contained in the Freedom of Information Act.[59] The Sunshine Act also outlines highly detailed

---

55. Buffalo Evening News v. U.S. Border Patrol, 791 F.Supp. 386, 20 Med.L.Rptr. 1553 (W.D.N.Y. 1992).

56. For a federal district court opinion finding 7(C) and 7(D) inapplicable, see Globe Newspaper Co. v. FBI, 21 Med.L.Rptr. 1013 (1992).

57. 5 U.S.C. § 552b.

58. See Energy Research Foundation v. Defense Nuclear Facilities Safety Board, 917 F.2d 581, 18 Med.L.Rptr. 1294 (D.C. Cir. 1990). Circuit court discusses criteria for determining when an entity is a federal agency covered by the FOIA.

59. See Natural Resources Defense Council v. Defense Nuclear Facilities Safety Board, 969 F.2d 1248, 20 Med.L.Rptr. 1564 (D.C. Cir. 1992).

procedures that must be followed if a meeting is to be closed. A decision to close must be accompanied by a written explanation. The agency must keep detailed minutes of closed meetings and make an edited version available as soon as possible. All agencies subject to the law have been required to draft regulations applying to their meetings and publish these in the *Federal Register.*

Federal courts have been asked in only a handful of instances to interpret the Sunshine Act. In *Public Citizen* v. *U.S. Department of Justice,* the Court held that the American Bar Association's Standing Committee on the Federal Judiciary is not an advisory committee within the meaning of the Federal Advisory Committee Act.[60] Therefore, the committee is exempt from the provisions of both the Government in the Sunshine Act and the Freedom of Information Act.

Public Citizen v. *U.S. Department of Justice,* **491 U.S. 440, 109 S.Ct. 2558, 105 L.Ed.2d 377 (1989).**

For more than thirty years, presidents and the Senate Judiciary Committee have relied on the bar group to screen nominees for federal judgeships and to assess their competence. In 1986 the Washington Legal Foundation, joined later by Public Citizen, sought access to meetings of the bar association's Standing Committee and to its records. When they were rebuffed on grounds that the committee is a private group not subject to federal access laws, they asked a federal district court to hold that it is a federal advisory committee. In part, the statute defines an advisory committee as any regularly constituted group "utilized by the President." Had they succeeded, at least some parts of the committee's deliberations might have been opened to public scrutiny.

When the case reached the Supreme Court, all eight justices who participated in the decision agreed that the Standing Committee is outside the reach of the Federal Advisory Committee Act. But they disagreed profoundly in their reasoning. Justice Brennan, writing for himself and four others, went through an exercise in statutory interpretation. Conceding that in the common usage of the term, the president and the Department of Justice do indeed "utilize" the committee in reaching decisions on judicial appointments, Brennan said that was not the end of the matter. When the literal reading of a statute would compel an odd result, courts must look to the legislative history to find out what Congress really meant. Brennan did that, starting with an executive order issued by President Kennedy in 1962. Brennan concluded that "there is scant reason to believe that Congress desired to bring the ABA Committee within FACA's net." Brennan said that he chose this route to his goal to avoid deciding constitutional questions raised by the act. Three other justices would have preferred to face those questions, which have to do with the president's power to appoint judges and other high-level federal officials. In their view, the Constitution gives the president sole power to make such appointments, subject only to the advice and consent of the Senate. A president's desire to consult others, including the American Bar Association's Standing Committee, is his or her business and is protected by executive privilege.

---

60.   5 U.S.C. § 1.

Earlier the Court of Appeals for the District of Columbia Circuit had held that the Chrysler Loan Guarantee Board was not an agency subject to the law. Although each of its members was an official appointed by the president and confirmed by the Senate, the appointments were to other positions within the federal government.[61]

There remain times, of course, when even the most dedicated government officials, acting in full awareness of the law's commitment to openness, feel compelled to sound the water before embarking on a potentially stormy sea of public controversy. There is no way of checking on telephone calls that are made from one board member to others in advance of a public meeting. Nor does the law forbid members of an administrative tribunal from talking with one another if they meet at a party or at lunch. On occasion, reporters have argued that because they saw a majority of a board's members having lunch together, the group was holding an unlawful meeting, but such complaints seldom get far. The fact remains that, taken together, the Sunshine Act and the Freedom of Information Act stand as remarkable commitments to public access to the activities and files of the federal government.

ACCESS TO STATE AND LOCAL DECISION MAKING

Problems of access to government information are not confined to the labyrinthine colossus that is the federal government. Reporters who cover the lowest level of local government engage in a daily battle to find out what's going on. Most issues of *Editor & Publisher*, a magazine covering the newspaper business, report one or more freedom of access cases every week involving state and local agencies of government. And there is not much public sympathy. The Society of Professional Journalists reported in its 1992 *Freedom of Information Report* that nearly half of Americans think freedom of information laws have gone too far in allowing access to government documents.[62]

In any case, reporters often find that the day-to-day reality of seeking newsworthy information from government officials is at odds with the policy of openness written into law by the legislatures of the fifty states. Statutes in all the states give reporters and the public access to most state and local records and to meetings of deliberative bodies, including such agencies as city and county councils, police departments, school boards, and the boards of trustees of state universities. Further, there is a long history of common law access to public records and meetings. Courts long have recognized that certain kinds of information must be readily available. If we are to know what the law is, we must have access to statutes enacted by legislatures, ordinances passed by city councils, and regulations adopted by administrative agencies. People

---

61.   Symons v. Chrysler Loan Guarantee Board, 670 F.2d 238, 7 Med.L.Rptr. 2363 (D.C. Cir. 1981).
62.   Lori Ringhand, "Backlash: Facing Public Privacy Fears, Some States Try to Legislate Away Our FOI Rights," *Quill,* October 1992, p. 10, quoting from a 1991 Louis Harris and Associates survey.

Dana Summers of the *Orlando Sentinel* satirizes Florida legislators after the Florida Supreme Court ruled in 1991 and again in 1992 that the state's open records law did not apply to the Florida legislature. *(Dana J. Summers)*

also need access to court decisions interpreting the law. If government is to be kept honest, records of money spent and received should be open to inspection. So should detailed election results. No prudent person would buy property without a rigorous title search. If taxes are owed on the land, or if the property is subject to an unpaid mortgage, the would-be purchaser needs to know. All these kinds of information, customarily and as a matter of legal right, have long been freely available. In some states, laws require that local governments buy newspaper advertising space to list their receipts and expenditures.

Other kinds of records—such as birth and death certificates, complaints filed with police, accident reports, welfare rolls—may or may not be freely available for public inspection. Access to such records depends on whether a law defines them as public records or whether courts, applying common law, have defined them as such. Because the common law definition of a public record has been incorporated into the statutes of some states, it is worth a look. *Corpus Juris Secundum,* a legal encyclopedia, states that definition as follows:

> A public record is one required by law to be kept, or necessary to be kept in the discharge of a duty imposed by law, or directed by law to serve as a memorial and evidence of some-

thing written, said or done, or a written memorial made by a public officer authorized to perform that function, or a writing filed in a public office.[63]

The problem with the common law definition has been that it requires a study of each record sought by a journalist or others to determine whether it qualifies as a public record. Sometimes, such a determination requires weeks of litigation. The public records statutes now in effect in each state attempt to define and classify state and local records, listing those that are freely available, those that may be made available at an official's discretion, and those that are not to be made public, because they might invade an individual's privacy, interfere with an investigation, or lead to other kinds of harm.

It is unusual for the federal government to interfere with state decisions about what is and what is not a public record, but in the mid-1990s Congress moved to block access to state motor vehicle records. Until passage of the Driver's Privacy Protection Act, motor vehicle records were readily available to the public in forty-two of the fifty states.[64] However, under the federal statute, states are allowed to provide access only to tow truck operators, toll collectors, private investigators, insurance companies, or individuals involved in litigation. As an alternative, states may set up an "opt out" program in which they can continue to make motor vehicle records generally available but must allow each motorist the right to exclude his or her record from general access. If a state adopts the opt out program, it is then required to notify each motorist of his or her rights and to make certain that it does not permit access to records of anyone who opts out. Failure to protect those records would be punishable by heavy fines and other criminal and civil penalties. The statute has been severely criticized by the news media, which for years have obtained information from state motor vehicle files, and by some states that view the federal statute as an unconstitutional intrusion into state government.[65]

At common law, there was also a right of access to most meetings of governmental bodies. State legislatures traditionally have opened their sessions to the public, although some committees might meet in secret occasionally. City and county legislative bodies usually have met in public, as have school boards. At the local level, however, governing bodies have made a practice of going into "executive session" (a euphemism for secret meeting) to discuss, and even come to conclusion on, sensitive matters. Such sessions usually involve sensitive issues that the members don't want to discuss in public.

The open-meetings laws now in effect in every state have been enacted in an attempt to end the practice of conducting public business behind closed doors. Such laws require legislative and administrative bodies to meet in public, with closed meet-

---

63. 76 C.J.S., Records, § 1, p. 112.
64. South Carolina made motor vehicle license records secret in 1995 in an amendment to the state's abortion bill. State legislators said that license records needed to be kept confidential to protect workers at abortion clinics from being identified and harassed by antiabortion advocates. Ron Chepesiuk, "Law Ends Media Access to S.C. Drivers' Records," *Editor & Publisher,* 8 April 1995, p. 13.
65. Jerome L. Wilson, "Keeping Motor Vehicle Records Open to the Press: It's Time to Go to Court," *Editor & Publisher,* 22 April 1995, p. 58.

ings permitted only for limited purposes. Most such laws define a public agency in broad enough terms to include any agency spending public funds. To enforce openness, these laws provide that any final action taken during an executive session is null and void. They also provide for use of the injunction to mandate openness.

An open-meetings law is of limited use if agencies can call special meetings with little or no notice. Therefore, most such laws require adequate advance notice of such meetings, usually forty-eight hours. News organizations that want to receive notice of special meetings sometimes provide agencies with addressed postcards that can be used for this purpose. Open-meetings laws also require that a notice of special meetings, including the topic to be considered, be posted.

Open-meetings laws narrowly restrict executive sessions. The Indiana law is typical.[66] It requires forty-eight-hour notice of such meetings and a statement, in general terms, of the topic to be discussed. Subject matter considered proper for closed meetings is limited to such things as the strategy to be followed in collective bargaining or in a pending legal action. The law also permits executive sessions to discuss possible purchase of land or buildings or to interview industrial or commercial prospects who may be thinking of locating in a community. Most such laws permit confidential discussion of some personnel matters, including complaints against individual employees. But any final action on matters discussed in executive session must take place at a subsequent open meeting.

Experience in two states, California and Ohio, indicates that exceptions written into open-meetings laws can be abused. California's original open-meetings law, like those in many other states, permitted local governing agencies to go into closed sessions to discuss legal strategy with an attorney. The legislature amended the provision to limit it to discussion of pending litigation. The California Newspaper Publishers Association strongly backed the change because member newspapers suspected that agencies were including their attorneys at meetings to justify closed discussions of issues that were not involved in lawsuits. A decision by the Ohio Supreme Court virtually wiped out provisions of the Cleveland city charter that permitted members of the city council to discuss business in private.[67] The court held that a meeting, as defined by the charter, is any gathering of a majority of the council or its committees at which public business is discussed. The decision overruled lower-court decisions holding that the state's open-meetings law did not apply to cities with home-rule charters.

No law, no matter how strongly worded, will ensure that the public's business is conducted in public or that records compiled by government agencies are open to public inspection. The *Media Law Reporter*[68] added more than seventy-five entries in 1995 to its growing list of appellate court opinions on access to records and meetings under state laws. Each issue of *Quill,* the magazine of the Society of Professional Journalists, contains a freedom of information section reporting on litigation and legislation. Such reports demonstrate that the right to know does not come easily.

---

66.   Ind. Code 5-14-1.5-1.

67.   Ohio, ex rel. Plain Dealer Publishing Co. v. Barnes, 38 Ohio St.3d 165, 527 N.E.2d 807, 15 Med.L.Rptr. 2083 (Ohio 1988).

68.   *Media Law Reporter* (Washington, D.C.: Bureau of National Affairs, 1995). There are now twenty-three volumes in the collection of court opinions affecting the media.

The constant struggle against secrecy reflected in the reports in *Quill* and elsewhere could lead observers to the unwarranted conclusion that most public officials are contemptuous of the public they serve. Some probably are. In reality, however, every day public officials freely offer a torrent of information to newspapers, broadcasters, and other private citizens. When public officials seek to withhold information, they frequently do so in the honest belief that they are complying with exemptions provided by law. Sometimes their concern, whether legitimate or not, is so narrowly focused on protecting personal privacy that it is hard for them to see the long-term societal interests at stake. Sometimes, too, officials are busy and resent disruptions by reporters, lawyers, and all the others who want to look at government records. Finally, some officials at all levels of government just do not understand that they are supposed to conduct the public's business in public. Sometimes they have to be reminded that openness is the general rule and exceptions should be exceptional.

SPECIFIC PROBLEMS IN JOURNALISTIC ACCESS

When records are clearly public and customarily open to inspection by anyone, journalists have no problems. But when records are not clearly defined as public, or when a journalist makes an unusual request for information, questions can arise. The most common of these are dealt with in the sections that follow.

Do Journalists Have Special Rights of Access to Records and Meetings?

Journalists are not singled out for special privileges. Public records laws provide a right of access for all persons. However, by earning the trust of their sources, reporters are often able to obtain access to records that the law defines as available only at the discretion of an official, or even to records defined as nonpublic.

Reporters also have no special rights of access to meetings of government agencies. As a courtesy, however, and in the interest of ensuring a greater degree of accuracy, governing bodies usually provide special seating for reporters where they can see and hear all that goes on. Governing bodies also commonly give reporters copies of proposed legislation and other documents scheduled for consideration. Reporters who are going to do more than cover the surface of events also seek to gain the confidence of individual members of government agencies. Only by doing so can they learn about the wider, and sometimes hidden, interests that mold government policy at all levels.

Do Journalists Have a Right to Inspect Police Records?

In all states, a secret arrest or imprisonment is illegal. Consequently, arrest records of adults are required to be kept as public records. Anyone can inspect the log, or "book," in which arrests are listed. Some state laws allow inspection during regular business hours. Others allow reporters to have copies of the records. Most police agencies develop their own policies concerning what information is public and who can release it, and occasionally these policies are at odds with the requirements of state law. Some states do not specify very clearly whether access is to the original police logs or to information in the logs. The difference can sometimes produce two sets of books, one for internal police use and a somewhat edited version for the public.

Police also receive and investigate many complaints that may or may not result in an arrest. Officers file written reports of such activities, and reporters may or may not be given access to these reports, depending on specific state and federal laws.[69] Police officers investigating crimes also prepare reports about leads, suspects, evidence, and witnesses. Access to those reports is generally, at least while the investigation is in process, at the discretion of the police. Unless a statute or court opinion requires disclosure of specific police records or defines citizen complaints or incident reports as public records, journalists have little legal recourse to force access.[70]

With some notable exceptions, however, the tendency has been for both state legislatures and courts to provide for as much access to police records as seems prudent. For instance, an Indiana law requires police to create and make available to the public a daily list of suspected crimes, accidents, and complaints. Only information that might interfere with an investigation or violate a right of privacy is exempt from disclosure. Moreover, the Indiana law says that if "a public record contains disclosable and nondisclosable information, the public agency shall separate the material that may be disclosed and make it available for inspection and copying."[71]

Federal courts have ruled that campus police cannot use the Family Education and Privacy Act[72] to deny access to information about crimes on college campuses.[73] In Wyoming, the state supreme court recognized both a statutory and constitutional right of access to police "case reports."[74] In Ohio, the state supreme court ruled that investigation records into shootings by police officers were not exempt as either "trial-preparation records" or "investigatory work product."[75] In Florida, an appellate court ruled that the public had a right of access to a sheriff's investigative records concerning the activities of a judge.[76]

Decisions also clearly indicate that courts are not willing to open all police records to public inspection. The *Lawrence* (Mass.) *Eagle-Tribune* was denied access to the

---

69. For a state-by-state guide to police record access, see Jodi L. Cleesattle and Zhao Xiao-hua, "Police Records, a Guide to Effective Access in the 50 States & D.C.," *News Media and the Law,* Fall 1992 19-page pullout section.

70. See, for example, Gallagher v. Marion County Victim Advocate Program, Inc., 401 N.E.2d 1362 (Ind.App. 1980).

71. Ind. Code 5-14-3 §§ 5 (c) and 6.

72. 20 U.S.C. 1232g. The Buckley amendment.

73. Bauer v. Kincaid, 759 F.Supp. 575 (W.D.Mo. 1991); Student Press Law Center v. Lamar Alexander, 778 F.Supp. 1227, 19 Med.L.Rptr. 1620 (D.D.C. 1991). See also Doe v. Board of Regents of the University System of Georgia, 215 Ga.App. 684, 452 S.E.2d 776 (1994).

74. Sheridan Newspapers Inc. v. Sheridan, 660 P.2d 785, 9 Med.L.Rptr. 2393 (Wyo. 1983).

75. Ohio, ex rel. NBC v. City of Cleveland, 38 Ohio St.3d 79, 526 N.E.2d 786, 15 Med.L.Rptr. 1853 (1988).

76. Tribune Co. v. Spicola, 543 So.2d 757, 16 Med.L.Rptr. 1169 (Fla.App. 1989).

evaluative records of Willie Horton, a state prison inmate who was accused of raping a Maryland woman while on furlough from a Massachusetts prison.[77] A Minnesota appellate court held that complaint forms about allegations of the use of excessive force by police officers were not subject to disclosure.[78] A Wisconsin appellate court ruled that a police department's inventory of the weapons it keeps in its arsenal did not have to be made public.[79]

These instances are only a few of the hundreds of actions, formal and informal, taken by citizens and the news media to access police information. The variety of outcomes serve as a reminder that police and court reporters need to be familiar with their state's access laws and should be able and willing to use them.[80]

Do Journalists Have a Right of Access to Juvenile Court Proceedings?

In general, journalists do not have a right of access to juvenile court proceedings, although many states give judges of such courts wide discretion over access to their proceedings. The juvenile justice system is a product of the idealism that suffused this country in the early part of the twentieth century. The system is based on the theory that youngsters go wrong not because they are evil, but because they have not been shown the right way to go. Therefore, the purpose of the system is seen as educational rather than punitive. Offenders are put on probation. If that doesn't work, they are sent to "reform schools." They are held in "detention facilities" rather than in jails. Traditionally, the system has been cloaked in secrecy, on the theory that publicity for juvenile offenders would stigmatize them and make it more difficult for them to go straight.

In the case of particularly vicious crimes, a juvenile court judge may order that offenders be tried as adults in the regular court system.[81] When that happens, there is no question about a right of access to the records and disposition of that particular offense. Legislatures also have given judges of juvenile courts authority to open their proceedings and records to inspection. In some states, juvenile courts release edited versions of their proceedings, designed to show the nature of the offense and the disposition by the court and to protect the identity of the offender. In part, such arrangements are a response to accusations that persistent offenders are not punished.

State laws designed to protect juveniles from publicity usually apply only to the courts, leaving police in many states free to release names if they wish. The Supreme

---

77. "Mass. Paper Cannot Get Info on Inmate," *Editor & Publisher,* 4 July 1987, p. 22.
78. Demers v. Minneapolis, 486 N.W.2d 828, 20 Med.L.Rptr. 1545 (Minn.App. 1992).
79. Wisconsin, ex rel. Schultz v. Bruendl, 482 N.W.2d 238, 20 Med.L.Rptr. 1193 (Wis.App. 1992).
80. For quick information to state access laws, see "Guide to State Access Laws," *Quill,* October 1992, pp. 27–38, and "Access to Electronic Records," *News Media and the Law,* Fall 1994, 28-page pullout section.
81. See Island Packet, ex parte, 417 S.E.2d 870, 20 Med.L.Rptr. 1166 (S.C. 1992). South Carolina Supreme Court finds that a family court's transfer hearing involving a fifteen-year-old murder suspect must be in open court, despite the defendant's anxiety about news coverage.

Court has held that neither a judge's order nor a state law can prevent publication of a juvenile offender's name, if it has been acquired legally.[82]

Do Journalists Have a Right of Access to the Scene of a Crime?

Access to the scene of a crime depends on the situation. The police investigation takes first priority. Whether the crime took place on public or private property, the police have a duty to protect the scene while evidence is being gathered. Thus, they can prevent access in the interest of preserving evidence. If a crime or accident takes place on public property, nothing prevents reporters and photographers from coming as close as the police will permit. And although it is not uncommon for police to attempt to forbid photography of particularly gruesome scenes, or of situations that may make them look bad, they have no legal right to do so. An officer who grabs the camera of a photographer who is not interfering with an investigation or who shoves the photographer has committed an assault and perhaps a battery. The news media can take prompt legal action in all such cases.

If the crime or accident takes place on private property, there is no right of access except that granted by whoever is in control of the property. Courts in Florida have held that if police or firefighters are in control of the property and are willing to admit reporters and photographers, they may do so.[83]

All police forces, no matter what the size, have policies regulating actions by officers at the scene of a crime. Usually these policies state that the news media shall be given information and be permitted to take photographs as long as they are not interfering with the investigation. However, reporters and photographers who refuse to obey a valid order by police in charge of the scene of a crime or accident risk arrest. For instance, the Wisconsin Supreme Court upheld a reporter's conviction for disorderly conduct based on his refusal to obey a police order to stay away from the scene of an airplane crash.[84]

Do Journalists Have a Right to Find Out What Grand Juries Are Doing?

Journalists do have a right to find out what grand juries are doing, a right that has been affirmed by the U.S. Supreme Court. But that right is hedged by limitations, both legal and ethical.

The grand jury is almost as old as English common law and had its origins in a need to temper the sometimes harsh and arbitrary authority of the king and his minions. Present-day grand juries are made up of persons, chosen at random, whose duty is to hear evidence indicating that a crime has been committed. If the jurors find reasonable cause to believe that a named individual has violated a specific law, they put their names

---

82. Oklahoma Publishing Co. v. District Court of Oklahoma County, 430 U.S. 308, 97 S.Ct. 1045, 51 L.Ed.2d 355, 2 Med.L.Rptr. 1456 (1977); Smith v. Daily Mail Publishing Co., 443 U.S. 97, 99 S.Ct. 2667, 61 L.Ed.2d 399, 5 Med.L.Rptr. 1305 (1979).

83. Fletcher v. Florida Publishing Co., 319 So.2d 100 (Fla.App. 1st Dist. 1975); 340 So.2d 914, 2 Med.L.Rptr. 1088 (Fla. 1977); cert. denied, 97 S.Ct. 2634 (1977).

84. Oak Creek v. Ah King, 148 Wis.2d 532, 436 N.W.2d 285, 16 Med.L.Rptr. 1273 (Wis. 1989).

to an indictment, or "charge." If the individual is not already in custody, the indictment serves as a warrant for that person's arrest. In federal courts, all felony charges must come from a grand jury. Most states give prosecutors authority to file charges without first submitting evidence to a grand jury. But if the evidence is in doubt or the case carries political freight, prosecutors may prefer to let a grand jury make the decision.

Since at least 1681, grand juries have met in secrecy. All states and the federal government prescribe secrecy for grand jury proceedings—by statute, by rule of court, or by common law.[85] There are several reasons for secrecy. Grand juries operate informally and, at the state level, have broad authority to look into what they will. They are not bound by the strict rules of evidence that guide a trial. Witnesses are free to report unfounded gossip, voice their suspicions, or even express views based on hatred or malice. Grand juries also may hear from witnesses whose lives would be in peril or who would be ostracized by their friends if word of their testimony became public. Secrecy also protects jurors from those who might try to influence them and protects those who have been investigated and cleared. Finally, if a grand jury does decide to indict persons who are not in custody, secrecy may be essential to keep them from fleeing.

Secrecy is enforced through an oath given to members of the grand jury and to stenographers or officers of the court who work with it. The record of the jury's deliberations, including the testimony it hears, is sealed. Thus, a juror who talks to a reporter about the proceedings or an official who leaks all or part of a transcript faces punishment for contempt if caught. Some reporters have been punished for contempt not for publishing information leaked from a grand jury, but for refusing to identify the source of the leak.

However, when a Florida prosecutor summoned reporter Michael Smith as a grand jury witness and then told him he could be jailed under state law if he ever published any part of his own testimony, the U.S. Supreme Court told the prosecutor that he and the state had gone too far. The effect of the order was to prevent Smith and his newspaper, the *Charlotte Herald-News,* from complete coverage of its own investigation into allegations of misconduct in the offices of the Charlotte County State Attorney and Sheriff. The newspaper's investigation had led to the calling of the grand jury.

Butterworth v. Smith, 494 U.S. 624, 110 S.Ct. 1376, 108 L.Ed.2d 572, 17 Med.L.Rptr.1569 (1990).

At issue in *Butterworth* v. *Smith* was a Florida law making it a crime for "any person knowingly to publish, broadcast, disclose, divulge, or communicate to any other person . . . any testimony of a witness examined before the grand jury, or the content, gist, or import thereof" unless it had been disclosed in court.[86] Smith, planning a book based on his investigation, asked a U.S. district court to declare the law unconstitutional. The court held that the legislature had acted within its powers in deciding that a permanent ban on disclosure of testimony was essential to proper functioning of the grand jury. The Eleventh Circuit Court of Appeals reversed, and the Supreme Court affirmed the reversal. However, the decision was a narrow one, applying only to the provision prohibiting a witness from disclosing his own testimony after the term of the grand jury had ended.

---

85. Yale Kamisar, Wayne R. LaFave, and Jerold H. Israel, *Modern Criminal Procedure,* 4th ed. (St. Paul, Minn.: West Publishing Co., 1974), pp. 884–893.
86. Fl. Stat., § 905.27.

Chief Justice Rehnquist noted that on several occasions the Court has upheld grand jury secrecy. But he also noted that there is a point at which such secrecy can impinge on freedoms guaranteed by the First Amendment. The complete ban imposed by the Florida law reached one of those points. He said that the state's interest in protecting witnesses ought not overcome the judgment of the witnesses themselves as to what they might choose to reveal to the public. Nor was the state's interest in protecting the reputations of persons who may be accused of, but not charged with, criminal activity sufficient to justify a prior restraint. Further, as applied in this instance, the law was subject to abuse because it could be used "to silence those who know of unlawful conduct or irregularities on the part of public officials." Justice Antonin Scalia would have gone further. In a concurring opinion he expressed doubt that a witness can be prevented, even while the grand jury is still sitting, from talking about what he or she knew before he or she entered the grand jury room.

Fourteen other states have laws similar to Florida's, the Court noted. Twenty-one states have directly or indirectly exempted witnesses from the secrecy that cloaks the jurors and the investigative process. The remaining fourteen states have remained silent on the issue.

Without relying on *Butterworth,* the Indiana Supreme Court, a week after the U.S. Supreme Court decision, held, three to two, that two reporters for the Hammond *Times* were not in contempt of court when they questioned former grand jurors two years after the grand jury had concluded an investigation.[87] The Lake County prosecutor had asked that the reporters be held in contempt for attempting to induce the grand jurors to violate their oath of secrecy. A trial court rejected the request, but the state court of appeals ruled that the reporters should be found in contempt. In reversing, the supreme court endorsed the need for grand jury secrecy but held that with the passage of time, the need to protect that secrecy diminishes. However, the Court cautioned that its decision did not establish a blanket rule. The majority said that courts would have to decide on a case-by-case basis whether reporters' attempts to question grand jurors might interfere with the administration of justice.

Thus, reporters are free to proceed with caution in their attempts to learn what grand juries have been told. Nothing prevents reporters from waiting outside the grand jury room and trying to talk to witnesses as they emerge. Nor does anything prevent reporters from identifying the individuals or officers under investigation and going after the news on their own. But in the states that impose an oath of secrecy on grand jury witnesses, reporters may risk being held in contempt if they induce *witnesses* to violate that oath before the grand jury's term ends. In any state and in the federal courts, reporters run a risk of being cited for contempt if they attempt to induce *grand jurors* to violate their oaths of secrecy.

One further note of caution: If a grand jury does not return an indictment, reporters who have produced stories about the investigation cannot rely on privilege as a defense if they are sued for libel. The record of the testimony will remain sealed and unavailable for use as evidence to support the accuracy of the story.

---

87.   Indiana v. Heltzel, 552 N.E.2d 31, 17 Med.L.Rptr. 1677 (Ind. 1990).

In the Professional World

David Morrissey, who, as a newspaper reporter, filed more than five hundred FOIA requests for such papers as the *Albuquerque Journal*, the *Idaho Argonaut*, and the *Anniston* (Ala.) *Star*, advises reporters who use the act to be persistent and patient.[88] He says that users should expect to encounter government bureaucrats who can be less than helpful. It helps to keep a sense of humor. Among the typical problems, Morrissey says, are these:

— Agencies that are slow to respond to requests

— Agencies that want to deny fee waivers

— Agencies that use inapplicable FOIA exemptions

— Agencies that improperly classify documents

Morrissey advises reporters who seek information from a federal agency to contact the agency's FOIA officer to get an insight into how the agency's files are compiled and what kinds of delays are likely. Before making a formal FOIA request, Morrissey suggests that a reporter:

— Research the subject as thoroughly as possible, making sure to look for government manuals that list and describe government agencies and for reports already published and catalogued in libraries holding government publications.

— Contact a variety of other sources, including known experts, university researchers, and investigators who are already dealing with the subject of the story or project.

— Be prepared to explain how and why the information is going to serve the public interest.[89]

This preliminary search may uncover documents containing other helpful information.

When the documentary sources have been identified, the next step is to file a formal request, which should be in writing. The statement should say that the request is being made under the terms of the Freedom of Information Act; it should identify the documents requested as specifically as possible, with titles and numbers if possible; and it should suggest some limit to the search and copying fees

---

88. David Morrissey conversation, November 1992. See also David H. Morrissey, *FOIA Case Study: USAF H-Bombs Albuquerque* (Honolulu: Society of Professional Journalists, University of Hawaii Chapter, 1989).

89. Abel Montez, "FOIA Helps Albuquerque Reporter Uncover Secret Biological Test, Nuclear Bomb Accident." In *F.O.I. Computer Access: Maze or Miracle* (Chicago: Society of Professional Journalists, 1990), p. 5.

the requestor is prepared to pay.[90] The law requires that such fees be "reasonable," but in instances where large numbers of documents are sought, fees can run into thousands of dollars. Often, if the request is from a reporter who is writing to inform citizens about government or to provide information that citizens can use to reach conclusions about how well government is working, the fees will be waived or reduced to modest copying costs.

But "[s]ometimes you have to be prepared to explain to government bureaucrats that they work for you. You don't work for them," said Morrissey. Sometimes you have to be ready to appeal up the line to agency heads or FOIA officers in Washington who understand what the law requires. Only twice, he said, has he had to ask for the help of a congressman. Never has he had to file suit in federal court.

Morrissey's use of the FOIA has produced important stories about a series of Army biological warfare tests conducted in the open air over an Alabama city, about a nuclear accident near Albuquerque, and about illegal drug use by an Air Force security unit assigned to guard a nuclear weapons storage depot. All of the records were available for the asking, but nobody besides Morrissey bothered to ask.

At the state and local levels, access procedures usually are less formal, in part because the volume of requests is not as great. Reporters also are more likely to have frequent contact with officials who control the release of documents. Ready access is more likely because many state press associations, individual publishers and broadcasters, and the Society of Professional Journalists have shown a willingness to go to court to enforce the terms of state open-records and open-meetings laws.

Because legal procedures can be slow, experienced reporters continue to cultivate other sources as well. Any controversy has losers as well as winners. The losers in an intra-agency battle over policy may be willing to carry an appeal to the public through a trusted reporter. Inefficiencies, and even corruption, in public agencies have been brought to light because a conscientious employee was willing to give information to journalists under a promise of confidentiality. In such instances, access laws can be used to obtain supporting or supplementary data.

Even in the economically tough times of the 1990s, many editors say they still are willing to meet any denial of access, either to meetings or to records, by asking the newspaper's lawyer to file a lawsuit. Usually the threat is enough to pry loose the sought-after information.

Beyond question, today's journalists have greater access to government meetings and information at all levels than at any other time in history. As the *Progressive* episode, discussed in Chapter 3, attests, this freedom includes the right to publish the nation's most highly guarded secrets, if they can be obtained. Nor is the right to publish restricted information confined to the workings of a hydrogen bomb or the labyrinths of foreign policy, as in the Pentagon Papers case,

---

90. A suggested request letter is included in "How to Use the Federal FOI Act," a publication of the FOI Service Center, 8090 18th Street, NW, Washington, DC 20006.

also discussed in Chapter 3. At the local level, the Supreme Court has held that journalists can publish the names of juvenile offenders, even when state laws say that those names aren't to be released. And as presidential campaigns repeatedly demonstrate, the media are free to poke as far as they can into the private lives of candidates for public office.

Does this mean that anything goes? Most editors say not. Most, for instance, won't publish the names of juvenile offenders unless the crime involved serious injury or death. Nor do many publications use the names of rape victims. Increasingly, editors and news directors have dropped long-established habits of identifying crime victims by name and address. Many, too, question blanket policies that identify by name and address every person arrested by police. Some news organizations, while continuing to publish routine arrests, advise readers that an arrest does not mean a person is guilty of a crime. A few newspaper editors now wait until persons arrested have been brought to court before reporting crimes.

The critical legal question is how much government information must be made available on request. The critical ethical question is whether available government information should be published. Journalists face that ethical question every day. The public's right to know means little if the media fail to insist that the right of access be honored. But the right to know also means little if the media fail to distinguish significant information from that which is trivial, misleading, or harmful. Editors and news directors, while ethically bound to insist on access to information, are also ethically bound to make informed judgments about the value of information to readers and viewers.

FOR REVIEW

1. What is meant by "First Amendment right of access"? How far does it seem to go?

2. What is the significance, with respect to a constitutional right of access, of the Supreme Court's decision in *Seattle Times Company* v. *Rhinehart?* Discuss the possible consequences if the Court's decision had gone the other way.

3. What is the Freedom of Information Act? What are its strengths? Its limitations?

4. Good reporters pride themselves on their ability to get information that government and other sources would prefer not to disclose. Why, then, should there be laws mandating access to most government records?

5. Define "agency record." Why is the term important?

6. Discuss the significance of the case in which the *Washington Post* sought access to the State Department's passport records.

7. Assess the right to obtain copies of records of investigatory agencies. To what kinds of records can journalists reasonably hope to gain access?

8. To what degree is there a right of access to police records? Given that most such records deal with incidents that are embarrassing to at least some of the participants, how much right of access to them should the public have?

9. How far can the media go in publishing information about juvenile offenders? How far should they go?

10. Should reporters respect the secrecy that cloaks the proceedings of grand juries? Why or why not? What legal problems may arise from attempts to penetrate grand jury secrecy?

11. If you could define an ideal relationship between journalists and government officials, what would it be? What does the public have a right to know? Who or what can best fulfill that right?

CHAPTER 10

OBSCENITY UNDER THE ROTH TEST
ROTH'S LEGACY: ANYTHING GOES
MILLER'S DEFINITION OF OBSCENITY
OBSCENITY LAW SINCE MILLER AND PARIS

Refining the Definition of Obscenity
Outlawing Child Pornography
Legal Alternatives to Criminal Obscenity Statutes

Zoning / Nuisance / Indecent Conduct / Racketeering / Licensing

OBSCENITY, INDECENCY, AND ELECTRONIC MEDIA

Broadcasting / Cable / Internet

The urge to censor portrayals of human sexuality has run deep in American society since colonial times. Courts have upheld such censorship as a necessary step to protect public morality in the belief that obscene depictions of human behavior lie outside the realm of ideas protected by the First Amendment. That belief was reinforced by the Supreme Court's 1931 decision in *Near* v. *Minnesota*,[1] in which Chief Justice Charles Evans Hughes wrote that "the primary requirements of decency" may permit prior restraint to prevent circulation of obscene materials.

The problem with the suppression of obscenity has been in defining obscenity. Throughout most of America's history, until after World War II, any description of sexual activity, no matter how delicately phrased, was likely to draw a censor's frown. James Joyce's *Ulysses,* now studied as a classic, was banned as obscene until a federal judge held in 1933 that it was literature, not pornography.[2] *Lady Chatterley's Lover* by D. H. Lawrence, the novels of Henry Miller, and Edmund Wilson's *Memoirs of Hecate County* were among the works that drew official disapproval. Even Norman Mailer had to be wary of the censor when he wrote *The Naked and the Dead,* a realistic account of small-unit combat in World War II. To avoid having his work labeled obscene, Mailer invented the word "fug" to substitute for one of the two most common epithets of the war. The four-letter version did not win the Supreme Court's ap-

---

1. 283 U.S. 679, 51 S.Ct. 625, 75 L.Ed. 1357, 1 Med.L.Rptr. 1001 (1931).
2. United States v. One Book Entitled "Ulysses," 5 F.Supp. 182 (D.N.Y. 1933).

OBSCENITY, INDECENCY, AND SEXUAL VIOLENCE

proval until 1971.[3] By that time the Court had lowered the barriers against literary and pictorial portrayals of sexual activity, but it had not abolished them.

Over the years, persistent attempts to suppress obscenity have pitted religious groups against civil libertarians; citizens' groups fearing human degradation against citizens' groups fearing suppression of healthy sexual expression; and prosecutors against a multibillion-dollar industry that makes and sells explicit sexual movies, videotapes, printed materials, and devices. An even larger flood of materials, including advertising, exploits sex appeal just short of the limits set by obscenity law. Many feminists have entered the fray, arguing that much explicit sexual material encourages rape by portraying women as inviting and enjoying the most degrading kinds of sexual assault. Cases requiring courts to interpret obscenity laws have divided judges as have few other issues. As we complete the last decade of the twentieth century, the legal attempt to suppress obscenity shows few signs of abating.

The controversy over the enforcement of obscenity laws centers on the fact that prosecutors seeking a conviction need not prove that anyone has suffered physical harm. The crime is one of the few that is committed in the mind. The Supreme Court has held that material is obscene if, among other things, it "appeals to a prurient interest in sex" by portraying "sexual conduct in a patently offensive way."[4] Traced to its Latin roots, "prurient" means literally "to itch," and therefore, figuratively, "to yearn for, to be lascivious." As the courts use it, the word means that material is considered obscene if a jury concludes that it arouses an obsessive or morbid interest in sex. Since virtually all humans feel, and even welcome, an interest in sex at some point, the critical determination is when an interest becomes obsessive.

Those who oppose the traffic in obscenity argue that it degrades society by corrupting the morals of persons who are exposed to it, particularly young people. Critics argue that the ready availability of magazines, movies, videotapes, and CD-ROMs devoted to infinite varieties of sexual gratification encourages sexual permissiveness and weakens the bonds that hold society together.[5] Scientific evidence to support such conclusions is mixed. In 1970 the President's Commission on Obscenity and Pornog-

---

3. Cohen v. California, 403 U.S. 15, 91 S.Ct. 1780, 29 L.Ed.2d 284 (1971) held that the four-letter word avoided by Mailer was protected speech when it was printed on the back of a man's jacket to show his opposition to the Vietnam war. Hess v. Indiana, 414 U.S. 105, 94 S.Ct. 326, 38 L.Ed.2d 303 (1973) held that the same word was not actionable when it was directed at a deputy sheriff during an antiwar demonstration.
4. Miller v. California, 413 U.S. 15, 93 S.Ct. 2607, 37 L.Ed.2d 419, 1 Med.L.Rptr. 1441 (1973).
5. Edwin McDowell, "The Critics Descend on Pornotopia," *Wall Street Journal,* 15 May 1973.

raphy concluded that there was no relationship between exposure to erotic materials and antisocial behavior.[6] On the other hand, Edward Donnerstein and Daniel Linz, psychology professors at the University of Wisconsin, reported that there is evidence that "exposure to even a few minutes of sexually violent pornography, such as scenes of rape and other forms of sexual violence against women, can lead to anti-social attitudes and behavior."[7] Then in 1985, a majority of a second government commission on pornography, this one appointed by President Reagan and headed by Attorney General Edwin Meese III, concluded that some sexually explicit material, especially that oriented toward sexual violence, was indeed related to behavior that caused physical and emotional harm. As a remedy, the Meese commission urged stricter enforcement of existing criminal obscenity laws.[8]

However, courts generally have chosen to sidestep the question of harm in dealing with allegedly obscene materials. They have focused on the value of content—or lack of value—of sexually explicit matter. In *Roth* v. *United States,*[9] the U.S. Supreme Court held that obscenity can be suppressed because it is devoid of idea content and therefore "not within the area of constitutionally protected speech or press." Materials are obscene, the Court said, if among other things, their dominant purpose is to arouse a prurient interest in sex in a patently offensive way. The Court has since noted in *Miller* v. *California* that the lack of "serious literary, artistic, political, or scientific value" is what deprives such sexually explicit material of any First Amendment protection. Not harm, but lack of serious value, is what condemns sexually oriented offensive speech.

This chapter will trace the development of obscenity law, focusing on the *Roth* and *Miller* decisions. Although the Supreme Court has decided numerous obscenity cases in the past thirty-five years, these two are the landmarks. In them, the Court established, as precisely as words can, the line at which sexually explicit materials leave the realm of ideas and pass beyond the pale of the First Amendment's protection. That line cannot be fixed with certainty, because the Supreme Court held in *Miller* that juries must apply their notion of community standards in determining whether sexually explicit materials are obscene. Thus, magazines, movies, and the like that are condemned as obscene in one community may be freely available in another a few miles away.

A word on meanings before we proceed further. Many students, and even some professors, make a distinction between obscenity and pornography. There is a difference, but many people, including the courts, often use the terms interchangeably. "Pornography" is of Greek origin, meaning literally "writing about prostitutes." In its current meaning, "pornography" applies to any portrayal of explicit sexual behavior. The Meese commission defined pornography as material that is "predominantly sexually explicit and intended primarily for the purpose of arousal." "Obscenity" is of Latin origin. In its primary meaning the term encompasses whatever may be offensive to accepted standards of decency or modesty. In its secondary meaning, "obscenity" ap-

---

6. *Report of the Presidential Commission on Obscenity and Pornography* (New York: Bantam Books, 1970).
7. Edward Donnerstein and Daniel Linz, "Sexual Violence in the Media: A Warning," *Psychology Today,* January 1984, p. 14.
8. Attorney General's Commission on Pornography, *Final Report* (Washington, D.C.: Government Printing Office, 1986).
9. 354 U.S. 476, 77 S.Ct. 1304, 1 L.Ed.2d 1498, 1 Med.L.Rptr. 1375 (1957).

plies to matter that incites lustful feelings or to lewdness. Thus, "obscenity" has both sexual and scatological connotations. In their decisions dealing with sexually explicit materials, the Supreme Court justices use the term "obscene" to describe patently offensive matter that appeals to the prurient interest and is so lacking in value that it lies outside the protection of the First Amendment.[10] It is in this sense that we use the term in this chapter.

Major Cases

- *Cruz* v. *Ferre*, 755 F.2d 1415 (11th Cir. 1985).

- *Federal Communications Commission* v. *Pacifica Foundation*, 438 U.S. 726, 98 S.Ct. 3026, 57 L.Ed.2d 1073, 3 Med.L.Rptr. 2553 (1978).

- *Fort Wayne Books, Inc.* v. *Indiana*, 489 U.S. 46, 109 S.Ct. 916, 103 L.Ed.2d 34, 16 Med.L. Rptr. 1337 (1989).

- *FW/PBS, Inc.* v. *City of Dallas*, 493 U.S. 215, 110 S.Ct. 596, 107 L.Ed.2d 603 (1990).

- *Hamling* v. *United States*, 418 U.S. 87, 94 S.Ct. 2887, 41 L.Ed.2d 590, 1 Med.L.Rptr. 1479 (1974).

- *Jenkins* v. *Georgia*, 418 U.S. 153, 94 S.Ct. 2750, 41 L.Ed.2d 642, 1 Med.L.Rptr. 1504 (1974).

- *Miller* v. *California*, 413 U.S. 15, 93 S.Ct. 2607, 37 L.Ed.2d 419, 1 Med.L.Rptr. 1441 (1973).

- *New York* v. *Ferber*, 458 U.S. 747, 102 S.Ct. 3348, 73 L.Ed.2d 1113, 8 Med.L.Rptr. 1809 (1982).

- *Paris Adult Theatre I* v. *Slaton*, 413 U.S. 49, 93 S.Ct. 2626, 37 L.Ed.2d 446, 1 Med.L.Rptr. 1454 (1973).

- *Pope* v. *Illinois*, 481 U.S. 497, 107 S.Ct. 1918, 95 L.Ed.2d 439, 14 Med.L.Rptr. 1001 (1987).

- *Roth* v. *United States*, 354 U.S. 476, 77 S.Ct. 1304, 1 L.Ed.2d 1498, 1 Med.L.Rptr. 1375 (1957).

- *Stanley* v. *Georgia*, 394 U.S. 557, 89 S.Ct. 1243, 22 L.Ed.2d 542 (1969).

---

10. See David Pritchard, "Beyond the Meese Commission Report: Understanding the Variable Nature of Pornography Regulation." In Susan Gubar and Joan Hoff, eds., *The Dilemma of Pornography,* (Bloomington, Ind.: Indiana University Press, 1989), p. 166.

OBSCENITY UNDER THE ROTH TEST ═══════════

Congress enacted its first obscenity law in 1873 at the urging of Anthony Comstock, who came out of Union Army service in the Civil War as a one-star general to devote the rest of his life to the suppression of vice. The law, which bears his name, is still in effect. It prohibits, subject to a fine of up to $5,000 and up to five years in prison, the mailing of "every obscene, lewd, lascivious, indecent, filthy or vile article, matter, thing, device or substance."[11] Even a cursory examination of the language illustrates the difficulty in prosecuting obscenity as a crime under the Comstock Law. Murder, for example, can be defined succinctly as the act of killing another person without justification; obscenity cannot even be defined as an act. Rather, obscenity is the nature of a communication.

The vagueness of the language, however, has not kept the Comstock Law from being enforced. For decades, trial courts translated its generalities by applying a standard borrowed from England. In 1868, in *Regina* v. *Hicklin,*[12] Lord Chief Justice Cockburn ruled that a work is obscene if "the tendency of the matter . . . is to deprave and corrupt those whose minds are open to such immoral influences and into whose hands a publication of this sort might fall."

In the United States, the test was made even stronger by rulings that it could be applied to isolated passages, even if they were taken out of context. A few lurid passages in any book, no matter how serious its overall purpose, could condemn the work as obscene. Criminal obscenity laws in every state supplemented the Comstock Law. Their combined effect was to drive the traffic in sexually explicit materials under the counter. Few wanted to try to argue that the First Amendment protected the lewd and the lascivious as well as the literary and the serious.

The first break in the high barriers against sexually explicit materials came in 1957, when for the first time the Supreme Court accepted two obscenity convictions for review. One of the cases, *Butler* v. *Michigan,*[13] involved a bookseller who had been fined $100 for violating that state's obscenity law. The judge had held that the book in question contained "obscene, immoral, lewd, lascivious language, or descriptions tending to incite minors to violent or depraved or immoral acts, manifestly tending to the corruption of the morals of youth." The Supreme Court found two things wrong with the judge's decision: (1) The book had been sold to an adult police officer, not a minor, and (2) the Michigan law, by defining obscenity in terms of material that would corrupt minors, would reduce the people of the state "to reading only what is fit for children." The Court added, "Surely this is to burn the house to roast the pig."

Later that year, the Court decided two cases as one and, for the first time, applied First Amendment theory to materials considered obscene. One case came out of New York City, where Samuel Roth had been found guilty in a U.S. district court of violating the federal law forbidding the sending of obscenity through the mails. The

Roth v. *United States,* **354 U.S. 476, 77 S.Ct. 1304, 1 L.Ed.2d 1498, 1 Med.L.Rptr. 1375 (1957).**

---

11. 18 U.S.C. § 1461.
12. 6 L.R. 3 Q.B. 360 (1868).
13. 352 U.S. 380, 77 S.Ct. 524, 1 L.Ed.2d 158 (1957).

other case came from Beverly Hills, California, where David S. Alberts had been found guilty in a state court of "lewdly keeping for sale obscene and indecent books" in violation of state law.

Justice William J. Brennan, Jr., wrote for himself and four others in upholding the convictions of both men. He began by asking "whether obscenity is utterance within the area of protected speech and press":

> Although this is the first time the question has been squarely presented to this Court, either under the First Amendment or under the Fourteenth Amendment, expressions found in numerous opinions indicate that this Court has always assumed that obscenity is not protected by the freedom of speech and press.

Brennan reviewed the history of laws curbing speech and came to the usual conclusion: The First Amendment is not absolute. The purpose of the Amendment, he said, is to protect "unfettered interchange of ideas" designed to bring about social and political change.

> All ideas having even the slightest redeeming social importance—unorthodox ideas, controversial ideas, even ideas hateful to the prevailing climate of opinion—have the full protection of the guarantees, unless excludable because they encroach upon the limited area of more important interests. But implicit in the history of the First Amendment is the rejection of obscenity as utterly without redeeming social importance. This rejection for that reason is mirrored in the universal judgment that obscenity should be restrained, reflected in the international agreement of more than 50 nations, in the obscenity laws of all of the 48 states, and in the 20 obscenity laws enacted by the Congress from 1842 to 1956. . . . We hold that obscenity is not within the area of constitutionally protected speech or press.

The Court then turned to distinguishing obscenity from the portrayal of sex:

> [S]ex and obscenity are not synonymous. Obscene material is material which deals with sex in a manner appealing to prurient interest. The portrayal of sex, e.g., in art, literature and scientific works, is not itself sufficient reason to deny material the constitutional protection of freedom of speech and press. Sex, a great and mysterious motive force in human life, has indisputably been a subject of absorbing interest to mankind through the ages; it is one of the vital problems of human interest and concern.

With that passage, Brennan made clear his belief that sex, in many of its aspects, is a matter of public concern that requires public discussion. Such discussion is within the realm of ideas protected by the First Amendment. Courts, then, must be on guard lest the prosecution of obscenity intrude into the realm of protected speech. If the material in question "does not treat sex in a manner appealing to prurient interest," it must be safeguarded. Brennan noted with concern that some American courts had adopted the *Hicklin* rule, under which a work was judged by the effect an isolated excerpt might have on particularly sensitive persons. The better rule, he wrote, would be to ask

> whether to the average person, applying contemporary community standards, the dominant theme of the material taken as a whole appeals to prurient interest.

Brennan's formulation has come to be known as the *Roth* test, and despite subsequent modifications, it remains a key to understanding what the Court means when it describes a work as obscene. In a footnote, Brennan cited previous decisions in federal and state courts as the source of the test, although he did not find the test mentioned explicitly in any of them. However, the fact that the test had not existed explicitly until Brennan wrote it in *Roth* didn't mean that a new trial was in order for Roth or for Alberts. The Court affirmed their convictions, finding that the trial judge had properly understood and applied the principles of obscenity law.

Brennan's opinion in *Roth* established an important precedent, but the concurring and dissenting opinions embodied deep differences that would divide the Court on obscenity cases for the next two decades.

Chief Justice Earl Warren sought to avoid having the Court decide whether materials were obscene. He argued that the critical test should be the suppliers' conduct. If they "were plainly engaged in the commercial exploitation of the morbid and shameful craving for materials with prurient effect," they should be charged with pandering. Justice John Marshall Harlan would have upheld Alberts's conviction under California law, but he would have reversed Roth's conviction under federal law, because he wanted to avoid adoption of a national standard for obscenity. Nor was Harlan comfortable with Brennan's willingness to let juries decide what might appeal to a prurient interest. He wrote that he could accept a jury's banning a book in one state—if it had any value, people still could buy it elsewhere—but he was not willing to run the risk of having a work like *Ulysses* or *The Decameron*[14] outlawed everywhere in the United States. Jury decisions on obscenity, he argued, should be reviewable by a judge to avoid suppression of such works.

Only Justices William O. Douglas and Hugo L. Black would have reversed both convictions. In a vehement dissent, Douglas raised questions that persist in obscenity cases to this day. He wrote:

> The tests by which these convictions were obtained require only the arousing of sexual thoughts. Yet the arousing of sexual thoughts and desires happens every day in normal life in dozens of ways. Nearly 30 years ago a questionnaire sent to college . . . women graduates asked what things were most stimulating sexually. Of 409 replies, 9 said, "music"; 18 said "pictures"; 29 said "dancing"; 40 said "drama"; 95 said "books"; and 218 said "man." Alpert, "Judicial Censorship of Obscene Literature," 52 Harv. L. Rev. 40, 73.
>
> The test of obscenity the Court endorses today gives the censor free range over a vast domain. To allow the State to step in and punish mere speech or publication that the judge or the jury thinks has an *undesirable* impact on thoughts but that is not shown to be part of unlawful action is drastically to curtail the First Amendment.

Douglas also deplored Brennan's willingness to let a jury determine a community's standards for tolerating portrayals of sexual activity. In his view, that would give jurors a free hand to "censor, suppress, and punish what they don't like."

Despite Douglas's protests, the decision in *Roth* settled one question: Materials found to be obscene do not have First Amendment protection. Because Roth and Alberts properly had been found guilty of selling such materials, they had to take their

---

14. *The Decameron* by Giovanni Boccaccio (1313–1375) is a collection of a hundred lighthearted Italian stories. The work is considered to be a masterpiece of the Italian Renaissance and was first translated into English in 1620.

punishment. The decision also established a test for obscenity: "whether to the average person (a jury), applying contemporary community standards, the dominant theme of the material taken as a whole appeals to the prurient interest." Further, the material must be, in Brennan's words, "utterly without redeeming social importance." The Court held that materials that fail the *Roth* test are outside the realm of ideas and therefore outside the realm of the First Amendment. The test does not require any proof that the materials in question harmed anyone. The effect of the materials is beside the point. If a work is obscene, that is enough. It can be condemned out of hand, and those who traffic in it can be punished.

ROTH'S LEGACY: ANYTHING GOES

Experience was to prove that the Supreme Court's decision in *Roth* raised more questions than it answered. Producers of sexually oriented materials studied the decision and found a challenge. How far could the producers go in linking portrayals of sex with ideas before crossing the line into a raw appeal to prurient interest?

They soon found they could go a long way. The decision came at a time when attitudes toward sexual activity and portrayals of sexuality were becoming more relaxed. Hugh Hefner founded *Playboy* magazine in 1953, four years before the Court decided *Roth*. *Playboy* was one of the first magazines of general circulation to feature photographs of bare-breasted young women. A nude Marilyn Monroe, photographed from the side and rear, was the subject of its first centerfold. Soon the magazine had many imitators that went far beyond it in portraying not only nudity but sexual activity. Explicit sexual movies, once seen only at clandestine all-male gatherings, began to make appearances on theater screens in the 1960s. So-called "adult" bookstores became thriving businesses. The proliferation of sexually oriented materials led to more than a dozen Supreme Court obscenity decisions in the fifteen years after *Roth*. Few of them are of more than historical interest, because only seldom could as many as five of the justices agree on any one point of law.

One case, *Memoirs v. Massachusetts*,[15] was important at the time because it greatly expanded the scope of permissible sexual portrayals. At issue was that durable classic of erotic literature, John Cleland's *Memoirs of a Woman of Pleasure,* commonly known as *Fanny Hill*. Although the book contains no vulgar, four-letter words, it abounds in descriptions of many kinds of sexual activity. In the 1820s, *Memoirs* was the subject of this nation's first reported obscenity decision,[16] and in the mid-1960s, Massachusetts courts again condemned it as obscene. The U.S. Supreme Court reversed that finding, but no more than three justices could agree on any one reason for doing so. The leading opinion, written by Brennan, tried to define the role of "redeeming social value" in the test used to measure obscenity. He said that a jury could not find a work obscene unless the prosecution proved it to be "utterly without redeeming social value." In this instance, several professors at esteemed New England

15.   383 U.S. 413, 86 S.Ct. 1975, 16 L.Ed.2d 1, 1 Med.L.Rptr. 1390 (1966).
16.   Commonwealth v. Peter Holmes, 17 Mass. 336 (Mass. 1821).

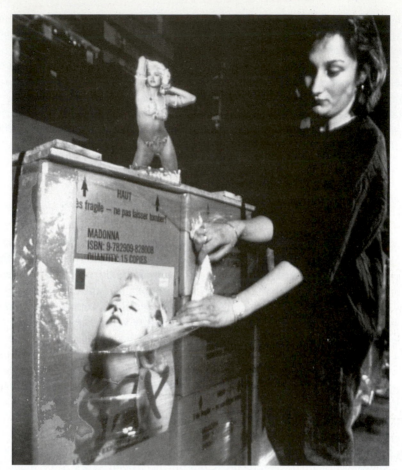

A bookstore employee unpacks a box of Madonna's book, *Sex.* The book hit the market in the early 1990s with a media splash that blatantly exploited her sexual image. It made the famous nude photos of Marilyn Monroe, which launched *Playboy* in the 1950s, seem quaint by comparison. *(Mathias Lacombe/Sygma)*

universities had testified that *Memoirs* was "a minor work of art," having "literary merit" and "historical value." One witness said that the book was redeemed by its moral, as expressed by Fanny toward the end of the book, that sex in marriage is more enjoyable than sex in a brothel.

The Court's decision seemed to signal a virtual end to successful prosecutions for obscenity, provided that care was taken in offering sexually explicit materials to the public. Within a year, that conclusion was reinforced by the *per curiam* decision in *Redrup* v. *New York,*[17] which reversed the convictions on obscenity charges of the operators of adult bookstores in several states. In reversing, the Court seemed to adopt the advice offered by Chief Justice Warren in his concurring opinion in *Roth.* The Court focused on the vendors' conduct. They had not offered their wares to minors.

---

17.   386 U.S. 767, 87 S.Ct. 1414, 18 L.Ed.2d 515 (1967).

They had not thrust sexually explicit materials on unsuspecting adults. There was no evidence of pandering. In short, they simply were catering to the tastes of adults who knew what they were after when they entered the stores.

Thereafter, courts in many jurisdictions read *Memoirs* and *Redrup* as virtually wiping obscenity laws off the books, particularly if sexually explicit materials were offered behind doors that were open to consenting adults but closed to minors. In its next major obscenity decision, the Supreme Court went a step further, holding that laws making the possession of obscene materials a crime were unconstitutional. The Court said that whatever people choose to see or read in the privacy of their homes is their own business.

The unwilling protagonist in the case was Robert E. Stanley, a suspected bookie.

Stanley v. *Georgia,* **394 U.S. 557, 89 S.Ct. 1243, 22 L.Ed.2d 542 (1969).**

Police obtained a search warrant authorizing them to enter his home to look for evidence that he was accepting bets on sporting events. The search found no such evidence, but in a desk drawer in Stanley's bedroom, an officer found three reels of eight-millimeter film. Using Stanley's projector and screen, police spent about fifty minutes looking at the film. That was enough to convince them that the film was obscene. Unable to make a gambling arrest, police arrested Stanley for possessing an obscene film, a crime under Georgia law. A county court found him guilty. The Supreme Court agreed to review the decision and reversed.

Writing for a majority of the Court, Justice Thurgood Marshall held "that the mere private possession of obscene matter cannot constitutionally be made a crime." Applying First Amendment principles to the facts of Stanley's arrest, Marshall found absolute protection for the "right to receive information and ideas." That protection is such that it forbids "state inquiry into the contents of a person's library." Marshall wrote: "If the First Amendment means anything, it means that a State has no business telling a man, sitting alone in his own house, what books he may read or what films he may watch. Our whole constitutional heritage rebels at the thought of giving government the power to control men's minds."

With cases like *Roth, Memoirs, Redrup,* and *Stanley,* it was not surprising that some authorities predicted an end to obscenity prosecutions in the United States.[18] A commission appointed by President Johnson to study the traffic in obscenity recommended in 1970 that the government give up its attempts to censor what adults might see or read. Twelve of the eighteen members said they had been unable to find any link between explicit sexual materials and sexual arousal, to say nothing of a link to anti-social behavior.

Richard Nixon, who was elected president while the commission was conducting its study, refused to accept its report. Then, in his first years in office, he appointed four conservative justices to the Supreme Court: Warren E. Burger, who replaced Earl Warren as chief justice of the United States; Harry L. Blackmun; Lewis F. Powell, Jr.; and William H. Rehnquist. Shortly after Burger's appointment, a *Wall Street Journal* reporter wrote that one of the chief justice's goals would be to use the obscenity issue

---

18.   Charles Rembar, *The End of Obscenity* (New York: Bantam Books, 1968). Rembar was counsel for G. P. Putnam's Sons in *Memoirs.*

to "reverse a major decision of the Warren Court"[19] and thus signal a more conservative approach to First Amendment law.

The prediction proved to be accurate. Three years later, Burger found an obscenity case behind which he could muster a majority of the Court. The decision, which he wrote, specifically repudiated *Memoirs* and *Redrup* and narrowed the scope of *Roth.*

MILLER'S DEFINITION OF OBSCENITY

In the late 1960s, the young manager of a restaurant in Newport Beach, California, was opening the day's mail while his mother stood near. He opened an envelope and found it stuffed with advertising brochures that were not like the usual "junk" mail. These brochures described a film, *Marital Intercourse,* and four books, *Intercourse, Man-Woman, Sex Orgies Illustrated,* and *An Illustrated History of Pornography.* The brochures were illustrated with photographs that left no doubt that the materials offered for sale portrayed sexual activity.

The manager and his mother gave the brochures to the police, who arrested Marvin Miller, the sender, on a charge of mailing unsolicited sexually explicit material, a violation of state law. A trial court found him guilty, and a state appeals court affirmed. A further appeal was taken to the U.S. Supreme Court. Chief Justice Burger had found his case. For the first time since *Roth,* sixteen years earlier, five justices would agree on a new definition of obscenity.

Like the decision in *Roth,* the new decision was to be laced with irony. The Court had upheld Roth's conviction, but its decision was to clear the way for others to do legally what Roth had been punished for doing. Now the Court would find that Miller's conviction had been improper because the California courts had used the wrong standard to determine obscenity. But in doing so, the majority would write a decision making it easier to obtain convictions in the future.

Miller v. *California,*
413 U.S. 15, 93 S.Ct. 2607,
37 L.Ed.2d 419,
1 Med.L.Rptr. 1441 (1973).

The chief justice himself wrote the decision in *Miller* v. *California.* He was joined by the three other Nixon appointees—Blackmun, Powell, and Rehnquist—and by Byron R. White, who had been appointed in 1962 by President Kennedy. The majority began by focusing on the origins of the case. "Aggressive sales action" had been used to thrust "sexually explicit materials" on an unwilling recipient. Burger wrote:

> This Court has recognized that the States have a legitimate interest in prohibiting dissemination or exhibition of obscene material when the mode of dissemination carries with it a significant danger of offending the sensibilities of unwilling recipients or of exposure to juveniles.

This statement was a reference to the Court's decision in *Redrup.* Burger turned next to a review of the decisions in *Roth* and *Memoirs,* noting that the latter had im-

---

19. Louis M. Kohlmeier, "High Court to Review Post Office's Power to Ban Obscene Materials from the Mails," *Wall Street Journal,* 3 March 1970.

posed a nearly impossible burden of proof on prosecutors in obscenity cases. Prosecutors were required to prove a negative, that is, "that the material was '*utterly* without redeeming social value.'" Burger noted that the *Memoirs* decision, like all other obscenity decisions since *Roth,* had been the product of a divided court. At no time had a majority of the Court endorsed the "utterly without redeeming social value" test. Nevertheless, the test had been used widely by lower courts, including, Burger said, the California court that had convicted Miller. Then came his clincher: "But now the *Memoirs* test has been abandoned as unworkable by its author, and no member of the Court today supports the *Memoirs* formulation."

That was the truth, but a somewhat misleading one. Brennan was the author of the plurality opinion in *Memoirs*. He had also written the *Roth* test. In *Miller,* he had written a strong dissent in which he had indeed abandoned the *Memoirs* formulation. But abandoning that test did not mean that Brennan wanted to make it easier for prosecutors to obtain obscenity convictions. On the contrary, he had moved close to the absolute position of Black and Douglas. In part, Brennan took this position out of revulsion against the Court's role as a "Supreme Board of Censors," which required it to look at sleazy books, photographs, and films to decide whether they would appeal to prurient interest. Brennan, joined by Marshall and Potter Stewart, urged the Court to adopt the decision in *Redrup* as its sole guide, thus making the test of obscenity the conduct of the vendors rather than the content of their wares.

The majority chose another course. It rejected the *Memoirs* test and then wrote its own three-point test to be applied by lower courts in future obscenity prosecutions. One of the purposes was to hand back to the states the major responsibility for controlling the traffic in pornography. States could control pornography without infringing on First Amendment freedoms, Burger wrote, if they acted under statutes specifically defining obscenity. Such statutes would have to be "carefully limited" and confined to "works which depict or describe sexual conduct." Further, a

> state offense must also be limited to works which, taken as a whole, appeal to the prurient interest in sex, which portray sexual conduct in a patently offensive way, and which, taken as a whole, do not have serious literary, artistic, political, or scientific value.

Within a paragraph, a majority of the Court had rewritten the law of obscenity. Lest that point be missed, Burger set down three guidelines for juries to apply:

> (a) whether "the average person, applying contemporary community standards," would find the work, taken as a whole, appeals to the prurient interest,
> (b) whether the work depicts or describes, in a patently offensive way, sexual conduct specifically defined by the applicable state law, and
> (c) whether the work, taken as a whole, lacks serious literary, artistic, political, or scientific value.

The newly proclaimed three-point test retained Brennan's formulation in *Roth* but rejected his plurality opinion in *Memoirs*. Henceforth, purveyors of sexually explicit materials could avoid an obscenity conviction only if they could prove that the items in question had some serious value to society.

The Burger majority offered advice to state legislatures in drafting statutes that would comply with the new test and to courts interpreting them. It listed "a few plain examples" of the kinds of works that would be obscene under "the standard announced in this opinion":

> (a) Patently offensive representations or descriptions of ultimate sexual acts, normal or perverted, actual or simulated.
>
> (b) Patently offensive representations or descriptions of masturbation, excretory functions, and lewd exhibition of the genitals.

The majority expanded on these examples:

> Sex and nudity may not be exploited without limit by films or pictures exhibited or sold in places of public accommodation any more than live sex and nudity can be exhibited or sold without limit in such public places. At a minimum, prurient, patently offensive depiction or description of sexual conduct must have serious literary, artistic, political, or scientific value to merit First Amendment protection. . . . For example, medical books for the education of physicians and related personnel necessarily use graphic illustrations and descriptions of human anatomy. In resolving the inevitably sensitive questions of fact and law, we must continue to rely on the jury system, accompanied by the safeguards that judges, rules of evidence, presumption of innocence, and other protective features provide, as we do with rape, murder, and a host of other offenses against society and its individual members.

The majority gave the jury a central role in obscenity cases. Jurors were to determine the standard of decency prevailing in their communities and decide what kinds of materials violated it. At the same time, the Court adopted the position that Harlan had taken in *Memoirs,* rejecting the idea that there can be a national standard for measuring obscenity. The standard would vary from community to community. Burger wrote:

> Under a National Constitution, fundamental First Amendment limitations on the power of the States do not vary from community to community, but this does not mean that there are, or should or can be, fixed, uniform national standards of precisely what appeals to the "prurient interest" or is "patently offensive." These are essentially questions of fact, and our Nation is simply too big and too diverse for this Court to reasonably expect such standards could be articulated for all 50 States in a single formulation, even assuming the prerequisite consensus exists. When triers of fact [a jury] are asked to decide whether "the average person, applying contemporary community standards" would consider certain materials "prurient," it would be unrealistic to require that the answer be based on some abstract formulation. The adversary system, with lay jurors as the usual ultimate fact-finders in critical prosecutions, has historically permitted triers of fact to draw on the standards of their community, guided always by limiting instructions on the law. To require a State to structure obscenity proceedings around evidence of a *national* "community standard" would be an exercise in futility. . . .
>
> It is neither realistic nor constitutionally sound to read the First Amendment as requiring that the people of Maine or Mississippi accept public depiction of conduct found tolerable in Las Vegas, or New York City. . . . People in different States vary in their tastes and attitudes, and this diversity is not to be strangled by the absolutism of imposed uniformity.

Thus, the Court sought to define "community" as the place from which a jury is drawn to hear an obscenity case. It also sought to define the "community standard" as the jurors' collective estimate of the level of sexual candor tolerated by them, their friends, and their neighbors.

Justice Douglas, writing in dissent, protested that the majority was giving juries of lay citizens a task for which even Supreme Court justices had shown remarkably little talent—that is, determining what is obscene. In his view, the new test "would make it possible to ban any paper or any journal or magazine in some benighted place." Douglas's protest had no effect. The Court returned the case against Miller to the California courts for retrial under the new standard.

On the same day, the Court decided *Paris Adult Theatre I* v. *Slaton,* an obscenity case aimed at an adult theater operator in Georgia. Again Chief Justice Burger was able to muster a majority, this time to repudiate the Court's *per curiam* decision in *Redrup.*

Paris Adult Theatre I v. Slaton, 413 U.S. 49, 93 S.Ct. 2626, 37 L.Ed.2d 446, 1 Med.L.Rptr. 1454 (1973).

Lewis R. Slaton, district attorney of Fulton County, Georgia, had brought a civil action to prevent the showing in an adult theater of two films, *Magic Mirror* and *It All Comes Out in the End,* which a judge had declared obscene. However, the judge had held that he could not prevent the theater from showing the films, because the theater operated within *Redrup* guidelines emphasizing conduct rather than content. The theater excluded minors and unsuspecting adults, and it did not pander. The Georgia Supreme Court overruled the judge, and the U.S. Supreme Court affirmed that decision.

The chief justice moved directly to the attack on *Redrup:*

> We categorically disapprove the theory, apparently adopted by the trial judge, that obscene, pornographic films acquire constitutional immunity from state regulation simply because they are exhibited for consenting adults only. . . . Although we have often pointedly recognized the high importance of the state interest in regulating the exposure of obscene materials to juveniles and unconsenting adults, . . . this Court has never declared these to be the only legitimate state interests permitting regulation of obscene material. The States have a long recognized legitimate interest in regulating the use of obscene material in local commerce and in all places of public accommodation, as long as these regulations do not run afoul of specific constitutional prohibitions. . . .
>
> In particular, we hold that there are legitimate state interests at stake in stemming the tide of commercialized obscenity. . . . These include the interest of the public in the quality of life and the total community environment, the tone of commerce in the great city centers, and possibly, the public safety itself. . . .
>
> If we accept . . . . the well nigh universal belief that good books, plays, and art lift the spirit, improve the mind, enrich the human personality, and develop character, can we then say that a state legislature may not act on the corollary assumption that commerce in obscene books, or public exhibitions focused on obscene conduct, have a tendency to exert a corrupting and debasing impact leading to antisocial behavior?

Lawyers for the theater had pointed to the Court's decision in *Stanley,* arguing that it established a right of privacy protecting the viewing of obscene materials. Burger replied that the decision in *Stanley* clearly confines that right to the home:

> The idea of a "privacy" right and a place of public accommodation are, in this context, mutually exclusive. Conduct or depictions of conduct that the state police power can prohibit on a public street do not become automatically protected by the Constitution merely because the conduct is moved to a bar or a "live" theatre stage, any more than a "live" performance of a man and woman locked in sexual embrace at high noon in Times Square is protected by the Constitution because they simultaneously engage in a valid political dialogue.

During the 1970s, *Deep Throat* became one of the classic porn movies enjoying considerable protection under Supreme Court decisions dating to the late 1950s. However, *Miller* v. *California* in 1973 gave local communities greater leeway to prosecute obscenity based on local community standards, and a federal jury in Memphis, Tennessee, found Harry Reems, one of the stars of *Deep Throat,* guilty of obscenity. *(Michael Weisbrot and Family/Stock, Boston)*

Redrup and the broader implications some had seen in *Stanley* had been torn to ribbons. States and localities might decide to tolerate adult bookstores and theaters if they wanted to, but if they chose to ban obscenity, the makers, sellers, and purveyors of such material could not look to the United States Supreme Court for help. All that was required to make obscenity a crime was for a state to statutorily define the crime in terms of the specific sexual or excretory conduct that could not be lawfully depicted. If the materials, taken as a whole, portrayed that activity in a manner that a jury found prurient and patently offensive, they could be condemned as obscene and the purveyors imprisoned. Not even a sign on a theater door marked "consenting adults only" could provide sanctuary. The only thing that could save the materials would be a finding that they had *serious* literary, artistic, political, or scientific value.

OBSCENITY LAW SINCE MILLER AND PARIS

In the immediate aftermath of the *Miller* and *Paris* decisions, two currents worked at cross purposes. Police and prosecutors moved against obscenity with renewed vigor. But some judges were still finding state statutes unconstitutional because the statutes did not define obscenity in terms of sexual conduct that were sufficiently explicit. A federal district court in Alabama ruled that the state's obscenity law was unconstitutional in a case involving *Last Tango in Paris,* a movie starring Marlon Brando.[20] In another case, the Minnesota Supreme Court struck down that state's statute, which included, word for word, the formulation in *Roth.*[21] Pointing to *Miller,* the court said that the law was flawed because it did not describe sexual conduct in specific enough terms.

It quickly became apparent that, even with its decisions in *Miller* and *Paris,* the U.S. Supreme Court had not succeeded in ridding itself of obscenity cases. The Court continued to do a steady business in appeals and in the years since has sometimes handed down as many as four obscenity opinions in a single term.

Refining the Definition of Obscenity

Justice William J. Brennan predicted that local juries would condemn as obscene some works that were recognized by juries in other places as being art. Even as he was writing that opinion in *Miller,* the case to prove him right began moving its way up to the Supreme Court from Georgia. A jury in Albany had found the movie *Carnal Knowledge* obscene. The exhibitor was fined $750 and placed on probation for a year. The film, starring Jack Nicholson, was a story about the sexual fantasies and subsequent problems of college friends who go their separate ways into early middle age. Most reviewers found the movie an honest look at the process and problems of maturing. Some thought well enough of it to place it on their list of the ten best films of the year. Nevertheless, the Georgia Supreme Court upheld the Albany conviction and its finding that the film was obscene. In light of its opinion in *Miller,* the Supreme Court of the United States agreed to review.

Jenkins v. Georgia, 418
U.S. 153, 94 S.Ct. 2750,
41 L.Ed.2d 642,
1 Med.L.Rptr. 1504 (1974).

In its decision in *Jenkins* v. *Georgia,* the Court reiterated two points it had made in *Miller:*

1. The Georgia Supreme Court was correct in holding that a jury need not be told to apply a statewide standard. Local standards of sexual candor are to be used in determining whether a film is obscene.

2. However, local juries do not have "unbridled discretion" in deciding what is obscene. Material can be obscene only if it depicts or portrays "patently offensive 'hard core' sexual conduct."

The jury was wrong about *Carnal Knowledge.* The movie was not obscene, because it was not patently offensive. Justice Rehnquist explained why:

---

20. United Artists Corp. v. Wright, 368 F.Supp. 1034 (M.D.Ala. 1974).
21. State v. Welke, 216 N.W.2d 641 (Minn. 1974).

While the subject matter of the picture is, in a broader sense, sex, and there are scenes in which sexual conduct including "ultimate sexual acts" is to be understood to be taking place, the camera does not focus on the bodies of the actors at such times. There is no exhibition whatsoever of the actors' genitals, lewd or otherwise, during these scenes. There are occasional scenes of nudity, but nudity alone is not enough to make material legally obscene under the *Miller* standards.

On the same day, in *Hamling* v. *United States,* the Court upheld prison terms imposed on two men who had mailed fifty-five thousand brochures advertising *The Illustrated Presidential Report of the Commission on Obscenity and Pornography.* The sample illustrations used in the brochure showed a wide variety of heterosexual and homosexual activity and of humans engaged in sexual activity with animals. The convictions had taken place in a federal district court and had been upheld by the court of appeals before *Miller* was decided. The Court held that in such instances convicted defendants are entitled to any help *Miller* might give them, but concluded that in this instance it gave them none.

**Hamling v. United States,
418 U.S. 87, 94 S.Ct. 2887,
41 L.Ed.2d 590,
1 Med.L.Rptr. 1479 (1974).**

Three points emerged from the decision:

1. Although federal laws define obscenity in general terms, they are made specific by the Supreme Court's decision in *Miller.* Under well-established principles of constitutional law, statutes mean what the courts say they mean. Thus, the federal law must be interpreted and applied in the light of the "few plain examples" provided by Chief Justice Burger in *Miller.*

2. Juries deciding obscenity cases brought under federal law are not required to apply a national standard. They are to draw on their knowledge of the standard of sexual candor prevailing in the communities from which they were selected.

3. Jurors are not required to pay attention to expert witnesses who testify as to what they believe the community standard is. The jurors are considered the experts on questions of community standards.[22]

The effect of *Hamling* was to strengthen the role of the locally drawn jury in determining standards. The jury's discretion in deciding what is obscene was limited only by the proviso, reinforced by *Jenkins* v. *Georgia,* that the material at issue must portray specific sexual activity in a patently offensive way that lacks "serious literary, artistic, political or scientific value."

Jurors are experts on community moral standards because they have firsthand knowledge of what their communities tolerate. However, the Supreme Court has held

---

22. It is possible in most courts to introduce public opinion surveys as evidence about local standards. Insofar as the surveys are helpful to the jurors in informing their knowledge of community standards, they are generally admissible, but jurors are also free to disregard the surveys or disagree with them.

that they are not experts in measuring a work's value to society. Rather, there is an objective standard that reasonable persons should apply to determine whether material has "serious value."

The case in question, *Pope* v. *Illinois,* came to the Court from Rockford, Illinois, where judges in two separate obscenity trials had instructed juries that they could find materials obscene if the average person in the community would believe them lacking in serious literary, artistic, political, or scientific value. Defendants in both trials were found guilty and the convictions were upheld by the Illinois Court of Appeals. The Illinois Supreme Court denied review. The U.S. Supreme Court took the case and reversed, five to four.

Justice White, writing for the majority, said that there was "no suggestion in our cases that the question of the value of an allegedly

Pope **v.** *Illinois,* **481 U.S. 497, 107 S.Ct. 1918, 95 L.Ed.2d 439, 14 Med.L.Rptr. 1001 (1987).**

obscene work is to be determined by reference to community standards." In *Miller,* White continued, the discussion of contemporary community standards had been linked to prurient interest and patent offensiveness, but not to the value of the material. In that decision, the Court had said that the First Amendment protects any allegedly obscene works "which, taken as a whole, have serious literary, artistic, political, or scientific value, regardless of whether the government or a majority of the people approve of the ideas these works represent." Such value does not vary from community to community and is not "based on the degree of local acceptance it has won. The proper inquiry is not whether an ordinary member of any given community would find serious literary, artistic, political, or scientific value in allegedly obscene material, but whether a reasonable person would find such value in the material."

The effect of the decision was to invite expert testimony as to a work's value and to place the ultimate decision about value in the hands of judges rather than juries. Presumably, judges are in a better position than jurors to discern the objective standard that reasonable people might use to measure the "serious literary, artistic, political, or scientific value" of a book, magazine, or film.

On another matter, Chief Justice Warren had urged as early as the *Roth* opinion that the Court consider the conduct of the defendant in determining whether a crime had been committed. Nine years later, in *Ginzburg* v. *United States,*[23] the Court, with Justice Brennan writing for the majority, affirmed that the manner in which materials were sold was relevant to deciding whether they were obscene. The same material that might not be obscene in one context could be obscene in another. The idea was that a defendant who pandered material as obscene provided powerful evidence against his own case. That idea has survived *Miller.* In *Splawn* v. *California,*[24] four years after *Miller,* the Court upheld a California judge who had told a jury that it could consider the seller's methods in coming to the conclusion that two reels of film were obscene. The decision meant that a seller who told customers his material would arouse their prurient interest was likely to be taken at his word if an obscenity prosecution resulted.

---

23.   383 U.S. 463, 86 S.Ct. 942, 16 L.Ed.2d 31, 1 Med.L.Rptr. 1409 (1966).
24.   431 U.S. 595, 97 S.Ct. 1987, 52 L.Ed.2d 606, 2 Med.L.Rptr. 1881 (1977).

Outlawing Child Pornography

Some adults see children as exciting sexual objects who can be exploited because of their immaturity and are willing to pay well for photographs of children engaged in sexual action. The traffic in such materials has led to passage by Congress of a statute providing for criminal prosecution of persons who knowingly distribute, receive, or reproduce such photographs "by any means including . . . computer."[25] Under the terms of this statute, violators can be sentenced to as long as ten years in prison for a first offense and property related to the crime can be confiscated. All fifty states have similar laws. Most such laws describe the crime of child pornography in terms of specific sexual acts. Even an isolated portrayal of a proscribed act is subject to prosecution if it involves a minor. For that reason, the laws do not precisely fit the *Roth-Miller* mold, which requires that a work charged with being obscene must be looked at as a whole.

In *New York* v. *Ferber,* the Supreme Court upheld that state's child pornography law and said that in protecting children from sex exploitation, states can go beyond the limits imposed by *Miller.* The Court held flatly that there is no First Amendment protection for portrayals of specifically described sex acts performed by boys or girls under sixteen years old. Justice White said that the Court could find no value in encouraging children to engage in sex. On the contrary, the Court would uphold the legislature in its conclusion that "the use of children as subjects of pornographic materials is harmful to the physiological, emotional, and mental health of the child. That judgment, we think, easily passes muster under the First Amendment."

New York v. Ferber, 458 U.S. 747, 102 S.Ct. 3348, 73 L.Ed.2d 1113, 8 Med.L.Rptr. 1809 (1982).

The decision is of further interest in that all nine justices agreed that *Ferber* should be punished. However, four of them wrote opinions in which they differed with White on some elements of his reasoning. Justices John Paul Stevens and William Brennan, for instance, did not join the part of the decision that held that all depictions of minors engaged in sexual activity are without First Amendment protection. These two justices would have held open the possibility that sometime, somehow, a work portraying sexual activity by teenagers might be a work of art.

Since *Ferber,* the Supreme Court has held that police can successfully prosecute a suspect merely for possessing child pornography, but that they cannot trap a suspect by excessively encouraging him to buy pornographic material.

The Court upheld an Ohio statute that made possession of child pornography, even in the privacy of one's home, a crime.[26] In doing so, the Court said that it was not repudiating the rationale it had used in *Stanley* v. *Georgia.* In that case, the Court had said that the First Amendment protects the right of individuals to read or view pornography, even that which might be legally obscene, in the privacy of their homes. However, the Court said, there was no First Amendment interest in protecting child pornography, even if it was not obscene by *Miller* standards. Referring to *Ferber,* the Court

---

25.   18 U.S.C. §§ 2251–2257 (1991).
26.   Osborne v. Ohio, 495 U.S. 103, 110 S.Ct. 1691, 109 L.Ed.2d 98 (1990).

said that the suppression of child pornography is justified by the state's interest in protecting minors from exploitation. Thus, the purpose of laws criminalizing traffic in child pornography is to cut off such materials at their source.

On the other hand, the Court threw out a child pornography conviction when it found that the defendant, fifty-six-year-old Keith Jacobson, had been entrapped by federal investigators.[27] The Court said that the government had overstepped the line between setting a trap for the "unwary innocent" and the "wary criminal" and had failed to show that Jacobson was independently predisposed to violate the Child Protection Act. Postal inspectors found Jacobson's name on a mailing list of a California bookstore that had mailed him two magazines containing photographs of nude preteen and teenage boys. The mailing occurred before the act took effect. However, investigators made Jacobson the target of a sting operation and began to send him mail from five fictitious organizations and a bogus pen pal to explore his willingness to break the law. After two and a half years of government mailings that included appeals to Jacobson's interest in civil liberties and inquired about his sexual interests, Jacobson was sent a catalogue listing pornographic materials that he could order. He responded by sending for a magazine depicting young boys engaged in sexual activities. He was then arrested and his home searched. The only pornographic materials uncovered in the search were those that had been sent by the government and the two magazines he had bought before the act became effective.

A majority of the Court said that although there is no dispute about the evils of child pornography or the difficulty of enforcing laws against it, the federal agents in this case went beyond simply providing the opportunity for Jacobson to break the law. The agents pursued him with twenty-six months of repeated mailings in a way that enticed him to break the law. That was entrapment, said the Court.

Of related concern to those who may inadvertently obtain sexually oriented photographs is that the Protection of Children against Sexual Exploitation Act makes a person responsible only if he or she knows that the persons portrayed are minors. Although the language of the statute appears to apply to anyone who "knowingly transports or ships" or "knowingly receives or distributes"[28] child pornography, the Court has interpreted that wording to mean that the prosecution must be able to prove that a defendant knew not only that the material was transported, shipped, received, or distributed but also that the defendant knew that the people depicted were under eighteen years old. Chief Justice William Rehnquist said in *U.S.* v. *X-Citement Video*[29] that when Congress wrote the law in 1977 and amended it in 1984, it had to be aware of Supreme Court precedent holding that obscenity laws are unconstitutional if they do not require the prosecution to prove that the defendant knew the nature of the material.

The *X-Citement* case involved a bookstore owner who sold forty-nine videos that actress Traci Lords had made before she was eighteen years old. The store owner, Rubin Gottesman, argued that because the teenage actress looked older than she was,

27. Jacobson v. United States, 503 U.S. 540, 112 S.Ct. 1535, 118 L.Ed.2d 174 (1992).
28. 18 U.S.C. § 2252(a)(1) and (2).
29. 115 S.Ct.464, L.Ed.2d 372 (1994). Linda Greenhouse, "Supreme Court Upholds Law on Child Smut," *New York Times,* 30 November 1994, p. A1.

he did not know she was a minor. The *X-Citement* holding was good news for librarians and store owners who might be reluctant to circulate works on sexuality. As for producers, Congress amended the act in 1990 to require those who produce a book, magazine, periodical, film, videotape, or other matter (such as a computer program) depicting "actual sexually explicit conduct" to find out, record, and make available the names and ages of performers.[30]

Legal Alternatives to Criminal Obscenity Statutes

Zoning

Zoning laws can be used to confine adult theaters and bookstores to specified parts of a city, but they cannot be used as a subterfuge to ban all such establishments. The Supreme Court's decisions in this area point up the variety of approaches to obscenity law made possible by *Miller* v. *California.* In some states, or even in parts of states, anything goes. Either there is no law that makes obscenity a crime, or if there is a law, local prosecutors do not bother to enforce it.[31] In other states and localities, obscenity laws are enforced strictly and juries return convictions regularly. Finally, some local authorities, more concerned about pandering and the quality of city life than about sexual explicitness, have turned to zoning laws to control the location of adult establishments.

In *Young* v. *American Mini Theatres,*[32] the Supreme Court upheld a Detroit ordinance that confined adult bookstores and theaters to commercial areas of the city. Its terms were held to be a reasonable restriction of time, place, and manner on First Amendment activities.

The Court also upheld a zoning ordinance in *City of Renton* v. *Playtime Theatres, Inc.,*[33] that prohibited adult theaters from locating within a thousand feet of any dwelling, church, park, or school. Thus, zoning laws may be used to concentrate sexually oriented businesses in a particular part of a city and to prevent them from expanding into designated neighborhoods.

However, the U.S. Court of Appeals for the Sixth Circuit found an unreasonable zoning restriction in Ann Arbor, Michigan, when that city adopted an ordinance that would have confined all sellers of sexually explicit materials to about one city block.[34] The court said that the city had acted unreasonably in confining adult establishments to such a small part of the city, especially when it had offered no valid reasons, such as preventing urban blight, for doing so.

And in *Schad* v. *Borough of Mount Ephraim,*[35] the Court said that a New Jersey community had gone too far when its zoning law forbade live entertainment. The

30.   18 U.S.C. § 2257.
31.   David Pritchard, Jon Paul Dilts, and Dan Berkowitz, "Prosecutor's Use of External Agendas in Prosecuting Pornography Cases," *Journalism Quarterly,* Summer–Autumn 1987, p. 392.
32.   427 U.S. 50, 96 S.Ct. 2440, 49 L.Ed.2d 310, 1 Med.L.Rptr. 1151 (1967).
33.   475 U.S. 41, 106 S.Ct. 925, 89 L.Ed.2d 29, 12 Med.L.Rptr. 1721 (1986).
34.   Christy v. City of Ann Arbor, 824 F.2d 489, 14 Med.L.Rptr. 1483 (6th Cir. 1987).
35.   452 U.S. 61, 101 S.Ct. 2176, 68 L.Ed.2d 671, 7 Med.L.Rptr. 1426 (1981).

law's target was an adult bookstore in which a woman danced in the nude behind a glass window. The Court said that the law was so broad that it could be used unconstitutionally to restrict other forms of expression.

Nuisance

Nuisance laws have been used successfully and unsuccessfully by local governments to control obscenity. The Texas legislature, for example, sought to combat obscenity by enacting a public nuisance law that permitted authorities to close theaters in which allegedly obscene films had been shown. The U.S. Supreme Court said the fact that theaters had shown movies found to be obscene in the past didn't mean that they would show obscene movies in the future.[36] In another decision, however, the Court upheld a California court's order closing an adult theater for one year on the grounds that it had become a public nuisance.[37] The California closure, unlike the one in Texas, was based on a judgment not about the content of films the theater offered, but about the type of patrons attending and their effect on the neighborhood.

In another case, the Court struck down an ordinance of the city of Jacksonville, Florida, forbidding outdoor theaters to show movies containing nudity.[38] The city argued that nudity on a screen that might be seen from a public place could be suppressed as a nuisance. However, the Court said that nudity in itself was not obscene and concluded that the city's content-based ordinance was overly broad. The ordinance condemned all nudity, however innocent, educational, or expressive.

Indecent Conduct

The Supreme Court noted, albeit in passing, that nudity in films such as those in the Jacksonville case could easily be distinguished from the type of nudity traditionally subject to indecent-exposure laws. In commenting on the distinction, the Court noted Justice William O. Douglas's dissent in the 1957 *Roth* case. Douglas had tried unsuccessfully in *Roth* to argue that erotic expression should be suppressed only to the extent that it is inseparable from illegal action. As an example of illegal action not protected by the First Amendment, he had cited "nudity in public places."

Douglas may have meant simply that he believed that expressive conduct should be protected and that nonexpressive conduct should not be protected. But most justices have been unwilling to live with any requirement that protects conduct just because it happens to be expressive. Consequently, during the late 1960s the Court developed a very different approach. In *United States* v. *O'Brien,* the Court said that if the

---

36. Vance v. Universal Amusement Co., 445 U.S. 308, 100 S.Ct. 1156, 63 L.Ed.2d 413, 5 Med.L.Rptr. 2553 (1980). See also Near v. Minnesota, 283 U.S. 697, 51 S.Ct. 625, 75 L.Ed.2d 1357, 1 Med.L.Rptr. 1001 (1931).
37. Cooper v. Mitchell Brothers' Santa Ana Theater, 454 U.S. 90, 102 S.Ct. 172, 70 L.Ed.2d 262, 7 Med.L.Rptr. 2273 (1981).
38. Erznoznik v. City of Jacksonville, 422 U.S. 205, 95 S.Ct. 2268, 45 L.Ed.2d 125, 1 Med.L.Rptr. 1508 (1975).

government regulation of expressive conduct furthered an important or substantial governmental interest, if the governmental interest was unrelated to the suppression of free expression, and if the incidental restriction on First Amendment freedoms was no greater than is essential to the furtherance of that interest, then the expressive conduct could be regulated.[39]

That ruling gave continued life to indecent-exposure laws, even if there were elements of protected expression involved in the indecency. Indiana, for example, successfully used its public indecency statute to stop women from dancing nude at an adult bookstore and at a bar. The state's prosecutors were careful to distinguish between the conduct of public nudity and the free expression of the dancers. The target of the statute was nudity, not obscenity and not expression. Indiana's interest in requiring people to wear clothes reflected only the moral disapproval directed at people appearing in the nude among strangers in public places. That interest, the Court said, was not related to the suppression of free expression. The erotic dancers were free to express themselves as erotically as they liked, short of being obscene or becoming completely nude. The only burden on their expressive conduct was to wear clothing, and by clothing Indiana meant only pasties and a G-string. The Court thought that such a restriction was a modest burden on erotic expression.[40]

Racketeering

In addition to using zoning, nuisance, and public indecency laws, authorities use racketeering laws, enacted originally to combat organized crime and drug dealing, to justify closing businesses that sell sexually oriented wares. Under these laws, officials can impose heavy penalties on individuals involved in a "pattern of conduct" pointing to repeated illegal activity. More important, the laws permit officials to seize at the time of arrest any assets earned by or associated with that activity. Typically, a "pattern of conduct" can be established by as few as two prosecutions for specified criminal offenses. In federal statutes and in at least fifteen states,[41] violations of obscenity laws are included among the predicate offenses. The criminal version of such laws is known as the Racketeer Influenced and Corrupt Organizations Act, or RICO. Some states provide also for civil actions to forfeit property under laws known as Civil Remedies for Racketeering Activity Acts.

---

39. United States v. O'Brien, 391 U.S. 367, 88 S.Ct. 1673, 20 L.Ed.2d 672 (1968).
40. Barnes v. Glen Theatre, 501 U.S. 560, 111 S.Ct. 2456, 115 L.Ed.2d 504 (1991).
41. 18 U.S.C. § 1961(1) (1982 ed., Supp. IV); Ariz.Rev.Stat.Ann. § 13-2301(D)(4)(u) (Supp. 1988–1989); Colo.Rev.Stat. § 18-17-103(5)(b)(VI) (1986); Del.Code Ann., tit. 11, §§ 1502(9)(a), (9)(b)(7) (1987); Fla.Stat. § 895.02(1)(a)(27) (1987); Ga.Code Ann. § 16-14-3(3)(A)(xii) (1988); Idaho Code § 18-7803(8) (Supp. 1988); Ind.Code § 35-45-6-1 (Supp. 1987); N.J.Stat.Ann. § 2C:41-1(e) (West Supp. 1988–1989); N.C.Gen.Stat. § 75D-3(c)(2) (1987); N.D.Cent.Code § 12.1-06.1-01(2)(d)(17) (Supp. 1987); Ohio Rev.Code Ann. §§ 2923.31(I)(1), (I)(2) (1987); Okla.Stat., tit. 22 § 1402(10)(v) (Supp. 1988); Ore.Rev.Stat. §§ 166.715(6)(a)(T), (6)(b) (1987); Utah Code Ann. § 76-10-1602(4)(fff)–(iii), (zzz) (Supp. 1988); Wash.Rev.Code § 9A.82.010(14)(s) (Supp. 1988).

In the first RICO obscenity case to reach the Supreme Court, *Fort Wayne Books, Inc.* v. *Indiana,* the Court found no problem with the enhanced penalty provisions of the law. Nor did it find anything wrong with defining the traffic in obscene materials as racketeering. But the Court said that RICO laws cannot be used to justify wholesale seizure of an adult bookstore's inventory at the time of the arrest, even if the requisite "pattern of conduct" has been established. Justice White, writing for a unanimous Court, noted that "this Court has repeatedly held that rigorous safeguards must be employed before expressive materials can be seized as 'obscene.'" At a minimum, there must be a jury trial, applying the *Miller* standards. The materials cannot be taken out of circulation unless, and until, that proceeding results in a finding that they are obscene. "It is 'the risk of prior restraint' that motivates this rule," White wrote.

Fort Wayne Books, Inc. v. *Indiana,* **489 U.S. 46, 109 S.Ct. 916, 103 L.Ed.2d 34, 16 Med.L.Rptr. 1337 (1989).**

The Court did not say that RICO's seizure provisions could never be used in obscenity cases. It assumed, without deciding, that bookstores and their contents could be forfeited like yachts and bank accounts where proper proof of their link to law violation was established. In this instance, however, the Court was not convinced that such a link had been established. Authorities had cleaned out the contents of the offending bookstore and had padlocked the building. It was likely, White wrote, that some of the contents were protected by the First Amendment. Books cannot be taken out of circulation simply because police have probable cause to believe that a crime has been committed. White concluded with the warning that "the State cannot escape the constitutional safeguards of our prior cases by merely recategorizing obscenity violations as 'racketeering.'"

Despite that aspect of the decision, the ruling was generally viewed as a victory for prosecutors who had been using RICO laws to combat obscenity.[42] A majority of the Court held that obscenity convictions could be considered racketeering. The majority also found nothing offensive to the Constitution in the fact that penalties for racketeering might involve longer prison terms and steeper fines than those for dealing in obscenity. And it did not close the door on using the law to seize the entire assets of dealers in obscenity. The Court said only that if those assets included materials arguably protected by the First Amendment, they could not be seized until a jury found them obscene.

After the *Fort Wayne* decision, some major bookstore owners said they were afraid that convictions in one of their stores for selling sexually explicit magazines in a conservative area could result in the forfeiture of their entire chain.[43] That fear was not an idle one. In Minneapolis the following year, a jury found the owner of a chain of bookstores, theaters, and video stores guilty of violating the RICO-obscenity law by selling four obscene magazines and three obscene videotapes. The owner, Ferris Alexander, was sentenced to six years in prison and fined $100,000 plus costs. In addition, under

---

42.   Stephen Wermiel, "Tactic to Fight Pornography Is Upheld," *Wall Street Journal,* 22 February 1989.

43.   Arthur S. Hayes and Bob Hagerty, "Obscenity Case May Affect Media Firms," *Wall Street Journal,* 8 July 1992.

the RICO statute, Alexander forfeited his $25-million business, and police confiscated the entire inventory of books and videotapes from his thirteen stores. On appeal, Alexander argued that seizing books and videotapes that had not been found to be obscene was a prior restraint in violation of the First Amendment and, moreover, that his punishment was disproportionate to his offense, a violation of the Eighth Amendment. The Eighth Circuit Court of Appeals affirmed the sentence and forfeiture order.[44]

On appeal, the U.S. Supreme Court, with Chief Justice Rehnquist writing for a five-to-four majority, held that the RICO forfeiture was not a prior restraint. "[T]he order in this case does not *forbid* petitioner from engaging in any expressive activities in the future, nor does it require him to obtain prior approval for any expressive activities. It only deprives him of specific assets that were found to be related to his previous racketeering violations."[45] The Court contrasted Alexander's situation with *Fort Wayne Books, Inc.* v. *Indiana.* In *Fort Wayne,* the seizure was premature because it was based only on a belief by the police and prosecutor that a RICO violation had occurred. In *Alexander,* however, the seizure followed a full criminal trial on the obscenity and RICO charges. Alexander had been convicted, and the forfeiture was part of his punishment for the crime.

Whether the punishment was too severe for the crime was another issue.[46] That question turned on how extensive Alexander's criminal activities were. The Court decided to send that question back to the Eighth Circuit Court of Appeals for reconsideration. However, Rehnquist wrote that he thought it misleading to characterize "the racketeering crimes for which [Alexander] was convicted as involving just a few materials ultimately found to be obscene." He noted that in the trial transcript the judge had described Alexander's business as "an enormous racketeering enterprise," a description that contrasted sharply with Alexander's portrayal of himself as a storekeeper who had been caught selling a few dirty books and tapes.

Licensing

As the preceding cases suggest, the Supreme Court has said, starting with *Near* v. *Minnesota,* that materials found to be obscene are not protected by the First Amendment and may be seized by police and destroyed. But the Court also has said that obscenity is not to be defined arbitrarily. Thus, the Supreme Court has established not only criteria for determining what is obscene and what is not, but also procedures to prevent arbitrary seizure and destruction of materials believed, but not proven, to be obscene. In doing so, the Court has on several occasions found itself at odds with police, prosecutors, and others who would prefer to apply their own standards individually or through boards empowered to preview and license sexually explicit material.

The landmark case is *Freedman* v. *State of Maryland.*[47] At issue was that state's film censorship law. The Court didn't say that the state could never set up a censorship

---

44. Alexander v. Thornburgh, 943 F.2d 825 (8th Cir. 1991); vacated and remanded, 113 S.Ct. 2766, 125 L.Ed.2d 441, 21 Med.L.Rptr. 1609 (1993).
45. Alexander v. United States, 21 Med.L.Rptr. 1609, 1612 (1993).
46. See Austin v. United States, 113 S.Ct. 2801, 125 L.Ed.2d 488 (1993); Bennis v. Michigan, 447 Mich. 719, 527 N.W.2d 483 (1994); cert. granted, 115 S.Ct. 2275, 132 L.Ed.2d 279 (1995).
47. 380 U.S. 51, 85 S.Ct. 734, 13 L.Ed.2d 649, 1 Med.L.Rptr. 1126 (1965).

board but held that if it did, decisions must be made promptly and be subject to "expeditious judicial review." In the event of a decision to deny a license to show a film, the state must first go to court to prove that the film was obscene beyond a reasonable doubt. The Court frequently has used the *Freedman* decision to remind overly zealous police and prosecutors that they cannot confiscate sexually explicit materials without first going to court and proving them obscene.

When officials in Dallas, Texas, adopted an ordinance providing for strict licensing and inspection of "sexually oriented businesses," the Court referred to *Freedman* in finding parts of the ordinance unconstitutional. The ordinance was aimed at a variety of businesses whose principal purpose was to offer the public entertainment or materials featuring "specified sexual activities."

FW/PBS, Inc. v. *City of Dallas*, 493 U.S. 215, 110 S.Ct. 596, 107 L.Ed.2d 603 (1990).

The ordinance defined the latter in terms drawn from *Miller.* Its target included adult book and video stores, adult theaters, cabarets, escort agencies, nude model studios, "sexual encounter centers," and motels renting rooms for less than ten hours. Justice Antonin Scalia saw the law as "one of an increasing number of attempts throughout the country . . . to prevent the erosion of public morality."

However, when a variety of challenges to the ordinance reached the Supreme Court, it held that the licensing provision violated the *Freedman* guidelines, although a majority could not agree on the extent to which it did so. Under the ordinance, police were supposed to reach a decision on whether to grant or refuse a license within thirty days. But they could not issue one until the premises had been approved by the fire and health departments and had been found by a building official to be in compliance "with applicable laws and ordinances." Because no time limit was fixed for completion of these approvals, the Court said that the ordinance imposed an unconstitutional restraint on businesses offering printed matter and films subject to First Amendment protection.

Justice Sandra Day O'Connor, writing for herself and two others, noted that simply by delaying any one of the required inspections, the city could deny a license indefinitely. Therefore, the ordinance violated the part of the *Freedman* guidelines that required a prompt decision on the licensing of First Amendment activities. However, she said that because the license applied to the right to do business rather than to "the content of any protected speech," the city would not have to go to court to justify the denial of a license.

Justice Brennan, writing for himself and two others, disagreed. In his view, denial of a license would serve as a prior restraint on arguably protected speech. Therefore, the city should be required to prove to a court's satisfaction that a denial was justified. Three justices found no First Amendment problems with the licensing scheme and, therefore, no need to refer to *Freedman.* Scalia took the most extreme position. In his view, the businesses covered by the ordinance were engaged in pandering to a prurient interest in sex and therefore could simply have been outlawed.

Despite these differences of opinion, the effect of the decision was to declare the licensing provision unconstitutional so far as it applied to businesses selling or displaying books, magazines, videotapes, movies, and other materials protected by the First Amendment.

In other cases, the courts have repeatedly held that performances cannot be forbidden merely because some municipal authority *thinks* they might be obscene. One case involved a ruling by Chattanooga, Tennessee, city officials preventing a performance of the rock musical *Hair* in a municipal auditorium.[48] Although the musical contained nudity and simulated acts of sexual intercourse and masturbation, it had not been held obscene by any court anywhere. Nor has it been since. Consequently, city officials could not interfere on the basis that the play was obscene until they first could prove that the performers were guilty of violating the criminal obscenity statute.

Another case involved the actions of Sheriff Nicholas Navarro in Broward County, Florida, who attempted to prevent the sale of the 2 Live Crew album *As Nasty As They Wanna Be*. The sheriff purchased a copy of the album and submitted it along with transcriptions of six of the album's eighteen songs to a Florida judge, who issued an order finding probable cause to believe that the album was obscene. Deputies from the sheriff's office then distributed copies of the order to music stores with a warning that sales of the album could result in arrests. The record company sued, and a federal judge ruled that the sheriff's actions were an unconstitutional prior restraint. However, the federal judge also found that the album was obscene.[49] On appeal, the Eleventh Circuit Court of Appeals affirmed that the sheriff's efforts to intimidate music retailers with a probable cause order was a prior restraint, and it reversed the obscenity finding, holding instead that obscenity, as defined by *Miller* v. *California,* had not been proven at trial.[50]

OBSCENITY, INDECENCY, AND ELECTRONIC MEDIA

Broadcasting

Although courts have shown a tendency to tolerate sexually explicit speech in print, as long as it is neither obscene nor exploits children, they have shown only limited tolerance for such speech in broadcast. Broadcasters can be punished, up to the point of revocation of their licenses, for airing language or sexual portrayals that would be clearly protected by the First Amendment in print, in a theater, or in a nightclub.

---

48. Southeastern Promotions v. Conrad, 420 U.S. 546, 95 S.Ct. 1239, 43 L.Ed.2d 448, 1 Med.L.Rptr. 1140 (1975).
49. Skywalker Records Inc. v. Navarro, 739 F.Supp. 578, 17 Med.L.Rptr. 2073 (D.C.S.Fla. 1990).
50. Luke Records, Inc. v. Navarro, 960 F.2d 134, 20 Med.L.Rptr. 1114 (11th Cir. 1992). The court said, "We reject the argument that simply by listening to this musical work the judge could determine that it had no serious artistic value." A petition for certiorari was denied by the U.S. Supreme Court in late 1992.

The case upholding the right of the Federal Communications Commission to regulate indecent broadcasts began when a disc jockey on the Pacifica Foundation's FM radio station in New York City played all twelve minutes of a George Carlin monologue entitled "Filthy Words." It was recorded before a nightclub audience that howled in appreciation as Carlin repeated in many contexts "the curse words and swear words . . . you couldn't say on the public, ah, airwaves, um, the ones you definitely wouldn't say." He proceeded to say them, and the station put them on the airwaves in the middle of a weekday afternoon. One listener, who was riding in his car with his son when the words came spilling out of the radio, was not amused. He complained to the FCC.

Federal Communications Commission v. Pacifica Foundation, 438 U.S. 726, 98 S.Ct. 3026, 57 L.Ed.2d 1073, 3 Med.L.Rptr. 2553 (1978).

The commission reprimanded Pacifica, holding that the Carlin monologue violated 18 U.S.C. § 1464, which forbids use on the air of any "obscene, indecent, or profane language." Although a reprimand is a mild form of censure, its potential harm lay in the fact that it would become a part of the station's file and would be a negative factor if someone were to challenge the renewal of the station's license. Pacifica took its case to the courts. There it argued that the controlling word in Section 1464 is "obscene." It further argued that, despite the sexually and scatologically explicit words in the monologue, it was not obscene, because the Court itself had held that such words do not in themselves appeal to a prurient interest.[51] A divided Supreme Court agreed that "Filthy Words" was not obscene, but it rejected Pacifica's first argument, upholding the FCC's reprimand, five to four.

Justice John Paul Stevens, writing for himself and two other members of the majority, said that the three kinds of language mentioned in Section 1464 must be looked at separately, not as a unit. Thus, a station could be punished for language that was indecent or profane, without being obscene. Upholding the commission's finding that the monologue was indecent, Stevens's plurality defined "indecent" as "nonconformance with accepted standards of morality."

Pacifica offered two other arguments in its defense: (1) Section 1464 imposes a form of censorship, directly violating Section 326 of the Communications Act, which forbids censorship of broadcasting stations by the FCC. (2) The definition of "indecent" was so broad that it might well include matter protected by the First Amendment.

The Court rejected both arguments. Looked at together, Sections 1464 and 326 mean that the FCC can't prevent stations from broadcasting "obscene, indecent, or profane" language, but the commission can punish stations if they do broadcast such material. The Court granted that there might be some First Amendment values in indecent language, even in Carlin's monologue, but, Stevens wrote, "surely [they] lie at the periphery of First Amendment concern." Such value as there might be was not

---

51.   Cohen v. California, 403 U.S. 15, 91 S.Ct. 1780, 29 L.Ed.2d 284 (1971); Hess v. Indiana, 414 U.S. 105, 94 S.Ct. 326, 38 L.Ed.2d 303 (1973).

enough to overcome the fact that "of all forms of communication it is broadcasting that has received the most limited First Amendment protection."

Stevens offered two reasons for upholding the FCC's right to punish indecent broadcasts:

1.   Unlike other forms of communication, broadcast messages come directly and unannounced into the privacy of one's home "where the individual's right to be let alone plainly outweighs the First Amendment rights of an intruder." Because viewers and listeners tune in and out of stations at will, "prior warnings cannot completely protect the listener or viewer from unexpected program content. To say that one may avoid further offense by turning off the radio when he hears indecent language is like saying that the remedy for an assault is to run away after the first blow."

2.   "[B]roadcasting is uniquely accessible to children, even those too young to read." The Court repeatedly has upheld the right of government to assist parents in protecting their children from exposure to indecent materials.[52]

The plurality ended by emphasizing the narrowness of its decision. It said it had no intention of making it impossible for a station to broadcast unexpurgated versions of Shakespeare's more earthy comedies. Nor was it saying that a taxi company could be punished if a frustrated driver uttered a curse into an open microphone. It was simply reminding broadcasters that their medium enters homes where children and unsuspecting adults might be listening. Therefore, discretion is in order. To many, the Carlin monologue would be a nuisance, which Justice George Sutherland had once described as "a right thing in the wrong place—like a pig in the parlor instead of the barnyard." To which Stevens added: "We simply hold that when the Commission finds that a pig has entered the parlor, the exercise of its regulatory power does not depend upon proof that the pig is obscene."

In *Pacifica,* the Court spoke to broadcasters at two levels. At one level, it was merely telling them that they run a risk at license renewal time if they persist in airing sexually oriented material when children are likely to be in the audience. At another level, the Court's decision gave support to those who believe that because of broadcasting's intrusive nature, and because of its potential for influencing conduct, government must retain some control over its content.

Broadcasters, for their part, read the *Pacifica* decision as permitting them to broadcast raunchy material when children are assumed to be in bed, between 10 P.M. and 6 A.M. For more than a decade, the FCC apparently gave the decision the same reading. Then, in 1987, reacting to more than twenty thousand complaints a year, the FCC issued regulations forbidding the broadcast over the airwaves of material at any time that described sexual topics in a "patently offensive way."[53] The commission relaxed its policy when, in *Action for Children's Television* v. *FCC,* the Court of Appeals for

---

52.   Ginsberg v. New York, 390 U.S. 629, 88 S.Ct. 1274, 20 L.Ed.2d 195, 1 Med.L.Rptr. 1424 (1968).
53.   Caroline E. Mayer (*Washington Post* Service), "FCC Cracks Down on Dirty Talk, Lyrics on Radio, Television," *Louisville Courier-Journal,* 17 April 1987.

the District of Columbia Circuit ordered it to provide a "safe harbor" for adult pro-graming.[54] In effect, that safe harbor became 8 P.M. to 6 A.M.[55]

At that point, Congress entered the fray, enacting legislation requiring the commis-sion to return to a twenty-four-hour ban on indecency, on the theory that children are always in the audience.[56] The commission announced that it would comply,[57] and in so doing it also refined its definition of "indecent speech." Sanctions would be limited, the FCC said, to "language or material that, in context, depicts or describes, in terms patently offensive, as measured by contemporary community standards for the broad-cast medium, sexual or excretory activities or organs." The definition was based on language from *Miller* v. *California,* but with three important differences: (1) The com-munity is that of the broadcast medium, not the whole community. (2) There is no re-quirement that the broadcast in question be looked at as a whole. The inference is that a broadcaster can be punished for airing an isolated outburst of profanity or a brief sexually explicit scene. (3) The material need not appeal to a prurient interest in sex.

Immediately thereafter, the commission asked three radio stations to respond to complaints about indecent programming.[58] All were cited on the basis of complaints about sexually explicit talk on the air during daytime hours. One of the stations, WFBQ-FM, Indianapolis, paid a $10,000 fine, although the station's general manager insisted that the program did not violate the city's community standards.[59] The pro-gram in question, *The Bob and Tom Show,* aired during morning commuting time and consistently ranked at or near the top of the Arbitron ratings of Indianapolis AM and FM radio stations.

In 1991 the federal appeals court for the District of Columbia Circuit rejected Con-gress's round-the-clock ban as unconstitutional.[60] Congress then passed a second law,[61] this time allowing broadcasters who broadcast twenty-four hours a day to carry indecent programming between midnight and 6 A.M., and public broadcasters who go off the air at midnight to carry indecent programming between 10 P.M. and midnight. When these restrictions were challenged in court, the District of Columbia Circuit said that the distinction between public and commercial stations could not be justified, but it approved limitations on indecent speech during daytime and evening hours and in-structed the FCC to permit the broadcasting of indecent material only between 10 P.M. and 6 A.M.[62]

Except for those nighttime hours, stations that broadcast materials defined as inde-cent by the FCC can be severely penalized. For example, three stations were fined

---

54. Action for Children's Television v. FCC, 852 F.2d 1332 (D.C. Cir. 1988).
55. Bob Davis, "Appeals Panel Rejects FCC Ruling Curbing Indecent-Broadcasting Hours," *Wall Street Journal,* 1 August 1988.
56. Pub. L. No. 100-459, 102 Stat. 2186 (1988).
57. "FCC, Following New Law, Bans Indecent Broadcasts," *Wall Street Journal,* 22 December 1988.
58. Jay Arnold (Associated Press), "FCC Warns Indy's WFBQ to Clean Up 'Bob and Tom Show,'" *Indiana Daily Student,* 25 August 1989.
59. Steve Hall, "WFBQ Owner Pays $10,000 Fine," *Indianapolis Star,* 23 September 1990.
60. Action for Children's Television v. FCC, 932 F.2d 1504 (D.C. Cir. 1991); cert. denied, 112 S.Ct. 1281, 117 L.Ed.2d 507 (1992).
61. Public Telecommunications Act of 1992, Pub. L. No. 102-356, 106 Stat. 949 (1992).
62. Action for Children's Television v. FCC, 58 F.3d 654 (D.C. Cir. 1995), cert. denied, No. 95-520 (1996). The FCC complied by amending 47 C.F.R. 73.3999 (1995). Linda Greenhouse, "Curb on Smut Is Allowed," *New York Times,* 9 January 1996, p. A5.

Howard Stern's explicit over-the-air discussions of masturbation, lesbian dating, and other sexual topics have been a regular target of listener complaints to the Federal Communications Commission. In 1995 Infinity Broadcasting, his employer, agreed to pay a record $1.7 million to settle five indecency charges brought by federal regulators between 1989 and 1994, the largest settlement ever involving accusations of indecent radio broadcasts. *(Reuters/Mark Cardwell/Archive Photos)*

$200,000 each for broadcasting Howard Stern's nationally syndicated talk show.[63] The commission acted after a woman in Los Angeles complained about an episode in which Stern talked about masturbation and lesbian dating. The woman told the FCC that she found Stern's "vicarious titillation of his own interests extremely repulsive." In 1995, Infinity Broadcasting, Stern's employer, agreed to pay the government $1.7 million to settle five indecency charges against Stern.[64]

Indecency, as defined by the FCC, means more than a few dirty words. Indecency is the kind of adult fare that uses sexual vulgarity and references to body parts and excretory functions to shock, titillate, and amuse. Curiously, indecency has not included the depiction of violence, but that may be changing. In 1995, Reed E. Hundt, chairman of the FCC, said that he believes "a record can be made that violent content on television is more dangerous to children than indecency."[65] In the wake of the D.C. Circuit Court's decision in *Action for Children's Television,* Congress began to consider legislation that would prohibit violent programs at times when children are believed to be watching. For example, a bill introduced by Senator Ernest F. Hollings, a Democrat from South Carolina, would require the FCC to treat violent programming in the same way that it treats indecency—channeling it to late-night TV. An alterna-

---

63. Stephen Chapman, "Shielding Our Ears from Shock Radio," *Indianapolis Star,* 27 January 1993.
64. Anthony Ramirez, "$1.7 Million to Settle Stern Radio Indecency Case," *New York Times,* 2 September 1995, p. 13.
65. Edmund L. Andrews, "F.C.C. Joining a Move to Curb Violence on TV," *New York Times,* 7 July 1995, p. 1.

tive proposed by other lawmakers would require broadcasters to code violent programs so that they could be blocked electronically by a computer chip installed in television sets and programmed by parents.[66]

Broadcasters have opposed expanding indecency regulations to reach programs depicting violence. Steve Bookshester, a lawyer for the National Association of Broadcasters, told a *New York Times* reporter that he believed it was wrong to make the jump from restrictions on indecency to restrictions on depiction of violence: "There's a big distinction between the sexual matter at issue here and violence. . . . If one cartoon character hits another one, is that violence? . . . What about news? What do you do with that?"

Cable

As in print and broadcast, the depiction of obscenity, as defined in *Miller* v. *California,* is a crime when transmitted over cable television. The Cable Communications Policy Act provides: "Whoever transmits over any cable system any matter which is obscene or otherwise unprotected by the Constitution of the United States shall be fined not more than $10,000 or imprisoned not more than 2 years, or both."[67] In addition, cable operators can be prosecuted for obscenity under state and local law.[68]

Indecency is another matter, however. Although the Supreme Court has upheld the authority of the Federal Communications Commission to punish radio and television stations for airing indecent programming, there is, at the moment, no similar restriction on cable systems. The Supreme Court affirmed, although without a written opinion, a lower-court decision striking down a Utah law aimed at limiting the sexual content of cable television programs.[69] Although the law closely followed standards that the Court had established in *Pacifica* and *Miller,* a U.S. district court in Salt Lake City held that Utah's cable decency act was preempted by the federal Cable Communications Policy Act, which allows for state prosecution of "obscenity" but not "indecency," and that, in any case, the definition of indecency was so broadly and vaguely written that cable operators would have no clear idea which programs might be offensive. The Court of Appeals for the Tenth Circuit upheld that ruling. The Utah statute banning indecency on cable television violated both federal law and the First Amendment.

Another challenge, this time to an ordinance banning indecent programming in Miami, Florida, produced a similar result.[70] The Court of Appeals for the Eleventh Circuit distinguished cable and broadcasting, noting that the authority for regulating indecency in broadcasting was based on the *Pacifica* case. But *Pacifica,* "it must be re-

---

66. "Simple V-Chip Could Spell Victory over T.V. Violence," *New York Times,* 11 July 1995, p. A12.
67. 47 U.S.C. § 559.
68. 47 U.S.C. § 558.
69. Community Television of Utah v. Wilkinson, 611 F.Supp. 1099, 11 Med.L.Rptr. 2217 (D.Utah 1985); affirmed, Jones v. Wilkinson, 800 F.2d 989, 13 Med.L.Rptr. 1913 (10th Cir. 1986); affirmed without opinion, 489 U.S. 986, 107 S.Ct. 1559, 94 L.Ed.2d 753 (1987). See also Community Television, Inc. v. Roy City, 555 F.Supp. 1164 (N.D. Utah 1982).
70. Cruz v. Ferre, 755 F.2d 1415 (11th Cir. 1985).

membered, focused on broadcasting's 'pervasive presence,' and the fact that broadcasting 'is uniquely accessible to children. . . .'' But cable "does not 'intrude' into the home. The Cablevision subscriber must affirmatively elect to have cable service come into his home." Unlike broadcasting, cable is an invited visitor. As for children, the court said that the government's interest in protecting children was "significantly weaker in the context of cable television because parental manageability of cable television greatly exceeded the ability to manage the broadcast media." The court cited the availability of detailed program guides for cable, parental discretion in subscribing to or refusing supplemental services, such as HBO, and the fact that the Cable Act requires operators to provide, on request, lock boxes that permit parents to block channels that might carry programs they would not want their children to see.

In the face of such decisions, Congress included new provisions about cable indecency in Section 10 of the 1992 Cable Television Consumer Protection Act.[71] The law gives cable operators the right to refuse to carry material they believe is indecent—that is, material that depicts sexual or excretory activities or organs in a patently offensive way as measured by contemporary community standards. Moreover, Congress directed the FCC to adopt rules that would require cable operators to move indecent programming to one leased access channel and make it available only to subscribers who requested to see it. The FCC did that in 1993,[72] but the rules were stayed pending court review.[73] In 1995 that review moved from the U.S. Court of Appeals for the District of Columbia, which upheld the indecency provisions, to the U.S. Supreme Court, where, at this writing, the case is pending the outcome of a petition for certiorari.[74]

Internet

Obscenity and child pornography are as illegal on the Internet as anywhere else. In fact, the federal child pornography statute specifically mentions computers as one illegal means of distributing child pornography,[75] and computer operators have been a clearly visible target in obscenity and child pornography prosecutions.[76]

Congress also has made it a crime to use the Internet

to display in a manner available to a person under 18 years of age, any comment, request, suggestion, proposal, image, or other communication that, in context, depicts or describes, in terms patently offensive as measured by contemporary community standards, sexual or

---

71. Pub. L. No. 102-385; 106 Stat. 1460, 1486; 47 U.S.C. 551, 532(h), 532(j), and 558.
72. Implementation of Section 10 of the Cable Consumer Protection and Competition Act of 1992: Indecent Programming and Other Types of Materials on Cable Access Channels, First Report and Order, 8 FCC Rcd. 988 (1993); Second Report and Order, 58 FR 19623 (1993).
73. Alliance for Community Media v. FCC, 10 F.3d 812 (D.C. Cir. 1993); Alliance for Community Media v. FCC, 15 F.3d 186 (D.C. Cir. 1994).
74. Alliance for Community Media v. FCC, 56 F.3d 105 (D.C. Cir. 1995); cert. filed, U.S.Sup.Ct. No. 95-227 (1995). A separate petition for certiorari was filed in Denver Area Educational Telecommunications Consortium v. FCC, U.S.Sup.Ct. No. 94-124 (1995).
75. 18 U.S.C. § 2252(a)(1). "Any person who knowingly transports or ships in interstate or foreign commerce by any means including by computer. . . ."
76. David Johnston, "Use of Computer Network for Child Sex Sets Off Raids," *New York Times,* 14 September 1995, p. 1.

excretory activities or organs, regardless of whether the user of such service placed the call or initiated the communication.[77]

What makes the Internet different from cable and broadcast is the difficulty of policing a globally diversified communications system that can exist without a centralized governing structure. With nothing more than the use of a common electronic language and a phone line, computer connections can blithely ignore national boundaries and political governments. For users, the Internet makes it as simple to connect to a sexually explicit—even obscene—database on the other side of the world as it is to connect to a library across town. There are no customs agents with which to contend—no declarations, no duties, no licenses, and no language barriers.

But although policing the Internet may be difficult, it is not impossible. Sometimes the Internet even makes prosecution easier. Posting on the Internet opens the possibility for prosecution anywhere that the Internet does "business," which is everywhere. For example, when federal prosecutors targeted a California couple who were maintaining a computer bulletin board offering a wide range of sexually explicit pictures and text, they found that the nature of the Internet made it possible to prosecute offenders nearly anywhere in the United States. After a Tennessee Internet user complained about the bulletin board, federal prosecutors in Memphis charged the California residents, Robert and Carleen Thomas, with transmitting obscenity through interstate telephone lines. Because obscenity is determined on the basis of local community standards, a successful prosecution was thought to be more likely in conservative Memphis, than in the place of origin—Milpitas, California.[78]

The Thomas case involved the transmission of *obscenity* over telephone lines, but system operators should be aware that FCC telephone regulations also deal with *indecency* over telephone lines and that Section 223(b) of the Federal Communications Act, while mainly aimed at "dial-a-porn" services, is worded broadly enough that it could include on-line computer systems.[79] The FCC has not yet treated Internet indecency as a form of dial-a-porn, but the groundwork has been laid.[80] In *Sable Communications of California* v. *FCC*[81] the U.S. Supreme Court held that although Congress could not entirely ban telephone conversations that were indecent, it could lawfully make it difficult for minors to gain access to dial-a-porn services by creating specific barriers, such as requiring that messages be encrypted and that users have coded access numbers. It is not altogether unreasonable to expect that eventually on-line system operators may be required to limit sexually explicit, Internet-accessible data to adults only.

---

77. Telecommunications Act of 1996, § 502 (47 U.S.C. 223).
78. Woody Baird (Associated Press), "Prosecutors Target Computer Porn," *Indiana Daily Student,* 21 July 1994, p. 13.
79. 47 U.S.C. § 223. "Whoever in . . . interstate or foreign communication by means of telephone . . . makes any comment, request, suggestion or proposal which is obscene, lewd, lascivious, filthy, or indecent . . . shall be fined . . . or imprisoned. . . . Whoever knowingly . . . by means of telephone, makes . . . any obscene communication for commercial purposes . . . shall be fined . . . or imprisoned. . . . Whoever knowingly . . . by means of telephone, makes . . . any indecent communication for commercial purposes which is available to any person under 18 years of age or to any other person without that person's consent . . . shall be fined . . . or imprisoned."
80. Lance Rose, *Netlaw* (New York: Osborne McGraw-Hill, 1995), p. 256.
81. 492 U.S. 115, 109 S.Ct. 2829, 106 L.Ed.2d 93, 16 Med.L.Rptr. 1961 (1989).

Moreover, there is a growing interest in enforcing existing laws against sexual harassment, stalking, and other forms of sexual violence on the Internet. Connecticut and Arizona, for example, are among the first states to make harassment by computer a crime.[82] Michigan's antistalking law specifically outlaws repeated and unwanted "mail or electronic communications."[83] A man in suburban Detroit was arrested and charged with stalking after several weeks of lovesick pleadings over the phone and on the Internet frightened his would-be girlfriend,[84] and a University of Michigan student was arrested when his sexually violent fiction on the Internet was thought to be intended as a threat against a female student.[85] In California, a junior college agreed to pay three students $15,000 each to settle charges of sexual discrimination and harassment after two women complained that they were the subject of anatomically explicit remarks posted on a computer bulletin board created by the school. The U.S. Department of Education's Office of Civil Rights said that the remarks were a form of sexual harassment that had created a hostile educational environment.[86]

Thus, in the last third of the twentieth century, few aspects of media law have led to more judicial and legislative consternation than has sexually explicit speech. No aspect of media law has divided people as has the law of obscenity. Even two presidential commissions, appointed to study the problem of pornography, disagreed on the danger of the problem. A majority of the commission appointed by President Johnson to study the effects of pornography found no evidence of such a tendency. But a commission appointed by Edwin Meese III, then President Reagan's attorney general, came to an opposite conclusion.[87] The Meese commission decided that exposure to certain kinds of pornographic materials, including those portraying physical abuse of women, causes an "increase in the incidence of sexual violence." This conclusion was based in part on testimony from law enforcement officers, who said they invariably found pornographic materials in the possession of sexual offenders, and on interviews with convicted offenders, half of whom said they were incited by such materials. Social scientists, too, told the commission that they thought pornography changes values, especially if sexual aggression is portrayed "as pleasurable for the victim."

Some scholars believe there is a link between pornography and the continuing problem of male assaults on women. Among them are Edward Donnerstein, Daniel Linz, and Steven Penrod, psychologists at the University of Wisconsin, whose experiments are summarized in *The Question of Pornography.*[88] That view is shared by feminist organizations who were able to persuade city councils in Minneapolis and Indi-

---

82. Jonathan Rabinovitz, "In Connecticut, Harassment by Computer Is Now a Crime," *New York Times,* 13 June 1995, p. 1.

83. Peter H. Lewis, "Persistent E-Mail: Electronic Stalking or Innocent Courtship?" *New York Times,* 16 September 1994, p. B11.

84. Ibid.

85. Peter H. Lewis, "An Internet Author of Sexually Violent Fiction Faces Charges," *New York Times,* 11 February 1995, p. A7.

86. Tamar Lewin, "Dispute over Computer Messages: Free Speech or Sex Harassment?" *New York Times,* 22 September 1994, p. 1.

87. Attorney General's Commission on Pornography, *Final Report.*

88. Edward Donnerstein, Daniel Linz, and Stephen Penrod, *The Question of Pornography* (New York: Free Press, 1987).

anapolis to adopt ordinances[89] treating obscenity as a violation of women's civil rights. They did so by attempting to redefine obscenity as the "graphic sexually explicit subordination of women." The mayor of Minneapolis vetoed that city's ordinance, acting in the belief that it was unconstitutional. The correctness of that belief was confirmed when the Indianapolis ordinance, challenged by the American Booksellers Association, was declared unconstitutional by a federal district court and affirmed on appeal.[90] The court said that the government must prevent sexual discrimination, but in light of the Supreme Court's specific guidelines in *Miller,* government cannot define as obscene those materials that are merely degrading and discriminatory.

With obscenity, the Supreme Court has taken the middle ground. Its decisions have held that at some point the portrayal of sexual activity can be punished or even suppressed, but only after a court has found such portrayal obscene, as the Court has defined that term. As for material that is not obscene but nevertheless sexually offensive, the Court has held that it is protected by the First Amendment except when it exploits children or is made readily accessible to children over the airwaves or phone lines, or when it is the very vehicle of the crime itself, as it might be when used to harass or threaten. The limits set by the Court strike some people as allowing much that is pornographic and socially harmful, but the Court has held, as it has with sedition and libel, that some harm will be tolerated to avoid suppression of speech that may contribute, however remotely, to the advancement of ideas.

In the Professional World

When the Supreme Court handed down its decision in *Miller,* a *New York Times* reporter talked to several major writers of fiction and found uneasiness among them.[91] Kurt Vonnegut, Jr., a Hoosier-born author of best-selling satire on middle-class mores, was one of several who thought that some jury, somewhere, might find one of their works obscene. Joyce Carol Oates predicted that the decision would lead to repression of the arts. Such fears have proved groundless. A Georgia jury found *Carnal Knowledge* obscene but was soon overruled by a unanimous Supreme Court. Since then, no work by any professional communicator of any stature has been condemned as obscene. One has only to read some of the best-selling fiction, go to an R-rated movie, or watch cable television to know that such a condemnation is highly unlikely.

The issue for most professional communicators is not obscenity; it is sex and violence. Professional communicators, ranging from news reporters through ad-

89. *An Ordinance of the City of Minneapolis,* amending Title 7, Chapters 139 and 141 of the Minneapolis Code of Ordinances, December 1983; *A General Ordinance,* amending Chapter 16 of the Code of Indianapolis and Marion County, Indiana, April 1984.

90. American Booksellers Association v. Hudnut, 598 F.Supp. 1316, 11 Med.L.Rptr. 1105 (S.D.Ind. 1984); 771 F.2d 323, 11 Med.L.Rptr. 2465 (7th Cir. 1985). The Supreme Court affirmed, six to three, without writing an opinion, 106 S.Ct. 1172 (1986).

91. Robert A. Wright, "Broad Spectrum of Writers Attacks Obscenity Ruling," *New York Times,* 21 August 1973.

vertising and public relations practitioners to recording artists, deal with the portrayal of sex and violence almost daily, sometimes without much thought for the consequences. A short discussion cannot cover all the questions raised by portrayals of sex and violence in the mass media, but it can point to some of the problems.

The spectrum begins with the treatment of words considered profane or vulgar. The Supreme Court has held that even the "strongest" of such words is protected by the First Amendment. However, the *Associated Press Stylebook* advises journalists not to use obscenities, profanities, or vulgarities "unless they are part of direct quotations and there is a compelling reason for them."[92] Many editors have learned that it may not be advisable even then. When the *Louisville Courier-Journal* ran an unexpurgated version of a report on the causes of the riot in Chicago during the Democratic National Convention in 1968, Norman Isaacs, executive editor, said he wrote hundreds of letters of apology to protesting readers who were offended by the report's frequent use of variations on the vulgarism for sexual intercourse.[93] When one federal employee directed the same kinds of words at another in the federal courthouse in Dayton, the target of his abuse shot him to death. The publisher of the *Dayton Journal Herald* thought the newspaper's readers should know the words that had provoked a public employee to such violence. Publication of the offensive words provoked protests from enough readers to get the publisher fired.[94] During the 1980s, the wives of several highly placed federal officials formed a nationwide organization—Parents' Music Resource Center, headed by Tipper Gore—to protest the use of explicit sexual language and hatefulness in rock music.[95]

Public concern about lyrics urging suicide, sexual violence, and antisocial attitudes has become so vocal that record companies now put warning labels on raunchy albums, some stores refuse to sell controversial recordings to minors, and some singers have withdrawn certain of their recordings from the market. Rapper Ice-T withdrew his song "Cop Killer" because of protests that it incited and glorified violence.[96] Only weeks earlier, Time Warner president, Gerald M. Levin, had refused to withdraw the record, saying: "[W]e believe that the worth of what an artist or journalist has to say does not depend on pre-approval from a government official or a corporate censor or a cultural elite. . . . [T]he test of any democratic society lies not in how well it can control expression but in whether it gives freedom of thought and expression the widest possible latitude, however controversial or exasperating the results may sometimes be."[97] That sentiment was not shared by at least one Florida sheriff, who warned record store

---

92. Christopher W. French, ed., *The Associated Press Stylebook* (New York: Associated Press, 1987), p. 155.
93. Interview with Norman Isaacs.
94. Interview with the former publisher.
95. Michael Cieply, "Records May Soon Carry Warning That Lyrics Are Morally Hazardous," *Wall Street Journal,* 31 July 1985.
96. Meg Cox, "Time Warner Recall of 'Cop Killer' Song Sparks Buying Rush," *Wall Street Journal,* 30 July 1992.
97. Gerald M. Levin, "Why We Won't Withdraw 'Cop Killer,'" *Wall Street Journal,* 24 June 1992.

owners in his area that they would be arrested for selling an album by another rap group, 2 Live Crew. The group responded with a lawsuit defending its recording *As Nasty As They Wanna Be,* against accusations of obscenity. The rappers won an injunction and a finding, on appeal, that the sheriff had not proven the album obscene under the *Miller* test.[98]

Questions of another kind are raised by portrayals of sex designed to sell products or attract viewers. A truism of both the advertising and entertainment worlds is that sex sells. Sex continues to sell, even though some church groups have organized campaigns against what they consider television's overexposure of women's breasts and buttocks.

One of the many valid questions about sex in the media is, To what extent does it contribute to reinforcing stereotypes about sexual roles? For example, what of the brewers' television ads that show trim, virile young men trooping off the job into a bar where they have a great time ordering beer by the pitcher? The only women in sight either are looking at the men adoringly or are waitresses, who not only serve the men but are the objects of their playful pranks. Or consider the plight, in another beer ad, of two young men condemned to live forever among a bevy of scantily clad women bearing their favorite brew. Four workers at the Stroh Brewery in St. Paul, Minn., sued their employer because of an Old Milwaukee beer ad featuring the "Swedish Bikini Team," a group of barely clad women who drop in on a male camping trip.[99] The workers, all women, alleged that Stroh's advertising contributed to a sexist attitude at their workplace. Their lawyer, Lori Peterson, said that the women viewed the advertising as a company endorsement of male behavior that subjected them to obscene and sexist comments by coworkers, men who liked to publicly display pornographic posters and slap women on the buttocks. Whether there is a link between the portrayal of women in advertising and sexist male behavior may be a tenuous proposition, and one that Stroh's denies, but many people believe that mass media reinforce harmful stereotypes, for which the media somehow should be accountable.

In the professional world there are no clear limits as to how far media managers will go in the exploitation of sex. Newspapers, and even some magazines, are reluctant to carry cigarette advertising, but they carry advertising for sexually explicit and highly violent movies. Many newspapers accept advertising from topless bars, massage parlors, lingerie modeling shops, and "escort services." Some newspapers won't publish the photographs and the dimensions of topless dancers, but others use photographs of seminude male and female performers, sometimes using an airbrush to clothe them barely within the limits of decency. Articles about sexual performance or medical problems related to sexual activity are increasingly apparent in newspapers and magazines, often tak-

---

98. Luke Records, Inc. v. Navarro, 960 F.2d 134, 20 Med.L.Rptr. 1114 (11th Cir. 1992); cert. denied, 113 S.Ct. 659, 121 L.Ed.2d 585 (1992).
99. "Stroh's Ads Targeted, Bikinis and Beer Lead to Harassment at Work, Suit Claims," *ABA Journal,* February 1992, p. 20.

ing a very straightforward approach to such once-taboo topics as oral sex and impotence. The necessity to inform readers about sexual transmission of AIDS from one person to another has led some publishers and broadcasters to discover that they can be comfortable with the word "condom." Advertising agencies for major clothing manufacturers, such as Calvin Klein and Jordache, have pushed the limits of sexual appeal in advertising, using models—sometimes very young ones—in provocative poses to attract buyers of underwear and jeans.

But whatever the limits of sexual explicitness, very few of the mainstream mass media will explicitly and graphically show the act of sexual intercourse. Even today, allusions to it are treated with great delicacy in newspapers, in general interest magazines, and on film.

Violence, however, is another matter. Much of the mass media, from news to entertainment, graphically portray violent death. Murder has been a staple of drama and fiction from earliest times. Homer's *Odyssey,* written three thousand years ago, describes in gory detail the manner in which Odysseus killed his wife's suitors when he returned home in disguise after the siege of Troy. And any well-performed version of Shakespeare's *Macbeth* drips with blood. Truman Capote's *In Cold Blood* is a modern murder classic, and Quentin Tarantino's violent film about professional killers, *Pulp Fiction,* has won major awards and critical acclaim.

Special-effects technicians have become experts in showing what happens when a chain saw cuts through flesh and bone, an ax cleaves a skull, or a bullet smashes through a brain. Films like *Texas Chainsaw Massacre, Maniac,* and *The Slumber Party Massacre* have become cult films. Although television producers, responding to pressure groups concerned about excessive portrayals of violence, now offer fewer deaths per evening of prime time viewing, popular police and medical dramas featuring various kinds of violence continue to dot the upper levels of the Nielsen ratings. Television viewers of *Murder, She Wrote* have learned that showing up at a party attended by Jessica Fletcher will be fatally hazardous to the health of at least one of the participants. Viewers of *NYPD Blue, ER, Chicago Hope,* and *CNN Headline News* can get a very real sense of the meanness of American life.

Statistics measuring the effects of violence in the media probably are no more reliable than are statistics measuring the effects of sexually explicit materials. Yet studies show that people who watch a lot of television tend to believe crime is more prevalent than it is,[100] and that exposure to filmed violence, especially when it is linked with sex, tends to desensitize the members of the audience toward sex crimes.[101] This is not to suggest, in a textbook devoted in large part to First Amendment freedoms, that obscenity laws should be broadened to include portrayals of violence. It is to suggest that professionals in a position to control what the media offer to the public may need to think beyond a consideration of

---

100. George Gerbner et al., "The 'Mainstreaming' of America: Violence Profile No. 11," *Journal of Communication,* Summer 1980, pp. 10–29.
101. Donnerstein and Linz, "Sexual Violence in the Media."

what sells. Sex and death are inescapable realities. Treated with respect, sex can unite two persons like no other force. Treated with respect, death can be a profound witness to the mystery of our mortality. Trivialized, both sex and the taking of life can become meaningless acts.

FOR REVIEW

1. Outline the arguments for and against restrictions on obscenity.

2. What is the nature of the crime of obscenity?

3. How did the Supreme Court define obscenity in *Roth* v. *United States?*

4. List and explain the changes in obscenity law resulting from the Court's decision in *Miller* v. *California.*

5. Outline and explain the role of the jury in obscenity cases. Is it true that a jury has unbridled discretion in determining what is obscene? Why or why not?

6. What is the "community" in an obscenity case? How are its standards of sexual candor determined?

7. Some people in your community become upset over two developments: the offering for rent of sexually explicit videotapes by video stores, and a cluster of massage parlors that are widely believed to be fronts for prostitution. The stores that rent the videotapes do not advertise them. Nor are scenes from them visible to the customers who come to the stores to rent other kinds of cassettes. The sexually explicit videos are kept in a locked room which is opened only at the request of a customer known to the manager. The city council is asked to adopt an ordinance placing strict license requirements on both kinds of enterprises. One provision in the proposed ordinance would give the police chief authority to revoke a license if the holder of it was believed to be in the business of purveying obscenity. You are asked to advise the council in drafting the final form of the ordinance. What advice would you give?

8. Assume that a licensing ordinance has been adopted. Assume also that the manager of one video rental store has twice been arrested for violating its terms. The police chief consults the prosecutor and concludes that under your state's law the store can be padlocked and its contents seized as the fruits of racketeering. Is that conclusion correct? Why or why not?

9. Make the same assumptions as in question 8 with respect to one of the massage parlors. How, then, would you answer the two questions in question 8?

10. On what rationale did the Supreme Court decide the *Pacifica* case? On the basis of your exposure to radio and television, give examples of what you might consider indecent programming.

11. Compare and contrast the accessibility by children to (1) television, (2) cable, and (3) the Internet. To what extent do you think the reasoning in *Pacifica* validly applies to each?

12. The courts seem to treat obscenity, pornography, indecency, and graphic violence in different ways. Do you think this approach is useful in deciding under what circumstances speech should or should not be allowed? Do you think there are other kinds of speech equally harmful as those discussed here? If so, should they be regulated in a similar way?

CHAPTER 11

Advertising, after word of mouth, is the most pervasive means of communication.
It makes up a substantial part of the content of newspapers and magazines. Without
advertising, radio, television, and cable systems would not exist in their present form.
Makers of commercial products, providers of services, and advocates of causes spend
in excess of $130 billion a year to catch the public's attention. About a third of this
amount is paid to the media for time or space.

Until recent times, advertising had little or no legal protection except that afforded
by the law of contracts and commercial transactions. As far as the First Amendment
was concerned, advertising was in exile, along with obscenity, fighting words, sedition, and other kinds of speech condemned by courts as lacking valid idea content.

ADVERTISING

Thus, unlike news and opinion, advertising could be subjected to prior restraint and other legal punishments with little hindrance.

This is not to say that advertising suffered from many restrictions. Any history student who has scanned the advertisements in turn-of-the-century newspapers has noted that any claim, no matter how preposterous, could be, and was, made for products such as patent medicines. Until well into the twentieth century, the rule in advertising was "anything goes," reflecting the age-old rule of commercial transactions: *caveat emptor* ("Let the buyer beware"). The law assumed that buyers and sellers, advertisers and their audiences, were of equal intelligence. Anyone who was stuck with a bad bargain or taken in by a flowery ad was out of luck. It was assumed that victims of sharp practices would learn from their experience and not be taken in the next time. Not until 1906 did Congress take a first small step toward control of deceptive advertising. In that year it passed the Pure Food and Drug Act, which gave a federal agency authority to regulate claims made on package labels. This legislation was followed in 1914 by the Federal Trade Commission Act. One of the duties of the commission was to regulate advertising claims. The Federal Trade Commission has become one of several weapons used against deceptive advertisers.

This chapter deals with four major themes of advertising law:

1. The Supreme Court's recognition in the 1970s that advertising is commercial speech entitled to limited First Amendment protection.

2. The role of the Federal Trade Commission in regulating advertising to prevent deception.

3. The media's right to refuse advertising, whether for selling a commercial product or for persuading others to adopt a point of view on a public issue.

4. The right of corporations to spend corporate funds on advertising intended to influence opinion on public issues.

Major Cases

- *Bates* v. *State Bar of Arizona,* 433 U.S. 350, 97 S.Ct. 2691, 53 L.Ed.2d 810, 2 Med.L.Rptr. 2097 (1977).

- *Central Hudson Gas & Electric Corp.* v. *Public Service Commission,* 447 U.S. 557, 100 S.Ct. 2343, 65 L.Ed.2d 341, 6 Med.L.Rptr. 1497 (1980).

- *First National Bank of Boston* v. *Bellotti,* 435 U.S. 765, 98 S.Ct. 1407, 55 L.Ed.2d 707, 3 Med.L.Rptr. 2105 (1978).

- *Metromedia, Inc.* v. *City of San Diego,* 453 U.S. 490, 101 S.Ct. 2882, 69 L.Ed.2d 800 (1981).

- *Morales* v. *Trans World Airlines, Inc.,* 504 U.S. 374, 112 S.Ct. 2031, 119 L.Ed.2d 157 (1992).

- *Posadas de Puerto Rico Associates* v. *Tourism Company of Puerto Rico,* 478 U.S. 328, 106 S.Ct. 2968, 92 L.Ed.2d 266, 13 Med.L.Rptr. 1033 (1986).

- *Shuck* v. *The Carroll Daily Herald,* 247 N.W. 813 (1933).

- *Virginia State Board of Pharmacy* v. *Virginia Citizens Consumer Council,* 425 U.S. 748, 96 S.Ct. 1817, 48 L.Ed.2d 346, 1 Med.L.Rptr. 1930 (1976).

- *Warner-Lambert Co.* v. *Federal Trade Commission,* 562 F.2d 749, 2 Med.L.Rptr. 2303 (D.C. Cir. 1977).

- *Zauderer* v. *Office of Disciplinary Counsel of Supreme Court of Ohio,* 471 U.S. 626, 105 S.Ct. 2265, 85 L.Ed.2d 652 (1985).

THE DOCTRINE OF COMMERCIAL SPEECH

Advertising and the First Amendment

Not until 1941 did the Supreme Court have occasion to consider the argument that advertising is protected by the First Amendment. And when it did, in *Valentine* v. *Chrestensen,*[1] the Court seemed to reject that argument out of hand. The issue involved was picayune. Police in New York City had arrested F. J. Chrestensen for violating an ordinance forbidding distribution of commercial handbills on city streets. However, the ordinance did not forbid distribution of handbills that promote a cause. Chrestensen had bought a submarine and was selling admission to it. He advertised by passing out handbills to people on the streets. When police told him he was breaking the law, he sought to avoid arrest by printing two-sided handbills. On one side was a message protesting the city's refusal to let him dock his submarine at one of its piers. On the other was a message informing people where the submarine was docked, the

---

1.   316 U.S. 52, 62 S.Ct. 920, 86 L.Ed. 1262, 1 Med.L.Rptr. 1907 (1942).

hours it was open to visitors, and the price of admission. The city's police and courts were not impressed. As they saw it, he was still using the city's streets to distribute advertising for his submarine. Chrestensen was ordered to pay a fine. He appealed all the way to the U.S. Supreme Court.

The Supreme Court was also unimpressed. A unanimous Court noted that the streets long have been considered proper forums for the communication of ideas, subject only to reasonable time, place, and manner restrictions. But with respect to commercial messages, the Court added: "We are equally clear that the Constitution imposes no such restraint on government as respects purely commercial advertising. Whether, and to what extent, one may promote or pursue a gainful occupation in the streets . . . are matters for legislative judgment."

In short, the Court said, state and local governments could decide for themselves how far they wanted to go in permitting commercial advertisers to use public property. If they wanted to forbid such use altogether, as New York City had, there was nothing in the Constitution to hinder them. For more than twenty years thereafter, legislators and judges assumed that the Court had held that "purely commercial advertising" was not the kind of speech protected by the First Amendment, putting it in the same category as "fighting words" and obscenity.

The first doubts about that assumption were raised in 1964 by the Supreme Court's decision in *New York Times* v. *Sullivan,*[2] which is discussed in Chapter 5. The basis for that case was an advertisement urging readers to support students at Alabama State College who were demonstrating against racial segregation. Lawyers for Sullivan cited *Chrestensen* in their brief, arguing that because the assertions allegedly defaming their client appeared in a paid advertisement, they were not protected by the First Amendment in any way. The Supreme Court disagreed. But it was careful to draw a line between the advertisement at issue in *New York Times* and other kinds of advertising. The former argued a cause of vital interest to the nation's welfare. People who might not be able to reach the public through other means had bought space in a leading newspaper to air their grievances. That their views appeared in an advertisement was beside the point. But it was to the point that publishers be encouraged to accept cause advertising. For that reason, the Court held that ads that express opinions on public issues are fully protected by the First Amendment.

However, the Court was silent on "purely commercial speech." It appeared, then, that the Court had divided paid communication into two classes, depending on the purpose of the ad. If the purpose was to sell an idea, the ad was protected by the First Amendment. If the purpose was to sell a product or a service, it was not.

This neat classification persisted for nearly a decade before another aspect of the civil rights movement raised questions about it. In the early 1970s, the Pittsburgh newspapers got into trouble with the city's Human Relations Commission because of the way they presented employment advertising. The newspapers said they were doing readers a service by listing some ads as of "male interest," others as of "female interest," and still others as "male-female." The commission disagreed. It held that the categories reinforced male-female stereotypes and encouraged sexual discrimination

---

2.   376 U.S. 254, 84 S.Ct. 710, 11 L.Ed.2d 686, 1 Med.L.Rptr. 1907 (1964).

in violation of a recently enacted city ordinance. When the newspapers were cited for violating that ordinance, they argued that editorial judgments were involved in deciding how to categorize the ads. Therefore, any attempt by the city to tell the newspapers how to label the ads would violate the First Amendment. Neither the commission nor a county court bought that argument. The newspapers were ordered to comply with the law. The newspapers carried their case to the Supreme Court, which upheld the lower court's decision.

However, in reaching its decision in *Pittsburgh Press Co.* v. *Pittsburgh Commission on Human Relations,*[3] the Supreme Court avoided the First Amendment question. The Court upheld the view that the newspapers' sexually oriented labels furthered discrimination on the basis of gender. Because such discrimination was illegal, the ads thus promoted an illegal act, making the newspapers law violators, too. However, in reaching its conclusion, the Court's majority conceded that "[u]nder some circumstances, . . . a newspaper's editorial judgments in connection with an advertisement" might be protected by the First Amendment. The degree of such protection would hinge on the content of the ad. In this instance, there was no protection, because the ads fostered an illegal purpose. Taken in context, the court's reasoning raised questions. What kind of advertising content might be protected? In *New York Times,* the ad in question discussed political and social issues. Are such issues the only kinds protected by the First Amendment? What about economic issues, which are frequently resolved in the marketplace? Is there not a public interest in knowing which goods and services are available and at what price?

Within two years, the Court began to answer the questions raised by *Pittsburgh Press.* The Court took a case that had been in and out of state and federal courts for four years. The dispute began when the *Virginia Weekly,* an underground newspaper at the University of Virginia, accepted an advertisement for an abortion clinic in New York City. At the time, which was before the Supreme Court's decision in *Roe* v. *Wade*[4] made abortion a matter of constitutional right, abortions were legal in New York but illegal in Virginia. Further, a Virginia law made it a crime to advertise abortion services. The weekly's editor, Jeffrey Bigelow, was found guilty of violating that law and was fined. Ultimately, the case reached the Supreme Court, which held, in *Bigelow* v. *Virginia,*[5] that the advertisement was protected by the First Amendment. Therefore, Bigelow could not be punished for publishing it. The service offered was legal in New York. Virginia could not punish women who went to New York to obtain an abortion. Therefore, it could not punish Virginia media for advertising legal abortion services. But again the Court stopped short of saying that all ads for legal goods or services contain ideas that the First Amendment will protect. Instead, the Court's majority rationalized its decision by focusing on what it saw as the abortion ad's informational content. By informing Virginia readers that other states had legalized abortions, the ad contributed to the debate on the issue.

---

3.   413 U.S. 376, 93 S.Ct. 2553, 37 L.Ed.2d 669, 1 Med.L.Rptr. 1908 (1973).
4.   410 U.S. 113, 93 S.Ct. 705, 35 L.Ed.2d 147 (1973).
5.   421 U.S. 809, 95 S.Ct. 2222, 44 L.Ed.2d 600, 1 Med.L.Rptr. 1919 (1975).

Within a year, the Court took another Virginia advertising case and this time held without apology that people find helpful ideas in straightforward product and price advertising. With its decision, the Court established the doctrine that even "purely commercial advertising" enjoys First Amendment protection if it is for a legal product. At issue in this case was the right of pharmacies to post the prices of prescription drugs. Under Virginia's laws regulating the practice of pharmacy, price advertising was banned as being unprofessional. Thus, a patient who required a prescription drug was, in effect, a blind buyer forced to pay whatever price was charged at the time of purchase. If all drug stores charged the same price for the same drug, there would be no problem, but prices vary greatly from store to store. The case report notes that the price of a commonly prescribed antibiotic ranged from $1.20 to $9.00 for the same number of capsules. Unless individuals had the time and persistence to go from store to store asking about prices, or could use the telephone, they had no way of knowing where to get the most for their money.

Virginia State Board of Pharmacy v. *Virginia Citizens Consumer Council,* 425 U.S. 748, 96 S.Ct. 1817, 48 L.Ed.2d 346, 1 Med.L.Rptr. 1930 (1976).

In its eight-to-one decision, the Court left no room for doubt about the status of advertising with respect to the First Amendment. It wrote:

> Here, in contrast [to the earlier cases], the question whether there is a First Amendment exception for "commercial speech" is squarely before us. Our pharmacist does not wish to editorialize on any subject, cultural, philosophical, or political. He does not wish to report any particularly newsworthy fact, or to make generalized observations even about commercial matters. The "idea" he wishes to communicate is simply this: "I will sell you the X prescription drug at the Y price." Our question, then, is whether this communication is wholly outside the protection of the First Amendment.

The answer was a resounding no. Justice Harry A. Blackmun, who wrote the decision, rationalized that in inflationary times, when prescription drug purchasers, many of them elderly pensioners, were being squeezed financially, price information is significant. Indeed, he wrote, the consumer's interest in prices "may be as keen, if not keener by far, than his or her interest in the day's most urgent political debate." Blackmun's opinion for the Court established the doctrine of commercial speech, holding that, as a minimum, the First Amendment protects the right to advertise any legal product or service.

Important questions remained unanswered. Chief Justice Warren E. Burger endorsed the Court's conclusion that pharmacies have a constitutional right to advertise the prices of prescription drugs. But he wrote separately to serve notice that he did not believe other professionals, especially lawyers and physicians, had a right to advertise. Justice Potter Stewart, also concurring in the result, wondered whether Blackmun had written so broadly as to nullify laws regulating deceptive advertising. Would the actual-malice rule born in *New York Times* permit advertisers to stretch the truth about their products? With the Court's ruling that price advertising for legal products and services is protected by the First Amendment, were state and local governments left without authority to regulate advertising? The answers to these questions are found in subsequent decisions of the Court.

Defining the Doctrine's Scope

For decades, lawyers and judges can move along serenely, unaware that a given area of law may offer legal or constitutional problems. All the questions seem to have been answered. Then, a court will be persuaded to accept and decide a case that challenges the comfortable assumptions of the status quo. The case will not quite square with precedents long taken for granted, and a bold court will strike out in a new direction. Soon, other courts will be persuaded to explore that new direction, leading to further expansion of the law. So it has been with commercial speech cases. A doctrine grudgingly recognized by the Supreme Court in the mid-1970s has expanded so rapidly that seldom since then has a Court term passed without producing one or more advertising cases. We will start by looking at the leading case defining the boundaries of the commercial speech doctrine and then see what has developed in three areas:

1. Advertising by professionals, particularly lawyers

2. The regulation of signs and billboards

3. The advertising of products that are themselves subject to regulation, notably cigarettes, alcoholic beverages, and gambling casinos

When Middle Eastern countries cut off oil exports to this country in 1973, New York State's Public Service Commission reacted by forbidding all advertising by electric companies that promotes the use of electricity. Its rationale was straightforward. Most of the electrical generating plants in the state burned fuel oil. If the companies sold less electricity, they would need less oil. Therefore, they should not be advertising to obtain more customers, or to urge their present customers to buy appliances that would use more electricity. The embargo was lifted in March 1974, but the New York advertising ban remained in effect.

The Central Hudson Gas & Electric Corporation, acting for itself and other New York State electric companies, asked a state court to

Central Hudson Gas & Electric Corp. **v.** *Public Service Commission,* **447 U.S. 557, 100 S.Ct. 2343, 65 L.Ed.2d 341, 6 Med.L.Rptr. 1497 (1980).**

end the ban. Looking at the Supreme Court's commercial speech cases, the utilities argued that the ban violated their First Amendment right to advertise. The state court disagreed, holding that there was a continuing need for oil conservation that was great enough to justify the restriction. When state appeals courts affirmed, Central Hudson carried its case to the Supreme Court, which reversed, with only one dissenting vote.

Justice Lewis F. Powell, Jr., writing for the Court, reviewed the commercial speech cases and found in them protection even for advertising that "communicates only an incomplete version of the relevant facts." The First Amendment, he said, "presumes that some accurate information is better than no information at all." Therefore, the state cannot prohibit all commercial speech, even though the Constitution gives it less protection than it does most other kinds of speech. The degree of protection for commercial speech, Powell wrote, "turns on the nature both of the expression and of the governmental interests served by the regulation." The Court has brought the First

Amendment into play to protect "the informational function of advertising." Thus, if a commercial message does "not accurately inform the public about lawful activity," it may even be suppressed, as in the *Pittsburgh Press* case.

If the commercial message does not mislead, and it concerns lawful activity, the government's power to regulate it is limited. Here, Powell outlined the points that must be taken into consideration in determining whether such regulation is proper:

> The State must assert a substantial interest to be achieved by restrictions on commercial speech. Moreover, the regulatory technique must be in proportion to that interest. The limitation on expression must be designed carefully to achieve the State's goal. Compliance with the requirement may be measured by two criteria. First, the restriction must directly advance the state interest involved; the regulation may not be sustained if it provides only ineffective or remote support for the government's purpose. Second, if the governmental interest could be served as well by a more limited restriction on commercial speech, the excessive restrictions cannot survive.

Powell wrote that the state cannot impose regulations that only indirectly advance its interests. Nor can it regulate commercial speech that poses no danger to a state interest. He concluded:

> In commercial speech cases, then, a four-part analysis has developed. At the outset, we must determine whether the expression is protected by the First Amendment. For commercial speech to come within that provision, it at least must concern lawful activity and not be misleading. Next, we ask whether the asserted governmental interest is substantial. If both inquiries yield positive answers, we must determine whether the regulation directly advances the governmental interest asserted, and whether it is not more extensive than is necessary to serve that interest.

Powell applied this four-step analysis to the New York commission's regulation and concluded that it violated the utility company's First Amendment rights. Clearly, Central Hudson's proposed advertising was not inaccurate, nor did it promote unlawful activity. But the utilities commission argued that Central Hudson, like all electric companies, was a monopoly. If people in its territory wanted electricity, they had to get it from Central Hudson. The New York courts had looked at that fact and concluded there was little point to advertising by electric companies. Therefore, such advertising was of little First Amendment value and must yield to a larger state interest in conservation.

Powell said that the lower courts had looked at the issue too narrowly. For some purposes, fuel oil and natural gas are in direct competition with electricity. And even in uses where there is no competition, advertising serves some purpose. The electric company may wish to offer new services or inform its customers of new terms of doing business. Further, it might wish to advertise new lines of appliances that use less energy than those now in use. Powell concluded that there are substantial reasons why electric companies should be permitted to advertise.

The state of New York had argued that it was serving two important interests by banning advertising: It was encouraging conservation of a scarce resource, and it was keeping rates lower than they otherwise would be. If the companies' advertising led to increased use of electricity, they would have to build new plants to meet peak demands. These building costs would be reflected in higher rates.

Powell conceded that both interests were substantial. But he dismissed the latter with a few sentences:

> The link between the advertising prohibition and Central Hudson's rate structure is, at most, tenuous. The impact of promotional advertising on the equity of [the company's] rates is highly speculative. . . . Such conditional and remote eventualities simply cannot justify silencing [its] promotional advertising.

He took the conservation argument more seriously, noting a direct link between promotional advertising and increased use of electricity. But it is well established, Powell said, that a restriction on speech cannot go beyond what is needed to protect a vital state interest. New York's ban was not limited to promotional advertising; it applied to all advertising by electric utilities. Thus, the ban swept too broadly and was in violation of the First Amendment. The utilities commission had not shown that it could not encourage conservation by a more limited restriction. Therefore, its broad ban on advertising must fall.

Powell made the four-part test look neater than it has proved to be. Even the first two parts of the test, which seem to be the most precise, have presented some problems. We can buy cornflakes, television sets, and clothing without breaking a law. These products and thousands of others can be, and are, advertised freely. But it is against the law to sell marijuana. Therefore, a publication that accepts an ad for "Acapulco gold," as some college newspapers have, is courting trouble. That much with respect to the first part of the test is reasonably simple. Beer, guns, and cigarettes also are legal products. However, all of them are subject to regulation by government. Further, all of them can be misused to break the law, and cigarettes have been held to be a major health hazard. Does the *Central Hudson* decision mean that advertising for such products can be regulated or even forbidden? Courts have differed in their answers to that question, depending on the product, but one subsequent Supreme Court decision seems to say that if the government can regulate a product or service, it can regulate the advertising for that product or service.

The second part of the test—whether an ad is deceptive—presents frequent problems. The Federal Trade Commission and other agencies at both the federal and state levels have procedures that are used to determine whether advertising has a capacity to mislead unwary consumers. If those procedures lead to the conclusion that an ad is deceptive, the ad may be banned, or the advertiser may be subject to other penalties.

Many problems in defining the scope of the doctrine have risen in connection with the last two prongs of the *Central Hudson* test. At what point does a state's interest in regulating advertising become substantial enough to justify a restriction on the advertiser's First Amendment right to promote a product or a service? Some people believe that the advertising of alcoholic beverages promotes overindulgence. Other people are offended by ads for condoms. Are such reactions enough to support laws that ban such advertising? If the state interest in forbidding or controlling advertising is great enough, how narrowly must the law be tailored to prevent it from harming other kinds of speech? These are questions on which courts have disagreed frequently.

Advertising by Professionals

In the *Virginia State Board of Pharmacy* case, then Chief Justice Burger agreed that it was proper for professional pharmacists to advertise the price of prescription drugs, but he said he did not think it proper for physicians and lawyers to advertise their services. At the time that he wrote, the codes of ethics of both professions condemned advertising as unprofessional. A listing by name in the yellow pages of the telephone directory was permitted, as was a discreet newspaper advertisement announcing the opening of an office or the formation of a partnership. Lawyers who were too overt in seeking clients ran a risk of being disciplined by their peers and could even be barred from their profession.

The old ways came under challenge in the 1960s with an explosive increase in the number of people applying for admission to law schools. The pressure led to increased enrollments and, inevitably, to an increase in the number of lawyers admitted to practice. In the resulting competitive atmosphere, the old ways of attracting clients no longer were good enough. John R. Bates and Van O'Steen, fledgling lawyers in Phoenix, Arizona, were among the first to challenge those methods. They did so by placing an ad in the *Arizona Republic* that went straight to the point. "DO YOU NEED A LAWYER?" it asked in big, bold type. In smaller type it proclaimed, "Legal Services at very reasonable fees." Under an illustration representing the scales of justice, the ad listed prices for half a dozen services, including uncontested divorces and bankruptcy. What the lawyers did flew in the face of the Model Code of Professional Responsibility of the American Bar Association and of the rules of court embedded in Arizona statutes. The president of the state bar himself filed charges alleging that Bates and O'Steen were soliciting clients in violation of the code of ethics. A hearing committee recommended that they be suspended from the practice of law for not fewer than six months. On appeal, the state supreme court reduced the penalty to censure. The lawyers took their case to the U.S. Supreme Court, which held that even censure was too much. Under the doctrine of commercial speech, the Court said, lawyers could advertise as long as they did not mislead the public about what they could do for their clients.

The decision struck at the foundations of the legal system by opening the way for radical changes in the way lawyers do business. For that reason, Justice Blackmun, who wrote for the Court, devoted a great many words to a discussion on the nature of the practice of law. What Blackmun's words boil down to is his conclusion that by remaining aloof from the marketplace, lawyers may have made themselves too remote and mysterious. Their clients tended to be corporations or persons of wealth who relied on their advice to keep out of trouble or to get them off the hook if worse came to worst. Not long before this decision was handed down, the Supreme Court had held that poor people accused of crime must have a lawyer at public expense. Congress also had established legal-aid societies to help the poor with civil court actions. But in Blackmun's view, the middle classes had hesitated to seek legal advice, perhaps out of ignorance as to what such advice could do for them, or out of fear that a lawyer might charge them more than they could afford. Blackmun reasoned that ads like the one run by Bates and O'Steen could help such

Bates v. *State Bar of Arizona*, 433 U.S. 350, 97 S.Ct. 2691, 53 L.Ed.2d 810, 2 Med.L.Rptr. 2097 (1977).

persons defend their legal rights when necessary. As it had in its earlier cases, the Court resorted to the rationale that whatever its commercial ends, the ad in question conveyed valuable information: "You, too, can afford a lawyer."

Blackmun also dealt with Stewart's reservation—in *Virginia State Board of Pharmacy*—that the doctrine of commercial speech might condone misleading advertising. He wrote:

> Advertising that is false, deceptive, or misleading of course is subject to restraint. . . . Since the advertiser knows his product and has a commercial interest in its dissemination, we have little worry that regulation to assure truthfulness will discourage protected speech. . . . And any concern that strict requirements for truthfulness will undesirably inhibit spontaneity seems inapplicable because commercial speech generally is calculated. Indeed, the public and private benefits from commercial speech derive from confidence in its accuracy and reliability. Thus, the leeway for untruthful or misleading expression that has been allowed in other contexts has little force in the commercial arena.

In other words, Blackmun was serving notice that there was no room in the doctrine of commercial speech for the *New York Times* rule. The First Amendment protection given to commercial advertising does not contain the "breathing space" for falsehood enjoyed by speech that comments on the activities of public officials and public figures.

At the time of the *Bates* decision, strict rules in effect in every state and in the federal courts prohibited lawyers from soliciting clients. But isn't advertising, even of the kind approved in *Bates,* a form of solicitation? How far can lawyers go in advertising their services without running afoul of the rules against solicitation? How far can they go without misleading prospective clients? To what extent can state bar associations or state courts regulate lawyer advertising without running afoul of the First Amendment?

These have proved to be vexing questions. Between 1978 and 1995, the Supreme Court decided eight cases in which it sought to define how far lawyers may go in advertising for clients.[6] The answer is, They can go pretty far, as anyone who watches television can testify. At this writing, the decisions seem to say that lawyers can solicit clients if they do so through the airwaves, in printed advertisements, or by letter, but they cannot do so in a face-to-face encounter.

It took less than a year for the first two post-*Bates* cases to reach the Supreme Court. One of them, *In re Primus,*[7] grew out of a letter from a lawyer, Edna Smith Primus, to a female Medicaid patient who had been sterilized without her consent. Primus, who was affiliated with the American Civil Liberties Union, spoke to a group of such patients and advised them that they had a right to sue. She then wrote a letter to one of the women, telling her that the ACLU would be willing to represent her without fee in a suit against the doctor who had performed the operation and the hospital that had permitted

---

6. In re Primus, 436 U.S. 412 (1978); Ohralik v. Ohio State Bar Association, 436 U.S. 447 (1978); In re R.M.J., 455 U.S. 191, 7 Med.L.Rptr. 2545 (1982); Zauderer v. Office of Disciplinary Counsel, 471 U.S. 626 (1985); Shapero v. Kentucky Bar Association, 486 U.S. 466 (1988); Oring v. State Bar of California, 489 U.S. 1092 (1989); Peel v. Attorney Registration and Disciplinary Commission of Illinois, 492 U.S. 917 (1990); Florida Bar v. Went For It Inc., 115 S.Ct. 2371, 132 L.Ed.2d 541, 23 Med.L.Rptr. 1801 (1995).

7. 436 U.S. 412, 98 S.Ct. 1893, 56 L.Ed.2d 417 (1978).

it. The state bar association found Primus guilty of unprofessional conduct in soliciting clients and reprimanded her. The Supreme Court held that the First Amendment protects what Primus had done. Her letter was not an in-person solicitation, and she would not profit from representing the woman. Justice Thurgood Marshall wrote separately to commend Primus. He said that she was acting "in accordance with the highest standards of the legal profession" by offering her services without charge to a woman who otherwise would have been unable to win redress against those who violated her rights.

In 1988 the U.S. Supreme Court held that any lawyer, even one not working on behalf of an important social cause, could write letters to potential clients without fear of being disciplined for improperly soliciting business. In *Shapero* v. *Kentucky Bar Association,*[8] the Court said that such letters could solicit specific individuals believed to be in need of legal services. At issue were letters that attorney Richard D. Shapero of Louisville had drafted for mailing to people whose home mortgages were being foreclosed.

This decision so broadened the field established by *In re Primus* that three justices protested. Sandra Day O'Connor, writing for Chief Justice William H. Rehnquist, Associate Justice Antonin Scalia, and herself, said that the decision could strip away the safeguards that make the practice of law a profession rather than a "trade or occupation like any other." As these justices saw it, there is little difference with respect to solicitation of clients between a personalized letter and a face-to-face encounter.

The majority, led by Justice William J. Brennan, Jr., held otherwise. Brennan said that there is no difference between a newspaper advertisement aimed at a specific group of potential clients and a letter sent to identified members of such a group. In either instance, the targets of the solicitations have the option of ignoring the appeal. In a portion of the decision in which he was joined by only three of his colleagues, Brennan wrote:

> The pitch or style of a letter's type and its inclusion of subjective predictions of client satisfaction might catch the recipient's attention more than would a bland statement of purely objective facts in small type. But a truthful and nondeceptive letter, no matter how big its type and how much it speculates can never 'shou[t] at the recipient' or 'gras[p] him by the lapels,' as can a lawyer engaging in face-to-face solicitation.

Justice O'Connor's misgivings about solicitation letters resurfaced in 1995, when the Court decided that letters seeking clients involved in accidents or disasters should not be mailed so quickly as to cause harm to victims who may be emotionally upset. The Court in *Florida Bar* v. *Went For It Inc.*[9] upheld a Florida rule requiring a thirty-day waiting period before lawyers could solicit victims of accidents and disasters. Justice O'Connor, writing for the majority, said that the bar's rule was reasonably well tailored to its goal of "eliminating targeted mailings whose type and timing are a source of distress to Floridians, distress that has caused many of them to lose respect for the legal profession."

Justice O'Connor's concern about damage caused by lawyers who contact emotionally vulnerable victims had its roots in a case decided on the same day as *In Re Primus*

---

8. 486 U.S. 466, 108 S.Ct. 1916, 100 L.Ed.2d 475 (1988).
9. 115 S.Ct. 2371, 132 L.Ed.2d 541, 23 Med.L.Rptr. 1801 (1995).

in 1978. In *Ohralik* v. *Ohio State Bar Association,*[10] the Court condemned in-person solicitation as a form of advertising by lawyers because, in the spirit of Justice Brennan's later rhetoric, it was advertising that grasped the lapels of victims and shouted in their faces. The Florida Bar in *Went For It* believed that an untimely letter addressed to an emotionally distraught accident victim was hardly different from a persuasive lawyer's visit to a hospital room, and that had been the situation in *Ohralik.*

When Albert Ohralik learned that a young woman with whom he was acquainted had been in an automobile accident, he telephoned her parents, learned she was in the hospital, and went to the hospital to see her. While he was there, he offered to represent the young woman on a contingency-fee basis. Learning that the woman had a friend who had been injured in the same accident, Ohralik called on her, too, and made a similar offer. The attorney tape-recorded both conversations and, when one of the women tried to dismiss him and accept an offer for settlement, used the recording as evidence in a suit for breach of contract. The state bar association charged Ohralik with unprofessional conduct. The Ohio Supreme Court held that Ohralik's direct solicitation of clients warranted an indefinite suspension of his right to practice law. The U.S. Supreme Court agreed.[11]

Most advertising efforts by lawyers are far less overreaching than in-person solicitation of accident victims. The advertising seen on television and in newspapers or magazines usually attempts merely to establish name recognition or tout available services. When that is the case, the Court, as the following cases illustrate, is highly protective of the free-speech interests of lawyer advertising.

In *In re R.M.J.,*[12] the Court struck down a Missouri Supreme Court rule that narrowly restricted the content of advertisements placed by attorneys. A lawyer was facing disbarment because his listing of practice areas did not use precisely the words prescribed by the rules. The intent of the Missouri courts in prescribing a list of words lawyers might use in indicating their preferred practice areas was to prevent deception. But a unanimous Supreme Court said that Missouri, to prevent possible deception, could not prevent lawyers from describing areas of specialty in their own terms. The Court said that the state's authority to regulate the content of an attorney's advertising is limited to actual instances of deception.

The Supreme Court, in a later content case, struck down an Ohio rule that forbade lawyers to use illustrations in their advertisements. Philip Q. Zauderer, a lawyer practicing in Columbus, had defied that rule by using a drawing of a Dalkon Shield, a birth control device, in a newspaper ad seeking clients who had suffered harm from its use. Large type immediately beneath the drawing asked, "DID YOU USE THIS IUD?" The text of the ad described the harm that some women said

Zauderer v. *Office of Disciplinary Counsel of Supreme Court of Ohio,* **471 U.S. 626, 105 S.Ct. 2265, 85 L.Ed.2d 652 (1985).**

---

10.   436 U.S. 447, 98 S.Ct. 1912, 56 L.Ed.2d 444 (1978).
11.   However, the Supreme Court took an entirely different position when the in-person solicitation was that of an accountant, rather than a lawyer. Finding a ban on in-person solicitation by accountants unconstitutional, the Court said, "Unlike a lawyer, a CPA is not a professional trained in the art of persuasion.' A CPA's training emphasizes independence and objectivity, not advocacy." Edenfield v. Fane, 113 S.Ct. 1792, 123 L.Ed.2d 543, 21 Med.L.Rptr. 1321 (1993).
12.   455 U.S. 191, 102 S.Ct. 929, 71 L.Ed.2d 64, 7 Med.L.Rptr. 2545 (1982).

they had suffered because of their use of the device. The ad concluded with Zauderer's offer to represent Dalkon shield clients on a contingency-fee basis—that is, for a percentage of such damages as a client might be awarded. The last sentence said, "If there is no recovery, no legal fees are owed by our clients."

The ad, placed in thirty-six newspapers, proved to be highly successful, drawing more than two hundred inquiries. Zauderer filed lawsuits on behalf of 106 of the women who wrote to him. The ad attracted the attention of the Office of Disciplinary Counsel, which filed a complaint against him. The Ohio Supreme Court found Zauderer in violation of its rules on advertising and subjected him to a public reprimand. On appeal, the U.S. Supreme Court held that all but the last sentence in the ad was protected by the First Amendment. The Court specifically struck down the part of the Ohio rules that forbade the use of illustrations. Writing for himself and five other Justices, Byron R. White said:

> The use of illustrations or pictures in advertisements serves important communicative functions: it attracts the attention of the audience to the advertiser's message, and it may also serve to impart information directly. Accordingly, commercial illustrations are entitled to the First Amendment protections afforded verbal commercial speech: restrictions on the use of visual media of expression in advertising must survive scrutiny under the *Central Hudson* test.

By that, White said he meant that the visual element in the ad must not be misleading. If illustrations or photographs used in advertising, including that by lawyers, are not misleading, they cannot be regulated unless the state can demonstrate some overriding interest in doing so. In this instance, there was no such interest.

However, the Court said that the last sentence in Zauderer's ad was misleading because it implied that clients would not have to pay him anything if he was unable to win a settlement or judgment for them. In reality, clients who retain lawyers on a contingency-fee basis may have to pay certain expenses incurred in the preparation of their case, and they may be responsible for court costs. The Court said that if the ad were to be completely honest, it should make clear the distinction between a lawyer's fees and costs, of which the latter usually are passed on to the client.

More recently, the Court held that three lines of type on an Illinois lawyer's letterhead did not deceive prospective clients.[13] Gary E. Peel, who practiced in Edwardsville, had tried to a verdict more than a hundred jury trials and had taken courses on trial advocacy. His letterhead included this information:

Certified Civil Trial Specialist
By the National Board of Trial Advocacy
Licensed: Illinois, Missouri, Arizona

On a complaint from the Illinois Attorney Registration and Disciplinary Committee, the state supreme court censured Peel, ruling that he was holding himself out to be a certified legal specialist in violation of a section of the Illinois Code of Professional Responsibility. The court said that the letterhead was misleading because Illinois had no official certification process for legal specialties. Further, the court said

---

13. Peel v. Attorney Registration and Disciplinary Commission of Illinois, 496 U.S. 91, 110 S.Ct. 2281, 110 L.Ed.2d 83 (1990).

that taken together, the three lines could lead the general public to believe that Peel had been licensed as a civil trial specialist in three states. By five to four, the U.S. Supreme Court overruled the Illinois court.

The Court said that the National Board of Trial Advocacy was established in 1977 to provide specialized training and certification for trial advocates, and that Chief Justice Burger had urged the creation of such an enterprise as early as 1973. The Board had set rigorous standards of experience and training. Certificates were issued for five-year periods and could not be renewed without additional training. The Court concluded that the certificate had meaning and that Peel was simply stating a fact in noting that he had been certified. The majority further held that the third line also stated a fact. Nor did the Court believe that people who are thinking of hiring a lawyer would be unable to distinguish between a certificate and a license. The letterhead's potential to mislead some consumers was not great enough to "satisfy the State's heavy burden of justifying a categorical prohibition against the dissemination of accurate factual information to the public."

The result was similar when another attorney, who also happened to be a certified-public accountant and a certified financial planner, used the designations CPA and CFP after her name on law firm stationery, on her business cards, and in her advertising.[14] This time however, it was not the bar, but the Florida Board of Accountancy, that complained. The Board argued that it was misleading for a lawyer to use such credentials to attract business to her law practice. A majority of the Court disagreed, saying that the designations were accurate and that there was no evidence that clients had been misled into thinking they meant something more than that she was a lawyer who also had been certified as a public accountant and a financial planner.

Regulation of Signs and Billboards

Shortly before the Supreme Court held that advertising by lawyers is protected by the First Amendment, the Court was asked to decide whether outdoor advertising enjoys First Amendment protection. The Court held, in *Linmark Associates* v. *Township of Willingboro,*[15] that it does, but the Court also held that signs can be regulated if government can demonstrate a sufficiently strong need to do so. In this instance, the government could not.

Willingboro, a New Jersey township, had forbidden the posting of "For Sale" or "Sold" signs in residential neighborhoods, in order to halt the flight of white homeowners from racially integrated neighborhoods. The Court ruled the law unconstitutional. White flight was not a sufficiently compelling reason to justify censorship. The Court noted that homeowners traditionally have used yard signs to tell others that their houses are for sale.[16] There are other ways of doing so, but all are more expensive and may not be as effective. If homeowners can be prevented from using the most direct

---

14. Ibanez v. Florida Department of Business and Professional Regulations, 114 S.Ct. 2084, 129 L.Ed.2d 118 (1994).
15. 433 U.S. 350, 97 S.Ct. 2691, 53 L.Ed.2d 810 (1977).
16. See also City of Ladue v. Gilleo, 114 S.Ct. 2038, 129 L.Ed.2d 36 (1994). Ordinance forbidding a homeowner from posting political signs on her property was found unconstitutional.

way to tell others that their house is for sale, Justice Marshall wrote, "then every locality in the country can suppress any facts that reflect poorly on the locality, so long
as a plausible claim can be made that disclosure would cause the recipients of the information to act 'irrationally.' "

That decision, inconsequential as it seemed at the time, was the first of a series of
important decisions in which the Supreme Court has sought to define how far communities can go to regulate or ban outdoor advertising.

The second case to reach the Court challenged an attempt by the City of San Diego
to ban billboards. A majority agreed that the at-
tempt violated the First Amendment, but no more
than three justices could agree on any one reason
why. All the justices agreed, however, that local
governments had the power to regulate or ban outdoor advertising if they could do it in an even-
handed way and offer a persuasive reason for the regulation.

*Metromedia, Inc. v. City of
San Diego,* **453 U.S. 490,
101 S.Ct. 2882, 69 L.Ed.2d
800 (1981).**

San Diego had enacted an ordinance banning most outdoor advertising, in an effort
to "to eliminate hazards to pedestrians and motorists brought about by distracting sign
displays" and "to preserve and improve the appearance of the city." The California
Supreme Court had held that those interests were important and that the city's decision to ban billboards was a reasonable means of addressing them. Three justices of
the U.S. Supreme Court said that they could have agreed with that conclusion if the
ordinance actually had addressed those important interests. But the ordinance allowed
some signs to continue to clutter and distract, while banning other signs, regardless of
whether they cluttered or distracted. For example, under the terms of the ordinance,
all outdoor advertising was banned unless the signs were erected on a business's own
premises or unless the signs were historical plaques, religious symbols, informational
signs at bus stops, or signs that displayed time, temperature, or news. As the plurality
saw it, if safety and aesthetic concerns were really serious problems, the ordinance
should have banned all signs, regardless of their content or business location. Instead,
the ordinance had banned unsightly signs that the city officials did not like, while continuing to allow unsightly signs that they apparently did like. Because the ordinance
turned on the content of the signs rather than on the effects that the signs had on motorists or on the environment, it ran afoul of the First Amendment.

Joining those three to form a majority, two justices, Brennan and Blackmun, agreed
that San Diego had the power to ban signs and billboards to promote traffic safety or
the city's aesthetic values, but they did not think that the city had proved that "billboards actually impair traffic safety" or that there was a substantial interest in promoting aesthetics in the city's commercial and industrial areas.

Three justices, on the other hand, would have upheld the ordinance regulating billboards as a reasonable way to try to improve the quality of urban life. Chief Justice
Burger found the plurality's position a bizarre example of federal power meddling
with local authority. Justice John Paul Stevens was convinced the city had proved its
case that the signs were a safety hazard. Justice Rehnquist was satisfied that aesthetic
grounds alone justified the city's regulation of billboards.

Although divided over the outcome in *Metromedia,* the justices agreed that a
carefully written regulatory statute intended to address an important local problem

could be justified under certain circumstances. Not surprisingly, within a year of *Metromedia,* the justices found those circumstances in a Los Angeles ordinance that forbade the posting of political campaign signs on public property. The case began when Roland Vincent, a candidate for city council, sued the city because his campaign signs were removed from utility poles by city employees. He took his case to the Supreme Court, which held, in *Members of City Council* v. *Taxpayers for Vincent,*[17] that the city has a right to protect aesthetic values by prohibiting advertising signs on public property as long as the ban applies to all types of signs. Unlike the ordinance in *Metromedia,* which arguably discriminated on the basis of the content of the signs for reasons that seemed insufficient to a majority of justices, the ordinance in *Taxpayers for Vincent* applied to all signs posted on public property, regardless of content, in an effort to reduce visual clutter.[18]

Courts continue to look to *Metromedia* for guidance, despite the fragmented nature of the decision. Laws that regulate billboards and other signs are often upheld if the rationale is sufficiently convincing. Courts are willing to uphold restrictions that are based on aesthetic considerations. For example, the Supreme Court of Arkansas upheld ordinances regulating the size and placement of billboards, despite testimony that the rules would increase the costs to the advertisers by more than 50 percent.[19] Courts also are willing to regulate outdoor advertising on the basis of health and safety considerations. For example, the Fourth Circuit upheld two Baltimore zoning ordinances that prohibited stationary, outdoor advertisements for alcoholic beverages and cigarettes in certain parts of the city.[20] The court found that the ordinances were carefully drafted to advance the city's substantial interest in curbing underage drinking and smoking in areas where minors were likely to be constantly exposed to alcohol and tobacco advertising. The ordinances essentially prohibited outdoor advertising of tobacco and alcohol in Baltimore's residential neighborhoods.

Advertising of Regulated Products or Services

For various reasons, government has seen fit to regulate the sale of certain products and services, or even to prohibit their sale altogether. Alcoholic beverages are a conspicuous example. During the early twentieth century, enough people became alarmed by the excessive consumption of such beverages to force adoption of a constitutional amendment outlawing their manufacture or use.[21] The amendment was so commonly violated that it was repealed by another constitutional amendment.[22] However, that amendment reserved to each state the power to continue prohibition, as some did un-

---

17.   466 U.S. 789, 104 S.Ct. 2118, 80 L.Ed.2d 772 (1984).
18.   See also Whitton v. Gladstone, Missouri, 54 F.3d 1400, 23 Med.L.Rptr. 1910 (8th Cir. 1995). Ordinance regulating political campaign signs on private property not content neutral and therefore unconstitutional.
19.   Donrey Communications v. City of Fayetteville, 280 Ark. 408, 660 S.W.2d 900 (1983); cert. denied, 466 U.S. 959, 104 S.Ct. 2172, 80 L.Ed.2d 555 (1984).
20.   Anheuser-Busch Inc. v. Schmoke, 63 F.3d 1305, 23 Med.L.Rptr. 2357 (4th Cir. 1995); Penn Advertising of Baltimore v. Baltimore, 63 F.3d 1318, 23 Med.L.Rptr. 2367 (4th Cir. 1995).
21.   The Eighteenth Amendment, ratified in 1919.
22.   The Twenty-first Amendment, ratified in 1933.

til recent times, and to regulate the conditions under which beer, wine, and liquor can be sold. Because the right to regulate alcoholic beverages is grounded in the Constitution, courts have held that advertising for such beverages can be regulated more strictly than can other kinds of commercial speech. Other products and services that are considered harmful have not been the subject of a constitutional amendment but have been regulated nevertheless. These include tobacco products, guns, gambling casinos, and houses of prostitution.

A decade before the Court held that commercial advertising is protected by the First Amendment, the surgeon general of the United States concluded that cigarette smoking causes serious health problems. At that time, tobacco companies were major television advertisers, spending about $250 million a year on commercials. A young lawyer in New York City, John W. Banzhaf, reasoned that the surgeon general's ruling made cigarettes the subject of a public controversy, as indeed it did. Banzhaf's persistence in his belief led to a ruling by the Federal Communications Commission that the fairness doctrine, then in force, required broadcasters to balance cigarette advertising by carrying public service messages calling attention to the health hazard.[23] These messages led to a significant drop in cigarette sales. Two years later, when Congress adopted a law banning cigarette advertising on "any medium of electronic communication subject to the jurisdiction of the FCC," the tobacco companies did not oppose it.[24] Although the Supreme Court has not yet ruled on cigarette advertising, the Court has decided cases involving advertising for alcoholic beverages and gambling casinos.

With respect to the advertising of alcoholic beverages, courts, generally, have held that the Twenty-first Amendment sanctions strict controls both on the sale of alcoholic beverages and on advertising for them.[25] In a frequently cited case, *Queensgate Investment Co.* v. *Liquor Control Commission,*[26] the Ohio Supreme Court held that the Twenty-first Amendment and a state interest in minimizing the consumption of alcohol justified a regulation prohibiting off-premises advertising of the prices of alcoholic beverages. Thus, the amendment condones prior restraint, which the U.S. Supreme Court has condemned in many other circumstances.

However, when the state of Oklahoma attempted to forbid advertising of any alcoholic beverage stronger than 3.2 percent beer, it encountered problems. Newspapers and other print media in the state had to comply with the law. Broadcasting stations within the state were required to refuse beer and wine advertising from local outlets but carried network programming that did include such commercials. Broadcasters in adjoining states whose programs could be seen or heard in Oklahoma also showed such commercials. Newspapers and magazines that were published elsewhere and distributed within the state carried liquor advertising. Cable systems presented a particularly vexing problem. They had offices in the state but routinely retransmitted pro-

---

23. WCBS-TV, 8 F.C.C.2d 381 (1967); affirmed, Applicability of the Fairness Doctrine to Cigarette Advertising, 9 F.C.C.2d 921 (1967); sustained, Banzhaf v. Federal Communications Commission, 405 F.2d 1082, 1 Med.L.Rptr. 2037 (D.C. Cir. 1968).
24. Public Health Cigarette Smoking Act, 15 U.S.C. § 1335 (1969).
25. Liquormart Inc. v. Rhode Island, 39 F.3d 5, 22 Med.L.Rptr. 2409 (1st Cir. 1994); cert. granted, 115 S.Ct. 1821, 131 L.Ed.2d 743 (1995).
26. 69 Ohio St.2d 361, 433 N.E.2d 138; appeal dismissed, 459 U.S. 807, 103 S.Ct. 31, 74 L.Ed.2d 45 (1982).

grams, many of them containing beer and wine commercials, that originated in distant states. Further, the rules under which they operated required them to pass along distant programming in its entirety, including commercials. For a while, state authorities required over-the-air broadcasters to block out beer and wine commercials but made no attempt to police cable systems. When the state attorney general ruled that those systems, too, would have to comply with the law, broadcasters and cable operators combined to challenge the law in court.

A district court judge held that the law was unconstitutional, but on appeal the circuit court reversed.[27] Citing the Twenty-first Amendment and *Queensgate,* the circuit court said that the state's interest in discouraging consumption of alcoholic beverages was sufficient under the *Central Hudson* test to overcome any First Amendment values the advertising might have. On further appeal, the U.S. Supreme Court reversed with respect to cable systems, but did so without reaching the First Amendment issue.[28] The Court noted that cable systems are regulated under federal law. That law requires them to retransmit in their entirety all programs the systems choose to carry. The Court held, applying long-established constitutional principles, that a state cannot impose its will in an area of law preempted by the federal government.

A year later, Oklahoma broadcasters, joined by the state's newspapers, went to court again and succeeded in having the law ruled unconstitutional in its continued application to them.[29] The court said that, by then, the law had so many holes in it that the remaining prohibitions violated the equal protection clause of the Fourteenth Amendment. In reaching that conclusion, the court listed twenty-seven ways through which beer, wine, and liquor advertising reached Oklahoma residents. Therefore, the court said, it was unfair to continue to enforce the ban against only two kinds of media. At the same time, however, the court reiterated that the Tenth Circuit's holding with respect to alcoholic beverage advertising and the First Amendment is still valid. The clear inference is that a regulation applying to all media would be upheld. The Fifth Circuit took that position in upholding a Mississippi law that forbade liquor advertisements originating within the state.[30] That court rejected an argument that the law violated the equal protection clause.

The Supreme Court held in a widely disputed decision that advertising for a regulated service, in this instance casino gambling, can be prohibited in any medium under a relaxed application of the *Central Hudson* test. Despite predictions at the time that the decision would be used to justify attempts to ban advertising for any product considered harmful,[31] and particularly for cigarettes and chewing tobacco, no such legislation has been enacted.

---

27. Oklahoma Telecasters Association v. Crisp, 699 F.2d 490, 9 Med.L.Rptr. 1089 (10th Cir. 1983).
28. Capital Cities Cable, Inc. v. Crisp, 467 U.S. 691, 104 S.Ct. 2694, 81 L.Ed.2d 580, 10 Med.L.Rptr. 1873 (1984).
29. Oklahoma Broadcasters Association v. Crisp, 636 F.Supp. 978, 12 Med.L.Rptr. 2379 (W.D. Okla. 1986).
30. Dunagin v. City of Oxford, Miss., 718 F.2d 738, 10 Med.L.Rptr. 1001 (5th Cir. 1983); cert. denied, 467 U.S. 1259, 104 S.Ct. 3553, 82 L.Ed.2d 855 (1984).
31. Debra Gersh, "Cigarette Company Exec Sounds Off on Ad Censorship," *Editor & Publisher,* 26 October 1986, p. 45.

At issue was a Puerto Rico statute and regulations forbidding advertising of casino gambling aimed at residents of Puerto Rico. The law, as construed by Puerto Rico authorities, permitted advertising of casinos in media directed at tourists and in hotels associated with the casinos. Posadas, operator of a Holiday Inn in San Juan, had twice been fined for violating the law and asked Puerto Rico courts to declare it unconstitutional. The commonwealth's courts held that the law, as modified by the Tourism Company, was constitutional.

Posadas de Puerto Rico Associates v. Tourism Company of Puerto Rico, 478 U.S. 328, 106 S.Ct. 2968, 92 L.Ed.2d 266, 13 Med.L.Rptr. 1033 (1986).

The U.S. Supreme Court agreed, five to four. Justice Rehnquist, writing for the majority, applied the *Central Hudson* test and concluded:

1. The advertising was for a legal product and was neither deceptive nor misleading. Therefore, it qualified for First Amendment protection.

2. The state's purpose in enacting the law was to reduce the demand for casino gambling among residents of Puerto Rico. "We have no difficulty in concluding that the Puerto Rico Legislature's interest in the health, safety, and welfare of its citizens constitutes a 'substantial' governmental interest."

3. As modified by the Tourism Company, to permit advertising in the kinds of materials that resort hotels provide for their guests, the law swept no further than necessary to serve the government's interest.

The majority noted that the commonwealth's legislature could have banned casino gambling altogether. That it chose instead to discourage such gambling by Puerto Rico residents was within its powers. The Court noted that several other kinds of gambling also are legal in Puerto Rico and that the law made no attempt to limit advertising for them. Residents of Puerto Rico may bet on horse races and cockfights, wager on games of chance at fiestas, or play the commonwealth's lottery. Rehnquist distinguished these forms of gambling from casino gambling by noting the trial court's holding that the former "have been traditionally part of the Puerto Rican's roots." Casinos are a recent development aimed at tourists from the mainland United States. Rehnquist said that the legislature's concern that most Puerto Ricans would not be able to cope with the more sophisticated games of chance offered by casinos was sufficient justification to meet the state-interest requirement of *Central Hudson*.

The dissenters were troubled by the majority's willingness to tolerate a prior restraint on advertising for a legal activity and to condone seemingly arbitrary regulations that permit such advertising in one medium while banning it in others. Justice Brennan said that he did not believe Puerto Rico could "suppress truthful commercial speech in order to discourage its residents" from engaging in only one of the several forms of gambling available to them. Justice Stevens also was struck by the inconsistencies implicit in the law. He wrote:

Unless the Court is prepared to uphold an Illinois regulation of speech that subjects *The New York Times* to one standard and *The Chicago Tribune* to another, I do not understand why it is willing to uphold a Puerto Rico regulation that applies one standard to *The New York Times* and another to the *San Juan Star.*

So far, there is little to indicate that the decision in *Posadas* did more than reinforce the principles embodied in the *Central Hudson* test, even though it applied them less strictly than it has in cases involving advertising for products or services that are not subject to regulation. In other cases, the Court has held that advertising can be regulated and even prohibited if the state interest justifying such restrictions is strong enough and the regulation does not sweep more broadly than necessary to achieve its purpose. The corollary that had begun to emerge even before *Posadas* is that an interest sufficient to support regulation of a product or service probably is sufficient to justify regulation of the advertising for it. The Court had held earlier, in *Village of Hoffman Estates* v. *Flipside, Hoffman Estates,*[32] that communities can regulate "head shops" and the advertising associated with them in order to discourage use of illegal drugs. In that instance, the Court said that authorities could look to the nature of advertising messages and even to the editorial content of publications offered for sale as guides to the purposes for which certain items were being sold. Justice Marshall, writing for the Court, pointedly noted that speech that promotes an illegal purpose may be regulated or banned entirely. In *Posadas,* the Court seemed to stretch that principle considerably to reach the advertising of an activity that had not been made illegal, but that could have been made so.

The stretch was so considerable, in fact, that by the mid-1990s the Court began to back away from it. In a footnote to a Supreme Court opinion invalidating a federal statute that forbade brewers from disclosing the alcohol content of their beers,[33] Justice Clarence Thomas, who wrote the majority opinion, flatly dismissed as unnecessary the Court's holding in *Posadas* that Puerto Rico "could ban promotional advertising of casino gambling because it could have prohibited gambling altogether." Justice Thomas explained that the Court in *Posadas* reached this argument only after it had already found that Puerto Rico's casino advertising ban had survived the *Central Hudson* test. In other words, the power to ban a harmful activity does not include the power to ignore entirely the principles set forth in *Central Hudson.*

The analysis in *Central Hudson* focused on the care in which government regulations attempted to control commercial speech. It is not surprising, therefore, that after *Central Hudson,* the Court struck down a law carried over from more prudish times. In 1983 the Court recognized reality by holding in *Bolger* v. *Youngs Drug Products Corp.*[34] that a federal law forbidding the mailing of condom advertising violated the First Amendment doctrine of commercial speech. Postal authorities argued that some persons might be offended if they opened their mail and found an advertisement for birth control devices. Justice Marshall responded by saying that if so, they could close their eyes and drop the ad in the wastebasket.

A common thread runs through these commercial speech cases: If a product or service causes substantial governmental concern about the harm it may cause, the adver-

---

32. 455 U.S. 489, 102 S.Ct. 1186, 71 L.Ed.2d 362 (1982).
33. Rubin v. Coors Brewing Co., 115 S.Ct. 1585, 131 L.Ed.2d 532, 23 Med.L.Rptr. 1545 (1994).
34. 463 U.S. 60, 103 S.Ct. 2875, 77 L.Ed.2d 469 (1983).

tising for it can be regulated or prohibited if the restriction is carefully designed to relieve that concern effectively and in a manner that minimizes any burden on free speech. With respect to cigarettes, the long-standing prohibition against radio and television commercials has been limited to media that are themselves subject to federal regulation as licensees. With respect to alcoholic beverages, the power to regulate advertising has been reinforced by the Twenty-first Amendment, but that alone is not sufficient to justify all restrictions on alcohol advertising. For the most part, the advertising of regulated services and products, even gambling, alcohol, tobacco, firearms, and prostitution, where it is legal, are governed by the principles announced in *Central Hudson.*

Advertisements That May Lead to Harm

Sometimes death or injury can be traced to an advertisement. For example, a teen-age girl suffered toxic shock syndrome from using Playtex Tampons advertised in *Seventeen Magazine,*[35] a man was injured by exploding fireworks advertised in *Popular Mechanics,*[36] and a twelve-year-old boy was killed by a rifle advertised in *Boys Life.*[37] In all three cases, plaintiffs sued the magazine because they believed that the magazine had a duty to investigate the safety of the product or at least warn consumers of the potential dangers. In each case, the courts recognized no such duty, unless the magazine took it upon itself to guarantee, warrant, or endorse the products.

However, publishers may be held accountable for harm that they know is likely to be caused by advertising. For example, when, *Soldier of Fortune* magazine published an ad for a mercenary and subsequently someone was murdered, the question for the court was not whether there was a duty to investigate the ad but whether the magazine had a duty to avoid a foreseeable harm.

Soldier of Fortune published this personal ad for John Wayne Hearn in its September, October, and November 1984 issues:

EX-MARINES—67–69 'Nam vets—ex-DI—weapons specialist—jungle warfare, pilot, M.E., high risk assignments U.S. or overseas. (404) 991-2684.[38]

The service offered turned out to be murder. The mother and teenage son of the victim sued the magazine, alleging that its editors should have known that an ad offering a "weapons specialist" seeking "high risk assignments" was likely to lead to harm. In response to the ad, Robert Black of Bryan, Texas, had offered Hearn $10,000 to kill his wife, Sandra Black, which Hearn did. A federal court jury in Texas awarded damages of $9.4 million. The judge said that the magazine had been negligent in accepting an advertisement that implied an offer to commit a crime.

---

35.   Walters v. Seventeen Magazine, 195 Cal.App.3d 1119, 241 Cal.Rptr. 101 (1987).
36.   Yuhas v. Mudge, 129 N.J.Super. 207, 322 A.2d 824 (1974).
37.   Way v. Boy Scouts of America, 856 S.W.2d 230, 21 Med.L.Rptr. 1684 (Tex.Ct.App. 1993).
38.   Eimann v. Soldier of Fortune Magazine, 680 F.Supp. 863, 15 Med.L.Rptr. 1026 (S.D.Tex. 1988). DI means Drill Instructor, the title of a military combat teacher; M.E. means multiple-engine aircraft.

Robert K. Brown, the publisher of *Soldier of Fortune,* holds a rocket casing at the magazine's headquarters in Boulder, Colorado. Brown packages male bravado and conservative politics in a manner that successfully attracts more than 100,000 readers a month. The magazine lost a battle against charges that a contract killer was hired through a classified ad in the magazine. Damages, originally set at nearly $14 million, were eventually reduced to $200,000. *(Michael Lewis/NYT Pictures)*

However, on appeal, the U.S. Court of Appeals for the Fifth Circuit reversed.[39] The court said that the news media have a duty to use "reasonable care" in screening ads for possible harm. In this instance, the court said, *Soldier of Fortune* had met that standard because the wording of the ad was too ambiguous to be read as a solicitation for criminal employment.

In 1985 and 1986 *Soldier of Fortune* published this personal ad for Richard Savage in its June through March issues:

GUN FOR HIRE: 37 year old professional mercenary desires jobs. Vietnam Veteran. Discrete [sic] and very private. Body guard, courier, and other special skills. All jobs considered. Phone (615) 436-9785 (days) or (615) 436-4335 (nights).[40]

---

39.   880 F.2d 830, 16 Med.L.Rptr. 2148 (5th Cir. 1989); cert. denied, 493 U.S. 1024, 110 S.Ct. 729, 107 L.Ed.2d 748 (1990).

40.   Braun v. Soldier of Fortune Magazine, 968 F.2d 1110, 20 Med.L.Rptr. 1777 (11th Cir. 1992); cert. denied, 113 S.Ct. 1028, 122 L.Ed.2d 173 (1993).

This time the magazine was sued by the surviving children of Atlanta businessman Richard Braun. A federal district court in Georgia awarded damages of $4.3 million, and the Court of Appeals for the Eleventh Circuit affirmed the judgment.[41]

Bruce Gastwirth, an Atlanta businessman, read the ad in *Soldier of Fortune* and hired Richard Savage to kill his partner. In affirming the award, the circuit court held that a publisher can be held liable for advertisements that contain "clearly identifiable unreasonable risks" and that this one did. When the Supreme Court refused to review the decision, the magazine agreed to settle with the plaintiffs. The magazine's attorney said that the alternative was to go out of business.[42]

Taken together, these decisions say that publishers have a duty at least to screen advertisements, using reasonable care to eliminate those that seem to present "unreasonable risks" of harm because of the nature of the offer. Because the ads at issue in the *Soldier of Fortune* cases were almost identical in their thrust, the distinction between a reasonable and an unreasonable risk becomes a jury question subject to review by an appellate court.

THE REGULATION OF ADVERTISING

The Federal Trade Commission

When the Federal Trade Commission (FTC) was established in 1914, its mission was to protect business firms from each other. It did so, in part, by seeking to stop deceptive advertising, which was held to give the offending firm an unfair advantage over its more honest competitors. This focus on unfair competition was reinforced by the Supreme Court when it held in *Federal Trade Commission* v. *Raladam*[43] that the law that created the commission did not give it the authority to act to protect consumers. Not until 1938 was the law changed to permit the FTC to act to protect consumers from deceptive advertising.

Even with that change, the FTC was destined to labor in obscurity for more than thirty years. The FTC was limited on one side by anemic budgets and on the other by news media that usually ignored its work. Its occasional findings that certain advertisements were deceptive and would have to be withdrawn or changed went largely unreported, except in a few consumer-oriented magazines of limited circulation.

That began to change in the 1960s when the same ferment that produced the civil rights and anti-Vietnam war movements also produced a consumer movement. Inflation, which became an uncomfortable factor of American life in the late 1960s, made everyone more conscious of value. Also during this time, authority generally was being questioned. Young people particularly were asking why those who were in charge of business firms and other institutions could not do things right. The media, especially television, contributed to the questioning mood. Most people took for granted a

---

41.   Ibid.
42.   "Military Magazine Gets Jury Judgment Reduced," *Wall Street Journal,* 1 March 1993; James Brooke, "For Soldier of Fortune, Bosnia Is Latest Front," *New York Times,* 12 December 1995, p. C5.
43.   283 U.S. 643, 51 S.Ct. 587, 75 L.Ed. 1324 (1931).

certain amount of puffery in print ads. Even children could see that sometimes there was a considerable difference between the way a product performed in a television commercial and the way it performed in actual use.

By 1969, under prodding from a special committee of the American Bar Association, both the president and Congress decided it was time to give the FTC the means to crack down on deceptive advertising. Thus began, in the early 1970s, a decade of what one observer called "trench warfare" between the FTC and the advertising business.[44] Toward the end of that period, the agency's own chairman said that it operated under such broad authority that "virtually any ad can be found to be deceptive."[45]

A look at the FTC's rulings in the early 1980s might lead one to that conclusion. A sampling includes the following:

— Kroger Co.'s "price patrol" advertising, featuring the results of comparison shopping, was held deceptive because it was not based on a broad enough sampling.[46]

— Sterling Drug Co. ads for Bayer, Bayer Children's Aspirin, Cope, Vanquish, and Midol were found to promise more than they could deliver in the way of headache and tension relief.[47]

— Standard Brands agreed to stop advertising that "every 15 seconds, a doctor recommends Fleischmann's" margarine. It could not produce valid survey results supporting the claim.[48]

— Control Data Corporation ads for its computer programming courses were found to be misleading. The ads had said that a college education is not an advantage in getting a job in the computer field.[49]

— Mobil Corporation agreed to warn users of its Mobil 1 oil, touted as reducing oil consumption up to 25 percent, that it might actually increase oil usage in some kinds of cars.[50]

These instances could be multiplied many times. Other targets of FTC deceptive advertising rulings during the decade included AMF bicycles and tricycles, Litton microwave ovens, Sears appliances, Bristol-Myers pain relievers, Sanka, Fresh Horizons, Wonder and Profile breads, Geritol tonic, Warner-Lambert's Listerine, STP oil

44. Bruce Fohr, "War: FTC v. Advertisers," Freedom of Information Center Report No. 535, School of Journalism, University of Missouri at Columbia, June 1976.
45. "New Chief of FTC Urges Congress to Limit Commission's Authority to Challenge Ads," *Wall Street Journal,* 19 March 1982.
46. "FTC Says Kroger's Ads Were Deceptive: Company Comparing Food Prices to Competitors'," *Wall Street Journal,* 1 October 1981.
47. "Sterling Drug, Inc., Gets Big Headache from an FTC Judge," *Wall Street Journal,* 11 February 1981.
48. Margaret Gerrard Warner, "Standard Brands Settles FTC Charges over Margarine Ads," *Wall Street Journal,* 7 January 1981.
49. "Control Data Settles with FTC on Claims for Computer Courses," *Wall Street Journal,* 9 October 1980.
50. "Mobil Agrees to Warn Consumers on Results of Synthetic Motor Oil," *Wall Street Journal,* 19 September 1980.

treatment, and the most common acne remedies. As the list suggests, the FTC managed to step on some very important toes in the business world.

It would be misleading, however, to suggest that the FTC was working wonders in that era. Its budget had been increased, but it was still minute in comparison with expenditures on advertising. It was receiving a great deal of attention in newspapers, many of which routinely covered FTC actions. But in many of the instances mentioned here, the advertising campaigns held to be deceptive had been discontinued months or even years before the finding was issued. Under its administrative procedures, the commission was always operating after the fact. It could do nothing until an allegedly deceptive advertising campaign was under way and had come to its attention. The FTC's investigation, and the hearings designed to meet the need for due process, usually took months to complete. Meanwhile, the advertisements in question would continue in use either until the campaign ran to its scheduled end or until just before an adverse commission ruling. The Kroger price patrol campaign, for instance, ended two years before the FTC held it to be deceptive. One of the concerns of the revitalized commission was to find procedures that would either forestall deception or permit it to be attacked and ended at an early stage.

Deceptive Advertising

Any action by the Federal Trade Commission begins with the question, Does the challenged advertisement have a capacity to deceive? If the commission's staff concludes that it does, a chain of procedures designed to end the problem is set in motion. The commission used varying standards to determine an ad's capacity to deceive consumers before settling on a policy statement adopted in 1983:

> The Commission will find an act or practice deceptive if there is a misrepresentation, omission or other practice, that misleads the consumer acting reasonably in the circumstances, to the consumer's detriment.[51]

This standard is known as the "reasonable person" test. Such persons are assumed to know enough about the ways of advertisers to tolerate a bit of puffery, as long as the claims are not demonstrably false.[52]

The law under which the FTC operates is written so as to give the staff considerable leeway in determining what might be deceptive. When the staff decides to act on a complaint, it looks not merely at the words of the ad, but at the overall impression it conveys. The basic test is the capacity, or tendency, to deceive. There need be no proof that the ad has deceived anyone. The FTC staff is not required to survey consumers, either for evidence of deception or to determine how the ordinary person perceives the ad. Thus, the staff has the initial authority to decide that an ad is deceptive. The law assumes that staff members are experts in the field, and their findings are to be given great weight.[53]

---

51. CCH Trade Regulation Reports ¶ 50, 455, p. 56,079.
52. Kircher, 63 F.T.C. 1282 (1963).
53. This paragraph and the next are based on 55 Am.Jur.2d § 740, pp. 51–53.

An advertisement can be literally true and still be considered misleading. Truth can be used, for instance, to create a misleading impression, to promise more than the product will deliver. If the ad conveys a misleading innuendo, it is in trouble. If a statement can be read two ways, one perfectly proper but the other misleading, the ad is to be judged by the latter interpretation. Finally, it makes no difference what the advertiser intended. Intent is not a factor in determining whether deception is present. The test is of the ad, and the meaning found in it by the staff of the FTC.

The catalogue of deceptive advertising listed in legal reference works such as *American Jurisprudence* and *Corpus Juris Secundum* is long and interesting.[54] Courts have held that widely advertised "free gifts" have costly hidden strings attached, that a product advertised at a ridiculously low price is bait designed to lure customers into the store so that salespersons can try to switch them to a higher-priced model, and that encyclopedia salespersons should not pose as pollsters. The decisions show that some "diet breads" have fewer calories per slice, not because of their ingredients, but because the slices are thinner than with regular bread. Courts also have held that despite advertising claims, no golf club in itself will convert a duffer into a low-handicap golfer; that "shockproof, waterproof" watches should not be worn in a shower (to say nothing of a snorkeling expedition); and that some "Havana" cigars were made in Pennsylvania after Fidel Castro came to power in Cuba. There is much, much more.

This is not to say that all advertising is deceptive. The great bulk of it is not. Advertising and public relations agencies subscribe to codes of ethics and usually follow them. Newspapers, magazines, broadcasting stations, and television networks have codes of acceptance designed to turn away fraudulent or misleading advertising. The problems occur at the fringes where sharp operators are to be found in any business, and in a genuine difference of opinion over the meaning of "deception" and as to whether a given ad has a capacity to deceive. The FTC takes a literal view of those terms. If a product is advertised as capable of removing "even the most stubborn sink stains with a single application," then it must do so, or the ad is subject to being ruled deceptive. But the FTC has been unwilling to find deception in ads that portray a mouthwash's ability to combat bad breath as the key to romance, even though most users will not be kissed by the next attractive man or woman they meet. Even in its most active period, the commission rejected suggestions that psychological manipulation of people's anxieties and desires might be a form of deceptive advertising. And in light of the First Amendment decisions discussed earlier in this book, the FTC clearly has no authority over political advertising, no matter how distorted or deceptive it may be.

Even within the rather narrow range in which the FTC operates, its authority to rule ads deceptive is limited by several safeguards. Staff findings are subject to review by administrative law judges, who, in turn, are subject to review by the commission itself. Beyond that, an advertiser who is displeased by the commission's verdict can go to the U.S. Court of Appeals for further review.

---

54.   55 Am.Jur.2d §§ 750–776, pp. 56–75; 87 C.J.S. §§ 92–120, pp. 325–405.

The FTC and Deceptive Advertising

The Federal Trade Commission is made up of five members, appointed by the president and subject to confirmation by the Senate, for seven-year terms. No more than three can be members of the same political party. The president designates one of the members to serve as chairperson. Although the term of each member spans almost two presidential terms, each president in recent times has been able to appoint enough members to have an influence on the commission's approach to its duties.

The FTC has concerns in two major areas. Its Bureau of Competition is concerned with antitrust law violations and with restraint of trade. The Bureau of Consumer Protection is concerned with deceptive advertising and unfair trade practices. Therefore, the commission is able to devote only a little more than half of its budget to deceptive advertising. Thus, staff and budget limitations require the agency to act largely in response to complaints.

If the staff decides that a complaint is worth investigation, it notifies the advertiser. At that point, the commission may be willing to settle for a *letter of compliance,* which is simply a written promise that the advertiser will change its ads to remove the alleged deception. The writing of such a letter does not involve an admission of deception on the part of the advertiser.

If the advertiser decides to contest the action, it is entitled to a hearing before an administrative law judge. The procedure is informal. The judge's conclusions are drafted as a *consent agreement,* outlining what the advertiser must do, if anything, to comply with the law. If the advertiser is willing to accept the terms of the agreement, the matter is ended. Again, acceptance of a consent agreement does not involve a confession of wrongdoing. It can mean no more than an unwillingness to go to the expense of further litigation. Or it can mean that the campaign in question has ended.

For practical reasons, advertisers and the FTC try to avoid going beyond the level of consent agreement. For an advertiser, further attempts at vindication not only become expensive but can result in protracted unfavorable publicity. For the government, the prospect of a court action can raise its level of proof from showing a capacity to deceive to showing that the advertisement at issue actually has deceived consumers. Circuit courts have varied on this point.[55] Whatever the reasons, however, about three-quarters of the actions begun by the FTC do not go beyond the level of consent agreement.

Advertisers who elect to proceed beyond the consent agreement begin to risk penalties. In the next step up the enforcement ladder, the commission may issue a *cease and desist order.* This is precisely what the name implies. The advertiser who gets such an order has only two courses open: immediate compliance or an appeal to the U.S. Court of Appeals. Failure either to comply or to appeal can lead to an injunction and fines.

Working within this framework, the FTC has relied on an early decision of the Supreme Court[56] to devise a wide variety of remedies designed to cope with deceptive

---

55. National Commission on Egg Nutrition v. Federal Trade Commission, 517 F.2d 485 (7th Cir. 1975); Federal Trade Commission v. Simeon Management Corp., 391 F.Supp. 697 (D.Cal. 1975); affirmed, 532 F.2d 708 (9th Cir. 1976).
56. Jacob Siegel Co. v. Federal Trade Commission, 327 U.S. 374, 66 S.Ct. 758, 90 L.Ed.2d 888 (1946).

advertising. Congress further strengthened its hand in 1975, at the height of the consumer movement, with passage of the Magnuson-Moss Warranty-Federal Trade Commission Improvement Act.[57] Some of its remedies are examined in the sections that follow.

Broadened Cease and Desist Orders

The traditional order merely forbade repetition of a specific deception by a single advertiser for a single product. As a result of the Supreme Court's decision in *Federal Trade Commission* v. *Colgate Palmolive Co.*,[58] the FTC has been able to issue cease and desist orders covering a specific deceptive practice, but applying to all advertisers who might be tempted to use it. Such orders have had their greatest effect on television commercials. If a product is demonstrated, it must be shown as is and under conditions of normal usage. If there is a time lapse between the application of that "new, improved" detergent and the disappearance of the stubborn grime, the announcer must say so, or a graphic must indicate it.

Affirmative Disclosure

Sometimes a truth is not the whole truth. When the Campbell Soup Company advertised that its chicken noodle and "most of" its other soups were low in fat and cholesterol and thus were helpful in fighting heart disease,[59] the FTC asked for its proof. The agency's complaint also said the ad failed to disclose that "soups are high in sodium and that diets high in sodium may increase the risk of heart disease." That failure made the ad deceptive, the commission charged. John MacLeod, director of the Bureau of Consumer Protection, said, "This case stands for the proposition that when you advertise a particular quality or characteristic of your product, you should disclose facts that tend to undermine or refute the specific claim that you have made. The message here is that the commission takes health claims seriously and will police the advertising of these claims."

Disclosure has been compelled in other contexts. Many stores sell appliances on a deferred-payment schedule. However, most merchants do not carry their own accounts. They sell their installment contracts to banks or finance companies. Thus, a purchaser of a faulty product may try to force the seller to make repairs by withholding payments, only to find that this has no effect except to elicit a nasty letter from the holder of the note. Stores did not used to have to tell customers what they did with their notes, but the FTC now requires affirmative disclosure of the sale of installment contracts to financial institutions.[60]

---

57. 15 U.S.C. §§2301–2312, 2345–2358.
58. 380 U.S. 374. 85 S.Ct. 1035, 12 L.Ed.2d 904 (1965).
59. Alix M. Freedman, "FTC Alleges Campbell Ad Is Deceptive," *Wall Street Journal,* 27 January 1989.
60. See, for example, Seekonk Freezer Meats, Inc., 82 F.T.C. 1019 (1973).

Affirmative Acts

Sometimes the fault lies not in the advertising, but in the advertisers' willingness to do what they promised to do. In such instances, the FTC has ordered specific performances to carry out the terms of an ad. This remedy has been applied most commonly to promotional games and contests, including the multitude of major prize offers that are sent to millions of persons through the mails. The FTC concluded that such promotions were being abused. For instance, winning numbers might be distributed only in cities where the promoter was pressed hard by competitors. Or the list of winners might be posted in an inconvenient place, so that most prizes would not be claimed.

The FTC looked into one promotion that was conducted by McDonald's fast-food chain. Advertisements said that the chain would give away 15,610 prizes, worth $500,000. The FTC learned that only 227 prizes, worth about $13,000, were claimed by McDonald's customers.[61] However, a divided commission rejected the staff's conclusion that advertising for the sweepstakes was deceptive. The majority concluded that if one accepted the literal meaning of the ads, McDonald's had not promised to give away all the prizes.

However, the investigation of that and similar sweepstakes led to adoption of a Trade Regulation Rule for Games of Chance in the Food Retailing and Gasoline Industries.[62] This regulation requires that customers be notified of the exact number of prizes to be given away in each category and the approximate odds against winning. If the sweepstakes continues more than thirty days, participants must be told how many prizes remain. Winning tickets must be distributed solely by chance, and the list of winners must be made available.

In addition, as a result of a case involving the Reader's Digest sweepstakes, the FTC held that if advertising promises that all prizes will be awarded, drawings must be continued until they are.[63]

Corrective Advertising

During the FTC's most active years, a group of law students at George Washington University in Washington, D.C., came up with a brilliantly original remedy for deceptive advertising: Why not require advertisers to confess and correct their deceptions? The students were outraged at television commercials for a new line of Campbell's Soups—Chunky Soups, so thick with meat and vegetables that the solid ingredients stuck up through the liquid in the bowl. What the camera did not show was the layer of marbles on which the meat and vegetables rested. The FTC staff accused Campbell of misleading advertising.

Into the fray charged the law students, calling themselves Students Opposing Unfair Practices, or SOUP. Why, they argued at the hearing, should Campbell, or anyone else, be permitted to profit from the impression left by a misleading ad campaign? Why not require errant advertisers to erase the impression by confessing their sins in

---

61. McDonald's Corp., 78 F.T.C. 606 (1971).
62. 16 C.F.R. § 419, 17 October 1969.
63. Reader's Digest Association, 79 F.T.C. 696 (1971); modified, 83 F.T.C. 1356 (1974).

subsequent commercials? This would be a form of penance that would carry a sting likely to make other would-be-sinners mend their ways. The commission, by a three-to-two vote, rejected the need for corrective advertising in this instance, but a majority agreed that it was an idea worth looking into.[64] Chairman Caspar W. Weinberger wrote

> We have no doubt as to the Commission's power to require such affirmative disclosure when such disclosures are reasonably related to the deception found and are required in order to dissipate the effects of that deception. . . . All that is required is that there be a "reasonable relation to the unlawful acts found to exist."[65]

Very shortly, the FTC began to carry the idea into effect. Several companies were even willing to accept consent orders requiring them to run corrective advertising. One of the notable pioneers was ITT Continental Baking Company, bakers of Profile bread, which was widely touted in television commercials as an aid in weight reduction. Eat two slices, plain or toasted, before lunch and dinner, the announcer said, and you, too, can lose weight. The FTC staff held that the ads conveyed the misleading impression that Profile bread had fewer calories than other kinds of bread and had some special value in taking off weight. In reality, bread is bread, and all brands of a given kind of bread contain essentially the same number of calories per ounce. If Profile had any value in a weight-reducing program, it was because it was sliced thinner than other breads.

ITT Continental agreed to a consent order requiring it to spend not less than 25 percent of its advertising costs for a year on messages proclaiming, "Profile is not effective for weight reduction, contrary to possible interpretations of prior advertising."[66] The effect was sobering. Sales of Profile bread dropped 20 to 25 percent.[67] Such an effect was noted by other prospective targets for corrective advertising, among them the Warner-Lambert Company, makers of Listerine antiseptic mouthwash. Confronted with a corrective order, Warner-Lambert fought the FTC all the way to the Supreme Court and lost. The case was a straightforward test of the FTC's authority to regulate commercial speech.

Warner-Lambert Co. v. Federal Trade Commission, **562 F.2d 749, 2 Med.L.Rptr. 2303 (D.C. Cir. 1977).**

Listerine has been on the market since 1879, with a formula that remained unchanged for a hundred years. Starting in 1921, it had been advertised as beneficial in preventing colds and sore throats, and in alleviating their symptoms. It became one of the most widely sold mouthwashes. Several times, the FTC had studied Listerine's advertising claims and had taken no action.[68] But in 1972, the commission

---

64. Gerald J. Thain, "Corrective Advertising: Theory and Cases," *New York Law Forum,* Summer 1973, pp. 1–34.
65. Campbell Soup Co., 77 F.T.C. 664, at 668 (1970).
66. ITT Continental Baking Co., Inc., 79 F.T.C. 248 (1971).
67. John Holusha, "Baking Firm Beats False Ad Charge," *Louisville Courier-Journal,* 28 December 1972. The headline referred to a subsequent FTC staff finding that ITT Continental had misrepresented the nutritional qualities of Wonder Bread and Hostess Snack Cakes. This time, ITT fought it out and an administrative law judge found in its favor.
68. Listerine's advertising was reviewed by the FTC in 1932, 1940, 1951, 1958, and 1962. Warner-Lambert Co. v. Federal Trade Commission, 562 F.2d 749, at 763, n.70, 2 Med.L.Rptr. 2303, at 2313, n.70 (D.C. Cir. 1977).

began another study that led to a formal complaint. Warner-Lambert asked for a hearing, which lasted four months and produced four thousand pages of testimony. The administrative law judge upheld the complaint, as did the full commission in 1975.

The commission found that Listerine did indeed kill millions of bacteria in the mouth and throat, but it left many millions more. However, this result had no effect on colds, because colds are caused by viruses, which are immune to the ingredients in Listerine. The commission therefore ordered Warner-Lambert to cease and desist from all advertising that claimed or implied that its mouthwash would cure colds or sore throats, or help its users avoid either ailment. Further, the FTC ordered the company to include, in future advertising, a corrective sentence: "Contrary to prior advertising, Listerine will not help prevent colds or sore throats or lessen their severity." Warner-Lambert was to run the corrective sentence until it had spent on such advertising a sum equal to its average annual expenditures on Listerine advertising during the preceding ten years—$10 million.

Warner-Lambert appealed to the Court of Appeals for the District of Columbia Circuit, arguing, in part, that the First Amendment protected its claims for Listerine and that the penalty was excessive. The result was a nearly complete victory for the FTC. A divided court held that the commission had not exceeded its powers in ordering corrective advertising. Nor could it find any relief for Warner-Lambert in the First Amendment. In the commercial speech cases decided up to that time, the Supreme Court had said several times that false or misleading advertising does not merit First Amendment protection. Warner-Lambert tried to take its case to the Supreme Court, but was denied certiorari.[69]

Long before the decision was handed down, Warner-Lambert had shifted the thrust of its advertising campaign for Listerine. Listerine was now being touted as the perfect remedy for bad breath, because it kills the bacteria that produce unpleasant odors in the mouth. The corrective sentence was incorporated as part of this new approach.

Relying on the *Warner-Lambert* decision, the FTC ordered other firms to use corrective advertising. Among them were two marketers of products designed to treat acne. Both were ordered to stop advertising their products until they had agreed to run specific corrective advertising. Hayoun Cosmetique of New York City had been advertising a kit offering four of its products as a cure for acne. It was ordered to stop suggesting that the products would eliminate the blemishes associated with the teenage affliction. Nor could it advertise in any way unless for the next six months its advertising clearly proclaimed, "No product can cure acne."[70] AHC Pharmacal of Miami, marketer of AHC Gel and Dr. Fulton's Acne Control Regimen, was the target of an even more specific order. The FTC said that AHC could not advertise further until it had run ads in Sunday newspaper supplements in six cities proclaiming in forty-eight point type, "No product can cure acne." The prescribed type is two-thirds of an inch high.[71]

---

69. 435 U.S. 950, 98 S.Ct. 1575, 55 L.Ed.2d 800 (1978).
70. Hayoun Cosmetique, Inc., 95 F.T.C. 794 (1980).
71. AHC Pharmacal, Inc., 95 F.T.C. 528 (1980).

Substantiation of Advertising Claims

Advertisers who make performance claims for products must be prepared to back them up. Advertising of gasoline mileage claims for automobiles offers one example. Because mileage can vary greatly with the way a car is driven, automobile manufacturers lean heavily on the ratings that the federal government requires for all new cars. But because these figures are products of laboratory tests, the FTC requires that their use in advertising be qualified by the notice that actual mileage will depend on the individual driver, road conditions, and weather.

Advertisers who claim that their product tastes better than others must be able to support that claim with data collected from a representative sampling of consumers. The FTC also requires that other kinds of claims for product performance be backed by valid survey results. The commission has taken a dim view of surveys conducted exclusively among dealers for a product, or by the manufacturer of a product.

Trade Rules

All the remedies mentioned thus far share a problem: None can be imposed until a complaint has been made and an investigation conducted by the FTC staff. If the advertiser resists, there is further delay until a hearing can be scheduled and conducted by an administrative law officer. Further resistance can lead to a hearing before the full commission, and thereafter the case can move into the federal courts. In the Listerine case, the procedure took six years. Thus, all remedies, except for corrective advertising, amount to little more than locking the garage door after the car has not only been stolen, but has been stripped and the remains sent to the crusher. Many television advertising campaigns, for instance, run for no more than thirteen weeks.

For the past twenty-five years, the FTC has been adopting trade regulation rules (trade rules) with the idea that they can be used to bring quick action against errant advertisers. Doubts about the commission's authority to do this were resolved by Section 18 of the FTC Improvement Act of 1975. However, the history of trade rules has been uneven. The procedure is as follows:

The FTC staff tries to identify misleading practices on an industrywide basis. It then proposes a set of rules that are designed to cope with such practices. These are published in the *Federal Register* and distributed within the affected industry with a request for comment. A hearing is scheduled. When all sides have been heard, the proposed trade rules are put into final form. These, too, are published and distributed. From that point on, the FTC acts on the theory that all of those involved know what the rules are and should be expected to obey them. Thus, an infraction is considered willful. If an infraction occurs, the FTC has the power to move at once with a cease and desist order backed by the ability to impose an injunction or fines that can run up to $10,000 a day.

In some areas, trade rules have met with little objection. In others, they have been fought. The oil industry, for instance, fought a trade rule requiring the posting of octane ratings on gasoline pumps. It lost.[72] The clothing industry, on the

---

72. National Petroleum Refiners Association v. Federal Trade Commission, 482 F.2d 672 (D.C. Cir. 1973); cert. denied, 415 U.S. 951, 94 S.Ct. 1475, 39 L.Ed.2d 567 (1974).

other hand, accepted a rule that requires cleaning instruction labels to be placed in garments.[73]

When the FTC tried to establish trade rules for the advertising of over-the-counter drugs, it ran into a storm of protest that led it, six years later, to retreat from the field.[74] At one point, the agency proposed that drug advertisers be required to use approved medical terms. Thus, a cough remedy would have to be described as an "antitussive." A mint tablet designed to quell digestive gases would have to be described as an "antiflatulent." Ads no longer could offer "relief for that burning sensation due to hyperacidity," nor could they present a remedy for "that bloated feeling due to excess gas."[75] After years of argument, the FTC abandoned the proposed regulation, in part because of its patent absurdity, and in part because the drug industry and its advertising agencies resisted vigorously.

An attempt to write rules regulating nutritional claims for food came to the same end after another six-year effort.[76] The agency was able, however, to write rules for claims that a food is "natural." That term can be used only for foods that contain no artificial ingredients and that have been subjected to no processing other than what could be done in a home kitchen.[77]

During the 1980s, the deregulation of business by government, begun by President Carter, was carried forward by presidents Reagan and Bush. In keeping with the policy, the FTC showed little interest in pursuing claims of deceptive advertising. Work on trade rules stopped and, in one instance, was reversed. In 1988 the commission repealed a requirement, in effect since 1971, that supermarkets keep enough stock on hand to meet the demand for advertised items.[78] The commission concluded that shortages of advertised items no longer are much of a problem and that the rule served little purpose other than to increase food stores' costs. Under the new rule, supermarkets can offer rain checks or substitute items, which most do. Or, if the ad states that supplies are limited, an item may be advertised without an alternative being offered. When the rule was adopted, studies showed that as much as 10 percent of advertised items were not on the shelves.

As the 1990s began, the FTC was prodded into new efforts to head off deceptive advertising. Responding to petitions from eleven trade associations, the commission issued nonbinding guidelines, rather than trade rules, designed to prevent deceptive claims that products are environment friendly. The trade associations and the commission acted, in part, to supplant guidelines developed by the attorneys general of eleven states that define acceptable environmental marketing terms. Under the FTC guidelines, advertisers must offer credible scientific evidence to support claims that products are biodegradable or will not harm the Earth's atmosphere. The FTC followed up by filing seven complaints against environment-based claims in advertising.[79]

---

73. Care Labeling of Textile Wearing Apparel, 16 C.F.R. § 423, 3 July 1972.
74. "FTC Kills Proposal on Ads for Drugs Sold over Counter," *Wall Street Journal,* 12 February 1981.
75. Burt Schorr, "How the FTC Plans to Cure Synonymity (Or Is It Synonymy?)," *Wall Street Journal,* 13 February 1978.
76. "FTC to End Six-Year Bid to Write a Rule on Nutrition Claims in Food Industry," *Wall Street Journal,* 3 April 1980.
77. "U.S. Issues Rules for Advertising 'Natural' Foods, *New York Times,* 13 October 1980.
78. "FTC Votes to End Supermarkets Rule on Advertised Items," *Wall Street Journal,* 22 April 1988.
79. Jeanne Sadler, "FTC Issues a 'Green-Marketing' Guide to Help Prevent Deceptive-Ad Charges," *Wall Street Journal,* 29 July 1992.

Other Means of Coping with Deceptive Advertising ═══════

Federal Agencies Other than the FTC

Although the Federal Trade Commission has been the most visible and most active agency dealing with deceptive advertising, the FTC is not alone in the field. Other federal agencies have some control over certain kinds of advertising. Agencies involved in financing housing and enforcing civil rights have adopted guidelines for real estate advertising placed in newspapers[80] to prevent discrimination based on race, religion, color, sex, or national origin of the buyer or renter. A federal district court judge held that a New York City real estate firm violated the law by distributing brochures and placing apartment rental ads in the *New York Times* that used white models exclusively. The court ordered the firm to pay $30,000 in compensatory damages to the plaintiffs, who were represented by the NAACP Legal Defense Fund.[81]

The Securities and Exchange Commission imposes narrow limits for advertisements of securities, including automated messages that report yield data by telephone.[82] Such messages must comply with guidelines imposed earlier on print advertising for mutual funds. In general, the guidelines require that yield data be reported for specified periods ranging from thirty days to ten years, depending on the nature of the fund. The purpose is to prevent the reporting of a current rate of return that does not accurately reflect performance over time. The telephone rule does not apply to live conversations with brokers.

Also at the federal level, agencies regulate the labeling of food and drugs; of alcoholic beverages; and of potentially dangerous tools, machinery, and appliances. The Food and Drug Administration took unusual action in 1987 and 1988, issuing statements alleging that advertisements for a prescription antihistamine and for aspirin might be misleading. Normally, advertising for such products is policed by the FTC, not the FDA, which is concerned with product labels. The FDA said that it was moved to action because the ads might lead to misuse of the products.

In one instance, the FDA released a letter that it had sent to Sandoz Pharmaceuticals Corporation charging that full-page newspaper advertisements for its antihistamine, Tavist-1, then available only by prescription, were "false and misleading."[83] The ads, which appeared in major newspapers, had been cleared in advance by the FDA. An agency official said that its drug-advertising branch was not aware "that some statements in the ad had been rejected as unproven by the FDA's medical-reviewing division." At issue was a claim that the product was less likely to cause drowsiness than other prescription antihistamines.

In the second action, the FDA expressed concern over aspirin advertisements that called attention to a study indicating that daily doses of aspirin may help prevent heart

---

80. *Publication Guidelines for Compliance with Title VIII of the Civil Rights Act of 1968,* 37 Fed.Reg. 6700 (1 April 1972); 45 Fed.Reg. 57102 (22 September 1980).

81. "Real Estate Firm Can't Run Ads Using Only White Models," *Wall Street Journal,* 27 August 1992.

82. Michael Siconolfi, "SEC Restricts Phone Messages That Cite Yields," *Wall Street Journal,* 27 May 1988.

83. Michael Waldholz, "FDA Calls Some Newspaper Ad Claims for Sandoz Drug 'False and Misleading,'" *Wall Street Journal,* 26 October 1987.

attacks.[84] FDA officials said they feared that the ads might lead some persons to take too much aspirin and others, suffering from illnesses for which aspirin can be harmful, to take the drug. An FDA official noted that, normally, the FTC has jurisdiction over such advertising but that the FDA could take action against the aspirin ads because they suggest "an intended use for which adequate directions are not given on the product label." The FDA's inquiry led to an agreement with aspirin makers to exercise voluntary restraint with respect to advertising aspirin as an aid for preventing heart attacks until more data are available.

The Food and Drug Administration has issued rules designed to implement the Nutrition Labeling and Education Act[85] and has asked for comment on a series of proposed rules. The rules are intended to limit the health claims that may be printed on food labels. They include definitions of such terms as "fat free," "low fat," "reduced fat," and other terms based on consumer preoccupation with prepared foods that are "good for you." The rules also would permit processors to state that there is an association between calcium intake and osteoporosis and that diets low in fat may reduce the risk of some types of cancer. However, processors could not state that there is an association between fiber intake and a reduced risk of cancer or heart disease.[86]

State Agencies

In the 1980s the FTC's inaction led others to move into the breach. State attorneys general, coordinating their activities through their national association, moved against major advertisers whom they believed guilty of deceptive advertising. Their targets included airlines, car rental agencies, insurance companies, McDonald's, and Sears. The vigor of the campaigns led to a protest from an FTC commissioner, who accused the attorneys general of "misdirected regulatory zeal" and of moving into an area best left to federal regulators.[87]

Airline advertising, particularly of discount fares and frequent-flier programs, was the first major target of the attorneys general. More than forty states announced that they had adopted standards for such advertising. At the time, the Department of Transportation had fined several carriers for lapses in their dealings with passengers, and Congress was considering an airline consumer protection bill.[88] Nevertheless, the state attorneys general issued standards that included ten limitations on airline advertising. One such limitation required that restrictions on bargain fares be stated in type at least one-third the size of the largest type in the ad. Another, applied to television commercials, required that restrictions be described orally rather than being reduced to a printed message briefly flashed across the screen. The limitations imposed by the state officials were more restrictive than those imposed by federal agencies.

---

84. Ronald Alsop, "Aspirin Makers Face FDA Scrutiny for Heart-Attack Prevention Ads," *Wall Street Journal,* 1 February 1988.
85. P.L. 101-535.
86. 56 FR 60366-60880 (No. 229, 1991).
87. Andrea Rothman, "Attorneys General Draw Fire of FTC in Turf War on Ads," *Wall Street Journal,* 15 December 1988.
88. Jonathan Dahl, "States Agree to Crack Down on Airline Ads," *Wall Street Journal,* 14 December 1987.

The airlines complained that the restrictions discouraged their attempts to publicize price competition. They sued to prevent enforcement of the state guidelines and obtained a temporary injunction, later made permanent, from a federal court in Texas.[89] The Fifth Circuit Court of Appeals affirmed,[90] as did the U.S. Supreme Court, five to three.

The Court held that the Airline Deregulation Act of 1978 exempts airlines' advertising from control by any agency other than the federal government. Therefore, the state attorneys general lacked authority to enforce their guidelines. Justice Antonin Scalia, writing for the majority, held that, in writing the Airline Deregulation Act, Congress had used language that clearly expressed its intent to make the regulation of airline advertising the sole province of the federal government. The statute does not say that in so many words. However, Section 1305(a)(1) expressly preempts the states from "enact[ing] or enforc[ing] any law, regulation, standard, or other provision having the force and effect of law relating to rates, routes, or services of any air carrier." Scalia focused on the statute's use of the words "relating to." In his view, those words bring advertising within the reach of the act because advertising, especially for cut-rate fares, bears a close relation to the ability of an air carrier to fill its seats and thus ensure that it stays in business. Engaging in a detailed analysis of the restrictions on advertising sought to be enforced at the state level, Scalia concluded that they would either discourage the offering of cut-rate fares or make it more difficult for users to learn about them. Either alternative would have an influence on fares, thus violating the purpose of the Airline Deregulation Act.

Morales v. *Trans World Airlines, Inc.,* **504 U.S. 374, 112 S.Ct.2031, 119 L.Ed.2d 157 (1992).**

Justice John Paul Stevens, writing for the minority, disputed that conclusion. He said he could find no evidence in the legislative history of the act that Congress intended to preclude the states from enforcing laws that regulate deceptive advertising or other trade practices. Nor could he agree that state enforcement of the advertising guidelines would have an effect on rates.

Because the decision was narrowly based on the Court's interpretation of a statute applying specifically to airlines, it has no effect on efforts by state attorneys general to act against allegedly deceptive advertising by car rental agencies, insurance companies, fast-food outlets, merchandisers, and other businesses operating across state lines.

Therefore, the state restrictions imposed on insurance company advertisements, particularly those using celebrities in pitches directed at the elderly, remain valid.[91] Attorneys general in California and Washington took the lead, challenging television commercials that featured Tennessee Ernie Ford, Art Linkletter, Ed McMahon, Dick Van Dyke, and Lorne Greene. Some of the celebrities promoted low-cost life insurance for the elderly. Others were selling medical care and hospitalization insurance.

---

89. Trans World Airlines v. Mattox, 712 F.Supp. 99 (W.D.Tex. 1989).
90. Trans World Airlines v. Mattox, 897 F.2d 773 (5th Cir. 1990); 949 F.2d 141 (5th Cir. 1991).
91. Ken Wells, "Insurance Ads Starring Celebrities Are Target of Crackdown by States," *Wall Street Journal,* 5 May 1988; Paul M. Barrett, "Attorneys General Flex Their Muscles: State Officials Join Forces to Press Consumer and Antitrust Concerns," *Wall Street Journal,* 13 July 1988.

State insurance regulators said that they had received many complaints about the policies being offered. As a result of the challenges, some of the commercials were taken off the air by court order. Insurance companies modified or withdrew others.

In Pennsylvania, a pharmaceutical company agreed, under prodding from state officials, to end an advertising campaign that promoted the Ascriptin brand of aspirin as "beneficial in the prevention of first-time heart attacks."[92] New York State's attorney general won agreement from the Kellogg Company that it would stop implying that the B vitamins in its Rice Krispies give consumers added vigor and energy.[93] In New York City, an action charging Sears with misleading price-cutting advertising led to an agreement on the phrasing of future ads.[94]

Civil Actions Brought by Business Firms against Competitors

Business firms moved into the void left by FTC inaction by filing civil court actions against competitors. Plaintiffs have asked courts to order competitors to stop or modify allegedly deceptive advertising campaigns. Some also have sought damages. In two notable decisions, courts have upheld the complaints. One of the legal actions involved charges and countercharges between Johnson & Johnson, the maker of Tylenol, and American Home Products, the maker of Anacin-3 and Advil, all highly advertised over-the-counter pain relievers. A U.S. district court judge in New York ruled that both firms were making exaggerated advertising claims for their products.[95] He went so far as to suggest how Johnson & Johnson could advertise Tylenol without being misleading: "For mild to moderate pain, you can't buy a more effective pain reliever without a prescription." The court ordered both companies to refrain from further deceptive advertising, but awarded no damages. The ruling came after four years of litigation. At about the same time, another federal district court in New York City ruled that Warner-Lambert Company had made false and misleading advertising claims for its "new improved e.p.t. Plus" home pregnancy test kit.[96] The lawsuit was brought by Tambrands, Inc., maker of a competitive home testing kit. The court imposed a permanent injunction forbidding future claims that users of the kit can know "in as fast as ten minutes" whether they are pregnant. The judge said that the test requires at least thirty minutes to give accurate results for most women. Also forbidden were further claims that the kit provides a "one-step" test and that it is the fastest test. The judge also ordered Warner-Lambert to pay Tambrands' legal expenses.

The examples that we have summarized are only a sampling of the lawsuits and state actions taken against allegedly deceptive advertising. This section serves as a re-

---

92. "Aspirin Unit Agrees to Stop Using Ad on Heart Attacks," *Wall Street Journal,* 13 July 1988.
93. Alex Kotlowitz, "Kellogg Agrees It Won't Run Some Cereal Ads," *Wall Street Journal,* 29 August 1988.
94. Robert Johnson and John Koten, "Sears Has Everything, Including Messy Fight over Ads in New York," *Wall Street Journal,* 28 June 1988; Robert Johnson, "Sears Drops Suit, Agrees to Change Ads in New York," *Wall Street Journal,* 10 January 1989.
95. William Power, "A Judge Prescribes a Dose of Truth to Ease the Pain of Analgesic Ads," *Wall Street Journal,* 13 May 1987.
96. Tambrands, Inc. v. Warner-Lambert Co., 673 F.Supp. 1190 (S.D.N.Y. 1987).

minder that attempts to control the content of advertising come from many sources. In the 1970s, the most notable control came at the national level from the Federal Trade Commission. When that agency retreated from the field in keeping with the deregulation policies of the Carter, Reagan, and Bush administrations, state governments and civil actions moved in. Although business firms argued, in some instances, that their advertising was protected by the First Amendment, courts reminded them that the Supreme Court has held that deceptive advertising does not qualify for such protection. The challenge facing those who prepare advertising is to know what the limits on puffery are and to work within them.

ACCESS TO THE MEDIA

The Right to Refuse Commercial Advertising

The news media, with few exceptions, are supported by advertising. Therefore, in the normal course of events, it can be assumed that the purpose of the advertising department of a newspaper, magazine, or broadcasting station is to sell as much advertising as possible. Yet, sometimes management feels compelled to refuse an ad. Most broadcasting stations, for instance, will not accept advertising for hard liquor. Some newspapers will not print cigarette advertising. Others have rules against advertising that is used to attack another business or an individual, or advertising on topics considered too controversial.

As long as advertising was considered to be without First Amendment protection, there was little question about the right to refuse advertising. Publishers could point to Article I, Section 10, paragraph 1 of the Constitution which states, in part: "No State shall . . . pass any bill of attainder, ex post facto law, or law impairing the obligation of contracts."

Advertising is sold under contract. If a state cannot impair a contract already made, it certainly cannot force an unwilling party to enter into one. That limitation ended the matter as long as most towns of any size had competing newspapers. With the advent of one-newspaper towns in midcentury, efforts were begun to change the rule. The argument was advanced that the news media are like common carriers—a bus line, the telephone company, or a ferry. If a newspaper is the only carrier of advertising in town, then it ought to be required to accept an ad from anyone who can pay the established price. One Ohio court had accepted that reasoning as early as 1919, in *Uhlman* v. *Sherman,*[97] but no other court has done so.

The classic case in this area is *Shuck* v. *The Carroll Daily Herald,* decided by the Supreme Court of Iowa. In that instance, the newspaper's agent went so far as to accept money for an ad brought in by the owner of a dry-cleaning store. The publisher then decided not to publish the ad and returned the money. The dry cleaner, Shuck,

Shuck **v.** *The Carroll Daily Herald,* **247 N.W. 813 (Iowa 1933).**

---

97.   31 Ohio Dec. 54 (1919).

sued to force the publisher to run the ad. The trial court refused, and the state supreme court affirmed unanimously. Rejecting the common-carrier argument advanced by Shuck and supported by reference to the *Uhlman* case, the court held:

> The newspaper business is an ordinary business. It is a business essentially private in its nature—as private as that of the baker, grocer, or milkman, all of whom perform a service on which, to a greater or lesser extent, the communities depend, but which bears no such relation to the public as to warrant its inclusion in the category of businesses charged with a public use. If a newspaper were required to accept an advertisement, it could be compelled to publish a news item. If some good lady gave a tea, and submitted to the newspaper a proper account of the tea, and the editor of the newspaper, believing that it had no news value, refused to publish it, she, it seems to us, would have as much right to compel the newspaper to publish the account as would a person engaged in business to compel a newspaper to publish an advertisement . . .
>
> Thus, as a newspaper is a strictly private enterprise, the publishers thereof have a right to publish whatever advertisement they desire and to refuse to publish whatever advertisements they do not desire to publish.

The many decisions since have added nothing to the principle. They have established that publishers and broadcasters can classify advertisements as they see fit[98] or can change an ad to meet their standards of acceptability.[99] However, to avoid conflict over whether a contract is in force, the wording of advertising contracts should reserve to the publisher, broadcaster, or advertising director the final right of approval and should state the kinds of advertising that are unacceptable. Any prospective advertiser should be given a copy of the terms at the first inquiry.

With respect to newspaper advertising, courts, generally, have recognized that some common acts signal acceptance of an ad. If an ad is received by telephone, as much classified advertising is, the copy is considered accepted at the end of the conversation. If copy for an ad is brought to a counter at the newspaper, the ad is considered accepted when the employee or the customer leaves the counter. If the copy is received by mail or fax, it is not considered accepted until it has been verified or the advertisement has been published.[100] If there is doubt as to whether an ad is acceptable, employees who take the copy should tell the customer that it cannot be used until they have checked with a supervisor. If the copy is deemed not acceptable, the customer should be told that the paper does not intend to use it. Lawyers recommend that in such instances, the less the employee says to the customer, the better. Any attempt at explanation may be used in court if a lawsuit should result.

What can happen if the terms of the contract are not clearly understood is illustrated by an Indiana Court of Appeals decision in *Herald-Telephone* v. *Fatouras*.[101] A candidate for a local school board paid for an ad that was to be run on the day before the election. She submitted the copy late, and the newspaper bent its normal deadlines to accept it. When the publisher's representative reviewed the copy, he rejected it on the ground that it made serious charges against persons who would have no opportunity to respond before voting began. The candidate persuaded a county judge to hold court

---

98.   Staff Research Associates v. Tribune Co., 346 F.2d 372 (7th Cir. 1965).
99.   Camp-of-the-Pines v. New York Times, 53 N.Y.S.2d 475 (S.Ct., Albany Co. 1945).
100. Peter J. Caruso, "Your Right to Refuse Ads," *Editor & Publisher,* 12 May 1984, p. 48.
101. 431 N.E.2d 171, 8 Med.L.Rptr. 1230 (Ind.App. 1982).

on Sunday evening to hear her argument that the publisher not only had refused to honor a contract, but had violated her First Amendment rights. Deciding that a contract had been reached when the candidate's money was accepted and the copy delivered to the newspaper, the judge ordered the ad to be run the following day. The newspaper ran the ad. The court of appeals eventually held that if a newspaper imposes conditions on the acceptance of advertising copy, advertisers must be told about them in advance.

The right to refuse advertising also is subject to antitrust law. The landmark case in this area is *Lorain Journal Co.* v. *United States.*[102] The case grew out of an attempt by the publisher of the *Lorain Journal* to freeze out a newly established radio station in an adjoining city. The publisher ordered the newspaper's advertising department to monitor the station and cancel the advertising contract of any Lorain merchant who bought time on the station. Because the newspaper's circulation reached 97 percent of the households in the area and the station could demonstrate nowhere near such coverage, this was a potent threat. The Supreme Court held that there was no doubt that the purpose of the policy was to preserve the newspaper's monopoly and, therefore, the policy was a violation of the law.

However, when there is no pattern of refusals that suggest an intent to monopolize, media may refuse commercial advertising for reasons of taste, politics, competition, space, or for no particular reason at all. The *Seattle Post-Intelligencer,* for example, rejected advertising from CompuServe that criticized Seattle-based Microsoft. Likewise the *Seattle Times* refused ads from Prodigy and America Online because it saw those companies as potential competitors with newspapers.[103] The three major commercial television networks said that they were complying with long-established policy when they refused advertising for birth control pills.[104]

The Right to Refuse Editorial Advertising

Privately Owned Media

In *New York Times* v. *Sullivan,*[105] the U.S. Supreme Court gave near-absolute First Amendment protection to editorial advertising. That decision predated by nearly a decade the Court's evolution of the commercial speech doctrine, extending only qualified First Amendment protection to other forms of advertising. Some legal scholars, foremost among them Jerome Barron, a professor of law at the National Law Center at George Washington University, read *New York Times* as implying a right of access to the media for persons and groups willing to buy space to plead a cause.[106] Although Barron acted as counsel in several cases testing his the-

---

102.   342 U.S. 143, 72 S.Ct. 181, 96 L.Ed. 162, 1 Med.L.Rptr. 2697 (1951).
103.   William Webb, "Seattle Daily Turns Down CompuServe Ad," *Editor & Publisher,* 23 September 1995, p. 33.
104.   "Major Networks Won't Air Ads for Birth Control Pills," *Providence Journal,* 3 November 1987.
105.   376 U.S. 254, 84 S.Ct. 710, 11 L.Ed.2d 686, 1 Med.L.Rptr. 1527 (1964).
106.   "Access to the Press—A New First Amendment Right," 80 *Harv.L.Rev.* 1641 (1967); *Freedom of the Press for Whom?* (Bloomington: Indiana University Press, 1973).

ory, courts at every level, including the Supreme Court, have rejected his argument except as it applies to state-owned high school and college newspapers and to public transit systems under narrowly defined circumstances. Otherwise, courts have held that any attempt to force an advertising medium to accept cause advertising violates both the Fifth Amendment's takings clause and the First Amendment's guarantee of freedom of the press.

With respect to privately owned newspapers, one case illustrates the general rejection of Barron's theory. When Chicago's newspapers refused to publish an advertisement that urged consumers to boycott stores selling imported clothing, a labor union asked a federal district court to compel the papers to do so. The union advanced two arguments. One compared newspapers to places of public accommodation, which are forbidden by law to refuse service on racial or religious grounds. The union said that the newspapers' refusal to accept its ad was a form of discrimination made illegal by the First Amendment protection given to cause advertising by *New York Times* v. *Sullivan.* The second argument was based on the thesis that newspapers enjoy so many favors from government that they have become a part of government. The union noted that local governments are required to advertise certain of their activities in newspapers. State and local governments, at the time, commonly gave newspaper reporters office space in police headquarters, city hall, county courthouses, and state capitols. In many cities, newspapers are the only product that can be sold legally on public streets and sidewalks.

A federal district court judge rejected both arguments.[107] With respect to the first, he said that the Supreme Court's purpose in *New York Times* was to encourage newspapers to publish cause advertising by offering them a high degree of protection against successful libel actions. The Court did not intend to stretch the First Amendment "to include the right to use the other fellow's presses."[108] With respect to the second, the court said that government and its officials make news, but they do not ordinarily publish it. "[T]here is no state press, no American equivalent to *Izvestia* or *Pravda.*" His reference was to the government-controlled newspapers in what was then the Soviet Union. In the United States, the judge added, "the press has long and consistently been recognized as an independent check on governmental power." His decision was upheld by the circuit court of appeals, and the Supreme Court rejected a request for a review of the decision.[109]

Government-Owned Media

The First Amendment stands as a barrier against government interference with media that carry news and opinion, and, to a lesser extent, with the advertising content of

---

107. Chicago Joint Board, Amalgamated Clothing Workers of America, AFL-CIO v. Chicago Tribune Co., 307 F.Supp. 422 (N.D.Ill. 1969); affirmed, 435 F.2d 470 (7th Cir. 1970); cert. denied, 402 U.S. 973, 91 S.Ct. 1659 (1971).

108. This restriction includes the other fellow's fax machine: Destination Ventures Ltd. v. FCC, 23 Med.L.Rptr. 1446 (9th Cir. 1995).

109. See also World Peace Movement of America v. Newspaper Agency Corp. Inc., 879 P.2d 253, 22 Med.L.Rptr. 2193 (Utah, 1994).

such media. As written, the amendment forbids Congress to make laws that abridge freedom of speech and press. Since the 1920s, the Supreme Court has interpreted the language of the Fourteenth Amendment as applying the First Amendment to most attempts by state and local governments and their officers to abridge freedom of speech and press. Further, the First Amendment has no application to decisions by private individuals who may want to prevent widespread public dissemination of someone's point of view. When editors decide not to use something, the decision is an editorial judgment, protected by the First Amendment.[110]

However, when media are owned by government, the application of First Amendment law changes. In the eyes of the law, many public high school and state university student newspapers are government-owned media, as is advertising space sold by public transit systems. When decisions on the content of such media are made by a government official, the power of government is brought into play. Thus, courts have held that an official's decision to prevent publication of cause-oriented content in some kinds of government-owned media under some circumstances is a form of prior restraint condemned by the First Amendment. The preceding sentence is phrased as carefully as it is because the Supreme Court's decision in *Hazelwood School District v. Kuhlmeier*[111] casts doubt on some of the earlier decisions holding that administrators and teachers could not control the content of public school newspapers. The *Hazelwood* decision is discussed in Chapter 3. The cases in point indicate that a right to buy editorial advertising in a public school or university newspaper, or any other government-owned medium of communication, depends on the answers to three questions:

1. If the publication is a public school newspaper, is it published independently, or as part of the staff's course work in journalism?

2. Whatever the medium, is it considered a public forum?

3. What is the status of the individual who makes decisions as to content?

In *Hazelwood,* the Supreme Court said clearly that if a high school newspaper is published as part of the school's course work in journalism, the teachers involved and the school principal have authority to determine its editorial content. Note that the Court avoided deciding whether the paper was a public forum. The U.S. Ninth Circuit Court of Appeals cited *Hazelwood* in upholding the right of school authorities to exclude certain advertisers from a high school newspaper and from athletic events programs.[112] The court noted that school authorities had reserved to themselves broad discretion to control school publications, making them nonpublic forums. Therefore, decisions to exclude advertisers had only to be reasonable to survive challenge on First Amendment grounds.

---

110. Miami Herald Publishing Co. v. Tornillo, 418 U.S. 241, 94 S.Ct. 2831, 41 L.Ed.2d 730, 1 Med.L.Rptr. 1898 (1974).
111. 484 U.S. 260, 108 S.Ct. 562, 98 L.Ed.2d 592, 14 Med.L.Rptr. 2081 (1988).
112. Planned Parenthood of S. Nevada, Inc. v. Clark County School District, 887 F.2d 935, 17 Med.L.Rptr. 1065 (9th Cir. 1991); affirmed *en banc,* 941 F.2d 817 (9th Cir. 1991).

If the newspaper is not tied to journalism courses, the rules are different. In recent decisions, courts have held that if state-owned media customarily carry views on controversial public issues, they are public forums. If so, a state employee's decision to reject content is subject to challenge on First Amendment grounds. Public school teachers and administrators are considered to be state employees. If the medium involved is a public school newspaper published independently of course work in journalism, the student editor has authority to reject both editorial content and advertising. These principles emerge from the cases summarized in the remainder of this section.

The Ninth Circuit ruled in an access case predating *Hazelwood* that a public high school governing board had violated the First Amendment by refusing to accept an ad from an organization that opposed registration for the draft.[113] The court held that the board had created a limited public forum by permitting the general public to buy advertising space in the school newspaper. It pointed specifically to armed forces recruiting advertisements as evidence that the board had opened its forum to speech by nonstudents, which is "both political and commercial with respect to at least one important and highly controversial topic—military service." Scattered earlier decisions by lower-level courts were to the same effect.[114] When student editors act on their own, without coercion from state employees, courts have upheld their right to make decisions on content. An editor can refuse to publish an article submitted by a would-be contributor.[115] Student editors also have been upheld when they have rejected cause advertising. In *Mississippi Gay Alliance* v. *Goudelock,*[116] the Fifth U.S. Circuit Court noted that the decision to reject an ad offering counseling and legal aid to gay students at Mississippi State University was the student editor's alone. Thus, the decision was not an exercise of state authority but was an editorial judgment protected by the First Amendment.

In several instances, courts have held that transit companies created public forums by accepting political advertising. Therefore, they could not reject advertising offered by controversial political organizations. A federal district court in New York State held that the Niagara Frontier Transit Authority could not deny space to an abortion rights group.[117] New York City's Metropolitan Transportation Authority was told that it could not deny *Penthouse* access to subway walls for an advertising poster.[118] The poster depicted Walter Mondale, then the Democratic presidential candidate, in a seminude pose. The Massachusetts Bay Transportation Authority was told that it could not refuse ads promoting the use of condoms to stop the spread of HIV.[119]

---

113. San Diego Committee against Registration and the Draft v. The Governing Board of Grossmont Union High School District, 790 F.2d 1471, 12 Med.L.Rptr. 2329 (9th Cir. 1986).
114. See, for instance, Lee v. Board of Regents of State Colleges, 306 F.Supp. 1097 (W.D.Wis. 1969); affirmed, 441 F.2d 1257, 1 Med.L.Rptr. 1947 (7th Cir. 1971), and Zucker v. Panitz, 299 F.Supp. 102 (S.D.N.Y. 1969).
115. Avins v. Rutgers, State University of New Jersey, 385 F.2d 151 (3d Cir. 1967); cert. denied, 88 S.Ct. 855 (1968).
116. 536 F.2d 1073, 1 Med.L.Rptr. 1949 (5th Cir. 1976); cert. denied, 430 U.S. 982, 97 S.Ct. 1678, 52 L.Ed.2d 377 (1977).
117. Coalition for Abortion Rights and against Sterilization Abuse v. Niagara Frontier Transportation Authority, 584 F.Supp. 985 (W.D.N.Y. 1984).
118. Penthouse International Ltd. v. Koch, 599 F.Supp. 1338 (S.D.N.Y. 1984).
119. AIDS Action Committee v. Massachusetts Bay Transportation Authority, 22 Med.L.Rptr. 2449 (1st. Cir. 1994).

However, the Supreme Court held in *Lehman* v. *City of Shaker Heights*[120] that public transit systems can reject cause advertising if no public forum has been created. The five-justice majority noted that the Court has been "jealous to preserve access to public places for purposes of free speech," but held that the system's buses were not public forums. Therefore, the city did not violate the First Amendment when it limited car card advertising to commercial messages.

Courts have held, then, that a right of access to state-owned media exists, but it is limited and rests on a narrow base. If the medium makes itself a public forum by accepting cause advertising, or even politically tinged advertising such as recruiting messages for the armed forces, it cannot refuse other such advertising if the decision is made by an agent of the state.

Corporate Political Speech

Because political speech lies at the core of First Amendment concerns, it enjoys almost absolute protection. The Supreme Court took note of that principle when it held, in *First National Bank of Boston* v. *Bellotti,* that corporations have a right to spend their stockholders' money to advertise a position on a public issue. In doing so, the Court struck down a Massachusetts law that made it a crime for a corporation to spend its funds to influence the outcome of a referendum unless the issue submitted to the voters would materially affect the corporation's business, property, or assets. The case began when Massachusetts residents were asked to change the state constitution to permit a graduated income tax. As it stood, the constitution required that all persons be taxed at the same rate. Officers of many financial institutions, including First National Bank of Boston, believed the proposal mistaken and sought to use corporate funds to oppose it. However, because the tax measure would not have a material effect on the institutions themselves, the law stood in their way. First National took the lead in asking state courts to declare the law unconstitutional, but they upheld it. The Supreme Court agreed to take the case.

First National Bank of Boston v. *Bellotti,* 435 U.S. 765, 98 S.Ct. 1407, 55 L.Ed.2d 707, 3 Med.L.Rptr. 2105 (1978).

The Massachusetts courts had acted on the theory that the Supreme Court's commercial speech cases give the state the right to restrict corporate speech. They had held that there was an overriding public interest in preventing corporations from spending funds to influence the outcome of a referendum. The Supreme Court said that that interpretation was a misreading of the commercial speech doctrine. At the heart of the issue, the Court said, was the nature of the speech in question. Its subject, in this instance, was taxation, a central concern of every citizen. Corporations, like other citizens, have a right to speak on public issues, through advertising or by other means. They do not have to prove, any more than a real person would, that the issue in question would have a material effect on them.

---

120.   418 U.S. 298, 94 S.Ct. 2714, 41 L.Ed.2d 770 (1974).

Two years later, in *Consolidated Edison Co.* v. *Public Service Commission*,[121] the Supreme Court expanded on that holding. At issue were bill inserts used by Consolidated Edison to argue its case for nuclear power. The Natural Resources Defense Council argued that the company should be compelled to permit the council to prepare inserts arguing against nuclear power. When that approach failed, the council succeeded in persuading the public service commission to ban all bill inserts of a political nature. The commission rationalized that utility customers hold widely divergent views and should not be made a captive audience for a company's opinions. The Court decided the case by direct application of the *First National Bank* precedent. It held that the state could regulate the time, place, and manner of corporate speech, but that it could not do so on the basis of the content of that speech. As long as Consolidated Edison did not lie to its customers, it could offer them its views on any subject.

The Court carried the protection of corporate speech an additional step by nullifying a California rule that required public utility companies to distribute bill inserts prepared by consumer groups.[122] In response to complaints about a newsletter mailed by Pacific Gas & Electric Company with its bills, the state's Public Utilities Commission ordered the company to include, four times a year, messages prepared by an organization opposing its rate-increase requests. Four of the five justices voting to strike down the order held that corporations, like individuals, cannot be compelled to associate themselves with views with which they disagree. However, the fifth justice focused narrowly on the company's envelopes, seeing them as private property to which it could deny access by others.

The effect of the three decisions is that corporate messages that advocate a position on public issues are placed at a level in the First Amendment hierarchy higher than that of messages designed to sell a product or service. The latter lie outside the realm of First Amendment protection if they promote an illegal product or promote a legal product in a deceptive way. Nondeceptive advertising for legal products is protected by the First Amendment, but still is subject to regulation if a substantial state interest requires it. But, in the three cases discussed in this section, the Supreme Court held that states cannot restrict a corporation's right to express a point of view on public issues, whether the corporation does so by advertisements in the media or by mailings to its customers. In the most recent case, the Court also held that states cannot compel corporations to become unwilling distributors of messages prepared by others.

In the Professional World

It would be misleading in the extreme to leave the impression that advertising claims are held in check only by the forces of law. This is no more true than the belief that the news staffs of the various media would engage in unbridled libel and invasion of privacy were it not for fear of lawsuits. All advertisers and

---

121.   447 U.S. 530, 100 S.Ct. 2326, 65 L.Ed.2d 319, 6 Med.L.Rptr. 1518 (1980).
122.   Pacific Gas and Electric Co. v. Public Utilities Commission of California, 475 U.S. 1, 106 S.Ct. 903, 89 L.Ed.2d 1 (1986).

media that accept advertising police themselves, applying professional standards of honesty and ethics that are products of experience and training. The several professional organizations that represent people who prepare advertisements have codes of fair practices. Newspapers, magazines, and broadcasters have adopted standards designed to screen out ads that are deceptive, fraudulent, or considered to be in bad taste.

To an extent unequaled by any other medium of expression, advertising operates in a fishbowl. The purpose of advertising is to call attention to a message designed to sell a product or service. Thus, advertising is likely to have more of an impact on more people than all but the most important news stories or commentary. If a reporter misstates a fact about an action taken by a city council, few aside from the persons immediately involved will know or care. If an advertiser makes overblown claims for a product, every dissatisfied user will know and care, and may take the further step of buying no more of that product or of any other products made by the same company. Not surprisingly, then, the guidelines adopted by the various advertising organizations focus on honesty and clarity. A typical code advises advertisers to be able to substantiate any claims made for a product, to avoid unfair disparagement of other products, and to give full price information. If gifts are offered as inducements, any conditions attached to the offer should be stated clearly. Because such codes are voluntary, they are not observed by all advertisers all of the time, but, given the huge volume of advertising messages, deliberate deception is rare.

Honesty is not solely a matter of ethics. There are good business reasons for it, as Eugene S. Pulliam, publisher of the *Indianapolis Star,* noted. He quoted, with approval, a statement made by Leonard S. Matthews, then president of the American Association of Advertising Agencies.[123] Pulliam endorsed Matthews's assertion that advertising "is much more honest than it has ever been," primarily because honesty is good business. Both also noted that today's "much brighter consumer of advertising," is not easily taken in.

Even a superficial survey of the literature leaves little doubt that advertising professionals are committed to the belief that honesty is the best policy. However, the same survey leaves no doubt that advertising, because of its pervasiveness and the role it therefore is believed to play in shaping society, remains controversial. Many of the questions raised probe at the professional's ethics. These questions lie in a realm where beliefs are strong, facts are evasive, and conclusions are subject to heated debate. The major points at issue can only be noted, not resolved, in a text of this kind.

One of the most persistent ethical questions is: At what point does advertising become offensive? For years, television networks refused ads for vaginal deodorants but had no qualms about ads for underarm deodorants, or for products designed to quell digestive gases or to "soothe that itch that is so private most of us will discuss it only with our doctor." Media of all kinds commonly use advertisements that hold out the promise of intimate romance to the users of the right shaving lotion, shampoo, makeup, or lingerie. It is a tru-

---

123.   Eugene S. Pulliam, "Publisher's Memo: Advertising," *Indianapolis Star,* 29 December 1985.

Editors of the *New York Times Magazine* found this attempt by Revlon to "equalize the gesture" too raunchy to use. Editors of eleven women's magazines did not. Some newspapers used it as a newsphoto to illustrate a story about the *Times*'s rejection. *(AP/Wide World)*

ism in the trade that sex sells. But when Revlon planned an advertising campaign to promote its Charlie perfume, the *New York Times Magazine* ruled that one of its ads was so sexy as to be in bad taste.[124] The ad featured a photograph of a young man and a young woman standing with their backs to the camera. The woman has her right hand on the man's left buttock. Both are not only fully clothed, but obviously expensively and conventionally clothed. The caption over the photo says, "She's very Charlie." In rejecting the ad, the *Times*'s advertising executives reasoned that readers would object if the ad showed a man patting a woman on the rear. Revlon said that the ad "equalizes the gesture." Eleven women's magazines found it acceptable. The generally conservative *Indianapolis Star* ran the photo three columns wide by nine inches deep—as news—with its article reporting the *Times*'s rejection.

---

124. "Ad Too Cheeky," *Indianapolis Star,* 31 July 1987.

This is but one example of sex-oriented advertising. An executive with Planned Parenthood in New York City estimated that each year, the three television networks broadcast twenty thousand sexually explicit references in their programs and commercials. But when the agency prepared a thirty-second commercial for its services, which started, "Four out of five young women who don't use birth control get pregnant before they want to," the city's three network-affiliated television stations rejected it.[125]

The AIDS epidemic has brought about some changes in advertising policies with respect to the use of condoms, for prevention of that disease if not for birth control. But even when condoms were presented as a means of preventing AIDS, one advertisement failed to pass muster with some media. Della Femina, Travisano & Partners created two versions of a condom ad with an AIDS-prevention theme. The print version showed the frightened face of a young woman. The copy said, "I enjoy sex, but I'm not ready to die for it. AIDS isn't just a gay disease, it's everybody's disease. And everybody who gets it dies." The ad suggested that smart women protect themselves by buying the advertiser's brand of condoms. In addition to promoting its business, the advertiser believed it was performing a public service. Acceptance executives at *Time, Newsweek,* and *People* magazines turned the ad down as offensive. *USA Today* and *New York* magazine used it. A television commercial based on the same theme was rejected by all three networks. Ad agency Chairman Jerry Della Femina commented, "What the networks are saying is, 'We don't care if people die. We have our policy.'"[126]

Does advertising reinforce stereotypes—about the young, the elderly, women, the mentally ill, and others? When the women's movement came to the fore in the 1960s, the National Organization for Women listed ten advertisements that it considered most insulting to women. These ads portrayed women as housewives whose greatest fear was that their husbands might find their coffee bitter, whose greatest concern was avoiding ring around the collar, and who lived in the kitchen, preparing food and washing dishes. Such ads appear on television with lesser frequency, but might there also be a stereotype in the well-groomed, physically attractive young woman who is always on the go, always involved in making major business decisions? The American Association of Retired Persons has objected to commercials that portray the elderly as frail, somewhat befuddled people who putter around until someone offers them a glass of lemonade, a powerful painkiller for their arthritis, a bowl of hot oatmeal, or a certain brand of ice cream. The National Stigma Clearing House, a group that monitors advertising for stereotypes of mental illness, has objected to a Nike television commercial that features Dennis Hopper as an obsessed football fanatic, given to tics, twitches, and manic laughter. In one scene Hopper rhapsodies about player Barry Sanders. "He does things on the field that make your

125.   Alfred F. Moran, executive director of Planned Parenthood of New York City, in "TV Advertising and Hypocrisy," a letter to the editor of the *Wall Street Journal,* 18 September 1987.
126.   Joanne Lipman, "Controversial Product Isn't an Easy Subject for Ad Copywriters," *Wall Street Journal,* 6 December 1986.

eyes go all crazy," Hopper says. "Sometimes I still see him when I sleep, and I don't sleep that much." In another scene, Hopper sneaks into the Buffalo Bills' locker room and removes Bruce Smith's Nike shoe from his locker. He takes a deep whiff. "You know what Bruce would do if he found me messing with this shoe?" he says. "Bad things, man, bad things." Those ads make *Advertising Age* columnist Bob Garfield laugh, but that doesn't mean he thinks they are appropriate. "Advertisers have a special obligation to observe the golden rule. No one asks to see a TV commercial. It just comes barging in. Advertising has to take special care not to be offensive or exploitative because it is completely unsolicited."[127]

Closely related to these issues is the way in which advertising influences behavior. Its purpose, of course, is to influence buying decisions. But what else does it do? What, for instance, are the consequences of portraying young men riding a water scooter up a waterfall, jumping a motorcycle over the crest of a sand dune, or driving a pickup truck at high speed up a rocky mountain trail? Or of Mercedes-Benz television commercials featuring cars driven at speeds in excess of one hundred miles per hour? Presumably, the commercials were made in Germany, where such speeds are legal, but the message is clear—this car is built for high speed. Other makers show their high-performance cars breezing through the curves on mountain roads, threading obstacles, or coming to panic stops inches short of the engineers who designed them. The fine-print message that advises viewers not to try to duplicate the maneuvers is on and off the screen in seconds. There is no way, of course, of telling which came first, commercials that encourage speeding and reckless driving or the prevalence of such driving. As one advertising executive noted, America's love affair with speed goes back to the time when people rode horses. Are these and similar commercials related to the fact that accidents are the leading cause of death among young people?

The Stroh Brewery Company made perhaps the ultimate stereotypical link among male bonding, good times, and sex in a series of television commercials for its Old Milwaukee beer. For years, Stroh's commercials had portrayed virile young males fishing, hiking, engaging in sports, and then, as evening came, drinking beer while one of the men said, "It doesn't get any better than this." But it did. At that point the "Swedish Bikini Team" arrived. The scantily clad, tall, buxom young women brought not only more beer but the promise of even better times. The campaign had several unanticipated side effects. The actresses who made up the team appeared on the cover of *Playboy* magazine, and they appeared uncovered on inside pages. Further, readers who called a 900 number could hear all but one of the women talk in phony Swedish accents about "tight buns" and Swedish men wanting "sex a lot quicker" than Americans. The one holdout, the mother of a two-year-old girl, said she didn't want to be associated with the call-in because "it's got the call-girl image or phone-sex image."[128] Nor

---

127. Laura Bird, "Critics Cry Foul at Nike Spots with Actor," *Wall Street Journal,* 16 December 1993, p. B7.

128. Joanne Lipman, "Stroh Ad Campaign Spins out of Control," *Wall Street Journal,* 12 December 1991.

was that all. Five female employees of Stroh's St. Paul, Minnesota, brewery sued their employer for sexual harassment, citing the ad series as an example of the company's mentality.[129] Further, a female employee sued Hal Riney & Partners, creators of the ads, alleging sexual harassment. Both the agency and the brewer said they had meant no harm; the ads were intended as a parody of the commercials commonly linking young males, beer drinking, and attractive women. Is it only a coincidence that abuse of alcohol is a major problem on most college campuses?

The *Soldier of Fortune* case stands as a warning that advertisers should not place, nor media accept, ads that can be construed as leading to harm. In that instance, the ad was crude and direct. A hired gun was looking for a job. But what happens if the harm is less direct but nevertheless real? Valid scientific evidence points to cigarette smoking as a leading cause of lung cancer and heart disease. Alcohol abuse is not far behind as a cause of disease. Each year, nearly two million people in the United States are victims of violent crime. One in every hundred deaths results from murder. Child abuse, spouse abuse, and AIDS also are frightening and seemingly pervasive problems. Some critics complain that advertising plays a contributing role in all of these hazards and point at five advertising campaigns as examples that raise serious ethical questions about the uses of advertising.

The first involved Calvin Klein's sensuous jeans ads. The campaign portrayed scantily clad teens in sexually suggestive poses mimicking cheesy adult videos. Angry critics, such as the American Family Association, compared the ads to child pornography and urged the Justice Department to investigate. Although it turned out that all the models were over eighteen years old, the Calvin Klein company withdrew the campaign, saying it was "taken aback" by the hostile reaction. On the heels of the jeans controversy, Calvin Klein came under fire again for its sensual ads promoting underwear. The ads featured a long-haired and scarcely clad young model named Joel West. In the ad, photographed in black and white, West is dressed only in tight gray briefs and is posed staring directly at the camera with his legs wide apart. Another ad portrays West, this time in white boxer briefs, as apparently sexually aroused. After articles about the ads appeared in *Newsweek, New York, The New York Observer, Women's Wear Daily,* and *USA Today,* the ads were pulled. Linda Warnaco, the chief executive of Warnaco, the company that owns the Klein underwear business, said that the company was "in the business to sell underwear . . . not in the business to have problems." But not everyone had a problem with West's underwear. Matthew Hanna, associate publisher of *Spin* magazine, described the ad as provocative and sexy. "But it's an underwear ad. It should be provocative. . . . We don't think our readers are taken aback by that type of advertising."[130]

---

129. George F. Will, "Of Lawsuits, Sexism and Beer Commercials," *Indianapolis Star,* 1 December 1991.

130. Stuart Elliott, "Calvin Klein Is Withdrawing, and Reshooting, Some Underwear Ads after More Complaints Are Heard," *New York Times,* 11 November 1995.

This controversial Calvin Klein advertisement was withdrawn after critics complained the ads were too sexually suggestive and the models too young. The company said it was surprised by the hostile reaction and that the models were all over 18 years old. *(Joel Gordon)*

The second controversy involves "Old Joe," the caricatured camel featured in RJR Nabisco's ads for Camel cigarettes. After the *Journal of the American Medical Association* published three studies showing that Old Joe was widely recognized by children, Surgeon General Antonia Novello and the association asked the company to drop the character from its ads, arguing that it was making smoking look attractive to minors.[131] One of the studies showed that among six-year-olds, Joe was almost as frequently recognized as Mickey Mouse. Magazine publishers laughed off Novello's request that they refuse ads with Old Joe. A spokesperson for Time-Warner's magazine group cited the First Amendment and said that it would continue to accept ads for legal products.[132] The FTC investigated and decided to leave Old Joe alone. The majority in the three-to-two decision said that "[a]lthough it may seem intuitive to some that the Joe Camel advertising campaign would lead more children to smoke, or lead children to smoke more, the evidence to support that intuition is not there."[133]

131. Joanne Lipman, "Surgeon General Says It's Time Joe Camel Quit," *Wall Street Journal,* 10 March 1992.
132. Joanne Lipman, "Surgeon General Hasn't Slowed Joe Camel," *Wall Street Journal,* 14 April 1992.
133. Stuart Elliott, "The F.T.C. Explains Its Joe Camel Decision," *New York Times,* 8 June 1994, p. C2.

The third controversial campaign was for the movie *Boyz N the Hood,* which was about a group of black friends growing up in a gang-ruled section of Los Angeles. The message was strongly antigang. However, television commercials promoting the movie focused on its relatively few episodes of violence. In cities across the country, the movie's opening attracted gang members, some of whom engaged in violence inside and outside the theaters. At the film's Los Angeles opening, one young man was shot in the back and paralyzed from the waist down. He sued Columbia Pictures, alleging that by ignoring the positive message of the film and focusing on violence, the commercials incited lawless activity, leading to his injury.[134] The movie's producer was quoted as attributing the shooting to the kind of violence that happens "every Friday and Saturday night in every single inner-city in America." He conceded that if the ads had focused on the film's positive elements, gang members might not have shown up for the openings. In that event, he said, they would not have been exposed to the movie's message.

The fourth controversial campaign was a television commercial for Colt 45 malt liquor, which the G. Heileman Brewing Company had promoted for years as a macho drink that held out the promise of a quick and inexpensive high. Its principal market was among young black males. The same company also made St. Ides, promoted by the rapper Ice Cube, and Crazy Horse, both high-powered malt liquors. In an attempt to dampen criticism aimed at its earlier campaigns, Heileman and its ad agency, Deutsch/Dworin, developed commercials in which an older black man, dressed in a white shirt and tie, sits on a front porch and talks to younger blacks about how he went to night school to get a college degree and the position he achieved as a result. The speaker and his friends are sipping Colt 45. Spokespeople for the Institute on Black Chemical Abuse and the Center for Science in the Public Interest condemned the ads as being in poor taste and using an aura of success to sell malt liquor, "right there on the street."[135] One spokesperson called the commercial cynical "because drinking these high-alcohol products frequently leads to the exact opposite result."

The fifth controversial campaign, for Virginia Slims cigarettes, was aimed squarely at young women. Philip Morris offered to give away black leather jackets and other articles, including leather backpacks, vests, sunglasses, and lighters. Advertisements, placed in the Sunday *New York Times, Glamour, Mademoiselle,* and other publications, used slender, laughing female models to show off the giveaway items. To get a free jacket, a woman needed only to buy 350 packs of Virginia Slims—seven thousand smokes—and send proof of purchase to Philip Morris. The purpose, said a spokeswoman, was to induce women to switch from other brands and build up a loyalty to Virginia Slims. The president of an organization that works in New York City schools to discourage smoking said that the campaign featured precisely the elements that appeal to teenagers. He said that the promotion "shows how low the tobacco in-

---

134. Joanne Lipman, "Issue of Ads Leading to Violence Is Raised in Suit Tied to Movie," *Wall Street Journal,* 27 April 1992.

135. Laura Bird, "Critics Shoot at New Colt 45 Campaign," *Wall Street Journal,* 17 February 1993.

dustry will stoop to addict young girls." The Philip Morris spokeswoman countered by calling attention to the coupon used to order items by mail. It contained a pledge certifying that the signer of the coupon is "a cigarette smoker 21 years of age or older."

Periodically, Congress has considered proposals that would ban cigarette advertising in all media, as it has been banned on television for thirty years. Advertising for alcoholic beverages operates under some restrictions, but outright bans in individual states are difficult, if not impossible, to enforce. Although commercial speech is protected by the First Amendment, those who invoke the Amendment's protection, be they advertisers pushing a product or writers pushing an idea, should not ignore the potential consequences.

FOR REVIEW

1. What is the meaning of "the doctrine of commercial speech"?

2. Explain the significance of the *Pittsburgh Press* case. On what rationale was it decided?

3. Outline the four-part test established by Justice Powell in *Central Hudson Gas* to determine when a commercial advertisement is protected by the First Amendment. With reference to one of the cases in the text, explain how each branch of the test is applied.

4. If you were advising a law firm that wanted to start an advertising campaign, what would you tell it? What could you do for the firm? What should you not do?

5. You are in the outdoor advertising business. Your community is considering an ordinance to restrict signs and billboards. Can it adopt such an ordinance? Why or why not?

6. Should advertising media be held responsible for harm attributed to the content of an advertisement? Why or why not?

7. What makes an ad deceptive? What standards are used by the Federal Trade Commission to determine whether an ad is deceptive? Illustrate with examples.

8. Define each of the following and assess its effectiveness: broadened cease and desist order, affirmative disclosure, affirmative acts, corrective advertising, advertising substantiation, trade rules.

9. How can the FTC's power to order corrective advertising be harmonized with the *Central Hudson* decision?

10. State attorneys general and lawsuits among competing advertisers can cope with deceptive ads more effectively than can the FTC. Agree or disagree? Discuss. Are there limits on state actions against deceptive advertising? Explain.

11. Explain the rationale that permits a medium of communication to refuse commercial advertising.

12. If you were adviser to a public high school or state university newspaper, what advice would you give the staff with respect to the public's right to place cause, or editorial, advertising in the publication?

13. If a corporation that manufactures and sells automobiles wants to run two advertisements, one promoting its new line of automobiles and one urging Congress to pass a balanced budget, which of the two ads would be subject to the commercial speech doctrine? What difference would it make? Explain.

CHAPTER 12

The drafters of the Constitution gave Congress the power to "promote the progress of science and useful arts, by securing for limited times to authors and inventors the exclusive right to their respective writings and discoveries." Copyright lawyers like to remind authors that the original purpose of this Constitutional right in Article 1, Section 8, was not primarily to reward authors but rather to secure for the country the benefits of their creativity.[1] One way to do that was to make sure that authors had the right to own whatever they created, at least for a while.

Since 1790, Congress has used its power to promote creativity by protecting authors with a series of Copyright acts and international treaties. The latest version of the Copyright Act passed Congress in 1976 and became fully effective in 1978. It has since been amended several times to keep up with advancing technology. The act reg-

---

1. Melville B. Nimmer and David Nimmer, *Nimmer on Copyright,* §1.03(A); Maser v. Stein, 347 U.S. 201, 74 S.Ct. 460, 98 L.Ed. 630 (1954).

COPYRIGHT AND TRADEMARK

ulates how persons with creative talent can protect their work from unauthorized use—whether by copying, performance, display, distribution, or production of derivative works, such as films or translations. The purpose of the law is to protect an author's ability to profit from talent and thus to encourage creativity. The law tries to do that by granting authors a monopoly for a fixed period over the uses that can be made of a protected work.

In a sense, then, copyright law complements the First Amendment. There might not be a vigorous marketplace of ideas if those with a talent for words, pictures, or other means of expression could not be sure of payment for their work. Copyright law encourages the exchange of ideas and viewpoints by talented individuals with the hope that the public will benefit.

From another point of view, however, copyright law places limits on the free marketplace of ideas. Publishers, broadcasters, and film producers cannot freely use any work they please in preparing their offerings. If they are going to make substantial use of copyrighted works produced by others, they must be prepared to pay. Copyright law makes it possible for authors to prevent others from publishing any of their work, especially things such as letters and diaries, during their lifetimes and for many years thereafter.

Although copyright is grounded in the Constitution, it is defined by federal statute.[2] Generally, the law protects any original work that is fixed in a tangible means of expression. If the work is an article, a book, a poem, or another form of written expression, the copyright covers the exact arrangement of words, phrases, sentences, and paragraphs. Courts have held that ideas, theories, historical incidents, standard forms, facts, and news are not generally protected by copyright. Copyright protection is not limited to the written word, however. Photographs, drawings, sculptures, computer programs, musical compositions, dance routines, and even pantomime can be protected from copying when fixed in a tangible form. By recording such major sports events as the Superbowl, the World Series, and the Masters golf tournament, producers fix these live contests in a copyrightable form.

The Copyright Act gives the owner of a copyrighted work almost complete control over its use. Copyright, like other forms of property, can be sold, assigned, or inherited. And it can be subdivided. Authors, for example, can grant performance rights but withhold translation rights. They can sell the right to publish in North

---

2. U.S.C., tit. 17, Copyrights.

America but withhold the right to publish in Europe. And just as others might have easements to drive across your land or be justified in using your property during an emergency, the law recognizes that some copying without permission is sometimes in the public interest, especially in such fields as history, biography, public affairs, and education. If copying is minimal and does not detract unduly from the commercial value of the original work, the law often allows it as a "fair use." If copying is substantial, or if it detracts from the commercial value of the original, it is likely to be an "infringement." Infringers are like trespassers in that they can be made to pay damages to the owners for using what does not belong to them. Moreover, infringers' copies can be confiscated, and they can be ordered by a court not to reproduce, perform, distribute, display, or make variations of the work. Copyright law is one of the few areas where expression can be subject to prior restraint.

In fact, the First Amendment plays only a peripheral role in copyright law. Alleged infringers sometimes have argued that the unauthorized reproduction of a work served a public interest of such importance that it was protected by the First Amendment. In 1985, in *Harper & Row, Publishers, Inc.* v. *Nation Enterprises,*[3] the U.S. Supreme Court rejected that argument. The Court held that whatever First Amendment interest there might be in the copying of a protected work, such copying is sufficiently protected by the "fair use" exception, which tries to balance competing public and private interests on a case-by-case basis.

Copyright questions arise frequently over the use of copying machines, video recorders, on-line data bases, and computer software. Other issues are raised by two topics closely related to copyright: trademarks (words or symbols that are a part of the identity of many businesses and their products) and misappropriation. Misappropriation is the unjust enrichment of oneself by exploitation of another's effort, even though the product of that effort might not be protected by copyright or trademark. The systematic copying by one news organization of news gathered by a competitor is a good example.

Trademark, unlike copyright, has no grounding in the Constitution. It is entirely a product of legislation and common law. The Federal Trademark Act protects many things left unprotected by copyright, such as slogans, titles of publications, colors, styles, sounds, and names. But the protection is limited to business uses. Whereas copyright is intended to preserve the economic rights of those who create new works, trademark is intended to forestall unfair competition and consumer confusion by identifying the origin of goods and services.

The subject matter of this chapter applies to persons working in all media of communications, including public relations practitioners, entertainers, and educators. Anyone who works with a tangible means of expression runs a risk of copyright infringement. Advertisers and public relations people, especially, deal with materials subject to copyright and trademark protections nearly every day.

---

3.   471 U.S. 539, 105 S.Ct. 2218, 85 L.Ed.2d 588 (1985).

Major Cases

- *Allen* v. *Men's World Outlet,* 679 F.Supp. 360, 15 Med.L.Rptr. 1001 (S.D.N.Y. 1988).

- *American Geophysical Union* v. *Texaco,* 60 F.3d 913 (2d Cir. 1994).

- *Carpenter* v. *United States,* 484 U.S. 19, 108 S.Ct. 316, 98 L.Ed.2d 275, 14 Med.L.Rptr. 1853 (1987).

- *Community for Creative Non-Violence* v. *Reid,* 490 U.S. 730, 109 S.Ct. 2166, 104 L.Ed.2d 811, 16 Med.L.Rptr. 1769 (1989).

- *Feist Publications, Inc.* v. *Rural Telephone Service Company, Inc.,* 499 U.S. 340, 111 S.Ct. 1282, 112 L.Ed.2d 358, 18 Med.L.Rptr. 1889 (1991).

- *Harper & Row, Publishers* v. *Nation Enterprises,* 471 U.S. 539, 105 S.Ct. 2218, 85 L.Ed.2d 588, 11 Med.L.Rptr. 1969 (1985).

- *Hoehling* v. *Universal City Studios,* 618 F.2d 972, 6 Med.L.Rptr. 1053 (2d Cir. 1980).

- *Jason* v. *Fonda,* 526 F.Supp. 774, 7 Med.L.Rptr. 2421 (C.D.Cal. 1981); affirmed, 698 F.2d 966 (9th Cir. 1982).

- *Maxtone-Graham* v. *Burtchaell,* 803 F.2d 1253, 13 Med.L.Rptr. 1513 (2d Cir. 1986); cert. denied, 481 U.S. 1059 (1987).

- *Rosemont Enterprises* v. *Random House,* 366 F.2d 203 (2d Cir.1966); cert. denied, 385 U.S. 1009, 87 S.Ct. 714, 17 L.Ed.2d 546 (1967).

- *Salinger* v. *Random House,* 811 F.2d 90, 13 Med.L.Rptr. 1954 (2d Cir. 1987); rehearing denied, 818 F.2d 252 (2d Cir. 1987); cert. denied, 108 S.Ct. 213 (1987).

- *Time Inc.* v. *Bernard Geis Associates,* 293 F.Supp. 130 (S.D.N.Y. 1968).

- *Universal City Studios* v. *Sony Corporation of America,* 465 U.S. 1112, 104 S.Ct. 1619, 80 L.Ed.2d 1480 (1984).

COPYRIGHT

The Copyright Act

The copyright of works in the United States is governed exclusively by a federal law that was revised extensively in 1976.[4] Under that law, the creator of any original work in any medium has a copyright from the moment it is put into a fixed form. It is not necessary to register the work to get a copyright; it exists from the moment of creation. Moreover, since 1989, when the United States signed a multinational copyright agreement called the Berne Convention, works are protected even if no copyright notice is displayed. However, for Americans who want the full value of the protection provided by the Copyright Act, it is best to do two things:

1. Register the work with the Copyright Office at the Library of Congress. To register a work, complete the proper application form, which is available for the asking from the Copyright Office; along with the application send two complete copies of the best edition of the work; and send the correct registration fee, at present $20.[5]

2. Put a notice of copyright on the work. The form of such notice is a C with a circle around it, followed by the date of first publication and the owner's name. The word "Copyright" or its abbreviation, "Cop.," may also be used.

Although a work is copyrighted even if not registered, the owner of a work that was created in the United States cannot sue for infringement without registration. Only foreign works created in a Berne Convention country do not require U.S. registration. Similarly, although notice is optional, the owner of a work might not be able to recover damages if absence of notice misleads an infringer into thinking that the work is unprotected.

Copyright does not last forever. It exists for the life of an author plus fifty years. If the work is for hire, the copyright belongs to the employer, not the author, unless terms of employment provide otherwise. If owned by the employer, the copyright is valid for a hundred years from the date of creation, or for seventy-five years from the date of publication, whichever is shorter. During the term of the copyright, the owner has the exclusive right to control the use of the work by others. The control of copyrights held by an author at death passes to the author's heirs.

Because copyright is a kind of property that can be bought, sold, and inherited, the owners are free to do all sorts of things with it that might produce income. They can license it; they can borrow against it; they can make it the subject of a contract that whittles it into television rights, merchandising rights, or even investment options.

---

4. This section is based on U.S.C., tit. 17, Copyrights. Because federal copyright law preempts only that state law which duplicates federal protection, some states provide copyright protection for unfixed works, such as conversations. See Cal. Civ. Code § 980(a)(1).
5. Deposit requirements can be modified when special concerns exist—for example, the work contains trade secrets or the work is a test. Best edition generally means most expensive edition.

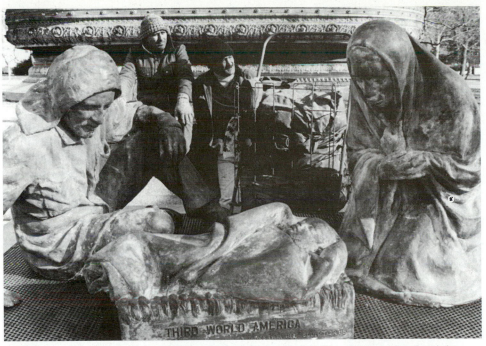

"Third World America" was created by sculptor James Earl Reid at the request of activist Mitch Snyder, in the background at the right, to dramatize the plight of Washington, D.C.'s homeless. When Snyder proposed that the sculpture be taken on tour to raise money for the homeless, Reid objected, leading to a dispute over copyright ownership that had to be resolved by the Supreme Court. *(Hugo Wessels/Photopress)*

Whatever they do, however, is best done with a written contract that describes who owns what and what can be done with it.

Works Made for Hire

***Community for Creative Non-Violence* v. *Reid*, 490 U.S. 730, 109 S.Ct. 2166, 104 L.Ed.2d 811, 16 Med.L.Rptr. 1769 (1989).**

Freelance creators especially should insist on a written contract, in light of the Supreme Court decision in *Community for Creative Non-Violence* v. *Reid.* In that case, the Court held that in the absence of a contract, the common law of agency governs whether creators are employees or independent contractors. The distinction is significant because it is the controlling factor in determining who is entitled to royalties from the work.

The case had unusual origins. In the fall of 1985, the Community for Creative Non-Violence, an organization calling attention to the plight of the homeless, decided to participate in the annual Christmas Pageant of Peace in Washington, D.C. Mitch Snyder, a trustee of the organization, conceived the idea of creating a sculpture that would dramatize his organization's cause. The trustees agreed to depict a modern Nativity scene in which two adult figures and an infant would appear huddled over a steam grate. James Earl Reid, a sculptor with a studio in Baltimore, agreed to create the work for not more than $15,000 to cover his expenses. There was no written contract. Reid, Snyder, and other members of the organization agreed on details of the design, which would portray the figures reclining on the grate, as homeless persons do to keep warm. The work was to be called "Third World America." During the two months it took Reid to complete the sculpture, Snyder and others went frequently to his studio to check on its progress and to coordinate the building of the base.

The work was delivered on Christmas Eve and remained on display as part of the pageant for a month. At the end of that time, Snyder proposed that the sculpture be taken on a tour of several cities to raise money for the homeless. Reid objected. He said that the material he had used would not stand such a trip. The figures were returned to Reid's studio for repair of minor damage incurred during their display.

In March 1986, Snyder asked Reid to turn the sculpture over to him and the Community for Creative Non-Violence. Reid refused. He filed an application for a copyright in his name and announced plans for a more modest tour than Snyder had suggested. Snyder countered by seeking copyright registration on behalf of his organization. He also filed suit in a federal district court asking for the return of "Third World America" and a resolution of the copyright dispute. The district court ruled that Reid had been hired to create the sculpture and therefore had no right to copyright it. On appeal, the U.S. Court of Appeals for the District of Columbia Circuit held that the arrangement between Reid and the Community for Creative Non-Violence did not make the sculptor an employee as defined by Section 101 of the Copyright Act. However, the circuit court sent the case back to the district court, suggesting that a closer look at the evidence might justify a conclusion that Reid and the Community had jointly created the disputed work, thus permitting them to share ownership of the copyright. On further appeal, the Supreme Court unanimously upheld the circuit court's decision.

The Supreme Court took the case to resolve conflicting circuit court opinions as to the meaning of Section 101. In its first part the section defines a "work made for hire" as a "work prepared by an employee within the scope of his or her employment." But the second part of the section attempts to define the circumstances under which "a work specially ordered or commissioned" will be considered as a "work made for hire." The language is so limited that it leaves many kinds of commissioned works, such as "Third World America," in limbo. The Court noted that how "work made for hire" is defined has "profound significance for freelance creators—including artists, writers, photographers, designers, composers, and computer programmers—and for the publishing, advertising, music, and other industries which commission their works."

After examining several cases in which it has made a distinction between employees and independent contractors, the Court concluded that the test most likely to bring about uniformity is that found in the common law of agency. Under that law, the examination begins with "the hiring party's right to control the manner and means by which the product is accomplished." The test proceeds to a study of the skill required to produce the work; the source and ownership of the tools and equipment used by the producer; the place at which the work is done; the duration of the relationship between the parties; whether the hiring party has a right to assign other duties to the producer; how much control the producer has over hours of work; the method of payment; the producer's control over the hiring and paying of assistants; whether the work is part of the regular business of the hiring party; and, indeed, whether the hiring party is in any business, the extent of employee benefits, if any, and the tax treatment of the hired party.

When those factors were examined in light of the arrangement between Reid and the Community for Creative Non-Violence, there was no doubt that the sculptor was an independent contractor, not an employee. Snyder and other trustees of the organization had conceived the idea and had provided occasional supervision, as well as the funding to cover Reid's expenses. But that ended it. As a sculptor, Reid was in a highly skilled vocation. He used his own tools and worked in his own studio. He was retained for about two months, a relatively short time. The Community had no right to expect him to do additional projects for it. He alone decided when and how long he would work, as long as he met the deadline. His payment was for a specific job. He alone decided to hire two assistants and determined how much he would pay them. The Community was not in business and certainly was not regularly engaged in creating works of sculpture. Finally, it provided Reid with no benefits and paid no taxes on his behalf. Therefore, the organization had no right to copyright "Third World America."[6]

Two cases early in the twentieth century defined the rights of photographers along these same lines. A photographer who was hired to take pictures of a newsworthy boxer found that the promoter who had hired him owned not only the copyright but also the negatives.[7] However, a photographer who had arranged to take pictures of members of a high school graduating class in the hope that he could sell enough of them to make a profit held a valid copyright on the class photograph.[8] Freelance photographers without written agreements run the risk of creating copyrights for other people, especially if they are satisfied to use someone else's film and chemicals or are told what to shoot, when, and how. Some neophyte wedding photographers have learned this the hard way after discovering that they could not charge for reprints because they had not made it clear that they, not the wedding couples who hired them, owned the copyrights.

Advertisers, too, need to be alert to copyright ownership. The U.S. Court of Appeals for the Fourth Circuit held that an advertiser who had asked a newspaper to prepare an advertisement and then had exercised no control over the creation of the ad could not claim a copyright on the ad.[9] The court said that the owner of the copyright was the newspaper unless a written contract specified otherwise. In this instance, the newspaper used its ownership of the copyright to prevent the advertiser from placing the ad with a competitor.

Finding the Owner

Copyrights are invisible and contracts are usually seen only by the parties involved. So most people do not really know who owns what rights when they see a film or a book or a magazine. Even the prominent display of copyright notice, while an important

---

6. See also Hi-Tech Video v. Capital Cities/ABC Inc., 58 F.3d 1093, 23 Med.L.Rptr. 2171 (6th Cir. 1995).
7. Lumiere v. Robertson-Cole Distributing Corp., 280 F. 550 (2d Cir. 1922).
8. Altman v. New Haven Union Co., 254 F. 113 (D.Conn. 1918).
9. Brunswick Beacon v. Schock-Hopchas Publishing Co., 810 F.2d 410, 13 Med.L.Rptr. 2030 (4th Cir. 1987).

device, does not always tell the whole story. Newspapers, for example, sometimes display a notice of copyright to advise competitors that they intend to control the rights to any staff-produced articles, photographs, advertisements, or any photographic reproduction of the paper. But such a notice of copyright does not mean that the newspaper owns the copyright to everything in its pages. It cannot claim, for example, a copyright to the news itself, or to anything published in the paper that is owned by others, such as letters to the editor, comics, syndicated columns, freelance stories, or news releases.

Magazines almost always display a notice of copyright and are more likely than newspapers to have purchased the copyright or part of it by a transfer clause in a contract. Yet magazines are compilations of material that may include works in the public domain, works that belong to individual authors, and works that were created for hire by the staff. A copyright notice on a magazine means only that the magazine claims a right to whatever it can claim as its own, which includes the way it chose to compile the magazine but not necessarily everything in it. A point worth remembering is that ownership always belongs to the author or to the employer unless it has been transferred in writing or is already in the public domain.

One place you won't find a copyright notice is on federal publications. There is no copyright protection for works created by the federal government, including reports by federal employees and opinions by judges. Their work belongs to the public that employs them. Consequently, such works are in the public domain and can be used by anyone.[10] Of course, some government documents are protected by a different sort of law—the classification of state secrets, a governmental power intended to protect interests far different from those protected by copyright.

Finding copyright owners can be a tiresome task, but you can at least begin with whatever notice has been attached to the work. If there is no notice, the job is harder but not impossible. The U.S. Copyright Office will allow you to search its collections on-line for materials dating from 1978, or you can search the Library of Congress card catalogue to identify the original owner. For a fee, you can use a searching service, such as the Copyright Clearance Center, a not-for-profit organization that helps obtain licenses for copyrighted materials. The Copyright Office is on the Internet at http://lcweb.loc.gov/copyright, and the Copyright Clearance Center is at http://www.copyright.com.

What Copyright Protects

Section 106 of the Copyright Act describes the rights that the copyright owner has in a work. Control over reproduction of the work is the first listed, but it is only one of the exclusive rights of an owner. Sometimes the other rights can be even more important. They are:

— The right to prepare derivative works, including translations, film documentaries, or any other subsequent work based on the original.

---

10.   17 U.S.C. § 105.

— The right to be the first person to distribute the work to the public. This right provides considerable control over unpublished manuscripts, letters, or other materials that have not been sold. Sometimes it is referred to as the right of first sale.

— The right to perform the copyrighted work publicly. This right is especially important for playwrights, composers, or writers of film documentaries.

— The right to display the copyrighted work publicly, including original photographs, paintings, sculptures, movies, and other works. Buying a collection of valuable photographs doesn't necessarily give the buyer the right to exhibit them publicly.

In 1990, Congress amended the act to include additional rights for visual artists. Although there are some exceptions, the protections consist of a lifetime right for an artist to control the use of his or her name and a right to prevent distortions, modifications, or mutilations of the work if it would be "prejudicial to his or her honor or reputation." These rights cannot be transferred but can be waived if waiver is specific and in writing.[11]

Section 102 of the Copyright Act describes the kinds of works that can be protected. Because the section is written in legal language, it is easier to understand if you look at each of its elements separately.

On a basic level, the work in question must be original with the creator. If the work borrows from others—say, by quoting extensively from a novel by Stephen King or from lyrics by John Cougar Mellencamp—the copyright does not cover the borrowed quotations. Further, the original work must be expressed in a tangible form "now known or later developed." This stipulation means that a writer must put words on paper or onto a computer disk; a photographer must make a photograph; a choreographer must diagram the positions of the dancers; a composer must take the notes pecked out on a piano and enter them onto a score; a broadcast news program must record the newscast. Whatever the form of the work, the creator must make possible the communication of the work to others, because it is at that point that the work becomes vulnerable to copying. For illustrative purposes, Section 102 lists seven categories of "works of authorship":

1. Literary works

2. Musical works, including any accompanying words

3. Dramatic works, including any accompanying words

4. Pantomimes and choreographic works

5. Pictorial, graphic, and sculptural works

6. Motion pictures and other audiovisual works

7. Sound recordings

---

11. 17 U.S.C. § 106A.

Computer Programs

The courts have long considered computer programs to fall into the category of literary works.[12] In 1980, Congress created an exception to allow copying of computer programs by permitting "owners of a copy of a computer program" to make a backup copy in case their original program would become damaged.[13] Almost all other copying of computer programs is an infringement of copyright.[14]

In 1988 the Copyright Office made it clear that it considered screen displays to be part of an overall computer program. Before that time, applicants frequently tried to protect a computer program as a literary work and its screen display as a separate pictorial or graphic work. The office decided that all copyrightable expression owned by the same claimant and embodied in a computer program, including the displays, should be a single work and should be registered on a single application form. In addition, the office said, in order to clarify copyright claims in computer screen displays, applicants could, if they wished, deposit visual reproductions of computer screens along with identifying materials for the computer code.[15] Today, the protection of the "look and feel" of a program turns primarily on whether the screen displays are being produced by an underlying program that is sufficiently original to be protected by copyright. But arguments about the protection of the screen displays continue to keep courts busy umpiring disputes among such familiar corporations as Atari, Nintendo, Apple, and Microsoft.

Originality is the key to the copyright protection of software, but originality can be elusive. For example, when Lotus Development Corporation sued Borland International for imitating its Lotus 1-2-3 spreadsheet "menus" in Borland's Quattro spreadsheet, a federal appeals court in Boston determined that the Lotus menus and commands, however original, were really just a "method of operation" like the buttons on a videocassette recorder or the QWERTY arrangement of keys on a typewriter. Methods of operation are specifically excluded from copyright protection under the 1976 act.[16] Courts can make fine distinctions between the part of the software that is an original contribution and the part that merely makes it work.

---

12. At least since the mid-1980s courts have held that programs are protectable by copyright whether in source or object code. Apple Computer, Inc. v. Formula International, Inc., 725 F.2d 521 (9th Cir. 1984); Apple Computer, Inc. v. Franklin Computer Corp., 714 F.2d 1240 (3d Cir. 1983). Also see June M. Besek, "Copyright Protection for Computer Software and Databases: An Overview." In *How to Handle Basic Copyright and Trademark Problems* (New York: Practising Law Institute, 1992).

13. In two controversial opinions, the Ninth Circuit has distinguished the rights of owners from the rights of licensees to copy software: MAI Systems Corp. v. Peak Computer Inc., 991 F.2d 511 (9th Cir. 1993), and Triad Corp. v. Southeastern Express, 64 F.3d 1330 (9th Cir. 1995).

14. 17 U.S.C. § 117. Section 101 defines a "computer program" as a "set of statements or instructions to be used directly or indirectly in a computer in order to bring about a certain result."

15. Copyright Office, *Circular 61, Copyright Registration for Computer Programs,* 1992. See also *Federal Register,* 10 June 1988, p. 21817.

16. Lotus Development Corp. v. Borland International Inc., 49 F.3d 807 (1st Cir. 1995); cert. granted, 116 S.Ct. 39, 132 L.Ed.2d 921 (1995). "A method of operation" is excluded from copyright protection at 17 U.S.C. § 102.

Video Clipping

Literary works can include "clippings" from newspapers or broadcast news programs. Of course, news events are not subject to copyright protection. No news medium can monopolize the reporting of a news event by attempting to register a copyright to the event. Neither do the notable facts of an individual's life nor the facts of history belong to anyone exclusively. On the other hand, a newspaper or television producer can register the copyright to its particular account of a news event, and an author who conducts research into an individual's life can register the copyright of his or her version of the events that made the individual interesting to the public.

Like newspapers and magazines, television stations own the copyright to all that is original in their news programs, including the way they have compiled and presented the information. However, they do not own items already in the public domain, or items expressed with such insufficient originality that they don't qualify for copyright, or items that belong to news sources. Ownership became an issue when Video Monitoring Services of America began to copy CNN's programs for clients who were willing to pay for "video clippings." CNN reacted by asking for and getting a temporary injunction to prevent commercial copying of its programs. On appeal, the monitoring service argued that the programs were made up of material that CNN did not own or could not legally register with the Copyright Office. A three-judge panel on the U.S. Court of Appeals for the Eleventh Circuit agreed, but it was a short-lived victory for the clipping service. CNN immediately asked that all the judges of the circuit meet to reconsider, and when they did they vacated the panel's opinion, dismissed the case, and let the injunction stand.[17] Even if CNN did not own the copyright to everything it collected and presented, it did own the copyright to the manner in which it had presented the things it had collected.

Shortly thereafter, a California case produced a similar result.[18] In *Los Angeles News Service* v. *Tullo,* the Ninth Circuit Court of Appeals upheld an injunction that prevented a video clipping service from recording television news programs and selling the "clips." The Los Angeles News Service had taped the sites of an airplane crash and a train wreck. The raw tape was later edited and used by its client television stations and networks. When Audio Video Reporting made recordings of those news broadcasts, the News Service sued for copyright infringement. The court rejected arguments that the raw footage was not sufficiently original to be protected by copyright or that there was a First Amendment or statutory right to record and sell clips of television news programs. The bottom line was that the News Service owned the copyright to the images, and the clipping service could not tape and sell them without permission.

---

17. CNN v. Video Monitoring Services, 833 F.2d 1472, 19 Med.L.Rptr. 1289 (11th Cir. 1991). The opinion was vacated on December 3, 1991, and the case was dismissed on April 4, 1992, when the trial court issued a permanent injunction protecting CNN.
18. 973 F.2d 791, 20 Med.L.Rptr. 1626 (9th Cir. 1992).

Telephone Directories

Originality should not be confused with hard work and enterprise. Sweat, tears, and long hours do not make a work original. And, of course, a work without that spark of originality is not protected by copyright, regardless of how great the effort was to create it.

In *Feist Publications, Inc.* v. *Rural Telephone Service Company, Inc.,* the U.S.

Feist Publications, Inc. v. Rural Telephone Service Company, Inc., 499 U.S. 340, 111 S.Ct. 1282, 112 L.Ed.2d 358, 18 Med.L.Rptr. 1889 (1991).

Supreme Court held that the facts found in the white pages of telephone directories are not original enough to be subject to copyright protection, no matter how hard it was to get and organize the information. At issue was an areawide directory of listings taken from smaller directories of eleven telephone companies in northwestern Kansas. This compilation was published by Feist and included both white pages, with the alphabetical telephone listings, and yellow pages made up of advertising arranged according to the service offered. The directory was sent without charge to all the persons or business firms listed in it.

In preparing its directory, Feist went to each of the eleven telephone companies and offered to pay for copying its white pages. Rural was the only one to refuse the offer. Feist took Rural's white pages anyway, weeded out those listings that fell outside the geographic range of its directory, and hired people to check the 4935 listings that remained. In addition to obtaining the data from Rural's white pages, Feist's checkers sought street addresses for each of its listings. In the end, 1309 of the listings were identical in both directories. Four of these were fictitious listings that Rural had included as a check on copying. Rural sued, arguing that Feist's copying was substantial enough to prove copyright infringement. A U.S. district court accepted the argument, and the U.S. Court of Appeals for the Tenth Circuit affirmed. A unanimous Supreme Court reversed.

Justice O'Connor, writing for the Court, started with a well-established principle of copyright law: Facts are never subject to copyright protection. The key to such protection, she continued, is originality. If it is to qualify for protection, a work must be independently created by the author and must have "at least some minimal degree of creativity; . . . even a slight amount will suffice." But no one "may claim originality as to facts . . . because they do not owe their origin to an act of authorship."

Rural argued that courts had long recognized a right to copyright compilations of facts. That is true, Justice O'Connor responded, but only when the compiler exercises choice as to the facts to be included and shows some originality or creativity in arranging them so that they may be used effectively by others. That limitation is reflected in Section 101 of the Copyright Act, which defines the kind of protection afforded to a compilation. The language makes clear that the law protects only compilations as a whole, not the individual facts that they comprise. The Court concluded that there is nothing original or creative in compiling the white pages of a telephone directory. Names are arranged in the only way that makes the listing useful, that is, in alphabetical order.

Rural also argued that the hard work that goes into compilations should make them eligible for copyright protection, but the Court rejected the idea. White pages listings,

Justice O'Connor wrote, are "not only unoriginal, [they are] practically inevitable. . . . [Copyright] rewards originality, not effort." Nowhere in the Copyright Act did the Court find any indication that Congress intended for hard work to stand as a substitute for originality.

Does that mean that a phone book or other directory can never be protected under copyright? No. A phone book—or a listing of sports scores, market reports, or some other compilation of facts—can be sufficiently original to be copyrightable, but hard work alone won't make that happen. The U.S. Court of Appeals for the Second Circuit, citing the *Feist* opinion, held that even a phone directory could meet the minimum criteria for originality under certain circumstances.[19] The court found those circumstances in a phone directory for New York City's Chinese-American community, which, the court said, was an original work because the compilers were selective in picking names to be included—businesses that in the judgment of the editors were not likely to stay in business were deleted—and the categories created for arranging the entries indicated a thoughtful effort to serve the interests of the Chinese-American community. The compilation included categories not found in other directories, for example: "BEAN CURD & BEAN SPROUT SHOPS."

Still, the court noted, it was the presentation and arrangement that was protected, not the hard work or the names and phone numbers. The latter are facts, and facts cannot be copyrighted.

Theories and Ideas

Ideas cannot be protected by copyright. And just as it is sometimes hard to see where facts end and a compiler's creativity begins, it is often equally difficult to separate an idea from its expression. For instance, can an original and imaginative theory about a historical event be copyrighted? The U.S. Court of Appeals for the Second Circuit said no. It held that a theory is an idea, not subject to copyright.

Hoehling **v.** *Universal City Studios, Inc.,* **618 F.2d 972, 6 Med.L.Rptr. 1053 (2d Cir. 1980).**

The case involved the explosion and fire that destroyed the German dirigible *Hindenburg* at Lakehurst, New Jersey, in May 1937, with the loss of thirty-six lives. That explosion has been the subject of considerable speculation for many years. The official verdict is that the fire probably was caused by static electricity that ignited the dirigible's highly flammable hydrogen. However, A. A. Hoehling spent years investigating the tragedy and came to a different conclusion. He concluded that a rigger, Eric Spehl, had planted a time bomb in one of the gas cells, intending to blow up the balloon after its passengers had disembarked. His purpose was to impress his girlfriend, an anti-Hitler Communist, in Germany. However, a thunderstorm delayed the ship's arrival, and Spehl was among those killed when his bomb went off. Hoehling described his theory in a book in 1962.

---

19.   Key Publications v. Chinatown Today Publishing Enterprises, 945 F.2d 509, 19 Med.L.Rptr. 1302 (2d Cir. 1991).

Ten years later, Michael Mooney took Hoehling's thesis and developed it into a fictionalized version entitled *The Hindenberg*. Universal City Studios bought the rights to Mooney's book and converted it into a motion picture that was released in 1975. Hoehling sued Universal for copyright infringement and lost. In upholding the district court's summary dismissal of the suit, the court of appeals said:

> [T]he protection afforded the copyright holder has never extended to history, be it documented fact or explanatory hypothesis. The rationale for this doctrine is that the cause of knowledge is best served when history is the common property of all, and each generation remains free to draw upon the discoveries and insights of the past. Accordingly, the scope of copyright in historical accounts is narrow indeed, embracing no more than the author's original expression of particular facts and theories already in the public domain. As the case before us illustrates, absent wholesale usurpation of another's expression, claims of copyright infringement where works of history are at issue are rarely successful.

The court held that Hoehling's thesis was not subject to copyright. His conclusion that Spehl had planted a bomb was simply one of many possible interpretations of historical data. The court added:

> To avoid a chilling effect on authors who contemplate tackling an historical issue or event, broad latitude must be granted to subsequent authors who make use of historical subject matter, including theories or plots.

The court said that its ruling would not excuse verbatim copying by one author of another's copyrighted work. But in this instance, it held, each author had developed the material in an individual way. In effect, the court sanctioned Mooney's and Universal's taking of Hoehling's idea but would not have sanctioned the taking of the language that Hoehling used to express that idea.

The U.S. Court of Appeals for the Seventh Circuit used the same reasoning in upholding the dismissal of a lawsuit that sought $10.5 million in damages from the producers of the television series *Simon and Simon*.[20] At issue was an episode in which Rick and A. J. Simon investigated the murder of a retired FBI agent who believed that John Dillinger, a onetime public enemy number 1, was not killed by police outside the Biograph theater in Chicago in 1934. Jay Robert Nash sued CBS Inc., MCA Inc., Universal City Studios, and others, alleging that they had violated his copyright on several books in which he maintained that Dillinger learned of the trap police set for him and induced a small-time hoodlum to take his place. The court concluded that the producers had indeed based the episode on Nash's books but ruled that the author's analysis of historical events was not protected by copyright. The court wrote: "The first person to conclude that Dillinger survived does not get dibs on history. If Dillinger survived, that fact is available to all."

---

20. Nash v. CBS, 899 F.2d 1537, 17 Med.L.Rptr. 1798 (7th Cir. 1990).

The Internet

The principles applied in the cases involving ideas also apply to information available on line. The Internet may be a difficult place to police copyright infringers, but it is not a place where copyright rules have been suspended. Original works of authorship are protected by copyright law in cyberspace as they are anywhere else.

Robert Penchina, a lawyer who specializes in copyright and First Amendment law in New York and Washington, D.C., offered some advice to newspaper publishers interested in using the Internet to gather or to report news.[21] He recommended the following:

— Any written or graphic material found on the Internet should be treated no differently from material found in rival newspapers: Do not republish it without express permission of the copyright owner.

— If you do not own the copyright to a work in your newspaper, do not post it on the Internet without permission of the copyright owner. For example, posting an entire newspaper on the net probably would violate some or all of your publication's agreements with wire services, feature syndicates, and advertising agencies, as well as with freelance authors, photographers, and graphic artists. Make sure contracts and licensing agreements include the right to distribute a work electronically.

— When posting anything of value on the Internet, prominently display copyright notice, and if access is limited to subscribers, specify the terms and conditions for subscribing to your electronic products. For example, you may want to specify that the works may be accessed only for personal, noncommercial use and may not be republished without prior consent.

Why all the limitations? Because copyright law is not dead on the Internet. Copyright owners, including Walt Disney, Paramount, Lotus, LucasArts, and BMI aggressively pursue infringers.[22] Playboy[23] and Sega[24] have shut down unauthorized electronic bulletin boards created to provide free copies of *Playboy* photos and Sega games. Business and professional newsletter publishers are especially aggressive about protecting copyrights. Those publishers pay bounties to informants who provide details about unauthorized copying. One $1,000 bounty produced a $100,000 settlement after Atlas Telecom, a software company in Portland, Oregon, was reported to be electronically redistributing about a dozen newsletters produced by Phillips Business Information across the country in Potomac, Maryland. Although Atlas Telecom had only one subscription to the newsletter, it had made hundreds of copies by putting the newsletter in its in-house database.[25]

---

21. Robert Penchina, "Venturing Online: Protecting You and Your Product in Cyberspace," *Editor & Publisher,* 24 June 1995, p. 15.
22. Lance Rose, "Is Copyright Dead?" In *Netlaw* (New York: McGraw-Hill, 1995), p. 88.
23. Playboy Enterprises Inc. v. Frena, 839 F.Supp. 1552 (M.D.Fla. 1993).
24. Sega Enterprises Ltd. v. Maphia, 857 F.Supp. 679, 30 U.S.P.Q.2d 1921 (N.D.Cal. 1994).
25. Junda Woo, "Electronic Copying May Bring Lawsuits," *Wall Street Journal,* 6 October 1993, p. B4.

In highly publicized cases, a songwriters association sued CompuServe for royalties after CompuServe subscribers began loading and downloading music from a CompuServe database.[26] The National Writers Union sued the *New York Times* and other periodicals, alleging a violation of copyright each time an article from the printed versions of their publications was electronically republished.[27] The Church of Scientology's Religious Technology Center sued Internet users in California, Colorado, and Virginia after they electronically posted church writings about spirituality.[28]

All of this high-profile litigation spurred the Clinton administration to propose amendments that would remove any lingering doubt among Internet users that transmission of books, magazines, and software through cyberspace is a form of copying covered by the Copyright Act. A presidential task force report in 1995 found that existing copyright law—which required distributors to obtain permission from copyright holders—was fundamentally adequate, but recommended changes to bring it in line with current technology.[29] Those changes, drafted into legislation by the House and Senate, make it clear that moving materials on or off the Internet is a form of copying that is protected by copyright.[30]

News Reports

These principles also apply to the coverage of news events. A reporter, like anyone else who reads about a newsworthy disclosure or sees an account of it on television, is not prevented from developing the same story. Reporters are free to go to sources mentioned in another's story and learn from them what they can. Reporters also can seek out other sources who know something about the event. As long as the resulting story does not quote substantially from the original story, or paraphrase it too closely without offering anything new, the reporter runs no risk of being penalized for copyright violation.

What reporters and others need to remember is that while facts, ideas, theories, and history belong to the public, an original work fixed in a tangible medium, even if that medium is only a computer memory, may be protected by copyright. It does not matter whether the work is a letter, press release, recorded conversation, interview, book, computer program, or term paper. To use it requires either permission, evidence that the work has passed into the public domain, or a demonstration that the use is a "fair use" in the public interest.

"Fair use" is the law's recognition that on occasion, even the most creative person cannot present something new without borrowing from a copyrighted work, even if the owner will not give permission. This recognition originally was established by the

---

26. Frank Music Corp. v. CompuServe, 93 Civ. 8153 (S.D.N.Y. 1993). Andrew Blum, "On-Line Music Copyright Case Settled," *National Law Journal* 8 January 1996, p. B1.
27. Rose, "Is Copyright Dead?" p. 103.
28. Mike Allen, "Dissidents on Computer Rile Scientology," *New York Times,* 14 August 1995, p. A7. James Brooke, "Ruling against Scientologists, Judge Orders Return of Seized Computer Files," *New York Times,* 14 September 1995, p. A11.
29. "Better Copyright Protection Urged for Electronic Networks," *New York Times,* 6 September 1995, p. C5.
30. NII Copyright Protection Act of 1995 (S. 1284 and H.R. 2441).

courts as the doctrine of fair use. Since 1978, that doctrine has been an explicit part of the Copyright Act.

The Doctrine of Fair Use

Fair use, as defined in Section 107 of the Copyright Act, permits one author, composer, or artist to borrow limited amounts of material from another without seeking permission. Fair use has nothing to do with the fact that honesty requires takers, no matter how inconsequential their taking, to give credit to their sources.

Section 107 says that copying another's work "for purposes such as criticism, comment, news reporting, teaching (including multiple copies for classroom use), scholarship, or research" is not an infringement, provided the use is fair. In determining whether a use is fair or not, Section 107 requires courts to consider the following factors:

1. The purpose and character of the use, including whether such use is of a commercial nature or is for nonprofit educational purposes

2. The nature of the copyrighted work

3. The amount and substantiality of the portion used in relation to the copyrighted work as a whole

4. The effect of the use upon the potential market for or value of the copyrighted work

Congress did not simply pick four principles out of the blue when it wrote Section 107 into the Copyright Act. Its definition of "fair use" was distilled from some court cases before 1978 that had recognized that the statute then in effect could not be enforced as it was written. Under its terms, any copying without permission, no matter how minor, was an infringement. Strict interpretation of the law would have stifled both scholarship and the market for popular literature, film, video and radio programming, and music. More than a century ago, courts began stretching the law to accommodate scholarly research and criticism of the arts. Thus, in 1841, in resolving a dispute between two biographers of George Washington, Justice Joseph Story wrote, "No one can doubt that a reviewer may fairly cite largely from the original work, if his design be really and truly to use the passages for fair and reasonable comment."[31]

Popular Works

Not until the middle of the twentieth century did courts become willing to extend the doctrine of fair use to protect works aimed at the popular market. The first case that did

---

31. Folsom v. Marsh, 9 F. Cas. 342 (C.C.D. Mass. 1841) (no. 4901).

so was *Rosemont Enterprises* v. *Random House.* In this case, the U.S. Court of Appeals for the Second Circuit established precedents on which Congress relied in drafting Section 107. The book involved in this landmark case was a biography of Howard Hughes.

At one time, Hughes was a highly visible public figure. Born to wealth, he enlarged his inherited fortune by providing services to the oil industry, by producing movies, and by building aircraft during World War II. Physically attractive, he was the companion of the most beautiful movie stars of the era. But in his later years, he retreated from public view, living in elaborately guarded hideouts and seeing no one except a few trusted associates. He protected his privacy with unmatched zeal and discouraged all attempts to pry into his life. This behavior made him even more a subject of public curiosity.

Rosemont Enterprises v. Random House, 366 F.2d 203 (2d Cir. 1966); cert. denied, 385 U.S. 1009, 87 S.Ct. 714, 17 L.Ed.2d 546 (1967).

In 1954, *Look* magazine capitalized on that curiosity by publishing a series of three articles recounting some of the more interesting episodes in Hughes's life. Nearly a decade later, Random House commissioned a writer to prepare a biography of Hughes that was aimed at the mass market. By that time, Hughes had become a recluse and refused all attempts to interview him. He tried to prevent publication of the Random House biography by buying the copyright to the *Look* articles and by filing a lawsuit for copyright infringement against the publisher. Pointing to the fact that the book, then in galley proofs, included accounts of incidents described in the magazine articles, he asked the court to issue an order forbidding the book from being published. Such prior restraint is one of the remedies provided by law against infringement.

A federal district judge in New York City ordered Random House not to release the book. He concluded that because it was aimed at a mass audience, it was not scholarly and therefore was not entitled to protection under the fair-use exception. The book contained only two direct quotations and one eight-line paraphrase that could be traced to language in the magazine articles. But the judge ruled that, given the popular nature of the book, even minimal copying was an infringement.

The court of appeals reversed, holding that the duplication of incidents did not prove infringement. Hughes was what he was and he did what he did. Biographers who portrayed him accurately obviously would describe many of the same incidents. As for the direct copying, the court held that it was minimal and, in any event, justified because the book dealt with a matter of public interest. Breaking new legal ground, the court said that when a book serves the public interest, it is protected by fair use, even though it is aimed at a mass audience. Hughes's life, the court said, reminds us that "initiative, ingenuity, determination and tireless work" are the keys to achievement "even in an affluent society."

Copying in the Public Interest

During the decade between the Second Circuit's decision in *Rosemont* and the revision of the Copyright Act in 1976, courts expanded the idea that the public interest protects some copying of another's work. One of the more notable cases involved admitted direct copying, albeit in another medium, of frames taken from a movie film of the assassination of President John F. Kennedy.

When Kennedy was shot to death on the streets of Dallas in 1963, Abraham Zapruder, a dress manufacturer, happened to record the event with his eight-millimeter movie camera. His film, in color, showed the president as the bullets struck him. *Life* magazine paid Zapruder $150,000 for exclusive rights to the film. Blown-up excerpts from it were used extensively by the magazine. Because there were no other photographs of the shooting itself, *Life* made copies of the Zapruder film for the commission named by President Lyndon B. Johnson to investigate the assassination. A number of still frames appeared in the final report, with the notation that *Life* held exclusive rights to their use.

While the commission held that the evidence pointed conclusively to Lee Harvey Oswald as the lone assassin, others speculated that the two bullets that struck the president had been fired from different locations. Among these theorists was Josiah Thompson, a professor of philosophy, who wrote a book called *Six Seconds in Dallas,* published by Bernard Geis Associates and distributed by Random House. Thompson tried and failed to get permission from *Life* to copy frames from the Zapruder film. However, his finished book was illustrated with charcoal drawings that were identified as "exact copies" of frames from the film.

Time Inc. v. Bernard Geis Associates, 293 F.Supp. 130 (S.D.N.Y. 1968).

When Time Inc., owner of *Life,* sued for copyright infringement, a U.S. district court in New York City made two important findings:

1. The film, even though it recorded a news event, could be copyrighted because Zapruder had taken enough care in selecting his vantage point that he had created an original composition.

2. The assassination, and Thompson's two-gunmen theory, were of great enough public interest to justify such copying as Thompson had done.

In any event, the court reasoned, Thompson's book was not likely to diminish the value of the film. If anything, it might stir enough interest in some people to lead them to seek a copy of the film itself.

Since its codification in the Copyright Act of 1976, the fair-use doctrine has continued to play an important role in determining when public interest should override protection for the ownership of expression. The Second Circuit Court of Appeals, for example, found that fair use justified the extensive copying of published interviews with women who had undergone abortions. The court came to this conclusion over the protests of the interviewer, who had refused to give permission to copy from her book. The court held that use of the interviews, like use of the rare Zapruder film, was a fair use in light of the nature and purpose of the publication.

In 1973, right after the Supreme Court had made abortions legal,[32] Katrina Maxtone-Graham interviewed seventeen women who had abortions, or who had considered having one, and published her findings under the title, *Pregnant by Mistake.* The book sold about twenty-two hundred copies before it went out of print. When it went out of print, Maxtone-Graham acquired the copyright from the original publisher.

Maxtone-Graham v. *Burtchaell*, 803 F.2d 1253 (2d Cir. 1986), cert. denied, 481 U.S. 1059 (1987).

In 1976, James Tunstead Burtchaell, a Catholic priest and professor of theology at the University of Notre Dame, wrote an essay entitled "Rachel Weeping," in which he quoted extensively from Maxtone-Graham's interviews and commented on them. The purposes of these two works were diametrically opposed. Maxtone-Graham supported the right to obtain an abortion. Burtchaell's purpose was to show that women who choose abortion suffer long-term, adverse psychological effects. When Burtchaell decided to include the essay in a book by the same name, he sought permission from Maxtone-Graham to quote from the interviews. When she refused, the priest decided on advice of counsel to publish anyway. Maxtone-Graham filed a copyright infringement action in a U.S. district court in New York City. That court granted summary judgment in favor of Burtchaell. On appeal, Judge Irving R. Kaufman, writing for a unanimous panel, conceded that "summary judgment on the question of fair use has been the exception rather than the rule," but held that it was justified in this instance.

The decision is of interest not only because it expanded the scope of fair use, but because it illustrates how courts apply the four principles in Section 107 of the Copyright Act. The court looked first at the nature of Burtchaell's book. It was commercial in the sense that it was written for a general audience. It was published in a hardcover edition in 1982 by Andrews & McMeel and in a softcover edition in 1984 by Harper & Row. By the time the case reached the court of appeals, about six thousand copies had been sold. However, the court found that the educational elements of *Rachel Weeping* far outweighed the commercial aspects of the book. Burtchaell's purpose in writing was criticism and comment. Maxtone-Graham had reported the interviews almost verbatim. Burtchaell had analyzed the women's accounts of their experiences with pregnancy and abortion and had organized the material "into a topical framework to make the case against abortion." In doing so, he had "applied substantial intellectual labor to the verbatim quotations, continually offering his own insights and opinions." The court concluded that Burtchaell's scholarship, even though it was flawed by taking some of the quotations out of context, outweighed the commercial purpose of his work. Thus, the first factor used in determining whether a use is fair was decided in his favor.

The court then turned its attention to the nature of Maxtone-Graham's work, *Pregnant by Mistake,* finding it essentially reportorial. This did not mean, the court said, that the book did not contain "elements of creative journalistic effort." It did, but as a whole "the book was essentially factual in nature." Referring to the *Rosemont* case, the court said, "Like the biography, the interview is an invaluable source of material

---

32.   The Supreme Court held in Roe v. Wade, 410 U.S. 113, 93 S.Ct. 705, 35 L.Ed.2d 147 (1973), that laws forbidding abortions violate a woman's constitutional right of privacy.

for social scientists, and later use of verbatim quotations within reason is both foreseeable and desirable." Thus, the second factor, too, favored Burtchaell.

The third factor, the amount and substantiality of the copying, presented a more difficult problem for the court. Burtchaell had copied extensively from Maxtone-Graham's book. He had directly quoted seven thousand words, or 4.3 percent of *Pregnant by Mistake*. There were only thirty-seven thousand words in the title essay of *Rachel Weeping*. Thus, nearly one-fifth of the essay was made up of material taken from Maxtone-Graham's interviews. As copyright infringement cases go, this amounted to a substantial taking.

But as the court noted, in weighing the third factor there are no absolute rules. In some instances, courts have condoned wholesale copying. In others, they have found infringement in the taking of only "a tiny portion" of the original work. The inquiry must focus on the nature of what was taken. In this instance, Burtchaell took quotations. He said that he had considered conducting his own interviews but had concluded that he could not because women who seek abortions probably would not speak freely to a priest. Thus, the credibility of such interviews as he might be able to conduct would be open to question. Therefore, he had decided to rely on verbatim quotations from Maxtone-Graham's book to make his discussion of the problems arising from abortions more credible. In light of those facts, the court concluded that the priest's taking was reasonable.

The fourth factor, the effect of the alleged infringement on the market for the original work, is "the single most important element of fair use."[33] In this instance, *Pregnant by Mistake* was out of print. Maxtone-Graham said that she intended to publish some copies on her own, but she had not done so. In any event, the two books served such different purposes that it was unlikely that one would have an adverse effect on the market for the other. The court concluded that readers of Burtchaell's book might even be led to try to buy *Pregnant by Mistake*.

With its conclusion that all four factors involved in fair-use analysis condoned Burtchaell's copying, the court ruled that the district court had acted properly in summarily dismissing Maxtone-Graham's infringement lawsuit.

A fair-use defense did not support Texaco, however, when it was sued by publishers who complained that a Texaco scientist had photocopied eight journal articles for his research files. Although Texaco argued that the scientist had made the copies for research purposes because the copying allowed him to write in the margins and avoid taking the originals into his messy lab, and because it sped circulation of the journals to colleagues, the court found that the copying was not a fair use.

American Geophysical Union v. Texaco, 60 F.3d 913 (2d Cir. 1994).

Texaco employs four hundred to five hundred scientists nationwide. Those scientists need access to research and technical journals to help them stay abreast of developments, and the company subscribes to journals and has its library circulate current issues to each scientist who places his or her name on a routing list. Most of the scientists photocopy or ask librarians and secretaries to photocopy the articles they

---

33. Quoting from Harper & Row, Publishers, Inc. v. Nation Enterprises, 105 S.Ct. 2218, 2234 (1985).

are most interested in having. In the aggregate, this amounts to the systematic copying of thousands of articles every month. The American Geophysical Union and eighty-two other publishers sued, claiming that Texaco's unauthorized photocopying was causing them significant financial harm. To simplify the case, the parties agreed to focus on one scientist chosen at random. That scientist turned out to be Dr. Donald H. Chickering II, who worked as a chemical engineer at Texaco's research center in Beacon, New York. From Chickering's files the court looked at eight articles copied from the *Journal of Catalysis,* a monthly publication of Academic Press, Inc., which owns the copyrights to each article published in its journal.

Texaco initially had only one subscription to *Catalysis* but increased that to two in 1983 and to three in 1988. All eight of the articles in Chickering's files had been photocopied from *Catalysis* in their entirety and kept for future reference. The critical question, said the court, was not whether an individual scientist could copy a few articles to aid in his scientific research. That might well be a fair use. The question was whether the practice of institutional, systematic copying for company employees, thereby increasing the number of copies available while avoiding the necessity of paying the cost of license fees or additional subscriptions, was fair. After reviewing the nature and purpose of the copying by Texaco, the amount taken, and the effect on the potential market, the court concluded that the copying was not fair.

First, the articles were copied, if Chickering was typical, primarily so that they would be conveniently available for reference when needed. Chickering, in fact, had never used five of the articles copied for him. If Chickering, said the court, "had asked the library to buy him a copy of the pertinent issue of *Catalysis* and had placed it on his shelf, and one day while reading it had noticed a chart, formula, or other material that he wanted to take right into the lab, it might be a fair use for him to make a photocopy." That, however, was not what happened here, and the first factor of analysis weighed against Texaco.

Second, the factual nature, rather than any artistic or creative attributes, of the articles was what made them useful to Chickering. Because copyright law recognizes the need to disseminate factual works, the second factor of analysis weighed in favor of Texaco.

Third, the fact that the amount copied was the entire content of the articles obviously weighed against Texaco.

Fourth, while the court agreed with Texaco that it wasn't likely that a few more subscriptions would have much impact on the market for scientific journals, it agreed with the publishers that there was a significant financial impact on the publishers. The court noted that because of the creation of the Copyright Clearance Center, the publishers were being deprived of a potential market for licensing revenues and fees. The Copyright Clearance Center is a nonprofit, central clearinghouse that was established in 1977, primarily by publishers at the suggestion of Congress, to license photocopying. The center maintains a variety of services, but primarily it provides a convenient mechanism for organizations like Texaco to obtain authorization to copy materials.[34] Accordingly, this final factor weighed against Texaco.

---

34. The Copyright Clearance Center is accessible on the Internet at htttp://www.copyright.com.

Six months after the court's decision, Texaco and the publishers agreed on terms to settle the dispute amicably. Texaco agreed to pay a seven-figure settlement and retroactive licensing fees to the Copyright Clearance Center and to enter into a standard annual license agreement with the center during the next five years.[35]

Unpublished Letters

The interplay among the four factors of fair-use analysis was dramatically illustrated in an instance involving the copying of unpublished letters that were publicly available in university libraries. The author who had penned the letters said that he had no intention of publishing them or of selling the rights to them, but the court concluded that if he changed his mind, his work could be worth thousands of dollars.

The case of the unpublished letters involved a biography of J. D. Salinger, author of *Catcher in the Rye.* The biography, like the one of Howard Hughes at issue in *Rosemont,* was of a public figure who had chosen, for more than twenty years, to reject public attention. Salinger continued that rejection by refusing to cooperate in any way with the biographer. However, over the years Salinger had written many letters to various individuals who had given them to research libraries for safekeeping. Like anyone who writes a letter, Salinger owned the copyright in those letters, but he said he had no intention of ever publishing them.

In 1983 Ian Hamilton, literary critic of the *London Sunday Times,* began work on a biography of Salinger to be published by Random House. Hamilton informed Salinger of the project and asked for his cooperation. Salinger refused, but the biographer discovered that between 1939 and 1961 Salinger had written letters to several persons, including a famous U.S. circuit court judge, Learned Hand, and a noted fellow author, Ernest Hemingway. Some of the recipients, recognizing the probable historical value of the letters, had given them to libraries at Harvard, Princeton, and the University of Texas. Hamilton was able to read the letters at the libraries, but he also had to sign agreements that he would not publish the letters without permission from the library or "the owner of the literary property rights." Under the 1976 version of the Copyright Act, that owner was Salinger. Section 106(3) protected unpublished works and gave their producers the right of first publication.

Salinger **v.** *Random House, Inc.,* **811 F.2d 90 (2d Cir. 1987); rehearing denied, 818 F.2d 252 (2d Cir. 1987); cert. denied, 108 S.Ct. 213 (1987).**

Nevertheless, Hamilton drew extensively in direct quotation and paraphrase from the letters in preparation of a version of the biography that reached the galley proof stage in May 1986. One set of the proofs was sent to Salinger for his comment. He reacted by registering seventy-nine of his unpublished letters for copyright protection and by telling his lawyer to object to publication of the book until all of the material taken from the letters had been removed.

---

35. "Texaco Finally Settles 1985 Infringement Case," *CCC On Line,* 22 December 1995.

Hamilton and Random House responded by revising the manuscript to remove all but about two hundred words of direct quotation. Passages that had been taken directly from the letters, using Salinger's words, were changed to close paraphrases. Proofs of the new version were sent to Salinger in October 1986. He identified fifty-nine instances of what he believed to be direct takings from his letters. He filed suit to prevent publication of the book. Judge Pierre Leval of a U.S. district court in New York City granted a temporary restraining order, then ruled after trial that because the copying was minimal, Hamilton's biography made a fair use of Salinger's letters. On appeal, the circuit court reversed.

Judge Jon O. Newman held that because the letters were unpublished, the presumptions must run against the claim that Hamilton's taking was a fair use. Applying the fair-use factors found in Section 107, he concluded that only one of the four factors—the nature of the biography—ran in Hamilton's favor. The book was, the judge said, a scholarly work, a product of research. The material taken from the letters discovered by that research would add materially to the public's insights into Salinger's literary career. Further, the judge said that Hamilton had every right to take facts and ideas from the author's letters because such content could not be copyrighted. But he had no right to take Salinger's method of expression, his "vividness of description." And judging from excerpts in the footnotes to this case, some of Salinger's description—of Charlie Chaplin and Wendell Willkie, for instance—was quite vivid indeed.

Newman said that the second factor in fair-use analysis—the nature of the copyrighted work—weighed heavily in Salinger's favor. The letters were unpublished. Even though they had been placed in libraries, Salinger had not lost control over them. Their content remained his. Only the physical form of the letters belonged to the recipients. The court said that until Salinger chose to publish the letters, he retained absolute control over their content.

On the third factor—the amount and substantiality of the taking—the circuit court disagreed with Judge Leval's conclusion that the taking was minimal. While relatively few of Salinger's words had been used in precisely the order in which he had written them, the paraphrases so closely followed the original passages as to constitute "a very substantial appropriation." "To a large extent, they make the book worth reading. The letters are quoted or paraphrased on approximately 40 percent of the book's 192 pages." Thus, this factor, too, weighed heavily in Salinger's favor.

As for the fourth factor, Salinger said that he had no intention of profiting by publishing the letters himself. But the circuit court said that was not material: "Salinger has the right to change his mind. He is entitled to protect his opportunity to sell his letters, an opportunity estimated by his literary agent to have a current value in excess of $500,000." Thus, this factor, too, weighed in Salinger's favor.

The court said that its ruling that the book infringed Salinger's copyright in his letters ought not prevent publication of a biography of the author. Judge Newman noted that the letters contain "a number of facts that students of his life and writings will no doubt find of interest, and Hamilton is entirely free to fashion a biography that reports those facts." And that is what Hamilton did. His book, *J. D. Salinger: A Writing Life,* was published by Random House in the summer of 1988.

The court's opinion was widely criticized by authors who saw it as an undue restriction on biographers.[36] Subsequent decisions in the Second Circuit, however, have made it clear that copyright protection for unpublished works does not automatically prevail in a fair-use analysis. The scope of fair use may be narrower with respect to unpublished works,[37] but that is only to say that the analysis is not mechanical. To emphasize that the scope is narrow is not to close it off entirely. That was the position of the Second Circuit in 1991 when it held that Dr. Margaret Walker's use of novelist Richard Wright's unpublished letters was a fair use.[38] Unlike the Salinger case, the taking was small, limited mostly to facts and ideas, and less threatening to the potential of any financial rewards of the copyright owner.

The cases in this section make abundantly clear that copyright law, as written by Congress and interpreted by the courts, condones some copying. Every writer about George Washington is not required to research government archives and major libraries for original documents bearing on his life. If the taking provides a public benefit, if no more is taken than necessary to provide that benefit, and if the taking does not harm the commercial value of the copied work, it is likely to be a fair use.

Parody

Although the Copyright Act does not specifically list parody as an example of a fair use,[39] the Supreme Court has made it clear that parody, even for a blatantly commercial purpose, is not excluded from consideration. When the rap group 2 Live Crew recorded its version of the Roy Orbison hit, "Oh, Pretty Woman," Acuff-Rose Music, Inc., the owners of the copyright, sued its record company, Luke Sykwalker Records, for copyright infringement.

Although Acuff-Rose refused permission to use the parody, 2 Live Crew included it anyway in a collection entitled *As Clean As They Wanna Be*. The album and compact disks had sold more than a quarter million copies by the time Acuff-Rose sued. The federal district court thought that the song was a fair use,[40] but the Sixth Circuit Court of Appeals reversed,[41] holding that the admittedly commercial purpose of the recording prevented the parody from being considered a fair use. The case reached the Supreme Court in *Campbell* v. *Acuff-Rose Music Inc.*

---

36. The Second Circuit Court of Appeals noted and disregarded the critical commentary in New Era Publications v. Carol Publishing Group, 904 F.2d 152, 17 Med.L.Rptr. 1915 (2d Cir. 1990).
37. New Era Publications International v. Carol Publishing Group, 904 F.2d 152, 17 Med.L.Rptr. 1913 (2d Cir. 1990). See Public Law 102-492, 24 October 1992, amending copyright law to clarify that the fair use doctrine applies to unpublished as well as published works.
38. Wright v. Warner Books, Inc., 953 F.2d 731; 19 Med.L.Rptr. 1577 (2d Cir. 1991).
39. The Copyright Act lists "criticism, comment, news reporting, teaching,…scholarship, or research." 17 U.S.C. § 107.
40. 754 F.Supp. 1150 (M.D.Tenn. 1991).
41. 972 F.2d 1429 (6th Cir., 1992).

Justice Souter, writing for the Court, said that he did not like bright-light rules that create presumptions of unfairness just because a work has a commercial rather than a political or artistic purpose. He said the four factors that must always be used to determine whether a use of someone else's work is a fair use should not be treated "in isolation, one from another. All are to be explored, and the results weighed together."

Campbell v. *Acuff-Rose Music Inc.,* **114 S.Ct. 1164, 22 Med.L.Rptr. 1353 (1994).**

As for the first factor—the purpose of the copying—Souter said that parody, like other comment or criticism, can claim fair-use status when it provides a public benefit "by shedding light on an earlier work, and, in the process, creating a new one."

We think it fair to say that 2 Live Crew's song reasonably could be perceived as commenting on the original or criticizing it, to some degree. 2 Live Crew juxtaposes the romantic musings of a man whose fantasy comes true, with degrading taunts, a bawdy demand for sex, and a sigh of relief from paternal responsibility. The later words can be taken as a comment on the naivete of the original of an earlier day, as a rejection of its sentiments that ignores the ugliness of street life and the debasement that it signifies. It is this joinder of reference and ridicule that marks off the author's choice of parody from the other types of comment and criticism that traditionally have had a claim to fair use protection as transformative works.

That the parody was commercial rather than nonprofit might weigh against a finding of fairness in some situations—for example, when a parody is used to advertise a product, but here the sale of the parody was for its own sake. What matters is not that it has a commercial purpose but rather what the commercial effect is likely to be on the copyright owner.

As for the second factor—the nature of the copyrighted work—the Court said that there could be no doubt that the song fell within the protective purposes of the Copyright Act.

As for the third factor—the substantiality of the amount taken—the Court said that what matters is that no more is taken than is necessary to produce the intended effect. In this case, it was necessary to copy the "heart" of the original—the opening riff and first line—to make the parody work. Justice Souter wrote:

This is not, of course, to say that anyone who calls himself a parodist can skim the cream and get away scot free. In parody, as in news reporting, . . . context is everything, and the question of fairness asks what else the parodist did besides go to the heart of the original. It is significant that 2 Live Crew not only copied the first line of the original, but thereafter departed markedly from the Orbison lyrics for its own ends. 2 Live Crew not only copied the bass riff and repeated it, but also produced otherwise distinctive sounds, interposing "scraper" noise, overlaying the music with solos in different keys, and altering the drum beat. This is not a case, then, where "a substantial portion" of the parody itself is composed of a "verbatim" copying of the original. . . .

Suffice it to say here that, as to the lyrics, we think the Court of Appeals correctly suggested that "no more was taken than necessary," . . . but just for that reason, we fail to see how the copying can be excessive in relation to its parodic purpose, even if the portion taken is the original's "heart."

As for the fourth factor—the effect on the potential market of the copyrighted work—the Court said that there was little evidence of harm in the only market that mattered: the market for rap versions of "Oh, Pretty Woman." The Court said that losses caused by mere criticism are not protected by copyright, and since it is unlikely that copyright owners would willingly harm themselves financially, the law does not recognize a market for self-parody. 2 Live Crew had not produced a verbatim rendition of "Oh, Pretty Woman" in an attempt to compete in the rock or pop markets. "It is impossible," said the Court, "to deal with the fourth factor except by recognizing that a silent record on an important factor bearing on fair use" means that 2 Live Crew is not entitled to summary judgment. "The evidentiary hole will doubtless be plugged on remand," concluded the Court.

Parody, then, like other forms of criticism, can be defended as a fair use, provided that it takes no more of the original than is necessary for an effective parody, and provided that it does not harm the market for the original work or harm the potential market for new versions of the original work. The ultimate burden is on the parodist. He or she must be able to demonstrate to the court how the nature of the original work, the purpose of the new work, the amount taken, and the effect on the market—all taken together—justify the use as fair.

Copyright Infringement

Access and Substantial Similarity

Courts considering copyright cases have recognized that it is possible for composers, authors, and artists working independently to create works that present the same themes in roughly the same way. Thus, evidence that two works are similar is not enough to prove infringement. There also needs to be a showing by the copyright owner who alleges harmful copying that the alleged infringer had the opportunity to see the work. Sonya Jason was able to prove neither similarity nor access and therefore lost an infringement action against Jane Fonda.

In 1972 Jason had written and published, at her own expense, the book *Concomitant Soldier—Woman and War.* About half the press run of eleven hundred copies was sold in New Jersey, where Jason lived. In 1977 some of the remaining copies were sold in southern California. The general theme of the book dealt with the return of an injured soldier from war and the effect of his injury on the women in his life.

Jason v. Fonda, **526 F.Supp. 774, 7 Med.L.Rptr. 2421 (C.D.Cal. 1981); affirmed, 698 F.2d 966 (9th Cir. 1982).**

Jane Fonda toured military bases and hospitals during the Vietnam war and became active in the movement against the war. Those experiences gave her and Bruce Gilbert an idea for a movie, which they outlined to a writer, Nancy Dowd, in 1972. Dowd submitted a script to Fonda and Gilbert the next year. They submitted it to other writers for revision. The result was a movie, *Coming Home,* which was produced in 1977. Its theme, too, dealt with the return of an injured soldier and his effect on the women in his life. United Artists released the film in 1978, and the movie was shown on the NBC television network the next year. Jason sued in the U.S. district court in Los Angeles, alleging copyright infringement.

The court dismissed the action, holding that Jason could not prove that anyone connected with the film had seen her book. Further, the time sequence made it clear that most of the photography had been completed before Jason's book went on sale on the west coast. Nor was there substantial similarity between the book and the movie. Although both dealt with the "effects of war on women, injured veterans and soldiers," these topics have been "the subject of countless works dating back for centuries." The book and the movie shared only themes, unprotectable ideas, and "commonly cited historical facts," none of which are subject to copyright.

What all this means is that access and substantial similarity are two pieces of circumstantial evidence that work in tandem. When works are nearly identical, a simple showing of an opportunity for access may be sufficient to convince a court of infringement, but if the works vary substantially, then it may be necessary to prove access. Of course, as in *Jason* v. *Fonda,* when there is neither similarity nor access, there is no evidence of infringement.

Yet sometimes there can be both access and substantial similarity and still no infringement, especially in the context of news reporting. William Russell, Jr., found out how that was possible when he complained that the *Gilpin County Advocate* was copying news from his *Weekly-Register Call.*[42] The *Call* was the only newspaper in Gilpin County, Colorado, until 1989, the year that Kay Turnbaugh started the *Advocate,* hired a reporter, and began to compete.

Turnbaugh admitted that she had access to the *Call.* The U.S. district court in 1991 even found that some of the articles were substantially similar. However, said the judge, copyright laws do not protect historical or contemporary facts, material traceable to common sources or in the public domain. Moreover, he said, authors may not claim copyright in statements made by others and reported or quoted in their work.

Of significance to the court was evidence that the articles in both papers were largely derived from press releases and issues raised at public meetings. The *Advocate,* in short, could show that its articles—although substantially similar in wording to those in the *Call*—were derived from its access to sources other than the *Call.*

The First Amendment and Fair Use

If the plaintiff in a copyright action can offer reasonable proof that the work was copyrightable and registered, that the alleged infringer had access to the plaintiff's work and that the works are substantially similar, the court then analyzes the competing works in light of the four factors found in Section 107 for fair use. If the defendant's taking does not qualify as a fair use, it is an infringement, and the court can either prevent further sales of the infringing work, or order its producer to pay damages to the plaintiff.

In the 1970s, however, some legal scholars and a few judges looked at the *Rosemont* and *Geis* decisions and found in them an intriguing element. In both in-

---

42.   Russell v. Turnbaugh, 18 U.S.P.Q.2d 1948, 18 Med.L.Rptr 2189 (D.C.Colo. 1991).

stances, the courts had held that the public interest justified a fair use under circumstances that might otherwise have been considered an infringement. In *Rosemont,* the public interest was found in the lessons people might learn by reading the biography of an unusual person who had built a fortune through hard work and enterprise. In *Geis,* the public had an interest in the theory that President Kennedy had been shot by two assassins rather than the lone gunman identified by authorities. In the minds of some, these decisions raised a question: Weren't the courts saying that First Amendment values protect more copying than the bare words of the law seem to justify? In one instance, a federal district court judge in Miami was explicit in holding that the First Amendment justified the *Miami Herald's* copying of a cover of *TV Guide.*[43] Other alleged infringers also invoked the First Amendment as a defense for their copying.

One of them was *Nation* magazine, which scored a journalistic coup in April 1979 by publishing excerpts from former President Gerald Ford's not-yet-released memoirs, *A Time to Heal.* The excerpts, including three hundred to four hundred words of direct quotation from Ford's book, gave new insights into former President Nixon's involvement in the Watergate burglary and into Ford's subsequent pardon of Nixon. The article also contained Ford's candid appraisal of some of the leading political figures of the day. Victor Navasky, the editor of *Nation* and author of the article, was correct in his belief that he had a newsworthy scoop. The article became the subject of widespread news stories and commentary.

The publication also had other effects. Harper & Row and the Reader's Digest Association, co-owners of the copyright on the book,

Harper & Row, Publishers, Inc. v. Nation Enterprises, 471 U.S. 539, 105 S.Ct. 2218, 85 L.Ed.2d 588, 11 Med.L.Rptr. 1969 (1985).

had obtained Ford's permission to sell excerpts from the book to magazines and newspapers in advance of its publication. One of the purchasers was *Time* magazine, which agreed to pay $25,000 for the right to publish a seventy-five-hundred-word excerpt dealing with the Nixon pardon. It had paid $12,500 in advance and had scheduled its article to appear in mid-April 1979. When the *Nation* article appeared, *Time* canceled the deal. Harper & Row reacted by suing *Nation* for copyright infringement. After a six-day trial, the U.S. District Court for the Southern District of New York found that there was indeed an infringement and awarded Harper & Row $12,500 in actual damages.

Nation appealed, arguing that the district court had not paid enough attention to the First Amendment value of its newsworthy scoop. The U.S. Court of Appeals for the Second Circuit, the same court that had decided *Rosemont,* agreed that the disclosures were "politically significant." It held that it is not "the purpose of the Copyright Act to impede the harvest of knowledge so necessary to a democratic state" or "chill the activities of the press by forbidding a circumscribed use of copyrighted words."[44] The court reversed the district court's decision, holding that when First Amendment interests were considered, *Nation's* article was a fair use, not an infringement.

The Supreme Court reversed the court of appeals, six to three. In doing so, it emphasized that no part of Ford's book had been released officially for publication

---

43. Triangle Publications, Inc. v. Knight-Ridder Newspapers, 445 F.Supp. 875 (S.D.Fla. 1978); affirmed on other grounds, 626 F.2d 1171 (5th Cir. 1980).
44. 723 F.2d 195, at 197, 209 (2d Cir. 1982).

When Victor S. Navasky, pictured here, scooped *Reader's Digest* and *Time* magazine with the story of President Gerald Ford's pardon of former President Richard Nixon, he found himself in the midst of a copyright infringement suit. The Court found Navasky's magazine, the *Nation,* did not have the right to quote major excerpts from Ford's soon-to-be-published autobiography without permission from his publisher, Harper & Row. *(William E. Sanro/ NYT Pictures)*

at the time the article appeared. The Court said that the right to control the release of one's work, and to prevent others from using it before release, is a key factor in fair-use analysis. The Court noted that the timing of release not only is important to the value of a work; it also assures authors time "to develop their ideas free from fear of expropriation." The latter consideration alone, the Court said, "outweighs any short term 'news value' to be gained from premature publication of the author's expression."

The Court also dealt with the First Amendment defense raised in the lower courts. The Court noted that *Nation* had sought to justify its copying of Ford's language "as essential to reporting the news story" embodied in his book. The magazine's lawyers argued in their brief that "the precise manner in which [Ford] expressed himself was as newsworthy as what he had to say." They argued further that the public's interest in getting that news as quickly as possible overrode the author's right to control the first publication of his autobiography.

Justice Sandra Day O'Connor, writing for a majority, rejected that argument. Adoption of the *Nation's* theory of the law, she wrote, "would expand fair use to effectively destroy any expectation of copyright protection in the work of a public figure." Copyright would mean little, especially to public figures, if its protections "could be avoided merely by dubbing the infringement a fair use 'news report' of the book." The infraction is particularly grave, Justice O'Connor added, when, as in this instance, it preempts the author's right of first publication.

Turning directly to the First Amendment question, the justice noted that "the Framers intended copyright itself to be the engine of free expression." By protecting authors' rights to profit from their work, "copyright supplies the economic incentive to create and disseminate ideas." At the same time, the law recognizes that First Amendment interests also are served by the permission of some copying under limited circumstances. Justice O'Connor summed up the Court's position:

> In view of the First Amendment protections already embodied in the Copyright Act's distinction between copyrightable expression and uncopyrightable facts and ideas, and the latitude for scholarship and comment traditionally afforded by fair use, we see no warrant for expanding the doctrine of fair use to create what amounts to a public figure exception to copyright. Whether verbatim copying from a public figure's manuscript in a given case is or is not fair use must be judged according to the traditional equities of fair use.

With that said, the majority proceeded to apply the four-step analysis used to discriminate between a fair use and an infringement. It found that there was news in *Nation*'s scoop, but that the magazine had exploited "the headline value of its infringement." Thus, the magazine's use of material from Ford's book was commercial. This judgment weighed against the magazine's claim for fair use.

The Court viewed Ford's book as "unpublished historical narrative or autobiography." Copyright law recognizes a greater need to disseminate such works than to distribute works of fiction or fantasy. But the Court also found that the fact that the book was unpublished was "a critical element of its 'nature.'" Justice O'Connor clearly saw this as the crucial question. She wrote:

> In the case of Mr. Ford's manuscript, the copyrightholders' interest in confidentiality is irrefutable; the copyrightholders had entered into a contractual undertaking to "keep the manuscript confidential" and required that all those to whom the manuscript was shown also "sign an agreement to keep the manuscript confidential." . . . A use that so clearly infringes the copyrightholder's interests in confidentiality and creative control is difficult to characterize as "fair."

The Court went on to find that while only 13 percent of Navasky's article quoted directly from Ford's manuscript, Navasky had extracted precisely those portions for which readers were most likely to buy the book. Further, his taking had led to direct economic loss through *Time*'s cancellation of its contract to publish an article based on the book. Therefore, *Nation's* use was an infringement for which it could be required to pay damages.

Justice William J. Brennan, Jr., writing for the Court's minority, protested that the decision resulted in "an exceedingly narrow definition of the scope of fair use." He predicted that it would "stifle the broad dissemination of ideas and information" and limit "the robust public debate essential to an enlightened citizenry." In the minority's view, Ford's book contained important historical information that neither he nor his publisher should be permitted to monopolize.

However, the decision stands as the Court's major pronouncement on the First Amendment aspects of the doctrine of fair use. In the majority's view, the Copyright

Act furthers First Amendment interests by protecting the right of creators to profit from their work, and thus it encourages free expression. The law also recognizes, through the doctrine of fair use, the public interest in ideas sometimes requires that creators share their work with others. In writing the doctrine, Congress and the courts have taken First Amendment interests into account. In *Harper & Row,* the Court said that those who would copy from the newsworthy works of important public figures have no First Amendment right to do so beyond that already included in the definition of fair use.[45] This is particularly true if the work has not yet been released to the public by the author or the owner of the copyright.

Penalties for Copyright Infringement

The victim of a copyright infringement is entitled to an award of damages. Section 504 of the Copyright Act also authorizes the use of an injunction to prevent further distribution of the infringing work. Thus, copyright is an area in which prior restraints are permitted, notwithstanding the language of the First Amendment and the Supreme Court's reluctance to approve them generally. Restraint is justified in copyright cases, on the theory that permitting authors to benefit from their writings for a limited time stimulates a greater flow of information. Moreover, justice would seem to demand that infringers ought not be permitted to prosper by passing off another's creative work as their own. The law permits courts to use two methods to calculate the damages an infringer must pay to the copyright owner. They are:

1. An award that makes good the copyright owner's losses from the infringement and takes the infringer's profits away. The copyright owner has the burden of proof in calculating the infringer's gross revenue. The burden is then on the infringer to prove deductible expenses and other factors that might reduce the profit attributable to the infringement. Courts have held, in cases involving movies, that some part of the profit can be attributed to the box office appeal of the actors and actresses. A magazine publisher could show that a major part of its profits came from subscriptions and advertising contracts that were affected little, if any, by an infringing article. Calculations of profit and loss involve many such intangibles. Thus, seldom can a loss be calculated with the precision of the *Harper & Row* case, in which the publisher could point to the $12,500 that *Time* refused to pay for the canceled article after *Nation* scored its scoop.

2. A statutory award fixed by the court. The copyright owner may elect this option at any time up to the point of final judgment. Such an award cannot be less than $250, unless the infringer was unaware of the taking, nor more than $10,000, unless the infringement is deemed willful, in which case the award can be raised to $50,000. If there are multiple infringements, the court may assess an award for each.

---

45. See also Los Angeles News Service v. Tullo, 973 F.2d 791, 20 Med.L.Rptr. 1626 (9th Cir. 1992).

Other Issues in Copyright

Changing technology almost always generates new questions about copyright ownership. Many of those questions are not easy to answer, and disputes over things such as the use of photocopy machines and digital recorders suggest that the prevention of some copying may be nearly impossible to enforce.

Areas of special concern have been the uncompensated use of amateur videos by news organizations, the widespread use of photocopying machines, especially in schools and libraries, and the pirating of television programming.

Amateur Video

When Abraham Zapruder filmed the assassination of John F. Kennedy in Dallas, he did it with an eight-millimeter movie camera designed for amateurs.[46] The camera was a simple device that required little technical skill. Yet there was a sufficient amount of creativity in the composition of the work—for example, deciding where to stand, what angles to shoot from, and what film to use—to qualify the work for copyright protection.

Eight-millimeter cameras have been replaced today by electronic video cameras that are even simpler to use and cheaper to operate. Focus and exposure are controlled electronically by the camera itself. All the photographer has to do is point and shoot. There isn't even any film to develop. The images are stored on videotape or disk and can be played back on any ordinary videotape player or computer. This simplification of the process has led some news organizations to argue that an amateur video recording of a news event is so mechanical and requires so little originality that it should not be protected by copyright.[47]

News organizations made that argument when two famous amateur videos became the subject of multimillion-dollar lawsuits. George Holliday, the plumbing store owner who taped the beating of Rodney King by police in Los Angeles, sued KTLA, CNN, and the three major networks, claiming that they had violated his copyright. Holliday said that he had given permission only to KTLA, but the station then fed the tape to a network, and it was copied and used many times over without his consent.[48] Holliday also sued film director Spike Lee over the use of the tape in his movie, *Malcolm X*. Lee settled the case for an undisclosed amount of money. In another lawsuit, the Los Angeles News Service, which taped Reginald Denny being beaten during the 1992 Los Angeles riots, claimed that news organizations violated its copyright by using the tape without permission.

---

46. Time Inc. v. Bernard Geis Associates, 293 F.Supp. 130 (S.D.N.Y. 1968).
47. Junda Woo, "Amateurs Sue Networks over Video Use," *Wall Street Journal*, 23 November 1992, p. B5. The argument about the mere mechanics of photography is an old one. See Burrow-Giles Lithographic Co. v. Sarony, 111 U.S. 53, 4 S.Ct. 279, 28 L.Ed. 349 (1884). The Court found that arranging the subject to be photographed was sufficient creativity. Also see Bleistein v. Donaldson Lithographing Co., 188 U.S. 239, 23 S.Ct. 298, 47 L.Ed. 460 (1903).
48. Holliday was paid $500 by KTLA. There was no written agreement concerning a transfer of rights. Woo, "Amateurs Sue Networks over Video Use," p. B5.

The news organizations argued in their defense that they did have permission, or, in the alternative, that the tapes were not copyrightable for lack of originality, or, again in the alternative, that the use was a fair use. The latter may turn out to be the most potent of the defenses in light of the minimal amount of originality required in the Zapruder case and in a decision by the Ninth Circuit Court of Appeals, *Los Angeles News Service* v. *Tullo*.[49] In *Tullo,* the court held that unedited videotapes that showed sites of an airplane crash and a train wreck were sufficiently original for copyright protection. The camera operator, riding in a helicopter, had decided what to tape and for how long, had selected the camera lenses, angles, and exposures, and had chosen the height and direction from which to view the wrecks.[50]

Many news organizations, wary of litigation over rights to news footage created by others, now attempt to prevent such suits by asking video makers to sign releases that transfer all or partial rights to the tapes they have made.

Photocopying

In the congressional hearings before passage of the 1976 Copyright Act, educators and librarians argued for free use of photocopy machines for classroom and research purposes. Publishers, particularly of specialized research journals, saw such free use as the road to their ruin.[51] Moreover, the discussion was shadowed by a decision of the U.S. Court of Claims that seemed to give public research libraries the right to copy journals on a wholesale basis. The four-to-three decision in *Williams & Wilkins Co.* v. *United States* in 1973[52] reversed a district court's finding that the National Institutes of Health and the National Library of Medicine had infringed the copyrights of four medical journals by taking thousands of copies of articles from them. The claims court held that the interest in furthering medical research was important enough to override copyright law. But the question was close. The Supreme Court took the case and split four to four, thus upholding the lower court's decision but leaving the door open to a different result in the future, as in *American Geophysical Union* v. *Texaco,* the 1994 case noted earlier in this chapter. In that case the Second Circuit Court of Appeals found that the copying of journal articles by Texaco researchers was not a fair use in light of the loss of licensing fees the Copyright Clearance Center could have collected for the journals.

Originally, publishers asked for a provision that would require makers of photocopy machines to pay an annual license fee on each machine in use, with proceeds to be split among copyright holders. This proposal foundered on its own complexities, but Congress did impose limits on copying by libraries and educators. These limits are

---

49. 20 Med.L.Rptr. 1626 (9th Cir. 1992).
50. Judge Learned Hand described in 1921 what still seems to be the prevailing judicial attitude toward originality in photography for copyright purposes: ". . . no photograph, however simple, can be unaffected by the personal influence of the author, and no two will be absolutely alike." Jewelers' Circular Publishing Co. v. Keystone Publishing Co., 274 F. 932 (S.D.N.Y. 1921), affirmed, 281 F. 83 (2d Cir. 1922). See Nimmer and Nimmer, *Nimmer on Copyright,* § 2.08(E)(1), at 2-126.3 (1992).
51. *Library Journal* followed the hearings on this point closely. See the issues of April through June 1976.
52. 487 F.2d 1345 (Ct.Cl. 1973) let stand by an equally divided Supreme Court, 420 U.S. 376 (1975).

found in Sections 107 and 108 of the Copyright Act, providing for fair use and for maintenance of library collections and copying for private study.

As Congress was debating the act, representatives of education and publishing organizations developed a set of guidelines that were then endorsed by the House and the Senate. The guidelines, while not a part of the act, are evidence of what those in attendance believed to describe a fair use of copyrighted materials for educational purposes. Not all, of course, agreed to the guidelines. Representatives of the American Association of University Professors and the Association of American Law Schools thought them too restrictive for classroom situations at the university and graduate school levels. In general, the guidelines provide that a teacher or student is permitted to make one copy of an article, a chapter from a book, or a sound recording for study purposes or for use in a classroom presentation. A teacher also can make multiple copies on a "spontaneous" basis for distribution to a class. But if such a copy is made a part of the syllabus and distribution becomes a planned part of the course, the use becomes an infringement because it obviously is not spontaneous. Libraries are not to engage in copying that would substitute for buying the publication involved.

Nebulous as these rules are, major publishers are serious about trying to enforce this understanding of fair use in education. In 1982 a group of publishers sued to restrain professors at New York University who allegedly were using a copying service to prepare collections of copyrighted works for student use.[53] The case resulted in an agreement to discontinue copying, except on a limited basis, without permission from the copyright owners.[54]

More recently, Kinko's Graphics Corporation lost a lawsuit brought by eight publishers of textbooks who complained that course packets prepared by Kinko's for professors were not a fair use of copyrighted material. As a result, Kinko's in 1991 agreed to pay $1.9 million in damages and court fees and promised not to photocopy textbook anthologies again without permission of copyright owners.[55]

While these suits against professors and copy shops were successful, a similar suit against a state university was not. The U.S. Court of Appeals for the Ninth Circuit ruled that state governments, including universities, can reproduce copyrighted works without permission and without incurring liability for money damages.[56] The case involved unauthorized copying of computer software by members of the faculty at the University of California at Los Angeles. The court held that the suit was barred by the Eleventh Amendment, which prohibits suits against states in federal court. Such suits are permitted where Congress explicitly authorizes them or where states have waived their immunities. The Ninth Circuit held that neither exception applied to actions brought under copyright law. Moreover, because copyrights are protected only by federal statute, infringement actions cannot be filed in state courts. Conceding that its decision left copyright owners virtually helpless to prevent copying by state institutions, the court said that the remedy was with Congress.

---

53. Bureau of National Affairs, *Media Law Reporter, News Notes,* 4 January 1983.
54. David Margolick, "Publishers and N.Y.U. Settle Suit on College's Photocopying Rights," *New York Times,* 15 April 1983.
55. Meg Cox, "Kinko's, Publishers Reach Settlement of Copyright Suit," *Wall Street Journal,* 18 October 1991.
56. BV Engineering v. University of California at Los Angeles, 858 F.2d 1394 (9th Cir. 1988).

Videocassette

When Congress revised the Copyright Act in 1976, its members could not foresee an advance in another technology that extended copying into a new dimension. This advance was Sony Corporation's development of Betamax, a video copying machine that sold for a few hundred dollars and could be operated by almost anyone. Betamax took the copying of television programs out of the studio and brought it into the home. This new capability raised the fear among producers of movies and television programs that their works would be copied and sold in violation of copyright law. Their fears were heightened by Sony advertisements that invited television viewers to "record favorite shows" and "build a library" of "classic movies," sports events, and other entertainment. Fearing loss of revenue, Universal City Studios and Walt Disney Productions went to court, seeking an order that would bar further sales of Betamax. They argued that every buyer of a video recorder was a potential copyright infringer. Conceding the difficulty of going into the purchasers' homes to find out what was being done with copied programs, the plaintiffs asked the court to find that Sony was contributing to copyright infringement.

The district court rejected their plea, but the U.S. Court of Appeals for the Ninth Circuit set Sony and other makers of home video recorders on their ears by holding that the devices did indeed contribute to copyright infringement. The circuit court passed the buck back to the district court to devise a suitable remedy. Sony reacted by asking the U.S. Supreme Court to intervene, which it did. After hearing two rounds of oral argument in separate terms, the Court decided, five to four, that the copying of programs for one's personal use was a fair use, not an infringement. The majority decision, in *Universal City Studios, Inc. v. Sony Corporation of America*,[57] was written by Justice John Paul Stevens. It concluded that most home copying is for convenience. Persons who cannot see a program when it is aired copy it so that they can see it at another time. This process is called "time shifting." As long as the copies are not sold or used for other commercial purposes, there is no infringement of copyright law.

In reaching its decision, the Court rejected outright the argument that Sony was contributing to copyright infringement by selling its video recorders. Justice Stevens called this argument "an unprecedented attempt to impose copyright liability upon the distributors of copying equipment." He added:

> One may search the Copyright Act in vain for any sign that the elected representatives of the millions of people who watch television every day have made it unlawful to copy a program for later viewing at home, or have enacted a flat prohibition against the sale of machines that make such copying possible.

The dissenters, led by Justice Harry A. Blackmun, saw the decision as an erosion of the control that the Copyright Act gives to authors over the use of their works. They were not satisfied that most copying is authorized by implication because it does no more than change the time at which the program is viewed. They would have remanded for another trial, at which the economic aspects of video recording could be explored more fully.

---

57.   465 U.S. 1112, 104 S.Ct. 1619, 80 L.Ed.2d 1480 (1984).

TRADEMARKS

Trademark law is a part of the law of unfair competition. It differs from copyright law in that it protects words, symbols, or images that identify a business or its products. Titles, short phrases, or surnames cannot be copyrighted, but if they are used in trade to identify the origin of goods or services, they might be protected as a mark—a trademark, a service mark, or a trade name.

The Federal Trademark Act[58] can be used to protect distinctive words or symbols that clearly identify a business firm and its products. Usually such marks must be registered with the Patent and Trademark Office if they are to be enforceable under the federal statute, and the owner must make an effort to prevent their unauthorized use.[59] But trademarks have been around since the dawn of civilization,[60] and legal protection for trade names and identifying marks has existed at least since the Middle Ages.

Unlike copyright, which is a right that exists in the very substance of the work created, trademark exists only with respect to some commercial activity. You get a copyright by creating a work; you get a trademark by using a distinctive mark in business. For example, Coke is a distinctive mark of the Coca-Cola Company. Competitors who use that mark to sell their own soft drinks compete unfairly with Coca-Cola by confusing their drink with that of another. They violate Coca-Cola's trademark because Coca-Cola is already using it to identify a product, and the public recognizes it as a distinctive name. But if Coca-Cola stops using the word "Coke"[61] or doesn't attempt to prevent others from using it, its trademark could cease to exist. Companies that do not successfully protect trademarks risk having them become generic terms that anyone can use. That has happened, for example, to aspirin, cellophane, thermos, elevator, escalator, lanolin, yo-yo, and trampoline. All of those terms were once the property of the companies that coined them. The quickest way for creators to lose trademarks is to forget, or let others forget, that a trademark is, by definition, an adjective modifying a noun. When "Kleenex tissues" become kleenex, "Xerox photocopiers" become a tool for xeroxing, or a "Frisbee flying disk" becomes a frisbee, trademarks like these run the risk of slipping into common usage.

A trademark can be almost anything—a word, a design, a color or a combination of colors,[62] a sound, a device, a style, a slogan—provided that it is distinctive. The mark doesn't have to convey any information about the product or the company. Some of the most successful marks have been entirely fanciful: Kodak, Xerox, Memorex, Exxon, Rolodex, Frisbee, Microsoft. The mark doesn't even have to include a company name or logo: "Don't leave home without it" (American Express); "You'll love the way we fly" (Delta Airlines); "You've got questions. We've got

---

58. 15 U.S.C. §§ 1051–1127, the Lanham Act, consisting of the Federal Trademark Act of 1946 and the Trademark Law Revision Act of 1988.

59. However, 15 U.S.C. § 1125 [Section 43(a)] provides federal protection even in the absence of a registered trademark. It provides a remedy for false advertising. See Allen v. Men's World Outlet Inc., 679 F.Supp. 360, 15 Med.L.Rptr. 1001 (S.D.N.Y. 1988), summarized below.

60. Building materials were among the first products with trademarks. The stone blocks of the Egyptian pyramids and bricks from ancient Mesopotamia were marked to indicate their origin.

61. Two consecutive years of nonuse raise a presumption of abandonment. 15 U.S.C. § 1052(d).

62. Qualitex v. Jacobson Products, 115 S.Ct. 1300, 131 L.Ed.2d 248 (1995). Linda Greenhouse, "High Court Ruling Upholds Trademarking of a Color," *New York Times,* 29 March 1995, p. A11.

answers" (Radio Shack); "When you are comfortable, you can do anything" (Marriott).

Words that are generic or descriptive—such as fresh apple pie—are not distinctive enough to be protected by trademark law. Neither are surnames, such as John Jones. But even descriptive words and common names can become distinctive by developing a secondary meaning, a meaning that identifies a specific product or company in the minds of consumers. For example, McDonald's is a valid trade name only because it has developed a secondary meaning. Its primary meaning is a family name, something that is not eligible for trademark registration; its secondary meaning, the one that is protected by trademark, is a kind of fast-food restaurant.

Does that mean that no other business can be called McDonald's? Can there be no McDonald's clothing store, no McDonald's grocery, no McDonald's swimwear? Not at all. Different firms can have the same name, provided that the similarity is not likely to cause consumer confusion about origin or quality.

Sometimes a trademark can shift from the identification of one product to the identification of an entirely different product. For example, the Haleakala Dairy in Hawaii printed the letters "POG" on bottle caps to identify a mix of passion fruit, orange, and guava juice. When children in Hawaii, and later in California, used the round, paper caps to play a popular sidewalk game, they called the game pogs. By the mid-1990s the children's game had become a $500 million manufacturing and licensing industry. The disks children played with were no longer discarded bottle caps, but were colorful wafers embossed with the images of sports figures, comic book heroes, and businesses willing to pay hefty licensing fees to get their logos on the disks. All of this became the grist for a months-long legal dispute about who, if anyone, owned exclusive rights to the word "pog." The dairy, which claimed "pog" as a trademark, licensed the use of the word to the World Pog Federation and became one of its owners. On the other hand, the rival Universal Pog Association claimed that Pog—the game, not the fruit juice—had been named, not by the dairy or the Federation, but by children at play, and therefore was a generic word describing the disks. In the end, World and Universal negotiated a settlement, giving World exclusive control of the trademark. Universal changed its name to Universal Slammers Inc., after the hard, metal disks used to hit the lighter, cardboard disks. And as for the children, they call the game and the disks whatever they want, but almost no one remembers that POG was originally a fruit drink.

Some trademarks are not eligible to be registered for federal protection. The federal statute forbids registration of immoral, deceptive, or scandalous matter, or matter that may disparage or falsely suggest a connection with persons, living or dead, institutions, beliefs, or national symbols, or bring them into contempt or disrepute.[63] Marks such as "Bubby Trap" for brassieres and "[o]nly a breast in the mouth is better than a leg in the hand" for a chicken restaurant have been held offensive.[64] The U.S. Patent and Trademark Office at first rejected but later reversed itself and accepted the Old Glory Condom Corporation's logo: an unfurled American flag shaped like a condom.[65]

---

63.   15 U.S.C. § 1052(a).
64.   In re Riverbank Canning Co., 95 F.2d 327 (Cust. & Pat.App. 1938). Bromberg v. Carmel Self Service, Inc., 198 U.S.P.Q. 176 (T.T.A.B. 1978).
65.   "Condom Trademark Too 'Scandalous,'" *Herald-Times,* Bloomington, Ind., 21 May 1992.

The company sells red, white, and blue "condoms with a conscience" in packages sporting the logo and a message that protecting lives by safe sex is patriotic. Of course, even if a mark is not eligible for federal registration, it can still be used, subject to the same regulations as any other kind of advertising.

Federal trademark registration lasts for only ten years, but it can be renewed easily.[66] The act says that any mark not used for two years is presumed to have been abandoned. That presumption of abandonment can be rebutted by a showing that there was an intent to resume its use.[67]

A case involving two clubs dedicated to serving young people illustrates both what a trademark is and how it can be protected. Officials of the Boys Clubs of America proposed changing the organization's name to the Boys and Girls Clubs of America. The purpose was to give a more accurate picture of the membership of the organization in an era when lines separating activities considered appropriate for boys and girls were being wiped out. The Girls Clubs of America began a trademark infringement action in a U.S. district court in New York City. The Girls Clubs said that its name was a trademark clearly identifying it and its activities in the minds of the public. The club argued that the proposed name change of the Boys Clubs might lead potential contributors to believe that the two organizations had merged. The court agreed that there was a likelihood of confusion and issued an order preventing the change until the trademark infringement action could be resolved.[68]

In this instance, the four words making up the name of the organization, "Girls Clubs of America," had become its trademark. If another's use of some part of that name could be shown to cause confusion in the public mind as to the identity of the two organizations, that use would be considered a trademark infringement. The National Geographic Society was able to win a partial victory in a trademark infringement action against a rival magazine publisher that took only one word, "traveler."[69] The publications involved in the dispute were the *National Geographic Traveler* and *Condé Nast's Traveler*. Both deal with travel and both had circulations of about 800,000. National Geographic's magazine was on the market first. When it sued the newer magazine for trademark infringement, the court held that it was not entitled to an injunction preventing Condé Nast from using the word "traveler" in its title, but it also held that Condé Nast should change its cover to give more prominence to the corporate name to avoid consumer confusion.

A U.S. district court in New York City extended the protection of federal trademark law to cover the imitation of an actor's physical appearance. The case illustrates how closely publicity rights and trademark rights are related.[70] In some states the action might have been successfully pursued as a common-law or statutory appropriation of publicity rights. That would have been difficult to do in the New York City case, however, because the actor's actual image was never used; only a clearly identified look-alike appeared in the ad campaign. As an alternative approach, the case was brought

---

66.   15 U.S.C. §§ 1058, 1059.
67.   15 U.S.C. 1127.
68.   Girls Clubs of America v. Boys Clubs of America, 683 F.Supp. 50 (S.D.N.Y. 1988).
69.   National Geographic Society v. Condé Nast Publications, 687 F.Supp. 106 (S.D.N.Y. 1988).
70.   See "Appropriation and the Right of Publicity" in Chapter 6, "Invasion of Privacy."

Some words are too common to be fully protected as trademarks. When both the National Geographic Society and Condé Nast used the word "traveler" in the title of their magazines, the court said they could both use it, but Condé Nast had to make sure there was no consumer confusion by displaying its corporate name prominently on the cover. *(Photo Works)*

under Section 1125 of the Trademark Act, a section that provides for protection even in the absence of trademark registration.

Woody Allen, an actor, musician, and producer of movies, became irked by advertisements that used a model who looked like him to promote a video rental chain and stores selling men's clothing at a discount. When the clothing stores placed ads in *Newsday,* a Long Island newspaper, Allen's attorney sued the men's store and its advertising agency to stop the ads, claiming trademark infringement. The court adopted his theory, holding that Allen was entitled to an injunction to prevent the clothing store and its advertising agency from using the look-alike in future advertising. The court held that the use of the look-alike created a likelihood of consumer confusion and therefore violated Section 1125(a) of the Trademark Act [Section 43(a) of the Lanham Act]. It was false advertising.

Allen v. *Men's World Outlet, Inc.,* 679 F.Supp. 360, 15 Med.L.Rptr. 1001 (S.D.N.Y. 1988).

The ad at issue showed Phil Boroff, who resembles Allen physically, holding a clarinet. Allen regularly played the clarinet with a jazz band at Michael's Pub in New York City. The court's decision said that the ad copy "evoked the 'schlemiel' persona Allen cultivated through his appearance in Annie Hall." Below Boroff's picture, "in small lightface type," was a sentence, "This is a Ron Smith Celebrity Look-Alike." The court said that that sentence kept Allen from successfully suing for appropriation of publicity rights under New York law. It was reasonably clear that the man in the ad was not Allen. But with respect to the trademark infringement claim, the court concluded that Allen did have a case. Boroff's resemblance to Allen, heightened by the copy, was sufficient to create an impression that Men's World clothing was somehow associated with Allen. The court held, in effect, that Allen's likeness was a form of trademark and that Boroff "resembles him strongly." Further, it was logical to assume that there was some overlap between purchasers of discounted men's clothing and people who go to Allen's movies. Thus, there was a group of people who might be confused by the ad. While there was no evidence that anyone had been confused by the look-alike, the Trademark Act requires only that there be the likelihood of confusion to support a finding of false representation. Given the diverse nature of *Newsday's* audience, some part of it would not have the sophistication to conclude that Allen was not associated with the ad, the court held.

The court said that Allen could not collect compensatory damages under the law, because he would have to prove actual consumer confusion. Nor could he obtain punitive damages, because the act makes no provision for them. But the court concluded that Allen was entitled to a permanent injunction.

OTHER LEGAL PROTECTION FOR LITERARY PROPERTY

The Allen case was a rather creative way to get at the problem of trading on a celebrity's fame for commercial gain. There are other ways. Bette Midler sued Ford Motor Company and its ad agency, Young and Rubicam, to stop the use of a sound-alike in a Ford commercial. Her argument wasn't that she had a trademark in her image, but that the agency had taken her image without her consent—the common-law tort of appropriation.[71] Bert Lahr sued Adell Chemical Company for a Lestoil commercial in which an imitation of Lahr's voice accompanied a cartoon of a duck. Lahr said that his style of vocal delivery was distinctive in pitch, accent, inflection, and sounds. The First Circuit held that Lahr had stated a cause of action for the common-law tort of unfair competition.[72] And Hugo Zacchini sued a news organization, Scripps-Howard Broadcasting, for broadcasting his entire performance, a dramatic flight from a cannon to a net two hundred yards away. The U.S. Supreme Court found that the act had been taken without Zacchini's consent, violating his Ohio common-law right of publicity. It didn't matter that the taking wasn't for a commercial purpose.[73] What mattered was that Zacchini owned what he had created and had the exclusive right to its use. Ohio's common law of publicity provided a kind of quasi-copyright/trademark protection that picked up where the federal statutes left off.

The torts of unfair competition and appropriation of publicity rights are the usual common-law protections for literary property. They are not limited to the redressing of damages caused by advertising or public relations efforts. They can affect news reporting as well.

Reporters often borrow from the work of other writers. Reporters who work on newspapers in areas served by more than one paper are sometimes asked by their editors to follow stories clipped from competing publications. Broadcasters occasionally read clips from newspapers on the air. News features sometimes begin in one newspaper and then make their way, in altered form with different authors, through several other papers, and, perhaps, into the wire services, and end as a special on the evening television news or as a book or a magazine article. It's part of the game, and as long

71. Midler v. Ford Motor Co. and Young & Rubicam, Inc., 849 F.2d 460, 15 Med.L.Rptr. 1620 (9th Cir. 1988); cert. denied, 112 S.Ct. 1513 (1992). Midler v. Young & Rubicam, Inc., 19 Med.L.Rptr. 2190 (9th Cir. 1991). Also see Waits v. Frito-Lay Inc., 20 Med.L.Rptr. 1585 (9th Cir. 1992).
72. Lahr v. Adell Chemical Co., 300 F.2d 256 (1st Cir. 1962).
73. Zacchini v. Scripps-Howard Broadcasting, 433 U.S. 562, 97 S.Ct. 2849, 53 L.Ed.2d 965, 2 Med.L.Rptr. 2089 (1977).

as reporters don't take too much, too often, all is well. But starting as far back as 1918, in *International News Service* v. *Associated Press,*[74] courts have penalized the systematic taking of news gathered by other reporters.

William Randolph Hearst established International News Service (INS) to offer his own newspapers and others an alternative to the Associated Press (AP) as a source of news. The AP alleged that many of the stories distributed by INS were thinly disguised rewrites of stories gathered by AP's reporters. Evidence supported the charge, and the courts condemned INS's piracy as a form of unfair competition. In a nice turn of speech, the Supreme Court said that the Hearst service was reaping where it had not sown; it was using the fruits of another's labor, which gave it an unfair advantage. Even though the AP news service was not copyrighted, and was widely used by its own members, the Court said that INS could not appropriate stories from that service and sell them as its own. Such an act is simply a misappropriation of another's property.

In the mid-twentieth century, courts in several states used the concept of unfair-competition by misappropriation to prevent radio stations from using in their newscasts descriptions of events taken from local newspapers[75] or to prevent one newspaper from copying advertisements from another. Implicit in all these decisions is the assumption that information is property. Thus the law of misappropriation is broader in scope than is copyright law, which focuses on protecting the fixed form in which information is presented, rather than the information itself.

In 1987 a majority of the Supreme Court decided an unusual misappropriation case that emerged not from the common law but from federal criminal law. The Court endorsed the concept that information is property, which its owner can protect against misuse and which the government can regulate to protect investors. The case was unusual in that it pitted a newspaper against two of its employees, who were charged with using unpublished information gathered in the course of their employment to make a profit in the securities markets for themselves and others. The newspaper was the *Wall Street Journal,* a financial newspaper with a circulation of more than a million. One employee was a reporter who frequently wrote the newspaper's "Heard on the Street" column, which discussed factors that might affect the price of a company's stock. The reporter, R. Foster Winans, noticed on occasion that share prices rose or fell significantly after his column had appeared in the morning newspaper. Because he knew what was going to be in the column, he decided to take advantage of that fact by trading in the affected stock before the market closed on the day before the column appeared. He enlisted David Carpenter, a copy clerk at the *Journal,* in the scheme.

Carpenter v. *United States,* 484 U.S. 19, 108 S.Ct. 316, 98 L.Ed.2d 275, 14 Med.L.Rptr., 1853 (1987).

The trading pattern of the two *Journal* employees soon was noticed by their stockbrokers, who proposed that they, too, benefit from the inside information by trading

---

74. 248 U.S. 215, 29 S.Ct. 68, 63 L.Ed.2d 528 (1918).
75. The most frequently quoted case is Pottstown Daily News v. Pottstown Broadcasting, 192 A.2d 657 (Pa. 1963).

on their own accounts and giving Winans and Carpenter a share of the profits. Over a four-month period, the brokers made a net profit of about $690,000 from information provided by Winans. The reporter's share was $31,000.

The trading pattern also was noticed by officials of the Securities and Exchange Commission, who began an investigation. As the net tightened, the participants in the scheme quarreled, and Winans and Carpenter told the SEC what had been happening. They and the brokers were charged with conspiracy to commit securities fraud through insider trading. One of the brokers pleaded guilty. A federal district court jury found the others, including Winans and Carpenter, guilty. The verdict was affirmed on appeal. The U.S. Supreme Court agreed to review the decision and affirmed it unanimously.

The Court upheld the view that the trio's use of information taken from the *Journal* was a form of theft of property. It made no difference that Winans, acting as a reporter, had obtained much of that information from sources on his own initiative. As the Court saw it, that information belonged to the *Journal,* not to Winans. Under *Journal* policy, the paper's employees are required to hold in confidence all information being prepared for publication. Justice Byron R. White, writing for the Court, said that the " 'intangible nature' [of the information] does not make it any less 'property' protected by the mail and wire fraud statutes." The Court said that there need not be proof that the taking had cost the *Journal* any monetary loss. "It is sufficient that the *Journal* has been deprived of its right to exclusive use of the information, for exclusivity is an important aspect of confidential business information and most private property, for that matter." Winans was sentenced to prison.

Seen at one level, the decision gave the government a strong new weapon to use against persons accused of insider trading—of profiting from advance knowledge of information that will affect the market. Indeed, it was hailed by the federal prosecutor in Manhattan, who said: "It gives prosecutors a very clear road map on how to proceed."[76] Using that map, U.S. attorneys prosecuted a number of insider trading cases, most of them against stockbrokers.

At another level, the case stands as a warning to anyone—including reporters, editors, advertising copywriters, corporate communicators, or public relations practitioners—who has knowledge of confidential information belonging to his or her employer. If that information is of the kind that could have an effect on securities markets, premature use of it can lead to prosecution. Only a year after the Supreme Court's decision in Carpenter, S. G. "Rudy" Ruderman, a former *Business Week* news broadcaster, pleaded guilty to mail fraud for trading on information from the magazine's "Inside Wall Street" column. As a radio broadcaster employed by the magazine, Ruderman had access to articles before the magazine reached the public. In two and a half years, he used that access to earn about $15,000 by trading in securities that moved up or down after *Business Week* reached its subscribers.[77]

---

76. James B. Stewart and Stephen Wermiel, "High Court Upholds Conviction of Winans, Two Co-Conspirators," *Wall Street Journal,* 17 November 1987.
77. Betty Wong, "Ruderman Pleads Guilty to Charges of Mail Fraud," *Wall Street Journal,* 9 December 1988.

The protection of literary property is a patchwork of federal and state law that covers in one way or another most property interests in communications. For example, while federal copyright law protects only fixed works, those that are not fixed may be protected by common law. State law also can protect works that are difficult to produce but are not original enough to gain copyright protection. While federal trademark law generally doesn't protect unregistered marks, Section 1125 of the Trademark Act condemns misappropriation of an unregistered mark in false advertising, and state law often protects unregistered trademarks. The complex pattern of laws covers property—whether that property is proprietary information or poetry—in a somewhat uneven manner. But for professional communicators, the pattern is clear: You take what belongs to others at great peril, and others take from you at their great peril.

In the Professional World

Professional creators in any field are far more likely to benefit from the Copyright and Trademark acts or the common law of misappropriation and unfair competition than they are to be restricted by them. Those who honestly attempt to do their own work—and they are in the majority—are unlikely to be infringers. Rarely does a court find that a reputable media organization has been guilty of copyright infringement. More common are cases that explore the outer limits of copyright law, as in the use of J. D. Salinger's readily available letters by his biographer, or *Nation* magazine's belief that a newsworthy "scoop" might justify copying from President Ford's memoirs.

Other cases have explored the limits of copying permitted by new forms of technology: computer software, data retrieval systems, and satellite dishes. Courts have held that it is a violation of copyright to copy a computer program without authorization.[78] Apple Computer filed a copyright action to protect the way its programs "look and feel" when information is displayed on a video screen.[79] A legal publisher fought a three-year court battle to win a settlement recognizing that page numbers that are part of a highly refined system of case

---

78. Whelan Associates Inc. v. Jaslow Dental Laboratory Inc., 797 F.2d 1222 (3d Cir. 1986), cert. denied, 479 U.S. 1031 (1987); Apple Computer Inc. v. Formula International Inc., 725 F.2d 521 (9th Cir. 1984); Apple Computer Inc. v. Franklin Computer Corp., 714 F.2d 1240 (3d Cir. 1983); E. F. Johnson Co. v. Uniden Corp. of America, 623 F.Supp. 1485 (D.Minn. 1985).

79. Apple Computer Inc. v. Microsoft Corp., 709 F.Supp. 925 (N.D.Cal. 1989); 717 F.Supp. 1428 (N.D.Cal. 1989); 759 F. Supp. 1444 (N.D.Cal. 1991). On April 14, 1992, a court order granted in part Microsoft's and Hewlett-Packard's motions for summary judgment. The court said that "if the Windows 1.0 'look and feel,' when supplemented with unprotectable expression leads naturally to the look and feel of the works in question, there is no infringement. If, however, the as yet-unspecified 'look and feel' of the Apple works is not the necessary result of the grafting of the unprotectable elements onto the licensed 'look and feel' of Windows 1.0, infringement may be shown. Court Order No. C-88-20149-VRW.

law analysis can be protected by copyright.[80] A court found copyright infringement in the use of a satellite dish to bring professional football games to a bar's patrons.[81]

However, for most who work in the professional world, considerations of copyright law start with asking whether formalities of complying with the act's registration terms should be observed. Since the law now assumes that works are copyrighted as soon as they take tangible form, why go to the bother and expense of registration with the Copyright Office? Not only does registration involve payment of a $20 fee, it also requires filling out a form and mailing it, along with two copies of the work, to Washington, D.C. The answer is that if a work has no market value, and the creator can be sure it is unlikely to have any, there isn't any point to registration. However, if a work does have value and is taken without consent, the owner of the copyright, except for owners of Berne Convention works that originate outside the United States, cannot sue for infringement until the work has been registered. Moreover, notice, while no longer required since the United States signed the Berne Convention, is still a good idea because failure to place a copyright notice on the work might offer the infringer a defense. An unknowing infringer is subject to minimum penalties.

The value of copyright protection for newspapers is debatable. Publishers vary in their use of the law. Most daily newspapers are not registered.[82] Others may register unusual stories, sometimes as a promotion device. Given the nature of most newspaper content, publishers often are not convinced that their publications are likely to have much market value beyond the initial price paid by the subscriber and advertiser. Publications of a more lasting nature, such as magazines or books, are almost always registered. In the entertainment field, music, plays, television programs, videocassettes, movies, and the like have such great potential value that they are always registered. In the business world, such things as catalogues, instruction manuals, and specialized computer programs are protected by copyright and are routinely registered.

The Woody Allen case is as noteworthy for the ethical questions it raises as for its value as a legal precedent. Should advertisers seek to capitalize on the value of popular entertainers or sports figures without paying them for their endorsement? Is it enough to explain in fine print that the reader is seeing only someone who resembles the entertainer? Might not some consumers conclude that a company that is willing to cheat in its advertising would also cheat in other ways?

---

80. West Publishing Co. v. Mead Data Central Inc., 799 F.2d 1219 (8th Cir. 1986), cert. denied, 479 U.S. 1070 (1987). Laurie P. Cohen, "Mead, West Publishing Are Expected to Settle 3 Suits over Legal Databases," *Wall Street Journal,* 26 July 1988.
81. National Football League v. McBee & Bruno's, 621 F.Supp. 880 (E.D.Mo. 1985).
82. Bureau of National Affairs, "New Copyright Rules Allow Group Newspaper Registration," *Media Law Reporter, News Notes,* 15 September 1992. Daily newspapers may now use a single application and fee to register all issues dated within the same month. 57 Fed.Reg. 39,615 (1992).

The Carpenter case also raises prickly ethical questions. When the editors of the *Wall Street Journal* learned that a reporter had shared with others information that he had gathered but that the newspaper had not yet published, they treated the matter as a gross breach of the newspaper's code of ethics. They took the position that all members of the newspaper's staff were bound by that code neither to profit from information gathered for the newspaper nor to disclose it to others before it was published. Others argued that the rules were not all that clear. In any event, who owns the bits and pieces of information that ultimately take form as a story? What happens if the reporter, or an editor, concludes that the bits and pieces do not add up to a story, but some of the bits point to what looks like a good investment? Should the reporter or editor have to forgo the investment? Or what happens if a reporter who is working on a long-range investigative project leaves one publication for another? Does the story, if it develops, go with the reporter? Or does it belong to the first employer? With the Supreme Court's holding that information gathered in the course of one's employment belongs to the employer, such questions are likely to spill out of the realm of ethics into the courts.

FOR REVIEW

1. What is the purpose of copyright law? How is that purpose carried into effect? How does copyright law relate to the First Amendment?

2. What can be copyrighted? What cannot be? Illustrate with examples.

3. Explain the degree of protection provided by copyrighting a newspaper or a news story. What precautions should be taken by a reporter who is assigned to follow up another medium's copyrighted news story?

4. Define "fair use." List and explain the elements that go into a determination of fair use. What is the significance of the *Rosemont Enterprises* decision with respect to the doctrine of fair use?

5. Compare and contrast the Supreme Court's decision in *Harper & Row* with the circuit court's decision in *Rosemont Enterprises* and the district court's decision in *Bernard Geis.* Collectively, what do these decisions say about the First Amendment in copyright infringement cases?

6. On balance, does copyright law enhance or inhibit First Amendment interests? Justify your conclusions.

7. Define and illustrate with reference to cases an infringement of copyright. What are likely to be the primary issues of concern for the court in making a decision?

8. What rationale did the Supreme Court use in deciding the home video recorder case?

9. What is a trademark? In what ways is a trademark related to copyright law? What are the significant differences?

10. What must a trademark owner do to retain title to the mark?

11. Discuss the legal and ethical aspects of an advertiser's use in commercials of models who sound or look like popular entertainers.

12. Define "misappropriation" as the term applies to communicators.

CHAPTER 13

Despite the seemingly absolute language of the First Amendment, speech and press in the United States have never been entirely free of government regulation. Advertising is regulated to prevent deception; obscenity is outlawed entirely, and news is subject to a variety of legal liabilities. Copyright restricts the use of work created by others. Sedition laws, though circumscribed, continue to be enforced. Moreover, the courts have long recognized that government regulation of the time, manner, and place of speech often is permitted within the First Amendment. For much of the twentieth century, the federal government has struggled to determine what, if any, regulation can be justified to maximize the potential of electronic communications, particularly broadcasting and cable television.

Although federal regulations have limited First Amendment freedoms of broadcasters, they also have been instrumental in allowing broadcasting to prosper. Today

ELECTRONIC MEDIA

there are far more radio stations and nearly as many television stations as there are daily newspapers.[1] Federal regulations helped broadcasters achieve these results chiefly by controlling competition within the industry, by restricting the ability of other media to buy broadcast stations, and by extending FCC regulatory power to control a medium that in the past decade has proven to be broadcasting's most serious threat, cable television.

The fundamental premise for broadcast regulation always has been that the electromagnetic spectrum is a scarce natural resource of such great value that it should be used in the public interest. But scarcity may have more to do with theoretical physics than with media practice. The rapid proliferation of electronic media—particularly media that maximize the electromagnetic spectrum by combining it with fiber-optic and microwave technologies—continually challenges the scarcity premise. The owner of even a cheap, portable radio can tune to any one of a dozen or more stations in most localities without risk of noise caused by station interference. Even without cable, most urban television viewers can receive five or more stations. With cable, the number of available channels can reach a hundred or more. In startling contrast, fewer than two dozen cities still have fully competitive newspapers, and, in most markets, avid readers may have a choice of no more than half a dozen local, regional, and national newspapers.

Because of the obviously broad choice of electronic media available, most FCC rules that required diversity in programming were abandoned in the 1980s. Commercial radio and television stations today operate with only minimal FCC programming requirements.[2] Even the fairness doctrine—a central tenet of broadcast regulation since 1949—was abandoned in 1985.[3] The fairness doctrine insisted that each station provide a variety of viewpoints and required broadcasters to document the diversity of their broadcast day. By the 1990s, the role of the FCC in regulating broadcast programming had diminished dramatically, and its mission began to shift from concerns about scarcity to concerns about overabundance.

---

1. There are about 9870 radio stations, 1151 television stations, and 1492 daily newspapers. The number of broadcasting stations licensed by the FCC is listed regularly in *Broadcasting* magazine.
2. Report and Order (BC Dkt. No. 79-219), 84 F.C.C.2d 968: reconsidered, 87 F.C.C.2d 797 (1981). Report and Order (BC Dkt. No. 81-496), F.C.C. 84-294 (1984).
3. Inquiry into Alternatives to the General Fairness Obligations of Broadcast Licensees, 102 F.C.C.2d 143 (1985). Syracuse Peace Council v. Federal Communications Commission, 867 F.2d 654, 16 Med.L.Rptr. 1225 (D.C. Cir. 1989); cert. denied, 493 U.S. 1019, 110 S.Ct. 717, 107 L.Ed.2d 737 (1990).

Even as Congress deregulated broadcasting, it simultaneously began a process of reforming and expanding telecommunications law to address new issues emerging from the rapid proliferation of electronic media. Those issues have focused on things such as the use of electronic media by children; the merging of computer, cable, telephone, and broadcast technologies; and consumer unhappiness about rapid rate increases by cable systems.

Beginning in 1984 with the Cable Communications Policy Act and culminating in 1996 with passage of the Telecommunications Act, Congress has restructured the government regulation of electronic media in a way that has preserved its traditional authority over broadcasting and telephony while firmly reasserting its authority over cable television and the Internet.

In this chapter we will look at some of the major issues that are unique to electronic media. We will begin by looking at history to see why broadcasting evolved as a regulated medium, and we will examine some of the major cases upholding regulations that are still in effect, including licensing of broadcasters and the use of broadcasting by candidates for public office. We will then examine some of the emerging issues involving government regulation of cable and computer networking.

Major Cases

- *CBS, Inc.* v. *Federal Communications Commission,* 453 U.S. 367, 101 S.Ct. 2813, 69 L.Ed.2d 706, 7 Med.L.Rptr. 1563 (1981).

- *City of Los Angeles* v. *Preferred Communications,* 476 U.S. 488, 106 S.Ct. 3034, 80 L.Ed.2d 480, 12 Med.L.Rptr. 2244 (1986).

- *Metro Broadcasting, Inc.* v. *Federal Communications Commission,* 497 U.S. 547, 110 S.Ct. 2997, 111 L.Ed.2d 445, (1990).

- *Miami Herald Publishing Co.* v. *Tornillo,* 418 U.S. 241, 94 S.Ct. 2831, 41 L.Ed.2d 730, 1 Med.L.Rptr. 1898 (1974).

- *National Broadcasting Co.* v. *United States,* 319 U.S. 190, 63 S.Ct. 997, 87 L.Ed. 1344, 1 Med.L.Rptr. 1965 (1943).

- *Red Lion Broadcasting Co.* v. *Federal Communications Commission,* 395 U.S. 367, 89 S.Ct. 1794, 23 L.Ed.2d 371, 1 Med.L.Rptr. 2053 (1969).

BROADCASTING

Under existing law, broadcasting stations are the only media that operate under licenses granted by the federal government. Holders of broadcast licenses must live with the possibility, however remote, that some individual or organization may some-day challenge their right to continue to operate.

Licensing has been in effect since 1927, when Congress passed the first Radio Act, at the request of broadcasters and the public to end the struggle for frequencies that had brought chaos to the fledgling industry. Commercial radio began in the early 1920s and soon became a popular form of entertainment, but because station opera-tors could use any AM frequency they pleased, with whatever power they could af-ford, electronic interference frequently made it impossible for listeners to hear the sta-tion of their choice.[4] Congress responded to the problem by creating the Federal Ra-dio Commission (FRC) and giving it authority to license broadcasters, requiring them to operate on an assigned frequency. The commission also specified the power, or electrical wattage, with which they could operate. These government controls were in-tended to enhance freedom of speech by replacing spectrum chaos with speech that at least could be intelligible. The regulations were based on the assumption that electro-magnetic frequencies are a scarce natural resource that belongs to all the people, and that government, acting on behalf of the people, has a responsibility to manage that resource in the public interest.

In the beginning, the government's main concern for broadcasting was merely the regulation of frequencies to prevent interference, but the focus soon shifted to other matters of public concern: assuring variety in programming, preventing broadcasters from becoming propagandists, and encouraging the healthy growth and continued vi-ability of the broadcast industry. During the 1930s, while the dramatically persuasive power of radio was being demonstrated by Adolf Hitler in Germany, the Federal Com-munications Commission, which replaced the FRC in 1934, adopted rules designed to prevent one political candidate, or one point of view on public issues, from dominat-ing the airwaves. Although these rules raised serious First Amendment questions, they were upheld by the courts, acting on the belief that diversity of opinion over the air-waves better served the public interest than did the protection of an individual license holder's freedom to be a demagogue. Thus was established the principle that licensees of broadcast frequencies do not enjoy the same editorial freedom as do the private owners of printing presses.

Licensing in the Public Interest

There is no doubt about the government's authority to regulate broadcasting in the public interest. The legal challenges to that authority were met and overcome more than fifty years ago.

The first questions were raised in the 1920s, when the government, in cooperation with Canada and Mexico, adopted an orderly process for assigning frequencies, pre-scribing limits on transmitter power, and setting hours of operation. Stations that were forced to change frequencies or reduce power if they were to retain their licenses chal-lenged the government's authority. The resulting court decisions held that broadcast-ers are engaged in interstate commerce and therefore are within the reach of federal

---

4. Erik Barnouw, *A History of Broadcasting in the United States,* vol. 1: *A Tower in Babel* (New York: Oxford University Press, 1966).

regulation.[5] Owners who were threatened with loss of their licenses because they refused to comply with the new regulations argued that the government was taking their property without due process of law, thus violating the Fifth and Fourteenth amendments to the Constitution. Courts held that a broadcasting license is not a form of property that belongs to the station owner. It is only a token of the station owner's right to use a frequency that belongs to the people. That right is valid only as long as the station owner serves the "public interest, convenience, and necessity."

Nor does the termination of a license necessarily violate a station owner's First Amendment right to freedom of speech, even when the decision is based on the content of the station's message.[6] In 1930 the FRC refused to renew the license of a Los Angeles radio station after hearing protests from more than ninety witnesses. The church-owned station had been used by its pastor to condemn gamblers, bootleggers, labor unions, judges, the bar association, Jews, and Roman Catholics. As he saw it, all were involved in ungodly immorality, and he said so in strong terms, using the station to spread his views. When the commission held that such usage violated the church's right to use the people's airwaves, the church appealed, arguing that the commission's action was a prior restraint of the kind that the Supreme Court recently had condemned.[7]

The Court of Appeals rejected that argument. The court said that a license to broadcast did not give the holder an unlimited right to spread hatred "from one corner of the country to the other." If licensees could do so, "then this great science, instead of a boon, will become a scourge, and the nation a theater for the display of individual passions and the collision of personal interests." The court said that the commission's action was "neither censorship nor previous restraint," nor was it "a whittling away of the rights guaranteed by the First Amendment." It was simply an exercise of the FRC's authority to make certain that the airwaves are used to serve a broad public interest rather than the narrow and abrasive private interests of the holder of the license.

These early lower-court decisions, handed down when broadcasting was in its infancy, proved influential in shaping judicial attitudes. They established that broadcasters must serve the public interest if they are to obtain and retain a license from the federal government. That license is merely a permit to use a frequency that belongs to the people as a whole. If a broadcaster uses the license in a one-sided way to spread a message that violates the public's concept of decency and fair play, the right to use a frequency can be taken away. Such a violation has not happened often, but the possibility has been there since 1932 and has had an effect on broadcasting for sixty years. Thus, almost from the beginning the courts have applied a different set of rules to broadcasters than to other media.

Broadcasting and the First Amendment

The idea of a different set of rules for broadcasters has been challenged repeatedly by broadcast licensees, but the Supreme Court has as often upheld those rules, finding

---

5. United States v. American Bond & Mortgage Co., 31 F.2d 448 (N.D.Ill. 1929).
6. Trinity Methodist Church, South v. Federal Radio Commission, 62 F.2d 850 (D.C. Cir. 1932).
7. Near v. Minnesota, 283 U.S. 697, 51 S.Ct. 625, 75 L.Ed. 1357, 1 Med.L.Rptr. 1001 (1931).

that the FCC has the authority to monitor and regulate the performance of broadcasters. In the 1940s and again in the 1960s the Court sustained the authority of the FCC to regulate broadcasting to serve the public interest. In the 1980s the Court supported the authority of the FCC to deregulate broadcasting to serve the public interest. Consistently, the Court has held that broadcasting, as a unique and pervasive medium, requires occasional tweaking and modulating by government if it is to be an effective First Amendment tool.

As early as the 1930s, companies such as the National Broadcasting Company and the Columbia Broadcasting System hit upon the idea of linking local radio stations to carry music, comedy, drama, sports, and news across the country. These networks could provide a nationwide audience for music and sports events, including New York's Metropolitan Opera and baseball's World Series. A ruckus over the broadcasting of the latter event gave the Supreme Court its first opportunity to review the powers of the Federal Communications Commission, which in 1934 had replaced the Federal Radio Commission.

The FCC became concerned enough about the growth of network broadcasting to propose regulations for bringing it under control. While it was considering the form the regulations should take, a new network, Mutual, bid for and obtained the right to broadcast the World Series of 1939, between the New York Yankees and the Cincinnati Reds. Because Mutual stations were relatively few, baseball fans in some parts of the United States were unable to hear the games. Stations affiliated with CBS and NBC were willing to air the games in areas not served by Mutual affiliates but were blocked by the terms of their network contracts. The resulting furor was reflected in the chain-broadcasting regulations drafted by the FCC to take effect in 1941.

The FCC conceded that it could not regulate the networks directly, because they did not require a license to operate. However, the commission proceeded on the theory that it could regulate network practices by imposing restrictions on the affiliated stations. The new rules said that any station that was a party to a network contract that contained certain prohibited conditions would not have its license renewed. NBC and CBS joined forces in asking a federal court to nullify the rules. The court dismissed their plea, and the Supreme Court affirmed, holding that to protect the public interest, the FCC can impose reasonable regulations on broadcasters consistent with the powers given it by Congress.

National Broadcasting Co. v. United States, **319 U.S. 190, 63 S.Ct. 997, 87 L.Ed. 1344, 1 Med.L.Rptr. 1965 (1943).**

The Court began its analysis by noting that NBC and CBS had gained an almost complete monopoly over programming, especially at night. Together, they controlled more than 85 percent of the nighttime wattage, a measure of a station's ability to reach its audience. The Court also took note of the fact that this control had prevented persons in some parts of the country from hearing the 1939 World Series.

Justice Felix Frankfurter, writing for five members of the Court, examined the alleged abuses of power by the networks and affirmed the remedies proposed by the FCC to correct them. The Court upheld a commission rule forbidding networks to require stations to enter into exclusive affiliation agreements. Because the FCC could not impose its will directly on the networks, the rule said that any station signing such an agreement would not have its license renewed. Stations also were given greater freedom to reject network offerings, to pick up network programs rejected by an affiliate serving the same market, and to set their own rates for advertising. The FCC's goal in imposing such rules was to give local network stations a better opportunity to tailor their programs and their commercials to serve the interests of their audience. The Court's decision also upheld the commission's right to limit the number of stations a network could own and to force NBC to divest itself of one of the two networks, the Red and the Blue, that it operated out of the same studios in Rockefeller Center in New York City. The divested network became the American Broadcasting Company.

The networks argued that these proposals went beyond the powers Congress had given the FCC and violated the networks' First Amendment freedoms. The Court disagreed. In doing so, it adopted and amplified the public interest theme that had run through the lower-court decisions.

Reviewing the history of radio, Frankfurter said that the old FRC had been brought into existence not merely to act as a sort of scientific traffic officer, policing frequencies and transmitter power, but to make certain that the new medium operated in the "public interest, convenience, and necessity." Those words, he wrote, were not an empty litany, but a grant of power authorizing the commission to use its judgment in coping with the medium's complications. He defined the "public interest" as "the interest of the listening public in 'the larger and more effective use of radio.'" In adopting the Communications Act of 1934, "Congress endowed the Federal Communications Commission with comprehensive powers to promote and realize the vast potentialities" of that medium.

Surely, the networks argued, that mandate did not extend to them. They were not licensed. They merely provided needed programming to stations that were. Frankfurter reminded the networks that their practices had denied some of that programming—the World Series—to people who had wanted it very badly. Thus, the FCC had intervened properly to make certain that the networks, too, served the public interest. To ensure that radio serves the public, Frankfurter wrote, Congress "gave the Commission not niggardly but expansive powers." This power included authority to impose special rules on stations "engaged in chain broadcasting."

Frankfurter turned next to the argument that the regulations proposed by the FCC would abridge the networks' freedom of speech. He wrote, "If that be so, it would follow that every person whose application for a license to operate a station is denied by the Commission is thereby denied his constitutional right of free speech." But that is not the case, the justice continued. Radio is not like newspapers or magazines. It operates in a medium that imposes physical limits on the number of stations that can use the available frequencies. It is not open to all who have the desire and the money to erect a transmitter. Some who would like to go on the air must be turned down. Congress gave the authority to make such choices to the FCC, acting for the people as a whole. Frankfurter said that if the FCC were to use the authority "to choose among applicants upon the basis of their political, economic or social views, or upon any other capricious basis," it would violate its trust.

But that was not the case in this instance, Frankfurter concluded. The FCC was using its licensing powers to strike down restrictive network rules that clearly had prevented member stations from serving the public interest. In doing so, he said, the FCC had acted well within the authority given to it by Congress. The reasonable use of that authority did not violate the First Amendment. The Court's decision was a solid victory for the FCC.

After World War II, the relatively new technology of television became a huge commercial success. Television's potential as an entertainer and educator was tremendous, and the FCC fashioned rules intended to help the medium become a stable and responsible agent of American political and popular culture. How successful those efforts were is not as important as the fact that they were made. The effort firmly established, with the support of Congress and the Supreme Court, the FCC's authority to monitor and impose on broadcasting expectations that were far different from those anyone dared to impose on print media.

Among those expectations was that broadcasters be fair. The FCC's fairness rules of the 1960s and 1970s grew from the belief that broadcasting had far more power than did the printed word to shape public opinion. Official concern over the power of broadcasting to inflame passions was rooted in the sometimes hysterical debate of the late 1930s about whether the United States should aid Great Britain in its war with Germany. In 1941, just months before the Japanese attacked Pearl Harbor, the FCC ordered broadcasters not to use their stations as platforms for personal views on public issues.[8] The ban lasted throughout the war and for several years afterward. When the FCC finally relaxed the ban eight years later, it permitted broadcasters to editorialize, but only if they also made air time available to persons holding other points of view.[9] This limitation led to a series of commission rulings that further refined that obligation, formulating what came to be known as "the fairness doctrine." In 1959, Congress gave the doctrine a nod of approval by amending Section 315(a) of the Communications Act to include this sentence:

> Nothing in the foregoing shall be construed as relieving broadcasters, in connection with the presentation of newscasts, news interviews, news documentaries, and on-the-spot coverage of news events, from the obligation imposed upon them under this Act to operate in the public interest and to afford reasonable opportunity for the discussion of conflicting views on issues of public importance.

For thirty years that doctrine shaped and, its critics say, limited the way in which radio and television stations presented news, documentaries, and discussions of public events. Under threat of losing their licenses—although that seldom happened—broadcasters were required (1) "to provide coverage of vitally important controversial issues of interest" in their communities, and (2) "to provide a reasonable opportunity for the presentation of contrasting viewpoints on such issues."[10]

The doctrine was grounded in the belief that those who are fortunate enough to obtain a license to use one of the nation's scarce frequencies should use it to serve the public interest. Many in Congress and in the courts believed that a most important public interest was the " 'uninhibited, robust, wide-open' debate on public issues."[11] If such issues were to be resolved logically and without violence, broadcasters had to

---

8. Mayflower Broadcasting Corp., 8 F.C.C. 333 (1941).
9. Report on Editorializing by Broadcast Licensees, 13 F.C.C. 1246 (1949).
10. Report Concerning General Fairness Doctrine Obligations of Broadcast Licensees, 102 F.C.C.2d143, 146 (1985).
11. New York Times v. Sullivan, 376 U.S. 254, quoted in the Introduction to the Fairness Report, 48 F.C.C.2d 1 (1974).

give truth and falsehood a fair chance to grapple by opening their microphones to all shades of opinion. The fairness doctrine was based on an affirmative theory of the First Amendment that perceived a responsibility on the part of government to encourage debate on public issues.

Among other things, the fairness doctrine protected persons who were targets of personal attacks on the air. Victims of such attacks had to be notified by the station that carried the offending broadcast. They also had to be given a tape or transcript of the offending remarks and offered time, without charge, for a reply.

A legal challenge to the personal attack rule led to a Supreme Court decision upholding not only that rule but also the fairness doctrine. The lawsuit leading to the decision was brought by Fred J. Cook, a journalist and author, who was the target of a fifteen-minute radio broadcast carried by more than three hundred stations. The speaker was the Reverend Billy James Hargis, a radio and television evangelist, who bought time to broadcast his "Christian Crusade."

In Hargis's eyes, Cook was a Communist sympathizer because he had written a *Red Lion Broadcasting Co.* **v.** *Federal Communications Commission,* 395 U.S. 367, 89 S.Ct. 1794, 23 L.Ed.2d 371, 1 Med.L.Rptr. 2053 (1969). campaign tract highly critical of Barry Goldwater, a conservative Republican who ran for president in 1964, and an article attacking J. Edgar Hoover, for years director of the Federal Bureau of Investigation. Cook, with his daughter's help, wrote to each of the stations that carried the Hargis Broadcast asking for reply time. Some offered time without question, but WGCB, in the small town of Red Lion, Pennsylvania, was among those that sent Cook a rate card. The station manager reasoned that because Hargis had paid for his time, Cook should have to pay for his response. Cook appealed to the FCC for an order requiring the station to give him time without charge. The FCC issued the order.

WGCB appealed to the U.S. Court of Appeals for the District of Columbia Circuit, which upheld the FCC's order. At about the same time, in a test case brought by the Radio-Television News Directors Association (RTNDA), the Seventh Circuit Court of Appeals in Chicago held that the personal attack rule and the fairness doctrine violated the broadcasters' First Amendment freedoms. The Supreme Court accepted both cases for review, combining them under the *Red Lion* title. The seven justices who heard the cases unanimously upheld the District of Columbia Circuit's decision in *Red Lion* and reversed the Seventh Circuit's decision in *RTNDA*.

Justice Byron R. White based the Court's decision squarely on the scarcity rationale. He wrote:

> Because of the scarcity of radio frequencies, the Government is permitted to put restrictions on licensees in favor of others whose views should be expressed on this unique medium. But the people as a whole retain their interest in free speech by radio and their collective right to have the medium function consistently with the ends and purposes of the First Amendment. It is the right of the viewers and listeners, not the right of the broadcasters, which is paramount. . . . It is the purpose of the First Amendment to preserve an uninhibited marketplace of ideas in which truth will ultimately prevail, rather than to countenance monopolization of the market, whether it be by the Government itself or a private licensee. . . . It is the right of the public to receive suitable access to social, political, esthetic,

moral and other ideas and experiences which is crucial here. That right may not be constitutionally abridged either by Congress or the FCC.

With that decision the Court endorsed the view, first advanced in lower-court decisions more than thirty years earlier, that owners of broadcasting stations are not to use the stations to promote their own political, social, or economic views. Rather, they are to operate their stations as a sort of community smorgasbord, laden with points of view and political arguments representing all shades of opinion on public issues. No one opinion is to be advanced over another, but all arguments are to be given a reasonable airing, leaving the viewers and listeners to decide which they will accept and which they will reject. And if some individual should be verbally assaulted—treated unfairly—during the debate, that individual must be given a reasonable amount of time to set the record straight.

This view was clearly at odds with the way in which First Amendment law treated print media, and it was only a matter of time before the Court was asked why a newspaper, a powerful medium controlled by the whims of a private owner, should not also be required to become a community smorgasbord, with all arguments getting a fair hearing and victims of verbal attacks getting a right to reply.

Five years after *Red Lion,* Pat Tornillo, a candidate for the Florida legislature, believed he had been treated unfairly—and personally attacked—by an editorial in the *Miami Herald.* The newspaper noted that Tornillo, an officer of a teachers' union, had called a strike in defiance of a law forbidding such actions. Its editorial called him a czar and a lawbreaker. Relying on Florida's long-unused right-of-reply law, Tornillo asked the newspaper to publish his defense of his actions. When the editors refused, he asked a county court to order them to do so. That court turned Tornillo down, holding that the law violated the newspaper's First Amendment rights. On appeal, the state Supreme Court reversed. On further appeal, a unanimous U.S. Supreme Court held that the right-of-reply law for newspapers was unconstitutional.

Chief Justice Burger, who wrote for the Court, endorsed the idea that the media should fairly reflect conflicting points of view. But he noted that any attempt to force the media to do so "necessarily calls for some mechanism, either governmental or consensual." If government provides that mechanism, "this at once brings about a confrontation with...the First Amendment." Burger offered four reasons to explain why any attempt by government to force newspapers to publish material their editors would reject violates the Constitution:

Miami Herald Publishing Co. v. *Tornillo,* **418 U.S. 241, 94 S.Ct. 2831, 41 L.Ed.2d 730, 1 Med.L.Rptr. 1898 (1974).**

1. In many previous decisions, the Court had held that an attempt to force publication of "that which 'reason' tells [editors] should not be published" violates the First Amendment. The chief justice added, "A responsible press is an undoubtedly desirable goal, but press responsibility is not mandated by the Constitution and like many other virtues, it cannot be legislated."

2. Compelled publication is a form of prior restraint. If editors are forced to put something into a newspaper, they will be forced to leave out something else. "Governmental restraint on publishing need not fall into familiar patterns to be subject to constitutional limitations."

3. The alternative to leaving something out is to increase the number of pages to accommodate the material mandated by government. This increases the publisher's costs for paper, ink, and composing time, thus imposing an economic penalty that amounts to a taking of property in violation of the Fifth Amendment.

4. Finally, a state-enforced right of reply might lead some editors to "conclude that the safe course is to avoid controversy and . . . political and electoral coverage would be blunted or reduced."

At the time, the Court had no reason to note that some of the reasoning it used in *Tornillo* applied with equal force to the facts at issue in *Red Lion*. The fairness doctrine, like the Florida personal attack rule, sometimes required broadcast news directors to air assertions that in their judgment should be rejected as fallacious, repetitive, or even trivial. Further, air time is even more restrictive than the page count of a newspaper. If several major news stories break on the same day, a publisher can add two or more pages to permit full coverage of the events. Try as they might, station owners cannot add even a second to the time available in any hour or any day. Time devoted to a reply or to fulfill a fairness obligation inevitably crowds off the air matter that an editor might consider more newsworthy. Finally, one of the arguments long advanced against the fairness doctrine was that some station owners consequently advised their news staffs to steer clear of controversy so that the station would not have to air unpopular points of view.

Eventually, the FCC and lawyers representing broadcasters noted the parallels between *Red Lion* and *Tornillo*. Ten years later, in response to a rising tide of discontent with the fairness doctrine, the FCC invited comment on it.[12] The result was the FCC's conclusion that the fairness doctrine was not serving the public interest as it had been intended to do. The FCC said its inquiry found that the doctrine actually may have inhibited debate, rather than encouraging it. Further, the doctrine gave government officials an unintended means to intimidate broadcasters. The FCC learned that President Richard Nixon had directed his staff on twenty-one occasions to "take specific action relating to what could be considered unfair news coverage."[13] An official in a Democratic administration said that its strategy "was to use the fairness doctrine to challenge and harass the right-wing broadcasters and hope that the challenges would be so costly to them that they would be inhibited, and decide it was too expensive to continue."[14]

Further, the FCC said that the *Tornillo* decision had cast doubt on the constitutional validity of the doctrine, and those doubts were reinforced by the Supreme Court's

---

12. Notice of Inquiry (Gen. Dkt. No. 84-282), FCC 84-140, 49 Fed.Reg. 20317 (1984).
13. Memorandum to H. R. Haldeman from Jeb S. Magruder, "The Shot-Gun versus the Rifle," 17 October 1969, reprinted in D. Bazelon, "FCC Regulation of the Telecommunications Press," 1975 *Duke L.J.* 213, 247–251 (1975).
14. Report Concerning General Fairness Doctrine Obligations, p. 54.

The Federal Communications Commission adopted the fairness doctrine because the commission believed it served First Amendment concerns about providing for a diversity of ideas. They abandoned the doctrine for the same reason. What had changed, besides politics, was the growth in the number of competing broadcast stations across the country. Cartoonist Bill Sanders depicts the fairness doctrine relegated to the trash and the FCC rediscovering the First Amendment. *(Bill Sanders)*

decision in *Federal Communications Commission* v. *League of Women Voters of California.*[15] The Court noted in that decision that the constitutional permissibility of the fairness doctrine was based on an assumption that it enhanced coverage of controversial issues. The Court said it would have to reevaluate the doctrine if the commission demonstrated the falsity of that assumption. The Court also noted that "[t]he prevailing rationale for broadcast regulation based upon spectrum scarcity has come under increasing criticism." The Court added:

> Critics, including the incumbent chairman of the FCC, charge that with the advent of cable and satellite television technology, communities now have access to such a wide variety of stations that the scarcity doctrine is obsolete. . . . [Citation omitted] We are not prepared, however, to reconsider our longstanding approach without some signal from Congress or the FCC that technological developments have advanced so far that some revision of the system of broadcast regulation may be required.

With its report, the FCC clearly sent that signal. What it needed was a case on which it could act. As it happened, two were already in process, and, prodded by the U.S. Court of Appeals for the District of Columbia Circuit, the commission declared the fairness doctrine dead.

A major question standing between the FCC and abolition of the fairness doctrine was whether the FCC had the authority to abolish the doctrine without congressional approval. If the doctrine was a product of the FCC's policy-making authority, the commission could abolish it if it had a good reason for doing so. But if the doctrine had been written into law by Congress, it could be repealed only by an act of Congress. At issue was the language of Section 315(a) as amended by Congress in 1959. That language says that broadcasters are expected "to operate in the public interest and to afford reasonable opportunity for the presentation of conflicting views on issues of public importance." In the eyes of some, that wording made the fairness

---

15.   468 U.S. 364, 104 S.Ct. 3106, 82 L.Ed.2d 278, 10 Med.L.Rptr. 1937 (1984).

doctrine a part of the Communications Act and therefore beyond the reach of an FCC bent on eliminating it.

The test of the commission's authority came about in an unusual way. In the late 1970s, several agencies experimented with an interactive communications system, known as "teletext," that operated in the intervals between the "pulses" of conventional television signals. Two newspaper giants, Knight-Ridder and the *Los Angeles Times,* were among the experimenters. Subscribers were provided with a device that permitted them to receive text and graphics on their television screens. The service included news, sports, weather, community events, the full texts of some government documents, airline schedules, shopping services, and whatever else the originating agency thought might be of value to its audience. Through a keyboard, subscribers could decide which items to call up for viewing.

The FCC took the view that the service was more like a print medium than like conventional broadcasting. Therefore, the commission concluded that none of the political access rules, including the fairness doctrine, should be applied to teletext. In reaching that conclusion, it took the position that the doctrine was an FCC policy, not a federal statute.

Two organizations—Telecommunications Research and Action Center, and Media Access Project—asked the U.S. Court of Appeals for the District of Columbia Circuit to review the order. That court held that teletext was broadcasting as defined in the Communications Act.[16] Therefore it must comply with the equal opportunities law. But the court also held that the commission had acted reasonably when it decided not to require teletext to offer access to candidates for federal office or to abide by the fairness doctrine.

The court held that the fairness doctrine was the product of FCC policy, which could be changed at the commission's will. In the court's view, the 1959 amendment to the Communications Act did not make "the fairness doctrine a binding statutory obligation; rather, it ratified the Commission's longstanding position that the public interest standard authorizes the fairness doctrine."

Thus, Congress had done nothing more than recognize the FCC's authority to impose the fairness doctrine on broadcasters. That left the commission free to exempt teletext from the fairness requirement if it had good reasons for doing so. The court concluded that it had. The commission had concluded on the basis of its reading of recent Supreme Court decisions that, because of the textual nature of teletext, any attempt to regulate its content would violate the First Amendment. Further, if the commission were to apply the fairness doctrine to teletext, it "might well impede the development of the new technology." Rather than risk the expense of fighting challenges to the fairness doctrine, teletext providers either would steer clear of controversy or would abandon their experiment. The court held that those two reasons were sufficient to support the FCC's finding that application of the fairness doctrine to teletext would not serve the public interest. The Supreme Court refused a request to review the decision.[17]

---

16.   Telecommunications Research and Action Center v. Federal Communications Commission, 801 F.2d 501, 13 Med.L.Rptr. 1881 (D.C. Cir. 1986).
17.   482 U.S. 919, 107 S.Ct. 3196, 96 L.Ed.2d 684 (1987).

Meanwhile, a direct challenge to the fairness doctrine was proceeding on another track. That challenge began when television station WTVH in Syracuse, New York, ran a series of advertisements arguing that a nearby nuclear power plant was a "sound investment for New York." The Syracuse Peace Council complained to the FCC that the station's owner, Meredith Corporation, had not adequately presented opposing viewpoints. The commission found that comments favorable to nuclear power outnumbered opposing arguments by ten to one and gave Meredith twenty days to explain how it would even the balance.[18] Meredith asked the FCC to reconsider. While doing so, the commission issued its 1985 Fairness Report, in which it concluded that the fairness doctrine no longer served the public interest.

Nevertheless, the FCC fudged on the *Syracuse* case. It refused to address constitutional questions raised by Meredith and held that the fate of the doctrine should be left up to Congress and the courts. Meredith took its case to the U.S. Court of Appeals for the District of Columbia Circuit, which reversed and remanded.[19] In doing so, the court reminded the commission that in *Telecommunications* it had held that the fairness doctrine was not mandated by Congress. The court also said that the commission could not "blind itself" to the constitutional questions raised by Meredith. In response to this prodding, the FCC broadened its inquiry by asking for public comment on its 1985 Fairness Report. The result was an FCC decision in Meredith's favor.[20]

Syracuse Peace Council appealed to the District of Columbia Circuit.[21] The court held that the commission had acted within its authority in holding that the fairness doctrine no longer serves the public interest. But despite its earlier chastisement of the FCC for dodging the First Amendment issues raised by the doctrine, the court also avoided these issues. It based its decision solely on its finding that, in abandoning the doctrine, the FCC was neither arbitrary nor capricious, nor had it abused its discretion. The Supreme Court refused a request to review the decision.[22]

In the end, the lessons in these court opinions may be simply that the constitutional differences between broadcasting and print are less significant in theory than in practice. In theory, government may regulate to enhance but not to abridge freedom of speech and press. In practice, government has long believed that broadcasting, unlike print, requires governmental intervention—if only by licensing—to enhance freedom.

Licensing Procedures and Policies

Only rarely is a new frequency made available to potential licensees, although some frequencies allocated to smaller markets have not been claimed because of doubt that a station can make a profit. More commonly, individuals or organizations wanting to get into broadcasting either buy a station and the right to its frequency from a

18. Syracuse Peace Council, 99 F.C.C.2d 1389 (1984).
19. Meredith Corp. v. FCC, 809 F.2d 863, 13 Med.L.Rptr. 1993 (D.C. Cir. 1987).
20. Syracuse Peace Council, 2 F.C.C.Rcd. 5043 (1987); reconsideration denied, 3 F.C.C.2d 2035 (1988).
21. Syracuse Peace Council v. Federal Communications Commission, 867 F.2d 654, 16 Med.L.Rptr. 1225 (D.C. Cir. 1989).
22. Cert. denied, 493 U.S. 1019, 110 S.Ct. 717, 107 L.Ed.2d 737 (1990).

licensee, or they launch a challenge to the renewal of a license. The latter course is the more difficult because licensees who are deemed to have operated in the public interest are given renewal preference by the FCC. To be successful, a challenger not only must offer convincing proof that the current holder has not operated in the public interest but also must convince the FCC that the challenger is likely to do so and is financially able to keep the station on the air for at least a year.[23] In 1996 Congress set the duration of a broadcast license at eight years but authorized the FCC to set a shorter period if, in its judgment, a short term better served the public interest.

Obtaining a License

Although the government charges nothing more than a modest filing fee for a broadcast license, getting a station on the air can be expensive. If there is competition for a new frequency, applicants will have to pay thousands of dollars in legal fees and, if successful in obtaining a license, additional sums for studios, offices, and a transmitter. Such costs can run well into six figures for an FM station in a city of 100,000. Low-power television stations can get on the air at a modest cost, but anyone contemplating starting a full-power station from scratch must count on spending millions of dollars.

Persons or organizations seeking a broadcasting license in a competitive proceeding must convince the FCC that they are best qualified to use the available frequency in the public interest. Several factors govern the commission's deliberations:[24]

1. Citizenship and character. The applicant must be an American citizen or an organization free from significant foreign control. Only in unusual circumstances will the FCC waive the citizenship requirement. Further, the applicant must report any convictions of felonies or serious misdemeanors and any adverse civil judgments, particularly those involving antitrust law or other questionable business practices.

2. Diversity of ownership. The commission's policy encourages competitive points of view. The Telecommunications Act of 1996 limits the number of radio and television stations that a company may own.[25] Television owners are permitted to reach as much as 35 percent of all national television viewers. A broadcast company is allowed to own five to eight radio stations in the same market, depending on the market size. It also may own both a television station and a cable system in the same market, but it is forbidden from owning more than one television station in a market and may not combine ownership of a newspaper with ownership of a television station, a radio station, or a cable system in the same market.

---

23. Television Deregulation, 98 F.C.C.2d at 1091–1096; 56 P & F Rad.Reg.2d at 1017–1020 (1984).
24. Policy Statement on Comparative Broadcast Hearings, 1 F.C.C.2d 393 (1965).
25. Telecommunications Act of 1996, § 202. Broadcast Ownership.

3. Financial and technical ability. The applicants must be able to show that they are financially able to build and operate a station, and that they have the technical skills to operate the station reliably.

4. Ownership by minorities and women. The commission has for many years encouraged license applications from ethnic minority groups and women. Racial and gender preferences were upheld by the Supreme Court in 1990.[26]

5. The past broadcast record of the applicants. Evidence of exceptional public service as a broadcaster is a plus factor; evidence of poor service, a minus. Average performance is not counted.

6. Programming. A prospective licensee must have a plan to offer programming that will serve the needs of the station's audience.

License Renewal

Normally, license renewal is automatic, or nearly so. The licensee need only send a form to the FCC.[27] The form asks the licensee to indicate that it has on file with the FCC its most recent Annual Employment Report, which documents the number of minorities and women in various job categories, and its Ownership Report, which lists owners and shareholders. The form also asks the licensee to affirm that he or she is an American citizen and to indicate the extent of any foreign control over the station. In addition, the Telecommunications Act of 1996 requires an applicant to attach a summary of any written comments received from the public that concern violent programming on the station. A small percentage of television and radio licensees are selected at random for more intensive scrutiny. Stations in this sample are asked to submit program audit forms designed to show how they operated in the public interest. They also are subject to on-site inspection of their public file, in which they supposedly have placed evidence of their public service.

In keeping with the commission's view that diversity is an important criterion for licensing, broadcasters must show that they not only hire minorities and women, but also promote them. The only exemptions are for small stations in areas in which minorities make up less than 5 percent of the population. The FCC's goal for broadcasters is employment equity—that is, a station staff that mirrors the racial and gender patterns of the community.[28] The commission may deny renewal of a license if it finds that the station has not served "the public interest, convenience, and necessity"; that the station has committed a serious violation of FCC rules; or that a station's repeated violations constitute a pattern of abuse.[29]

---

26. Metro Broadcasting, Inc. v. Federal Communications Commission, 497 U.S. 547, 110 S.Ct. 2997, 111 L.Ed.2d 445 (1990).
27. Memorandum Opinion and Order, 46 Fed.Reg. 26236 (1981).
28. Nondiscrimination in the Employment Policies and Practices of Broadcast Licensees, 60 F.C.C.2d 226 (1976).
29. Telecommunications Act of 1996, § 204(k)(1).

Challenging License Renewal

The Federal Communications Commission and its staff cannot subject each request for license renewal to strict scrutiny to determine whether the holder has operated in the public interest. Nor does the FCC try to. Moreover, for many years it was not willing to listen, in a formal way, to people who might not be satisfied with the way a station served their particular public interest. Not until the 1960s, and then only under orders from a federal court, did the commission agree to do so. In a case that grew out of blatantly discriminatory programming decisions by a television station in Jackson, Mississippi, the U.S. Court of Appeals for the District of Columbia Circuit told the FCC that it should listen to complaints from a station's audience when considering license renewal.[30] Previously, the commission had ignored such complaints, holding that under its rules members of a station's audience lacked the standing to participate in licensing decisions. Judge Warren E. Burger, then three years away from becoming chief justice of the United States, overruled the commission. He reasoned that if viewers could intervene at license renewal time, broadcasters would have an additional incentive to be "responsive to the needs of the audience." He also reminded the commission and station owners that when a "broadcaster seeks and is granted the free and exclusive use of a limited and valuable part of the public domain," he accepts a "franchise . . . burdened by enforceable public obligations."

On remand, the commission listened to the complaints, then renewed the station's license. Again there was an appeal. Judge Burger rebuked the commission, withdrew the license, and invited new applicants for the frequency.[31]

This episode is unique in broadcasting history and has had one lasting effect: Licensees are required to announce well ahead of the expiration date that they will seek renewal and to invite public comment. Normally, nothing happens. But on occasion, an individual or an organization will be unhappy enough with some part of a station's operation to intervene by seeking to obtain the license to start up a new station or by filing a petition to deny renewal of the license.

If a challenger offers evidence of fraudulent operations or of a gross abuse of the broadcaster's public service obligation, the FCC may require the station to defend itself in a hearing. Rarely do such challenges succeed.

Despite all the emphasis in broadcast law on serving the public interest, a licensee's character and business practices are far more likely to get him or her in trouble with the FCC than are deficiencies in programming. A study of the sixty-four revocations or failures to renew between 1970 and 1978 showed that lying to the commission was the most common reason for the action. Only eleven of the revocations or failures to renew were for departures from promised programming.[32]

---

30. Office of Communication, United Church of Christ v. Federal Communications Commission, 359 F.2d 994 (D.C. Cir. 1966).
31. Office of Communication, United Church of Christ v. Federal Communications Commission, 425 F.2d 543 (1969).
32. Fredric A. Weiss, David Ostroff, and Charles E. Clift III, "Station License Revocations and Denials of Renewal, 1970–78," *Journal of Broadcasting,* Winter 1980, p. 69.

Programming Quality and License Renewal

Theoretically, at least, a broadcaster's devotion to serving the public interest is the justification for its right to possess a valuable portion of the people's airwaves. In reality, the FCC has wobbled all over the lot in trying to assess programming quality and applying a quality assessment to licensing proceedings. Moreover, the Supreme Court has held that the FCC's role in seeking to influence the quality of programming should be minimal.[33]

That decision by the Court, coming when the FCC commissioners already were committed to deregulation, accelerated a hands-off policy toward broadcast programming. The FCC's minimalist approach means there are no fixed quotas for the amount of time that must be devoted to news, public affairs, or public service announcements. Instead, the commission rewards, in contested renewals, licensees who have provided "meritorious or substantial service." Such reward is known as a renewal expectancy, meaning that stations that provide some public service programming can expect their licenses to be routinely renewed, even if there is a challenge.

In most communities, however, listeners seem content with stations that offer no local public affairs programming at all. FM radio stations in particular have adopted successful programming formats limited to a single kind of recorded music, such as pop, rock, or country and western, occasionally interrupted for a minute or so of news from a satellite service. AM stations have taken over much of the "public affairs" role, but only by giving themselves over to "talk radio," a kind of programming in which listeners can call in to discuss the problems of the day with an announcer.

In 1990, concerned about the apparent decline in the quality of programming for children, Congress passed into law the Children's Television Act. A major provision of that law limits the amount of time a broadcaster can devote to commercials during programs for children. The law also instructed the FCC to draft rules that would encourage broadcasters to develop more programming for children. In response, the commission directed broadcasters and cable operators to provide educational and informational programming for children sixteen years old and younger and to keep records of the children's programs aired by them for review at license renewal.[34]

Limitations on Ownership

FCC rules forbid any single entity from monopolizing the media in the country or in a community. The regulations change from time to time, but in 1996, for example, a radio broadcaster could own as many stations nationwide as he or she wanted, but was not permitted to control more than eight radio stations serving the same market. The Telecommunications Act of 1996 provides the following:[35]

---

33. Federal Communications Commission v. WNCN Listeners Guild, 450 U.S. 582, 101 S.Ct. 1266, 67 L.Ed.2d 521 (1981).

34. Mary Lu Carnevale, "FCC Adopts Rules on Children's TV; Critic Calls Them 'Barest Minimum,'" *Wall Street Journal,* 10 April 1991, p. B6.

35. Telecommunications Act of 1996, § 202(a)(1).

— In a radio market with more than forty-four commercial stations, a company may control up to eight stations, not more than five of which are either AM or FM.

— In a radio market with between thirty and forty-four commercial stations, a company may control up to seven stations, not more than four of which are either AM or FM.

— In a radio market with between fifteen and twenty-nine commercial stations, a company may control up to six stations, not more than four of which are either AM or FM.

— In a radio market with fourteen or fewer commercial stations, a company may control up to five stations, not more than three of which are either AM or FM, if it does not control more than half of the stations in the market.

Television broadcasters may own as many stations nationwide as they want, as long as the national audience share does not exceed 35 percent. FCC regulations limit a broadcaster to one television station per market, but Congress has asked the FCC to reconsider that restriction in the future.[36]

A company may own both a television station and a cable system in the same market. However, newspaper/broadcast combinations are restricted by the commission. Generally, a broadcast station may not own the daily newspaper in its community. However, newspapers owned by broadcasters before 1975 have been allowed to continue, and the FCC usually grants a temporary waiver to allow time for a company to sell a newspaper if it acquires a station where it already owns the paper.

Legal Restraints on Broadcast Content

The Equal Opportunities Law

Beginning with the Radio Act of 1927, the statutes have contained language designed to prevent radio, and now television, from being dominated by any political candidate or party. Currently, Section 315 of the Communications Act of 1934 defines what is known as the equal opportunities requirement. Under its terms, a station that permits any candidate for public office to use its facilities to reach an audience must stand ready to permit equivalent use by the candidate's opponents. "Use" is defined in terms that exclude "bona fide" newscasts, documentaries, news events, and news interviews. As a practical matter, then, a political "use" is limited to paid messages in which the candidate is a participant, and to appearances in nonnews programming, whether it be entertainment or a talk show not normally devoted to newsworthy issues. Under Section 315, no station is required to permit itself to be used by any candidate. If it does so, it cannot censor the content of the

---

36.   Telecommunications Act of 1996, § 202(c)(2).

candidate's message and it must be willing to provide, on request, comparable time to the candidate's opponents.

Other provisions of Section 315 require stations that elect to sell time to political candidates to do so at the lowest rate offered to commercial advertisers. "Broadcasting stations" are defined to include cable television systems. After the 1990 election, about fifty candidates, including candidates for governor in California and Georgia, sued stations, alleging that the stations had overcharged them. They acted after an FCC audit of twenty stations in five markets showed that sixteen had billed candidates for something more than the "lowest unit charge" paid by commercial advertisers.[37]

A subsection of Section 312, not to be confused with Section 315, requires broadcasting stations to sell "reasonable amounts of time" to candidates for federal elective offices, which includes the presidency and both houses of Congress. Refusal to do so can result in loss of license. The section was enacted because some television stations in large metropolitan areas, which might be carved into as many as a dozen congressional districts, refused to sell time to candidates for Congress, to avoid creating equal opportunities obligations that might use up all available commercial time. Obviously, Sections 312 and 315 impose on broadcasters both duties and restrictions with respect to political campaigns that are not imposed on newspapers and magazines.

Broadcasters have chafed at these duties and restrictions. They have argued that they could do a more meaningful job of covering political campaigns if they did not have the FCC looking over their shoulders and applying a stopwatch to each use by a candidate.

To qualify for access to air time under Section 315, a candidate must meet three criteria:

1. He or she must be eligible for election to the office sought. In one instance, the FCC held that a thirty-one-year-old was not a legally qualified candidate for president because the Constitution says that a president must be at least thirty-five.

2. He or she must be an announced candidate.

3. He or she must have taken the steps required by law to qualify for a place on the ballot. Candidates who seek write-in votes must show that they are conducting a campaign.

These criteria apply equally to primary and general elections. A primary is a preliminary election at which members of a political party select their candidates for office. If nominations are made by convention or caucus, the candidate must make a serious showing of an effort to win the nomination.

In legal terms, a political spot announcement is a "use" if the candidate or the candidate's voice is identifiable in it. On the other hand, a political commercial of any length is not a "use" if the candidate's likeness or voice is not a part of it. The key to a use that will trigger Section 315 is the candidate's identity. If the candidate can be rec-

---

37. Milo Geyelin, "Broadcasters Sued on Campaign Ad Rates," *Wall Street Journal,* 11 November 1991, p. B3.

ognized by the viewer or listener, and the appearance is not covered by one of the four exemptions listed in the act, it is a "use." If the candidate did not pay for such a use, his or her opponents are entitled to a similar free use if they ask for it. It makes no difference if the original candidate's use had nothing to do with politics. For example, a Michigan television station triggered an equal opportunities requirement when it ran an old Ronald Reagan movie during that state's primary campaign in 1980.

"Equal opportunities" goes beyond a counting of minutes. It starts there—if one candidate for governor buys thirty minutes of air time, the station must be willing to sell thirty minutes to each opponent—but also takes into account the potential audience. Thus, thirty minutes at 1 A.M. is not equal in opportunities to thirty minutes at 8 P.M. Usage must be scheduled so that each candidate can reach approximately the same number of persons. If a station offers help to one candidate in preparing for a use—in staging, graphics, or anything else—it must offer the same help to each opponent. However, none of these provisions is self-triggering. A candidate who seeks to balance an opponent's use, free or paid, must apply to the station within seven days of that use.

The equal opportunities provision balances paid time against paid time, free time against free time. There is no crossover between the two. If one candidate is able to buy a great deal of time, and the other can afford little or none, the station is under no obligation to balance the scales by giving the latter free time. If it were to do so, it would be obligated to give the first candidate free time if he or she asked for it, as almost certainly would happen.

The FCC has been quite liberal in defining bona fide news programs subject to the four exemptions. Any station's regular news programs are exempt from equal opportunities requirements. When one candidate for office was interviewed on the same station's newscast five days in a row, the FCC ruled that Section 315 could not be invoked.[38] NBC's *Today*[39] and CBS's *60 Minutes*[40] are examples of bona fide news programs.

A "bona fide news interview" must take place during a regularly scheduled, continuing series of programs devoted to newsworthy topics. Thus, long-established programs such as *Meet the Press* or *Face the Nation* are exempt from the equal opportunities requirement. A call-in show, such as *Larry King Live* on CNN, is exempt if it is regularly scheduled and is under the control of the station's news department. But talk shows not devoted primarily to newsworthy topics do not qualify for exemption from Section 315. The commission looked at one such program and found that its content had ranged from "monsters in films to sexual fantasies to psychic healing and TV soap operas." Therefore, it held, a candidate's appearance on the program had not resulted in a "bona fide news interview,"[41] and therefore was a "use."

There has been little dispute over the meaning of a "bona fide news documentary." If such programs are under the control of a station's or network's news department and are devoted to a newsworthy topic, they qualify for exemption.

---

38. Letter to Citizens for Reagan (WCKT-TV), 58 F.C.C.2d 925 (1976).
39. Lar Daly, 40 F.C.C. 314 (1960).
40. Letter to CBS, 58 F.C.C.2d 601 (1976).
41. Socialist Workers Party, 65 F.C.C.2d 234 (1976).

The meaning of "on-the-spot coverage of bona fide news events," however, has generated controversy. Some complaints have grown out of broadcasts by presidents to announce or comment on news events when they were candidates for reelection. In such instances, the commission generally has upheld the broadcaster's "reasonable, good-faith judgment" that the occasion was newsworthy. Debates among candidates for the same office are considered bona fide news events, even when they are arranged by a broadcaster, and may be covered without triggering the equal opportunities requirement.[42] Press conferences held by candidates for public office also are considered news events.

Few cases interpreting the equal opportunities provision have reached the courts. Two of the more interesting raised the following question: Should persons who earn their living performing on radio or television have to give up their jobs if they decide to run for office? In each case, the answer was yes. In one instance, Pat Paulsen, a comedian, argued that no one else must give up his or her occupation when he or she becomes a candidate. As he saw it, Section 315 discriminates against TV and radio performers. Paulsen's problem began when he entered the New Hampshire primary as a candidate for the Republican nomination for president. His purpose was to poke fun at the news media's heavy focus on a midwinter primary that usually involved fewer than 200,000 voters. Shortly before his flirtation with politics, Paulsen had signed a contract with Walt Disney Productions to appear in a TV series, *The Mouse Factory*. One episode would be telecast during the primary campaign. When the producer learned of Paulsen's candidacy, he asked the FCC whether that would raise equal opportunities problems. The FCC ruled that it would. Disney canceled Paulsen's contract. The actor appealed first to the FCC and then to the U.S. Court of Appeals for the Ninth Circuit. In *Paulsen* v. *Federal Communications Commission*,[43] the court upheld the producer and the FCC.

The Court said that the purpose of Section 315 is to require broadcasters to treat all candidates alike. Paulsen argued that he should be treated differently because his appearance in *The Mouse Factory* would be nonpolitical, he would have no control over the script, and, because he already was well known, the program would have no effect on his candidacy. The court said that if it were to accept Paulsen's arguments, it would plunge the FCC into passing judgment on program content to distinguish between political and nonpolitical appearances. Further, it also would open a loophole that ingenious candidates could exploit by creating entertainment programs for no other purpose than to help them win election.

The U.S. Court of Appeals for the District of Columbia Circuit used similar reasoning in holding that a Sacramento television reporter would have to stay off the air if he chose to run for town council.[44] William Branch, a general assignment reporter for KOVR, argued that his appearances on his station's newscasts were part of bona fide news events and therefore should not be considered a use as defined in Section

42. The Law of Political Broadcasting and Cablecasting: A Political Primer—1984 Edition, 100 F.C.C.2d 1476.

43. 491 F.2d 887 (9th Cir. 1974).

44. Branch v. Federal Communications Commission, 824 F.2d 37, 14 Med.L.Rptr. 1465 (D.C. Cir. 1987).

315. Whenever he reported such events, he was simply doing his job as a reporter, not campaigning for office. KOVR's management, seeking to avoid equal opportunities requests, told Branch he'd have to choose between his job and his political aspirations. The reporter appealed to the FCC, which told him the same thing.

In rejecting Branch's further appeal, the circuit court said that Congress had amended Section 315 in 1959 to remove any doubt about its application to on-the-air journalists. Their job is to cover bona fide news events. If a political candidate is involved in the event, his or her appearance on the air is not considered a use. Reporters who cover the event are not a part of it, the court said, "for the event would occur without them and they serve only to communicate it to the public. . . . There is nothing at all 'newsworthy' about the work being done by the broadcaster's own employees, regardless of whether any of those employees happens also to be a candidate for public office."

The court, echoing the Ninth Circuit's decision in *Paulsen,* also rejected the argument that Section 315 unduly interfered with Branch's right to run for office. The court said that he could run for office if he wished, but he could not remain on the air unless the station's management was willing to provide time, on request, to his opponents. The court added, "[N]obody has ever thought that a candidate has a right to run for office and at the same time to avoid all personal sacrifice."

Political Candidates and Censorship

Section 315 of the Communications Act flatly forbids broadcasters to censor a political candidate's use of their stations. Until 1984, the FCC and the courts interpreted that provision to mean exactly what it says, no matter how crude or libelous the candidate's remarks. In that year, an unusual candidate, Larry Flynt, publisher of *Hustler* magazine, said that he would include sexually explicit episodes in his campaign messages. This announcement prompted an FCC staff conclusion that broadcasters could not be required to use obscene or indecent political advertisements.[45] The staff analysis said that Section 312(a)(6) "carve[d] an exception" to the law forbidding broadcasters to censor political uses by candidates. Under that section, the FCC can revoke the license of a station that broadcasts obscenities.

A modified version of that exception came into play in 1992 when more than a dozen candidates for office sought air time for political advertisements showing aborted fetuses. One of them, Daniel Becker, Republican candidate for Congress in Georgia's Ninth District, tried to buy time on WAGA-TV in Atlanta for a thirty-minute message, including a four-minute segment depicting a surgical abortion. He specified that his message be aired immediately following an Atlanta Falcons–Los Angeles Rams football game on the Sunday afternoon before the election. Because the station had received an unusual number of protests when it had aired previous political messages showing aborted fetuses, it asked a federal district court judge for a ruling that would permit it to refuse Becker's request without violating the reasonable access law.

---

45.   Memorandum by FCC Staff, 6 January 1984; "Stations Needn't Show Political Ads with Obscenities," *Wall Street Journal,* 26 January 1984, p. A38.

The station's lawyers argued that Becker's advertisement was indecent, and that if it were shown, the station would violate a criminal statute forbidding the broadcast of "obscene, indecent or profane language,"[46] as well as risk losing its license.

Judge Robert Hall, citing the FCC staff memorandum in *Flynt,* said that he would be guided by the agency's interpretation of the access statute. He also said that after viewing Becker's message in its entirety, he had concluded that it violated Section 1464: "[T]he videotape contains graphic depictions and descriptions of female genitalia, the uterus, excreted uterine fluid, dismembered fetal body parts, and aborted fetuses. This portion of the videotape depicts these activities and materials in a manner which is patently offensive according to contemporary community standards."[47]

However, Hall did not agree to the station's request to keep the message off the air. Referring to several decisions reflecting the FCC's concern with preventing children from being exposed to the broadcasting of indecent material, he said that Becker still could buy time from the station, but it would have to be between midnight and 6 A.M., when few children are believed to be in the audience. Hall's decision was handed down on the Friday before the election. Becker filed an immediate appeal with the Eleventh Circuit Court in Atlanta, asking it to stay Hall's order. That court bucked the request to Supreme Court Justice Anthony Kennedy, who oversees the Eleventh Circuit. On Sunday, he refused Becker's request for a stay.[48] As a result of the weekend's flurry of litigation, some stations decided to air election-eve graphic antiabortion commercials during the early hours of the morning, while others aired them at the times requested by the candidate, along with a warning that the subject matter might be harmful to children. Nathan Deal, a Democratic incumbent, defeated Becker, 113,924 to 79,792.

The FCC has ruled in numerous instances that political advertisements cannot be censored for containing derogatory racial epithets[49] or even what the *New York Times* called "a barnyard expletive."[50]

The Supreme Court held in 1959 that a station cannot be sued for a libel spoken during a political use. Ruling in *Farmers Educational and Cooperative Union of America* v. *WDAY,*[51] the Court said that lawsuits must be directed at the candidate. The case grew out of a demand for equal opportunity by a minor candidate for United States senator from North Dakota after WDAY had given time to the two major-party candidates. The speaker devoted part of his time to an attack on the farmers' union, accusing it of trying to establish "a Communist Farmer's Union Soviet right here in North Dakota." The union, which was a farmers' cooperative marketing organization and a strong political force in the state, sued both the candidate and the station for libel. When state courts dismissed the suit against the station, the Supreme Court

46. 18 U.S.C. § 1464.
47. Gillett Communications of Atlanta, Inc. v. Becker, 807 F.Supp. 757, 20 Med.L.Rptr. 1947 (N.D.Ga. 1992).
48. Rebecca Perl, "High Court Lets TV Block Abortion Ad," *Atlanta Constitution,* 2 November 1992, p. B2.
49. Atlanta N.A.A.C.P., 36 F.C.C.2d 635 (1972), is an early example.
50. Bernard Weinraub, "One Word Is Worth a Thousand Speeches to Obscure Presidency Hopeful," *New York Times,* 16 October 1980, p. B8.
51. 360 U.S. 525, 79 S.Ct. 1302, 3 L.Ed.2d 1407 (1959).

agreed to take the case. It upheld the state courts, five to four. The majority noted that, in writing Section 315, Congress had given broadcasting stations no option. If they gave or sold time to one candidate for political office, they had to be willing to give or sell time on request to his or her opponents. The law also said that stations could not censor a candidate's remarks; therefore, stations could not be held accountable for those remarks.

The "Reasonable Time" Requirement

Section 312(a)(7) of the Communications Act requires broadcasters to sell reasonable amounts of time to candidates for federal offices. Congress wrote sharp teeth into the law. The penalty "for willful or repeated failure to allow reasonable access or to permit purchase of a reasonable amount of time" is revocation of the offending station's license. Further, the Supreme Court has held that the law serves a First Amendment interest, although in doing so the Court said that stations could refuse to honor a specific request for time if they acted on some rational basis.

The test case grew out of a request by the Carter-Mondale Presidential Committee to buy a thirty-minute spot on all three networks during the first week of December 1979. The purpose was to announce the start of President Carter's reelection campaign. For various reasons, including the assertion that it was too early to start the 1980 political campaign, the networks refused to sell the requested time. The committee complained to the FCC, which ruled that the networks had violated Section 312(a)(7) by denying reasonable access to the airwaves. The networks took their case to the court of appeals, which affirmed the FCC's ruling. On further appeal, the Supreme Court did likewise.

Chief Justice Burger, writing for the Court, held that the networks did not have the right to determine when a political campaign ought to begin. That is a decision to be made by politicians. However, the majority held that stations could refuse time to candidates for federal offices if they had good reasons for doing so. The Court said that "to justify a negative response, broadcasters must cite a realistic danger of substantial program disruption—perhaps caused by insufficient notice to allow adjustments in the schedule—or of an excessive number of equal time requests." In weighing requests for time, the Court said that broadcasters should consider such factors "as the amount of time previously sold to the candidate, the disruptive impact on regular programming, and the likelihood of requests for time by rival candidates under the equal opportunities provision." The Court also advised broadcasters to explain their reasons for any refusal of time or for making a counteroffer. If they can show that they acted "reasonably and in good faith, their decisions will be entitled to deference even if the Commission's analysis would have differed in the first instance."

CBS, Inc. **v.** *Federal Communications Commission*, **453 U.S. 367, 101 S.Ct. 2813, 69 L.Ed.2d 706, 7 Med.L.Rptr. 1563 (1981).**

The Court brushed aside CBS's argument that the reasonable access provision violated its First Amendment rights. Section 312(a)(7) was written, Burger said, to enhance the ability of candidates for federal office to present their views to the voting public. Thus, it served the more important First Amendment interests of the people in receiving "information necessary for the effective operation of the democratic process."

CABLE TELEVISION

Cable, which began as a means of bringing programming from distant stations to hard-to-reach areas, has become a giant of an industry, reaching more than sixty million subscribers, 63 percent of homes with television sets.[52] Cable began simply by retransmitting commercial television programs. Today, cable companies produce their own twenty-four-hour news, sports, movies, music, weather, shopping, and political programming. To protect the viability of broadcasting, the FCC requires cable owners to carry local broadcast stations, but the competition between cable and broadcast networks is keen, with both sides clamoring for government protection and congressional revision of existing telecommunications law.

The Regulation of Cable

When the first community antenna television system (CATV) brought signals from Philadelphia stations into the mountain valley towns of western Pennsylvania, less than half a century ago, the new technology was seen as a handy tool, giving viewers access to the entertainment and sports offered by the few VHF television stations then on the air. The owners of those broadcast stations saw CATV as a means of extending their audiences, thus making the stations more attractive to advertisers. Sponsors of network programming saw such systems as a means of extending the reach of their advertising messages. The only grumblers were the creators of television programming, who saw the cable systems as freeloaders, dodging payment of copyright royalties. But when United Artists Television sued to force antenna systems in Clarksburg and Fairmont, West Virginia, to pay for the retransmission of movies that it had licensed to the television networks, the U.S. Supreme Court turned it down.[53] The Court held that CATV was simply a remote antenna, an extension of the individual viewer's television set, doing no more than delivering signals from over-the-air television stations to viewers who might not otherwise be able to receive them.

At the time, that was a fair description of cable television. In 1965, fewer than fourteen hundred cable systems served a small percentage of the homes with television sets.[54] Only about 10 percent of those systems originated any programming. Today, three decades later, the description is far from accurate. "Remote antennas" have become a communications medium of satellites, coaxial cable, and fiber optics, reaching

---

52. Joseph R. Dominick, Barry L. Sherman, Gary A. Copeland, *Broadcasting / Cable and Beyond,* 3d ed. (New York: McGraw-Hill, 1996), p. 194.
53. Fortnightly Corp. v. United Artists Television, 392 U.S. 390, 88 S.Ct. 2084, 20 L.Ed.2d 190 (1968).
54. Thomas Whiteside, "Onward and Upward with the Arts: Cable—1," *New Yorker,* 20 May 1985, p. 45.

more than sixty million subscribers, 63 percent of the households with television sets.[55] Further, cable networks today originate more programming, both in variety and in quantity, than do broadcast networks. As a consequence, cable has whittled away at the broadcast share of the audience, reducing it to less than two-thirds of the viewers tuned in at any one time.[56]

In the beginning of cable television, both the FCC and Congress treated cable as the Supreme Court had in *United Artists,* a remote antenna. But in the 1960s, as cable operators began charging viewers for special programming, mainly sports events and movies, the climate changed. Over-the-air broadcasters came to see cable systems as competitors for both audience and advertising. At the time, such regulation as there was came primarily from local governments. Cable systems, like the telephone and the electric companies, could provide service only by stringing wires over or under public streets or through easements obtained from owners of private property. These restrictions made cable subject to franchises granted by local governments. In return for the right to operate in a community, local officials could and did impose conditions that the system must meet. Typically, the franchise agreement might specify the quality of service and the number of channels to be offered, the fee to be charged subscribers, and particular stations that must be carried. Bidding for the right to serve a community sometimes became intensely competitive and tinged with politics.

Beginning in 1965, the FCC asserted its authority over cable programming. The commission acted on the same rationale that it had used in the 1940s to bring the broadcast networks under its supervision. It had intervened then to make certain that broadcasting could continue to serve the public interest, and it intervened now for the same reason. Because cable used and enhanced the work of licensed broadcasters, cable operators were to be treated, generally, as though they were broadcasters, too. The FCC subsequently required cable systems to carry local broadcast stations, to meet the FCC's standards for hiring and promoting minorities and women, and, for those cable operators producing their own programs, to satisfy FCC regulations governing political campaigns, fairness, and decency.

Although cable operators complained that local government franchises kept rates too low to be profitable, the demand for service grew steadily during the 1970s and 1980s. Those years also brought changes in the legal status of cable. In 1984, Congress passed the Cable Communications Policy Act "to establish a national policy concerning cable communications."[57] The act permitted local governments to continue to franchise cable systems, but it limited the fees that they could charge cable operators and took away their ability to mandate programming. The act ended, in most instances, the power of local governments to control the rates that cable systems could charge customers. In 1992, after complaints about rapid rate increases by cable systems, Congress authorized the FCC to control increases by setting standards for determining when a cable operator's charges for basic services are "reasonable."[58] In

---

55. Dominick, Sherman, and Copeland, *Broadcasting/Cable and Beyond,* p. 194.

56. Lawrie Mifflin, "Cable TV Continues Its Steady Drain of Network Viewers," *New York Times,* 25 October 1995, p. B1.

57. Pub.L. 98-549, 98 Stat. 2779, codified in scattered sections of 47 U.S.C., starting with § 521 (1984).

58. S. 12, 102d Cong., 2d Sess. (1992).

1996, Congress freed cable rates again from government control—for small systems immediately and for the rest of the industry by March 31, 1999.[59]

The Cable Communications Policy Act of 1984

The debate about competition among the media has a home in the Congress. Since the early 1980s, the House and Senate have been revising telecommunications law in ways that reflect the intense pressure from cable, phone, and computer companies to merge their technologies, if not their companies. In 1984 and 1992, Congress adopted legislation intended to establish "a national policy concerning cable communications."[60] In 1996, Congress overhauled the Communications Act of 1934 to permit greater competition among electronic media of all kinds, but particularly cable and telephone companies.[61]

One of the goals of the cable legislation, like the regulation of broadcasting, is to "assure that cable communications provide and are encouraged to provide the widest possible diversity of information sources and services to the public." On a more mundane level, the Cable Communications Policy Act of 1984 attempted to establish "an orderly process for franchise renewal which protects cable operators against unfair denials of renewal." The act established standards for quality of service which, if met, would ensure franchise renewal.

The act permits authorities to require operators to set aside channels for public, educational, or government use. If such a requirement exists, the operator is forbidden to exercise editorial control over the content of those channels. Further, systems that offer more than thirty-six channels must set aside some of them for commercial use by others, which could include newspaper publishers. Cable operators can charge reasonable fees for such use but are forbidden to exercise editorial control over the content. However, franchising authorities may forbid programming that is obscene or "is in conflict with community standards in that it is lewd, lascivious, filthy, or indecent or is otherwise unprotected by the Constitution." Another section of the act provides for stiff penalties for use of a cable system to transmit obscene materials.

Local governments retain the authority to grant and renew franchises. However, local governments are not permitted to treat cable systems as common carriers for purposes of regulation. This restriction exempts cable systems from rate-setting procedures with which public utilities must comply. However, the act requires franchising authorities to "assure that access to cable service is not denied to any group of potential residential cable subscribers because of the income of the residents of the local area in which such group resides."

Local governments also retain the authority to require cable operators to pay a franchise fee for the privilege of doing business. However, the Cable Communications Policy Act has taken from local governments all authority to reg-

---

59. Telecommunications Act of 1996, § 301(b).
60. 47 U.S.C. § 521.
61. See the Telecommunications Act of 1996 and the Communications Decency Act of 1996.

ulate rates charged for cable service except in those areas where cable systems have no competition, either from over-the-air stations or from another cable system.

The act strips from local governments all authority over services, facilities, and equipment of cable operators. It gives the FCC authority to establish technical standards for equipment and, thus, for the quality of video pictures delivered to subscribers. It denies local government the authority to require operators to carry specified "video programming or other information services."

Cable operators are permitted to change the terms of their franchise if they can demonstrate that it is "commercially impracticable" to continue to comply with the current terms. Thus, operators may propose to drop a channel if the fee charged by the provider is raised, or if subscriber fees drop below the break-even point. However, such proposals must be submitted to a public hearing.

If a local government is dissatisfied with a cable operator's service and therefore is not likely to renew the operator's franchise, it must schedule a hearing three and a half years prior to the termination date. At that time, officials must identify the future cable-related needs and interests of the community and review the performance of the current operator. If the operator seeks renewal, its request must be granted unless further hearings result in an adverse finding in one or more of four areas:

1. The operator has not "substantially complied with the material terms" of the existing franchise.

2. The quality of service, "including signal quality, response to consumer complaints, and billing practices," is unsatisfactory.

3. The operator is unable, because of financial, legal, or other problems, to provide the service called for in the franchise.

4. The operator's proposal for meeting the community's needs, as identified in the earlier proceeding, is unreasonably inadequate or expensive.

A local government that decides not to renew a cable franchise must issue a written decision giving its reasons. That decision is subject to appeal to the courts. The law says that "the court shall grant appropriate relief" if the franchising authority failed to comply with the prescribed procedures or if its findings in any of the four areas above are "not supported by a preponderance of the evidence." The language of the section creates a strong presumption that franchises are to be renewed.

If the franchise is not renewed, the law requires the franchising authority or the new franchisee to pay the operator the "fair market value" of the physical property "valued as a going concern." No value is to be allocated to the franchise itself. If a franchise is revoked for cause, the new owner is required to pay "an equitable price." The difference between "equitable price" and "fair market value" is not explained. In the few cases that have tested this procedure, courts have held that once begun, the procedure must be carried to a conclusion unless the parties reach agreement in informal negotiations.

The Cable Television Consumer Protection and Competition Act of 1992

Beyond question, the Cable Communications Policy Act of 1984 benefited cable system operators. However, five years after it took effect, some members of Congress began to ask whether it was as good for cable system subscribers, for television broadcasters, and for other competitors in the information and entertainment sectors. Some charged that one effect of the act had been to deregulate the cable industry in a way that created a powerful cable monopoly that was gouging the public with high rates and poor service.[62] Witnesses told the Senate Commerce Committee that rates in some Tennessee cities had increased by more than 100 percent in three years.[63] The average monthly rate for basic service rose from about $7.50 in 1980 to $16.00 in 1990. Committees of both houses of Congress drafted legislation designed to bring cable operators under control.

A four-year battle in which lobbyists for cable operators, broadcasters, public interest groups, and others contended for favor in Congress ended in October 1992 with passage, over President Bush's veto, of the Cable Television Consumer Protection and Competition Act. Its principal selling point was a provision giving the FCC authority to review rate increases and cap those deemed unreasonable. Rate regulation would be most strict on a cable system's basic tier of services, which would include most over-the-air stations, along with public, government, and educational channels. Rates on a second tier of services, which typically might include ESPN, CNN, and other programming not available over the air, could be regulated if more than 70 percent of a system's viewers subscribed to a second tier.

The act also permitted local television stations to charge cable systems for carrying their signals, required cable operators to maintain telephone lines to receive service complaints twenty-four hours a day, and forbade operators from forcing users to subscribe to a second tier of service in order to subscribe to premium channels such as HBO or Cinemax.

Despite a flurry of lawsuits, the FCC moved forward with the drafting of rules to implement the law.[64] One of the first rules defined the must-carry provisions. Cable systems that offer twelve or fewer channels must carry one noncommercial educational station and at least three local commercial stations. Systems with thirteen to thirty-six channels must carry as many as three local noncommercial stations and devote up to one-third of the channels to local commercial stations.

---

62. Jack J. Valenti, "Is Cable Monopolizing Television? How Congress Created a Cable Monster," *New York Times,* 24 May 1987, p. C2; Mary Lu Carnevale, "Congress Seeks to Rein In Cable TV," *Wall Street Journal,* 11 December 1989, p. B1; and Dennis Kneale, "Why Viewers Would Like to Zap Their Cable Firms," *Wall Street Journal,* 19 March 1990, p. B1.
63. "Cable Takes a Hit in the House," *Broadcasting,* 2 July 1990, p. 19.
64. Mary Lu Carnevale, "FCC Adopts Regulations on Service, Use of Local Signals by Cable Industry," *Wall Street Journal,* 12 March 1993, p. B8.

United States District Judge Harold H. Greene poses in his chambers in Washington, D.C. Judge Greene oversaw the breakup of AT&T's Bell Telephone System in the 1980s. The dismemberment of the giant communications corporation led the way to competition in long-distance telephone service and the entry of phone companies into other aspects of the communications business. *(Andrea Mohin/NYT Pictures)*

The Telecommunications Act of 1996

One reason cable television could grow into an industry of its own was that, until the 1990s, competition from broadcasters and telephone companies was severely limited by antitrust law and FCC regulations. Had it been otherwise, telephone companies, already connected to most homes in their service areas, might have enjoyed a significant advantage. By simply upgrading from telephone wires to coaxial cable or fiber optics, telephone companies had the potential to become not only the dominant carrier of voice and digital messages, but also the primary carrier for cable television, and, more significantly, a potential competitor in the electronic news and advertising business.

However, the nation's telephone companies were kept out of the cable business. Moreover, in the 1980s, the biggest phone company, AT&T, came under attack from the Justice Department because of its near monopoly over telephone services. The Justice Department led an effort to break up AT&T and in 1984 succeeded. Judge Harold Greene of the U.S. District Court for the District of Columbia approved an agreement, called a consent decree, that directed the dismemberment of the giant corporation into independent, regional telephone companies and, in addition, invited competitors into the business of long-distance telephone service. Thus, AT&T entered a new world of competition with energetic long-distance providers such as MCI and Sprint.

The break up of AT&T changed everything. In a climate of competition, government regulators had fewer fears that new, smaller phone companies could dominate national media. For example, when the new AT&T began to suggest that it would like to make its *Yellow Pages* available over interactive television, newspaper publishers joined cable operators in an effort to persuade Judge Greene to bar AT&T from providing electronic information services to customers. But in the end, Judge Greene said that he would allow the entry of a phone company into the information business if the company could show "there was no substantial possibility" that it could use its monopoly power to impede competition.

On appeal, the Circuit Court for the District of Columbia told the judge that even this standard—"no substantial possibility"—was too strict.[65] The appeals court said that phone companies should be permitted to provide information services if doing so is in the public interest. Judge Greene then said he would permit phone companies to offer information services as long as he could be convinced that the effect of such an offer was not anticompetitive.[66] Newspaper publishers asked the Supreme Court to stay Judge Greene's order, but the Court refused to do so.[67]

Congress ratified and encouraged this new era of competition in 1996 with passage of the Telecommunications Act. The act made major revisions to the Communications Act of 1934 and replaced much of Judge Greene's consent decree. Under the new act, phone companies may expand their involvement in electronic publishing, albeit indirectly, by working with separated affiliates and joint-venture companies.[68] More importantly, perhaps, the act allows cable and telephone companies to compete with each other in a full range of telephone, video, and high-speed data communication services—including television. In 1996, AT&T announced its entry into television for the first time in its 111-year history with plans to compete with cable by beaming 175 channels from orbiting satellites.[69]

The 1996 Telecommunications Act not only allows telephone companies to enter the cable business; it allows cable companies to enter the telephone business, and both to own competing stations and systems in the same community and throughout the country. Moreover, the act frees cable companies, at least by the year 1999, to regain control over setting rates. The eventual results of this litigation are impossible to predict, but even before Congress cleared the way for multimedia competition, the cable industry had witnessed a dizzying array of corporate positioning by its potential competitors: AT&T split itself into three separate companies, one of which is devoted entirely to exploiting new opportunities in communications; two of the nation's four major television networks merged with multimedia companies—CBS with Westinghouse Corporation, and Capital Cities/ABC with the Walt Disney Company; two of the seven Bell telephone companies, Nynex and Bell Atlantic, proposed a merger that would give them dominant access to local telephone and cellular systems from Virginia to Maine. Representative Edward J. Markey, a Massachusetts Democrat, called it a "digital free-for-all."[70]

---

65. United States v. Western Electric Co., 900 F.2d 283 (D.C. Cir. 1990); cert. denied, 111 S.Ct. 283 (1990).
66. United States v. Western Electric Co., 767 F.Supp. 308 (D.D.C. 1991).
67. "Supreme Court Clears Way for Baby Bells on Data Businesses," *Wall Street Journal,* 31 October 1991, p. B4.
68. Telecommunications Act of 1996, § 274.
69. Mark Landler, "AT&T Enters TV Business via Satellite Broadcasting," *New York Times,* 23 January 1996, p. C1.
70. Edmund L. Andrews, "Congress Votes to Reshape Communications Industry Ending a 4-Year Struggle," *New York Times,* 2 February 1996, p. A1.

Cable Systems and the First Amendment

Although cable systems have been the subject of court decisions for more than thirty years, courts have reached no firm position as to their First Amendment status. At times, courts have given cable no more First Amendment protection than they have given broadcasters. At other times, courts have suggested that cable systems have more in common with newspapers than with broadcasters. The present tendency is for courts to treat cable systems as offering a mixture of speech (the programming) and conduct (the system itself). In theory, then, cable television is a form of symbolic speech. The leading case in that area of First Amendment law is *United States* v. *O'Brien,*[71] in which the Supreme Court established a four-part test for determining when government may regulate speech laced with conduct. Many courts hold that a specific restriction can be imposed on a cable system only if:

1. It is within the constitutional power of the government. Whatever the restriction is, it must be something that the government unit involved has authority to impose.

2. It furthers an important or substantial government interest. The government must be acting to advance a goal that will benefit significant numbers of people.

3. The government interest is unrelated to the suppression of free expression. Government cannot impose restrictions on a cable system for the sole purpose of preventing the expression of unpopular ideas.

4. The incidental restriction on alleged First Amendment freedoms is no greater than is essential to the furtherance of that interest. Government cannot ban all sexually oriented programming from cable systems simply because some of it might be obscene.

This four-part test has been used in decisions about the granting of exclusive franchises to cable systems, about rules that require cable systems to carry designated stations, and about state and local laws that forbid indecent programming.

Cable Systems and Antitrust Law

Stringing coaxial cable, even in densely populated neighborhoods, costs a considerable amount of money per subscriber. To protect their investment, cable operators seek and often obtain exclusive franchises to serve a community or a well-defined part of a community. Early court decisions upheld such franchises on the ground that the "apparent natural monopoly characteristics of cable television provide . . . an argument for regulation of entry."[72]

Exclusive franchises, however, may be on the verge of becoming history. The Telecommunications Act of 1996 clearly reflects Congress's interest in encouraging

---

71. 391 U.S. 367, 88 S.Ct. 1673, 20 L.Ed.2d 672 (1968).
72. Omega Satellite Products v. City of Indianapolis, 694 F.2d 119 (7th Cir. 1982).

competition in the television cable business. Just how far the federal government will go to foster local competition remains to be seen, but even before Congress moved to allow phone companies into the cable business, the U.S. Supreme Court held that a city's authority to grant an exclusive franchise is limited by the First Amendment's interest in fostering a robust competition of ideas.

The case began when Preferred Communications sought to install a cable system in a part of Los Angeles already served by another op-

City of Los Angeles v.
Preferred Communications,
**476 U.S. 488, 106 S.Ct.
3034, 80 L.Ed.2d 480, 12
Med.L.Rptr. 2244 (1986).**

erator franchised by the city. The city and its Department of Water and Power refused to let Preferred use poles or underground conduits to string its cable, although both agreed that there was space to install another service. Preferred appealed to a U.S. district court for relief, arguing that its rights had been violated under the First Amendment and federal antitrust law. The court granted the city's motion to dismiss. The court of appeals affirmed the dismissal of the antitrust complaint, but reversed on First Amendment grounds, holding that the city's grant of an exclusive franchise in an area where existing pole systems could support more than one cable restricted freedom of speech. The Supreme Court affirmed, but remanded the case to the trial court to resolve undisputed questions of fact.

In its argument to the Court, Preferred compared cable television service with newspapers and magazines. Its business, like theirs, it said, is to provide subscribers with a mixture of news, information, and entertainment. Like newspapers, it does so by using some of its space to retransmit material provided by others, at the same time originating content on its own. Justice William H. Rehnquist, writing for the majority, gave partial endorsement of that argument:

> [T]hrough original programming or by exercising editorial discretion over which stations or programs to include in its repertoire, respondent seeks to communicate messages on a wide variety of topics and in a wide variety of formats. We recently noted that cable operators exercise "a significant amount of editorial discretion regarding what their programming will include."[73] Cable television partakes of some of the aspects of speech and the communication of ideas as do the traditional enterprises of newspaper and book publishers, public speakers and pamphleteers. Respondent's proposed activities would seem to implicate First Amendment interests as do the activities of wireless broadcasters, which were found to fall within the ambit of the First Amendment in *[Red Lion]*, even though the free speech aspects of the wireless broadcasters' claim were found to be outweighed by the government's interests in regulating by reason of the scarcity of frequencies.

Three justices concurred in the Court's decision but wrote separately to note their understanding that, because the factual basis for the dispute had not been resolved by the courts below, the First Amendment status of cable was left open. It still is.

The unresolved facts, required for an *O'Brien* analysis, involve the interests that the city sought to protect by granting exclusive cable franchises. The city said it sought to minimize the demands cable systems make on the use of public property, prevent "a permanent visual blight" resulting from Preferred's stringing of "nearly

---

73.   United States v. Midwest Video Corp., 406 U.S. 649, 92 S.Ct. 1860, 32 L.Ed.2d 390 (1972).

700 miles of hanging and buried wire," and avoid traffic delays caused by cuts in city streets.

On remand, Preferred renewed its lawsuit in district court to force city officials to grant it a franchise. City officials continued to oppose the company's ten-year effort to bring competitive cable to Watts and other nearby areas populated largely by blacks. In 1991 the court ruled against Preferred, granting the city's motion for summary judgment. The company's lawyers appealed to the Ninth Circuit Court, arguing that the lower court had erred in upholding franchising procedures used by the City of Los Angeles to reject Preferred's attempt to establish a competing cable system.[74]

Direct competition among cable companies serving the same area is rare. A senior analyst with Paul Kagan and Associates, a media research firm, estimated that only two or three dozen communities have allowed second companies to compete for cable subscribers.[75]

The U.S. Court of Appeals for the Eighth Circuit read the Supreme Court's decision in *Preferred* as permitting exclusive franchises in smaller cities where the size of the market makes competing systems impractical.[76] In such instances, the appeals court said, the First Amendment interest in a competitive marketplace for ideas can be served by opening a franchise for competing bids at the end of the current holder's term. A U.S. district court judge in California held that the scarcity rationale used by the Supreme Court in *Red Lion* clearly does not apply to cable systems, because they have "the potential of providing a virtually limitless number of channels."[77] Therefore, "unless cable television differs in some material respect from the print media, the First Amendment standards that apply to newspapers apply with equal force to cable." The court concluded that the city of Santa Cruz could not grant an exclusive franchise to one cable operator but could require that a potential competitor prove its financial ability to install and maintain a system.

Courts have held in several cases that franchising authorities can permit a competing company to "overbuild" by installing cable in territory already served by another operator, if that operator was not given an exclusive franchise.[78] A court also has upheld the right of a municipality to operate its own cable system in competition with a franchised cable operator.[79]

Clearly, the law condones competition among cable systems serving the same area. The economic feasibility of such competition is another matter.

Must-Carry Programming

Cable operators, broadcasters, the FCC, Congress, and the courts have been jousting over must-carry rules since the 1960s. Such rules require cable operators to carry

---

74.   Brief of Appellant in No. 91-55625, Preferred Communications, Inc. v. City of Los Angeles, California, filed 13 September 1991.
75.   John R. Emshwiller, "Prying Open the Cable-TV Monopolies," *Wall Street Journal,* 10 August 1989, p. B1.
76.   Central Telecommunications v. TCI Cablevision, 800 F.2d 711 (8th Cir. 1986).
77.   Group W Cable v. City of Santa Cruz, 669 F.Supp. 954, 14 Med.L.Rptr. 1769 (N.D.Calif. 1987).
78.   Triad CATV, Inc. v. City of Hastings, 916 F.2d 713 (6th Cir. 1990); Storer Communication of Northern Kentucky, Inc. v. The Boone County Fiscal Court, No. 89-193 slip op. (E.D.Ky. 1992); James Cable Partners, L.P. v. City of Jamestown, 818 S.W.2d 338 (Tenn.Ct.App. 1991).
79.   Warner Cable Communications, Inc. v. City of Niceville, 911 F.2d 634 (11th Cir. 1990).

stations designated by the franchising authority or by the FCC, which at one time required cable systems to carry any local station or any station "significantly viewed," if it requested carriage. The principal beneficiaries were public television stations and independent UHF stations, which were assured of an opportunity to reach a broader audience than they might otherwise attract.

More than a decade ago, cable system operators began an attack on must-carry rules, first with the FCC and then in the courts. One case began when the FCC fined a cable system in Quincy, Washington, $5000 because the system had ignored an order to carry television stations in Spokane, Washington. On appeal, the U.S. Court of Appeals for the District of Columbia Circuit ruled in *Quincy Cable TV* v. *Federal Communications Commission*[80] that the must-carry rules violated the First Amendment rights of cable system operators. Applying the *O'Brien* test, the court concluded that the FCC had not proved that the rules furthered a substantial government interest.

Broadcasters and interest groups representing television viewers protested. They feared that cable operators would drop poorly viewed local stations, including public television stations, to show more popular fare. The National Cable Television Association entered into negotiations with broadcasters to seek agreement on a revised set of must-carry rules that both sides could live with. With a push from Congress, the FCC adopted a compromise. It was challenged almost immediately, leading to an appellate court decision in *Century Communications Corp.* v. *Federal Communications Commission*[81] that also held that the rules violated the First Amendment. Dennis Patrick, then FCC chairman, said that the decision justified the commission's reluctance to renew the must-carry rules. "It's difficult to square the First Amendment with any must-carry regime in the absence of actual evidence of harm," he said.[82]

As noted previously in this chapter, First Amendment concerns have not prevented Congress and the FCC from trying to revive the must-carry rules. Sponsors of the 1992 law said that it was crafted to meet objections raised by the circuit court in *Quincy* and *Century.* The law and the FCC rules designed to carry it into effect prescribe only the number of local stations that must be carried. The choice as to which stations, if there are more local stations than the mandated number, is left to the cable operator. Supporters of the law argued that such freedom of choice, limited as it might be in some instances, preserves the First Amendment rights of cable system operators.

The Supreme Court in 1994 considered the constitutionality of the 1992 act and the must-carry rules, but although it upheld the act, the Court sent the must-carry challenge back to the lower court. In a sharply split decision, a majority of the justices held that the must-carry rules might or might not violate the First Amendment, depending on whether the government could provide sufficient evidence to justify the assumption that the rules were necessary to protect broadcasting from economic ruin.[83] On remand, a three-judge district court panel, with Judge Stanley Sporkin writing for the court, upheld the must-carry rules, concluding that there was substantial evidence in the con-

---

80. 768 F.2d 1434, 12 Med.L.Rptr. 1001 (D.C. Cir. 1985).
81. 835 F.2d 292, 14 Med.L.Rptr. 2049 (D.C. Cir. 1987).
82. Bob Davis, "Court Throws Out FCC's Requirement That Cable-TV Carry Broadcast Outlets," *Wall Street Journal,* 14 December 1987, p. A5.
83. Turner Broadcasting v. Federal Communications Commission, 114 S.Ct. 2445, 22 Med.L.Rptr. 1864 (1994). Linda Greenhouse, "Justices Back Cable Regulation," *New York Times,* 28 June 1994, p. C1.

gressional investigations and analysis to find that local broadcasting was threatened by the growing cable industry. Judge Thomas Penfield Jackson concurred but said that he would have preferred the issue to go to trial. Judge Stephen Williams dissented.[84] Attorneys for the cable companies promptly headed back to the Supreme Court.[85]

Public Access Channels

About fifteen hundred communities require their cable systems to provide a public access channel open without charge to anyone who wants to try to reach the public with a noncommercial message. The cable operator is required to provide a studio, video camera, and other assistance needed to get the message on the air. Some cable operators cover such events as high school athletic awards dinners, band concerts, and service club speakers, presenting them either as they happen or on a delayed basis. The original idea was that the channel could become a public forum for the airing of opinion on local issues.

The channels also have been discovered by groups such as the Ku Klux Klan, American Nazis, and other fringe groups. Some of these groups have produced taped programs and offered them through their members to public access channels on a regular basis.[86] The presumption is that such channels are public forums which must be open to all points of view, no matter how offensive to some members of the community. The Cable Communications Policy Act forbids censorship except to prevent obscene programming. Some communities have reacted to hate broadcasts by organizing discussion groups to present arguments that rebut extremists of any persuasion.

The city council in Kansas City, Missouri, took another course to counteract cable use by the Klan. It abolished the public access channel called for in its franchise with American Cablevision. The Klan, helped by the American Civil Liberties Union, sued on grounds that it was being denied freedom of speech. Although there are no cases directly in point, the city's lawyers concluded that they could not win the lawsuit. The council voted to restore the channel,[87] leaving the legal status of public access requirements unresolved.

Cable and Access to Private Property

Companies that provide water, electricity, natural gas, or telephone service gain access to private property through concessions known as easements. The theory is that the essential nature of the services makes them of such value that landowners will

84. Turner Broadcasting v. Federal Communications Commission, 1995 U.S. LEXIS 18611, (D.D.C. 1995). "Judges Uphold 'Must Carry' Cable-TV Rule," *New York Times,* 14 December 1995, p. C7.
85. Turner Broadcasting v. Federal Communications Commission, No. 95-992 (U.S. Supreme Court); cert. granted, 21 February 1996. Linda Greenhouse, "Justices Reconsider Law Requiring Cable TV to Carry Local Stations' Signals," *New York Times,* 21 February 1996, p. A8.
86. Charles McCoy, "White Supremacists Find a TV Platform via Public Access," *Wall Street Journal,* 12 July 1988, p. B38.
87. "Klan Wins a Battle for Cable TV," *New York Times,* 16 July 1989, p. A20.

grant these companies rights of way in order to receive the services. In some instances, utilities pay a nominal fee for an easement.

The Cable Communications Policy Act seems to place cable systems on the same footing. It says, in part, that any "franchise shall be construed to authorize the construction of a cable system over public rights-of-way, and through easements . . . within the area to be served by the cable system and which have been dedicated for compatible uses."[88] However, courts have differed in their assessment of the right of access by cable operators to private property through existing easements. Some have held that the language quoted here created a federal right to use both public and private easements.[89] Others have held that the right to use private easements can be exercised only if the easement is dedicated for general use by utilities.[90] Under the latter interpretation, a cable operator could not string a line through an easement granted specifically to an electric company or a telephone company without coming to terms with the owners of the land beneath the line.

Extension of cable to multiple dwelling units also raises legal questions. The Supreme Court has held that a franchise's requirement that apartment owners permit installation of cable service was a taking of property for which the owners should be compensated.[91] On remand, the New York Court of Appeals upheld the right of the state cable television commission to fix the amount of the fee.[92]

THE INTERNET

Cable, telephone, and broadcast companies had been talking about some kind of interactive, on-screen communication for years, but video phones and two-way television never quite caught on with the American public. What caught on instead was the computer network. For anyone who has invested in a personal computer, adding a simple modem and some communications software is relatively inexpensive, and linking it with a global computer network costs no more than a subscription to a cable television service.

The Internet is little more than a lot of little computers connected to a lot of big computers connected to other big computers connected to a lot of little computers. The connections are often as simple as threads of copper telephone wire, but anything that can transmit digital information will work, including coaxial or fiberoptic cable, ISDN phone lines,[93] and broadcast frequencies. What makes the Internet so amazing is that all the computers connected to the network contain enormous amounts of information—news, weather, books, poetry, pornography, music, advertising, propaganda, software,

---

88. 47 U.S.C. §541(a)(2).
89. Cable TV Fund 14-A, Ltd. v. Property Owners Association Chesapeake Ranch Estates, 706 F.Supp. 422 (D.Md. 1989); Mumaugh v. Diamond Lake Area Cable TV Co., 456 N.W.2d 425 (Mich.Ct.App. 1990).
90. Cable Holdings v. McNeil Real Estate Fund VI, Ltd., 953 F.2d 600 (11th Cir. 1992).
91. Loretto v. Teleprompter Manhattan CATV Corp., 458 U.S. 419, 102 S.Ct. 3164, 73 L.Ed.2d 868, 8 Med.L.Rptr. 1849 (1982).
92. Loretto v. Teleprompter Manhattan CATV Corp., 459 N.Y.S.2d 743 (N.Y. 1983).
93. ISDNs (integrated services digital networks) are a new generation of high-capacity telephone lines.

Allison Davis, a former producer for the television program *Today,* has gone from television to cyberspace. She is in charge of an NBC News venture on the Internet called NBC Supernet distributed on, and underwritten by, the Microsoft Network. She and her staff, whom she calls cyber-journalists, provide on-line news, background material, and access to the NBC News archives. *(Fred Conrad/NYT Pictures)*

films, and sometimes on-line experts willing to give advice on everything from computer technology to sex therapy. Without all that information the Internet would be little more than an alternative way to send a message, but with it, the Internet is an enormous encyclopedia and an agent for influence and power. Information providers include the full range of powerful and would-be powerful forces in the global world of entertainment and politics. Players include the United States Congress, the Disney Company, *Playboy,* the Vatican, the *New York Times,* and a gamut of hate groups, guerrilla armies, universities, and elementary school children. That is a mix that can't help but attract attention.

It is not entirely true that the Internet is an unregulated frontier. Internet users are global travelers and subject to the laws of more than 160 countries. As we have seen in earlier parts of this text, the laws of copyright, defamation, and invasion of privacy apply to the Internet as well as to print or broadcast media. It is still a crime to threaten the life of the President, whether by phone, letter, or E-mail. Obscenity laws apply to materials on the Internet with as much force as anywhere else. But the Internet also is a frontier that is difficult to police, short of outright censorship. For example, German officials, unhappy with some two hundred sex-related forums, pressured CompuServe in the United States to cut off access worldwide. CompuServe officials said that it had no way to prevent the offensive material from being read in Germany without censoring it everywhere else.[94]

---

94. Peter H. Lewis, "Limiting a Medium without Boundaries," *New York Times,* 15 January 1996, p. C1.

In the United States, an estimated 5.8 million adults are connected directly to the Internet, and another 3.9 million are connected through commercial on-line services, such as CompuServe, America Online, and Prodigy. Of the estimated thirty million users worldwide, the United States accounts for about half. Some research indicates that the typical user is a male between eighteen and thirty-four years old with a median household income between $50,000 and $75,000. He is most likely to be working in education, sales, or engineering.[95] Those kinds of figures make the Internet look like a place where commercial businesses might like to be, and the figures have not been lost on the cable industry, with its ready supply of coaxial cable, or the telephone industry, with its global switching capabilities. For example, Time Warner Cable in upstate New York has packaged an Internet service that offers cable subscribers access to their local newspaper, library, and community college, as well as the rest of the world. Tele-Communications Inc., the largest cable operator, is scrambling to get into the business and has begun an ambitious plan to link its cable systems with each other and, in turn, to the Internet. Comcast, the third largest cable operator, is planning to offer Internet service to its customers, beginning with Baltimore. Phone companies, until now merely the local conduit to an Internet access provider, are likewise beginning to talk about entering the access business.[96]

All this activity raises serious policy questions about the role of government in regulating the Internet. Cable, phone, and broadcast companies already operate under the watchful, if tolerant, eye of the FCC. To what extent, if any, should the FCC attempt to regulate access to the Internet by these merging technologies? To what extent should Internet users—whether giant corporations or teenagers—be protected by the First Amendment?

The Telecommunications Act of 1996 makes it clear that the federal government is not about to completely turn away from the opportunity to have something to say about Internet operations and content. The Internet may exist in the wild frontiers of cyberspace, but it is the product of electronic technology and a sibling of cable, broadcast, and telephony. It is the policy of the United States, said Congress,

- to promote the continued development of the Internet . . .;

- to preserve the vibrant and competitive free market that presently exists for the Internet . . .; unfettered by Federal or State regulation;

- to encourage the development of technologies which maximize user control over what information is received by individuals, families, and schools who use the Internet . . .;

- to remove disincentives for the development and utilization of blocking and filtering technologies that empower parents to restrict their children's access to objectionable or inappropriate online material; and

---

95. Steve Lohr, "Who Uses Internet? 5.8 Million Are Said to Be Linked in U.S.," *New York Times,* 27 September 1995, p. C2. Other estimates range from 10 million to 24 million users in the United States and Canada. See Peter H. Lewis, "Report of High Internet Use Is Challenged," *New York Times,* 13 December 1995, p. C5.
96. Mark Landler, "Where on Line Is on Cable," *New York Times,* 31 January 1996, p. C1.

■   to ensure vigorous enforcement of Federal criminal laws to deter and punish trafficking in obscenity, stalking, and harassment by means of computer.[97]

The policy statement reflects some of the ambiguity inherent in Congress's desire to deregulate electronic communications and control them at the same time. Still, the Internet remains mostly unregulated, and Congress has indicated no interest in licensing access providers or users. Instead, it appears that Congress hopes to steer the medium toward a course of self-control primarily by enforcing laws that protect minors, copyright owners, and the victims of on-line harassment.

In the Professional World

Rapid technological change has done far more than alter the nature of the electronic media. It also has changed the way news is gathered and presented. Electronic news-gathering techniques have made it possible for digital cameras to go almost anywhere and, with the help of microwave links and satellites, have put news on the air as it is happening. The live remote has become a staple of broadcasting and cable news.

"Live" can also mean "on-line." Reporters routinely monitor computer bulletin boards, web sites, and chat services for tips and press releases. Reporters can share information and interview sources on the Internet, and in some cases subscribers can read newspapers on-line and ask questions of reporters who are covering breaking stories. Such on-line communication is often spontaneous and unedited, and almost always interesting and immediate.

Within hours after a bomb exploded near a federal building in Oklahoma City on April 19, 1995, the Internet was humming with eyewitness accounts, rumors, and speculation about Arab terrorists, motives, and death tolls. Some of the information was correct and useful. Some of it was wrong. All of it was immediate and rang with the note of credibility that always comes with the sense of being present and participating in a news event.

When the space shuttle *Challenger* exploded seconds after liftoff, television viewers shared the shock and surprise of the event. They also shared the intrusion into the privacy of the next of kin of the astronauts as the cameras shifted focus to record their stunned reaction to the tragedy. In the hours that followed, viewers who stayed tuned also shared the tedium as the networks strove to fill time between interviews with officials who speculated on what had gone wrong, or with persons who wanted to talk about the victims.

The ability to present the news raw, before it can be tested and refined to an approximation of truth by the checking and rechecking of skilled reporters and editors, raises special ethical considerations. Electronic media professionals live

---

97.   Telecommunications Act of 1996, §509 (47 U.S.C. 230).

with the knowledge that their technology has an infinite capacity to distort the news. Tom Pettit, an award-winning television newscaster and executive vice president of NBC News, warned, "Today, technology permits producers to speed up or slow down actual events, actual voices. This is alteration of reality akin to forging a check."[98] Technology allows photos to be altered without trace, words to move around the world without thought, and half-truths and guesses to gain a respect they don't deserve.

To forestall such forgery in television, the news divisions of networks and many local television stations adopt codes of ethics that often are even more specific than the general code of their professional organization, the Radio-Television News Directors Association (RTNDA). The RTNDA code starts with an assertion that the primary purpose of broadcast journalists is "to inform the public of events of importance and appropriate interest in a manner that is accurate and comprehensive." That purpose, the code says, overrides all others. The code also says that stories should be given sufficient background to make them meaningful and should not be sensationalized. Further, it says that broadcast journalists "shall at all times display humane respect for the dignity, privacy and the well-being of persons with whom the news deals."

At this point the code seems to part company with the realities generated by the intense competition among television news organizations. The television reporter who thrusts a microphone at the grieving survivors of disaster victims to catch their response to "How do you feel?" has become a cliché. That approach to news and the infamous ambush interview used on some news shows have contributed to the public's perception that reporters are callous invaders of privacy. There is enough truth in that perception to make some journalists sensitive to the complaint and to adopt more detailed codes, such as those at CBS and NBC News, which advise against interviewing survivors on the air unless their permission is obtained in advance, and then only if the interview produces information essential to a proper telling of the story.

Fred Friendly, a former president of CBS News who became a professor at Columbia University, once told WBBM-TV that the ambush interview "is the dirtiest trick department of broadcast journalism."[99] In such interviews, a subject suspected of having something to hide is confronted suddenly in front of a live camera and is asked a question akin to "When are you going to stop cheating on your taxes?" or "Why are you ripping off your customers with this phony sale?" Even persons with nothing to hide can appear startled, angry, evasive, and guilty when trying to respond spontaneously. Producers of television news shows are divided in their opinions as to the propriety of such an approach.[100] All concede that it can be abused, but many argue that there

---

98.   Richard D. Yoakam and Charles T. Cremer, *ENG: Television News and the New Technology* (New York: Random House, 1985), p. 248.
99.   Interviewed on *Watching the Watchdog* documentary, WBBM-TV, Chicago, 20 April 1981.
100. H. Eugene Goodwin, *Groping for Ethics in Journalism* (Ames: Iowa State University Press, 1983) pp. 181–182, 301.

are times when it should be used with public officials or business leaders who are accountable to the public for their performance and who need to be put on the spot.

Later, Friendly used even stronger language to condemn a much more serious lapse in broadcast journalism ethics. ABC News used an actor to portray a U.S. diplomat passing a briefcase to a supposed Soviet KGB agent, also an actor. The videotape, as shown on the evening news with Peter Jennings, was grainy, as hidden-camera tape or video often is. It included an electronic time code and cross hairs. The tape was labeled "Exclusive" and was introduced by Jennings as "a harsh reminder that secrecy sells." Nothing was said about the whole episode's being a reenactment of an event that may never have happened. Four days later, Jennings apologized on the air for not labeling the tape as a reenactment. He attributed the lapse to a "production error." At any event, the diplomat, who was named in the story—and in many other news accounts—was not charged with any offense, let alone espionage.

Friendly called the ABC News episode a "fraud," which it was, and "an outrageous demonstration of shameful journalism."[101] That story and stories in other media were based on leaks from the State Department, the FBI, and other government agencies. Using the information at all was questionable ethics, but to stage an event as though it had actually happened and pass it off as news, Friendly said, could "not be excused as dramatic license."

Dramatic license has become the stock-in-trade of tabloid TV, where it is easy to recognize, but it also springs up occasionally on mainstream television news magazine programs. One incident involved *Dateline NBC,* with Jane Pauley and Stone Phillips as anchors. *Dateline* devoted a fifteen-minute segment to General Motors pickup trucks and called it "Waiting to Explode?" GM trucks manufactured between 1973 and 1987 carried their fuel tanks behind the cab on the outside of the truck's chassis. The program's thesis was that this placement made the tanks vulnerable to being punctured and set afire if the truck were struck from the side by another vehicle. In fact, this had happened in some instances, and the bulk of the program was devoted to interviews with survivors of GM truck fires. The segment concluded with a one-minute demonstration that showed a GM truck being struck from the side and bursting into flames. Coincidentally, GM at the time was defending itself in an Atlanta courtroom in a suit brought by a couple who contended that their son had been burned to death because the truck he was driving was poorly designed. A jury agreed with the parents, awarding them $105.2 million, most of it in punitive damages.[102]

Immediately after the NBC broadcast, General Motors did two things. It announced that its top executives would discuss the case at a press confer-

---

101. Fred W. Friendly, "News, Lies and Videotape," *New York Times,* 6 August 1989, p. B1.
102. GM later settled with the parents for an undisclosed, but presumably smaller, amount of money. Andrew Blum, "GM Settles Suits: Turmoil Remains," *National Law Journal,* 25 September 1996, p. A6.

ence, and it filed a libel suit against NBC News and its corporate parent, General Electric. At the press conference, Harold J. Pearce, GM's general counsel, presented detailed evidence that proved beyond doubt that the truck crash shown on *Dateline NBC* was a composite of two truck crashes that had been staged on a rural road outside Indianapolis, Indiana; that the gas tanks had not been ruptured; that model rocket engines had been attached to the vehicles to act as detonators; that there was no cap on the gasoline tank of one of the trucks involved, permitting fuel to spill on impact; and that despite all this, the crashes had produced only one fire, which burned out in fifteen seconds. The true nature of the demonstration was confirmed by videotapes taken by volunteer firefighters who were standing by to put out the expected big fire, and by detective work that enabled GM's Indianapolis attorneys to find the vehicles, with the burned-out rocket engines still attached, in a salvage yard.[103]

NBC's top executives watched the press conference on television in their headquarters in New York City. Before the day was out, their lawyers were talking to GM's lawyers. Agreement was reached on a settlement that night. NBC would pay all the expenses, estimated at $2 million, incurred by GM in establishing the truth about the staged truck crashes. On the following night's *Dateline NBC,* Pauley and Phillips read "a long and somber apology to their viewers and to GM." Michael Gartner, then president of NBC News, said the decision to settle was his. He was quoted as saying he was still proud of the segment, aside from the one-minute staged crash. Of that, he said, "When you make a mistake, you've got to stand up to it." Less than a month later, he announced his resignation.[104]

News personnel at other television networks, as one might expect, were vocal in condemning NBC for not disclosing that it had rigged the trucks with detonators.[105] However, two newspaper columnists saw in all fifteen minutes of "Waiting to Explode?" a larger ethical question. Steve Hall, television columnist of the *Indianapolis Star,* wrote that the program "showed a peculiar idea of fair play."[106] The executive and the lawyer who presented GM's case had been interviewed in what appeared to be an office. Relatives of several victims of crashes in which GM trucks caught fire had been interviewed in their homes. Pictures of the victims had been shown. Eyewitnesses had described how the victims died, sometimes as a voice-over while the screen showed a charred corpse in a wrecked vehicle. Hall's point was that "a company's denial of fault

---

103. "How GM One-Upped an Embarrassed NBC on Staged News Event," *Wall Street Journal,* 11 February 1993, A1.

104. Elizabeth Jensen, "NBC News Seeks Successor to Gartner, Who Quit as President Due to GM Fiasco," *Wall Street Journal,* 3 March 1993, p. B11.

105. Elizabeth Jensen, "Some Journalists Join GM in Criticizing NBC's Treatment of Truck-Crash Story," *Wall Street Journal,* 10 February 1993, p. B1.

106. Steve Hall, "NBC Report Put Unfair Slant on Facts," *Indianapolis Star,* 12 February 1993, p. C7.

does not carry the emotional impact of the picture of a dead child—or a truck turning into a fireball." Hall concluded that "the visual slanting of news stories" is "something that's going to blow up in another TV news organization's face— and they won't need toy rockets to start it."

John Leo, a contributing editor to *U.S. News & World Report,* has pointed to other television news programs that have used photos, some also rigged, to make an emotional point.[107] One such broadcast, on *NBC Nightly News,* purported to show large numbers of fish that had died of pollution caused by clear-cutting of trees along the stream. In reality, the fish had been stunned by forestry officials so that they could be counted and checked for disease. Leo quoted Richard Reeves, also a syndicated columnist, as saying that pressure for ratings, coupled with a decline in ethical standards among younger journalists, has led to an emphasis on dramatic effects rather than on truth.

Not just television raises issues about the ethical use of drama in electronic media. When the United States was engaged in the Gulf War, cable proved its ability not only to carry that faraway conflict directly into our homes, but to do it hour after hour with live and dramatic coverage from behind enemy lines. Broadcast television can make news immediate and emotional, but cable television can make news immediate, emotional, and continuous—adding greatly to the tedium and the suspense of real-time news. Cable's ability to focus our attention for months on a war, or a trial, in real time is a new experience. What are the ethical responsibilities of reporters live and on the air behind enemy lines, such as the CNN crew in Baghdad during the Gulf War? How much should they show? How can they separate news from propaganda? Is it possible for them to be neutral, loyal, and truthful all at the same time?

Cable's continuous coverage of the O.J. Simpson murder trial was yet another example of cable television's ability to preempt the public agenda with continuous live coverage. Those who watched faithfully learned a great deal about a particular criminal case. Was it too much? Was it fair?

Other aspects of cable television also can be troubling. Cable is a fragmenting medium, as conventional broadcasters are discovering to their sorrow. Subscribers to the basic channels on a cable system have a choice at any one time of a bewildering array of programming. They can surf the channels to look for a movie, listen to a symphony, and catch the news before going to bed. But it is just as easy for them to lock themselves away into programming exclusively devoted to sports, old movies, rock music, country music, religion, or merchandising. They can use their leisure time to immerse themselves in the fare of their choice, to the exclusion of all else. Those who are turned off by the world's troubles need, if they choose, never be troubled by them. They can create their own world from the choices available on cable.

Young people already show a lack of interest in national and international news.[108] One survey of young adults showed that the younger generation

---

107.   John Leo, "Spicing Up the (Ho-hum) Truth," *U.S. News & World Report,* 8 March 1993, p. 24.
108.   Debra Gersh, "Age of Indifference," *Editor & Publisher,* 7 July 1990, p. 10.

"knows less, cares less, and reads newspapers less. It is also a generation that votes less and is less critical of its leaders and institutions than young people in the past."

The survey was conducted in the immediate aftermath of the overturn of Communist governments in eastern Europe, climaxing in the breaching of the Berlin Wall. For older people who had spent their lives thinking of the Soviet Union and communism as powerful forces that shaped twentieth-century history, those events were breathtaking. Yet the study found that only 42 percent of the sample under thirty years old said that they were interested in the story of the wall, and only 19 percent said that they were interested in news about the execution of the Communist dictator and his wife in Romania. News of subsequent events in eastern Europe attracted as few as one in twenty young people. In contrast, 58 percent of the sample over age 50 followed the news about the Berlin Wall and one-third said that they were "engaged" by stories from Romania. The study also found that people aged thirty to forty-nine "are almost as likely to be tuned out" to news about domestic and international political matters as are younger people. Young people showed significant interest only in sports events, major catastrophes, and news about the attempts to make abortions illegal again.

The study examined surveys conducted by other polling organizations since 1944 to discover whether indifference to political and government news among young people is a recent phenomenon. The authors concluded that it is. This declining interest is reflected in a decrease in newspaper readership and in the viewing of television news programs. In 1965 a Gallup poll reported that 67 percent of adults under thirty-five said that they had read a newspaper the day before. The *Times Mirror* survey found only 20 percent who said they had. Viewing of television news fell from 52 percent in 1965 to 41 percent in 1990.

The survey also asked young people about their interest in political campaigns. The authors concluded: "The 30-second commercial spot is a particularly appropriate medium for the MTV generation. . . . Sound-bites and symbolism, the principal fuel of modern political campaigns, are well-suited to young voters who know less and have limited interest in politics and public policy. Their limited appetites and aptitudes are shaping the practice of politics and the nature of our democracy."

What that shape and nature will become cannot be known, because we cannot be certain what electronic media are going to look like, even in the next few years. The Internet, for instance, was the little-known province of academic and government researchers before it burst into national prominence within eighteen months in the middle of the decade. Broadcasting, cable, and the Internet, with all its computers and telephone lines, are shaped as much by the people who use them as the users are shaped by the technology. That is all the more reason why the well-being of a democratic society depends, at least in part, on the ethical values of media professionals responsive to the need for careful, truthful, and balanced reporting in a chaotic world of conflict and escapism.

FOR REVIEW ▬▬▬▬▬▬▬▬▬▬▬▬▬▬▬▬▬▬▬▬▬▬▬▬▬▬▬▬▬▬

1. What is the rationale for the regulation of broadcasting? Is it a valid rationale? Explain your answer.

2. Compare and contrast the First Amendment rights of broadcasters and of print publishers.

3. If you were a member of the FCC, how would you determine whether a broadcasting station is serving the public interest? If you owned a station, what factors would you want the FCC to consider in determining whether you were operating in the public interest? As a listener and a viewer, which of the stations you listen to or watch regularly best serves the public interest? Justify your answers to each part of this question.

4. List the principal provisions of the equal opportunities sections of the Communications Act of 1934. To whom do they apply? Under what circumstances? How much discretion does a station owner have in deciding whether to grant time to a candidate for public office? Can a station owner exercise control over the content of a political use? Why or why not?

5. List reasons for giving local franchising authorities the sole right to regulate cable television systems, for giving the FCC that right, and for exempting cable television systems from government regulation. On balance, what degree of regulation, and by whom, strikes you as fair?

6. Outline the major provisions of the Cable Communications Policy Act of 1984, the Cable Television Consumer Protection and Competition Act of 1992, and the Telecommunications Act of 1996 as they relate to cable. To what extent do you think this legislation helps or harms the cable industry?

7. Describe the First Amendment status of cable system operators as defined by court decisions.

8. Some Internet system operators have argued that they are more like newspapers than like broadcasters or cable operators for regulatory purposes. Are they? Explain. Why is this distinction important?

CHAPTER 14

The First Amendment protects news, opinion, and advertising, but it does not grant the media immunity from laws that regulate business operations. At one time, some publishers attempted to argue that such things as minimum wage and antitrust laws restrict freedom of the press, but the courts have held otherwise. The general rule is that in their business operations, publishers, broadcasters, filmmakers, cable operators, advertisers, and public relations firms must obey the same rules as nonmedia businesses. They are subject to antitrust laws if they use predatory business practices to harm their competitors. They must comply with wages and hours laws as well as employment discrimination laws. They must pay the same kinds of taxes that apply to other business entities. However, if business regulations are used as a substitute for censorship or to unduly burden freedom of the press, courts have held that the First Amendment remains a powerful protector.

This chapter first examines antitrust law as it applies to media. The law is often used to challenge the legality of advertising rates or the fairness of competition among daily newspapers and free-circulation, advertising publications. And for years, antitrust law has provided a congressional forum for debate about the decline in the number of competing daily newspapers. Thirty years ago Congress enacted an important exception to antitrust law, hoping to help failing newspapers survive and compete in the marketplace of ideas. That effort has been largely unsuccessful in stemming the growth of newspaper chains, one-newspaper cities, and the loss of big-city dailies. The Federal Communications Commission also has tried to ensure

THE MEDIA AS BUSINESS

the survival of competing voices in a community by limiting the number of broadcast stations and newspapers that can be owned by the same entity in the same city. These efforts to engineer and encourage a marketplace of ideas have been the primary, if not always the most successfully achieved, goal of antitrust law in the context of mass media.

This chapter also examines the role that the First Amendment has played in protecting the financial interests of mass media. More than fifty years ago, a persistent religious group, Jehovah's Witnesses, endured considerable persecution to establish that the First Amendment protects the right to distribute ideas door to door or in public places. Today, the principles forged then protect the right of newspaper publishers to place coin-operated newspaper racks nearly anywhere that people are likely to pass by. The First Amendment also plays a role in how media are taxed. Because taxation influences decisions about the use of financial resources, tax policy can affect how and what kind of information and entertainment is available. In Chapter 2 we discussed John Milton's seventeenth-century argument against the licensing of printing in England. In this chapter we examine twentieth-century warnings that restrictions on the dissemination of ideas and discriminatory taxation that are aimed at media might still be used, as they were then, to suppress ideas considered harmful by government officials.

But no issue causes the manager of a media organization more day-to-day concern than decisions about the fairness of hiring, firing, harassment, and discrimination. Media are subject to the same employment and civil rights regulations as other American businesses are. So this chapter ends with a look at some of the employment concerns of media workers. To ignore them or be ignorant of them is to ask for expensive litigation, poor public relations, unhappy employees, and poor performance.

Major Cases

- *Associated Press* v. *United States,* 326 U.S. 1; rehearing denied, 326 U.S. 802, 65 S.Ct. 1416, 89 L.Ed. 2013, 1 Med.L.Rptr. 2269 (1945).

- *Citizen Publishing Co.* v. *United States,* 394 U.S. 131, 89 S.Ct. 927, 22 L.Ed.2d 148, 1 Med.L.Rptr. 2704 (1969).

■ *City of Lakewood* v. *Plain Dealer Publishing Co.,* 486 U.S. 750, 108 S.Ct.2138, 100 L.Ed.2d 771, 15 Med.L.Rptr. 1481 (1988).

■ *Discovery Network Inc.* v. *Cincinnati,* 946 F.2d 469, 19 Med.L.Rptr. 1449 (6th Cir. 1991).

■ *Federal Communications Commission* v. *National Citizens Committee for Broadcasting,* 436 U.S. 775, 98 S.Ct. 2096, 56 L.Ed.2d 697, 3 Med.L.Rptr. 2409 (1978).

■ *Grosjean* v. *American Press Co.,* 297 U.S. 233, 56 S.Ct. 444, 80 L.Ed. 660, 1 Med.L.Rptr. 2685 (1936).

■ *Kansas City Star Co.* v. *United States,* 240 F.2d 643 (8th Cir. 1975); cert. denied, 354 U.S. 923 (1957).

■ *Leathers* v. *Medlock,* 499 U.S. 439, 111 S.Ct. 1438, 113 L.Ed.2d 494, 18 Med.L.Rptr. 1953 (1991).

■ *Minneapolis Star and Tribune Co.* v. *Minnesota Commissioner of Revenue,* 460 U.S. 575, 103 S.Ct. 1365, 75 L.Ed.2d 295, 9 Med.L.Rptr. 1369 (1983).

■ *Simon & Schuster* v. *New York Crime Victims Board,* 502 U.S. 105, 112 S.Ct. 501, 19 Med.L.Rptr. 1609 (1991).

■ *Syracuse Broadcasting Corp.* v. *Newhouse,* 319 F.2d 683 (2d Cir. 1963).

ANTITRUST LAW AND THE MEDIA

When Congress adopted the Sherman Antitrust Act in 1890, its main targets were John D. Rockefeller's Standard Oil Company and Andrew Carnegie's United States Steel Company. These entrepreneurs had cut prices on a selective basis to freeze out competitors. They had made exclusive deals with favored customers. Their purpose was to establish monopolies that would let them charge what they pleased. Other targets of the act were burgeoning monopolies in whiskey distilling, in the making of white lead paints, and in sugar refining. Cartoons of the era picture such businesses as giant octopuses with tentacles reaching out across the nation. The original 1890 act did much to curb abuses, and it was revised and strengthened in 1914 by the Clayton Act and in 1936 by the Robinson-Patman Act.

Along with labor and contract law, antitrust law forms the basic legal structure for doing business in the United States. But it is doubtful, even when the Clayton Act was adopted, that anyone thought of antitrust laws as applying to newspapers or magazines. First, there were no national newspapers in 1914, nor was there a dominant magazine. Second, publishing was a highly competitive business. As late as 1923, there were competing newspapers in 502 of the 1297 cities with daily papers. Finally, it was generally presumed that newspapers, like other small firms, did not do business beyond state lines and therefore were beyond the reach of federal laws governing interstate commerce.

The Supreme Court demolished that assumption with its decision in *Indiana Farmer's Guide Publishing Co.* v. *Prairie Farmer Publishing Co.*[1] The Court held that any publication that uses material, such as advertising or news reports, created in another state, or that sells copies by mail to residents of another state, is engaged in interstate commerce and therefore is subject to federal laws. The Court also held that to become a monopoly, a business firm need not be a giant seeking to control a national market. A publishing company is to be judged by the extent to which it dominates its market area. Because circulation of most newspapers is concentrated in a local retail trading zone defined by the shopping practices of subscribers, the *Indiana Farmer's Guide* decision brought even the smallest newspapers within reach of antitrust law.

The Court expanded the scope of this decision when it rejected the argument that the First Amendment gives the news media immunity from antitrust laws. In this instance, the owner of the *Chicago Tribune,* the legendary Colonel Robert R. McCormick, had used his veto power as a director of the Associated Press (AP) to deny that agency's news service to Marshall Field's newly established morning *Sun.* The AP bylaws then in effect made it difficult and expensive for owners of a new newspaper to obtain the service if they were in direct competition with an existing member. This did not mean they would be left without a wire service. At least two others, United Press and the International News Service, were then in competition with the AP. However, Field took the position that the AP was the best of the three, and that his newspaper would not be competitive without it.

The Department of Justice took up Field's cause and charged the Associated Press with violating antitrust laws. The government asked that AP's restrictive membership rules be declared illegal. The news agency offered two arguments in its defense, both grounded in the First Amendment:

Associated Press **v.** *United States,* **326 U.S. 1; Rehearing Denied, 326 U.S. 802; 65 S.Ct. 1416, 89 L.Ed.2d 2013, 1 Med.L.Rptr. 2269 (1945).**

1.   Because the AP was engaged in the business of gathering and disseminating news, it should be granted immunity from antitrust law unless the government could show that its actions represented a clear and present danger to a vital government interest.

2.   Because the AP considered itself a cooperative news-gathering agency, any government interference with its method of choosing members violated its First Amendment freedom of association.

A United States district court in New York City rejected both arguments and ruled in the government's favor. The AP took its case to the Supreme Court which, in *Associated Press* v. *United States,* upheld the district court's ruling five to three. Writing for the majority, Justice Hugo L. Black used reasoning that continues to be applied to

---

1.   293 U.S. 268, 55 S.Ct. 182, 79 L.Ed.2d 356 (1934).

the news media, not only in antitrust cases, but in other cases dealing with their business aspects. With respect to the first argument, he wrote:

> Member publishers of AP are engaged in business for profit exactly as are other businessmen who sell food, steel, aluminum, or anything else people need or want. . . . All are alike covered by the Sherman Act. The fact that the publisher handles news while others handle food does not . . . afford the publisher a peculiar constitutional sanctuary in which he can with impunity violate laws regulating his business practices.
>
> Nor is a publisher who engaged in business practices made unlawful by the Sherman Act entitled to a partial immunity by reason of the "clear and present danger" doctrine which courts have used to protect freedom to speak, to print, and to worship. . . . Formulated as it was to protect liberty of thought and of expression, it would degrade the clear and present danger doctrine to fashion from it a shield for publishers who engage in business practices condemned by the Sherman Act.

Justice Black was equally blunt in dismissing the AP's second argument. He noted that the news agency was founded as a cooperative; that is, it was formed by newspapers who did no more than share local news of regional or national interest with one another. This sharing of news was a principle of the AP's operation in the 1940s and continues today. At the time of this case, the AP's membership rules made it difficult and expensive for a direct competitor of an established member to enter the cooperative. The reasoning was simple: Why should an established newspaper be required to share its news with an upstart competing medium? In defending its rules, the AP argued that if everyone who wanted the service had to be admitted to membership, the flow of news would be diminished. Where competition existed, no one would share news with the wire service until it no longer was news; otherwise, the medium that got the news first would be giving away its own scoop. Thus, as the AP saw it, any change in the membership rules would restrict First Amendment freedoms. Justice Black disagreed:

> It would be strange indeed . . . if the grave concern for freedom of the press which prompted adoption of the First Amendment should be read as a command that government was without power to protect that freedom. The First Amendment, far from providing an argument against application of the Sherman Act, here provides powerful reasons to the contrary. That amendment rests on the assumption that the widest possible dissemination of information from diverse and antagonistic sources is essential to the welfare of the public, that a free press is a condition of a free society. Surely, a command that the government itself shall not impede the free flow of ideas does not afford non-governmental combinations a refuge if they impose restraints upon that constitutionally guaranteed freedom. Freedom to publish means freedom for all and not for some. Freedom to publish is guaranteed by the Constitution, but freedom to combine to keep others from publishing is not. Freedom of the press from governmental interference under the First Amendment does not sanction repression of that freedom by private interests. The First Amendment affords not the slightest support for the contention that a combination to restrain trade in news and views has any constitutional immunity.

This decision made an important point: The main concern of the First Amendment is the protection of the dissemination of news and opinion. It cannot be stretched to give those in the business of disseminating news and opinion an exemption from laws that generally regulate business activities.

Some Disapproved Business Practices

Section 1 of the Sherman Act prohibits every contract, combination, or conspiracy that restrains trade or commerce. Over the years the courts have found certain media practices to be so anticompetitive that they are presumed to be unlawful even if the motives are well intentioned or the effects minimal. Examples include agreements among competitors to fix prices, to allocate customers and territories, and to organize group boycotts. Many other media practices also can violate the Sherman Act if they suppress competition. To decide if they do, courts examine all the circumstances to determine if the anticompetitive effects of the practice outweigh any procompetitive benefits. By "all the circumstances," the court means financial records and reports, office memos, employee conversations, and just about anything else that could help determine motives, interpret facts, or predict consequences. Defendants, even eventual winners, describe the experience of an antitrust suit as disruptive and expensive. Losers run the risk of business failure, and winners pay dearly in legal fees.

Section 2 of the Sherman Act prohibits the attempt to acquire or use power to control prices or exclude competition. In short, it prohibits monopolization, attempts to monopolize, or conspiracies to monopolize. The Supreme Court in *United States* v. *Grinnell Corp.*[2] said that to prove monopolization under Section 2, two things must be shown:

1. That the company possesses monopoly power in its market—that is, it has the ability to fix prices or exclude competitors

2. That the company willfully acquired or maintained that power by means other than that which could be attributed to a superior product, business acumen, or historic accident

Courts have often made it clear that merely having monopoly power is not a violation of the law. The nature of the market may be such that only one competitor can succeed financially, or perhaps a media owner can corner the market by superior skill and intelligence. What is illegal is anticompetitive conduct by a media owner who has the power to exclude others from entering the market or enlarging their market share. Examples of illegal behavior include any of the practices that would be illegal under Section 1, such as price fixing, or such other things as charging unreasonably low prices or refusing to deal with competitors or with customers or suppliers who deal with competitors.

Media that have apparent monopoly power—such as daily newspapers in cities with only one daily paper—often find their business behavior scrutinized more carefully than that of their upstart competitors when a complaint is filed or there is suspicion of anticompetitive practices. One of the notable newspaper antitrust cases to reach the Supreme Court was *Lorain Journal Co.* v. *United States.*[3] By systematically refusing to sell advertising to merchants and others who bought time on a competing

---

2.   384 U.S. 563, 86 S.Ct. 1698, 16 L.Ed.2d 778 (1966).
3.   342 U.S. 193, 72 S.Ct. 181, 96 L.Ed. 162, 1 Med.L.Rptr. 2697 (1951).

radio station, the publisher of the *Journal* engaged in "bold, relentless, and predatory commercial behavior" clearly designed to harm the station. All of this took place in a limited market area served by both the newspaper and the broadcaster. There was little question that the publisher's actions tended to promote a monopoly, thus violating the Sherman Act. Lower courts have cited the case as a precedent in condemning similar refusals to accept advertising in Las Vegas, Nevada,[4] and in Haverhill, Massachusetts,[5] where the complaining parties were competing newspapers; and in Providence, Rhode Island,[6] where the plaintiff was a rental information service.

Taken together, the cases suggest that care be taken in exercising the right to refuse advertising. If refusals are based on established standards of acceptance, and those standards are applied with an even hand, legal problems are unlikely. But if the pattern of refusals points to a conspiracy to harm a competing medium, or to harm a firm in competition with a favored advertiser, it might be possible to prove a violation of antitrust law.

Home Placement Service v. *Providence Journal* raises a special note of caution with respect to advertising offered by a competing medium. Home Placement charged its customers a fee for providing them with a listing of available rental housing. This service put Home Placement in competition with the *Providence Journal,* which sold classified advertising to owners of rental property who were seeking tenants. When Home Placement sought to advertise its service in the *Journal,* it was told it could not unless it agreed not to charge customers the usual fee for its service. Home Placement complied with the condition, but the U.S. Court of Appeals for the Second Circuit held that the newspaper's act violated antitrust law.

Media that have achieved dominant positions in their markets must always take particular care in any actions that might adversely affect competitors, including setting advertising and circulation rates. The abuse of that dominance may result in an antitrust suit. For instance, the U.S. Court of Appeals for the Eighth Circuit held that the Kansas City Star Company's advertising and circulation policies tended to create a monopoly. In an action brought by the U.S. government, the court struck down a series of all-or-nothing package deals, coupled with a diligently enforced advertising policy that helped the Star Company dominate Kansas City's advertising market in the early 1950s. The company published three newspapers, the morning *Times,* the afternoon *Star,* and the *Sunday Star,* and owned radio station WDAF and the city's first television station, WDAF-TV. People who wanted to subscribe to one of the newspapers were required to buy all three. Advertisers likewise had to buy space in all three papers to get space in one. Star executives rationalized the arrangement by contending that they published only one newspaper with thirteen issues a week. There also were advertising tying arrangements between the newspaper and the television station. In some instances, advertisers who wanted to buy time on WDAF-TV were told they could do so only if they bought space in the newspapers.

---

4.   Greenspun v. McCarran, 105 F.Supp. 662 (D.Nev. 1952).
5.   Union Leader Corp. v. Newspapers of New England, 284 F.2d 586 (1st Cir. 1960).
6.   Home Placement Service v. Providence Journal Co., 682 F.2d 274, 8 Med.L.Rptr. 1881 (1st Cir. 1982).

The arrangement was profitable. It also had a devastating effect on competing media. A publisher of a competing newspaper had gone out of business during World War II, leaving the *Times* and *Star* alone. Seven other dailies continued to publish in the metropolitan area, but the largest of these, the *Kansas City Kansan,* had a circulation of only 27,873 in 1951. In contrast, circulation of the three Star Company newspapers exceeded 350,000 a day. In 1952, those newspapers received 94 percent of the money spent on newspaper advertising in the Kansas City area. With broadcasting revenues included, the company accounted for 85 percent of the total advertising revenue billed by all media.

Kansas City Star Co. v. United States, **240 F.2d 643 (8th Cir. 1957); cert. denied, 354 U.S. 923 (1957).**

In a criminal proceeding, the Department of Justice charged the Star Company with unfair competitive practices in violation of the Sherman Act. Witnesses told a district court jury that the newspaper's advertising executives had used threats and intimidation to discourage advertisers from using competing media, to the latter's harm. *Star* advertisers who ignored the warning found their advertisements placed in poor positions. A major-league baseball player, who also owned a flower shop in Kansas City, was the target of another kind of threat. When he placed an ad in a competing newspaper, an advertising sales representative told him that even if he hit a hundred home runs a year, his name would never appear in the newspapers' sports pages except in the box scores.

A jury found that the unit advertising system "was used . . . with the intent and effect of excluding competition." It also found that an effect of the unit circulation policy was to discourage subscribers from taking any other newspaper. Therefore, the Star Company was guilty of violating the Sherman Act. The court ordered the newspaper to pay a fine of $5,000 and the advertising director, $2,500. In addition, the company was ordered to stop its unit sales of advertising and subscriptions, to stop tie-in sales between the broadcasting stations and the newspaper, and to stop threatening advertisers who did business with competing media. The company appealed.

The newspapers argued that the government's action was an attempt to intimidate a free press and therefore violated the First Amendment. The appeals court disposed of that argument:

> Publishers of newspapers must answer for their actions in the same manner as anyone else. A monopolistic press could attain in tremendous measure the evils sought to be prevented by the Sherman Antitrust Act. Freedom to print does not mean freedom to destroy. To use the freedom of the press guaranteed by the First Amendment to destroy competition would defeat its own ends, for freedom to print news and express opinions as one chooses is not tantamount to having freedom to monopolize. To monopolize freedom destroys it.

The decision came at a time when formerly independent morning and evening newspapers were coming under the same ownership, even in cities with a population of 100,000 or more. The decision sent a message: Publishers must not force advertisers or subscribers to take both publications or none. If it offers a unit advertising rate, a publisher must leave the way open for an advertiser to choose one newspaper or the other. And it must not use its dominant position to try to squeeze out suburban newspapers or other kinds of advertising media that might emerge in response to changing patterns of urban living.

In the aftermath of the Kansas City case, the Star Company and the Justice Department entered into a consent agreement that is still looked to for guidance in setting advertising rates in cities where one owner owns two newspapers, two broadcasting stations, or any combination of media companies. The agreement forbade compulsory combinations of the kind condemned by the court, but it permitted the publisher to offer substantial discounts to firms that were willing to place ads in more than one newspaper.[7] As long as such combination rates are not set unreasonably low, so as to make it impossible for other media to compete economically, and as long as they are not manipulated with intent to harm a media competitor, they do not violate antitrust law.

The principles established in the *Kansas City Star* case were reinforced by the U.S. Court of Appeals for the Second Circuit. In its decision, *Syracuse Broadcasting Corp.* v. *Newhouse,* the court said that Newhouse was simply using good business practices to buttress its position as the dominant advertising medium in Syracuse, New York. The company owned both newspapers in the city, along with WSYR-TV and its companion radio station, WSYR.

Syracuse Broadcasting Corp. v. Newhouse, 319 F.2d 683 (2d Cir. 1963).

Syracuse Broadcasting Corporation, owner of WNDR radio, suffered financial problems that it blamed on the Newhouse combination. It filed a civil antitrust suit, alleging:

1. That WSYR stations got a better break in the newspapers, in both the news columns and in advertising, than it did. One of these breaks, it said, was free advertising space.

2. That the newspapers had established a joint advertising rate so low that it was particularly attractive to national advertisers who might otherwise buy radio time.

3. That the newspapers were picking on WNDR by publishing unfavorable news stories about its financial problems.

A federal district court held that Syracuse Broadcasting had not proved its case, and, on appeal, the circuit court agreed, holding that "inequality of treatment (in news and advertising) is not sufficient to prove a violation of antitrust laws." It was reasonable to believe that the newspaper's editors might pay more attention to their publisher's broadcasting stations than to others. Syracuse Broadcasting would have to show that it had been frozen out of the news columns altogether or that the publisher had told the editors to suppress news about its station. Also the plaintiff could not prove that WSYR stations were getting free advertising. More likely, the court concluded, there was a trade-off between the newspapers and the Newhouse stations that ended up as a bookkeeping transaction. The complainant did not prove there was any-

---

7.   United States v. Kansas City Star Co., 1957 Trade Cas. (CCH) §68.857 (W.D.Mo. 1957).

thing unreasonable about the joint advertising rate. As for the news stories, they merely reflected a truth—that WNDR was having newsworthy financial problems. Therefore, Newhouse was acting reasonably and was not in violation of antitrust law.

Obviously, what is reasonable is a matter of opinion. The media market in any community has become extremely complex and highly competitive. Talk of a monopoly press stems from the obvious fact that all but a few cities in the United States are served by only one daily newspaper owner. But few daily publishers are without stiff competition from other media that seek business from retail advertisers. The spread of population into suburbs has led to a proliferation of weeklies that cater to the news and advertising needs of specific neighborhoods. Some weekly publishers have found it highly profitable to print publications devoted almost completely to advertising and to distribute them at no charge to readers. Moreover, in the face of competition from direct mail advertising, most daily newspapers have reluctantly become the distributors of glossy, full-color advertising supplements designed and printed by others. Where they once were in the business of selling large amounts of advertising display space to local retailers, dailies now sometimes simply charge retailers for the right to use their distribution system. Competition for the advertiser's dollar and for the consumer's attention also comes from billboards, point-of-sale advertisements, local magazines, zoned editions of national magazines and national newspapers, and telephone yellow pages.

All of this says nothing of the electronic delivery of advertising. A city with one newspaper may have three or more television stations, several times that many radio stations, and one or more cable systems, all vigorously seeking to sell time to advertisers. Because television stations particularly can point to research findings that the average person spends more time watching or listening to electronic media than reading newspapers, competition from this quarter is formidable.

For all of these media, the setting of advertising rates is a delicate matter. The rates must be competitive, or the medium will be bypassed by advertisers seeking maximum results for each dollar spent. But the rates must be high enough to cover expenses and return a profit, or the advertising medium eventually will fail. In addition, the owner of any medium that has achieved a substantial share of the market must be aware of possible antitrust action. Every policy concerning advertising rates, even such seemingly harmless practices as placing the ads of favored advertisers in favored positions or time slots, is always subject to challenge.[8] Most complaints fail, but the possibility of antitrust action, civil or criminal, is a factor to be considered in any rate decision.

Antitrust Law and Joint Operating Agreements

"To monopolize freedom destroys it," wrote the U.S. Court of Appeals in the *Kansas City Star* case in 1957. Already by then, however, the nature of media com-

---

8. See Conrad M. Shumadine, Walter D. Kelley, Jr., Gary A. Bryant, and Mark D. Stiles, "Antitrust and the Media," In *Communications Law 1992,* vol. 3 (New York: Practising Law Institute, 1992), pp. 437–809.

petition was being rapidly redefined. Most cities in the United States were becoming one-newspaper towns. In 1923, 39 percent of the cities with daily newspapers had competing ownerships. By 1930, that number had declined to 20.6 percent. Thirty years later, as John F. Kennedy was running for the presidency of the United States, only 61 cities, or 4.2 percent of the 1461 that had daily newspapers, had competing ownerships.[9]

In 1960 more than half the nation's daily newspapers were still independently owned, often by families. The long-established corporate chains—Hearst, Scripps-Howard, Knight-Ridder, Newhouse, and Cox—had stabilized their newspaper holdings and were diversifying into other media. Yet at the same time a new phenomenon was developing: Small, family-owned newspapers of little interest to the corporate giants were quietly being purchased by new, emerging companies. The leaders were Gannett and Thompson, but there were others, bearing family names such as Lee, Nixon, Booth, and Worrell.

In part, the rapid growth of newspaper chains was a factor of heredity. The children and grandchildren of patriarchs who had founded newspapers early in the twentieth century either lost interest in journalism or found it necessary to let estate administrators sell property-rich but cash-poor newspapers to raise money for inheritance taxes. Whatever the reasons, the once vast role of the press as a player in the marketplace of ideas appeared to be diminishing in the dust of mergers and buyouts. Even television, in the eyes of the Kennedy administration, was becoming a "vast wasteland" controlled by networks and rocked by scandal.[10] And to the Justice Department, the rapid growth of newspaper chains with fewer and fewer owners smelled darkly of anticompetitive activity.

The trend toward chain ownership and one-newspaper towns was enough to convince the Kennedy administration that something needed to be done. As the President and his advisers saw it, people in too many cities were becoming a captive audience to a few owners. Increasingly, those owners were not individuals who lived in their communities, but faceless corporations, with headquarters elsewhere, that were interested in only one thing: profit. Thus, the marketplace of ideas was becoming not a robust exchange for all kinds of political news and views, but a flabby monopoly offering only one point of view, or, even worse, no point of view. The President ordered the Antitrust Division of the Department of Justice to take action to preserve as much of the marketplace of ideas as still existed and try to restore what already had been lost.

President Kennedy died before the Justice Department could investigate newspaper mergers and monopolies, but his brother Robert carried on as attorney general under President Lyndon B. Johnson and, with the President's support, began to move against newspaper owners in places like Tucson, Los Angeles, and Cincinnati, where newspapers had formed joint operating agreements.

---

9.   Raymond B. Nixon, "Half of Nation's Dailies Now in Group Ownerships," *Editor & Publisher,* 17 July 1971, p. 7.
10. FCC Chairman Newton N. Minow, "The Vast Wasteland." Address to the National Association of Broadcasters, Washington, D.C., 9 May 1961.

The Tucson agreement was one of the earliest, dating to 1940, and was typical of the way such arrangements operated. At the

Citizen Publishing Co. v. *United States,* **394 U.S. 131, 89 S.Ct. 927, 22 L.Ed.2d 148,1 Med.L.Rptr. 2704 (1969).**

time it was formed, two owners were in head-to-head competition. The *Tucson Star* was making a modest profit, but the *Citizen* had dropped into the red. The two owners reached an agreement and organized a third company, Tucson Newspapers, Inc., which, in effect, became the city's only newspaper publisher. The company sold advertising for and distributed both newspapers. It operated the printing plant. As publisher, it decided what to charge for advertising and set the subscription rates. Profits were pooled and distributed to the two owners according to a formula on which they had agreed at the time the joint operation began. Executives of the two papers were bound by an agreement not to take part in a competing newspaper in the Tucson area, even if they lost their current jobs.

The arrangement worked for more than twenty years. Then the family who owned the *Star* lost interest, and the paper was offered for sale. The small Brush-Moore chain of Canton, Ohio, offered to buy. William A. Small, Jr., owner of the *Citizen,* exercised his option to buy under the operating agreement. The Justice Department filed suit under Section 7 of the Clayton Act and Section 1 of the Sherman Act to prevent that sale and to require that the *Star* be sold to anyone but Small. The resulting legal battle went to the Supreme Court, which not only upheld the department, but held in *Citizen Publishing Co.* v. *United States*[11] that the joint operating agreement violated antitrust law. The decision raised doubt about the legality of each of the twenty-two other agreements then in existence and sent shock waves through the newspaper business.

Justice William O. Douglas, writing for the Court, found three fatal flaws in the Tucson agreement. Tucson Newspapers' control of advertising and circulation rates amounted to illegal price fixing. Profit pooling, with distribution by formula, also violated antitrust law. So did the restrictions on participation in competing newspapers. That was market control. The Citizen Publishing Company could defend the arrangement only if it could prove that the *Citizen* not only had been failing at the time of the original agreement in 1940, but that there was no other buyer who might have saved it. Douglas held that the evidence did not support such a conclusion. If the *Citizen* had been failing in 1940, why would the publishers of the *Star* be willing to enter into an agreement giving it a fixed share of the profits?

The joint operating agreement could survive, the Court said, only if it was rewritten to permit each newspaper to set its own advertising and circulation rates, to distribute profit in a manner that reflected performance, and to eliminate the restrictions on future employment. The effect of the Supreme Court's decision was to make each party to a joint agreement sink or swim on the basis of individual performance. Both could still operate from the same printing plant, but if advertising and circulation rates were to be set independently, the owners almost certainly would have to separate those vital operations.

---

11.   394 U.S. 131, 89 S.Ct. 927, 22 L.Ed.2d 148, 1 Med.L.Rptr. 2704 (1969).

Some publishers anticipated the Supreme Court's decision. After all, as ill-defined as antitrust law might appear, it did clearly prohibit price fixing and agreements to control markets. Moreover, the primary defense for the merger—that the *Citizen* had been failing in 1940—was difficult to prove. Publishers began to lobby Congress for legislation that would provide an antitrust exception for newspapers. Sixteen months after the *Tucson* decision, President Richard M. Nixon signed the Newspaper Preservation Act.[12]

That law allows competing newspapers to make joint operating agreements under certain circumstances and with the written consent of the Justice Department. With the passing of this act, Congress approved agreements then in existence and restored the Tucson agreement, except for the section that forbade executives from joining a competitor. In any future proposal for a joint operating agreement, the proponents would have to show that one of the newspapers was in "probable danger of financial failure," a standard of failure somewhat less strict than that usually applied under general antitrust law governing anticompetitive mergers. Once the proposal was approved, newspapers in the same community could merge business operations and share profits, provided that they maintained competitive editorial and reportorial voices in the community. Thus, the Newspaper Preservation Act was a compromise intended to ease government concern about a diminishing market of ideas while allowing greater financial power for publishers and their shareholders.

The constitutionality of the Newspaper Preservation Act has withstood challenge in the courts.[13] The *Bay Guardian,* a monthly newspaper in San Francisco, attacked the act in a suit asking that the joint operating agreement between two other newspapers, the *Chronicle* and the *Examiner,* be dissolved. Judge Oliver J. Carter of the federal district court in San Francisco held that no constitutional issue was involved. The antitrust laws are an act of Congress, and what Congress does in one era it can modify in another to meet changing conditions. The Newspaper Preservation Act merely grants newspapers an exception from antitrust law under certain narrowly drawn conditions. The agreement in San Francisco met those conditions, Carter held.

However, finding that Congress and the President did not violate the Constitution by making an exception to antitrust law is not quite the same as saying that joint operating agreements immunize all anticompetitive business behavior. Judge Carter also held that the suit against the *Chronicle* and the *Examiner* should continue on its merits to determine whether the newspapers' advertising and circulation practices violated the Sherman Act. The *Bay Guardian* and its publisher, Bruce Brugmann, were joined by other plaintiffs, including a department store owner who said that the joint advertising rates were so high that he had been forced out of business because he could not afford to advertise in the newspapers. The suit was settled when the defending newspapers agreed to pay seventeen plaintiffs $1.35 million.[14]

---

12. 15 U.S.C. § 1801. President Nixon initially opposed the bill, but reportedly changed his mind after lobbying by newspaper publishers. Keith Naughton, "JOAs: Is It Time to Lay the Funeral Wreath?" *Quill,* January/February 1993, p. 16.
13. Bay Guardian Co. v. Chronicle Publishing Co., 344 F.Supp. 1155 (N.D.Calif. 1972). See also America's Best Cinema Corp. v. Fort Wayne Newspapers, Inc., 347 F.Supp. 328 (N.D.Ind. 1972).
14. Earl W. Wilken, "S.F. Printing Co. Settles Monopoly Suits Out-of-Court," *Editor & Publisher,* 31 May 1975, p. 7.

Thus, although the court held that joint operating agreements do not in themselves violate the antitrust act, the case stands as a reminder that the Newspaper Preservation Act does not immunize participating newspapers from the workings of antitrust law. If newspapers take advantage of the act to set rates that harm a competitor or freeze out potential advertisers, they are vulnerable to an antitrust action.

The Marketplace of Ideas Today

With the benefit of nearly thirty-five years of hindsight, we can now see that the effort to stem diminishing newspaper competition has failed. The trend toward one-ownership cities and newspaper chains has intensified. Whether the marketplace of ideas has been diminished by that trend can be debated. A great deal depends upon how one defines the market and identifies the sources of ideas competing for attention.

If the focus is on the entire range of mass media available for disseminating political and commercial information, the marketplace is a colorful bazaar of competing ideas. But if the focus is only on daily newspapers, the facts are clear. The number of cities with competing daily newspapers is approaching the vanishing point, and more than 70 percent of the nation's 1492 dailies are owned by fewer than 135 newspaper companies, which control more than 80 percent of the total daily newspaper circulation.

Even in Tucson, where the two newspapers still operate under a joint operating agreement, the ownership of the newspapers has been passed on to out-of-state corporations. The *Star* is owned by Pulitzer, whose primary newspaper property is the *St. Louis Post Dispatch,* and the afternoon *Citizen* is one of Gannett's eighty-four dailies.[15]

Gannett is perhaps the most noteworthy newspaper group today. Frank Gannett founded the firm in 1906 when he bought a newspaper in Elmira, New York, but it was under the leadership of Al Neuharth in the 1970s and 1980s that the company gained international attention. In 1982, Gannett founded a national daily newspaper, *USA Today,* which, despite not making a profit for more than a decade, reached a circulation of more than 1.5 million by 1993.[16] In the mid-1980s the Gannett group of mostly small-town newspapers shed its minor-league image by buying the *Cincinnati Enquirer,* the *Detroit News,* the *Louisville Courier-Journal,* and the *Des Moines Register.* These purchases helped the company pass Knight-Ridder and Newhouse in the number of newspapers sold each day. Gannett is now the largest newspaper publisher in the United States in terms of circulation, with more than five million papers published in more than eighty cities each day.[17]

Gannett, moreover, is a good reminder that large, daily newspaper companies are not just newspaper companies. Gannett also owns nondailies in fourteen states and op-

---

15. *Editor & Publisher Yearbook 1992.* The yearbook annually publishes data on all U.S. daily newspapers and a listing of newspaper groups with their affiliated newspapers.
16. Associated Press, "'USA Today' Records Its First Profit Ever," *Herald-Times,* Bloomington, Ind., 27 January 1994, p. B5.
17. John C. Busterna, "Trends in Daily Newspaper Circulation," *Journalism Quarterly,* Winter 1988, p. 831; "Groups Still Own Most U.S. Dailies," *Editor & Publisher,* 28 April 1984, p. 76.

erates ten television stations and fifteen radio stations. It is the largest outdoor advertising company in North America.

As group-owned newspapers have increased in number, cities with competing separate ownerships have decreased. In 1970 there were sixty-six cities with two or more dailies owned by separate companies. In 1990 there were only forty-three, and more than half were publishing under joint operating agreements. The number of households that read two or more papers a day has declined from 25 percent in the 1970s to about 12 percent in 1991.[18] Large cities served by only one newspaper owner, and in many instances by only one newspaper, include Atlanta, Baltimore, Cleveland, Houston, Indianapolis, Kansas City, Miami, Milwaukee, Minneapolis, Philadelphia, Phoenix, St. Louis, and San Diego. The trend reflects economic realities. The inflation of the 1980s and the recession of the early 1990s limited the extent to which newspapers could increase their advertising rates. Further, in cities with competing newspapers, advertisers tend to buy space in the paper that reaches the most customers. To be number 2 can mean being left with too little advertising to support a newspaper. As a result, more than thirty dailies closed or merged with other newspapers between 1991 and 1995. In 1993 the total of daily newspapers in the United States reached a low of 1492, compared with 1701 in 1983, and 1785 in 1953. Among those that have discontinued publication are some of the nation's oldest, including the *State-Times* of Baton Rouge, Louisiana, founded in 1842; the *Dallas Times Herald,* founded in 1879; the *Hudson Dispatch* of Union City, New Jersey, founded in 1874; the *Arkansas Gazette,* founded in 1819; the *Daily Journal* of Elizabeth, New Jersey, founded in 1779; the *Union* of Sacramento, California, founded in 1851; the *Evening Post* of Charleston, South Carolina, founded in 1894; and the *Houston Post,* founded in 1884. The closing of the *Houston Post* left Houston with the distinction of being the largest city in the United States with only one daily newspaper.

Not even joint operating agreements have worked consistently to save financially troubled newspapers. Two notable examples are the *St. Louis Globe-Democrat,* owned by the Newhouse group, and the *Miami News,* owned by Cox Enterprises. Newhouse's continued heavy losses forced the closing of its St. Louis paper in the early 1980s. Another publisher bought the paper but ceased its publication in 1986, ending 133 years of *Globe-Democrat* publication. Cox Enterprises closed the *Miami News* in the late 1980s, ending twenty-two years of publication under a joint operating agreement with Knight-Ridder, publisher of the *Miami Herald.*[19] Cox said that the newspaper's losses were $9 million during the year that it closed, despite the joint operating agreement.

Joint operating agreements are not a guarantee of profitable operation. At best, they give two owners who are willing to work at it an opportunity to coexist as competing news operations and survive as business entities. Their continued existence in seventeen cities is evidence that some publishers are willing to give them a try.[20]

---

18. Joseph Ungaro, "Newspapers I: First the Bad News," *Media Studies Journal,* Fall 1991, p. 104.
19. Martha Brannigan, "Cox to Close the Miami News at Year End," *Wall Street Journal,* 17 October 1988.
20. George Garneau, "Kiss of Death? Countdown to 1998 JOA Expiration at Evansville Press Begins; Scripps Serves Notice That It Will Not Extend the Agreement," *Editor & Publisher,* 8 January 1994, p. 11.

This focus on the problems of daily newspaper competition should not suggest a overly gloomy assessment of the future of newspapers. Despite notable failures of dailies in some of the nation's big cities, closings often have been balanced by start-ups of highly profitable suburban dailies and new Sunday newspapers. Suburban weeklies, many of them devoted almost exclusively to advertising, have proliferated rapidly. Moreover, surviving daily newspapers continue to be profitable. For them, being the only daily in town has helped, but other factors have been important, too. Electronic composition and pagination has greatly decreased the costs of composition. New presses have given newspapers the ability to print high-quality color, rivaling that found in magazines. Computer-generated graphics have given editors a powerful way to present visual information, and reporters and editors have seen salaries improve over the past ten years.[21]

Still, the reality is clear. Most cities in the United States have only one daily newspaper, and there are more than two chances out of three that that newspaper is part of a chain. Neither antitrust law nor the Newspaper Preservation Act, which permits joint operating agreements, has succeeded in preserving newspaper competition. Today, most dailies compete with cable television, computer data services, and broadcast stations, rather than with other daily newspapers.

Joint Ownership of Newspapers and Broadcasting Stations

In the early days of broadcasting, many newspapers established radio stations and used them for promotion and as an additional outlet for news. In time, these stations became profitable in their own right, and many of the newspaper-owned broadcasters became pioneers in television. By the mid-1970s, there were 176 newspaper-radio combinations and eighty-three newspaper-television combinations.

In 1974 the Justice Department, again acting out of concern for the marketplace of ideas, asked the Federal Communications Commission to refuse to renew broadcast licenses owned by newspapers in St. Louis and Des Moines.[22] Later, the request was expanded to include newspaper-broadcast combinations in Milwaukee and Salt Lake City. The Justice Department chose to act through the FCC rather than through the courts because its attorneys believed that they would have more success proving that these combinations were not in the public interest—thus violating the Federal Communications Act—than they would proving that they were anticompetitive—thus violating the Sherman Act. The Justice Department was unsuccessful in its effort to convince the FCC to deny license renewals, but it was successful in getting the FCC's

---

21. The median income for journalists on daily newspapers in 1991 was $35,180. That is nearly $10,000 more than the median income for television journalists, who made $25,625. David Weaver and G. Cleveland Wilhoit, "Who Are We? A Brief Status Report on Jobs and Work," *Quill*, January/February 1993, p. 45.
22. "Justice Agency Urges FCC to Deny Licenses to 6 Stations It Says Are Newspaper Owned," *Wall Street Journal,* 4 January 1974.

attention, which proceeded with its own study of the problems of cross-ownership of newspapers and broadcast stations.[23]

By the mid-1970s, the FCC had agreed on the main thrust of a proposed regulation: No newspaper would be permitted to start a new broadcasting station or buy the license of an existing station in its own community. All of the then existing cross-ownerships would have to be ended within five years. This proposed regulation provoked such a storm of protest that it led to additional hearings. In the end, the FCC decided that diversity might not be the only goal worth achieving. It found that some newspaper-broadcast combinations were doing a good job in serving the public interest, and in most cases these combinations were faced with vigorous competition from other broadcast stations. So when the regulation took final form, it had been significantly modified. While it still forbade future newspaper acquisitions in the same city, it limited the divestiture provision to those cities in which the only daily newspaper also owned the only broadcast station. The FCC identified eighteen such communities, eight involving television stations. It ordered divestiture in sixteen.[24]

That divestiture order came under fire from two directions. The stations involved thought it went too far. A consumer advocate group, the National Citizens Committee for Broadcasting, on the other hand, didn't think it went far enough. The Justice Department agreed with the citizens' group, arguing that if diversity of ownership is essential to a robust marketplace of ideas, as the FCC recognized in principle, then that principle ought to be carried as far as was practicable.

Federal Communications Commission v. *National Citizens Committee for Broadcasting,* **436 U.S. 775, 98 S.Ct. 2096, 56 L.Ed.2d 697, 3 Med.L.Rptr. 2409 (1978)**

Both sides appealed to the Circuit Court of Appeals for the District of Columbia, which agreed with the position of the Justice Department and the consumer advocates' group and decided against the FCC. The court ruled that no newspaper-broadcast combination could stand unless the owner could prove that it qualified for an exemption under rules laid down by the FCC. The FCC joined the losing owners in going to the Supreme Court.

Ruling in *Federal Communications Commission* v. *National Citizens Committee for Broadcasting,* the Court upheld the rule against future acquisitions and reversed the appeals court on divestiture. Justice Thurgood Marshall, writing for a unanimous Court, held that the FCC had acted reasonably and within its power in concluding that forced divestiture, if carried too far, might weaken the marketplace of ideas. Surviving newspapers or surviving broadcast stations might in some instances be too weak economically to provide truly independent voices if forced to compete. They might not be able to afford a vigorous news and public affairs staff any longer. Even worse, given the realities of broadcast and newspaper ownership patterns, a strong independent local owner might be replaced by an outside chain owner. The Court concluded

---

23. "Broadcast Licenses Renewed in Rebuff to Justice Agency," *Wall Street Journal,* 25 October 1976. Further Notice of Proposed Rule Making (Docket No. 18110), 22 F.C.C.2d 339 (1970).
24. *Second Report and Order,* as amended upon reconsideration, 53 F.C.C.2d 589 (1975), 47 C.F.R., §§ 73.35, 73.240, 73.636 (1976).

that the FCC had acted rationally in regulating combinations and at the same time limiting its divestiture order to only sixteen cities.

The FCC regulates not only newspaper-broadcast combinations in a market, but also the number of broadcast stations—television, AM radio, and FM radio—that a company can own. As technology has made the use of the electromagnetic spectrum more efficient and competition among broadcasters has increased, Congress and the FCC have been willing to make ownership rules more liberal. Currently, a broadcast company may own as many television stations as it wants, as long as it does not reach more than 35 percent of all national television viewers. A company also may own as many radio stations as it wants, as long as it does not own more than five to eight stations in the same market, depending on market size. A company may own both a television station and a cable system in the same market, but it cannot own more than one television station in a market or combine ownership of a newspaper with that of a television station, a radio station, or a cable system in the same market.[25]

REGULATING THE DISTRIBUTION OF INFORMATION: TIME, MANNER, AND PLACE

One place where competition doesn't seem to be a problem is on the streets of Chicago. In one city block, the block where the federal courthouse is situated, nineteen vending machines offer eleven different publications. Chicagoans can find such diverse titles as *Investor's Daily,* the *Chicago Tribune, Chicago Woman,* and the *Relcon Apartment Directory.*[26] The distribution of news, opinion, and advertising by means of sidewalk vending machines is common in every American city. In Cincinnati, for example, there are nearly two thousand news racks along city streets.[27] But not everyone likes it. Many urban planners consider the boxes unsightly—the sidewalk equivalent of a highway billboard—and dangerous. Nearly all city governments regulate newspaper vending machines by restricting their size, design, and location. Some cities require publishers to pay license fees and buy liability insurance. A few ban the boxes altogether.

The distribution of publications from coin-operated machines along public walks, as well as in airports and subway stations, has given rise to a generation of First Amendment litigation over the power of government to license and regulate the distribution of information. As a general matter, the Supreme Court has been careful to draw a line between the distribution of products or services and the distribution of ideas. Local governments may regulate and even prohibit the former. They cannot entirely prevent the latter, even if the ideas are obnoxious. Court decisions involving churches, labor unions, civil rights advocates, political demonstrators, and news racks have established an important principle of First Amendment law: Government cannot prevent the dissemination of ideas, but it can impose restrictions of

---

25. The Telecommunications Act of 1996, § 202, Broadcast Ownership.
26. Chicago Observer v. Chicago, 929 F.2d 325, 18 Med.L.Rptr. 1974 (7th Cir. 1991).
27. David Frum, "How About Free Speech for Business, Too?" *Forbes,* 12 October 1992, p. 108.

time, place, and manner on their dissemination, provided that the restrictions are "reasonable."

Justice Byron R. White, in *Heffron* v. *International Society for Krishna Conscious-ness,*[28] outlined the characteristics of a reasonable time, manner, and place restriction in this way:

— The restriction must be based neither on the content nor on the subject matter of the speech.

— The restriction must serve a significant government interest.

— The restriction must be the least drastic means of accomplishing the government's interest.

— There must be alternative forums available for disseminating the message.

If a regulation attempts to restrict an expressive activity but fails any part of Judge White's test, the regulation is an unreasonable and unconstitutional prior restraint.

One dispute in Ohio over the manner and place of newspaper vending machines made it all the way to the U.S. Supreme Court and produced an unusual four-to-three decision.[29] Although not all the justices in the case were willing to concede that placing vending machines on side-walks is a form of speech, enough of them did to find that a city ordinance that left the regulation of news racks to the unbridled discretion of public of-

City of Lakewood v. Plain Dealer Publishing Co., **486 U.S. 750, 108 S.Ct. 2138, 100 L.Ed.2d 771, 15 Med.L.Rptr. 1481 (1988).**

ficials was unconstitutional on its face. Justice William J. Brennan, Jr., who wrote the plurality opinion for the Court, said that disseminating news through vending machines was a fully protected expressive activity and that leaving decisions about restrictions in the hands of a mayor was an invitation to censorship. Justices White, John Paul Stevens, and Sandra Day O'Connor, in a vigorous dissent, argued that placing a vending machine on a public sidewalk is not an expressive activity at all. Rather, they said the issue was whether a private newspaper vendor could permanently appropriate a piece of public property for his or her own business purposes. From their point of view, anchoring vending boxes to a public sidewalk was no more expressive than de-ciding where to locate the newspaper's printing plant.

Moreover, the dissenters grasped the opportunity to blunt any temptation by pub-lishers to read too much into Brennan's opinion. They pointed out, correctly, that de-ciding that an ordinance is too vague to be constitutional is not the same thing as es-tablishing an absolute right for publishers to place news racks on city sidewalks. Even if all the justices agreed that the placement of vending machines was an expressive ac-tivity, the city could still rewrite its ordinance to ban news racks entirely in the inter-est of safety, aesthetics, or some other public need, as long as there were alternative ways to disseminate the news. Even the most liberal view of the First Amendment would require only that restrictions on news racks be content neutral, be tailored nar-

---

28.   452 U.S. 640, 101 S.Ct. 2599, 69 L.Ed.2d 298, 7 Med.L.Rptr. 1489 (1981).
29.   Chief Justice Rehnquist and Justice Kennedy did not take part in the decision.

rowly to a significant government interest, and be sensitive to protecting alternative forums for getting the news.

Still, it is Brennan's powerful condemnation of arbitrary power for which the case is best remembered. Brennan wrote that the "expressive activity" at peril in this case was "the circulation of newspapers." An ordinance that regulated the placement of news racks was "a close enough nexus to expression, or to conduct commonly associated with expression, to pose a real and substantial threat" of censorship. That threat, he said, came from language in the ordinance that gave the mayor authority to grant or deny applications for annual news rack permits. To get a permit, the design of the newspaper rack had to be approved by the Lakewood Architectural Board of Review before installation. The rack's owner had to agree to hold the city free from any liability resulting from its placement and to provide at least $100,000 in insurance. But most important, the ordinance said that the publisher had to comply with any "other terms and conditions deemed necessary and reasonable by the Mayor." Those lines are what the Sixth Circuit found objectionable and the Supreme Court plurality condemned. The Court said that nothing in the ordinance required the mayor to do any more than hold that a request for a news rack permit was not in the public interest. As Brennan saw it, that reason could be a convenient mask to hide a mayor's real motive for rejecting a permit—disdain for the newspaper's policies or opinions. And because a mayor's permission would have to be secured annually, it was reasonable to expect a prudent publisher to soften news coverage of the mayor's administration rather than risk losing the lucrative right to place news racks on busy sidewalks.

Lower courts, applying whatever guidance they are able to find in *City of Lakewood,* generally have agreed that the right to distribute newspapers by whatever means—including news racks—is protected by the First Amendment as being closely and necessarily linked to protected speech. They also generally have agreed that the protection is subject to reasonable time, place, and manner restrictions. Of course, what is reasonable necessarily depends on the facts of a particular case. For example, a U.S. district court in New Jersey held that the port authority could ban newspaper vending boxes from Newark International Airport. The court agreed with the authority's argument that since newspapers were already available to travelers at the airport newsstands, the ban served the airport's interest in ensuring public safety, making the airport aesthetically pleasing, permitting the free flow of pedestrian traffic, and protecting the revenue of airport newsstands, which paid the authority a percentage on sales.[30] *USA Today* lost a challenge to an ordinance that regulated the placement of its vending boxes on public sidewalks in Pennsauken, New Jersey. The court there thought that the regulation, which required boxes to be thirty feet from intersections and bolted to the sidewalk, was a rule tailored specifically to the city's interest in aesthetics.[31] The *Chicago Tribune,* however, was able to prevent the city of Chicago and an airline company from removing its vending boxes in an airport passenger concourse. The airline argued unsuccessfully that the boxes would take revenue from its

---

30. Gannett Satellite Information Network v. Berger, 716 F.Supp. 140, 16 Med.L.Rptr. 2057 (D.N.J. 1989).

31. Gannett Satellite Information Network v. Township of Pennsauken, 709 F.Supp. 530, 16 Med.L.Rptr. 1673 (D.N.J. 1989).

rent-paying concession stands and were a security threat. Passengers, however, complained that, although the airport was busy twenty-four hours a day, the concessions were closed late at night and no newspapers were available. The restrictions, although content neutral, had failed to account for the fact that there were no alternative sources for news and information after the concessions closed.[32] Finally, in Arizona, a federal district court judge awarded Phoenix Newspapers $66,000 in legal fees after it won the right to place its vending machines in the Tucson airport. The court said that the airport authority's attempt to regulate and charge rent for placement of the machines violated the First Amendment when it gave employees unbridled discretion to fix fees and determine locations for the boxes.[33] Not surprisingly, the judge cited *City of Lakewood* v. *Plain Dealer Publishing Co.*

At issue in the news rack cases is not only the First Amendment protection for the distribution of news, but also protection for the distribution of advertising—whether displayed on the news racks themselves or in the commercial handbills distributed from them.

The notion of a sidewalk billboard caught the imagination of entrepreneurs at the *Chicago Observer,* and they created something they called the AD BOX, an oversized news rack that measured thirty-four inches wide and fifty-two inches high. A nine-inch open slot was reserved for access to the tabloid-size, folded *Chicago Observer.* The rest of the exterior surface was sold as advertising space. The city of Chicago responded with an ordinance banning off-premises ads on the public way, banning off-premises ads attached to news racks, and limiting the size of news racks. An off-premises ad was defined as a sign that advertised a business more than twenty feet away. That ordinance effectively put the AD BOX out of business.

The Seventh Circuit upheld the ordinance, finding it to be a reasonable time, place, and manner restriction on advertising.[34] Judge Frank A. Easterbrook wrote that Chicago had a significant interest in curtailing visual clutter and that the ordinance did not regulate the viewpoint of publications nor make any exceptions for favored causes. He noted that Chicago left ample channels for communications: "Chicago teems with ads and with publications," he said. Responding to the *Chicago Observer*'s objection that the size restrictions were arbitrary, Easterbrook wrote:

> True, the City's maximum sizes are arbitrary. All lines—all rules—are arbitrary. Chicago had to use bright-line rules, given *Lakewood* v. *Plain Dealer,* which finds discretion constitutionally objectionable. . . .
>
> If, as the *Observer* says, the City tailored the dimensions in the ordinance to freeze out its boxes while not affecting others, what of it? The *Observer*'s " AD BOXes" were nonpareil. No newspaper has the right to demand that burdensome, and unnecessary, regulation be fixed on others. Courts abjure government to use the least restraint essential to the task. Chicago did so and deserves praise rather than condemnation.

---

32. Chicago Tribune Co. v. City of Chicago, 705 F.Supp. 1345, 16 Med.L.Rptr. 1333 (N.D.Ill. 1989). See also Multimedia Publishing Co. v. Greenville-Spartanburg Airport District, 774 F.Supp. 977, 19 Med.L.Rptr. 1081 (D.S.C. 1991).
33. Phoenix Newspapers v. Tucson Airport Authority, 16 Med.L.Rptr. 1500 (D.C.Ariz. 1989). See also Sentinel Communications Co. v. Watts, 936 F.2d 1189, 19 Med.L.Rptr. 1097 (11th Cir. 1991); Hays County Guardian v. Supple, 969 F.2d 111, 20 Med.L.Rptr. 1681 (5th Cir. 1992).
34. Chicago Observer Inc. v. Chicago, 929 F.2d 325, 18 Med.L.Rptr. 1974 (7th Cir. 1991).

Meanwhile, in Cincinnati, Discovery Network and Harmon Publishing Company obtained permits to place vending racks at downtown street corners. Discovery distributes catalogues for adult education classes and social events. Harmon advertises local houses for sale or rent. Several months later, the city council voted to deny permits to everyone except "publications primarily presenting coverage of, and commentary on, current events."[35] It instructed the Department of Public Works to enforce an ordinance that forbade the distribution of "commercial handbills" on public property.

That ordinance prevented Discovery and Harmon from distributing their advertising from vending boxes, and they sued, arguing that the restrictions were an unconstitutional prior restraint. The federal district court, the Sixth Circuit Court of Appeals, and the U.S. Supreme Court all agreed.

Discovery Network Inc. v. Cincinnati, **946 F.2d 469, 19 Med.L.Rptr. 1449 (6th Cir. 1991).**

The Sixth Circuit in its ruling reviewed previous U.S. Supreme Court opinions concerning First Amendment protection for commercial speech, particularly *Central Hudson Gas & Electric Corp.* v. *Public Service Commission of New York*[36] and *Board of Trustees of State University of New York* v. *Fox.*[37] Those cases provide an analysis that is similar, although not identical, to the time, manner, and place rules. Under *Central Hudson,* the four-part analysis goes like this:

— Commercial speech must first of all concern a lawful activity and not be misleading to be protected by the First Amendment.

— The restriction imposed must serve a substantial government interest.

— The restriction must directly advance that government interest.

— The restriction must not be more extensive than is necessary to serve that interest.

In the *Fox* case, the Court said that a regulation is not more extensive than necessary when it is a reasonable fit between the ends sought and the regulatory means chosen. The regulation need not be the "least restrictive means" available.

The Sixth Circuit found that although Cincinnati had a substantial interest in safety and aesthetics, the ordinance prohibiting the distribution of commercial handbills while allowing the distribution of other material that differed only in content was not a regulation reasonably fitted to the city's goals. For example, a regulation that required *all* boxes be bolted to the sidewalk would have solved the security problem; a regulation that established color and design limitations for *all* boxes would have solved the aesthetics problem; and a regulation that limited the *total* number of boxes permitted on the sidewalks to a first-come-first-served basis would have solved any

---

35. David Frum, "How About Free Speech for Business, Too?" p. 108.
36. 447 U.S. 557, 100 S.Ct. 2343, 65 L.Ed.2d 341, 6 Med.L.Rptr. 1497 (1980). See Chapter 11, "Advertising."
37. 492 U.S. 469, 109 S.Ct. 3028, 106 L.Ed.2d 388 (1989).

overcrowding problem. The current regulation merely burdened advertisers without any appreciable effect on safety or visual clutter.

As for time, manner, and place, the court said that if the ordinance was not crafted carefully enough to pass muster under *Central Hudson* and *Fox,* it hardly had a chance under a test that required it to be content neutral and narrowly tailored. In the court's opinion, an ordinance that could be understood only by reference to the commercial content of the publications it regulated was not content neutral. Moreover, when there are so many other less restrictive options for accomplishing the city's significant interests, the ordinance can hardly be said to be tailored narrowly.

Cincinnati immediately appealed to the U.S. Supreme Court, which held, six to three, that Cincinnati had violated the First Amendment rights of the two companies. Justice John Paul Stevens wrote that there was not a reasonable fit between the city's regulation and the goal it was supposed to accomplish. Removing sixty-two of the two thousand boxes would not have made a dent in the city's sidewalk clutter problem, and the city's distinction between advertising and news had no bearing on the problem of clutter.[38]

TAXATION AND THE FIRST AMENDMENT

The Supreme Court has held that the news media, as businesses, can be taxed as other businesses are taxed. But it also has held that any tax that singles out media for special treatment, favorable or unfavorable, violates the First Amendment guarantee of freedom of the press.

Grosjean v. *American Press Co.,* 297 U.S. 233, 56 S.Ct. 444, 80 L.Ed.2d 660, 1 Med.L.Rptr. 2685 (1936).

In its earliest media tax case, *Grosjean* v. *American Press Co.,* the Supreme Court struck down a tax that was clearly designed to punish daily newspapers whose editorials opposed a state governor's rise to power. The governor, Huey P. Long, was one of the most flamboyant political figures of the twentieth century. In the 1920s, he established a political machine in Louisiana that permitted members of his family to rule that state for more than forty years. Long went on to become a U.S. senator and an aspirant for the presidency. His career was cut short by an assassin in 1935.

In 1934, at Long's request, the Louisiana legislature enacted what appeared to be a general tax law. It imposed a 2 percent levy on the gross receipts of newspapers, magazines, periodicals, or books that had a circulation within the state of more than twenty thousand copies a week. In actuality, the tax applied to only nine publishers of thirteen daily newspapers, all of whom had editorialized against Long's regime. The publishers promptly asked a federal district court to declare the tax void as a violation of the First Amendment. When the court did so, the state appealed to the U.S. Supreme Court, which affirmed unanimously.

Justice George Sutherland, whose writing style usually could be described as dull, wrote an eloquent essay on the meaning of freedom of the press. He went

---

38.   Linda Greenhouse, "Rights of Commercial Speech Affirmed," *New York Times,* 25 March 1993, p. A11.

back to Milton and examined the history of attempts to control the press. One such method was through taxation. In some instances, the British sovereign had used the threat of taxation to bring publishers into line. If that failed, taxes could be imposed at such a level as to drive publishers out of business. The American Revolution, Sutherland recalled, was in part a protest against the Stamp Tax, which had newspapers and pamphlets among its targets. Such taxes, he wrote, properly were called "taxes on knowledge":

> That the taxes had, and were intended to have, the effect of curtailing the circulation of newspapers, and particularly the cheaper ones whose readers were generally found among the masses of the people, went almost without question, even on the part of those who defended the act.
>
> . . . [T]he dominant and controlling aim was to prevent, or curtail the opportunity for, the acquisition of knowledge by the people in respect of their governmental affairs.

This tax was no different. Its purpose clearly was not to raise revenue as much as it was to punish Long's political opponents. The levying of such a tax could be as vicious as direct censorship in diminishing the flow of vital information to the people. Therefore, the Court held, the tax was unconstitutional. But that did not end the matter:

> It is not intended by anything we have said to suggest that the owners of newspapers are immune from any of the ordinary forms of taxation for support of the government. But this is not an ordinary form of tax, but one single in kind, with a long history of hostile misuse against the freedom of the press.
>
> . . . The newspapers, magazines, and other journals of the country, it is safe to say, have shed, and continue to shed, more light on the public and business affairs of the nation than any other instrumentality of publicity; and since informed public opinion is the most potent of all restraints upon misgovernment, the suppression or abridgment of the publicity afforded by a free press cannot be regarded otherwise than with grave concern. The tax here is bad not because it takes money from the pockets of appellees. If that were all, a wholly different question would be presented. It is bad because, in the light of history and of its present setting, it is seen as a deliberate and calculated device in the guise of a tax to limit the circulation of information to which the public is entitled. . . . A free press stands as one of the great interpreters between the government and the people. To allow it to be fettered is to fetter ourselves.

Those last two sentences should be engraved in the minds of every American. The First Amendment, Sutherland was saying, is not a special privilege for those whom fortune has placed in journalism. Journalists are protected because they are the only independent interpreters of what those in government do for us or to us.

Nearly fifty years after the *Grosjean* decision, the Supreme Court again rejected an attempt to impose a special tax on publications. This tax was not prompted by political vindictiveness, but by the state of Minnesota's need for revenue, tempered by special treatment for newspapers. Minnesota adopted a retail sales tax on most items, but excluded newspapers. To protect the sales tax, it imposed a use tax on items bought outside the state but consumed in Minnesota. The legislature amended the use tax to include the cost of paper and ink used in publication. No other items used in the manufacture of a retail product were subject to the tax. The law was further amended to exclude the first $100,000 worth of paper and ink consumed by a publication in any calendar year. The effect was to exclude all but eleven publishers who produced fourteen of the 388 paid-circulation newspapers in the state. Two-thirds of the revenue produced by the tax was paid by the Minneapolis Star and Tribune Company.

The newspaper company challenged the tax in the state courts and lost. Arguing *Minneapolis Star and Tribune Co. v. Minnesota Commissioner of Revenue, 460 U.S. 575, 103 S.Ct. 1365, 75 L.Ed.2d 295, 9 Med.L.Rptr. 1369 (1983).* that it was the victim of a special tax much like that in *Grosjean,* it carried an appeal to the Supreme Court. In *Minneapolis Star and Tribune Co.* v. *Minnesota Commissioner of Revenue,* the Court held that this tax was different from the one in *Grosjean,* but that it still violated the First Amendment.

Justice O'Connor, writing for seven members of the Court, said that the tax would have been proper had it been applied evenly to all kinds of business firms. As it was, the tax targeted a small group of speakers, raising concerns about censorship. When the press is singled out for special taxation, Justice O'Connor continued, the state must prove that it has a compelling government interest for doing so. The power to tax is a "powerful weapon" that can weaken or cripple a target that stands by itself. But when all are treated equally, the realities of politics restrain the hand of the tax collector.

Minnesota said that it had imposed the tax not to harm the press but to raise needed revenue. But that reason, standing alone, was not enough, O'Connor said. The same amount of revenue could have been raised by a slight increase in a levy applying to all business firms. Or, she suggested, the revenue could have been raised by applying the sales tax to the price of newspapers. The state further argued that the use tax gave the press favored treatment, imposing levies on it at a lower rate than those paid by other businesses. That made no difference, the Court held. The point was that the press was given differential treatment. This point was highlighted by the fact that even within the press, most publishers paid no tax, while a few carried most of the burden. O'Connor concluded:

> Whatever the motive of the legislature in this case, we think that recognizing a power in the State not only to single out the press but also to tailor the tax so that it singles out a few members of the press presents such a potential for abuse that no interest suggested by Minnesota can justify the scheme.

The Supreme Court confronted another example of discriminatory taxation when Arkansas decided to apply its 4 percent sales tax to general-interest magazines while exempting religious, professional, trade, and sports journals, and newspapers.[39] One of the taxed magazines, the *Arkansas Times,* asked to be exempted on the grounds that it published occasional articles on religion and sports. The commissioner of revenue refused the request and was upheld by state courts. The U.S. Supreme Court agreed to review the request and reversed the state courts. Relying heavily on the rationale of *Minneapolis Star and Tribune,* the Court said that the tax was unconstitutional be-

---

39.   Arkansas Writers' Project v. Ragland, 481 U.S. 221, 107 S.Ct. 1722, 95 L.Ed.2d 209, 13 Med.L.Rptr. 2313 (1987). See also Dow Jones & Co. Inc. v. Oklahoma Tax Commission, 787 P.2d 843, 17 Med.L.Rptr. 1401 (Okla. 1990), discrimination on the basis of sales price unconstitutional.

cause it treated some magazines less favorably than others. The discrimination was "particularly repugnant to First Amendment principles," the Court said, because "a magazine's tax status depends entirely on its content."

The following year, in *Texas Monthly* v. *Bullock,* the Court struck down a Texas law that exempted religious periodicals from the state's sales tax.[40] This time the Court relied on the "establishment" clause of the First Amendment rather than on the "free press" clause. The Court's majority held that the effect of the exemption was to subsidize certain publications solely because they served a religious purpose. The Court said that Texas could impose a general sales tax on religious publications if it wanted to, or it could exempt all publications from the sales tax, but it could not single out a publication because of its religious content and exempt it from a tax that other publications had to pay.

In all of these cases the Court was concerned primarily about the use of taxation to burden or reward a few publications that had been singled out for special tax treatment. What was left unanswered by the Court was whether a tax that differentiated among types of media, rather than among specific media organizations, would also be unconstitutional. For example, would it be unlawful to require a sales tax on all cable television subscriptions but not on any newspaper subscriptions? By 1990, courts in some states were already beginning to confront the issue, but with mixed results. The Oklahoma Supreme Court, for example, held that taxing broadcasters while exempting newspapers from similar taxes violated the First Amendment.[41] Similarly, the Tennessee Supreme Court held that taxing magazines but not newspapers violated the First Amendment.[42] But in Iowa, the state supreme court held that taxing magazines but not newspapers did not violate the First Amendment.[43] And in California, an appellate court held that taxing advertising publications but not news publications was not a First Amendment violation.[44]

The U.S. Supreme Court took up the issue in *Leathers* v. *Medlock,* with Justice O'Connor again writing the majority opinion. She said that Arkansas had not violated the First Amendment when it decided to impose its sales tax on fees paid by all cable television subscribers, despite an exemption that applied to newspapers and magazines. The tax was one of general application to the cable medium and therefore was constitutional.

Leathers v. *Medlock,* **499 U.S. 439, 111 S.Ct. 1438, 113 L.Ed.2d 494, 18 Med.L.Rptr. 1953 (1991).**

The case began when the Arkansas legislature amended the state's Gross Receipts Act in 1987 to impose its 4 percent sales tax on cable television. Counties could impose an additional 1 percent and cities could impose another 0.5 percent. The legislature let stand an exemption for receipts from newspaper subscriptions and over-the-counter sales, and from magazine subscriptions. Daniel Medlock,

---

40. 489 U.S. 1, 109 S.Ct. 890, 103 L.Ed.2d 1, 16 Med.L.Rptr. 1177 (1989).
41. Oklahoma Broadcasters Association v. Oklahoma Tax Commission, 17 Med.L.Rptr. 1994 (Okla. 1990).
42. Newsweek Inc. v. Celauro, 789 S.W.2d 247, 18 Med.L.Rptr. 1134 (Tenn. 1990).
43. Hearst Corp. v. Iowa Department of Revenue and Finance, 461 N.W.2d 295, 18 Med.L.Rptr. 1241 (Iowa 1990).
44. Redwood Empire Publishing Co. v. California State Board of Equalization, 255 Cal.Rptr. 514, 16 Med.L.Rptr. 1257 (Cal.App. 1989).

a cable television subscriber, along with a cable television operator and an organization representing the state's cable operators sued in state court to block the extension of the tax. They argued that the expressive activities of cable systems are comparable to those of newspapers and magazines and that the disparate treatment of the media violated cable operators' rights under the First Amendment and the "equal protection" clause of the Fourteenth Amendment. The state courts did not agree that the tax scheme was unconstitutional, but they were uncertain how to explain it. The trial court held that because cable television is granted the use of public rights of way, it could be taxed differently from other media without the Constitution being violated. The state supreme court rejected that holding, but said that the tax did not violate the First Amendment as long as it did not discriminate among members of the same medium. The U.S. Supreme Court agreed to grant certiorari.

Justice O'Connor reviewed the Court's media taxation cases and concluded that they demonstrated "that differential taxation of First Amendment speakers is constitutionally suspect when it threatens to suppress the expression of particular ideas or viewpoints" or when it "discriminates on the basis of the content of taxpayer speech." She said there was nothing in this case to indicate that the tax on cable television was suspect on either ground. It is a general tax, applying to all one hundred cable operators, and is not based on the content of anyone's speech. Since the tax didn't single out a small group or try to punish or reward certain kinds of messages, there was no danger that imposition of the tax would suppress expression of any particular ideas.

Justice Marshall, joined by Justice Harry A. Blackmun, protested that the majority seemed to be ignoring what they saw as the thrust of the Court's decision in *Minneapolis Star and Tribune.* They read that decision as requiring states to apply an even hand in taxing the media. In this instance, Marshall wrote, the Court was condoning a tax imposed on one segment of the information market while exempting another. Such discrimination, he said, "triggers the central concern underlying the nondiscrimination principle: the risk of covert censorship."

In light of the *Leathers* decision, courts subsequently have held that it does not violate the First Amendment to classify cable television for tax purposes as a utility, thus subjecting it to higher taxes than print media[45] or to classify newspaper and advertising publications as different media for tax purposes, even if both are produced in similar ways with similar materials.[46]

Shortly after the *Leathers* decision, the Supreme Court examined another kind of "tax" on media. This one singled out a class of authors who had one thing in common: They all were profiting by writing or talking about crimes for which they had been accused.

---

45. Sacramento Cable Television v. Sacramento, 19 Med.L.Rptr. 1532 (Cal.Ct.App. 1991). Cox Cable Hampton Roads Inc., 19 Med.L.Rptr. 1656 (Va.Sup.Ct. 1991).
46. Gallacher v. Connecticut Commissioner of Revenue, 602 A.2d 996, 19 Med.L.Rptr. 2140 (Conn. 1991). Maryland Pennysaver Group Inc. v. Maryland Comptroller of the Treasury, 19 Med.L.Rptr. 1937 (Md.Ct.App. 1991).

Simon & Schuster v. New York Crime Victims Board, 502 U.S. 105, 112 S.Ct.501, 19 Med.L.Rptr. 1609 (1991).

The Supreme Court drew heavily from its *Leathers* decision in striking down New York's "Son of Sam" statute, which had been enacted in 1982 after an accused serial killer, known as Son of Sam, sold his story to a publisher.[47] The law required anyone contracting with an accused or convicted person for a depiction of the crime to submit a copy of the contract to the Crime Victims Board and to turn over any income under that contract to the board. Sums collected were to be held in escrow for the benefit of any victim who, within five years, sued and obtained a civil judgment for damages against the criminal. The New York law had been used to collect funds earned by Mark David Chapman, who killed John Lennon; Jean Harris,[48] who fatally shot the doctor-author of *The Scarsdale Diet,* Herman Tarnower; and R. Foster Winans, the former reporter found guilty of selling information gathered during the course of his employment by the *Wall Street Journal.* Similar laws were in effect in forty-one other states and at the federal level.

Simon & Schuster mounted its challenge to the New York law in 1986 when the Crime Victims Board sought to collect the proceeds from *Wiseguy,* a book written by Nicholas Pileggi and based on extensive interviews with Henry Hill, an admitted gangster. Hill's most notable exploit was his involvement in the theft of $6 million from Lufthansa Airlines in 1978. After his arrest in 1980, Hill was granted immunity from prosecution in exchange for his testimony against other mobsters. He assumed a new identity and dropped from sight. At the time the board approached Simon & Schuster, the publisher had paid Hill's literary agent $96,260 in advances and royalties and was holding another $27,958 for payment to Hill. Simon & Schuster sued in a federal district court in New York City, asking that the Son of Sam law be declared unconstitutional. That court found nothing in the law that violated the First Amendment. The U.S. Court of Appeals for the Second Circuit affirmed. A unanimous Supreme Court reversed.

The decision, written by Justice O'Connor, treated the New York law as a form of taxation of the media. And because the tax was imposed on only one kind of speech— accounts of crime produced by, or in cooperation with, the criminals or suspects involved—it clearly was content based. Citing *Leathers,* O'Connor wrote: "A statute is presumptively inconsistent with the First Amendment if it imposes a financial burden on speakers because of the content of their speech."

O'Connor, quoting from *Arkansas Writers' Project,* said that for New York to justify a statute that placed financial disincentives on speech based on its content, New York would have to show that its regulation served a compelling state interest and was narrowly drafted to achieve that interest. She said that New York did have a compelling interest in ensuring that victims were compensated by those who harmed them and even in seeing to it that criminals did not profit from their crimes, but this statute

---

47. New York's law was never actually used to capture earnings by Son of Sam, an alias used by David Berkowitz. Berkowitz was found to be incompetent to stand trial, and at that time the statute applied only to criminals who had been convicted.

48. Mrs. Harris was paroled in early 1993 after serving twelve years in prison. She had been convicted of second-degree murder.

Wiseguy is a book based on the life of Henry Hill, a self-declared gangster who was granted immunity from prosecution in exchange for his testimony against criminal colleagues. The Supreme Court ruled that a New York statute, called the "Son of Sam" law and which would have prevented Hill from collecting earnings from the book, is unconstitutional. New York has since redrafted the statute.

was so poorly drafted for those ends that it would have included anyone who admitted or was accused of criminal wrongdoing. Had such a statute been in effect at the place and time of publication, it would have escrowed payments to Malcolm X, Henry David Thoreau, Saint Augustine, Emma Goldman, Martin Luther King, Jr., Sir Walter Raleigh, Jesse Jackson, and Bertrand Russell. It was so overly inclusive that even an elderly writer's brief recollection of a youthful crime, despite the fact that the statute of limitations had long since run out, would transfer the writer's income from these remembrances to the board for five years.

O'Connor's reliance on the *Leathers* and *Arkansas Writers' Project* opinions drew a strong objection from Justice Anthony Kennedy, who nevertheless concurred in the result. He said that her quotation from *Arkansas Writers' Project* conceded too quickly that tax statutes can single out the media for special treatment if the state can "show that its regulation is necessary to serve a compelling state interest and is narrowly drawn to achieve that end." In Kennedy's view, this statement could "be read as a concession that states may censor speech whenever they believe there is a compelling justification for doing so." He added, "Our precedents and traditions allow no such inference." Had he been writing for the Court, he would have ruled "that the New York statute amounts to raw censorship based on content, censorship forbidden by the text of the First Amendment and well-settled principles protecting speech and the press. That ought to end the matter."

Justice Blackmun also expressed a reservation while concurring in the result. In his opinion, O'Connor had understated the problems with the statute. As he saw it, the New York statute "is both under inclusive and over inclusive and . . . we should say so." Under settled First Amendment principles, either fault would be enough to condemn the law. Such a holding, he said, would have given lower courts better guidance in considering what to do with the laws in effect in other states.

In response to the Court, the New York legislature in 1992 approved a revised Son of Sam law. The new statute attempts to avoid the Court's First Amendment objections by requiring judges to order defendants to pay reparations, regardless of their ability to pay or the sources of their income. Instead of taxing criminals for their speech, the statute would make criminals the debtors of their victims. The court order for reparations would act as a lien on any assets related to the crime—not just books and writings about the crime—and would give victims priority over other creditors in collecting from those assets. The statute also extends the time a victim has to file for civil damages from one to seven years.

Where the validity of other state statutes has been left in doubt because of the Court's decision in *Simon & Schuster,* crime victims have used their own initiative to capture earnings or discourage criminals from profiting from crime stories. For example, the parents of a twelve-year-old girl who was tortured and burned to death sued the killers for $1 billion in an attempt to discourage them from trying to cut a financially rewarding deal with the media. The convicted killers were two teen-aged girls whom the court sentenced to sixty years in prison. "Obviously, we will never collect $1 billion in damages," the parents' attorney told the Associated Press. "But when considering the value of Shanda's life to her family, why should we consider anything less . . . ?"[49]

MEDIA EMPLOYMENT PRACTICES ———————

As we have seen, the media are subject to the same rules that apply to businesses in general. Only if those rules have the effect of threatening the widespread and robust dissemination of ideas will the First Amendment intervene. Regulations that single out some media for adverse treatment or regulations based on the content of messages are suspect. But most business regulations do neither. Most business regulations are concerned with protecting a market-based economic system by manipulating its fundamental elements—capital investment, competition, innovation, and labor.

All media managers need to be concerned to some extent with antitrust and intellectual property law, and with the rules involving marketing, insurance, securities, banking practices, and taxes. But it is with the regulations that involve labor that they frequently find themselves spending a disproportionate amount of energy. Competent managers of newspapers, magazines, advertising agencies, public relations firms, or broadcast stations need to know something about the rights of organized as well as unorganized labor; they need to know something about making employment contracts;

---

49. Associated Press, "Torture Victim's Parents Sue Girls," *Herald-Times,* Bloomington, Ind., 8 January 1993, p. C1.

and they need to know something about the rights of employees to be treated without discrimination or harassment.

The overall vastness of business law is beyond the scope of this text, but it is worth pausing for a bit to look at three areas that seem to have the most immediate impact on media employees and their managers—hiring and firing, overtime pay, and discrimination.

Hiring and Firing

A San Antonio television reporter was fired because, in the view of his station management, he was rude to President George Bush during a press conference.[50] A newspaper editor in Pennsylvania was fired because he insulted a congressman.[51] An editor and a reporter in Iowa were fired because they were active in a right-to-life group at their church.[52] An editorial writer for the Associated Press was fired for engaging in union activity.[53] A telemarketer for the *Milwaukee Journal* and the *Milwaukee Sentinel* was fired for falsely claiming that she had found a syringe in a can of Pepsi at work.[54] A reporter for NBC News was fired for refusing an assignment in the Balkans.[55]

There are many reasons why an employee can be fired—tardiness, drug use, incompetence, insubordination, misuse of funds, conflict of interest, to name a few. A decision to fire an employee is always a serious matter, but not an uncommon one. Even among the most diligent reporters, designers, copywriters, and public relations practitioners, job security is uncertain in an industry that is constantly changing technologically and constantly demanding that employees perform—sometimes publicly—under great pressure.

The legal rule that for centuries has defined the basic relationship between an employer and an employee is the doctrine of employment "at will." Employment at will means that employers have the right to fire with impunity, for any or no reason, workers who are not otherwise protected by contracts or statutes. Although this continues to be the basic rule, it has been greatly eroded during the past thirty years, as employees have complained to the courts about how their bosses treated them.

Most employers today who think they can fire workers for any reason or no reason are in for something of a shock. In a nutshell, some of the major exceptions to employment at will are discussed in the following sections.

THE MEAN EMPLOYER.   An employee who is fired may sue to recover damages for the tortious conduct of his employer. For example, a case for intentional infliction of emotional distress might be made because the manner of termination was outrageous

50. Associated Press, "Reporter Fired after Questioning Bush," *Herald-Times,* Bloomington, Ind., 1 March 1992, p. A5.
51. "Fired Editor Files Lawsuit," *Editor & Publisher,* 5 March 1994, p. 19.
52. Pam Hoffman, "Pro-Life Editor, Reporter Sue Former Employer," *Editor & Publisher,* 9 March 1991, p. 37.
53. Associated Press v. National Labor Relations Board, 301 U.S. 103, 57 S.Ct.650, 81 L.Ed. 953, 1 Med.L.Rptr. 2689 (1937).
54. "Fired Employee Gets Prison in 'Tampering,'" *Editor & Publisher,* 18 December 1993, p. 30.
55. "NBC News and Kent Settle Lawsuit," *New York Times,* 17 March 1994, p. B4.

and caused serious emotional distress. A case for defamation might be made because the termination was accompanied by derogatory statements made to people with no need to know. A case for negligence might be made because the employer failed to advise the employee in a timely manner that he was to be terminated.[56] A case for fraud might be made because an employer deceived the employee in order to get him or her to act in a way that was injurious to the employee.

THE VINDICTIVE EMPLOYER.   An employee who is fired may sue to recover damages on public policy grounds. For example, a case might be made that the employee was fired because he or she reported unlawful conduct of the employer, such as failing to comply with FCC regulations; refused to do something illegal, such as price fixing or committing perjury; exercised a legal right or privilege, such as filing a workers' compensation claim; satisfied a legal duty, such as serving on a jury; or refused to take a polygraph test.

THE UNFAITHFUL EMPLOYER.   An employee who is fired may sue to recover damages for the breach of an implied contract. For example, a case might be made that the employer created an implied contract by orally agreeing not to fire the employee except under certain circumstances, such as unsatisfactory performance or misconduct.[57] Since not all employment contracts have to be in writing, promises that are made to induce an employee to work for the company or stay on the job can be as binding as if they were formally produced.

Or a fired employee may consider suing the employer because a handbook or brochure given to employees implied that jobs were secure and that no one would be fired except for cause. As simple a thing as a handbook's troublesome phrase referring to employees as "permanent" could lead to such a lawsuit. Courts have held that employers are bound by any policy manuals they publish and distribute to employees, even if there are no other contractual arrangements.[58]

THE UNFAIR EMPLOYER.   A few states, notably Massachusetts, New Hampshire, and California, have recognized a covenant of good faith and fair dealing.[59] Employees have recovered damages because they were sexually harassed, because they were fired so that an employer could avoid paying commissions or pensions, and because they were fired without a reason, despite long-time employment and dedication to the company.[60]

Many broadcast personalities refuse to work without a written contract that clearly spells out the terms of employment. Often they hire agents to negotiate the terms for them. The same is true of many book authors. Some newspaper employees work under collective-bargaining agreements, but most work at the discretion of employers, tempered somewhat by published company policies. In any case, employers and

---

56.   Chamberlain v. Bissell, Inc., 547 F.Supp. 1067 (W.D.Mich. 1982).
57.   Phillip Perry, "Terminating Employees," *Editor & Publisher,* 9 March 1991, p. 48.
58.   Rodgers v. Flint Journal, 779 F.Supp. 70 (E.D.Mich. 1991). See Ralph H. Baxter, Jr., "Avoiding Liability in Firing Employees," *National Law Journal,* 12 September 1983.
59.   See Esther S. Bushman, "Wrongful Discharge," *Case & Comment,* May–June 1989, p. 3.
60.   Ralph H. Baxter, Jr., *Manager's Guide to Lawful Terminations* (New York: Executive Enterprise Publications Co., 1983).

employees in the media are wise to be aware of the pitfalls when expectations are unclear or motives are dishonest. Management consultants advise media managers never to fire an employee in anger or without compassion. They suggest that managers who are unhappy with the performance of an employee might avoid problems if they do the following:

— Keep records. A file that documents the employee's unsatisfactory conduct—his intoxication, insubordination, conflicts of interest, disorderly conduct, unexcused absences, dishonesty, neglect of duty, revealing of confidential information, inaccuracy, or missed deadlines—may convince a worker that protesting a dismissal is futile.

— Use progressive discipline. A file that shows that the employee was warned and was given opportunities to correct or improve will go far to head off complaints of surprise or deceit. The record would do well to show that there were informal meetings and oral reprimands, followed by written deficiency notices and formal evaluation conferences. Assuming that those devices failed to improve performance, the record might show further attempts short of firing, such as unsatisfactory-performance evaluations and suspension without pay.

— Terminate humanely. That the end is coming should be no surprise to the employee. He or she may not like it, but it shouldn't be something out of the blue. The manager should be as unemotional as possible and should explain simply that things have not worked out, citing the previous meetings. It is not a good idea to be apologetic, to rehash past sins, or to suggest that there are other, undocumented, reasons for the decision. It is a good idea to make arrangements immediately for the employee to be paid whatever salary, severance, vacation, or sick pay is owed.

Overtime Pay

The media are not exempt from the requirements of federal labor laws, including the National Labor Relations Act (NLRA), which governs union activity, and the National Labor Standards Act (NLSA), which governs time and wages.[61] The NLSA has been of particular interest to broadcast and print journalists because it requires overtime pay for employees who work more than forty hours a week, with one important exception: Section 213(a)(1) exempts employees who occupy "bona fide executive, administrative, or professional" positions. News organizations have argued repeatedly that reporters, copy editors, assignment editors, directors, and producers are professionals, administrators, or executives and thus don't have to be paid overtime. They have had little success with that argument.

Nineteen general-assignment reporters, producers, directors, and assignment edi-

---

61. Associated Press v. National Labor Relations Board, 301 U.S. 103, 57 S.Ct. 650, 81 L.Ed. 953, 1 Med.L.Rptr. 2689 (1937) (the National Labor Relations Act). Mabee v. White Plains Publishing Co., 327 U.S. 178, 66 S.Ct. 511, 90 L.Ed. 607 (1946) (the Fair Labor Standards Act), 29 U.S.C. §§ 201–219 (1988).

tors sued KDFW-TV in Dallas-Fort Worth, Texas, on the grounds that the station had violated the NLSA by requiring them to work more than forty hours a week without overtime pay.[62] The trial court found for the journalists, and KDFW appealed. The Fifth Circuit Court of Appeals noted that the Labor Department's interpretation of the exception for professionals required employees to have as their primary duty the kind of work that is "original and creative in character in a recognized field of artistic endeavor," the success of which depends "primarily on the invention, imagination, or talent of the employee." In the case of the reporters, the court agreed with the trial judge that the KDFW reporters did from time to time do original and creative work. Nevertheless, the approach they took to their day-to-day jobs was mostly dictated by management, and the stories they produced were not analytic, interpretive, or original.

As for the news producers, the court said that they produce their work in a well-defined framework of management policies and editorial convention. "To the extent that they exercise discretion," said the court, "it is governed more by skill and experience than by originality and creativity." The facts did not support KDFW's contention that its producers were creative professionals.

Nor were they exempt as administrators. The court noted that the producers' responsibilities began and ended with their ten- to twelve-minute portion of the newscast. They were not responsible for setting business policy, planning objectives, negotiating salary or benefits with personnel, or any of the other activities that might be typical of administrators. Their duties were more closely related to production than to administration.

As for the directors and the assignment editors, the court found the former to be highly skilled coordinators but not managers and the latter to have no real authority at all. Neither type of employee was exempt, as KDFW argued, as administrators or executives.

The *Washington Post* did somewhat better than KDFW. It convinced a U.S. district court to issue a summary judgment finding that thirteen reporters and editors at the *Post* were not entitled to time-and-a-half pay for overtime because they were professionals.[63] Judge Gerhard A. Gesell said that the employees produced "original and creative writing of high quality within the meaning of the regulations; they have far more than general intelligence; they are thoroughly trained before employment; their performance as writers is individual, interpretative and analytical both in the writing itself and in the process by which the writing must be prepared; and their performance is measured and paid accordingly."

It was a short-lived victory for the *Post,* however. On appeal, the District of Columbia Circuit Court said that the trial judge was wrong in granting summary judgment, because there were unresolved factual questions as to whether the work by the reporters and editors was original or creative.[64] The circuit court noted that one reporter, Thomas R. Sherwood, specifically contested the *Post*'s assertion that the journalists' work was predominantly original, creative, or analytical. Sherwood's description of the reporter's job was considerably more modest than that described by Judge

---

62. Dalheim v. KDFW-TV, 918 F.2d 1220, 18 Med.L.Rptr. 1657 (5th Cir. 1990).
63. George Garneau, "Judge Says Reporters Are Professionals," *Editor & Publisher,* 23 January 1988, p. 25.
64. Sherwood v. Washington Post, 871 F.2d 1144, 16 Med.L.Rptr. 1665 (D.C. Cir. 1989).

Gesell. "If you are accurate, brief, and clear, then you have performed your job to report information." Sherwood said that the *Post* separately labeled news stories that were creative or analytical as "news analysis" or "commentary," and he had few of the latter. The *Post,* on the other hand, said it expected all its reporters and editors to "produce original and creative reporting on news events." Clearly, said the court, there is a factual dispute about whether the work is or is not original or creative, and it remanded the case for trial.

Whether specific employees are in the category of professionals, administrators, and executives for purposes of overtime pay depends on the facts of a particular case. What are the responsibilities and expectations of the job? How closely aligned is the job with management functions? What kind of authority and discretion does the employee have? A bureau chief who has no authority to hire, fire, or evaluate employees, for example, is not a supervisor;[65] but a sports editor who has the discretion to discipline employees in his or her department and to authorize overtime pay is a supervisor.[66] Editorial writers are so closely aligned with management and policy that they likely qualify as executives even if they do not have authority over other employees.[67] An employee whose primary responsibility is analysis or commentary is also likely to qualify as a creative professional.

But the people on a publications or broadcast staff who are the most likely to be called on to work overtime—reporters, copy editors, producers, directors, and photographers—will most likely not be considered "creative professionals." That evaluation may be a blow to their egos, but it is generally a help to their pocketbooks.

Discrimination

The Equal Employment Opportunity Commission (EEOC) handles an average of sixty thousand job-related complaints a year.[68] About 30 percent of the complaints are based on charges of sexual harassment or gender discrimination, 40 percent are based on discrimination because of race, and the remaining 30 percent are based on age, religion, or physical disabilities.

The EEOC is the agency that enforces Title VII of the Civil Rights Act, which prohibits employment discrimination because of race, color, religion, sex, or national origin.[69] The agency also enforces laws that ban employment discrimination because of age[70] or physical disability.[71] An exception to such laws is a decision to discriminate that is based on a bona fide occupational qualification necessary to operate the enterprise. For example, choosing men to play male roles as actors and hiring Catholics to

65. Passaic Daily News v. NLRB, 736 F.2d 1543, 10 Med.L.Rptr. 1905 (D.C. Cir. 1984).
66. NLRB v. Medina County Publications, 735 F.2d 199 (6th Cir. 1984).
67. Wichita Eagle & Beacon Publishing Co. v. NLRB, 480 F.2d 52 (10th Cir. 1973), cert. denied, 416 U.S. 982 (1974).
68. Richard Kell (Associated Press), "Discrimination Complaints Rise," *Indiana Daily Student,* 2 December 1992, p. 12.
69. 42 U.S.C. § 2000e-2.
70. 29 U.S.C. § 621.
71. 42 U.S.C. § 12112.

teach in Catholic elementary schools are considered decisions that are based on bona fide occupational qualifications.

If a business employs at least fifteen workers, it is bound by Title VII and the regulations of the EEOC. Thus, nearly all media companies, even some very small newspapers or radio stations, are concerned about the legal consequences of practices that produce differences in pay or opportunity among employees.

GENDER DISCRIMINATION. The EEOC guidelines make it clear that no employment decision can be based on assumptions about the characteristics of people in general— for example, that the turnover rate among women is greater than among men, or that men are less capable of assembling intricate equipment, or that women are less capable of aggressive salesmanship. Even if such generalizations could be established as statistically true, they would not justify discrimination in a particular case. The guiding principle is that individuals are to be treated on the basis of their individual capacities and not on the basis of any characteristics generally attributed to the group.

For publishers, the commission has a special warning against the use of help-wanted advertisements that indicate a gender preference, unless gender is a bona fide occupational qualification for the particular job involved. Classified advertisements that list job opportunities under columns headed "Male" or ""Female" are considered by the EEOC as discriminatory.[72]

SEXUAL HARASSMENT. The EEOC describes sexual harassment as unwelcome sexual advances, requests for sexual favors, and other verbal or physical conduct of a sexual nature when

1. Submission is made a condition of employment.

2. Submission or rejection is the basis of employment decisions.

3. Such conduct interferes with work performance or creates an intimidating, hostile, or offensive working environment.

This definition says that two different kinds of harassment are possible, and both are wrong: The first is *quid pro quo harassment,* in which an employee typically is pressured to submit to sexual advances as a condition for receiving job benefits. The second is *hostile-environment harassment,* which involves conduct of a sexual nature severe enough that it creates a hostile or offensive workplace. Hostile-environment harassment includes such things as repeated and offensive leers, stares, whistles, sexist language, dirty jokes, pinup pictures, sexual propositions, offensive touching, and office promiscuity.[73] If an employer knows or should have known of sexual harassment

---

72. 29 C.F.R. § 1604.5. The Supreme Court has upheld the view that gender-based labels further discrimination and are not protected by the First Amendment. Pittsburgh Press Co. v. Pittsburgh Commission on Human Rights, 413 U.S. 376, 93 S.Ct. 2553, 37 L.Ed.2d 669, 1 Med.L.Rptr. 1908 (1973). See Chapter 11, "Advertising."

73. Kingsley R. Browne, "Sexual Protectionism in the Work Place?" *Detroit News,* 20 October 1991, p. B3. Nina Burleigh and Stephanie B. Goldberg, "Breaking the Silence," *ABA Journal,* August 1989, p. 46+.

and fails to take immediate, corrective steps, the employer, as well as the offending party, is liable.[74]

AGE AND RELIGION.   In 1992, the EEOC recovered $65.6 million from employers in settlements. Most of it ($50.7 million) was paid to settle age discrimination suits.

The federal Age Discrimination in Employment Act, as well as many state statutes, prohibits employers from discriminating against individuals because of age when hiring, promoting, or deciding compensation.[75] The act was intended to prevent arbitrary age barriers and to encourage managers to base opportunities on merit and ability.[76] It is intended to protect those people who are most likely to be discriminated against, those between 40 and 65 years old. As with gender, the EEOC warns publishers that certain wording in job advertisements can violate the act. Such limiting terms and phrases as "age 25 to 35," "young," "college student," "recent college graduate," "boy," or "girl" may deter the employment of older persons. The EEOC likewise warns against terms such as "age 40 to 50," "age over 65," "retired person," or "supplement your pension" because they discriminate against others within the protected group of 40- to 65-year-olds.

Title VII of the Civil Rights Act requires employers to accommodate the religious practices of an employee unless the employer can demonstrate that accommodation would result in an undue hardship on the business. The EEOC has made it clear that it reads "religious practices" broadly and includes moral or ethical beliefs about what is right or wrong, if held sincerely and with the strength that others hold traditional religious views.[77] The EEOC guidelines suggest that employers generally can accommodate their employees' religious beliefs by helping employees obtain substitutes to cover job responsibilities, by providing flexible work schedules, such as staggering work hours or allowing an employee to make up time lost, or by changing job assignments or making lateral transfers. If there is more than one means of accommodating an employee, the commission reserves the right to determine whether the one chosen was reasonable.[78]

NATIONAL ORIGIN.   The EEOC says that discrimination based on national origin includes not only discrimination based on an individual's ancestry or place of birth, but also discrimination based on physical, cultural, or linguistic characteristics that a person shares with a national group. The commission guidelines indicate, moreover, that the EEOC is concerned about behavior that denies employment opportunities because a person is married to or associated with a person of a national origin group, or because a person's name, school, or church is associated with a national origin group.[79]

The commission has warned that certain job selection criteria may be discriminatory, including height or weight requirements that exclude certain ethnic groups, fluency in English, or an American education. The commission presumes that any com-

---

74. For more on sexual harassment in media, see American Society of Newspaper Editors, "Harassment: It's about Power, Not Sex," *Bulletin,* January/February 1992.
75. 29 U.S.C. § 621; 29 C.F.R. § 1625.
76. Martha McCarthy, *Discrimination in Employment: The Evolving Law* (Topeka, Kan.: National Organization on Legal Problems of Education, 1983), pp. 50–56.
77. See United States v. Seeger, 380 U.S. 163 (1965) and Welsh v. United States, 398 U.S. 333 (1970).
78. 29 C.F.R. § 1605.
79. 29 C.F.R. § 1606.1.

pany rule that requires employees to speak only English at all times in the workplace violates Title VII of the Civil Rights Act. A person's primary language is often an essential national origin characteristic. However, an employer may require that English be spoken at those times when there is a business necessity for English.

As with gender, harassment on the basis of national origin can result in liability for media managers. Ethnic slurs are harassment, under EEOC guidelines, when they have the purpose or the effect of creating a hostile working environment, or interfere with an individual's work performance or employment opportunities.

DISABILITIES.   The Americans with Disabilities Act was signed by President George Bush in 1990.[80] That year the unemployment rate for people with disabilities was about 65 percent,[81] and of those who were working, not many were in media jobs. A survey by the American Society of Newspaper Editors in 1992, for example, found that only about one-third of 326 responding newspapers employed people with disabilities.[82]

According to the act, businesses must be prepared to hire qualified disabled people and integrate them into the workplace. The law prohibits discrimination against qualified persons with disabilities in job applications, hiring, firing, advancement, compensation, job training, or in any other conditions or privileges of employment. The law describes a qualified disabled person as one who, with reasonable accommodation, can perform the essential functions of a job. Reasonable accommodation includes things such as making existing offices readily accessible, restructuring or reassigning jobs, changing work schedules, buying or modifying equipment, adjusting examinations and training materials, and providing readers or interpreters. For some media, reasonable accommodation has meant new elevators, ramps, chair rails along walls, cups at drinking fountains, and clipboards with pens for people who cannot reach a counter. Employers are not required to make changes that would require significant difficulty or expense when considered in light of the employer's size, financial resources, and the nature of the operation. Employers are not expected to lower quality to accommodate someone with a disability, nor are they required to provide personal items such as glasses or hearing aids.

RACE.   It goes almost without saying that a manager who discriminates among employees or potential employees because of their race runs afoul of the Civil Rights Act. Yet it is astounding that as the twentieth century closes, American media—particularly American newspapers—have made such little progress in diversifying the racial composition of their organizations. Sidmel Estes-Sumpter, the president of National Black Journalists, noted grimly in 1992 that if the newspaper industry hoped to meet the hiring goals set by other industry groups, the number of African-Americans would have to triple in newsrooms by the year 2000.[83] In 1995, minority journalists made up 10.91 percent of newsroom employees, compared with 8.7 percent in 1991.[84] Forty-five per-

---

80. 42 U.S.C. § 12112.
81. William G. Stothers, "Where's Disability (Wo)man? . . . Tick, Tock, Tick, Tock. Time's Up!" *Quill,* May 1992, p. 18.
82. William G. Stothers, "Tips for Improving Our Performance," *Quill,* May 1992, p. 19.
83. "Industry's Diversity Action Plan Nets Warm but Cautious Response," *Quill,* June 1992, p. 14.
84. William Glaberson, "Slight Increase Is Reported for Minorities in Newsroom," *New York Times,* 5 April 1995, p. A14.

cent of all daily newspapers employ no minorities.[85] Broadcast is doing somewhat better. Minorities make up 17.4 percent of all television news personnel. In radio, the number is 12 percent.[86] But television management is surprisingly lacking in racial diversity. A study by the *Morris Memo* indicates that in 1992 there were only five minority news directors and four vice presidents of news at the 260 commercial TV stations in the hundred largest markets.[87]

This chapter has reminded us that media are like people with split personalities. In one part of their being, the media are privileged vehicles for the dissemination of news and opinion protected by the First Amendment. We saw earlier that the media are free to criticize government officials in the strongest terms, even to the point of calling for their overthrow. And the First Amendment's protection is not limited to publications that are true, fair, or dedicated to a noble purpose. Freedom of the press protects some falsehoods so that a strict insistence on truth won't dampen the fire of public debate. The media are protected even though they choose to deal in what many members of society consider trashy portrayals of sexual activity that borders on the obscene, of violence, and of repugnant ideas. Even advertising, long considered beyond the reach of the First Amendment, now is protected unless it is false or seeks buyers for an illegal product or service. In short, because of the First Amendment, the content of the media is almost beyond regulation except by the forces of the marketplace.

In the other part of their being, the media are subject to regulation, not only by the marketplace but by the government. Almost all media are profit-seeking business organizations. They must take in enough money from customers and advertisers to cover their costs, or they will go out of business. Some media have become giant conglomerates with revenues from circulation, advertising, and the sale of products running into billions of dollars a year. Annual pretax profits reaching 10 to 20 percent—even in times of recession—have been common in the industry.

Therefore, it is not surprising that courts have held that in their business operations the media are to be treated like anyone else. More than forty years ago the Supreme Court said that the First Amendment does not protect the news media from laws that regulate their business aspects. In that instance, the Court held that publishers could not treat the Associated Press like a private club. Their attempt to deny the service's news report to publishers who were in competition with them violated antitrust law. The Court later rejected joint operating agreements as a business arrangement, as it would have for other businesses. The power of Congress and the Newspaper Preservation Act were required in order to make joint operating agreements a legal exception to the antitrust laws. Even then, the Newspaper Preservation Act was at its heart an attempt to preserve competing voices, not failing businesses. Such arrangements today are controversial and remain in effect in only seventeen cities.

Even in their business aspects, however, the media are not completely without First Amendment protection. In two sensitive areas, circulation and taxation, the Supreme Court has limited the power of government. Because of the early efforts of the Jehovah's Witnesses, the Supreme Court has said that people have a right to dissemi-

---

85. Ibid.
86. Ed Avis, "Broadcast Media Need the Color, Too," *Quill,* January/February 1993, p. 25.
87. "Minority TV Managers Rare," *Quill,* June 1992, p. 15.

nate—even sell—ideas in public places. In modern times, this ruling has led to decisions holding that the First Amendment protects the right to place news racks on public property, subject only to narrowly tailored regulations designed to protect the quality of city life and the right of others to use the streets and sidewalks safely.

The Supreme Court has held that a discriminatory tax imposed on media violates the First Amendment. The Court said that if it were to recognize a right to tax the media in ways not applied to other kinds of businesses, it would open the door for government to use the power to tax to influence or destroy its critics. That, said Justice Sutherland, would restore the licensing power condemned by John Milton in *Areopagitica*.

Finally, we have seen that the media are exempt neither from the provisions of the Civil Rights Act nor from the other federal provisions designed to assure all Americans of the opportunity for employment in an environment free from sexual or racial harassment and discrimination. The media as businesses are expected to behave at least as well as other businesses in their hiring and firing practices and in paying employees for the extra work they do. The protections afforded media by the First Amendment do not exempt them from their obligations to compete fairly and honestly in the business world.

In the Professional World

In the 1960s, President John F. Kennedy became concerned about what he saw as the disappearance of the marketplace of ideas. In part, his concern was political. Few newspapers had supported him editorially in his campaign for the presidency in 1960. He also knew that no Democratic presidential candidate, not even Franklin D. Roosevelt in the midst of World War II, had ever won much backing from newspaper publishers. But Kennedy also noted a steady decline in the number of cities with two truly competing daily newspapers, and a growth in newspaper chains. Thus he embarked on what has proved to be a losing battle to encourage competing independent newspapers. Today, only a handful of cities support two newspapers, and more than two-thirds of all newspapers are part of a chain.

With the benefit of hindsight, we see that President Kennedy's view of the marketplace of ideas clearly was too narrow. The fewer than fifteen hundred daily newspapers still in business are only a small part of the marketplace in which all media, print and electronic, scramble for an audience and for advertising revenue. Daily newspapers are outnumbered by more than twelve thousand radio and television stations. They are outnumbered three to one by weekly newspapers, which enjoy continued growth in the suburbs. However, the popular belief that the daily newspaper in a one-newspaper town is a news and advertising monopoly is an idea that continues to persist unabated.

For that reason, publishers of daily newspapers, no matter the size of their market, must operate with awareness of the antitrust implications that flow from their decisions. Failure to do so can lead to the unproductive expense of fighting an antitrust suit. In recent years, publishers have come under attack because competitors have complained of the practice of selling advertising space below cost, and advertisers have complained of gouging and tying arrangements that pushed advertising rates too high. Publishers have learned to be careful and circumspect about publishing weekly advertising products with free distribution and cut-rate advertising, or establishing zoned editions with discounted advertising, lest they be seen as attempts to drive competitors out of business. Publishers also have encountered antitrust problems when they have attempted to change from juvenile to adult carriers or when they have insisted that carriers sell the paper for the price set by the publisher.

Entanglement in the antitrust thicket is not confined to newspaper publishers. Cable television franchising arrangements and decisions by cable operators to carry some stations, but not others, have led to antitrust actions.

Thus, in the professional world there is a vigorous marketplace—for ideas and entertainment, to be sure, but especially for advertising. And judging from the court cases, that marketplace contains many operators who are on the alert for practices that seem to give others an unfair competitive advantage.

The competition for advertising is linked to equally intense competition for audiences. All media use market surveys not only to determine the nature of their audience, but to probe its likes and dislikes, its varied interests, and its spending habits. Television programs literally live or die by the Nielsen Ratings. Newspapers, in a move to improve their own ratings, have moved to shorter stories and greater use of graphics and color. Some have developed whole sections that resemble magazines, sections on recreation, dining, travel, sports, and business—all of this to meet the expectations of particular segments of the audience. Some idealistic editors claim to feel uncomfortable with such a blatant marketing approach to news, arguing that it is pandering to the tastes of the unwashed. But most have accepted it, concluding that if some adjustments can ensure a financially secure newspaper, then they can afford to give their readers what they need along with what they say they want.

With newspapers, the competition for an audience has affected circulation methods, too. Traditionally, dailies, particularly those outside the major metropolitan areas, have relied on subscriptions for 95 percent of their circulation. However, the same marketing surveys that probed reader interest in content also led to the discovery that a considerable number of people neither read nor want to read a newspaper every day. They want to be able to buy a newspaper whenever they feel like it. That discovery, coupled with the rise of national and regional newspapers, has led to the proliferation of news racks. In many cities that have only one daily newspaper, it is not unusual for shoppers to confront batteries of racks offering the local paper, *USA Today,* the national edition of the *New York Times,* the *Wall Street Journal,* and three or four regional newspapers. Single-copy sales have become so important to publishers that it has been worth spending money to protect their access to city sidewalks, subways, and airports. For that reason publishers have been willing to challenge attempts by local government to license or restrict racks. However, litigation usually is a last resort. Negotiation, coupled with a reminder that newspaper distribution is a protected First Amendment activity, is the cheaper and the preferred course. Lawyers advise publishers to cooperate with any reasonable regulations and to respond quickly and positively to complaints about service or potential hazards. It is not only good business, it is good citizenship. No publisher should want to contribute to the ugliness and congestion of urban life by littering the public ways with discordant distractions.

No business issue is more important than the treatment of employees. Media organizations—whether newspapers, broadcasters, advertising agencies, or public relations firms—are called to a new sensitivity toward the people who have joined their enterprise. No one likes to work for a boss who is mean, who teases and harasses, or who is preoccupied with his or her personal appetites for power, greed, or sex.

Job satisfaction among journalists has declined dramatically since 1971. Indiana University professors David Weaver and G. Cleveland Wilhoit reported in early 1993 that only 27 percent of journalists said they were very satisfied with their jobs, compared to almost 50 percent twenty years earlier. African-Americans and Asian-Americans were the least likely to be very satisfied.[88] Unhappy workers are not the kind of people who are likely to take the time to do all they can to serve their company or their public. Media managers face the task of finding ways to ensure that good people are encouraged, trained, respected, retained, and rewarded.

FOR REVIEW

1. Three principles applied by the Supreme Court in the *Indiana Farmer's Guide* and *Associated Press* cases have made virtually all media subject to antitrust law. What are those principles and what is their meaning?

2. Can a commercial newspaper refuse advertising in all circumstances? Why or why not?

3. What rule of law is applied by the courts to determine whether advertising rates or other business practices are in compliance with antitrust law?

4. What factors seem to have motivated President Kennedy's attempt to use antitrust law to preserve a marketplace of ideas? Was his view of that marketplace valid? What is the nature of the marketplace today?

5. Define a joint operating agreement. What is the purpose of such an agreement?

6. What did the Supreme Court say about joint operating agreements in the *Citizen Publishing Co.* case? With the benefit of hindsight, what has been the long-range effect of that decision?

7. What is the law in respect to joint ownership of newspapers and broadcast stations in the same city?

---

88. Weaver and Wilhoit, "Who Are We? A Brief Status Report on Jobs and Work," p. 45.

8. What is the test to determine valid time, manner, and place regulations? How does this test differ from the test used in the *Central Hudson* and *Fox* cases to test the validity of a commercial speech regulation?

9. What principles with respect to taxation of the media were established by the Supreme Court in the *Grosjean* and *Minneapolis Star and Tribune* cases?

10. How does the EEOC define sexual harassment? Can you think of some examples of what would make an office become an intimidating, hostile, or offensive working environment? Do you see any First Amendment problems with regulations that attempt to control hateful speech in a work environment because of its content?

GLOSSARY

acquit In contract law, to release from an obligation; in criminal law, to release from a charge of guilt.

actual damages; actual injury See compensatory damages.

actual malice The publication of defamatory material with reckless disregard for the truth or knowledge of its falsity. Actual malice should be distinguished from "malice" or "ill will."

adversary hearing A legal procedure in which evidence is heard from opposing parties. An adversary hearing should be distinguished from an ex parte hearing, in which evidence is heard from only one party.

affidavit A written account of facts, sworn to as true.

agency record A body of documents in physical possession of a federal agency and subject to the Freedom of Information Act.

antitrust laws Statutes designed to prevent businesses from conspiring, contracting, combining, or using monopoly power to interfere with free trade among competitors. The most important antitrust laws are the Sherman Act and the Clayton Act.

appeal A plea to a higher court to alter or overturn a judgment of a lower court because of error or injustice.

appellate court See court of appeals.

arraignment A hearing in which a criminal suspect is advised of his or her rights and asked to plead to the charges against him or her. Sometimes an arraignment is called a preliminary hearing or initial appearance.

bail Money or a bond posted to release someone from jail.

beyond a reasonable doubt The standard of proof in a criminal case, which requires that the jury be satisfied to a high degree of certainty that the crime was committed by the defendant. This standard is higher than that for most civil cases: preponderance of the evidence.

blasphemy Spoken or written words that insult a divine power.

burden of proof The duty to prove a claim in an adversary proceeding.

cause of action The legal basis of a lawsuit.

censorship The prohibition of public distribution of written, printed, filmed, spoken, or other material that is considered offensive, immoral, or dangerous to the public welfare.

certiorari An order in the form of a writ from a higher court authorizing an appeal to proceed. Often referred to simply as "cert."

circuit court In the federal system, an appellate court with jurisdiction over several judicial districts. In a state system, often, a trial court of original jurisdiction. "Circuit court" initially referred to a court system with multiple sites served by a single judge who traveled the circuit to have hearings at each site.

class action suit A legal action brought by some injured parties on behalf of themselves and all others similarly injured.

classified material Information that is restricted in access to a particular group of people. Usually applied by government to documents considered vital to national security.

clear and convincing evidence   A standard of proof sometimes used in civil lawsuits and in regulatory agency cases. This standard is higher than "preponderance of the evidence" but lower than "beyond a reasonable doubt."

commercial speech   A form of communication that is intended to promote a business or sell a product or service. Forms of commercial speech, including advertising, are entitled to more limited protection under the First Amendment than are forms of political speech.

common law   In the United States, law that is derived from judicial decisions based on usage and customs, some of which date to ancient principles recognized in English courts before the American Revolution. Common law should be distinguished from statutory law.

common pleas court   A trial court with original jurisdiction over civil and criminal cases.

commute   To change or reduce a prison sentence.

compensatory damages   Payment in money to reimburse a plaintiff for actual loss.

common carrier   An organization such as a telephone company, a bus line, or a ferry that must do business with all would-be customers.

constitutional law   The area of law that focuses on the interpretation, violation, and enforcement of a state constitution or the federal Constitution.

constitutional privilege   See constitutional right.

constitutional right   A right guaranteed in a state constitution or in the U.S. Constitution. An example of such a right is freedom of speech or assembly. Other rights not found in a constitution may be guaranteed in legislation—for example, the U.S. Civil Rights Act.

contempt   Behavior that interferes with court proceedings, impugns a court's dignity, or violates an order of a court. A judge has inherent power to punish for contempt if there is a clear and present danger to the administration of justice.

contract   A legally binding agreement in which one party makes an offer to perform certain acts, and another party accepts that offer in exchange for some kind of consideration. The consideration may be money but can be anything of value, such as information or documents.

copyright   Federal statutory protection of the ownership of an original work that has been fixed in a tangible medium of expression.

court of appeals   A court that reviews the judgments of courts of original jurisdiction.

criminal information   A document, filed by a prosecutor, that formally accuses a person of a crime. A criminal information should be distinguished from an indictment.

Criminal Syndicalism Act   A law that forbids individuals to associate for the purpose of advocating violent changes in the form of government.

cross-examination   The questioning of witnesses by the opposing party.

declassification   The process by which previously restricted information is made more widely available.

defendant   The party against whom a lawsuit is brought by a plaintiff or who is accused of a crime.

deposition   Testimony given under oath outside a trial or proceeding.

dictum   A written opinion from a judge that is not about an issue essential to deciding the case at hand. Dicta are not binding as precedent for later court actions but are often influential.

directed verdict   A court decision in favor of one side because that side's evidence is compelling or because the other side has not clearly prevailed. A directed verdict orders the jury to return a verdict in accord with the judge's order.

discovery   The pretrial process in an adversary proceeding by which participants must answer all questions and produce all documents concerning the facts of the case.

district court   In the federal system, a trial court of original jurisdiction. The United States has ninety-four federal district courts, at least one in each state.

diversity The legal basis for proceeding with a civil case under state law but in federal court because the parties are from different states.

double jeopardy The trial of a person more than once for the same crime. A new trial won by a defendant because of error in the first trial is not double jeopardy.

due process The legal principle, guaranteed by the Fourteenth Amendment, that a person may not lose rights or have interests compromised unless he or she has had an opportunity to defend those interests. In practice the principle may be merely concerned with procedure, such as the right to a hearing, but in cases where fundamental rights are at stake, due process often involves the court in a substantive determination of those rights.

entrapment An act by police, government agents, or other public officials that induces a suspect to commit a crime.

equal opportunity For the general population, the legal requirement that everyone has the same rights to benefits such as jobs. For political candidates, the federal statutory right to reach the public by radio or television.

ex parte Describing a judicial action such as a hearing, order, or injunction on behalf of one party without notice to the person adversely affected.

fair use The doctrine in copyright law holding that minimal copying of another's original material for the benefit of the public is permissible if it does not detract unduly from the commercial value of the original.

felony A serious crime. A felony should be distinguished from a misdemeanor.

grand jury A body of citizens that evaluates evidence about a crime to determine whether a suspect should be charged with having committed the crime. The grand jury should be distinguished from a petit jury.

hearing A legal proceeding during which evidence is heard so that the facts of a case may be established.

hearsay Information not personally seen or heard but based on something heard or seen by someone else. Hearsay is not admissible as evidence, because its truth cannot be tested by cross-examination.

immaterial Describing evidence that is not admissible, because it makes no difference in the case at hand.

impeach To accuse or charge a public official with wrongdoing. In legal proceedings, to raise questions about the truth of a witness's testimony.

indictment A document, filed by a grand jury, that charges a suspect with a crime. An indictment should be distinguished from a criminal information.

infringement In copyright law, the substantial copying of another's original work or copying that detracts unduly from the original's commercial value.

injunction See temporary injunction and permanent injunction.

innocent Describing a person who is free from sin, evil, or guilt. "Innocent" is not a legal term. The court can find a person guilty or not guilty of a crime, but it cannot determine whether the person is innocent. News media often use "innocent" and "not guilty" as synonyms, but such use is journalistic license rather than legal precision.

instructions The judge's directions to the jury at the close of a trial about the law and about the jury's authority to determine the facts and to draw inferences from the facts so that it can reach a verdict.

interrogatories Written questions in a civil case that are put to parties who must answer under oath. Interrogatories should be distinguished from a deposition.

intrusion Behavior that violates a person's right to privacy, for which a plaintiff may win damages.

invasion of privacy The violation of a person's right to be free from outside interference or publicity.

joint operating agreement   In antitrust law, an agreement between newspaper owners to conduct the business of two newspapers in concert. A joint operating agreement is considered legal unless it harms a competitor or freezes out potential advertisers.

jurisdiction   A court's authority to hear a case.

landmark case   An appellate court case that is often quoted by a lower court. A court case that acts as a turning point in the law.

law of contracts and commercial transactions   The area of law that governs agreements in which one party assumes the obligation to perform certain acts and the other party agrees to give consideration for that performance.

libel   A false statement, fixed in a tangible medium, that harms a person's or an organization's reputation. See slander.

matter of law   A case that raises a question that can be resolved if the law is applied to the facts.

misdemeanor   A crime that is considered less serious than a felony and punishable by a short jail term, a fine, or both.

mistrial   A trial canceled by a judge while it is going on because of an error by one of the parties or because the jury is unable to agree on a verdict.

motion to quash   A request to a court to make void a subpoena, indictment, or other order.

natural rights   According to John Locke, a seventeenth-century political philosopher, the personal rights that belong to people in the free state of nature.

negligence   Failure to exercise the care justly expected of a reasonably prudent person.

neutral reportage   The privilege of news media to report evenhandedly the claims and counterclaims in highly charged controversies without investigating each accusation. The privilege exists even when the news organization doubts the truth of the claims it reports.

not guilty   A plea by a defendant in criminal cases, or a jury's verdict of acquittal. Such a verdict means that the prosecution has failed to prove the defendant's guilt beyond a reasonable doubt; it does not mean that the defendant is innocent.

obscenity   Works which, taken as a whole and applying contemporary community standards, appeal to the prurient interest in sex, portray sexual conduct in a patently offensive way, and lack serious literary, artistic, political, or scientific value.

ordinance   A city or municipal law.

original jurisdiction   A court's authority to try a case in the first instance. Original jurisdiction generally refers to a trial court, although appellate courts under certain circumstances can originate a case and thus exercise original jurisdiction.

pardon   An order by the president or a governor to release a person who has been accused of or found guilty of a crime.

per curiam **decision**   A written opinion from a multijudge court that expresses the opinion of the court as a whole rather than the opinion of any particular judge on the panel.

permanent injunction   A court order that requires some action to be taken, or some party to refrain from taking action. See temporary injunction.

petit jury   The ordinary jury of twelve (sometimes six) citizens who serve at the trial of a civil or criminal action. The members of the petit jury are the judges of the facts and make factual determinations about what happened in the case. The petit jury should be distinguished from a grand jury.

plaintiff   A party who brings a lawsuit against a defendant.

plea   An admission or denial of guilt in a criminal case.

pleadings   Written documents, such as a complaint, answer, and reply in a civil case, that inform the court of the claims at issue. Also, the manner of making an argument in court. Pleadings should be distinguished from a plea.

plurality opinion   A judicial opinion offered by the greatest number of judges, but by less than a majority, of a multijudge panel.

police power   The inherent authority of the state to protect the health, safety, morals, and general welfare of its residents.

precedent   A judicial decision that is cited as controlling the outcome of a similar case.

preferred position   The status imputed by court decisions to First Amendment rights and certain other rights guaranteed by the Bill of Rights to protect against government attempts to prevent "harmful" speech; a doctrine used as a weapon against censorship.

preliminary hearings   Legal proceedings, preliminary to a trial, during which evidence is heard so that the facts of a case may be established. See pretrial proceedings.

preponderance of the evidence   A standard used in civil law to determine which side's evidence has been sufficient to allow it to prevail.

pretrial proceedings   Hearings held before the beginning of a trial, during which evidence that might not be admissible at a trial may be offered. See preliminary hearings.

previous restraint   See prior restraint.

prior restraint   Any attempt by government or courts to mandate the content of a medium; a form of censorship that violates the First Amendment guarantee of freedom of speech and press.

privilege   A form of legal immunity from compelled disclosure in court. Privilege generally refers to confidential communications that are protected by law.

probation   The court-ordered requirements of behavior in lieu of jail time for a party convicted of a crime.

public domain   In copyright law, material that is not protected by copyright and can be used by anyone.

punitive damages   An award made by a court to a complainant that exceeds his or her actual loss; the purpose is to punish the offender.

restraining order   A court order that temporarily forbids a party from committing some act; a form of injunction.

retraction   A statement that confesses to a mistake in an earlier statement.

right of publicity   The right of people, particularly celebrities, to control how others use their names or images.

right to know   The right, imputed to the public, of access to information about what their government is doing.

search warrant   A court order, authorized for good cause by a judicial magistrate, that allows a search of private property.

sedition   The crime of acting to overthrow the government or urging others to do so.

seditious libel   The crime of questioning the wisdom of a ruler's policies.

sentence   A judgment imposed upon a person after his or her conviction of a crime. A sentence states the punishment that is to be inflicted.

separation of powers   The doctrine that allocates to the legislature the power to make the law, to the executive the power to put it into effect, and to the judiciary the power to settle disputes arising under the law.

sequester   To isolate a jury.

shield law   A statute under which journalists are entitled to protect the confidentiality of their sources and/or their notes.

slander   A false statement, not fixed in a tangible medium, that harms a person's or an organization's reputation. See libel.

standing   The legal right to sue based on an assertion that a plaintiff's interests have been threatened or injured.

statutory law   A law passed by a state or federal legislature and signed by the chief executive officer of the state or the nation.

subpoena   A court order that requires someone to appear in court to testify or to produce documents.

summary judgment   A decision by a judge that is based on the pleadings. A summary judgment circumvents a jury trial because the judge has found that there is no dispute among the parties about the facts of the case, and consequently there is no need for a jury to decide the facts.

superior court   A state trial court, usually distinguished from various inferior courts, such as traffic courts or small claims courts.

temporary injunction   A court order that requires some action to be taken, or some party to refrain from taking action, until the court decides whether to issue a permanent injunction.

temporary restraining order   A court order that forbids or requires action until the court may hold a hearing. Usually of a very short duration, the temporary restraining order should be distinguished from a temporary injunction.

tort   A civil wrong, other than a breach of contract, for which one may recover damages or seek an injunction.

trade rules   Regulations that govern certain industries and that are proposed and published by the Federal Trade Commission after administrative hearings.

trier of fact   Usually the jury, but sometimes a judge, appointed to hear evidence and determine the truth from it.

unconstitutional   Forbidden by the Constitution of the United States or by a state constitution.

verdict   The finding for or against a defendant by a jury after it has determined the facts and weighed them according to the judge's instructions regarding the law. A verdict may be a general finding of liability or guilt, or it may be specific findings of fact. The latter is called a special verdict, the former a general verdict.

voir dire   The process of questioning potential jurors so that each side and the court may decide whether to accept or reject individuals for jury duty.

warrant   A court order that gives a police officer the power to arrest someone or conduct a search.

writ of certiorari   See certiorari.

writ of mandamus   A court order that commands a lower court or a nonjudicial official to perform an official duty.

CASE INDEX

Note: Major cases are in **boldface.**

SUBJECT INDEX

Note: Page numbers in **boldface** refer to illustrations.